Perceptions of the Press in Nineteenth-Century British Periodicals

Advance Reviews

"This is an invaluable aid to researchers and historians seeking insights into how the various aspects of the press were addressed and written about in nineteenth-century British periodicals. The compilation of sources and annotations collected here allow the modern researcher to gauge how journalism as practiced by many hands in the nineteenth century was perceived."

—*Tamara Baldwin, Chair and Professor of Mass Media, Southeast Missouri State University*

"Anyone interested in nineteenth-century journalism will covet this unique reference work. It is of enormous value to historians considering journalism during the century in which British power and influence reached around the globe. Its concise annotations also offer an absorbing read for anyone interested in knowing how the Victorian-era press established journalism standards still widely accepted in the twenty-first century."

—*Ross F. Collins, Professor of Communication, North Dakota State University*

"Building on her previous outstanding work on nineteenth-century journalism, the author provides us with an incredibly rich and meticulous overview of how journalism was discussed in a wide range of periodicals throughout the century. The result is a treasure-trove of information, a vital insight into the formation of a field of scholarship and a commercial activity."

—*Martin Conboy, Professor of Journalism History, University of Sheffield*

"During the nineteenth century, the British periodical press took the world for its subject. Fuelled by growing literacy rates and advances in techniques in printing and distribution, the press grew exponentially. By turns brilliant, wide-ranging, analytical, opinionated, and informative, the press for the most part managed to avoid that great sin of dullness. It's hard to think of a major decision or policy in which the press did not play a significant role. And so what the press thought about its role, what individual periodicals thought about their own mission, and how they perceived other papers is central to any attempt to understand both the press and nineteenth-century life more broadly. With *Perceptions of the Press*, E. M. Palmegiano has given scholars a most valuable tool to understand that extraordinary entity that came, one might almost say, to rule public life."

—*Robert Scholnick, Professor of English and American Studies, College of William and Mary*

"E. M. Palmegiano's *Perceptions of the Press in Nineteenth-Century Periodicals* has given the scholar and the curious researcher together a welcome and extremely rich literary treasure which will enhance the comprehension of the role and influence of the historical British Press right to modern times."

—*David R. Spencer, Professor of Information and Media Studies, University of Western Ontario*

Perceptions of the Press in Nineteenth-Century British Periodicals

A Bibliography

E. M. Palmegiano

ANTHEM PRESS
LONDON · NEW YORK · DELHI

Anthem Press
An imprint of Wimbledon Publishing Company
www.anthempress.com

This edition first published in UK and USA 2012
by ANTHEM PRESS
75-76 Blackfriars Road, London SE1 8HA, UK
or PO Box 9779, London SW19 7ZG, UK
and
244 Madison Ave. #116, New York, NY 10016, USA

British Library Cataloguing-in-Publication Data
A catalogue record for this book is available from the British Library.

Library of Congress Cataloging-in-Publication Data
Palmegiano, E. M.
Perceptions of the press in nineteenth-century British periodicals : a bibliography / E. M. Palmegiano.
p. cm.
Includes bibliographical references and indexes.
ISBN 978-0-85728-439-6 (hardback : alk. paper)
1. Journalism–Great Britain–History–19th century–Periodicals–Bibliography.
2. Journalism–Great Britain–Language–Periodicals–Bibliography.
3. Press and politics–Great Britain–History–19th century–Periodicals–Bibliography.
4. Great Britain–Politics and government–19th century–Periodicals–Bibliography.
5. English periodicals–Bibliography. 6. British periodicals–Bibliography. I. Title.
Z6956.G6P35 2012
[PN5114.P4]
016.072'09034--dc23

2011046559

ISBN-13: 978 0 85728 439 6 (Hbk)
ISBN-10: 0 85728 439 8 (Hbk)

This title is also available as an eBook.

Preface

Nineteenth-century British periodicals regarded the press as a phenomenon of the age. Contemporaries considered it ubiquitous, competing everywhere with pulpits and governments to become the voice of the people. Given the approximately 100,000 publications in the United Kingdom and the volume of publications outside, this conclusion was logical. Commentary on press activity matched its productivity. Those penning for serials did not confine their remarks to domestic developments, frequently measuring ones in other areas, albeit with a British yardstick. Although onlookers saw the press from numerous vantage points, everyone cast it as a major player in the culture of a society. Spotlighting the press gave it status, deserved or undeserved. This bibliography shows how writers *in* the press shaped the discourse *on* the press by offering a substantial sample of opinion on common concerns, specific journals, and individuals.

What was this press that fascinated so many? Essayists then and this book now categorize "the press" as anything published regularly: annuals, quarterlies, monthlies, fortnightlies, weeklies, and dailies. Catalogers increasingly reserved the term journalism for the newspaper. From the 1820s through the 1890s, the decades mainly covered here, observers recorded at length how and why the press changed dramatically. Nationally, they watched as elite reviews and great London newspapers waxed and waned, legions of specialized monthlies and weeklies opened and closed, penny and then halfpenny gazettes in the country and in the city challenged and sometimes vanquished older ones, and annuals died ingloriously. Columnists noted how intrusions by officials slowed or ceased, how journalists shed the veil of anonymity, how readers increased, and how readership shifted the market. Probes of the international press complemented or contradicted these happenings. Generalizations notwithstanding, dialogue was disparate occasionally in the same organ and regularly from generation to generation. Schooling, sect, penchants, prejudices, and politics surely account for differences, as could occupation. Authors might have full-time positions in the press, but they were as likely to be casual or constant freelancers with or without other employment. Their diversity probably explains the range of their epithets for the press, from the laudatory "palladium of liberty" to the wary "engine of evil" with the neutral "agora" between.

Any bibliography must strive to be comprehensive, but one drawn from nineteenth-century periodicals must acknowledge the limitations inherent in their study. Their numbers and their fluidity, resulting from mastheads capriciously altered, contents mysteriously labeled, and parts lost, complicate inquiry. These factors, together with the bulk of texts on the press and the variety of interpretations of it, make any attempt to encompass everything futile.[1] Hence this book surveys 48 publications, selected because they embodied sundry political, economic, religious, social, and literary perspectives, and most lacked subject indexes. This roster comprises 15 quarterlies, 22 monthlies, six weeklies, one quarterly turned monthly, one bimonthly, one fortnightly turned monthly, and two weeklies turned monthlies. Among them are relevant ones in *The Wellesley Index to Victorian Periodicals*, chosen because of their availability and utility as sources for research in several disciplines and its indication of editors and omission of a subject index. Since *Wellesley* captions spoke primarily to upper and upper middle/middling class readers, organs that addressed otherwise underrepresented audiences, such as *Chambers's Journal* and *Hogg's Instructor*, have been added. Further criteria for incorporation were prominent editors or publishers and/or known contributors.[2]

An introduction summarizes recurrent issues in the serials, cited alphabetically with title modifications in subheadings. Dates for the *Edinburgh Review*, the *New Monthly Magazine*, and *Tait's Edinburgh Magazine* coincide with the *Wellesley Index*; dates for the rest correspond to the years of their runs between 1824 and 1900. Each caption has a preamble synopsizing editors or owners/sponsors of titles not in the *Wellesley Index*, predecessors and successors, mergers, audience, and themes. Entries are chronological; annotated, with original grammar, spelling, and punctuation in quotations, and signed as printed. Other authorship attributions come from the *Wellesley Index*; Eileen M. Curran, "The Curran Index: Additions to and Corrections of *The Wellesley Index to Victorian Periodicals*" (http://victorianresearch.org/curranindex.html); Anne Lohrli, Household Words: A Weekly Journal, *1850–1859: Conducted by Charles Dickens* (Toronto, 1973); Ella Ann Oppenlander, *Dickens'* All the Year Round: *Descriptive Index and Contributor List* (Troy, NY, 1984); E. M. Palmegiano research. Listings do not include fiction, miscellaneous "notes," and material on press stances on policies or events unrelated to journalism.

The author index has pseudonyms but not initials. The subject index identifies topics related to the kingdom at large and London. Postings for other English cities, Ireland, Scotland, Wales, the Channel Islands, regions of the British Empire, and those under foreign control are inclusive. Place names refer to the nineteenth century, and indexes, to entry numbers.

Many people have contributed to this book, and I wish to thank all those who have done so. A few deserve special mention. The staffs of the British Library and Newark (NJ) Public Library showed much skill and patience in locating missing periodicals. Saint Peter's College supported this project by funding time away from teaching, travel to distant collections, and research assistants. The work of these students, Katrina Luckenback, Maria Dela Paz, Thomas Cleary, and especially Nicholas Lambrianou, has been invaluable. Also at Saint Peter's College, Kerry Falloon and David Hardgrove in O'Toole Library and Maryann Picerno and Carlo Macaraig in Information Technology responded quickly and capably to my countless requests for help. My colleagues Jerome J. Gillen and David S. Surrey very generously shared their expertise with me. My editor Janka Romero exemplified professionalism and kindness. I am grateful to one and all and to my family and friends who have tolerated with grace my absorption in this venture.

Notes

1 For a brief overview of the nineteenth-century British press, *see* E. M. Palmegiano, "'The Fourth Estate': British Journalism in Britain's Century," in *The Rise of Western Journalism, 1815–1914*, ed. Ross F. Collins and E. M. Palmegiano (Jefferson, NC and London, 2007), 139–72.

2 Among the most useful modern reference works on the Victorian press are *Dictionary of Nineteenth-Century Journalists*, general editors Laurel Brake and Marysa Demoor (London, 2009); The Research Society for Victorian Periodicals: "Biennial Bibliography" (http://www.rs4vp.org/bib.html); "Victorian Periodicals – Aids to Research: A Selected Bibliography," prepared by Rosemary Van Arsdale (http://www.victorianresearch.org/periodicals.html); *The Waterloo Directory of Newspapers and Periodicals, 1800–1900*.

Introduction

Overview

Contributors to nineteenth-century British periodicals perceived the press as the principal medium of public conversation. Convinced of its real or potential power, they examined it thoroughly. They discovered its roots in ancient Rome, Renaissance Amsterdam, or the English Civil Wars. They described its adolescence in the eighteenth-century western world and delineated its maturity in Britain, if not the empire and foreign realms, during the Victorian epoch. They attested, not always with enthusiasm, to the evolution of the domestic press from an aristocratic to a democratic institution and emphasized its standing internationally, supposedly due to accurate and impartial news gathering and thoughtful commentary. Discussion ranged broadly, but persistent motifs were the nexus between the press and government; changes in newspapers, magazines, and reviews; the definition of journalist and its consequences for training and reward; how these circumstances compared or contrasted with those in other places.

The Impact of Government

Serials of all persuasions noticed Parliament's history of interference with the press. Pieces surfaced on the stamp duty passed in 1712, the subsequent imposts on advertising and paper, the resistance of Members to admitting reporters, the press curbs in 1819, and the ongoing prosecutions for seditious or blasphemous libel and subventions from cabinets. Writers simultaneously and retrospectively protested or celebrated these actions and similar ones of colonial governors and Continental governments. In this discourse, taxes either inhibited "news" papers for the poor and fattened the treasury, or deterred uprisings; Ireland consistently typified prosecutions and Russia, censorship; India and France inconsistently typified both.

When the campaign to end the "taxes on knowledge" commenced at home, fierce controversy flared in articles from the 1830s until the mid-century abolition of these levies. While Commons had opened its doors before 1801 and some editors had the ear of ministers after, observers nevertheless routinely aired how widely official tentacles reached. Legislation on copyright, partnership, and postal charges; nationalization of telegraphy; bureaucratic leaks and patronage exemplified the effects on content, revenue, and access.

Newspapers

Pundits spotted the hand of authority most often in the newspaper, whose purpose and performance they gauged extensively in the reviews and magazines of this bibliography. Sketches of London's stamped morning dailies operating since the eighteenth century distinguished them from their unstamped weekly brothers. Earning stature from their rapid and reliable intelligence during the Napoleonic wars, the metros emerged as the paramount sources of news in 1815. With party affiliation fueling subscriptions, editorializing initially appeared as a tool to reinforce loyalty, then for shaping opinion on anything and everything. The notion that journals directed as well as reflected reasoned judgment, a concept *The Times* came to represent, was extremely popular in the 1850s and 1860s. Thereafter the construct of the "newspaper as echo" triumphed, but savants perennially underscored the clout of *The Times*. Because they acknowledged it as the paradigm for the newspaper, they devoted far more energy to it than to its peers.

Much about the newspaper engrossed bystanders. A section that enthralled generations was advertisements, bygone and current. Contemporaries, anticipating today's economists, sociologists, psychologists, and historians, pictured inserts as a flooding stream of income, a broadcast of human wants and desires, and a master key to the past. Another aspect of the newspaper closely tracked was its connection to technology that hastened production and distribution, chiefly improvements of steam-powered printing and railroads. But the advent of telegraphy, coinciding as it did with the mid-century launch of penny dailies and Reuters, gained greater coverage as the wires transformed the contour and circulation of news.

Awareness of speed went beyond technology. Essays also conveyed how readers feeling "rushed" affected content and layout. As time allegedly became an obsession, newspapers accommodated cursory reading, originally by shrinking paragraphs and stressing terseness, soon replacing words with illustrations and enlarging headlines. Although Victorians applauded brevity, they argued about the intellectual advantages of these adaptations that, many averred, had already corrupted American gazettes. After the enactment of compulsory education in 1870, disagreement sharpened.

Scrutinizers of dailies' behavior in a highly competitive market deplored or endorsed the race to capture graduates by pirating sensationalism from the Sunday herald and intimacy from the American interview. Scribes bickered about the merits of space allocation, whether papers should reduce details and interpretations of British and international policies in order to grow sports pages and to inaugurate ladies' pages. Admirers reckoned that this "new journalism" made for a perkier press, but their opposites damned renovations as unworthy of journalists. The gimmickry of the halfpenny capped the conflict, which had raised a fundamental question: was the press primarily a public entity to enlighten the citizenry, or a private enterprise to enrich some citizens?

Columns about weeklies, from the elite to the inexpensive, mirrored their diversity. The first group, said to cater to an educated and affluent but narrow audience seeking weightier literary, political, and social analyses, contained the *Athenaeum*, *Spectator*, *Saturday Review*, and their ilk. Workers' tribunes, which ordinarily had fleeting lives, apparently drew more readers and certainly drew more remarks. In the early decades of the century, the minority of this press urging lower class rebellion terrified those associated with Tory and Whig organs.

According to chroniclers, pessimists need not have worried since the majority of the unstamped were apolitical, confined by choice or law in their information transfer, and gradually trumped by the generic weekend paper. Working and lower middle class audiences reputedly turned to it because the pressure of labor precluded perusal of a daily, the Sunday highlighted graphic felonies, and the Saturday harbored data of all sorts. Stopping at pubs, reading rooms, and libraries, readers sought guidance passively by scanning and actively by submitting queries on a plethora of subjects, thereby confirming the pontificate of the press.

Evaluators did not overlook the country, where the weekly prevailed until the 1860s. They saluted papers with seniority or cachet, as the *Manchester Guardian*, and welcomed neophyte dailies. After the enlargement of suffrage in 1867, calls for partisan sponsorship of dailies outside London intensified. Narrators nonetheless expected rural weeklies, even those with small staffs, to endure because they monopolized local advertising and news.

Insiders and outsiders outlined how Scotland and England paralleled patterns of development and exchanged personnel; how political and economic crises hamstrung Ireland and linguistic differences, Wales; how the Channel Islands hovered on the journalistic periphery.

Reviews and Magazines

Commentators throughout the century hailed the *Edinburgh Review* as the model of quality for its genre. They accepted the review as appropriate for maintaining fidelity to a political party, religious belief, or literary canon when adherents paid the bills. Spewing out scathing criticism of opponents on any of these three fronts and interspersing it with scholarly dissertations, reviews garnered fans and foes until their influence began to evaporate in the 1850s. Then lack of timeliness, lengthy and occasionally labyrinthine articles, and high prices purportedly reduced the review's sway over powerbrokers and a populace who increasingly opted for monthly and weekly magazines.

From the 1830s people recognized the proliferation of magazines that targeted everything: the trades and the professions, God and mammon, household organization and imperial management, the arts and the races, maternity and quasi-pornography, staid hobbies and hot adventures, and any other topic that would sell. Arbiters conventionally deemed cheap miscellanies dedicated to "instruction" and "amusement" clones of the *Penny Magazine*. The entertaining squibs, poems, and lore that these periodicals cobbled together captivated some referees, but others worried about less wholesome captions full of subtle sexuality and flagrant criminality. When mid-brow magazines such as *Temple Bar* and the *Cornhill* arrived in the 1860s, judges extolled their better fiction and trenchant expositions but predicted that the appetite for currency would ultimately doom them as it had the annuals of the 1830s.

Journalists

Ideas about journalists shifted dramatically over the century. Before and after journeyman newspaper editor Gibbons Merle in 1833 labeled their efforts "journalism," they were an indeterminate lot. What journalism was, profession or trade, vocation or avocation, and what its relationship to literature was seemed clearer to its participants than to observers. They enrolled in its ranks leader-writers, Parliamentary reporters, penny-a-liners, "special" correspondents, critics, illustrators, essayists, editors and their minions, and proprietors. Given this spectrum, it is hardly surprising that a squabble about prerequisites followed. Counselors eventually pitted the university against apprenticeship for newspaper positions but never articulated guidelines for magazine drop-ins, from experts requiring no pay to losers in former endeavors surviving on it.

Sages quarreled too about anonymity, which diminished journalists' status and salaries but sustained the force of the editorial "we." While top quarterlies could usually afford talented contributors and London dailies could hire some staff, these persons and their compatriots stood in the shadows because of the custom of anonymity, until William Howard Russell made the war correspondent a star. Although the legions of unknowns far outnumbered the score or so of famous military correspondents, their exploits quickly sparked contention about the scope of reporting in a free society. According to their enemies, they were spies, analogous to the interviewers of "new journalism" in disclosures of secrets.

Stories showcased individuals besides war correspondents. Featured were pioneers from Daniel Defoe to John Wilkes and their heirs. Among the prominent in the nineteenth century were owners and editors of London's newspapers, as James Perry, William Cobbett, John Walter II, Leigh Hunt, and John Delane, and of pricey magazines and reviews, as William Blackwood, Francis Jeffrey, and John Gibson Lockhart.

Onlookers likewise rescued the anonymous, either by naming them or by elucidating their roles. Commemorated, for instance, were firebrands of the 1830s and wordsmiths in every decade, printers with sideline newspapers, and skippers of underfunded publications. Yet paragraphs on editors of dailies, leader-writers, Parliamentary reporters, and literary and theatre critics predominated. Authors might dismiss the average journalist as a semi-literate ready to pen anything for money, or honor his caste as crusaders and champions for the voiceless. With the cancellation of press taxes, the birth of inexpensive dailies, the sprouting of myriad magazines, and the multiplication of autodidacts after 1850, press watchers logged the expansion of this job market, particularly the influx of women.

Readers

Who read the press and why they did so stumped nineteenth-century assessors as much as later historians. There were plenty of assertions about which folks read what and how they got the press. But the talk of readership was just that: talk. Few accounts presented hard evidence, probably because audience surveys did not exist. Still these fuzzy attempts at profiling indicate who witnesses guessed constituted audience. They classified readers around the globe under several headings: age, sex, education, employment, faith, and social grade; format preference (dailies to annuals, leaders to letters, visuals to treatises); location (urban, rural, imperial, foreign); interests (politics, business, religion, advertising, advice, fiction, the arts, poetry, sports, gossip, and the affairs of colonials and strangers). These characterizations were neither rigid nor coherent, but they do verify the breadth of readership.

Writers claimed that customers' creativity in accessing the press demonstrated their fascination with it and its hold on them. Thus, many articles spelled out pathways, among them subscribing alone or in concert, buying or renting from vendors, borrowing from neighbors and distant contacts, utilizing literal and figurative open arenas with news announcers, and consorting with smugglers.

The Press around the World

Serials measured the press outside the United Kingdom by its standards. The products of France and the United States were the pets of columnists who vacillated between complimenting and condemning others. Characterizations of French journalists sympathized with those deprived of liberty in the 1820s and 1850s and castigated those who prioritized political careers, engaged in bribery, and incited or benefited from revolutions in July 1830 and February 1848. Alternatively, the men of the *Journal des Débats* and the *Revue des Deux Mondes* won respect whatever the regime. Notes on Americans commended them for their ingenuity in finding news, success in attracting newspaper buyers, and skill in illustrating magazines but decried gazettes' layouts, editors' crudeness, and proprietors' blatant partisanship or raw capitalism. Epitomizing good and evil were Horace Greeley of the *New York Tribune* and James Gordon Bennett of the *New York Herald*. Communities to the north of the United States and to the south, from Mexico to Argentina, rated only rare nods.

People did not foreground most Europeans beyond France except for the Germans, Italians, and Russians. Censorship threaded through the compositions on their presses, but otherwise estimates of their output varied. The deeds of Otto von Bismarck distressed appraisers of the German press, the heritage of Rome and Venice impressed those of the Italian press, and the underground sheets of the Nihilists divided those of the Russian press. Glances at the Scandinavians, Dutch, Belgians, Spanish, Portuguese, Swiss, Slavs, and Greeks were intermittent. Probes of the Ottoman Empire's press touched on its European and Arab components, mainly in Egypt. Other African lands had little mention. Even the late-century war in South Africa did not stimulate serious attention to its press.

Actual and imaginative travelers did focus on some of the empire. Items on the Raj centered on the press in what are modern India, Pakistan, and Bangladesh. Whether run by locals or interlopers, organs sparked apprehension sporadically throughout the century. Ironically, the events of 1857–1858 did not exacerbate the fear of all reviewers but did catalyze justifications to restrain the press. The frightened blamed it for provoking insurrection, while the calm pointed out the illogic of a free press where despotism ruled. These rationales recurred in the multiple subsequent debates about the burgeoning, vibrant vernacular press in the subcontinent. Adjacent and remote Asian regions lured a mere handful of investigators. Infrequent musings on China dealt with the indigenous imperial press and the British on-scene one. Glimpses of the Japanese press were scarcer.

In the Pacific, the press of the New Zealand colonies accumulated fewer plaudits than that of the Australian settlements. Journals in Sidney and Melbourne received the highest marks, and their journalists, the greatest publicity.

Conclusion

By Queen Victoria's death, British periodicals had done more than shed light on the press of her era. They had crafted a record of its origins and had linked it to its kin across the planet. If this self-study tipped in favor of assets, it did not neglect liabilities. But considered from the perspective of the twenty-first century, it failed to resolve a crucial issue, namely how a free press functions when entry to a forum is easy but entrants may not have the wisdom to separate use and abuse of it. From the tabloid to texting is really just a short jump.

Ainsworth's Magazine, 1842–1854

Planned as light reading by William Ainsworth, who oversaw the *New Monthly Magazine* after 1845, *Ainsworth's* press coverage had an international flavor.

1. [Ainsworth, W. H.]. "Preliminary Address." 1 (1842): i–iv.
Pledged that *Ainsworth's*, with "real responsibility in *literary* hands," would "give greater freedom to writers." Papers with "bold and original inquiry" and without politics and "scandal" would evidence that *Ainsworth's* goals were "a higher tone of literary speculation" and "a more steadfast moral endeavour."

2. Cruikshank, George. "A Few Words to the Public about Richard Bentley." 1 (1842): verso, i.
Cruikshank denied that he was the illustrator of *Bentley's Miscellany* but acknowledged that it had one of his etchings every month and promoted his nephew, an engraver, as an illustrator.

3. [Ainsworth, W. H.]. "To the Subscribers to *Ainsworth's Magazine*." 1 (1842): recto, i.
Justified a price rise to two shillings to pay for more engravings as articles increased. Sales were "large," and press approval of the magazine was "unequivocal and emphatic."

4. [Ainsworth, W. H.]. "To Our Readers." 2 (1842): i–ii.
Excused a switch to smaller typeface, which writers and readers disliked, because commissioned articles were so numerous.

5. "A Paper on Puffing." 2 (1842): 42–47.
Classed many current book reviews as "preliminary," "negative," "mysterious," "deprecatory" or "pugnacious," unfortunate because the 'reading,' not 'thinking' public adopted press opinion. Evening papers "boldly fling off every trammel of respectability and truth."

6. [Ainsworth, W. H.]. "To Our Readers." 3 (1843): i–iv.
Asserted that *Ainsworth's* success attracted talented contributors (listed).

7. Nimrod [C. J. Apperley]. "The First Word in the Morning and the Last at Night." 3 (1843): 219–23.
Periodical writer preferred "obvious" as well as "unthought of or unknown" grammar.

8. [Ainsworth, W. H.]. "To the Readers of *Ainsworth's Magazine*." 4 (1843): 1–2.
Assured that *Ainsworth's* accommodated "in excess" the public interest in illustrations.

9. "Lever and *Arthur O'Leary*." 5 (1844): 362–64.
Essay on Charles Lever said that he recorded conversations with "forty-reporter power."

10. A Matter of Fact-or. "The Hum of Men." 6 (1844): 109–13.
Disdained "the stereotyped scraps and scrips of penny-a-line *belles lettres* picked up by the vulgar in the daily papers"; "a sort of editor of the lady's magazinish-influence," and "a dealer in light articles for heavy reviews."

11. "*New South Wales*." 6 (1844): 413–16.
Noted that there were "several rival and abusive newspapers published in Sydney."

12. The Author of *Mornings in Bow Street* [John Wight]. "The Court and the Court Circular – An Anecdote of 'Old Townshend.'" 6 (1844): 498–502.
Deemed the newspaper *Court Circular* dull. George IV, annoyed that his court was "infested" by "mercurial out-scouts of journalism," asked John Townshend to set up the "COURT NEWSMAN" as "the only *authentic*" source of court news.

13. [Ainsworth, W. H.]. "The Late Mr. Laman Blanchard." 7 (1845): 217–25.
Discussed Blanchard's writing in *Ainsworth's* and the *New Monthly Magazine*.

14. Brooks, Shirley. "The Country Editor." 8 (1845): 89–92.
Believed that "the most energetic man in any county" was the newspaper editor. Known by name, unlike his London counterpart, the local editor of a "respectable" paper was "usually a highly educated man, who possesses two pre-essentials – a keen intellect and a ready pen." He needed "great energy," "indomitable pluck," and tact. He read every line of London dailies, then scissored and added his own notes. He also reviewed the columns of London and local correspondents, consulted the local noble, and solicited businesses for advertising. At elections he might pen a candidate's address and design his placards before reporting the vote.

15. A Travelling Satellite of Queen Victoria. "Glimpses of Germany, with a Glance at France." 8 (1845): 317–21.
Reporter with a royal tour revealed that "French journalists…were almost as much the rage at Bonn as the royalties." The "*feuilletonists*" and Jules Janin were very popular. He was "a sort of bourgeois dandy, with a great deal of consequence, and very little conversational wit to support his claims." Janin exemplified that "nothing is too absurd for a thorough-going French journalist." Because the French "printed everything they heard," they were "utterly untrustworthy of the high and responsible function which they usurp."

16. [Ainsworth, W. H.]. "Alexandre Dumas and His Romances." 11 (1847): 241–52.
Remarked that Dumas, *père*, had five romances simultaneously in five newspapers for which he was underpaid. Exhausted from this journalism, he tried to stop. Two Paris newspapers, the *Constitutionnel* and *Presse*, sued him for breach of contract.

17. [?Ainsworth, W. H.]. "Pope Pius IX and the English." 13 (1848): 88.

Prefaced a letter of thanks from Pius IX, for Thomas Roscoe's article (December, 1846) on papal sovereignty of Rome, by saying that the pope had a "high-minded regard for public opinion, and for its organ, a free press."

18. "French Almanacks." 14 (1848): 461–69.

Declared that French almanacs "reflect the details of character and the spirit of the times" like "so many tiny mirrors." Named several and quoted the *Almanach Comique* and *Almanach Prophétique et Pittoresque*.

19. White, Mrs. [Caroline Alice]. "A Chapter on Puffs and Advertisements." 16 (1849): 42–46.

Described newspaper advertising as "a social history of the times." "Cheapness and appearance," as well as an appeal to "ordinary motives," were the keys to luring buyers. Aside on "[b]revity…the soul of periodical writing."

20. White, Mrs. [Caroline Alice]. "Man *versus* Metal." 16 (1849): 309–13.

Paraphrased a writer living hand-to-mouth after he abandoned a year's commission at a monthly because that editor did not feature his work and payment was late for "last month's articles, though the magazines have been out these three weeks." Postponements were common because serial novels had priority over articles. Worse, some periodicals offered one fee for articles and then paid less, while others never paid because insolvencies were frequent.

21. "Life of the Editor of a Manchester Newspaper." 19 (1851): 234–39.

Review of Archibald Prentice's *Historical Sketches and Personal Recollections of Manchester* stated that he wrote for the *Manchester Guardian* "during the epoch of Hunt radicalism" and "assumed to himself the task of directing the opinion of reformers, hitherto represented by Cowdroy's *Manchester Gazette*."

22. "An Evening with Some Socialists." 21 (1852): 120–24.

Alluded to "editors of revolutionary journals who had been forced to fly from Prussian persecution."

23. "The Mighty Rumour of the City." 21 (1852): 299–300.

Averred that "penny-a-liners ready to dish up…scandal or horror" spread rumors.

24. Anthony, Joseph, Jr. "Rough Notes from My Diary: Valparaiso to San Francisco." 22 (1852): 415–25.

Found in English and German reading rooms in Valparaiso, Chile, several English dailies, weeklies, and magazines.

25. Anthony, Joseph, Jr. "Rough Notes from My Diary: San José." 23 (1853): 22–32.

Discovered that Stockton (CA) had two papers, the *Republican* and the *Journal*, both of which "display much talent."

26. Dumas, Alexandre, [*père*], Collaborator. "Dumas and the Revolution of 1830." 24 (1853): 50–62.

Review of the *Memoirs* of Alexandre Dumas, *père*, recalled events in July, 1830, when "the police met with some resistance in executing their orders to seize a newspaper," while contributors to the *National* were creating a provisional government.

27. Rowsell, E. P., Esq. "My London Newspaper in the Country." 24 (1853): 340–42.

Condemned country readers who abhorred 'London and its bustle' but read its papers.

28. [?Ainsworth, W. H.]. "German Popular Literature." 25 (1854): 147–56.

Concluded, after perusal of German almanacs, that "Germany cannot boast of any cheap literature at all to be compared with" that in Britain.

29. Allen, John Naule. "The Model Editor: Mr. Scribbler's Day Dream – Freely Rendered." 25 (1854): 248–53.

Painted the ideal editor as powerful, a guardian of the shrine to genius, and contented when his periodical gained subscribers. He sped through his own writing, answered letters immediately and respectfully, paid contributors promptly and well, and put their material into the next number.

30. Allen, John Naule. "All Sorts of Readers." 25 (1854): 352–59.

Categorized readers of the press. The "reader plain" liked leaders in dailies; the "candid reader," journals of criticism; the "indulgent reader," everything.

All the Year Round, 1859–1895

Superseding *Household Words*, *All the Year Round* kept the layout of its predecessor. Commanded by Charles Dickens, father and son, its principal interest was the newspaper, from London parish to Australian settlement.

1. [Collins, Wilkie]. "Sure To Be Healthy, Wealthy, and Wise." 1 (1859): 5–10; response, 251.

Satirized newspaper advertising with unbelievable promises. Denounced moneymaking schemes "especially in the cheap newspapers, which have plenty of poor readers hungry for any little addition to their scanty incomes." Letter confirmed fraudulent advertising.

2. [Hollingshead, John]. "Right Through the Post." 1 (1859): 190–92.

Watched newspaper transmittal: "Local papers going to London to set an example to the metropolitan press; London papers sucked dry by provincial politicians, and sent across the country to some fourth or fifth day readers."

3. "*All the Year Round* at the Post-Office." 1 (1859): 442.

Announced that the law (18th Victoria, cap. 2) required the date and title of a periodical on each page for post office registration, thence transmission to other countries and the empire.

4. [Hollingshead, John]. "*Great Eastern* Postscript." 1 (1859): 546–52.

Defined 'our own correspondent' as "a profession...which hangs upon the skirts of literature without being literature." Pay paralleled risks for "men who live only in action, who feed only upon excitement." Correspondents covering the *Great Eastern* explosion were "running historians for running readers."

5. [Sala, George Augustus]. "Since This Old Cap Was New." 2 (1859–60): 76–80.

Labeled as new the railroad station newsboy with "his rapid shuffle, keeping pace with the moving train, his astonishing shrill slurring of the names of the newspapers."

6. "The *Foo-Chow Daily News*." 2 (1859–60): 86–88.

Scanned a handwritten Chinese paper with imperial and regional information copied "from a placard daily affixed to the governor's office."

7. [Dickens, Charles]. "The Tattlesnivel Bleater." 2 (1859–60): 226–29.

Criticized the typical London correspondent for a local paper because this "blockhead" wrote about things "he cannot possibly know."

8. [Yates, Edmund]. "Holding Up the Mirror." 3 (1860): 595–600.
Profiled the "well conducted and highly respectable...chronicle of the theatrical, musical, and 'entertaining' world" with many advertisements. Its theatre critics went to their offices – rather than to taverns as before – to pen reviews.

9. "On the Parish." 4 (1860–61): 273–76.
Assumed that a London parish paper was a good source for news of "local affairs" and advertisements. Among the several listed was the *City Press*, "the largest of the district penny papers." Readers wanted exact reports of meetings and speeches without attempts to make the "vulgar" "genteel." Leaders were to "instruct or amuse," but advertisements conveyed a sense of neighborhood.

10. "The Queen of the Blue Stockings." 5 (1861): 82–87.
Story on Hester Lynch Salusbury Thrale Piozzi pictured eighteenth-century newspapers as gossipy.

11. "A Two-Year Old Colony." 5 (1861): 294–97.
Announced that Brisbane had two newspapers, the *Moreton Bay Courier* and *Queensland Guardian*, in addition to the *Government Gazette*.

12. "Almanacs." 6 (1861–62): 318–21.
Testified that almanacs, often supplements of illustrated newspapers or comic magazines, were very popular. English, French, and American almanacs varied.

13. [Dickens, Charles]. "The Young Man from the Country." 6 (1861–62): 540–42.
Reprinted from Dickens' *American Notes* that most newspapers were "licentious," engaged in "ribald slander." Although some had "character," they all catered to "an enormous class" of voters who only read newspapers.

14. "A Literary Life." 7 (1862): 115–20.
Drew information on Leigh Hunt's theatre criticism from his autobiography and letters. With the vast expansion of periodical literature, authors moved to that market. More than one "literary man finds himself speedily lapsing into the journalist" if they had moral and common sense and breadth of knowledge.

15. [Blanchard, Sidney L.]. "Punch in India." 7 (1862): 462–69.
Looked at the *Delhi Sketch-Book*, which had crude typography and illustrations. Because of the distance of authors from the press, there was little opportunity for editing. Entries reflected the interests of the military and civilian officials who were its contributors and buyers.

16. [Halliday, Andrew]. "Tragic Case of a Comic Writer." 7 (1862): 469–71.
Halliday bemoaned that he never had the opportunities to write a "sensation story" and to review serious books. Instead, his editor assigned him "monthly parts of the penny periodicals, concerning which I am expected to say that they sustain their reputation, and are fully up to their usual standard."

17. "Princely Travel in America." 8 (1862–63): 174–80.
Ranked the American press as a "second order" of literature, with stereotyped articles and "crude compilations, weighty accumulations of false or veritable facts, ridiculous hoaxes, childish

declamation, without judgment, wit, or intellect." To fill "twenty immense columns of microscopic type" meant verbosity. Aside that New York state's 600 dailies relied on telegraphy for news.

18. [Linton, Eliza Lynn]. "John Wilson." 8 (1862–63): 272–76.
Noticed Wilson's "strong literary criticism, almost savage" and his "masterly" *Noctes Ambrosianae* in *Blackwood's Magazine.*

19. "Small-Beer Chronicles." 9 (1863): 404–08.
Speculated that advertising for the middling classes mirrored value shifts.

20. "*Punch* in Australia." 9 (1863): 610–16.
Assessed Melbourne's *Punch*, which mimicked London's in paper, type, woodblocks, and cover (although the colonial Mr. Punch was younger with different attire). The colonial version, mainly on Melbourne with some material on the rest of Victoria, was catholic in its ridicule.

21. [Yates, Edmund]. "Gazetting Extraordinary." 10 (1863–64): 58–61.
Indexed the press as dailies, weeklies, and illustrated, sponsored, or interest-directed serials. Among the last were the *Pawnbroker's Gazette* (news, advertising, letters) and *Hue and Cry.*

22. "China Ornaments." 10 (1863–64): 419–21.
Touched on the *North China Herald* (Shanghai), "the weekly organ of British and commercial interests" of which four-fifths was advertising.

23. "England over the Water." 10 (1863–64): 461–63.
Thought that Melbourne's "press is very active," with three-penny "heaps of weekly," digging, and "upcountry journals." Also popular were religious, agricultural, and sports papers, and the local *Punch*, though its illustrations were uneven, but other illustrated journals usually failed. "*The Argus*, the best paper in the colony, sometimes contains really excellent articles."

24. [Yates, Edmund]. "My Newspaper." 11 (1864): 473–76.
Summarized a London daily's content: Parliament, society, sports, commerce, foreign affairs. In a daily's office, the subeditor and reporters had access to telegraphy, "an enormous boon to all newspaper men," especially for leader topics. Compositors, on duty from four in the afternoon until two in the morning, earned three or four guineas weekly. The Hoe was the principal printer. Newsboys were important in distribution.

25. [Wills, W. H.]. "Forty Years in London." 13 (1865): 253–57.
Remembered evening papers, sold by newsboys tooting horns, that scavenged "[a]ny scrap of news" for another edition; the *Mirror of Literature, Amusement, and Instruction*, the two-penny "modest precursor of cheap periodicals," which died when competition developed; and "*Forget-Me-Not*, [which] set the fashion for illustrated annuals."

26. "Writing for Periodicals." 14 (1865–66): 200–04.
Regretted that so few editors valued contributors, "a distinct and recognized profession." They were often underpaid for their intense intellectual endeavor. While they could write from

anywhere at any pace and with some "cramming" on any subject, they had to be as accurate as a photograph and as coherent as a machine. Although the periodical was "art – and its object is to instruct and elevate," it had to sell. Contributors had to fit its format, and editors had to vary its content. Compositors and proofreaders were also important.

27. "The Fenians." 14 (1865–66): 300–04.
Swore that the Fenian press was "harmless enough, though amusing" with advertising, general news, and letters, even though some of its Dublin peers thought otherwise.

28. [Parkinson, Joseph Charles]. "The Roughs' Guide." 14 (1865–66): 492–96.
Centered on William Ruff's *Guide to the Turf*, a penny biweekly with advertising, letters, leaders on horseracing, and columns on hunting, sculling, and dogs.

29. "A Recent Lounge in Dublin." 14 (1865–66): 516–20.
Referred to newsmen in the streets, placards in front of newspaper offices, and machines producing many sheets.

29a. [Halliday, Andrew]. "The Parish Organ." 15 (1866): 69–72.
Introduction synopsized contents of the average London parish paper.

29b. [Parkinson, Joseph Charles]. "The Genii of the Ring." 15 (1866): 230–35.
Rehabilitated the personnel of sports newspapers, portraying owners as men of decorum and staffers as neither "slangy" nor loud.

30. [Sala, George Augustus]. "Shocking!" 15 (1866): 585–89.
Graded the "the *New York Times*, a paper of very high character and respectability" and its editor, "Henry Raymond, one of the most distinguished of living American politicians."

31. [Parkinson, Joseph Charles]. "What Is Sensational?" 17 (1866–67): 221–24.
Confirmed that newspapers' sensational writing echoed sensational events.

31a. "Very Old News." 18 (1867): 6–10.
Described ancient Rome's *acta diurna* as "honest and reliable" sheets that circulated swiftly throughout imperial provinces. Aside from Cicero on the Roman Empire's sports press.

32. "The Cabman's Guide." 18 (1867): 63–66.
Opened with a new penny periodical for cabmen, *The Whip*.

33. "The French Press." 19 (1867–68): 127–32.
Traced French press history from Théophraste Renaudot's *Gazette de France*, blessed by Armand de Richelieu. Quoted extensively from the preface of this successful weekly. Thereafter, many papers were suppressed, but not Jacques Loret's *Gazette*. Under Louis XV and Louis XVI, even with censorship the press displayed "a recklessness of invective and a licentiousness of speech." Discussed government press policies from the French Revolution through the reign of Louis

Philippe and journalists' role in the July Revolution. Napoleon III controlled the political press by restrictions, such as signature and caution money that made publication expensive. "Printer, editor, journalist," all were liable to fine and imprisonment, though the recent softening of regulations was a good sign.

34. "Some Very Light Literature." 19 (1867–68): 319–23.
Examined an old (undated) issue of the *Belle Assemblée* to prove how rapidly periodicals were stale. Its tone was not suitable for the present, correspondence was absurd, and biographies were fluff, but its fashions were excellent. This very weak link between the *Tatler* and the nineteenth century evidenced the bad taste of the 1830s.

35. "Nothing Like Example." 19 (1867–68): 583–87.
Objected to news vendors' sheets that highlighted brutal crimes.

36. "Telegraphs under Government." 20 (1868): 37–41.
Measured the impact on the press of government takeover of telegraphy.

37. "A Special Wire." 20 (1868): 331–34.
Recorded that the Scottish and Irish morning newspapers relied on telegraphy. Three Irish and four Scottish papers had special wires at night from London to Dublin or Glasgow. Midnight to two a.m. was the peak time for receiving from London staff breaking news and related leaders or correspondents' columns. The typical subeditor, with pencil on ear and penknife in mouth, was under pressure as he rearranged the jumbled sentences from the wires. "The newspapers which do not depend on 'sensation' and titles of eight lines in large type" spent less than their American, and particularly New York, counterparts.

38. "Far-Western Newspapers." 20 (1868): 349–56.
Focused on the American frontier, where every town from Omaha west had a paper that relied on advertising. San Francisco had ten dailies, eight monthlies, one semiweekly, one triweekly, three annuals, and three papers in German, three in Spanish, two in French. Many local editors, some of them women, had "good ability and even refinement" but were casual about work. They also accepted travel perks for praising hotels. Worse, their "scurrilous" and personal attacks on each other could lead to violence. Sometimes printer-editors laced local news with opinion. Their papers had "personality" but looked bad because of typographical and contextual errors.

39. "Old Newspapers." 20 (1868): 569–70.
Contrasted advertising in early newspapers, as the seventeenth-century *Commonwealth Mercury*, and the 1868 "leaders and well-written articles" that proved the "march of intellect."

40. "New Lamps for Old Ones." n.s., 1 (1868–69): 33–36.
Reckoned that advertising in the "*Exchange and Mart*, a weekly periodical" for personal sales, matched buyers and sellers.

41. "Caricature History." n.s., 1 (1868–69): 184–89.
Considered eighteenth-century newspaper caricature.

42. "A Gentleman of the Press." n.s., 2 (1869): 132–37, 156–61.
Identified Daniel Defoe as "a journalist of rare powers" who in the nineteenth century would probably edit a "great daily or weekly" or pen "powerful leading articles." For his *Review*, he did all the work "in the midst of great difficulties" for nine years. He also edited the *Edinburgh Courant* and, as a foreign news translator, allegedly manipulated *Mist's Weekly Journal* and other papers.

43. "Saint Martin-le-Grand's Adopted Child." n.s., 2 (1869): 324–28.
Compared private companies, which leased special wires and "collect, edit, and transmit intelligence to the press," and the post office, which only transmitted messages collected and edited by individuals or press associations.

44. "An Unsubjected Woman." n.s., 2 (1869): 497–501.
Starred Elizabeth Carter, who died in 1806 at 89 and whose father's friend, Edward Cave, published her verses in his *Gentleman's Magazine.*

45. "Jovial Journalism." n.s., 3 (1869–70): 514–16.
Branded *Cigarette* the most popular French newspaper, one with a large Paris circulation. Although it ignored news, it had fresh and lively gossip, a descriptive style, theatre and finance columns, and many clever advertisements. It was very different in writing and charm from its British equivalents.

46. "T.S." n.s., 5 (1870–71): 227–32.
Title was abbreviation for Telegraph Street, where the central station of the Postal Telegraph Department was located. Representatives of the Central Press and the Press Association had some space, and papers with special wires had a separate room for use after 7 p.m. by their London correspondents.

47. "Leaves from Old London Life: 1664–1705." n.s., 5 (1870–71): 232–36.
Pirated from several broadsheets news ranging from naval battles and dangerous storms to stories of witches and ghosts.

48. "Thoughts on Puffing." n.s., 5 (1870–71): 329–32.
Viewed newspaper advertisements as appeals to desire, not intellect. Because of their proliferation, "newspapers are swelling into vast unmanageable advertising sheets."

49. "An Old Project and a New One." n.s., 5 (1870–71): 570–72.
Proposed that the post office carry all literature free, as it did newspapers, with their "current history and opinion."

50. "A State of Siege in Cuba." n.s., 5 (1870–71): 610–13.
Delineated Cuban newspaper censorship and stereotyped columns of advertising from the United States; the "localista" or general reporter and the subeditor, and an official journal, presumably to balance Cuba's coverage by American reporters.

51. "How Paris Mourns." n.s., 6 (1871): 150–55.
Spotted among the mementos of the Franco-Prussian War, many newssheets sold in 1871 at inflated prices.

52. "Old Satirical Prints." n.s., 6 (1871): 269–73.
Studied Stuart era-illustrated broadsheets with their news of politics and war and satirical gossip in "strong language."

53. "Chronicles of London Streets: Five Fleet-Street Taverns." n.s., 6 (1871): 349–56.
Believed that the coffeehouse was the source for political news by the late seventeenth century. Aside that Oliver Goldsmith "drudged" for the *Monthly Review*.

54. "Mail Day in the West." n.s., 6 (1871): 534–39.
Sketched "steamer day" in Victoria (Vancouver Island) when local newsmen lifted material from incoming periodicals for their special editions. Citizens paid a shilling to send these summaries of ten to 14 days of news on the steamer. After it departed, the locals "grind up the editorial scissors" for their own papers, adding news of arriving passengers and goods. Aside on the newsboy in San Francisco, "the sharpest of his race," who could sell old issues of the *New York Herald* because Eastern papers were in demand.

55. "A Bill of the Play." n.s., 6 (1871): 606–10.
History of the playbill opined that with "the growth of the press came the expediency of advertising the performances of theatres in the columns of newspapers." Because early papers had no leaders or Parliamentary coverage, foreign news was hard to get, and local was censored, editors paid managers for theatre advertising. Papers devoted to theatre advertising and information generally failed.

56. "Wanted in Clerkenwell." n.s., 7 (1871–72): 250–53.
Explained that London parish papers, akin to country journals, were the consequence of the repeal of stamp and paper duties. These gazettes provided neighborhood news and low-cost advertising.

57. "Among the Tipsters." n.s., 8 (1872): 156–58.
Sampled advertisements in sports papers by people who promised to call winners.

58. "The White Hat and Its Owner." n.s., 8 (1872): 510–13.
Followed Horace Greeley from printer to *New York Tribune* owner. Greeley purportedly had as little capital initially as James Gordon Bennett had when he launched the *New York Herald*.

59. "The Almanack Crop." n.s., 9 (1872–73): 112–17.
Concluded from French almanacs that they frequently promoted periodicals.

60. "An Australian Mining Township." n.s., 9 (1872–73): 352–57.
Headlined Quartzborough (near Melbourne), whose local paper was similar to those of other towns. The gazette had "an inch of telegram," local council and police news, and a leader. Its editor earned 250 pounds annually but, like others "up-country," had no intellectual stimulation.

61. "Press Telegrams." n.s., 9 (1872–73): 365–69.
Endorsed government takeover of telegraphy because private companies determined what was sent and charged too much for it. Detailed regulations and prices for individual newspapers, but most relied on news organizations, which collected and edited material for about 320 towns.

62. "Dublin Life in the Last Century." n.s., 10 (1873): 155–62.
Of Irish newspapers, 1763–1800, *Faulkner's News-Letter*, *Saunders' News-Letter*, and the *Freeman* were "very creditable," and the last two were still publishing. Printed "distinctly and correctly" on well-sized quality paper and in good ink, they had home and foreign news, leaders, "sensible correspondence," and many accident reports.

63. "News of the Past." n.s., 10 (1873): 441–45.
Analyzed *The London Spy Revived* (1736) by Democritus Secundus, which had no leaders, parliamentary and law reports, or literary and theatre reviews but had stories on thefts, wonders, and pantomimes alongside a few personal and goods advertisements and poetry.

64. "Forty Years Ago." n.s., 11 (1873–74): 161–64.
Reviewed William Maginn's *A Gallery of Illustrious Literary Characters* (originally printed in *Fraser's Magazine* and accompanied by portraits). Many of Maginn's subjects were connected to the press of the 1830s. The prediction then that a cheap press would lead to "unbridled licentiousness" proved inaccurate.

65. "New Year's Day in London a Hundred Years Ago." n.s., 11 (1873–74): 224–28.
Skimmed small two-penny dailies of "poor paper, clumsy type, bad ink" with advertising, gossipy letters, and a smattering of news. More expensive monthlies specialized, as the *Lady's Magazine*, or had no "solid stuff."

66. "Advertising in New York." n.s., 12 (1874): 425–27.
Condensed New York newspaper advertising on sales of realty and goods, employment, and services from astrologers to dance instructors.

67. "Christmas in London a Hundred Years Ago." n.s., 13 (1874–75): 252–57.
Imagined that eighteenth-century press reports of weddings stimulated gossip and matrimonial advertising, which, together with inserts on jobs, goods, and services, were good indicators of society.

68. "Criticism Extraordinary." n.s., 13 (1874–75): 558–63.
Sneered at the American press for its "comical" and panegyric criticism.

69. "Among the Advertisers." n.s., 14 (1875): 485–90.
Observed that business and personal advertisements in morning papers offered much hyperbole, by publishers about their books and individuals about their qualifications.

70. "How We Get Our Newspapers: A Day with Messers. W. H. Smith and Son." n.s., 15 (1875–76): 305–09.
Tracked distribution of the press. Smith received dailies "in bulk, unfolded, wet" from printing and organized them for early trains. Weeklies were folded for the post, and periodicals were sorted for subdistributors whose orders varied by title.

71. "Some Strange Reports." n.s., 15 (1875–76): 495–99.
Attributed journalism's errors to typographical and stenographic slips, hasty descriptions of calamities, and inadequate fact checking. While the American reporter was "a chartered libertine, licensed to misuse old words and manufacture new ones," in London weeklies and London letters for local heralds, writers of "tittle-tattle" columns on "everybody who is anybody" were not much better.

72. "Italian Almanacs." n.s., 16 (1876): 150–54.
Enlightened that Italian almanacs varied (science, household, religious, comic) but the majority were instructive.

73. "Who's Lloyd?" n.s., 16 (1876): 201–05.
Silhouetted Edward Lloyd, the insurer who in 1696 started *Lloyd's News*, "a tiny newspaper," a two-page penny triweekly. Suspected that news on politics and government caused him problems because the press was not yet the Fourth Estate.

74. "'Knowledge is Power.'" n.s., 17 (1876–77): 351–55.
Opened with women's newspapers, "useful and instructive journals" filled with letters on every subject. Respondents, who might advise only friends on certain topics, answered strangers' every query and bore the costs of paper and stamps. Guessed that having serious problems solved in the press discouraged women from thinking and that airing personal or frivolous ones demeaned their sex.

75. "From the States." n.s., 18 (1877): 7–12.
Avouched that American newspapers, with slangy writing in "narrow columns of small type" broken by big headlines and directed by editors ready to hint about scandal without verifying it, truly pictured the United States.

76. "Harriet Martineau." n.s., 18 (1877): 126–32.
Disclosed that when Martineau was 19 years old, no London editor would look at her work, so she wrote as V. for the *Monthly Repository*, first for nothing and then for very little. She later penned articles for *Household Words* and, more significantly, leaders for the *Daily News*.

77. "A Japanese Newspaper." n.s., 18 (1877): 207–09.
Presented the *Yokohama Daily News* (20 February 1873), which devoted two of its four pages to news, business, social scandal, and weather, and two to advertising and a lottery. The "favoured newspapers" received copy from the imperial court.

78. "Wanted Particularly." n.s., 19 (1878–79): 294–97.
Averred that advertisements for heirs, prizewinners, creditors, and missing family and friends validated journalism's social utility.

79. "The Press of the Trades." n.s., 19 (1877–78): 389–94.
Targeted both established "prominent and honourable" trade journals and recent "businesslike" ones.

80. "French Almanacks." n.s., 20 (1878): 63–68.
Contended that French almanacs were not bothered by government unless they ridiculed it.

81. "What Is Public Opinion?" n.s., 20 (1878): 77–82.
Guaranteed that if an English newspaper confirmed readers' general views, they respected its "good sense" and accepted its guidance. Radical papers were really escapist, no threat because worker-readers were sensible.

82. "School-Board Journalism." n.s., 20 (1878): 224–30.
Spotlighted education periodicals, as the *School Board Chronicle*, *Pupil Teacher*, and *Scholastic Register*.

83. "Interviewing Extraordinary." n.s., 20 (1878): 305–08.
Broadcast that interviewing was a "regular duty of a newspaper reporter" in the United States but not yet in the United Kingdom.

84. "Advertisers and Advertisements." n.s., 21 (1878): 34–37.
Centered on all-advertising heralds. Morning papers also published many advertisements since they were an important revenue stream.

85. "Caricature in America." n.s., 21 (1878): 298–302.
Scrutinized the style and impact of Thomas Nast in the widely circulated *Harper's Weekly* and Frank Bellew in *Harper's Bazaar*. *Frank Leslie's Illustrated Weekly* was "less distinguished" than previously, and Leslie's *Budget of Fun* and *Jolly Joker* depended on borrowed as well as original caricature. New York's *Daily Graphic* had the most pictures, which complemented the news. The paper copied European prints and produced its own with "photo-lithography."

86. "All in Half a Century." n.s., 22 (1878–79): 185–88.
Recollected that *The Times* of 1828, four pages at seven pence because of stamp, paper, and advertising duties, printed 5,000 copies daily. In 1878 the typical morning paper sold for a penny and printed 250,000 copies.

87. "On the Tramp, from the Pacific to the Atlantic." n.s., 22 (1878–79): 277–82, 299–303.
Delighted that a station in Paraiso (Panama) had the *New York Herald*, *Harper's Weekly*, and *Frank Leslie's Illustrated Weekly*, all arriving regularly.

88. "Telephonic Reporting of the Press." n.s., 24 (1879–80): 65–68.
Divulged that *The Times* was ready to link its office by telephone to Parliament's Reporters' Gallery to save time and labor, but other London papers needed machine typesetting first. Reporters for the locals still used shorthand and telegraphy.

89. "The 'Puzzle Mania.'" n.s., 24 (1879–80): 114–16.
Studied puzzles, supposedly very popular in newspapers and magazines.

90. “English as Spoken at Radha Bazaar.” n.s., 26 (1880–81): 343–48.
Quoted language in stories and letters in several Indian newspapers.

91. “Sunday in Shoreditch.” n.s., 27 (1881): 108–14.
Glanced at newsboys with “sheafs of *Lloyd's* [*Weekly Newspaper*] and [*Weekly*] *Dispatches*” delivering to “a population given to Sunday papers.”

92. “Blunders in Print.” n.s., 29 (1882): 447–49.
Pinpointed press errors due to reporters' mishearing or misunderstanding and printers' mistakes.

93. “We and Our Fathers.” n.s., 34 (1884): 105–09.
Postulated that the current era was more “intellectual” than before but that pressure of time and lack of ability accounted for the popularity of magazines, which simplified ideas in “a seductive and digestible form.”

94. “Literature in the Scottish Capital.” n.s., 35 (1884–85): 61–68.
Nodded to the eighteenth-century Edinburgh press, from James Watson's *Courant* before the Act of Union to the 1728 *Evening Courant* (extant), the *Edinburgh Review*, and *Blackwood's Magazine*.

95. “The Cries of London.” n.s., 36 (1885): 33–37.
Heard among the criers were newsmen, who shouted about “alarming news,” whereas eighteenth- century men, as “Old Bennet, the News-Cryer,” sometimes used horns to get attention.

96. “American Newspapers.” n.s., 36 (1885): 340–45.
Drew on the United States Census Commission's data on newspaper circulation. Of the 78 pre-revolutionary journals (some named), 39 were extant in 1885 when the *Hartford Courant* was the oldest. Real growth was from 1840. In 1851 every town of 15,000 had a newspaper, and two were common in towns of 20,000. By 1880, when every hamlet had a herald, there were 771 dailies, 8,633 weeklies, 133 semiweeklies, 73 triweeklies, 40 biweeklies; 1,167 monthlies, 160 semimonthlies, two trimonthlies, 13 bimonthlies; 116 quarterlies, and six semiannuals. Newspapers devoted to ‘news, politics, and family reading’ numbered 8,863; religious, agricultural, commercial, professional, trade, juvenile, fashion, and literary numbered 2,451.

Aside that Mexico published the intensely religious newspaper, *Gazette de Mexico*, in the seventeenth century.

97. “The Paris Claque.” n.s., 36 (1885): 441–45.
Bruited that newspaper theatre critics were less influential in Paris because of the prevalence of their claques.

98. “Corners.” n.s., 39 (1886–87): 203–08.
Among the symbolic corners was the “Poets' Corner” in local newspapers, a space customarily open to all.

99. “Old Eton Days.” n.s., 39 (1886–87): 322–26.
Starred the *Eton College Magazine* and *The Kaleidoscope*, both short-lived but “well conducted” with some anonymous contributions of “considerable ability.”

100. "'Answers to Correspondents.'" n.s., 40 (1887): 11–12.
Blared that answers were a "prominent feature" in weekly magazines and newspapers. The most widely-circulated weeklies featured legal and medical questions, usually fairly answered but sometimes biased about products. Answers were especially popular in girls' papers because readers regarded editors as "infallible." Boys' papers did not publicize male concerns but rather information on hobbies and the military.

101. "A Century of Newspapers, 1688–1788." n.s., 42 (1888): 85–91.
Survey from the *Universal Intelligencer* to *The Times* registered that by 1692 there were 26 newspapers, some short-lived. Anne's reign brought the daily, stamp, and advertising duties, and the first generation of important writers, Daniel Defoe, Joseph Addison, Richard Steele, and Jonathan Swift. By 1714 there was a growing interest in news just as the stamp purged the press. Only "men of character and responsibility" survived. After 1715 caricature and advertising flourished, and marriage and obituary notices surfaced. Henry Fielding wrote excellent political ridicule in his *True Patriot*, Oliver Goldsmith penned for the *Public Ledger*, and John Wilkes and Junius were active. Yet the November 1758 *Tatler* quoted Samuel Johnson that newsmen lied for profit. In 1745 the all-advertising *Daily Advertiser* arrived and in 1770 the first theatre criticism. Previously, editors paid for such news, so critics encountered "much hostility." The *Gentleman's Magazine*, reputedly the oldest in the British Empire and maybe the world, was famous for its columns on Parliament.

102. "Thirty Years Ago." n.s., 42 (1888): 295–96.
Called John Delane the "supreme head" of journalists because he and *The Times* had much influence although other newspaper editors were energetic.

103. "Fifty Years Ago." n.s., 43 (1888): 30–34.
Recalled that there were many dailies, magazines, and reviews in 1838 but no illustrated newspapers, *Punch*, or telegrams.

104. "The Agony Column." n.s., 43 (1888): 275–78.
Decoded personal advertisements.

105. "American Types." 3d ser., 2 (1889): 126–29.
Singled out New York newsboys for their slang and the *New York Evening Post* as "the leading evening journal in the city and the representative of the highest culture and literary talent in the country."

106. "Slips of the Pen." 3d ser., 4 (1890): 64–66.
Explained that many newspaper printing errors occurred because "the pressure of rapid work in modern journalism is so great."

107. "Curios from the Daily Press." 3d ser., 4 (1890): 208–10.
Conceded that dailies, even with "excellent management," contained "blunders" due to haste, reporters' bad copy, and printing flubs.

108. "An Incorrigible Joker." 3d ser., 4 (1890): 377–81.
Biography of playwright Samuel Foote referred to "George Faulkner, printer of the *Dublin Journal*," as "a decent, quiet man."

109. "Writers and Reviewers." 3d ser., 6 (1891): 341–44.
Categorized reader press tastes: City men liked the daily's business section and maybe "heinous murder"; artisans liked self-help and sporting gazettes; clergy liked the "public prints" for which they also wrote; women liked the penny serials with novels and fashion. Tradesmen read little. Newspapers generally sold for their news, particularly if "spiced."

110. "John Leech." 3d ser., 7 (1892): 84–88, 100–06.
Review of W. P. Frith's *John Leech, His Life and Work* declared that his first *Punch* drawing (7 August 1841) on "Foreign Affairs" led to a circulation decline because few readers wanted overseas news. Thus, it was not until 1844 that he was a regular for the serial.

111. "A Day at the London Free Libraries." 3d ser., 7 (1892): 305–09.
Visited several local libraries, among them St. Martin's. It had a well-lit and well-occupied newsroom, a magazine room with fewer readers, and an evening boys' room where children aged five to 12 queued on Monday because there was entertainment. Every library had magazines and "newspapers of all kinds." Newsboys sparked reading of evening papers for sports, but men also read job advertisements. Curates looked for ideas in religious journals; women, for clothes in fashion ones.

112. "Charles Keene." 3d ser., 8 (1892): 177–81.
Review of George Layard's *The Life and Letters of Charles Samuel Keene* observed that he sketched for *Punch* for 40 years after 1851. He also illustrated *Once a Week*. Keene, John Leech, and John Tenniel made *Punch* a success, although Keene's work was less inventive than that of Leech. He did not sign his drawings C. K. until 1854 because, unlike modern journalists, he had no desire to see his name in print.

113. "The Penalties of Greatness." 3d ser., 8 (1892): 245–50.
Recognized that some readers coveted press coverage even though it often deprived an individual of freedom of action.

114. "Interviewers and Interviewing." 3d ser., 8 (1892): 422–26.
Berated American interviewers who, unlike English, harassed subjects and selectively printed their responses. In the United States, refusing an interview could lead to threats. In England, the "lackey type," a "hero-worshipper," was typical. Thus, British interviews of the great read like home furniture catalogues.

115. "Short Stories and Long." 3d ser., 9 (1893): 79–84.
Posited that critics castigated magazines of "scraps" because they "debauch" the many readers addicted to "shreds and patches," although short stories might be a fad.

116. "Anonymity." 3d ser., 9 (1893): 112–13.
Insisted that anonymity was less crucial than accuracy for the integrity of the press. Signed leaders supposedly reduced the writer's influence, but audiences should always form, never borrow opinions. Anonymity was a first chance for an unknown of quality, and anonymous criticism of their work was no disincentive for really great authors. Because subjects could not respond, publishing unsigned poison pen letters was inappropriate.

117. "The Reporter of the 'Evening Despatch'" 3d ser., 9 (1893): 301–03.
Satirized the modern reporter as rather "seedy," a person who fed on "[g]ossip and sensation" to earn a living but faced dismissal for a headline not fact-based.

118. "Circulating Libraries." 3d ser., 11 (1894): 488–90.
Logged that Liverpool's library began in 1758 when a group of men bought the *Monthly Review* and then shared other periodicals.

119. "A Century of Feminine Fiction." 3d ser., 12 (1894): 537–40.
Deemed the *Lady's Companion* an "eminently practical and common-sense little magazine."

Bentley's Miscellany, 1837–1868

Conceived by Richard Bentley for the amusement of a comfortable and literate audience, *Bentley's* emphasized British literary reviews, French newspapers and almanacs, and German almanacs.

1. Boz [Charles Dickens]. "Editor's Address on the Completion of the First Volume." 1 (1837): iii–iv.

Enthused that *Bentley's Miscellany* was "inundated with orders" and had invited "many of the very first authors of the day" to contribute.

2. [Maginn, William]. "Prologue." 1 (1837): 2–6.

Proclaimed that the goal of *Bentley's Miscellany* was to be witty, not to challenge other monthlies or to study politics.

3. [Mackay, Charles]. "Periodical Literature of the North American Indians." 1 (1837): 534–40.

Centered on Cherokee newspapers, especially the *Indian Phoenix* published by tribal editors. The *Phoenix*, published in English in Washington, allegedly circulated among "roving aborigines" and employed printers with the same skills as their peers at English local papers and better than the Germans or Portuguese.

4. Jones, John [Thomas Gaspey]. "Grub-Street News." 2 (1837): 425–28.

Based on evidence in the State Paper Office, credited George Iland as the father of *Grub-Street News*, which "fabricated intelligence."

5. [Beazley, Samuel]. "Lions of the Modern Babylon." 7 (1840): 80–88.

Mentioned that "one of those extraordinary daily papers with which the modern press teems" highlighted London pleasures.

6. Taylor, Dr. W. C. "Moral Economy of Large Towns: Liverpool." 8 (1840): 129–36.

Part of a series, this section recorded that workers found the pub "a comfortable place" to read newspapers on Sunday. Recommended opening reading rooms to offer "time and opportunity for quiet reflection" and to counter the pub's "depraving" environment.

7. "Theodore Edward Hook, Esq." 10 (1841): 320–24.

Touched on Hook's tenure as editor of *John Bull* where, "besides holding a share in the property, he was allowed, as we have heard, a handsome weekly salary for this duty." "[H]is lavish talent raised the publication at once into a high degree of popularity and profit."

8. [Forrester, C. R.]. "The Philosophy of Punning." 12 (1842): 316–24.
Observed that the *Morning Post* circulated puns from people of "notoriety in the circles of the aristocracy."

9. [Kenealy, E. V. H.]. "The Late Dr. Maginn." 12 (1842): 329–30.
Obituary of William Maginn cited his work for *Blackwood's Magazine*, the *Quarterly Review*, and *Bentley's* and swore that his contributions to the first "established his name as a writer of first-rate ability."

10. Poyntz, Albany [Catherine Gore]. "Clubs and Clubmen." 14 (1843): 453–63.
Agreed that "[c]lubs may be estimated as the fourth estate of the British Constitution: a moral exchange for the traffic and barter of opinion."

11. "Some Account of Miss Ray: Selwyn Correspondence." 14 (1843): 511–16.
Assumed from George Selwyn's letters that eighteenth-century journalists were different from those in 1843 "who now enrich the daily and weekly press with knowledge, and the excellences of their composition."

12. [Sinclair, Catherine]. "An [*sic*] Universal Newspaper to Suit All Tastes and Opinions: *The Whig and the Tory*." 15 (1844): 590–95.
Essay was set up as a newspaper with columns of news and advertisements and a promise to be impartial.

13. Murray, J. Fisher. "The Physiology of London Life: Business of the House." 16 (1844): 61–64.
Monitored reporters' reactions to a dull speaker in Parliament.

14. Murray, J. Fisher. "The Physiology of London Life: The Fourth Estate." 16 (1844): 275–85.
Declared that the daily newspaper was a necessity in London for information on business and pleasure. Men read their own copies whereas in the country a copy passed through many hands. Newspapers were "like clouds, gathering and sucking up the impalpable vapours of public opinion," which their leaders reflected while spreading knowledge. Leaders could paraphrase, promote, or rise above politics because anonymity assured that the text would be judged on its merits. News came from correspondents everywhere. Advertisements were merely the news of wants. Literary quality could win fame for a paper as in France.

15. [Pearce, Robert Rouière]. "The Rev. Sydney Smith." 17 (1845): 379–94.
Alluded to Smith's early connection to the *Edinburgh Review* whose first issue reputedly went to four editions and "created a great sensation" with its original articles.

16. "The Rev. Richard Harris Barham." 18 (1845): 198–200.
Noted that Barham "contributed much, during many years, to several popular periodicals – the *Edinburgh Review, Blackwood's Magazine*, and the *Literary Gazette* among the number; but his most popular series of papers was given to this *Miscellany*."

17. A Middle-Aged Man [Katharine Thomson]. "A Literary Retrospect: Dr. Maginn." 18 (1845): 587–92.

Detailed William Maginn's duel in consequence of an article in *Fraser's Magazine*. "No modern writer in periodicals has ever given to satire a less repulsive form of personality." "He wrote when our periodical literature was at its zenith."

18. K[enney], C[harles] L[amb]. "Memoir of Albert Smith." 18 (1845): 620–21.

Commemorated Smith's work for "the *Literary World* – a little periodical…started by [John] Timbs, the editor of the *Mirror* [*of Literature, Amusement, and Instruction*]," as well as for *Punch* and *Bentley's*.

19. The Author of "Second Love" [J. P. Simpson]. "The *Flâneur* in Paris." 21 (1847): 70–78.

Aside on sellers of Paris evening papers.

20. An American Lady [Elizabeth Wormeley]. "The Eventful Days of February 1848 in Paris." 23 (1848): 408–16.

Reported that Paris newspapers, such as the *Presse*, with "scraps" of news, "sold at famine prices" in February 1848.

21. Ward, James. "The Career of M. Guizot." 23 (1848): 435–47.

Revealed that the *Globe*, for which François Guizot wrote in 1828, "exercised considerable influence upon the rising generation of France."

22. [Sinnett, Jane]. "*Literary Statistics of France for Fifteen Years.*" 23 (1848): 456–64.

Review of Charles Louandre's book maintained that before 1848 France had about 500 newspapers. After the July Revolution, most emphasized politics, later trade. The larger ones kept or added subscribers with "the deplorable introduction of the *feuilleton*." France also had fringe papers, many specialized periodicals, and "a few reviews and magazines on the English plan."

23. Sinnett, Mrs. Percy [Jane]. "Gossip from Paris." 23 (1848): 636–39.

Grieved that French "[j]ournalism of course goes on at an awful rate, some 'Citizens' writing whole papers 'out of their own heads,'" such as the *Journal des Honnêtes Gens* and *Ami du Peuple*, and the women's *Voix des Femmes* and *Cause du Peuple* (George Sand's paper).

24. [Lewes, G. H.]. "Memoir of Sir E. Bulwer Lytton, Bart." 24 (1848): 1–10.

Recalled Bulwer-Lytton's editing of the *New Monthly*, "which flourished under his care as a Magazine, but did not flourish so well as a commercial speculation" and his "capital articles" in the *Edinburgh Review* and elsewhere.

25. The *Flâneur* in Paris [J. P. Simpson]. "The Republican Newspapers of Paris." 24 (1848): 147–54.

Dated a French free press from the February 1848 revolution, which ended the stamp duty and "caution money" paid by editors as "a guarantee for their respectability." However, mobs threatened papers, such as the *Constitutionnel* and *National*, that opposed the new government because cheap papers, multiplying even before the revolution, had turned workers toward a republic of "terror."

Gazettes, using lies to sell like those in the seventeenth-century Civil Wars, posted copies around Paris and at newsstands, "wooden booths or sheds" cropping up everywhere. Worse were the public criers, vendors whose "screaming fills the air."

26. Marvel, I. K. [D. G. Mitchell]. "Street Views in Paris from My Window, During the Late Insurrection." 24 (1848): 178–84.
Cited Paris newspapers published in February 1848.

27. Mathews, Mrs. [Anne]. "Our Times: *Un Peu de Déraison*." 24 (1848): 621–25.
Assured that "the freedom and infallibility of the press" were axiomatic even though commentary sometimes was misleading.

28. The *Flâneur* in Paris [J. P. Simpson]. "The Mirror of the French Republic; or, the Parisian Theatres." 25 (1849): 369–78.
Bowed to the "small daily satirical journals of Paris," such as *Charivari*.

29. "Memoir of William Cooke Taylor, LL.D." 26 (1849): 498–503.
Referred to Cooke Taylor's many essays in the *Athenaeum*.

30. "Literature: The Press During the Past Year." 27 (1850): 93–98.
Presumed that the press, "the mighty Press, so ambitious and so laborious," served as "a ready tool" for all interests, good and bad. *The Times*, with 30,000 copies daily and a corps of "able writers," was incomparable for "usefulness" and "completeness." "The Press of England is yearly doing wonders, in enlarging the knowledge, in refining the taste, in promoting the civilization and happiness of the human race." London publishers were "united and resolute" in their goal "to keep the press pure," so the few who pushed "trash" were disdained.

31. Bell, Robert. "The Stage as It Is in 1850." 27 (1850): 298–303.
Hoped that theatre critics would acquire "more knowledge and independence" and thereby regard reviewing not as an occupation but as a study of an art form.

32. "The Metropolis on Sunday." 27 (1850): 587.
Counted as one London Sunday activity "reading of the vile and blackguard portion of the periodical press."

33. [Bell, Robert]. "The History of Newspapers." 27 (1850): 596–97.
Review of F. Knight Hunt's *The Fourth Estate* contended that press history was important in tracing the liberty to print. Hunt's book was invaluable for its "repertory of facts," though it had some gossip.

34. [Chastel de Boinville, Alexander]. "The Past and Present State of France." 28 (1850): 172–79.
Disparaged Napoleon I because, during his reign, "[t]he press was reduced to the most abject slavery…the daily papers became the instruments of imposition and falsehood."

35. Crowquill, Alfred [A. H. Forrester]. "Our Pen and Ink Gallery: Lord Brougham." 28 (1850): 215–17.

Resurrected Henry Brougham's defense of John and Leigh Hunt on a charge of libel while editors of the *Examiner*.

36. [Mahony, Francis]. "Young England's Onslaught on *Young Italy*." 28 (1850): 298–306.

Review of A. D. R. Cochrane's book labeled the *Contemporaneo* "a remarkable journal" while disdaining the premier of the Papal States in 1849 who wrote newspaper articles "but would not tolerate other journalists in reply." Aside that the *Quarterly Review* no longer had "a permanent effect" on readers.

37. [Boissier, G. R.] "The Press of 1850." 29 (1851): 107–09.

Examined only books because "the daily press and the weekly and monthly periodicals" were a separate class, "too important an influence" to be dismissed with a few observations."

38. [Bell, Robert]. "Robert Southey." 29 (1851): 115–30.

Characterized Southey as a writer who reaped a good income from periodicals. In the first 97 issues of the *Quarterly Review*, he published 89 articles. His articles were varied, but he purportedly did research quickly and resented editorial changes to his work. The *Quarterly* earned respect and popularity even though its partisanship may have affected its quality.

39. [Bell, Robert]. "Literary Men of the Last Half Century." 29 (1851): 343–54.

Review of *Memoirs of a Literary Veteran* by Robert Gillies, founder of the *Foreign Quarterly Review*, questioned whether the public appreciated "the masculine power and wide-reaching knowledge poured out with such freshness and unfailing fertility in the columns of the daily papers" or by the "nameless labourers in the thousand and one periodicals" that instructed and amused. Neither Gillies as editor nor reviewers were paid well. Anonymity meant no reputation, so writers specialized and placed articles in many serials to survive. However, their literary careers were allegedly "wrecked in newspapers and magazines."

Both *Blackwood's Magazine* and the *Edinburgh Review* influenced reading, but the *Edinburgh* significantly shaped the canon of criticism. It was "consistently able, and luminous," whereas the *Monthly Review* and the *Gentleman's Magazine* were adequate. With new print technology, cheaper newspapers aired fast but less worthwhile criticism.

40. Hobbes, Robert G. "Calcutta." 30 (1851): 361–68.

Discussed the six English newspapers in Calcutta, all with editors "of experience and talent, who know how to suit the appetites of their customers." Papers were one-third leaders and local news, one-third advertising, one-third from London magazines. This press was no worse than the British and impacted government which it "fearlessly" criticized. Aside that there were 40 periodicals in the presidency.

41. [Creasy, E. S.]. "Memoir of the Right Honourable Thomas Babington Macaulay." 31 (1852): 1–6.

Literary biography noticed Macaulay's early work in *Knight's Quarterly Magazine* but credited his *Edinburgh Review* essays for making his name.

42. [Kaye, J. W.]. "Society in India." 31 (1852): 242–49.
Logged that the arrival of fortnightly newspapers and occasional reviews kept the English in India well informed about home affairs.

43. [Crowe, E. E.]. "Reminiscences of a Man of the World." 31 (1852): 273–80.
Doubted that in 1815 the newspapers, even *The Times*, had any war correspondents.

44. "The Late Baroness von Beck." 31 (1852): 314–19.
Article on alleged spy accused the public of blindly following "the dictation of the press of the privileged classes."

45. "*The Memoirs of Mallet du Pan*." 31 (1852): 553–57.
Reviewed a book by Jacques Mallet du Pan (b. 1749) on his career as a journalist. In 1784 he commenced editing the *Mercure de France* which he made famous. In the 1790s he was in exile in Switzerland but by 1799 was in London editing the *Mercure Britannique*.

46. [Crowe, E. E.]. "Paris in 1852." 31 (1852): 682–97.
Bared French middle class discontent with imperial press control, which "gagged and mutilated" the *Constitutionnel* and *Siècle*, though readers did not mind restraints on the socialist press. Even though official policy cost jobs, many people thought that this press had abused power but not Emile de Girardin's well-written *Presse*. It and Louis Véron of the *Constitutionnel* were remarkable good at undermining the emperor's "pretensions." The *Journal des Débats* and *National* were weak, and the requirement of signature sapped the spirit of journalists.

47. [Creasy, E. S.]. "Francis Jeffrey." 32 (1852): 127–31.
Biography of the editor of the early *Edinburgh Review* believed that it, the *Quarterly Review*, and *Blackwood's Magazine* set an example for "periodicals of vigour and entertainment," inspiring others that now gave "employment to so large a literary portion of the age; and from which the great majority of our educated classes form their literary opinions almost entirely, and, to a very great extent, their political opinions also."

48. [Crowe, E. E.]. "Memoirs of a Man of the World." 32 (1852): 257–72.
Profiled the literary men of Francis Jeffrey's Edinburgh world before commenting on the *Revue Française*, which failed because of "no sale, no influence, no reputation." An "enterprising printer" planned the more successful *Globe*, a "literary and philosophical paper" later edited by a Saint-Simonian, and a rival of the *National* of Adolphe Thiers and Armand Carrel. Thiers had written for the *Constitutionnel* when its owners were "timid bourgeois."

49. "*Autobiography of Alexandre Dumas*." 32 (1852): 471–78.
Stressed that the *Presse* owed "its great vogue and sale" to the serial work of Dumas, *père*.

50. Smith, Albert. "To the Readers of *Bentley's Miscellany*." 33 (1853): 1–2.
Reminisced about a first submission to *Bentley's* with "fear and anxiety" and the "great pride" on publication. Recently returned from the East, Smith promised to pen "light *pablum*" for the *Miscellany*.

51. Russell, W[illiam] H[oward]. "Dining Out for the Papers." 34 (1853): 143–50.
Times writer traced his career development from covering his first dinner party. Aside that newspaper offices were "interiorily seedy."

52. B[urgoyne], M[argaret] A., Our Own Correspondent. "Affairs in Turkey." 35 (1854): 593–603.
Testified that London papers sent special correspondents to war zones.

53. Monkshood [Francis Jacox]. "John Gibson Lockhart." 37 (1855): 27–31.
Saluted *Quarterly* editor Lockhart for raising "the tone and character" of the *Review* although in style he was a "heavy transgressor."

54. "The German Almanacks for 1855." 37 (1855): 176–85.
Alerted that in the German states, with a periodical press "almost in its infancy" because of censorship, almanacs' influence was akin to that of dailies in England. There were 13 in Prussia, four in Austria, two in Saxony, and one in Bavaria and in Hanover, but the most popular was Austria's *People's Almanack*. The *Illustrated Leipzig News* published the *Illustrated Almanack*.

55. "French War Pamphlets." 37 (1855): 451–66.
Perused one pamphlet that justified imperial legislation regulating the press because the papers had used their liberty for personal attacks, for "calumny," "injustice," and "exaggeration." The French resorted to pamphlets to criticize government rather than risk suppression of a newspaper, which would result in layoffs at dailies and ruin owners of small gazettes.

56. Monkshood [Francis Jacox]. "Prosings by Monkshood about the Essayists and Reviewers." 37 (1855): 479–93, 638–52; 38 (1855): 96–110, 129–36, 432–40, 462–73; 39 (1856): 430–40; 40 (1856): 104–10, 208–20, 316–30, 538–50, 640–52; 41 (1857): 563–70; 45 (1859): 581–92.
Remarked that periodical critics in the 1850s had to write an "original disquisition" on a book or a "critical appreciation of a new intellectual tendency" apparent in several texts; show how a new work was unique in its "mode of thought," or paint a literary portrait of "some representative man." Analyzed the style and topics of numerous periodical contributors and of *The Times*. Commented that J. W. Croker was the best example of "the slashing critic"; Leigh Hunt was less successful in managing periodicals than were Robert and William Chambers or Charles Dickens, and the *Foreign Quarterly Review* once courted Robert Southey. Wished that *Blackwood's Magazine* had published information on its contributors as *Fraser's Magazine* had done.

57. [Ainsworth, W. H.]. "How We are All Getting On." 38 (1855): 1–6.
Editor-owner (since 1854) expressed "utmost satisfaction" with *Bentley's* past work and confidence about its future quality.

58. "The Mormons in Utah." 38 (1855): 61–70.
Glanced at the Mormon press in Europe, France's *Etoile du Deseret* and Hamburg's *Banner of Zion* (three numbers only in 1851).

59. “Gilfillan’s *Portrait Gallery*.” 38 (1855): 136–40.
Review of George Gilfillan’s *A Gallery of Literary Portraits* informed that he contributed to the *Critic* as Apollodorus.

60. “Beaumarchais and His Times.” 39 (1856): 171–85, 293–303.
Biography of Pierre Augustin Caron cited the *Gazette Cuirassé*, a scandal paper published in England, and London’s *Courrier de l’Europe* and *Journal de Paris*.

61. “Lord Cockburn’s Memorials.” 40 (1856): 45–57.
Essay on Henry Cockburn, based on his *Memorials of His Time*, said that the early *Edinburgh Review* paid 10–20 guineas for a review page.

62. “The Newspaper in France.” 40 (1856): 457–69.
Review of Eugene Matin’s *Histoire du Journal en France, 1631–1853*, opened with Théophraste Renaudot, the physician who published the *Gazette de France* in 1631 and other papers of the age. Decided that the power of the press was not realized until 1789, but then liberty gave way to “libertinism” with language “only worthy of a revolutionary epoch.” The Directory suppressed “a parcel of useless journals.” The July Revolution spurred many short-lived papers, and the 1848 Revolution even more. This pattern confirmed that “the character of a nation is well depicted in the history of its press,” which in France seesawed from control to excess. In 1856 there were 14 newspapers, among them the *Journal des Débats*, which existed by “the grace of the Emperor” to show that the press was still free.

63. “Paris in 1856 – The French Almanacks.” 40 (1856): 477–87.
Tagged Amédée de Noé, known as Cham, “the Cruikshank of the French Almanacks.”

64. “What We Are All About.” 40 (1856): 487–94.
Alluded to the influence of *The Times* and the *Morning Post*.

65. [Wraxall, Lascelles]. “The Second Empire.” 42 (1857): 1–14.
Pondered the role of several newspapers in the February 1848 Revolution in France.

66. “Louis Philippe and His Times.” 42 (1857): 111–29.
Review of *History of the Reign of Louis Philippe* by Victor de Nouvion emphasized the press part in the July Revolution.

67. “Our Indian Empire.” 42 (1857): 258–65.
Opposed constraints on the Anglo-Indian press since it was “the most competent to judge the real condition of India.”

68. “French Almanacks for 1858.” 42 (1857): 535–46.
Centered on themes in French almanacs.

69. "German Almanacks for 1858." 43 (1858): 38–44.
Categorized German almanacs as "comic…amusing…instructive" and equal to the French in style but with more impact.

70. "The Causes of the Indian Mutiny." 43 (1858): 60–68.
Identified as one cause of the uprising the Anglo-Indian press from which Indian journals pirated criticism of the government. Sermonized that because India was "a subjugated country," a free press was illogical.

71. "Eugene Sue: His Life and Works." 44 (1858): 54–66.
Touched on Sue's literary contracts with the *Constitutionnel*, *Presse*, *Siècle*, and other publications.

72. "The French Almanacks for 1859." 44 (1858): 517–30.
Posited that French almanacs mirrored popular "fancies."

73. "German Almanacks for 1859." 44 (1858): 563–70.
Among a survey of German almanacs, called Berthold Auerbach's "informative and entertaining."

74. [Wraxall, Lascelles]. "A Frenchman in Kentucky." 45 (1859): 179–86.
Told of a former French soldier who in 1859 edited the *Semi-Weekly Messenger*, Oaksburg (KY).

75. [Ainsworth, W. H.]. "The State of Affairs: Political and Literary." 45 (1859): 221–24.
Deemed Alexander Andrews' *History of British Journalism* impartial and accurate with "rare information."

76. [Ainsworth, W. H.]. "Here and There." 46 (1859): 1–4.
Lauded briefly Charles Oliver who opted to be "a miscellaneous writer in the periodicals."

77. [Wraxall, Lascelles]. "Honoré de Balzac." 46 (1859): 148–56.
Included Balzac's editing, in the 1830s, of the short-lived literary review, *Chronique de Paris*.

78. [Ainsworth, W. H.]. "A Glance at Passing Events." 46 (1859): 331–34.
Considered French imperial policy on the press.

79. "The French Almanacks for 1860." 46 (1859): 460–69.
Examined contents of French almanacs.

80. "German Almanacks for 1860." 46 (1859): 567–73.
Rated German almanacs mediocre but significant for their wide circulation in "remote districts," whereas the French offerings were getting duller.

81. [Ainsworth, W. H.]. "The Epilogue to 1859." 46 (1859): 651–52.
Underscored the success of *Bentley's Quarterly Review* and the quality of *Bentley's Miscellany*.

82. "A German in London." 47 (1860): 55–61.
Rejected Julius Rodenberg's dismissal of newspaper advertisements because German journalists, unlike American journalists, did not appreciate their value.

83. "A Vacation Tour of Spain." 47 (1860): 412–22.
Pointed out a Valencia newspaper, the *Diario Mercantil*.

84. "The French Almanacks for 1861." 48 (1860): 458–70.
Skimmed contents of French almanacs.

85. "German Almanacks for 1861." 48 (1860): 615–21.
Broadcast that German almanacs had little or old news and humor pirated from *Punch* but surpassed the French in knowledge if not wit.

86. [Ainsworth, W. H.]. "The Present State of Literature." 49 (1861): 215–19.
Averred that literary periodicals recruited "the first men of the day" and that the genre stimulated the German though not the French press.

87. R. "Mems. [?Memorials] of an Unreported Meeting." 50 (1861): 74–79.
Commended "reporters for the public press" for giving sense and style to speakers, though perhaps missing audience nuances at a meeting.

88. "Count Cavour." 50 (1861): 88–94.
Recollected that Camillo di Cavour spent some time "hard at work as a journalist."

89. "The French Almanacks for 1862." 50 (1861): 480–90.
Held that French almanacs were neither as specialized nor as "business-like" as English ones.

90. "The German Almanacks for 1862." 50 (1861): 591–98.
Applauded German almanacs because they were "more national in their tone."

91. [Wade, John]. "Letters of Junius under Their Comic Aspect." 50 (1861): 611–19.
Assessed the style and sway of Junius in the *Public Advertiser*, where he was "the most bold and accomplished gladiator that ever figured in journalist columns."

92. Kohl, J. G. "The American Athens." 50 (1861): 620–32.
Pictured Boston's literary press. "There are upwards of 100 printing-offices, from which a vast number of periodicals issue. The best and oldest of these is the *North American Review*."

93. "The Moral Condition of the French." 51 (1862): 55–66.
Graded "the lighter and less moral productions of the French press" accurate but not representative of French character.

94. "Social Science and Sunny Scenes in Ireland." 51 (1862): 162–72.
Reporter at the Social Science Association meeting in Dublin heard "Miss Emily Faithfull with plain good sense describe the working of the Victoria Press, by which so many females are employed in a trade hitherto believed to be only fitted for men."

95. [Wraxall, Lascelles]. "A Real American." 51 (1862): 210–21.
Biography of William Walker reminded that he edited the New Orleans *Crescent*, then the San Francisco *Herald* before going to Central America.

96. [Wraxall, Lascelles]. "Travels in Equador [*sic*]." 51 (1862): 371–79.
Enlightened that Quito had a single paper, "the *Nacional*, which is the official journal of the government, and merely reprints ministerial decrees."

97. "Both Sides of the Atlantic." 52 (1862): 157–66.
Aside on poet Carl Heinzen who "edits the notorious *Pioneer*."

98. "A German in London." 52 (1862): 412–20.
Review of Julius Rodenberg's *Day and Night in London* abridged his ideas on the number of newspapers and their advertisements, the format of *Times* leaders (first on the topic of the day; second and third on contemporary history; fourth on London), and Reuters. Telegrams, once demeaned as "trickery and humbug," were popular. Many papers used Reuters, such as Paris' *Moniteur* and Cologne's *Zeitung*.

99. Knight, Brook J. "A Summer in America, VII." 52 (1862): 480–94.
Marked the *Church Chronicle for the Diocese of Montreal*, established in 1860.

100. "The French Almanacks for 1863." 52 (1862): 581–92.
Mused about contents of French almanacs.

101. "German Almanacks for 1863." 53 (1863): 26–34.
Excerpted contents of German almanacs.

102. Lessing, A. von "A German in Dublin." 54 (1863): 95–102.
Thought that Dr. Daniel Cahill, a Catholic priest, wrote "the best articles in the *Catholic Telegraph*."

103. "Gibson's *Miscellanies*." 54 (1863): 247–48.
Praised the work of William Sidney Gibson, a periodical author "so agreeable, so contemplative, and so competent."

104. "Chronicles of Paris." 54 (1863): 529–37.
Acknowledged the *Indépendance Belge*.

105. "The French Almanacks for 1864." 54 (1863): 577–92.
Announced that French almanacs ignored politics.

106. "German Almanacks for 1864." 55 (1864): 25–33.
Branded German almanacs dull.

107. "The French Almanacks for 1865." 56 (1864): 575–87.
Survey of French almanacs hypothesized that the "exceeding increase in the number of cheap papers in Paris" caused "excessive competition."

108. Jacox, Francis. "The Unwelcome News-Bringer." 56 (1864): 637–46.
Discussed the plight in history and literature of the bearers of false or bad news.

109. "Specimens of German Humour." 57 (1865): 310–22.
Looked at "the Prussian *Punch*," *Kladderadatsch*, whose large circulation meant good pay for its talented authors.

110. "Dudley Costello." 58 (1865): 543–50.
Hailed the quality of Costello's criticism, notably in the *New Monthly Magazine*.

111. "The French Almanacks for 1866." 58 (1865): 585–95.
Accepted the unvarying formula of French almanacs because it stimulated "pleasant… reminiscences."

112. "The German Almanacks for 1866." 59 (1866): 28–46.
Extracted at length from several German almanacs.

113. "Sketches of Sunny Scenes and Social Science in Switzerland." 60 (1866): 193–202, 319–30.
Sampled matrimonial advertisements in Thun's *Intelligenz-blatt*.

114. "The French Almanacks for 1867." 60 (1866): 597–612.
Contrasted serious and amusing French almanacs with aside on the competition among "halfpenny papers."

115. "The German Almanacks for 1867." 61 (1867): 94–110.
Found "more freshness and variety" in 1867 German almanacs but nothing on the Austro-Prussian War.

116. Estagel, John. "A Glance at New York." 62 (1867): 412–40.
Appraised the New York press. Dailies were printed "in meagre type, with pale ink, and on wretched paper." A *Pall Mall Gazette* would not last in United States because of its paper, print, and quality writing. The *New York Times* had some articles that were "well reasoned, excellent in taste, and written with force and spirit" but had recently had a dispute with the *New York Tribune* about 'doing English.' Although the *New York Herald* claimed to "lead journalism on the American continent," it was not as good as a British local. Conversely, American trade journals were solid, "edited in a practical and creditable manner." Monthlies were similar to the *London Journal* and *Family Herald*

but not as cheap and copied much from English papers. Quarterlies were "respectably edited and decently printed."

117. "Dufton's *Abyssinia*." 62 (1867): 487–98.
Review of Henry Dufton's *Narrative of a Journey Through Abyssinia, 1862–63*, aired that many areas of Africa and Asia lacked newspapers, but news spread nonetheless, usually in coffeehouses and bazaars.

118. "The French Almanacks for 1868." 62 (1867): 598–612.
Quoted several French almanacs.

119. "The German Almanacks for 1868." 63 (1868): 33–49.
Singled out a German almanac.

120. "Fenianism in America." 63 (1868): 129–33.
Imagined that New York dailies were a quasi-Fenian press.

121. "The Atlantic and Pacific Railroad." 63 (1868): 284–92.
Starred "our cosmopolite contemporary, the *Illustrated London News*."

122. "Indian Sporting Literature." 63 (1868): 527–39.
Estimated that Indian sporting periodicals were weak until the *Calcutta Sporting Review*, established in 1844, which contained "able and genuine articles."

123. B., M. V. "From London to Lahore." 64 (1868): 70–79.
Spotlighted an article from *Bentley's* in *Zapiski dla Chtenai*, a St. Petersburg review.

Bentley's Quarterly Review, 1859–1860

Richard Bentley founded *Bentley's Quarterly*, which touched on fiction in British serials and restrictions on the French press.

1. [Mozley, Anne]. "*Adam Bede* and Recent Novels." 1 (1859): 433–72.
Alluded to the opportunity to publish novels in "a popular periodical."

2. [Austin, Sarah]. "France." 1 (1859): 508–49.
Called the press of the Second Empire "crushed and fettered."

Blackwood's Edinburgh Magazine, 1824–1900

Established by William Blackwood with a Tory bias, *Blackwood's* contained myriad essays on the press, especially its influence everywhere. Other themes were literary criticism and newspapers' quality.

1. N., C. [J. G. Lockhart]. "Note on the *Quarterly* Reviewers." 15 (1824): 83–85.
Reckoned that the last number was the *Quarterly's* "very best" notwithstanding the departure of editor William Gifford and was especially satisfying, as the "cowardly ruffians" at some other periodicals had predicted that the review would suffer without him. The *Quarterly* "seems to have paid-off a host of heavy worthies…a dead-weight upon the spring of intellect" and turned to new writers, "people of the world." Aside on an *Edinburgh Review* contributor as "an inferior scribe."

2. [Maginn, William]. "Letters of Timothy Tickler, Esq. to Eminent Characters. To C. North, Esq., Etc. No. XIII: Mr. Theodore Hook." 15 (1824): 90–93.
Expressed "contempt for the people connected with the London newspapers" except those associated with *John Bull.*

3. [Lockhart, J. G.]. "Letters of Timothy Tickler, Esq. to Eminent Literary Characters. No. XIV: To Francis Jeffrey, Esq. on the *Westminster Review*, Etc." 15 (1824): 144–51.
Described writers in the *Westminster* as "clever, determined, resolute, thorough-going," some as educated as *Edinburgh Review* authors and as "well skilled…in the arts of communicating," and the neophyte review as "written well, with distinctness and vigour almost throughout, and occasionally very considerable power and eloquence."

4. Y., Y.Y. [David Robinson]. "*The Edinburgh Review*, No. LXXVIII, Articles I and IX: 'The State of Europe' and the 'Holy Alliance.'" 15 (1824): 317–33.
Painted the *Edinburgh* as "a blushless, lawless, furious, fanatical party publication." "The *Edinburgh* ostensibly exists as one of the supreme censors of the British press. Its avowed object is to sit in judgment upon the literature of the country" in articles by anonymous scribes who conformed to its opinions or faced suppression.

5. [Maginn, William]. "A Running Commentary on *The Ritter Bann*, A Poem, by T. Campbell, Esq." 15 (1824): 440–45.
Grumbled that there was "a dirty spirit of rivalry afloat at present among the various periodicals," except *Blackwood's* and the *Gentleman's Magazine*. *Blackwood's* promoted periodical literature, whereas the *New Monthly Magazine* was notorious for puffing.

6. "Office of the Lord Advocate of Scotland. *Edinburgh Review*." 15 (1824): 514–22.

Deprecated an *Edinburgh* article (January 1824) as "the work of a very coarse hand; at once commonplace in statement and feeble and inclusive in reasoning," full of "a farrago of contradictions" and "trash."

7. [Maginn, William and J. G. Lockhart]. "Letters of Timothy Tickler, Esq. to Eminent Literary Characters. No. XV: To Francis Jeffrey, Esq. on the Last *Westminster* and *Quarterly Reviews*." 15 (1824): 558–66.

Responded to James Mill's critique of other periodicals in the *Westminster* (April 1824). Supported a strong libel law to stop the "virulent publications which swarmed from the polluted press of London." Added that recent *Quarterly* essays (March 1824) were by "people who are absolutely and totally in a state of Cimmerianism." *See Westminster* 1: 206.

8. [Maginn, William]. "Letters of Timothy Tickler, Esq. to Eminent Literary Characters. No. XVI: To Christopher North, Esq. on the last *Edinburgh Review*." 15 (1824): 702–05.

Stamped another *Edinburgh* number (March 1824) "as stupid as usual...leavened by an extra portion of spite and malignity." Denied that "scribing for a newspaper...is a circumstance greatly to be rejoiced at."

9. [Maginn, William]. "Profligacy of the London Periodical Press." 16 (1824): 179–83, 438–39.

Pontificated that many magazines contained "filth, stupidity, or ignorance" and that "three-penny critics," like penny-a-liners, were jealous of their more successful colleagues. Among the offenders were the "idiots of the *New Monthly* [*Magazine*] who find evidences of a conspiracy against the liberties of the country in the Scotch novels" and the "VERMIN" in the *London Magazine* who targeted Walter Scott because he penned for *Blackwood's*. The *Westminster Review* admired authors who made women the butt of jokes and libeled those in public life. Rebutted a *London Magazine* retort by repeating earlier points.

10. [Maginn, William]. "Letters of Timothy Tickler, Esq. to Eminent Literary Characters. No. XVII: To Christopher North, Esq. on the Last *Westminster Review*." 16 (1824): 222–26.

Evaluation of a *Westminster* number (July 1824) assayed one article, "Travels in the United States," as "shabby trash."

11. [Lockhart, J. G.]. "Letters of Timothy Tickler, Esq. to Eminent Literary Characters. No. XVIII: To Christopher North, Esq. on the Last *Edinburgh* and *Quarterly Reviews*, and on Washington Irving's *Tales of a Traveller*." 16 (1824): 291–304.

Reacted to recent numbers of the *Edinburgh* (July 1824) and the *Quarterly* (January 1824) with "feelings of tedium and disgust" partly because these publications and the *New Monthly Magazine* pushed the books of their publishers.

12. Z., X. Y. [John Neal]. "American Writers." 16 (1824): 304–11, 415–28, 560–71; 17 (1825): 48–69, 186–207.

Profiled, among others, several journalists in a nation where "newspapers are everything" so the "ablest men write" for them, but magazines were increasingly original. Among people selected (others listed) were A. H. Everett, editor of the *North American Review*; Paul Allen, the first editor of the Maryland *Telegraph*, and Robert Walsh, Jr., whose *National Gazette* was "one of the very best papers."

13. Σ. [William Stevenson]. "On the Reciprocal Influence of Periodical Publications, and the Intellectual Progress of this Country." 16 (1824): 518–28.

Assessed contemporary newspapers as better for "power of thought...correctness of taste...elegance, and vigour of style" than those of 50 years before, but magazines had "common-place topics," worrisome because "periodical publications...are a surer index of the state and progress of the mind than works of a higher character." Serials had become more numerous, varied, and accurate since 1793, when war with France demanded greater "exertion of intellect." One example of the shift was the *Monthly Magazine*, a miscellany that gave way to specialized journals of more talent. Magazines with large circulations should "display fine or eloquent writing and leave readers with their taste purified, their comprehension enlarged, their judgment rendered stronger, and their habits of observation and reflection quickened and confirmed." Reviews, as the *Edinburgh*, *Quarterly*, and *Westminster*, were the leaders in literature.

14. A Constant Reader [William Maginn]. "MS. Notes on the Articles Concerning Ireland, the West Indies, Etc. in the Last Number of the *Edinburgh Review*." 17 (1825): 461–75.

Deemed the January 1825 *Edinburgh* "[a] poor Number upon the whole."

15. A Constant Reader [William Maginn]. "MS. Notes on the Last Number of the *Quarterly Review*." 17 (1825): 475–80.

Lauded prior *Quarterly* editor William Gifford though he occasionally was biased. The new man, John Taylor Coleridge, might be an excellent writer, but his choice of an opening article (March 1825) was not fit for the *London Magazine*, much less the *Quarterly*.

16. [Maginn, William]. "Letters of Timothy Tickler, Esq. to Eminent Literary Characters. No. XXI: To Malachi Mullion, Esq., M.D., F.R.S. Sec. of C. North, Esq. E.B.M." 17 (1825): 604–09.

Insisted that the *Westminster Review* "sells wretchedly" irrespective of its good writing. With less on politics and more on science and literature, it could crush the *Edinburgh Review*. Aside that libel laws "invest scoundrels with the character of martyrs."

17. [Maginn, William]. "Note-Book of a Literary Idler." 17 (1825): 736–44; 18 (1825): 233–40, 587–95.

Referred to a periodical writer as a "journalist."

Commented that the *Classical Journal* had limited sales but was not "ill executed," the paper and typography of the *Journal of Science* made it "almost as slovenly in appearance as the German periodicals," and the *North American Review* could improve.

18. "Letters of Timothy Tickler, Esq. to Celebrated Literary Characters." No. XXII: To John Murray, Esq., Publisher of the *Quarterly Review*." 18 (1825): 132–36.

Chronicled that the *Quarterly* declined after William Gifford's editorship and would need more than its "vigorous pace" to recover. The *Edinburgh Review* was "stupid," with falling sales, but still had influence. The recent number (June 1825) had poorly placed, untimely, and dull articles.

19. [Lockhart, J. G.]. "Remarks on Mr. Coventry's Attempts to Identify Junius with Lord George Sackville." 18 (1825): 164–77.

Review of George Coventry's *A Critical Enquiry Regarding the Real Author of the Letters of Junius* said less about Junius than about the *Edinburgh Review*.

20. N[eal, John]. "Late American Books." 18 (1825): 316–34.

Portrayed the *North American Review* as "a stout, serious quarterly" whose first six years did "little good, and less harm," but a "hug" from the *Edinburgh Review* indicated that the *North American* was not taken seriously.

21. [Maginn, William]. "French Literature of the Day." 18 (1825): 715–19.

Recognized the *Mémorial Catholique* as "a Periodical of talent and popularity" and the *Globe* as an impartial journal that was "grave, sensible, dignified" with "original and first-rate" criticism. *See* 19: 205.

22. [Wilson, John, William Maginn, David Robinson, and John Galt]. "Preface." 19 (1826): i–xxx.

Dated *Blackwood's* birth at a time when the *Quarterly Review*'s political influence was weak, the *Edinburgh Review* and the monthlies were anti-government, and *The Times* ignored "truth and decency." The *Examiner* was the "only readable Sunday paper," yet it published "unmixed infamy" and thirdhand stories written in "prurient language." John Scott insulted other periodicals to promote his *London Magazine*, and provincial papers were politically inconsequential. The *Monthly Review* was adequate. *Blackwood's* articles were controversial but revolutionized literary criticism by undermining "tenth-rate literary scribblers without head or heart" and "literary prostitution." Anonymity was acceptable because critics were known writers and egocentrics preferred attack to neglect. *Blackwood's* tried to help talented tyros and would print their work as space permitted. Although the editor was the "mildest of men," he was a despot about when and where to insert articles.

23. N., C. [William Maginn]. "The French *Globe* and *Blackwood's Magazine*." 19 (1826): 205–10.

Quoted the *Globe* reaction to *Blackwood's* tribute (18: 715). Confessed that *Blackwood's* liked to torment the *Edinburgh Review* and to support the *Quarterly Review* even when the latter did not reciprocate. Aside that foreign periodicals ignored the *New Monthly Magazine*.

24. L. "The *New Monthly Magazine* and the Margravine of Anspach." 19 (1826): 470–73.

Opined that Thomas Campbell, editor of the *New Monthly Magazine*, highlighted frivolity because he lacked the capacity for drudgery and the wit and power necessary to sustain a periodical. Captioned article (January 1826) certified the *New Monthly's* degraded level.

25. [Croly, George]. "Greece." 20 (1826): 824–43.
Petitioned for a public press to unite and educate Greeks and to defend liberty, as did the British press, by exposing government oppression and corruption.

26. [Robinson, David]. "The Change of Ministry." 21 (1827): 745–62.
Translated press political partisanship as being a "slave" to government.

27. [Robinson, David]. "Mr. Huskisson's Speech on the Shipping Interest." 22 (1827): 1–17.
Swore that newspapers were "a disgrace and a scourge to the country."

28. [Robinson, David]. "The Faction." 22 (1827): 403–31.
Objected to the contents of the *Edinburgh Review* (June 1827) and the claims to "omniscience" by the *Morning Chronicle* and *The Times*.

29. [Wilson, John]. "A Preface to a Review of the *Chronicles of the Canongate*." 22 (1827): 531–56.
Placed reviewing "at the lowest possible ebb" because the decline of professional, if cruel critics meant lower pay for the less abusive but less talented, "the menial, the flunky reviewing race." The *Edinburgh Review* originally "assumed the dictatorship, not only of taste, but of genius," but in 1827, it, the *British Critic* together with the "Reviews – only in name," the *Quarterly* and the *Westminster*, flourished.

30. [Croly, George]. "Sentiment." 23 (1828): 194–95.
Assumed that life in London sired newspapermen of common sense, while country weeklies spawned the sentimental without "sagacity or skill."

31. [Wilson, John]. "*Lord Byron and Some of His Contemporaries*." 23 (1828): 362–408.
Review of Leigh Hunt's book discussed the *Liberal*, "the poorest of all Periodicals," because Hunt was not at his best and Lord Byron sent only his secondary works there.

32. McGillicuddy, Phelim, A Suffering Papist. [Edward Johnston]. "The Reviewer Reviewed." 23 (1828): 917–21.
Charged the *Edinburgh Review* with bias.

33. [Robinson, David]. "The 'Breaking in upon the Constitution of 1688.'" 25 (1829): 503–24.
Stated that the "more influential" country newspapers and the London press were "directly opposed." Country gazettes were "sound in principle, and in respect of talent" and circulated more viewpoints than London morning papers. They were all "ably written," but individual heralds were slanted because the same person penned leaders irrespective of topic.

34. [Wilson, John]. "Monologue, or Soliloquy on the Annuals." 26 (1829): 948–76.
"Periodical Literature – how sweet is the name!" Attributed more reading to the impact of early periodicals, such as the *Gentleman's Magazine*, *Monthly Review*, *Critical Review* and *British Critic*, and the later

Edinburgh Review and *Quarterly Review*. Based on *Forget-Me-Not* (with "extensive circulation") and others, commended annuals' engravings. Marked "Alaric Watts as the Father of the Annuals."

35. N., C. [John Wilson]. "Notice." 27 (1830): 539–40.
Counseled contributors to *Blackwood's* to submit essays that were original and fit its format.

36. [Wilson, John]. "Notices to Correspondents." 28 (1830): 136–44.
"A rejected contributor is the bitterest of all enemies – but likewise the most impotent." Hinted that *Blackwood's* rejected many manuscripts because authors needed more talent to write for a "first-rate periodical" than for a quality book. Only six women met its standards: Felicia Hemans, Caroline Norton, Caroline Bowles, M. R. Mitford, Geraldine Jewsbury, and one unnamed. Others should mail their papers elsewhere, possible since Great Britain and Ireland had about 100 monthlies and weeklies, about the same as France and the German states. Among men, the Scots were "too philosophical," so few "first-rate contributors" came from Edinburgh.

37. [De Quincey, Thomas]. "France and England." 28 (1830): 699–718.
Realized that leader-writers for dailies had "little time for reflection" unlike those for weeklies and that editors could not admit mistakes for "ruin would follow the confession of an error." Asides on "the endless caprices of *The Times*" and the *Standard's* celebration of the July 1830 revolution spearheaded by the press.

38. [De Quincey, Thomas]. "Political Anticipations." 28 (1830): 719–36.
Opposed ending stamp and postal charges on newspapers, despite growing pressure to eliminate them, because they stopped "ruinous diffusion of political irritations" to the poor. Abolition, coupled with print technology, would bring a flood of "smaller, coarser" journals, as in the United States. Country gazettes, "more amenable to the court of public opinion," might "retain some deference to the decencies of life, but the "London newspaper will abandon itself to a ruffianism worse by much, because more ingenuous and elaborately varied, than that of Kentucky." "The press, the incendiary press, is on the eve of a great revolution," although the cost (c. 5,000 pounds) to establish a newspaper might make radicals think like capitalists.

39. [Alison, Archibald]. "On the Late French Revolution." 29 (1831): 36–45, 429–46, 745–62, 919–35; 30 (1831): 281–95, 765–81.
Cautioned that the growth of a "liberal and radical" press was synonymous with a "diffusion of errors" because all newspapers confirmed some opinions and shaped others by topic selection. To urban masses incapable of forming rational opinions, journals had the authority of the Bible. This audience was particularly susceptible to widely circulated papers that preached change. As the United States proved, editors catered to such readers with ideas of democracy and equality that drove out ideals of "virtue or talent." Quoted the *Memoirs* of Thomas Jefferson (IV: 38) that such a press was in a "putrid state" with writers of "malignity, vulgarity, and malicious spirit." Aside that the earlier French *Ami du Peuple* was "inflammatory."

40. [Robinson, David]. "The Local Government of the Metropolis, and Other Populous Places." 29 (1831): 82–104.
Expressed anxiety about the press, one of the "guides of public opinion" of upper-class readers and increasingly the mirror of the rest in order to sell. Adding lower-class readers tended to "emancipate

the press from the control of public men." Previously, the government and the opposition had their own newspapers "to correct the press by means of the press." Since Lord Liverpool, both sides bribed privately owned journals, often in the hands of Scots and Irish "hostile to England" and of businessmen who prioritized profit rather than issues. Simultaneously, reviewers had become "literary mechanics," disdaining morals in their critiques, and London Sunday papers, equally immoral and also irreligious, had acquired too much clout.

41. [Wilson, John]. "Reformers and Anti-Reformers – A Word to the Wise from Old Christopher." 29 (1831): 721–31.

Thundered that most London dailies were full of "trash and falsehood" about politics, so the Tories had to support the *Standard*, *Morning Post*, and *John Bull*.

42. [Johnston, William]. "Parliamentary Sayings and Doings." 29 (1831): 732–44.

Avouched that people read *The Times* "occasionally" for news and advertising because the style of its commentary was not good.

43. [Wilson, John]. "The Lord Advocate on Reform." 29 (1831): 980–1010.

Reiterated that the Tory press was ineffective.

44. The Whig-Hater [William Johnston]. "The Late Elections in England." 29 (1831): 1011–16.

Viewed newspapers as "great engines of political influence" because they reached people in villages and alehouses who read or were read to by others. Tribunes, both in London and the country, might direct middle-class opinion but promoted revolutionary ideas among workers because they "flatter the people and their prejudices" with "agreeable lies."

45. The Author of 'Parliamentary Reform and the French Revolution' [Archibald Alison]. "Remote Causes of the Reform Passion." 31 (1832): 1–18.

Imagined that the "extraordinary prevalence of magazines and reviews and the immeasurable increase of the daily press" were signs of a "restless temper." Because popular journals lied and even talented contributors aroused emotions, the press corrupted not only its growing mass audience but also upper-class readers.

46. [Eagles, John]. "What Caused the Bristol Riots?" 31 (1832): 465–83.

Answered the title question by saying that one factor was the influence of the press. The local press was "revolutionary," and the London was "foolish" about politics.

47. Satan [John Eagles]. "The Art of Government Made Easy." 31 (1832): 665–72.

Warned that liberty of the press could be a mighty weapon against enemies, especially when used by the seditious anxious for power.

48. [Alison, Archibald]. "Dumont's *Recollections of Mirabeau*." 31 (1832): 753–71.

Review of Etienne Dumont's book classified most readers of dailies as "either totally incapable of forming a sound opinion on any subject of thought, or so influenced by prejudice as to be inaccessible to the force of reason, or so much swayed by passion…or so destitute of information" to be logical.

49. [Alison, Archibald]. "Salvandy on the Late French Revolution." 31 (1832): 965–80.

Review of N. A. Salvandy's *Seize Mois, ou La Révolution et Les Révolutionaires* borrowed from it on the role of the French press in the July Revolution.

50. [Alison, Archibald]. "*Memoirs of the Duchess of Abrantés*." 32 (1832): 35–54.

Review of a book on France, 1789–1815, pirated that editors of papers opposed to Napoleon I were "delivered over to military commissions" and their presses thrown into the Seine.

51. [Alison, Archibald]. "The Fall of the Constitution." 32 (1832): 55–75.

Noted the political influence of the press in Britain.

52. [Alison, Archibald]. "The Spanish Revolution." 32 (1832): 328–42.

Held the local press partly responsible for the recent revolutions in Spain.

53. [Alison, Archibald]. "Prospects of Britain under the New Constitution." 32 (1832): 343–58.

Touched on the "taxes on knowledge." Bemoaned that the Tories supported the "higher departments of literature," as the *Quarterly Review*, but not dailies and weeklies, which reached more people.

54. [Alison, Archibald]. "Foreign Affairs." 32 (1832): 614–38.

Quoted the *Life of Lafayette*, by his aide-de-camp Sarrans, that a free press during the French Revolution eroded state authority.

55. H., T. W. [William Johnston]. "On Affairs in General." 32 (1832): 684–92.

Fretted that British "freedom of the Press was certainly the most abused freedom that the world ever saw –falsehood is diffused – truth is withheld."

56. [Alison, Archibald]. "The French Revolution of 1830." 32 (1832): 931–48.

Affirmed that the French press, whenever unfettered after 1789, was a destructive force in society.

57. An Inhabitant of the Island. "A Short Statement of the Causes That have Produced the Late Disturbances in the Colony of Mauritius." 33 (1833): 199–205.

Blamed local gazettes, controlled by lawyers who eluded restrictions on the press, for stirring up unrest against the government in Mauritius.

58. [Croly, George]. "The Life of a Democrat: A Sketch of Horne Tooke." 33 (1833): 963–83; 34 (1833): 206–31.

Biography of John Horne Tooke in which Part I centered on his opposition to John Wilkes; Part II tracked newspapers from the *acta diurna* to the Venetian *gazetta*, then English development during the Civil Wars. Robert Walpole was in a "perpetual newspaper war," but by the reign of George III, "newspapers [were] a general indulgence of the nation." Junius reinvigorated the press with his "singular felicity of language."

59. [Alison, Archibald]. "America. No. I." 34 (1833): 285–308.
Review of Thomas Hamilton's *Men and Manners in America* agreed with him that American newspapers were inferior to English. American heralds, in a "ruffian vocabulary," aired "villainy" however "gross or improbable" about political opponents rather than enlightened people about politics. Because papers were cheap, they drew buyers from the ignorant. In England, a higher price meant more educated readers and writers of ability and knowledge. Without a stamp, there would be two presses, rich and poor, and with democracy would come the "perpetual…debasement of the press, which is the great modeler of public thought."

60. [Alison, Archibald]. "France in 1833." 34 (1833): 641–56, 902–28.
Declared that liberty of the press was the only freedom to survive the July Revolution but had generated licentiousness and sedition despite government prosecutions. However, officials avoided censorship or suppression since those led to the 1830 upheaval. English dailies were run by persons "of great ability but in general of inferior grade in society" while French were the reverse. French politicians penned for or conducted papers because those roles had more prestige than membership in the Chamber of Deputies, turning Paris journalism into a "wild and intemperate republican press."

61. [Alison, Archibald]. "Progress of Social Disorganization." 35 (1834): 228–48.
Accused British "lower journalists" of "incessant pandering" to the "corrupt and vicious inclinations" of the masses, fanning discontent, and printing "innumerable falsehoods." Some penny magazines amused or shared practical information but not moral guidance; others disseminated the ideas of Thomas Paine, the *Black Dwarf*, or *The Woman of Pleasure*. Feared that Britain would "sink under the vulgarity of American journalism or the corruptions of French sensuality" now witnessed in London's "licentious periodicals."

62. [Wilson, John]. "Whig Prosecutions of the Press." 35 (1834): 295–*310.
Endorsed restraints on the press if it threatened political stability in dangerous times, but prosecution for seditious libel of the *True Sun* was not valid. While the paper's advice was "rash and wrong," it did not advocate physical force. Equally wrong was the attack, purportedly sanctioned by some Whig papers, on the editor of the *Newcastle Journal* (for anti-Whig handbills and paragraphs) by "a gang of five ruffians." Asides that *John Bull* was "the wittiest of the witty" and the *Standard* was "a paper unsurpassed in principle and unequalled in power."

63. [Alison, Archibald and Arnout O'Donnel]. "Results of the Triumph of the Barricades." 36 (1834): 209–27.
Contrasted British press freedom with French after the July Revolution, the first restraining aristocracy and the second encouraging democracy.

64. [Alison, Archibald]. "The Influence of the Press." 36 (1834): 373–91.
Linked "great changes of recent times" to the press but bewailed its effects on "the lower orders" and "the depraved principles of our nature." "Higher branches" of periodicals addressed to the "really educated" were exceptions but had small audiences. The majority read papers that "laud their wisdom, and magnify their capacity, and flatter their vanity," conveying a sense of power to them. Dailies were driven by numbers of readers; "[e]ditors and journalists," by gain. To counteract this trend, papers should be subject to state supervision of standards. *See Westminster Review* 21: 498.

65. [Lockhart, J. G.]. "Death of Mr. Blackwood." 36 (1834): 571–72.
Obituary of William Blackwood stated that his goal in establishing *Blackwood's* was to restore quality to magazine literature, so he was directly involved in its publication. A man who adhered to his principles, he inspired the "respect and confidence" of contributors.

66. [Moir, George]. "A Glance at the German Annuals for 1835." 37 (1835): 386–90.
Scanned German annuals from the eighteenth-century *Hinkende Bote*, previously an almanac to which famous German authors contributed. Compared to the excellent illustrations in the *Literary Souvenir* of A. A. Watts, German engravings were poor except for *Minerva* in 1831. Most German almanac scribes (several named) wrote badly. The annuals from Vienna, as *Vesta* and *Huldigung der Frauen*, were better than most. *Vergiss-Mein-nicht* showed talent but not taste. Among others were *Taschenbuch der liebe unde Freundschaft*, *Urania*, *Cornelia*, and *Penelope*.

67. [Wilson, John]. "Mant's *British Months*." 37 (1835): 684–98.
Review of Richard Mant's titled work suspected that millions read *Blackwood's* in Britain and "hundreds of thousands" in Ireland.

68. [Alison, Archibald]. "Change of Ministry." 37 (1835): 796–814.
Signaled that newspapers and magazines increasingly supported order, not revolution in politics.

69. [Alison, Archibald]. "Conservative Associations." 38 (1835): 1–16.
Maintained that a society with many readers was "democratical," acceptable when balanced by property, education, and rural loyalty. With urbanism, the "revolutionary hydra in the periodical press" was dangerous. Conservatives should purchase the "ablest" papers and circulate them among workers and continue the "higher" Conservative periodicals, as the *Quarterly Review*, and magazines, as the *New Monthly*, *Fraser's*, and the *Dublin University*.

70. [Bell, George Hamilton]. "India." 38 (1835): 803–08.
Worried that the free press, a "blessing" in England, would be a tool to disseminate revolution in India. Cancellation of press restrictions would "proclaim to every native of India that a hundred millions of men are held in subjection by about 30,000 foreigners."

71. [Badham, C. David] "Paris Mornings on the Left Bank of the Seine: The Sorbonne of 1835." 39 (1836): 296–312.
Profiled, among others, St. Marc Girardin, editor of the *Journals des Débats*.

72. [White, James]. "Hints to Authors. No. VII: On the Critical." 39 (1836): 607–18.
Satirized styles of literary criticism, especially the "accurate" and the gossiping," and advised on how to write it.

73. [Croly, George]. "The World We Live In." 40 (1836): 609–26; 41 (1837): 33–48; 42 (1837): 309–30, 506–25, 796–814.
Essay on many topics alerted that, as the press was "the great organ of public reason," people must watch who played it. A free press was fine unless it promoted rebellion against a legitimate king (Charles X) or tolerated tyranny (Louis Philippe). In all British newspapers, for country papers

followed London, leaders were "solemn and sarcastic"; foreign departments "subtle and sagacious"; accident columns "startling" but often "merciless invention" in hyperbole. Alternatively, American gazettes were "a powerful instrument" with "irresistible" descriptions. They were "the national food" prepared by "dashing, daring" editors who "combine Hibernian effrontery, English nonchalance, and French coxcombry." Readers who disagreed with editors did not send letters, as in England, but cancelled their subscriptions. Asides on the circulation of the *New York Herald* (30,000–40,000) and the difficulties of getting American subscribers to pay for their newspapers.

74. [Alison, Archibald]. "Democracy." 41 (1837): 71–90.
Guaranteed that *Blackwood's* stopped revolution in 1831 while other Tory publications did little. The *Morning Post*, though it supported *Blackwood's*, had few able journalists and was the newspaper read in a "fashionable lady's boudoir."

75. [Swinton, Archibald C.]. "A Word in Season to the Conservatives of Scotland." 41 (1837): 241–51.
Reminded that periodicals survived on subscriptions and advertising.

76. W[arren, Samuel], An Old Contributor. "Pegsworth: A Press-Room Sketch." 41 (1837): 523–28.
Recorded press reactions to an execution.

77. [Wilkes, John]. "Thiers." 43 (1838): 311–30.
Glanced at Adolphe Thiers' work for the *Constitutionnel.* The French press was more influential than English dailies because it spoke to "light" rather than "reflective" readers. English audiences read papers to get information in order to form their own opinions "conscientiously and individually adopted"; French, to receive opinions developed by others. French journalists advanced their own political careers rather than national principles.

78. "Colonial Misgovernment." 44 (1838): 624–37.
Perceived Malta as nothing but a Mediterranean fortress whose people "were disaffected" and unready for the free press which they sought.

79. [Alison, Archibald]. "Secular and Religious Education." 45 (1839): 275–86.
Was uneasy about the impact of the "Radical Press" on workers with only a secular education.

80. [White, James]. "Literature in the Jungles." 47 (1840): 342–54.
Posited that the *Oriental Sporting Magazine* (Bombay), penned by soldiers who wrote on hunting, exemplified how British "sporting magazines, Old and New, contain some of the best writing of the present day."

81. [Smith, William Henry]. "Wild Oats – A New Species." 47 (1840): 753–62.
Announced that the press was the "only fit organ of communication" for literary failures.

82. [O'Donnel, Arnout]. "Progress of Protestantism in France." 47 (1840): 763–78.
Pointed out that "journalism" was the name "under which all periodical publications are included," but that "where there is a newspaper there is power." Called for a European-wide Protestant daily to complement the French *Esperance*.

83. [Maginn, William]. "The Tobias Correspondence." 48 (1840): 52–63, 205–14.
Satirized topics of newspaper leaders and remarked about newspaper language and layout.

84. [Jones, H. Longueville]. "France." 48 (1840): 522–34.
Discerned that young men in England entered business and in France went to "that worst portion of the literary world, the public political press," as critics, "*feuilletonists*," or "paragraph-mongers."

85. [De Quincey, Thomas]. "Foreign Politics." 48 (1840): 546–62.
Speculated that readers of dailies might doubt the validity of all reports because the press regularly printed inaccurate news of foreign affairs.

86. [O'Donnel, Arnout]. "France *versus* England." 49 (1841): 457–75.
Registered that France "lately prosecuted certain journals."

87. [Murray, J. Fisher]. "The World of London." 50 (1841): 327–39, 477–89, 767–78; 51 (1842): 639–53.
Part of a series examined the press. The newspaper was "a reflex of the public mind, a *camera* fixing upon its broad sheet the evanescent images of the day," and a "grand medium of publicity" thanks to advertising. Local papers had more unanimity and less trivia than metros. Among journalists, the middle-class Irishman was often "reporting for the public press, for which he has established a reputation of peculiar talent." His compatriots were also subeditors and even editors, though rarely owners of local papers and wrote for magazines and reviews, where a classical education was important. Newspaper theatre critics exercised power, sometimes ruining a career by praising early work.

88. [Finlay, George]. "The Bankruptcy of the Greek Kingdom." 54 (1843): 345–62.
Applauded the Greek free press, which included newspapers.

89. A Designing Devil [Catherine Gore]. "The New Art of Printing." 55 (1844): 45–49.
Welcomed illustrations, even in the "scandalous Sunday" newspapers whose goal was "unveiling their libels in caricature," because people were too busy to read periodicals and dailies. Prophesized that pictures would soon dominate sports reporting and advertising, MPs would supply press photos, and penny-a-liners would go.

90. William, John [Samuel Phillips]. "News from an Exiled Contributor." 55 (1844): 184–96.
Delineated Melbourne newspapers: the *Patriot*, *Herald*, and *Gazette*, all twice weekly with many advertisements resulting in owners' profits of 4,000–5,000 pounds a year.

91. [Smith, William Henry]. "M. Louis Blanc." 56 (1844): 265–77.
Review of Blanc's *Histoire de Dix Ans* singled out "M. Louis Blanc, a democratic journalist, with all, and perhaps more than the usual talents of the Parisian journalist."

92. [Hardman, Frederick]. "Letters and Impressions from Paris." 60 (1846): 411–27.
Based on the ideas of Karl Gutzkow, spotlighted some French journalists. Emile de Girardin led a *Presse* with talented writers. Jules Janin, "the feuilletonist of the *Débats*" and "a professed critic," was "a journalist, and a journalist only; he aspires to be no more." By contrast, many theatre critics and actresses traded favors, and duels were a tool to destroy competitors.

93. An Old Contributor [Samuel Warren]. "Things in General; A Gossiping Letter from the Seaside to Christopher North, Esq." 60 (1846): 625–44.
Characterized newspapers as "a very great honour to Great Britain" because of their "ability, energy, accuracy, and amazing promptitude" in gathering world news. "The public is this vast creature – the press are the tentacles." All institutions benefited from press scrutiny and from morning dailies that commented on the prior evening's parliamentary speeches quickly with logic and style, thus influencing opinion.

Spain's press was silenced, its personnel fined and imprisoned. In the United States, newspapers were generally "pandering to the vilest passions." When the London press went in this direction, the public acted as a censor. Journalists served as a further check on each other for accuracy.

94. [Coxe, Cleveland]. "'Maga' in America." 62 (1847): 422–31.
Indicted Americans for pirating *Blackwood's*, at first through some reprints in "literary periodicals… and daily newspapers," but in 1847 "Reprint and Company" republished whole volumes at a cheaper price. No one bought the *Edinburgh Review* except "clannish provincials in Boston," but *Blackwood's* circulated widely. Reprints warned of "SPURIOUS AND HIGHLY PERNICIOUS IMITATIONS" even though the reprints themselves were not authorized and realized their profits without cost or effort.

95. [Coxe, Cleveland]. "American Copyright." 62 (1847): 534–46.
Reported that American dailies regularly carried unauthorized local reprints of British periodicals, as *Blackwood's*, perhaps because periodicals and dailies were "great manufacturers and exponents of public opinion." William Cullen Bryant was "active, as editor of the *New York Evening Post*," on the copyright issue. Aside that the American *Literary World* was "a periodical of the *Spectator* class."

96. [Bristed, C. A.]. "The Periodical Literature of America." 63 (1848): 106–12.
Postulated that British audiences knew about American newspapers from extracts in their own press, but less about American periodicals though they numbered 4,000 and were relatively cheap (four to five dollars per year). "[O]ne of the superficial peculiarities of American magazines is that the names of *all* the contributors are generally paraded conspicuously on the cover." Magazine style was bad but not "disfigured by the violence and exaggeration" of dailies. Monthlies were crude; quarterlies, soporific. Magazines did not pay or paid their contributors poorly because editors had little money. The results were that no effort was put into literary criticism and "unity of tone" was impossible without a "permanent corps of writers." Contributors without a broad liberal education apparently could not be independent in the face of democracy, powerful interests, and provincialism. International copyright would boost original work. Aside that the *Courier and Enquirer* was the best New York daily.

97. [Neaves, Charles]. "*Blackwood* and Copyright in America." 63 (1848): 127–28.
Pleaded for international copyright of periodical materials. *Blackwood's* was the "champion of the rights of authors" in the United States. By fighting cheap reprints of elite British periodicals, from which "weekly pirates" stole, it encouraged the growth of quality American serials.

98. [Simpson, J. P.]. "Republican Paris: March, April 1848." 63 (1848): 573–88.
Witnessed in Paris, spring 1848, "old established newspapers…submerged in this deluge of republican prints" as a wide range of journals were hawked.

99. [Alison, Archibald]. "How to Disarm the Chartists." 63 (1848): 653–73.
Bowed to the *Glasgow Daily Mail*, "conducted with much ability," and the *Jamaica Despatch*, which reflected the views of island whites.

100. [Moir, George]. "American Feeling Towards England." 63 (1848): 780–84.
Reassured that "among the higher organs of periodical literature" in the United States and the United Kingdom there was a feeling of "mutual respect."

101. Ernest [Cleveland Coxe]. "American Thoughts on European Revolutions." 64 (1848): 31–39; 65 (1849): 190–201.
Indicated the impact of telegraphy on journalism.

102. [Hardman, Frederick]. "*Eighteen Hundred and Twelve*: A Retrospective Review." 64 (1848): 190–207.
Review of Lewis Rellstab's book unveiled him as an outstanding music critic for and editor of several newspapers.

103. [Hardman, Frederick]. "Satires and Caricatures of the Eighteenth Century." 64 (1848): 543–56.
Review of Thomas Wright's *England under the House of Hanover* referred to essays and reviews in eighteenth-century publications, as the *North Briton* of John Wilkes.

104. [Hardman, Frederick]. "What Is Spain About?" 64 (1848): 627–31.
Spotted Barcelona's *Constitucional* as "one of the few remaining papers in Spain which now and then venture to speak the truth" until suppressed.

105. [Aytoun, William E.]. "Modern Biography – Beattie's *Life of Campbell*." 65 (1849): 219–34.
Review of William Beattie's *Life and Letters of Thomas Campbell* mentioned his writing for the *Morning Chronicle* and editing of the *New Monthly Magazine* and *Metropolitan*.

106. [Alison, Archibald]. "Macaulay's *History of England*." 65 (1849): 383–405.
Deemed eighteenth-century periodical essays "elegant and amusing." Those in the *Edinburgh Review* were different, with "vigour of thought, fearlessness of discussion, and raciness of expression." The *Edinburgh* not only revised literary criticism but introduced the critical historical essay, masked as a review, full of thought and knowledge but shorter to read than a book. Featured such early contributors as Francis Jeffrey, Sydney Smith, and T. B. Macaulay.

107. [Alison, Archibald]. "Lamartine's *Revolution of 1848*." 66 (1849): 219–34.
Review of Alphonse de Lamartine's book credited the press for French revolutions in 1830 and 1848.

108. [Hogan, J. S.]. "Civil Revolution in the Canadas." 67 (1850): 249–68.
Regarded the *Boston Atlas* as "the great leading journal of the New England states," with statesmen as writers as in England.

109. An Old Stager [William E. Aytoun]. "A Lecture on Journalism." 68 (1850): 691–97.
Questioned the expertise and impartiality of younger literary critics, less knowledgeable than their predecessors but with their "general slashing style." Yet defended anonymity to sustain journalism's respectability.

110. [Alison, Archibald]. "The Dangers of the Country. No. I: Our External Dangers." 69 (1851): 196–222.
Grumbled that press owners only listened to subscribers or shareholders and that the masses were indifferent to journalism because of their "misery."

111. [Smith, William Henry]. "Southey." 69 (1851): 349–67, 385–405.
Review of Robert Southey's *Life and Correspondence* revealed that he was uncomfortable about the restraints of the *Quarterly Review* but it offered him "constant employment," as had the *Annual Register* previously.

112. [Hardman, Frederick]. "Transatlantic Tourists." 69 (1851): 545–63.
Review of travel books borrowed data, from X. Marmier's *Lettres sur l'Amérique*, on the 'immense number of newspapers' in the United States. Many reprinted French and British serials or contained 'personal diatribes,' 'puffs,' 'puerile anecdotes,' and advertisements. Except for the New Orleans *Bee* and the *Courier of the United States*, not even the best paper (reputedly the *New York Evening Post* edited by William Cullen Bryant) could compare to French provincial gazettes because there were too many American sheets and too few 'able writers.' Papers survived because of party support and advertising.

113. [Eagles, John]. "The Submarine Telegraph." 70 (1851): 562–72.
Forecast how telegraphy would affect the press.

114. [Croly, George]. "English Administrations." 71 (1852): 320–34.
Review of *The Grenville Papers*, edited by W. J. Smith, Esq., studied John Wilkes and the *North Briton*.

115. [Aytoun, William E.]. "The Reform Measures of 1852." 71 (1852): 369–86.
Guessed that in "periodical literature" most cheap journals were anti-establishment.

116. [Smith, William Henry]. "Jeffrey." 72 (1852): 269–84, 461–78.
Biography of Francis Jeffrey drew from Henry Cockburn's *Life of Lord Jeffrey* and Jeffrey's articles in the *Edinburgh Review*. Considered the founding of the *Edinburgh* "the most important event" in Jeffrey's life because the *Review* extended to many the knowledge of a few. "This is one of the chief functions of periodical literature." "[T]heir great and constant service is the diffusion over the whole community of the taste, judgment, reasoning, and knowledge of an educated and cultivated class," creating "a watchful and enlightened audience." The *Edinburgh* did this in a "novel, a most effective, and incomparable manner" in contributions that "peculiarly display the intellectual character, the

power and the opinions of its able editor." Yet Jeffrey, who also pursued a career in law, was haunted by a sense that "in his literary avocations there was something that disparaged the dignity of the lawyer and of the Judge."

117. [Hardman, Frederick]. "Paris on the Eve of Empire." 72 (1852): 724–35.
Speculated that few French read British papers because the Second Empire excluded them and many French people did not know English.

118. [O'Meagher, J. B.]. "A Few Words on France." 73 (1853): 718–29.
Outlined how the Second Empire controlled the press. This policy was acceptable because of "unjustifiable excesses" after February 1848 when many of the 1,200 Paris newspapers catered to the ignorant and brutal, whereas English readers of "improved taste and sounder judgment" curbed any tendency toward the vulgar.

119. [Eagles, John]. "Thackeray's Lectures – Swift." 74 (1853): 494–518.
Recalled that *Edinburgh Review* editor Francis Jeffrey complained that he was unable to "restrain his ardent writers," but his defense of "personal libels" shocked at least one contributor.

120. Vedette [Frederick Hardman]. "A Letter from the Boulevards." 74 (1853): 662–77.
Spotlighted Louis Véron, of the *Constitutionnel*, who founded the *Revue de Paris* in 1829 with François Guizot as the first editor. The *Revue*, revived by Théophile Gautier, was the oldest extant French literary periodical in 1853. It had theatre commentary and "pleasant and readable," occasionally "serious articles" but "not the weight of the *Revue des Deux Mondes*."

121. [Hardman, Frederick]. "*Fifty Years in Both Hemispheres*." 75 (1854): 203–25.
Review of Vincent Nolte's book claimed that one of the first New Orleans papers was the *Telegraph*, 1806–07, which appeared in French and English.

122. [Johnston, F. W.]. "London to West Prussia." 75 (1854): 572–92.
Skimmed marriage advertisements in the *Berliner Intelligenz Blatt*.

123. [Moir, George]. "Death of Professor Wilson." 75 (1854): 629–32.
Lauded John Wilson's writing style and contributions to *Blackwood's*.

124. Vedette [Frederick Hardman]. "The Insurrection in Spain." 76 (1854): 151–65.
Recorded that Spain suppressed newspapers – the *Clamor Publico* "ably conducted" by Fernando Corradi and the *Nacion* edited by Rua Figueroa – and confiscated copies of the *Diario Espagnol* and *Epoca* because of news as well as commentary while government organs, the *Madrid Gazette* and *Heraldo*, were not bothered.

125. [Robertson, T. C.]. "The Gangetic Provinces of British India." 76 (1854): 183–205.
Ranked the *Friend of India*, edited by J. C. Marshman, "the ablest of the Calcutta journals."

126. [Johnson, G. B.]. "The Coming Fortunes of Our Colonies in the Pacific." 76 (1854): 268–87.
Registered that the "excellent digest of Australian news" in Melbourne's *Argus* and the *Sydney Morning Herald* was "sent by every Government mail."

127. Vedette [Frederick Hardman]. "The Spanish Revolution." 76 (1854): 356–70.
Listed new halfpenny newspapers since the Spanish revolution.

128. [Finlay, George]. "King Otho and His Classic Kingdom." 76 (1854): 403–21.
Supposed that previously, under Bavarian ministers, the Greek press had a degree of liberty with few restraints on newspapers. Since 1838, under Greek officials, freedom of the press had spawned 16 newspapers in Athens, enabling every group to malign government with "unrestrained license."

129. [Eagles, John]. "Civilisation [*sic*] – The Census." 76 (1854): 435–51, 509–24; 77 (1855): 21–39, 309–30.
Trumpeted that the "glory of the Nineteenth Century is the Press" but merely quoted periodicals on specific topics.

130. Vedette [Frederick Hardman]. "Spanish Politics and Cuban Perils." 76 (1854): 477–92.
Graded the *Diario Espagnol* "one of the best written and best informed of the Madrid journals."

131. Warren, Samuel. "A Few Personal Recollections of Christopher North." 76 (1854): 731–36.
Paean to John Wilson mentioned his work in *Blackwood's*.

132. [Aytoun, William E.]. "Revelations of a Showman." 77 (1855): 187–201.
Review of *The Life of P.T. Barnum*, his autobiography, disclosed that he established a newspaper, the *Herald of Freedom*, and had been fined and imprisoned for libel. Barnum's book purportedly exposed "newspaper puffery" and misuse of the "prodigious" power of the press.

133. [Smith, William Henry]. "*The Life of Lord Metcalfe*." 77 (1855): 202–20.
Review of William Kaye's book explained that Charles Metcalfe, as Governor-General of India, granted full press freedom because he thought that banishment to England was not an effective penalty for journalists who broke press laws and that instructing Indians was desirable.

134. [Oliphant, Margaret]. "Charles Dickens." 77 (1855): 451–66.
Rued that *Household Words*, "a powerful organ," did not offer enlightenment to the poor.

135. [Oliphant, Laurence]. "Notes on Canada and the North-West States of America. No. VI." 78 (1855): 322–38.
Touched on the *Minnesota Pioneer*, launched in 1849 in St. Paul, "a community worthy of being represented by a press." In 1855 the city had four dailies, two triweeklies, and two weeklies. Aside on the problems in establishing a newspaper.

136. [Aytoun, William E.]. "Light Literature for the Holidays." 78 (1855): 362–74.
Regretted that newspapers wasted ink and paper on much that was inconsequential, but *Bell's Life in London* was a good holiday read.

137. [Hamley, E. B.]. "North and the *Noctes*." 78 (1855): 395–408.
Analyzed the content and style of John Wilson's material in *Blackwood's*, signed with many names.

138. [Swayne, G. C.]. "Death of the Rev. John Eagles." 78 (1855): 757–58.
Saluted Eagles, a long-time *Blackwood's* contributor.

139. [Patterson, R. H.]. "Public Lectures – Mr. Warren on Labour." 79 (1856): 170–79.
Boasted that in the nineteenth century, the "mighty Engine of the Press" reached "full power." Although newspapers, whose primary goal was to sell papers, were less impartial and accurate than books, they provided information faster in a more varied format.

140. [Hamley, E. B.]. "Lessons from the War." 79 (1856): 232–42.
Talked about the scope of reports on the Crimean War: private letters "extensively published," copy of special correspondents of dailies reprinted elsewhere, and many columns of commentary. English dailies circulated writing of "great literary power" and good stories on life in the field but were not as clear on the military campaign as the French *Moniteur*.

141. [Nicolson, Alexander]. "Biography Gone Mad." 79 (1856): 285–304.
Focused on Horace Greeley and the elder James Gordon Bennett as prototypical newspaper editors of the penny press, many of the 3,000 in the hands of men with no other options. In the United States, unlike Britain, this press represented "quackery, virulence, and indecency." People equated coarseness and strength, scurrility and "smartness." Success came from quick news delivery. Followed Greeley from his early journalism to the *New York Tribune*, examined in depth here. Bennett symbolized "audacious scheming, impenetrability to shame," a man who served readers thirsty for scandal. His *New York Herald* showed "minimum literary ability" and "maximum moral worthlessness."

The British press was free and fair, its power derived from anonymity. Because journalism was "more and more of a recognized profession – a profession too calling for special gifts and training," it should not be a refuge for literary rejects. Sometimes editors lacked the nature or education to influence. A good editor had to know employees and what they could do, have confidence and perseverance, and work hard. Journalism's pursuit of profit did not mean that editors abandoned principle.

142. [Oliphant, Margaret]. "Sydney Smith." 79 (1856): 350–61.
Biography marked Smith as the "originator" of the *Edinburgh Review*.

143. Tlepolemus [G. C. Swayne]. "Touching Temporalities: A Letter to Irenaeus." 80 (1856): 592–603.
Essay on the Anglican Church compared advertisements of *The Times* and the *Ecclesiastical Gazette*.

144. [Aytoun, William E.] "Mrs. Barrett Browning – *Aurora Leigh*." 81 (1857): 23–41.

Fumed that current literary press critics were powerless but numerous and annoying with their "barking."

145. Phosphorus [William E. Aytoun]. "Letters from a Lighthouse. No. I." 81 (1857): 227–42.

Yearned for quarterlies that formerly balanced profundity and humor because their articles in 1857 were "too learned" for most readers.

146. [Oliphant, Margaret]. "Picture-Books." 81 (1857): 309–18.

Decreed that the "days of annuals are over."

147. Vedette [Frederick Hardman]. "Memoranda from the Manzanares." 82 (1857): 358–72.

Divulged that the Spanish read only newspapers. Madrid had 23 dailies, and rural areas had some periodicals. Gazettes were not ably done or informative, especially about foreign news. The leader was on a controversial topic; the rest was trivia or a feuilleton.

148. [Oliphant, Margaret]. "The Byways of Literature: Reading for the Million." 84 (1858): 200–16.

Related that cheap magazines delivered useful information alongside tales of the rich to the "lower orders," but little that was original. Of the most popular, the *London Journal* was less "edifying" than *Cassell's Illustrated Paper*. The *Family Herald* was "blandly narrative" in contrast to the "severely instructive" whose authors imagined that they were "the only true teachers of a benighted world."

149. [Dallas, E. S.]. "Popular Literature – The Periodical Press." 85 (1859): 96–112, 180–95.

Enthused that the "rise of the periodical press is the great event of modern history." "[I]t gives every one of us a new sense – a sort of omniscience, as well as a new power – a sort of ubiquity." "A periodical is a creature of the day. Periodical literature is essentially popular literature" that required a large audience because its shelf-life was short. Fueling the rise of periodicals were the steam press, the end of taxes on newspapers and advertisements, better illustrations, telegraphy, and railroad and post transmission.

The "Fourth Estate" was important because, absent universal suffrage, the press represented the people and influenced Parliament. The press also offset the intellectual tensions of civilization with "an increased relaxation in pleasure." The key to the position of the press was "the multiplicity and specialty of its divisions." "The newspaper is the elemental form of modern literature," so everyone read it. Its simple language did not mean superficiality. "[T]he simplicity and the clearness which are the essentials of periodical writing frequently imply a much more perfect grasp of the subject… than…more ambitious performances. Truth is generally simple and can be simply told."

All who wrote, amateurs or regulars, were part of the press. Anonymity was not secrecy but an opportunity for every class or interest to express itself, unlike in the United States. Anonymity protected private citizens from public pressures, checked journalists' egotism, and restrained bombast.

The press was commercial but not corrupt and, like other businesses, its good products tended to last.

150. [White, James]. "Review of a Review." 85 (1859): 750–64.
Perused *The News from the Republic of Letters*, established in 1654 and published by Peter Bayle in Holland.

151. [Aytoun, William E.]. "The Anglo-Gallican Budget." 87 (1860): 381–96.
Mused briefly about the duties on paper.

152. [Ballard, J. A.]. "Our Only Danger in India." 88 (1860): 688–97.
Opposed freedom of the press in India because that would be incompatible with despotic government and would open the door to sedition.

153. [White, James]. "*Italy*: by Marc Monnier." 89 (1861): 403–20.
Essay on Italian intellectual life cited several periodicals: Milan's *Conciliatore*, a literary review c. 1820 that was suppressed, and its *Italian Library*; Florence's *Antologia*, which preceded the *Revue des Deux Mondes* but shared the same format and was suppressed after several years, and the monthly *Tutor's Guide* on education. The Florentine serials were published by J. P. Vieusseux in a building that housed his presses on the lowest floor and a library of periodicals from around the world and his staff on the upper floors.

154. [Aytoun, William E.]. "The Ministry and the Budget." 89 (1861): 517–36.
Recognized that abolition of paper duties benefited newspaper owners but that the poor cared less about press taxes than those on tea and sugar.

155. [Atkinson, J. B.]. "Social Science." 90 (1861): 463–78.
Article on the Dublin meeting of National Association for the Promotion of the Social Sciences quoted Henry Brougham that a cheap price increased newspaper circulation.

156. [Fergusson, James]. "Some Account of Both Sides of the American War." 90 (1861): 768–79.
Condemned "common" suppression of Northern American newspapers when Southern ones, as the *Charleston Mercury*, were free to criticize authorities.

157. [Oliphant, Margaret]. "John Wilson." 92 (1862): 751–67.
Asserted that when *Blackwood's* was established, the *Edinburgh Review* was "a triumphant periodical" and the *Quarterly Review* "a sufficiently promising opponent." Because the *Edinburgh Monthly Magazine* was "tame," its editors were "bought off" and the brilliance of Wilson and J. G. Lockhart shaped the new *Blackwood's* even though they signed articles with an alias or the names of "dull but well-known men."

158. [Osborn, Sherard]. "Progress in China." 93 (1863): 44–60, 133–48.
Despaired that without the check of an "independent press" and the public opinion it printed, Chinese political morals were "debased."

159. [Oliphant, Margaret]. "Henri Lacordaire." 93 (1863): 169–87.
Borrowed from J. B. Lacordaire's biographer, the Count C. de Montalembert, information on his role in the launch of the *Avenir* and *Ere Nouvelle*, which was "neither so long-lived nor so brilliant as the *Avenir*."

160. [Seymour, E. A.]. "The Peripatetic Politician – in Florence." 93 (1863): 321–29.
Chronicled that Florence had many newspapers "for a country town," about 12 dailies and two triweeklies that dealt with national matters, and several periodicals. The *Gazetta del Populo* had the largest circulation (3,000 daily) but lost about 25 percent due to politics and competition. The *Censor*, a "thoroughly Tuscan paper," lost buyers when it raised its price. Even with censorship, the press had "latitude," but officials still sequestered editors.

161. [Gleig, G. R.]. "Charles James Blomfield." 93 (1863): 731–49.
Starred the Anglican bishop who founded the *Museum Critic*, "which sustained a sickly existence from 1813 to 1832" and was often in conflict with the *Classical Journal.*

162. [Paget, John]. "George Cruikshank." 94 (1863): 217–24.
Surveyed Cruikshank's work, including his sketches for the *Comic Annual.* Aside on James Gillray.

163. [Smith, William Henry]. "Mr. Knight's Reminiscences." 95 (1864): 412–25.
Based on Charles Knight's *Passages of a Working Life*, decided that when he was owner-editor (1812) of the *Windsor and Eton Express*, journalism was hazardous because of the libel law, since tempered by Lord Campbell's Act. Knight was also associated with the *Etonian* before he started *Knight's Quarterly Magazine*, which featured T. B. Macaulay but was too narrow to secure a large circulation.

164. [Paget, John]. "John Leech." 97 (1865): 466–71.
Commemorated a famous *Punch* illustrator.

165. [Collins, W. Lucas]. "Etoniana, Ancient and Modern - Conclusion." 97 (1865): 471–88.
Part of a series on Eton said that it was the first public school with a magazine, *Microcosm*, which George Canning edited and Charles Knight published after paying 50 guineas for the copyright. Both it and the later *Miniature* were short-lived and didactic, but the *Etonian* was lighter. Others followed (several listed) until the current *Eton College Chronicle* (established 1863), which was a "school newspaper."

166. [Hardman, Frederick]. "Notes and Notions from Italy." 97 (1865): 659–74.
Remarked that Piedmont had too many journals and one Turin morning paper was edited by a Jew.

167. [Gleig, G. R.]. "The Government and the Budget." 97 (1865): 754–72.
Complained that abolition of the paper duty cost the government revenue and benefited only cheap magazines, not "respectable" publishers.

168. [Neaves, Charles]. "The Death of William [E.] Aytoun." 98 (1865): 384–88.
Memorialized Aytoun, long-time *Blackwood's* writer (120 articles on many subjects), who was also professor of Rhetoric at Edinburgh.

169. [Oliphant, Margaret]. "French Periodical Literature." 98 (1865): 603–21.
Admired the "admirable, elaborate, learned, and weighty" articles in the *Revue des Deux Mondes.* French magazines were "ponderous," and many illustrated French weeklies were "in the *genre* of the *London Journal* and the *Family Herald.*"

170. Borcke, Heros von. "Memoirs of the Confederate War for Independence." 99 (1866): 83–102.

Touched on British correspondents covering the American Civil War, Francis Lawley, the reputedly well-known reporter for *The Times*, and Frank Vizetelly, with his "clever pencil," for the *Illustrated London News*.

171. [Gleig, G. R.]. "The Position of the Government and Their Party." 99 (1866): 382–402.

Aside that the circulation of the *Irish People* was 8,000 weekly.

172. [Smith, William Henry]. "Life of Steele." 99 (1866): 726–46.

Review of Henry R. Montgomery's *Memoirs of the Life and Writings of Sir Richard Steele* portrayed the *Tatler* as part newspaper and the *Spectator* as unique because it was a daily.

173. [Lever, Charles]. "Cornelius O'Dowd." 100 (1866): 380–92, 517–34; 105 (1869): 438–48; 106 (1869): 344–62.

Series on many topics noticed the press. "French newspapers are not only more able in style, and more eloquent in tone, than the Italian, but they possess a far wider range of knowledge," so the Gallic had much influence in Italy. Among the British journals, the *Standard* was an "excellent contemporary." However, the universal newspaper habit of publishing letters from those seeking "momentary publicity" taught readers that writers were wiser than rulers. Alternatively, prudent war correspondents were an asset for "our great journalism." Ruminated about why and how periodicals introduced a new series.

174. [Collins, W. Lucas]. "Light and Dark Blue." 100 (1866): 446–60.

Essay on Oxford and Cambridge referred to the *Oxford Undergraduates' Journal*, a broadsheet on current events, and *Harlequin*, which aped *Punch*, as well as Cambridge's *Light Blue*. Most university magazines had brief lives because capable students were otherwise engaged or could publish elsewhere, but *Knight's Quarterly Magazine* was an exception.

175. [Smith, William Henry]. "*The Gay Science*." 101 (1867): 149–65.

Review of E. S. Dallas' book condensed his ideas on literary criticism.

176. [Mackay, Charles]. "Manhood Suffrage and the Ballot in America." 101 (1867): 461–79.

Rated New York's *World* "as highly respectable a paper as any published in England."

177. [Mackay, Charles]. "Transatlantic Fenianism." 101 (1867): 590–605.

Calculated that New York's *Herald* had the largest circulation in the United States.

178. [Gleig, G. R.]. "The Progress of the Question." 102 (1867): 109–24.

Tagged the *Pall Mall Gazette* "semi-aristocratic" and "clever."

179. [Hamley, E. B.]. "The Death of Sir Archibald Alison." 102 (1867): 125–28.

Revered Alison as one of *Blackwood's* "great contributors."

180. [Mackay, Charles]. "The Impending Crisis in America." 102 (1867): 634–52.
Stamped Kentucky's *Louisville Journal* "one of the ablest newspapers in America."

181. [Gleig, G. R.]. "The Government and the Press." 102 (1867): 763–83.
Insisted that dailies and weeklies, as well as monthlies and quarterlies, had shifted political loyalties. "Between 1800 and 1830 the tone of the public press in this country was almost universally Tory," but thereafter Whigs let young writers know that advocacy would earn them patronage.

182. [Mackay, Charles]. "Modern Cynicism." 103 (1868): 62–70.
Denigrated literary critics who reviled authors. These "smaller critics" replaced an earlier generation in mutual admiration societies and eschewed reviews, whose impact was declining.

183. [Gleig, G. R.]. "*Memoirs of Sir Philip Francis*." 103 (1868): 150–65.
Review of book by Joseph Parkes and Herman Merivale discussed Junius and John Wilkes.

184. [Gleig, G. R.]. "Opposition Tactics." 103 (1868): 367–82.
Categorized the *Tablet* as "the great Roman Catholic organ."

185. [Collins, W. Lucas]. "William Edmondstoune Aytoun." 103 (1868): 440–54.
Evaluated some articles of Aytoun, a long-time *Blackwood's* contributor.

186. [Mozley, Anne]. "Clever Women." 104 (1868): 410–27.
Focused on clever women who had to work. Options "very appropriate for female talent" – as long as a woman had "definiteness of aim, independence of thought, and freshness and accuracy of style" – were to pen "lighter periodical literature," intended for those "too lazy or too restless" to engage in "good talk," and articles for the "didactic" press, "designed for children and the poor" and readers of "immature taste and judgment."

187. [Mackay, Charles]. "A Great Whig Journalist." 106 (1869): 457–87.
Credited Daniel Defoe with writing the forerunners of leaders, "short and racy disquisitions upon public affairs." Defoe was "accustomed to unburthen his mind in newspapers," and his *Review* was the model for the papers of Joseph Addison and Richard Steele.

188. [Oliphant, Margaret]. "New Books." 107 (1870): 628–51.
Opened what became an ongoing *Blackwood's* feature by commenting that literary journals, though numerous, had little effect on literature or readers. They distrusted critics whose reviews were too often done because an author had a connection with a periodical or an editor demanded favoritism.

189. [Hamley, E. B.]. "Note to Our Review of *Lothair*." 108 (1870): 129–32.
Grieved devaluations of literary criticism.

190. [Mackay, Charles]. "Strangers in the House." 108 (1870): 478–92.
Tracked Parliamentary reporting, which Members initially resisted, from the "dry summaries" in the *London Gazette* of Charles II to the breakthrough by the *Gentleman's Magazine* in the 1730s, notably in the copy of William Guthrie, "a Scotsman, a *litterateur* of varied acquirements, and with a tenacious

memory." In 1769 the *Morning Chronicle*'s William Woodfall, with his "wonderful power of memory," expanded coverage. Other papers followed, and Parliament acquiesced. In 1810 Parliament threatened to remove reporters, but R. B. Sheridan explained that they were well educated and impartial and that their columns were in the public interest. In 1870 Parliament expected reporters to take notes but retained the right to close the House. The new penny daily, accelerated by the abolition of newspaper duties, was a "marvelous product of our modern civilization" and "mighty" for good.

Asides on early influential journalists Daniel Defoe, Joseph Addison, Richard Steele, John Wilkes, and Junius.

191. [Neaves, Charles]. "The Late George Moir." 109 (1871): 109–17.
Referred to the articles of Moir, a Scottish lawyer, in the *Edinburgh Review*, the *Quarterly Review*, and *Blackwood's*, to which he was "a regular and frequent contributor" from 1831.

192. [Oliphant, Margaret]. "A Century of Great Poets, from 1750 Downwards. No. IV: Samuel Taylor Coleridge." 110 (1871): 552–76.
Revisited Coleridge's "curious little newspaper-magazine," the *Watchman*, that died after ten numbers.

193. [Marshall, Frederic]. "The Situation in France." 111 (1872): 609–26.
Gloried that *The Times* Paris correspondent (Laurence Oliphant) sent "the most masterly and truthful pictures" of France after the Franco-Prussian War.

194. [Oliphant, Margaret]. "A Century of Great Poets, from 1750 Downwards. No. VII: Lord Byron." 112 (1872): 49–72.
Catalogued the *Edinburgh* in 1807 as a "big and popular Review, then at the very zenith of its greatness."

195. [Lockhart, Laurence]. "Charles James Lever." 112 (1872): 327–60.
Presented Lever as a *Blackwood's* contributor and editor of the *Dublin University Magazine*.

196. [Oliphant, Margaret]. "William Smith." 112 (1872): 429–38.
Essay on Smith, a *Blackwood's* contributor, 1839–71, justified anonymity in magazines and reviews because it gave writers freedom to be fair and to "communicate to thousands the opinions and sentiments which are their best part" even if it cost scribes fame.

197. [Tulloch, John]. "Montalembert." 112 (1872): 595–609.
Review of *Memoir of Count [C.] de Montalembert* by Margaret Oliphant remembered his early work in the *Revue Française* when François Guizot was editor and his direction of the *Avenir*. Swore that he was "[d]riven from his career as a journalist by Papal disapproval," although in 1858 he did write for the *Correspondant*.

198. [Blackwood, John, revised by Charles Neaves]. "The Death of Lord Lytton." 113 (1873): 255–58.
Assured that the writing of E. G. Bulwer-Lytton in *Blackwood's* never exhibited negligence.

199. [Cowell, Herbert]. "The Founders of Modern Liberalism." 116 (1874): 501–18.
Review of W. F. Rae's *Wilkes, Sheridan and Fox* characterized John Wilkes as "a vulgar libertine, without knowledge or capacity of any mark...elevated into a champion of liberty and...idolised by the whole nation" because of #45 of the *North Briton*.

200. [Lockhart, Laurence]. "Lord Lytton's *Speeches*." 117 (1875): 279–304, 570–99.
Abridged E. G. Bulwer-Lytton's reasons for opposing the newspaper stamp duty. They sparked "contraband publications" with inaccurate news and social and political theories that could have a "dangerous and depraving influence upon the ignorant classes." They deprived people of information and of a mode of "mental training." Knowledge was better than punishment as a 'political agent,' and newspapers "familiarized uncultured minds" with the habit of reading.

201. [Marshall, Frederic]. "France and Germany." 117 (1875): 765–76.
Aired an accusation by the French press that *The Times* created a scare to drive down Bourse prices but concluded that Gallic newspapers displayed "intemperance and ignorance" because they were jealous that they did not print the story first.

202. [Fletcher, H. C.]. "A Sketch of Canada as It Now Is." 118 (1875): 44–59.
Labeled the press "the greatest exponent of public opinion." Canadian newspapers had "a far higher tone than the generality of those in the United States." Canadians were "still too personal in their attacks on public men...in language which is more forcible than elegant." Because every town had two newspapers, small circulation meant less money to pay for "high talent." Magazines, penned by Canadians who were as good as English writers, faced competition from the United States and Great Britain.

203. [Oliphant, Margaret]. "Macaulay." 119 (1876): 614–37.
Review of G. O. Trevelyan's *Life and Letters of Lord Macaulay* alluded to T. B. Macaulay's early pieces in *Knight's Quarterly Magazine* and the invitation to write for the *Edinburgh Review*.

204. [Shand, Alexander Innes]. "Speculative Investments." 120 (1876): 293–316.
Warned that press rumors gleaned from telegrams could affect finance but conceded that the British press, unlike the French, had "independence and honesty." Finance columnists should resist "sensational writing," not letting "imagination run daily riot." They should practice "caution and judicious reticence" until they had enough facts to give "sound advice."

205. [Cowell, Herbert]. "Review of the Session." 120 (1876): 383–98.
Pushed for more detailed Parliamentary reporting, primarily in "the daily newspapers, which derive support from classes yet trained or at leisure to appreciate debates." Argued that one column for a few hours of debate was inadequate so that even brilliant speeches by private members had little space.

206. [Brackenbury, Henry]. "Philanthropy in War." 121 (1877): 150–74.
Highlighted the *Bulletin International des Sociétés de Secours aux Militaires Blessés*, an international quarterly (Geneva) that indexed aid periodicals.

207. [Oliphant, Margaret]. "Lord Neaves." 121 (1877): 380–90.
Article on Charles Neaves, a *Blackwood's* contributor, considered its early material, notably from John Wilson, "the Jove of modern criticism," and J. G. Lockhart, more humorous than its essays in 1877.

208. [Oliphant, Margaret]. "Harriet Martineau." 121 (1877): 472–96.
Review of Martineau's *Autobiography* indicated her work for the *Monthly Repository*, *Daily News*, and *Household Words*.

209. [Allardyce, Alexander and John Blackwood]. "Samuel Warren." 122 (1877): 381–90.
Underscored Warren's many papers published in *Blackwood's*.

210. [Oliphant, Margaret]. "The Opium-Eater." 122 (1877): 717–41.
Recorded Thomas De Quincey's ties to *Blackwood's*, which paid well and offered a venue to men of genius; to the *Quarterly Review*, and to the *Westmoreland Gazette* (Kendal), which he edited. He reputedly transformed the *Gazette* from a paper to enlighten and amuse "simple dalesmen" to "an organ of philosophical thought" for the learned, proving that he was unsuited to be a country editor.

211. [Shand, Alexander Innes]. "*Vienna and Viennese Life*." 123 (1878): 603–24.
Review of Victor Tissot's book averred that prior to 1848 Vienna had no newspapers except the *Official Gazette* but soon had "an infinity." About 217 started, but some were quickly suppressed. In 1878 the *Neue Freie Presse* had much foreign correspondence and feuilletons of merit, the *Politische Correspondenz* got news from Berlin, and the *Fremdenblatt* was the "most lucrative." All "leading journals," with two editions daily, showed talent and honor and had good relations with government. Aside that the *Tagblatt* put its advertisements in French for wider circulation.

212. [Shand, Alexander Innes]. "Contemporary Literature. I: Journalists." 124 (1878): 641–62.
Contrasted early 'broad-sheets' with "almost illegible type" and the contemporary press. In 1878 local newspapers challenged the London gazettes, even with their money, prestige, and connections, because local news appealed to readers. All newspapers had a range of occupations. Anonymity was useful to hire people with past or future careers elsewhere. Rarer were those who made journalism a career. They needed general knowledge, humor, logic, good health, and the ability to write in plain language under pressure, especially from telegrams that left little time to check facts or get full details. Foreign correspondents should become a power "by fear or flattery" yet maintain "an evident reserve of self-respect." Special correspondents, of whom the best were war correspondents, were easier to identify: they had expertise, a readiness to go anywhere, and a sense of drama. With much news, dailies reduced reviewers of culture to penning "stop-gaps that may serve to pad an issue on occasion." "Critical weeklies" therefore should keep their reviews current.

213. [Shand, Alexander Innes]. "Contemporary Literature. II: Journalists and Magazine-Writers." 125 (1879): 69–92.
Earmarked society and financial journals. The motto of the first, "nothing is sacred as nothing is secret," earned them publicity from libel suits based on stories by contributors who affected "airs of omniscience" based on talk with servants. Financial papers were "carefully" and "judiciously conducted" and City (financial) editors, some experts, were highly regarded by readers.

Staffing a new magazine was hard because experienced people were unwilling to move. However, more magazines meant more jobs. "Padding" in "lighter" magazines was suitable for new readers. For the serious, quarterlies provided "occasional articles of special value" because they usually had good editors.

214. [Shand, Alexander Innes]. "Contemporary Literature. III: Magazine-Writers." 125 (1879): 225–47.

Certified *Blackwood's* as a model for magazines because its emphasis on *belles lettres* was lighter than quarterlies as its writers (named) exemplified. The goal of "a leading magazine" should be "not merely to enlighten the public, but to direct them." Magazine contributors should speak to a variety of readers; editors should rein in experts, and magazines should abandon book reviews to the literary weeklies. Many magazines flourished thanks to serial novels, but the best of this genre were the religious, whose contents were "curiously mixed."

215. [Shand, Alexander Innes]. "Contemporary Literature. IV: Novelists." 125 (1879): 322–44.

Hypothesized that serializing a novel in "a leading magazine" could ensure success. Magazines of fiction, illustrated journals, and society and literary weeklies were also excellent venues as were those with editors who liked installments. The local press formed groups to publish novels for readers unlikely to go to libraries. Theft by the American press was an ongoing problem.

216. [Shand, Alexander Innes]. "Contemporary Literature. VII: Readers." 126 (1879): 235–56.

Presumed that there was "no getting beyond the reach of the press" because "localities, interests, trades have their special organs" and railroads moved London dailies quickly at a "trifling cost." Described the offices of "a great daily paper" from midnight to dawn. Reporters were trying to write "calmly, consecutively, and reflectively under an excess of high pressure." Editors were attempting to "procure at least a creditable semblance of consistency" while avoiding libel or commitment to some dangerous policy. "The solid walls and floors are sensibly vibrating to the ceaseless revolutions of the steam-engines...Nimble fingers are moving by instinct about the compartments of the type-boxes, mechanically translating thought into metal."

217. [Shand, Alexander Innes]. "Contemporary Literature. VIII: Newspaper Offices." 126 (1879): 472–93.

Alleged that pressure of time was not harmful to publishing news but limited creativity. Competition among newspapers was more intense since telegraphy. American papers seemed more interested than the British in making profit "the chief object of journalism." Hence, the *New York Herald* was willing to pay well for "sensations." Nonetheless, British press advertising was expanding "on a scale that would have seemed reckless insanity" in the past.

New York housed newspapers well but not Paris because editors, with money from other careers, wrote in their mansions. *The Times*, "with its irrepressible enterprise and its practically inexhaustible resources," took the lead in offices for the London press. The *Daily News* lost money for some time so perhaps could not afford better ones. Asides on newspapers in Germany and Vienna.

218. [Allardyce, Alexander]. "Whig Reviewers, as Painted by Themselves." 126 (1879): 562–73.

Review of *Selections from the Correspondence of the late Macvey Napier*, the *Edinburgh Review* editor, 1829–47, affirmed that his letters did not flatter but did not hurt the *Edinburgh's* reputation based on later "able management" and "less reckless writing."

219. [Lockhart, Laurence]. "The Late John Blackwood." 126 (1879): 767–77.
Obituary of *Blackwood's* editor/publisher itemized his editorial qualifications, as a broad education and good judgment in weighing articles on their merits rather than on authors' credentials. He usually initiated a series, then chose an appropriate writer whose identity he shielded. He treated all contributors with tact and respect. His care in monitoring shifts in public taste increased *Blackwood's* circulation and influence.

Aside on John Delane's success as editor of *The Times*.

220. [Northcote, H. S]. "Conservative Reorganization." 127 (1880): 804–10.
Demanded inexpensive Tory country papers with news and well-written leaders to counter the "scurrilous personalities which too often are the feature of the minor Radical newspapers." Reading the latter, "the partially educated artisan" suffered "the deleterious effect of moral dram-drinking." Cities should have "large papers with correspondents everywhere, with ample telegraphic and general news, and with skilled editors and leader-writers" to promulgate Conservative ideas.

221. [Oliphant, Laurence]. "The Unloaded Revolver–The Diplomacy of Fanaticism." 128 (1880): 647–66.
Reckoned that the *Journal des Débats* was "one of the most judicious and calm exponents of public opinion on the Continent."

222. [Cowell, Herbert]. "Mr. Kinglake's New Volume." 128 (1880): 689–709.
Review of A. W. Kinglake's *The Invasion of the Crimea* branded the war correspondent "that *enfant terrible* to all military commanders." In Crimea, he was "under no restraint except that of his own sagacity and good feeling," so some disclosures helped the enemy. Whether a paper should disclose information depended on the news itself and its impact. About Crimean blunders, *The Times*, like ministers and the public, did not know where the blame lay, but the paper energized investigation of them.

223. [Allardyce, Alexander, revised by William Blackwood, III, Joseph Langford, and E. B. Hamley]. "George Eliot." 129 (1881): 255–68.
Tribute to Eliot spoke of her articles in the *Westminster Review* and *Blackwood's*, where she was always "the most careful and accurate among authors."

224. [Montague, W. E.]. "Besieged in the Transvaal: The Defence of Standerton." 130 (1881): 1–20.
Noticed the *Standerton Times*, a "new and interesting" gazette with some humor and much advertising that served a small isolated community.

225. [Skelton, John]. "The Late John Hill Burton." 130 (1881): 401–04.
Talked about Burton's articles in *Blackwood's* and his friendship with its editor, John Blackwood.

226. [Oliphant, Laurence]. "The Adventures of a War Correspondent." 130 (1881): 724–44.
Retelling his own activities during the Franco-Prussian War, Oliphant stated that "[p]ersonal modesty is perhaps the most remarkable quality of the modern war correspondent," unknown unless daring gave him fame.

227. [Montague, W. E.]. "The Boers at Home: Jottings from the Transvaal." 130 (1881): 753–70.

Aside on English illustrated papers.

228. An Ex-Member of the Fenian Directory [Alfred Aylward]. "Fenianism – Its Force and Its Feebleness." 131 (1882): 454–67.

Blared that Ireland's "Fenian press is well, even if coarsely, conducted; and the newspapers of the most advanced type command an extensive circulation."

229. [Shand, Alexander Innes]. "The Lights of 'Maga.' I: The Heroes of the *Noctes*: Wilson – Lockhart – Hogg." 131 (1882): 747–73; II: "Lockhart," 132 (1882): 116–31; III: "Hogg," 132 (1882): 355–73.

Designated John Wilson, J. G. Lockhart and James Hogg as the "fathers" of *Blackwood's*. It "gave them the freest scope for the exercise of powers which were stimulated in a brilliant and general fellowship." Wilson's *Noctes* covered all topics of "the journalism of to-day and the literature of all ages" though they were somewhat provincial. Lockhart, who published 110 articles in the *Quarterly Review*, was less known, but his use of satire made him some enemies. Hogg's narratives were "agreeable interludes to the political and literary articles of Wilson and Lockhart."

230. [Montague, W. E.]. "The Late Campaign." 132 (1882): 654–74.

Declared that the war correspondent was "tightly muzzled" while the generals' broadcast "twaddle." Once correspondents were free, coverage that was at first "the gilt of fiction" became "the gingerbread of fact." Aside that newspaper proprietors reaped fortunes by selling "special editions shrieked for sale every hour at the street-corners by ragged little boys."

231. [Northcote, H. S.]. "The True State of the Opposition." 132 (1882): 811–18.

On politics, society journals printed "the tattle of a few idle young men"; the *Fortnightly Review* was an anomaly, "an extreme Radical periodical issued under Tory editorship," and the *Spectator* was serious.

232. [Skelton, John]. "A Little Chat about Mrs. Oliphant: In a Letter from an Island." 133 (1883): 73–91.

Endorsed anonymity because it allowed critics to "promote and consolidate a sound public judgment" without being "arbitrary and personal."

233. [Oliphant, Margaret]. "American Literature in England." 133 (1883): 136–61.

Identified magazines as the latest American invasion. Some had "excellent illustrations" and "freshness of flavour," even if not the highest literary quality. The *Century Magazine* was the best of *Blackwood's* competitors.

234. [Collins, W. Lucas]. "*Autobiography* of Anthony Trollope." 134 (1883): 577–96.

Touched on Trollope's stories in the *Cornhill Magazine* and the money he received for them.

235. [Hamley, E. B.]. "*The Life of Lord Lytton.*" 135 (1884): 310–22.
Review of *The Life, Letters and Literary Remains of Edward Bulwer, Lord Lytton* by his son, reiterated Bulwer-Lytton's idea that an author could renew public interest in his work by writing for periodicals.

236. [Oliphant, Margaret]. "The Sons of the Prophets: Two Representatives of the Catholic Faith." 135 (1884): 529–53.
Bruited that articles in the Salvation Army *War Cry* were impolite, narrow, and written badly.

237. [Lindau, Rudolph]. "Berlin in 1884." 136 (1884): 1–20, 230–49.
Articulated that among the "legion" of periodicals and newspapers available in Berlin was the best one in Germany, Cologne's *Zeitung*. It had a "numerous staff of regular contributors and reporters" in the capital and a special wire. Berlin had other well-informed gazettes and two monthlies, *Rundschau* and *Nord und Sud*. However, because of the plethora of journals, notably dailies since the 1860s, it was easy for anonymous journalists to abuse newspaper power with a little cleverness and "the facility of style so much appreciated by newspaper editors." All politicians realized the sway of the press and used it to start a discussion or indicate the direction of a policy. The paper devoted to Otto von Bismarck's interests, the *Norddeutsche Allgemeine Zeitung*, was therefore widely read in Europe.

238. [Gleig, G. R.]. "The Right Hon. John Wilson Croker." 136 (1884): 553–78, 799–816.
Review of Croker's *Correspondence and Diaries* traced his journalistic career. He "occasionally" advised *Quarterly Review* editor J. G. Lockhart about how to deal with politics and criticism. Croker thought that *Blackwood's* should have more information, fewer reviews, and a lighter tone, that newspaper writing required an "epigrammatic style," and that French journals were the "effective" political literature of politician-editors whereas English editors were "needy adventurers."

239. [Shand, Alexander Innes]. "Outlying Professions. " 136 (1884): 579–91.
Defined journalism as a "profession." London leader-writers, men and women who worked three or four nights a week, and country editors had good salaries and some sway. Critics and essayists also had influence, but "the romance of the profession" was the "ingenious and dashing" war correspondent to whom the military was "civil" because of his clout. Although he wrote anonymously, his paper made him known lest he go elsewhere. His dangerous life paid because he could make a "small fortune" writing signed articles and lecturing.

240. [Hamley, E. B.]. "The Life and Letters of George Eliot." 137 (1885): 155–76.
Alluded to Eliot's periodical writings.

241. [Allardyce, Alexander]. "Russia in Search of a Frontier." 137 (1885): 549–57.
Cautioned that the Indian vernacular press could weaken the British position in Asia.

242. [Oliphant, Margaret]. "The Late Principal Tulloch." 139 (1886): 414.
Eulogized *Blackwood's* contributor John Tulloch. *See* 139: 415, 144: 736.

243. Oliphant, M[argaret] O. W. "Principal Tulloch." 139 (1886): 415–41.
Expanded 139: 414. Reminded that Tulloch wrote for several periodicals, "chiefly" the *North British Review*. Invited to edit *Fraser's Magazine* in the hope that "his name and inspiration" would revive the periodical, which had not retained its original popularity." He was temperamentally unsuited for the job. *See* 139: 414, 144: 736.

244. [Hamley, E. B.]. "Mr. Hayward and His Letters." 141 (1887): 37–44.
Review of *A Selection from the Correspondence of Abraham Hayward, Q.C.*, edited by H. E. Carlisle, recalled that Hayward edited the *Law Magazine* "for some years" and penned "careful articles" for the *Edinburgh Review* and a variety of essays for the *Quarterly Review*.

245. [Oliphant, Margaret]. "The Old Saloon." 141 (1887): 291–315, 416–45, 737–61.
Series on current literature noted the *Century*, "one of the best-known of American magazines"; the impact of John Wilson on *Blackwood's*; the "glittering phalanx" of early *Edinburgh Review* writers, and the growth of newspapers with the concurrent evolution of the "profession of journalism."

246. [Oliphant, Margaret]. "The Rev. W. Lucas Collins." 141 (1887): 734–36.
Saluted *Blackwood's* contributor Collins whose "whole literary career was thus woven in with that of this Magazine." He and other anonymous essayists "gave up their own credit and praise to the honour of the ensign under which they did their work." Anonymous literary criticism was a means to review friends' work without pressure and to create essays with "power" because "personality" was hidden.

247. [Allardyce, Alexander]. "Retrospects of the Reign." 142 (1887): 388–99.
Verified that the British press "within the last twenty-five or thirty years has caught to a very considerable extent the accents of Parisian journalism; and our 'society' papers and kindred periodicals are a happy imitation."

248. Mackay, Charles. "English Slang and French Argot: Fashionable and Unfashionable." 143 (1888): 690–704.
Thundered that stories on crimes, accidents, and "prurient scandals" proliferated in "newspapers which enjoy the largest and most profitable circulation." These stories encouraged slang, akin to the "usage of the careless and semi-educated writers of the inferior English and American press." Penny-a-liners favored stock phrases, but worse was the language "of the pretentious literary Reviews, whose editors assume to be the arbiters of taste and style." Contributors to these serials should set an example, not pen in the style of *Bell's Life in London*.

249. [Knatchbull-Hugesson, E. H., 1st Baron Brabourne]. "The Second Half of the Session." 144 (1888): 297–310.
Commented on *O'Donnell v. Walter*, a libel suit against *The Times*.

250. H[amley], E. B. "The Death of Mr. Gleig." 144 (1888): 311–14.
Lauded G. R. Gleig, one of *Blackwood's* "stoutest and staunchest…friends" who wrote many articles for it. He also penned for some "Quarterlies" and was among the "well-known" scribes of *Fraser's Magazine*.

251. [Story, R. H.]. "Mrs. Oliphant's *Life of Principal Tulloch.*" 144 (1888): 736–56.
Review of Margaret Oliphant's book listed John Tulloch's journalism, such as writing for the *British Quarterly Review* and the *North British Review* and editing the *Record*, a religious organ, and *Fraser's Magazine*. *See* 139: 414, 415.

252. [Kebbel, T. E.]. "Lord Chesterfield." 147 (1890): 206–21.
Review of the *Letters of Philip Dormer*, 4th Earl Chesterfield, observed that attention to the *Tatler* and *Spectator* shadowed other eighteenth-century journals. While the *Tatler* and *Spectator* had "uniform high excellence," others, such as *Mist's Weekly Journal* and the *Craftsman*, were intermittently good.

253. Lexophilus [George Brooks]. "What I Learned in Ireland." 147 (1890): 269–90.
Fretted that "Irish Unionist journals" in Tipperary used "Parnellite correspondence" to save money and that English reporting, which "merely records facts," was adopting the "vicious practice" of Irish and American journals wherein political opinion appeared "in every column – almost every paragraph."

254. [Cowell, Herbert]. "The Report of the Commission." 147 (1890): 430–48.
Defended *The Times*, "the leading public journal," for stories alerting the public to danger that it believed true without "strictly legal evidence"; "it was wilfully imposed upon by falsehood and forgery emanating from the camp of its opponents" while the *Irish World*, *Irishman*, and *United Ireland* promoted agitation.

255. [Oliphant, Margaret]. "Lord Lamington." 147 (1890): 449–50.
Obituary of Alexander Cochrane-Baillie, a "valued" writer for *Blackwood's*, guessed that he would probably be gratified to have his articles identified.

256. Trench, F[rederick] Chenevix, Major-General. "The Russian Journalistic Press." 148 (1890): 115–26.
Emphasized that the Russian authorities viewed the press as an "essentially pernicious force," so they enforced strict censorship in the provinces. Harassed by petty restrictions and dictates on topics, most papers were careful since government was their only news source and serious opposition led to suppression. Although the daily *Golos*, with a circulation of 30,000, was "the most influential and best conducted paper ever published in Russia," circulation and sponsors of other papers (data given) in St. Petersburg and Moscow were important because many people were still without a gazette.

257. [Allardyce, Alexander]. "John Murray and His Friends." 149 (1891): 717–31.
Essay apparently drew from Samuel Smiles' *A Publisher and His Friends: Memoir and Correspondence of John Murray*. Silhouetted *Quarterly Review* publisher Murray who purportedly founded it because the *Edinburgh Review* displayed "autocratic conduct," "reckless criticism," and "unscrupulous politics." The *Quarterly's* early success was due to Robert Southey's essays and William Gifford's editing, though his "conscientious" and "careful" "abridgments" of articles seemed like "mutilation" to their authors. Also studied the tenure of J. G. Lockhart as *Quarterly* editor, his relations with William Blackwood whose magazine Lockhart expected would fail, and Murray's daily, the *Representative*.

258. [Allardyce, Alexander]. "Laurence Oliphant." 150 (1891): 1–20.
Glanced at Oliphant's work for *Blackwood's* and *The Times*.

259. [Willcocks, William]. "The Egyptians and the Occupation." 150 (1891): 696–711.
Logged that when the British occupied Egypt, "the Arabic press was entirely in the hands of interested Syrians."

260. Skelton, John. "A Chapter of Reminiscences: Lord Rosebery's *Pitt.*" 151 (1892): 136–50.
Returned to the "brilliant essayists" of the early *Edinburgh Review* who could be "grotesquely unscrupulous" about politics and to the *Edinburgh Guardian*, a weekly with "admirable writing" in the 1850s. Among its staff was E. S. Dallas, "later for many years the leading critic of *The Times*."

261. [Bannatyne, D. J.]. "Civilisation, Social Order, and Morality in the United States of America." 151 (1892): 617–37.
Described American newspapers as factually accurate but otherwise full of "sensational filthy reading matter."

262. [Griffin, Martin J.]. "Election Week in America." 152 (1892): 892–907.
Bemoaned that American newspapers "fan the fever of excitement" of an election whose results morning papers carried irrespective of telegraphy.

263. [O'Conor-Eccles, Charlotte]. "The Experiences of a Woman Journalist." 153 (1893): 830–38.
O'Conor-Eccles delineated her own career, beginning with country papers as a subeditor, proof reader, reporter, and ladies' columnist, all "irregular and precarious" assignments compared to magazine writing. In London a letter of introduction to a "journalistic great" was unproductive, so prowling Fleet Street came next. Most editors, accustomed to being "dunned" by the "incompetent and self-opinionated," perceived a woman as "a nuisance, an untried fledge being very much in the way." Letters finally resulted in a request from a 'society' journal for articles, "the naughtier the better," and the offer was rejected. The Ladies Employment Bureau was no help, but advertising sparked other offers, from a "new high-class monthly" that promised low pay and no publicity and from a "literary sweater," a correspondent for London and colonial papers who hired young women to write columns in which they mentioned popular shops (by whom he was paid) and a ghost writer for magazines, who paid women to do the work. Both of these were also rejected. Learned the ropes of journalism from the Writers' Club sufficiently to pen short and perky pieces on fashion for the London edition of the *New York Herald* for three guineas per week and subleaders, children's columns, and answers to correspondents, as well as proofread, for a weekly paying 30 shillings.

264. [Shand, Alexander Innes]. "General William Hamley." 153 (1893): 879–84.
Nodded to Hamley's brother, E. B. Hamley, a *Blackwood's* contributor of versatility and sparkling style.

265. Escott, T. H. S. "Thirty Years of the Periodical Press." 156 (1894): 532–42.
Reminisced about associates: George Augustus Sala, the "Ulysses of London journalism"; Laurence Oliphant, a major influence on the "best contributors to the periodical press in the last half-century"; James Mure, editor of the *Edinburgh Courant*, to which Escott sent London reports; Douglas Cook, *Saturday Review* editor; several at the *Daily Telegraph* where Escott covered Parliament in the early 1870s; journalists he met at their local haunts. In 1893 journalism was less congenial and more competitive.

Construed society journalism as the extension of local newspapers with their gossip and the *World* the heir of Oliphant's *Owl.* Aside on the evening press before the *Pall Mall Gazette*.

266. [Oliphant, Margaret]. "John Stuart Blackie." 157 (1895): 662–64.
Celebrated Blackie as a *Blackwood's* contributor since 1832.

267. Stutfield, Hugh E. M. " 'Tommyrotics.'" 157 (1895): 833–45.
Branded the nineteenth-century *Spectator* "grave and sedate."

268. [Oliphant, Margaret]. "The Looker-on." 157 (1895): 902–29.
Averred that the newspaper was "a very great and important institution, as we all know," one that depended on "a great public shock, a distinguished death, an alarming and terrible accident" for existence. "[B]y copy alone we live or die" was the current press motto, copy repeating matters in which the public had little interest. Women's pages had plenty of copy, mostly on fashion. These columns were useful to "the general crowd of women, who are not of very much account save in their own private and immediate surroundings and have little or nothing 'to do' as men – at least young men, reckon – no games, no sports, no pastimes, no clubs."

The press shaped public policy because "no one has the power of contradicting" it. "It can make a passing folly look like a genuine aspect of society – and not only look, but in time be so, by persistent assertion and reiteration – a very curious and most dangerous power." When a paper did not sell, an owner ended it quickly.

269. [Allardyce, Alexander]. "*Life of Sir E. B. Hamley*." 158 (1895): 583–608.
Reviewed books by Alexander Innes Shand, "one of the most brilliant contributors" to *Blackwood's*.

270. [Allardyce, Alexander]. "Professor Blackie." 158 (1895): 715–33.
Review of Anna M. Stoddart's *John Stuart Blackie* singled out his articles in the *Foreign Quarterly Review* and *Blackwood's*, where he wrote with "freshness" and "modesty," 1835–42, and as "a recognized oracle" thereafter.

271. [Millar, J. H.] "The Life of *Punch*." 158 (1895): 866–79.
Review of M. H. Speilmann's *The History of Punch* referred to W. M. Thackeray's article on *Punch* in the *Quarterly Review* (96: 75). His contributions to the magazine were "incomparably superior in literary quality" to those of Douglas Jerrold. Shirley Brooks was the best editor of *Punch* and Tom Taylor the worst. Assessed the work of prominent contributors and outstanding artists because "the greatest feature of *Punch* is the pictures." In 1895, while other magazines lifted French themes, honest people were not ashamed to read *Punch*. Aside that anonymity was a "valuable characteristic of English journalism" but a disappearing one.

272. [Collins, Clifton W.]. "Oxford in Faction and Fiction." 158 (1895): 880–904.
Showcased the 1895 *Oxford Magazine*, where "the literary talent of aspiring undergraduates" and varied contents earned a good circulation in contrast to many earlier ephemeral journals (named), with their "stale gossip and scurrilous anecdotes." One exception was the 1867 *Oxford Spectator*.

273. O[liphant], M[argaret] O. W. "The Anti-Marriage League." 159 (1896): 135–49.
Registered that the leaders in Paris' *Figaro* were "amusing," but those in British papers were "political discussions."

274. [Millar, J. H.]. "Recent Celtic Experiments in English Literature." 159 (1896): 716–29.
Differentiated between early and late nineteenth-century literary reviewers. "Our great-grandfathers took to task, corrected, castigated, condemned with freedom, and praised but sparingly; our contemporaries discover a new genius once-a-month."

275. Skene, Felicia M. F. "Some Episodes in a Long Life." 159 (1896): 828–50.
Bared that Walter Scott disliked son-in-law J. G. Lockhart's "sharpness" in periodical writing.

276. [Meldrum, D. S.]. "The Novels of John Galt." 159 (1896): 871–82.
Review of *Works of John Galt*, which Meldrum edited, linked Galt's novels and *Blackwood's*.

277. [Shand, Alexander Innes]. "Fortunes of Paris: for the Last Fifty Years." 160 (1896): 336–49.
Review of Capt. D. Bingham's *Recollections of Paris* posited that press influence was increasing in Paris because the papers offered more stability than the legislature. No longer was "the sparkling leader-writer" anticipating office. Thanks to signature, "pressmen" had power through their journals. The "firebrands" who "pander to the blind passions of the populace" could compete for high salaries. Young provincials seeking a "career" in journalism needed to attract the notice of "an omnipotent manager" in Paris. Asides that Felix Whitehurst covered the Second Empire for "the *bourgeois* readers of the *Daily Telegraph*," that Laurence Oliphant resigned as *The Times* correspondent when the Commune became bloody, and that "great Hebrew capitalists" financed "many of the journals, like the railways" in France and Germany.

278. [Oliphant, Margaret]. "John Gibson Lockhart." 160 (1896): 607–625.
Review of Andrew Lang's *The Life and Letters of John Gibson Lockhart* rejected Lang's interpretation of Lockhart's connection to *Blackwood's* and the notion that editing the *Quarterly Review* was much better than editing *The Times* at a moment when *The Times* was at "its zenith of influence and power."

279. Saintsbury, George. "Twenty Years of Reviewing." 161 (1897): 21–36.
Guaranteed that the multitude of journals in 1897 meant that none had a "commanding reputation or influence," but the *Edinburgh Review*, with "fair pay," ensured quality literary criticism.

280. [Cowell, Herbert]. "*Forty-One Years in India*." 161 (1897): 297–316.
Review of a book by Field-Marshall Lord Roberts of Kandahar sanctioned a regulated vernacular press in India because Indian gazettes engaged in "persistent misrepresentation and calumny."

281. [Oliphant, Margaret]. " 'Tis Sixty Years Since." 161 (1897): 599–624.
Recollected that in 1837 only London had a daily press, most country papers were weekly because of the difficulty of getting news quickly, and penny-a-liners proclaimed wonders, not reported events.

282. Greenwood, Frederick. "The Newspaper Press: Half a Century's Survey." 161 (1897): 704–20.
Testified that the reputation of the press improved about 1860 because the *Saturday Review* hired excellent *Morning Chronicle* writers when the paper died; the *Pall Mall Gazette* brought to the daily the thought of a review; the evening papers revived; and newspapers developed their own linguistic

style, albeit losing "charm" in the process. By 1897 there were more and better country papers, and, overseas, Melbourne's *Argus* was second only to *The Times* among English-language papers, but many highlighted the "abominable" side of humans.

As newspapers multiplied, government could be indifferent to an individual paper unlike earlier ministries' fear of powerful metros and desire to "stand well" with them. Proliferation discouraged good writing by pressuring leader-writers, but the "independence, courage, incorruptibility" first seen in foreign and war correspondents were in 1897 characteristic of British journalism generally.

283. [Lobban, J. H. and William Blackwood, III]. "Mrs. Oliphant." 162 (1897): 161–64.
Honored Margaret Oliphant, "the most accomplished periodical writer of her day," less appreciated because she opted for anonymity.

284. [Zimmern, Helen]. "Italian Journalism as Seen in Fiction." 162 (1897): 207–19.
Announced that Italians read many papers. Although the press was "venal and insincere," manipulated by the government or a patron, it had "far-reaching influence."

285. Simpson, J. Y. "The Political Prisoner in Siberia." 162 (1897): 320–44.
Among cases cited was that of "the editor of perhaps the most influential paper in Siberia." Arrested because he knew members of a secret society, he depended on his wife to continue "the paper for him." Even with censorship, some political prisoners could subscribe to newspapers or receive the occasional magazine, but officially none of foreign origin.

286. [Seton-Karr, W. S.]. "The Native Press in India." 162 (1897): 579–86.
Passed from removal of press restraints in the 1830s to their reinstitution in 1857. In the interval, several papers surfaced, though "native journals were then of very small account." In the 1860s easing of restrictions spawned many papers, soon checked by 1870s legislation whereby "[j]ournalists became moderate in tone and language." When Lord Ripon, Viceroy after 1880, "unmuzzled" the vernacular press, "shameful licence" but not influence followed because few of the papers reached 25,000 in circulation. A "seditious, disloyal, false, and unchecked" vernacular press undermined British prestige and proved that grafting Western forms on Asian societies impeded progress.

287. [Lobban, J. H.]. "'Maga' and Her Publishers." 162 (1897): 860–72.
Review of Margaret Oliphant's *Annals of a Publishing House* covered the founding of *Blackwood's*, akin to the *Tatler* in style, and many contributors. Nominated the *Gentleman's Magazine* as the trendsetter for the "miscellaneous magazine" at a time not "ripe" for "anonymous magazine writing."

288. An Oxonian [Clifton W. Collins]. "Cambridge." 163 (1898): 33–51.
Skimmed undergraduate journals. "The two best-known – and longest-lived" were *Granta* and the *Cambridge Review* while some, as the *Cambridge Tatler* and *Gadfly*, died quickly.

289. [Hannay, David]. "The Spanish Crisis." 163 (1898): 238–53.
Alerted that the editor of Cuba's *Nacional* could afford to be "bold" because, as a legislative deputy, he could not be prosecuted without the Cortes' consent.

290. [Whibley, Charles]. "Disraeli the Younger." 163 (1898): 583–97.
Retold Benjamin Disraeli's role in the launch of John Murray's *Representative*.

291. [Millar, J. H.]. "Among the Young Lions." 163 (1898): 729–42.
Essay on novelists who first penned for periodicals relied on public library statistics as evidence of reader interest in journalism. The most popular serials amused and instructed. Their literary criticism was sometimes "hasty" but "independent" because of anonymity. Usually, "in the best of the cheap illustrated magazines, [the] 'sexual problem' novel is conspicuously absent." In 1898 newspaper journalists wrote "straightforwardly and vigorously" if perhaps "slangy," but advertisements with endorsements by the anonymous or "experts" were suspect.

292. [Whibley, Charles]. "A New School." 163 (1898): 779–87.
Scorned French Naturists who praised each other's work in their journal, the *Revue Naturiste*.

293. [Hannay, David]. "The End of an Old Song: Confessions of a Cuban Governor." 164 (1898): 422–35.
Review of *Mi Pólitica en Cuba* by the Marquis of Polevieja counseled against stealing from the "American yellow press." Cuba's *Tribuna*, the supplement to the *Lucha* edited by Don Agustin Cervantes, was free as demonstrated by its "scandalous language" and insults of private and public people. Because the law held the writer, not the owner, accountable for libel, Cuban journalists might each face a multitude of libel charges at any moment.

294. [Watson, W. L.]. "The Press and Finance." 164 (1898): 639–50.
Postulated that newspapers could significantly impact finance, and not for the better. Financial advice was a great responsibility because the press symbolized information and morality. London evening papers were "frankly financial" but were not accurate. All City (financial) editors were pressured by time to skip fact checking, and neophytes lacked expertise. They detracted from the newspaper's reputation, although sixpenny weeklies were more trustworthy.

295. [Millar, J. H.]. "Old Whig and New." 164 (1898): 682–91.
Review of John Knox's *Memoirs of the Life and Correspondence of Henry Reeve* condensed Reeve's work for *The Times*, 1840–55, when he wrote 2,402 leaders as circulation increased from 13,000 to 62,000. *The Times* had clout because its "information was early, exclusive, and accurate," but its supremacy ceased with the advent of the penny press. Reeve later edited the *Edinburgh Review* where he recruited quality writers and supported anonymity.

296. [Whibley, Charles]. "The Sins of Education." 165 (1899): 503–13.
Anguished that, since compulsory education, the English periodical press had become the worst in Europe. Blamed new editors for "the weekly or monthly rag-bags of gossip and sensation." Whereas their predecessors forced readers to accept higher quality, the men of 1899 catered to audiences in order to sell serials. They bowed to the public, "a peevish imbecile" demanding short and light articles with "crisp" paragraphs. Pages full of "superfluous knowledge" interspersed with photographs of "exalted personages" or "ancestral halls" prevailed in magazines; newspapers displayed indiscretion and Americanisms that were "a mixture of slang and headlines." The result of large circulations was "government by journalism." Unlike John Delane, irresponsible editors used numbers, not intelligence, to evidence their power over people who worshipped print. The American "Yellow Press" confirmed the danger. The old journalist was "reputed a blackguard"; the new was "well-educated, and more often than not polished by a University training" yet had neither style nor a sense of standards, disconnecting journalism from literature.

297. [Michie, Alexander]. "A Year's Diplomacy in Peking." 165 (1899): 773–80.
Thanked the "leading organs of public opinion" for "their diligence in supplying the best information and the best reasoned comments" during the "Chinese crisis." Summaries, from diverse sources and "in a few terse words," by *The Times* correspondent, "a man of capacity who has risen to the occasion," were especially valuable.

298. [Millar, J. H.]. "The Record of a Life." 165 (1899): 895–904.
Considered Margaret Oliphant's style of periodical writing and commitment to anonymity.

299. [Bealby, J. T.] "The Downfall of Finland: An Object-lesson in Russian Aggression." 166 (1899): 1–15.
Appreciated that Michael Katkoff "formed and guided public opinion in Russia with an influence that was little less powerful than that of the Czar," but "journalistic writers" of his ilk biased the press against the Finns.

300. Millar, A. H. "William Lauder, the Literary Forger: An Unrecorded Episode in His Life." 166 (1899): 381–96.
Analyzed the contents of the *Gentleman's Magazine* in the 1740s with respect to the controversy about Lauder.

301. [Macdonald, J. H. A.]. "France To-Day." 166 (1899): 543–55.
Contrasted British papers, which supplied news in "moderate language," presented both sides of an issue, and eschewed "private characters besmirched," and the French press on the Dreyfus case. Several gazettes were "unscrupulous, base, and abominable," resorting to "foul language" for their personal attacks. Even "news columns" were "utterly devoid of common decency." Their editors "believe...their modes, which are abhorrent to all decency," sold papers. The *Petit Journal*, with its circulation of over a million per day, seemingly verified this belief.

302. [Brackenbury, Henry]. "Lord Lytton's Indian Administration." 166 (1899): 852–70.
Review of Lady Betty Balfour's *The History of Lord Lytton's Indian Administration, 1876–80*, scrutinized the Vernacular Press Bill, 1878, that dealt with newspapers in "oriental languages." The bill required printers and publishers to post a bond not to circulate anything "to excite...dissatisfaction" with government or "antipathy" among races, castes, and religions and to refrain from using the press for extortion. Violations resulted in a warning from local government followed by seizure of materials, but appeal was possible. In 1882, repeal of this legislation caused "venom" to pour from the vernacular press. Thus, in 1897, the Penal Code was amended along the lines of the 1878 bill.

303. [Cowell, Herbert]. "Is This War a Necessity?" 166 (1899): 891–909.
Review of J. P. Fitzpatrick's *The Transvaal from Within* recorded that Boers financed newspapers in France and Germany.

304. [Whibley, Charles]. "The Victorian Drama." 167 (1900): 98–108.
Review of *The Drama of Yesterday and To-Day* by Clement Scott, once theatre critic of the *Daily Telegraph*, spoke about him and other theatre reviewers.

305. Hare Court [T. E. Kebbel]. "The Old Tavern Life of London." 167 (1900): 111–22.

Enlightened that eighteenth-century taverns were places where journalists gathered information to print, as in the *Tatler*, and nineteenth-century ones were sites where journalists gathered to socialize.

306. Boyd, Mary S. "From a Country-House in New Zealand." 167 (1900): 220–33.

Underscored the "omnipresent press" in New Zealand and the value of society papers for local belles.

307. [Whibley, Charles]. "Musings Without Method." 167 (1900): 275–87, 420–30; 168 (1900): 394–404, 757–67, 915–26.

Agreed that all journalists were patriots but wondered if their determination to report and comment on the South African War aided the enemy by publishing information or complaints from the ranks. Blamed John Delane, *Times* editor during the Crimean War, for setting this precedent of open journalism, but all war correspondents hurt Britain when they attacked military censorship and favored some officers only to amuse readers and earn more money. Ridiculed magazine contributors who wrote quickly for profit, subordinating their own tastes to those of editors or readers. These people, often semieducated but armed with typewriter, twine, paper clips, cheap camera, bottle of gum, scrapbook, and scissors, succeeded in the popular press if they were unscrupulous. They penned trivia while pledging their devotion to literary work. Sneered at the American yellow press. Asides on W. T. Stead, Richard Harding Davis of the *New York Journal*, and Paris' halfpenny papers.

308. [Michie, Alexander]. "China." 168 (1900): 405–15.

Wondered why the British daily press published minutiae of fact and fiction on China since correspondents under any siege would probably not waste time telegraphing "inane twaddle."

309. [Stoddart, Anna M.]. "*Helena Faucit (Lady Martin).*" 168 (1900): 906–14.

Review of Theodore Martin's book identified him as one of the oldest living *Blackwood's* writers. Aside that modern interviewers filled newspapers columns with more talk about themselves than about their subjects.

The British and Foreign Review, 1835–1844

With a multicultural bent, the *British and Foreign* ranged from domestic press taxes to European press censorship.

1. [Bird, Christopher]. "Introduction." 1 (1835): 5–16.
Declared that the *British and Foreign* planned "as much to learn as to teach" about many topics from an international perspective in contrast to other reviews "conducted with partial and limited views."

2. [Brougham, Henry]. "Lord Brougham's Speech: Taxes on Knowledge." 1 (1835): 157–72.
Brougham repeated his ideas that the high cost and pre-payment of a newspaper stamp deprived the public of essential knowledge. The established press ignored the subject or warned that repeal would bring "seditious and blasphemous papers." Owners of top metros feared that cheap papers would rob them of advertising profits. Because London gazettes "give a tone in good measure to the Provincial Press," readers thought repeal was unimportant or dangerous. London papers also influenced MPs, particularly those from rural areas. However, "the respectable and intelligent middle classes" thought for themselves and read country papers that were "less tainted." Since illegal malicious and treasonous papers already existed, new inexpensive ones would be an improvement. Pleaded also for lowering the paper duty. *See New Monthly Magazine* 44: 485.

3. "France." 1 (1835): 492–512.
Deplored recent French "laws against the press," laws violating Louis Philippe's principles and promises at accession.

4. "Lord Bolingbroke." 2 (1836): 209–32.
Alluded to the writing style of Henry St. John in the *Craftsman*.

5. [Sheil, Richard Lalor]. "Orange Lodges." 2 (1836): 328–94.
Mentioned the *Dublin Evening Mail* and William Motherwell, editor of the *Glasgow Courier*.

6. [Grattan, Thomas Colley]. "The Political, Social, and Commercial State of Belgium." 3 (1836): 1–23.
Noted that government prosecution of the press had ceased in Belgium.

7. "The Germanic Confederation: Its Political Character and Influence." 4 (1837): 169–213.
Condemned German Confederation support for a "Carlsbad Censorship" because it implied that opposition to government was always the byproduct of 'an unbridled press.'

8. [Wallace, William]. "Memoirs, Reminiscences and Travels: Light Literature." 4 (1837): 367–410.

Attributed the growth of periodical literature about 1815 to the impact of the Romantics who started journals to counter two trends. "The two principal Reviews were, no doubt, warped by political bias," and criticism in weeklies and monthlies went from mere notices or extracts of books to "the instrument of party hate or personal favour."

9. "The Political Press in France." 4 (1837): 410–41.

Broadcast that French papers had recently emerged from a long struggle with the authorities. "From 1789 to 1831, the ordinary condition of the Press was a rule of censorship and oppression." After 1789 few had the literary or technical skills to produce a paper, so by 1815 there were more magazines than dailies. In 1837 the reverse was true because dailies in the departments had been growing since 1830. Although their news was secondhand, advertising covered operating costs. Early 1830s Paris papers focused on politics had more influence than new arrivals prioritizing profit. Gain was easier than in London because expenses were lower in Paris. "The correspondence which *The Times* maintains at Paris alone costs more than the whole editorial business of a French paper." However, competition, legislative "fiscal burdens," and outmoded "internal organization" were handicaps. French political tribunes should ape England and the United States, emphasizing advertisements and news and leaving opinion to the reviews.

10. "The Recent French Elections." 6 (1838): 371–95.

Assayed the power of the *Journal des Débats*, *Constitutionnel*, *Siècle*, and other newspapers.

11. [Cole, Henry]. "The Justice and Profit of a Uniform Penny Postage." 8 (1839): 451–89.

Yoked postal rates to circulation of "cheap periodicals."

12. [Banfield, Thomas Collins]. "The Turkish Treaty." 9 (1839): 247–72.

Despised Russian pressure for press censorship, and torture for any breach, in Wallachia and Moldavia.

13. "The Political Opinions of the Germans." 10 (1840): 25–49.

Decried German restraints on press freedom. Aside that the *Allgemeine Zeitung* was "one of the most important public organs, and perhaps the best conducted in Europe."

14. "Popular Literature of the Day: *Jack Sheppard*." 10 (1840): 223–46.

Review of W. H. Ainsworth's novel contended that this genre's "personality and sarcasm" affected cheap newspapers. They might be "the guide as well as the mirror" of opinions and "tastes," but these papers printed "poisonous and abominable trash." In their sensational police reports, illustrations, and advertising of quack medications, they demonstrated their disinterest in "public morals." Their denunciations of unacceptable conduct were so "coarse and graphic" as to be advocacy of it.

15. "Austria in Italy: *Memoirs of a Prisoner of State*." 10 (1840): 644–75.

Aside, in Alexander Andryane's book work, that Austria closed Italy's *Subalpino* and several literary periodicals, as the earlier *Conciliatore* (Milan) and *Antologia* (Florence) had been silenced.

16. [Banfield, Thomas Collins]. "Austrian Statistics." 14 (1843): 218–87, 554–628; 15 (1843): 529–59.

Decided that Austrian anxiety about the press was an acknowledgment of its power. Suppressing journals was dangerous because they were a vent for public dissatisfaction and their disappearance would exacerbate suspicions about government. Even Russia issued monthly ministerial bulletins.

17. [Lewes, G. H.]. "State of Criticism in France." 16 (1844): 327–62.

Stated that French press influence came from numbers. Criticism was formulaic, often replete with "journalistic vices – shameless venality, reckless partisanship, cruel flippancy, and astonishing ignorance." French critics were "witty" but not very talented. Among those profiled were Jules Janin, important in the *Journal des Débats* and in demand from "the gayest to the gravest" periodicals, a man who could be cruel to get a laugh; Théophile Gautier, who scribbled for money and fame in the *Presse*; Paul Forgues, who as "Old Nick" wrote frequently and severely for the *National* and as Léon Durocher for the *Revue de Paris*; Eugene Guinot ("Pierre Durand"), one of the most agreeable of the *feuilletonists*"; Eugene Briffaut, whose "Revues de Paris" in the *Siècle* were "wordy and ungrammatical." Still, Italian criticism was purportedly worse, though German was cosmopolitan.

18. [Lewes, G. H.]. "Eugene Sue: *Les Mystères de Paris*." 18 (1844): 217–38.

Grieved that the "moral press" of England had no words about Sue while the *Journal des Débats*, "the high conservative, constitutional, and moral journal of France," and its ilk abhorred his work. Because English press power was "immense," it could crush or exalt any literary form.

The British Quarterly Review, 1845–1886

Devised for middle-class Dissenters, the *British Quarterly* prioritized French journalism but ran occasional and equally serious pieces on English gazettes.

1. [Vaughan, Robert]. "The Priesthood of Letters." 3 (1846): 283–319.
Articulated that the best British literature of Queen Anne's day was in periodicals. "Periodical literature, as distinguished from mere periodical news, owes its origin to this country." By the end of the eighteenth century, 200 periodicals had come, and many had gone in England and Scotland but had influenced the upper and middle classes. The *Edinburgh Review*, with its talented writers, rejuvenated literary criticism but soon faced the *Quarterly Review* in a political war. Cheaper serials, aiming to educate but "light, elegant, and amusing in their style," attracted readers of all classes. Although some periodicals still showed "inanity and bad taste," the demand for quality was growing. Newspapers, better since Roger L'Estrange's *Observator* and Daniel Defoe's *Review*, were by 1846 "models of condensation, clearness, accuracy, and power" and used their power for "salutary and humane" purposes, not to corrupt.

2. [Kirwan, A. V.]. "Journalism in France." 3 (1846): 468–524.
Tracked French journalism from the seventeenth-century *Mercure Français*, when "*Gazetier* signified the Editor of a periodical paper, as well as the Publisher." The eighteenth-century English *Monitor* (1759) reputedly inspired the "moral and political articles" of the *Moniteur* (1760), later the official mouthpiece. *Nouvelles à la Main* (c. 1750) was an early scandal sheet, but the press of the French Revolution was worse.

Spotlighted the contents, major writers, and circulation (12,000 subscribers in 1826–27) of the *Journal des Débats*, with less detail on other newspapers. Since 1830 every Paris newspaper was known by its politics, but greed rather than high startup costs due to press laws apparently motivated publication of serialized novels that lured readers and advertisers and destroyed the newspaper. French gazettes had less prestige because of the perception that they were not in the national interest in contrast to British, which were equally capitalist. The "powerful" British newspaper was "a successful commercial establishment, having large capital at its command, which capital enables it to obtain correct, copious, and early intelligence." Hence, British ministers tried to bribe proprietors; the French, journalists.

French journalists had a "strong *esprit de corps*" because the public valued good newspaper writers and editors, compensating Parisians well. The French, unlike the English, had more time to craft leaders. However, journalists were losing power as education spread and losing reputation as papers of poor quality multiplied. *See* 38: 126; *Fraser's Magazine* 33: 674, 42: 74 (which reprinted p. 513 of this essay), and 43: 350; *Hogg's Instructor* 3: 411.

3. [Kirwan, A. V.]. "Modern Spain." 4 (1846): 143–79.
Aired that Spanish dailies appeared at 10 a.m. and 7 p.m. but most had been suppressed by 1846.

4. [Kirwan, A. V.]. "Newspaper Press, and Political Literature of Spain." 6 (1847): 315–32.

Chronicled that 1800 Madrid had two official newspapers and from 1812 to 1822, several journals. During the "constitutional government" after Ferdinand VII, papers were unsophisticated. In 1847 Madrid had morning and evening dailies with 30,000 readers and 15,000 buyers. Like the United States, more papers meant less influence, but, unlike the American, Spanish papers had few advertisements. The Madrid press did not represent "great parties" unlike in Paris or great capitalists and scribes unlike in London. Madrid borrowed feuilletons from the French, but the Spanish press lacked the "soul" and "substance" of the Gallic. Madrid's humor was "coarse and obscene." Provided content analysis, subscription prices, and proprietors of major papers.

"The reporters of the Spanish press are a very hilarious, hirsute, filthy-looking race, smelling rancidly of garlic, tobacco, and bad *quardiente*." "A low-lived, boozy, debauched, jolly set of dogs are these Spanish stenographers, somewhat resembling the British penny-a-liners." Consequently, pay was low.

5. [Kirwan, A. V.]. "Public Men of France." 7 (1848): 123–47.

Noticed "Mme. Pauline de Meulan, who edited a periodical called the *Publiciste* with the greatest success" and for which François Guizot wrote. She also helped to found the *Revue Française* "that did so much to enlarge the views of Frenchmen, and to elevate the tone of their periodical criticism." Adolphe Thiers wrote articles of "vigorous thought" and "purity and pungency of style" for the *Constitutionnel* and cofounded with Armand Carrel the *National*, a catalyst of the July Revolution.

6. [Jones, Martha]. "Samuel Warren – *Now and Then*." 7 (1848): 378–404.

Touched on Warren's many articles in *Blackwood's Magazine*.

7. [Lushington, Henry]. "Italy: Its State and Prospects." 7 (1848): 464–95.

Skimmed liberty of the press in Italy.

8. [Kirwan, A. V.]. "French Revolution of 1848." 7 (1848): 496–527.

Alluded to the French Association for the Defence of the Liberty of the Press in the 1830s.

9. [Vaughan, Robert]. "Sterling's Life and Writings." 8 (1848): 176–203.

Recognized John Sterling's columns in the *Athenaeum* as responsible for its initial reputation and in the *Quarterly Review*, *Westminster Review*, and *Blackwood's Magazine*.

Literary criticism in periodicals suffered from a demand for the "showy"; pressure to produce quickly, if not ably; the temptation to be partisan that sired "disputatious and dogmatic" pieces; and anonymity.

10. "Europe in 1848." 8 (1848): 516–53.

Praised the "courage and eloquence" of French newspapers during the 1848 revolution.

11. [Lewes, G. H.]. "T. B. Macaulay – *History of England*." 9 (1849): 1–41.

Analyzed Macaulay's style, first shown in his 1824 articles in *Knight's Quarterly Magazine*, which drew many "young and able writers."

12. [Kirwan, A. V.]. "State of Opinion and Parties in France." 9 (1849): 272–95.

Evaluated the sway of the *National* and *Réforme* in France.

13. "Fame and Letters." 10 (1849): 75–98.
Centered on Junius.

14. [Masson, David]. "Douglas Jerrold." 10 (1849): 192–208.
Featured Jerrold's humor writing in newspapers and in *Punch*, where he was one of its "principal contributors."

15. [Edwards, Edward]. "Libraries and the People." 11 (1850): 61–80.
Lectured that American newspapers sometimes sparked other reading, but British gazettes frequently superseded it. The English and Scots supplemented the newspaper only with novels or romances from libraries, and it was the sole reading of the Irish lower classes.

16. "Eastern Europe and British Policy." 11 (1850): 230–65.
Urged the press to be "more studious and reflective" in writing on foreign affairs rather than publishing "mere bluster and gossip," which put English journalism "far behind that of France." During 1848–49, the *Daily News* tried to get "accurate and ample information," but *The Times* was "less noble and generous" in covering "every moment of social importance."

17. "Newspapers – and the Stamp Question." 15 (1852): 135–62.
Based on the report of the Select Committee on Newspapers, concluded that the "doom of the newspaper stamp duty is sealed." The Board of Inland Revenue was arbitrary about deciding which publications required a stamp, and the post office had inconsistent rates for newspapers and other periodicals, although only one-fifth were mailed. Lower postage would benefit "highly useful cheap weekly publications," such as *Chambers's Journal*, *Household Words*, and the *Family Herald*, and would encourage more. The result would give workers a "taste for reading," as Horace Greeley noted in the United States. Some, as W. H. Smith and Mowbray Morris, *The Times* manager, opposed repeal because it might lead to an immoral or dangerous press; others, because it could hurt circulation (with data for London dailies). *The Times* had overwhelming superiority in numbers because advertising paid for good writers and news gathering. The *Morning Chronicle* could be a competitor if it returned to the course set by James Perry. Without the stamp, more papers would surface in the country because even large locals could not possibly cover all the news of surrounding towns. *See Chambers's Journal* n.s., 17: 329.

18. "Travels in South America." 15 (1852): 338–61.
Aside called the *New York Express* "a most authentic paper."

19. [Kirwan, A. V.]. "Napoleonism – Its Present and Its Prospects." 15 (1852): 555–73.
Denounced the Second Empire where "[a]ll the democratic newspapers have been suspended or suppressed." When the government "extinguished" the *National* and other papers, "many writers, reporters, compositors, folders, pressmen, distributors, book-keepers, clerks" lost their jobs; some committed suicide, and a few were sent to prison or executed.

20. [Vaughan, Robert]. "Lord Jeffrey – Our Periodical Press." 16 (1852): 152–96.
Review of Henry Cockburn's *Life of Jeffrey* introduced Francis Jeffrey as the first editor of the *Edinburgh Review* but shadowed the press from the *Orange Intelligencer* of William III and *Daily Courant* of Anne. Early eighteenth-century papers, such as the *Tatler* and *Spectator*, blended literature

and politics and added a "considerable batch of printed news." By the 1760s John Wilkes' *North Briton* and the "Letters of Junius" signaled more politics and fewer essays. While the *Monthly Review* and *Gentleman's Magazine* were dull, Jeffrey's *Edinburgh* was innovative, famous for the "bold and slashing style" of its outstanding authors. Anonymity was acceptable to promote a "freer and more fair-play spirit in politics, literature, and everything else."

Since 1829 the political influence of newspapers had increased because London journalists had shown "amazing talent" in responding to the demand for prompt opinions on important questions. Consequently, by 1852 the British had outgrown the *Quarterly Review* and *Blackwood's Magazine* on politics.

21. [Kirwan, A. V.]. "French Literature under the Restoration." 19 (1854): 233–59.
Glanced at François Guizot who wrote for the *Globe* and "more for the *Constitutionnel*, whose proprietors were timid." The *Globe* commenced in 1823 as a literary journal. Guizot started the *National* with Armand Carrel and Adolphe Thiers in 1830. Aside that Napoleon I paid the editor of the *Journal des Débats* to support the government and the Roman Church.

22. [Kirwan, A. V.]. "Portraits of French Celebrities." 20 (1854): 220–47.
Painted French journalism as almost "inanimate" because of the "strict censorship" that left only the government *Moniteur* – and perhaps the *Pays*, formerly edited by Alphonse de Lamartine – safe. The *Journal des Débats*, *Siècle*, and *Constitutionnel* had no "vitality." Even if the press "exercised its powers wantonly," from 1830 to 1848 there was no need to tighten restrictions on political discussion. While London was superior to France for political reporting, the capital was "very inferior…in the character and tone of its literary and critical articles." Most notable was the work of Charles Sainte-Beuve who penned for the *Globe*, *Revue des Deux Mondes*, *Revue de Paris*, and *Constitutionnel*. Aside that Emile de Girardin was "notorious."

23. [Masson, David]. "Present Aspects and Tendencies of Literature." 21 (1855): 157–81.
Classified British reading matter in 1855. 1) "True or High": "In our periodicals, and in our own best newspapers, we have frequently beautiful specimens of disquisition put forth anonymously." 2) "Wholesome Popular": Great demand for this genre induced "some of the best minds," as Charles Dickens in *Household Words*, to write for this press. *Chambers's Journal* had an "elevating style…and contents." 3) "Trash and Garbage": Five or six periodicals, with 200,000 copies sold every Saturday to the poor, had scraps of news and articles pirated from others, answers to correspondents, medical advice, "jests," and "stunning fiction," the staple of this genre.

24. "*Memoirs of James Montgomery*." 21 (1855): 513–39.
Recorded that Montgomery became editor of the *Sheffield Iris* when he had little political or literary experience. The late eighteenth-century country newspaper "was rather a conveyance for news than a leader of opinion" because most relied on scissors and paste. Montgomery soon inserted commentary and also penned for the *Eclectic Review* at a time when critical essays were shorter than in the 1850s.

25. "The Know-Nothings: American Prospects." 22 (1855): 45–75.
Informed that American newspapers widely disseminated ideas. Dailies, weeklies, and other serials printed 426,409,978 copies annually in the United States, although 33,645,485 were "avowedly religious."

26. [Vaughan, R. A.]. "Life of Sydney Smith." 22 (1855): 172–201.
Weighed Smith's role in launching the *Edinburgh Review* and making it significant by his many articles on political and social abuses. In contrast to Smith's pages, those of editor Francis Jeffrey were more analytical but less humorous.

27. "*Lands of the Slave and the Free*." 22 (1855): 412–28.
Review of H. A. Murray's book disclosed that the United States had 2,526 newspapers circulating 427 million copies, "many of these broad sheets…of the most despicable description." Literary and religious periodicals were allegedly better, but the political press had the "foulest mouths" and appeared on "wretched paper," although many locals had clout.

28. [Kirwan, A. V.]. "*Beaumarchais and His Times*." 23 (1856): 519–48.
Review of Louis de Lomenie's book whispered about the writing of Pierre de Beaumarchais in the *Revue des Deux Mondes*.

29. [Vaughan, R. A.]. "Piedmont and Italy." 24 (1856): 507–38.
Singled out Lorenzo Valerio, "leader of the liberal opposition" in the Piedmontese parliament, who published *Letture Popolari* and *Letture di Famiglia*, journals to spread knowledge among "the lower classes."

30. "American Democracy and the Slave Power." 25 (1857): 190–211.
Called the *New York Evening Post* "[o]ne of the most moderate American newspapers."

31. "The Government of India and the Mutinies." 26 (1857): 476–504.
Advocated suppression of the Indian press because it promoted civil rights for local people.

32. "Gustave Planche and French Fine Art Criticism." 27 (1858): 340–61.
Noted that Planche contributed to the *Artiste*, *Revue des Deux Mondes*, and *Journal des Débats*.

33. [Kirwan, A. V.]. "Guizot's *Memoirs*." 28 (1858): 149–80.
Based on François Guizot's book, explicated his work for the *Globe* and *Revue Française*. The French press, 1815–51, used its liberty well. Paris had about 15 morning and seven evening varied newspapers, while London had six morning and about five evening gazettes. In 1858 the *Journal des Débats*, *Constitutionnel*, and other newspapers had leaders "far more tastefully and spiritedly written than any appearing in the London papers." Aside on a duel involving journalists of *Figaro*.

34. "Serf-Emancipation in Russia." 29 (1859): 151–85.
Estimated that *Kolokol*, a "clever audacious radical" Russian-language paper published fortnightly in London by Alexander Herzen, circulated 2,000 copies in Russia read by intellectuals and abolitionist owners.

35. [Kirwan, A. V.]. "France and England." 29 (1859): 215–38.
Proclaimed that the French press was "dead" unlike 1815–51, when it was powerful if sometimes malicious. In the Second Empire, censorship, warnings, and suppression resulted in unemployment for many in Paris and the provinces. Among the Paris victims was the *National*. Even the *Progres du Pas de*

Calais, for which Napoleon III once wrote, had disappeared. The *Journal des Débats* was independent, but it and the *Siècle* had been warned. The French also confiscated English dailies and weeklies, even "the twaddling *Observer*." Only the pro-imperial *Constitutionnel* was secure. Paris correspondents at home and abroad were careful. Count C. de Montalembert, writing for the *Correspondent*, "a monthly review addressed to the gentry and better intellects," had been imprisoned.

36. "Cheap Literature." 29 (1859): 313–45.
Contended that abolition of the stamp duty on newspapers, coupled with advances in printing and telegraphy, resulted in new widely read penny papers. Often sold at railway stations, they showed "moderation and good taste." London also had vibrant parish and émigré papers as well as specialized ones.

Cheap periodicals aimed to instruct and amuse, but the *Family Herald*, *London Journal*, *Reynolds's Miscellany*, and their ilk emphasized fiction more than information in contrast to the "more solid" *Leisure Hour*. Readers must decide whether the cheap press was elevating. Aside that George Augustus Sala at *Welcome Guest* was akin to Charles Dickens at *Household Words*.

37. "Henry Lord Brougham." 32 (1860): 3–42.
Attributed to Brougham, Francis Jeffrey, and their colleagues the introduction in the *Edinburgh Review* of "a new type of periodical literature," one by great minds writing on law, politics, and literature. Brougham published many articles on a plethora of topics but was undistinguished in style and thought.

38. "The Government Machine." 34 (1861): 184–203.
Stressed that newspapers provided information to MPs on which they based decisions. Since identifying issues already in the public eye raised sales, top papers preferred to echo readers rather than to explore new topics. Deciding what to print marked an editor's skill.

39. "Camillo Benso di Cavour." 34 (1861): 234–54.
Cited Cavour's journalism: articles in the *Revue des Deux Mondes* and creation of the *Giornale Agrario* and – with others – the *Risorgimento*, which Caesar Balbo edited.

40. "French Protestantism." 36 (1862): 338–70.
Categorized as part of the French Protestant press the Paris daily *Temps* and the *Revue Chrétienne*.

41. "The Ethics of Periodical Criticism." 37 (1863): 277–92.
Gloried that the press was "never in better condition." Papers, even the penny, had "disquisitions" of "ability and elaboration." Although some writing showed "flippancy and incompetence," the "newspaper is regarded as an infallible authority, both for opinions and facts." One flaw was that gazettes' literary critics had power but were often wrong by intent or ignorance. Because the public made them "indispensable," the "journalist…should not pander to the worst and meanest part of a nature he should be doing his best to exalt and correct."

42. "Christopher North." 37 (1863): 365–410.
Suggested that John Wilson was well suited to periodical work as his 8,234 pages in *Blackwood's Magazine* proved. When it emerged, the *Edinburgh Review* had already lost "freshness," and the *Quarterly Review* was "pompous." *Blackwood's* early articles paralleled American sensationalism. The "insolent swash-buckling style" and the maligning of others, chiefly *Edinburgh* reviewers, were due to "inexperienced" authors. In 1863 *Blackwood's* was "solid in matter and lively in style."

43. "De Quincey and His Writings." 38 (1863): 1–29.
Surveyed Thomas De Quincey's work for the *Literary Gazette* and *Tait's Edinburgh Magazine.*

44. [Kirwan, A. V.]. "France – the Press, Literature, and Society." 38 (1863): 126–68.
Referred to 3: 468. Recalled that the French "Press of 1815, of 1820, of 1830, of 1840, and 1848 – was a great and free instrument" and from 1830 to 1848 "a great intellectual instrument" even if "prejudiced," "corrupt," or manipulative. In 1848, with a rush of papers, "[m]any women aspired to become Journalists," among them George Sand, Eugénie Mboyet, editor of the "socialist" *Voix des Femmes*, and Amandée DeCésena, editor of the "democratic" *Triomphe du Peuple.* With the advent of low prices, standards dropped. Much of the writing was "milk for babes and not meat for men." Suppressions soon increased, such as of the *Univers*, whose editor Louis Veûillot was "the ablest writer among the more modern Journalists." Alternatively, the *Moniteur*, the "official Journal of the Empire," gained a higher circulation and more advertising. Detailed the contributors and circulation, sometimes ownership and production, of the *Journal des Débats*, *Constitutionnel*, *Presse*, *Siècle*, and *Patrie*, "the most popular evening paper in Paris." Asides on weeklies and recent confiscations of the *Saturday Review*, *Daily News*, and *Fraser's Magazine* in France and on Sir John Easthope, a profit-minded owner of the *Morning Chronicle*, who lowered its standards.

45. "Home in Poland." 38 (1863): 368–83.
Aside on the *Dziennik Poznanski*, a Polish newspaper.

46. [Vaughan, Robert]. "*Modern France*." 39 (1864): 191–201.
Quoted extensively A. V. Kirwan's book, captioned here, the first half of which was on French journalism.

47. "The English Post Office." 40 (1864): 79–101.
Mentioned that the 1836 reduction in the newspaper stamp duty led to an "enormous increase" of newspapers in the post. Vividly described late-day arrival of newsboys.

48. "Charles Knight's Personal Recollections." 40 (1864): 423–40.
Sketched, using Knight's books, his career from 1812 when he reported for London's *Globe* and started the *Windsor and Eton Express* even though workers could not afford respectable papers. In 1820 he published the *Etonian* before founding *Knight's Quarterly Magazine* with its fine writers. His *Penny Magazine*, whose goal was to "whet the appetite" for knowledge, sold 200,000 copies per week within two years of inception.

49. [Collins, Mortimer]. "Matthew Arnold, Poet and Essayist." 42 (1865): 243–69.
Sighed that though Eton, 1825, had quality magazines, the 1865 "*Eton College Chronicle* was a mere school newspaper."

50. [Collins, Mortimer]. "Praed and His Works." 43 (1866): 339–66.
Literary biography of Winthrop Mackworth Praed marked J. G. Lockhart as "one of the few men in whose editorial hands a review or magazine becomes a power" and the *Owl* as "a curious periodical" whose "contributors combined a good deal of recondite, political, and fashionable information, with a pleasant vein of the poetry of society."

51. [Pressensé, Edmond de]. "The Ecclesiastical Crisis in the Reformed Church of France." 43 (1866): 479–529.

Catalogued French Protestant journalism: the *Archives du Christianisme*, *Semeur*, *Esperance*, the "witty and sarcastic" *Réformation*, the small *Disciple de Jésus Christ* and the *Protestant Libéral*, and *Lien*, edited by Etienne Coquerel and for which Albert Réville wrote "witty and informed articles." Controversy between the religious and political journals generated "passionate articles."

52. [Porter, Noah]. "The United States since the War." 45 (1867): 178–214.

Deplored that the American South before 1860 had "no free journalism."

53. [Lawrance, Hannah]. "Recollections of Thomas Hood." 46 (1867): 323–54.

Trailed Hood's journalistic career. In 1821 he went to the *London Magazine* to "assist in editorship." That role meant "little more than arranging the order of the articles, and seeing them through the press" because of "the well-known ability of the whole staff of contributors." Hood, although a "young and unknown writer," also handled "a department strictly belonging to the editor – the answers to correspondents" and corrected proofs as "a labour of love." In 1830 he began the *Comic Annual*. During the 1830s he contributed to the *Athenaeum*, *Punch*, and the *New Monthly Magazine*, of which he was later editor. He eventually raised enough money to establish the monthly *Hood's Magazine*, whose first number sold 1,500 copies, a sale "unprecedented" according to "an eminent publisher," and which later attracted articles from prestigious authors, such as Charles Dickens.

54. [Hutton, James]. "British India under Three Administrations." 48 (1868): 350–76.

Emphasized that Governor-General Charles Canning censored the press because all his advisers agreed that it was not a good time to allow the Anglo-Indian papers to demand vengeance for the 1857 uprising or to challenge government. Their words were "certain to be freely rendered into the native languages and diffused far and wide."

55. "In Memoriam – Rev. Dr. Vaughan." 49 (1869): 160–88.

Summarized Robert Vaughan's editing of the *British Quarterly* and its tensions with the *Eclectic Review*.

56. [Pressensé, Edmond de]. "Roman Catholicism in France on the Eve of the Ecumenical Council of 1869." 49 (1869): 391–435.

Highlighted several French Catholic periodicals of the 1860s as well as Louis Veûillot, "the too notorious editor" of the *Univers*, and Count C. de Montalembert, once "the impetuous editor" of the *Avenir*.

57. [Keltie, J. S.]. "The Later Life of DeFoe[*sic*]." 50 (1869): 483–519.

Charged Daniel Defoe with exploiting journals, among them *Mist's Weekly Journal*, for political purposes. Defoe was purportedly the first writer after John Milton to appreciate the force of public opinion and how to use it.

58. [Allon, Henry and H. R. Reynolds]. "The Hundredth Number of the *British Quarterly Review*: A Retrospect and a Prospect." 50 (1869): 520–39.

Abridged the *British Quarterly's* position on numerous issues.

59. "The American Press." 53 (1871): 1–26.
Postulated that the "progress of the press becomes historically the most constant and faithful indication of the general progress of a nation." While the press was essential for progress because it supported public safety and morals and fostered "healthy and independent public opinion," it also headlined "the wicked, the worthless, and the shallow" in "false, distorted, and narrow" stories.

Tracked American newspapers from the seventeenth century. In 1775 there were 34; in 1800, 200; in 1871, 5,244, among them the *New York Times*, "one of the most respectable and powerful newspapers." Yet the United States had "not even produced a single great newspaper writer." The famous New York "capital editors" were the elder James Gordon Bennett, Horace Greeley, and Henry Raymond, but they were "greatly inferior" to Hugh Miller (*Edinburgh Witness*) and Albany Fonblanque (*Examiner*) "in that art of scholarly, dignified, and tasteful leader-writing, which gives such a power and charm to London journalism." In the United States, identifying an editor linked "the authority of the journal with the personal influence of the editor." American journalists vulgarized English and indulged in factionalism and exaggeration as had the British earlier. Like the French, American scribes did not seek to instruct but to advance themselves politically. The United States needed more writers who prioritized the country's welfare, avoided flattery, and eschewed hoaxes.

Except for the *North American Review*, the United States "never produced a Quarterly worthy of the name." Other magazines, general and specialized, did not measure up to British publications except for religious journals.

60. [Richard, Henry]. "The Established Church in Wales." 53 (1871): 139–79.
Registered that most religious literature of Wales was Nonconformist. Of "about 30 periodicals, quarterlies, monthlies, and weeklies, at present published in the Welsh language," all but three were Dissenter owned or edited.

61. "The Downfall of Bonapartism." 53 (1871): 409–41.
Indicted Paris journalists for misleading the public in 1870 by flaunting French power.

62. "The Modern Newspaper." 55 (1872): 348–80.
Averred that British newspaper history had yet to be written and then traced its roots from the *acta diurna* to the eighteenth century. Papers flourished dramatically after the 1855 repeal of the newspaper stamp. "[T]he modern newspaper is a moral daguerreotype reproducing the moral physiognomy of a people" but depended too much on advertising. Reuters' telegraphy homogenized news and reduced editorial responsibility. Although leaders were still good, Parliamentary coverage was less clear than that of the French Chamber because speeches were handled by a local correspondent or special reporter, not a "regular and responsible attaché" of a paper. Cheapness would kill evening papers that did not attract big audiences.

The local press sprouted slowly in the eighteenth century. Before 1760 there were about 30 mostly "miserable sheets" pirating material from London to supplement neighborhood advertising. In 1871 Mitchell's *Newspaper Press Directory* put the number at 70 in England, Scotland, and Wales. These gazettes were full of discussion and accurate local news because country journalists exaggerated less than London penny-a-liners. "Original writing is not the strong point of provincial journalism," but people read it because of editorial "enterprise, ability, and care."

Scanned *Punch*, the illustrated and parish papers, and journals in Ireland, India, Australia, and Canada. Contrasted British and Continental papers with respect to format, production costs, and journalists, who in Britain were not recognized as professionals. Checked French provincial papers, which did not equal British except for their outstanding leaders, and German, Belgian, and Russian heralds, the last modeled on Britain.

63. "Mazzini and New Italy." 58 (1873): 103–44.
Spoke about Giuseppe Mazzini's writing in Florence's *Antologia* and his persuading the editor of the *Indicatore Genoese*, an advertising journal, to include literary articles, which caused problems with the censors.

64. "Mr. Mill's *Autobiography*." 59 (1874): 195–215.
Review of John Stuart Mill's book judged the *Edinburgh Review* and the *Quarterly Review* "able and influential" journals that gave "intelligence and vigour" to political and literary discussions. The first number of the *Westminster Review* did the unusual by publishing "a criticism upon another review," an article by James Mill on the *Edinburgh*, but the *Westminster* founders were not "pleased with the *Review* as a whole."

65. "Authors and Publishers." 59 (1874): 313–42.
Cited Daniel Defoe's *Review*, the *Tatler*, *Spectator*, *Gentleman's Magazine*, and the *Monthly Review*, *Quarterly Review*, and *Edinburgh Review*.

66. "The Electric Telegraph." 59 (1874): 438–70.
Guaranteed that since the post office takeover of telegraphy, news supply was no longer "scanty, inferior, and fitful" and was cheaper. About 20 newspapers had special wires, so some locals published London news the same morning as the metro papers.

67. "The Tory Administration and Its Whig Admirers." 60 (1874): 171–94.
Portrayed the early *Edinburgh Review* as a serial "where the sentences of [Henry] Brougham run like fire along the ground" and T. B. Macaulay "flings the fine lightning of his scorn."

68. [Japp, Alexander H.]. "Edgar Allan Poe." 62 (1875): 194–218.
Considered Poe's editing of the *Southern Literary Messenger* from which he was apparently fired for drinking, his writing for New York's *Mirror*, where he was "cheerful and obliging" and labored with "regularity," and his long "angry feud" with the *North American Review*.

69. [Ralston, W. R. S.]. "The Progress of Reform in Russia." 63 (1876): 382–405.
Trumpeted that Russian censors who privately alerted editors about topics that the government deemed "unfit for publication" negated the 1865 law on press freedom. Ignoring a warning could result in disaster, as *Besseida* learned when its issues were burned.

70. [Ralston, W. R. S.]. "Russia." 65 (1877): 448–75.
Panicked that Russian papers published in Geneva and London, notably "[Alexander] Herzen's famous *Kolokol*," promulgated revolution.

71. "*Thomas De Quincey*." 66 (1877): 415–33.
Review of H. A. Page's book connected De Quincey to *Blackwood's Magazine*.

72. [Trowbridge, T. C.]. "The Americans in Turkey." 67 (1878): 28–59.
Observed that American missionaries published "a number of newspapers" in "Constantinople and Beirut, in the Arabic, Armenian, Armeno-Turkish, Greco-Turkish, and Bulgarian languages." In Constantinople, "circulation by subscription" accounted for "6,591 copies."

73. [Mayer, S. R. Townshend]. "Bryan Waller Procter." 68 (1878): 63–82.
Studied Proctor's writing in the *Literary Gazette* and *London Magazine*, with brief notes on other *London* scribes, such as T. G. Wainwright whose pen name was Janus Weathercock.

74. Rae, John. "England and the Greek Question." 70 (1879): 177–200.
Perceived that with the large population of well-educated people in Greece, "the press is daily assuming greater and greater influence." There were 129 newspapers and periodicals "conducted with great ability and spirit." Although "severe and plain-spoken" about politics, the papers rarely resorted to "absolute scurrility." Since the 1864 end of censorship, they had helped to develop "a healthy and vigorous public opinion."

75. Rae, John. "The Revolutionary Movement in Russia." 71 (1880): 394–442.
Assumed Alexander Herzen's *Kolokol* and Michael Katkoff's *Moscow Gazette* verified that the Russian press was a powerful organ of opinion. *Kolokol*, written with "vigour and ability…and wit," had a huge circulation in Russia where anonymity added importance to journalism and secrecy added more.

76. C[roskery], T[homas]. "The Irish Land Question." 73 (1881): 418–41.
Asserted that "the most important and influential communications from Ireland" were Charles Russell's columns in the *Daily Telegraph*.

77. Palmer, H. S. "Recent Japanese Progress." 76 (1882): 1–34.
Focused on the remarkable growth of the "native newspaper press" that began in Japan around 1860, pre-dated by magazines of small circulation. In 1871 the first daily commenced in Yokohama and the government *Shimbun Zasshi* opened in Tokyo. "In 1873 a high-class paper called the *Miroku Zasshi* was brought out by a society of prominent and able literary men," including Mori Arinori, minister to Great Britain in 1882. It was soon "the leading journal" thanks to journalists who were "fairly well-informed, and gaining rapidly in experience and knowledge." Special correspondents during uprisings faced "danger and hardship." The 1873 press laws were supplemented by more severe ones in 1875 and 1876 because of the "extreme and dangerous license" of a few editors and writers. The laws were mild compared to those in Europe but could result in fines and imprisonment. Still the press blossomed, reaching 112 dailies and 130 periodicals, which together had an annual circulation of over 33 million copies.

78. "George Eliot." 81 (1885): 316–33.
Mentioned Eliot's tenure as *Westminster Review* assistant editor and writer of articles of "considerable merit."

79. "Toryism of the Last Half-Century." 81 (1885): 386–415.
Regarded J. W. Croker's *Quarterly Review* articles as "more remarkable for the malignity of their spirit than for the force of their reasoning."

Chambers's (Edinburgh) Journal, 1832–1900

Addressing the lower social ranks, *Chambers's Journal*, the product of brothers William and Robert Chambers, publicized the press extensively. Significant in this output were a pioneer history of newspapers and an ongoing concern about country gazettes.

1. Chambers, William. "The Editor's Address to His Readers." 1 (1832–33): 1–2.
Promised that *Chambers's* would provide knowledge and amusement but not news because of the stamp duty.

2. "Popular Information on Literature." 1 (1832–33): 99–100, 122, 220.
Depicted Robert Southey as a hardworking, wide-ranging author in the *Quarterly Review* and William Gifford and J. G. Lockhart as its editors who ensured its quality criticism in contrast to Thomas Campbell, a less energetic editor of the *New Monthly Magazine*. In the eighteenth century, distinguished writers established periodicals that generated little interest; in the nineteenth, anonymity produced "literary hypocrisy" but opened doors to tyros.

3. "Printing and Stereotyping." 1 (1832–33): 278.
Explained that *Chambers's* use of stereotyping kept costs down.

4. [Chambers, William]. "*Chambers's Edinburgh Journal*." 2 (1833–34): 1–2.
Assessment of *Chambers's* first year listed introduction of stereotyping; issuance in the United States and some colonies; employment of seven writers with "practice and experience in letters" to complement borrowed material; rejection of illustrations in order to appeal to "understanding," not the "senses," or present the "endless, meaningless flippancy" of many periodicals. Condemned the "desperate trash" of unstamped political tribunes while *Chambers's* commercial success legitimated its moral goal of education. In Scotland, 35 newspapers produced 1,733,500 sheets per year and *Chambers's* produced 2,600,000.

5. "The New Knowledge." 2 (1833–34): 196–97.
Objected to newspapers' attempts to convince readers that the only knowledge was in their pages. Journalists shielded by anonymity often made snap judgments on public questions, reported trivia, and promoted the books of publishers who supported the paper or the goods of its frequent advertisers. For their collusion, the rewards of "sages," the editors, were few.

6. "*Chambers's Edinburgh Journal*." 2 (1833–34): 296.
Complained that most newspapers disliked *Chambers's* because of its wide circulation, good pay for writers, and refusal to include 'trash,' but the *Dumfries and Galloway Courier*, "one of the cleverest and certainly the most amusing of our provincial prints," was a fan.

7. "New South Wales." 2 (1833–34): 342.

Measured the "march of intellect" in New South Wales by its six newspapers and periodicals plus the *Government Gazette* and the *Australian Almanack.*

8. "Western States of America: Ohio." 2 (1833–34): 381–82.

Bruited that Cincinnati had three dailies, two semiweeklies, six weeklies, and a variety of periodicals.

9. "*Chambers's Edinburgh Journal.*" 3 (1834–35): 1–2.

Provided data on *Chambers's* sales by towns in England and Scotland and the number of its sheets compared to quarterlies and monthlies. Alleged that it circulated among the lower classes and succeeded by returning to the eighteenth-century style of the "moral or didactic" essay.

10. "Popular Information on Literature: American Literature." 3 (1834–35): 27.

Centered on American newspapers from 1704: by 1776 there were 35; 1810, 358; 1843, 1,200. Without a stamp duty and with a cheap post, newspapers were popular. Most seemed morally sound but literarily weak and "degraded" by political bias.

Periodicals from Benjamin Franklin's *General Magazine* developed slowly because there were few writers and publishers. Of the 24 in 1810, *Portfolio*, edited by Joseph Dennie in Philadelphia, was important. Among reviews, the *North American*, edited by A. H. Everett in Boston, and the *American Quarterly*, edited by R. Walsh, in Philadelphia, had well-earned circulations of 3,000–4,000. The *New York Mirror*, a weekly literary gazette, had original art and engravings.

11. "Popular Information on Literature: Newspapers." 3 (1834–35): 113–14, 130–31, 146–47, 193–94, 242–43, 306–307, 322.

This seven-part history of newspapers, reputedly by 1834 the "monitors" of government, covered Scotland in depth. Less attention went to English locals and Irish gazettes.

Opened with Roman editors, far more straightforward about news of disasters than their 1834 peers, and Venetian officials, so suspicious of reporting that they were reluctant to reduce it to writing. The roots of advertising were postings of French wants in public places, but Théophraste Renaudot fathered the Gallic press. In England, the publications of Nathaniel Butter and Marchamont Nedham were groundbreaking. The initial impetus for the press was the Civil Wars followed by the American and French revolutions.

The journals of the Restoration had bizarre titles, notably in the plague years, and Roger L'Estrange reputedly suppressed several sheets of "evil-disposed persons." By century's end, advertising was rife as papers multiplied. The eighteenth-century *Tatler* and its progeny were "a new species," which the *Spectator* particularly embodied. Besides Joseph Addison and Richard Steele, Daniel Defoe, Jonathan Swift, Henry Fielding, and the "notorious" John Wilkes were important. Edward Cave and his friends took notes in Parliament for his *Gentlemen's Magazine*, 1731–38. When challenged by a Member, Cave commissioned Samuel Johnson to pen under the title "Debates in the Senate of Great Lilliput." Needing money, Johnson did so but was apparently uncomfortable in the work. Other magazines copied the *Gentleman's* practice of quoting Members with false appellations.

The early English country press included papers in Norwich, Leeds (*Mercury*), Gloucester, Manchester, Oxford, Preston, and Liverpool. In 1833 there were about 150–160 locals, almost all published weekly in contrast to Scotland where several appeared oftener. In England, newspaper taxes, higher startup costs, and proximity to London inhibited locals. Alternatively, their ongoing expenses were less since London proprietors had to pay more for editors and compositors in "combination." Locals also survived on other printing jobs and advertising, much higher in relation to circulation than in Scotland. Owners, often Scots, reaped 2,000–3,000 pounds annually.

The Scots reprinted a London diurnal, *Mercurius Politicus*, in 1653, but Thomas Sydserf produced the first local in Edinburgh in 1660. The *Mercurius Caledonius* was a weekly quarto, but James Watson's *Edinburgh Gazette* from 1699 and his *Edinburgh Courant* from 1705 dominated the Scottish market. In 1718 the *Evening Courant* of James M'Ewen published foreign news directly from abroad rather than through London, so it was surely the first Scottish newspaper, notwithstanding the claim of the *Caledonian Mercury* of 1720. Glasgow's press dated from its 1715 *Courant*. During the Forty-Five rising, insurgents took presses and furniture of several printers in the city. The premier issue of James Chalmers' *Aberdeen Journal* in 1746 printed the news of Culloden and by 1826, with a steam press, was "the most lucrative" in Scotland. The *Dumfries and Galloway Courier* was third, with about the same number of advertisements and circulation (1,500) as the second-place *Glasgow Herald*.

"Civil commotion appears to have been in Ireland, as in England and Scotland, the origin of newspaper intelligence." For example, at the time of the Union, no printer would work for the government press. *Freeman's Journal*, a daily, was a leader in quality. In 1766 Esther Crawley produced the halfpenny *Waterford Journal*. The oldest newspaper still printing was Belfast's *News Letter*, dating from 1737.

12. "Biographic Sketches: Thomas Chatterton." 3 (1834–35): 174–75.
Biography of writer and poet Chatterton commented that he first published in a Bristol newspaper. By 1770 he was working for London gazettes and magazines, one of which paid him four guineas per month when he died at age 18.

13. "The Canadian Press." 3 (1834–35): 254–55.
Described Canadian newspapers as four-page folios of coarse paper, "miserably printed." In Lower Canada, they were bilingual. Most towns had a paper that pirated from English and Scottish counterparts except at elections and abounded in advertisements and articles meant to lure immigrants.

14. "The Annuals: Story of an East Indian Boy." 3 (1834–35): 333.
Considered annuals "pretty picture books" without much "literary value" and costly to produce. *Jennings's Picturesque Annual* was "elegant"; the *Oriental Annual*, with 'exceedingly fine engravings," was readable.

15. "The London Newspaper." 3 (1834–35): 389–90.
Concentrated on the morning daily that required about 50,000–60,000 pounds to start. Salaries of the editor and subeditor, ten to 14 reporters, 30–35 compositors, readers and reading boys, printers, the publisher, and clerks amounted to 200 pounds per week. With other expenses, owners needed advertising to cover costs. Conceded that evening papers, without Parliamentary reporters, were cheaper to run.

16. "*Chambers's Edinburgh Journal*." 4 (1835–36): 1–2.
Sensed that more people were reading *Chambers's*, which strived to maintain moral and literary standards and to replace superstition with knowledge.

17. "Dippings into Old Magazines – the *Gentleman's* for 1731." 4 (1835–36): 7–8.
Returned to the first number of the *Gentleman's Magazine*, a 42-page octavo that abstracted articles in the *Craftsman* and other serials and added a "Monthly Intelligencer" on births, marriages, and deaths and news ranging from libels to lotteries.

18. "The London Press: Editorial Department." 4 (1835–36): 18–19; "Mechanical Department," 46.

Categorized penning leaders and original criticism and reporting Parliament as the "[i]ntellectual" work of newspapers. Editors reviewed evening and foreign papers and parliamentary reports, prepared leaders, and authorized express boats to get overseas news quickly. Subeditors had to be careful because choice of copy affected a paper's reputation, particularly a 'family newspaper.' Only a half dozen of the 70–80 parliamentary reporters used shorthand, but they all arranged their notes in an anteroom before going to the office to write. Reporters were "men of talent, information, and superior education"; many were "gentlemen." Penny-a-liners might earn three pounds for a half-column if every morning paper bought a story. Asides on printing and the stamp, advertising, and paper duties.

19. "Mechanism of *Chambers's Journal*." 4 (1835–36): 149–51.

Included compositing, proofing, stereotyping, and steam printing as aspects of the production of *Chambers's*.

20. "*Chambers's Edinburgh Journal*." 5 (1836–37): 1–2.

Reiterated *Chambers's* determination to inform, amuse, and raise taste as sales went from 50,000 to 58,000 in one year.

21. Russell, Lord John. "The Diffusion of Literature." 5 (1836–37): 31.

Quoted Russell's speech on the increase of periodicals and the 'ability' mirrored in *Edinburgh Review* and *Quarterly Review* articles.

22. "Biographical Sketches: Sir Richard Steele." 5 (1836–37): 109–10.

Articulated that the *Tatler* was the first to feature ongoing articles on "the reformation of society," the "decencies of life," and "taste." Its predecessors were small and mainly focused on politics, though Daniel Defoe made "comments on manners." Aside that Joseph Addison was more serious than Steele, who penned humor.

23. "The *North Pole Gazette*." 5 (1836–37): 333.

Recorded that Capt. W. Edward Parry's expedition published "a jocular newspaper" that parodied home coverage of news, reviews of drama and fine arts, and advertisements.

24. "*Comic Almanack* for 1837." 5 (1836–37): 407–08.

Tagged the *Almanack* a "droll publication" with engravings by the "inimitable George Cruikshank."

25. "Editorship of Morning Newspapers." 5 (1836–37): 411–12.

Excerpted from James Grant's *The Great Metropolis* information about editors of London dailies whose time went to business meetings, correspondence, and visits from amateur writers. Metro editors needed "consummate sagacity, coupled with great facility in writing" to do their jobs. Their country colleagues were under pressure to obtain an 'exclusive,' especially of neighborhood news.

26. "Pastoral Life in the South of Scotland." 6 (1837–38): 21–22.

Divulged that Scottish shepherds read only religious matter and newspapers.

27. "A Few Hints about Newspapers." 6 (1837–38): 28–29.
Regretted that there was too much local news in London and Edinburgh newspapers and too little on the empire. London gazettes had a plethora of police reports and theatre reviews; Edinburgh journals were full of long leaders, speeches, and letters. The British could learn from the colonial press, as Sydney's *Colonist*, which was "skilfully conducted." If newspapers were one-third world views, one-third instruction, and one-third "home news" broadly defined, carried no advertising, and cost three pence, they would sell well.

28. [Grant, James]. "Magazine Day." 6 (1837–38): 89–90.
Discussed the distribution center (Paternoster Row, London) of magazines on the last day of the month unless it was a Sunday. Booksellers arrived at noon to place their orders, but copies also were dispatched to the country. Authors came to read their reviews. Included data on copies purchased (always in cash).

29. "New System of Postage." 6 (1837–38): 131–32.
Spelled out postal charges for newspapers and magazines.

30. "London Coffee-Houses." 6 (1837–38): 181–82.
Aired that some London coffeehouses had 60–70 newspapers, all the metro and many of the local, and charged for access to back issues. Everyone read a paper, but there was a quick turnover of readers.

31. "Rejected Contributors." 6 (1837–38): 336.
Printed poems hitherto rejected because persistent authors wore down editorial resistance and their works were examples of bad writing to alert future contributors.

32. "*Jennings's Picturesque Annual* for 1838." 6 (1837–38): 364–65.
Profiled *Jennings's* as "[o]rnamented," published at a "moderate price" by an "accomplished man of letters" and "the very first of British architectural artists."

33. "Editorial Notice." 6 (1837–38): 376.
Swore that *Chambers's* always attributed borrowings but those who took from it did not.

34. "The French Newspapers." 6 (1837–38): 412–13.
Cited the *Encyclopedia Britannica* as the best source on French newspapers, "this important subject." From 1789 their problems with government, literary criticism, and feuilletons were important. Aside on subscription statistics for the Paris press.

35. "Cincinnati." 7 (1838–39): 60.
Took as a sign of Cincinnati's intellectual life the proliferation of daily and weekly newspapers.

36. "*Chambers's Edinburgh Journal*." 8 (1839–40): 8.
Rejoiced that *Chambers's* averaged 68,300 sheets per week, perhaps because, in an era of "great social jars," readers found it "soothing."

37. "The Athens of America." 8 (1839–40): 12–13.
Focused on Boston, where everyone read a newspaper. The city had a "flourishing" and profitable press of ten to 12 dailies. Penny papers "conducted with respectable ability," sold on the street, but others were by subscription. Boston also had semi, tri, and biweeklies, monthlies, a "highly respectable magazine," the *Christian Examiner*, and the quarterly *North American Review*. Aside that New York sold 30,000 penny papers per day on the street.

38. Merle, Gibbons. "The Social System of Fourier." 8 (1839–40): 268–69.
Biography of Charles Fourier explored his *Phalanstre* and his followers' *Chronique du Mouvement Social* and *Nouveau Monde*, whose writers were French, British, and Polish.

39. "How We Encourage the Fine Arts." 8 (1839–40): 287.
Appraised the *Art-Union* as a new monthly with "useful information."

40. "The Annuals." 8 (1839–40): 383.
Trailed annuals from *Forget-Me-Not* to a current peak, according to the *Art-Union*. A. A. Watts improved their contents in his *Literary Souvenir*, and competition among these journals led to better quality paper and binding. These changes justified their high price.

41. "Occasional Notes: Anonymous Writing in Country Towns." 9 (1840–41): 4–5.
Bared that people using an alias sent to country newspapers untrue birth, marriage, and death announcements that were anguishing or libelous and letters on politics as "base" as those in the American press.

42. "Notices of Monthly and Quarterly Journals." 9 (1840–41): 13–15.
In response to reader requests, planned to reprint book reviews that were of "value," penned with "talent" and without "severe and sarcastic remarks."

43. "*Tait's Magazine* for April." 9 (1840–41): 117–18.
Painted *Tait's* as a magazine with literature of "high character" and less expensive than its compatriots.

44. "Correspondents." 9 (1840–41): 193–94.
Declined submissions from tyros because *Chambers's* received too many "mediocre" pieces by the "unskilled" that took too much time to edit. It did print some manuscripts to gratify a few contributors and to illustrate errors. *Chambers's* also refused to publish letters on its typographical and format mistakes, those seeking information and advice on trivia or on subjects of extensive research, and missives venting personal troubles. *See* 9: 221.

45. "Uninvited Contributions." 9 (1840–41): 221–24, 255–56.
Reiterated that weak writing had little merit. *See* 9: 193.

46. "Malta, by a Traveller." 9 (1840–41): 2[illegible]–29.
Imagined that the Maltese were not yet sufficiently educated to appreciate the worth of a press.

47. “Biographical Sketches: M. Thiers.” 9 (1840–41): 291–92.
Mentioned that Adolphe Thiers derived some wealth from his share in the *Constitutionnel* but, unhappy about its “somewhat antiquated tone,” started the *National* with Armand Carrel.

48. “The *Renfrewshire Annual*.” 10 (1841–42): 79–80.
Observed that the *Renfrewshire Annual* (Paisley) “contains a fair show of agreeable miscellaneous readings…printed and embellished in an exceedingly handsome manner.” Although they were important for the “diffusion of literary taste,” annuals did not do well in the country.

49. “Occasional Notes: Some Small Country Newspapers.” 10 (1841–42): 125.
Enthused that more monthlies of local news and advertising encouraged a taste for literature and careful language in public speaking. If they did not require a stamp, their startup costs were small, so they could sell for a penny. Abolition of the advertising duty would spur their growth. *See* n.s., 1: 121, n.s., 2: 287, n.s., 7: 59.

50. “Biographical Sketches: Letitia Eliza Landon.” 10 (1841–42): 163–64.
Peeked at Landon’s connection to the *Literary Gazette*.

51. “Botanical Periodicals.” 10 (1841–42): 300–01.
Classified the expensive *Ladies’ Magazine of Gardening* as an “elegant monthly” with a “beautiful colour-plate.” The *Florist’s Journal* was “a cheaper monthly” with “very tolerable coloured engraving.” *Paxton’s Magazine of Botany, and Register of Flowering Plants* had “resplendent coloured prints and wood engraving.”

52. “Joseph Sturge’s *Visit to the United States*.” 11 (1842–43): 116–17.
Review of Sturge’s book accepted his evaluation of the American monthly *Lowell Offering* as a tool to “spread intellectual cultivation.”

53. “A Backwoods Editor.” 11 (1842–43): 184.
Plagiarized a story from the *Louisville* (KY) *Advertiser* on the hazards resulting from editorial criticism of locals and its implications for the editorial “we.”

54. “The Literary Profession.” 11 (1842–43): 225–26.
Delineated the “Literary Profession” as “wide,” with different rewards for the “useful class of writers” who penned articles on “controversial politics in newspapers” and for “conductors and contributors to literary and periodical works.” The current “commercial community…looks down” on all writers, so journalists needed a good basic education and the ability to produce quality regularly in accord with sound “business principles.”

55. “Favourite Phrases of the Press.” 11 (1842–43): 237.
Distinguished newspaper language, as the current “the masses” and “clique,” from the earlier “people” and “fudging.”

56. “Hints for Picture Criticism.” 11 (1842–43): 292–93.
Hoped that as more local papers printed fine arts reviews, critics would display taste and learning, not blandness.

57. "The Periodicals." 11 (1842–43): 375.

Limned the *Foreign Quarterly Review*, which had a "merited reputation" for criticism of taste that introduced British readers to unknown works. Quoted the *Review* (30: 466) on the American press.

58. "*Friendship's Offering* for 1843." 11 (1842–43): 379–80.

Called the titled annual "one of the most respectably conducted" and Camilla Toumlin one of its "earnest and efficient corps" of writers.

59. "Periodical Literature of France: *Review of the Two Worlds*." 11 (1842–43): 383–84.

Portrayed the *Revue des Deux Mondes* as a journal whose depth of coverage of Britain was atypical for a French serial. It also printed fiction, criticism, and essays moderate in politics and knowledgeable in history and science. Aside that the feuilleton verified that French readers placed amusement ahead of information in a newspaper.

60. "Biographic Sketches: Alan Cunningham." 11 (1842–43): 388–89.

Biography of a poet who penned for *Blackwood's Magazine* and a London newspaper stated that Cunningham disliked the "late hours and slavish labour of reporting."

61. "Kohl's *Russia* – Moscow." 12 (1843): 19–20.

Review of J. G. Kohl's book labeled *Viedomoski* "the celebrated newspaper of Moscow." Begun in 1761, it had 2,000 subscribers by 1812 and 12,000 in 1842.

62. "Thomas Carlyle and His Writings." 12 (1843): 37–38.

Named Carlyle a "constant contributor to *Fraser's Magazine*," where his articles revealed his talent and established his reputation.

63. "A Schoolboy Newspaper." 12 (1843): 83–84.

Singled out the *Tulketh Hall Mercury*, a halfpenny quarto, as evidence of the 'march of intellect.' Written and printed by boys at a private academy who used the editorial "we" with "grace and dignity," this daily contained "moral, instructive," and occasionally critical articles, advertisements, general information, school news, and letters from students to maids.

64. "Provincial Literature." 12 (1843): 93.

Believed that it was important for a town to have a newspaper, even a partisan or an advertising sheet. Britain, in contrast to the Continent, had a solid local press much better than the "paltry and distempered prints" of the United States. Scottish papers were adequate on literature and somewhat too political or sectarian but featured no "vulgar demagogues or insidious quacks." Towns of 3,000–4,000 often had literary periodicals or annuals. The periodicals frequently failed because they were too ambitious in relation to available resources and writers but would succeed if they stuck to local themes and light literature.

65. "Visit to *The Times* Printing-Office." 12 (1843): 169–71.

Toured *The Times* composing room, locking-up room with corrected pages set, press room, and reporters' and editors' spaces. "*The Times* is a power in Europe" because of its purported "indifference."

Its correspondents, scattered worldwide or stationed, as in Paris, received six pounds for ordinary expenses, 35 for risky assignments. About 20 reporters covered Parliament, the courts, and meetings in London and beyond for about five pounds per week. Parliamentary reporters typically summarized bad speakers, and leader-writers worked at home. Editor Thomas Barnes received 1,200 guineas per year. Advertising increased after the duty decreased in 1833.

66. "The *Lowell Offering*." 12 (1843): 260–61.
Thought that the American *Lowell Offering*, a small octavo of 350 items of prose and poetry, was not well written but showed that its female authors, better paid than their British counterparts, had some education, breeding, and taste.

67. "Illustrated Periodicals." 12 (1843): 275–76.
Realized that wood engravings were very popular in London crime journals and that the cylinder press improved printing. Referred to the *Illustrated London News*, *Pictorial Times* (whose literature paralleled that of the "best weekly"), and the *Illuminated Magazine* as outstanding for both engraving and writing. The last was edited by Douglas Jerrold, aided by "Mark Lemon, the clever farce writer, and a host of literary sketchers."

68. "Occasional Note: Merits and Rewards in Literature." 12 (1843): 276–77.
Mused that editing a newspaper or a periodical reaped a steadier income than authoring books.

69. "Reviewers." 12 (1843): 393–94.
Avouched that early nineteenth-century literary criticism was less savage than that of the eighteenth century.

Chambers's Journal

70. "*The Gift*, an American Annual." n.s., 1 (1844): 6–9.
Concluded that annuals were dying in Britain because of the "trashiness of their literature" and "completely overdone" format for which elegant covers did not compensate. Although *The Gift* was a "handsome octavo" from Philadelphia, its average prose presaged the same outcome for American annuals.

71. "*Friendship's Offering* for 1844." n.s., 1 (1844): 25–26.
Graded the captioned annual "one of the most respectable" because of its quality pictures and type and "generally good" literature from Camilla Toumlin and Anna M. Hall.

72. "Biographic Sketches: Dr. Maginn." n.s., 1 (1844): 92–94.
Remembered that William Maginn was a regular, anonymous, and unpaid contributor to *Blackwood's Magazine*, 1819–21, then Paris correspondent for the *Representative*. His earnings from newspapers, magazines, and annuals were "scanty" until 1829. Later, he was appointed joint editor, with William Gifford, of the evening *Standard*, wrote for *John Bull*, and had a hand in starting *Fraser's Magazine*.

73. "Occasional Notes: Small Country Papers." n.s., 1 (1844): 121.
Enlightened that monthly magazines with information, fiction, poems, and advertising were multiplying. The Scots published several agricultural monthlies "of a superior character." All had

signed articles and served farmers who wished to share agricultural innovations. *See* 10: 125, n.s., 2: 287, n.s., 7: 59.

74. "Charlotte Corday." n.s., 1 (1844): 125–26.
Logged that the Jacobins bought the presses of Jean-Paul Marat's *Ami du Peuple* after his death in order to prevent "less worthy" people from getting them.

75. "*Hood's Magazine* – 'The *Maison de Deuil.*'" n.s., 1 (1844): 190–91.
Deemed the first numbers of *Hood's* "a most agreeable mélange of light literature," as the title story indicated.

76. "Occasional Notes: Periodical Works." n.s., 2 (1844): 24–25.
Counseled that with the multiplication of periodicals the only roads to success were to address a niche market, recruit "a writer of remarkable gifts," or adopt a political bias, each of which could confer a "distinct and uniform character."

77. "Jottings on the Colonies: Adelaide, South Australia." n.s., 2 (1844): 184–85.
Borrowed from Adelaide's *Observer* the news that the colony had four weeklies. The *Observer*, which promised to be "printed and edited with skill and care," contained many advertisements, local news, and business information.

78. "Small Country Papers." n.s., 2 (1844): 287–88.
Guaranteed that towns could afford monthly penny newspapers with advertising, agricultural matter, and literature if they shunned other news and thus paid no stamp duty. They should be well printed on good paper, bar engravings, and guard against puffery in advertisements. *See* 10: 125, n.s., 1: 121, n.s., 7: 59.

79. "Newspapers." n.s., 2 (1844): 296–97.
Reveled that newspapers were unique, an "ephemeral record of history." Even though they could intrude on privacy, confuse true and false, cause "smiles and tears," they noted the "habits and tastes" of everyone.

80. Hay, William. "Reading Aloud in Workshops." n.s., 2 (1844): 335–36.
Boasted that workmen in Scottish mills subscribed to one local and one Edinburgh, Glasgow, or London paper, which they discussed and then exchanged for one purchased by another shop.

81. "Temperance Papers." n.s., 2 (1844): 350–51.
Introduced the new *Oddfellows' Journal* on the Isle of Man, which had more temperance news than its rivals. The *National Temperance Advocate*, with a circulation of 10,300, was "well managed" and filled with advertising and news.

82. "Missing the Post." n.s., 2 (1844): 383.
Quoted the *Glasgow Citizen* that a newspaper must reach subscribers on time.

83. "Advertising as an Art." n.s., 2 (1844): 401–03.
Compared the eighteenth-century *Public Advertiser* of ten to 15 listings to the 1844 *Times* of 700–1,000 (with samples).

84. "A Few Words to Our Readers." n.s., 3 (1845): 1–3.
Updated that *Chambers's* printed 90,000 copies while other popular magazines printed 6,000–9,000 copies. Because it was the first to offer "respectable literature" cheaply, it had secured a wide audience.

85. "The Newspaper Press in America." n.s., 3 (1845): 33–36.
Avowed that "[i]n no other country in the world, perhaps, is the newspaper press so powerful an engine" as in the United States. All Americans read papers that addressed every interest. Town dailies, typically morning and evening, and village weeklies created local pride, and thanks to advertising, they were cheap. Their political columns were violent, and their literature was not respectable. Run by editor-owners who wanted to be first with a story, "men of bustling enterprise, not talent and education," gazettes were often "slovenly" and without unity, "of enormous bulk, but of no elevation." Libel was rare even though these men were well known.

86. "View of Canada and the Colonists." n.s., 3 (1845): 61–63.
Highlighted London (Ontario) whose library had *Blackwood's Magazine*, *Bentley's Miscellany*, the *Dublin University Magazine*, and *New Monthly Magazine* in cheap New York reprints and *Chambers's* and the *Penny Magazine*, both circulating widely.

87. "Penny-a-Liners." n.s., 3 (1845): 65–68.
Designated penny-a-liners as "stragglers of the London press" who cost major London papers about 1,000 pounds per year. Penny-a-liners reported fires, crime, accidents, and sports by depending on tips. If they traveled outside London, they were welcomed because they said good things about the locals in the metro press. Most penny-a-liners were accurate and able writers, but some took money to suppress a story and then published it under another name or fabricated stories. This behavior brought "aspersions" on journalists, but those who covered coroners' inquests were lowest in status.

88. "The Curler's Annual." n.s., 3 (1845): 120–22.
Showcased the contents of the *Annual* of the Royal Caledonian Curling Club.

89. "Discoveries in Printing." n.s., 3 (1845): 137–38.
Detailed the printing of the *Art-Union*, principally the transfer of steel engravings to plates.

90. "Railway Literature." n.s., 3 (1845): 177–80.
Scrutinized railroad newspapers, all "conducted by scientific men, with a high degree of respectability and independence" who promoted or panned schemes. The serials had nothing but railway news. Less specialized papers had a column on trains, except the *London Gazette* because Parliament ordered railway information printed there.

91. "Advertisements of *The Times*." n.s., 3 (1845): 199–202.
Recommended advertisements on personal matters and goods as excellent sources for social history.

92. "Biographical Sketches: The Rev. Sydney Smith." n.s., 3 (1845): 233–36.
Praised Smith for conceiving and penning articles for the *Edinburgh Review*.

93. "Notice of Two Old Periodical Works." n.s., 4 (1845): 34–37.
Examined *The Rêveur* (November 1737) and *Letters of the Cricket Club* (monthly 1738). Although both came from Edinburgh, neither had much on Scotland. *The Rêveur* had essays of "good sense, tolerably well expressed," while its counterpart stressed satire.

94. "Newspapers from 'Foreign Parts.'" n.s., 4 (1845): 123–25.
Perused the *Sandwich Island Gazette* (advertising); *Friend* (a Hawaiian semimonthly "neatly printed on good paper" with general and temperance news); *Hawaiian Cascade and Miscellany* (amusing); *China Mail* (a Hong Kong paper that had trouble finding able compositors); and *Mechanic Apprentice* (an American monthly without personality).

95. "Want of Reading-Rooms in London." n.s., 4 (1845): 152–53.
Petitioned for more London reading rooms to emulate *Peel's*, which carried the London and major country press and charged a small fee. In Edinburgh, a penny gave access to about 700 titles, London and Edinburgh papers, English and Scottish locals, foreign gazettes, and domestic monthlies and quarterlies. *See* n.s., 5: 175.

96. "Biographic Sketches: Theodore Edward Hook." n.s., 5 (1846): 91–93.
Noticed that Hook edited *John Bull* for 2,000 pounds a year.

97. "Working Men's Evenings – the Hampstead Reading Rooms." n.s., 5 (1846): 175.
Welcomed the Hampstead reading room, where a subscription cost two pence. *See* n.s., 4: 152.

98. "The Last Number of the *Foreign Quarterly*." n.s., 6 (1846): 109–10.
Noted that the *Foreign Quarterly Review* was not exclusively interested in foreign topics.

99. "The Magazines." n.s., 6 (1846): 253–55.
Theorized that the magazine and review era was over because these serials had undeservedly lost their clout. *Blackwood's Magazine* was wise, droll, and "less violent." *Tait's Edinburgh Magazine* had "solid and world-like" articles unlike its "metropolitan brethren." *Bentley's Miscellany* was still "lively," and the *New Monthly Magazine* was an "old favourite." The sectarianism of the *Dublin University Magazine* limited its circulation.

100. "An Importation." n.s., 6 (1846): 334–35.
Touched on American reprints of *Chambers's*.

101. "Fifteen Years Ago." n.s., 7 (1847): 15–16.
Commemorated *Chambers's* anniversary by repeating that its priority was to educate.

102. "Small Country Papers." n.s., 7 (1847): 59–60.
Generalized that most small-town penny papers, edited by "literary amateurs," were "respectably conducted." Gazettes varied from original materials to reprints, but they did not scissor enough on science and industry from metro and local papers or open enough space to letters from women and mechanics. *See* 10: 125, n.s., 1: 121, n.s., 2: 287.

103. "Quack Advertisements." n.s., 7 (1847): 62–63.
Chastised newspapers for condoning fraud by running advertisements for spurious medicines and treatments.

104. "Our Correspondents." n.s., 7 (1847): 77–79, 221–22.
Catalogued contributors' correspondence to *Chambers's* from "snappish," often anonymous complainers and, increasingly, from Irish women.

105. "The *Art-Union.*" n.s., 7 (1847): 95–96.
Explored the writing and engraving in the "well-known" *Art-Union.*

106. "The English in India." n.s., 7 (1847): 118–21.
Remarked that the Anglo-Indian press commenced with the eighteenth-century *Hicky's Gazette*, but in 1847 many newspapers and other serials circulated throughout India. One was the *Calcutta Review*, a quarterly literary journal priced at six shillings. "[S]ome of its best articles are written by native contributors" who stimulated the intellectual interests of other Indians.

107. "The Contributor." n.s., 7 (1847): 330–33.
Sighed that while periodicals gave literary employment and "respectability to letters as a profession," "impenetrable anonymity" hid most journalists.

108. "The *Art-Union Journal.*" n.s., 8 (1847): 238–40.
Hailed S. C. and Anna M. Hall for sponsoring the monthly *Art-Union* as a means to promote taste in the arts.

109. "The Late Proprietor of *The Times.*" n.s., 8 (1847): 284–87.
Recognized John Walter II, for saving the "languishing paper" of his father. Quoted *The Times* that the son inherited a "well-organized corps of reporters" but raised the level of literary criticism and expanded foreign news while dealing with strike threats that could shut down printing.

110. "Newspapers in France." n.s., 8 (1847): 365–67.
Dated the French press from the seventeenth-century *Gazette* of Théophraste Renaudot and the *Burlesque Gazette*, edited by Jacques Loret, "a courtier." The monthly *Mercure Galant* had a modern style but a duodecimo format and many famous contributors before it died as the *Mercure de France* in 1815. In 1777 the *Journal de Paris*, the first daily, was about the size of one *Times* column. The French Revolution inspired many journals (listed), but censorship afterward limited proliferation. With a loosening of restrictions in the 1830s, the press flourished. In 1847 Paris had 26 dailies with 180,000 subscribers, an increase allegedly due to feuilletons. Aside that the word gazette derived from *gazza*, magpie.

111. "The Anglo-Indian Press." n.s., 9 (1848): 31–32.
Tracked the Anglo-Indian press from *Hicky's Gazette*, which was "full of infamous scandal." Thereafter, Anglo-Indian papers were a "salutary check" on government and famed for their "respectability," but the Indian journals were replete with personal and political satire. In 1848 there were 27 papers in India, five in Singapore and the Straits, and three in China. Calcutta had three dailies, four weeklies,

and two fortnightlies; the *Christian Advocate and Hindoo Intelligencer* specialized in educating Indians. Bombay had a daily, biweekly, and weekly; Madras had a daily and two biweeklies; Ceylon had a biweekly. Both the *Straits Times* and *Friend of China* were biweekly. The *Kurachee Advertiser* had lithographs. In London, the *Indian News* and *Indian Mail* published news quickly but lacked the quality of the *Asiatic Journal.*

112. "Early Newspaper Advertisements." n.s., 9 (1848): 158–60.
Sampled the *Impartial Intelligencer* (1648), then the more sophisticated *British Apollo* (1710) whose advertising encompassed wants, cures, and investments. Suspected that charging for advertising began in the *Jockey's Intelligencer* (1683) and the *Country Gentleman's Courant* (1706) popularized the practice.

113. "Our Correspondents." n.s., 9 (1848): 190–92.
Classed *Chambers's* correspondents as seekers of information, critics of its "blunders," the incoherent, the young, and the "begging." *See* n.s., 11: 301.

114. Ritchie, Leitch. "Article Literature." n.s., 9 (1848): 193–95.
Construed writing for periodicals as a new branch of literature because of pressure of time. Articles were popular because they were terse, enlightened or entertained, and bared more of the author's persona than did books. Essays, even in cheap organs, were an important part of the intellectual world.

115. "Dippings into Old Magaznes: The *Gentleman's* for 1748." n.s., 9 (1848): 249–51.
Noticed that the *Gentleman's Magazine*, with "dark paper, coarse print, and homely engravings," excerpted eighteenth-century newspapers.

116. "Adventures of an Author of the Last Century." n.s., 9 (1848): 343–47.
Essay on Oliver Goldsmith confessed that he penned for pay in the *Monthly Review*.

117. "*Art-Journal* – The Vernon Gallery." n.s., 11 (1849): 107.
Featured the engravings of the Vernon collection in the *Art-Journal*.

118. "A Curiosity in Literature." n.s., 11 (1849): 157–58.
Averred that the Welsh, more than the Highland Scots, supported newspapers and other serials, as "*Amserau*, a popular Welsh newspaper," demonstrated.

119. S., A. "Literary Aspirants." n.s., 11 (1849): 257–59.
Cautioned tyros that the manuscripts of unknown contributors swamped periodical editors and that penning for periodicals was "very wearing work."

120. "Our Correspondents." n.s., 11 (1849): 301–04.
Grumbled that letter-writers to *Chambers's* were still too numerous and too critical. Aside on *The Olive Branch, a Journal for the Work Table*, which was free with a purchase of Hall's Wisbeach Sewing Cotton. *See* n.s., 9: 190.

121. "English Newspapers and Foreign News." n.s., 11 (1849): 351–52.
Quoted the *Hampshire Advertiser* that the British press was superior to the Continental because it retained foreign correspondents or agents and resorted to express boats and telegrams in order to be first with foreign news.

122. R[itchie], L[eitch]. "What Is Criticism?" n.s., 11 (1849): 353–54.
Dismissed anonymity but not the influence of publishers as a problem in literary criticism.

123. "London Morning Newspapers." n.s., 12 (1849): 85–90.
Held that the public knew little about the captioned press, such as its "vast capital," "high degree of enterprise and worldly shrewdness," "highly skilled and intelligent manual labour," and above all, "great, and keen, and cultivated, and flexible intellectual power."

Editors were the commanders. At their desks from 10 p.m. to 5 a.m., they decided matters of major import and suggested leader topics. Subeditors worked from 8 p.m. to 4 a.m. meeting minor business visitors but primarily scanning all the material of a paper except leaders and foreign correspondence handled by a special subeditor.

Leader-writers were cloaked in secrecy, so they rarely came to the office to work. Financial reporters likewise penned separately in the City. Educated parliamentary reporters went from the House to legal and literary careers, though some were content to be skilled shorthand men. A 45-minute turn meant four hours of labor for two columns of close type. Reporters condensed and clarified most speeches, though not of ministers. Generally, the Gallery was a "pleasant and a merry place" to work.

Foreign correspondents abridged the local papers at their posts and visited officials, but their real job was to decide whether breaking news was important enough to warrant a special courier or pigeons. 'War' reporters, "quite a new class," had to be cool, self-reliant linguists.

Penny-a-liners, with a nose for news but no "real tangible footing" in the press, were essential for stories of disasters and crimes. These "waifs and strays" might be "dissipated" reporters or semiliterates who otherwise might do manual labor. While they could earn a good income, they were "improvident" so sometimes spun a hoax for money.

Since the daily was an "intellectual and moral engine," its compositors were important. These well-paid people deserved their salaries not only for their technical skill but for their ability to decipher scribbling done in haste.

124. "*The Maori Messenger*." n.s., 12 (1849): 111.
Headlined a New Zealand newspaper with alternate columns in English and Maori.

125. "The Taxes on Knowledge." n.s., 12 (1849): 318.
Argued that abolition of the stamp and other duties would sire many newspapers, which telegraphy would abet, with no more "foulness" than their cheap American brothers.

126. "The Fourth Estate." n.s., 13 (1850): 321–23.
Reassured that newspaper power, though without the "usual checks or responsibilities" of other institutions, was curbed by public opinion. Most papers showed "a spirit of fairness and veracity," but each had a unique personality. Signature generally and rejection of favors by theatre critics specifically would secure individual responsibility. Aside that without duties, newspapers would grow.

127. "Philosophy of Journalism." n.s., 13 (1850): 404–06.
Review of F. Knight Hunt's *The Fourth Estate* despaired that the "history of journalism is still unwritten." Knight was the "Herodotus of Journalism" – not a historian but "an industrious collector and an agreeable narrator" of original and useful information without a moral context. The newspaper was the "voice" of readers; the journalist, their "mouthpiece," collected what suited them and echoed their ideas. Journalists knew the role "instinctively." If some did "pander" to vice, they merely reflected those of low taste in need of elevation. The press was therefore a gauge of both the "shortcomings" and "advance" of a nation.

In the early seventeenth century, only the rich could afford "news-writers." Propelled by civil war, but not yet an instrument of warfare, the press soon became the tools of government and its enemies. John Milton was the first of many important writers to pen for the press, whether the newspaper or the literary journal. Because political libels were frequent and papers were multiplying, the government wished to control journalism. In Anne's reign, there was a "general repugnance" to overt censorship, so the stamp and advertising duties seemed ideal solutions. In the eighteenth century, the character of newspapers changed: with theatre criticism, they earned money from advertising instead of paying for news and secured the right to cover Parliament. The startup capital required was always sufficiently high to ensure that only a few papers would be in the forefront, the *Public Advertiser* in Junius' day, the *Morning Chronicle* in James Perry's, and *The Times* in 1850. That paper often recruited and always paid its talented scribes well, some originally authors of letters to *The Times*. Most of its London peers had about 100 employees for printing and management alone. Weekly expenses for a morning daily were: 220 pounds for editing, 100 pounds for correspondence, and 200 pounds for printing and general outlays.

In 1849 newspapers numbered 113 in London, 223 in England, 11 in Wales, 85 in Scotland, 101 in Ireland, and 14 in the Channel Islands.

128. R., A. B. "London Newspapers and London Theatres." n.s., 14 (1850): 41–44.
Castigated theatre critics who accepted perks for doing their jobs when most had "a recognized literary position" and who were unfair when they knew the actors or were playwrights.

129. C[hambers], R[obert]. "State Burdens on Literature." n.s., 15 (1851): 17–19.
Examined the costs of the advertising duty for *The Times* and the *Athenaeum* with a gloss that the paper duty inhibited circulation in contrast to the United States.

130. "Curiosities of Advertising Literature." n.s., 15 (1851): 55–58.
Dipped into advertisements in *The Times*.

131. "Journalism Beyond the Rocky Mountains." n.s., 15 (1851): 349–50.
Silhouetted Utah's *Deseret News*. *See* n.s., 19: 153.

132. "Telegraphy of Thought." n.s., 16 (1851): 31–32.
Saluted the *Revista Britannica* (Florence), which introduced English ideas into Italian society by reprinting excerpts of British periodicals, and the *Lyttleton Times* (New Zealand), "a well-printed paper." It proved that the English opened a newspaper wherever they settled.

133. "The French Press." n.s., 16 (1851): 169–70.
Perceived the newspaper as the "intellectual telegraph of civilized life." In the Ottoman Empire, it was an "infant"; in Russia and Austria, a "slave"; in Italy, a "dwarf"; in Spain, a "muffled desperado"; in France, a weapon, and in England, an investment for capitalists. English papers were businesslike;

French, personal. Even with the advertising duty, English gazettes had more advertising than French. French journals were inexpensive because they paid no paper duty, but few cheap serials prospered because of government restrictions.

134. "A Newcastle Paper in 1755–6." n.s., 17 (1852): 105–07.
Revisited the *Newcastle Chronicle* that had social and business news, advertisements, and miscellaneous articles but no leaders or political news.

135. "Margaret Fuller Ossoli." n.s., 17 (1852): 322–25.
Review of the *Memoirs of Margaret Fuller Ossoli* gleaned that she edited the *Dial* and contributed regularly to the *New York Tribune*.

136. "The Taxes on Knowledge." n.s., 17 (1852): 329–31.
Anticipated that removal of stamp, advertising, and paper duties would spawn more country papers. Even if their material was "deleterious," they would meet local needs and train critical readers. Referred to the *British Quarterly Review*, 15: 135, on taxes.

137. "A London Newspaper in 1667." n.s., 17 (1852): 334–35.
Scan of the *London Gazette*, 1667–81 noted that until the 1790s newspapers developed slowly in Britain.

138. "Mr. Jerdan's *Autobiography*." n.s., 17 (1852): 375–78.
Review of William Jerdan's book spanned his career at the *Morning Post* and as *Sun* editor but not as editor of the *Literary Gazette*.

139. "*The Advocate*, and Its Author." n.s., 18 (1852): 275–77.
Honored Edward Cox who conducted the *Advocate*, *Law Times*, *Magistrate*, and *County Courts' Chronicle* and penned for the *Critic*, which had "more than usual proportion of thought" and "small superficial cant."

140. "Magazines of the Last Century." n.s., 18 (1852): 334–36.
Surveyed magazines of the 1780s, among them the *Gentleman's*. For a shilling, the *European* offered elegant engravings and music. The *New Lady's*, at sixpence, was really "an illustrated monthly newspaper." Most magazines covered Parliament and domestic and foreign news but were weak in literature because "hacks" dominated their pages. When the French Revolution caused newspapers to burgeon, magazines switched to more literature and improved once the *Edinburgh Review* raised the bar by paying for talent.

141. "Ideas about the Diggings." n.s., 19 (1853): 39–42.
Broadcast that the Australian press was growing faster than that of the English countryside. Colonial papers, as Melbourne's *Argus* and the *Geelong Advertiser*, were large and cheap because they paid no duties.

142. "Journal of the City of the Great Salt Lake." n.s., 19 (1853): 153–55.
Expanded on the *Deseret News*. *See* n.s., 15: 349.

143. "The Newsboy's Day." n.s., 19 (1853): 305–08.
Shadowed the newsboy. In the morning, he delivered papers or sold them on streets; in the afternoon, he exchanged the unsold for ones sent by evening post to the country.

144. "History of a Contributor." n.s., 20 (1853): 72–74.
Outlined the career of T. G. Wainwright, on the staff of the *London Magazine* as Janus Weathercock.

145. "Secrets Exposed." n.s., 20 (1853): 161–63.
Deciphered cryptic messages in advertisements in *The Times*.

146. "The Columns of Society: A New Gauge of Progress." n.s., 20 (1853): 420–23.
Gave statistics on pages, charges, arrangement, and content of advertising in "*The Times*, the colossus of the press."

147. C[hambers], W[illiam]. "Things as They Are in America: New York." 3[d.] ser., 1 (1854): 355–59; "Rhode Island," 3[d] ser., 2 (1854): 6–11, "Philadelphia," 167–72.
Observed that American newspapers were cheap, so everyone bought them. Their emphasis on advertising and personalities, as well as scissoring from large metro gazettes, was similar to British local papers. Unlike in Britain, American newspapers were everywhere, and "stereotyping by electric process" was popular. New York was the leader, thanks to its *Herald*, *Tribune*, and *Evening Post*. The city's *National Magazine* was "respectable." Among other magazines, *Putnam's* had better literature and *Harper's Monthly* had a circulation of 100,000. Philadelphia had about 12 dailies, 40 weeklies, and many magazines on art and science.

148. "Convict Literature." 3[d] ser., 1 (1854): 388–90.
Aired that convicts on a transport ship created a weekly.

149. "A Laudation of Trash." 3[d] ser., 2 (1854): 31–32.
Raved that multiplication of inexpensive periodicals fostered reading even if they published trash. Real competition was among higher journals: they had to specialize to survive.

150. "Jottings from the Cape." 3[d] ser., 2 (1854): 76–77.
Assumed that newspapers everywhere were a gauge of society. The *Mercantile Advertiser, or Shopkeeper's Journal*, published triweekly in Cape Colony, had information on shipping, goods, and local politics but existed on advertising.

151. "The Reformer of Turkey and His Gazette." 3[d] ser., 2 (1854): 124–25.
Congratulated Sultan Mahmud II for sponsoring in 1831 the *Tatler of Events*, whose wide circulation in the Ottoman Empire and inclusion of foreign news opened many of his subjects' minds.

152. "The Bringing Forth of the Daily Newspaper." 3[d] ser., 2 (1854): 129–33.
Toured a daily's office, deserted until late afternoon. Previously, when the race among London dailies for influence was "fiery" and "the destinies of the country seemed to hang upon the press," editors talked with "men of official rank." Then, news gathering was exciting. Money went for getting news first; in

1854 owners sought profit and frequently cross-examined editors about their choice and placement of material. Only papers with large returns or proprietors rich enough to sustain gazettes for other purposes freed editors from such conversations, which should have been with the new business managers.

Editors got an overview of the paper from subeditors but were ready, unlike the French, to shift contents for the latest happenings. Editors also dealt with incoming letters, those to *The Times* particularly well written. The well-paid subeditor was usually exhausted by the drudgery of shaping up the text of penny-a-liners. He could only scissor a little from local papers because they rarely commented on serious national matters. Special correspondents were everywhere. Parliamentary reporters faithfully took shorthand of entire speeches, so the clarity and wit of previous summaries was missing. The "headed" articles depended on "chance" contributions. Those in the *Morning Post* were "gay, graphic"; in the *Daily News*, full of statistics; in the *Morning Advertiser*, on "jobs and abuses." Except at *The Times*, critics were inexpert staff already burdened. Theatre reviewers were the worst, pressured to say something immediately. The English should copy the French, having all reviews for a week in a single article. Printers with "tact" often prioritized contents to ensure a good appearance.

153. "A Honolulu Newspaper." 3d ser., 3 (1855): 34–37.
Skimmed the *New Era and Weekly Argus*, a Hawaiian weekly with good paper and bad print. It contained many advertisements and some local and foreign news but no crime, literature, and births, marriages, and deaths.

154. "Horace Greeley." 3d ser., 3 (1855): 212–15.
Tailed Greeley from printing to locals to owner and editor of the *New York Tribune*, where he crusaded for social improvement and against abuse.

155. "Paternoster Row and Magazine-Day." 3d ser., 3 (1855): 400–04.
Petitioned for sites elsewhere replicating London's magazine distribution center.

156. "Life and Conversation of the Rev. Sydney Smith." 3d ser., 4 (1855): 19–23, 36. 40.
Review of *A Memoir of the Rev. Sydney Smith* by his daughter, Lady Holland, touched on his tie to the *Edinburgh Review*.

157. "Scottish Newspapers from an English Point of View." 3d ser., 4 (1855): 56–59.
Said that the average Scottish weekly dealt with local news, so it had a small staff. The editor, who typically earned 80 pounds a year, performed many tasks. He had to be informed, patient, prudent, energetic, and able. Good editors soon moved to better jobs. The subeditor had to select material from the London press with care, and the reporter had to know shorthand to cover meetings well. A larger gazette, as the *Inverness Courier*, might have a London correspondent.

158. "The Penny Daily Paper." 3d ser., 4 (1855): 223–24.
Predicted that not all the new unstamped papers would improve the "national mind."

159. "Lurking Literature of London." 3d ser., 5 (1856): 58–60.
Included in titled group *The Aristocrat*, a weekly of the scissors-and-paste school, and *Bawker's Magazine*, which pirated from morning newspapers and American periodicals. Excluded the "*Hue and Cry* – interesting to rogues and vagabonds," police, crime victims, and trade journal readers because it identified lost and stolen property.

160. "The Spirit Faith in America." 3d ser., 5 (1856): 81–83.
Analyzed Boston's *New England Spiritualist*.

161. "Material and Intellectual Life In Brussels." 3d ser., 5 (1856): 314–16.
Categorized as Brussels' free press: the *Indépendance Belge*, with the largest circulation and Russian and French editions; the Catholic *Emancipation Belge* and *Journal des Bruxelles*; *Sancho*, *Figaro* and *Mephistophiles*, inspired by the French "*petite presse*."

162. "Matrimonial Correspndence." 3d ser., 7 (1857): 93–95.
Targeted the personal advertisements in New York's illustrated *Ledger of Romance*.

163. "Answers to Correspondents." 3d ser., 7 (1857): 129–31.
Hypothesized that weeklies were more likely to answer correspondence than busier dailies and magazines or quarterlies with their long intervals between issues and readers "of education and high tone of taste and thought."

164. "All for a Penny." 3d ser., 9 (1858): 415–16.
Cited the *Tottenham and Edmonton Advertiser*, a monthly with metro train schedules and local news and advertising, as evidence that the London parish press was valuable.

165. "A Glance at an Old Newspaper." 3d ser., 10 (1858): 232–34.
Focused on the *Westminster Journal and London Political Miscellany* (28 June 1794), with its coarse paper, poor typography, and small size. It echoed the *London Gazette* but without details on Parliament, the royals, crime, and accidents. A newspaper pictured its era, and those in 1858 reflected Victorian progress. *The Times*, the model, was a "living power" with "polished" leaders of literary and moral influence whose letters came from correspondents with "a keen eye" on society and government.

166. "The Newspaper World." 3d ser., 10 (1858): 274–76.
Probed newspaper personnel. Editors, metro and country, were born with talents to "scent out the libel," distinguish puffing from informing, and select columns that raised circulation. While large towns had penny dailies run with "spirit and ability," and the *Manchester Examiner and Times* produced 15,000 copies per hour for its daily sales of 28,000, most of Britain's 800 local gazettes had small staffs. In the capital, reporters covered Parliament, and penny-a-liners sniffed out other stories. Subeditors chose material from these sources, other papers, letters, telegrams, and foreign correspondence. Business managers worried about the costs of buying and maintaining machinery and lawsuits from penny-a-liner "fictions."

166a. "Dr. Elizabeth Blackwell." 3d ser., 10 (1858): 350–52.
Aside that the *English Woman's Journal* was a "clever and promising aspirant of the periodical press."

167. "Their Rejected Contributors." 3d ser., 11 (1859): 33–36.
Specified that periodicals rejected submissions primarily because of plagiarism, illegible handwriting, and bad style. Editors should be kind and should realize that angry, insolent, or humiliated contributors were likely to increase as more professional men, "intelligent mechanics," and women writers sent in their work.

168. "Parochial Newspapers." 3d ser., 11 (1859): 353–55.
Abridged the local newspaper with its news, weather, and advertisements.

169. "Sydney and Its Suburbs." 3d ser., 12 (1859): 296–99, 318–20.
Visited Sydney's *Morning Herald*, whose office was more attractive than London's *Morning Post* and more spacious than *The Times*. Its editor, junior editor, subeditors, reporters, and London correspondents earned salaries akin to their *Times* colleagues, reputedly because the *Herald* had 20,000 pounds in profit per year.

170. "A German Newspaper." 3d ser., 12 (1859): 381–83.
Investigated Vienna's inexpensive *Neue Tagblatt*, chiefly its advertising and obituaries.

171. "Reporting." 3d ser., 13 (1860): 263–65.
Review of C. J. Gratton's *The Gallery* traced parliamentary reporting from seventeenth-century letters to the *Gentleman's Magazine*. Thereafter, William Radcliffe and William Woodfall memorized Members' speeches, and James Perry inaugurated relays of "quick-witted but vulgar Irishmen," as Mark Supple. In 1860 the number of parliamentary reporters varied, but most took about two or three hours to transcribe a 30-minute turn.

172. "Manchester Free Libraries." 3d ser., 13 (1860): 340–43.
Rejoiced that the newspaper room (70 by 50 feet) of Manchester's Campbell Library received 1,929 people a day perusing British, American, and imperial gazettes.

173. "Fielding's Newspapers." 3d ser., 14 (1860): 142–44.
Stated that Henry Fielding's *True Patriot*, 1745, paralleled Joseph Addison's *Spectator*, 1715, insofar as both commented on politics and society and published births, marriages and deaths but little on crime and accidents.

174. "Nobody's Newspapers." 3d ser., 15 (1861): 124–26.
Fussed that newspapers sent from another place were of no interest to the recipient, such as advertisements in the *Sydney Intelligencer* for an English reader.

175. "Newspapers under the Paper Duty." 3d ser., 16 (1861): 308–10.
Logged that London had 210 newspapers: 20 daily (13 morning, seven evening) and 190 weekly (the bulk specialized). Local papers, many with small audiences, numbered 180. The oldest were supposedly the *Worcester Journal* (1709), *Nottingham Journal* (1710), and *Newcastle Courant* (1711). Londoners influenced the politics of country papers and wrote scandal for them. Wales had 32 papers (mostly in the South), Scotland had 150, Ireland had 138, and the Channel Islands had 13, including Guernsey's French official paper. The total paying the paper duty in the United Kingdom was 1,142.

176. "Newspaper Maps and Maps of Newspapers." 3d ser., 16 (1861): 390–92.
Alerted that papers decoyed buyers by adding an extra sheet, illustrations, or maps to raise circulation. The latest fad was a map locating tribunes whose names were rather repetitive. The country press, which was bigger than London's though smaller than the American, excelled in advertising. *The Times* profited from its advertisements (about 4,000 per issue) and its public service reporting (as on the Crimean War), but also counted on technology (as the steam press) and events (Great Exhibition

52,000; Wellington funeral 70,000 for which the *Illustrated London News* sold 400,000 of a double number) to sell more copies.

177. "Between London and Paris." 3^{d} ser., 17 (1862): 177–80.
Deplored that the French emperor restricted entry of foreign periodicals, a problem for the British in Paris who wanted *The Times*, *Illustrated London News*, *Daily News*, and *Daily Telegraph*.

178. "A Sandwich Islands' Newspaper." 3^{d} ser., 17 (1862): 279–80.
Plumbed Abraham Fornander's *Polynesian*, a Honolulu weekly with local and Pacific but little British news. Advertisements from hair dye to bowling-alleys demonstrated the "social condition" of the area.

179. "The *Monthly Chronicle*." 3^{d} ser., 17 (1862): 388–91.
Contrasted the eighteenth-century *Monthly Chronicle*, which had some advertising but little news, to the 1862 "sensation paragraphs" of Reuters and of foreign correspondents in every capital.

180. "News." 3^{d} ser., 18 (1862): 225–27.
Followed news transmission from the Egyptians to newspapers and their relation to a free press.

181. "Literature of the American War." 3^{d} ser., 18 (1862): 321–25.
Regarded American newspapers as an "avenue for all communication" during the Civil War. The *New York Herald* paid 30 correspondents 20 dollars per week to cover the conflict. Some journalists enlisted to get the news because the South expelled many journalists. The South had no popular magazine except the *Southern Literary Messenger*. The North had several: *Harper's Monthly* and the *Atlantic Monthly* had "enormous sales." The "*New York Ledger*, a sensational weekly," once sold 250,000; the *New York Herald*, 150,000 until competition developed. The Sunday *Mercury* sold 120,000. Philadelphia, Chicago, and Cincinnati papers had comparable records.

182. "A Romance of a Non-Combatant." 3^{d} ser., 19 (1863): 321–26.
Quoted a *New York Herald* correspondent that the paper paid its staff well, did not interfere in their work, and deserved its reputation for news gathering irrespective of Europeans' disdain.

183. "Penny-a-Liner's English." 3^{d} ser., 20 (1863): 11–13.
Satirized penny-a-liner language as verbose and gushing like French reporting.

184. "Early Advertisements." 3^{d} ser., 20 (1863): 355–57.
Pondered advertisements on lost goods and new jobs in the *Mercure Politicus* (1652), *Moderate* (1649), and *London Gazette* (1680s); on quack cures in the *Postman* (1697); and on theatre in the *Flying Post* (1699).

185. "Trade Newspapers." 3^{d} ser., 20 (1863): 369–71.
Included numerous specialized newspapers and magazines.

186. "Popular Reading-Rooms." 3^{d} ser., 20 (1863): 411–12.
Requested reading-rooms with newspapers, magazines, and reviews that allowed patrons to relax while gathering information.

187. "Occasional Notes: Anonymous Journalism." 4th ser., 1 (1864): 127.
Contended that signed journalism had "less public weight" and caused readers to abandon their own principles for another's opinion but reduced "slanders and exaggerations" and boosted circulation. Anonymity concealed inferiority, obvious when an author was not good enough to have the work republished with a signature.

188. "Forty Years in America." 4th ser., 1 (1864): 212–15.
Review of Thomas Low Nichols' *Forty Years of American Life* chronicled that the United States had many newspapers (450 dailies, 4,000 weeklies, 356 fortnightlies and monthlies in 1861). If a paper ran counter to opinion, it might be 'mobbed.' New York was the hub of dailies that circulated nationally. The *Herald* had the biggest numbers because of James Gordon Bennett's emphasis on the "exclusive." One way to raise circulation was to pay well for a popular column. Fanny Fern received 20 pounds for every column because 3,000 newspapers carried it.

189. "Thackeray." 4th ser., 1 (1864): 277–79.
Peeked at the contributions of W. M. Thackeray to *Fraser's Magazine* and his role in the 1836 launch of the *Constitutional and Public Ledger*, which did not sell.

190. "A Glance at Dunedin." 4th ser., 1 (1864): 344–46.
Boasted that New Zealand's *Otago Daily Times* was as big as *The Times* and had many advertisements.

191. "Advertisement Romance." 4th ser., 1 (1864): 449–51.
Abstracted personal advertisements in *The Times*.

192. "Arrival of the Mail in Melbourne." 4th ser., 1 (1864): 598–600.
Monitored Adelaide reporters who boarded European steamers, then telegraphed news to papers in other Australian regions. The *Argus*, "the leading journal of Melbourne," quickly had an extra ready for hawking by newsboys. The *Home News*, published in London, sold in Melbourne by "unwashed children of the street" for twice its home price. In colonial bookshops, several London newspapers and periodicals were popular.

193. "The Early Newspapers of Modern Europe." 4th ser., 1 (1864): 636–40.
History went from ballads to the early seventeenth-century German *Aviso* and *Franfurter-Oberpostamts-Zeitung*, Antwerp *Nieuwe Tijdinghe* (with woodcuts), Nathaniel Butter's *Weekely News*, the French press of the 1630s, and the Italian of the 1640s.

194. "On Bank-Service in Canada." 4th ser., 1 (1864): 673–78.
Appreciated that the local press acquainted citizens with the methods of a suspected swindler.

195. "The Most Popular of Periodicals." 4th ser., 2 (1865): 113–14.
Highlighted almanacs.

196. "Modern Criticism." 4th ser., 2 (1865): 433–35.
Judged literary critics of the 1860s inferior to the biased but learned scribes in the early *Edinburgh Review* and *Quarterly Review*. Contemporary critics merely wished to showcase "their own wit."

Many were ill-paid because book reviews were not popular. Periodicals should emulate the *Saturday Review*, identifying books of merit and rejecting publishers' promotions.

197. "The Penny Newsroom." 4th ser., 2 (1865): 545–547.
Discovered a variety of holdings in one reading room. Among them were London dailies; Scottish country papers perused by newshounds; imperial newspapers ranging from Melbourne's *Argus*, the *Sydney Morning Herald*, and *Cape Argus* to papers of the sugar colonies full of stale or stolen copy; German papers; Alexander Herzen's *Kolokol*, and trade magazines.

198. "How We Get Our Newspapers." 4th ser., 2 (1865): 769–74.
Explicated the printing and distribution of *The Times*.

199. "An Undiscovered World." 4th ser., 3 (1866): 209–13.
Unearthed advertisements in "penny weekly newspapers, of which 'the respectable classes' know nothing," although such gazettes had big circulations.

200. "Critical Blunders." 4th ser., 3 (1866): 476–78.
Gave examples of errors in newspapers.

201. "Some Old Advertisements." 4th ser., 3 (1866): 506–07.
Drew, from seventeenth- and eighteenth-century newspapers, advertisements for lost goods, cockfights, information, and sales.

202. "Literary Partnerships." 4th ser., 3 (1866): 609–12.
Included the press partnership of Joseph Addison and Richard Steele because their humor was neither "coarse" nor scurrilous and their essays exhibited talent.

203. "The P. & O." 4th ser., 4 (1867): 57–59.
Linked extra editions of Australian newspapers to steamer arrivals.

204. "Our Leading Columns." 4th ser., 4 (1867): 449–51.
Differentiated leader-writers at major papers, where a cadre assigned topics endured revision of their work, from the country editor who had more freedom because the audience was less critical than in London. Aside that leader-writers snubbed metro subeditors as scissors men.

205. "The Press at Sea." 4th ser., 4 (1867): 488–91.
Ruminated about weeklies published aboard ships on long voyages. The *Lightening Gazette and Ocean Advertiser*, en route from Liverpool to Melbourne, printed events, news, and advertisements.

206. "Aytoun." 4th ser., 4 (1867): 648–52.
Review of Theodore Martin's *William Edmondstoune Aytoun* mentioned his essays in *Blackwood's Magazine*.

207. "Scissors and Paste." 4th ser., 4 (1867): 785–88.
Condensed the work of the newspaper subeditor, which consisted principally of reviewing letters, reports, penny-a-liner stories, and telegrams and dealing with printers. Because the

subeditor supervised the paper except for leaders, the person could play favorites. However, a good subeditor was born with "a peculiar journalistic instinct" for separating the important from the mundane, for understanding what interested readers. To keep such a marvel, editors of dailies maintained that a gulf permanently separated this position from the "superior rank of journalists," namely themselves and leader-writers.

208. "Our Own Reporter." 4th ser., 5 (1868): 33–36.
Portrayed the reporter as "unobtrusive," yet ubiquitous, so shorthand was essential. Reporters could be "eager" and "flowery" in language, but few were "dissipated." They might go from being a 'devil' on a country weekly to reporting for a minor urban daily, finally to subediting or editing a small paper or sitting in the parliamentary gallery, "easier work and better pay."

209. "Our Special Wire." 4th ser., 5 (1868): 433–36.
Theorized that the 1850s size, accuracy, and technology (Hoe's press and telegraphy) of penny papers were remarkable for their price. By 1868 Edinburgh and Glasgow dailies had special wires to London, and many papers had subeditors and reporters there. These journalists made Scottish papers cosmopolitan but also susceptible to errors from transmissions done in haste.

210. "In the Gallery." 4th ser., 5 (1868): 737–40.
Illuminated parliamentary reporting, from the comfortable quarters for scribes to the gallery where numbers varied and short turns generated slips taken by messengers to the papers. Paid about five guineas per week, some reporters sidelined the work.

211. "American Newspapers." 4th ser., 7 (1870): 406–09.
Lectured that newspapers guided opinion based on common ideas or characteristics, so they were the index of a nation. English newspapers symbolized logic and deliberation; French, the sensational in short paragraphs and drama; American, the variety of the people. The "great New York dailies" were the *Herald*, *Tribune*, *Times*, and *World*. Their Associated Press reduced telegraphic costs. The *Herald*, whose only goal was to sell, was first with the news but "fickle, coarse, and blustering." The *Tribune* had political influence under Horace Greeley. The *World* was a "bitter, partisan paper." All four gazettes had many advertisements but few literary or art reviews. The *New York Evening Post* of William Cullen Bryant was the "best daily literary paper in the United States." Among other excellent papers were those in Boston and Philadelphia, the *Providence Journal*, *Toledo Blade*, and *Louisville Journal*. *The Nation* was as good as the best English weekly. Aside that some editors entered politics.

212. "The Electric Telegraph." 4th ser., 7 (1870): 545–48.
Noted that P. J. Reuter transmitted news by pigeon at Aix-la-Chapelle in 1849, four years after the *Morning Chronicle* carried the first telegraphic report to a newspaper.

213. "The Balloon and Pigeon Posts." 4th ser., 8 (1871): 129–34, 154–56.
Revealed that the siege of Paris tested the ingenuity of newspapers. The *Daily News* used horsemen; the *Journal des Débats* man swam the Seine; the *Journal Officiel* sent photographic reductions by balloons; pigeons carried *The Times* to Paris, and calico balloons covered with linseed oil and oxide of lead came from the French provinces.

214. "A Good Correspondent." 4th ser., 8 (1871): 169–74.
Lauded G. T. Robinson who covered the siege of Metz for the *Manchester Guardian*.

215. "German Advertisements." 4th ser., 8 (1871): 219–20.
Excerpted the German *Tagblatt*, a small quarto of 8–48 pages of advertising.

216. "Postal Telegraph." 4th ser., 8 (1871): 287–88.
Surmised that government takeover of telegraphy reduced costs and left news collecting to news associations with unlimited messaging compared to private companies' selected texts.

217. "A Specimen of Feminine Journalism." 4th ser., 8 (1871): 433–36.
Exulted that women editors in Britain were not associated with the political press, but in the United States, Victoria Woodhull and Tennessee Claflin ran *Woodhull and Claflin's Weekly* with leaders, stories, and advertisements.

218. "At the Reporter's Table." 4th ser., 8 (1871): 449–51.
Alluded to the haphazard seating available to reporters at public meetings.

219. "The Youth of Dickens." 4th ser., 9 (1872): 17–21, 40–45; "The Middle Age." 4th ser., 10 (1873): 74–79; "Dickens's Life: Conclusion." 4th ser., 11 (1874): 177–80.
Review of John Forster's *The Life of Charles Dickens* talked about his tenure as a parliamentary reporter, his early magazine articles in the *Old Monthly* for which he was never paid, and his editing of the *Daily News*, which he called a "Daily Nuisance."

220. "*Chambers's Journal*." 4th ser., 9 (1872): 65–66.
Celebration of *Chambers's* fortieth anniversary referred to penny serials that had not survived, notably the "meritorious" *Penny Magazine* that began with a large circulation, Leigh Hunt's 1834 *London Journal*, and cheap weeklies "with considerable literary taste and scholarship."

Reiterated *Chambers's* original pledge to serve all classes, emphasize literature, and avoid politics and religion and its belief that the "cheap and respectably conducted" periodical was "an engine of social improvement." In its early years, *Chambers's* was bought by workmen but was also read by boys now grown who testified that it gave them "their first elevation of sentiment." As more juvenile magazines surfaced, *Chambers's* addressed adults who were increasingly educated. After Robert Chambers died in 1871, James Payn, long "editorially connected," became editor. *Chambers's* eschewed "staff" writers because they preempted the "literary aspirant" and made a serial stale. Instead, it depended on submissions, in 1872 about 200 contributions per month, mostly poems and mostly rejected.

221. "A Poet's Autobiography." 4th ser., 9 (1872): 373–76.
Review of *Life of Thomas Cooper* resurrected his early work for a Lincoln newspaper that paid him 250 pounds per year with free rent and coal and his launch of the *Midland Counties Illuminator*. His Chartist, not his journalistic endeavors, landed him in jail.

222. "Slips of the Press." 4th ser., 9 (1872): 433–36.
Marked errors in British and American newspapers.

223. "The Special Staff." 4th ser., 10 (1873): 17–20.
Centered on the special staff at the London telegraph office, who handled correspondents' copy. Because newspapers did "represent the general public," the staff had to know press deadlines and journalists' phrasing and to accommodate journalists who drew on their paper's account to pay for messages (with data on pricing for individuals and press associations). Aside that telegraphy pressured special correspondents to write quickly and well.

224. C[hambers], W[illiam]. "Horace Greeley." 4th ser., 10 (1873): 49–52.
Examined Greeley's work as a periodical contributor, compositor, and newspaper editor. His editing of the *New Yorker* made his reputation, soon enhanced by the "purity" of the *New York Tribune.*

225. "The Penny-a-Liner." 4th ser., 10 (1873): 113–16.
Saw the penny-a-liner and the special correspondent as the two literary extremes of London dailies. The special had "prolonged duty," as with an army in the field. Below him were "regular reporters," local correspondents, and finally penny-a-liners. They gathered news bits and embellished them with "eloquence and sensationalism." Some were specialists; all had an instinct for news. Paid for what appeared, they had uncertain incomes. Editors relied on them because they recorded information on minor events quickly and were generally truthful but sometimes suppressed "painful" or "discreditable" stories for money.

226. "Speaker and Reporter." 4th ser., 10 (1873): 193–95.
Commiserated with parliamentary reporters who had to take notes on boring speeches.

227. "The 'Press' of 1873." 4th ser., 10 (1873): 285–87.
Idolized the press as "a modern marvel" based on information about newspapers and magazines in C. Mitchell's *The Newspaper Directory and Advertisers' Guide.*

228. "George Grote." 4th ser., 10 (1873): 437–40.
Review of *The Personal Life of George Grote* by his wife, Harriet Grote, divulged that her *Westminster Review* articles supported the couple in the early days of their marriage and that he also penned for the periodical.

229. C[hambers], W[illiam]. "A Word about Otago." 4th ser., 10 (1873): 573–74.
Spelled out the contents of Otago's *New Zealand Gazette* and Dunedin's *Morning Star.*

230. "A Versatile 'Special.'" 4th ser., 10 (1873): 597–98.
Review of Archibald Forbes' *Soldiering and Scribbling* decreed that all war correspondents have courage, intelligence, patience, vitality, "good temper," and "adaptability." Forbes' writings on war and "some social subjects" were not "polished," but he was apparently a good interviewer.

231. "Experiences of a Literary Aspirant." 4th ser., 10 (1873): 827–29.
Narrated a personal struggle to publish in periodicals that culminated in an appointment to a comic journal, "essentially demoralizing for the journalist" because it relaxed the nerves. The successful contributor was "modest, "compliable," "respectful," and ready to listen to senior writers.

232. "The Street News-Boys of London." 4th ser., 11 (1874): 113–15.
Silhouetted the newsboy, typically aged ten to 18, as a person without capital, trade, or a future but with the English "commercial character." Before his time, newsmen sometimes sold their own papers to buyers. In 1874 newsboys were helpers, ordinary sellers, and agents who negotiated between street boys and publishers. Sellers needed cash (amounts here) to buy quires, but agents received papers on trust and could return some. The boys sold where people walked. *Punch's Almanac* had a big street sale, but the *Echo* and *Globe* attracted the most buyers between 2 p.m. and 8 p.m.

233. "Wretched Writers." 4th ser., 11 (1874): 163–65.
Castigated bad penmanship, as Horace Greeley's *New York Tribune* submissions.

234. "*History of Advertising*." 4th ser., 12 (1875): 131–34.
Review of Henry Sampson's book averred that all newspapers derived the "bulk of their income" from advertising. *The Times*, followed by the *Daily Telegraph*, *Standard*, and *Daily News*, were the most profitable in London. Manchester and Liverpool papers had many advertisements, but Glasgow was the leader outside the capital. Advertising took space from news except in the specialized sheets dating from the 1657 *Public Advertiser*. Since the 1700s, British journals had more personals, while American had more humorous entries. Aside that John Walter II made *The Times* "the first newspaper of the world."

235. "Reporters' Mistakes." 4th ser., 12 (1875): 639–40.
Attributed errors to style, reporters' mishearing and haste, and compositors' mishandling of copy. Aside that London journalists made fun of their country colleagues.

236. "Deceptive Advertisements." 4th ser., 14 (1877): 70–72.
Branded as the most deceptive advertisements those for medical remedies, easy loans, and moneymaking schemes.

237. "Odd Notes from Queensland." 4th ser., 14 (1877): 824–27.
Bruited that the *Darling Downs Gazette* lacked leaders and the *Queenslander* fired reporters who engaged in character assassination.

238. "Sensational Reporting." 4th ser., 15 (1878): 150–52.
Pontificated that press writing was a "responsibility," mainly for the penny daily whose large circulation made it "one of the most potent agents for good or evil which our generation possesses." The press acted for the moral welfare of readers, so stories on crime should alert readers but not be "exciting" or graphic. Giving offenders "meretricious glory" was inappropriate but sold newspapers.

239. "Story of George Cruikshank." 4th ser., 15 (1878): 161–64.
Examined Cruikshank's work in *Ainsworth's Magazine*, *Bentley's Miscellany*, and his own *Omnibus*, edited by Laman Blanchard, and popular *Comic Almanac*.

240. "Drolleries in Advertising." 4th ser., 15 (1878): 551–53.
Starred the variety of advertisements in the 1820s *Morning Herald*, the personal listings in the *Matrimonial News* and the 'Agony' column of *The Times*, and "smart" American inserts in *Harper's Weekly*. Flagged the dangers of advertisements by swindlers and quacks.

241. Chambers, W[illiam], LL.D. "*Chambers's Journal*, 1879." 4th ser., 16 (1879): 16.
Confirmed that *Chambers's* did not rely much on advertising but serialized fiction to increase sales and that American newspapers stole *Journal* articles, which British local gazettes recopied. Aside that the "sub or acting editor" was Robert Chambers II.

242. "Recollections of Thackeray." 4th ser., 16 (1879): 341–43.
Claimed that the first issue of the *Cornhill Magazine*, edited by W. M. Thackeray, sold 110,000 copies.

243. C[hambers], W[illiam]. "Literary Work." 4th ser., 16 (1879): 353–55.
Praised the *Edinburgh Review* and the *Quarterly Review* because they "stimulated the public taste for literature." In 1879 readers of inexpensive magazines, which employed "thousands of skilled writers," looked for humor, common sense, and impartiality.

244. "A Newspaper Institute." 4th ser., 16 (1879): 395–97.
Introduced Alexander Mackie's Newspaper Institute at Crewe to train journalists. Intended to replace the drudgery of apprenticeship, Mackie's six-month program included typesetting, proofreading, reporting (punctuation and style), subediting, and bookkeeping. Alleged that American editors were calling for universities to teach journalism.

245. A London Sub-Editor. "Sub-Editing a London Newspaper." 4th ser., 16 (1879): 663–64.
Explained that a subeditor at a London daily had to review telegrams and copy from reporters and correspondents; to summarize foreign news; to select copy after meeting with the editor about leaders, articles, reviews, and correspondence; to determine headlines; and to consult the printer. The subeditor's first assistant reviewed police reports, often badly written; a second wrote obituaries; a third checked the *Scotsman*, *Glasgow Herald*, and *Irish Times* for items; a fourth did sports columns based on telegrams. The subeditor was usually an energetic man in his forties or fifties with substantial journalism experience. "He is not ordinarily one of your press Bohemians, but quiet, severe, and respectable." Although the job was hard, the wages kept a person comfortable in retirement.

246. "The Telephone Exchange." 4th ser., 16 (1879): 695–96.
Glanced at *The Times* use of telephones.

247. "Tales of the Telegraph." 4th ser., 17 (1880): 126–28.
Excerpted from the *Java Bode*, *Swiss Times*, and *The Times* examples of how editors misread telegrams.

248. "New Reporting Arrangements in the House of Commons." 4th ser., 17 (1880): 822–23.
Pictured the new facilities for parliamentary reporters, such as a larger gallery so that local papers, as well as London ones and press associations, could have seats. To get enough time to transcribe their shorthand, local reporters rotated taking notes, then penned their own stories so that the wires to each paper were different.

249. "Concerning Reporting." 4th ser., 18 (1881): 36–39.
Brooded that there were more journalists than jobs, so candidates needed to master shorthand, to write well, to stay calm, to be impartial, to concentrate, to know current events, and to understand what was important.

250. "Literary Beginners." 4th ser., 18 (1881): 65–68.
Review of *Journals and Journalism* by John Oldcastle [Wilfrid Meynell] advised magazine neophytes to pen carefully, to ask a mentor to edit their work, to submit material that fit a journal because editors had no time to critique anything unless it was clearly publishable, and to submit a stamped return envelope. *See* 5th ser., 1: 48.

251. "Some Curiosities of Journalism." 4th ser., 18 (1881): 123–25.
Trumpeted that "[l]ike other marketable things, news is occasionally dressed up for sale" often in smart paragraphs that did not conceal ignorance. While the American press tolerated "purely personal reflection on anyone," the English had "purity and influence."

252. "William Lloyd Garrison." 4th ser., 18 (1881): 188–89.
Tracked Garrison's press career from anonymous articles as A[n] O[ld] B[achelor] to joint editor with Benjamin Lundy of *The Genius of Universal Emancipation* but had little on the *Liberator*.

253. "Dornbusch." 4th ser., 18 (1881): 430–32.
Profiled George Dornbusch, owner and editor of the twice-daily, expensive *Dornbusch's Floating Cargoes List*, a "privately circulated newspaper…for corn and seed trade."

254. "Some Curiosities of Reporting." 4th ser., 18 (1881): 510–12.
Indicted the editor, subeditor, and compositor for newspaper errors, but the chief culprit was the reporter, who summarized badly or incompletely or was ignorant, careless, or expansive in writing.

255. Chambers, W[illiam]. "Our Jubilee Year." 4th ser., 19 (1882): 49–59.
Combined personal reminiscences of and reader reactions to the *Journal* on its fiftieth anniversary.

256. "Mortimer Collins." 4th ser., 19 (1882): 242–43.
Honored Collins as a contributor to *Punch*, *Fraser's Magazine*, and the *Dublin University Magazine*.

257. An Englishman [?H. W. Wilson]. "Anglo-Americans." 4th ser., 19 (1882): 280–84.
Realized that journalism, "to a certain extent," was following other businesses by moving from individual to corporate control.

258. "Some Curious Advertisements." 4th ser., 19 (1882): 399–401.
Spotlighted employment, personal, and sports advertisements in several eighteenth-century newspapers.

259. "Newspaper Editors and Their Work." 4th ser., 19 (1882): 585–87.
Attested that newspapers were becoming "a greater power" every year, one that required editors of talent, judgment, and "special training." More than in other professions, journalists rose by merit,

difficult because of the great competition. Editors of dailies had power but many duties. They had to write commentary as the news broke, decide what to exclude when space was tight, and deal with a variety of people who might deliver important stories. Although editors were anonymous, most had peer recognition and some, the acquaintance of the famous.

260. "Obituary Curiosities." 4th ser., 19 (1882): 701–03.
Discovered interesting obituaries in such magazines as the *Gentleman's* and *Scots*.

261. "Hints to Young Writers." 4th ser., 20 (1883): 3–6.
Advised new periodical authors on how to choose a subject, to compose with accuracy and style, and to learn from rejections.

262. "A Wonderful Index." 4th ser., 20 (1883): 143–44.
Acclaimed William F. Poole for his *Index*, which showed the "immense literary activity" of British periodicals and the plagiarism of American.

263. "Curious Marriage Advertisements." 4th ser., 20 (1883): 526–28.
Culled matrimonial advertisements from the eighteenth-century *Scots Magazine*.

264. "Another Word to Literary Beginners." 5th ser., 1 (1884): 48–49.
Detailed that from August 1882 to August 1883 *Chambers's* received 3,225 manuscripts (2,065 prose) from Britain and the empire and accepted 14 percent of prose, 3 percent of poetry. Rejections were sometimes due to space constraints, but having an occasional piece published did not provide a living wage. *See* 4th ser., 18: 65.

265. "Occasional Notes: American Literary Piracy." 5th ser., 1 (1884): 274–75.
Accused American periodicals of lifting articles from *Chambers's* and cheaper British magazines of compounding the crime by reprinting these pieces.

266. "Erratic Pens." 5th ser., 1 (1884): 313–15.
Excused journalists for their jargon because they had no time for careful writing and the 'press-reader' was casual.

267. "American Newspapers on Themselves." 5th ser., 1 (1884): 714–16.
Postulated that advertising supported American newspapers, especially locals that promoted their towns. Named the *Sacramento* (CA) *Bee* "the spiciest, ablest, most brilliant and most independent journal on the Pacific coast." Listed gazettes that had Native American and English words in their titles, such as the *Klickitat* (WA) *Sentinel.*

268. "The Future of Telegraphs and Telephones." 5th ser., 2 (1885): 39–40.
Predicted that the telephone would not displace telegraphy for news transmission because telegrams were so cheap.

269. "Post-Office Notes." 5th ser., 2 (1885): 591–92.
Informed that 143,674 newspapers were posted in Britain, April 1884–85.

270. "Make-Believes." 5th ser., 2 (1885): 806–09.
Vilified "respectable magazines" for advertisements that promised educated women, upon remittal of a fee, instruction useless for remunerative work or publication in a nonexistent magazine.

271. "The *Board of Trade Journal*." 5th ser., 3 (1886): 720.
Deduced that the captioned *Journal* would be valuable to manufacturers and merchants.

272. "Some Odd Advertisements." 5th ser., 4 (1887): 91–92.
Excerpted personal advertisements, as on male escorts, in eighteenth-century English and Scottish newspapers.

273. "Winged War-Messengers." 5th ser., 4 (1887): 353–56.
Pleaded for retention of pigeons to carry news, as they had in the Franco-Prussian War, in case other modes of transmission fell to an enemy.

274. "American Newspaper Headlines." 5th ser., 4 (1887): 396–97.
Gloated that British reporters avoided the "sensationalism," "smartness," and originality of American headlines, which were often bigger than the story. London leaders had no headlines except in the *Daily News*.

275. "The 'B. M.' Newspaper Room." 5th ser., 4 (1887): 727–28.
Presented the British Museum wing, recently opened with money from William White, where readers could peruse bound volumes of newspapers.

276. "In Memoriam: Robert Chambers." 5th ser., 5 (1888): 272.
Obituary of Robert Chambers II recalled his "goodness and generosity to contributors."

277. "Two Cities of the Far West: Vancouver and Victoria." 5th ser., 5 (1888): 327–29.
Registered that Victoria had "[s]everal daily newspapers…which are enterprising enough in the supply of news, but essentially American in style, and lacking dignity of tone."

278. "BABY – BEER – BULLETS!!! A Western Sketch." 5th ser., 5 (1888): 460–63.
Title referred to a headline with "staring capitals and exclamation points" in the *Denver Daily News*, "the leading daily of Denver," as an example of American journalistic style.

279. "The Rounds of the Press." 5th ser., 5 (1888): 705–06.
Comprehended that press associations meant the same paragraphs in many London morning papers, from which the evening, country, and American press borrowed. However, the evening also telegraphed opinions about current events to locals whose London correspondents penned weekly columns based on society papers. Many sheets copied the same paragraphs of miscellany and literature to fill space, but careless editing produced contradictions. Aside that in the United States, an 'exchange' editor handled the scissors.

280. "News-Transmission Fifty Years Ago." 5th ser., 5 (1888): 748–49.
Recollected that before railroads and telegraphy, London papers left one page blank so that a local journal could insert a late report of a speech in its area.

281. "An Old Newspaper." 5th ser., 5 (1888): 779–81.
Unearthed the *Royal Cornwall Gazette* (Truro, 9 November 1805), once "the chief newspaper of the west country" whose printer and editor was Thomas Flindell. The issue contained word of Trafalgar and a few liquor advertisements but no leaders.

282. An Australian Journalist. "The Daily Press at the Antipodes." 5th ser., 5 (1888): 805–08.
Chronicled Australian dailies, each of which had greater circulation, proportional to population, than did any London paper, with Adelaide in the lead. All emphasized local news and sports. Leaders were broad unless a major event occurred or a local issue was hot. Editors earned 500–1,000 pounds per year, and some were also owners. Subeditors received eight to 12 pounds per week. Staff leader-writers were paid 400–700 pounds per year for five leaders per week; outsiders were paid by the column. The financial editor, whose pay ranged widely, worked outside the office. Reporters, with Adelaide's the best trained, received seven to ten pounds per week. They had varied assignments. Every paper had a person who talked daily with ministers ready to welcome journalists because the Australian press had "enormous power." If the weekly edition was not an abstract of the daily, it had a sports editor who earned ten pounds per week and was on staff whereas drama or music critics were not. Country correspondents on agriculture were paid a pound per column. A "good daily" had two London correspondents, one for cables and one for newsletters. These journals also had people in Paris, New York, San Francisco, and Port Louis. A university degree counted little; a smart person with colonial experience and shorthand, ready to work hard, could move easily from journalism to politics.

283. "The Post-Office on Wheels." 5th ser., 6 (1889): 234–37.
Alluded to newspaper transmittal by post.

284. "Heard and Overheard: Jottings from a Reporter's Note-book." 5th ser., 7 (1890): 623–24.
Unveiled that reporters often jotted down emotional reactions that they could not weave into their stories.

285. "Button's Coffee-House." 5th ser., 7 (1890): 705–07.
Noted that Richard Steele, when editing the *Guardian*, made Button's coffeehouse "his editorial office."

286. "Some Early Colonial Newspapers." 5th ser., 7 (1890): 811–12.
Looked at the *Sydney Gazette and New South Wales Advertiser*, a weekly of official announcements and old news. Among the problems of early Australian papers were scarcity of paper, poor type and ink, and printer-editors with little experience. Labeled the *Derwent Star and Van Diemen's Land Intelligencer* (1810), without local politics but with British news, the first Tasmanian paper, followed in 1816 by the government's *Hobart-Town Gazette and Southern Reporter*. The island's press was free by 1824.

287. "How Some Popular Institutions Began." 5th ser., 8 (1891): 122–24.
Observed that P. J. Reuter initially failed to supply news to London but that his later success was a precedent for the Press Association. Formed by owners after government takeover of telegraphy, it had people everywhere in 1891.

288. "Some Methods of Modern Journalism." 5th ser., 8 (1891): 317–20.
Presumed that journalism was sometimes slow in adopting new technology in news transmission because rural districts still sent sports news by pigeon. However, printing, telegraphy, and telephone advances forced reporters to be energetic though news from those covering speeches on the stump might also go by special train.

289. "The Postal System of India." 5th ser., 9 (1892): 108–10.
Footnoted Indian arrangements for newspaper postal 'privilege,' of prepayment for up to three months.

290. "A Visit to the Post-Office." 5th ser., 9 (1892): 502–03.
Described journalists' use of special post, in red or orange envelopes, and special wires, with messages sent to all along the route after 6 p.m.

291. "A Few Words about Reading." 5th ser., 10 (1893): 225–27.
Sermonized that most people had "an almost superstitious veneration" of their gazettes and no independent judgment, so the "awful power of the omnipotent daily paper as an engine for good or evil can hardly be over-estimated."

292. "Strange Messengers and Modes of Communication." 5th ser., 10 (1893): 235–37.
Mentioned that the *Daily Graphic* recently relied on pigeons to get the results of the Oxford-Cambridge boat race.

293. "Landmarks of a Literary Life." 5th ser., 10 (1893): 801–03.
Declared that longtime *Chambers's* contributor Camilla Toumlin, Mrs. Newton Crossland (b. 1802), was as well known in her time as were women columnists in 1893.

294. "A New Land of Promise." 5th ser., 11 (1894): 97–99.
Broadcast that some journalists went with Australian strikers to Paraguay to establish a "socialistic colony on Communist principles." The leader, William Lane, English born and American educated, had "edited a couple of democratic newspapers in Queensland."

295. "Some Memories of Books, Authors, and Events." 5th ser., 12 (1895): 17–19.
Paraphrased the reminiscences of James Bertram, who wrote for *Tait's Edinburgh Magazine* and *Hogg's Instructor* before editing Edinburgh's *North Briton* (1855), "one of the first penny newspapers." He was "one of the earliest disciples of the 'New Journalism' school." Aside that *Tait's* editor, Christian Johnstone, did not put Thomas De Quincey's material in every issue lest it become "commonplace."

296. "Some Notable Beginners in *Chambers's Journal.*" 5th ser., 12 (1895): 33–35.
Documented the flood of periodical submissions. In 1872 *Chambers's* had 200 per month; in 1882, 3,225 with 330 printed. The *Journal*, widely read in libraries, had always welcomed tyros, as Arthur Conan Doyle, whose first story it published in 1879.

297. "The State and the Telegraphs." 5th ser., 12 (1895): 161–63.
Updated that press telegrams had increased since state control. In 1895 the Press Association sent 500 columns per night, and London and some local papers had special wires.

298. A Journalist. "Newspaper Obituaries." 5th ser., 12 (1895): 353–55.
Specialist confessed to penning obituaries of the famous in advance. Misidentification or misinformation could bring a libel suit, so creating background files was essential.

299. "The Humours of Newspaper Enterprise." 5th ser., 12 (1895): 423–26.
Recited that it took "labour," "ingenuity," and capital to produce the daily that the public took for granted in 1895. Earlier gazettes spent money to hire special correspondents or boats to best each other. The *New York Herald* also displayed ingenuity in commissioning Henry Stanley, and Archibald Forbes scooped rivals with his 1874 *Daily News* interview of the survivors of the burned ship *Cospatrick.*

300. "The Return of the Rejected – How Editors Send Back Manuscripts." 5th ser., 13 (1896): 431–32.
Itemized editors' reasons for rejecting a manuscript, namely unsuitable or uninteresting topics, length, and illegibility. Replies went from gracious to form letters.

301. "The Biographer of Sir Walter Scott." 5th ser., 13 (1896): 737–40.
Review of Andrew Lang's *Life and Letters of J. G. Lockhart* opined that he and John Wilson were "the ruling spirits in the early days" of *Blackwood's Magazine*. Lockhart declined the editorial chair of the *Representative* before editing, with "fairness and ability," the *Quarterly Review*, whose circulation was 9,000–10,000.

302. "Journalistic Remuneration." 5th ser., 13 (1896): 753–54.
Assured that the remuneration of journalists had improved. *The Times* paid five to ten guineas for a freelancer's piece or rejected it promptly and courteously if a self-addressed envelope accompanied it. Most other morning papers paid two guineas except the halfpennies. Morning dailies had regular staffs so ignored freelancers. Of the evening press, the *Pall Mall Gazette* gave two guineas, but the rest of the evening press and the weeklies paid less. *Tit-Bits* took outside material only for its prize-story for which it sent a guinea. In the United States, payment paralleled acceptance; in Britain, it was monthly. "[H]igh class trade journals" were the rudest in their rejections. *See* 5th ser., 14: 161.

303. Phillips, Ernest, Author of *How to Become a Journalist.* "Journalistic Remuneration: The Other Side of the Picture." 5th ser., 14 (1897): 161–63.
Contradicts 5th ser., 13: 753 on the ground that journalism was "overcrowded." Freelancing, where only a few succeeded notwithstanding the opportunities offered by the myriad of serials, was at best supplementary income because "innumerable trashy publications" stole material.

304. "Producing a Great Daily Paper." 5th ser., 14 (1897): 319–20.
Underlined the efforts of the entire staff of a morning daily, every hour of every day. Great papers were well organized but flexible. Leaders were easy to place and departments had rigid column allocations, but space had to be found for late news, chiefly foreign that bumped everything else. When Parliament was not sitting and politicians were everywhere, local correspondents sent volumes of telegrams that subeditors polished. The really competent editor was "rare," a person knowledgeable about policy and grammar, calm, patient with staff, and whose "liver must be in good order."

305. "The Press Association." 5th ser., 14 (1897): 516–17.
The Press Association, formed about the time of government takeover of telegraphy, was the "leading news-collecting agency in the kingdom, a cooperative association of newspaper proprietors." Prior to its existence, local papers lacked funds to gather news adequately. The Press Association fee scale fit publication schedules, and its journalists, "some of the ablest in London," were impartial in news gathering. Local material often came from penny-a-liners; foreign, principally from Reuters that dispatched Press Association news of England around the world.

306. "Christmas Numbers Old and New." 5th ser., 14 (1897): 640–43.
Scanned *All the Year Round*, the *Illustrated London News*, and other serials. Charles Mackay, the *Illustrated London News* editor, inaugurated a Christmas number, double the paper's regular size, with an illustration by Mason Jackson that increased sales. Preparation of a Christmas issue took time, so some serials charged a higher price. When James Payn edited *Chambers's*, he printed Christmas numbers, but the *Journal* had not had one in 27 years until 1897.

307. "Some Early Contributors to *Chambers's Journal*." 5th ser., 14 (1897): 708–11.
Agreed that successful periodicals, as those of George Newnes, served readers what they wanted. Most magazines, particularly the illustrated, were quick to copy trends. Although many 1897 journals pursued and handsomely paid well-known authors for fiction, *Chambers's* always opened its doors to everyone. William Chambers was "sternly practical"; his brother Robert had "literary grace" and chose articles that fit public taste and could "instruct and elevate" readers. Among famed contributors were Camilla Toumlin and Thomas De Quincey. James Payn had "a good team," thanks to his kindliness as an editor.

308. "Blackwood's: The History of a Publishing House." 5th ser., 14 (1897): 753–56.
Assessed the early *Blackwood's Magazine* as dull, then "hostile journalism." Its pivotal contributors were William Maginn, J. G. Lockhart, and John Wilson, the last "most trying" but too important to lose. Thomas De Quincey was frequently late with his articles but he, like the majority of *Blackwood's* scribes, was loyal to the publisher.

309. "Some Notables at Play." 6th ser., 1 (1897–98): 289–91.
Headlined the leisure activities of editors.

310. White, Arnold. "The Jew in Modern Life." 6th ser., 1 (1897–98): 401–04.
Rumored that the "Jewish capture of newspapers all over Europe" was obvious from "the great Pest newspaper, the *Pester Lloyd*" that had only one Christian on staff.

311. Edwardes, Charles. "Life in Madrid." 6th ser., 1 (1897–98): 468–70.
Saw newsboys, clamoring about telegraphic news, in every Madrid café.

312. "Writers for the Young." 6th ser., 1 (1897–98): 716–20.
Glanced at George Manville Fenn, "journalist," owner of *Once a Week*, and frequent contributor to *Chambers's*, and L. T. Meade (Mrs. Toumlin Smith), who penned for the *Sunday Magazine* for six years and edited *Atalanta*.

313. "A Great Editor: John Blackwood." 6th ser., 2 (1898–99): 83–85.
Narrated that Blackwood enjoyed editing *Blackwood's Magazine* but never wrote for his publication unlike Douglas Cook of the *Saturday Review*. Blackwood recruited a range of contributors and preferred anonymity to signature. He supervised all writers but favored those who took "his hints."

314. "Feuilletons." 6th ser., 2 (1898–99): 509–11.
Sneered that the inexpensive Paris *Petit Journal* captured the world's largest journalistic circulation by feeding readers the "mental pabulum for which their souls are supposed to yearn."

315. MacDonagh, Michael. "The Proof-Reader." 6th ser., 2 (1898–99): 513–15.
Accented proofreaders' importance for newspaper accuracy, so they had to be "intelligent and widely read, diligent, and painstaking" and comfortable working in a small space. Authors in weeklies and monthlies did their own proofreading.

316. A Working Man. "My First Investment in *Chambers's Journal*." 6th ser., 3 (1899–1900): 316–18.
Purchaser of *Chamber's* since 1847 remembered that there were few other periodicals in Scotland at that time. The "*Aberdeen Journal*, the oldest newspaper in the north of Scotland," was read by wealthy farmers alone or by tradesmen aloud to friends. In 1899 everyone had morning and evening papers and access to a library with "every month a flood of periodicals." People were excited when the *Illustrated London News* appeared, but *Chambers's* had always been worth the price, "a perfect treasure."

317. "Obituary Notices from Their Humorous Side." 6th ser., 3 (1899–1900): 334–36.
Pointed out one American editor who wrote his own obituary, another who threatened nonpaying customers with obituary notices unless they settled accounts, and death columns in British and Spanish papers.

318. "About Some of Our Latest Contributors." 6th ser., 3 (1899–1900): 807–12.
Acknowledged that to please mass audiences in 1900 the newspaper purloined from the magazine, "an illuminated scrap-book for an idle hour, without much intellectual sediment or stimulus." *Chambers's* always opposed illustrations as distractions. Its contributors, among them John Morley, James Payn, and several others cited, also penned for newspapers and other magazines.

319. "Bargain-Sales and Advertisements." 6th ser., 4 (1900–01): 61–64.
Learned social history from advertisements.

The Contemporary Review, 1866–1900

The *Contemporary*, started by Alexander Strahan also of *Good Words*, circulated pivotal articles on the profession of journalism and the anonymity of journalists. Its most famous columns, on press power, came from W. T. Stead's pen.

1. Kinnear, J. Boyd. "Anonymous Journalism." 5 (1867): 324–39.
Confirmed that "[j]ournalism has gained a position so important and wields now a power so immense that an examination of the soundness of the principles on which it is conducted becomes a matter of urgent necessity. It represents the real thinking part of the nation." If journalism was "to inform, to advise, and to direct," it could not be anonymous without having its honesty and trustworthiness questioned. Newspapers were no longer advocates but judges who spoke in "authoritative" and "impartial" language. Yet anonymity allowed them to misrepresent, garble, and even falsify news without taking responsibility. A paper expressed an editor's ideas in a leader, so there was no need for secrecy. Political articles, criticism, and commentaries on finance and foreign policy should be signed to facilitate fair discussion and rewarded for "excellence and high principle." Opposition to signature rested on habit, insecurity, and the avarice of owners unwilling to pay for merit. The French mandated signature as an instrument of official control; the British should promote voluntary signing monitored by public opinion. Aside that censorship kept the French press from being worse than it was.

2. [Maurice, C. E.]. "Rome at the Close of 1867." 7 (1868): 21–35.
Deemed the Roman press unreliable. The "*Osservatore Romano* and *Giornale di Roma* do not scruple to falsify the known facts." They were outdated and "filled with violent attacks" on opponents.

3. [?Alford, Henry]. "The London Press: the *Spectator*, the *Guardian*, the *Nonconformist*." 7 (1868): 98–107, 262–76; "The *Pall Mall Gazette*," 578–85.
Insisted that newspapers showed decency, but not kindness, and the "*conceit of certainty*" based on a scientific spirit, scientific "in its hardness, in its positiveness, and in its distrust." They symbolized "crowd-worship" even though the "*personnel* of journalism is mixed" with men from other professions or by accident. The *Saturday Review* commenced a new era of newspaper writing that displayed the "culture and *esprit de corps* of the highly-educated Englishman," a man of talent. The *Pall Mall Gazette* was "the most powerful organ of the reaction of culture." Its articles presented many views expressed by scribes of talent and expertise in straightforward language. With its strong staff and large resources, the paper acted as "a social and literary police."

Aside that a London daily cost 40,000 pounds to start.

4. Thorold, Anthony W. "The Evangelical Clergy of 1868." 8 (1868): 569–96.
Bowed to the *Children's Friend* and *Friendly Visitor* as the "first cheap religious periodicals" and the *Visitor* as the "first school for clergymen's daughters."

5. Tyrwhitt, R. St. J. "Skilled and Literary Art-Criticism." 11 (1869): 101–18.
Decried two species of art critic, the amateur "pressman who hangs about studios, and reads a day or two at the British Museum" and the specialist, the "*litterateur*," who saw himself as the authority for artists as *The Times* was for bishops and the *Saturday Review* was for "ladies."

6. Strahan, Alexander. "Our Very Cheap Literature." 14 (1870): 439–60.
Dismissed much cheap literature as such trash that the post office recently cancelled its low rate for all magazines to the colonies. Among the inexpensive listed were the *Family Herald* and *London Journal*, whose notices to correspondents were entertaining, while others featured inferior fiction.

7. V[enturi], A. E[milie]. "Joseph Mazzini: What Has He Done for Italy?" 15 (1870): 383–407.
Cited systematic suppression of newspapers and imprisonment of editors in Piedmont.

8. Collet, Sophia D. "Mr. Richard H[olt] Hutton as Critic and Theologian." 16 (1870–71): 634–50.
Essay on *Spectator* editor Hutton drew from his *Essays, Theological and Literary*, originally printed in the *National Review*.

9. Mazzini, Joseph. "The Franco-German War." 17 (1871): 1–14.
Bemoaned that the "observation of daily chroniclers was inevitably superficial, and coloured by party feeling," notably war reporting with its "exaggerated expressions" and "epithets."

10. Mazzini, Joseph. "The Commune in Paris." 17 (1871): 307–18.
Aside on the old journalistic habit of making anything French news.

11. Mozley, J. R. "The Use of Modern Literatures in the Higher Education." 17 (1871): 559–68.
Grieved that the failure of English universities to teach about other nations led a major English newspaper to an "absurd mistake" in a leader.

12. Horne, R. H. "The United States of Australia." 18 (1871): 174–88.
Segmented Australian journalism. "The daily and weekly journals of Melbourne and Sydney are conducted with great ability and sometimes contain articles worthy in all respects of comparison with the best of those which appeared in the great leading journals of Europe." Because no Australian books sold and "nothing of an intellectual kind is 'believed in'...the finest articles of their press are comparatively thrown away...the great mass of the people, like some of their long-enduring ministries, *do not know one thing from another*." Identified Edward Wilson as the "chief proprietor" of Melbourne's *Argus*.

13. Wright, Thomas. "The People in Relation to Political Power and Opinion." 18 (1871): 351–61.
Grumbled that workers lacked experience and knowledge for "getting up, supporting, and 'inspiring' press organs." Workers needed "a leading daily paper" comparable to other groups so that their views counted among the "opinions of the press." New labor journals could be 'slashing' and 'scathing'

but should eschew the "blatant abuse" in weekly working-class papers that addressed politically uninformed readers.

14. Wright, Thomas. "The Composition of the Working Classes." 18 (1871): 514–26.
Broadcast that the latest generation of workers tended to read "the wide-spreading press," from *The Times* to *Lloyd's Weekly Newspaper* and the *Beehive*, on "working-class questions."

15. Littledale, Richard Frederick. "The Secular Studies of the Clergy." 19 (1871–72): 55–81.
Pointed out that journalists were "largely recruited" from the clergy, yet "the sensational leaders of the *Daily Telegraph*" were examples of "the worst possible English style." Clerics should study "really good criticism, not of such shallow censors as Lord [Francis] Jeffrey."

16. Gibb, John. "Prince Bismarck and the Ultramontanes." 20 (1872): 172–83.
Whispered that some news of Prussia came from Belgian papers.

17. Strahan, Alexander. "Norman Macleod." 20 (1872): 291–306.
Obituary of Macleod told of reading his work in the *Scotsman* and offering him the editorship of *Good Words*. Macleod had already edited the *Edinburgh Christian Magazine* for ten years at a "heavy loss." His first issue of *Good Words* paralleled the birth of the *Cornhill Magazine* with its instant popularity. However, by 1867, *Good Words* was a success, achieving the highest circulation of the monthlies. Macleod was also connected to the *Contemporary Review* and the *Sunday Magazine*.

18. [Evans, Albert Eubule]. "Constitutional Germany." 20 (1872): 839–59.
Considered press suppression, in Baden in 1849 and the German states generally. Until 1863 gazettes could not print news of internal politics and were constrained by "degrading regulations" that left them to "demoralize" rather than to educate readers.

19. Michaud, Eugene. "The Political Situation in France." 22 (1873): 957–72.
Tied several papers to politics.

20. Murphy, Arthur. "The Tory Press." 23 (1873–74): 822–40.
Professed that journalism, followed here from Queen Anne to 1873, was part of literary history, albeit contemporary journalists might not reach readers' fundamental instincts, such as the desire for repose and the love of progress. Among the upper classes, journalism was not popular as a career even though the profession had more dignity than most and influenced 100,000 readers daily. Political journalism was fascinating because of its immediate effect on opinion, its "epigrammatic style," its mystery. Most Conservative papers emphasized matter rather than manner, unlike the French. The Tories needed better style and leader-writers, scholars of "punctuality, sobriety, and discretion," who had common sense, could write with "wit and humour," and were ready to work hard for 400–500 pounds per year and remain anonymous. If journalists had status and commensurate reward, journalism would improve, particularly the rural press that did not encourage moral and mental habits appropriate for journalism. Because Liberal magazines outweighed Conservative in number and quality, the Tories required new journals of literary criticism and possibly a weekly newspaper.

21. Lytton, [E. R. Bulwer]. "The French Constitutional Monarchy of 1830: An Enquiry into the Causes of Its Failure." 24 (1874): 856–74.
Defended the "defiant, petulant, provocative" press of the July Monarchy because it represented all interests and "enlisted some of the profoundest, and some of the most brilliant writers." Its journalists reaped "fame" and "power" from this "Golden Age" of French journalism.

22. Tulloch, John. "The Author of *Thorndale*." 25 (1874–75): 377–96.
Memorialized William Smith, whose writings in the *Quarterly Review* earned high praise from its editor, J. G. Lockhart. Smith also penned for *Blackwood's Magazine* and resuscitated the *Literary Gazette* before it merged with the *Athenaeum*.

23. Strahan, A[lexander]. "Bad Literature for the Young." 26 (1875): 981–91.
Theorized that 'penny-dreadfuls' could inspire crime or self-help. Most were "garbage," read by youths whose parents perused the *Illustrated Police News*. Nonetheless, even the respectable classes bought periodicals that should have been "beneath their notice." English juvenile gazettes should disdain the American model of teen romance and promote service and religion in action.

24. [Rands, William Brighty]. "The Higher Controversy and Periodical Literature." 29 (1876–77): 516–17.
Sanctioned specialized periodicals that offered "open council" on important matters even though magazines were burgeoning.

25. [Rands, William Brighty]. "Editing." 29 (1876–77): 517–20.
Thought that good periodical editors, such as François Buloz of the *Revue des Deux Mondes*, balanced contributions from celebrities and neophytes, both of whom "editorial alteration" might irritate. Anonymity was better than signature because "stars" or experts had too much influence on readers.

26. [Rands, William Brighty]. "The Rationale of Reviewing." 29 (1876–77): 1144–47.
Discussed the role of the periodical reviewer for the general and literary reader.

27. [Rands, William Brighty]. "Parliamentary Reporting." 30 (1877): 165–67.
Credited parliamentary reporters for changing perceptions about speeches; their importance no longer derived from delivery but from reading by thousands. Yet reporters were still in the House by "sufferance" so could still be removed. Ideal MPs "speak slowly, in ordinary words and intelligible sentences." For the rest, journalists should "*avoid* accuracy, and cook the speeches." As newspapers reduced space for speeches, parliamentary reporters were less qualified but should be people of "*bright* as well as accurate minds, and of *versatile* culture" who read widely.

28. *** [Buchanan, Robert W.] "Signs of the Times: I. The Newest Thing in Journalism." 30 (1877): 678–703; with note, 1054.
Thundered that papers were full of 'opinions' and "tittle-tattle" instead of news in "naked English, clean and unashamed." Although there were plenty of gazettes, the latest headlined scandal, epitomized by *Vanity Fair* with its "coloured caricature" on the cover. It typified "the vulgar-genteel journal [which] deals less in plain statement than in secret inference, more in sly, diabolical suggestion than in bold, unvarnished decency." Publication of "absolutely idiotic" acrostics proved the low "intellectual

caliber" of this genre. Although the *World* printed interviews of the famous and their friends, it at least reported on Parliament and the Stock Exchange. Among other "new pests of journalism" were *Truth*, which showcased the "new journalist" who had "self-confidence" in his own opinions, and the unrefined *Whitehall Review*, aimed at "meretricious women." Note responded to the statement in the *World* that anger about lost circulation generated Buchanan's article.

29. Monod, Gabriel. "Contemporary Life and Thought in France." 31 (1877–78): 183–201, 391–407, 633–49.

Recorded the birth in France of new "learned" reviews and other scholarly periodicals and the cessation in dailies of high quality literary criticism. The *Revue des Deux Mondes*, a serial of authority not shaken by the century's revolutions, had a well-paid staff and 20,000 subscribers.

30. S., T. [Elizaveta Bezobrazova]. "Contemporary Life and Thought in Russia." 31 (1877–78): 620–32.

Alluded to the Russian press, including *Golos* and the *Moscow Gazette*.

31. [Rands, William Brighty]. "Government Officials and Literature." 31 (1877–78): 660–61.

Justified the right of officials to publish articles. If they breached trust by penning in "society journals," they would be stigmatized.

32. Gubernatis, Angelo de. "Contemporary Life and Thought in Italy." 31 (1877–78): 841–55.

Indicated major Italian papers, as Rome's *Diretto* and *Civiltà Cattolica*, Genoa's *Corriere Mercantile*, Milan's *Perseveranza*, and Florence's *Nazione*, as well as reviews, the *Rassegna Settimanale*, modeled on the *Saturday Review* and the "most eminent and trustworthy" *Nuova Antologia*.

33. S., T. [Elizaveta Bezobrazova]. "Contemporary Life and Thought in Russia." 32 (1878): 599–624.

Noted Russian censorship of the press except the *Moscow Gazette*.

34. "Anonymous and Signed Writing." 32 (1878): 835–36.

Suspected that signature resulted in more "bitterness" though less "coarseness" in controversies among critics.

35. Gubernatis, Angelo de. "Contemporary Life and Thought in Italy." 33 (1878): 155–65.

Titled Angelo Brofferio an independent journalist and Filippo de Boni an "ex-monk" who was a "virulent journalist."

36. S., T. [Elizaveta Bezobrazova]. "Contemporary Life and Thought in Russia." 34 (1878–79): 594–604.

Silhouetted a Russian monthly, *Zemlia i Volia*. Recently begun by revolutionaries after police seized their first printing office, it was a gazette of style and variety. Aside that Michael Katkoff, editor of the *Moscow Gazette*, was a sycophant of government.

37. Monod, G[abriel]. "Contemporary Life and Thought in France." 35 (1879): 339–60, 923–42.

Mused about new French Protestant and republican newspapers, as the *Signal* and the *Réformateur Anti-Clérical et Républicain*, and the art journals, the *Art* and *Vie Moderne*.

38. Blind, Karl. "Conspiracies in Russia." 35 (1879): 422–57, 875–902.

Reminded that the Russian press was always censored whenever it showed "firmness," as the 1860s case of the *Great Russian* evidenced.

39. Browne, Matthew [William Brighty Rands]. "Mr. Macvey Napier and the *Edinburgh* Reviewers." 36 (1879): 263–73.

Review of *Selections from the Correspondence of the Late Macvey Napier, Esq.*, edited by his son, concluded that 1879 reviews were no better or worse than those in the early *Edinburgh Review*. Discussion of science and politics was freer in 1879, but, because the press was more "commercial," a "tendency to compromise in the expression of opinion" left contemporary articles with less clout.

40. Osborn, Robert D. "India under Lord Lytton." 36 (1879): 553–73.

Labeled the Vernacular Press Act of 1878 a gag because the Press Commission distributed "worthless" material to the Anglo-Indian papers or withheld information that criticized officials, as the *Calcutta Statesman* proved.

41. Monod, G[abriel]. "Contemporary Life and Thought in France." 36 (1879): 697–714.

Scorned *Père Duchesne*, a "filthy and bloodthirsty paper" edited in 1871 by Alphonse Humbert.

42. S., T. [Elizaveta Bezobrazova]. "Contemporary Life and Thought in Russia." 37 (1880): 156–66.

Rued that Russia's "[l]iberal journalism," encumbered by financial restraints, died from lack of subscribers in contrast to the *Moscow Gazette*.

43. Stuart, Roberto. "Contemporary Life and Thought in Italy." 37 (1880): 167–76.

Commented on the recent introduction in Italy of newspaper Sunday supplements. They carried "articles purely literary in character," such as in Rome's *Fanfulla*, edited by Ferdinando Martini, "one of the best modern Italian writers."

44. Lethbridge, Roper. "The Vernacular Press of India: An Historical Sketch." 37 (1880): 459–73.

Lethbridge, former editor of the quarterly *Calcutta Review*, dated the English press in India from *Hicky's Gazette*, with "an infinite amount of scurrility and scandal, varied only occasionally by lucid intervals of fair and sensible journalism." In 1823 the only native paper in Serampore belonged to missionaries; in 1835 there were 12 serials. From 1822 to 1878 the local press had a "slow but steady growth" in number and circulation (with statistics). In 1850 there were 28 papers in the North; in 1878–79, 60. Urdu papers, the most numerous, were written with "considerable ability" but were "not skillfully edited." Bengali gazettes devoted much space to English literature, so they did not reflect the intellect of Indians, but these journals passed through many hands. Maratha papers had a reputation for sedition; Gujarati, for "good sense and enlightenment"; Tamil and Burmese were "politically unimportant." Most Indian heralds had no advertising so depended for survival on patrons or delayed payment of editors and printers. The Press Act of 1878 gave reporters access to government and abolished prior permission but had warnings and fines. By replacing punitive with preventive measures, the new system would discourage martyrs and bring this press to "maturity."

45. An American Statesman [?Gamaliel Bradford]. "Party Politics in the United States." 38 (1880): 761–72.

Evaluated the "influence of the press" in the United States. Washington papers in 1880 did not sway the city, much less the country, in contrast to those in 1840. American gazettes were only "*news*papers" without a political editor. Widely circulating New York ones were less provincial, but their weak leaders had less impact than those in the 1860s. Most metro tribunes were not well edited but had less "personal abuse" than their predecessors. Monthlies offering political education were not read by the public. Magazines with "light literature and richly illustrated" were popular, and "weekly illustrated papers" had "very wide influence" and were "a power in the political world." The religious press was apolitical.

46. Knighton, W[illiam]. "Young Bengal at Home." 38 (1880): 888–97.

Stamped the *Indian Mirror*, *Hindu Patriot*, and *Bengali* (Calcutta newspapers), and the *Oriental Miscellany* (monthly) publications of quality comparable to "more pretentious" British ones.

47. MacColl, Malcolm. "Young Ireland." 39 (1881): 129–47.

Explicated the relationship between Ireland's *Nation* and Young Ireland in the 1840s.

48. Wright, Thomas. "On a Possible Popular Culture." 40 (1881): 25–44.

Posited that compulsory education graduated buyers of the "lower types of weekly newspapers." An earlier generation's "garbage" was counteracted by cheap quality serials, as the *Penny Magazine*, *Eliza Cook's Journal*, and *Chambers's Journal*. In 1881 workers supplemented local papers, less exciting in "comparatively weak piping times of peace," with penny dreadfuls. They did not necessarily criminalize or demoralize but did displace better reading. One of the worst was the *Illustrated Police News*. Women were better off than men because they had no dreadfuls and no interest in newspapers.

49. MacColl, Malcolm. "Are Reforms Possible under Mussulman Rule?" 40 (1881): 257–81.

Digressed at length about "Scrutator" (*The Times*, c. 1871), a "literary hack" according to the *German Correspondent*.

50. A Non-Resident American [George Washburn]. "City Life in the United States." 40 (1881): 710–25.

Highlighted big New York dailies that traded insults but saw themselves as different from *The Times* only because of their huge circulations. They spent money to get news, much of it sensational that lowered public taste. Since the Civil War they displayed less party bias and more editorial personality. The city's religious weeklies matched dailies in influence.

51. Booth, William. "The Salvation Army." 42 (1882): 175–82; Frances Power Cobbe, 182–89; Randall T. Davidson, 189–99.

Booth verified that the *War Cry* and *Little Soldier* had a combined circulation of 180,000 weekly. Cobbe considered the "startling" articles in the *War Cry* inappropriate. Davidson found the *Little Soldier* full of "pernicious stuff."

52. Evans, Arthur J. "The Austrian War Against Publicity." 42 (1882): 383–99.

Evans, who referred to himself as a former foreign correspondent for the *Manchester Guardian* and the *Pall Mall Gazette*, claimed that Austrian officials suppressed "independent news" of Eastern Europe. Censors checked telegrams and postings, marked articles published internally "unsuitable" for British readers, and generally harassed correspondents. Their information came from government or Vienna newspapers controlled by the authorities.

53. Osborn, Robert D. "Representative Government for India." 42 (1882): 931–53.

Characterized the *Umrita Bazaar Patrika* as "the most influential native journal in India."

54. Monod, G[abriel]. "Contemporary Life and Thought in France." 43 (1883): 157–78.

Noted that Louis Blanc wrote from London for the *Temps* (1860–70).

55. Baxter, William Edward. "The Business of the House of Commons." 43 (1883): 629–35.

Urged London dailies and locals to stop printing Commons speeches in full because the coverage encouraged long and boring orations. Worse, Members, after reading their words in the morning papers, devoted too much question time to journalistic commentary on them.

56. O'Donnell, Frank Hugh. "Fenianism – Past and Present." 43 (1883): 747–66.

Classified some newspapers in Ireland and New York as Fenian.

57. Stepniak [S. M. Kravchinsky]. "Russia after the Coronation." 44 (1883): 317–30.

Swore that the Russian government listened to the European press.

58. Lang, A[ndrew]. "Literary Forgeries." 44 (1883): 837–49.

Admitted that periodicals even of the rank of *Blackwood's Magazine* and the *Spectator* were duped by contributors.

59. Besant, Walter. "The Amusements of the People." 45 (1884): 342–53.

Observed that workers read papers regularly, especially those "red-hot on politics."

60. Adams, Charles Kendall. "Contemporary Life and Thought in the United States." 45 (1884): 734–50.

Bowed to George W. Curtis, the "accomplished editor" of *Harper's Weekly*.

61. Monod, G[abriel]. "Contemporary Life and Thought in France." 46 (1884): 127–43.

Believed that *Figaro* reflected the "boulevard" while the *Temps* was "the most earnest of all the Parisian journals." *See* 48: 887.

62. Monod, G[abriel]. "Contemporary Life and Thought in France." 48 (1885): 887–901.

Contrasted the Parisian *Figaro*, a "literary and society paper," and the *Temps*, with "the widest circulation of all the political journals." *See* 46: 127.

63. Stead, W. T. "Government by Journalism." 49 (1886): 653–74.

This famous article perceived the newspaper as "a mirror reflecting all the ever-varying phases of life in the locality" and representing current concerns better than did Parliament. As a "necessity of life," the newspaper lent importance to speeches; as a "gauge of public opinion," it allowed politicians to sound out policy more effectively than did less frequent public meetings even if ministers often misled reporters instead of confiding in them. The press was more timely than Parliament, had access to more experts, and paid attention to the "disinherited." Newspapers lifted the minds of workers to a "higher sphere of thought and action," so an editor was "the uncrowned king of an educated democracy" particularly when the Cabinet divided. Editors did not appreciate their power (e.g., to print or exclude speeches, generate interest in an issue, prioritize policy), which was akin to the former sway of religion but with "the priesthood of Comte." They should accept leadership but should exercise "civic responsibility…as a watchman." Reporters should master facts and interview people, then use the sensational, "the very material of life," to spur reform, not rouse emotions. *See* 50: 663.

64. Dowden, Edward. "The Interpretation of Literature." 49 (1886): 701–19.

Personified "professional interpreters of literature…scribes who expound the law from their pulpits in the reviews, weekly, monthly, quarterly," as judges castigating quality writing because authors were unknown. Even Francis Jeffrey, an extraordinary critic, was guilty, but not Leigh Hunt, whose newspapers and essays were nicknamed 'signpost criticism.'

65. Marvin, Charles. "Batoum – and After." 50 (1886): 267–76.

Peeked at the influence of Michael Katkoff, the editor of *Moscow Gazette*, and at the informative Russian *Official Journal* and other newspapers.

66. Williams, Charles. "Alexander I of Bulgaria." 50 (1886): 501–08.

Ranked "A. von Huhn, Paris correspondent" of Cologne's *Zeitung* as "one of the very first, if not the first, of living war correspondents."

67. Pennell, Elizabeth Robins. "The Modern Comic Newspaper: The Evolution of a Popular Type." 50 (1886): 509–23.

Regarded *Punch*, *Fun*, and others as "successors of the old masques" and *Ally Sloper's Half Holiday* as "eminently a publication for the people" though some thought it "vulgar."

68. Stead, W. T. "The Future of Journalism." 50 (1886): 663–79.

Complement of 49: 653 maintained that a competent newspaper editor, one informed about opinion in and outside London, could be very influential. He should depend on "trustworthy assistants" who knew key people connected to ministers, "ambassadors, judges, generals, and great financiers"; on reporters who could find news, and on people throughout the country who could keep him current on popular views. '[J]ournalistic travelers' would check on these pollsters at least annually. An editor should be "universally accessible" and should reach out to learn the problems of the masses. His goal should be to make the newspaper "a civic church and a democratic university." If owners would take less profit, staffs could grow. Until then editors would be "overworked" and reporters would be "hard-pressed."

69. Monod, G[abriel]. "Contemporary Life and Thought in France." 50 (1886): 728–43.

Referred to "Henri des Houx, the late director of the *Journal de Rome*," a new book titled *Souvenirs d'un Journaliste Français à Rome*, and the 100 year old M. E. Chevreul, "the great chemist" and "the only member on the management of the *Journal des Savants* who does not go to sleep during the sittings of the editorial committee."

70. Marzials, Frank T. "M. Zola as a Critic." 51 (1887): 57–70.

Remarked that "French criticism seems certainly to have passed the meridian of its palmist day," but articles by Hippolyte Taine, Ernest Renan, and "the younger writers of the *Revue des Deux Mondes* revived "a literary mood."

71. Haggard, H. Rider. "About Fiction." 51 (1887): 172–80.

Predicted that because of literary plagiarism the only original American literature would soon be in the "columns of a very enterprising daily press." It printed 'full and special' reports of scandals but was critical of novelists who portrayed real life.

72. Boglietti, Giovanni. "Contemporary Life and Thought in Italy." 51 (1887): 274–94.

Noticed *Rosmini*, a recent periodical named for "the celebrated philosopher," Antonio Rosmini.

73. Traill, H. D. "Our Self-Conscious Selves." 51 (1887): 654–67.

Scoffed at "the host of light periodicals" with "so-called 'literary gossip,'" which was really self-advertising by their writers.

74. Rogers, J. E. Thorold. "Confessions of a Metropolitan Member." 51 (1887): 681–94.

Member of Parliament feared that London voters were "entirely indifferent to the leading articles of the newspaper" because they lived "too near the workshop of what is called public opinion." Although some gazettes circulated news that was "full and honest," the "London daily press counts for next to nothing in the development of public opinion."

75. Thompson, Stephen. "Australian Literature." 52 (1887): 401–14.

Glanced at Marcus Clark's early writing in the *Australasian*, the 'weekly' of Melbourne's *Argus*.

76. [Monod, Gabriel]. "Contemporary Life and Thought in France." 52 (1887): 428–47.

Singled out, among "[t]he most heedless and irresponsible, the most scandalous and implacable of the Paris journals," the *Lanterne*.

77. An English Resident in Russia [E. J. Dillon]. "Michael Katkoff." 52 (1887): 504–22.

Determined that before Katkoff became editor of the *Moscow Gazette* in 1850, it was "an obscure daily newspaper owned by the University." In 1855 he left to start the monthly *Russian Messenger* with contributions from great writers. He ran it until 1863 when he returned to the *Gazette* where he received the advertising revenue, about 15,000 pounds a year. While he was editor, the standards for a respectable newspaper (facts, fair play, no personal abuse) did not apply to the *Gazette*. He pushed government to end the quality *Golos* and the monthly *Memoirs of the Fatherland*, thus abetting intellectual decline in Russia. In 1887 the *Gazette* was "the most serious and respectable newspaper in Russia."

78. Adams, Charles Kendall. "Contemporary Life and Thought in the United States." 52 (1887): 724–34.

Alluded to George W. Curtis, "editor of *Harper's Monthly* [*Magazine*] and *Harper's Weekly*, two journals which have an enormous circulation among the most intelligent people" in the United States.

79. Geffcken, F[riedrich] H. "Contemporary Life and Thought in Germany." 52 (1887): 880–94.

Reported that Frankfurt's *Zeitung* was doing interviews and the *Norddeutsche Allgemeine Zeitung* was "the Chancellor's paper." Asides on "the Russian-inspired paper at Brussels," the *Nord*, and the influence of Michael Katkoff while *Moscow Gazette* editor.

80. Duffy, C. Gavan. "An Australian Example." 53 (1888): 1–31.

Veteran journalist explained that type was once scarce in Sydney and "type-founding an unknown art," so the *Port Phillip Patriot* was in manuscript as Louis Kossuth's *Pesti Hirlap* had once been. William Wentworth bought "a printing press to found an independent newspaper."

81. Morgan, G[eorge] Osborne. "Welsh Nationality." 53 (1888): 84–93.

Grieved because London papers except the *Daily News* ignored the Welsh.

82. Monod, G[abriel]. "Contemporary Life and Thought in France." 53 (1888): 902–20.

Denigrated the "disreputable *Lanterne*" and other papers that "represented no serious political opinion" but only "scandal, calumny, and extortion." Asides that *Petit Journal* circulation was over a million and that "a clever journalist and vaudevillist" was once minister of public information.

83. Underwood, F[rancis] H. "The Awakening of New England." 54 (1888): 257–78.

Saluted New England as the center of American thought, spearheaded by the *North American Review*, although magazines surfaced throughout the United States. Aside on John Greenleaf Whittier as a newspaper editor and writer.

84. Hunter, W. W. "The Present Problem in India." 54 (1888): 313–34.

Recognized that English dailies, weeklies, and monthlies made it impossible to ignore India. "The special Monday telegrams of *The Times* form one of the most striking feature [*sic*] of English journalism in our age." One recent transmission had 2,414 words. The "native Press" was "vigorous," almost a "political power." Although "higher class" papers were "generally moderate and loyal," Anglo-Indian journals headlined those that were "foolish and violent." *The Voice of India*, a monthly summary of the Indian press, was "fair and complete."

85. Hunt, W. Holman. "Reminiscences of John Leech." 54 (1888): 335–53.
Recalled contacts with Leech whose colleague, Kenny Meadows, was an early "ruler among the illustrators of *Punch*."

86. Lang, Andrew. "A Dip in Criticism." 54 (1888): 495–503.
Mandated that a critic who hinted that a writer was "an untruthful person and literary thief" sign the review.

87. Gallenga, A[ntonio]. "France and Italy." 54 (1888): 587–99.
Disclosed that Italian Premier Francisco Crispi was "an old journalist" and that Italians often read French papers, as *Figaro*, since there was little else to peruse in the cafés.

88. Monod, G[abriel]. "Contemporary Life and Thought in France." 54 (1888): 897–916.
Insisted that France's "really representative papers are far more fair and moderate" than either Berlin's *Norddeutsche Allgemeine Zeitung* or Cologne's *Zeitung*.

89. Hamerton, P. G. "The Political Situation in France: II. The Immediate Future." 55 (1889): 495–507.
Comprehended that wherever newspapers were "very active, monotony in government is sure to breed dissatisfaction."

90. Besant, Walter. "The First Society of British Authors (1843)." 56 (1889): 10–27.
History of an earlier authors' group revealed that members (some listed) pledged to reduce "malignant" reviewing in journalism, "a branch of literature."

91. Farrar, F. W. "'The Nether World.'" 56 (1889): 370–80.
Opened with a critique of reviewers whose "sense of superiority" and "anonymous arrogance" caused them to pen a "contemptuous condemnation" of any and all books.

92. Pennell, Joseph. "A New Profession Wanting Professors." 58 (1890): 121–32.
Deduced that the standards of British illustrated journals were "deplorably low" and "illustrated daily journalism at the present time in every country is simply amateurish" because the majority of illustrators were self-taught. *See* 58: 256.

93. Thomas, Carmichael. "Illustrated Journalism." 58 (1890): 256–60.
Responded to 58: 121 that Pennell did not understand journalism. Just as dispatches were rewritten into columns, so sketches were altered under pressure of time, robbing "'black-and-white' artists who work so hard and conscientiously" of plaudits.

94. Jennings, L. J. "Behind the Scenes in Parliament." 59 (1891): 55–68.
Counseled that a "judicious reporter" could make a reputation by improving his writing style.

95. Heaton, J. Henniker. "Postal and Telegraphic Reforms." 59 (1891): 327–42.
Condensed postal regulations on the transmission of newspapers. About 100,000 addressed to the colonies and foreign countries were "confiscated annually" for insufficient postage and sold as waste paper.

96. Gosse, Edmund. "The Influence of Democracy on Literature." 59 (1891): 523–36.
Applauded London and some local papers for the quality and completeness of their book reviews, important because newspapers were "the most democratic of all vehicles of thought."

97. Spielmann, M[arion] H. "*Punch* and His Artists: A Chapter in the History of English Comic Draughtsmanship." 60 (1891): 52–69.
Surveyed *Punch* illustrators by name. They were particularly significant when the young periodical had "political weight" because it seemed moderate compared to its predecessors.

98. Murray, David Christie. "The Antipodeans." 60 (1891): 293–312, 450–68, 608–23.
Deemed Australian gazettes "amongst the best in the world." Those in Melbourne and Sydney were "models of newspaper conduct...for extent and variety of information, for enterprise, liberality, and sound adhesion to principle, or for excellence of sub-editing arrangement, or for force, justice, and picturesqueness in the expression of opinion." The *Sydney Bulletin* was "very capably written and edited" with the "brightest Australian verse," "best Australian stories," and excellent illustrations. Although the *Bulletin* was influential, its ideas made it the "most mischievous journal in the world." Both Australia and New Zealand had quality papers in several towns. Weeklies focused on local news but added columns on popular interests, such as literature, fashion, and chess, because small populations could not support specialized periodicals as in Britain. Aside on Sir Henry Parkes, journalist and politician.

99. Morgan, George Osborne. "Are We Really So Bad? A Word on Lady Jeune's 'London Society.'" 62 (1892): 85–91.
Response to an article in the *North American Review* (May, 1892) mentioned that the number of women in journalism was "daily increasing."

100. Lanin, E. B. [E. J. Dillon]. "The Tsar Alexander III." 63 (1893): 1–24.
Warranted that Alexander III read the *Moscow Gazette* daily and had read to him extracts of other Russian and some European papers.

101. Blowitz, [H. G. A. Opper de]. "Journalism as a Profession." 63 (1893): 37–46.
Questioned whether journalism could be taught because it was not a "normal career." Unlike others, it had "no body of doctrine, no series of fixed rules, apparently no possible method of instruction." Because "journalism governs the world," its practitioners should be incorruptible. Yet it attracted men who failed elsewhere because it rejected the bureaucratic structure of other professions. One could treat the news according to one's own inclinations, "own personal temperament." Although this approach might confuse readers, the "chance journalist" believed himself a "god." Journalists

should regard their work as a vocation; be able, with some investigation, to write about any field in "generally intelligible language"; have a "love for truth," "boundless curiosity," "facility of rapid assimilation and comprehension"; good health and a first degree; and speak two other languages. Then they should study for two years history, geography, literature, economics, and the military and learn to box, shoot, and ride a horse. After examinations, they should travel for three years to other schools of journalism, which should be federated and guarantee fixed fees, scholarships, and employment at one of the "serious leading journals in the neighbourhood."

French journalists had 'talent,' "wit, gaiety, imagination," but they lacked knowledge of foreign affairs. In general, the European press, "where journalism is marked by pride and passion which lead to irresponsible utterances," aggravated tensions among states. To counteract this threat, a professional editor at the helm was essential. Every nation should also have a paper, *The Judge*, in which "a competent committee above suspicion" would print errors of other papers, which would pay its maintenance.

102. Blowitz, [H. G. A. Opper de]. "Reminiscences of a Journalist." 63 (1893): 228–35.

Sighed that the public did not celebrate journalists who worked hard on their stories and settled for public belief in their veracity as recompense. Aside that those interviewed frequently later denied they had spoken on the record.

103. Lanin, E. B. [E. J. Dillon]. "Constantine Pobedonostseff." 63 (1893): 584–608.

Ridiculed "instantaneous journalistic photographers" who sped through Russia identifying and quickly solving its problems in their columns.

104. Crawford, Emily [J.]. "Journalism as a Profession for Women." 64 (1893): 362–71.

Guessed that journalism seemed easy, so many women entered it without the requisite energy, health, and "staying power" necessary to cope with competition, pressure of telegrams, and night work. Candidates did not need shorthand because it only filled columns with "dull speeches" but should learn typing and acquire habits of "close observation and punctuality." They should have "presence of mind and courage," "[a]daptibility," "moral sense," "an appetite for books," and no conceit. Among journalists' rewards were good salaries and contact with interesting people. Women, unless they were second or third-rate writers without taste and judgment, put more life into stories.

French journalism was almost closed to women except for the feuilletons of Mme. Emile de Girardin, "which made the fortune of *La Presse*," and of Mme. Claude Vignon in the *Temps* and *Moniteur*. Vignon was also a political journalist. "There never was a quicker, more exact, punctual, and indefatigable parliamentary reporter" of the Versailles National Assembly for *Indépendance Belge*. Caroline de Remy, who wrote as Séverine and was the "secretary of an ill-conditioned, penniless Communist of genius, Jules Vallès," founder and editor of the *Cri du Peuple*, initially succeeded him when he died. She was soon forced out by jealous men who resented her popularity as a leader-writer for *Figaro* and other Paris and provincial papers.

105. Hamerton, P. G. "The Foundations of Art Criticism." 64 (1893): 405–14.

Author who published in the *Fine Arts Quarterly* depicted the New Criticism as anonymous like its predecessor, but more technical, less literary, and less intellectual.

106. Monod, Gabriel. "The Political Situation in France." 64 (1893): 613–28; 67 (1895): 592–608.

Proclaimed that the "Panama affair has thrown light on the profound corruption of the press" in France. "The newspapers, of which there are far too many, are either in the hands of financiers or are themselves so many financial ventures, often of a dreadful character." Even *Justice*, of which Georges Clemenceau was "the director," was subsidized by financiers seeking to gain the benefit of his political clout. Asides on the *Petite République*, the "principal organ" of the Socialists, and *Père Peinard*, of the anarchists.

107. Courtney, W. L. "Dramatic Criticism." 64 (1893): 691–703.

Doubted that theatre critics, who had to be in print within three or four hours of a performance, could be "sensitive, receptive, appreciative" and "reflect with unerring accuracy." The unfriendly called the critic "a reporter," but journalism's "proper" role was to "picture the world in the last twenty-four hours," to inform about particulars, not theatre. Theatre criticism should move from dailies to weeklies or better, monthlies because journalistic criticism incorrectly emphasized the actor instead of the play.

108. Norman, Henry. "Urgency in Siam." 64 (1893): 737–48.

Skimmed the *Siam Free Press*, a Bangkok newspaper. Aside that English readers made judgments about important issues based on photographs in illustrated newspapers.

109. Besant, Walter. "Literary Conferences." 65 (1894): 123–39.

Article on the July 1893 Chicago Literary Congress quoted in part H. D. Traill's paper, "The Relations of Literature and Journalism." Work for "a newspaper or monthly magazine" might pay better than penning for other literary venues, but material was edited and owned by the journal. Magazines were increasing because they printed "wholesome literature," not works "pandering to the brutal mob." *Chambers's Journal*, with its circulation of 250,000, was "always in the very front rank of journals, always conducted with the greatest skill to discover what people like, and the strongest sense of responsibility…the model for fifty years of what a popular journal should be." Unfortunately, other cheap and accessible periodicals filled with "rubbish" were the recreation of many juveniles.

110. Blind, Karl. "The Rise and Development of Anarchism." 65 (1894): 140–52.

Singled out Michael Katkoff, editor of *Moscow Gazette*, "the organ of old Russianism"; Arnold Ruge, "the foremost champion of Young Hegalianism in a democratic sense" and the editor of the *Deutsche Jahrbücher*, and the *Prolétariat*, "the organ of the Socialist Federation of French Workers."

111. A Fogey [?Andrew Lang]. "The Young Men." 65 (1894): 177–88.

Praised newspaper criticism "written by men interested in their work," not "mere scribblers of paragraphs on books they have not read." Newspapers should give more attention to literature "than hacks can afford, more knowledge than lady amateurs can bestow."

112. Conway, W. M. "An Alpine Journal." 66 (1894): 210–24.

Bruited that to Italian border guards the *Piedmontese Gazette* was "really a good paper."

113. The Author of "The Policy of the Pope." [E. J. Dillon]. "Intellectual Liberty and Contemporary Catholicism." 66 (1894): 280–304.

Listed Russia's "semi-official" *Novoe Vremya*, Rome's Jesuit-influenced *Civiltà Cattolica*, and Vienna's "anti-Catholic" *Neue Frie Presse*.

114. Smith, Goldwin. "*If Christ Came to Chicago*." 66 (1894): 380–89.
Disagreed with W. T. Stead's opinion, in his title book, that the Chicago press was "already in a state of servile subjugation" to the rich.

115. Sellers, Edith. "Our Most Distinguished Refugee." 66 (1894): 537–49.
Followed Peter Kropotkin to England in the 1870s where he published papers on "scientific subjects" in *Nature* and "notes on Siberian affairs for *The Times* and other periodicals" to support himself but left before he launched the *Révolte* in 1877.

116. *** "The Late German Crisis." 66 (1894): 829–34.
Discussed the relationship of the German press with the official Press Department and the press role in repressive legislation dealing with 'subversion.' Aside that Cologne's *Zeitung* was "an irresponsible daily."

117. A. "The Experiences of an Anglican Catholic." 67 (1895): 396–414.
While living in Spain appreciated the *Church Times*, a "useful publication."

118. Quilter, Harry. "The Gospel of Intensity." 67 (1895): 761–82.
Blared that it was "ridiculous to talk about the power of the Press, and its claims upon our admiration and gratitude, if that power is not to be exerted beneficially in matters which are distinctly of public importance." In 1874 the *World* introduced indecency as part of "sensational journalism," and others aped its "unscrupulous" behavior. "Exaggeration is the very essence of the modern journalistic art, the very use of the headline (footnoted "from America") almost enforces it." Even *Punch* was moving in that direction. The "game of brag," with interviews and illustrations, was most noticeable in stories on actors. Editors went along because they were "men of business."

A major change was in "journalistic criticism," from the "ladies and gentlemen, who are kind enough to instruct us, in the columns of the daily Press." Criticism had gone from "indiscriminating, vehement, and unmeasured laudation" to condemnation. Neither was "ennobling." Recent criticism was very biased except in "the great daily papers." The worst appeared in the evening and illustrated tribunes that "degrade art, and excite the animal appetites" in order to be "up-to-date." The new illustrated sheets were "vulgarizing England" because London set the tone for the locals.

Anticipated that sensational journalism and its effects would soon fade. *See Macmillan's* 42: 391.

119. Heaton, J. Henniker. "Ten Years' Postal Progress: An Imperial Plan." 68 (1895): 1–14.
Congratulated the press for lifting "its invincible arm" for social reform but opposed, as against public policy, postal rates that effectively repressed magazines with their expertise and favored dailies with their gossip, sports, and crime.

120. Boborykine, Peter. "English Influence in Russia." 68 (1895): 50–57.
Assumed that Nihilism was "fostered by the Russian revolutionary press," which had learned the power of journalism from the English.

121. Ouida [Marie Louise de la Ramée]. "The Crispi Dictatorship." 68 (1895): 241–55.
Denounced Italian officials who checked domestic newspapers' language and confiscated foreign journals that were anti-government. *See* 68: 384.

122. Stead, W. T. "Jingoism in America." 68 (1895): 334–47.
Tagged Chicago's *Times-Herald* "one of the most influential and enterprising of all the newspapers in America."

123. Riccio, Vincenzo. "Crispi's Administration." 68 (1895): 384–94.
Rebutted 68: 241 on the ground that it merely echoed "the worst journals" of the Opposition in Italy.

124. Wedgwood, Julia. "Richard Holt Hutton." 72 (1897): 457–69.
Painted Hutton as an honest, not bitter editor whose *Spectator* flourished under "his guidance."

125. Stoddart, A[nna] M. "The House of Blackwood." 72 (1897): 632–48.
Review of Margaret Oliphant's *Annals of a Publishing House* probed *Blackwood's Magazine*, its operation and contributors.

126. "The Demoralisation of France." 73 (1898): 305–25.
Aired that the *Revue des Deux Mondes*, edited by Ferdinand Brunetière, was "patronized by the aristocracy and the army."

127. Murray, David Christie. "Some Notes on the Zola Case." 73 (1898): 481–90.
Headlined attempts by French journals to pressure the jury in an action arising from the Dreyfus case.

128. Guyot, Yves. "The Dreyfus Case." 73 (1898): 618–27.
Spotlighted the roles of several newspapers in the Dreyfus case.

129. A Financial Journalist. "The Art of Blackmail." 74 (1898): 196–205.
Decried the influential "high-class periodicals, daily and weekly, which are corrupt either through their proprietors or their City staffs or both" more than the "dirty City weeklies with no *bona fide* circulations." Some promoters purchased the silence of the "gutter press," but the autocratic city editors of "respectable" weeklies were as ready to sell their good will. The current price was 100–500 pounds and a bonus on all subsequent business. Promoters often manipulated circumstances to seem as if any journalist who opposed them had been bought. The great financial papers, secure in their profits and reputations, had to counter this corruption.

130. "France, Russia, and the Nile." 74 (1898): 761–78.
Peeped at the French *Éclair*, which "possesses mysterious ways and means of acquiring interesting information…absolutely inaccessible to other newspapers," and "very widespread and respectable" *Journal*.

131. Kinnear, Alfred. "The Trade in Great Men's Speeches." 75 (1899): 439–44.
Reported that every Saturday, newspapers could order from news agencies copies of Parliamentary speeches scheduled for the following week. Orders cost ten shillings per column whether they were 'verbatim,' 'full,' or 'summary.' The last was popular because readers preferred information from the Divorce Court to that from Parliament.

132. Shorter, Clement K. "Illustrated Journalism: Its Past and Its Future." 75 (1899): 481–94.

Attributed the multiplication of illustrated journals (from five in 1890 to 12 in 1899) to cheaper printing, more newspaper buyers, and more faith in advertisements. In the past, the *Swedish Intelligencer* (London, 1632) had occasional illustrations, but the *Mercurius Circus* was the first to print them regularly. William Clement, the *Observer* owner in 1791, was "the first hero of illustrated journalism"; Herbert Ingram, the father of the *Illustrated London News* in 1842, made the "first systematic attempt to illustrate news." Ingram was also instrumental in getting the newspaper stamp and paper duties repealed. Prophesized that artists would remain important irrespective of photography and that Sunday supplements would expand but would not publish "masses of illustrations" as did New York's *World* and *Journal*.

133. D., E. "The Situation in France." 76 (1899): 41–50.

Returned to the French press, including the *Petit Journal*, in the aftermath of the Dreyfus case.

134. A Heretic. "The Anglo-Indian Creed." 76 (1899): 272–81.

Juxtaposed restrictions on the Indian press and informal official pressure on Anglo-Indian journals, different perhaps because British authorities believed that the vernacular press should not criticize its "betters."

135. Hosken, William. "Ten Years in Johannesburg." 77 (1900): 472–79; rejoinder, 662–68.

Objected to Boer enforcement of restrictive press laws on the British but not the "government-subsidized Press." *See* 77: 656 to which rejoinder reacts.

136. Hobson, J. A. "The Testimony from Johannesburg." 77 (1900): 656–62.

Replied to 77: 472 that the Boer Press Law of 1896 was less drastic than British press controls in Ireland and India. No government would tolerate the sedition of the *Transvaal Leader*.

137. Guyot, Yves. "The Psychology of the French Boerophiles and Anglophobes." 77 (1900): 777–92.

Parts two and three chronicled how the French press exaggerated.

138. Bigelow, Poultney. "Germany, England, and America." 77 (1900): 881–91.

Declared that the "peculiar form of patriotism known as Jingoism is essentially a product of the Press," a technique that newspapers in Berlin, New York, and London employed to increase sales.

139. A Russian Publicist. "The Secret Springs of Russian Policy." 78 (1900): 497–501.

Briefly memorialized Michael Katkoff, editor of the *Moscow Gazette*, as "the most celebrated Russian editor of his day."

140. Brooks, Sydney. "Bryanism." 78 (1900): 633–42.

Fumed that British correspondents, primarily stationed in New York, paid little attention to other American news and views, merely reprinting trivia from heartland gazettes.

The Cornhill Magazine, 1860–1900

Intended as recreational, the *Cornhill* under W. M. Thackeray and his editorial descendants showcased the impact of journalism on public opinion and the characteristics of journalists.

1. [Hunt, Thornton]. "A Man of Letters of the Last Generation." 1 (1860): 85–95.
Honored Leigh Hunt who "established a reputation for cultivation, consistency, taste, and independence and originated a style of contemporary criticism unknown to the newspaper press." His *Examiner* set the "style, tone, and sentiment for the press," a "cultivated style, elegant tone, and independent sentiment." Asides on his *Reflector* and *Indicator*.

2. [Sala, George Augustus]. "William Hogarth: Painter, Engraver, Philosopher." 1 (1860): 177–93, 264–82, 417–37, 561–81, 716–35; 2 (1860): 97–112, 225–41, 354–69, 438–61.
Subtitled "Essays on the Man, the Work, and the Time," Sala's essay connected publisher William Hone to the eighteenth-century *Grub-street Journal*, *Daily Courant*, and *London Gazette*; Theodore Hook's "scurrilous" writing to *John Bull*; and George Canning's jokes to the *Anti-Jacobin*.

3. [Merivale, Herman]. "A Few Words on Junius and Macaulay." 1 (1860): 257–63.
Focused on T. B. Macaulay's interest in identifying Junius.

4. [Thackeray, W. M.]. "The Four Georges: Sketches of Manners, Morals, Court and Town Life." 2 (1860): 1–20, 175–91, 257–77, 385–406.
Cited the *Tatler* and *Spectator* as reflecting eighteenth-century "town life." Aside on the *Royal New York Gazette* in 1778.

5. [Thackeray, W. M.]. "Thorns in the Cushion." 2 (1860): 122–28.
Mused about letters to a periodical editor concerning submissions.

6. [Thackeray, W. M.]. "Roundabout Papers, No. VI: On Screens in Dining Rooms." 2 (1860): 252–56.
Disapproved of criticism in the *Saturday Review* and *New York Herald* that addressed the personality of an editor rather than his work.

7. [Stephen, James Fitzjames]. "The Morality of Advocacy." 3 (1861): 447–59.
Impugned the press for its unfavorable portraits of barristers and stories on trials. "People read newspapers, and especially the trials reported there, almost exclusively for amusement" because gazettes favored cases of "a slightly scandalous kind."

8. Thackeray, W. M. "On a Chalk-mark on the Door." 3 (1861): 504–12.
Disliked women contributors who sent manuscripts to editors' homes.

9. [Stephen, James Fitzjames]. "Keeping Up Appearances." 4 (1861): 305–18.
Emphasized that the "great peculiarity of periodical literature is that it reflects, with minute exactness, the moral and intellectual features of the society in which it exists." "In good newspapers," political articles were "usually written in a careful, straightforward, business-like manner, with as much talent as the resources and standing of the paper enable it to obtain." For example, *The Times* printed leaders that generated responses from which the editor extrapolated ideas for new columns. Newspapers "sugared over with conventional geniality" nonpolitical issues and printed personal letters that might amuse but could injure.

10. [Stephen, James Fitzjames]. "Journalism." 6 (1862): 52–63.
Pontificated that the "enormous reputation for both power and ability which our leading newspapers possess is due in a considerable degree to the impatience which everyone feels of being governed in a prosaic way. People look for something more striking [than Commons] and they find it in the notion of an invisible power called 'Public Opinion.'" Yet the press operated for profit. Dailies had more news; weeklies, more "original matter." News was serious or amusing; original matter included leaders and reviews. Leaders determined "standing and influence." They had to be timely, "perfectly clear, attractively written, and relevant throughout to some one well-marked point." The "best" were "nothing more than samples of the conversation of educated men on passing events." Their authors were about a hundred educated men, many lawyers and clerics, for whom gathering and organizing opinion were technical skills. The goal of leader-writers was to be unbiased lest readers discount their views. Hence, British scribes opted for anonymity rather than "notoriety" unlike the French.

Journalism was not difficult if a paper had money. Editors were paid a salary; contributors might be. Editors made assignments based on their understanding of the public, which made *The Times* worth its price. Most staff needed no unique talent except the special correspondent, lower in rank than the leader-writer. Journalists could work their way up, but those who stopped midway spent their lives penning nonsense, as club gossip.

11. [Lewes, G. H. and Frederick Greenwood]. "Our Survey of Literature, Science, and Art." 6 (1862): 103–20.
Inaugurated a regular column by disavowing "newspaper gossip," particularly that about the private lives of authors and publishers.

12. [Richardson, Coke]. "The Sharpshooters of the Press: in England, France, and Germany." 7 (1863): 238–51.
Differentiated French journalists, who garnered influence from signature, and English leader-writers, who achieved it by serving an "interest or principle." The French fought more wars of words; the English stretched the facts or exhibited bias. The French newspaper displayed "elegant impertinence"; the English, "trenchant aggressiveness" demonstrated in its choice of title, as *Viper* or *Scorpion*.

13. [Wilberforce, Edward]. "Newspaper Writers in Germany." 7 (1863): 748–55.
Summarized restrictions on the press in the German states. Although controls eased after 1848, editors still signed all papers. The multiplicity of German states caused a diffusion of capital and talent. Editors

acted as correspondents for other papers. Writers, with jobs or interests outside journalism, penned or scissored articles for several gazettes. Many volunteers paid by the line used initials to identify their entries, frequently done in great haste. The "most generally circulated of all German newspapers" was the *Allgemeine Zeitung*. Viennese tribunes were more akin to British, albeit Austrian publishers and editors (allegedly many Jews) were wealthier and journalists were more in harmony.

14. [Greenwood, Frederick]. "To Correspondents." 7 (1863): 801–04.
Satirized the job of a periodical editor, chiefly dealing with the volume of work and the promise of new authors.

15. H[amerton], P. G. "Art Criticism." 8 (1863): 334–43.
Decried newspaper reviews of art exhibitions that were neither "entertaining" nor "attractive reading" but merely showcased the value of fine arts. Paris critics need not be as well-trained as their theatre colleagues because readers had less expertise about art than drama.

16. [Lewes, G. H.]. "Publishers Before the Age of Printing." 9 (1864): 26–32.
Recorded that ancient Roman newspapers were perused throughout the empire "with great avidity."

17. Trollope, Anthony. "W. M. Thackeray." 9 (1864): 134–37.
Eulogized Thackeray as an editor kind to his contributors.

18. [Stephen, James Fitzjames]. "Sentimentalism." 10 (1864): 65–75.
Disputed a *Saturday Review* assessment of a *Cornhill* article ("Marriage Settlements") as "sentimentalism."

19. Arnold, Matthew. "The Literary Influence of Academies." 10 (1864): 154–72.
Justified a literary academy as a safeguard of language. Without one, the British newspaper tended to be aggressive and unsophisticated "with its party spirit, its thorough-goingness, its resolute avoidance of shades and distinctions, its short, highly-charged, heavy-shotted articles."

20. [Dallas, E. S.]. "John Leech." 10 (1864): 743–60.
Biography of Leech, an illustrator for *Bentley's Miscellany* and *Punch*, contained many of his drawings. "*Punch* was singular in being the product of men of genius, true and rare," such as Leech, Theodore Hook, Douglas Jerrold, and W. M. Thackeray.

21. Boyes, J[ohn] F[rederick]. "A Memorial of Thackeray's School-Days." 11 (1865): 118–28.
Remembered that the young W. M. Thackeray read *Blackwood's Magazine*, the *New Monthly Magazine*, and the *Literary Gazette*, "then in nearly their first glory and full of excellent articles." His first periodical contributions were in magazines because the *Edinburgh Review* and the *Quarterly Review* were "too high and dry."

22. [Hannay, James]. "Provincialism." 11 (1865): 673–81.
Certified that local newspaper editors were more accessible than those in London and their gazettes were more personal, less independent.

23. [Parker, Francis]. "The Profession of Advocacy." 12 (1865): 105–15.
Fretted that newspapers lowered esteem for barristers by printing their scandalous, not their significant cases.

24. Arnold, Matthew. "My Countrymen." 13 (1866): 153–72.
Chastised the *Saturday Review* and *Morning Star* as well as French and German papers for stereotyping language.

25. [Wright, Thomas]. "A Working-Man on the Education of the Working-Classes." 14 (1866): 283–98.
Guessed that educating working class boys would produce readers of an "agitation newspaper" or a "sensation serial."

26. [Kaye, J. W.]. "The Peace-Conflicts of India." 14 (1866): 422–31.
Thundered that the Anglo-Indian press devoted no more space to scandal than the home gazettes, but in India these columns had a greater impact because of the nature of Anglo-Indian society.

27. [Stephen, James Fitzjames]. "The Law of Libel." 15 (1867): 36–46.
Introduced the captioned topic with reference to a suit against the *Pall Mall Gazette* by a reputed quack.

28. [Turner, S. W.]. "Canning and the *Anti-Jacobin*." 15 (1867): 63–74.
Glanced at George Canning's journalism in the *Anti-Jacobin* and other periodicals.

29. [Elton, C. I.]. "Early English Newspapers." 18 (1868): 119–28.
Considered newspapers "one of the chief pillars of our modern civilization" but also significant earlier. Nathaniel Butter purportedly took the idea of "a weekly newspaper from the Venetian gazettes," and Charles I quickly understood its value. He was the patron of the *Mercurius Aulicus*, but many heralds sprouted during the 1640s. Journalists were regarded with increasing contempt, so the appointment of a censor in 1673 was logical. The appointee, Roger L'Estrange, ran the "readable" *Public Intelligencer* only to supplement his government pay. He employed spies as correspondents and "mercury-women" to hawk the paper. From the cessation of censorship after 1688 until the enactment of the newspaper stamp in 1712, papers blossomed. This legislation put a duty on news sheets partly because government associated a cheap press with revolution.

30. A Cynic [Leslie Stephen]. "Our Rulers – Public Opinion." 21 (1870): 288–98.
Concluded that as newspapers were the real rulers, letters to the press could supersede the cost and trouble of elections. Rallying support for an issue might be difficult, but an editor could create or prioritize a question. Anonymity would keep journalists honest and unsusceptible to flattery. Newspapers might be "gushing" or "cynical." The first was optimistic, born of the "loftiest motives" but not organized, affording the second the opportunity to act superior by censuring bad planning.

31. [Kaye, J. W.]. "Some Recollections of a Reader." 22 (1870): 437–50.
Admitted reading "most of the best serial stories in the monthly magazines, and some also in the weeklies."

32. Thornton, W. T. "National Education in India." 23 (1871): 282–95.
Affirmed that "the *Hindoo Patriot* and other like newspapers [were] designed to be vehicles and reflectors of native thought," but the people of Lower Bengal preferred their gazettes in English.

33. [Dennis, John]. "Daniel Defoe." 23 (1871): 310–20.
Characterized Defoe as a journalist from his youth, an able political writer second only to Jonathan Swift in the *Examiner*. It was reprinted, whereas Defoe's *Review*, preceding the *Tatler*, was not.

34. Merivale, Herman. "The Last Phase in the Junius Controversy." 23 (1871): 668–87.
Identified Junius from his style and the handwriting analyses done by others.

35. [Colvin, Sidney]. "Théophile Gautier." 27 (1873): 151–69.
Placed Gautier as an art critic at Paris' *Presse* (1837–55), then the *Moniteur*.

36. [Grenville-Murray, E. C.]. "The French Press." 27 (1873): 703–31; 28 (1873): 411–30; 29 (1874): 154–71, 535–52.
Traced Gallic interest in news from the Roman Empire to medieval chroniclers in every town and troubadours who incited rebellion as effectively as some later editors. The religious wars bred handbills, and better roads and the post accelerated dissemination. In early seventeenth-century France as in England, gossipy handwritten newsletters were popular, but Théophraste Renaudot's *Gazette de France* had items from Armand de Richelieu and advertising. The *Gazette* staff translated news from abroad and added well-written commentary. Many serials discussed here surfaced during the Fronde, but Jacques Loret introduced the *Musé Historique* to amuse. By 1762 the *Gazette* was a typical biweekly whose editor earned 600 pounds per year. Investigated the publications in the reign of Louis XIV, as the literary *Journal des Savants*, social *Mercure*, and political *Gazette*. The *Mercure* reputedly sold favors, setting a pattern for French journalism. The king preferred French to foreign papers if there had to be a press.

In the eighteenth century, a feud developed between "gazetteers" of the licensed political press and journalists of the literary. Perhaps because provincial journalism was poor, the Encyclopedists were not sympathetic to the press. Still, by 1774 there were 28 papers in Paris. As the press became more anti-royal, the throne tried unsuccessfully to control it. The *Courrier de l'Europe*, published in London, spread British ideas of liberty. Journalists of the French Revolution were inaccurate and ignorant. The papers of Count H. Mirabeau were "wild" but not as scurrilous as later ones. J. M. Marat typified "rabid journalism." The result was that people regarded the press as an "unmitigated nuisance," which excited instead of checked the "bad passions" of the Revolution.

The French press, unlike the British, had not by 1873 improved in the amount, variety, or veracity of news except for the *Journal des Débats*. Even this paper, limited by restrictive legislation during the century, had become insecure.

Aside that the word "gazette" came from a Venetian coin.

37. [Lathbury, D. C.]. "The Casuistry of Journalism." 28 (1873): 198–206.
Title referred to journalists' "rules" on what and where to write. The public thought that journalists were "exempt from professional restraints" yet acknowledged their influence. Leader-writers did not need to identify completely with a paper's stance, though that helped circulation because there was "much difference of opinion now-a-days." An editor could ask for neutrality on a topic or an endorsement of his views but not for betrayal of a writer's convictions. In contrast to the partisan

press, the independent press shaped opinion. Journalists had to choose which organ suited them. Ideally, they should agree with its political and religious positions and approve of the morality of its methods. Anonymity guaranteed integrity.

38. [Grenville-Murray, E. C.]. "Parisian Journalists of Today." 28 (1873): 715–32.
After a preface that stereotyped the journalism of several countries, turned to leading French journalists.

39. [Stephen, Leslie]. "Hours in a Library: Dr. Johnson's Writings." 29 (1874): 280–97.
Evaluated Samuel Johnson's style in the *Gentleman's Magazine* and the *Rambler*.

40. [Warre-Cornish, F. W.]. "Thoughts of a Country Critic." 30 (1874): 717–27.
Local art critic denied that he was parochial since he was familiar with art reviews and reviewers.

41. [Smith, George Barnett]. "Shelley: Politician, Atheist, Philanthropist." 31 (1875): 345–65.
Claimed that P. B. Shelley had "a keen interest in newspaper warfare" and wrote letters to several, including one on freedom of the press. He also spoke for John and Leigh Hunt in the *Examiner* case involving the Prince Regent.

42. [Grenville-Murray, E. C.]. "Jacques Girard's Newspaper; or the Trials of a French Journalist." 32 (1875): 691–710.
Featured Girard, subeditor and then editor of the *Indépendant*. Believed that French journalists were ignorant, unscrupulous, emotional, dogmatic, inaccurate, yet influential because French laws prohibited attacks on government, not private individuals.

43. D[ennis], J[ohn]. "Sir Richard Steele." 34 (1876): 408–26.
Skimmed Steele's journalism in the *Tatler*; the "wonderfully popular" *Spectator* where Joseph Addison surpassed him in style; the *Guardian* done alone; the *Englishman*; and the *Plebian* as well as his attacks on Jonathan Swift columns in the *Examiner*.

44. [Stephen, Leslie]. "Thoughts on Criticism by a Critic." 34 (1876): 556–69.
Imagined that the goal of university education in journalism was to graduate those who could pass "competitive examinations" and write "a smart review." Anonymous criticism was "more independent" even if "less responsible" as long as it was not "slashing."

45. [Medhurst, Walter H.]. "Posting and Post-Offices in China." 38 (1878): 95–102.
Quoted the *Pall Mall Gazette* that the Japanese post transmitted 7,372,536 newspapers, June 1876–June 1877.

46. [Stephen, Leslie]. "Hours in a Library: The First *Edinburgh* Reviewers." 38 (1878): 218–34.
Concurred with the *Westminster Review* (1: 206) that early *Edinburgh Review* articles were so "amateurish" that "a first-rate periodical" in 1878 would reject them. Men from other fields penned them merely for money. Exceptions were Sydney Smith, Francis Jeffrey, Henry Brougham, Francis Horner, and T. B. Macaulay. Smith's work was creative, but Jeffrey's criticism was "random" and

Brougham's essays were "ephemeral" because he was distracted by politics. Soon the *Edinburgh* provided a forum for "independent discussion" by talented well-paid writers.

47. Kebbel, T. E. "The Eighteenth Century." 38 (1878): 540–58.
Disagreed with Thomas De Quincey that "[p]olitics and journalism have no doubt a tendency to debase literature." Journalism, "if injurious to the dignity of literature, is favourable to the cultivation of style," as Jonathan Swift, Junius, and others evidenced. T. B. Macaulay adapted the "journalistic" style of Samuel Johnson.

48. [Kebbel, T. E.]. "Cobbett." 39 (1879): 427–41.
Concentrated on William Cobbett's *Political Register*, allegedly the most important periodical of its time for the lower middle class. Although it was popular and profitable, his expenses were so high that he eventually was bankrupt. Aside on his *Porcupine*.

49. [Stillman, W. J.]. "New Lamps for Old Ones." 41 (1880): 96–103.
Criticized briefly Italian views of the press, one where journalists "control or express the little public opinion which exists in Italy."

50. Jones, Harry. "The Homes of Town Poor." 42 (1880): 452–63.
Noticed that the urban lower class discovered the "refinements of life" in newspapers and magazines.

51. [Stephen, Leslie]. "Rambles among Books: The Essayists." 44 (1881): 278–97.
Looked at essays in the eighteenth-century *Spectator* and *Rambler*, among other writings.

52. [Grenville-Murray, E. C.]. "Political Spies." 44 (1881): 713–24.
Divulged that European governments often sent spies to join "Radical newspapers," as Berlin's *Hacknesser*, or created a "private organ," as Adolphe Thiers' *Bien Public*.

53. Whittle, J. L. "A Glimpse of the United States." 46 (1882): 427–39.
Sketched American newspapers as numerous, frequently with "able" staffs but without sway because readers did not believe them.

54. [Trollope, T. A.] "A Roman Penny-a-Liner in the Eighteenth Century." 46 (1882): 584–601.
Recounted that eighteenth-century Rome had no newspapers but had illegal *avvisi* who reported for money. Conte or Abate Enrico Trivelli (b. 1709, Naples) went to Rome to seek his fortune and made a career as an *avviso*. For "the composition of malicious and seditious writings," he was "condemned to be decapitated and to perpetual infamy."

55. [Richards, James Brinsley]. "Memories of Léon Gambetta." 47 (1883): 160–70.
Related that Gambetta did not tolerate editing of his journalism but did laugh at his mistakes in print. As the "conductor" of the *République Française*, he apparently contradicted himself in leaders. Aside that André Gill was a "spiteful caricaturist."

56. [Allen, Grant]. "A Scribbler's Apology." 47 (1883): 538–50.

Reckoned that the "newspaper in the abstract is a beneficial and useful institution" but in the "concrete it has many defects." One was its "slipshod literary style." The craving for news justified "the printers, the reporters, the editors, and possibly even the leader-writers" but not "the tootlers" who penned "nothing in particular for the mere gratification of idle people." This journalist of questionable ethics wrote not to enlighten, improve, or amuse those who labored but to tickle the upper classes and earn money to supplement some other position, such as footman. Columnists should be honest and knowledgeable since everyone read the dailies.

57. [Child, Theodore]. "The French Newspaper Press." n.s., 1 (1883): 124–35, 243–54.

Commenced with the Restoration press. The *Journal des Débats* read like a review so had a small audience. In the 1830s Emile de Girardin launched the less expensive *Presse*, a daily with advertisements and a feuilleton, which lured women unconcerned about events and issues of the day. Then, as in 1883, a female audience was vital for journalism. Although the *Presse* subordinated ideas to advertising, it did entertain. In 1848 the "petite press" arrived with *Figaro*. Initially a cheap political venue, after 1852 its trivia "appealed to the most wretched passions of the lower middle classes." Because it was widely read, it reaped profit but degraded taste. Most French gazettes stressed rapid, not necessarily accurate news; treated the courts and politics as diversion, and promoted financiers who owned the papers. Disseminating less news than the British meant a slower pace conducive to better writing. Alluded briefly to Gallic costs of and laws affecting publication as well as circulation.

The French had no elite critical reviews akin to those in Britain and the United States partly because critics took bribes.

French journalists were of three types: "the soldier of an idea," "mercantile," or "gossipy."

58. [Payn, James]. "Some Literary Recollections." n.s., 1 (1883): 631–44; n.s., 2 (1884): 33–41, 148–59, 244–61, 361–74, 486–505, 584–92; n.s., 3 (1884): 41–58, 150–70.

Recalled publishing a first article in *Household Words*, where W. H. Wills, assisting Charles Dickens as editor, "was conscientious to his contributors." At the same time, Payn wrote for *Chambers's Journal* under editor Leitch Ritchie, "a man of somewhat severe culture and fastidious taste." Penning regularly for both serials increased Payn's income. As the *Journal's* subeditor, he worked with Robert Chambers. His encounters with a variety of contributors taught him much about human nature. Writers, for example, might cite their age and connections or pledge originality to get into print. Anonymity gave novices a chance but concealed the fraudulent and the pathetic. Throughout his career, Payn encouraged tyros, recommending that they reprint their articles to introduce themselves to the public and other editors. Those rejected flooded him with letters. Aside on Alexander Russel's tenure as editor of the *Scotsman*. *See* n.s., 23: 34, *et seq*.

59. [Norris, W. E.]. "Englishmen and Foreigners." n.s., 3 (1884): 587–98.

Judged that English dailies, "weekly reviews," and *Punch* pictured politics and thought better than French newspapers.

60. [Frith, Walter]. "Trade Journals." n.s., 7 (1886): 512–37.

Estimated that trade journals with articles and advertising were about 30 years old. Not subject to passion or censorship, this press aimed "to educate, to advise, to help, to protect" like the former trade guilds.

61. [Robinson, G. D.]. "The Pigeon as a War Messenger." n.s., 8 (1887): 600–08.
Valued pigeons as news carriers in emergencies, as the siege of Paris in 1870–71.

62. [Harrison, F. Bayford]. "Our Small Ignorances." n.s., 10 (1888): 60–74.
Dated, not always accurately, early news sources: *acta diurna* (c. B.C.E. 623), *notizie scritte* (Venice, c. 1536), and *London Gazette* (1666). Named as the first real newspaper *King Pau*, or "chief sheet" (Peking, 911).

63. [Miller, W. C.]. "Some Mistranslations." n.s., 10 (1888): 412–16.
Regarded the incorrect translation of *Our Mutual Friend* in Paris' *Opinion Nationale* as serious because "the feuilleton of a French journal is a most important department of it, and on the merits of which its circulation depends."

64. [Jones, Harry]. "Afterthoughts." n.s., 14 (1890): 161–78.
Guessed that *Punch* took the lead among comic papers largely because John Leech could get anyone to smile.

65. [Ballantyne, Alick]. "French-English." n.s., 14 (1890): 279–86.
Aired errors in British and French periodicals whose book reviewers attempted translations.

66. [Watson, John]. "Couriers of the Air." n.s., 15 (1890): 502–23.
Underscored the worth of pigeons as carriers of news and photographic negatives.

67. [Wilkinson, W. H.]. "Advertising in China." n.s., 17 (1891): 257–67.
Skipped through advertisements in the "Chinese vernacular press," the dailies in Canton, Shanghai, and Tientsin, to learn local "manners and morals" previously evident on placards. The best inserts were in the *Shanghai Gazette*. They dealt with theatre, books, house rentals, cargo auctions, patent medicines, and lotteries, the last two the most popular. Most listings had bizarre Sino-English grammar and incorrect punctuation. Alleged that the Central News Agency circulated an advertisement translated by the author for the *North China Herald*.

68. [Edwardes, Charles]. "The Balearics." n.s., 18 (1892): 423–38.
Mentioned that in the Balearics, the Saturday paper "constitutes the press."

69. [Williams, Mrs. E. Baumer]. "Concerning Leigh Hunt." n.s., 18 (1892): 480–506.
Based on letters to or by Hunt, discussed his press activities, notably his prison sentence in the *Examiner* case.

70. [Lowry, R. W.]. "The Russians at Home." n.s., 19 (1892): 174–91.
Confirmed that all Russian journals were subject to some censorship. Most towns had newspapers of lesser quality and greater price than those in Britain. Some "fair weekly illustrated papers" were available but only by annual subscription. Russian journalists resented foreign press criticism of Russia.

71. [Edwardes, Charles]. "Barcelona." n.s., 19 (1892): 291–302.
Bumped into newsboys all over Barcelona's Rambla.

72. Payn, James. "Gleams of Memory; With Some Reflections." n.s., 23 (1894): 34–60, 138–63, 255–80.

Returned to early journalistic experiences, as a neophyte at *The Picture* when the owner died, then a regular staffer at *Household Words*. By the 1890s weekly reviews had more clout than quarterlies, and the "despotism of editors" was no longer "so arbitrary." *See* n.s., 1: 631, *et seq*.

73. [Watt, J. H.]. "An Editor's Letters." n.s., 24 (1895): 21–28.

Quoted the letters of Francis Jeffrey when he was *Edinburgh Review* editor.

74. [Symonds, Emily M.]. "The Old Criticism." n.s., 24 (1895): 151–57.

Deplored the severity of early nineteenth-century periodical criticism of books by novice authors.

75. [Symonds, Emily M.]. "The Advance of Advertisement." n.s., 25 (1895): 505–13.

Located the first advertisement in a German newsbook (1591). Although the 1640s had many newsletters, the first English listing was in the *Mercurius Politicus* (January 1652). By 1657 the *Public Advertiser* was almost exclusively advertising. Frivolous inserts disappeared in the wake of the plague and Great Fire in the 1660s, and theatre ones purportedly began in the July 1700 *Flying Post*. In the eighteenth century, an advertisement was ordinarily eight lines of narrow measure selling for a shilling. The *Tatler* highlighted advertising in a 1710 article, and in the later *Idler*, Samuel Johnson opined that the "trade of advertising" was "near perfection." Further impetus to newspaper advertising came from the nineteenth-century reduction, then abolition of the duty on it.

76. [Jones, Harry]. "The Awakening of London." n.s., 26 (1896): 75–78.

Remarked that "newspaper trains start at five o'clock for their daily sowing of the land with type."

77. Ritchie, Mrs. Richmond [Anne]. "The First Number of *The Cornhill*." 3[d] ser., 1 (1896): 1–16.

Retrospective, which included letters about articles, reminded that the *Cornhill's* shilling price was atypical.

78. Withers, Hartley. "The Mysteries of Money Articles." 3[d] ser., 2 (1897): 684–91.

Alerted that financial and sports reporters assumed that their readers were knowledgeable.

79. Duffield, W. B. "John Wilkes (Died December 25, 1797): An Anniversary Study." 3[d] ser., 3 (1897): 723–37.

Retold the story of the *North Briton*, No. 45. Credited Wilkes (while a magistrate in the City) for the release of printers charged with publishing Commons' debates, which led to a struggle with a House that considered reporting its proceedings a privilege. Aside on Wilkes' correspondence with Junius.

80. Stephen, Leslie. "James Payn." 3[d] ser., 4 (1898): 590–94.

Noticed Payn's recent articles in the *Illustrated London News*.

81. Duffield, W. B. "The *Anti-Jacobin* (Last Number Published July 9th, 1798): An Anniversary Article." 3d ser., 5 (1898): 17–32.
Logged William Pitt's efforts to silence hostile journalists during the French Revolution.

82. Duffield, W. B. "Daniel O'Connell: A Study." 3d ser., 6 (1899): 29–38.
Recollected that *The Times* published 300 leaders on O'Connell. When reporters would not record his speeches, he would clear the house of these "strangers."

83. MacDonagh, Michael. "The Bye-Ways of Journalism." 3d ser., 6 (1899): 395–406.
Focused on penny-a-liners whose name was an insult, suggesting a "disreputable" journalist. These "poorly educated and unambitious" or failed journalists, who ranged far beyond staff to sniff out news, should be called liners. Low pay mandated verbosity, but custom also dictated that the first liner to report a story had all its proceeds. Liners specialized, men covering fires and crime, and women covering society. On dull days, liners invented news.

84. Harte, Bret. "The Rise of the 'Short Story.'" 3d ser., 7 (1899): 1–8.
Pioneer of the short story while editing the *Western Magazine* maintained that American humor, polished in the press, was "an essential feature of newspaper literature" in 1899.

85. Lucas, E. V. "Concerning Catalogues." 3d ser., 7 (1899): 195–201.
Cited advertising in several periodicals.

86. Gwynn, Stephen. "The Sensibility of the Critics." 3d ser., 7 (1899): 229–33.
Narrated reactions of "literary journalists" to sensibility in novels.

87. MacDonagh, Michael. "At the Reporters' Table." 3d ser., 7 (1899): 505–18.
Contended that the "ubiquitous" reporter was the most important person on a newspaper's staff. The good reporter needed an instinct for important news and a tolerance of danger. Editors' demands for "plain, simple English" curbed wordiness and corrected the quaint or incorrect language of tyros. Abstracting speeches meant better columns. Errors occurred because many reporters could not read their own notes or had misheard.

88. Payn, James. "An Editor and Some Contributors." 3d ser., 7 (1899): 577–83.
Rated Charles Dickens a better editor of periodicals than W. M. Thackeray or Anthony Trollope because of his "passionate attachment to the profession." Editors had to be just. If they accepted bad writing, they wasted an owners' money. They should choose contributors for expertise, however unexpected, as a woman penning on hunting. Contributors should practice clear handwriting and resist sending long letters with their manuscripts.

89. "The Leading Article." 3d ser., 7 (1899): 797–811.
Traced the evolution of the leading article. Eighteenth-century newspapers were all news, but their successors tried to "mould or direct opinion" with leaders (named for the leads or spaces between the lines). By 1824 leaders were a regular feature. A paper's prestige came from its leaders; its revenue, from advertising. Many large local papers were excellent news gatherers but sometimes did not have

the weight of smaller journals. A leader helped busy people to form opinions. "In a word, the average leader-writer must follow, while he seems to lead," that is capture and present coherently the chief ideas of the community. At an influential paper, the editor, subeditor, and leader-writers selected topics. These were assigned on the basis of interest/expertise, but every column had to fit the paper's policies and its readers' ideas. Since topics varied, writers had to be "well-read," with "common sense and sound judgment," "without crochets, without conceit." They must write precisely and well because revision was not rigorous unless the scribe deviated from the paper's positions. Among important leader-writers were Henry Reeve (*The Times*, 1840–55) who wrote 2,482 leaders for 13,000 pounds and James Macdonell (*The Times*, 1870s) whose biography by Dr. Robertson Nicoll was supposedly the only one of a journalist.

90. Birrell, Augustine. "Is It Possible to Tell a Good Book from a Bad One?" 3^d^ ser., 8 (1900): 305–17.

Denounced newspapers that promoted a book in which they had a financial interest.

The Dark Blue, 1871–1873

Created by Oxonians, the *Dark Blue* noticed the press across the globe.

1. Lang, Andrew. "Théophile Gautier." 1 (1871): 26–35.
Biography of Gautier, the French poet, critic, and journalist, noted his late entry into journalism but only specified his work for the *Chronique de Paris*, edited by Honoré de Balzac.

2. "*The Life and Times of Henry, Lord Brougham*, Written by Himself." 1 (1871): 253–54.
Credited Brougham for much of the success of the early *Edinburgh Review*.

3. Rawlins, W. D. "The '*Tatler* in Cambridge.'" 1 (1871): 628–29.
Welcomed a new triweekly quarto that had "literary merit."

4. [Quin, W. T. W., 4th] Earl Dunraven. "Personal Reminiscences of a War Correspondent at Versailles." 2 (1871–72): 549–56, 715–29.
Recalled a sojourn at Versailles, during the Franco-Prussian War, when "anxious correspondents endeavoured to weave 'copy' from the casual observations of diplomatic lips." The careful correspondent, "who writes contemporaneous history," helped to separate truth from error, so it was "a very great evil that the public should expect from war correspondents a never-failing supply of interesting letters, full of ghostly horrors or picturesque scenes, and resonant with the din of battle." Correspondents should provide the facts impartially, and a war editor, which every paper needed, should write the stories.

5. "Oxford Chit-Chat." 3 (1872): 474–77.
Noticed among Oxford weeklies the informative *Oxford Times* on Friday and the *Oxford Guardian* on Wednesday. Aside that "street arabs" daily pressured people to buy London's *Echo*.

6. Laurie, Colonel W. F. B. "Periodical Literature in India." 3 (1872): 506–14, 628–49; 4 (1872–73): 63–78.
Surveyed Indian and Anglo-Indian journalism. The initial Anglo-Indian paper was the eighteenth-century *Hicky's Gazette*. In 1818 the *Sumachar Durpun* represented "the first efforts to improve the native mind by education, and by periodical literature in the shape of a native newspaper." Once government lessened restrictions on the press, "several Bengali newspapers" and a magazine emerged. "The stars of Anglo-Indian periodical literature" were the *Meerut Universal Magazine* and *Calcutta Literary Gazette*, but the *Calcutta Review* was as important to Indian literature as were the *Edinburgh Review* and *Quarterly Review* to British. Also examined religious, scientific, and comic serials and those of Ceylon.

7. Rossetti, Dr. [W. M.]. "Pasquale De'Virgilii." 4 (1872–73): 123–26.
Disclosed that De'Virgilii "conducted the *Constituzione*" (1848) and *Nuova Italia* (1860).

8. Tipping, J. W. "Francis Deak: A Memoir." 4 (1872–73): 184–93.
Alluded to Louis Kossuth's paper, *Pesti Hirlap*.

9. Jerrold, Evelyn. "Théophile Gautier." 4 (1872–73): 277–82.
Denigrated Gautier's work in the *Presse* because his commitment to the feuilleton made him "the prey of journalism" but praised his criticism in *Figaro*, the *Revue de Paris*, and the *Artiste*.

10. Tipping, J. W. "Russia and Pansclavism [sic]." 4 (1872–73): 285–94.
Essay on Panslavism pointed to "[s]ensational paragraphs in Czech journals" that were seditious and the Russia *Moscow Gazette* and *Aurore Sclave*, published in Vienna.

11. Laurie, Col. W. F. B. "Sir Henry Lawrence: A Biographical Study." 4 (1872–73): 536–48.
Based on H. B. Edwards' *Life of Sir Henry Lawrence* and J. W. Kaye's *Lives of Indian Officers* described Lawrence as "a writer of elaborate essays, 'gravid' with important matter, on a variety of subjects for the *Calcutta Review*, or of sketches for the newspapers."

The Dublin Review, 1836–1900

Aimed at an English constituency, the Romanist *Dublin* featured the European press. Additional motifs were press liberty and *Dublin* rivals.

1. [Robertson, James B.]. "Gerbet on the Eucharist." 1 (1836): 200–21.
Review of *Considerations sur la Dogme* by Abbé Ph. Gerbet tagged him as the editor in 1824 of the monthly *Mémorial Catholique*, "a journal distinguished not less for its literary talents than for its excellent principles."

2. [Quin, M.J.]. "Wraxall's *Memoirs*." 1 (1836): 343–67.
Review of Sir N. W. Wraxall's book aired his quest to identify Junius.

3. [Howitt, William]. "Literature of the Aristocracy, and the Literature of Genius." 2 (1836–37): 111–29.
Highlighted the "sudden" proliferation of serials from which readers acquired much knowledge. "Every class of people has its periodical organ of enquiry and intelligence." Expensive annuals shaped taste, but many suffered from poor writing done by amateurs, often friends of the publisher. Cheap offerings, principally the *Penny Magazine* and *Chambers's Journal*, relied on the steam press to publish practical information gleaned from many sources.

4. [Russell, C. W.]. "The Dublin Society." 2 (1836–37): 226–44.
Illuminated the Royal Dublin Society "news-room" valued by its members.

5. [O'Connell, John]. "Recent Opinions upon America." 2 (1836–37): 354–67.
Verified that many articles in British newspapers headlined the United States.

6. [Wiseman, Nicholas]. "Summary Review of French Catholic Literature, from September 1836 to March 1837." 2 (1836–37): 588–603.
Sermonized that "modern Reviews" only gave a "partial view" of literature, especially foreign. Overlooked in the year captioned were the French Catholic *Europe*, a daily edited by the Marquis de Jouffroy and capitalized at 750,000 francs; the fortnightly bishop-sponsored *Revue religieuse et édifiante*; and the projected *Catholicisme*.

7. [Stapleton, Miles T.]. "Montémont's *London*." 3 (1837): 113–33.
Review of Albert Montémont's book opined that French newspapers were more influential than better-written English ones because Gallic gazettes were the only medium for public communication.

8. “Summary Review of Italian and German Catholic Literature, from January to June 1837.” 3 (1837): 249–53.

Glanced at Italian but not German periodicals, namely the *Annali delle Scienze Religiose*, a Roman quarterly edited by Abate de Luca; the *Propagatore Religioso* (Turin); *Pragmalogia Cattolica* (Lucca); and *Memorie di Religione, di Morale e di Litteratura* (Modena).

9. [Chapman, H. S.]. “The Irish in America.” 3 (1837): 452–68.

Calculated that New York had 13 or 14 newspapers, among them the “well-conducted” *Times* and papers that stereotyped certain groups.

10. [Wiseman, Nicholas]. “Summary Review of French Catholic Literature, from March to September 1837.” 3 (1837): 550–57.

Announced a new periodical, the *Revue Français et Etrangère*, edited by Baron Ferdinand d’Eckstein and P. - S. Ballanche and capitalized at 100,000 francs.

11. [Coux, Charles de]. “Saint-Simonism.” 4 (1838): 138–79.

Scrutinized Saint-Simonian journals, the *Productive*, a monthly with “remarkable articles upon political economy and history,” and its successor, the *Organizateur*, as well as the French *Globe*, so well capitalized in 1831 that it circulated without charge.

12. “Summary Review of French and Italian Catholic Literature, from September 1837 to March 1838.” 4 (1838): 543–58.

Closed with the table of contents (December 1837) of the French *Université Catholique*.

13. [O’Connell, John]. “*Memoirs of* [*Sir Walter*] *Scott*.” 5 (1838): 377–407.

Review of J. G. Lockhart’s book on Scott decried the religious bias of the London press except the *Sun*.

14. “Summary Review of French Catholic Literature, from October 1838 to April 1839.” 6 (1839): 545–55.

Welcomed the *Revue du Nord de la France*, a Lille monthly “conducted with much ability”; the *Tablettes du Chrétian*, an inexpensive weekly; and the *Ami des Sourds-muets*, a Nancy publication of M. Piroux, “director of the deaf and dumb asylum.”

15. [Robertson, James B.]. “German Catholic Literature.” 7 (1839): 253–63.

Listed several new Catholic periodicals: Frankfurt’s *Katholische Kirchenzeitung* that had already achieved “considerable success”; *Zeitschrift fur Theologie*, a quarterly; and *Historisch-Politische Blätter*, which “exerts great influence on public opinion.”

16. [?Cooper, C. P.]. “The Liberty of the Press.” 7 (1839): 518–40.

Surveyed the history of libel and supported proposed legislation requiring proof of falsehood and express malice. Counted on judicial construction and press political debate, modeled on the exchanges between Jonathan Swift and Joseph Addison/Richard Steele, to protect individuals and reduce prosecutions.

17. [Russell, C. W.]. "Prejudices of Our Popular Literature." 8 (1840): 56–105.
Differentiated the *Edinburgh Review*, "the foe of intolerance in all its forms," from the *Quarterly Review*, with its "indulgence of party spleen, and the gratification of sectarian animosity."

18. [Steinmetz, John]. "Civil and Religious Education in Belgium." 8 (1840): 373–414.
Mourned that since Belgian independence, the press was free from "official prosecutions" of its "vomit...disgusting calumnies" about the authorities.

19. [Chapman, H. S.]. "New Zealand." 9 (1840): 189–214.
Bruited that presses and type from Adelaide made possible the publication of the *New Zealand Gazette* and *New Zealand Journal*.

20. [Quin, M. J.]. "Mental Epidemics." 10 (1841): 348–82.
Castigated newspapers for their graphic stories on suicide because they inspired murderers and demoralized other readers. These columns were the product of penny-a-liners anxious to inflate their pay and editors and proprietors anxious to sell papers.

21. [Robertson, James B.]. "Moral and Intellectual Condition of Catholic Germany." 11 (1841): 53–104.
Saw some lessening of censorship in Prussia and Austria, where the *Allgemeine Zeitung* had "the widest and most unlimited circulation."

22. [De Morgan, Augustus]. "Jones on the Value of Annuities, Etc.: Society for the Diffusion of Useful Knowledge." 11 (1841): 104–33.
Title referred to a text published by the captioned Society, which also sponsored the *Penny Magazine*, largely designed by publisher Charles Knight. Its success allegedly fueled the campaign against the stamp duty. The Society for Promoting Christian Knowledge sired the competing *Saturday Magazine*.

23. [Anstey, T. C.]. "Van Diemen's Land under the Prison System." 11 (1841): 426–77.
Nodded to the *Hobarton Advertiser*, "edited by an emancipist" in Van Diemen's Land.

24. [Leahy, J. P.]. "Switzerland – Convents of Argau." 12 (1842): 446–66.
Named numerous Swiss Protestant journals, among them the *Semeur*, "a leading periodical amongst the French Protestants," *Gazette of Upper Germany*, *Protestant Gazette*, and *Helvétie*.

25. [Kenealy, E. V. H.]. "Life of Flood." 13 (1842): 100–55.
Biography of Henry Flood, an eighteenth-century MP, abridged his speeches on press liberty in reference to the libel case of *Dublin Magazine* publisher Peter Wilson, speeches given when journalism was in "a lowly condition."

26. [O'Connell, John]. "Why is Ireland Exempted from the Income Tax?" 13 (1842): 155–206.

Singled out Dublin's *Morning Register*, a paper "of long-established reputation"; *Evening Post*, "equally high"; and *Freeman's Journal*, "another most able, influential, and patriotic public organ."

27. [McMahon, Patrick]. "Laing's Travels." 14 (1843): 277–320.

Review of Samuel Laing's *Notes of a Traveler* mentioned that there were "many newspapers published at Copenhagen," but a few had "merit." Those with "talent [were] hampered by the jealousies of the court, and by laws," but Denmark produced 180 periodicals. Sweden also had press censorship.

28. [Murray, P. A.]. "The Persecution of Slander: *Edinburgh Review*; [George] Borrow's *Bible in Spain*." 14 (1843): 443–80.

Retort to *Edinburgh Review* article (February 1843) howled that religious bias existed in the elite reviews. While their goals were "to instruct, to amuse," they resorted to "ridicule" and "sarcasm" masked by an "affectation of impartiality" in such paragraphs. The *Edinburgh*, because of its "high literary character" and "advocacy of certain liberal views," sowed "reckless bigotry" with ease.

29. [Renouf, Peter]. "Carlyle's *Past and Present*." 15 (1843): 182–200.

Review of Thomas Carlyle's book referred to William Hamilton's articles in the *Edinburgh Review*.

30. [Russell, C. W.]. "*Life of Gerald Griffin*." 15 (1843): 387–415.

Review of a biography by "His Brother" quoted Griffin on William Maginn's able work in *Blackwood's Magazine* and L. E. Landon's in the *Literary Gazette*.

31. [Crolly, George]. "The Life and Writings of Miss Brown, the Blind Poetess." 17 (1844): 517–60.

Essay on Frances Brown catalogued her contributions to the *Irish Penny Journal*, *Athenaeum*, *Keepsake*, and *Hood's Magazine*.

32. [Wiseman, Nicholas]. "Spain." 18 (1845): 370–485.

Footnoted the *Pensamiento de la Nacion*, an 1844 weekly with 16 pages of politics, literature, and Catholic news. Directed by James Balmez, a "young and able ecclesiastic," it was "calm, moderate, and grave" with a "pure and elegant" style. Balmez had previously run the *Sociedad*, a Barcelona newspaper, 1843–44.

33. [Wiseman, Nicholas]. "Brownson's Conversion." 19 (1845): 390–400.

Avowed that it was unusual for one periodical to borrow from another but that the *Dublin* excerpted Orestes Brownson's *Quarterly Review* because *Dublin* readers would not otherwise see its valuable contents. Aside that Brownson had previously penned for the *Christian Examiner*.

34. [Wiseman, Nicholas]. "The Religious Movement." 19 (1845): 522–38.

Concluded with Wiseman's perspective on the *Dublin Review*.

35. [?Ward, John]. "Foreign Lotteries." 20 (1846): 408–27.

Ridiculed British Sunday papers that branded foreign lotteries swindles but carried racing sweeps and advertised raffles.

36. [Dasent, J. B.]. "Adventures in the South Seas." 23 (1847): 341–63.
Review of Herman Melville's *Omoo* defined advertisements as "rubbish" in disguise.

37. [McCabe, W. B.]. "The Austrian Revolution and Its Results." 25 (1848): 40–71.
Realized that British press readers disliked "details which are not dabbled with human gore."

38. [Robertson, James B.]. "Political State of Germany." 26 (1849): 481–522.
Applauded prosecutions to control "an inflammatory press" in Vienna and "an incendiary press" in France.

39. [Robertson, James B.]. "France since the Revolution of February." 27 (1849): 91–122.
Imputed the February 1848 revolution to the *National* but bowed to the "able" *Revue des Deux Mondes*.

40. [Wiseman, Nicholas]. "The Art of Puffing." 27 (1849): 146–62.
Focused on advertising content, such as personal entries in *The Times*.

41. [Oakeley, Frederick]. "Ways and Means of the Church: The Offertory." 27 (1849): 267–91.
Honored the *Rambler* for "far exceeding in depth and solidity the ordinary run of magazines, yet preferring no claim to the more substantial character of a Review." Although marred by fiction and occasional "sentimentality," it attracted a broad audience.

42. [Crolly, George]. "Irish Factions, Parsons, and Landlords." 27 (1849): 468–511.
Denigrated "the largest portion of the Irish press, of all shades and colours – a press conducted for the most part without character and ability" – one ready to distort facts to serve faction.

43. [Wiseman, Nicholas]. "The Industry of the Poor." 30 (1851): 484–532.
Review of Henry Mayhew's *London Labour and the London Poor* reprinted its findings that the uneducated listened to Sunday papers read aloud in beer shops and illiterate costermongers purchased illustrated serials. Warned that any reading of the poor might cause "disaffection, combination, and anarchism."

44. [Russell, C. W.]. "The Moralities of Legislation – 'The Italian Church.'" 31 (1851): 218–58.
Lamented that *The Times* shunned "truth, justice, and common honesty" when covering a topic that it hated.

45. [Allies, T. W.]. "The Catholic University." 31 (1851): 529–88.
Lectured that journalism was the "new ruler of our modern world." "What was once mere communication of news threatens to absorb into itself all powers of civil government; to dictate decisions on all questions…to wield all moral influences…[to be] a despotism." In Britain, France, and the United States, newspapers were everywhere, and everywhere they ruled. This "leveling and superficial literature" endangered stability because no part of life was "free from its prying search and imperious decision."

46. [Crolly, George]. "Jeffrey's Life and Correspondence." 32 (1852): 464–511.
Review of Henry Cockburn's *Life of Lord Jeffrey, with a Selection from His Correspondence*, accepted Sydney Smith's account of the birth of the *Edinburgh Review*. Editor Francis Jeffrey was "the soul" of the *Review*, writing and soliciting many essays. He penned with "accuracy and elegance" over 200 and read, corrected, even rewrote others, demonstrating that editing was drudgery. A man of ability, patience, and prudence, he lost no contributors and raised the reputation of the *Edinburgh*. During his tenure, it displayed "delicacy and decorum" in contrast to the "exceedingly prosy and stupid" *Quarterly Review*. While "writing constantly for a periodical publication" was "laborious and irksome," it was a "marketable commodity." By the *Edinburgh's* fourth issue, contributors were paid.

47. [Robertson, James B.]. "Count de Montalembert's *Catholic Interests in the Nineteenth Century*." 34 (1853): 139–74.
Book review charged the Archbishop of Paris with wounding the *Avenir*, edited by C. de Montalembert. Aside that Louis Veûillot would be an "excellent" subeditor for the *Univers*.

48. [Finlason, W. F.]. "The Case of Achilli." 34 (1853): 244–314.
Diverted from a legal case involving J. H. Newman to classify *Bell's Messenger* as "speaking for the coarse sections of the middle classes" and the *Spectator* as a "philosophical and reflective" journal. Averred that author anonymity was no deterrent to periodical reading.

49. [Oakeley, Frederick]. "Cardinal Wiseman's *Essays* – Periodical Literature." 34 (1853): 541–66.
Attested to the multiplication and impact of serials in England, 1800–50. Periodical literature was the child of the nineteenth century because the eighteenth lacked serious reviews. They furnished a forum and organized views, but to have influence a periodical's contents must "harmonize." Because many contributors were interested in popularity, not truth, anonymity was ideal, an "intermediate between the boldness of profession and the cowardice of concealment."

50. [Wiseman, Nicholas]. "Our Ministry of Public Instruction." 35 (1853): 199–229.
Indicted journals, particularly dailies, for their silence on or opposition to sensitive topics. Papers suppressed letters, manipulated leaders, and hired biased foreign correspondents.

51. [Abraham, G. W.]. "Richard Lalor Sheil." 38 (1855): 321–54.
Nodded to Sheil's articles in the *New Monthly Magazine*.

52. [Finlason, W. F.]. "The Action Against the Cardinal." 39 (1855): 146–64.
Based on the case of *Boyle v. Wiseman*, studied many English and French Catholic serials.

53. [Crolly, George]. "Sidney [*sic*] Smith." 39 (1855): 244–72.
Flagged Smith as one of the "ablest contributors" to the *Edinburgh Review*.

54. [Wiseman, Nicholas]. "Italy and the Papal States." 41 (1856): 171–226.
Petitioned for "foreign correspondents" who were "honest, honourable, trustworthy, and truthful." Aside that the *Morning Star* was "one of the most successful penny papers."

55. [Wiseman, Nicholas]. "The Present Catholic Dangers." 41 (1856): 441–70.
Complained that no "Catholic newspaper" noticed the *Dublin* but praised and excerpted the *Rambler*. It had "a circulation equal to more than an average one in such a straitened circle as Catholic society" but no real influence because it did not defend Catholic positions. *See Rambler* 2[d] ser., 7: 140 and 8: 216.

56. [Oakeley, Frederick]. "The Latest Phenomena of Anglicanism." 42 (1857): 95–123.
Presented some of the Anglican press, among them the *Union*, "a weekly newspaper"; *Record* (full of "twaddle"), and *Christian Remembrancer* and *Guardian*, "two periodicals of undoubted ability."

57. [Wetherell, T. F.]. "Catholic Unity and English Parties." 43 (1857): 172–206.
Reported that many writers of the *Oxford Union Herald* had moved to the *Union*.

58. [Oakeley, Frederick]. "Religious Disabilities of Catholic Prisoners." 44 (1858): 485–501.
Marked the *Tablet* "our able contemporary."

59. [Finlason, W. F.]. "Platform Slanderers and Newspapers Libellers." 45 (1858): 413–28.
Pointed out that a newspaper proprietor's responsibility for libel was less clear than that of an editor or scribe. Because newsmen were unsure what constituted libel, their best protection against conviction was probably a sympathetic jury.

60. [Oakeley, Frederick]. "Cardinal Wiseman's Tour in Ireland in 1858." 46 (1859): 499–510.
Review of Nicholas Wisemen's *Sermons, Lectures, and Speeches* defended newspapers as "servants of the English public," with *The Times* and *Saturday Review* among the "distinguished."

61. [Finlason, W. F.]. "The Massacre of Perugia." 47 (1859–60): 168–264.
Condemned the Piedmontese government for trying to muzzle the press.

62. [Donnelly, Thomas]. "Modern Humorists." 48 (1860): 107–49.
Spotlighted *Punch*, once on "a brilliant course" but in 1860 replete with "slanderous sneers and indecent caricature of the Catholic religion and its dignitaries." Those who used freedom of the press in this way would only harm themselves.

63. [Purcell, Edmund S.]. "Bonapartism." 49 (1860–61): 104–46.
Considered Italian religious press circulation small compared to France's secular *Siècle* (500,000 subscribers), *Monde* (13,000), *Journal des Débats* (10,000), and others cited.

64. [St. John, M. Georgina S.]. "Book Hawking." 49 (1860–61): 146–55.
Hoped that Catholic literature would lure juveniles from the cheap press, as *Lloyd's Weekly Newspaper*, *Reynolds's Miscellany*, and the *London Journal*.

65. [Donnelly, Thomas]. "Thomas Hood." 49 (1860–61): 300–47.
Peeked at Hood's work for the *London Magazine* and *Hood's Magazine*.

66. [Gainsford, R. J.]. "Austria and Hungary." 50 (1861): 349–96.
Found English newspapers partisan except *The Times*, "a huge commercial undertaking" but not coherent because it followed current trends.

67. [Donnelly, Thomas]. "Modern Periodical Literature." 51 (1862): 275–308.
Revealed that penning for a serial ordinarily started as a sideline. Nonetheless, magazines, as *Blackwood's*, *Fraser's*, and *Bentley's Miscellany*, contained "valuable matter in many departments"; and reviews, as the *Edinburgh*, *Quarterly*, and *Monthly*, produced "some of the finest writing, some of the deepest learning, and some of the acutest criticism." The father of modern magazines was *Household Words*, which was inexpensive and edited by "a favourite and successful writer." Examined it and its successors, *All the Year Round* and *Once a Week*, as well as their reputed rival *Cornhill Magazine*. Neither the *Cornhill* nor *All the Year Round* added much to literature because their material was largely "injurious." Analyzed *Macmillan's Magazine* but dismissed *Temple Bar* because it was not distinctive. Most other periodicals were "below mediocrity" except *Chambers's Journal*, which rejected "sensation" and fostered literature. In the 1830s, when few good serials were cheap, *Chambers's* offered an "elevating influence," helping workers to achieve success as independent citizens. By 1862 masses of periodicals left readers with "no opportunity for reflection" and compelled "hasty composition" by writers "sacrificed to expediency."

68. [Purcell, Edmund S.]. "Sicily: The Italian Revolution and the Papacy." 51 (1862): 481–509.
Blared that Italians did not read newspapers.

69. [Wiseman, Nicholas]. "On Responsibility." 52 (1862–63): 155–84.
Stressed that people quoted morning papers by name because they trusted them. Yet their leader-writers, deriving authority from anonymity, were not necessarily better educated or informed than readers and might alter facts to underpin a paper's position. Foreign correspondents were "notoriously worthless." Though many wrote well, they were ready to sell themselves because there was no retribution for misrepresenting the truth. Even if they signed articles, like the French, they could be inaccurate, like the French.

70. [O'Reilly, Myles]. "The Duty of the State, Its Rules and Limits." 52 (1862–63): 245–71.
Review of E. Ducpetiaux's *Mission de l'état* measured liberty of the press: in Belgium it was broad enough that outsiders could run papers; in France, nonexistent; in Britain, wide except for the posting of security for libel and other criminal actions.

71. Delta. "The French Elections." n.s., 1 (1863): 191–219.
Talked about the launch of *France* (1861), edited by A. de la Guéronnière. A journalist who could "mould himself into any shape," he previously edited a country paper, then moved to the *Presse*. Aside on other editors, Léonor Havin of the *Siècle* and Emile de Girardin of the *Presse*.

72. [Thompson, E. H. and Harriet]. "Foreign Periodical Literature." n.s., 1 (1863): 262–74, *et seq.*

This entry was a regular feature beginning with the new series of the *Dublin* but changed its title to "Our Contemporaries" from n.s., 3.

73. "Prison Ministers Act." n.s., 1 (1863): 356–97.

Observed that *Times* writers of "unquestionable ability" could be fair – or not.

74. [Murray, P. A.]. "Theological Errors of the Day. Brownson's *Review.*" n.s., 2 (1864): 58–95.

Asserted that Orestes Brownson's *Quarterly Review* was very popular among American Catholics.

75. "The Santiago Catastrophe and Its Critics." n.s., 2 (1864): 419–32.

Added a gloss on the *Saturday Review* as the leader of the 'intellectual press.'

76. [Coleridge, H. J.]. "Our Contemporaries." n.s., 2 (1864): 512–22.

Postulated that good periodicals in 1864 were easily accessible. Although they were occasionally biased, they had a major impact on public opinion by providing "the most active and influential minds…a ready and convenient mode of working upon the intelligence of the public."

77. [Ward, William G.]. "Rome and the Munich Congress." n.s., 3 (1864): 64–96.

Recorded the Papal closing of the *Home and Foreign Review*, which "exhibited a vast amount of learning and mental activity" but "anti-Catholic principles."

78. [Manning, H. E.]. "Memorial of His Eminence Cardinal Wiseman." n.s., 4 (1865): 267–78.

Paean to Nicholas Wiseman nominated him as "the ablest and most illustrious supporter" of the *Dublin* and quoted this "joint founder" on the details of its birth.

79. [D., B.]. "The Celtic Language and Dialects." n.s., 5 (1865): 69–87.

Depicted "the native Welsh press" as "constantly active: it teems periodicals, weekly, monthly, quarterly, on all subjects of general interest or necessity." "The national newspaper press not only lives, but flourishes in Wales," as evidenced by the "select" monthlies and quarterlies listed. Papers in South Wales were in Welsh and English.

80. [Ward, William G.]. "Mr. Oxenham and the *Dublin Review.*" n.s., 5 (1865): 319–51.

Alluded to the 'short notice' in periodical literary criticism.

81. [Ward, William G.]. "Irish Writers on University Education." n.s., 7 (1866): 88–101.

Argued that the *Dublin* was no more an Irish publication than the *Edinburgh Review* was a Scottish one.

82. [Wilberforce, H. W.]. "Jamaica." n.s., 7 (1866): 362–414.

Demonstrated the influence of newspapers from their reports on Edward Eyre's governance in Jamaica.

83. [Ward, William G.]. "Pius IX and the *Civiltà Cattolica*." n.s., 7 (1866): 414–32.

Lauded the *Civiltà Cattolica*, a periodical "conducted with such consummate wisdom, learning, and industry," the *Osservatore Cattolico* (Bologna), the *Univers* (Paris), and "a courageous Central American journal, whose name escapes."

84. [Ward, William G.]. "Two Criticisms on the *Dublin Review*." n.s., 8 (1867): 164–72.

Denied that the "tone" of the *Dublin*'s new series was "too peremptory and overbearing."

85. [Hoey, J. C.]. "The State of Ireland." n.s., 8 (1867): 482–92.

Discovered that "Italian revolutionaries managed to get on the staff of several of the London leading journals," and the American press was "in a great measure written by Irishmen, and the Irish-Americans are almost all Fenians."

86. [Vaughan, H. A.]. "Popular Education in England." n.s., 10 (1868): 131–65.

Assured that the press "speaks out freely its own mind."

87. [Ward, William G.]. "Principles of Catholic Higher Education." n.s., 12 (1869): 86–106.

Recognized that all manner of periodicals were blossoming but that at least one "penny sporting paper" had "foul advertisements."

88. [Ward, William G.]. "Catholic Controversy." n.s., 13 (1869): 377–92.

Admonished the Catholic *Month* for its "habit of publishing reprehensive and somewhat sharply-expressed remarks" about the *Dublin*.

89. [Hoey, J. C.]. "Is Ireland Irreconcilable?" n.s., 14 (1870): 451–81.

Feared the implications of repressive press policy, such as suppression of Irish papers and prosecution of staff. Because Dublin juries tended to convict "national journalists," Irish gazettes should eschew "coarseness" and copy the *Nation*, which had "disowned" rebellion.

90. [?Wilberforce, H. W.]. "Protestant London." n.s., 15 (1870): 1–26.

Fumed that "licentious penny newspapers" circulating 250,000 copies weekly corrupted the young, hardly appropriate for a free press.

91. [Hoey, J. C.]. "The Fall of the French Empire." n.s., 15 (1870): 479–95.

Peeped at the *Journal des Villes de Compagnes*, a well-known Paris paper c. 1840.

92. [Hoey, J. C.]. "Paris and France." n.s., 16 (1871): 428–47.

Disputed that Napoleon III prosecuted many journalists and suppressed many journals.

93. [Hoey, J. C.]. "The Situation in France." n.s., 22 (1874): 204–10.

Commented on French official suspension of the *Univers*.

94. [Hoey, J. C.]. "The Fall of the Duc de Broglie and the Crisis in France." n.s., 23 (1874): 133–59.

Spoke about the role of the French press in shaping politics.

95. [?Vaughan, H. A.]. "The Pilgrimage to Pontigny." n.s., 23 (1874): 378–412.

Challenged the notion that "newspapers never err" by highlighting mistakes of facts and in translations due to haste, ignorance, or bias.

96. [Ward, William G.]. "A Few Words on Dr. Brownson's Philosophy." n.s., 26 (1876): 36–55.

Grieved that Orestes Brownson's *Quarterly Review*, which had "so notable and important a career," had ceased publication.

97. [Hoey, Frances Cashel]. "Paris." n.s., 26 (1876): 55–73.

Decided that Paris morning dailies outnumbered London because every circle had a journal. Since French journalists signed articles, a "clever writer" could build a political career. The country papers were "obscure" because all the better journalists left for Paris. Gazettes did not care about consistency. They were thriving because they served readers who liked "immoral" feuilletons, light jests on serious subjects, and scandals. If newspapers reflected a population, Parisians lacked virtue and decorum.

98. [Ward, William G.]. "Father O'Reilly on Society and the Church." n.s., 26 (1876): 73–96.

Starred Russell O'Reilly, S.J., editor of the *Irish Monthly Magazine*, with its "homely style."

99. [Hoey, J. C.]. "The Republican Victory in France." n.s., 27 (1876): 198–213.

Yoked the French Radical and Belgian Liberal presses.

100. [Hoey, J. C.]. "The Cloud in the East." n.s., 28 (1877): 181–91.

Pictured the French *Nord* as "the oracle of Russian news, views, and ideas in Western Europe," doing so with "much ability and unflagging zeal."

101. [Hoey, J. C.]. "General Ignatieff." n.s., 29 (1877): 68–93.

Aside that the Russian press had some freedom and influence in the 1860s.

102. "Modern Ideals and the Liberty of the Press." n.s., 29 (1877): 191–222.

Interpreted freedom of the press as "a shibboleth of the present century," "a Liberal war-cry" because it did not yet exist in Rome, Berlin, Paris, St. Petersburg, and Ireland, as the 1860s suppression of the *Irish People* proved. In a society prone to synthesizing ideas, this liberty was "an evil and a snare."

103. "Catholic Fiction." n.s., 31 (1878): 439–62.

Concluded that periodicals, with their regular appearance and low price, lured more readers than books. In the United Kingdom and in the United States, Catholic serials had multiplied since the 1830s.

104. [Hedley, J. C.]. "To Our Readers." 3d ser., 1 (1879): 1–2.
Justified the *Dublin's* third series on the ground that "[n]ews, in these days, accumulates so fast, and every topic is written on so quickly and completely" that a quarterly had to "take *wider* views than the other periodicals." Commenced a regular column, "Notices of Catholic Continental Periodicals."

105. "Thomas Moore." 3d ser., 1 (1879): 323–68.
Supposed that Moore "vastly promoted his popularity and improved his finances" by penning "political squibs" in the *Morning Chronicle*, "edited by his friend Mr. [James] Perry," and *The Times*, edited by "Mr. [Thomas] Barnes, another personal friend." Moore earned 500 pounds per year as he "fearlessly lashed...political corruption, religious bigotry, and intolerance."

106. "The Letters of Charles Dickens." 3d ser., 3 (1880): 409–38.
Evaluated Dickens as editor of *Household Words* and *All the Year Round*. Although he equated editing with torture, he appreciated the work of others so his critiques were "expert and keen but kindly."

107. "The Religious Press." 3d ser., 6 (1881): 1–29.
Spanned religious newspapers from Anglican to Unitarian, excepting Catholic, with attention to advertising (primarily quack medicine listings) and circulation. While the breadth of this press signaled public willingness "to absorb a practically unlimited quantity" of periodicals, reading secular ones was not "a sign of a growing intelligence" but of "decay of patriotism, of public spirit, and of public morality" and of "increasing frivolity." Referred to *Macmillan's Magazine* 43: 385.

108. "Literature for the Young. Part I: Periodical Literature." 3d ser., 6 (1881): 354–77.
Stamped the genre of juvenile periodicals "completely modern." Of the 80 or so magazines in 1881, many were well established. Dealt with boys' serials because "the reading appetite [was] universal among boys" and girls' journals were neither numerous nor influential. The worst boys' papers were 'penny awfuls' with criminal heroes. Somewhat better were crude and absurd sheets with "feverish passion and wild adventure" that substituted "insolent vulgarity for manliness" and "imbecility for chivalry." *Sunshine* and a few others checked the materialism and "low-level thoughts and animal instincts" of urbanites. Aside that magazines were successful thanks to illustrations, amusing paragraphs, verisimilitude in fiction, and information in articles and in answers to letters.

109. "Ireland: Her Friends and Foes." 3d ser., 9 (1883): 181–200.
Endorsed prosecution of journalist "William O'Brien, the proprietor of *United Irishman*," because the paper had commented on the unfairness of some local trials of murderers. Named as the chief Irish papers the *Nation*, *Irish Times*, and New York's *Irish World*. Aside that *The Times* reprinted "conversation of the London clubs."

110. Blundell, Charles Weld. "Democracy – Whither?" 3d ser., 13 (1885): 393–405.
Pinpointed the danger of an ignorant press in a society where readers were multiplying. Newspapers did not spend money for educated staffs when "lively imagination and an elastic conscience," "flippancy and flattery," sufficed. Editors were capitalists who served "newspaper garbage" to "illiterate electors." Leader-writers repeated political gossip or "pseudo-philosophy." Penny-a-liners criticized "the high and good and respectable." Interviewing, with its "[t]ransatlantic vulgarity" of exposing private wrongs, compounded the subversion of "national mind and morals."

111. Wegg-Prosser, F. R. "The Church and Liberalism." 3[d] ser., 15 (1886): 58–68.
Featured F. de Lamennais, one-time editor of the *Avenir*, on liberty of the press.

112. Vaughan, John S. "Social Disturbances – Their Cause and Cure." 3[d] ser., 16 (1886): 335–51.
Cited the *Freiheit* as "the great Anarchist organ."

113. Amherst, William J., S.J. "Frederick Lucas." 3[d] ser., 16 (1886): 392–428.
Named Lucas as founder, editor, and co-owner of the *Tablet*, a paper preceded by the stamped and short-lived *Beacon* and *Phoenix*. The *Tablet* reputedly gained more cachet after its 1849 move to Dublin, where it fit better than in England as the spokesman for the Irish. Although Lucas was a good journalist, John Lemoinne of the *Journal des Débats* represented "perfection" in newspaper style and impartiality.

114. Britten, James. "The Catholic Truth Society." 3[d] ser., 17 (1887): 400–13.
Catalogued the Catholic press that shared the captioned Society's goals.

115. Jeffrée, [F.]. "The Jews in France." 3[d] ser., 18 (1887): 323–50; 3[d] ser., 19 (1888): 34–61.
Anti-Semite reviewed several books including *La France Juive*. Author Edouard Drumont, "by profession a journalist," drew on Jewish periodicals, as the *Univers Israélite*, and *Bulletin d'Alliance Israélite Universelle*. Jeffrée purported that Jews published seditious papers, as the *Freiheit*, owned or edited many in Paris and the French provinces, and generally monopolized the European press. By controlling the major news agencies, as Reuters and Havas, they could spread rumors that jeopardized continental diplomacy and markets. "Absolute masters" of the press, they flattered mass passions reaping "immense power over public opinion, which they manipulate as they please." "The unthinking part of mankind, which, after all, forms the majority, take from the newspapers their political creed, and very often their principles of right and wrong, of honor, of virtue, of uprightness, of patriotism." Newspapers were the idol directing "what to adore and what to burn." Examples of their impact were the "*Lanterne*, edited by the Jew Meyer [Eugene Mayer]"; [Edouard] Lockroy, "a penny-a-liner on some gutter paper" who later became French minister of commerce, and *The Times* Paris correspondent, "the Jew [H. G. A. Opper de] Blowitz."

116. Clerke, Ellen M. "*Memoirs of a Royalist.*" 3[d] ser., 20 (1888): 22–42.
Review of a book by the Count de Falloux assessed the influence of French Catholic journals, such as the *Univers*.

117. Britten, James. "Art and the People." 3[d] ser., 21 (1889): 377–89.
Enthused that good art was available in periodicals as more depended on illustrations to attract buyers. Works in expensive serials had "real art value." Boys' papers had "greatly improved of late years," and "comic and other weekly illustrated papers, if not always refined, are at any rate decent." Even advertising was artistic, although art should educate, not sell goods. The *Illustrated Police News*, "with its weekly tale of crime and horror, graphically presented on its front page," was offensive.

118. "The Pope and Catholic Philosophy in England." 3[d] ser., 25 (1891): 272–89.
Affirmed that the monthly of 1891 was the "literary bread" of the upper and upper middle classes as the daily had been in 1801. The "innocuous" and "agreeable" articles on various subjects in most

monthlies won the "superficially educated," resulting in big circulations and profits. Occasional essays on serious topics might be well written but were too short to have any depth.

119. Wilberforce, Wilfrid. "William George Ward." 4th ser., 6 (1894): 1–29.
Headlined Ward as a former *Dublin* editor and *British Critic* contributor.

120. Clerke, Ellen M. "Mrs. Augustus Craven." 4th ser., 7 (1895): 120–35.
Biography of Pauline de la Ferronay noticed her writing for the French Catholic press.

121. Devas, Charles S. "*Catholic Socialism*." 4th ser., 9 (1896): 117–28.
Review of F. S. Nitti's book highlighted "a social science review of extreme vigour and competence, namely, *Revista Internazionale de Scienze Sociali*," published monthly in Rome since 1893.

122. Casartelli, L. C. "Our Diamond Jubilee." 4th ser., 9 (1896): 245–71.
Celebrated the *Dublin* whose early 'quarterly' style," "grave, dignified, erudite," gave way in the "busy" era of later years. W. G. Ward changed the *Review's* appearance and "tendency," moving away from the founders' goals in the second series. Book reviews grew larger and short notices (on science, exploration) appeared. Important players in the *Review's* development were Daniel O'Connell, Nicholas Wiseman, and Charles Russell, a long-time contributor.

Thanked Matthew Russell, S. J., "the genial and gifted Editor of the *Irish Monthly*," for publishing (vols. 21–3, 1893–95) a history of the *Dublin* with its editors and authors. Identification of contributors to the second series was not as complete, perhaps because they did not wish to be named. By the third series, "old-fashioned anonymity" had ended.

123. Bridgett, T. E., C. SS. R. "Monuments to Cardinal Wiseman." 4th ser., 13 (1898): 245–74.
Commemorated Nicholas Wiseman by analyzing some of his *Dublin* articles.

124. Kent, W. H., O. S. C. "William Ewart Gladstone." 4th ser., 14 (1898): 1–40.
This piece on Gladstone's articles in serials counseled periodical reviewers to discuss a book's contents and judge its merits impartially.

125. Kent, W. H., O.S.C. "Dr. Fairbairn on *Catholicism*." 4th ser., 15 (1899): 384–407.
Review of a book by A. M. Fairbairn, who penned for the *Contemporary Review*, discerned a recent spurt in periodical essays collected and published as books.

126. Blakelock, R. B. S. "Montalembert and French Education." 4th ser., 17 (1900): 102–20.
Touched on the Count C. de Montalembert's work for the *Avenir*.

127. "The Justice of the Transvaal War." 4th ser., 18 (1900): 1–44.
Fumed that the "vernacular Press of India" approached sedition "in its criticism of the British administration."

The Dublin University Magazine, 1833–1880

Catering to Anglo-Irish subscribers, the *Dublin University* and its heir, the *University Magazine*, 1878–80, disseminated plenty of sentences on the press at home and elsewhere. Two of its favorite topics were newspapers and literary periodicals.

1. [O'Sullivan, Samuel]. "The Present Crisis." 1 (1833): 1–14.
Thought that "a little spice of inconsistency" did not hurt a journal and that Robert Southey's essays enhanced the *Quarterly Review*, a "noble periodical."

2. [Stanford, Charles Stuart]. "New Year's Day; or, Our First Number." 1 (1833): 87–90.
Editor hoped that the *Dublin University*, by instructing and amusing, would win an audience in spite of "a prejudice against Irish periodicals." The English and Scottish attracted "talented contributors," but Dublin had "the stigma of never having supported a good general Magazine." Because "[v]ariety was the very essence" of a magazine, he recruited local talent from many fields.

3. N., Y. "England in 1819 and Ireland in 1833." 1 (1833): 436–50.
Linked the "licentious and infidel" English cheap papers in 1819 and the "penny vehicles of sedition and irreligion" in 1833 Ireland.

4. R[owley], H[arry]. "Familiar Epistles from London." 1 (1833): 575–82; 2 (1833): 155–65, 339–48.
Rambling article stereotyped journalist Harriet Martineau as "that odious man-woman"; some newspapers as subversive of workers' "reverence" for religion, and the rich, in their country houses, as eager readers of morning dailies.

5. [Stanford, Charles Stuart]. "At the Close of the Year." 2 (1833): 1–8.
Editor thanked the printer of and the women "critics and contributors" of the *Dublin University* for their work.

6. "Literary Reform." 2 (1833): 530–35.
Proposed that reviews reject promotions by authors; newspapers "diametrically opposite" refuse to hire the same reviewer; reviewers read books under review and avoid hackneyed quotations; contributors eschew duress to get their material published; owners pay adequately for ideas, not the number of lines or pages; editors have a liberal education; and subeditors be literate.

7. [Ferguson, Samuel]. "The Sixpenny Manifesto." 3 (1834): 253–63.
Title referred to *Companion to the Newspaper*, a "political retrospect" published in 1833 by Charles Knight as a supplement to such cheap journals as the *Penny Magazine*. It undersold serials from

which it had plagiarized popular but not very useful material. It did not form a "liberal sentiment" among readers because of its "confusion of ideas, dissipation of mind, and undue confidence in their competency" and did not empower workers because it failed to reach the "grimed artizan's garret," unlike the *Satirist* and *Poor Man's Guardian*.

8. "Twenty-Two Illustrations of 'Humbug.'" 4 (1834): 235–36.
Included statements prioritizing *Blackwood's Magazine* and *Fraser's Magazine* above the *Dublin University*.

9. [Johnston, William]. "Passages from the Diary of Terence O'Ruark, A.M." 5 (1835): 312–19, 432–38, 580–90, *et seq.* not relevant.
Discursive piece understood that newspapers were timelier than pamphlets on "political controversy." Parliamentary reporters might miss or mishear speeches, immaterial when Commons did "routine business" about which readers reputedly cared little.

10. [Butt, Isaac]. "The Close of the Year." 6 (1835): 708–11.
Contrasted the success of the *Dublin University* and the "failure of every preceding Irish periodical," a success based on "liberty of the press" but not "licentiousness." Listed several Irish newspapers that had complimented the *Magazine*.

11. "Irwin, Western Australia." 7 (1836): 149–62.
Review of F. C. Irwin's *The State and Position of Western Australia* alluded to the *Tasmanian* and the *Sydney Herald*.

12. "Willis' *Pencillings by the Way*." 7 (1836): 314–27.
Review of N. P. Willis' book challenged his description of J. G. Lockhart as a critic of "malice" and "ignorance." Criticism in the *Quarterly Review* was impartial and well written. "There is certainly no periodical to which the purity of English literature owes so much."

13. [Anster, John]. "*Literary Remains of Hazlitt*." 8 (1836): 406–23.
Review of William Hazlitt's writings, which title had notes by E. G. Bulwer-Lytton, recalled Hazlitt's early days as "a reporter of the [parliamentary] debates and a writer of dramatic entertainments," a time when his drinking was the result of a journalist's irregular hours and income.

14. "*The Church of England Quarterly Review*." 9 (1837): 230–33.
Expected the captioned periodical to counter the "seeming moderation" of elite serials, whose superficial "fairness" had "the effect of deceiving some, and slackening the zeal of others." One example was the *Edinburgh Review*, whose "ability, moderation, and a large qualification of sound criticism and high feeling" drew a big audience that conferred on it "a proportional power to do evil."

15. [O'Sullivan, Samuel]. "Past and Present State of Literature in Ireland." 9 (1837): 365–76.
Urged Dublin writers not to flee to the London press. The Irish should stay home and create literary taste as the Scottish had done in Scotland. Good manuscripts that flooded the *Dublin University* offices already raised its circulation.

16. "Present State of America." 9 (1837): 507–19.
Painted American newspapers as weapons of politicians in battle. Gazettes would likely increase as government "democratized" and closed off opportunities for "the more silent and gentle influences of taste and reason."

17. [O'Sullivan, Samuel]. "Lockhart's *Life of Scott*." 10 (1837): 142–57, 292–312, 385–402; 11 (1838): 667–88.
Review of J. G. Lockhart's book discussed Walter Scott's connection with the early *Quarterly Review*.

18. [O'Sullivan, Samuel]. "The Government Pacificators for July – The Press and the Police." 10 (1837): 217–23.
Charged the *Dublin Evening Post* with bias.

19. [Butt, Isaac]. "Memoranda from Our Tablets of the Month." 10 (1837): 230–40, 361–68, 483–96, 622–31, 749–60, *et seq.*
Refocused a regular column to include excerpts from and evaluations of newspapers. For example, the *Carlow Sentinel* was "a provincial journal of the highest character," and the country press "frequently supply very important information relative to the state of Ireland, which some of the metropolitan journals are not always prompt in extracting and arranging."

20. [O'Sullivan, Samuel]. "Lord Mulgrave's Government and the *Edinburgh Review*." 10 (1837): 692–703.
Whispered about the *Edinburgh's* wide circulation and solid reputation.

21. M'Glashan, James. "To Correspondents." 11 (1838): *verso* Table of Contents.
Alerted those who submitted material to the *Dublin University* that rejections might be due to lack of space or merit. Responses were in the publisher's office where individuals could retrieve them.

22. "Australia – Second Article – Van Diemen's Land." 13 (1839): 176–86.
Deduced that Van Diemen's Land was civilized because it had a press.

23. "Social, Moral, and Political State of Sweden." 13 (1839): 693–707.
Review of Samuel Laing's *Tour in Sweden* recorded that Sweden had about 80 newspapers, 19 "published in the metropolis" and all subject to a small stamp duty but none for paper or advertising. Many journals were not "political" but were full of local advertisements and "amusing tales." The papers of the middle and lower classes were available everywhere. The chief herald, the *Aftonblad*, had 4,000 subscribers. The more conservative had no advertising, "proof that they are not the papers of the people."

24. [Ferguson, Samuel]. "Our Portrait Gallery. No. I: Rev. Caesar Otway." 14 (1839): 396–97.
Narrated that in 1832, "to gratify the demand…for cheap literature" and "to aid in the diffusion of useful information" among the poor, Otway and George Petrie, Esq., conducted the *Dublin Penny Journal* for a year. *See* 14: 638.

25. "Our Portrait Gallery. No. II: Doctor Anster." 14 (1839): 544–46.
Opined that John Anster penned literary critiques "in an easy and pointed style."

26. [Ferguson, Samuel]. "Our Portrait Gallery. No. III: George Petrie, R.H.A., M.R.I.A." 14 (1839): 638–42.
Pegged Petrie as coeditor, with Rev. Caesar Otway, of the *Dublin Penny Journal*. *See* 14: 396.

27. "The Way We Do Things." 15 (1840): 66–74.
Sketched the contents of a typical review: a "Leading article...of dogmatic severity"; a "German extravaganza"; something on antiquities and a tour; a personal narrative; a poem; and book reviews. "Reviewing is the foundation of all periodical writing," but it took genius to weave assessments of many books together. Because reviews affected sales, bias of contributors was a factor. They included the serious writer with "sentences of fearful length"; the fashionable, with "insipid jargon"; the logical, with statistics; the "ideal college student," who "smokes inveterately and occasionally ventures on opium" leaving readers in "a state of excited confusion"; the poetry reviewers who "cannot utter a sentence but in extremes."

28. [Ferguson, Samuel]. "*The Dublin Penny Journal*." 15 (1840): 112–28.
Responded to a charge in *Saunders' News-Letter* (3 December 1839) by Philip Dixon Hardy, proprietor of the captioned journal, that the *Dublin University* was trying to ruin his reputation and trade by claiming that the *Journal* deteriorated after he became owner. From excerpts of the *Journal*, Ferguson concluded that under Caesar Otway it was "distinguished for lively and agreeable writing" and under George Petrie circulation "shot up." Hardy offered plagiarized matter and "Irish legend of the lowest kind," but his ill health, not a drop in circulation, caused the *Journal's* demise.

29. "Gallery of Illustrious Irishmen. No. XI: Jonathan Swift." 15 (1840): 131–44, 333–44, 538–56, 634–61.
Judged that Swift ran the *Examiner* with energy during his seven months as editor. Because his appointment came as Joseph Addison retired as editor of the *Whig Examiner*, Swift had no conflict with a friend though newspapers had not yet replaced pamphlets as a political medium.

30. [Butler, W. A.]. "Our Portrait Gallery. No. X: Mrs. S. C. Hall." 16 (1840): 146–49.
Underscored Anna M. Hall's "numerous contributions" to periodicals, many in "an elegant style."

31. [Ferguson, Samuel]. "Our Portrait Gallery. No. XI: the Rev. Charles Stuart Stanford." 16 (1840): 266–68.
Honored the first editor of the *Dublin University*.

32. [O'Sullivan, Samuel]. "Our Portrait Gallery. No. XIII: Isaac Butt, Esq., LL.D., Professor of Political Economy in the University of Dublin." 16 (1840): 506–10.
Mentioned Butt's essays in the *Dublin University*.

33. [Otway, Caesar]. "Our Portrait Gallery. No. XV: William Carleton." 17 (1841): 66–72.
Skimmed Carleton's work for the *Dublin University* and *Christian Examiner*.

34. [M'Glashan, James]. "Postscript to Our Hundredth Number." 17 (1841): 528–32.

Editorial history of the *Dublin University* claimed that its goal was to promote Irish interests but that its readers came from Ireland and beyond. Aside that most newspapers displayed "honest impartiality" in literary reviews if not in political columns.

35. [Lever, Charles]. "Our Portrait Gallery. No. XXI: William Hamilton Maxwell." 18 (1841): 220–25.

Marked Maxwell's work in the *Dublin University* and *Bentley's Miscellany*, where his articles were some of "its best."

36. Editor [Charles Lever]. "Our Contributors at the Brunnens." 18 (1841): 500–08.

Smiled at the departure of *Dublin University* writers for German spas.

37. Lorrequer, Harry [Charles Lever]. "Introduction." 19 (1842): 423–24.

New editor planned to publish more varied articles and book reviews for those with time to read only a magazine. The *Dublin University* "journalist" came from the "highest walks of periodical literature." Because "stipendiary" contributors sent enough material, others should not submit long unsolicited manuscripts.

38. [Butler, W. A. and Charles Lever]. "The Late Rev. Caesar Otway." 19 (1842): 546–58.

Memorialized Otway's work for the *Dublin University* and *Christian Examiner.*

39. [Starkey, D. P.]. "Our Portrait Gallery. No. XXXI: The Right Hon. John Wilson Croker, L.L., F.R.S." 19 (1842): 796–800.

Looked at Croker's articles in the *Quarterly Review*. Aside that all periodical writing was "miniature labour."

40. Printer's Devil [Charles Lever]. "The Sub-Editor's Snuggery." 20 (1842): 123–26.

Satirized the newspaper subeditor faced with letters that ranged from compliments to complaints, from job hunting to advice seeking.

41. [Lever, Charles]. "Continental Countries. No. I: Belgium." 20 (1842): 403–14.

Investigated the Belgian press. The literary journals – the *Artiste*, *National*, and *Edinburgh Review of Belgium* – had a "range of information" by "most accurate reasoners." The dailies were weak, and the journalists were mostly "third and fourth rate contributors of Parisian journals" who substituted "license" for wit.

42. [Lever, Charles]. "Continental Countries. No. II: Holland." 21 (1843): 224–31.

Avowed that Holland had a free press since 1840. The *Handelsbad* was the chief paper with 4,000 subscribers. Next, with 2,000 subscribers, was the *Avonbode* edited by a man of "high literary character," but the *Haarlem Chronicle* was the oldest journal in Europe.

43. [O'Sullivan, Samuel]. "A Biographical Sketch of the Late John Sydney Taylor." 21 (1843): 232–48.

Tracked Taylor's press career from columns in the *Morning Chronicle*, a leading paper thanks to James Perry's "zeal, skill, and true liberality." Taylor next started the *Talisman* before managing the *Morning Herald*. He then divided his time between being a barrister and "a public journalist."

44. [Taylor, W. C.]. "Mormonism; or, New Mohammedanism in England and America." 21 (1843): 283–98.

Unmasked the *Millennial Star* as a Mormon paper launched by Parley Pratt in Liverpool.

45. B[utler, W. A.]. "Sydney Smith's *Works*." 21 (1843): 540–54.

Reckoned that Smith was not a strong "public instructor," although his humor publicized abuses. Periodical writers should not reprint their articles as collections because books could not recapture the topic's original excitement and could expose "sameness of style." Those who published in elite journals should not aim for "individual fame" but "luster" for their journals.

46. [Graves, Robert J.]. "Wilde's *Austria*." 22 (1843): 89–101.

Review of J. R. Wilde's book conveyed that 15 Austrian cities had access to the official *Provinzial Zeitung* as well as every government department's *Amsblatt*. Major imperial newspapers were the *Austrian Observer* and *Magyar Kurir*. Of Vienna's half dozen journals, the *Wiener Zeitung* had the largest circulation. Foreign news came from the *Allgemeine Zeitung* and foreign papers. In 1833 the German states sent 252, France 116, the Italian states 35, and England 20, but there were fewer in 1843 because of stricter censorship. Austria also had "higher periodical literature," 76 mostly based in northern Italy that reflected a variety of interests. The "Austrian journal of eminence" was the *Jahrbücher der Literatur*.

47. H[olmes], M[rs.] D[alkeith] [Augusta]. "The Feuilletonists of France." 22 (1843): 701–19.

Singled out Delphine Gay, who adopted the alias Vicomte de Launay for her weekly "Courrier de Paris" in her husband's *Presse*; Eugene Sue, "the most prolific" feuilletonist, who wrote about the vilest citizens; and Jules Janin, the critic.

48. [Kenealy, E. V. H.]. "Our Portrait Gallery. No. XXXIV: William Maginn, LL.D." 23 (1844): 72–101.

Extolled Maginn's "libelous" articles in *Blackwood's Magazine* for their "profusion of wit and learning." In 1824 Maginn moved to Paris as foreign editor of the *Representative*. After the paper died, he contributed to magazines, annuals, and newspapers until he became editor of *Fraser's Magazine*, a position that marked the "zenith" of his career. Maginn authored most of its "Gallery of Literary Portraits." These essays, "the most original and sparkling" of his work, were accompanied by the sketches of Daniel Maclise. *Fraser's* "soon attained a circulation the most extensive and respectable of any of the London published periodicals," but a quarrel with the publisher, James Fraser, forced Maginn to withdraw until Fraser died in 1841. Aside on Maginn's other press writing.

49. [Lever, Charles]. "*Paris and Its People*." 23 (1844): 102–11.

Review of James Grant's book pontificated that "newspapers of every country, even where most powerful, are rather the 'indices' than the suggestors of public sentiment."

50. [Hayman, Samuel]. "*Life of Gerald Griffin*." 23 (1844): 157–70.
Review of a book by "His Brother" enlightened that Gerald Griffin had at age 18 edited a Limerick newspaper, the *Advertiser*. Then he supported himself by "reporting trials for newspapers" and penning for periodicals, where his anonymous articles garnered "high praise" from editors. He next was a parliamentary reporter until the *Literary Gazette* retained him.

51. "Girardin's *Cours de Littérature [Dramatique]*." 23 (1844): 589–99.
Review of St. Marc Giradin's book remarked that "his great reputation rests upon his political writing in the [*Journal des*] *Débats*." There he was akin to *The Times* "Thunderer," a man of party, not of the classics.

52. [Anster, John]. "*Life and Writings of the Late William Taylor of Norwich*." 24 (1844): 152–62.
Review of a book compiled by J. W. Robberds quoted him that Taylor directed the foreign department when the *Monthly Review* was at its peak. He reputedly set the standard for periodical reviews that went beyond mere analysis of a book, a standard midway between the useless and the detailed, the latter typical of the *Edinburgh Review* and *Quarterly Review*. Letters between Taylor and the editor of the *Monthly Review* demonstrated how the "editor of a popular review condescended to correspond with one of his authors." Taylor also penned 800 articles, 1796–1825, for the *Monthly Magazine*.

53. "Our Portrait Gallery. No. XXXVI: The Right Hon. Francis Blackburne." 24 (1844): 470–78.
Synopsized Attorney-General Blackburne's prosecution of the owner of the *Pilot* for publishing a letter of Daniel O'Connell.

54. [Ferguson, Samuel]. "Eugene Sue." 24 (1844): 702–17.
Cautioned that British readers disliked "the indiscriminate censure and panegyric which sordid interests have substituted for honest criticism in most of our metropolitan organs."

55. [Lever, Charles]. "*Memoirs of the Reign of George the Third*." 25 (1845): 227–41.
Review of Horace Walpole's book revisited John Wilkes.

56. [Hayman, Samuel]. "The Late Mrs. James Gray." 25 (1845): 327–31.
Silhouetted Mary Ann Brown Gray, the wife of a founder of *Blackwood's Magazine* and herself a periodical writer who preferred anonymity.

57. [Ferrari, Giuseppe]. "The Insurrections and Insurgents of Italy." 27 (1846): 304–14, 409–26.
Article from the *Revue des Deux Mondes* denigrated eighteenth-century Naples' officials who sentenced readers of Florence's *Gazetta* to six months in jail. In 1831 the city's *Antologia* was suppressed.

58. [Walsh, John Edward]. "Ireland Sixty Years Ago." 27 (1846): 543–62.
Unearthed the eighteenth-century *Cooney's Morning Post* and *Dalkey Gazette*, papers of Dalkey Island in the bay of Dublin.

59. [O'Sullivan, Samuel]. "Bell's *Life of Canning*." 28 (1846): 109–26.
Review of Robert Bell's book on George Canning broadcast that he penned considerable 'scurrility' in the *Anti-Jacobin*.

60. "Paris in 1846." 28 (1846): 179–86.
Exclaimed that "[j]ournalism is carried to an extraordinary extent in Paris" thanks to 40 papers, 20 of news and politics. Although many had less news and certainly fewer advertisements than a typical London daily, the French serials were more intellectual irrespective of the feuilletons. The daily and Sunday, available in inexpensive reading rooms, had bigger circulations than those of London.

61. A[nster, John]. "*Life and Correspondence of John Foster*." 28 (1846): 491–508.
Review of Foster's book tagged him "a diligent contributor" to the *Eclectic Review*.

62. [Kenealy, E. V. H.]. "Laman Blanchard." 28 (1846): 509–24.
Selected Blanchard as an example of "magazine scribblers" and "clever men who exhaust their mental wealth on newspapers and reviews" to get "ready pay from that great, shallow-headed patron, the 'reading public.'" He was subeditor of the *Monthly Magazine* and coeditor of *True Sun*. After 1832 he supported himself in a variety of venues. He was editor of "George Cruikshank's clever magazine, the *Omnibus*"; subeditor of *Ainsworth's Magazine* after it merged with the *Omnibus*; and a contributor to Henry Colburn's *New Monthly Magazine*, which like all "monthly magazines craved incessantly for new 'copy.'" After his death in 1845, Colburn gave Blanchard's friends the copyright for the *New Monthly* articles and these, with his *Ainsworth's* essays, were republished.

63. [O'Sullivan, Samuel]. "Adolphe Thiers." 28 (1846): 553–71, 635–47.
Abridged Thiers' journalism: writer for the *Courrier Française*; part owner of the *Constitutionnel* when it was "the most influential journal on the continent of Europe"; and a founder of the *National* that figured prominently in the July Revolution. Aside that J. F. Cotta, owner of the *Allgemeine Zeitung*, was honest.

64. [O'Sullivan, Samuel]. "Guizot." 29 (1847): 265–76.
Article on François Guizot mentioned Pauline de Meulan, editor of the *Publiciste* for which he was a leader-writer while she was ill.

65. A[nster, John]. "Leigh Hunt's *Men, Women, and Books*." 30 (1847): 386–97.
Analyzed Hunt's book that was "a selection of papers, written from time to time, in the popular London and Edinburgh journals, reviews of books, and notices of one kind or other of such matters as a periodical writer, from some incident of the day or hour, or from some passing humour of his own mind, might think likely to attract the attention of an unoccupied reader." "Let no man think lightly of periodical literature," which had been "reforming and refining" society since the days of Joseph Addison, Richard Steele, and Samuel Johnson.

66. "The French Revolution of 1848." 31 (1848): 523–36.
Explained that the French government portrayed journalists as "[l]icentious, anarchical," but some were able, even courageous.

67. "*Paddiana.*" 31 (1848): 715–27.
Review of R. F. Walond's book on Irish life saw *The Times* as "a mighty organ of English opinion."

68. "Theodore Hook." 33 (1849): 81–89.
Defended Hook against his critics, among them J. G. Lockhart in the *Quarterly Review* (72: 53) and many whose political careers or social standing he advanced. Hook was not a literary man, and his "severe reviews" in *John Bull*, the newspaper started in 1820 to defend George IV, were sometimes retaliatory. Hook earned 2,000 pounds per year from his share in that journal and "a liberal salary as editor." Aside that Henry Brougham had a "servile devotion" to "the newspaper press."

69. "No one [O'Sullivan, Samuel]. "A Provision for the Roman Catholic Clergy Considered, in a Letter to the Editor of the *Quarterly Review.*" 33 (1849): 102–17.
Lauded the *Quarterly* as "a publication which commands an extensive circulation and exercises a powerful influence over the national mind." Its "moral character" was "deservedly high, and its judgment upon important and critical subjects often such as to influence the decision of the legislature in matters seriously affecting the public weal."

70. Kappa [A. V. Kirwan]. "France: A Retrospect of the Year 1848." 33 (1849): 134–50.
Spotted "habitual conspirators" at the *Réforme* and *National*. They were "editors, printers" who gave authority to the February 1848 government and received patronage in return. Aside that *The Times* had "unparalleled power in securing early and speedy intelligence."

71. [O'Sullivan, Samuel]. "*The Times* and the 'New Irish Poor-Law.'" 33 (1849): 221–27.
Resented "editorial dictum" from *The Times* about Irish affairs even if it was a "great journal."

72. A[nster, John]. "The Poet Campbell." 33 (1849): 245–62.
Disclosed that Thomas Campbell's "fixed engagements with the *Philosophical Magazine* and the *Star* newspaper" netted him 200 pounds a year. As editor of the *New Monthly Magazine* after 1820, he earned 500–600 pounds a year but left in 1829 to edit the *Metropolitan*.

73. Kappa [A. V. Kirwan]. "France – The Inauguration of 1849." 33 (1849): 265–80.
Charged that during the June Days, the government jailed many editors, some because the *National* wished to punish its enemies.

74. [Boyd, Percy]. "Our Portrait Gallery. No. LI: James W. Whiteside, Q.C." 33 (1849): 326–39.
Glanced at Whiteside's essays in the *Literary Gazette* and "Irish periodicals now extinct."

75. [O'Sullivan, Mortimer]. "*The Times*, Lord Brougham, and the Irish Law Courts." 33 (1849): 478–83.
Indicted *The Times* publisher for sedition and "inducement of a depraved public opinion." "While Irish journalists have been prosecuted, with exemplary rigour, for seditious and pernicious publications, the Attorney-General for England has never proceeded against *The Times*, for these mischievous

libels in which the Queen's English and Irish subjects have been daily, for several years back, excited to mutual hostility in the columns of that journal." Aside on the *Press*, "a new Dublin paper."

76. "Our Portrait Gallery. No. LV: Thomas Crofton Croker, F.S.A., M.R.I.A" 34 (1849): 202–16.

Bowed to Croker's short-lived 1820 *Talisman*, and his "active and regular" contributions to *Fraser's Magazine* in the 1830s.

77. [Waller, J. F.]. "Doctor Cooke Taylor." 34 (1849): 495–96.

Remembered William Cooke Taylor's many essays for the *Dublin University* and his work for "the *Evening Post*, the Irish government paper."

78. [O'Sullivan, Samuel]. "Canada." 35 (1850): 151–68.

Chronicled that the "Canadian people have been taught to look to *The Times* as an exponent of the feelings of the British people." Yet it and others were "insulting, sneering" in some Canadian columns, a bias the *Montreal Herald* and *Montreal Gazette* deplored.

79. [O'Sullivan, Samuel]. "*Life and Correspondence of Robert Southey*." 35 (1850): 236–53; 36 (1850): 113–21; 37 (1851): 37–52.

Review of a book edited by C. C. Southey glided over the contributors to and celebrity of the early *Edinburgh Review*.

80. [O'Sullivan, Mortimer]. "The Orangemen and the *Quarterly* and *Edinburgh Reviews*." 35 (1850): 254–69.

Omitted an appraisal of the *Edinburgh* but not the *Quarterly*: "that great publication claims the highest position in the British periodical press."

81. [Anster, John]. "Leigh Hunt." 36 (1850): 268–86.

Review of Hunt's *Autobiography* etched his *Examiner* as unpartisan, one whose "writers were honest men, not well-informed, very confident, very clever, very witty, and doing business in a style exceedingly likely to vex the persons whom they – more for the fun than anything else – were in the weekly habit of showing up for ridicule." "The *Examiner* gave offence to people in power, and it was indicted more than once for libel." Hunt, who was in contact with Theodore Hook and other editors, ran or contributed to several other papers (listed).

82. "Lord Clarendon's Policy in Ireland." 37 (1851): 136–58.

Labeled the *Tablet* the organ of Roman Catholics and the *World* a satirical serial whose editor took bribes.

83. [Masson, David]. "William and Robert Chambers." 37 (1851): 177–90.

Scrutinized *Chambers's Journal* at length. Although preceded by a "cheap, weekly sheet" of Leigh Hunt and faced with early competition from the *Penny Magazine* of Charles Knight, William and Robert Chambers produced an inexpensive periodical "of a superior tone, carefully prepared, and with comprehensive views as regarded popular enlightenment," a serial that aired "solid, clear matter of a miscellaneous character." The *Journal's* circulation (1832: 50,000; 1840: 72,000) rose, notably after a change in format from folio to octavo in 1844 (1845: 90,000), but never reached the numbers of the *Penny Magazine*, "cheaper, and also embellished with woodcuts." After it and the *Saturday Magazine* ended, the *People's Journal*, *Hogg's Weekly Instructor*, *Eliza Cook's Journal*, *Household Words*, and others entered the ranks as well as the *Family Herald*, albeit "of a somewhat different class." The numerous authors committed to *Chambers's* goals to instruct and amuse cost 1,000 pounds annually. Many writers of quality penned for cheap "popular periodicals" because the pay was better than for "dear literature."

84. "Johnston's *England as It Is*." 37 (1851): 351–69.
Excerpted William Johnston's book on how to establish a London morning paper, from initial capital required (50,000 pounds) to securing staff, printing, and distributing.

85. "Roche's Varieties of Literature." 37 (1851): 454–67.
Pirated from James Roche's *Critical and Miscellaneous Essays* that the priorities of leader-writers in the dailies were "actuality," "freshness of sentiment," and "direct reference to what is passing through the heads of the readers or of the public at large." To be *au courant*, these writers sought information from "first hand sources, or from approved 'go-betweens.'" Style was secondary.

Classed as journalists "proprietors, managers, editors, and leader-writers of a daily." Newspapers were not merely "the transcript and utterance of popular and passing emotion" but "the thinking aloud of a nation." Newspapers bared the "character and ideas" of a people, "the convictions of society," "the wishes, if not the wants, of an age."

86. [Waller, J. F.]. "The Late Rev. Samuel O'Sullivan, D.D." 38 (1851): 504–08.
Acknowledged that O'Sullivan's articles gave the *Dublin University* "a high place in literature." He also contributed to *Blackwood's Magazine* and *Fraser's Magazine*.

87. "John Sterling and His Biographers." 39 (1852): 185–99.
Stated that Sterling's father Edward was part owner of and perhaps a foreign correspondent for *The Times*.

88. "Ireland under Lord Clarendon." 39 (1852): 237–76.
Decreed that the *World* "had neither character, political influence, nor circulation" though it hit 6,000 weekly. It dealt primarily in private scandal but offered an occasional political piece. In 1848 money began to come from Lord Clarendon, perhaps as a payoff.

Questioned an earlier prosecution of the *United Irishman* for treason in newspaper articles that advocated no overt action. Eventually, its papers were seized, its presses broken. Its successors, *Felon* and *Treason*, were more dangerous.

89. [Anster, John]. "*Life of Lord Jeffrey*." 39 (1852): 625–39, 722–30.
Review of Henry Cockburn's book recounted the birth of the *Edinburgh Review*, whose editor, Francis Jeffrey, understood that the press was a shaper of opinion.

90. D[owe], W[illiam]. "Touching the Identity of Junius." 40 (1852): 1–18.
Referenced attempts to identify Junius, as in the *North British Review* (19: 475).

91. "Autobiography – Jerdan and Miss Mitford." 40 (1852): 289–306.
Concentrated on William Jerdan, "editor of a publication – half newspaper, half magazine – called the *Literary Gazette*," who had previously had "a good deal of experience in the management of political newspapers." "The *Literary Gazette*, if not conducted with any great ability, was certainly remarkable for its general kindliness of tone."

92. [Waller, J. F.]. "Our Past, Our Present, and Our Future." 41 (1853): 1–8.
Editor, on the twentieth anniversary of the *Dublin University*, reiterated that its purpose was to serve Ireland in the way that *Blackwood's Magazine* and the *Edinburgh Review* served Scotland. Saluted several contributors by name, many of whom began their careers in the periodical.

"The British press is the most candid, the most enlightened, the most incorruptible…in the world," and "while it exists, freedom of speech and freedom of thought shall ever be secured to us." "Long may popular opinion thus find its legitimate exponent and its legitimate guide."

93. "Our Portrait Gallery. No. LXXI: Thomas Colley Grattan, Esq." 42 (1853): 658–65.
Marked Grattan as a "constant contributor to the English periodicals." Although he lived in Paris, he wrote for the *Edinburgh Review*, *Westminster Review*, *New Monthly Magazine*, and *North American Review*, the "great literary authority in America."

94. [Waller, J. F.]. "Editorial Embarrassments." 43 (1854): 369–78.
Confessed that many contributions to the *Dublin University* were not read, so it published some poems by lot.

95. [Patterson, R. H.]. "Professor Wilson – 'Christopher North.'" 43 (1854): 615–24.
Gushed that John Wilson, whose articles were full of "zest," was the "intellectual Atlas" of *Blackwood's Magazine*.

96. "American Ambition and Europe's Dilemma." 44 (1854): 111–28.
Aside on "the Madrid correspondent of the *Morning Herald*."

97. [Wilde, Jane F.]. "*The Countess of Blessington*." 45 (1855): 333–53.
Review of R. R. Madden's book peeked at Marguerite Blessington's pieces in the *New Monthly Magazine* but stressed her work for annuals. Her title helped annuals, whose basis was "personal vanity" embodied in the pictures of beautiful noblewomen, to sell. As an editor she received 2,000 pounds per year, but authors, unless of great reputation, were not paid. Aristocrats were always ready to write for annuals but were not popular with readers.

98. [Jeaffreson, J. Cordy]. "Daniel De Foe [*sic*]." 48 (1856): 57–71.
Testified that Defoe's *Review*, of which he was the sole scribe, was "the parent" of the *Tatler*, *Spectator*, and *Rambler*.

99. "Lord Brougham." 48 (1856): 113–26.
Reviewed Henry Brougham's *Contributions to the Edinburgh Review*.

100. [Brady, Cheyne]. "Popular Education in the British Empire." 48 (1856): 240–52.
Bruited that Robert Raikes had a newspaper, the *Gloucester Journal*, in the 1780s.

101. [Corkran, J. F.]. "Lamartine, *Homme de Lettres*." 48 (1856): 408–23.
Itemized Alphonse de Lamartine's press career. He wrote the entire monthly *Conseiller du Peuple* (later *Civilisateur*); essays for another monthly, the *Cours Familier de Littérature* (circulation 20,000); and columns for the *Siècle*, *Constitutionnel*, and *Presse*.

102. [Lever, Charles]. "How must Sardinia Fight Austria?" 48 (1856): 505–13.
Logged that Piedmont had no free press, only the official *Monitore* filled with exchange rates, theatre notices, and "carefully culled passages from French and English newspapers."

103. "Slavery." 48 (1856): 675–90.
Thundered that newspapers in the American South, as the *Muscogee* (AL) *Herald*, read "more like the ravings of delirious than the reasonings of determined men."

104. "Our Antipodean Neighbours." 48 (1856): 735–48.
Review of *Two Years in Victoria* by William Howitt and *A Residence in Tasmania* by Capt. H. Butler Storey registered that Melbourne had "several daily and other journals" and its own *Punch*.

105. "Realities of the Late War." 49 (1857): 229–37.
Regarding Crimea, "the Press is accused of having pandered to the popular clamour against the aristocracy, of having exaggerated such mismanagement as existed, and, through ignorance of military affairs, having confounded the inevitable hardships of warfare." *The Times* "acrid hostility" to the staff officer who wrote *Letters from Head-Quarters*, which exposed "unavoidable and pardonable misrepresentations" by the paper, might be fodder for enemies of press liberty.

106. "Transportation." 49 (1857): 322–34.
Fumed that *The Times* 'fashions its doctrines to the varying hour' instead of guiding opinion.

107. J[errold], W. B. "Madame Puff." 49 (1857): 456–60.
Scorned periodical writers, particularly women fashion columnists, who excessively promoted goods.

108. [Tupper, Martin F.]. "The Rides and Reveries of Mr. Aesop Smith, No. VI." 49 (1857): 621–30.
Satirized how an editor coordinated journalists, each with "name and fame," "temperament and talent," all bent on success and convinced of their own influence. The tempting advertisements of local newspapers might corrupt "rustics"; the leaders in *The Times* did inspire people to raise themselves in society. Aside that the newspaper was a 'history of the world for to-day.'

109. C[ole], J. W. "William Howard Russell, *The Times* Special Correspondent in the Crimea." 50 (1857): 279–92.
Premised that a "considerable preponderance of living literary talent is engaged in the leading magazines, reviews, and newspapers." "The remuneration is ample and immediate, the labor

comparatively light, the subjects diversified, the demand perpetually on the increase, and the competition great."

Russell, an Irishman, was a journalist of accuracy and style who first wrote for *The Times* in 1843 when he covered Daniel O'Connell's meetings. In 1845 he worked on railroad reports before he was appointed to the paper's permanent staff and dispatched to Ireland. He went to the *Morning Chronicle* in 1847 but soon returned to *The Times*. His postings from Crimea galvanized public opinion enough to move the government and catalyzed a debate about whether reporters should be at a war front, that is, whether to prioritize press liberty or patriotism.

110. "How We Talked about the Indian Mutiny: An Extract from the Journal of a Public Servant." 50 (1857): 625–38, 742–57.

Sanctioned suspension of the press in times of crisis because Indian journals copied false information about government from Anglo-Indian sheets.

111. "A Week with *The Times*." 51 (1858): 40–50.

Contended that leaders in *The Times*, though many and excellent, were quickly forgotten or hard to access, so abstracted them for the week beginning Thursday, 3 December 1857. Penned by those who "learned to think from the great masters of antiquity," these columns of contemporary history were "rarely personal, never immoral or irreligious" and created "a national taste for good English."

112. [Corkran, J. F.]. "*A Year of Revolution*." 51 (1858): 50–56.

Review of book by C. H. Phipps, Marquis of Normanby and British ambassador to France in 1848, asserted that French reporting and commentary were sophisticated. Descriptive writing seemed "to have caught its inspiration from the daguerreotype."

113. "British Stokers and Italian Sympathies." 51 (1858): 157–66.

Unveiled how a *Times* correspondent adopted "various disguises" to get "early, exclusive, and authentic information."

114. [Corkran, J. F.]. "Pierre Jean Béranger." 51 (1858): 437–50.

Review of Béranger's *Memoirs* designated *Minerva* (NY) "a journal of considerable reputation."

115. "The Times and *The Times*." 51 (1858): 663–67.

Reveled that in Britain "there is no stronger instance of this vitality in our constitution, energizing, leavening, and leading the masses, than the power of the Press." "The free press is the viceroy of a free people." By contrast, French papers vacillated between being the "exponent of anarchical licence and of abject submission," and other Continental governments controlled their journals.

116. [Kent, Charles]. "The Right Hon. Sir Edward Bulwer Lytton: His Career, His Genius, and His Writings." 52 (1858): 34–56.

Described E. G. Bulwer-Lytton as a hardworking editor who aimed to make the *New Monthly Magazine* "a critical and political organ." A "genial and sagacious" writer, he authored many quality essays for the *Monthly Chronicle*, *Edinburgh Review*, *Foreign Quarterly Review*, and *Westminster Review*. In Parliament he campaigned for reduction of the stamp duty and the "grinding" one on advertising.

117. [Dobbin, O. T.]. "The Works of the Rev. R. A. Vaughan." 52 (1858): 559–67.
Assessed several articles by Vaughan, who edited the *British Quarterly Review* and wrote "lighter papers" for *Fraser's Magazine* and elsewhere.

118. [Kennedy, Patrick]. "Irish Archeological Publications." 52 (1858): 629–40.
Deemed the *Ulster Journal* the "most successful" of the titled genre.

119. [Corkran, J. F.]. "M. de Montalembert on the Indian Debate." 53 (1859): 118–28.
Revealed that Count C. de Montalembert, in his "panegyric" pamphlet on England, praised its press mainly for the freedom apparent in discussions of issues. Corkran believed that *The Times* and *Saturday Review* reports on India had "a masculine vigour and a fearless eloquence."

120. "Massy's *History of England*." 53 (1859): 192–206.
Review of William Massy's book dismissed late eighteenth-century newspapers as "feeble and inefficient," leashed by law as the case of John Wilkes evidenced.

121. [Brooke, Stopford]. "New Novels." 53 (1859): 483–95.
Observed that the defunct *Irish Metropolitan Magazine* was "spirited and clever" and "marked in a high degree by taste and scholarship."

122. [Heard, J. B.]. "Italy, Seen Through French Spectacles." 53 (1859): 750–62.
Calculated that nine of ten Englishmen read *The Times*, and the rest perused the *Daily News*, *Globe*, *Morning Post*, *Morning Chronicle*, or *Morning Herald*.

123. [Bigg, John S.]. "Heinrich Heine." 54 (1859): 590–98.
Flagged Heine's work in the *Revue des Deux Mondes* and the *Allgemeine Zeitung* for which he was Paris correspondent.

124. [Kent, Charles]. "W. M. Thackeray – Satirist and Humorist." 54 (1859): 630–40; 55 (1860): 22–35.
Detailed that Thackeray's stepfather directed London's *Constitutional* for which Douglas Jerrold was theatre critic and Laman Blanchard, literary. Dudley Costello reported foreign affairs, and Thackeray was Paris correspondent before moving to *Fraser's Magazine* and *Punch*.

125. [Heard, J. B.]. "France, England, and Italy." 54 (1859): 754–62.
Confided that the French government asked the British to suppress "irritating articles" about France. Aside on the *Revue Indépendante*, a London monthly published by "Jeffs, the intelligent foreign bookseller of the Burlington Arcade."

126. [Corkran, J. F.]. "On Advances Towards Liberty in France." 55 (1860): 131–44.
Welcomed greater freedom for the French press as long as it did not lead to licentiousness.

127. [Heard, J. B.]. "Our Political Chorus." 56 (1860): 226–36, 500–08.
Likened British newspapers to a Greek chorus, "a running commentary on the action," important because of Britain's global influence.

Speculated about the impact of penny prints on *Times* circulation after abolition of the paper duty. (Heard expanded his perception of the effect of cheap dailies in a regular column [57: 760]: "trivial twaddling journalism" of a "run-and-read system.")

128. [Heard, J. B.]. "Political Chronicle." 56 (1860): 329–38.
Noticed articles, by St. Marc Girardin in the *Revue des Deux Mondes*, on restraint of the French press. French officials differed from British who considered government responsible to public opinion expressed "through the Press."

129. "The Vice of Our Current Literature." 56 (1860): 515–28.
Defined the captioned vice as wordiness. "No one would seek in the *London Journal* or the *Family Herald* for fine samples of close reasoning and careful English." Yet a "penny-a-liner's account of a dreadful accident or a mysterious occurrence has its charm for many who would be slow to appreciate the beauties of a leading article in *The Times*," whose faults came from the pressure of producing a daily. Aside that anonymity in journalism was decreasing as new serials emerged.

130. [Brady, Cheyne]. "Anon, Anon, Sir!" 57 (1861): 284–89.
Emphasized that until recently journalists were anonymous, but people guessed their identities because "[u]nderneath the kindly veil of the anonymous the witchery of good writing could not be hidden." Anonymity allowed public opinion to be based on an idea, not a person; encouraged young authors; kept the genius in bounds; and, most importantly, protected the minority in a democratic state. "The Press is the great – ay the only organ by which the minority can make their voice heard." Signing, as the French discovered, was "a cunning device to break down the power of the Press" and wrongly permitted personality to shape opinion. Better to have the anonymous in the *Saturday Review* "criticise professional people in an unprofessional way" than to ape Americans using signature to sell papers. Current "prying curiosity into personal details" did not justify intruding on journalists' private lives.

131. [Hall, J.]. "China." 57 (1861): 560–69.
Doubted that *The Times* and *All the Year Round* filed accurate China reports.

132. [Trotter, L. J.]. "A Batch of Last Year's Novels." 59 (1862): 396–409.
Bewailed that *Reynolds's Miscellany* and the *London Journal* had "grosser fare" than a novel by W. M. Thackeray and that the *Morning Star* was full of "democratic hatred, malice."

133. [Scott, J. A.]. "The British Newspaper: The Penny Theory and Its Solution." 61 (1863): 359–76.
The newspaper, "the symbol and citadel of free institutions," "made thoughtful patriots." It was "a bulwark of aggression from the lower orders, a guarantee against excesses among the higher." Because British journalism was "untrammeled," "competent to lead and influence," and resistant to bribery, it had "the confidence of the community." "It is itself under effective control, and serious irregularities are practically impossible. Its leading writers are men commonly of sound judgment, large experience in affairs, honest purpose, and scrupulous honour." Its victims probably deserved censure.

The British press was better than the press elsewhere, "unequaled…in its literary power, in its copiousness of intelligence, in the universality of its correspondence, in its very mechanical arrangements." The French press functioned under despotism. The American was neither informed nor instructive. By 1798, as *The Times* proved, the newspaper had a format (advertising, leader, news) but not the impartiality that soon made "its independent and important position." The Napoleonic wars and Catholic and reform "agitators" boosted sales. After 1832 they dropped until the "Corn Law controversy," which demonstrated the significance of the country papers. With more revenue from advertising, gazettes made greater efforts "to secure the early possession of news, to combine commercial departments with political, and to obtain more powerful writing." Wealthy dailies were able to encompass "every public interest."

Since about 1859 British journalism had "gone through what it is no exaggeration to call a terrible tempest, and has not even yet got into settled waters again." From 1861 to 1863, the number of newspapers rose from 1,102 to 1,206. Of these, London had 239, English localities 639, Ireland 134, Scotland 142, Wales 37, Channel Islands 15. England had 46 dailies with 21 in London; Ireland had 14, with six in Dublin; Scotland had nine. This proliferation, due mainly to abolition of duties, spawned "unhealthy and unscrupulous competition" among the inexperienced who envisioned the press as a source of power, wealth, and status. In three years, "*a quarter of a million sterling*" was lost in failed newspapers "by old defending and new squandering." London "speculators went crazy for a time on penny papers," but there was also competition in the country. A charge of slightly more than a penny would keep journalism from being "gambling." Dependence on advertisements was a problem when advertisers refused to pay or cancelled when business dipped and readers' tastes changed. Costs were high for production and the original writing that replaced earlier scissored columns, but both expenses were essential to compete.

Opponents of taxes had hoped that more journals would educate as had the American press, but attacks on older papers, usually foes of abolition, ended the dream. Many people expected the penny paper to have the same quality as the more expensive, but some accepted "congeries of penny-a-liners' reports and sensational canards." In the United States, James Gordon Bennett and his confreres were "public nuisances." "[I]n order to make American papers pay, the editors are obliged to appeal to, and systematically inflame the passions of democracy." "Crime is favoured with glowing records." "The accounts of the smallest matter of daily life are pitched in the highest key." Papers on the "western borders" were "miserable," edited by men of no experience, full of advertisements but not much news so that "public conscience is abased, a cool practical judgment upon matters of importance is rendered impossible." Americans turned to magazines and reviews when secession showed the "utter helplessness of a cheap and degraded press in a national crisis."

Some British penny gazettes had well-paid "first class" contributors, but even this press did not diminish the clout of the *Morning Post*, *Morning Herald*, *Daily News*, and *The Times*, "whose position is exceptional." The substantial country papers temporarily reduced their price or formed management alliances to survive; the rest were mostly advertising sheets. Unlike their American brethren, local papers "resist disturbing agitations at their inception."

The public had to pay for a quality press. Sheets "of flimsy paper and smutted printing" only benefited opticians, not readers or advertisers. In the country the penny might appeal to passers-by anxious to scan the telegrams or "fast writing" but carried no local news or analysis by "men of knowledge and experience."

Journalism should not be merely "a vehicle for Mr. Reuter's summaries and *canards*." "The journalist's is a profession of high honour, but it is also a business demanding uncommon attention, careful management of details, and a constant practical sagacity." Even before the penny press, it was not for amateurs.

Predicted that democracy would bring mass audiences and large profits to a few.

134. [Collins, Mortimer]. "Political Pasquinade and Comic Literature." 62 (1863): 363–72.

Esteemed pasquinades in the *Anti-Jacobin* and *John Bull* but not the "generally contemptible" ones in current comic periodicals, such as *Fun* and *Punch*. Dickens allegedly "gave the first impulse to this love of mere comicality and caricature." His influence on "small writers increased by his establishment of a cheap journal [*Household Words*]," which also exhibited "sham pathos." Aside that the *Saturday Review* was "self-conceited."

135. [Scott, J. A.]. "Half a Century of Literary Recollections." 63 (1864): 456–60.

Centered on publisher Charles Knight's *Windsor and Eton Gazette*, where he was "reporter, manager, editor," and *Knight's Quarterly Magazine*, written largely by a "brilliant set of Cambridge students." Aside that, c. 1819, the cheap *Black Dwarf* and its ilk were "vehicles of seditious and infidel opinions."

136. [Scott, J. A.]. "Phases of Life in Federal America." 63 (1864): 471–80.

Characterized American newspapers as unparalleled for "mischievous extravagance."

137. [Kennedy, Patrick]. "Léon Gozlan – A Word about His Life and Writings." 63 (1864): 673–84.

Touched on Gozlan's work in *Figaro*, edited by Nestor Rocqueplan, and other serials.

138. [Trotter, L. J.]. "Life in Munich." 63 (1864): 696–702.

Announced that Bavarian newspapers neglected politics, earlier assigning space to theatrical gossip and in 1864, to society chat.

139. [Kennedy, Patrick]. "A Triad of French Writers." 64 (1864): 330–41.

Starred Edmond About, who conducted the "*Gazette de Franche Comté*, a legitimatist journal, for twenty years" and published in the *Journal des Débats*, *Siècle*, and *Revue des Deux Mondes*.

140. [Scott, J. A.]. "Poland During the Insurrection of 1863–4." 64 (1864): 436–46.

Saluted correspondent W. H. Bullock for his hazardous work covering the captioned insurrection.

141. "Charles Lever's Essays." 64 (1864): 459–62.

Spoke of Lever's articles in the *Saturday Review* and *Blackwood's Magazine* and his writing as Harry Lorrequer and Cornelius O'Dowd.

142. [Scott, J. A.]. "England and Her Colonies." 64 (1864): 483–96.

Singled out Quebec's *Union Nationale* and *Daily News* as well as Toronto's *Globe*.

143. [Fitzgerald, Percy]. "About Charles Lamb, His Friends and Books." 65 (1865): 123–36.

Relayed that in Lamb's era, Leigh Hunt could "chatter pleasantly" in his serials while a coterie of his generation puffed each other. The *Literary Gazette* printed "trifling criticism, done in a flippantly slashing style," and the *Monthly Review* sank into "a sort of toothless dotage."

144. [Scott, J. A.]. "A Group of New Novels." 65 (1865): 339–51.
Accented that newspapers, which people read "extensively," aided novels' sales by circulating prompt reviews and advertisements.

145. [Scott, J. A.]. "Another Cluster of Novels." 65 (1865): 570–81.
Scorned novel reviews with "hackneyed" or dishonest judgments.

146. [Kennedy, Patrick]. "London." 66 (1865): 32–41, 544–52.
Cited the eighteenth-century *Public Advertiser*; Edward Cave's *Gentleman's Magazine* that gave "healthy employment to many a pamphleteer;" and the "cobbler of Cripplegate" in the *London Chronicle*, his era's *Punch*.

147. [Kennedy, Patrick]. "The Man Without a Vocation." 66 (1865): 206–11.
Headlined Louis C. Barbara, a Frenchman who penned for the *Revue de Paris*.

148. [Scott, J. A.]. "The Relations of England with America." 66 (1865): 709–16.
Hypothesized that American newspapers developed a "soberer style of writing" during the Civil War. Like the British press, the American press was "guided by public opinion" but molded it more than the British.

149. [LeFanu, J. S.]. "Fenianism." 67 (1866): 116–20.
Pondered the seizure of the *Irish People* and the trial of its principals for conspiracy in 1865.

150. [Scott, J. A.]. "The Fenian Conspiracy in America and in Ireland." 67 (1866): 464–80.
Investigated the seizure of the *Irish People* and the escape and subsequent arrest of its founder, James Stephen. The paper lacked the "ability" of the *Nation* but was "more pungent." Its editor, John O'Leary, was "the most vigorous though not the most refined" of writers.

151. [Hill, O'Dell T.]. "Balzac: His Literary Labours." 70 (1867): 510–29.
Informed that the *Revue de Paris* paid Balzac 250 francs per sheet, but its editor, François Buloz, complained that correcting, often rewriting Balzac's articles drove up expenses.

152. [Kennedy, Patrick]. "William Edmonstoune Aytoun." 70 (1867): 587–600.
Analyzed Aytoun's writing in *Blackwood's*, *Fraser's*, and *Tait's* magazines.

153. [Kennedy, Patrick]. "George Petrie." 73 (1869): 363–81.
Trailed Petrie from the *Dublin Examiner* in 1816, where he wrote leaders and fine arts columns. In 1832–33, with Caesar Otway and John Donovan, he "supported the valuable *Dublin Penny Journal*, and in 1840–41 he edited the *Irish Penny Post*." Both were the "best cheap periodicals" of Ireland and circulated in England.

154. [Kennedy, Patrick]. "A Century of English Caricature." 74 (1869): 3–28.
Resurrected the *Craftsman*, "conducted by Nicholas Amhurst" under the fictitious name, Caleb Danvers.

155. "A Set of National French Novels: the Erckmann-Châtrian Novels." 74 (1869): 363–77.

Ordained that writings akin to those in *Bow Bells* or the *Young Englishwoman's Magazine* did not belong in "a grave periodical like the *Revue des Deux Mondes*."

156. "Exclusive Intelligence – Reminiscences of an Elderly Member of the Fourth Estate: Fonthill Abbey." 76 (1870): 196–99.

Remembered that covering a local story once meant paying the costs of overnighting at inns.

157. [Kennedy, Patrick]. "Some Parisian Eccentrics." 77 (1871): 121–38.

Sketched Eugene Briffault, a feuilletonist, whom Paris editors highly regarded.

158. "*Vox Populi*, as Represented in Valentines." 77 (1871): 184–94.

Condemned journalistic anonymity that licensed a critic to lie to friends about the value of their work and an MP to manipulate the local press.

159. P[icciotto,], J[ames]. "The Prospects of Europe." 77 (1871): 322–33.

Aired that some journalists suppressed "unpleasant facts" relating to the Prussian invasion of France.

160. [Kennedy, Patrick]. "Irish Life Pictures of Yesterday." 77 (1871): 361–81.

Unmasked J. G. A. Prim as an early "proprietor and editor of the *Kilkenny Moderator*."

161. [Wraxall, Lascelles]. "Gambling-Houses in Germany." 77 (1871): 466–76.

Considered the German press "a power, at least in social matters," such as gambling. Its advertisements surfaced in the chief Frankfurt papers as well as the *Allgemeine Zeitung* and *Indépendance Belge*, but word of gambling was also "smuggled into the most respectable papers" in travel columns and feuilletons. Aside that Paris papers paid writers by the piece.

162. [Kennedy, Patrick]. "Two Centuries of Irish Literature." 78 (1871): 1–20.

Drew from R. R. Madden's *History of Irish Periodical Literature* for data on early newspapers, as the *Dublin News Letter* (1685), *Dublin Gazette* (1689), and *Dublin Intelligencer* (1690–94). The *News Letter* was a double-side folio with some advertisements while the *Intelligencer* was one-sided. *See* 80: 121.

163. Picciotto, James. "United Italy." 78 (1871): 241–56.

Enthused that "new political journals, new magazines, and periodicals of every imaginable character," many of "high literary merit," were cropping up regularly in Italy.

164. P[icciotto], J[ames]. "An Old Newspaper." 78 (1871): 557–68.

Perused the eight-page *London Chronicle* (Tuesday, 2 July 1771) containing letters, advertisements, essays and reviews, gossip, "foreign intelligence," and much news of the John Wilkes case. Among the periodicals advertised in the *Chronicle* were the *Town and Country Magazine*, *Oxford Magazine*, *Gentleman's and Lady's Magazine*, and *Wheble's Ladies Magazine*, with its "interesting articles." Aside that the British at home read Indian and Australian papers to learn about the British overseas.

165. "M. Thiers." 79 (1872): 92–100.
Glided over Adolphe Thiers' writing in the *Constitutionnel*.

166. [Elliott, Charles W.]. "San Francisco." 79 (1872): 218–28.
Warranted that San Francisco sold 500,000 copies of newspapers and magazines, such as *Harper's Monthly*, *Putnam's*, the *Atlantic Monthly*, and the locally published *Monthly Medical Journal* and *Occident*, "a weekly religious paper." There were 47 dailies and weeklies, "which as a whole aim high" and had "not fallen into the fashion of pandering to the baser propensities, nor made themselves the champions of the lower classes," although there were a few "despicable sheets," such as *Varieties*. "The leading papers, the *Evening Bulletin*, the *Alta Californian*, and the *Times*, rank high." They cost ten cents, whereas the *Morning Call*, with "an immense circulation and a great influence," charged two cents. There were also gazettes in French, Italian, German, and Spanish.

167. "The Cutting Style of Writing." 79 (1872): 415–25.
Dated the slashing style of political and literary press criticism from the Restoration, but among its later practitioners were Junius, William Hazlitt, J. G. Lockhart, J. W. Croker, and "the most renowned and the most vehement" in the nineteenth century, Theodore Hook, "a wit of the first water." He edited *John Bull*, the epitome of the genre. The paper "was intended for the perusal of the highest classes; was in a manner the organ of the Court, and was a triumph of successful journalism." The style persisted in *The Times* until the 1840s. With more and freer newspapers, slashing declined but was still alive in local papers and "medical" and "clerical" journals.

As serials multiplied, journalism emerged as an authentic and well-paid profession because journalists "feel the restraint of etiquette and honourable understanding." Writers, especially for "better periodicals," realized that shaping opinion gave them power, so they had no need to slash in contrast to New York newspapers.

168. "Charles Lever." 80 (1872): 104–09.
Evaluated Lever's writings in and direction of the *Dublin University* where he was very popular as editor.

169. [Kennedy, Patrick]. "Dublin Newspapers of Last Century." 80 (1872): 121–31, 241–47.
Borrowed, as in 78: 1, from R. R. Madden, whose contents' analyses and library location of eighteenth-century periodicals were apparently invaluable. A newspaper embodied the "spirit of its locality," whether the long-lived *Pue's Occurrences* (1703–92) or short *Postman*. *Walker's Hibernian Magazine* and the *Antologia Hibernica* were "equal in ability and entertainment to the best English periodicals, their contemporaries."

170. D[obson], W.T. "Benjamin Disraeli." 80 (1872): 511–15.
Elucidated Disraeli's tie to the *Representative*.

171. N., L. M. "Thomas Hood." 81 (1873): 99–112.
Alluded to Hood's writing for the *Comic Annual* and editing of the *New Monthly Magazine* (for 300 pounds per year) and his own *Hood's Magazine*.

172. [Elliott, Charles W.]. "Peking and the Chinese." 81 (1873): 384–93.
Declared that in China "[n]o newspapers exist and the *Peking Gazette* is only printed to give forth the imperial decrees of the Emperor and the news of the government."

173. [Waller, J. F.]. "Patrick Kennedy." 81 (1873): 581–82.
Eulogized Kennedy, a writer of the *Dublin University* and "our able contemporary, the *Dublin Review*," a man who preferred anonymity because he was "too humble, too retiring, and too modest." His articles on Dublin's press (78: 1, 80: 121) "showed…painstaking erudition."

174. "*Ireland in 1872*." 81 (1873): 631–45.
Review of James Macaulay's book objected to its section on the Dublin press. "The *Daily Express* is eulogized, the *Freeman's Journal*, the *Irish Times*, and *Saunders' News-Letter*, each come in for prominence; but the [*Dublin Evening*] *Mail*, one of the ably edited, certainly the least oscillating in its tone, and obviously the safest authority on politics and literature of the Irish press, is comparatively overlooked."

175. Dobson, W. T. "Literaria: Authors, Printing, and Printers." 82 (1873): 153–65.
Grumbled about reporters' poor penmanship, inability to spell or punctuate, and lack of style, and telegraphy's cheap paper and clerical abbreviations, all of which caused errors in newspapers "hurriedly produced."

176. The London Hermit [Walter Parke]. "Essays and Sketches: The Mysteries of Literary Speculation." 83 (1874): 309–11.
Warned that too many inexperienced people 'start a paper.' They counted on advertising to recoup initial investments, but early losses precipitated selling or closing journals.

177. [Webb, Thomas E.]. "Our Portrait Gallery, 2d ser. No. 2: John Francis Waller." 83 (1874): 312–16.
Commemorated Waller, long-time editor of the *Dublin University* as well as a "constant and prolific writer" for it. Aside that Young Ireland had a "brilliant newspaper, the *Nation*."

178. "The Education of Women." 83 (1874): 583–91.
Comprehended that readers pressed for time favored magazines and newspapers.

179. [Dunlop, Durham]. "Notes on Passing Events: The Fenian Convicts." 83 (1874): 633–36; "The New Betting Bill," 636–39.
Opposed suppression of the Fenians as long as their "folly was confined to the pages of their so-called patriotic press." Approved legislation to curb fraud in horseracing advertisements.

180. One Who Knows. "On the State of Education among the Roman Catholic Clergy in Ireland." 84 (1874): 562–64.
"A devout Catholic," the author refused to write for a Catholic periodical that would not print criticism of the Roman Church.

181. Clive, Arthur [Standish O'Grady]. "*Kottabos*." 84 (1874): 565–79.
Introduced *Kottabus*, the "witty and spirited little periodical issued at the commencement of each term" at Dublin University.

182. "Our Portrait Gallery, 2d ser. No. 13: Alexander Edward Miller, Esq., Q.C." 85 (1875): 152–59.
Biography of a candidate for representation of Dublin University appreciated that, as editor of the *Solicitor's Journal and Weekly Reporter*, Miller "fully sustained…its well-deserved reputation" in the legal profession.

183. Purves, James. "Edgar Allan Poe." 85 (1875): 336–51.
Chronicled that Poe's writing in the *Southern Literary Messenger* sent its circulation "from seven hundred to as nearly many thousands. On the order of the publisher, he commenced the practice of writing sharp and biting critiques of living little authors, which increased the periodical's circulation, but made him many unknown enemies." Poe next penned for the *New York Quarterly Review* before editing a Philadelphia magazine that went "from five to fifty-two thousand" sales. He published in *Graham's Magazine* and the *American Review*, but his own magazine failed because he was not a good financier. In 1848 he circulated a prospectus for the *Stylus* – a review of literature, fine arts, and drama – but lured no backers.

184. Bouverie, J. Fortrey. "Good for Evil." 85 (1875): 407–19.
In a story on the transformation of an Irish newspaper from Tory *Irreconcilable* to Radical *Moderator*, yarned that opponents of the *Moderator* once got the staff drunk enough to prevent regular publication of an issue but not a special edition when they sobered.

185. "Dublin a Hundred Years Ago." 85 (1875): 447–53, 703–08.
Celebrated 1780s *Morning Post* editor Peter Cooney who was sentenced to one hour in the pillory, then six months in jail "for asserting the liberty of the press by publishing a paragraph from the London papers."

186. The London Hermit [Walter Parke]. "The Physiology of 'Penny Awfuls.'" 86 (1875): 364–76.
Scoffed at penny serials that attracted many, largely uneducated buyers of "depraved taste."

187. "Our Portrait Galley, 2d ser. No. 21: James Wills, D.D." 86 (1875): 404–25.
Spotlighted a cleric, poet, and essayist who contributed to *Blackwood's Magazine*, the *Dublin University*, and *Dublin Penny Journal*, which had "considerable value in the book market owing to the distinguished men who wrote for it, and the scarceness of the work." Wills, a friend of John Sydney Taylor, editor of the *Morning Herald*, also played a part in the launch of the *Irish Quarterly Review*.

188. "Our Portrait Gallery, 2d ser. No. 22: The Right Rev. William Alexander, D.D., Lord Bishop of Derry and Raphoe." 86 (1875): 534–42.
Mentioned Alexander's essays in the *Christian Remembrancer* and the *Contemporary Review*.

189. "Our Portrait Gallery, 2d ser. No. 24: The Very Rev. John Tulloch, D.D." 87 (1876): 34–47.
Peeked at Tulloch's articles in the *North British Review* and the *British Quarterly Review*.

190. "Our Portrait Gallery, 2^d ser. No. 25: The Right Rev. William Connor Magee, D.D., Lord Bishop of Peterborough." 87 (1876): 168–80.
Flew past Magee's work in the *Contemporary Review*.

191. Bowie, Archibald Granger. "The Post-Office Telegraph Finances." 87 (1876): 330–35.
Endorsed preferential treatment for the press in Clause 16 of the 1868 Telegraph Act. "[T]he Press should be afforded every facility and help for the collection of news so eagerly thirsted after by the public."

192. Purves, James. "Noms de Plume." 87 (1876): 595–604.
Tolerated anonymity only when the consequences of signature would be "very unpleasant," as for Junius. The "disguised contributors" of dailies and weeklies too often expressed opinions different from their own. Assigned authors to several periodical articles published with pseudonyms or Greek letters.

193. "Our Portrait Gallery, 2^d ser. No. 29: His Excellency Baron Lytton, G.C.S.I., Viceroy and Governor-General of India." 87 (1876): 654–68.
Stated that E. R. Bulwer Lytton had penned anonymously for "high-class periodicals" in his youth.

194. "Our Portrait Gallery, 2^d ser. No. 30: Sir Bernard Burke, C.B., LL.D., M.R.I.A." 88 (1876): 16–24.
Tribute to the Keeper of the Irish State Papers trumpeted that "he conducted and largely sustained by his literary fertility" two volumes of *St. James's Magazine*.

195. Knowles, Richard Brinsley Sheridan. "The Personality of Goldsmith." 88 (1876): 352–67.
Documented that Oliver Goldsmith wrote for "the *Bee*, framed on the model of the *Rambler*," and for the *Public Register*. Salary and fame came after "one [Ralph] Griffiths, publisher of the *Monthly Review*, an acute man of business," recruited him.

196. "Literary Cliques and Critics." 88 (1876): 620–23.
Deduced that "the strictures passed by journalists in Ireland being based upon purely party grounds" were worthless for literary criticism. Editors, who "must cater to their publics," published the "vulgar and commonplace" of literary lions leaving little space for the work of neophytes. Anonymous critics faced with masses of material cheered everything in their newspaper reviews, which sentences then appeared as advertisements in monthlies.

197. [Curtis, Ella J.]. "The Essence of Agony." 88 (1876): 760–63.
Highlighted the personal advertisements in the 'agony columns' of morning dailies.

198. Wallis, C. J. "French Political Journalism." 89 (1877): 289–303.
Disputed that French journalism originated in the seventeenth century because only a licensed few could publish official news and commentary. The *Gazette de France* and others paralleled the Roman *acta diurna* and the Venetian "*Foglietti*, small news sheets." Nathaniel Butter's *Weekely Newes* was the "earliest attempt to establish a political periodical newspaper." Although it lacked the quality

of the French, it had "freedom of political utterance." In 1777 the first French daily, the *Journal de Paris*, surfaced; during the French Revolution, the first independent political journal, the *Patriote Français*, appeared. The revolutionary press was "foul-mouthed and bloodthirsty," but the Royalist had previewed "gross impurity, violence, and outrageous invective." The *Actes des Apôtres*, with its satires, and the *Vieux Cordelier*, edited by Camille Desmoulins, were exceptions to mediocre, often scurrilous sheets. Although journalism was free, 800 journalists were executed in 1793–94. The Directory tightened the leash, and Napoleon closed 73 of the 86 papers in 1800. Censorship persisted until 1819. The *Journal des Débats*, born in 1789, was "the semi-official organ" of the July Monarchy, which put up with the *Constitutionnel* and *Siècle* but was jealous of the *National's* power. When Emile de Girardin, "the most enterprising and conspicuous of French journalists," commenced the *Presse* in 1836, fear of cheap papers resurfaced. The *Presse* was half the cost of others that watched its circulation rise from 10,000 to 20,000 in a few months when it transformed feuilletons from literary or philosophical pieces to "enervating and demoralizing effusions of a crowd of novelists." During the 1848 Revolution, the volume and abuse of the press was similar to the National Convention years. In 1850 the new Napoleon halted this trend by mandating stamp and signature. Press laws in 1877 were still restrictive. Papers exhibited a "pale cosmopolitanism" in foreign news but partisanship in domestic, which lowered their sales compared to London dailies. John Lemoinne, at the *Journal des Débats*, was unusual, "an exceptionally dispassionate, unprejudiced, and judicious journalist." With fewer buyers, the French relied on news agencies instead of correspondents to keep costs down. Among the nonpolitical organs, *Figaro*, started in 1826, was weak until Henri de Villemessant became editor. Independent criticism by well-paid contributors who penned "well-spiced and not overscrupulous gossip" made the journal very popular.

Signature brought competition: Henri Rochefort, who earned 18,000 francs per year, went to the *Soleil* for 24,000 francs. Anonymity conferred more power on British leader-writers who addressed practical matters, whereas the French preferred theoretical.

199. Prester John. "Terrorism in Ireland." 89 (1877): 390–95.

Coupled Ireland's 1798 *Union Star* and *Press* of 1798 and New York's 1877 *Irish World*, widely circulated in Ireland. Aside that the *Daily Express* did not publish sensationalism.

200. "Our Portrait Gallery, 2d ser. No. 39: The Rev. James Martineau, D.D., LL.D., Etc." 89 (1877): 434–49.

Noted Harriet Martineau's "long and intimate connection with the *Daily News*" and her brother's "almost numberless" varied periodical essays.

201. "Our Portrait Gallery, 2d ser. No. 40: Sir William Thomson, LL.D., D.C.L., F.R.S., Etc., Professor of Natural Philosophy in the University of Glasgow." 89 (1877): 560–67.

Earmarked Thomson's articles in the *Cambridge and Dublin Mathematical Journal* and *Journal de Mathematiques*.

202. Sheehan, John, of the Inner Temple. "Our Portrait Gallery, 2d ser. No. 43: Tom Taylor." 90 (1877): 142–58.

Sheehan reminisced about reporting from Spain for a London morning daily before editing the *Cambridge Independent*. Taylor, a Cambridge Apostle, scribbled leaders for the *Morning Chronicle* and *Daily News* and columns for *Punch*, where he was "a leading writer."

203. C[ook], K[eningale and] M[abel]. "Early Days of Mortimer Collins." 90 (1877): 340–56, 474–98.

Followed Collins from his days as a "reading-boy" for the *Gentleman's Magazine* in 1838. First his poems, then many essays appeared in the *Bath and Cheltenham Gazette*. In 1847 he also wrote for the *Westmoreland Gazette*, *Fraser's Magazine*, and *Felix Farley's Journal* (Bristol), which abandoned its scissors for his original columns. His poetry was in the *Lancaster Gazette*, *British Quarterly Review*, and *Saturday Review*. After 1851 he was a regular contributor to the *Dublin University*. *See* 90: 561.

204. Hopkins, Tighe. "Our Portrait Gallery, 2[d] ser. No. 45: The Rev. Hugh Reginald Haweis, M.A." 90 (1877): 396–414.

Certified that Haweis, while at Cambridge, "floated and edited, under the title of the *Lion*, a somewhat crude and pompous journal, which brought down swift retribution in the shape of the *Bear*." Haweis also published in the *Contemporary Review* at editor Henry Alford's request, *The Times*, the *Quarterly Review*, *Spectator*, *Daily Telegraph*, *Globe*, and *Good Words*, and edited *Cassell's Magazine*.

205. C[ook], K[eningale and] M[abel]. "Journalism and Poetry of Mortimer Collins." 90 (1877): 561–93.

Continued 90: 340. Remarked that it was hard to be a poet and a journalist because journalism "uses up the intellectual machinery." In 1856 Collins helped to establish the *Idler*, a six-penny journal "devoted to the idealistic school of young Tories" and the *Leamington Mercury* to compete with a newspaper "of a somewhat sober type." His *Mercury* opened a "new and livelier era in provincial journalism" with leaders that were "usually a succession of lively unconnected paragraphs." In the 1850s he edited the *Plymouth Mail*, then the *Nottingham Guardian*. In the 1860s he published in *Temple Bar* and was joint editor of the *Globe*. Aside that the first Paris magazine of light literature was the seventeenth-century *Mercure Galant*.

The University Magazine

206. Bagwell, R[ichard]. "Home Rulers at Home." n.s., 1 (1878): 207–19.

Criticized *Freeman's Journal* for publishing telegrams of country editors as leaders, a practice exposed by the editor of *Saunders' News-Letter* but not before *The Times* Irish correspondent had used the columns.

207. Ruskin, Prof. [John]. "My First Editor: An Autobiographical Reminiscence." n.s., 1 (1878): 385–91.

Thanked W. H. Harrison, a "literary godfather" who edited Ruskin's articles for the *Architectural Magazine* at a time when *Blackwood's Magazine* and *Fraser's Magazine* were in "modest browns" and quarterlies were in "majesty." By 1878 British periodicals had an aura of authority, so editors were pressured to print current and original studies. *See* n.s., 2: 235.

208. Harrison, W. H. "Notes and Reminiscences." n.s., 1 (1878): 537–47, 698–712; n.s., 2 (1878): 56–67, 221–34, 309–23, 433–51, 613–18, 705–36.

Memorialized acquaintances, among them Robert Bell, "[n]ovelist, dramatist, critic, and journalist"; Thomas Gaspey, *Sunday Times* editor when it had "a distinctive notoriety as the medium of matrimonial negotiations"; William Jerdan of the *Literary Gazette*, which declined because of rivalry with the *Athenaeum*; and Francis Mahony, "the Father Prout of *Fraser's Magazine*."

209. "Alphonse Karr, Gossip and Gardener." n.s., 2 (1878): 207–20.
Condensed Karr's career as scribe, then editor of *Figaro* in 1835; contributor to the monthly *Guêpes*, "a newspaper, critical, literary, and social," and editor of the *Journal* in 1848.

210. "Ephemeral Literature." n.s., 2 (1878): 235–42.
Sermonized that the "average intellect...overburdened by the calls made upon its attention," turned to light literature. Magazines were an obvious choice because, as n.s., 1: 385 articulated, elite periodicals were too intense. Magazines tended to restrict high quality, although "the more dignified" dependent on subscribers published serious material in parts. Unlike the "[s]olid magazines," the light captured a large audience because they could be read long after the issue date. Periodicals should leave a blank page between articles so that a reader could add related material and should index their contents.

211. Cox, Henry F. "Charles Lamb at Edmonton." n.s., 2 (1878): 469–73.
Hinted at Lamb's work for the *Quarterly Review*, *Examiner*, and *Morning Chronicle* when it hired few journalists.

212. [Cook, Mabel]. "Margaret Fuller." n.s., 2 (1878): 542–51, 686–704.
Probed Fuller's editing of the *Dial* but not her work for the *New York Tribune*.

213. "Contemporary Portraits. No. 11: William Morris, M.A." n.s., 2 (1878): 552–68.
Publicized Morris' efforts for the *Oxford and Cambridge Magazine*, a monthly of "solid excellence" started by "a few choice spirits."

214. C., E. "Contemporary Portraits. No. 14: Miss Emily Faithfull." n.s., 3 (1879): 173–81.
Congratulated Faithfull for operating the successful *Victoria Magazine*, where women trained as compositors for jobs in London and the country, and for editing the weekly *London Express*.

215. "Contemporary Portraits. No. 15: Robert Browning." n.s., 3 (1879): 322–35, 416–43.
Divulged that Browning's grandfather (d. 1866) was "an authority on the 'Letters of Junius.'"

216. Autolycus. "'Gentlemen of the Press.'" n.s., 3 (1879): 513–30.
Designated the reporter as "the historian of his day, the universal man," who transmitted the new even more than the news to the public. The reporter in 1879 was "a wholly unpicturesque, practical person," not "wild, free, careless," or partisan. Having "somewhat too close a peep into the seamy side of life," reporters were indifferent to politics. The contemporary reporter, often a failure elsewhere, had to be physically sound; a master of shorthand; knowledgeable about many things; adaptable to an editor's summons; capable of "gently worming out of a person information"; and able to judge what was important and summarize it in "presentable newspaper English."

The London press was "literally swarming" with Irish reporters who, though not always sober or reliable, were versatile, thus good special correspondents. Because specials had to write quickly and well on the spot, they shared information irrespective of party or religion. As "one of the remarkable products of modern newspaper enterprise," the special had to have "descriptive literary power" and to know the reading public and public life as much as an issue. At a local paper, the "Man-of-all-work" was a typical job and a beneficial apprenticeship.

The penny-a-liner's position was "not only honourable but lucrative in the extreme." The liner was "the most thoroughly independent" journalist, not a "shorthand writer" who was "slovenly" or "wonderfully cute in making the most of a paragraph." Because journalism allowed the journalist to control how work was done, a keen subeditor had to watch for signs of alcoholism. As the profession expanded, there was less bonding but still "*camaraderie*."

Since proprietors were no longer speculators but men trained for the business of journalism, the newspaper was a "great commercial concern." While "the editor reigns supreme," stories had to lure buyers dear to advertisers. "Literary editors" were relegated to "old-fashioned monthly magazines." Reporters moved to war correspondence, leader-writing, press management, direction of institutions, and law. Aside that interviewing, more prevalent in the United States, invaded privacy.

217. "Contemporary Portraits. No. 17: Rev. J. Llewelyn Davies, M.A." n.s., 3 (1879): 583–602.

Identified Davies, a cleric, as a contributor to *Fraser's Magazine*, *Macmillan's Magazine*, *Good Words*, and the *Contemporary Review*.

218. "Contemporary Portraits. No. 18: J. J. Garth Wilkinson," n.s., 3 (1879): 673–92.

Communicated that Wilkinson, a physician, "wrote a little for the newspapers" and the *Monthly Magazine*. His brother, W. M. Wilkinson, edited the *Spiritual Magazine*, "a periodical now either defunct or attenuated."

219. "Isaac Butt, M.P." n.s., 3 (1879): 710–15.

Pointed out that Butt was a founder of the *Dublin University* as well as the *Protestant Guardian*, "later amalgamated with the *Warder*," and penned for many journals in Ireland and England.

220. "Contemporary Portraits. No. 20: Justin McCarthy, M.P." n.s., 4 (1879): 182–94.

Assayed the career of McCarthy, a reporter for the *Cork Examiner*, edited by John Francis Mulgrave, and a later unnamed Liverpool gazette. After publishing in the *Westminster Review*, McCarthy became a parliamentary reporter, then foreign editor of the *Morning Star*, edited by John Bright's son-in-law until McCarthy succeeded him. He also wrote "bright, clever, interesting" articles for British and American magazines. In 1879 he was the parliamentary leader-writer for the *Daily News*.

Worried that "regular newspaper work" took "so much of the brain and energy of our literary men."

221. [Hawthorne, Julian]. "Biography, New Style: Mr. Julian Hawthorne." 3[d] ser., 1 (1880): 54–57.

American athlete admitted that by 1870 he had developed the "deleterious practice of writing short stories for magazines," although he also published in the *Contemporary Review*.

The Edinburgh Review, 1802–1900

With an early Whig proclivity and seniority among nineteenth-century reviews, the *Edinburgh* probed the journalism of numerous societies. Some of its strongest language was on the freedom of and taxes on the press.

1. "Lichtenberg's *Miscellaneous Works*." 3 (1803–04): 343–54.
Review of George C. Lichtenberg's book on German literature revealed that he penned for almanacs, reviews, and magazines that "had an extensive circulation through the whole German empire for thirty-six years."

2. [Jeffrey, Francis]. "*Correspondence and Memoirs of John Wilkes*." 5 (1804–05): 477–89.
Denied that John Wilkes extended "private liberty."

3. "*Journal des Mines*." 8 (1806): 78–86; 9 (1806–07): 67–83.
Headlined a French periodical that dealt with minerals.

4. [?Mill, James]. "Filangieri on the *Science of Legislation*." 9 (1806–07): 354–73.
Review of Gaetano Filangieri's book emphasized that liberty of the press was "the most inestimable security...of a people, because it gives that tone to the public feelings on which all liberty must ultimately rest." Yet press freedom existed not by law but by "connivance." *See* 18: 98.

5. [Allen, John]. "*Mercurio Peruano*." 9 (1806–07): 433–58.
Plumbed a Lima periodical, 1791–94, published by a private society, *Amantes de Lima*, until its sponsors returned to Spain. Its goal was to present criticism and information. Aside on the Peruvian *Guia*, an annual.

6. "Janson's *Stranger in America*." 10 (1807): 103–16.
Review of Charles W. Janson's book referred to its chapter on American newspaper advertisements, no more measures of taste than the 'eccentric' ones in London and country papers.

7. [Jeffrey, Francis]. "Cobbett's *Political Register*." 10 (1807): 386–421.
Much-quoted article avowed that Cobbett's *Register* had more influence "than all other journalists put together" because of "the force of his personal character." The *Register*, "written with great freedom, and often with great force of argument," deserved its preeminence among journals addressed to the class "just above the lowest." *See New Review* 9: 362 and *Tait's Edinburgh Magazine* n.s., 2: 491.

8. [Smith, Sydney]. "Ingram on Methodism." 11 (1807–08): 341–62.
Review of Robert J. Ingram's *Causes of the Increase of Methodism, and Dissension* listed several periodicals, such as the *Methodist Magazine*, *Evangelical Magazine*, *Instructor*, and *Eclectic Review*, and alluded to their advertisements.

9. [Brougham, Henry and Francis Jeffrey]. "Semple's *Second Journey in Spain*." 15 (1809–10): 384–96.
Review of Robert Semple's book on Spain in the spring of 1809 castigated authors and booksellers who selected for their advertisements the one sentence of approval from the many of censure in an *Edinburgh* article or altered words for these promotions.

10. [Napier, Macvey]. "Ashe's *Travels in America*." 15 (1809–10): 442–53.
Quoted Thomas Ashe that "Irish and Scotch journalists" who reported on Congress captured the spirit of a speech and then abstracted it in "a language interesting to read."

11. [Mill, James]. "Liberty of the Press." 18 (1811): 98–123.
Repeated the theme of 9: 354. In 1811 press freedom was in jeopardy because libel law "was at utter variance with the sentiments of every class and denomination of men" and was arbitrarily enforced by judges and government ministers. A press inciting anarchy was less dangerous than despotism because a truly free press could deter revolutionary excesses. The immoderation of the French press after 1789 was the consequence, not the cause of a revolution wherein papers were tools of the "domineering faction."

12. [Brougham, Henry]. "Abuses of the Press." 22 (1813–14): 72–88.
Centered on "uncertainty in the execution of the law of libel" and critiques of press "licentiousness." Libel was popular but only prosecuted when the accused was "obnoxious on other accounts." Comments on licentiousness did not mean it was rising but that the authorities were censoring more. Jonathan Swift, Joseph Addison, and others faced a similar situation in the eighteenth century. Those who attacked "private character" or exhibited "personal malice" to feed "the diseased appetite of the public" deserved punishment. *See* 27: 102.

13. [Mackintosh, James]. "France." 24 (1814–15): 505–37.
Nodded to the suppression of the press by Louis XIV and its manipulation by Napoleon I.

14. [Mill, James]. "Liberty of the Continental Press." 25 (1815): 112–34.
Blared that the press was "the *palladium* of civilized society." Because most periodicals enlightened, even when restrained, they helped humans to improve. A free forum did not breed revolution but rather stopped it by allowing for "sound discussion." No one should fear press liberty because people were not naturally anti-government unless they were ignorant, not likely with many journals. Press prosecutions tended to deal with 1) religion (unnecessary because rationality would triumph); 2) "sexual delicacy" (best left to private repudiation); 3) institutions of government (unthreatened because of the force of custom); 4) governors (whose abuses of power should be exposed); 5) private persons (acceptable to motivate good behavior). The law should prosecute those who libeled the poor because it was impossible for them to respond. Ruminated about the future press in a France that linked liberty to excess and in Holland and the German states that did not prioritize press freedom.

15. [Brougham, Henry]. "Liberty of the Press and Its Abuses." 27 (1816): 102–44.
Focused on how to secure the most discussion in the press while protecting the stability of the community and the "safety of private character." The law of libel was central even though, as 22: 72 said, prosecution was uncertain. Civil prosecutions that awarded damages did not penalize but rewarded guilty newspapers because cases usually expanded sales. Victims did not bring criminal prosecutions because they dreaded loss of reputation. Both action and inaction encouraged habitual offenders and gave journalism a bad reputation. Whether truth was available as a defense was significant, particularly when private citizens were involved.

16. [Brougham, Henry]. "Dangers of the Constitution." 27 (1816): 245–63.
Underscored the value of the press in publicizing government proceedings and opinion on them. *See Westminster Review* 1: 505.

17. [Brougham, Henry]. "Junius." 29 (1817–18): 94–114.
Recounted numerous attempts to identify Junius.

18. "French Law of Libel." 32 (1819): 192–208.
Explained that the French distinguished private and public libel and had a better provision for defamation than the British. Aside that representative assemblies required "salutary" publicity. *See Household Words* 1: 238.

19. [Brougham, Henry]. "The Recent Alarms." 33 (1820): 187–225.
Warned that the government used the press "weekly and daily to repeat, with gross exaggeration, and even all the resources of the most shameless fabrication, the tale of terror."

20. [Jeffrey, Francis]. "Dispositions of England and America." 33 (1820): 395–431.
Aside on Robert Walsh's views, in *An Appeal from the Judgments of Great Britain Respecting the United States of America*, about bias in the *Edinburgh* and *Quarterly Review*.

21. [Brougham, Henry]. "Constitutional Association." 37 (1822): 110–21.
Resisted return of the press to earlier "excessive restraint, almost approaching to persecution" after "a season of total indifference." The government was capricious in its prosecution of newspaper printers and editors. Officials ignored gazettes that incited "rebellion, mutiny, and assassination" and supported those that were "the vehicle of private defamation and obscene ribaldry." The purpose of the Constitutional Association was to curb "licentiousness" in journalism.

22. [Hazlitt, William]. "The Periodical Press." 38 (1823): 349–78.
Divided periodicals into newspapers, magazines, and reviews. Of the London dailies the *Morning Chronicle* was "best for amusement and instruction" thanks to the style of editing and writing inaugurated by James Perry. *The Times* was influential but "pompous, dogmatical, and full of pretensions," so hardly "readable." Its leaders mirrored interests of the moment rather than a commitment to principles. Other dailies merited less attention. Of the weeklies, William Cobbett's *Political Register* was "first in power and popularity." Next was the *Examiner*, with "a much greater variety." The *Observer* had more "murders, assaults, robberies, fires, accidents" than the others.

Of the magazines, the *Gentleman's* was "the last lingering remains of a former age"; the *New Monthly* was very similar to and more popular than the *Monthly*. Most magazines were not refined, a dangerous tendency as their audiences grew.

In reviews criticism was improving, though the author of light literature in the 1820s "renounces eternal fame for a newspaper puff." Politics might be overdone but made reviews "palatable to the ordinary taste." The only contributors not starving were "anonymous critics" known by their reputations and political essayists.

The "Ministerial Press," modeled on the defunct *Anti-Jacobin*, denounced individuals, catering to the "vulgar appetite for slander" rather than to the passions or even prejudices of audiences. Officials tried to "gag" the opposition and "hoodwink" readers who were "timid, indolent, and easily influenced by a little swaggering and an air of authority."

23. [Brougham, Henry]. "Quin's *Visit to Spain*." 40 (1824): 44–67.

Review of Michael J. Quin's book pirated statistics on Spanish newspapers. Before 1820 there were two in Madrid (one government, one advertising, neither selling 2,000 copies). By 1824 there were several, among them the *Universal* (7,000 copies), *Espectador* (5,000 copies), and for the "lower ranks," *Telegrapho*.

24. [Denman, Thomas]. "Law of Evidence – Criminal Procedure – Publicity." 40 (1824): 169–207.

Noticed 'gentlemen of the press,' notably newspaper reporters of criminal trials whose stories rumored about a defendant's past or encouraged "sentimental admiration" for criminals. This coverage was inappropriate because "the Press is the organ of public opinion, but of public opinion acting upon facts selected and conveyed by the same organ."

25. "Italy." 40 (1824): 207–25.

Quoted Joseph Pecchio's *Letter to Henry Brougham, Esq., M.P.* on Vienna's censorship of the Italian press.

26. [Smith, Sydney]. "America." 40 (1824): 427–42.

Opined that American authors were sensitive to British literary criticism, being "flung into such convulsions by English Reviews and Magazines."

27. [Brougham, Henry]. "Parliamentary History." 44 (1826): 458–90.

Signaled that the influence of the newspaper on politics surpassed that of the pamphlet.

28. [Macaulay, T. B.]. "The Present Administration." 46 (1827): 245–67.

Vilified government for its "dexterous use of secret-service money" to buy the favor of London's "able and respectable journals." Other papers were either "slang uttered by drunken lads" and gossip-mongers or all advertising.

29. [Carlyle, Thomas]. "Signs of the Times." 49 (1829): 439–59.

Equated newspaper editors and preachers because both displayed zeal for their causes yet desired personal success.

30. [Hazlitt, William]. "Wilson's [*Memoirs of the*] *Life and Times of Daniel Defoe*." 50 (1829–30): 397–425.

Review of Walter Wilson's book claimed that Defoe's *Review* was the forerunner of the essays and "dramatic sketches" in the serials of Joseph Addison and Richard Steele.

31. [Macaulay, T. B.]. "Mr. Robert Montgomery's *Poems*, and the Modern Practice of Puffing." 51 (1830): 193–210.

Explicated how publishers used their periodicals to promote their books, circulating good evaluations that magazines, then newspapers echoed. The more respectable reviews labeled this puffery advertising or endorsement.

32. [McCulloch, J. R.]. "Taxes on Literature." 53 (1831): 427–37.

Essay on the stamp, advertising, and paper duties defended the stamp. Even though it was oppressive, publishers should know how many copies to print. All duties should be proportional to a paper's price so that cheaper journals could attract "men of talent and principle" and a more specialized press could replace the "omnivorous system" of 1831.

33. [Empson, William]. "The Americans and Their Detractors." 55 (1832): 479–526.

Scorned American newspapers read by all as second-rate, secondhand, and "scurrilous."

34. [McCulloch, J. R.]. "Stuart's *Three Years in North America*." 56 (1832–33): 460–81.

Review of James Stuart's book doubted that a free press existed in the American South.

35. [Brougham, Henry]. "Progress of the People – The Periodical Press." 57 (1833): 239–48.

Highlighted the *Penny Magazine* (200,000 sales), *Saturday Magazine* (60,000), and *Chambers's Journal* (60,000) because they educated readers to be "more capable of judging soundly and charitably upon matters of controversy, whether civil or religious." These magazines, which inculcated "regular habits" and transmitted "sound information," disproved that the lower classes were only interested in "ribaldry and libel" in contrast to the "[h]igher classes."

The London dailies worried that abolition of newspaper duties would multiple cheap gazettes, yet their only harm to others was plagiarism. Expensive dailies, often careless about facts and irresponsible in attacks on "public men," only became organs of the people when the public lost confidence in the "Old Parliament." In 1833 these papers no longer wished to reflect opinion but "sometimes try to excite and to guide it." With more newspapers and thus a more informed community, their sway would likely diminish. Reduction of duties would also spawn more "provincial papers, perhaps the most important part of the periodical press."

36. [McCulloch, J. R.]. "Complaints and Proposals Regarding Taxation." 57 (1833): 434–48.

Graded advertising duties unfair to the press.

37. [Brougham, Henry]. "Tory Views and Machinations." 58 (1833–34): 457–68.
Deplored Tory promises of lavish newspaper patronage and repeal of the libel law, both important because the press was already a power in politics. Endorsed the French requirement that journal conductors publicly identify themselves.

38. [Brougham, Henry]. "Newspaper Tax." 61 (1835): 181–85.
Swore that London papers vetoed repeal of the newspaper stamp because it kept prices high and reduced competition. Abolition of a duty that impeded the public right to know and obstructed the spread of "*general* knowledge" would fuel new "innocent and beneficial" serials to counter London's dominion. Abolition would not cause a decline in revenue because there would be more sales subject to the advertising duty or an increase in "sedition, profaneness, and immorality" because the "vile" already were unstamped. *See* 62: 126.

39. [Brougham, Henry]. "French Parties and Politics." 61 (1835): 216–20.
Abhorred French "prosecutions against the Press, now proceeding with unrelenting and most impolitic severity" notwithstanding the "excesses" of Paris papers, because the press was "so great an engine of improvement, so essential a safeguard of freedom."

40. [Brougham, Henry]. "Taxes on Knowledge." 62 (1835–36): 126–32.
Repeated the thesis (61: 181) that London newspapers objected to repeal of the newspaper stamp in order to maintain their monopoly. Unlike their activism about other monopolies, London papers suppressed news of abolitionists, ignoring "three of the greatest public meetings ever held in the metropolis." Even though local papers were loud for repeal, the "liberal and literary" government had no sense of this demand because of London's silence. Unstamped country weeklies without a printer's name were selling in London because "people are determined to read newspapers." Attempts to print unstamped dailies failed for "want of due preparations." Aside that French authorities were "chaining" the cheap press because of an alleged royal assassination plot.

41. [Merivale, Herman]. "Hazlitt's *Literary Remains*." 64 (1836–37): 395–411.
Review of book collection of William Hazlitt's writings flagged his antipathy to the *Quarterly Review*.

42. [Bulwer-Lytton, E. G.]. "Chateaubriand on the Literature of England." 64 (1836–37): 506–36.
Noted that the impact of the eighteenth-century *Spectator* was underrated.

43. [Empson, William]. "Fonblanque's *Seven Administrations*–Newspaper Literature." 65 (July, 1837): 196–213.
Review of Albany von Fontblanque's *England under Seven Administrations* regarded the newspaper as "an essential element" and "peculiar symbol" of British civilization, a medium that reached all fields. It communicated ideas and guided opinion. The newspaper, the principal means for "political education of the majority of the population," could have influence as long as it did not treat an opponent as "either rogue or fool." Journalists, however, had little control over the "moral and intellectual character of their contemporary public." Readers without taste meant that the level of writing in the cheap press was not high, although education should produce better quality.

Journalism was becoming a profession, so writers should strive to write good critical reviews and political essays, not emulate the "violence and exaggeration" of the Americans. William Cobbett raised the intellectual but lowered the moral reputation of the press unlike Albany Fonblanque. Yet reprinting articles, as in his *England under Seven Administrations*, seemed worthless because news was temporal and styles of writing were "close, personal, and contentious," "quick, antithetical, and dramatic," appropriate for immediate, not long-term sales.

Cited the *Liberia Gazette* as an example of the newspaper's role in a free society, the American press on mass circulation, and the *Examiner* on press benefits.

44. [Brougham, Henry]. "Abuses of the Press: George the Fourth and Queen Caroline." 67 (1838): 1–80.

Concentrated on the law of libel. The press was an "engine of public instruction and a vehicle above all, of political discussion," but there was always tension between a free press and "licentiousness." Since covering Caroline's case, the press had been "unbridled and violent" in its attacks on government and on individuals, often as revenge. If a person was important, other papers copied the story. Those who did not respond to libel were assumed guilty; those who did answer did not know their enemies. The press hid behind anonymity, refused to acknowledge errors, and harassed victims or took bribes to kill stories. Editors should dismiss libelers whose attacks stemmed from grudges, and the upper class should disdain libel. *See Fraser's Magazine* 18: 1.

45. [Rich, Henry]. "Claims of the Whigs and Tories." 67 (1838): 202–09.

Respected *Quarterly Review* essays on "general literature" but not on politics, which were done "in a spirit, temper, and language more befitting the lowest organs of its party."

46. [Tremenheere, H. S.]. "Laing's *Tour in Sweden*." 69 (1839): 349–65.

Review of Samuel Laing's book recorded the recent grant of press freedom in Sweden.

46a. [Mill, John Stuart]. "*Democracy in America*." 72 (1840): 1–47.

Review of Alexis de Tocqueville's book held that the press was an "agora." Telling people what others felt helped to develop public opinion and established newspapers as the unions of politics.

47. [Macaulay, T. B.]. "Warren Hastings." 74 (1841–42): 160–255.

Added a gloss on the identity of Junius.

48. [Spedding, James]. "Dickens's *American Notes*." 76 (1842–43): 497–522.

Review of Charles Dickens' book assumed that the "character" of newspapers anywhere depended on the costs of printing, paper, and taxes. In Britain the tone of London dailies and the stamp duty checked inexpensive scurrilous sheets, so "respectable proprietors" flourished. Still, papers spread rumors and misrepresented facts because new readers liked contention and "licentiousness." American journals, of which Dickens was critical, were worse but less accountable because respectability was not so valued in United States. Wondered how well-educated Americans could read their gazettes. *See Foreign Quarterly Review* 31: 250.

49. [Hayward, Abraham]. "The Advertising System." 77 (1843): 1–43.

Sampled advertising for products and services (especially professional) and on religious and personal concerns.

50. [Moir, George]. "*Recreations of Christopher North.*" 77 (1843): 72–104.
Assessment of essays originally in *Blackwood's Magazine*, here edited, attested to a shift in style in reviews' political articles and literary criticism.

51. [Macaulay, T. B.]. "Life and Writings of Addison." 78 (1843): 193–260.
Stated that Richard Steele originated the *Tatler* but Joseph Addison was a master satirist with "grace" and "moral purity" and a "gazetteer" with access to fast and accurate foreign intelligence. His work allowed the *Tatler* to disseminate foreign news as well as literary and theatre criticism to the country. In 1709 the *Tatler* was more popular than any prior periodical but changed character with a new government. The *Spectator*, with 4,000 copies, was full of Addison's work but died with the advent of the stamp duty. The *Guardian*, with fewer columns by Addison, was less successful. Neither Addison's weekly *Spectator* of 1714 nor Steele's *Englishman* was as good as the original *Spectator*.

Aside that a shorthand reporter in 1843 could produce paragraphs on Parliament so quickly that a speech given at 4 a.m. was on "30,000 tables" by 10 a.m.

52. [Macaulay, T. B.]. "Barère's *Memoirs*." 79 (1844): 275–351.
Review of Bertrand Barère's book reckoned that his *Mémorial Antibritannique* never reached more than 1,500 subscribers, mostly Gasçons. The problem was not that Paris was pro-British but that he was not a talented writer. Alternatively, the *Journal des Débats* under "able management… had a circulation of at least 20,000 copies."

53. [Macaulay, T. B.]. "Early Administrations of George III: The Earl of Chatham." 80 (1844): 526–95.
Condemned George Grenville's "war on the press" in the John Wilkes case. The *North Briton*, "written with some pleasantry, and great audacity and impudence, had a considerable number of readers." After No. 45 was seized and Wilkes sent to the Tower, there was "popular rage" that turned to "delight" when his arrest was ruled unlawful.

54. [Forster, John]. "Charles Churchill." 81 (1845): 46–88.
Biography of a writer and poet discussed his role at the *North Briton*, where he was "not a good prose satirist," and the controversy over its No. 45. Aside that William Hogarth did an unpleasant sketch of John Wilkes in retaliation for the *North Briton's* caricature of a Hogarth drawing in *The Times*.

55. [Forster, John]. "Daniel DeFoe [*sic*]." 82 (1845): 480–532.
Described Defoe's *Review* as a weekly quarto with wide print, then half a sheet with smaller print and double columns. The *Review* was unique in its inclusion of "personal and public themes," politics, morals, the serious, and the entertaining. "Remarkable for its rich and various knowledge, its humour, its satire, its downright earnestness, it is a yet more surprising monument of inexhaustible activity and energy." It fathered the *Tatler* and reasoned better than Jonathan Swift in the *Examiner*. Very popular but often pirated, the *Review* had modest profits.

56. [Denman, Thomas]. "Parliament and the Courts." 83 (1846): 1–47.
Recollected instances of exclusion of reporters, as "strangers," from Parliament. In 1810 they were lambasted while they were out of Commons.

57. [Milnes, R. M.]. "Political State of Prussia." 83 (1846): 224–39.
Petitioned for Prussian liberty of the press in order to temper the police and to open the courts even if journals had the "vices of the infancy of freedom."

58. [Hayward, Abraham]. "Ford and Hughes on Spain and the Spaniards." 84 (1846): 175–95.
Review of books by Richard Ford and J. M. Hughes unmasked Spanish Prime Minister Don Luis Gonzalez Bravo as a former editor of a newspaper of sarcasm and scandal. In Spain persons "of the highest rank" penned and edited newspapers and took bribes to suppress stories. Heavy censorship and penalties, as deportation, stopped some; destruction of presses by victims and their friends halted others. The chief Spanish paper was the *Eco de Comercio*, akin to *The Times*, *Journal des Débats*, and *Allgemeine Zeitung*.

59. [Hayward, Abraham]. "Thackeray's Writings." 87 (1848): 46–67.
Judged W. M. Thackeray a failed editor but a successful "writer for respectable magazines and newspapers," such as *Fraser's Magazine* and *Punch*. Periodical scribes were responsible for "most of the great steps in taste, criticism, correct feeling, and social improvement" and for circulating "many a valuable truth." Yet the British, unlike the French, did not honor writers because of the custom of anonymity.

60. [Christie, W. D.]. "Coleridge and Southey." 87 (1848): 368–92.
Aired that S. T. Coleridge started the short-lived *Watchman* in 1796 and penned for the *Morning Post*. Robert Southey authored the "history part" of the *Edinburgh Annual Register* in 1809.

61. [Bruce, John]. "William Allen and Mrs. Fry: Modern Quakerism." 87 (1848): 503–34.
Cited the 1810 launch of the Quaker *Philanthropist*, "intended to stimulate the active benevolence of the public."

62. [Bulwer-Lytton, E. G.]. "Goldsmith." 88 (1848): 193–225.
Revealed that Oliver Goldsmith received board and a "small salary" from Ralph "Griffiths, the bookseller" and publisher of the *Monthly Review*. Its rival was the *Critic*, set up by Archibald Hamilton with Tobias Smollett.

63. [Rogers, Henry]. "Sydney Smith's *Sketches of Moral Philosophy*." 91 (1850): 356–77.
Lauded Francis Jeffrey, the early *Edinburgh* editor, for his "taste, skill, and energy."

64. [Spedding, James]. "The United States." 92 (1850): 339–71.
Quoted Daniel Webster on the "foolish and violent paragraphs in the press" of the United States.

65. [Greg, W. R.]. "England as It Is." 93 (1851): 305–39.
Heralded that wages of compositors at London morning papers went from 40 shillings per week in 1800 to 48 per week in 1836.

66. [Donne, W. B.]. "Southey's *Life and Correspondence*." 93 (1851): 370–402.
Review of a book edited by C. C. Southey considered Robert Southey's periodical writing as his "sheet anchor." He earned 400 pounds a year for his contributions to the *Edinburgh Annual Register* and penned 100 articles in 30 years for the *Quarterly Review*.

67. [Peyronnet, Caroline de]. "A Few Words on International Copyright." 95 (1852): 145–52.
Supported a proposed law that would permit reprint of newspaper or periodical material if the source was cited and the author did not object.

68. [Merivale, Herman]. "Mallet du Pan." 95 (1852): 481–517.
Profiled Jacques Mallet du Pan who wrote when eighteenth-century newspaper writing compared favorably with nineteenth-century "political intelligence." He penned for the *Annales Politiques et Littéraires*, published in London, Brussels, Geneva, and Paris, and relocated as its editor, S.-H. Linguet, "caused heat." In 1783 Mallet du Pan commenced the *Memoirs Politiques et Littéraires*, which was full of "shrewd common sense." In 1784 he was the chief political scribe for the *Mercure de France*, which paid him 7,200 livres per year plus 1,200 for any literary articles. During the French Revolution the paper was Royalist until war with Austria ended its run. By 1798 he was in Britain editing the *Mercure Britannique*. French journalists were an "irregular corps" created by the early Revolution, but they had real influence. Under Napoleon III they were "objects of jealousy and superstition." Aside that the United States, unlike France, did not welcome journalists of quality to public office.

69. [Colborne, John]. "Jervis's [*The*] *History of* [*the Island of*] *Corfu, and* [*and of the Republic of the*] *Ionian Islands*." 97 (1853): 41–86.
Review of H. J. W. Jervis' book, with abbreviated caption, differentiated the "new crop of editors of newspapers" who flattered legislators from the "despicable" journalists of "rabid" papers in the early days of the free press. Throughout the British Empire the press still engaged in "political tirades," but it was unnecessary to enforce censorship when responsible editors were available "at a cheap rate."

70. [Russel, Alexander]. "The Newspaper Stamp." 98 (1853): 488–518.
Analyzed the taxes affecting the British newspaper press, the best in the world and the "only free one in Europe" because it knew that popularity was more profitable than partisanship. While the paper duty was a necessary evil for national revenue, the end of the advertising duty was a boon to newspapers. The stamp was not a tax but a charge for cheap postal transmission. Readers often sent London papers to the country after they finished reading; the country papers relied on the post for circulation but not news. Thanks to telegraphy, locals could print before the London papers arrived, which raised a complex issue of copyright, namely news as "exclusive property." Removal of the stamp would not reduce costs except for those who never posted. Penny papers would not survive because the nation did not have enough readers with leisure or funds to buy them. Canceling the stamp would result in more cheap locals or fewer capitalist ones. The first would abet parochialism and the second would homogenize opinion. Richard Cobden wanted the British to follow the American model, more news and less discussion, but the latter was the "life-blood" of the British political system, the "chief engine" of multiple and peaceful reforms, and a bastion "against crudities and quackeries."

71. [Conington, John]. "Hermann's *Aeschylus*." 100 (1854): 80–115.
Review of Godofredus Hermann's book had a long footnote on the *Journal of Classical and Sacred Philology*.

72. [Lewis, George Cornewall]. "Parliamentary Opposition." 101 (1855): 1–22.

Assured that "the daily press exercises a most important influence upon the character of the [parliamentary] debates themselves, and upon the conduct of the speakers" because Members grasped that they were really addressing the public, not each other.

73. [Greg, W. R.]. "Modern French Literature." 101 (1855): 92–120.

Counseled aspiring politicians and authors in France to write first for political journals. While the "excellence" and influence of British newspapers was "peculiar to our times," French journalists had a more direct effect on government.

74. [Mangles, R. D.]. "Statesmen of India." 102 (1855): 147–78.

Posited that a free press was "a great agent of knowledge and civilisation," exposed abuses, and promoted reforms in governance.

75. [Hayward, Abraham]. "The Rev. Sydney Smith.: His Life, Character, and Writings." 102 (1855): 236–74.

Admitted that Smith took credit for envisioning the *Edinburgh* and editing the first number, but the serial had no formal editor until its fourth number. Its authors, among them Smith with seven of the 29 articles in the first number, were anonymous but "speedily recognized."

76. [Greg, W. R.]. "The Newspaper Press." 102 (1855): 470–98.

Tracked "journalism," which had grown slowly, from Nathaniel Butter, printer of the *Weekely News*, and Marchamont Nedham, the "patriarch" of newspapers. After censorship ended, more and more "able" papers surfaced. In the early eighteenth century, journalists were often men of power. A period of decline culminated in the "scurrility" of John Wilkes' *North Briton*, but Junius rehabilitated the press by setting the standards for accuracy and style found in contemporary quality papers though without his biased and unscrupulous attacks. By the nineteenth century newspapers had superseded pamphlets, but the libel law was bothersome.

Gazettes gradually evolved into powerful instruments for news gathering, providing information to ministers faster than their official channels in 1855. More importantly, newspapers with a "high and pure character" were the "guardian of free institutions," keeping voters "*au courant*" and airing critiques by the "best qualified intellects." They always had to be on guard that they were not the pawns of politicians. They might be the tools of government to "instruct" the people, but they were also the instruments of its control. They represented those without a vote and presented to voters issues for which Parliament had no time. They were a "safety valve" for society and an advocate for those with individual grievances for whom the courts were too slow. They elevated public taste with their leaders penned by barristers waiting for or ceasing from a practice, young politicians, and "men of trained and cultivated minds" interested in a literary career writing politics.

Anonymous scribes, who had less access to public office than did their French colleagues of signature, spoke for all and encouraged the public to read all, not just the notorious. Although some columnists were warped by biases, most were not corrupt. Their unsigned attacks were less hurtful and exposed many ills.

The Times, read by everyone, had the greatest clout. The locals might counteract its voice, and weeklies, as the *Illustrated London News*, were also "correctives," but the best deterrent to its overweening power was its own staff. Even without a stamp, it was unlikely that the penny paper would flourish until the poor formed the habit of daily reading, albeit telegraphy already made London news cheaper for the locals to report.

77. [Reeve, Henry]. "The Results of the Campaign." 102 (1855): 572–92.
Saluted William Howard Russell for covering the Crimean War "with fearless independence, strict veracity, and considerable judgment." He was a credit to *The Times*, "the powerful journal which employed him."

78. [Greg, W. R.]. "French Judgments of England: Montalembert and Rémusat." 103 (1856): 558–90.
Reviewed books by Charles de Rémusat and his articles, collected in a volume, from the *Correspondant*, "a semi-religious periodical." He was formerly in the Chamber of Deputies and interior minister but by 1856 penned for the *Revue des Deux Mondes*, "the most influential and highly reputed publication in France." Aside that English papers, including some of the "most powerful," "needlessly exaggerated and extravagantly coloured" problems in Crimea, whereas French reports were less volatile.

79. [Kaye, J. W.]. "India." 106 (1857): 544–94.
Justified why Lord Charles Canning "shackled the Indian press. The native journals had, for some time, been unscrupulously mendacious in their statements, and seditious in their tone." The Anglo-Indian newspapers, speaking for colonials and "half-castes," "contained much which had tended greatly to irritate the public mind, and to embarrass the government." The gag caused a fury in Europe but had no effect on the press in India. Its language would not be tolerated at home where men without "temper" and with "discretion" directed a press of "great ability."

80. [Russell, C. W.]. "The Hawkers' Literature of France." 107 (1858): 232–47.
Abstracted popular French publications, including almanacs.

81. [Procter, B. W.]. "Edgar Allan Poe." 107 (1858): 419–42.
Alluded to Poe's failure as a journalist generally and as an editor of the *Richmond Magazine*, *Graham's Magazine*, and his own *Stylus*.

82. [Forsyth, William]. "*The Speeches of Lord Brougham*." 107 (1858): 443–64.
Aside on the libel case against John Williams, editor of a Durham newspaper, for his story on the failure of church bells to ring at the death of Queen Caroline.

83. [Hayward, Abraham]. "Canning's Literary Remains." 108 (1858): 104–35.
Commented on George Canning's work for the *Anti-Jacobin* as well as his role in establishing and his contributions to the *Quarterly Review*.

84. [Mill, John Stuart]. "Centralisation." 115 (1862): 323–58.
Publicized the *Revue des Deux Mondes*, renowned for its voluminous contents and its writers who were the "first minds in France," and the *Revue Nationale* for the quality of its "principal articles."

85. [Head, Edmund]. "Sir George Cornewall Lewis on Forms of Government." 118 (1863): 138–66.
Recalled that Lewis wrote for the *Edinburgh* and other periodicals named.

86. [Hayward, Abraham]. "Macknight's *Life of Lord Bolingbroke*." 118 (1863): 404–38.
Review of Thomas Macknight's *The Life of Henry St. John, Viscount Bolingbroke*, assayed Jonathan Swift's contributions to the *Examiner*.

87. [Morris, W. O'C.]. "Phillimore's *Reign of George III*." 118 (1863): 523–42.
Review of John George Phillimore's book cited the case of John Wilkes.

88. [Hayward, Abraham]. "Diaries of a Lady of Quality." 119 (1864): 305–39.
Paraphrased *Diaries and Commonplace Books of a Deceased Lady of Quality* (Miss Williams Wynn) on the identity of Junius.

89. [Brickdale, M. F.]. "*The Queen's English*." 120 (1864): 39–57.
Review of Henry Alford's book lamented the "Editorialism" that required anonymity in a periodical in order to suggest that it was an "infallible oracle." This custom might be appropriate for authors in elite journals but not for second-class writers whose egoism and dogmatism it inflated.

90. [Milnes, R. M.]. "*Charles Lamb*." 124 (1866): 261–74.
Review of B. W. Procter's book evaluated Lamb's contributions to Leigh Hunt's *Reflector* and the *London Magazine*, "which held a high place in the literature of its time" and counted among its other contributors William Hazlitt, Thomas Carlyle, and Thomas De Quincey.

91. [Bayley, C. J.]. "*Memoirs of Sir Philip Francis*." 127 (1868): 166–212.
Weighed evidence that suggested Francis was "Candor" and Junius in the *Public Advertiser*.

92. [Croskery, Thomas]. "The Irish Abroad." 127 (1868): 501–37.
Accused Irish-American newspapers of delaying Irish assimilation in the United States. This primarily urban press, allegedly the puppet of Catholic bishops and therefore 'ultramontane,' was republican on American politics, revolutionary on Irish, and reactionary on Continental. The Irish also monopolized the staffs of some "leading American newspapers." Both ethnic and other gazettes were the "sole mental pabulum" of Irish readers, not uplifting them but "rousing their worst passions." Orestes Brownson's *Review* was "the only really able and powerful representative of American Romanism."

93. [Reeve, Henry]. "*Letters and Speeches of Léon Faucher*." 128 (1868): 191–200.
Indicated that Faucher was "one of the principal editors" of the first *Temps* and after 1834 editor-in-chief of the *Courrier Français*, "a journal which was for many years identified with his own opinions."

94. [Peyronnet, Caroline de]. "Victor Jacquemont's *Letters*." 130 (1869): 57–84.
Echoed the 1830s opinion of Jacquemont that American newspapers, 'prodigious in number,' educated 'to a certain degree the mass of the nation' but deterred 'the more enlightened' from reading other and better material.

95. [Geffcken, Friedrich H.]. "Count Bismarck." 130 (1869): 417–58.
Lectured that Prussian press liberty was "extremely illusory." Since 1852 every newspaper could be seized pre-publication. Likewise, after three warnings, the government could "stop, suspend,

or suppress" any paper threatening the "public weal," a policy "borrowed from the administrative despotism of Imperial France."

96. [Wynter, Andrew]. "Postal Telegraphs." 132 (1870): 209–49.
Clarified how "several associations engaged in collecting and forwarding news to the provincial papers" used "news-express wires." "The press wires are at work from 7 p.m. to 3 a.m." Men with expertise in a foreign language were essential employees, but women clerks, supposedly hard to silence, sometimes divulged messages even though doing so was a misdemeanor.

97. [Merivale, Herman]. "Earl Stanhope's Reign of Anne." 132 (1870): 519–54.
Review of James Stanhope's *History of England* maintained that the essays in eighteenth-century periodicals were unequaled because their habit of careful correction of texts was obsolete by 1870. Daniel Defoe was "the prototype of the prolific, versatile, indefatigable class of slaves to the press whom modern facilities of production have created." He produced singlehandedly his *Review* five times a week for nine years and wrote "homely-wise leaders in *Mist's Journal*." Aside that Joseph Addison penned 240 essays for the *Spectator* between March 1711 and December 1712.

98. [Wynter, Andrew]. "Applications of Photography." 133 (1871): 338–58.
Rhapsodized that "a carrier pigeon…by the aid of microscopic photography" carried to Paris during the Franco-Prussian War "upwards of 35,000 messages and dispatches in the space of three inches rolled in a quill fixed to the middle feather of the tail." *The Times* was also sent this way. Quoted the editor of the *British Journal of Photography* that color photography was imminent.

99. [Wood, Henry H.]. "Suppressed and Censured Books." 134 (1871): 161–94.
Peeked at John Wilkes' *North Briton*, No. 45.

100. [Reeve, Henry]. "Communal France." 134 (1871): 250–90.
Indicted the Paris Commune for ending liberty of the press.

101. [Stigand, William]. "The Commune of Paris." 134 (1871): 511–63.
Denounced Communard suppression of most French newspapers. Although many had survived other nineteenth-century regime changes, now only gazettes run by friends of the Communards circulated: "a more wretched bundle of trash could hardly be collected in Mexico or the states of South America." The most influential, *Père Duchesne*, was "vile and scandalous."

102. [Merivale, Herman]. "*The Works of John Hookam Frere*." 135 (1872): 472–501.
Review of a book edited by H. and B. Frere followed J. H. Frere's career from the *Microcosm*, an Etonian journal to which George Canning also contributed and which Winthrop Praed's later *Etonian* surpassed. Frere also wrote for the *Anti-Jacobin* and had an article, "one of the very ablest which ever appeared in any English periodical," in the *Quarterly Review*, started by "clever Tories" to instruct their fellows and to counter the *Edinburgh*.

103. [Massey, W. N.]. "*The Life and Times of Henry, Lord Brougham*." 135 (1872): 502–49.
Review of Brougham's autobiography attributed to Sydney Smith the idea for and to Francis Jeffrey the planning of the *Edinburgh*. Smith supplied "energy and perseverance" when Jeffrey

had doubts about the project as had Brougham who was "with difficulty brought back" to it. Early numbers sold quickly, and a "large permanent circulation" was soon achieved. The major early authors were Smith, Jeffrey, Brougham, and Francis Horner. Paraphrased Brougham that the *Edinburgh* increased the influence of periodical criticism because reviewers were severe but not malicious.

104. [Alcock, Rutherford]. "Reform in Japan." 136 (1872): 244–69.
Referenced notions in the American *Japanese Herald* and *Japanese Mail* about Japanese development.

105. [Bridge, Cyprian]. "The Cuban Insurrection." 138 (1873): 395–425.
Aside on letters in *The Times* and *Daily News*.

106. [Reeve, Henry]. "*Autobiography* of John Stuart Mill." 139 (1874): 91–129.
Categorized the *Westminster Review* initially as "the organ of the most advanced opinions of the Utilitarian school," so editor John Bowring was disliked as a "spurious Benthamite." John Stuart Mill and his father, James, were both contributors. Because the early *Westminster* was financially insecure, many writers were volunteers.

107. [Lorimer, James]. "Memoirs of Archibald Constable." 141 (1875): 149–78.
Review of Thomas Constable's *Archibald Constable and His Literary Correspondents* enlightened that he published the *Edinburgh*, *Scots Magazine*, *Farmer's Magazine*, and *Medical Journal*. The "minor reviews and ephemeral literary periodicals which now constitute so large an element in the pabulum of the reading public" were absent in Constable's era, which also had no *Athenaeum* or the "literary portions" of the *Saturday Review* and *Spectator*.

108. [Hill, Arthur]. "Post Office Telegraphs." 143 (1876): 177–88.
Sputtered that legislation giving newspapers "a right of transmitting or receiving no less than seventy-five words in the night for one shilling" was an "inordinate concession" to them, "improvident and unjust." News, the business of papers, was delivered by night telegraph clerks paid at public expense. "The provincial press has been literally created by the Telegraphs, which enable it to anticipate the arrival of the metropolitan journals," so local papers could and should bear the salaries of these employees. "The Press in England is too powerful and too rich to require or to desire to be subsidized in this manner by the State."

109. [Reeve, Henry]. "*Life and Letters of Lord Macaulay*." 143 (1876): 544–81.
Review of G. O. Trevelyan's book spoke of T. B. Macaulay's articles in *Knight's Quarterly Magazine* and the *Edinburgh*, ones commended by editor Francis Jeffrey.

110. [Reeve, Henry]. "Wallace's *Russia*." 145 (1877): 358–82.
Review of D. Mackenzie Wallace's book glanced at the *Moscow Gazette*.

111. [Dempster, Charlotte]. "*Souvenirs* of Countess d'Agoult." 146 (1877): 339–61.
Biography of Marie de Flavigny (alias Daniel Stern) skimmed her contributions to the *Revue des Deux Mondes* and *Indépendante*.

112. [Massey, W. N.]. "The Constitution and the Crown." 148 (1878): 262–94.
Surmised that the public was as well informed as officials thanks to "the incessant action of the press, the platform, and the telegraphy." Aside that the *Quarterly Review* was "read by the educated classes."

113. [Froude, J. A.]. "The Copyright Commission." 148 (1878): 295–343.
Thought that copyright law was "inconsistent and imperfect" about periodical articles. Without copyright protection "able" writers would go to "popular journals, which already bid high for their assistance." Magazines and reviews addressed contemporary "sentiments, or passions, or interests"; newspapers, "epidemic excitements." Journalists of both genres had little time for contemplation.

114. [Dempster, Charlotte]. "*Memoirs of Mrs. Jameson.*" 149 (1879): 84–104.
Review of Geraldine Macpherson's *Memoirs of the Life of Anna Jameson* acknowledged her series on art in the *Penny Magazine* and article in the *Art Journal*.

115. [Stebbing, William]. "Walpole's England in the Nineteenth Century." 149 (1879): 168–210.
Review of Spencer Walpole's *A History of England from the Conclusion of the Great War in 1815* underscored the maturing of the press. Earlier "newspapers were regarded for the most part as disseminators of libels," and "reviews had little influence." An example of the first was the *Black Dwarf* with its 'miserable libels' and 'scurrilous nonsense.' "The institution of the *Edinburgh* was at once a literary and a political revolution." Often penned by men in power, the *Edinburgh* and the *Quarterly Review* "gave credit and dignity to the newspaper press." Anonymity "was best suited for the utterance of a collective judgment."

116. [Stebbing, William]. "William Cobbett." 149 (1879): 458–99.
Determined that Cobbett was not consistent because he mirrored readers; he inflamed rather than quelled "class feuds" but exposed official hypocrisy. His *Porcupine*, begun at a time when the "newspapers fought…against each other like famished wolves," failed because he treated it as an "enlarged pamphlet" when readers wanted news. Alternatively, his *Political Register* opened an epoch in the history of journalism. The paper, "really a weekly essay by Cobbett," led to his jailing for libel. Originally a fortnightly with 300 subscribers paying ten pence, by 1803 it had 4,000 subscribers and 40,000 readers and by 1809, it had 6,000 subscribers. The cheap version of the *Register* spoke to the new mill-hands, who purchased 44,000 copies of the two-penny edition. The large audience meant that Cobbett "became a power in the State," but the sway of the *Register* declined as the Whigs moved toward reform. By 1816 it printed only 1,600 copies, but parts were republished monthly in 1830 as *Twopenny Trash*.

117. "Germany since the Peace of Frankfort." 150 (1879): 301–38.
Delineated how a German Privy Councilor collected the weekly news from the ministries and published the "semi-official *Provinzial-Correspondenz*," sent free to "all official local papers." This person also fabricated leaders and correspondence for German and foreign papers. The government controlled telegraphy, and Otto von Bismarck had two 'independent' papers, the *Norddeutsche Allgemeine Zeitung* and the *Post* to propagate his policies. Bismarck, who exhibited "a womanish susceptibility to the criticisms of the press," had opposition gazettes "rigorously prosecuted on the slightest pretext."

118. [Stebbing, William]. "Bigelow's *Life of Benjamin Franklin*." 151 (1880): 321–58.

Review of an autobiography edited by John Bigelow labeled Franklin "a struggling printer" who learned good English from the *Spectator* and later circulated the *Craven Street Gazette*.

119. [Reeve, Henry]. "England and Ireland." 153 (1881): 274–304.

Discovered that the *Irish World*, printed in New York, circulated "largely among the peasantry" in Ireland.

120. [Toyne, Frederick E.]. "Methodism." 154 (1881): 1–37.

Learned from the *Methodist Almanac* that there was an "immense stream of periodical literature" for that faith. Its four quarterlies and about 150 other journals ranged from the long-running *Wesleyan-Methodist Magazine* to the recent *Experience*.

121. [Croskery, Thomas]. "Irish Discontent." 155 (1882): 155–85.

Declared that there was no Irish press before the 1842 "racy journalism" of Charles Gavan Duffy in the *Nation*. Newspapers thereafter educated the Irish politically. Of the 153 in 1882, 59 domestic and New York's *Irish World* were nationalist as was the *Freeman's Journal*, the most important Catholic tribune. It was fair, often printing opinion from English serials. Most newspapers emphasized sedition and eschewed independence, honesty, and impartiality; they were "illiberal, narrow, and degrading."

122. [Lyall, Alfred]. "Government of the Indian Empire." 159 (1884): 1–41.

Mused about India's "native newspapers" that spoke for opponents of government. The British regime of foreigners making mistakes was a good target for "sharp-witted journalism." Because even petty papers were important, they were all translated for officials. Leading Indian newspapers demonstrated "ability and moderation," but many others "reflected the disturbed surface of the public mind, without representing the deeper currents of native opinion and prepossessions. The press often appeals in the same breath to the primitive prejudices of Indian religion, and to the latest notions of European civilisation." The Indian press was "more untrammelled" than the press at home because it developed few rules of etiquette and its victims did not understand libel law. The Raj needed the press to explain its actions but should not endure constant misinterpretations of its policies. If a free press survived in India, it would be a good example for autocracies in Europe.

123. [Shand, Alexander Innes]. "The Literary Life of Anthony Trollope." 159 (1884): 186–212.

Recounted that Trollope authored magazine articles systematically, always filling the space allotted him.

124. [Walpole, Spencer]. "The Croker Papers." 161 (1885): 1–37.

Review of J. W. Croker's *Correspondence and Diaries*, edited by Louis J. Jennings, contended that Croker's "virulent and intemperate language [in the *Quarterly Review*] imparted a deplorable tone and temper to literary criticism." One of the first to recognize "the growing power of the press," he penned for Robert Peel's government. "The Minister was supplying the fact, and he was applying the tact."

125. [Conder, Francis R.]. "Secret Papers of the Second Empire." 161 (1885): 245–72.

Announced that the French government manipulated the 1869 elections by paying "modest" amounts to several named newspapers and sending writers to favored gazettes and items to Havas for rapid circulation.

126. [Oliphant, Margaret]. "The Life and Letters of George Eliot." 161 (1885): 514–53.

Chronicled that "in the autumn of 1851 Miss Evans went to London permanently as assistant editor of the *Westminster Review*, taking thus at once a position in the literary world." *Romola* was "the only one of her longer books which was published in a magazine," the *Cornhill*.

127. [Johns, B. G.]. "The Literature of the Streets." 165 (1887): 40–65.

Concluded that with compulsory education had come more cheap sensational periodicals very different from the wholesome *Penny Magazine* of the 1830s. The new "penny broadsheets, mostly newspaper size," were full of "slang" and "exaggeration." Less offensive were weeklies with scraps of information and "gleanings from American newspapers" or "Society" papers that indulged in "scandalous slander." An exception was the *Family Herald*, which handled letters with "skill and intelligence," characteristics also evident in its quasi-leaders.

The "chief newspapers" were "the voice and wish of the people, interpreted and uttered by able and upright men" ready to "guide public opinion," men who would maintain the dignity of the press and consequently its influence. "English journalism, taken as a whole, holds a position of which it may well be proud, won by fearless independence, honesty of motive, and unqualified regard for truth." Because it had millions of readers it should not let a small segment act as a "blot on its fair fame."

128. [Gallenga, Antonio]. "The Correspondence of Gino Capponi." 165 (1887): 388–413.

Believed that Capponi was "for many years the only journalist in Italy" whose work was worthy of inclusion in an English quarterly. He corresponded with *Edinburgh* editor Francis Jeffrey and wrote for the *Giornale Agrario*.

129. [Johns, B. G.] "The Education of Women." 166 (1887): 89–114.

Despaired that "no one special periodical or journal" existed for middle-class girls aged 15–18 that equaled in quality the ones for boys of the same rank and years.

130. [Lyall, Alfred]. "India under the Marquis of Dufferin." 169 (1889): 1–43.

Postulated that the "English government...created journalism in India." The government gave the vernacular papers importance by translating them to hear the "voice of India," but this treatment encouraged the "extravagance of minor journalists" who abused the "privilege of free anonymous writing." These newly educated men founded papers that required little initial capital or intellectual depth yet conferred a certain "notoriety." The leading gazettes were "so well written, so generally moderate, and so practical in their views and demands"; the new, not restrained by public opinion, the law courts, or the competition of a solid government press, engaged in constant criticism of the Raj. Their "editorials are smart and sensational, loose-tongued and unmannerly; the official papers occasionally published in reply are dull, accurate, and dignified." If the authorities were unwilling to restrict the press, they had to tolerate its abuses.

131. [Reeve, Henry]. "The Literature and Language of the Age." 169 (1889): 328–50.
Fretted that "the immense extension and influence of the newspaper press, supplying to countless millions the only form of literature with which they are acquainted," was corrupting the English language. Particularly at fault were the inferior country gazettes and those of the British Empire and the United States.

132. [Conder, Francis R.]. "The Railways of England." 170 (1889): 36–68.
Explained that London morning dailies expected railroads to deliver the 25 rolls of paper required every two days. Railroads warehoused a fortnight's supply to guard against accidents at the mills and handled the paper carefully lest a roll damage a press.

133. [Roscoe, E. S.]. "The New Series of State Trials." 172 (1890): 350–71.
Abridged, among other trials, the case of William Cobbett for seditious libel in his *Political Register*.

134. [Prothero, R. E.]. "American Fiction." 173 (1891): 31–65.
Bruited that American "newspapers and magazines usurp the place of books; the best men become editors instead of authors."

135. [Reeve, Henry]. "The Correspondence of John Murray." 174 (1891): 121–31.
Review of Samuel Smiles' *A Publisher and His Friends: Memoirs and Correspondence of John Murray* tagged the commencement of the *Quarterly Review* as a significant event in Murray's life. Although the London agent of the *Edinburgh*, on which he modeled his serial, Murray was a Tory. The "main conductor" of the *Quarterly*, he suggested topics and "pursued writers of ability," but editor William Gifford also shaped the *Review*. Murray's only failure was the *Representative* that he hoped would rival *The Times*.

136. [Kebbel, T. E.]. "*The Life and Works of Dr. Arbuthnot*." 177 (1893): 174–201.
Review of George A. Aitken's book on John Arbuthnot, M. D., mentioned that he "helped...with the *Grub-street Journal*." Aside that Lord Bolingbroke inaugurated the *Craftsman*.

137. [Elliot, Arthur]. "The Great Irish Conspiracy." 177 (1893): 247–81.
Deemed New York's *Irish World* an 'organ of dynamite.'

138. [Roscoe, E. S.]. "The Commonwealth and Protectorate." 181 (1895): 140–72.
Quoted S. R. Gardiner on the *Mercurius Elenctius*, *Mercurius Pragmaticus*, and *Man in the Moon*, newspapers after 1649 that flourished as Royalist papers despite government attempts to gag them.

139. [Owen, John]. "*Erasmus*, by the Late Professor Froude." 181 (1895): 173–205.
Revisited J. A. Froude's tenure as editor of *Fraser's Magazine*, the "well known monthly." As editor, Froude showed "unfailing courtesy" and "sympathetic consideration for young beginners" whose style he pruned. His goal was to make *Fraser's* "an organ for novel and profound thought, with as much diversity and light matter interspersed as might help its forward movement."

140. [Clarke, G. S.]. "Crimean Letters." 182 (1895): 326–50.
Imagined that the press did not originally understand the impact of telegraphy, especially in the hands of "ignorant or reckless correspondents" during war. In Crimea war correspondence was in its

"infancy," so "both writers and editors were doubtless ignorant of the injury which they combined to inflict upon the army." Similarly, General W. T. Sherman "bitterly complained of the license permitted to Northern newspapers" during the American Civil War. Alternatively, the Japanese had recently utilized the press to military advantage.

141. [Roscoe, E. S.]. "*Life of Sir Fitzjames Stephen*." 182 (1895): 418–39.
Review of Leslie Stephen's book on his brother, James, targeted his journalism for the *Morning Chronicle* and *Saturday Review*, where he "was one of the very able staff of writers who gave that periodical, for a number of years, a unique position among English journals." Even with many talented contributors, the *Saturday Review* was not influential because each number circulated "individual opinions," not a "collective and continuous appeal to the public mind, dictated by a general and systematic policy." The journal criticized but did not create opinion.

142. [Walpole, Spencer]. "The Reign of the Queen." 183 (1896): 1–27.
Broadcast that in 1839, 70 million stamped newspapers passed through the post.

143. [Elliot, G. J. M. K., Viscount Melgund, 4th Earl Minto]. "War Correspondents." 183 (1896): 129–42.
Starred G. L. Gruneisen, in Spain in 1835–37 for the *Morning Post*, as the first war correspondent. The job formally began in Crimea where inexperienced journalists jeopardized the troops. Because reporters were "cold-shouldered" by the military, they relied on gossip or their own "untutored eyes" in preparing telegrams. Errors arose from ignorance, not lack of patriotism, and reporters did publicize the needs of the army. In 1896 war correspondence was a highly paid profession offering a "chance for distinction" to those with "energy, ability, and courage." Yet these journalists still did not realize that their allegiance to news might endanger military operations. News was "subservient" to a military campaign irrespective of the "evil influence of the American press" in the Civil War. Greater government concern prompted War Office rules (excerpted from Archibald Forbes' *Memoirs*) for the Afghan campaign in 1879 and the Egyptian in 1882, but civilian reporters were preferable to military press spokesmen.

144. [Lecky, W. E. H.]. "Henry Reeve." 183 (1896): 267–71.
Honored long-time *Edinburgh* editor Reeve who was knowledgeable and committed to a high standard of style. "He had a strong sense of the responsibility of an editor, and especially of the editor of a Review of unsigned articles."

145. [Lyall, Alfred]. "English Letter-Writing in the Nineteenth Century." 183 (1896): 306–35.
Prefaced that the eighteenth century had few newspapers and those "neither good nor trustworthy" and no magazines or reviews of note before 1750. Letters were more reliable sources before the "copious indefatigable journalism" of the nineteenth century, when gazettes were replete with news and correspondence and monthly reviews, with signed articles full of "valuable ideas and information."

146. [Grant Duff, M. E.]. "Manning and the Catholic Reaction of Our Times." 184 (1896): 1–36.
Hinted about bigotry in the French Catholic press, as the *Univers*.

147. [Elliot, Arthur]. "Newspapers, Statesmen, and the Public." 185 (1897): 215–33.
Review of *An Editor's Retrospect* by Charles Cooper of the *Scotsman* introduced its founders and editors. It started in 1817 as a ten-penny weekly with eight small pages. By 1823 it was a biweekly for seven pence; in 1836 it offered for four pence news from 'liners' who were specialists in fires, murders, and accidents, and it pioneered the 'special wire' and 'special train.' In 1897 most readers wanted an independent press, easier to achieve outside London. Country gazettes were "papers of high standing and great influence," so the *Scotsman* was not the exclusive "expression of national opinion" though perhaps the broadest. Because competition to be first was keen, "the Press steadily improves."

148. [Shand, Alexander Innes]. "*Annals of a Publishing House*." 187 (1898): 40–66.
Review of Margaret Oliphant's book avouched that Oliphant became a regular contributor to *Blackwood's Magazine* because she was dependable, able to write on many topics at short notice. "John Blackwood was a singularly able editor of a periodical of world-wide celebrity." His contributors shared a "fraternal solidarity," a kinship fostered by founder William who always looked for "latent talent." Launched to rival the *Edinburgh*, *Blackwood's* prized, among many outstanding authors, J. G. Lockhart, John Wilson, Samuel Warren, and Frederick Hardman, earlier a foreign correspondent for *The Times*.

149. [Lyall, Alfred]. "Thackeray." 188 (1898): 378–409.
Biography of W. M. Thackeray rated his 1837 "Yellowplush Papers" in *Fraser's Magazine* "his earliest contribution of any length or significance" in periodicals. In the early 1830s he was a newspaper correspondent in France and scribbled for *Punch*, which by 1898 seemed "a dreary and deleterious specimen of misplaced farce."

150. [Elliot, Arthur]. "The *Memoirs* of Henry Reeve." 188 (1898): 516–43.
Pronounced Reeve, long-time *Edinburgh* editor, an excellent author. "As an anonymous writer of first-class ability, he exercised for a long series of years much influence over the public opinion of his countrymen." He penned articles for the *Edinburgh* and *Quarterly Review* and columns on foreign affairs for *The Times* in "its palmiest years" under John Delane. In the 1840s, before the advent of penny dailies, *The Times* was allegedly the only British paper read abroad. By 1898 it had even better coverage of news and variety in contents as well as "literary power" in a decade when Britain prided itself on the independence of its press.

151. [Laughton, J. K.]. "*Autobiography of the Third Duke of Grafton*." 189 (1899): 489–514.
Bowed to Junius and John Wilkes.

152. [Gwynn, Stephen]. "The Life and Writings of Mrs. Oliphant." 190 (1899): 26–47.
Stressed Margaret Oliphant's voluminous journalism, which displayed style and breadth, in *Blackwood's Magazine*.

153. [Blennerhassett, Charlotte]. "Montalembert." 190 (1899): 209–43.
Tracked Count C. de Montalembert's journalism from the *Avenir*, which was suppressed in 1832. In the 1840s he helped to establish the *Univers Catholique* and *Correspondant*. The first was a Paris version of Rome's *Civiltà Cattolica*. Aside that *Eos* was the "organ of Bavarian Catholics."

154. [Gwynn, Stephen]. "Some Tendencies of Prose Style." 190 (1899): 356–76.
Speculated that anonymous reviewing done by people of talent in an "impersonal manner" made 1800–40 the heyday of the "serious" journals.

155. [Birrell, Augustine]. "Copyright." 191 (1900): 141–56.
Compared British copyright law to that of other countries. The 1824 Act did not clarify whether a newspaper was a periodical, but the 1881 legislation protected its "original articles." What was needed was protection for stories secured at great expense and purloined by rivals.

Although the British were not as proud of the "Fourth Estate" in 1900 as previously because they knew its secrets, they acknowledged that it still served the public by presenting the news, mirroring opinion, and circulating much that was 'uplifting.' Its 'press men' were journalists of "feverish activity and more than feminine susceptibility."

156. [Roscoe, E. S.]. "James Russell Lowell." 191 (1900): 157–81.
Reminded that Lowell was the first editor of the *Atlantic Monthly*. "He worked upon the new literary venture with steadfast diligence, watching over it with extraordinary interest. Thus he is markedly identified with the rise of the periodical literature of the United States, which has now so much influence and circulates so widely over the Continent." He was later joint editor of the *North American Review*.

157. [Fletcher, Julia C.]. "M. Edmond Rostand and the Literary Prospects of the Drama." 192 (1900): 307–21.
Gushed that "[j]ournalism, the ideal of journalism, consists in formulating brilliantly what the man in the street was on the verge of saying." Many plays, even the successful, never rose above "smart and workmanlike journalism – of journalism which is to literature what a wall-paper is to a picture."

The Foreign Quarterly Review, 1827–1846

True to its title, the *Foreign Quarterly*, later affiliated with the *Westminster Review*, focused on the Continental press.

1. [Gillies, R. P.]. "Schubert's *Travels in Sweden, Etc.*" 1 (1827): 189–214.
Review of Friedrich Schubert's book documented a Swedish "war of periodical writers" around 1800 between the *Literary and Theatrical Journal* and the *Lyceum*, *Polypheme*, *Aurora*, and *Phosphorus*. Among other Swedish serials were *Iduna* on history and *Svea*, a miscellany. Two Privy Councilors edited periodicals.

2. [Gillies, R. P.]. "The German Pocket-Books for 1828." 1 (1827): 641–46.
Examined 15 German annuals while waiting for others, apparently with better articles, to arrive.

3. [Vieusseux, André]. "Italian Literature of the Eighteenth Century." 2 (1828): 621–61.
Reported that the "establishment of periodical publications or journals in Italy dates from the seventeenth century." The first was in Rome (1668) followed by a literary journal in Parma (1686) and the *Gallery of Minerva* in Venice (1696). In the eighteenth century, the *Journal of Letters*, among others, circulated in Venice (1710) and the *Café*, conducted by Pietro Allessandro Verri, in Milan.

4. [Rumy, K. G.]. "Language and Literature of the Magyars." 3 (1828–29): 28–76.
Asserted that the "most distinguished" Magyar periodicals were the *Transylvanian Museum*, edited by Gabriel Döbrentei, *Life and Literature*, and the *Scientific Magazine*. Also worthwhile were the *Magyar Museum* of Kasinczy Szabó, the *Universal Magazine*, *Iris*, *Orpheus*, and *Uranus*. Most, with 200–800 subscribers, had little valuable criticism because modest editors were afraid of offending authors.

5. [Merivale, Herman]. "French Histories of the English Revolution." 3 (1828–29): 76–92.
Footnoted the French *Revue Trimestrielle*, "which evidently possesses the assistance of several writers of considerable ability, and, on domestic subjects, of extensive information."

6. [Ward, John]. "Present State of the Netherlands." 5 (1829–30): 365–419.
Assured that newspapers were a "means of disseminating information," not a distraction from important study. In the Netherlands, there was one newspaper per 100 people; in England, one per 184; in France, one per 437. Netherlands papers, as French, prioritized politics above profit. The "young men of talent who endeavour to lead, rather than follow, the public opinion" ran the nongovernmental. No reviews or magazines existed except those imported or about trade. The imprisonment of Belgian *Argus* writers for joking about the authorities evidenced that suppression only made the press stronger.

7. [Robertson, T. C.]. "The English in India." 6 (1830): 148–80.
Opposed removal of all restrictions on the press because it would set the English against one another when Anglo-Indian papers criticized officials. "[U]nreserved and public discussion on every topic" was illogical under despotism and unnecessary because India's press was already freer than in imperial territories closer to Britain, as Malta.

8. [Lewis, George Cornewall]. "French Revolution of 1830." 6 (1830): 473–91.
Rooted the July Revolution in royal efforts to curb newspapers, culminating in the destruction of some presses.

9. [Southern, Henry]. "The Belgian Revolution." 6 (1830): 497–515.
Contended that the Belgian press derived its power from its opposition to government. The *Argus* provoked restrictions because the Dutch, less used to periodicals than the Belgians, tied journalism to sedition.

10. [Tufnell, Henry]. "The United States." 7 (1831): 194–233.
Opined that the "publication of *newspapers* is carried on in the United States to an extent unparalleled in any other quarter of the globe." This "vehicle for the communication of ideas" spread education but displayed "abandoned licentiousness" more commonly than British and certainly French gazettes. The American "abusive tone" mirrored citizens' "party spirit" and "unintellectual character." Because "light reading, which is too apt to degenerate into slander, is the prevailing taste" and cities had different interests, one could not know the United States from its press. Washington's papers focused on government; Philadelphia's and Boston's on literature; New York's on commerce. "The establishment of some leading newspapers" might improve journalism, but it was hard to "induce a person of high intellectual attainment to devote his time and talents to the drudgery of daily composition." In 1831 even the better papers selling 2,000 copies filled space with advertising. The reviews, such as the *American Quarterly* and *North American*, did attract talented scribes, but they frequently demeaned Britain in contrast to the fairness of their British peers.

11. [Moir, George]. "German Pocket Books for 1831." 7 (1831): 234–42.
Scanned 11 German annuals in which, unlike their British counterparts, "distinguished authors" wrote long articles. Deemed illustrations in some publications better than those in the *Comic Annual.*

12. [Vieusseux, André]. "Poland in 1830." 7 (1831): 519–32.
Lamented that Article 16 of Poland's 1815 constitution, which guaranteed "liberty of the press," was no barrier to the "strict censorship" since 1819.

13. [Ward, John]. "Diffusion of Knowledge in France: Necessity of Public Instruction." 8 (1831): 431–38.
Featured the *Sentinelle du Peuple*, "established for the sole purpose of setting before the lower orders, plainly and truly, passing events." Priced at 12 francs per year and with contents similar to other Paris papers, the *Sentinelle* appeared Sundays in Paris and Thursdays in the country. The 48-page monthly *Père de Famille*, the chief organ of the *Société d'Instruction Public*, charged 12 francs per year for a subscription in Paris, slightly more in the departments. Aside that French magazines succeeded better than newspapers.

14. [Buller, Charles]. "Letters of a German Prince." 9 (1832): 290–312.
Catalogued styles of literary criticism. The *Quarterly Review* published "vulgar ribaldry" or avenging, even dishonest paragraphs. The *Edinburgh Review* had better language but was equally unfair, and the *Westminster Review* was "candid."

15. [Moir, George]. "The German Ultra-Liberal Press: Börne and Heine." 10 (1832): 150–62.
Blamed the press for inciting revolutions in the German states as well as Belgium and France in 1830. German revolutionary serials multiplied as they catered to popular taste. Ludwig Börne, "who edited several journals," and Heinrich Heine, who wrote for others, adopted a "disguise of an affected and exaggerated liberalism" that discredited it and its press. "[T]heir incoherent ravings, their gross inconsistencies, their planless speculations, their contempt for taste and decency" proved that the power of the press could be harnessed for evil.

16. [Southern, Henry]. "The Revoution of 1830: Government of Louis-Philip [*sic*]." 10 (1832): 514–40.
Denigrated French journalists who "regard insurrection...as a legitimate expression of public opinion" instead of altering views "without the violation of public order." "The press is the universal adviser, corrector, and abuser" in France, but too many writers in too many papers with too many views endangered stability. Since "persecutions of the press" would merely "till the land of sedition" and prosecutions of journalists were difficult, government should convert them or operate journals.

17. [Moir, George]. "Present State and Prospects of French Literature." 11 (1833): 181–200.
Accepted French public opinion as the creature of dailies in Paris and the provinces. Their "hyperbole" impacted government, but official gazettes were an antidote.

18. [Lister, T. H.]. "Rush's Residence in England." 12 (1833): 209–35.
Review of Richard Rush's *A Residence at the Court of London* concurred with him that not only the "cheap, unstamped" but also the "highest and most powerfully supported" British papers attacked their own and other governments.

19. [Busk, Mary Margaret]. "Swedish Periodical Literature." 13 (1834): 314–40.
Centered on *Svea* although the *Foreign Quarterly* did not ordinarily review periodicals, even those with original material.

20. [?Lloyd, Hannibal Evans]. "Post Office Communication Between England and Foreign Countries." 13 (1834): 397–405.
Argued that the "Foreign Office was the principal obstacle to an arrangement for the circulation of newspapers in Great Britain and France respectively, either free, or at a moderate rate of postage" because its clerks did not want to lose this revenue. Aside that freer exchange of serials would diminish old enmities.

21. "*Ionian Anthology*." 13 (1834): 442–44.
Greeted a new periodical produced by people "of weight and consequence" in the Ionian Islands. The British should encourage islanders' "spirit of inquiry," "thirst for knowledge," and desire to overcome their sense of inferiority. The editor should not pirate ancient Greek or modern cheap publications but reprint English and French texts of quality and limit light material until civil society developed.

22. "Present State of Theatricals in France and England." 15 (1835): 266–88.
Lectured theatre critics of French "public journals," who were quick to label a play "trash," that it was "far more easy and profitable to supply the papers with trash than the theatres." Equally bad was British readers' perception of journals as "oracles."

23. [Leeds, W. H.]. "Russian Annuals." 16 (1835–36): 445–50.
Enlightened that Russia published about the same number of annuals as England or the German states. The Russian, with essays and criticism, were more akin to the "general literary periodical." The *Polar Star* (editors and contributors listed) was the source of an article penned by John Bowring in the *Westminster Review* (1: 80). After the editors of the *Polar Star* were implicated in a conspiracy and hanged in Siberia, *Russian Antiquity* and *Thalia* commenced.

24. [Urquhart, David]. "Character and Opinions of Travellers in Turkey." 17 (1836): 176–209.
Alluded to the *Courrier de Smyrne*, Alexander Blacque's journal concentrating on the Greeks. Blacque and "one of the highest dignitaries among the Ulema" later founded "a government Gazette" printed in Turkish for locals and French for Europeans.

25. "Thibaudeau's Memoirs of Napoleon." 17 (1836): 317–61.
Review of A. C. Thibaudeau's *Le Consulat et l'Empire* recounted that the Consulate licensed 16 political journals in Paris. Papers opposing the government or the French people could be suppressed, as was the *Ami du Lois* for ridiculing the Scientific Academy. "The *Moniteur* proclaimed itself the only official journal."

26. "Foreign Policy and Internal Administration of the Austrian Empire." 18 (1836–37): 257–304.
Pointed to the Polish *General Remembrancer of Art and Science*, *Cracow Themis*, and *Quarterly Review of the Fine Arts*, 1833–35. Aside that Austrian newspapers communicated little information to Europe.

27. [Leeds, W. H.]. "Grecian and Italian Architecture Contrasted." 19 (1837): 377–97.
Confessed that some critics in the *Foreign Quarterly* lacked expertise but averred that anonymity did not always conceal ignorance.

28. [Leeds, W. H.]. "Present State of Art in Russia." 20 (1837–38): 328–39.
Recognized Russian art journals, the new *Gazette of Fine Arts*, 1837, and the short-lived *Journal of the Fine Arts*, c. 1825. The *Gazette*, edited by Nestor Kukolnick, featured biographies. Russian art journals usually had more success than British art journals, which suffered from inept publishers

or untalented editors. German periodicals, as the *Berliner Kunstblatt*, contained "profound and instructive criticism."

29. "The Abbé de Lamennais." 21 (1838): 118–31.
Spotlighted the *Avenir*, a journal with which F. de Lamennais was associated. First promoted by Rome, it had problems with the pope as it became more "democratic."

30. [Pote, B. E. and a Collaborator]. "Late Proceedings in India: English Usurpation of Oude." 23 (1839): 93–116.
Skimmed the *Oriental Herald*, "a publication of extraordinary talent and interest," as well as the *Agra Ukhbar* and *Calcutta Englishman*.

31. "School for Journalists." 25 (1840): 113–30.
Review of *L'Ecole des Journalistes* by Mme Emile de Girardin, the wife of the publisher of the *Presse*, relayed how it "highlights the abuses of journalism" without distinguishing between "the clever journalist and the venal scribbler." Many French ministers and "all good writers in France" began as newspaper scribes or editors. French gazettes were "powerful and universal engines" for "truth and calumny" as well as texts of "general interest." The press could be "useful, honourable, and beautiful," could enlighten, or could be "guilty of much injustice, of numerous cruelties."

32. [Blackie, John Stuart]. "Lessing's Life and Writings." 25 (1840): 233–53.
Saluted periodicals of the "Berlin school of criticism," the *Bibliotek der schönen Wissenschaften* (1757), *Litteratur-Briefe* (1759), and *Allgemeine Deutsche Bibliotek* (1765). These journals developed "when periodical literature all over Europe was in its infancy."

33. [Kater, Edward]. "Printing and Publishing at Home and Abroad." 26 (1840–41): 95–126.
Looked at the König press used to print *The Times*.

34. [Gallenga, Antonio]. "Copyright in Italy." 26 (1840–41): 289–311.
Pondered the effect on periodicals of a recent copyright agreement between Piedmont and Lombardy-Venetia. Aside that a "higher tone of daring opinion and free discussion" was evident in the most popular Italian serials, such as Naples' *Progresso* and Milan's *Revista Europea.*

35. [Gallenga, Antonio]. "Education in Italy." 27 (1841): 297–327.
Heralded that Italy, imitating England, had numerous penny magazines. While some amused "with idle inanities" or corrupted with immoral fiction, others taught. Among the last was "the oldest and most deserving" *Guida dell'Educatore*, "conducted by Abate Raffaello Lambruschini, an evangelical as well as a Catholic priest." The *Guida*, a monthly born in 1835, by 1841 had reached "the highest plenitude of success and popularity." Among its "distinguished writers" were Pietro Thouar, Niccolo Tommaso, and Enrico Mayer. While the French education journals *Ruche* and *Education practique* had died, the *Guida* was still "vigorous," even publishing an appendix, *Letture pei fanciulli*, for the young. Equally "praiseworthy" was *Letture Popolari* (Turin), but it might be suppressed as had been *Subalpino*, a literary journal, in 1839.

36. "*The Convention of July 13.*" 28 (1841–42): 206–32.
Review of Prosper Duvergier de Hauranne's book rated the "*Courrier Français* one of the most influential of the nine or ten Paris journals" of the July Revolution.

37. "Kohl's *Sketches of St. Petersburg.*" 28 (1841–42): 398–434.
Review of J. G. Kohl's book announced that Russian journal writers were well paid, getting money "for merely giving their names to periodicals."

38. "The Baltic Provinces of Russia." 29 (1842): 32–68.
Registered six Baltic newspapers, at Riga, Reval, Dorpat, Pernau, Mitau, and Libau. "There are six or seven periodicals of a light literary character, and there is one, the *Inland* of Dorpat, which makes some pretensions to science, and has published many valuable articles in illustration of the history and statistics of Russia."

39. [Pardoe, Julia]. "On the Rise and Progress of Magyar Literature." 29 (1842): 204–27.
Returned to 1781 when "Matthew Ráth, a man of excellent principles and information, succeeded in establishing a Hungarian newspaper, which was speedily followed by several others in the same language."

40. [Bulwer-Lytton, E. G.]. "The Reign of Terror: Its Causes and Results." 29 (1842): 274–308.
Speculated about why the French "attached such affectionate importance" to a press whose situation shifted regularly. "[I]n a popular crisis it can inflame passions better appeased – in ordinary times it is exposed to persecutions the virulence and impunity of which are a scandal."

41. [Thackeray, W. M.]. "The Last Fifteen Years of the Bourbons." 29 (1842): 384–420.
Stressed "the astonishing spirit of rancour and falsehood of every organ of the French press" in the 1840s.

42. "The American Envoy and the King of the French." 29 (1842): 484–90.
Review of Louis Cass' *France, Its King, Court, and Government* noticed that the *Temps*, one of the papers instrumental in bringing Louis Philippe to power, was recently suppressed by his officials.

43. "French Criticism of English Writers." 30 (1842–43): 1–12.
Observed that in 1815 the French read literary criticism in newspapers. The *Constitutionnel* stood for the Enlightenment and the *Globe* for romanticism. The *Globe* presaged the *Deutsche Jahrbucher* insofar as both were noncontroversial in politics and religion until the Saint-Simonians bought the *Globe* in 1830 to promulgate their doctrines. Aside that critic Philarète Chasles was an expert on English literature unlike his colleague, Jules Janin.

44. [Forster, John]. "The Newspaper Literature of America." 30 (1842–43): 197–222.
Thundered that "the more respectable the city in America, the more infamous, the more degrading and disgusting, we have found its Newspaper Press." In Britain, only a few London papers reflected the same "social dregs and moral filth which *will* deposit somewhere in so large a city."

The *New York Herald*, a penny "broadsheet of lies and filth" from its wide network of correspondents, sold 30,000 daily irrespective of its dreadful paper, print, and format "jumble." New York's *Courier and Enquirer* was equally "adept at filth" as was the *Louisville Gazette*. The *New York Evening Post*, *Washington Intelligencer*, and *Boston Daily Advertiser* hired "men of character and of great ability," but respectability was secondary to popularity for American newspapers whose stock cry was "Party." Libel suits were rare because they blackened the reputation of plaintiffs seeking to stay in office. Consequently, newspapers assailed politicians at will, destroyed their privacy, and aroused "frightful restlessness and active hatred" among the "half-educated." *See* 31: 250.

45. [Kirwan, A. V.]. "Charles Gutzkow's Paris." 30 (1842–43): 316–30.
Review of Gutzkow's *Letters from Paris* revisited the launch of the *National* and the changes in the *Globe*.

46. [Corkran, J. F.]. "The Newspaper Press of France." 30 (1842–43): 466–98.
Presumed that French newspapers no longer swayed politics because a recent election had discredited Adolphe Thiers, the minister and former journalist who "flattered, seduced, and bamboozled" the gazettes to win power. He also tried to control the weekly *Revue de Paris* and fortnightly *Revue des Deux Mondes*, "the great gun of French periodical literature." The "ably conducted…first paper in France," the *Journal des Débats*, was an exception to the many anti-English journals, such as the *Presse* and *National*, that exacerbated irritations between the two countries. French journalists should abandon their diatribes and put their talents to secure journalism's liberty and regain its clout. Aside on the attempt to charge the editor of the *Journal du Peuple* for regicide because of a letter he printed. *See Chambers's Journal* 11: 375.

47. "Balzac on the Newspapers of Paris." 31 (1843): 182–87.
Review of Honoré de Balzac's *Monographie de la Presse Parisienne* charged it with inflating the ills of the press in its criticism of journalists.

48. [Thackeray, W. M.]. "Thieves' Literature of France." 31 (1843): 231–49.
Linked periodical serialization of crime literature to higher sales.

49. [Forster, John]. "The Answer of the American Press." 31 (1843): 250–81.
Retorted to editorials in New York's *Herald* and *Courier and Enquirer* and an article in the *Westminster Review* (39: 146) in response to Forster's essay on American newspapers. Reiterated ideas in 30: 197 that these tribunes "level, to an undistinguishable mass, the educated, the ignorant, and the base." The *Westminster* put *The Times* and *Standard* on the same level as American gazettes, but British reporters did not invade privacy or bully. Britain had only two newspapers that paralleled United States "recklessness and indifference" but without the Americans' success. Referred to the *Edinburgh Review* (76: 497).

50. [Thackeray, W. M.]. "French Romancers on England." 32 (1843–44): 226–46.
Bemoaned that "[a]buse of England is the daily bread of the French journalist. He writes to supply his market."

51. "The German Newspaper Press." 33 (1844): 371–87.
Conveyed that the foreign press rarely affected the German except for the *Allgemeine Zeitung*. Its quality and broad coverage by a large, well-paid staff guaranteed a big circulation and an influence unmatched by other German papers. The Germans had no national press, but governments shaped the

political press everywhere. Each region had censorship "interwoven" into every aspect of publication, from license to pre-publication review of format and writing.

52. "Domestic Life in the Slave States." 34 (1844–45): 104–29.

Review of G. W. Featherstonhaugh's *Excursion Through the Slave States* raged that the American press abused press liberty. The "great sign of American civilization, the cheap newspaper," was common because in the United States everyone read the papers. Little Rock had three for a population that in England could not support "a printer of occasional hand-bills." A town's "newspaper office is the grand rendezvous," made easy in Little Rock where the editor of the "principal gazette" owned the general store and ran the post office from the same site as his publication business.

53. [Lewes, G. H.]. "French Literary Journals." 36 (1845–46): 70–73.

Situated the *Revue des Deux Mondes* as dominant in "serious periodical literature" because it had "learning and careful writing." When French newspapers added feuilletons, it lost its best authors and some sales. In 1845, smaller but with quality restored, "[i]n its subjects, it has approached our Reviews; in its treatment, it has often surpassed us." Alternatively, the *Revue Nouvelle* lacked consistency, mixing the popular and the serious.

54. "Political Rights of the German Nation." 36 (1845–46): 168–78.

Review of *Important Documents on the Political Rights of the German Nation* emphasized the chilling effect on the press of the Carlsbad Decrees, so severe that even the "*Allgemeine Zeitung*, so moderate in its tone," was still publishing foreign news and science but little of "public concern."

55. [Taylor, Philip Meadows]. "Indian Railways and the Indian Press." 36 (1845–46): 306–23.

Stereotyped the Anglo-Indian press as "whimsical and extravagant," one given to printing inaccuracies. The *Friend of India* was an exception, "a paper generally remarkable for the calmness of its tone, and the fairness of its course of argumentation."

56. "The Political Prospects of Our Empire in the East." 36 (1845–46): 486–505.

Whined about Anglo-Indian press coverage of military campaigning.

The Fortnightly Review, 1865–1900

Without a commitment to party or religion, the *Fortnightly* revealed journalism's breadth. Entries spanned such diverse subjects as British foreign correspondence; imperial, European, and American newspapers; and the women's press in and out of the kingdom.

1. Editor [G. H. Lewes]. "Robert Buchanan." 1 (1865): 443–58.
Noted that book reviews were often hastily done.

2. Trollope, Anthony. "On Anonymous Literature." 1 (1865): 491–98.
Commended French journalistic signature because it created professionals with honor. Britain's anonymity suited a newspaper's "prevailing spirit" on politics, but signing other articles would catalyze more careful writing and eliminate the "eulogistic" writing typical of periodical criticism.

3. Gurney, Archer. "France as It Is." 1 (1865): 721–32.
Flagged French "seizure of English papers," among them the "respectable *Morning Herald*"; Charles de Remusat and other admirable writers in the *Revue des Deux Mondes*; and the political alignment of Paris newspapers.

4. Pelly, Lewis. "British India." 2 (1865): 31–42.
Spelled out that the British in India once read only the *Army List*, *Gazette*, and "a local paper."

5. Editor [G. H. Lewes]. "Criticism in Relation to Novels." 3 (1865–66): 352–61.
Fretted that "[e]ven in the best journals," criticism of novels was too laudatory. The press did not judge novels as literature but by the "ordinary canons which would be applied to a history, an article, or a pamphlet."

6. Editor [G. H. Lewes]. "Causeries." 4 (1866): 503–09.
Disdained anonymous criticism because responsibility for it might attach to any writer of the journal where it appeared. Anonymity allowed a critic to pan or praise arbitrarily. "Signatures would not prevent injustice, would not create sympathy, could not substitute knowledge for ignorance; but they would check insolence and carelessness, and in checking these would greatly improve criticism."

7. Editor [G. H. Lewes]. "Causeries." 5 (1866): 241–46.
Generalized that critical "opinions of the press" were frequently "puffs," which a public no longer gullible quickly recognized.

8. Schlesinger, Max. "Count Bismarck." 5 (1866): 385–405, 600–23.
Juxtaposed the freedom of "feudal and semi-official papers" in 1860s Prussia and the seizure of Liberal papers or the capricious prosecution of their owners and editors.

9. Benni, A. W. "Russian Society." 6 (1866): 549–66, 729–44.
Calculated that 1859 Russia had about 300 periodicals. "Literature being in Russia almost identical with journalism, and consequently of an almost exclusively political character," most journals quickly died because they hired the uninformed. The survivors included the *Moscow Gazette*; Moscow's *Day*, a weekly of the Slavophiles edited in 1866 by Ivan Aksakov; and two Nihilist monthlies in St. Petersburg: the *Contemporary*, started by Alexander Pushkin, and the *Russian Word*, owned by G. A. Kushelev-Bezborodko. Singled out Michael Katkoff, former Moscow University professor, who edited its monthly *Russian Messenger* and its daily *Moscow Gazette*. When the government instituted "correctional censure" for all periodicals, the *Gazette* defended the state as did the *Northern Post* and *Invalide*.

10. Editor [G. H. Lewes]. "Causeries." 6 (1866): 757–62.
Preferred anarchy to rules for journalistic criticism.

11. Editor [G. H. Lewes]. "Farewell Causerie." 6 (1866): 890–96.
Saw periodical criticism as "a great civilising influence very much in need of vigilance" because it depended on sincerity rooted in a sense of personal responsibility. Most anonymous critics wished only to unmask others' faults. *See* n.s., 32: 511.

12. Editor [John Morley]. "Causeries." n.s., 1 (1867): 100–03.
Applauded the *Pall Mall Gazette*, "a journal which is exerting so very wide and admirable an influence upon the periodical mind."

13. Wilson, John. "M. Guizot's *Own Time*." n.s., 2 (1867): 257–71.
Presumably a review of François Guizot's memoirs stamped the *Journal des Débats* a "highly influential newspaper" and the *Revue Retrospective* the child of the February 1848 Revolution.

14. Editor [John Morley]. "Anonymous Journalism." n.s., 2 (1867): 287–92.
Oft-quoted article held that the press, "the most important of social influences" not be a "secret society." Most leader-writers, contrary to the stereotype, were thoughtful and knowledgeable and penned for more than money. Anonymity encouraged them to repeat a journal's views rather than to think. Signature would make controversy "more sincere," force writers to exercise self-control, and serve readers who perceived writers as "oracles." *See New Review* 1: 513 and *Westminster Review* 88: 381.

15. Merivale, Herman. "Junius, Francis, and Lord Mansfield in December, 1770." n.s., 3 (1868): 250–56.
Focused on efforts to identify Junius.

16. Rae, W. F[raser]. "John Wilkes." n.s., 4 (1868): 260–76.
Rehabilitated Wilkes, misjudged by later writers who either "underrate his importance" or "deny his sincerity." "Less polished than [Joseph] Addison and less incisive than Junius, he had the art of stating a case with a clearness that rendered it intelligible to every reader, and he had the audacity requisite for putting in plain terms the most unpalatable truths." Wilkes established the *North Briton* "with the express object of ridiculing Scotchmen and opposing Lord Bute," but use of a general warrant in his case was a blow to press liberty.

16a. Editor [John Morley]. "Old Parties and New Policy." n.s., 4 (1868): 320–26.
Rebuked journalists for irresponsibly using their power to supervise government and ratify or veto its decisions. Deprecated press readers who adopted journalistic opinions rather than form their own.

17. Dowden, Edward. "Lamennais." n.s., 5 (1869): 1–26.
Biography of F. de Lamennais connected him to the *Mémorial Catholique* and the *Avenir*, which "struggled against overwhelming odds."

18. Blind, Karl. "The Condition of France." n.s., 6 (1869): 651–64.
Revealed that "better treatment of the Press" in France had sired 150 new anti-government periodicals more "fiery" than Paris journals except the *Réveil* and *Rappel.*

19. Editor [John Morley]. "The *Fortnightly Review* and Positivism: A Note." n.s., 8 (1870): 118–20.
Response to a *Saturday Review* article (11 June) on the *Fortnightly's* stance avowed that many periodicals represented an interest. The *Fortnightly* was, except for the *Westminster Review*, the only periodical to give ideas "fair play." The *Saturday Review* should pay more attention to "careful fidelity of facts" and less to "promiscuous and universal sneering."

20. Editor [John Morley]. "France and Germany." n.s., 8 (1870): 367–76.
Prescribed a "salutary shock of tribulation" for French newspapers with "their blood-thirsty levity, their unchivalrous and brutal disparagement of their enemies."

21. Laveleye, Emile de. "The Future of France." n.s., 8 (1870): 615–30.
Posited that the French press "forms opinion, and public opinion is the true sovereign." French gazettes published no foreign news, and bias dominated domestic. Those with the widest circulation "live on scandal and falsehood." "[B]etween the English newspapers and those of other countries, the distance is enormous." France needed a "well-informed, reasonable, and influential" paper on the English model.

22. Harrison, Frederic. "Bismarckism." n.s., 8 (1870): 631–49.
Denounced press reports of the Franco-Prussian War because their tone debased readers. "For months the journals have filled our minds with the loathsome cant of the camps."

23. Dicey, Edward. "Paris after the Peace." n.s., 9 (1871): 485–94.
Witnessed a marked improvement in the "social," if not the "political" tone of the Paris press. During the Second Empire the papers with the largest circulation, the *Gaulois* and *Figaro* and "their innumerable minor imitators," lived on gossip. In 1871 the French concentrated on national news and polished leaders published anonymously.

24. Harrison, Frederic. "The Revolution of the Commune." n.s., 9 (1871): 556–79.
Despised French journalism's "wild stories" and "ridiculous" commentary about the Commune. The *Journal des Débats* was "one of the least corrupt of the French newspapers, the organ of the Orleanists and the rich bourgeois."

25. Harrison, Frederic. "The Fall of the Commune." n.s., 10 (1871): 129–55.
Accused Paris reporters even of the "best known newspapers" of "willful lying" to goad the public.

26. Hillebrand, Karl. "The Prospects of Liberalism in Germany." n.s., 10 (1871): 387–420.
Broadcast that the German press had a wide berth but did not use this freedom and lacked "French good taste and elegance of form, and English sound common sense." The British press was less influential than the French, but the German had no clout. Unlike British gazettes the German had no letters to the editor or much beyond political topics. Germany had no large middle class to read "first-class papers" or reviews, so only "commonplace local papers for a respectable hum-drum bourgeoisie" and "scientific special periodicals" for savants circulated. Aside that the Belgians and Swiss had fewer correspondents and a less organized telegraphy than the British.

27. Castelar, Emilio. "The Republican Movement in France." n.s., 11 (1872): 668–91; n.s., 12 (1872): 1–18, 166–90, 325–38.
Branded Léon Gambetta's newspaper, the *Réforme*, "persecuted."

28. Booth, Arthur J. "Fourier." n.s., 12 (1872): 530–53, 673–91.
Biography of Charles Fourier studied his 1836 journal, *Phalanstère, ou la Réforme Industrielle*. Another serial, the *Phalange: Journal de la Science Sociale*, appeared thrice monthly, 1836–37, then monthly until 1840, and thrice weekly until 1843 (as the *Démocratie Pacifique*). There were Fourier journals in England and the United States. The English *Morning Star* was known as the *London Phalanx* in 1841, the same year that the Buffalo (NY) *Phalanx* commenced. Then Albert Brisbane started New York's *Future* and after was a columnist for the *New York Tribune*. Purported that the *Dial* and others endorsed Fourier's ideas so that by 1843 there were three papers in New York and at least one in 40 states as well as reviews.

29. Editor [John Morley]. "The Death of Mr. Mill." n.s., 13 (1873): 669–76.
Obituary of John Stuart Mill thought that the "better sort of journalists educated themselves on his books, and even the baser sort acquired a habit of quoting from them."

30. Bowen-Graves, Francis. "Marat." n.s., 15 (1874): 43–74.
Sketched the *Ami du Peuple* as a small octavo of eight to 12 pages with varied type, many errors, and repetitions but no coarseness. French authorities, in retaliation for their denunciation by J. P. Marat, its editor/writer and printer/publisher, seized its press. Marat then wrote and published the *Junius Français* until he introduced in 1792 his *Journal de la République*, later captioned the *Publiciste de la République*.

Aside that "a daily newspaper" was "a medium adequate enough for negative criticism."

31. Colvin, Auckland. "The Indian Famine and the Press." n.s., 15 (1874): 484–95.
Aside on the usual style of "cool reason" of *The Times*.

32. Parsloe, Joseph. "Railway Rates and Fares." n.s., 18 (1875): 75–92.
Remarked on the incoherence of fees for newspaper transmission by rail.

33. Dicey, Edward. "The Copyright Question." n.s., 19 (1876): 126–40.
Groaned that without copyright protection of magazine articles, British periodicals lost revenue because the Americans stole essays, thus stifling their own talented authors.

34. Saintsbury, George. "Modern English Prose." n.s., 19 (1876): 243–59.
Disagreed that "the prevalence of journalism" accounted for bad writing even though newspaper prose was poor. While "the better class of newspaper" aimed for excellence, it was hard to achieve because pressure of time meant repetitive, albeit picturesque language. Scrutinized style in *The Times*, *Spectator*, *Saturday Review*, and the quarterlies.

35. Abbott [Abbot], Francis E. "The Catholic Peril in America." n.s., 19 (1876): 385–405.
Skipped through American religious journalism, such as the Louisville *Catholic Advocate* and the New York Evangelical Protestant *Christian Union and Independent*. The *Catholic World* was "the leading periodical of the Church published in America." The Protestant *Christian Statesman* was the organ of a movement to amend the United States Constitution to include a reference to God, a movement opposed by the *Liberal and Index*, a Boston weekly. Aside that New York's *Irish World* also publicized ideas of the Roman Church.

36. Bunce, J. Thackray. "James Northcote, R.A." n.s., 19 (1876): 861–76.
Mentioned Northcote's art essays in the *Artist* (c. 1807) and other articles, which showed "freshness," in the *New Monthly Magazine*.

37. Wedderburn, David. "English Liberalism and Australasian Democracy." n.s., 20 (1876): 43–59.
Gloried that "the leading papers in Australia…rank with the high-class journals in England, which they appear to have chosen as their models, and I certainly do not know any American newspaper which can be favourably compared with the *Melbourne Argus* or the *Sydney Morning Herald*."

38. Courtney, Leonard. "Political Machinery and Political Life." n.s., 20 (1876): 74–92.
Believed that the press "exercises an enormous influence in diffusing and popularizing" parliamentary ideas, but "its opportunities of original action are and must be rare."

39. Dilke, Charles Wentworth. "English Influence in Japan." n.s., 20 (1876): 424–43.
Divulged that in Japan "the new men who rule the country show a great impatience of the criticism of the Press," notably in the *Hochi Shimbun* and *Akebono Shimbun*. The government enforced a "severe press-gagging law" and persuaded the British to jail British publishers of Japanese papers in the treaty ports, but not the English-language *Yokahama Punch*.

40. Appleton, C. E. "American Efforts after International Copyright." n.s., 21 (1877): 237–56.
Speculated that local American newspapers often shaped a Congressman's views "perhaps [because] he owes his seat" to them.

41. Simcox, G. A. "Miss Martineau." n.s., 21 (1877): 516–37.
Profile of Harriet Martineau cited her work for the *Monthly Repository*, which after 1829 paid her 15 pounds per year for "reviewing" "when no other magazine would look at her articles." She later penned for the *Westminster Review*, *Household Words*, and the *Daily News*.

42. Campbell, G[eorge]. "The Farther Outlook in the East." n.s., 21 (1877): 803–19.
Grieved that the free press in India sometimes wrote "in language which in Europe would be called seditious."

43. Wallace, D. Mackenzie. "Secret Societies in Russia." n.s., 22 (1877): 149–69.
Peeked at "*Kolokol*, a Russian paper published in London by [Alexander] Herzen and strictly prohibited by the Press-censure," yet "read by thousands" in Russia.

44. Hyndman, H. M. "Cavour." n.s., 22 (1877): 219–43.
Bowed to Camillo di Cavour as a founder and editor of the *Risorgimento*.

45. Hutton, R[ichard] H[olt]. "Walter Bagehot." n.s., 22 (1877): 453–84.
Remembered Bagehot's work for "the *Inquirer*, which then was and still is the chief literary and theological organ of the Unitarian body" and for the *Fortnightly*. This knowledgeable editor of the *Economist* "brought life" to "dry subjects" but deplored the "intolerable and fatiguing cleverness" of French reviews.

46. Pattison, Mark. "Books and Critics." n.s., 22 (1877): 659–79.
Outlined the order in which people dealt with the mass of literary criticism in 1877. First they scanned the dailies, which scattered literary columns between politics and commerce, and then the literary weeklies. The *Saturday Review* was no longer "froth and frivolity" but "highly instructive." The exclusive literary weeklies, as the *Athenaeum*, had "current opinion." Next readers perused monthly reviews, "the most characteristic and pithy part of our literary produce." These periodicals flourished because people did not want to wait for quarterlies, the "venerable" *Edinburgh Review* and *Quarterly Review* that the *Fortnightly*, *Contemporary Review*, and the *Nineteenth Century* overshadowed because they had the "best writers." To be a critic required "comprehensive study," but some were lazy or incompetent people paid to fill pages.

47. Harrison, Frederic. "The Republic and the Marshal." n.s., 22 (1877): 747–72.
Underscored French official harassment of republican journals prior to 1877 when sales in public and in "places of public resort" were prohibited. This policy, done at the behest of provincial authorities, may have echoed their concern that the *Bulletin des Communes* converted from a local gazette transmitting official documents to a "scurrilous party" weekly.

Aside that an English free press was still subject to the laws of libel and sedition.

48. Editor [John Morley]. "Memorials of a Man of Letters." n.s., 23 (1878): 596–610.
Essay on Macvey Napier, editor of the *Edinburgh Review*, 1829–47, paralleled managing a great periodical and a great opera house because each required dealing with stars. Signature meant less responsibility for editors because they could recruit the talented rather than training tyros but also meant that writers, once known by their interest, might be less forthright. Anonymity lent serials

more political cohesion. A scribe who submitted a "disorderly manuscript" burdened the editor and printers, "more meritorious persons than fifth-rate authors."

49. Grant Duff, M. E. "Emilio Castelar." n.s., 23 (1878): 816–34; n.s., 24 (1878): 46–73.

Marked Castelar as a contributor to British and American periodicals.

50. Grant Duff, M. E. "Henry Murger." n.s., 24 (1878): 231–49.

Supposed that Murger, who edited *Castor* and wrote for the *Artiste*, edited by Arsène Houssaye, never made much money because he worked slowly. During the last years of Murger's life "there was no journal which was not only too glad to have him."

51. Laveleye, Emile de. "Prince Bismarck." n.s., 24 (1878): 765–86.

Recorded that in the Franco-Prussian War Otto von Bismarck employed two journalists to write his press releases. Thereafter, he authorized the *Correspondance de Berlin* for the foreign press. Printed in French on yellow sheets, it was easy to scissor.

52. Trollope, Anthony. "George Henry Lewes." n.s., 25 (1879): 15–24.

Tribute to Lewes, the first *Fortnightly* editor, summarized his contributions to many periodicals, as *Blackwood's Magazine*, *Fraser's Magazine*, the *Cornhill Magazine*, the *Edinburgh Review*, and the *Leader*, which he edited from 1851 to 1854. As editor of the *Fortnightly*, he was "indefatigable and enthusiastic" and more eclectic than his successor. A man who did this job while he penned his "great work," Lewes upheld the *Fortnightly's* goals to be "strictly impartial and absolutely honest" and to get the best literature by paying for it.

53. Harrison, Frederic. "First Impressions of the New Republic." n.s., 25 (1879): 353–72.

Noticed that exiles who returned to France authored newspaper articles but were "poor writers" whom "nobody reads."

54. Pearson, Charles H. "The Functions of Modern Parliaments." n.s., 26 (1879): 68–81.

Rooted the modern press in Puritan pamphlets and eighteenth-century dailies, the first censored and the second stamped. During the Napoleonic Wars *The Times* and *Morning Chronicle* "borrowed the assistance of trained writers to give a better literary form to the leading articles," inaugurating a new press era. British journalism, unlike French, did not typically lead to a legislative seat, probably good because an editor who was a Member of Parliament would likely refrain from policy statements in the House.

55. Colvin, Sidney. "Art and Criticism." n.s., 26 (1879): 210–23.

Lauded the *Pall Mall Gazette*, which had "honorably distinguished" itself since 1874 in the field of art criticism.

56. Giles, Herbert A. "Present State of Affairs in China." n.s., 26 (1879): 362–84.

Aired that scandals and abuses of the Chinese government only surfaced in "local foreign newspapers or in Chinese newspapers guarded by some foreign flag."

57. Minto, William. "Edgar Allan Poe." n.s., 28 (1880): 69–82.
Abridged Poe's work for the *Southern Literary Messenger*, *Gentleman's Magazine* (Philadelphia), and *Graham's Magazine*, which reputedly did not fire him for negligence or "debauchery." He usually reviewed books for the *Messenger* and *Graham's*. More tales in the last periodical would have brought more income, but he wrote slowly because he was scrupulous.

58. Reid, T. Wemyss. "Public Opinion and Its Leaders." n.s., 28 (1880): 230–44.
Contrasted how London and local papers handled political commentary. The metros, some professing to be "authorised and infallible interpreters of public opinion," were smug about their political acumen and biased or erroneous about public wants. London gazettes formed "a mutual admiration society." They "ignored, with a severity" that which tended "to crush out any spark of independence or self-respect by which they may chance to be distinguished," the country press. But in 1880 the locals were increasingly more accurate as the political center shifted out of the capital. Among the best were the *Scotsman*, *Glasgow Herald*, *Manchester Guardian*, and *Birmingham Post*. Metro journals had either to reduce their foreign news or reprint the country in the evening to compete.

59. Smyth, P. J. "Young Ireland." n.s., 28 (1880): 696–707.
Assessed the impact of the *Nation* when Charles Gavan Duffy was its editor.

60. Statham, F. Reginald. "How to Get Out of the South African Difficulty." n.s., 29 (1881): 285–301.
Former editor of a Natal journal informed that the *Zuid Afrikaan*, a Capetown paper, had the largest circulation in the region. Its editor and the editor of the *Natal Mercury* were both involved in politics.

61. Schuster, Ernest. "The Anti-Jewish Agitation in Germany." n.s., 29 (1881): 371–84.
Insisted that Jews were not the only group controlling the press in Germany. Listed several papers, among them Cologne's *Zeitung* and the *Allgemeine Zeitung,* that had "hardly any Jews on their staff." Journalists of many identities lacked tact and fine feeling.

62. Stevenson, Robert Louis. "The Morality of the Profession of Letters." n.s., 29 (1881): 513–20.
Regretted that "the American reporter or the Parisian *chroniquer*, both so lightly readable… touch upon all subjects…with the same ungenerous hand; they begin the consideration of all, in young and unprepared minds, in an unworthy spirit." All reporters should be factual even if they had different perspectives; investigate thoroughly, and take time to develop their ideas because every "scribbler" had the chance to educate at least one reader.

63. Woodberry, George Edward. "The Fortunes of Literature under the American Republic." n.s., 29 (1881): 606–17.
Woodberry, an American, averred that in the United States, democracy had sired schools whose graduates' reading taste could be measured in 1881 by Sunday newspapers with "sensation." The United States had scarcely "a half-dozen organs of critical opinion," but this genre educated, a

prerequisite for national excellence. Aside that British magazines learned from the widely circulating *Harper's Monthly* and *Scribner's*.

64. Niven, Robert. "William Lloyd Garrison." n.s., 31 (1882): 247–63.
Followed Garrison from printer's apprentice at the *Newburyport Herald* to journalist elsewhere, then junior editor of the *Genius of Universal Emancipation* and ultimately the soul of the *Liberator*, which he produced "with the help of one white man and a negro boy." He published the paper, which faced "daily threats," using type from the newspaper where he worked as a compositor.

65. Allen, Grant. "The Decay of Criticism." n.s., 31 (1882): 339–51.
Separated literary critics by generation. Earlier reviews relied on specialists, men who felt responsible for an article and for the serial. In 1882 there was no discipline or "common sentiment" among ignorant and pretentious critics who could write on anything. Quality criticism still existed in elite journals, but newspaper reviews counted for nothing except in "a few steady-going" gazettes that printed "careful and deliberate" columns. The rest were the products of reporters taking inventory. Penned in simple language and without rancor, this criticism enhanced bad books or penalized promising young authors. But the public liked this style, and newspapers mirrored the public.

Thanks to compulsory education, more newspapers emerged, and journalism became an open profession. It "no longer demands…special aptitude, special training, or special function." Because everyone quickly got a job, there was no apprenticeship or "reflection…all is haste."

66. "Some Irish Realities: An Historical Chapter." n.s., 31 (1882): 380–99.
Returned to the 1850s when the *Irishman* tried to increase its circulation at the expense of the *Nation* and "all the essentially Catholic Irish newspapers." The *Irish People* had a scribe who, though talented and "of good heart," was "a violent writer," causing him many problems with the police.

67. Editor [John Morley]. "The Life of James Mill." n.s., 31 (1882): 476–504.
Review of *Memorials of the Life of James Mill* pointed out that he edited the *Literary Journal*, "a shilling weekly," and the *St. James's Chronicle* in addition to writing many review articles.

68. Aylward, Alfred. "Africa and the Empire." n.s., 31 (1882): 505–17.
Communicated that the *Express*, a Bloemfontein paper, was in Dutch and English, whereas the majority of Southern African papers were only in English.

69. Gallenga, A[ntonio]. "Finland." n.s., 31 (1882): 602–11.
Contended that the Finns opposed a free press on two grounds: it was better not to compete with established Swedish papers, and Swedes in Finland would tap fellow Scandinavians for their staffs, leaving the Finns isolated.

70. Editor [John Morley]. "Valedictory." n.s., 32 (1882): 511–21.
Editorial farewell observed that periodical literature lost its freshness rapidly notwithstanding eminent named contributors. Gloss on G. H. Lewes' ideas on anonymity (6: 890) maintained that signature had positive and negative effects. Signing meant more experts who were narrower or ready to be 'stars.' Newspapers would soon have signatures as editors developed views not tied to party and as MPs looked to journals not just for support or as barometers but for "ideas, guidance, and counsel,"

functions closer to their French peers. The *Fortnightly* and its brethren, putting serious ideas before the public, were "more powerful pulpits, in which heretics were at least as welcome as orthodox" scribes.

71. Collings, Jesse. "A Radical in Russia." n.s., 33 (1883): 205–20.
Alluded to Russian censorship of domestic newspapers and restrictions on or deletions from foreign ones.

72. [Barrère, Camille and Hector Depasse]. "Gambetta." n.s., 33 (1883): 285–97.
Bared that Léon Gambetta derived his wealth from shares in two newspapers he inspired, the *République Française* and *Petite République*.

73. Sinnett, A. P. "Anglo-Indian Complications and Their Cause." n.s., 34 (1883): 407–21.
Editor of the *Pioneer* for ten years swore that it was "generally regarded in India as its leading journal."

74. Griffin, Lepel. "A Visit to Philistia." n.s., 35 (1884): 50–64.
Sighed that "American reporters are very apt to record the questions they may ask as being the answers they have received."

75. Escott, T. H. S. "Mr. Hayward." n.s., 35 (1884): 414–25.
Eulogized Abraham Hayward, the founder of the *Law Magazine* and a regular contributor to the *Quarterly Review*. *See* n.s., 35: 549.

76. Kebbel, T. E. "The Tory Party under Wyndham and Bolingbroke." n.s., 35 (1884): 495–509.
Stamped the *Craftsman* "the most powerful and influential party paper which has ever existed." Although it did not circulate like a modern penny gazette, its "political journalism" rested on "authentic information."

77. [Cartwright, W. C., *et al.*]. "Mr. Hayward Postscripta." n.s., 35 (1884): 549–56.
Continued n.s., 35: 414 with a note that Abraham Hayward made a good living at the *Morning Chronicle*.

78. MacColl, Malcolm. "Russia Revisited." n.s., 35 (1884): 593–610.
Suspected that Russia's prohibition of a free press did not stop "clandestine" sheets but did prevent the people from having an "organ for articulate expression."

79. Bowles, Thomas Gibson. "Newspapers." n.s., 36 (1884): 17–29.
Referred to 1870 and 1881 legislation that defined a newspaper as a publication of "current topics" at least weekly with title and date. Alleged that news had to be "new, unexpected, and calculated to satisfy curiosity" but could be false.

Narrated the newspaper's history from the Roman *acta diurna* to the Italian gazette and eventually to Nathaniel Butter's *Weekely News*. The Civil Wars spawned numerous mercuries, and in 1655 the *Perfect Diurnall* had the first advertisement. From the 1773 *Morning Post*, papers multiplied with 2,000 by 1884. The early ones were akin to contemporary society journalism but without their personal scandal. The end of duties (1853 advertising, 1855 stamp, 1861 paper) catalyzed more and cheaper publications. Newspapers were still sent by post at the same charge per copy but should be charged by weight. If, as on Saturday, 14 June 1884, *The Times* had more advertising than news, it should pay the book rate.

The "press is now a great power in the nation" because journalists were worthy. As suffrage expanded, people anticipated that the press would guide them about issues. The 'leader' "overshadowed the news in importance" because editors told readers what to think, "rather to instruct than to inform, rather to proselytise than to instruct." Editorial priorities could result in neglect of news gathering, impede "the honest and unreserved publication" of news gathered, and induce reporters to slant their stories. Leader-writers, together with "foreign Correspondents, reporters, and penny-a-liners, have an enormous power of previous instruction in any matter, and an almost unlimited power of subsequent exaggeration of that matter." Readers would be better served by news only, with time to formulate their own opinions, and a press undivided by competition and politics might have its power "fully honoured."

Newspapers were censored in Germany and Russia; were "without enterprise and very trivial" in Spain, and were "trivial or venal or both" in Italy. The French press, "while inferior in the quantity and quality of its news, is far superior to the English in respect of its comments and handling of many subjects." American newspapers displayed "far greater enterprise, far greater readiness to understand and to hit the taste of the moment than the English," but they were free from "corruptibility by money" and trustworthy in their news.

Calculated the costs of writing and producing a newspaper, the first paid by sales and the second, by advertising. A journal "buys the attention of its readers by its news and sells that attention to its advertisers for their money."

80. Blunt, Wilfrid Scawen. "Ideas about India: Race Hatred." n.s., 36 (1884): 445–59.
Guessed that a leading newspaper or magazine was "intellectually superior" to statesmen's speeches in England but that the reverse was true in India.

81. Jebb, R. C. "Ancient Organs of Public Opinion." n.s., 36 (1884): 569–88.
Delineated ancient ways of spreading news from Homer through later Greeks and Romans. Greek oracles were forerunners of modern answers to correspondents. The Roman Lucilius was "a slashing journalist." Julius Caesar launched the "regular gazette of official news."

In the eighteenth century the *Tatler* dealt with "manners, letters, and politics," and the *North Briton* symbolized a free press more representative of opinion than Parliament. In 1884 "the double power wielded by the newspaper press, at once as the ubiquitous instructor and the rapid interpreter of the national mind," was obvious. Journalism was an "inestimable gain" for society because of its "quickness in seeking and supplying information – continual vigilance of comment – electric sympathy of social feeling" even if journalists sometimes "abused" their influence or used an "objectionable…tone."

82. Healy, T. M. "The Irish and the Government." n.s., 36 (1884): 649–56.
Yoked press laws of India and official treatment of the *Kerry Sentinel*.

83. Kebbel, T. E. "John Wilson Croker." n.s., 36 (1884): 688–702.
Situated Croker as "the principal political writer in the *Quarterly Review* for nearly a quarter of a century."

84. Escott, T. H. S. "Men of Letters on Themselves." n.s., 36 (1884): 834–46.
Drew from the autobiographies of Edmund Yates, James Payn, and Antonio Gallenga. Yates and Gallenga, who were "prompt, accurate, persevering, graphic," were in the "first rank" of journalism. Yates and Payn started their careers at *Household Words*. Gallenga, who later worked for John Delane at *The Times*, discovered that journalism was not easily accessible to a foreigner. However, in 1884, "Gallenga occupies a prominent place in the brilliant galaxy of special and war correspondents, the other bright particular stars of which are W[illliam] H[oward] Russell, [George Augustus] Sala, [Archibald] Forbes, and [John A.] Cameron of the *Standard*." Telegraphy robbed correspondents of their authority, but *The Times*, *Morning Post*, *St. James's Gazette*, and *Globe* still offered "instructive commentary."

Aside that as periodicals emphasized business, they lost their "freshness" and "fun."

84a. [Arnold, Arthur]. "Redistribution by Different Lights: Seats or No Seats." n.s., 37 (1885): 37–43.
Mused about specialized art periodicals and art critics who "relieve dry columns of leading journals" and popularize art.

85. Colvin, Sidney. "Fleeming Jenkin – In Memoriam." n.s., 38 (1885): 120–22.
Obituary of an engineer sidelined his articles in the *North British Review*.

86. Child, Theodore. "The Paris Newspaper Press." n.s., 38 (1885): 149–65.
Imagined that the "newspaper business in Paris is at present far from prosperous." There were about 150 dailies, some profitable, led by the *Journal des Débats*, "faithful to the traditions of the French press before cheap papers were introduced," and *Figaro*, "one of the most wonderful productions of the century." Because common printers and three advertising agencies kept down expenses, French papers proliferated, serving every interest. The small might run a deficit, but influential businessmen owned the large.

"[T]he Parisian press strikes one as a strange mixture of seriousness and frivolity, of loyalty and deceit, of sincerity and roguery, of irredeemable defects and brilliant qualities." The French did not have the British "mania for news because it is news," but some of the newer gazettes moved in that direction. The second *Temps*, with "dull and heavy" anonymous articles, close text, and inelegant makeup, was the "model of the grave French journal." Foreign correspondence and "unadulterated fact" made it "a thoroughly respectable newspaper." To satisfy readers, French papers needed the literary qualities of *Figaro*. The *Petit Journal*, selling about a million daily, had only moderate clout and depended, like many others, on feuilletons. Glided over the Radical and provincial press.

Journalists in France had considerable independence. *Chroniquers* specializing in interviews earned 15,000–20,000 francs per year. Foreign correspondents kept the French informed when their own press was gagged during the Second Empire. In 1885 British correspondents (several named) presented narrow views; Americans were more tolerant, except at the *New York Herald*, "which is proverbially the worst written paper in the world" and "spends immense sums" to get news five minutes before others.

87. Archer, William. "Norway To-Day." n.s., 38 (1885): 413–25.

Announced that Norway had "no controversial journalist of any mark" covering politics but only the "impotent virulence of a handful of nameless editors."

88. Marlborough [G. C. S. Churchill, 8th Duke]. "Cant in Politics." n.s., 38 (1885): 585–90.

Labeled *The Times* "that organ and protector of corporate and respectable wealth," one that "writes gloomily" while "the penny press fans the flame" of change.

89. Linton, E[liza] Lynn. "A Retrospect." n.s., 38 (1885): 614–29.

Counseled that friendships with editors and critics were useless for journalistic success but that "camaraderie" among journalists and protecting a source were important. "I have written a great deal for the Press, both the daily and weekly – few women more, or so much; but I have never got to the back of things – have never seen how the wires were pulled, nor how patronage was to be had, nor favoritism secured." Once "a famous firm of printers" offered a bribe for silence about "the details of a bit of sharp practice" learned from a "confidante," but Linton rejected the offer and protected her source.

90. Child, Theodore. "The American Newspaper Press." n.s., 38 (1885): 827–39.

Concentrated on New York with its "lean and nervous street-arabs howling or mumbling the titles of newspapers" and elevated trains crowded with readers of gazettes and strewn with those discarded. Manhattan had 23 important dailies with circulations from the *Herald's* 190,000 to the *Evening Post's* 5,000–15,000. Nearby Brooklyn and Jersey City had ten evening dailies and Newark, four morning and three evening dailies, but the press was everywhere in the United States. The country had 1,183 dailies and 10,082 weeklies or one paper for every 6,000 people in 1860. Many heralds were in European languages, a few in Chinese, and one in Cherokee. However, there was no hub press akin to London or Paris.

Papers were of two types: "the respectable and somewhat sleepy ones which exercise careful supervision over both reading matter and advertisements" (papers of 40,000–50,000 sales); and "the enterprising and money-making journals which are less scrupulous" read by the masses (with 100,000+ sales). The *Springfield* (MA) *Republican*, whose editor Samuel Bowles respected readers and the English language, was an example of the first type.

The mass press was generally "trivial, sensational, and essentially vulgar," contained bad writing, and exuded "a taint of provincialism." These characteristics were consonant with immigrant readers unrestrained by tradition and eager for wealth, but all gazettes portrayed politics as "a struggle for office" and foreign policy as inconsequential. About 1880 New York's *World* began the "sensationalism" that complemented the indecency in personal advertisements meant to boost sales. The *Sun* was "the best written and the best edited journal" even though it carried trivia to boost circulation. Sunday papers, very large since the Civil War, proved American "admiration of mere size, bigness, immensity" and their "fidgety and purposeless civilisation, without dignity or repose, running eagerly after one toy and then after another."

The United States had no "tradition of high-class journalism." In 1885 there were few "trained and highly educated writers" or "great editors of the mental and moral calibre of the famous editors of the past," as Horace Greeley and the elder James Gordon Bennett. His son paid too much for insignificant news for the *Herald*. The "average intellectual standard of the American journalist is not sufficiently high to enable him to be an adviser," much less a critic of the arts or theatre. Alternatively, the financial columns were "models of conciseness, fullness, exactitude, and impartiality." Because of the emphasis on reporting, leaders were short but politically influential and occasionally penned by competent men at the *New York Times*, *Tribune*, and *Sun*. Anonymity conveyed an editorial view; signature, better paid and more responsible, was appropriate for higher journalism.

While advertising produced profits, the trade depression curbed indiscriminate spending by Western papers that wanted Eastern news and Eastern gazettes that sought European information. The Associated Press and telegraphy were assets in the race for news.

Recommended Frederick Hudson's *History of Journalism in the United States* on the early press.

91. Llana, M. G. "Political Parties in Spain." n.s., 39 (1886): 106–20.
Commemorated Emilio Castelar's early career in "militant journalism" when he apprenticed at the *Discussion* "under the direction of Don Nicholas Maria Rivero." Castelar soon won a reputation for "his eloquent defences in press cases," a reputation he carried to his newspaper, *Democracia*.

92. Escott, T. H. S. "Small Talk and Statesmen." n.s., 39 (1886): 121–40.
Elucidated how Abraham Hayward, a writer, and John Delane, the editor, planned a column for *The Times*.

93. Salmon, [Edward] G. "What Boys Read." n.s., 39 (1886): 248–59.
Sermonized that "boys' magazines, with a few notable exceptions" as the *Boy's Own Paper*, "are in every way objectionable." Yet the masses did not buy *Every Boy's Magazine* and *Young England* and other good serials causing many to die quickly. Speculated that works "of an obtrusively preachy kind" drove youths to the penny dreadfuls corrupting the young, but neither the public nor the clergy noticed. Magazines of this ilk defeated the goals of compulsory education and taught children to admire criminals. Freedom of the press was valuable but so were children's minds.

94. Beatty-Kingston, William. "Foreign Correspondents." n.s., 39 (1886): 371–87.
Declared that foreign correspondents, by 1886 "trained journalists," confirmed British interest in the politics of others. These scribes, who sent interesting but rarely startling news, got information by gaining the confidence of foreigners willing to speak on the record. After newspapers printed the truth, foreign officials habitually disavowed it and accused the correspondent of "dishonesty" or "imbecility."

The foreign correspondent (current named with specialties) should be "a gentleman," a linguist, a man of "[d]iscretion, tact, and imperturbable temper," in order to overcome his known flaws of being British and a journalist. Earlier he could enlighten readers at length, but telegraphy had changed his reports. Correspondents usually did not move from a paper that paid them a steady income, had editors who would back them, and readers who trusted them more than a foreign mouthpiece press.

95. Child, Theodore. "Society in Paris." n.s., 39 (1886): 480–99.
Characterized the Paris press as "largely literate" in a society where important writers and politicians customarily began as journalists. These included Edouard Hervé, "editor of the Orleanist *Soleil* and a member of the French Academy"; Ernest Renan, who wrote for the *Journal des Débats*; and Alphonse Daudet, who published in *Figaro*. "The mere title of journalist in itself speaks but little in a man's favour in Paris; everything depends upon the individual journalist." Aside that Mme Edmond Adam was the "fair editor of *La Nouvelle Revue*."

96. Hozier, H. M. "Lloyd's." n.s., 39 (1886): 528–39.
Documented that *Lloyd's News* commenced in 1696 and published for 76 months before it was censored. It resumed in 1726 as *Lloyd's List* so was the oldest British newspaper after the *London Gazette*.

97. Dykes, Thomas. "Ocean Steamers." n.s., 39 (1886): 680–96.
Mentioned how transatlantic steamers impacted news transmission from the United States, where "smart and daring journalistic feats" enabled a paper to be first to telegraph a story around the country. Yet in 1865 "a golden opportunity in journalism was lost forever" when no one telegraphed news, accessible in newspapers aboard the *Nova Scotia* running ahead of the mail steamer, that Abraham Lincoln was dead.

98. Burnand, F. C. and Arthur à Beckett. "History in *Punch*." n.s., 40 (1886): 49–67, 737–52; n.s., 41 (1887): 546–57.
Starred the establishment of *Punch* as a "memorable day in journalism." Divided its history into three periods: 1841–54, 1854–60, since 1860.

99. Heaton, J. Henniker. "Universal Penny Postage." n.s., 40 (1886): 533–41.
Registered the costs of mailing newspapers.

100. Stepniak [S. M. Kravchinsky]. "The Mir and the Police." n.s., 41 (1887): 237–48.
Noted that the *Official Messenger* and other government papers circulated everywhere in Russia's territories. After June 1878 editors of newspapers and other serials were prohibited from censuring the police, but in the 1881 interlude of press liberty, papers except the *Moscow Gazette* criticized authorities. Aside that *Zemstro* had "responsible editors."

101. Edwards, H. Sutherland. "Mr. Katkoff and the *Moscow Gazette*." n.s., 42 (1887): 379–94.
Conceded that Michael Katkoff was a very influential journalist after 1857 in a country without a free and political press. By 1881 he and Alexander Herzen were the major journalists. Katkoff penned for the literary *Russian Athenaeum*, launched the *Russian Messenger*, and edited the *Moscow Gazette*, making a serious newspaper a power. The *Messenger* had top writers and original material, much on England. Although the *Messenger* was initially reformist, it and the majority of the press changed after the Polish rebellion. That event, first covered by the Slavophile *Day*, shaped Katkoff's career, showing that an "independent journalist" could survive in Russia. Aside on the Nihilist secret press.

During the reign of Nicholas I the only periodicals known outside Russia were the *Russian Invalid*, the Ministry of War organ; *St. Petersburg Gazette* of the Academy of Sciences; *Journal de St. Pétersbourg*, published in French by the Ministry of Public Affairs; and *Moscow Gazette* of Moscow University. Significant magazines and reviews were the *Telegraph* (1827), *Moscow Messenger* (1827), *Telescope*, *Library for General Reading* (1835), *Contemporary* (1836), and *National Annals* (1838). Among the private serials were *Child of the Land*, "a small sheet with a large circulation" that was "perfectly harmless," and the *Russian Bee*, edited by a "Russianized German" and a Russian Pole who cultivated "notoriety" but were ignorant and venal.

102. Rochefort, Henri. "The Boulangist Movement." n.s., 44 (1888): 10–23.
Logged circulation of several French papers, among them the *Lanterne*, which sold 500,000 daily. Asides on the editor of the *Presse*, Georges Laguerre, and the new *Cocarde*.

103. Knollys, W. W. "A Hundred Years Ago." n.s., 44 (1888): 373–80.
Celebrated the birth of *The Times* as "memorable."

104. Wilde, Oscar. "Pen, Pencil, and Poison: A Study." n.s., 45 (1889): 41–54.
Lionized T. G. Wainwright, whose mother was a daughter of the founder of the *Monthly Review*. With an invitation from *London Magazine* editor John Scott, Wainwright, as Janus Weathercock and Egomet Bonmot, contributed material on art and theatre criticism until his activities as a forger and a murderer resulted in his transportation. "Modern journalism" was similar to his "Asiatic prose… pictorial epithets…pompous exaggeration" and journalists' intrusion of their own personalities into stories.

105. Dowden, Edward. "Hopes and Fears for Literature." n.s., 45 (1889): 166–83.
Praised newspapers and "humbler periodicals" for the "democratising of literature" by tempting many to read.

106. Ingram, J. [T.] Dunbar. "*Two Centuries of Irish History*: A Review." n.s., 45 (1889): 229–44.
Review of a book by several authors resurrected c. 1800 Irish papers, such as the *Belfast News-Letter* and *Dublin Journal*.

107. "The Trade of Author." n.s., 45 (1889): 261–74.
Lamented that "[h]alf the ablest writers in England are wasting their energies daily, I do not doubt, on very ill-paid and laborious journalistic handicraft. They are writing paragraphs" without a chance to publish elsewhere.

108. A Former Resident in Russia [?E. J. Dillon]. "Some Truths about Russia." n.s., 46 (1889): 274–92.
Saluted the *Russian Gazette*, a Moscow newspaper, and *Russian Thought*, a review.

109. Lanin, E. B. [E. J. Dillon]. "Russian Characteristics." n.s., 46 (1889): 410–32, 573–88, 722–36, 854–68; n.s., 47 (1890): 256–75.
Groaned that Russian journalists, plagued by censors, learned hypocrisy from officials. The authorities sometimes approved an article, then forced an author to denounce it if it had "real merit." Journalists adopted artifice to survive. For example, a former Odessa editor who forged items for his next employer, the *New Russian Telegraph*, was later a "respected" member of the staff of "the most widely circulated daily newspaper in all South Russia" with plans to continue forging. Nevertheless, newspapers and magazines ordinarily pictured Russian life accurately.

110. Dowden, Edward. "Literary Criticism in France." n.s., 46 (1889): 737–53.
Unveiled essays in the *Revue des Deux Mondes* on literary criticism.

111. Day, William. "The Evil of Betting and How to Eradicate It." n.s., 47 (1890): 343–60.

Associated horse racing with gambling, abetted by the "sporting" papers the *South American* and *Sporting Life*.

112. Runciman, James. "King Plagiarism and His Court." n.s., 47 (1890): 421–39.

Charged that Rider Haggard stole Runciman's ideas in the *Pall Mall Gazette* for a story Haggard published in the *Illustrated London News*.

113. Linton, E[liza] Lynn. "Literature: Then and Now." n.s., 47 (1890): 517–31.

Memorialized contributors who once wrote according to "conscience," scribes of the *Edinburgh Review*, *Quarterly Review*, and the original *Saturday Review*. In 1890 the "new journalism," with "all its sensationalism, all its rant, and all its personality," depended on journalists less accurate because they were less thoughtful and cultured, mirroring modern "tastes" learned by being "offensive" in interviews. Authors followed no rules, so their essays lacked order and proportion in the "superficial" periodicals multiplying as fast as the new readers who demanded their rubbish.

114. "A National Want: A Practical Proposal." n.s., 47 (1890): 595–600.

Urged the government and the military to publish a journal akin to France's *Revue Militaire de l'Etranger*.

115. Bourchier, James D. "A Glance at Contemporary Greece." n.s., 47 (1890): 864–80.

Abhorred typical Greek dailies that maligned the government for personal reasons. One editor was angry because his attempt to get a staff member into office was rebuffed; another, because his profitable "gambling-den" was closed by authorities. Papers were full of "diatribes," dangerous because "at least a third of the newspapers find their way into the country districts." There they were read aloud to the unsophisticated who took them seriously unlike urbanites who found them "amusing." And, unlike the Germans, the Greeks had no official press to counter such talk. Only one Athens gazette, in French, covered foreign news.

116. Gosse, Edmund. "The Protection of American Literature." n.s., 48 (1890): 56–65.

Article on American copyright law remarked that British newspapers carried less telegraphic information from the United States than from "Philippoli."

117. Lanin, E. B. [E. J. Dillon]. "Armenia and the Armenian People." n.s., 48 (1890): 258–73.

Deplored Russian press censorship of Armenia's three monthly reviews and two dailies whereby "whole pages are cut out of the reviews, long paragraphs suppressed."

118. [Geffcken, Friedrich H.]. "The Change of Government in Germany." n.s., 48 (1890): 282–304.

Decided that the daily press was more important in Germany than elsewhere, although journalism was widely "influential in forming and guiding public opinion." In Britain, parties had their papers; in Germany, the goal of Otto von Bismarck was "making the Press subservient to his policy" irrespective of his journalistic background. In the 1850s he wrote for the *Kreuzzeitung*, which supported him in the 1860s as did the *Norddeutsche Allgemeine Zeitung*, "afterwards his own special organ." He tried unsuccessfully to place articles in the French press. In 1874 he sponsored legislation mandating editors to give police every issue of their serials at publication. These faced suppression unless the name and address of editor and printer appeared. The same penalty applied for airing forbidden news in wartime or columns inciting treason or violence anytime. The law also permitted judicial punishment for sedition and degradation of a person, including the chancellor. Foreign correspondents who offended him could be expelled. Yet the government press could print anything. Cologne's *Zeitung* was servile, and Hamburg's *Nachrichten* was a 'reptile.' Local papers received cash or "special information" to support the Reich. Because they got their news and views from Berlin, the country papers saved money, making competition difficult.

119. Lanin, E. B. [E. J. Dillon]. "The Jews in Russia." n.s., 48 (1890): 481–509.
Castigated the Russian press for extreme bias.

120. Lanin, E. B. [E. J. Dillon]. "Finland." n.s., 49 (1891): 38–68.
Observed that "the semi-official organ of the Russian government," the *Novoe Vremya*, was known to impress the tsar.

121. Meath [Reginald Brabazon, 12th Earl]. "Anglo-Saxon Unity." n.s., 49 (1891): 615–22.
Listed periodical exchange as one of many factors that created a common mindset among the people of the United Kingdom, its empire, and the United States.

122. Harrison, Frederic. "Editorial Horseplay." n.s., 49 (1891): 642–55.
Chastised *Nineteenth Century* editor James Knowles for publishing "an article on an international question, written in good faith by an old contributor," then three months later admitting it was a hoax. Knowles thus redefined the editor's role, alienating future contributors who feared possible public denunciation.

123. Lanin, E. B. [E. J. Dillon]. "The Russian Censure." n.s., 49 (1891): 798–824.
Explained how Russian censors operated. Foreign periodicals mailed and registered usually arrived; local periodicals were available at a censor's discretion. Among the latter were the weekly *Universal Illustration*, *Memoirs of the Fatherland* for the provinces, and the officially subsidized *Grazhdanin*.

Russian journalism required little capital, but papers generated none because of the threat of censorship. Pre-publication rules forced editors to self-censor, but officials still tore out pages and ordered reprints. Editors then pasted mostly inferior material that had passed muster. Telegrams and advertisements were also checked. In towns without a censor, delays raised costs.

124. Crawfurd, Oswald. "The Future of Portugal." n.s., 50 (1891): 149–62.
Maligned Portuguese newspapers, allegedly urban recruiters for mobs, as "the most flimsy, trivial, and the lowest in price of any journals of any country in Europe."

125. Adams, Francis. "Social Life in Australia." n.s., 50 (1891): 392–407.
Graded Sydney's *Bulletin* "the one really talented and original outcome of the Australian press," which was very powerful. Journalists owned the newspaper, whose profits kept it "pure." The editor, J. F. Archibald, was freer than any editor in Britain or the Eastern or Central United States. He was "the one

journalist of genius in Australia" and "the only mouthpiece of originality in Australia," unlike many who demonstrated "pseudo-intellectualism" that masked ignorance and superficiality. The *Sydney Morning Herald*, the richest paper, was politically cautious but had integrity. Melbourne's *Argus* showed more "temerity." The *Age* had the largest circulation, "over 80,000" because of its "popular crazes." Brisbane's only two-penny morning paper was the *Courier*. Most Australian gazettes aped London and circulated only in their regions, but the *Bulletin* was widely read. *See* 51: 194.

126. Dowden, Edward. "The Interviewer Abroad." n.s., 50 (1891): 719–33.
Focused on Jules Huret's interviews in *Echo de Paris* of French "men of letters." Underscored that Huret always prepared questions.

127. Adams, Francis. "Some Australian Men of Mark." n.s., 51 (1892): 194–212.
Repeated (50: 392) that J. F. Archibald, the editor of Sydney's *Bulletin*, was the "one Australian journalist of genius" but added that Frederick Ward, "who 'made' the Sydney *Daily Telegraph*," and Kinnaird Reid of Brisbane's *Courier* were also outstanding. Proprietors increasingly emphasized business, not literature in journalism. The wealthiest owners were John Fairfax (*Sydney Morning Herald*) and David Syme (*Age*), who was the "most powerful." He started by setting, then writing copy. Both Melbourne's *Argus* and the *Morning Herald*, edited by men of intelligence but with little "free play," had a "higher literary standard" than the *Age* but less political impact. Marcus Clarke was the Australian Horace Greeley because he typified "editing managers, or managing editors" of an "average influential colonial newspaper" like any found in the United States in the 1840s and 1850s. Clarke eschewed party support and favors, such as free theatre tickets.

128. Griffin, Lepel. "The Place of the Bengáli in Politics." n.s., 51 (1892): 811–19.
Fumed that Bengal newspapers incited sedition or engaged in blackmail while the British government talked about a free press in India.

129. Adams, Francis. "Two Australian Writers." n.s., 52 (1892): 352–65.
Headlined Marcus Clarke, who set the standard for Australian journalists, penning for several journals including the *Melbourne Revue*.

130. Hodgson, W[illiam] Earl. "Our Weekly Reviews." n.s., 52 (1892): 508–16.
Distinguished literary newspapers of 1892 and their predecessors. Eighteenth-century organs, such as the *Tatler* and *Spectator*, had to deal with fewer topics and be more "expository" in the absence of many morning dailies. In the 1860s the only weekly of note was the *Saturday Review* but, as magazines burgeoned, more "men of high literary accomplishment" entered journalism. In 1892 weeklies assumed that readers got their facts from dailies, with "their strenuous outpourings of practical instruction on the questions of the day." "[T]he new function of the Reviews is to set the fashion in matters of intellectual moods and tastes," to provide "a mental relaxation after the febrile exhaustion of the flying day." Weekly reviews gave the reader time to weigh facts before forming opinions. The paragraphs in the *Saturday Review* were full of "rapid movement" and in the *Spectator* were graver.

131. An Englishman. "Politics and Finance in Brazil." n.s., 53 (1893): 80–90.
Rated the *Journal do Commercio* "the principal Brazilian newspaper."

132. Curzon, George N. "Politics and Progress in Siam." n.s., 53 (1893): 454–67.
Alerted that Siam's Royal Library had copies of *The Times, Athenaeum, Review of Reviews*, and *Truth*.

133. Smalley, George W. "A Visit to Prince Bismarck." n.s., 54 (1893): 1–27.
Interviewer realized that Bismarck did not perceive the differences between German and English or American journalism. This failure was irrelevant since he disregarded all press criticism of his policies.

134. X. [Harold Frederic]. "The Ireland of To-day." n.s., 54 (1893): 686–706.
Asserted that Irish journalism, in decline from the days of John Mitchie and Thomas Davis, was more active outside than within Ireland. Nonetheless, Irish readers in 1893 were "easily swayed" by such newspapers as *Freeman's Journal*.

135. X. [Harold Frederic]. "The Rhetoricians of Ireland." n.s., 54 (1893): 713–27.
Proclaimed the *Nation* the model for "the popular partisan newspaper…a novel engine of warfare" in Ireland. The current *United Ireland*, with too many exclamation points and italicized words, seemed merely overzealous.

136. An Observer [Marie Louise de la Ramée]. "L'Uomo Fatale." n.s., 55 (1894): 355–64.
Anguished that copies of Milan's *Italia del Populo* and *Secolo*, "a courageous and well-written daily," and Sienna's *Martinello del Calle* were seized and their editors imprisoned. The British press was silent about these actions, but the German press condemned them.

137. Carrel, Frederic. "English and French Manners." n.s., 55 (1894): 680–92.
Pronounced the "French Press…the brightest, the most interesting, and the most literary press in the world – a leisurely press" that relied more on writers' abilities than on getting news. The French handled politics with "witty condensation," personal scandals with discretion, and literary criticism with politeness. Writers, especially specialists, were popular heroes. The *feuille de chou* were "the pests of French journalism" because they printed false, if clever and amusing stories that often resulted in duels. Conversely, London dailies, with their anonymity, sober outlook, and small type, were not "cheerful." They also suffered from too many advertisements, "hideous typographical displays." Local gazettes, published for profit unlike the French, were better than those of the French boulevard but not as free to speak. The English reporter was an anonymous recorder of "facts in careful language"; the French was an "artist" who signed his work.

138. Stanford, C. V. "Some Aspects of Musical Criticism in England." n.s., 55 (1894): 826–31.
Presumed that music criticism was inferior because dailies wanted speedy reviews. Analysts for weeklies, such as Henry F. Chorley, had more time to think. Dailies should either eliminate criticism about which editors knew little or designate a special day for publishing reviews. Critics, victims of "unwholesome hours and hard labour," had to pen for numerous serials to earn a living in this journalistic specialty, undervalued because of anonymity.

Aside that the *Journal des Débats* was "a typical Parisian daily paper of the best order."

139. Johnston, H. H. "The Boer Question." n.s., 56 (1894): 161–69.
Bruited that the "preponderance of the press is English" in the Dutch South African areas.

140. Runciman, John F. "Musical Criticism and the Critics." n.s., 56 (1894): 170–83.
Nominated J. W. Davison (*The Times*, 1840s–70s) as the first paid music critic, one whose writing was "beneath contempt" because of his "ignorance" and "petty spite." The critics of the 1880s were "literary men" who raised the bar. Among them were E. F. Jacques, editor of *Musical World* and "the most brilliant editor of the *Musical Times*," and his colleagues at the *Magazine of Music*, *Musical Standard*, and *Scottish Musical Monthly*. George Bernard Shaw shifted from reviewing based on canons to reviewing drawn from personal tastes. Shaw's columns in the *World* were in stark contrast to the dull ones in the *Athenaeum*, *Truth*, *Standard*, *Daily News*, and *Daily Chronicle*. Editors of dailies treated criticism, usually done by amateurs, like crime reports. A few critics "graduated from blacklegs into full-fledged 'professionals,'" but turnover and coercion by editors, advertising managers of smaller papers, artists' agents, readers, and acquaintances kept standards low. Signature might eventually drive out the incapable, but those who were mercenaries, librettists, or employees of impresario owners would be hard to budge.

141. Malato, Charles. "Some Anarchist Portraits." n.s., 56 (1894): 315–33.
Classified Peter Kropotkin's *Révolte* as a journal of "morality." Aside on the French *Union Socialiste*.

142. Graham, William. "Side-Lights on the Second Empire, II." n.s., 56 (1894): 498–512.
Reasoned that "few contemporary documents" existed on the Second Empire because Napoleon III ""'muzzled" the French press.

143. Carrel, Frederic. "In Syria." n.s., 56 (1894): 562–73.
Conjectured that press censorship in Syria, limiting newspapers to translations of European gazettes, discouraged "native talent."

144. Phillipps, Evelyn March. "Women's Newspapers." n.s., 56 (1894): 661–70.
Incorrectly stated that the *Lady's Own Paper* (instead of the *Ladies' Newspaper*) became the *Queen* in 1863. The *Queen*, with royal and general news, advertisements, needlework, and cookery, generated other women's fashion weeklies (cited). "Writing upon dress has become an art in its way." Writers helped business by "pushing goods and awakening a craving for a hundred luxuries." Some authors took money from shops to promote goods or blackmailed proprietors to get free clothes. Clothing advertisements, useful guides for those in the country, paid the bills for papers whose editors disdained but printed society news. The *Queen's* outside page cost 40–50 pounds.

Among the most popular features was the correspondence column. "It is hard to believe that this sort of stuff can please some adults, but apparently it exactly suits a certain portion." Women's papers should publish more stories on jobs for females and fewer on their health, paragraphs that were "mischievous" and promoted quack remedies. Children's pages sometimes overemphasized competition or trivialized subjects but did prize juvenile achievements.

Almost all women's papers were edited by men, "a deplorable fact" when much of the labor was women's. Editors were constantly trying to secure more talent and variety. The *Lady's Pictorial* series on women journalists showed the success of this effort.

Women's papers in the United States were "sensible and useful" but addressed mostly the young. Those in Australasia spoke to the same audience but without American quality. France and Germany had "excellent" domestic serials. Papers for a 'cause' were not popular anywhere, but women's papers should cover important issues affecting women.

145. Davey, Richard. "Turkey and Armenia." n.s., 57 (1895): 197–210.

Peeked at London's *Anglo-Armenian Gazette*, "a little newspaper."

146. Escott, T. H. S. "London Pen and Gown in the Sixties and Since." n.s., 57 (1895): 238–49.

Spotlighted some journalists. George Augustus Sala maintained "a uniform level of literary excellence" irrespective of pressure. He symbolized a "higher type of journalistic literature" while many colleagues reaped an "absurd contempt for popular journalism." Charles Dickens invented, in *Household Words*, the "modern leading article in its lighter form" and welcomed special reports from abroad. He affected the press broadly because he and his associate, W. H. Wills, trained many journalists, among them Sala. Abraham Hayward was "the most accomplished reviewer and essayist of the last half of this century," a man of stature in the press. Escott yarned here about former confreres and several papers.

Since the 1860s, journalism was "more of a profession," more accessible to competent aspirants. Journalists in the 1890s had greater "independence, public usefulness, and respect" if less "camaraderie." As writers moved from "literary organs" to edit papers, they became "journalistic masters of ceremonies." Aside that some Anglican clerics were originally journalists.

147. Chisholm, Hugh. "How to Counteract the 'Penny Dreadful.'" n.s., 58 (1895): 765–75.

Raged that some issues of the *Illustrated Police News* were obscene.

148. W. "The Two Eastern Questions." n.s., 59 (1896): 193–208.

Regarded one Maynard, a foreign correspondent for *Figaro*, as "the most influential journalist of his day."

149. Archer, William. "George Henry Lewes and the Stage." n.s., 59 (1896): 216–30.

Highlighted the theatre criticism of Lewes, as "Vivian," in the *Leader*, 1850–54.

150. Blaze de Bury, Yetta. "Jules Lemaître." n.s., 59 (1896): 547–61.

Noticed Lemaître's work for the *Revue Bleue* (1884) and *Journal des Débats* (1888), the center of French "critical arts."

151. "The Integration of the Empire." n.s., 59 (1896): 738–50.

Reckoned that *Britannia* was an excellent monthly and a tool for imperial intellectual integration.

152. Sellers, Edith. "Wilhelm Liebknecht: The Veteran Leader of the German Socialists." n.s., 59 (1896): 997–1008.

Probed Liebknecht's tenure as "chief of the foreign department" of the *Norddeutsche Allgemeine Zeitung*, edited by his friend, August Brass. Liebknecht joined the *Allgemeine Arbeiterverein* to prevent it falling under Otto von Bismarck's hand.

153. "Luck or Leadership?" n.s., 60 (1896): 199–206.

Showcased press impact on the House of Commons.

154. Blaze de Bury, Yetta. "Edmond de Goncourt." n.s., 60 (1896): 333–49.

Glanced at Goncourt's work, 1852–53, for *Paris*, his brother's paper until an imperial 'ukase' closed it.

155. Ouida [Marie Louise de la Ramée]. "Italy: The Marquis di Rudini and Italian Politics." n.s., 60 (1896): 350–62.

Declaimed that in Italy "absurd Press laws continue, out of date and intolerable though they are." For example, the *Corriere di Napoli*, "a moderate and monarchial journal," suffered from the legislation. Although the Italian press could be corrupt, it was not "outspoken." The country needed a free press for a "liberal national life."

156. Bell, [H. T.] Mackenzie. "William Morris: A Eulogy." n.s., 60 (1896): 693–702.

Recollected that Morris published in and financially supported the *Oxford and Cambridge Magazine*.

157. Blind, Karl. "Young Turkey." n.s., 60 (1896): 830–43.

Surveyed the journalism of Young Turkey: *Mukhbir*, published in London and Paris, 1867–68, and edited by Mustafa Fazil Pasha, "the well-known statesman"; *Mesveret*, published in French and Turkish in Paris by Ahmed Riza; *Mizan*, published in Cairo by Murad Bey; *Hurriyet*, edited by Selim Faris as "Djioanpire"; *Avenir*, published in Athens and edited by one Dagues; *Hakikat*, published in French in Geneva and edited by Munif Bey. Halil Ganem, who first edited *Hilal* and then *Jeune Turquie*, wrote for *Mesveret*.

158. Reed, Edward J. "Dr. Cornelius Herz and the French Republic." n.s., 61 (1897): 1–20.

Positioned Herz as a frequent contributor to the Paris *Globe* for which he wrote on politics and medicine to pay his way through medical school. He later started and edited the "first scientific reviews on electricity," the *Lumière Electrique* and *Journal d'Electricité*.

159. O'Grady, Standish. "Ireland: The New Irish Movement." n.s., 61 (1897): 170–79.

Summarized *Times* style in its Irish coverage as "sneers, taunts, insults, menaces."

160. Baillie-Grohman, W. A. "The Shortcomings of Our Sporting Literature." n.s., 62 (1897): 233–43.

Whined about errors in sports reporting in the *Badminton Magazine* and *The Times*.

161. Vandam, Albert [D.]. " 'The King of the Journalists.' " n.s., 62 (1897): 259–76.
Crowned Emile de Girardin, father of the *Presse*, who had a "spirit of enterprise, a craving for daring innovation, a fertility of invention, and a true conception of the part democracy will eventually be cast to play in the drama of civilisation." This spirit sometimes brought trouble, as a duel with Armand Carrel of the *National* in which Carrel died. Still, de Girardin and his writers were always accessible to the public.

162. Bhownaggree, M. M. "The Present Agitation in India and the Vernacular Press." n.s., 62 (1897): 304–13.
Attributed Indian unrest partly to journals without moderation, accuracy, and a sense of responsibility, journals that surfaced after repeal of the press laws. Most were small: the Bombay Presidency had 211, but only 38 had more than 1,000 subscribers and 26 had no subscribers. However, men loyal to Britain no longer controlled the papers. Editors of the top gazettes only earned 12–18 pounds per month, and reporters worked for pennies. Both were blackmailers or tools of the "irresponsible, vulgar, and unscrupulous."

163. Lafargue, Paul. "Socialism in France from 1876 to 1896." Trans. Edward Aveling. n.s., 62 (1897): 445–58.
Singled out Jules Guesde who edited *Droit de l'Homme*, then established *Egalité*, the first socialist journal in France since 1849. Aside on the *Commune*, begun and edited by Felix Pyat in Paris in 1871.

164. Stein, C. [John Cecil Russell]. "*Annals of a Publishing House*." n.s., 62 (1897): 853–61.
Review of Margaret Oliphant's book on the Blackwood family studied some editors of and contributors to *Blackwood's Magazine* and its relationship to the *Edinburgh Review*. Aside on the *Black Dwarf*.

165. Hogarth, Janet E. "The Monstrous Regiment of Women." n.s., 62 (1897): 926–36.
Included journalism among jobs available to women. The "average woman-journalist" had to struggle for a living because females purportedly did not understand "the necessity of accepting the most humdrum and distasteful tasks, the trials of the interviewer, and the endless subterfuges of the society reporters." Tyros might see the names of famous female journalists, but very few women were as successful as men. A female usually sold "the chatty article" or bits of information to a variety of general gazettes or penned columns for women's papers that bordered on illiteracy.

166. Wolf, Lucien. "Anti-Semitism and the Dreyfus Case." n.s., 63 (1898): 135–46.
Shared that Edouard Drumont, the founder and "fire-eating editor" of the *Libre Parole*, who commenced his career at *Liberté*, was the "protégé of the Jewish brothers [Emile and Isaac] Pereire." He next edited *Inflexible*, the journal of the Imperial police. In 1894 he opened the *National*. The *Libre Parole*, which had come two years earlier, was "widely read" but had little clout until the Dreyfus case.

167. Steuart, John A. "Authors, Publishers, and Booksellers." n.s., 63 (1898): 255–63.
Discounted dailies as an 'advertising medium' for books because few readers perused the "interminable columns of publishers' announcements" that were "so prominent a feature of the morning papers." Referred readers to an article on the topic in *Chapman's Magazine*.

168. Thring, G. Herbert. "Recent Attempts at Copyright Legislation." n.s., 63 (1898): 461–67.
Scrutinized a copyright bill that incorporated magazines but not newspapers as had an earlier version.

169. Ouida [Marie Louise de la Ramée]. "Felice Cavallotti." n.s., 63 (1898): 601–03.
Honored an Italian journalist noted for his political columns.

170. MacDonagh, Michael. "Can We Rely on Our War News?" n.s., 63 (1898): 612–25.
Dated war correspondence from William Howard Russell in Crimea, but in 1898 it was "a regular branch of journalism" filled by "men of daring, resource, and ability, who are attracted by the fascination of war." Although it paid well, the job required "physical strength," "iron nerves and mental vigour, sound sense and rapid judgment, a quick observant eye," and "a ready, vivid pen." Correspondents who risked their lives not just for the story but for the campaign's success were duly honored.

The War Office by 1898 recognized this job but worried that its practitioners leaked secrets. The result was a set of official "Rules for Newspaper Correspondents at the Seat of War," which authorized censorship of dispatches and control of telegraphy. The Rules penalized more the civilian journalists, who were independent and accurate reporters, than retired soldier-commentators. Even the Germans in the Franco-Prussian War and the Russians in the Russo-Turkish War had been "more lenient."

War correspondents did not shake the confidence of the troops since they already knew the bad commanders. Reporters could cause readers to jump to conclusions but only somewhat faster than they did in earlier wars after receiving personal letters. Rarely did a "civilised" enemy benefit from British war reporting and never did "the uncivilised who rely entirely on their own powers of observation." The public was "not likely to tolerate any unreasonable attempt" by the War Office to restrict reporters because readers desired "early and vivid and independent newspaper accounts from the seat of the war."

171. Jane, Frederick T. "The '*Maine*' Disaster and After." n.s., 63 (1898): 640–49.
Feared that the *Daily Chronicle*, with a pro-American bias, might be misconstrued as representing British journalism and public opinion.

172. Dicey, Edward. "Egypt, 1881 to 1897." n.s., 63 (1898): 681–99.
Relayed that English, French, Greek, and Italian journals circulated in Egypt in proportion to their nation's populations there. The "enormous increase in the home newspaper postal service," which went from two to seven million in 15 years, "must be found in the large circulation of the native Arabic newspapers." Before 1881 there was only the *Official Gazette*; by 1897 "large towns" had streets "filled with newsboys selling native papers." The character of the serials might not benefit readers, but the numbers evidenced greater "intellectual activity."

173. Hirst, Francis W. "A Dissolving Empire." n.s., 64 (1898): 56–71.
Essay on the Austrian Empire acknowledged "K., the brilliant editor of *Die Zeit*" in Vienna.

174. Sharp, William. "Edward Burne-Jones." n.s., 64 (1898): 289–306.
Marginalized Burne-Jones' work for the *Germ* and *Oxford and Cambridge Magazine*. The Brasenose copy of the second identified authors but apparently not always correctly.

175. Vandam, Albert D. "The Spy-Mania and the Revanche Idea." n.s., 64 (1898): 396–409.

Testified that 1870 French newspapers kept Otto von Bismarck apprised of the French situation; the 1880 Paris *Gil-Blas*, *Gaulois*, and *Paris Journal* broke the story that French secrets were being sold to the Germans, and the 1898 press, determined to get every detail about national defense, engaged in "journalistic blackmail" by paying generals for articles.

176. Escott, T. H. S. "Mr. Henry Reeve." n.s., 64 (1898): 703–14.

Reviewed J. K. Laughton's *Memoirs and Correspondence of Henry Reeve, C.B.* Reeve, whose father contributed to the *Edinburgh Review*, was its long-time editor (1855–95). He previously wrote, under John Delane for *The Times*, "a species of polite and leisurely pamphleteering rather than journalism." His sources were not the 'flimsy' of telegrams but letters from "distinguished foreigners" and discussions with "the best informed contemporary statesmen." When Reeve assumed the *Edinburgh* editorship, periodicals were party organs, so he cut material that did not fit his review's stance. Aside that E. G. Bulwer-Lytton helped Antonio Gallenga, "the great *Times* leader-writer and correspondent as he afterwards became," to get a foothold at the paper.

177. An Anglo-Parisian Journalist [Emily J. Crawford]. "France of To-Day." n.s., 64 (1898): 810–20.

Outlined journalism's part in the Dreyfus Case. The army leaked information to the *Libre Parole* even though six other Paris papers were more important. Aside that anti-Semitism stemmed from panic about Jewish control of Léon Gambetta's *République Française*.

178. Bentwich, Herbert. "The Progress of Zionism." n.s., 64 (1898): 928–43.

Bowed to Claude G. Montefiore, "the learned co-editor of the *Jewish Quarterly Review*."

179. Pennell, J[oseph] and E[lizabeth] R[obins]. "The Centenary of Lithography." n.s., 64 (1898): 968–83.

Indicated earlier journals that had lithographs, the relatively cheap *Parthenon* (1826) and *Monthly Sheet of Caricatures* and *Mirror* (1826, Glasgow) and the more expensive *Artiste* (1845–65) as well as a piece on lithography in the *Gentleman's Magazine* (1808).

180. [Pareto, Vilfredo]. "Vilfredo Pareto on Italy." n.s., 65 (1899): 475–85; with postscript by Ouida [Marie Louise de la Ramée].

Postscript stressed that the Italian government had ended liberty of the press. "Several editors and journalists" were in jail, owners paid fines, and new restrictive legislation was looming.

181. Coubertin, Pierre de. "France since 1814." n.s., 65 (1899): 572–85; n.s., 66 (1899): 977–90.

Article in a series (other pages irrelevant) specified French press censorship in 1827 and press influence in the planning of the Panama Canal.

182. An Anglo-Parisian Journalist [Emily J. Crawford]. "Bonapartism." n.s., 65 (1899): 680–93.

Opined that Parisians "allow journalists and the Chamber to think and speak for them."

183. Bain, R. Nisbet. "Finland and the Tsar." n.s., 65 (1899): 735–44.
Reminded that Russia employed "preventive censorship" of dailies and weeklies.

184. Shelley, H. C. "Thomas Hood's First Centenary." n.s., 65 (1899): 987–1003.
Tracked Hood's journalistic career. As subeditor of the *London Magazine* (1821) he printed "facetious" answers to letters. As editor of the *New Monthly Magazine* he earned 300 pounds a year. A dispute with publisher Henry Colburn led Hood to start his own serial, *Hood's Magazine*, a success shortened by his death soon after its inauguration.

185. Jacobs, Joseph. "The Mean Englishman." n.s., 66 (1899): 53–62.
Warranted that the average working class man purchased no dailies and only occasionally 'snippet' weeklies.

186. Bastide, Charles. "M. Brunetière." n.s., 66 (1899): 500–09.
Lauded Ferdinand Bruntière's "able subediting, then editing of the *Revue des Deux Mondes*."

187. Foxcroft, Helen C. "The 'Dreyfus Scandal' of English History." n.s., 66 (1899): 563–75.
Paralleled the Popish Plot and the Dreyfus Affair with respect to the press. "The nascent form of journalism of the seventeenth century seemed contaminated in its source; Grub Street pamphleteers performed the hireling services of the modern 'reptile' Press," with its lack of propriety and ignorance exemplified by French coverage of the Dreyfus Affair.

188. Reid, Andrew. "History in Advertisements." n.s., 66 (1899): 576–88.
Centered on seventeenth-century advertising from the days of the *Mercurius Politicus*. During the 1665 plague, many inserts for quack cures surfaced, some supposedly penned by the king. Advertisements for boxing matches portrayed men and women participants, but slave inserts c. 1700 were "pregnant with political and social history." "The historian...could write a very decent story of England from newspaper advertisements."

189. Ouida [Marie Louise de la Ramée]. "Unwritten Literary Laws." n.s., 66 (1899): 803–14.
Recited a litany of problems in 1899 journalism: the "vulgar ridicule" in the caricature of the eminent in famous journals spurred artists of "intellect" to avoid the "public arena"; some illustrated journals used worn wood-blocks or new ones that did not match text; most serial thefts of parts of novels went unprosecuted because plagiarism was hard to prove and costs of a suit were high; an editor committed a "betrayal of trust" when soliciting a "well-known writer" to comment on a "political or public question," then showing proofs of the article to another author so that a contradictory article was ready for the next issue; the anonymous "we" might connote authority but masked ignorance. The "anonymous press acquires a dignity and importance which are not its own; it is unfair and harmful; it protects exaggeration, hyperbole, flattery, and calumny" but served "the great financiers." Anonymous journalism had "its chief influence" on the public, so opinion had less and less "moral and honourable feeling." Signature would require "candour and courage."

190. Thring, G. Herbert. "Lord Monkswell's Copyright Bill." n.s., 67 (1900): 453–63.
Prefaced discussion of captioned bill with an excellent history of copyright legislation. The new bill (approved by the Select Committee of the House of Lords, 1899) extended protection to magazine material that could be published elsewhere after two years but created copyright problems for newspapers that took "cuttings" from their peers.

191. Davey, Richard. "A Few French Facts." n.s., 68 (1900): 268–84.
Scoffed at the "blasphemous and indecent" French press, whose effect on the lower classes was detrimental unlike the "intensely respectable" British *Advertiser*, "one of the few newspapers in pubs." *Gil Blas* published pornography daily, and too many political gazettes were either "Voltairian" or "clerical." Among those with a lighter style was the "very brilliantly written" *Echo de Paris* with leaders of "high tone." Quoted Horace Greeley that refusing to buy bad papers protected freedom of the press.

192. Y. "England and Belgium." n.s., 68 (1900): 753–64.
Touched on Belgium's important and "half-penny journals."

Fraser's Magazine for Town and Country, 1830–1882

Leaning conservative at first and at last and providing a plethora of material on the press, *Fraser's* was the child but not the namesake of publisher James. The magazine's unique and usually illustrated mini-biographies called attention to its well-known and unknown personnel.

1. [Maginn, William]. "Our 'Confession of Faith.'" 1 (1830): 1–7.
Editor assumed that magazines gained initial buyers from a prospectus, however inelegant.

2. [Maginn, William and ?J. A. Heraud]. "Fashionable Novels." 1 (1830): 318–35.
Denounced Henry Colburn, owner of the *Court Journal*, *New Monthly Magazine*, *Naval and Military Magazine*, and *Sunday Times* and co-owner of the *Literary Gazette*, for using them to push books he published, books that critics in other serials graded "trash."

3. [Maginn, William]. "The Election of Editor for *Fraser's Magazine*." 1 (1830): 496–508, 738–57; 2 (1830–31): 238–50.
Mentioned numerous past and present periodical editors.

4. Pungent, Pierce [Thomas Powell]. "Literary Characters. No. II: The Bard of Hope." 1 (1830): 563–71.
Biography of Thomas Campbell, editor of the *New Monthly Magazine*, classed it as "one of the most influential of the third-rate organs of public opinion." It was superficial, full of puffery and criticism without "manliness of language." Praise of his administration by the *Edinburgh Review* probably spoiled Campbell.

5. [Maginn, William]. "The *Edinburgh Review*: Mr. Thomas Babington Macaulay and Mr. Southey." 1 (1830): 584–600.
Sneered that the *Edinburgh* was "driveling into dotage" when Macaulay began writing for it.

6. [Maginn, William]. "Gallery of Illustrious Literary Characters. No. 1: William Jerdan, Esq., Editor of the *Literary Gazette*." 1 (1830): 605–06.
Titled series had a drawing of the "literary character," in this case Jerdan. Trailed him from the *Sun* to the *Literary Gazette*, which he managed "admirably well" so that it was "wholly free from spite and rivalry." He solicited talented writers for this "pleasant paper" but was slow to pay them.

7. [Maginn, William]. "Gallery of Illustrious Literary Characters. No. 2: Thomas Campbell, Esq., Editor of the *New Monthly*." 1 (1830): 714.

Touched on Campbell's tasks as the *New Monthly* editor, among them reading article proofs.

8. [Maginn, William]. "Gallery of Illustrious Literary Characters. No. 3: John Gibson Lockhart, Esq., Editor of *The Quarterly*." 2 (1830–31): 77.

Hoped that Lockhart was "a gentleman of too much sense and acuteness not to fall into the regular editing habit of never reading any such rubbish as the papers sent by contributors" so would stem publication of "literary atrocities."

9. "Eugenius Roche." 2 (1830–31): 118.

Obituary of a subeditor of the *Morning Post* and editor of other papers depicted him as a man of "considerable talent, kindly disposition," and "the most unwearied industry." Yet at his death he had a 5,000-pound loan for a small share of one paper, payment of which took his whole estate.

10. Culpepper, Ned [William Maginn and ?J. A. Heraud]. "Place-Men, Parliament-Men, Penny-a-Liners, and Parliamentary Reporters." 2 (1830–31): 282–94.

Trumpeted that MPs wanted to be reported fully in newspapers but had "fear" of and "contempt" for reporters because of press partisanship. Only three London papers, *The Times*, *Morning Chronicle*, and *Morning Herald*, promised "a fair and full account of the debates." Papers recruited men of good judgment and broad knowledge to be parliamentary reporters. They earned 300–400 pounds per year for taking 45 minutes of notes that required four hours of writing. Being grouped with penny-a-liners was disparaging.

11. "The *Edinburgh Review* versus [John] Galt's *Life of Byron*." 2 (1830–31): 467–68.

Scoffed at a Henry Brougham review (October 1830) as "a petty bit of tradesmanlike spite and critical sniveling" that *Edinburgh Review* editor Francis Jeffrey should have rejected.

12. "France and England." 2 (1830–31): 469–83.

Commented on an official French report on press liberty during the July Revolution, with an aside that *Blackwood's Magazine* supported press censorship in such circumstances.

13. "The Annuals." 2 (1830–31): 543–54.

Overview of annuals equated their contents intellectually with the poems, puzzles, and letters filling space in newspapers. The *Amulet* was one of the best, and the *New Comic Annual* one of the worst. A. A. Watts should focus on a single publication.

14. [Southern, Henry]. "Belgium: By an Eye-Witness." 2 (1830–31): 604–11.

Held that "the Belgian revolution is a newspaper revolution, as was that of Paris," in response to official suppression of "organs of discontent." "Lebry Bagnano, the editor of the *National* and a printer," was a key player.

15. "Narratives of the Late French Revolution." 2 (1830–31): 673–86.

Revisited the role of the press in the July Revolution.

16. [Lockhart, J. G.]. "Gallery of Illustrious Literary Characters. No. 8: The Doctor." 2 (1830–31): 716.
Protagonist was William Maginn, associated here only with the *Standard*.

17. A Looker-on. "Stray Notes on the *Anti-Slavery Monthly Reporter*." 3 (1831): 205–08.
Accused the *Anti-Slavery Reporter* of bias.

18. [?Maginn, William]. "Mr. Sadler and the *Edinburgh Review*." 3 (1831): 209–21.
Essay on T. B. Macaulay's review (July 1830) of Michael Sadler's *Law of Population* indicted the *Edinburgh* for publishing "palpable trickery" and "deliberate misrepresentation."

19. [Maginn, William]. "Gallery of Literary Characters. No. 11: John Wilson, Esq." 3 (1831): 364.
Scanned Wilson's writings as Christopher North in *Blackwood's Magazine*.

20. [?Maginn, William]. "To Petrus Maximus, on the Ejectment of Jeffrey: A Monologue." 3 (1831): 391–94.
Snarled that the "business" of the *Edinburgh Review* was "to depress by sneer and ridicule every man of true genius."

21. [Maginn, William]. "*The Metropolitan*: A 'Prospect'-ive Puff of a New Periodical." 3 (1831): 493–95.
Derided the *Metropolitan* prospectus for its "insincerity and stupid composition" and its bias against the *New Monthly Magazine*. Thomas Campbell, the *Metropolitan* editor, formerly had the same post at the *New Monthly* but reputedly took orders from proprietor Henry Colburn about book reviews. Campbell either exercised no "careful and conscientious superintendence" or colluded in "bibliopolist cupidity," which was an "odious prostitution of name and influence." *Fraser's* gave no such 'false impressions of new publications,' to which the *Athenaeum* supposedly testified. The *Spectator* was "conducted generally with great ability," but the *New Monthly* had little merit. Nonetheless, admitted that literary criticism in newspapers and weekly reviews was not replacing that in magazines.

22. [?Maginn, William]. "*Autobiography* of Edward Lytton Bulwer, Esq." 3 (1831): 713–19.
Challenged L. E. Landon's views in the *New Monthly Magazine* (31: 437) and those she quoted of E. G. Bulwer-Lytton on anonymity.

23. Y., O. [William Maginn]. "An Apology for a Preface to Our Fourth Volume." 4 (1831–32): 1–7.
Castigated the *New Monthly Magazine*, *Literary Gazette*, and *Blackwood's Magazine* for their partiality when reviewing books offered by the serial's publisher or penned by a volume's author.

24. "The March of Humbug." 4 (1831–32): 85–93.
Classified newspaper advertising, especially for books and patent medicines, as humbug.

25. "Influence of the Newspapers." 4 (1831–32): 127–42, 310–21.
Asserted that newspapers, as "mere echoes of public opinion," published rumors. So-called "licentiousness" of "private character" was merely repetition of gossip, which publicity diluted. The papers and the law gave the injured a way to vindicate their reputations, the first by printing retractions and the second by libel suits. Most gazettes avoided party or personal abuse, the "rancour of journalists," because it reduced credibility, although *The Times* slandered the "dead or powerless" incapable of response. Using its influence for gain or malice degraded the press, abetted ignorant or fearful proponents of censorship, and ignored the feelings of the wrongfully slandered.

News of vice and crime was different. Readers desired this "light reading"; the press, a business, responded to buyer demand but fostered a decline in morals, for example by covering brutal prizefights or by corrupting women whose only source of instruction was the press.

The morning dailies had the greatest circulation, several reaching the middle and lower classes. To maintain this audience, whose only reading was often the newspaper, editors printed the "vulgar." London papers, with free postage, had infected the country though expensive overseas mailing checked this fallout. Since the profit margin per paper was low, sales had to be high. But the stamp duty, intended to limit news to the masses, spurred their pub-going and the political clubs of the middle class as readers shared the cost of access. Repeal of the stamp and advertising duties and a change in domestic postal rates would breed a cheap, free press of talent and moderation.

Because "the lower classes were the most voracious readers" and easily roused by the press, "the journalist" had the potential for great political influence by exploiting the envy of the mob for the upper ranks or by propagating party or proprietor bias. Anonymity allowed leader-writers to be inconsistent or worse, so men no longer looked to the newspapers for information to form political opinions. Even *The Times* contained "hasty and muddled arguments" propounded by columnists who were tired or dumb. To make the newspaper respectable, editors had to be fairly paid, parliamentary reporters had to be careful, and the "subordinate class" of reporters had to be subject to legal restrictions on access.

26. [Maginn, William]. "Peter Robertson *versus* the *Edinburgh Review*." 4 (1831–32): 180–86.
Conceded that the *Edinburgh* displayed "considerable learning and ability."

27. [Maginn, William]. "Gallery of Literary Characters. No. 16: Right Hon. John Wilson Croker." 4 (1831–32): 240.
Glided over Croker's work for *John Bull* and the *Quarterly Review*.

28. [Maginn, William]. "The Briareus of the Press." 4 (1831–32): 490–95.
Situated the Irish among the most talented journalists in the United Kingdom press. David Curtayne, editor of the *Cork Sentinel*, was the ideal single voice, the "briareus." Aside that adoption of the steam press was common.

29. "The Reaction Against Reform." 4 (1831–32): 502–12.
Articulated that monthly magazines could not compete with dailies or weeklies for "rapidity of comment" but could for analysis because their writers had time to think.

30. Roughhead, Robin [William Maginn]. "Epistles to the Literati. No. 1: Letter to Edward Lytton Bulwer." 4 (1831–32): 520–26.
Conceptualized the *New Monthly Magazine* as full of "twaddle"; the *Westminster Review* as clever; the *Metropolitan* as questionable, and the *Edinburgh Review* as irrelevant for the times.

31. [Maginn, William]. "The Great and Celebrated Hogg Dinner." 5 (1832): 113–26.

Underscored that Scots edited the "leading journals," the *Quarterly Review*, *Edinburgh Review*, and *Blackwood's Magazine*, but that *Edinburgh* editor Francis Jeffrey never helped any talented Scottish writers. Aside that parliamentary reporters were biased.

32. Yorke, Oliver. "John Black's 'Lord Plunkett' and John Galt's 'Archibald Jobbry.'" 5 (1832): 244–46.

Called John Black of the *Morning Chronicle* "the only independent journalist in town" and the paper "marvelously honest and consistent."

32a. "*The Altrive Tales*." 5 (1832): 482–89.

Review of a work by James Hogg wondered why in his introductory autobiography he had said little about his relations with William Blackwood and J. G. Lockhart, *Blackwod's Magazine* and the *Quarterly Review*. Aside on J. C. Robertson of the *Mechanics' Magazine*.

33. [Maginn, William]. "Gallery of Literary Characters. No. 27: Edward Lytton Bulwer, Esq." 6 (1832): 112.

Demeaned Bulwer-Lytton's novel, *Henry Pelham*, as "smart magazine papers" suitable for the *New Monthly Magazine* or *Fraser's* "in a dull month."

34. Y., O. [?William Maginn]. "Regina and Her Correspondents." 6 (1832): 255–56.

Explained that the similarities between *Fraser's* and *Blackwood's Magazine* were due to having many contributors in common, but *Blackwood's* had lost some men of "high genius."

35. [Maginn, William]. "The Late Sir James Mackintosh and the *Law Magazine*." 6 (1832): 307–12.

Glanced at Mackintosh's career as a leader-writer for both the *Morning Post* and a politically opposite paper.

36. "A Dish of Wholesome Proverbs." 6 (1832): 499–508.

Tagged William Motherwell the "trusty and well-beloved" editor of the *Glasgow Courier*. Aside that the *Paisley Magazine* was not well known.

37. "The *Friendship's Offering*, *Amulet*, *Book of Beauty*, and Annual Pocket-Books." 6 (1832): 653–72.

Characterized editors of annuals as gentlemen who knew how to "please the most scrupulous of contributors and the public."

38. Yorke, Oliver [?William Maginn]. "Address to Contributors and Readers." 7 (1833): 1–15.

Shared with *Fraser's* readers that "[m]agazine literature, in London, was at a low ebb when we appeared." The majority, exemplified by the *New Monthly Magazine*, were "ingenious puffs of extensive bookselling establishments. Their tales were silly and sentimental – their verse...namby-pamby – their criticism hireling and worthless." Literary weeklies were as bad, and even the *Edinburgh Review*'s criticism was biased. *Fraser's*, by being impartial in all areas, had become popular at home and from Iceland to China. Charges that it was "scurrilous" and "vain" came from enemies jealous of its "eminence."

The Irish, Scots, Americans, French, Italians, Spanish, Russians, and Germans submitted material to *Fraser's*. Contributors constantly challenged editorial decisions. "Dull, stupid, drowsy articles, sent us by men of genius," were usually returned in the hope that rejections would inspire submission of better work or fill the pages of *Blackwood's Magazine*, *Tait's Edinburgh Magazine*, or the *New Monthly*. The lesser author when rejected became "the most malignant creature in existence" turning to a "petty publication" such as *Tait's* to vent anger.

39. "The Last *Quarterly*." 7 (1833): 112–15.
Deemed the December 1832 *Quarterly Review* "one of the most brilliant numbers."

40. [Maginn, William and John Churchill]. "The Fraser Papers." 7 (1833): 620–32.
Recommended consulting newspaper proprietors about the stamp duty since their investments in the press had the same protection accorded other businesses.

41. [Maginn, William]. "Gallery of Literary Characters. No. 37: Thomas Carlyle, Esq." 7 (1833): 706.
Declared that Carlyle's essays in the *Edinburgh Review* lent it "a Christian and honourable tone."

42. Y., O. [Maginn, William]. "A Wind-up for Our Seventh Volume, Literary, Political, and Anti-Peelish." 7 (1833): 750–52.
Averred that *New Monthly Magazine* sales were down and that *Blackwood's Magazine* was "jealous" of *Fraser's*, which exposed "Puffers" among the literary critics.

43. "Political Unions." 8 (1833): 28–35; 9 (1834): 65–71.
Supposed that the Northern Political Union (NPU) fathered the Newcastle press, the *Courant*, *Chronicle*, and *Mercury*. The editor of the *Tyne Mercury*, William Andrew Mitchell, an NPU member, had a "writing mania" but could be "amusing." Thomas Doubleday, the NPU secretary, was a "strong writer of that flaming patriotic *Magazine* named of *Tait*." Aside that the *Black Dwarf* kept readers in "a constant state of excitement."

44. [Maginn, William]. "Gallery of Literary Characters. No. 39: George Cruikshank, Esq." 8 (1833): 190.
Divulged that Cruikshank was not always well paid for his press work.

45. [Maginn, William]. "Gallery of Literary Characters. No. 40: Doctor Moir." 8 (1833): 290.
Saluted George Moir for his writings of "simple perspicuity of style" and "good sense" in *Fraser's* and *Blackwood's Magazine*.

46. "The Press and the Tories." 8 (1833): 330–38.
Highlighted "the immense influence of the press" and "the great change which it has wrought in the destinies of mankind." "The objects of the press are, principally, to disseminate the knowledge of facts, and to communicate opinions." Most people were "too dull, too eager, or too idle, to think upon

a public question." Even the more thoughtful did not always distinguish fact from fiction or reason correctly. The press served readers by being accurate and guiding opinion although many perceived the newspaper, with its "venality and licentiousness," as an instrument of evil. People interested in order had left politics to "the disaffected," so London gazettes spread the "vicious opinions" of the "depraved rabble," the "unenlightened," and the "profligate" to the country and reiterated them so loudly that country readers accepted them. *The Times* fed lower- class envy of the upper class in order to prove that the paper led opinion. To counter this sway, the Tories had to finance new papers until they built a sufficient circulation to secure advertising revenue.

47. [Maginn, William]. "Gallery of Literary Characters. No. 42: Miss Harriet Martineau." 8 (1833): 576.

Besmirched Martineau "the idol of the *Westminster Review*" and other periodicals that were a "nauseous mixture of the absurd and the abominable."

48. [Maginn, William]. "Gallery of Literary Characters. No. 48: Charles Molloy Westmacott, Esq." 9 (1834): 536.

Designated Westmacott, a pivotal editor of the *Age*, as the "antagonist" of Edward Bulwer-Lytton, editor of the *New Monthly Magazine.*

49. Yorke, Oliver [?William Maginn]. "Mr. Duncombe and Mr. Fraser." 10 (1834): 494–504.

Discussed *Fraser's* alleged libel of Thomas Duncombe and London press reaction to the matter. Aside that the *Morning Herald* was twaddle.

50. [Maginn, William]. "Gallery of Literary Characters. No. 54: James Smith, Esq." 10 (1834): 538.

Yawned at Smith's "monotonous" articles in the *New Monthly Magazine.*

51. Cornwall, Barry [B. W. Procter] and The Man of Genius [John Churchill]. "Two Articles on the Annuals: Judgment of the Annuals." 10 (1834): 604–09, 610–23.

Churchill, author of the second essay, portrayed conductors of annuals as "harmless, simple-minded, and soft-hearted" and *Friendship's Offering* and *Forget-Me-Not* as "accustomed mediocrity."

52. [Maginn, William]. "Gallery of Literary Characters. No. 59: Miss Jane Porter." 11 (1835): 404.

Lauded Porter who penned for *Fraser's.*

53. Galt, John. "Anonymous Publications." 11 (1835): 549–51

Fumed that dailies driven by malice or party printed "gross libels" by unidentified leader-writers. Weeklies, an "ephemeral class of periodicals," were guiltier because their anonymous scribes had more time and less pressure to write. Monthly magazines, untouched by libel, often insulted authors instead of letting bad books die of neglect and impugned critics who signed articles as vain. Signature in newspapers would diminish "licentious" columns by making journalists as liable as proprietors and printers.

54. [Maginn, William]. "Gallery of Literary Characters. No. 61: Mr. Alaric Attila Watts." 11 (1835): 652.

Followed Watts' career as a "scribbling man" of gossip and slander in the *Literary Gazette* to the *Leeds Intelligencer*, then to the *Literary Souvenir* as editor.

55. Rattler, Morgan [P. W. Banks]. "Of Politicians, Public Opinion, and the Press." 12 (1835): 32–42.

Warned that "the Radical press of London" was dangerous because of its ideas and its influence on local papers. As busy people increasingly sought guidance from newspapers, a free press could alter the social system.

56. [Mahony, Francis]. "Gallery of Literary Characters. No. 63: Henry O'Brien, A.B." 12 (1835): 154.

Dismissed the *Edinburgh Review* in 1835 as a "rickety go-cart of dwelling dotage."

57. [?Maginn, William]. "Cobbett." 12 (1835): 207–22.

After a review of William Cobbett's journalism, rated him an ignorant writer.

58. [Maginn, William]. "Gallery of Literary Characters. No. 65: William Cobbett, M.P. for Oldham." 12 (1835): 430.

Belittled *Edinburgh Review* contributors who sold essays for high fees and later contradicted their own theses in articles equally pricey.

59. "Mr. Alaric *Alexander* Watts." 13 (1836): 129–31.

Speculated that as the result of a quarrel with *Fraser's*, Watts might find employment at a two-penny press but never a monthly. *See* 13: 132.

60. "The Speech of William Erle, Esq., K.C., in the Case of Watts v. Fraser and Moyes." 13 (1836): 132–42.

Explicated an 1835 case in King's Bench. *See* 13: 129.

61. [Maginn, William]. "Willis's *Pencillings* [*by the Way*]." 13 (1836): 195–202.

Review of a book by N. P. Willis, whose ideas originally surfaced in the *New York Mirror*, opined that the *Quarterly Review* under editor William Gifford was biased and the *Edinburgh Review* was "somnolent."

62. "The Morning and Evening Papers." 13 (1836): 620–31.

Catalogued *The Times* as the "*leading journal of Europe*"; the *Morning Chronicle* as the "chief organ of government" but declining in influence and style; the *Morning Post* as the "fashionable paper," the 'Pet of the Petticoats'; the *Morning Herald* as a gazette with a "very extensive circulation"; the *Standard* as defender of the High Church with honor; the *Globe* as the government's evening paper; the *Sun* as having a "good circulation" and being "well conducted"; the *True Sun* as less on both counts; the *Morning Advertiser* as popular with London's "licensed victuallers"; and the *Public Ledger* as a "rising authority" on commerce. Aside that "the balance of newspaper *power* is uncontestably in favour of the Conservative party."

63. "*England in 1835*." 13 (1836): 631–38.
Review of Frederick von Raumer's book expressed annoyance that a German press censor from a region that restricted circulation of English newspapers evaluated the British press.

64. [Maginn, William]. "Mr. Grant's *Great Metropolis*." 14 (1836): 710–19.
Review of James Grant's book blared that he knew "nothing of the actual governing powers of the newspapers" and provided faulty data about editors, writers, and owners of journals but quoted him that contributors to *Fraser's* were 'numerous and talented,' 'a happy brotherhood.'

65. G., T. [R. A. Willmott]. "A Scourging Soliloquy about the Annuals." 15 (1837): 33–48.
Overview of annuals painted *Friendship's Offering* as replete with "flashy tales and watery rhymes."

66. "The Trial of Fraser v. Berkeley and Another, and Berkeley v. Fraser." 15 (1837): 100–37.
Dealt with a slander case arising from a *Fraser's* review (August 1836) of Grantley Berkeley's *Berkeley's Castle*. *See* 15: 137.

67. Maginn, William, Esq., LL.D. "Defence of *Fraser's Magazine* in the Berkeley Affair." 15 (1837): 137–43.
Amended 15: 100 with information about the repercussions of the review cited. Defended anonymity in magazines and newspapers because the use of "we" mirrored the literary and political views of many people and readers knew the identity of writers in the major serials.

68. [Heraud, J. A. and ?William Maginn]. "One or Two Words on One or Two Books." 15 (1837): 498–514.
Remarked that W. S. Landor's *A Satire on Satirists* criticized *Blackwood's Magazine* reviewers.

69. Menenius [D. P. Starkey]. "To T. P. Thompson, Esq., Ex-M.P. for Hull." 16 (1837): 390–99.
Surmised that the *Westminster Review* was "impotent in effect" because it was not well planned or executed.

70. [Thackeray, W. M.]. "A Word on the Annuals." 16 (1837): 757–63.
Discovered that several annuals, each determined to please the public, had similar contents.

71. "The Newspaper Press of Paris." 17 (1838): 50–61, 208–29.
Lectured that the French press as Fourth Estate meant the Paris newspapers, where Deputies went to correct proofs of their speeches and news typically took two-thirds of a page with the rest for feuilletons, the arts, and science. Dailies and weeklies might be political; "half-Political, half-Amusing, and Theatrical"; "Literary, Theatrical, and Miscellaneous without politics," or legal. The *Moniteur*, which sent copies to Deputies, was likewise free in libraries and cafés but otherwise available by subscription. People read it for official news, not foreign, scientific, or literary content. The *Journal des Débats* (costs/advertising rates cited in this article) suffered in competition with cheaper papers. Its newest editorial staffer was Michel Chevalier, a proponent of women's rights. The *Presse* was

the "giant-killer of the old press." Considered at length here were the price, circulation, advertising rates, staff, quality of writing, and layout of the *Presse* and other dailies. Most French editors worked harder than British editors because French dailies published on Sunday. Low pay meant journalists were untalented and immoral or amoral. Since Paris evening papers appeared late and the post was inefficient, the provinces, whose papers ignored politics unlike British locals, received news slowly.

Monthlies and quarterlies ordinarily specialized.

72. [Thackeray, W. M.]. "Half-a-Crown's Worth of Cheap Knowledge." 17 (1838): 279–90.

Surveyed 15 publications costing a penny or two. Cheap papers catering to the urban lower class had changed since the stamp duty decreased. Most no longer instructed, except the *Poor Man's Friend* and the *Moral Reformer*, a "very well executed" organ. The rest stole information, as the *Penny Satirist*'s medical advice, and literature. The "graceful, fantastic, sarcastic" *Fly* was akin to the French *Charivari* and the *Town*, the best guide to drinking and gambling haunts. These publications confirmed that licentiousness was no longer the domain of the aristocratic press.

73. [Maginn, William]. "Gallery of Literary Characters. No. 81: The Rev. Sydney Smith." 17 (1838): 468–70.

Pontificated that the *Edinburgh Review* "gave a new aspect to the whole of periodical literature – nay, to the general opinion, doctrine, and character of the time" because of its learning and principles. Smith, who was a founder, sponsored talented tyros.

74. [Anderson, William]. "The Newspaper Press of Scotland." 17 (1838): 559–71; 18 (1838): 75–85, 201–09.

Studied both active and "defunct" newspapers in Edinburgh, Glasgow, Aberdeen, and elsewhere and some editors, from Daniel Defoe to George Houy. The *Caledonian Mercury* borrowed its name from a seventeenth-century gazette, and the *Glasgow Courant* was that city's first newspaper. In 1838 there were 57 newspapers in Scotland, one all advertising, most dominated by self-made men. Because the Conservative press was the best written, it had the most advertising. The reduction in the stamp duty spawned Radical papers that spoke to the desperately poor and undermined the respectability of the press.

75. "The *Edinburgh Review*, Lord Brougham, and the Press." 18 (1838): 1–28.

Responded to Henry Brougham's essay in the *Edinburgh* (67: 1) by defining the *Diary Illustrative of the Times of George IV* as a vindication, not a libel, of Caroline and accusing Brougham of reversing himself on press liberty. He should introduce legislation that would enable writers and publishers to plead truth as a defense in libel cases. Such a statute would restore respect for a press that frequently printed scandal to sell papers.

76. [Anderson, William]. "The Religious Periodical Press." 18 (1838): 330–38.

Believed that religious serials had "an extensive circle of readers," most of whom they influenced positively. Provided data on affiliation/circulation of several Protestant newspapers.

77. "Sporting Literature." 18 (1838): 481–88.

Flipped through the *Old Sporting Magazine*, "a drowsy periodical" with stories on theatre, adventure, and crime as well as sports, and the *New Sporting Magazine* (1831), which pioneered "sporting Fiction."

78. [Thackeray, W. M.]. "Our Annual Execution." 19 (1839): 57–67.

Assayed numerous annuals, as the "dumpy" *Forget-Me-Not.*

79. [Merle, Gibbons]. "A Newspaper Editor's Reminiscences." 20 (1839): 588–603; 22 (1840): 336–45, 415–30; 23 (1841): 699–710.

Merle recollected that as a youth he read the newspaper to his father. The editorial "we" then suggested power, but as an adult editor he understood it did not mean "greatness." He started as a correspondent on "fashionable movements of my place of residence," but the sentence of a corporal to 1,000 lashes drew him into a campaign against this punishment. He moved to the *White Dwarf* whose 300 subscribers hardly matched the thousands of the *Black Dwarf* until the Home Office took 100, then 1,000 copies. Misunderstanding about an article led to editing an English paper abroad. He returned to London, eventually as an editor, a post with "vanity" but not much "gratification." He learned that Cabinet officers sent contradictory messages and other powerbrokers disclaimed a connection with the press publicly but solicited its backing privately. London gazettes, but for the few of "malevolence and falsehood," were far more independent than French.

Parliamentary reporters, of whom Merle was not one, paid for their legal educations from this salary. They took notes only on "leading points," later fleshing them out from memory. A reporter without shorthand but with style was one Proby, a man of "good humour" with a "portly figure," "rubicund countenance," and "powdered hair" who always carried an umbrella, a man "brought down by a fondness for good living and the bottle."

Part II of the "Reminiscences," on theatre, observed that readers rejected London theatre critics who played favorites; Part III, on British and French politics, and Part IV, on poetry, are irrelevant here except for an aside that Merle first published in the *Poetical Magazine* and claimed that he had to resign as editor of a daily when he rejected the poetry of a shareholder.

80. An Old Journalist. "How to Make a Newspaper, Without Credit or Cash." 20 (1839): 746–52.

Swore that newspapers burgeoned in London after reduction of the stamp duty. The exploits of Robert Herron, in connection with the *Globe*, verified that neither capital nor credit was necessary to purchase a share of a journal. Herron immediately sold his share to others, then became editor. Because he was "a wretched farrago, destitute of taste, talent, and intelligence," he was soon fired.

81. "Characteristics of the Nineteenth Century." 21 (1840): 147–64.

Pigeonholed as superficial the knowledge disseminated by cheap serials, as the *Penny Magazine* and those of the Chambers brothers.

82. One of the Reviewed. "On the Present State of Literary Criticism in England." 21 (1840): 190–200.

Stereotyped literary critics who penned for the press. The German critics were "vain and pedantic"; the French were "supercilious and presuming"; the British put everybody above British writers. French dailies printed some literary criticism, but the French had no "purely critical journal." The *Revue des Deux Mondes* was the equivalent of a "third-rate English periodical"; the *Revue Germanique*, acceptable; the *Revue du Nord*, "inferior"; the *Revue Britannique*, "contemptible." The *Edinburgh Review* and the *Quarterly Review* were not up-to-date. The *Foreign Quarterly Review* was a "collection of essays." The *Metropolitan* and *New Monthly Magazine* were "mere booksellers' puffs." The *Monthly Chronicle* had "some very fair critical sketches." *Blackwood's Magazine*, particularly articles signed Christopher

North, had "spirit and excellence." Newspapers of criticism, the *Athenaeum* and *Literary Gazette*, had mixed success. The writing in British dailies, such as *The Times*, *Standard*, *Morning Post*, *Morning Herald*, and some locals, was better than in French gazettes, but Gallic journalists had more power. *The Times* was an exception because its good review could sell a book. Many dailies, though not the *Sun*, only printed reviews when the editor had space and a friend to write them. Critics in 1840, though still deprived of fame by anonymity, were gentlemen unlike an earlier generation. Aside that the lower classes perused only "newspapers of violent democratic tendency."

83. Scupper, Nelson Tattersall Lee, Esq. [W. M. Thackeray]. "Epistles to the Literati. No. 14: On French Criticism of the English and Notably in the Affair of the *Vengeur*." 21 (1840): 332–45.

Imagined that Paris' centrist press, as the *Journal des Débats*, *Constitutionnel*, and *Siècle*, had considerable sway in politics.

84. "The History and Mystery of Secret Societies and Secret Political Clubs." 21 (1840): 542–53; 22 (1840): 243–52.

Regretted that copies of the *Journal de la Societé de Jacobins* were "rare."

85. "A Batch of Almanacks for 1841." 23 (1841): 101–08.

Sampled *Oliver and Boyd's Edinburgh Almanack*, "the fullest and cheapest" of its time, and the *Comic Almanack* of 1841, which was worthy of George Cruikshank. Aside on the advertisements in the *Caledonian Mercury* (1734) and *Edinburgh Courant* (1745).

86. Tackletoo, Ephraim. "Specimen Leaders of a Would-Be Editor." 23 (1841): 433–50.

Satirized the style of leaders in several London dailies and weeklies.

87. [Mathews, Anne]. "To the Messieurs of the Diurnal Press: An Unpublished Letter Found in the Desk of a Deceased Editor." 24 (1841): 234–36.

Considered the newspaper "one of the daily necessities of life" but disliked its scandalous "*Private Correspondence*," "*low*" police reports, and unreliable theatre criticism. Skipped its politics, advertisements, and columns on court and fashionable life but not those on births, marriages, and deaths, bankruptcies, accidents, and the "London markets," reports that were almost incomprehensible.

88. "A Chapter on Tailors." 24 (1841): 288–96.

Urged "the journalist…to aim at expanding the intellects and amending the morals of his countrymen."

89. [Mathews, Anne]. "Theodore Edward Hook." 24 (1841): 518–24.

Warranted that while Hook edited *John Bull*, his talent pervaded its leaders and its "witty and playful portions." As editor of the *New Monthly Magazine* he "added weight and attraction to it."

90. "The Late Mr. Fraser." 24 (1841): 628–30.

Obituary of publisher James Fraser incorporated tributes from other serials.

91. [Thackeray, W. M.]. "Dickens in France." 25 (1842): 342–52.
Bowed to Jules Janin, "the critic of France," whose weekly feuilleton in the *Journal des Débats* was full of "brilliancy and wit" that combined "impudence" and "good feeling," "honesty" and "falsehood."

92. [Kenealy, E. V. H.]. "The Late William Maginn, LL.D." 26 (1842): 377–78.
Memorialized Maginn for bringing "early success" to *Fraser's* and rendering "valuable services" to it thereafter, but, "as to editorial management of the Magazine, in that he never took part."

93. [Wilks, John]. "Reminiscences of Men and Things." 26 (1842): 730–42; 27 (1843): 289–301, 687–704.
Profiled Armand Carrel, coeditor of the Paris *National*, and his colleague, Adolphe Thiers, during the journalists' protests of July 1830; A.-E. Génoude, editor of the royalist *Gazette de France*, which endured "numberless seizures and prosecutions" after 1830 but "continued its manly and straightforward course"; and Heinrich Heine, when he wrote for the *Allgemeine Zeitung*.

94. [Kenealy, E. V. H.]. "Oliver Yorke at Home." 27 (1843): 1–35.
Rambled that *Fraser's* was "the best paying Magazine," a power unlike editor Macvey Napier's *Edinburgh Review*, and printed more on Ireland than its own press.

95. [Willmott, R. A.]. "Joseph Addison." 28 (1843): 143–59, 304–20.
Swept past the eighteenth-century *Tatler*, *Examiner*, and *Spectator*, which "was not only to diffuse the name of Addison over the civilised world, but was also to replenish his exhausted treasury."

96. [Cunningham, Peter]. "Campbelliana." 30 (1844): 342–52.
Bruited that Thomas Campbell did little editing at the *New Monthly Magazine*, but his name and a "good brigade of writers" increased the *New Monthly* audience.

97. [Willmott, R. A.]. "The Writings of the Late John Foster." 30 (1844): 684–702.
Appraised Foster's work, including some of the 185 essays he wrote for the *Eclectic Review*, 1806–18.

98. "Public Patronage of Men of Letters." 33 (1846): 58–71.
Comprehended that political views could separate literary men, as the editors of the *Edinburgh Review* and *Quarterly Review*, *The Times* and *Morning Chronicle*.

99. [Thackeray, W. M.]. "A Brother of the Press on the History of a Literary Man, Laman Blanchard, and the Chances of the Literary Profession." 33 (1846): 332–42.
Dwelt on Laman Blanchard's *Sketches from Life*, notably his essay "The Penny-a-Liner," and E. G. Bulwer-Lytton's memoir of Blanchard in the same volume. Aside that journalism was the literature of the day. Etonians read *Punch* more regularly than schoolbooks, and *The Times* was a giant miscellany. Journalists amused and instructed but endured low pay and little respect.

100. Blunt, Benjamin, Formerly a Bencherman and Trencherman in the Inner Temple, Now a Rentier of the Rue Rivoli [A. V. Kirwan]. "A Letter to Oliver Yorke on French Newspapers and Newspaper Writers, French Farceurs and Feuilletonists, French Duellists, French Actresses, Etc." 33 (1846): 674–83.

Shortened version of a *British Quarterly Review* article (3: 468) divided French journalists into "riff-raff" and the intellectually, morally, and socially outstanding. The French press, though not so respected or well run as in 1826, was still quite good. One example was the *Journal des Débats*, directed by "gentlemen and men of letters." They had none of the "blackguardism" of the managers of the *Presse* who debased journalism and demoralized journalists, many well paid but living beyond their means. Feuilletonists and penny-a-liners obeyed editors. Originally feuilletons were "clear, correct, candid, and learned criticism" on the arts, but in 1846 they were tales for "vulgar appetites" that lured readers and advertisers by substituting melodrama for style. If the British copied this format, liberty of the press would cease. Aside that the *Siècle*, with 42,000 subscribers, had the largest circulation.

101. "Brougham's *Men of Letters and Science*." 34 (1846): 67–84.

Review of Henry Brougham's work, volume II, resurrected Samuel Johnson's parliamentary reports in the *Gentleman's Magazine*, reports less of speeches in the House than of talk in coffeehouses.

102. "English Journalism." 34 (1846): 631–40.

Alleged that after 1832 newspapers shifted away from party scandals and trite language. Leaders that were "abusive or personal" gave way to those of "salient piquancy, sportive humour, and even argumentative eloquence." By 1846 journalism was a profession with influence. Leader-writers of the established and independent papers were people of "education, information, and ability," "earnestness, eloquence, and brilliance," who fulfilled the mission of the press with "dignity and integrity." They exceeded the "erudition, reflectiveness, and judgment" of two-thirds of their readers. Because they raised public taste their gazettes had a reputation for quality, one that even the Americans acknowledged. British audiences expected and accepted expertise from scribes yet consigned them to anonymity, a "curse" that shielded the libeler and the liar who discredited decent journalists. While they used their power to critique "factious license and popular passions," their confreres exalted themselves by pandering to the dispossessed. The widely read *Sun* writers were "vulgar in their ideas and the most virulent in their style." Others of this genre were "venomous" or "morbid." They tried, like French journalists, "to excite and to please, not to convince or to conciliate." No surprise that men who failed in law or medicine were more ashamed of being journalists. Party leaders needed to shore up morale at their tribunes, and every paper should pay fairly lest the unhappy take their talents to reform journals funded by the wealthy.

103. [Francis, G. H.]. "Literary Legislators. No. 1: Mr. B. Disraeli." 35 (1847): 79–95.

Detected similarities only of approach in Benjamin Disraeli's "Letters of Runnymede" in *The Times* and Junius's columns in the *Public Advertiser*. Disraeli's paragraphs "subverted" history, but readers relished their "flippancy" and "insolent smartness."

104. [Lewes, G. H.]. "The Condition of Authors in England, Germany, and France." 35 (1847): 285–95.

Posited that periodicals, "a potent instrument for the education of the people," offered employment to those who could pen short pieces. Contributors were a profession, albeit one neither honored nor respected. The British essayist wrote more than the French, but the Gaul had a copyright that permitted remunerative reprints. Because British authors typically penned for many serials to earn a living, people incorrectly assumed that this behavior "sacrifices truth to effect," "substitutes brilliancy for solidity." Asides on the pay scales of English and French quarterlies and of French and German newspapers.

105. [Kirwan, A. V.]. "Chronique de Paris; or, the Restoration and the Revolution Compared." 35 (1847): 418–28.

Suspected that in the 1830s French officials paid for newspaper articles from "secret service money." Government controlled the news except for the small press, as *Charivari*, and the foreign, as *Eco del Comercio* (Madrid). Theatrical journals, as *France Théâtrile*, *Furet*, and "*Corsaire Satan*, said to be the property of that intriguing priest, Abbé [A.-E.] Génoude," attacked critic Jules Janin. *Corsaire Satan*, with "more talent, wit, and subscribers," was the first he sued for libel.

106. [Kirwan, A. V.]. "The Girondists, Jacobins, and M. [Alphonse] de Lamartine, Deputy for Macon." 36 (1847): 253–76.

Alluded to Emile de Girardin as "the clever editor of the *Presse*."

107. [Francis, G. H.]. "Some New Members of the New Parliament: Mr. J. Walter, Mr. Feargus O'Connor, Mr. G[eorge] Cornewall Lewis." 37 (1848): 167–76.

Revered *The Times* because it was "what a newspaper should be...an organ of intelligence, and of political, commercial, and economic opinion." John Walter II made the paper the exemplar of "THE POWER" of the age and of the independent press by keeping it a "delicate barometer of public opinion." Walter senior separated his views from the journal but whether his son, an MP, could do the same was debatable. Aside that O'Connor tried unsuccessfully to buy the *Cork Southern Reporter*.

108. "Romance of Portuguese Revolution." 37 (1848): 272–85.

Caricatured "the government organ, the *Lisbon Gazette*," as "a half-sheet of blotting paper."

109. "The French Revolution of 1848: Its Causes and Consequences." 37 (1848): 371–87.

Congratulated Paris *Tribune* editor Armand Marrast for leading a campaign that exposed government patronage in the 1830s.

110. [Thomson, Katharine]. "Publishers and Authors." 38 (1848): 411–20.

Asserted that the early *Spectator* made "light reading fashionable." Eighteenth-century publishers critiqued submissions previously checked by censors. Still, Edward Cave sheltered "an army of hack-writers" at the *Gentleman's Magazine*. Aside that the *Paris Gazette* dated from 1622.

111. Nerke [Cyrus Redding]. "London from the Crow's Nest." 39 (1849): 58–64.

Boasted that *The Times*, with its "train of dependents...at nocturnal labours" who satisfied the public "hunger and thirst" for news, epitomized a joint "effort of capital and activity."

112. [Wynter, Andrew]. "The Post-Office." 41 (1850): 224–32.

Rhapsodized about the "enormous" number of newspapers posted morning and evening in London, including "[s]everal vans full of *The Times*." The 70 million newspapers annually went, irrespective of size or weight, free except for a penny news stamp, and magazines less than two ounces cost only another penny. There was "speedy transmission of news to all parts of the kingdom and its colonies."

113. "A Batch of Biographies." 41 (1850): 443–59.

Reviewed R. H. Barham's *Life and Remains of Theodore Edward Hook* and William B. Scott's *Memoirs of David Scott, R.S.A.* Hook successfully edited *John Bull*, whose first numbers caused an "electrical sensation." Although he earned 2,000 pounds per year there, overspending compelled him to edit the *New Monthly Magazine*. Scott's articles in *Blackwood's Magazine* were "obsolete and egotistical."

114. [Kirwan, A. V.]. "Ledru-Rollin's *Decline of England*." 42 (1850): 74–85.

Review, echoing the *British Quarterly Review* (3: 468), said that A. A. Ledru-Rollin purloined his ideas from the London press. Aside that *The Times* was "not the journal of the English aristocracy, but the journal of the monied, mercantile, and middle classes."

115. "The Age of Veneer." 42 (1850): 437–45; 44 (1851): 332–39; 45 (1852): 87–93.

Rued that newspapers in 1850 followed instead of led opinion. The great journals formerly championed public matters and influenced statesmen validating the press as the Fourth Estate. Overconfidence cost papers the respect essential to shape opinion. Columns that appealed to "lower and lower orders of intelligence" and manipulation of a "public used to thinking for themselves" further decreased clout. Aside that morning dailies were an excellent venue for advertising.

116. [?Whewell, William]. "A Gossip about the Christmas Books." 43 (1851): 37–46.

Recalled how popular annuals were in the 1830s.

117. "Lord Holland's *Foreign Reminiscences*." 43 (1851): 220–36.

Review of Richard Holland's book corrected that the editor of the *Courrier de Provence* was P. E. Dumont, not Count H. de Mirabeau.

118. [Kirwan, A. V.]. "*History of French Journals, and Biography of French Journalists*." 43 (1851): 350–66.

Review of Edmond Texier's volume repeated ideas in the *British Quarterly Review* (3: 468). Seventeenth- and eighteenth-century French papers with "the most learned and able men" as writers and women as managers printed much scandal. Government warned, then sent to convents the worst slanderers. The power of modern French journalism developed from the *Journal des Débats* of Francis and Lewis Bertin. The paper's feuilletons, criticism, "learning, "wit," and "independence" in 1851 accounted for its 10,000–12,000 circulation. The *Constitutionnel*, with equally able writers, peaked in 1830 when it reached 23,000 subscribers and again in the 1840s. The men of the *National* played a pivotal part in the July Revolution. Also discussed here were the scribes of the *Moniteur*, *Siècle*, *Presse* and *Globe*, "some of the ablest and most instructed men." By 1851 French journalists were inferior to London leader-writers, who combined "talent, energy, information, readiness, and compression," but the Parisians were superior in influence and "social and literary consideration" though they earned less money. Paris had many papers because French readers were more concerned about "public affairs" and "foreign policy" than were British. Aside that newspaper writing was so exhausting that journalists everywhere relied on "set phrases" and "pet ideas."

119. [Kirwan, A. V.]. "Chronique de Paris." 43 (1851): 682–89.

Glimpsed "signs of revival in the Paris press" that was in decline since 1845. Alphonse de Lamartine wrote for the daily *Pays*; Adolphe Thiers, for *Ordre* and "his own *Messager des Chambres*," and François Guizot, for the *Assemblée Nationale*.

120. [Kingsley, Charles]. "Little Books with Large Aims." 44 (1851): 26–40.

Confided that it was the "routine of journalism" to review books short on quality as a group or to neglect them.

121. "Notes on the Newspaper Stamp." 44 (1851): 339–54.

Reacted to the Report of the Select Committee on the Newspaper Stamp. The stamp applied to "public" news sheets, not "private" or specialized, but affected advertising papers by limiting their size. The "liberty of the press is one of the necessities of the people," but price was a problem in Britain before 1836. The four-penny stamp denied the "humble" access to practical information. After reduction of the duty, newspaper circulation tripled, and newspapers retained their "literary or moral character." But abolition of the duty would destroy small London papers, spur locals of political "detraction and vituperation," and encourage the cheapest to serve the "lowest orders" a diet of "rabid politics" and crime. Abolition would not benefit the poor who already had a variety of magazines, would result in substandard newsgathering, and would pressure a post that already transmitted 120,000–260,000 papers daily in London.

Repeal of the pesky and minute paper duty would have no deleterious outcome.

122. [Kirwan, A. V.]. "*History of the Restoration of Monarchy in France*." 44 (1851): 355–74.

Review of Alphonse de Lamartine's book theorized that the Chamber of Deputies of Louis XVIII accepted some limits on press freedom because members were tired of revolution.

123. [Francis, G. H.]. "Henry, Lord Brougham; His Career and Character." 44 (1851): 458–72.

Noticed Brougham's writing in the *Edinburgh Review* when that "great literary periodical" dominated criticism.

124. Kirwan, A. V., Esq., Barrister-at-Law. "The Coup D'Etat in France: A Letter to the People of England." 45 (1852): 110–26.

Damned the press censorship of Napoleon III, whose plans for expansion threatened journalism in neighboring states.

125. "Modern History, and Other Matters, at Cambridge." 45 (1852): 170–82.

Aired that university fellows whom Cambridge could not afford to hire as professors penned leaders of "knowledge of life and good sense" in *The Times* and *Morning Chronicle*.

126. [Kirwan, A. V.]. "State and Prospects of France and the Continent of Europe." 45 (1852): 352–62.

Boomed that the French press was "utterly and entirely extinct." "All the republican, democratic, liberal, and Orleanist papers are destroyed – their writers in exile, their printing offices shut up, their types scattered." The *Constitutionnel*, "once the sentinel of public liberty," was "the fulsome flatterer" of Napoleon III. The *Journal des Débats* was politically discreet; the *Siècle* had no leaders because Louis Jourdan, Pierre Bernard, and Emile de Labédollière had been silenced. Every article had to pass the censor, an office abolished in 1791 except for drama but restored by the emperor. Recent press legislation not only curbed the French but also the foreign press, which needed permission to circulate. Domestic papers had to purchase a stamp and deposit caution money, intended not merely to stop the scurrilous but even serials of high quality. Penalties for violations were fines and suppression.

Aside that Louis Véron, an early writer for *Quotidienne*, purchased a share in the *Constitutionnel* in 1838 and promptly engaged Eugene Sue to pen the feuilletons that raised circulation from 3,000 to 30,000.

127. "Lord Jeffrey's Life." 45 (1852): 557–63.

Review of Henry Cockburn's *Life of Lord Jeffrey* reminded that during his era as editor of the *Edinburgh Review*, articles were very short. He earned 2,000 pounds a year; writers, ten guineas, then 16, and finally 20–5 a sheet.

128. "Neglected French Authors: Chamfort." 46 (1852): 291–304.

Biography of Nicholas Chamfort, of the *Mercure de France*, realized that times of unrest put journalists in the limelight because they worked unceasingly. Their efforts detrimentally affected health and raised "deadly enemies."

129. [Craufurd, John]. "The Ionian Islands and Their Government." 46 (1852): 593–608.

Attributed recent restrictions on journalism in the Ionian Islands to the "calumny" of the free press since 1849.

130. "Thomas Moore." 47 (1853): 1–17.

Saluted Moore as "a distinguished contributor to the *Edinburgh Review*."

131. "American Statesmen." 47 (1853): 31–39.

Broadcast that many Americans read dailies of "moderate ability" and "verbosity." The "better class" of papers paralleled English gazettes in the "style, tone, and temper of their leading articles."

132. Small, John [W. M. Thackeray]. "Mr. Thackeray in the United States." 47 (1853): 100–03.

Peeked at the *Broadway Delineator*, a New York newspaper with "a fabulous circulation."

133. [Kirwan, A. V.]. "Napoleon III – Invasion – French Pamphlets and the English Press." 47 (1853): 135–48.

Opened with information on A. de la Guéronnière, who commenced his journalistic career in the provinces, at the *Avenir* (Limoges) and the *Journal de Clermont* before joining the "*Bien Public* of Maçon." When that paper merged with the *Pays*, he moved to its Paris staff where he became prominent when Alphonse de Lamartine was ill. Because of a difference of political opinion Lamartine left the paper that Guéronnière then transformed into a Bonapartist herald.

134. [Kirwan, A. V.]. "Dr. Véron's *Memoirs*." 49 (1854): 19–30.
Review of Louis Véron's book recited his journalistic activities: founder and editor of the *Revue de Paris*, shareholder of the *Constitutionnel*, and scribe for the *Moniteur*. *See* 51: 676.

135. [?Kirwan, A. V.]. "Paris Gossip." 49 (1854): 195–98.
Chatted about Paris papers with little hard news.

136. L[indo], M. P. "Researches in Dutch Literature." 50 (1854): 95–105, 663–76.
Dated the Dutch periodical from Justus van Effen, who published the *Spectator*, 1731–35, modeled on the British one and as popular and influential. In 1854 the Dutch had many journals, among them literary, theological, and archeological organs. Even with good writing, most averaged 400 subscribers. The monthly *Guide* published severe criticism, and the *Mirror of the Times* published essays and reviews. The dailies did not cover politics and economics well and engaged in "personal attacks" in stories on church-state relations.

137. [Strachey, George]. "Russian Defeats and Their Effect on Europe." 50 (1854): 594–606.
Argued that the press should be open in war as long as journalists reported the news, refrained from criticizing or advising the military, and remembered that their stories could offend soldiers' families.

138. "Massey's *History of England* [during the Reign of George III]." 51 (1855): 127–44.
Review of William Massey's book paraphrased him on eighteenth-century papers, as John Wilkes' *North Briton*, Tobias Smollett's *Briton*, and the *Auditor* of Arthur "Murphy, a man of considerable literary talent."

139. [Kirwan, A. V.]. "Recent French Literature." 51 (1855): 676–93.
Reiterated the theme of 49: 19, stressing that Louis Véron resuscitated the *Constitutionnel* by hiring Eugene Sue.

140. A Manchester Man, R[obert] L[amb]. "An Essay on Humbug." 52 (1855): 30–41.
Rejoiced that advertisements in "leading journals" were "mirrors of domestic life," not humbug.

141. The Author of 'The Upper Ten Thousand,' C. A. B[risted]. "The English Press and the American Public." 52 (1855): 42–47.
Focused on press criticism, except in the *Westminster Review* and *Daily News*, of American laws and customs. Even though British reports were accurate and leaders were well-written satire, they offended American readers who were more sensitive than French. British banter was not malicious and applied as frequently to citizens as foreigners, but Americans took this talk seriously. Yet such papers as the *New York Herald* and *New York Tribune* disseminated "wholesale fabrications" in contrast to the British practice, "to omit or slur over counterbalancing facts." In Britain, "scandalous" papers were dying from lack of sales; in the United States, libel boosted circulation.

142. "Parliament, the Press, and the War." 52 (1855): 115–22.
Preferred a 'ribald press' that exposed military abuses to a muzzled press because, as Crimea demonstrated, war correspondents could spur government to increase military funding and citizens to aid soldiers.

143. R[obertson], J. C. "*Noctes Ambrosianae*." 52 (1855): 363–78.
Reckoned that John Wilson and *Blackwood's Magazine* benefited from his work for it. Aside that editor J. G. "Lockhart used to smarten up the articles of his *Quarterly* [*Review*] contributors."

144. "Hugh Miller." 52 (1855): 588–93.
Spotlighted Miller, who edited the newspaper of the Scottish Free Church party. Aside that editing any newspaper was "harassing."

145. B[risted], C. A. "The Political Press of America." 52 (1855): 678–85.
Prefaced an essay on the American press with comparisons. The English newspaper was "a faithful representative of the English people – not of this or that class, but of the people, the intellectual and moral *momentum* of the nation." The French version, 1840–50, was not a picture of French life.

American newspapers, inferior in type, paper, and layout, had many misprints, few and stale leaders, and inaccurate domestic news but were cheap and easily folded. Since the 1830s the penny press had lured big audiences by "pandering" to slander, scandal, and violence instead of fulfilling journalists' duties "to instruct and elevate the public." Signature kept "quiet, sensitive men" from seeking editorial jobs, opening the field to editors of little "talent, education, taste and character" but much sway because the United States had a small "intellectual aristocracy." In New York the *Herald* editor was an "epicurean blackguard"; the *Tribune*, a "fanatical blackguard" whose paper carried the "newest popular delusions"; and the *Sun*, willing to run hoaxes. New York papers circulated widely in and outside the United States, but those in Boston and Washington were of some interest.

146. "The United States, Cuba, and Canada." 53 (1856): 522–33.
Pointed out that the "influence of the broadsheet is immense" in the United States where untaxed newspapers were not a luxury but a necessity. Every group sponsored a paper, and large towns could have ten or more dailies.

147. [Kirwan, A. V.]. "M. Montalembert and John Wilson Croker; or *Traduttore Traditore*." 53 (1856): 563–83.
Associated Croker, "long the bully and the bravo of the *Quarterly Review*," also with the *Standard* and *John Bull*. Aside on the "self-complacent, reckless, and too often ignorant criticisms" of 'Our Own Correspondent' during the Crimean War.

148. "Lord Cockburn's *Memorials*." 54 (1856): 79–89.
Review of Henry Cockburn's book tapped Francis Jeffrey's "delightful articles" in the *Edinburgh Review* and its relation to Scottish literature; the "personality" and able scribes of *Blackwood's Magazine*; and the *Beacon's* "scandalous" paragraphs.

149. [Boyd, A. K. H.]. "James Montgomery." 54 (1856): 457–73.
Trailed Montgomery, who was a "fairly educated" clerk, then a writer for the *Sheffield Register* before buying and renaming it. As the "editor, proprietor, printer, and publisher of the *Sheffield Iris*," a

weekly that started as a "Radical newspaper" in 1794 and that he sold in 1825, he conducted the paper "reasonably" but lacked the "energy" to keep circulation high.

150. [Hurlbert, W. H.]. "What Are the United States Coming To?" 54 (1856): 611–22.
Scanned several American newspapers, among them the *Richmond Enquirer*, "a prominent journal of Virginia," and *Richmond Examiner*. Quoted "a Canadian journal," the *Kennebuc Journal*, on the merits of the *South Side Democrat* (VA), *Charleston* (SC) *Standard*, *Muscogee* (AL) *Herald*, and other papers prominent in their regions.

151. [Donne, W. B.]. "John Mitchell Kemble." 55 (1857): 612–18.
Recalled that Kemble wrote for *Fraser's*, the *Foreign Quarterly Review*, and *British and Foreign Review*, which he edited, 1835–44.

152. "The Press and the Public Service." 55 (1857): 649–62.
Rated "ready resort to the Press…one of the most noticeable characteristics of the age" but doubted that anonymous letters accorded with a press of public service. In such correspondence military officers could attack their seniors with impunity and civil service officers, their department heads. Editors should suppress information obtained because of the writer's official position unless the person's supervisor approved the release. Journalists should not be required to reveal their sources in a government inquiry because they were responsible to the public, not the state.

153. I., K. P. [A. K. H. Boyd]. "Edgar Allan Poe." 55 (1857): 684–700.
Described Poe as a "hack-writer" whose journalistic career took him from a Virginia paper to editing Philadelphia's *Gentleman's Magazine*. In this position, as in other journalistic endeavors, he had no sense of organization. By 1845, when he owned and edited the *Broadway Journal*, he suffered from alcoholism.

154. [?Kirwan, A. V.]. "A Few Words on France and French Affairs." 56 (1857): 157–61.
Accepted suspension of the *Assemblée* and *National* as proof that Napoleon III was arbitrary in his treatment of the press.

155. P[arker, John W., Jr.]. "David Charles Badham." 56 (1857): 162–63.
Celebrated C. David Badham as a "valued" author for *Fraser's*, a "graceful pen" who also wrote for *Blackwood's Magazine*. He was unusual in that he signed articles with an initial instead of remaining anonymous.

156. A[ndrews], A[ugustus]. "The Indian Army." 56 (1857): 164–72.
Implied that the press of educated Indians was a factor in the rebellion of some troops.

157. I., K. P. [A. K. H. Boyd]. "About Edinburgh." 56 (1857): 505–20.
Review of Robert Cutlar's *Edinburgh Dissected* communicated that its information on newspapers was incorrect and that Edinburgh was no longer a leader in periodicals because the *Edinburgh Review*, *North British Review*, *Titan*, and *Blackwood's Magazine* had no Scottish writers. Aside on the monthly *Macphail's Journal*.

158. P[attison], M[ark]. "The Birmingham Congress." 56 (1857): 619–26.
Assumed that a newspaper, however powerful, was "the creature of public opinion." To sell, its views had to be popular unlike those expressed at the Birmingham meeting of the National Association for the Promotion of the Social Sciences.

159. [Kirwan, A. V.]. "Lord Normanby and *A Year of Revolution*." 56 (1857): 724–35.
Review of a book by C. H. Phipps, Lord Normanby, on the 1848 French Revolution stamped the *Journal du Palais*, owned in part by A. A. Ledru-Rollin, a "flourishing professional paper." Armand Marrast, the editor of the *National*, was "a neat and pointed writer, not deficient in elegance" but "insufferably arrogant."

160. [Arnold, W. D.]. "India in Mourning." 56 (1857): 737–50.
Assessed the effect of the uprising by Indian troops on Anglo-Indian papers. At first they issued "Extras," then were silent. The *Delhi Gazette* was "plundered, the staff was murdered"; the *Mofussilite* could not distribute its copies because of the violence; the *Lahore Chronicle* received daily from government "an epitome of the most important public news" in the style of "penny-a-liner." To dispel "false rumours," the epitome was printed on a "small quarter sheet" and sent wherever the post reached.

161. [Keightley, Thomas]. "On the Life and Writings of Henry Fielding." 57 (1858): 1–13, 205–17, with postscript, 762–63.
Bared that in 1752 Fielding edited the *Covent Garden Journal*, published two or three times weekly.

162. G., D. [Theodore Martin]. "A Word about Our Theatres." 57 (1858): 231–41.
Protested that "editors of our leading journals" published kudos for "trash" but overlooked good plays. Theatre critics did not denounce "vicious management" because they were dishonest, unlike those who wrote on "social questions."

163. "Cyrus Redding's *Personal Recollections*." 57 (1858): 242–53.
Followed Redding's career, including stints writing for *Gould's Naval Chronicle* and editing *Galignani's Messenger* in Paris. As subeditor of the *New Monthly Magazine* he encountered "a strange medley of politics and chance articles" circulated by Henry Colburn, "half bookseller, half publisher." Redding went with editor Thomas Campbell from the *New Monthly* to the *Metropolitan*, which soon failed. Aside on William Gifford as editor of the *Anti-Jacobin* and *Quarterly Review*.

164. P[arker, John W., Jr.]. "Robert Stephen Rintoul: In Memoriam." 57 (1858): 611–13.
Honored Rintoul as a "responsible editor" of the *Spectator* because he raised "the tone of journalism and journalists," many of whom he trained.

165. [Kirwan, A. V.]. "Recent French Memoirs." 57 (1858): 673–85.
Opined that the 1830 law granting liberty to the French press promoted open discussion and trained journalists for public service.

166. B[oyd], A. K. H. "Concerning Work and Play." 58 (1858): 253–65.
Valued a man who could do many things, from fix a kite to write an article for *Fraser's* or a leader for *The Times* or *Spectator*.

167. H[ughes], T[homas]. "Richard Ford: In Memoriam." 58 (1858): 422–24.
Eulogized Ford, a contributor to the *Quarterly Review*.

168. B[oyd], A. K. H. "Concerning the Art of Putting Things: Being Thoughts on Representation and Misrepresentation." 59 (1859): 19–35.
Ruminated about style in journalism, in an essay and in the "plain matter-of-fact way, like *The Times*' reporter."

169. [Parker, John W., Jr.]. "William John Broderip: *In Memoriam*." 59 (1859): 485–88.
Alluded to Broderip's work for *Fraser's*, the *Quarterly Review*, and *New Monthly Magazine* and his friendship with the editor of the last, Theodore Hook.

170. H[obart, V. H.]. "Thoughts on Modern English Literature." 60 (1859): 97–110.
Searched for progenitors of the "copious stream" of periodicals in 1859. Their timeframe may have originated with Richard Steele, but the *Tatler* and *Spectator* were examples of "polished dullness and prim pleasantries," not the light reading common in magazines of the 1850s.

171. [?Martin, Theodore]. "Much Ado about Nothing." 60 (1859): 361–72.
Estimated that two-thirds of the public "believe whatever they see in print" because of "the infallible 'we' of the daily press."

172. Stuart, J. Montgomery. "England's Literary Debt to Italy." 60 (1859): 697–708.
Flagged Ugo Foscolo as an author known for "plain speaking" in such reviews as the *Edinburgh*, *Quarterly*, and *Westminster*.

173. H[obart, V. H.]. "Points of View." 61 (1860): 228–37.
Mused that the *Edinburgh Review* was "one of our oracles, resorted to by the faithful in no ordinary degree" in matters of public controversy.

174. Verax. "A Plea for Truth in Advertisement." 62 (1860): 108–12.
Pondered advertisements for houses, food, and drugs and publishers' blurbs for books.

175. A Man on the Shady Side of Fifty [A. V. Kirwan]. "Social and Political Life Five-and-Thirty Years Ago." 62 (1860): 113–32.
Juxtaposed London morning and evening newspapers, 1824–25, and those of 1860. The earlier gazettes, with news from the coffeehouses and brutal satire, were inferior in "paper, type, size, form" and "taste, tact, judgment, good tone, and literary ability." In 1860 *The Times* had more world news and more leaders penned by those with "literary ability" and a "mastery of subjects." Its art and literary criticism were still excellent but not its parliamentary reports.

176. "*In Memoriam*." 62 (1860): 810–13.
Tribute to *Fraser's* editor, John W. Parker Jr., talked about his skills in that position. He not only recruited experts to write articles but supported them intellectually and psychologically.

177. [Bullock, T. H.]. "A Blue Mutiny." 63 (1861): 98–107.
Alerted that the Anglo-Indian press was suppressing news about the unrest among indigo workers.

178. C., J. E. "Saint Saturday." 64 (1861): 116–23.
Despaired that workers read only crime reports or the fiction in *Reynolds's Miscellany*.

179. "Something about Modern Arabic." 64 (1861): 504–16.
Perused "learned" Arabic newspapers whose zeal for a "classical type" of journalism led to peculiar translations of the European press. Arab journals should hire European editors with "the qualities of a merchant" because locals resisted buying newspapers, a fact noticed by the *Garden of News* (Beirut, 1859), or should ape the *Mercury* (Algiers), a weekly subsidized by Napoleon III. It tried to win readers by a "respectful" attitude on religion and variety in content. Recommended that the British government sponsor a cheap one-page weekly without politics but with alternate columns of information in Arabic and English in order to convert and civilize Arabs.

180. An Old Apprentice of the Law [A. V. Kirwan]. "Editors and Newspaper Writers of the Last Generation." 65 (1862): 169–83, 595–609; 66 (1862): 32–49; letter, 49–53 by John Leycester Adolphus.
Recited a litany of deceased editors and reporters. Among those in Part I were William Cobbett; Thomas Barnes, law student turned reporter and editor of *The Times*; John Black, reporter, then editor of the *Morning Chronicle*; John S. Taylor, owner and editor of the *Sun*; Peter Finnerty, the editor of the *Irish Press* occasionally jailed for libel before he went to the front in 1809 as the *Morning Chronicle* special correspondent; James Murray, *Times* reporter in Portugal with the British army before he became the paper's leader-writer and a contributor to the *Foreign Quarterly Review*.

Part II included John Adolphus, lawyer and knowledgeable theatre critic who was a "frequent contributor to the journals and periodicals." Harry Clifford, reporter for the *Morning Chronicle* and later counsel for *Independent Whig* editors in a libel case, was an example that the press chose ex-journalists as counsel in libel suits. Sir James Mackintosh, who penned for the *Monthly Review* and *British Critic*, covered the libel trial of a French journalist for attacking Napoleon I in the British *Ambigu*, at a time when the prejudice against reporters was worse than in 1860. "[I]ntimately connected with journalism," Mackintosh had "a wise and gentlemanly horror of demagogism" that made him Daniel O'Connell's opponent.

Part III chronicled among others James Perry, editor of the *Morning Chronicle* when it was the "first paper of the day" with a large circulation; James Silk Buckingham, owner and editor of the *Oriental Herald*, then founder of the *Athenaeum*, whose work was "wanting in nerve and sinew" and the "compactness necessary to good periodical writing"; Horace Twiss, parliamentary reporter for *The Times* for 35 years and a scribe for the *Quarterly Review* and *John Bull*; Mr. Thwaites, owner and editor of the *Morning Herald*, which c. 1828 was "second only in circulation to *The Times*." Thwaites was not a journalist, so his leaders were "inconsequential and illogical" as well as ungrammatical. He did other things better: prioritized news, shortened parliamentary reports that were often "slovenly and ungrammatical," published "truly graphic and amusing" crime reports and "pithy and pungent" theatre criticism, and spiced foreign correspondence with anecdotes. He favored as owners and editors English men of business; as critics and reporters, the Scots and Irish because they were alert, clearheaded, and flexible about assignments.

Letter by John Leycester Adolphus corrected errors about his father and specified that he contributed to the *British Critic* and *British Magazine*, a "highly respectable but short-lived magazine of the old school."

181. "*North America*." 66 (1862): 256–64.
Review of Anthony Trollope's book graded Orestes Brownson's *Quarterly Review* "an unpretending Roman Catholic periodical of much ability."

182. [Hill, M. D.]. "The Post-Office." 66 (1862): 319–36.
Deduced from the increase of delivery of serials, from 45 million in 1839 to 72.5 million in 1861, that the post office abetted the growth of the periodical press by cheap and rapid transmission.

183. "The Late Lady Morgan and Her Autobiography." 67 (1863): 172–91.
Review of the *Memoirs* of Sydney Owenson culled from it her work for *Freeman's Journal*, the *Hibernian Magazine*, and *New Monthly Magazine*, whose publisher Henry Colburn used it to puff books. Aside that Leonard Macnally, editor of London's *Public Ledger*, was a friend of her father.

184. [Kebbel, T. E.]. "Bolingbroke as a Statesman." 67 (1863): 687–702.
Referred to Henry St. John's *Craftsman* and *Examiner*.

185. [Kirwan, A. V.]. "A Fortnight in Paris in the May of 1863." 67 (1863): 807–22.
Pictured many French "news-writers, editors, and contributors" as Jews who spent their mornings running railroads or trading on the Bourse.

186. "Liberty of Criticism, and the Law of Libel." 68 (1863): 35–45.
Based on the case of Dr. Campbell v. the *Saturday Review*, investigated the relationship of libel law and literary criticism.

187. "The Periodical Press of the United States of America." 68 (1863): 325–34.
Held that the United States, with 450 dailies, over 4,000 weeklies, and 356 fortnightlies and monthlies, had periodicals for every taste (with data on some cities and states and rural distribution). American newspapers were cheap to launch and subject to local mob pressure. Country papers, charging six to eight shillings per year for news and cuttings from magazines, typically had a printer-editor and a circulation of 500–2,000.

Many Eastern papers were sent to the West. In New York the *Herald*, the largest in the city, was an immoral but commercially accurate gazette. It focused on hot news, global events, and scandal. Horace Greeley, at the *Tribune*, was an able, conscientious, and honest but not smart man who loved causes. Alternatively, other papers had ousted editors favoring a cause. The *New York Ledger* was "a refined sensation weekly" in contrast to the city's religious press, notably the Unitarian with writers of knowledge and style. Most metropolitan editors were not well educated, so they were sensitive to criticism but garnered respect if their columns were reprinted in London. Editors and proprietors reaped the rewards of influence, especially political appointments.

188. [Kirwan, A. V.]. "A Fortnight in Belgium in the June and July of 1863." 68 (1863): 335–52.
Concentrated on Brussels' widely circulated *Etoile Belge*; the bigger and more expensive *Echo du Parlement*; the popular *Journal de Bruxelles*; the "bombastic" *National*; and the "well-known" *Indépendance Belge*, owned by "Jewish bankers" and edited by Léon "Berardé, a Frenchman of talent, high honour, and liberal sentiments." Antwerp also had many papers. The *Précurseur d'Anvers*

sold 1,700–800 copies; the *Journal d'Anvers*, 1,000–200, and the *Escaut*, 1,500. In Flemish were the *Grondwet* (700–800 subscribers) and *Handelsblad* (1,400–500).

189. [Stephen, James Fitzjames]. "England and America." 68 (1863): 420–37.
Denigrated *The Times* New York correspondent who greatly influenced British views of the Civil War when he quoted "every blackguard rant of the *New York Herald*."

190. [Martin, Theodore]. "Plays, Players, and Critics." 68 (1863): 767–76.
Sneered at the journalistic theatre critics, authors of "flimsy comediettas," who condemned anything of better quality.

191. W[hyte]-M[elville], G[eorge]. "A Week in Bed." 69 (1864): 327–35.
Listed as joys of convalescence reading the dailies' "subtle arguments" in leaders and the births, marriages, and deaths and overlooking foreign news, crime reports, and advertisements.

192. Cobbe, Frances Power. "The Morals of Literature." 70 (1864): 124–33.
Placed the literary critic as a "medium" between the author and reader and, if gifted, as a writer of literature. "Of the multitude of criticisms which issue every week from the periodical press, how many are conscientiously written?" Material in "colourless" serials was "only fair," laced with stereotypes, sarcasm, and puffery, and in "higher journals" "prejudice conquers truth" though in a more gentlemanly fashion than the old *Quarterly Review* or *Blackwood's Magazine*.

193. Tennent, J. Emerson. "Mr. Whitworth and Sir Emerson Tennent." 70 (1864): 133–34.
Defended the "conventional rules of the press" that authorized criticism of books without opportunities for authors to respond.

194. An American Abolitionist [Moncure D. Conway]. "President Lincoln." 71 (1865): 1–21.
Mentioned the "*Louisville Journal*, the leading newspaper of Kentucky," and the *National Anti-Slavery Standard*.

195. "Richardson." 71 (1865): 83–96.
Depicted the eighteenth-century press. The *Novelists' Magazine* was full of "licentiousness," and the *Critical Review*, "rubbish." "In the columns of the newspapers, in the pages of the popular periodicals which only dressed what the journals first present raw" were crime and immorality.

196. [Martin, Theodore]. "The Drama in London." 71 (1865): 124–34.
Welcomed theatre criticism in "daily and weekly papers" that called bad plays bad.

197. [Stanley, Arthur P.]. "Theology of the Nineteenth Century." 71 (1865): 252–68.
Commended the *Home and Foreign Review* for its "calm, dignified, respectful" closing article.

198. [Conway, Moncure D.]. "Virginia, First and Last." 71 (1865): 277–94.
Denominated John Daniel, the *Examiner*, and J. R. Thompson, the *Southern Literary Messenger*, as journalist friends of Edgar Allan Poe.

199. [Solly, Henry]. "Working Men's Clubs and Institutes." 71 (1865): 383–95.
Suggested to titled institutes, already the subjects of the *Working Man's Club and Institute Magazine*, that they open newspaper and magazine reading rooms in order to induce workers to leave pubs.

200. "The Court of Rome: Its Parties and Its Men." 71 (1865): 403–20.
Paralleled the political influence of the *Civiltà Cattolica*, a Jesuit organ with 12,000 subscribers, in Rome and of the *Moniteur* in France even though the *Civiltà Cattolica* faced competition from Carlo Passaglia's weekly *Mediatore*.

201. Rossetti, W. M. "The Royal Academy Exhibition." 71 (1865): 736–53.
Reasoned that because artists did not pen art criticism, they disregarded it, but the "outside critic" should hesitate to guide public taste.

202. An American Abolitionist [Moncure D. Conway]. "The Assassination of President Lincoln." 71 (1865): 791–806.
Jumped from the topic of Abraham Lincoln's assassination to a Georgia offer of a reward of 5,000 dollars for the arrest of the *Liberator* editor.

203. [Conway, Moncure D.]. "Mannahatta." 72 (1865): 269–87.
Enlightened that "New York has always been the center of the most influential journalism of the United States. The newspapers are crowded together in one district of the city, pretty much as they are in London, and sometimes the editorial rooms of eight or ten of them are in one building." "The great Dailies," whose editors could make or break politicians, had their own buildings. "For a long time, the *New York Herald* was the ruling paper...started by a shrewd, half-educated, and utterly unscrupulous Scotchman – James Gordon Bennett – with 'carroty' hair, cross-eyes, and generally repulsive exterior" that reflected his morals. He colluded with scoundrels and used blackmail to build his fortune. In a paper that was "the sewer of New York," he sold cheaply the sensation stories for which he paid well. Horace Greeley went from typesetter to owner and editor of the *New York Tribune*, shaping it into "the leading newspaper in America" by his ability and industry. He hired able writers, such as Margaret Fuller and George Ripley, but penned leaders daily. The *New York Times*, under editor Henry Raymond, followed the "golden mean." The city's *Evening Post*, edited by William Cullen Bryant, was literary. For years New York had only one literary weekly, the *Century*, but in 1865 had the *Round Table* and *Nation*. *Harper's Weekly*, conducted by George W. Curtis, was similar to the *Illustrated London News*, but the majority of the weeklies were "sectarian." The ablest was Henry Ward Beecher's *Independent*, but Parker Pillsbury edited with vigor the *Anti-Slavery Standard*. The quality evident in English newspaper leaders and monthly articles materialized in sermons, not the press, in the United States.

204. [Kebbel, T. E.]. "Writings of Bolingbroke." 72 (1865): 475–91.
Featured Henry St. John, "the first man who made 'journalism' a power in the State" in the *Examiner* and then the *Craftsman*. Previously, "shoals of papers" issued from "men of no mark or education,

the Grub-street gang." Bolingbroke wrote some for the *Examiner*, much for the *Craftsman*. His essays displayed knowledge and irony. Junius emulated him, by which time the dailies "began to acquire their modern shape, weight, and respectability." The *Examiner*, also with Jonathan Swift, inspired Joseph Addison's *Whig Examiner*. The *Craftsman*, edited by Nicholas Amherst (as Caleb Danvers), had a larger circulation than the earlier *Spectator*. The *Craftsman*, which took journalism "from infancy to adolescence at a bound," fathered the *Anti-Jacobin* and *John Bull*. "All members of the profession of journalism, therefore, as well as all believers in the usefulness of the press, are bound to respect Lord Bolingbroke" who later took the pseudonym Humphrey Oldcastle.

205. [Hayward, Abraham]. "Politics and Prospects of Spain." 72 (1865): 671–91.
Grumbled about the "license" in Spanish journalism, mainly in the *Diario Español*, *Discussion*, and *Español*.

206. [Conway, Moncure D.]. "The Queen of the West." 73 (1866): 42–68.
Essay on Americana singled out Fanny Wright, editor and writer of the New Harmony (IN) *Gazette*; the *Spiritual Register*, the organ of spiritualism; and the *Republikaner*, a Cincinnati German-language daily started by August Willich who left Europe in 1848.

207. G[airdiner], J[ames]. "Sundays, Ancient and Modern." 73 (1866): 264–76.
Complimented Norman Macleod, "the accomplished editor of *Good Words*, and the *Spectator*, which was "so intelligent a newspaper."

208. [Hayward, Abraham]. "Clubs." 73 (1866): 342–67.
Review of John Timbs' *Club Life of London* broadcast his plagiarism of the *Spectator*.

209. [Conway, Moncure D.]. "Thoreau." 73 (1866): 447–65.
Cited H. D. Thoreau's contributions to the quarterly *Dial*.

210. [Grant Duff, M. E.]. "Belgium." 73 (1866): 795–816.
Recorded that Belgium abolished "the newspaper stamp" in 1843, but the press was still subject to a censorship sometimes warranted. In 1865 the *Journal de Liége* was "one of the oldest papers," owned by the same family that opened it in 1765. Ghent's *Bien Public* showed "considerable vigour and ability." The *Indépendance Belge* was "edited by a man of unremarkable intelligence, M. [Léon] Bérardé," and was more European than Belgian. Among other newspapers were the *Journal des Bruxelles* and its satellite, *Emancipation*, *Echo du Parlement*, and *Paix*. Joining them were the periodicals *Revue Trimestrielle* and the "respectable" *Revue Générale*.

211. Burton, Richard F. "From London to Rio de Janeiro." 74 (1866): 159–78.
Last episode in a travel series unveiled Dr. Vasconcellos as "the health officer and editor of the *Jornal do Recife*."

212. [Conway, Moncure D.]. "Washington." 74 (1866): 327–46.
Recollected that the *National Era* published *Uncle Tom's Cabin*.

213. "Heinrich Heine." 74 (1866): 588–609.
Shadowed Heine from England, 1827, to Munich where he accepted J. F. Cotta's offer to edit the *Politische Annalen*. Ludwig Börne "gave him some paternal advice as to his new office as editor of a political paper," but in 1828 he resigned. Heine enthused that the July Revolution was 'sunbeams wrapped in newspapers.' He and Börne "went to Paris as newspaper correspondents." Heine wrote first for the *Allgemeine Zeitung* but "soon became a constant contributor to *Europe Littéraire*, the *Revue Rétrospective*, and the *Revue des Deux Mondes*. He preferred to pen for established and influential serials and to accommodate himself occasionally to the views of his editors and the public instead of starting like Börne a hole-and-corner paper, in which he certainly might have spoken without the least restraint, but also without the authority and influence of an old-established and recognised organ of public opinion." "German governments were terrified at the bold tone of their foreign newspaper correspondents," so officials pressured publishers not to print their stories and the Diet to limit liberty of the press in 1835, the restrictions lasting until 1842.

214. Shirley [John Skelton]. "Mr. Dallas, *The Gay Science* – The Laws and Functions of Criticism." 74 (1866): 771–86.
Positioned as "prizes" in literary criticism "the applause of the *Quarterly* [*Review*] or the *Edinburgh* [*Review*]."

215. "*The Foul Smells of Paris*." 75 (1867): 370–80.
Review of a book by Louis Veûillot, editor of the *Paix* (1838) and *Univers Religieux* (1843, later suppressed), joined him in castigating French newspaper gossip but discerned the same evil in English, Scottish, Irish, and Belgian gazettes.

216. Walker, Patricius, Esq. [William Allingham]. "Rambles." 76 (1867): 474–90.
Biography of William Cobbett announced that he was already known as a journalist from his American writing before he started the daily *Porcupine*. His *Political Register* was a "thorn in the side of the ministry – of every ministry in turn" and earned him fines and imprisonment for libel, but his *Poor Man's Friend* was the symbol of his life.

217. "Turkey and the Crimean War: With Variations." 76 (1867): 503–17.
Rued that Turkey had no "periodical literature" to mirror opinion.

218. [Hayward, Abraham]. "More about Junius." 76 (1867): 794–813.
Review of *Memoirs of Sir Philip Francis, K.C.B., with Correspondence and Journals*, a work begun by Joseph Parkes and completed by Herman Merivale, noted an article in the *Quarterly Review* (90: 91) on the identity of Junius but concluded that Francis was not the man.

219. "Australia." 77 (1868): 642–54.
Acclaimed the *Australasian* as "the best written and the most widely read paper in the southern hemisphere."

220. R[obinson], J[ohn]. "A Voice from the Colonies on the Colonial Question." 79 (1869): 202–16.
Cheered that colonists had "the highest respect" for British serials and were "immensely uplifted by the slightest notice" of the colonies in those journals.

221. "Modern Preaching." 79 (1869): 254–68.

Cautioned that periodicals could be inaccurate and illogical, so reliance on them was unwise.

222. J[erdan], W[illiam]. "The Grand Force!" 79 (1869): 380–83.

Designated the newspaper as the "Grand Force" that fueled the election of MPs but also had power elsewhere. Its advertisements sold shoddy or adulterated goods, promoted "bubble companies," sustained bad theatre and periodicals, and publicized ideologies, "monster meetings," and "nonsense."

223. A Scoto-Celt. "Scottish Characteristics: A Prelection." 79 (1869): 451–65.

Affirmed that the *Edinburgh Review*, which "still holds its own," set the standard for literary reviews and *Blackwood's Magazine*, which "still occupies a foremost place," did the same for magazines.

224. [Braddon, Edward]. "Life in India: India Eighty Years Ago – A Retrospect." 79 (1869): 585–601.

Mulled over the *Calcutta Gazette and Oriental Advertiser*, edited by W. S. Seton-Karr, president of the Bengal Record Commission, 1784–97. Published with the government's blessing, the weekly was a monopoly "but a very puny literary dwarf" and inconsistent with the notion of a free press. The *Gazette* contained news from Indian governments and Britain, translations of local poetry, "feeble witticism," theatre reports, and advertisements for slaves and goods.

225. [Braddon, Edward]. "Life in India: The Natives of the Country." 80 (1869): 326–47.

Bewailed that Eurasians got their ideas of Englishness from the pages of the *Overland Mail*.

226. [Donne, W. B.]. "Henry Crabb Robinson." 80 (1869): 522–36.

Mentioned that Robinson was *The Times* correspondent in Holstein in 1807, then Spain and later its foreign editor. Aside that the *Monthly Review*, *Edinburgh Review*, and *Quarterly Review* set the "canons of taste" in the early nineteenth century.

227. [Braddon, Edward]. "Life in India: The Rulers, the Public, and the Press." 80 (1869): 704–21.

Hypothesized that India had "no adequate expression of public opinion" because papers in the local languages and in English did not represent the "*vox populi*." Most Indian journals lacked a consistent policy although their editorial quality was improving. Their chief problems were that they overlooked important issues, employed incompetent writers, and published in a society with few readers, chiefly in the villages. The Anglo-Indian press of penny-a-liners spoke for rulers with little nonofficial input. This press amused readers or advertised their needs and wants. Editors were government workers or ill-educated men unable to guide the public. Most small papers had a leader, scraps of news on Europe and the outstations, reports of the law courts, and columns on the military, sports, amateur theatre, and trivia.

228. W[hittle], J. L. "Irish Elections and the Influence of the Priests." n.s., 1 (1870): 44–58.

Underscored that Catholic journals headlined meetings of priests in order "to train the laity to await their nod in all political action."

229. G[reg], W. R. "The Cost of a Napoleon." n.s., 1 (1870): 474–88.
Recounted that Napoleon III "gagged the press – and that in England is a heinous wrong." Although he left "first-class reviews wholly unfettered," he exercised "rigid and arbitrary control" of other publications. Some restriction was appropriate because "French radical newspapers," like "Irish national ones," printed lies and bred "incendiarism."

230. M[acdonell, James]. "Irish Politics and Irish Priests." n.s., 1 (1870): 491–99.
Distinguished the "Rebel Priest" who sent letters to the *Irishman* and *Nation* about an eventual Irish uprising from the "West-British Priest" who ignored these Dublin papers and read London's *Weekly Dispatch* but conceded that Irish journals were generally popular with the clergy.

231. [Hayward, Abraham]. "The Personal History of Imperialism in 1870." n.s., 2 (1870): 637–51.
Starred Archibald Forbes, the "bold, active, and accurate" *Daily News* correspondent of the Franco-Prussian War, and an unnamed colleague at the *Journal des Débats*.

232. "Touraine in April 1871." n.s., 4 (1871): 43–61.
Urged newspapers to print verified information, not confuse readers by expressing opinions.

233. S[cott], W[illiam] B. "The Art Season of 1871." n.s., 4 (1871): 182–92.
Aside on the "systematically mendacious" French *International* and *Situation*.

234. F[agan], H. S., A Vicar of the Church of England. "At Paris, Just Before the End." n.s., 4 (1871): 230–48.
Paris visitor during the Commune encountered "newsboys…as active as usual," peddling papers without picking pockets unlike their peers in New York.

235. T. "The Constitution of Sweden." n.s., 4 (1871): 765–75.
Relayed that the Swedish press had "little or no restraint," so newspapers were free to criticize government.

236. "The Early Life of Charles Dickens." n.s., 5 (1872): 105–13.
Review of John Forster's *The Life of Charles Dickens* tagged Dickens' father, John as "a newspaper parliamentary reporter" whom Charles emulated in his youth. He covered both Commons and public meetings throughout the country, gaining a reputation for accuracy and speed of transcription while simultaneously publishing articles.

237. "Parisiana." n.s., 5 (1872): 477–90.
Opted for many Paris papers rather than a single "International" one that could lead to an "ugly dictatorship." During "the palmy days of *The Times*," Britain came too close to this outcome. Even if the *Journal des Débats*, *Figaro*, and others assumed facts, they were less dangerous. Equally threatening to society was the official hunt in 1872 for journalists who were Communists.

238. "John Hookam Frere." n.s., 5 (1872): 491–510.
Biography of Frere returned to his affiliations with Eton's *Microcosm* and the *Anti-Jacobin*, a serial important in literature and politics under editor William Gifford. His insistence on accurate news and "wit" made the journal an "immense and immediate success."

239. C., A. "Irish Nationality." n.s., 5 (1872): 525–40.
Touched on the role of the *Nation* in developing Irish national identity.

240. C[onway], M[oncure] D. "Horace Greeley." n.s., 6 (1872): 474–90.
Trailed Greeley from his days as a Vermont printer to his New York journalism, notably editing his *Tribune*. Initial capital, 1,000 dollars for expenses and 1,000 dollars for equipment, came from the publisher and 500 subscribers. Greeley promoted causes before they were popular. Not the best stylist, he wrote "vigorously, concisely, and clearly" leaders that were never dull and hired talented journalists like Margaret Fuller.

241. Wright, Thomas, the 'Journeyman Engineer.' "Mis-Education." n.s., 6 (1872): 641–50.
Registered that Standard VI in the new compulsory education system established the newspaper as the test for reading and writing.

242. S. "A Sketch of M. Thiers." n.s., 7 (1873): 94–100.
Talked about the launch of the *National* by Adolphe Thiers and Armand Carrel and its role in the July Revolution.

243. F[itzpatrick], W[illiam] J. "A Sketch of Charles Lever." n.s., 7 (1873): 190–96.
Appraised Lever's work for the *Dublin University Magazine* first as contributor, then editor, 1842–45.

244. M[arshall], C[harles], A Visitor to Salt Lake City. "The Original Prophet." n.s., 7 (1873): 225–35.
Essay on Joseph Smith disclosed that in 1844 some Mormons ransacked the Illinois office of William Law's *Expositor* as an earlier mob had destroyed the *Star* offices in Missouri.

245. Alcock, Sir Rutherford, K.C.B. "The *Peking Gazette*." n.s., 7 (1873): 245–56, 341–57.
Earmarked the *Gazette* as the "official organ of the Government of China." It published official appointments and promotions but little news. Reports of mass disasters were secondary to trivia about the court. The *Gazette* had no leaders but printed criticism of officials, unlike Russian publications that censored such statements. Each issue had 20–40 pages of cheap paper with a "dingy yellow wrapper." The first copy, a manuscript with the day's decrees, went to government offices. Subscribers, who paid six dollars a year, received an edited version printed from wood type. Both versions had no style, a fact noted by the Shanghai *Cycle*, "a paper of great ability." The *Gazette* could amuse and instruct, sometimes inadvertently by revealing local corruption. Begun in the late 900s, it was the only journal

that circulated throughout the Empire even though the Chinese scooped up the Shanghai locals and the translated foreign ones. However, most Chinese still got their news and views in tea-shops.

246. Cluseret, G. [P.], General. "The Paris Commune of 1871." n.s., 7 (1873): 360–84.
Grieved that publicizing the capitulation of Paris in the *Combat* nearly cost Félix Pyat his life. The French government denied the news in the *Official Journal*, and then confessed its lie. During the peace negotiations in 1871 several newspapers were suppressed and new ones were forbidden.

247. Gosse, Edmund. "The Present Condition of Norway." n.s., 9 (1874): 174–85.
Summarized the press in Norway where every town had a *Folktidende*. Norway had 72 newspapers, 12 in Oslo. There were three north of the Artic Circle, *Hammerfests Tidende* the most distant. Those in Danish were "exceptionally well printed and edited" and as good as any in Europe except Britain. The first Norwegian paper, the *Norske Intelligenz-Seddeler* (May 1763), had no "character or colour." The major paper, the *Morgenbladet*, began in 1819 with gossip and paragraphs on the arts, but in 1831 "an able and enlightened editor" faced with competition added the political coverage that gave it influence. In 1874 it attracted "some of the most promising of the younger writers." Reviews were short-lived, so literature was in the hands of subeditors. The *Skilling Magazin*, emerging in 1834, was like the *Penny Magazine*, cheap, "useful," but not "original."

248. Bowie, Archibald Granger. "The Postal Telegraph Service." n.s., 9 (1874): 437–49.
Thought that the "the effecting of a free trade in the collection of news for the press" was a benefit of the nationalization of telegraphy. Thereafter the Press Association and the Central News Agency gathered news for transmission by the Post Office Intelligence Section, whose Press and News Section handled press accounts (with journalists using vouchers). The Press Association had three categories of subscribers: Class I received all the news; Class II, a condensed version, and Class III, a summary. The Central News Agency divided its costs by services.

249. Escott, T. H. S. "Political Novels." n.s., 9 (1874): 520–36.
Postulated that "the great secret of the success of the cartoons in *Punch*" was that they were "pictorial expositions of a more or less prevailing idea," caricature that exemplified "moderation" and "taste."

250. "Scott and His Publishers." n.s., 9 (1874): 559–68.
Certified that the early *Edinburgh Review* "could make or mar any literary project."

251. "The Father of Universal Suffrage in France." n.s., 9 (1874): 610–19.
Essay on A. A. Ledru-Rollin logged that in 1849 London he coedited the *Proscrit*, a paper with writers of many nationalities, among them Giuseppe Mazzini.

252. Escott, T. H. S. "The Place of Albany Fonblanque in English Journalism." n.s., 9 (1874): 635–44.
Enthused that the anonymous English journalist was no longer a "hireling" or a "scurrilous pen" unlike some predecessors who may have deserved the epithets. By 1874 "the spirit of journalism… has inspired our best prose writers," a spirit springing from John Milton, Daniel Defoe, Jonathan Swift, Joseph Addison, and Richard Steele. Fonblanque was aware of the bias against journalism

when he entered it, but he knew that being a critic or a "firebrand" paid well. Although mainly "a paragraphist" without breadth or philosophy, he tried to rise above partisanship, writing carefully and with integrity.

The eighteenth-century press had little impact because people got their news in coffeehouses and local markets. Once parties developed, readers desired commentary, and once the Empire grew, they wanted international news. The result was "popular journalism – meaning by the word that combination of facts and criticism of which journals now consist." Early information was unreliable, and criticism was "carping" and "offensively personal." Serious writers penned pamphlets, so journalism was "seriously retarded." In the 1820s the Whigs were "nursing the newspapers, metropolitan and provincial," but the Tories shunned the press because they previously suffered from its "personal ridicule and coarse satire." After 1832 journalism became authoritative, no longer in a position of "political distrust and social disparagement." Unlike in France where journalism trained for government and the United States where it trained for democracy, in Britain the press emerged as a significant institution. Its reputation improved because the public recognized its support for social reforms, its talented writers recruited from other fields, its quality reviews, and its incorruptibility.

253. "Mr. Disraeli's *Letters of Runnymede*." n.s., 10 (1874): 254–68.

Rehashed Benjamin Disraeli's letters to the press written in the eighteen months before he was first in Commons and published in *The Times* (18 January–13 May 1836). The letters occasionally slipped beyond the "permissible limits of political invective." For example, he dismissed the *Globe* as 'rheumy rhetoric' after it refused to publish his critique of its editor.

254. Hawkins, J. M. "'Junius' and His Time." n.s., 10 (1874): 325–44.

Dubbed the *Public Advertiser* of Junius' time "the most current newspaper of the day," one whose letters others copied. Libel in 1874 was primarily the tool of disgruntled authors against critics, but in the eighteenth century it was a symbol of the "court's resentment" of newspaper articles. The charges against Junius were baseless but confirmed his popularity, underpinned by his masked audacity. He exhibited "malignity" when he spread rumors but took no pay, appearing as an "ardent patriot" rather than a "mercenary scribbler." Aside on the John Wilkes case.

255. Newman, Francis William. "The Dangerous Glory of India." n.s., 10 (1874): 448–64.

Traversed time, from 1857 when *The Times* correspondent reported "the cruel outrages of the European" to 1874 when members of the Civil Service penned the *Calcutta Review*.

256. C[annon], J[ohn]. "The Literary Partnership of Canning and Frere." n.s., 10 (1874): 714–27.

Replayed the journalism of schoolboy friends George Canning and John Hookam Frere from Eton's *Microcosm* to the *Anti-Jacobin*. The goal of the second was "to combat the so-called Jacobin press," but editor William Gifford supplemented its "ridicule and fierce abuse" with news, poetry, and advertising.

257. E[scott, T. H. S.]. "Politics and the Press." n.s., 12 (1875): 41–50.

Avouched that relations between press and Parliament were the subject of much discussion in the recent session. The London press, the "echo" of Parliament, could no longer hoodwink a public capable of forming its own judgments. Even *The Times* could not mold political views in 1875, but it was the only morning daily that could "reflect opinion with authority." It covered events better and circulated them wider than any of its European peers. Its assets were its coverage of religion and its commentary. Whatever political sway it had came from "its known independence." The penny press, except for "fanatic sectarians" and "visionary enthusiasts," admired it. Among other papers, the *Pall Mall Gazette* was respected for its independence; the *Daily News*, for its editing, talented scribes, and timely, often exclusive news; the *Daily Telegraph*, for its writing. The *Standard* was the biggest of a press that was a force on social issues and the guardian of efficiency in service and business. In general, British papers famous for their "originality, freshness, ability, vigour, and variety" had less political impact than French papers. France had "no symbol of national unity" similar to *The Times*, but its "host of petty prints" had clout. "English journalism represents interests, French journalism represents opinions." French journalism spawned political careers in the 1830–40s as had English papers in Queen Anne's reign. In 1874 British statesmen penned for the quarterlies, not the penny press, and owners, not reporters, sat in Parliament.

258. [Betham-Edwards, Matilda]. "The International Working Men's Association." n.s., 12 (1875): 72–87, 181–94, 300–11.

Surveyed the journalism of Karl Marx and his cohorts: Marx editing the *Rheinische Zeitung* that culminated in banishment and collaborating with Heinrich Heine on *Vorwärts*, published in Paris; the *Tribune du Peuple*, the International Working Men's Association organ published in Belgium; the *Volkstimme* and *Gleichheit*, both suppressed in Vienna in 1869; the *Wochenblatt*, edited in Prussia by W. Liebknecht. Aside on the British *Naval and Military Gazette*.

259. O[rmsby], J[ohn], One of the Electors. "Remarks on a Recent Irish Election." n.s., 12 (1875): 233–42.

Glanced at John Mitchel, the purportedly powerful editor of the *United Irishman* in 1848.

260. B[oyd], A. K. H. "Norman Macleod." n.s., 13 (1876): 497–505.

Quasi-review of Donald Macleod's *Memoir of Norman Macleod* lauded him for resisting an 1835 scheme, "by narrow-minded students" who had already succeeded in barring the *Edinburgh Review* from Divinity-Hall Library, to exclude *Blackwood's Magazine*. Macleod penned many columns for *Good Words* and edited others of contributors well paid by publisher Alexander Strahan, whose energy in soliciting advertising gave the serial a "vast circulation."

261. Blyden, Edward W. "Christianity and the Negro Race: By a Negro." n.s., 13 (1876): 554–68.

Flitted past the *American Missionary*, *Spirit of Missions*, *Independent*, and *American Citizen*, an African-American newspaper in Lexington (KY) but not such "popular and influential periodicals as *DeBow's Review* and the *Richmond Examiner*."

262. Stutzer, Albert. "Some Remarks Respecting the Purchase of Books in Germany." n.s., 13 (1876): 569–72.

Encompassed German illustrated periodicals that addressed every class and taste. "The foremost" was "*Ueber* [*sic*] *Land und Mer*," run by F. W. Hackländer, "called the German 'Boz.'" It excelled in both drawing and writing. The next in rank was the *Illustrirte Welt*. Both periodicals had circulations of 150,000, apparently an enormous number for Germany and surpassed only by the *Gartenlaube*, "excellently conducted by Mr. E. Kiel, the proprietor and editor." This "Family Paper of Germany" reached 300,000. H. Schoenlein's *Illustrated Journal*, directed to the lower middle and lower classes, was "inferior" in literature and pictures but only cost 19 pence for 13 issues, much cheaper than the *Illustrated London News*. However, the British had access to serials in free libraries, by shared-cost subscriptions, and in pubs, where newspapers supposedly satisfied the minds of tradesmen.

263. Blind, Karl. "The Life and Lays of Ferdinand Freiligrath." n.s., 13 (1876): 659–74.

Sidelined Freiligrath's contributions in 1849 to Cologne's *Neue Rheinische Zeitung*.

264. X. [T. Wemyss Reid]. "Modern Newspaper Enterprise." n.s., 13 (1876): 700–14.

Testified that journalism in the 1870s was a well paid, acceptable but impersonal career in a highly competitive arena.

P. J. Reuter earlier facilitated foreign news gathering by organizing correspondents with accessibility to telegraphy, but during the Franco-Prussian War the "feverish eagerness for news" impelled British gazettes to send correspondents to the front, men who competed for exclusives, very dicey when telegraph lines were destroyed. After the war most papers lacked the resources to ape *The Times*, which had its own wire rather than a leased 'special' (priced 500 pounds per year for transmissions between 6 p.m. and 6 a.m.). The *Times* wire, "the most remarkable achievement of newspaper enterprise," soon forced others to follow at considerable expense.

To capture buyers, the papers introduced "new-fangled" approaches, lifting from the *New York Herald* the model for adventure. However, the metros, except the *Daily News*, thought the interview was alien to British "social habits." The latest addition to the gazettes was the weather chart, which, thanks to technology, was precisely and easily produced. The greatest technological aid was the faster presses that printed 14,000 copies every hour, still not enough for tribunes with circulations in excess of 100,000. These innovations, as well as ingenuity, energy, and outlay, were essential in an era of increasing newspaper rivalry, particularly as the local press gained greater access to telegraphy and their London correspondents, no longer "Grub-street hacks" or the 'lounger at the clubs,' sent more and varied news.

265. ?H[ughes], T[homas]. "Last Century Magazines." n.s., 14 (1876): 325–33.

Disputed that the "extraordinary" growth of periodicals in the nineteenth century was a sign of "superficial culture" because they served many interests. In the eighteenth century the *Gentleman's Magazine*, *London Magazine*, and *Scots Magazine* were the principal ones in years of the short-lived serial. These three originally abridged articles in newspapers but then recruited regular contributors, as Samuel Johnson in the *Gentleman's*. Essays in later magazines never matched those of Joseph Addison, Richard Steele, and other "authors of eminence and genius" because the newcomers copied too much from newspapers dominated by "hack writers." Poems were inartistic; parliamentary reports were "very free versions" of speeches; political articles were full of invective; lists of books were interrupted by titles of pamphlets and "small trumpery publications"; pages were replete with poor spelling, peculiar words, and coarse language. The obituaries, ironically, were invaluable, often the only records of many people.

266. Kilian, Dr. E. H. "The Bulgarians." n.s., 14 (1876): 537–60.

Counted 14 newspapers for Bulgarians, among them *Istoch no Vreme*, "edited by an Englishman" in Constantinople.

267. Hewlett, Henry G. "Heinrich Heine's Life and Work." n.s., 14 (1876): 600–23.
Evaluated Heine's work in 1831–32 and 1840–43 for the "respectable" *Allgemeine Zeitung*, the *Revue des Deux Mondes*, and an international review new in 1832, *Europe Littéraire*, edited by Victor Bohain.

268. B[oyd], A. K. H. "Charles Kingsley." n.s., 15 (1877): 254–68.
Paean remembered Kingsley's writing for and editing of *Fraser's* (in spring 1867 when J. A. Froude was away).

269. Turner, C. E. "Studies in Russian Literature. No. 7: Karansin." n.s., 16 (1877): 186–95; "No. 9: Kriloff," 348–57.
Labeled Nicholas Karansin the architect of the *Moscow Journal* whose 300 subscribers provided him with the funds and reputation to start the *European Messenger* in 1802. It featured literature, politics, Russian history, famous Russians, and Western European society. Ivan Krilov began a "satirical paper, *Letters from Below*," in 1788 and later the *Spectator* and *St. Petersburg Mercury* but had little success as a journalist.

270. S., S. "Count Cavour." n.s., 17 (1878): 185–99.
Noted that Camillo di Cavour was a founder and editor of the *Risorgimento.*

271. J[ennings, Kate V.]. "Louis Börne." n.s., 17 (1878): 617–31.
Silhouetted Louis Börne, a physician who edited the monthly *Wage* in 1818 when the German periodical press was "pitiful." He also wrote theatre criticism, so after the journal closed in 1819 he worked in Paris with F.-V. Raspail on the "short-lived *Réformateur*."

272. B[etham]-E[dwards], M[atilda]. "Jean Reynaud: French Mystic and Philosopher." n.s., 17 (1878): 718–28.
Skimmed Reynaud's articles in the *Magasin Pittoresque* and *Revue Encyclopédique*, which he coedited with Pierre Leroux. When the *Revue* died from lack of contributions, Reynaud edited the *Encyclopédie Nouvelle*.

273. "'Frisco.'" n.s., 18 (1878): 679–96.
Rated the *Chronicle* "the best commercial newspaper" in San Francisco. While it had "a very large circulation," the respectable did not allow it in their homes. It insulted the editors of the *Call*, *Bulletin*, and *Alta California*, "papers of a higher moral standard," and attacked the politics and "private character" of prominent persons. *Chronicle* reporters often prepared stories, then promised to withhold them if their subjects paid blackmail, and *Chronicle* pages brimmed with slang and questionable advertisements, especially of fortunetellers.

274. Smith, G[eorge] Barnett. "Mr. Walpole on England in the Nineteenth Century." n.s., 18 (1878): 713–25.
Quoted Spencer Walpole's *A History of England from the Conclusion of the Great War in 1815* on the newspaper from Nathaniel Butter's 1622 *Weekely Newes* through the 1816 *Times* with a circulation of 8,000. Editor Thomas Barnes, a man of "ability and discretion," enhanced the paper's reputation, and the steam press sped printing dramatically. Because press power was "acknowledged and feared early in the century," people despised journalists, even the distinguished staff of the *Morning Chronicle*.

275. Smith, G[eorge] Barnett. "Walter Bagehot." n.s., 19 (1879): 298–313.
Review of Bagehot's *Literary Studies* considered his essay, "The First *Edinburgh* Reviewers," "a tribute" to those who "fearlessly attacked abuses." Bagehot focused on Francis Horner, Sydney Smith, and Francis Jeffrey, whom he regarded as an author of only average ability.

276. [Allingham, William]. "Some Fifty Years Ago." n.s., 19 (1879): 790–800.
Editorial retrospective classified reviews in *Fraser's* first volumes as "of the slashing order."

277. The Editor [John Tulloch]. "Our Past and Our Future." n.s., 20 (1879): 1–12.
History of *Fraser's* painted its original scribes as "a bright set" with "good taste, refinement, and moderation" on a variety of topics. Editor William Maginn, a man of "versatility and genius," also used his "facile pen" for the *Globe* and *Blackwood's Magazine* and as Rome correspondent for the *Daily News*. By the late 1840s his work was "higher if less sparkling and vivacious in tone." After 1849 *Fraser's* published less mirth but more "healthy criticism." George Whyte-Melville, who "delighted in writing," did his best work for *Fraser's*.

Since a magazine was "an organ of literary expression," it could inform or amuse but should "elevate" the taste and "quicken" the mind. Although the multitude of periodicals in 1879 did not do so, their "dilettantism" probably captured those who might otherwise miss literary study.

278. [Reid, T. Wemyss]. "Gossip and Gossip." n.s., 20 (1879): 90–102.
Marked the eighteenth-century *Spectator* as the "quintessence of an age of gossip," akin to some papers in 1879. The earlier journal was "plainer" about foibles, whereas the gazettes of the 1870s reinvented gossip as "a lucrative and flourishing trade." Unlike *Spectator* scribes, later ones resorted to no artifice and exempted no aristocrat or politician from their scope. This style was amusing unless it dredged up personal news of private people, whereas social tidbits of foreign correspondents were merely dribble, "garbage" hardly worth a look.

279. Shairp, J. C. "The Late Canon Mozley." n.s., 21 (1880): 174–80.
Confided that J. B. Mozley's "real vocation" was writing. "He hated showiness, looseness, slovenliness of thought," which his articles in the *British Critic* and in the *Christian Remembrancer*, where he was coeditor (1844–54), proved.

280. Irby, A. P. "A Russian Lady's Book." n.s., 21 (1880): 612–18.
Review of Olga de Novikoff's *Russia and England from 1876 to 1880* presented her as a scribe for the *Northern Echo* (Darlington) and Russian journals. The British did not learn much about Russia from "the masses of misrepresentation which reach our press from the Jewish correspondents of foreign journals" or censored Russian serials.

281. Graham, H. G. "Russel of *The Scotsman*." n.s., 22 (1880): 301–17.
Intoned that a "journalist's fame is slowly won, and quickly lost," apparently not applicable to Alexander Russel, long editor of the *Scotsman*. He contributed to *Tait's Edinburgh Magazine* edited by Christian Johnstone, the wife of his friend John who edited the *Inverness Courier*. "Adopting journalism as a profession," Russel edited the *Berwick Advertiser* in 1839 where he received 70 pounds per year to extract news from other tribunes and write on literature and politics. In 1842 he edited the *Fife Herald* during its political war with the *Fife Journal* edited by James Bruce, "an able, genial, accomplished man." In 1844 Russel edited the new *Kilmarnock Chronicle* in Glasgow.

In 1845 he joined the *Scotsman* as subeditor and reporter when Charles Maclaren, a "hard-headed, sagacious, unhumorous" man was editor. By 1849 Russel was the official editor although he had been doing the job since 1846. He made the *Scotsman* a very important northern paper even in the face of an 1856 libel case that the paper lost, paying 400 pounds in damages. At first the *Scotsman* was a biweekly but shifted to daily publication after the stamp duty ended. Editing a daily was a "high pressure" job, but Russel contributed to the *Edinburgh Review*, *Quarterly Review*, and *Blackwood's Magazine* even when he worked every night at the *Scotsman*.

282. Northbrook, [Thomas G. Baring, 1st Earl]. "The Natives of India." n.s., 22 (1880): 721–24.

Praised the *Hindoo Patriot*, a Calcutta paper in English, and others of this genre that "hold their own well with the Anglo-Indian journals."

283. B[oyd], A. K. H. "Lord Campbell." n.s., 23 (1881): 334–52.

Borrowed from John Campbell's autobiography, *Life of John, Lord Campbell*, that this Lord Chancellor left a post as a country vicar to become a parliamentary reporter for the *Morning Chronicle* while he trained for the law.

284. "A Stormy Passage in Politics." n.s., 23 (1881): 411–22

Nodded to "the daily press, which lives on popular excitement."

285. Lang, Andrew. "Mr. Carlyle's *Reminiscences*." n.s., 23 (1881): 515–28.

Review of Thomas Carlyle's book conveyed his anger on being overlooked for the editorship of the *Westminster Review*, but he penned anonymously for *Fraser's*.

286. "Léon Michel Gambetta." n.s., 24 (1881): 28–41.

Narrated that Gambetta worked as a correspondent for Frankfurt's *Journal de l'Europe* for the money. Much later he established the *République Française* with 50,000 francs lent by friends.

287. "Robert Southey and Caroline Bowles." n.s., 25 (1882): 206–13.

Review of the Southey-Bowles *Correspondence*, edited by Edward Dowden, registered Southey as a contributor to the *Quarterly Review* and Bowles, to *Blackwood's Magazine*, the *Keepsake*, and other annuals.

288. "Clôture." n.s., 25 (1882): 253–60.

Wondered why British journalists frequently quoted the German press when "a variety of subservient journals" were the parrots of Otto von Bismarck.

289. Noble, J[ames] Ashcroft. "A Pre-Raphaelite Magazine." n.s., 25 (1882): 568–80.

Headlined the *Germ*, its founders and writers because, though hard to locate, it was important in the area of "pictorial and literary art."

290. A Foreign Liberal. "The Irish Difficulty." n.s., 26 (1882): 120–40.

Admitted that Dublin's *Irishman* and *United Ireland* carried the same articles because both came from the Irish National Newspaper and Publishing Company.

Good Words, 1860–1900

Bridging the gap between the sacred and the earthly, *Good Words* was edited for decades by Norman and then Donald Macleod. With a connection to the *Contemporary Review*, it went from stories on Jewish serials in Paris to Indian ones in Bengal, from printing technology to war artists.

1. "Protestantism in France." 1 (1860): 27–29, 41–42.

Plumbed French Protestant periodicals, of which there were 17, with 11 in Paris. Most were "practical and edifying," "one or two" for youths. Some were "intellectual," as the *Archives du Christianisme*, established in 1818 and edited in 1860 by Frederick Monod. The *Revue de Théologie et de Philosophie Chrétienne* and the *Revue Chrétienne* were similar in style to the *Quarterly Review*. Among others were the *Bulletin de la Société de l'Histoire du Protestantisme Français* and *Journal des Missions*.

2. ?L[udlow], J. M. "Aspects of Indian Life During the Rebellion." 1 (1860): 250–53.

Review of William Howard Russell's *My Diary in India* heralded that he went to India on terms "unparalleled in newspaper annals" paid by a *Times* famed for its "smartness and...scene-painting, which must have spoilt as many a pen as they have trained."

3. ?M[artin], B. "The Newspaper." 3 (1862): 117–20.

Announced that the "newspaper is the grand climax of our age," more important than steam and electricity because everyone read and "appreciated" columns that imparted knowledge of others, broke the daily monotony by their variety, and "think for us" on every subject.

4. Stevenson, W. Fleming. "Matthew Claudius, *Homme de Lettres*." 3 (1862): 425–31.

Aired that Claudius wrote for Hamburg journals, 1768–70, before joining the *Wandsbeck Messenger*, which paid him a much-needed salary.

5. The Editor [Norman Macleod]. "Rambling Notes on a Ramble to North Italy." 3 (1862): 449–54.

Observed that Italians "seem fond of newspapers, and eagerly devour them."

6. Smith, Alexander. "Literary Work." 4 (1863): 740–42.

Contended that periodical writing in 1863 was "not distinguished at this moment by style in any rich and characteristic way." It was all alike, as the same cleverness in the "much read, much admired, and much feared...weekly Review" demonstrated.

7. A Stenographic Reporter. "The Work of the Stenographer." 5 (1864): 314–19.
Attributed errors in parliamentary coverage to reporters' mishearing as they strained to catch details of a speech with technical terms or by a poor speaker.

8. Dean of Canterbury [Henry Alford]. "Letters from Rome." 5 (1864): 469–81.
Noticed that *Osservatore Romano* published all foreign and domestic news of interest to Romans but could intrude on journalistic privilege. When the *Journal des Débats* criticized the Roman courts, the *Osservatore Romano* demanded that the paper reveal its source.

9. Kaye, J. W. "Our Indian Heroes. No. 1: Sir Henry Lawrence." 6 (1865): 69–80.
Conveyed that Lawrence wrote two or three articles without literary style but with plenty of facts for each issue of the quarterly *Calcutta Review*.

10. Verney, Edmund Hope. "An Overland Journey from San Francisco to New York." 7 (1866): 378–93.
Stopped at Salt Lake City, which had two newspapers, the weekly *Deseret News* and an unnamed daily. A "Christian" journal, the *Vidette*, came from a nearby military camp.

11. Holland, Henry W. "Evasions of the Law." 7 (1866): 413–18.
Balanced press crime coverage. Dailies exposed the scope of lawbreaking, while the *Hue and Cry* taught criminals how to escape the law.

12. Nicholson, Alexander. "Alexander Smith." 8 (1867): 171–78.
Detailed that poet Smith published prose in numerous periodicals to earn money. In a style that was "intelligent and eloquent," he produced some of his best articles for the Edinburgh press. Aside that the *Critic* of 1850 was "a weekly journal of some mark."

13. Gilbert, William. "The Jews in Paris." 8 (1867): 458–65.
Skimmed the *Universe Israélite*, edited by S. Bloch, and *Archives Israélites*, edited by Isidor Cohen. These "two periodicals, conducted with great ability," were far above average in literary quality, but their sectarianism precluded public acclaim.

14. Strahan, Alexander. "Charles Knight, Publisher." 8 (1867): 615–21.
Delineated Knight's journalistic ventures, among them Eton's *Microcosm*; the *Eton and Windsor Gazette*, which had difficulty because of the stamp duty and libel law; the *Etonian*; and *Knight's Quarterly Magazine*. The last, full of humor and the "clear and earnest thinking" of "gifted young men," had a "refined spirit" that attracted educated buyers but few others. He later launched the *Penny Magazine*. An immediate success with 200,000 weekly sales by the end of its first year, the *Penny* blended original and pirated material and boosted reading by the poor.

15. "Sadie: In Memory of an Esteemed Contributor." 9 (1868): 379–83.
Eulogized Sarah Williams, a contributor to *Good Words* and other serials before dying when 30 years old.

16. The Editor [Norman Macleod]. "Peeps at the Far East. No. 4: From Bombay to Madras." 10 (1869): 324–37.

Satirized the "fine writing in classical English" of the *Weekly Journal of Prabu News*.

17. S., F. R. [H. A. Page]. "Michael Farraday." 12 (1871): 121–27.

Flagged Farraday as the father of the *Quarterly Night*, a magazine in 1816.

18. Gilbert, William. "Maria S. Rye." 12 (1871): 573–77.

Alluded to Rye's connection with the *English Woman's Journal*.

19. Hogg, Lewis M. "Religion in Italy." 12 (1871): 753–60.

Catalogued papers dealing with Papal power, the French *Univers* and several Italian publications.

20. Stanley, Arthur P., D.D. "Norman Macleod, D.D." 13 (1872): 505–08.

Memorialized the editor of *Good Words*.

21. Smith, Walter C., D.D. "Norman Macleod, D.D." 13 (1872): 509–17.

Opined that Macleod's periodical writing had a "sketchy, unfinished character."

22. Smith, Walter C., D.D. "William Allan." 14 (1873): 196–201.

Spotlighted a working man who was a one-time reporter and subeditor of the *Newry Herald*.

23. Winkworth, Catherine. "A Ladies' Congress in Germany." 14 (1873): 554–58.

Article on the Second Congress of the *Lette-Verein*, the alliance of many societies, reported that it published a Berlin monthly, the *Frauenanwalt*, edited by Jenny Hirsch. One Congress society, the General Union of German Ladies, also had a journal, *New Paths*.

24. Allardyce, Alexander. "The Calcutta Natives." 15 (1874): 201–06, 371–75, 444–48.

Limned the Indian vernacular press. In the late eighteenth century there were few newspapers, so on "journal day" they passed around every village. The 1818 "*Mirror of News*, a small Bengalee [*sic*] journal issued from Dr. Carey's press," was the first forum of public opinion in India. Lord C. Canning gave a "great impetus to Bengalee journalism" when, at the urging of Rev. James Long, he appointed an "official reporter upon vernacular newspapers." In 1874 Bengal had a strong and "respectable" vernacular press that operated in almost every country town. Calcutta's *Som Prukash* was outstanding, a newspaper with "thoughtful, decisive articles" for all Bengal. The city also had papers in English under "native management," such as the *Hindoo Patriot*, the British Indian Association journal of "ability and influence"; the *Indian Mirror*, the organ of "progressive Brahmists"; and the *Bengalee*. The English did not read many of these gazettes because they focused on "interpreting native opinion." Although there was no direct communication between the Anglo-Indian and vernacular presses, they did cover some of the same public issues. As education spread, and local papers became more original and wholesome, journalism could be a "lucrative profession." Aside that Ram Mohun Roy began his literary career in 1821 when he started the *Brahminical Magazine*.

25. Smiles, Samuel. "The Story of Robert Nicoll's Life." 16 (1875): 313–18, 414–19.

Profiled a poet and writer whose articles appeared in *Johnstone's Edinburgh Magazine* and the *Dundee Advertiser* before he edited the *Leeds Times* at the age of 22. Nicoll believed that newspapers should correct prejudice and error but found writing leaders for a country tribune stressful because it had greater influence than an urban one with many competitors. To supplement his editor's income of two pounds a week, he wrote for a Sheffield paper and the *Monthly Repository*.

26. Alexander, William. "Literature of the People – Past and Present." 17 (1876): 92–96.

Designated William and Robert Chambers and Charles Knight as "pioneers of a healthy and instructive secular literature for the people." In the 1830s the elite worker read their serials while the majority perused those of a lower "moral tone." In 1876 country weeklies addressed "the wants and tastes" of laborers. Thanks to the end of the stamp and advertising duties, penny papers "perfectly free from anything like coarseness or indecency" circulated widely. However, they did "pander" to bad taste with their sensational fiction. Countering this content was the material of the Religious Tract and Book Society that annually sold over a million copies, most for a penny. Aside that servant girls as well as men bought the *British Workman*.

27. The "Journeyman Engineer" [Thomas Wright]. "Readers and Reading." 17 (1876): 315–20.

Swept over a plethora of expensive reviews and newspapers available at mechanics' institutes because employers paid for subscriptions. Aside that Eliza Cook was a popular writer for the *Weekly Dispatch* and owner of *Eliza Cook's Journal*.

28. Page, H. A. "Philanthropic Work in Birmingham." 17 (1876): 352–60.

Cheered that the Birmingham library had numerous dailies, weeklies, and magazines, with many readers but few thefts.

29. The "Journeyman Engineer" [Thomas Wright]. "The Service of Steam. No. 3: The Walter Press." 17 (1876): 688–94.

Traced speedy printing of periodicals from 1790 when William Nicholson, editor of the *Journal of Natural Philosophy*, obtained the first patent for mechanization. The König and other presses followed, culminating in the Walter, the product of "elaborate and costly experiments" over three years. The Hoe press, imported from the United States in 1857, was good, but the Walter in 1876 allowed *The Times* to print 72,000 sheets per hour followed by machine folding. The *Daily News*, *Scotsman*, and *New York Times* used the Walter.

30. Stevenson, Rev. W. Fleming. "The Mission Fields of India, China, and Japan. No. 4: Among the Missions." 20 (1879): 324–30.

Calculated that the Japanese press comprised 14 dailies, with a total circulation of 52,000, and over 200 weeklies, fortnightlies, and monthlies, with such titles as *News of Wind and Willow* and *Fashionable Intelligence*.

31. Hutton, R[ichard] H[olt]. "Thomas Carlyle." 22 (1881): 282–88.

Wondered if a style shift in Carlyle's *Edinburgh Review* articles was due to "corrections" made by editor Francis Jeffrey.

32. Smith, Walter C., D.D. "Reminiscences of Carlyle and Leigh Hunt; Being Extracts from the Diary of the Late John Hunter, of Craigcrook." 23 (1882): 96–103.
Quoted Hunter on Edward "Sterling, the principal writer in *The Times*," and John "Forster, the critic of the *Examiner*."

33. Smith, Walter C., D.D. "Dr. John Brown." 23 (1882): 446–51.
Remembered Brown's articles in *Good Words* and the *North British Review*.

34. Kaufmann, Rev. M[oritz], M.A. "Christian Socialists. No. 1: Lamennais." 23 (1882): 576–83; "No. 2: Charles Kingsley," 673–79; "No. 3: Victor Aimé Huber," 786–92.
Noted the work of F. de Lamennais for the *Avenir*, the contributions of Kingsley to *Fraser's Magazine*, and the editing by Huber of *Janus*, a Berlin organ of limited circulation, perhaps due to its official subsidy or Berliners' intellectual apathy.

35. Oliphant, Mrs. [Margaret]. "Anthony Trollope." 24 (1883): 142–44.
Recalled that in 1863 editor Norman Macleod rejected Trollope's first submission because it was "unsuitable" for *Good Words*. This decision was a "large pecuniary sacrifice" for the magazine that thereafter published Trollope until his death. *See* 25: 248.

36. Garnett, Mrs. Charles [Elizabeth]. "With the Salvation Army." 24 (1883): 246–51.
Declared that the touching facts in the Salvation Army periodical, *War Cry*, sometimes shocked readers.

37. Montagu, Irving. "Adventures of a War Correspondent." 24 (1883): 643–49.
Reminisced about reporting the Carlist campaign in Spain in 1874.

38. Editor [Donald Macleod]. "Anthony Trollope." 25 (1884): 248–52.
Unveiled negotiations between the editor of *Good Words* and Trollope for a story, followed by the rejection of "Rachael Ray." *See* 24: 142.

39. Kaufmann, Rev. M[oritz]. "The 'State Socialists.'" 25 (1884): 613–18.
Mentioned the *Christian Socialist*, *Christian Social Correspondence*, and *State Socialists*, the short-lived press of parliamentary socialists in Berlin.

40. Walker, R[obert]. "John Tenniel and Caricature Art." 25 (1884): 815–22.
Celebrated *Punch's* "honourable" career as the best comic paper in Europe. *Punch* was "healthy, manly, and honest," whereas its French peers were "ferocious and indecent." John Tenniel, who also drew for *Sharpe's London Magazine*, gave an impetus to caricature. Editor Mark Lemon invited him to join the *Punch* staff where he became one of its best artists. John Leech, perhaps the best, was hired in 1851 when Richard Doyle resigned because he believed *Punch* to be anti-Catholic. After Leech died in 1864, Tenniel dominated the field.

41. Johnston, Henry. "The Making of a Newspaper." 26 (1885): 363–68.
Assigned responsibility for a newspaper to several areas: business management; editing and subediting; reporting (including local correspondence); case-room, stereotyping, and printing. 1) Business: advertising was essential because profit from sales was "trifling." Since an established paper had to lead, management

had to pay for special trains and post at home and additional expenses overseas. London papers, closer to government, had somewhat less expenditure than country ones. 2) Editing: editors maintained the "character" of papers. They supervised specialists, as theatre and art critics, though typically left literary reviews to outsiders. Editors allocated space to parallel public interests but left subeditors to deal with printers about the specifics of placement. Subeditors helped with leaders and reviewed telegrams and columns from other gazettes. 3) Reporting: morning dailies had four to eight reporters headed by a chief. Domestic reporters took down speeches verbatim and abridged them with discrimination. Special correspondents had to go anywhere, have courage, and stay cool. They might use telegrams or pigeons for their dispatches, but local reporters relied on express trains and telegrams. 4) Case-room: personnel ensured that type was stored carefully for stereotyping and kept the subeditor updated on the amount of space still available in an issue. Printing was ever faster: the 1814 steam press produced 1,000 copies per hour; the 1885 rotary, 12,000. Errors resulted from the pressure on leader-writers and reporters penning under a deadline as much as from printing. Aside that the *Daily News* had the world's largest circulation.

42. Heath, R[ichard]. "Two Years in Paris. No. 3." 26 (1885): 732–37.
Announced that Paris had a vast number of newspapers, four times more than London, but they tended to "demoralize and degrade" readers.

43. Howitt, Mary. "Reminiscences of My Later Life." 27 (1886): 52–59.
Part of a series championed husband William Howitt who was in 1846 the editor and part owner of the *People's Journal*, a "cheap weekly journal, exclusively devoted to the instruction and improvement of the people." Legal problems with co-owner John Saunders led to a break and the birth of *Howitt's Journal*. Aside that Howitt helped Edward Youl get a job at 200 pounds per year for a three-day work week penning leaders for a John Cassell paper.

44. Editor [Donald Macleod]. "Principal Tulloch." 27 (1886): 239–41.
Honored John Tulloch, once "admirable editor" of *Fraser's Magazine*, who found his position difficult because the periodical was published in London and he held a post at St. Andrew's in Scotland.

45. Underwood, F[rancis] H. "John Greenleaf Whittier." 28 (1887): 29–34.
Recorded that Whittier, when 21 years old, edited a Hartford paper. While he was editor of the Pennsylvania *Freeman*, a pro-slavery mob sacked its offices. He was also the corresponding editor of the *National Era*, a Washington abolitionist paper, and a contributor to the *Liberator*.

46. M[artin], B. "W[illiam] Fleming Stevenson: In Memoriam." 28 (1887): 71–72.
Starred a long-time contributor to *Good Words*.

47. Underwood, Francis H. "Oliver Wendell Holmes." 28 (1887): 298–304.
Rooted the early success of the *Atlantic Monthly* in Holmes' "thought and style."

48. Swain, Joseph. "Frederick Walker, A.R.A." 29 (1888): 471–77.
Posited that Walker, like many artists, began his career drawing for periodicals. His work appeared in the *Cornhill Magazine*, *Once a Week*, *Good Words*, and *Punch*. In 1888 the *Graphic* was popular.

49. Swain, Joseph. "Charles Henry Bennett." 29 (1888): 589–94.
Referred to Bennett's sketches for *Punch*.

50. Swain, Joseph. "George John Pinwell." 29 (1888): 814–17.
Praised Pinwell's drawings in the 1860s for *Good Words*, *Once a Week*, and the *Sunday Magazine*.

51. Underwood, Francis H., LL.D. "Charles Dudley Warner." 30 (1889): 190–95.
Asserted that young writers struggling for recognition submitted "frantic and farcical" pieces to newspapers and magazines. Their work was not unlike American "fatuous or absurd" 'funny' columns. Warner, by contrast, produced quality writing. During his college years, he published in the "*Knickerbocker* and *Putnam's Magazine*, two popular periodicals." In 1860 he edited the *Hartford Press* where he earned a fine reputation. In 1867, when the *Press* merged with the *Hartford Courant*, "a long-established and influential paper," he edited the *Courant*. His leaders were lucid, but he knew that to succeed an editor needed "good sense, an instinctive knowledge of public tastes and prejudices, and patient labour" more than literary skills. Although the newspaper guaranteed him income, he penned for other venues.

52. Symington, A. Macleod, D.D. "William Fleming Stevenson, D.D." 30 (1889): 311–15.
Talked about Stevenson's early association with the *Edinburgh Christian Magazine* and his longer one with *Good Words*, which, with "other magazines of kindred spirit," was a sign of the public's spirituality.

53. Tulloch, Rev. W. W., B.D. "'Delta.'" 30 (1889): 394–99.
Identified Delta as David M. Moir who wrote for the *Edinburgh Literary Gazette* and *Fraser's Magazine*. His most important journalism was for *Blackwood's Magazine*, where he published 370 articles, some analyzed here.

54. Swain, Joseph. "Frederick Eltze." 30 (1889): 671–77.
Described Eltze's illustrations in *Punch* in the 1860s. He also drew for *Good Words*, the *Sunday Magazine*, Birmingham's *Illustrated Midland News*, and *Once a Week*, the only weekly that could afford artists of "high standing," such as John Tenniel, John Leech, and J. E. Millais.

55. Picton, J. Allanson, M.P. "Richard Steele." 30 (1889): 736–41.
Review of George A. Aitken's *The Life of Richard Steele* said that periodical literature once meant "polished essays and smart comments on contemporary persons" that required "higher intellectual gifts" to pen than articles in 1889. Steele "made his main mark" in journalism. The *Tatler* was similar to 1889 society papers except that it had less personal gossip and more literary articles. After its demise, Steele began the *Spectator* on the same model. He would probably not succeed in 1889 because the great demand for information limited dailies to printing "absolutely necessary news."

56. Nicol, John. "Professor Elmslie: In Memoriam." 31 (1890): 39–44.
Esteemed W. Gray Emslie, D.D., who wrote for *Good Words* and other religious periodicals (named).

57. Flint, Professor [Robert], D.D., LL.D. "Socialism. No. 2: Its History." 31 (1890): 263–68.
Listed the socialist press in 1890 as *To-day*, *Justice*, *Commonweal*, *Freedom*, the *Socialist*, *Church Reformer*, and *Christian Socialist*.

58. Horton, Rev. R[obert] F., M.A. "The Responsibility of Reading." 32 (1891): 28–31.

Advised readers to check for bias in the "daily and weekly press."

59. Editor [Donald Macleod]. "John Nichol." 32 (1891): 268–69.

Honored a long-time staff member and then subeditor of *Good Words*. Nichol also penned for the *Contemporary Review*, *Sunday Magazine*, and other journals and was the publishing manager of Isbister and Co.

60. Hutton, John. "Miss Linskill." 32 (1891): 477–82.

Printed the obituary of Mary Linskill, "for many years a large contributor" to *Good Words*.

61. Sinclair, W. "David Robertson, F.G.S., F.L.S." 32 (1891): 737–41.

Biography of Robertson, a naturalist, peeked at his articles in the *Glasgow Herald* and *Scotch Reformers' Gazette*.

62. Buckland, Rev. A. R., M.A., Morning Preacher at the Foundling Hospital. "London Street-Life." 33 (1892): 86–94, 240–46, 468–74, 742–49.

Glimpsed aspects of London journalism. In daylight the newsboy was ubiquitous on the capital's crowded streets. At night Fleet Street was hectic because the telephone and telegrams delivered a steady stream of news for metro and local subeditors to handle. By 3 a.m., the morning dailies ready for trains were bound for suburban news agents. "Most of the great morning papers in the provinces publish a late edition which contains the cream of the news and the points of the leaders of the London dailies" that local subeditors still scissored.

63. Hall, Rev. Newman, LL.B. "Charles Haddon Spurgeon." 33 (1892): 233–37.

Commended preacher Spurgeon for his *Sword and Trowel*, "a monthly magazine."

64. Burnett, Rev. William, M.A. "The Early Days of French Newspapers." 33 (1892): 266–69.

Abstracted journalism history from the *acta diurna* and Venetian gazettes through the sixteenth century when French nobles had their own badly-paid journal writers. In 1631 Théophraste Renaudot, inspired by his patients' letters from abroad, started the *Gazette de Paris*. Always careful about politics, the paper grew from four to eight to 12 pages. While the London *Daily Courant* appeared in Anne's reign, the first French daily, the *Journal de Paris*, did not arrive until 1777. The impetus for the political press was Count H. de Mirabeau's *Journal des Etats Généraux*, 1789, soon suppressed. Its successor, the *Courrier de Provence*, lasted a few months. Napoleon I sanctioned the *Moniteur* but leashed the *Journal des Débats* and thirty others. Louis XVIII penned for the *Journal de Paris*, but Louis Philippe reigned during "the most brilliant period of French journalism" when the quality and tone of writing were high. Advertising slowly but surely led to lower prices until in 1863 the *Petit Journal* sold for a sou. In 1891 France had 5,178 papers (3,180 in the provinces, 1,998 in Paris) whose enormous total circulation vastly enriched owners and whose exploitation of press freedom brought it close to licentiousness. This result was unfortunate because the newspaper was "an absolute necessity of our modern civilisation."

65. S., H. M. "Bishop Harley Goodwin." 33 (1892): 305–09.
Earmarked Goodwin as "a frequent contributor" to the *Contemporary Review* and the *Nineteenth Century*.

66. Layard, George Somes. "Millais and *Once a Week*." 34 (1893): 552–58.
Communicated that J. E. Millais had a reputation as an artist when he was invited to join John Leech, John Tenniel, and others illustrating *Once a Week*. Its first editor was Samuel Lucas who hired a "brilliant…array of black and white artists." Millais also drew for the *Cornhill Magazine* and *Good Words*, which introduced the technique of drawing directly on the block.

67. Walker, Robert. "John Pettie, R.A." 34 (1893): 750–57.
Recognized Pettie as an artist who illustrated *Good Words*.

68. Aitken, George A. "The Proof Sheets of Macauley's Essays." 35 (1894): 26–30.
Discussed proof sheets for two of T. B. Macaulay's essays in the *Edinburgh Review*: "Sir James Mackintosh's *History of the Revolution*" (July 1835) with reference to Macvey Napier's editing and Macaulay's response; and "Lord Bacon" (July 1837).

69. Murray, John, III. "Some Authors I Have Known." 36 (1895): 87–93, 165–70.
Mused about some "pillars" of the *Quarterly Review*, such as J. W. Croker and J. G. Lockhart, and their colleagues, Francis B. Head, Lady Elizabeth Rigby Eastlake with her brilliant reviews, and L. J. Jennings, a "constant" contributor. He edited the *Friend of India* before moving to the *New York Times* where "he succeeded in breaking up the notorious 'Tammany Ring' – a task requiring nerve and insight of no ordinary kind." *Quarterly* editor William Smith and Murray's father apparently had close ties.

70. Howitt, Margaret. "Some Letters from Miss Mitford." 36 (1895): 377–84.
Essay on letters to Mary Howitt avouched that H. F. Chorley was "a valued member of the literary staff" of the *Athenaeum* and Thomas Noon Talfourd penned "masterly articles" for the *New Monthly Magazine*.

71. Moulder, P. E. "The Literature of Factory Workers by One of Them." 37 (1896): 530–31.
Labeled *Home Notes* and the *Young Ladies' Journal* among the "favourite weeklies" of factory girls. Boys read too many penny dreadfuls. Both sexes liked the publications of the Religious Tract Society, the *Girl's Own Paper* and the *Boy's Own Paper*, each with a circulation of 150,000–200,000 per week.

72. Pike, G. Holden. "'General Readers' in East London." 37 (1896): 668–70.
Headlined the many workers who went to Bethnal Green Free Library in the evening to read newspapers and magazines, among which trade journals were extremely popular.

73. Walker, Robert. "Old Glasgow." 37 (1896): 678–87.
Returned to Glasgow, 1715–1850, when the city published about 200 newspapers and other periodicals, some still in existence. The *Glasgow Courant* (1715) became, after its third issue, the *West Country Intelligencer*. The *Glasgow Advertiser and Evening Herald* (1782) was the *Herald and Advertiser* after 1802 and appeared in 1896 as the *Glasgow Herald*.

74. King, Jessie Margaret. "At the International Women's Congress." 38 (1897): 635–40.

Chronicled a Berlin meeting attended by Lina Morganstern who in 1874 began a "journal for housewives," the *Hausfrauen Zeitung*; Mina Cauer, who edited the *Frauenbewegung*, and Belva Lockwood, "editor of the *Peacemaker*, an American journal now in its twenty-ninth year."

75. Layard, George Somes. "On Some Caricature – Portraits of Thackeray by Pen and Pencil." 38 (1897): 702–08.

Perused articles on W. M. Thackeray in *Punch*; the *Month*, "a very fascinating monthly" founded in 1851 by Albert Smith and John Leech; and *Fraser's Magazine*, where Thackeray was one of William Maginn's "Fraserians."

76. Smith, Harry. "The Science of Anonymity." 39 (1898): 99–104.

Chose Junius as the forerunner of the anonymity common in the nineteenth century. Periodical authors wanted their work judged on its merits, but some authors were easy to identify because they provided their initials, variations on their names, or an alias.

77. Wright, H. C. Seppings. "The War Artist." 39 (1898): 119–25.

Seppings discoursed about his experiences, supplemented by his own drawings, as a war correspondent in West Africa. The job was always fascinating, sometimes pleasant, irrespective of disease, bullets, sand, insects, and heat. To be "a war correspondent," a journalist needed "a strong constitution…a good kit…a good stout heart." The reporter should present credentials under the Military Discipline Act, "which is most leniently interpreted in the case of correspondents." Censors guarded against slips in dispatches and spies.

78. Lillingston, Leonard W. "Carrier Pigeons." 39 (1898): 310–15.

Indicated stories on pigeons in the "sporting" papers and a paper on the homing variety. Pigeons were reporters' tools to send late-breaking sport results until the telephone and were still used to transmit illustrations. Shooting to steal a story was "a little too unscrupulous to square with the ethics of even the most go-ahead journalism" but occurred.

79. Mackenzie, William C. "Lloyd's.'" 39 (1898): 346–50.

Rediscovered *Lloyd's News*, a 1696 newspaper, short-lived because its "unpalatable references" did not pass "press censorship…which was rigorously exercised." In 1726 Edward Lloyd's company started *Lloyd's List*, the second oldest newspaper in England after the *London Gazette*.

80. Watt, J. H. "Some Unpublished Letters to Lord Jeffrey." 39 (1898): 563–67.

Glossed the letters of William Hazlitt about the *Edinburgh Review*, editor Francis Jeffrey who was a harsh critic but a kind person, and contributors.

81. Robinson, Phil. "How I Landed in Cuba." 39 (1898): 678–84.

Reporter for the *Pall Mall Gazette* grumbled that the United States censor in Cuba, who would not approve true stories about American activities, mutilated Robinson's telegrams. Aside that the *Standard's* man, one Whigham, had a press photographer.

82. Bayliss, Sir Wyke, F.S.A., P.R.B.A. "Sir John Everett Millais.: The Painter of Men and Women." 40 (1899): 94–102.

Thought that Millais' work, in the 1850s and 1860s for *Once a Week*, *Good Words*, and the *Cornhill Magazine*, helped elevate readers' taste in art.

83. Sharp, William. "Mr. Alfred Austin." 40 (1899): 406–10.

Highlighted Austin as a writer, poet, and journalist for the *Standard*, but neglected his editing of the *National Review*.

84. Freshfield, Frances Heath. "The Book Trade in the Good Old Times." 41 (1900): 106–10.

Surmised that newspapers were "already a power" by the late Stuarts because every coffeehouse had nine journals. Despite these sales, printer-publishers paid their editors and writers low wages.

85. Pendleton, John. "Diversions of a Newspaper Life." 41 (1900): 157–59.

Exulted that journalists of 1900 were fearless, "level-headed," "original and trenchant" scribes. Earlier prejudices against leader-writers and parliamentary lobbyists and gallery men had evaporated. While war correspondents were ready for danger, interviewers needed more patience. Aside that major London dailies had three to 12 reporters who knew shorthand and busy subeditors who faced piles of reports, news items, and telegrams.

86. Pendleton, John. "The Diversions of an Editor." 41 (1900): 332–35.

Underscored that the responsibilities of dailies' editors caused them anxiety. They should be cool in crises and in the face of critics. One exemplar was John Delane of *The Times*, who was always outwardly calm. Delane had a "news-getting instinct," ever alert for potential exclusives, and "sound judgment." Because of the competition among London morning dailies in 1900, a paper had to print speedily news that was gathered and written by an able staff, headed by leader-writers and special correspondents, and to tolerate literary reviewers whose severity stemmed from the mounds of rubbish they had to sort. *See* 41: 781.

87. Ralling, George. "The Cape in Time of War." 41 (1900): 374–83.

Deduced from the *Cape Argus* special edition on Majuba that newspaper sales were a "fair gauge of popular feeling in South Africa" but contained no troop news because of military prohibition.

88. Pendleton, John. "The Autocrat of the Night." 41 (1900): 781–84.

Reiterated how the pressure of issuing a daily affected an editor. *See* 41: 332.

89. Ellis, G. Stanley. "'Agony' Advertisements." 41 (1900): 827–30.

Sampled personal advertisements in newspapers.

Hogg's (Weekly) Instructor, 1845–1856

With a Christian outlook and a low price, James Hogg's *Instructor*, the forerunner of *Titan*, neatly profiled press scribes of the eighteenth and nineteenth centuries.

1. "Thoughts at Starting." 1 (1845): 1–3.
Proclaimed that *Hogg's* "motive" was "purer and better" than being distinguished or profitable. Driven by religion that other journalism ignored and aware that "nameless contributions in a cheap weekly miscellany" did not make a reputation, it planned to print solid literature and information.

2. "Biographical Sketches: Thomas Campbell." 1 (1845): 83–86, 98–102.
Swore that while Campbell edited the *New Monthly Magazine*, "it became the most popular of the monthlies."

3. "Biographical Sketches: Robert Nicoll." 1 (1845): 114–16.
Headlined Nicholl as an editor of the *Leeds Times*, a writer for newspapers and magazines, and a friend of publisher William Tait.

4. "Biographical Sketches: Sydney Smith." 1 (1845): 130–32.
Deemed Smith a "witty" critic who neither produced a master work nor created a school of literature.

5. "Eminent Living Authors: Thomas Noon Talfourd." 1 (1845): 210–12.
Reminded that Talfourd was the theatre critic for the *New Monthly Magazine* and a writer for the *Edinburgh Review*, *London Magazine*, and other serials.

6. "Portrait Gallery: Thomas Hood." 1 (1845): 275–76.
Centered on Hood's humor.

7. "Biographical Sketches: Joseph Addison." 1 (1845): 307–10.
Claimed that Addison's best work was in the *Tatler* making it more popular in 1709 than any prior paper. Its successor, the *Spectator*, was an "immense success."

8. Ellis, Mrs. [Sarah]. "Thoughts on Popular Literature." 1 (1845): 353–54.
Assured that a multitude of periodicals in 1845 served every interest. While each sect had its own serial, cheap miscellanies should weave in religion without bias as the "ablest" papers integrated politics. The inexpensive should also blend quality amusement and instruction, not make the imagination of workers "a manufactory of miseries."

9. "Portrait Gallery: Rev. David Welsh, D.D." 1 (1845): 371–72
Biography of Welsh, an editor of the *North British Review*, designated it as "a periodical which professes to combine the highest literature and scientific merit with sound morality and evangelical religion." Because Welsh recruited talented contributors, he probably would have made the *Review* one of the most popular and influential had his tenure been longer.

10. "A Gossip about Well-Paid Authors." 2 (1845–46): 203–05.
Bared that Christian Johnstone had "a very handsome income by her contributions to the periodical literature" and Mary Howitt received 70 pounds for a short story.

11. "Biographical Sketches: Francis Horner." 2 (1845–46): 291–94.
Earmarked Horner as a cofounder of and frequent author in the *Edinburgh*. He and his colleagues had such little faith in the *Review* that they only ordered 750 copies for the first number.

12. "Biographical Sketches: Henry Fielding." 2 (1845–46): 339–42.
Respected Fielding for supporting his family by penning for the *Champion* and later for establishing the *True Patriot*, which showed "considerable ability" and some humor as did its heir, the *Jacobite Journal*.

13. "Biographical Sketches: James Beattie, LL.D." 3 (1846): 2–4.
Unearthed that Beattie early in life scribbled "fugitive pieces" for the *Scots Magazine*.

14. "Biographical Sketches: Letitia E. Landon." 3 (1846): 19–21.
Glanced at Landon's work in *Fisher's Drawing-Room Scrap-Book*.

15. "General Characteristics of Modern British Literature." 3 (1846): 198–202.
Rejoiced that more reviews and magazines were focusing on religion. Aside that *Punch* forced readers to think by exposing humbug under the guise of humor.

16. "The Newspaper Press." 3 (1846): 337–40.
Commenced a history of the newspaper with the notion that it once relieved the dreariness of life by its stories of monsters and miracles. This history progressed from the *acta diurna* to the German *Ersalungen*, newsletters first numbered and registered in 1612. By then Venetians were perusing *gazettas*. In England, the newspaper path went from Nathaniel Butter through the Civil Wars to London's *Evening Post* and the *Tatler* in 1709. Soon the *Gentleman's Magazine* provided abstracts of weeklies, of which there were about 200. The earliest outside London were the *Stamford Mercury* (1695); Edinburgh's *Caledonian Mercury* (1660), although the government *Edinburgh Gazette* dated from 1600; and the *Dublin Evening Post* from 1725. This press depended on advertising to fill space.

In 1846 the kingdom had 550 serials (12 daily) that employed many. *The Times* had a large staff supervised by a powerful editor. There were 25 parliamentary reporters, more than half Irish, who earned seven guineas per week, which they supplemented by practicing law or acting as metro correspondents for local serials. *The Times* also used outsiders: penny-a-liners (paid more than a penny) as well as reviewers on the arts and literature and foreign correspondents whose expenses were large, all recompensed by revenue from advertising. Leader-writing in all London papers showed "great ability" even though scribes worked under pressure.

17. "The Newspaper Press: The French Journals." 3 (1846): 411–13.
Accepted that the press was powerful everywhere because of its political advice, exposure of fraud, redress of wrongs, and capacity to excite public opinion.

Ran through French journalism from Théophraste Renaudot and the *Mercure Galant* (1672). In 1846 the *Moniteur*, staffed by men of ability and power, was the official organ. The *Journal des Débats* gained fame with Julien Geoffroy, "almost worshipped" by readers for his light literature. The *National*, so important in the July Revolution, was particularly solid in the 1830s under Armand Carrel, "one of the ablest writers." The *Constitutionnel* was "flourishing and influential" in 1846, but the *Presse* and *Siècle* had high circulations. In most papers the feuilleton stole space from book reviews but not politics and the arts. Quoted the *British Quarterly Review* 3: 468.

18. "Female Authors." 4 (1846–47): 1–4.
Starred Christian Johnstone as "the most accomplished editress and female critic" although some of her work displayed the "negligence of...execution" and "dashing levity of style" of many magazine writers.

19. "Pigeon Expresses." 4 (1846–47): 11–12.
Noticed that pigeons were not frequent news carriers in 1846.

20. "A View of English Literature Between 1727 and 1780." 4 (1846–47): 67–69.
Alluded to Junius.

21. "Revival and Progress of National Literature in Scotland." 4 (1846–47): 271–72.
Nodded to the *Gentleman's Magazine*, first a news abstract, then a miscellany.

22. Gilfillan, Rev. George. "Popular and Cheap Literature." 4 (1846–47): 280–81.
Determined that William Cobbett built a journalistic career from founder of a small but influential weekly. In 1846 most of this genre neglected politics and religion in order to amuse and instruct the poor as well as introduce them to good manners.

23. "The Newspaper Stamp." 5 (1847): 58.
Borrowed from the *Penny Magazine* that Joseph Addison and Richard Steele were ready to publish in the face of the stamp duty. Aside on news vendors in the streets in the early eighteenth century.

24. "Biographical Sketches: Thomas Moore." 5 (1847): 104–08.
Revived Moore's 1806 challenge to duel Francis Jeffrey because the *Edinburgh Review* editor had published adverse criticism of Moore's work.

25. "Stamped Covers for Newspapers and Periodicals." 5 (1847): 116–17.
Backed abolition of the newspaper stamp because it and the paper duty discouraged newspapers and forced local buyers to share a gazette. Without a stamp, more subscriptions in the country would generate more advertising whose duty would compensate government for the loss of profits due to cancellation of the other two taxes.

26. "Classes: In Relation to Modern Tendencies. No. 2: The Literary Classes." 5 (1847): 347–49.

Included "the popular journalist" as a "man of letters."

27. "Literature of the Scottish Bar. No. 2: Lord Jeffrey." 6 (1847–48): 129–33, 153–56.

Postulated that the original goal of the *Edinburgh Review* was to cover many subjects and to demonstrate "independent judgment." By making literary criticism livelier and worthwhile, it improved literature. Francis Jeffrey, a cofounder and long editor of the *Review*, was more qualified to lead it than another of its sires, Sydney Smith. Under Jeffrey's direction, it undertook "courageous and independent investigation" that established its position as a 'Fourth Estate.' Jeffrey was also a good critic except in the sciences, but he lacked Smith's wit and Henry Brougham's power in political articles. The competition of the *Quarterly Review* and *Blackwood's Magazine* gradually eroded the *Edinburgh's* sway. In 1847 it was no longer a "literary censor" because it did not take the initiative in identifying and reviewing works with new ideas.

28. Oldmakenew, Richard. "The Old Newspaper." 6 (1847–48): 179–82, 237–39, 363–65.

Flipped through the contents of an unnamed review of 1756 before honing in on 1805 newspaper clubs whose members read, at each other's homes, highly priced but generally dull and stale journals. In 1847, because of anonymity, neither writers nor editors gained recognition for their efforts. Editors especially worked long and hard writing frequent leaders and coordinating their gazettes.

29. Gilfillian, George. "Portrait Gallery: William Cobbett." 6 (1847–48): 353–57.

Contrasted the styles of Cobbett and Junius, the first loud and the second quieter and deadlier in effect.

30. "Woman and Her Advisers." n.s., 1 (1848): 135–36.

Learned from the *Boston Journal* that American newspapers and magazines teemed with advice for women.

31. Gilfillan, George. "Gallery of Literary Divines. No. 2: Dr. George Croly." n.s., 1 (1848): 161–64.

Peeped at Croly's periodical articles of "various merit."

32. "Metropolitan Advertisements." n.s., 1 (1848): 276–78.

Fretted that advertisements in London gazettes reflected too much interest in and spurred too much expenditure on "artificial" wants but were amusing, whether about events, instruction, sales, or employment.

33. "Portrait Gallery: Thomas Hood." n.s., 2 (1848–49): 209–12.

Charted Hood's migration from the *Dundee Magazine* to the *London Magazine* and *Comic Annual*, full of the sophisticated humor that marked the peak of his periodical work.

34. Gilfillan, George. "Gallery of Literary Divines. No. 4: William Anderson, Glasgow." n.s., 2 (1848–49): 280–84.

Opened with a digression on Gilfillan's father, Samuel, who penned for the *Christian Magazine*.

35. "Samuel Drew, A.M." n.s., 3 (1849): 8–11.
Resurrected Drew's 1805 appointment as "metaphysical reviewer" for the *Eclectic Review* and his employment in 1818 to edit the new *Imperial Magazine.*

36. "Parliamentary Sketches. No. 1: Preliminary." n.s., 3 (1849): 17–19.
Pictured the Reporters' Gallery as narrow, with two rows of seats for current note takers and their replacements. The "withdrawing room" was a lounge where reporters between shifts criticized or joked about MPs to relieve the pressure of straining to listen to their speeches. The majority of reporters were Irish, but Scots were entering the field. The Irish were noisy and inaccurate; the Scots, cool; the English, independent and good-humored.

37. "The New Spirit of Criticism." n.s., 3 (1849): 273–75.
Ruminated about the shift in newspaper treatment of the Crown.

38. "Portrait Gallery: William Cullen Bryant." n.s., 4 (1849–50): 81–83.
Fixed on Bryant's journalistic ventures from the *New York Review and Athenaeum Magazine* in 1825 to his appointment as chief editor of New York's "*Evening Post*, one of the oldest established and most influential of the American newspapers." He also coproduced (1827–29) the *Talisman*, "a celebrated American annual" and published poetry in the *North American Review.*

39. "Portrait Gallery: Charlotte Elizabeth." n.s., 4 (1849–50): 145–47.
Extolled Charlotte E. Tonna who edited the *Christian Lady's Magazine* in the 1830s and the *Protestant Magazine* in the 1840s.

40. "Gilfillan's *Second Gallery of Literary Portraits*." n.s., 4 (1849–50): 326–29.
Review of George Gilfillan's book evaluated E. G. Bulwer-Lytton as editor of the *New Monthly Magazine*, "when it approached our ideal of a perfect magazine; combining as it did, impartiality, variety, and power." Unlike Bulwer-Lytton, Gilfillan sanctioned anonymity to protect tyros learning their craft; to enable the mature writer, "out of himself," to do his best work; to pique readers; and to "denounce wrong, with greater safety and effect."

41. "Notes of a Ten Years' Residence in New South Wales." n.s., 5 (1850): 129–33, 147–50.
Saluted Thomas Brisbane, governor, 1821–25, for ending official restraint of the New South Wales press.

42. "Lacordaire." n.s., 5 (1850): 305–09. 329–33.
Biography of J. B. Lacordaire pirated ideas in the *Galerie des Contemporains Illustres* about his connection with the *Avenir*. Among his associates was Count C. de Montalembert. The *Avenir* favored democracy and civil rights, but the French bishops opposed it because it attacked the Gallican Church. The pope allegedly suppressed it because he did not want the French Church or French king challenged by "zeal-devoured journalists" who might target him next.

43. "Portrait Gallery: Bernard Barton." n.s., 5 (1850): 353–55.
Biography of an eighteenth-century poet warranted that the early "*Edinburgh* [*Review*] stood almost alone as a sterling organ of criticism." In 1850, with more quarterlies, monthlies, weeklies, and

dailies, the "force of individual decisions upon literature" was "at a low point." Critics were no longer superior to readers because the "genteel level has been raised immensely."

44 "Portrait Gallery: Rev. John Pye Smith, D.D., LL.D., F.R.S, F.G.S., Theological Professor, Homerton College, London." n.s., 5 (1850): 401–03.

Certified that Smith edited the *Sheffield Iris* while its regular editor, James Montgomery, was in jail for libel.

45. "Portrait Gallery: Thomas Carlyle." n.s., 7 (1851): 81–86.

Avouched that the early *Edinburgh Review* "attacked ignorance and promoted social activities."

46. "Portrait Gallery: Rev. Thomas Price, LL.D., Editor of the *Eclectic*." n.s., 7 (1851): 289–91.

Graded Price, who purchased the *Eclectic Review* in 1835 from Josiah Conder, Esq., a "talented and cultivated editor" who attracted writers of "commanding intellect and extensive acquirements."

47. "The Present State of Hungary." n.s., 7 (1851): 373–75, 392–94.

Exposed subterfuges that journals used to circulate news in the face of censorship, as that encountered by the daily *Pesti Naplo*. The press should be "the public standard of truth," but in Hungary most papers were afraid to show anything but "servitude and dissimilation" for fear of penalty. When a paper for "ladies," *Hölgy Futár*, published a poem on Magyar bravery, its publisher was jailed.

48. "Literary and Philosophical Societies of Edinburgh During the Eighteenth Century." n.s., 8 (1851–52): 43–46.

Spotlighted Edinburgh's Mirror Club, one of whose members, Henry Mackenzie, edited its "two elegant and classical periodicals, the *Mirror* and the *Lounger*." Named contributors to both.

49. "The Mormonites." n.s., 8 (1851–52): 107–09.

Skimmed Mormon newspapers, the *Evening and Morning Star* and the *Upper Missouri Advertiser*, and the anti-Mormon *Expositor*, whose Illinois office was leveled because of its stance.

50. Swisshelm, Mrs. [Jane Grey]. "Magazine Fashion Plates." n.s., 9 (1852): 76–77.

Villified fashion magazines as "a curse of humanity" because their counsel to women caused lung ailments and undermined female honor.

51. "Cockburn's *Life of Jeffrey*." n.s., 9 (1852): 200–01, 210–13.

Review of Henry Cockburn's book dubbed Francis Jeffrey "the first stationary salaried conductor" of the *Edinburgh Review*, who initially persuaded friends to write. He once came close to a duel with Thomas Moore who objected to *Edinburgh* criticism of his poetry though the two were later friends.

52. "*The Autobiography of William Jerdan*." n.s., 9 (1852): 259–61; n.s., 10 (1852–53): 73–75.

Review shadowed Jerdan from his "apprenticeship to journalism," a seven-year stint as a reporter. In 1813 he edited the *Sun*, co-owned by John S. Taylor, for 500 pounds a year and a one-tenth share of the paper. In 1817 he began editing the *Literary Gazette*, the first journal to print literary columns in a newspaper.

53. "Theodore Hook." n.s., 10 (1852–53): 20–23.

Featured Hook's journalism, chiefly his editing of *John Bull*, soon notorious for its "wit" and "invective." At the height of its popularity, Hook earned 2,000 pounds per year but no fame as the editorship was "kept strictly private."

54. "Who Was Junius?" n.s., 10 (1852–53): 193–96.

Weighed the evidence on the identity of Junius.

55. "Too Much Reading." n.s., 10 (1852–53): 480.

Observed that newspapers got bigger as readers' interests expanded.

56. A Scottish Emigrant. "Spiritualism in America." n.s., 10 (1852–53): 499–502.

Sidelined the New England spiritualist journal, *New Era, or Heavenly Opener*.

57. "The Bourbon Bubble Burst." 3d ser., 1 (1853): 56–60.

Scoffed at George Putnam's attempt to entice American readers to buy his new monthly magazine by headlining that Louis XVII was alive and well in the United States.

58. "The Life and Writings of Edgar Poe." 3d ser., 1 (1853): 97–106.

Portrayed the United States as a "land of journalism, and not of great books." The chief requirements to succeed in journalism were talent and perseverance. Because Poe lacked the second, he had trouble as a writer and an editor. Aside that all periodicals could benefit from more editing.

59. Gilfillan, George. "Modern British Orators. No. 3: Lord Brougham." 3d ser., 2 (1854): 41–49, 216–21.

Categorized the majority of newspapers and periodicals as intellectually "dull" in contrast to Henry Brougham's articles. Alluded to Brougham's role in the birth of the *Edinburgh Review* and to one of its essayists, John Foster.

60. "Popular Amusements." 3d ser., 2 (1854): 362–69.

Commended *Leisure Hour*, which balanced amusement and instruction.

61. Gilfillan, George. "Prospective Periodical Literature." 3d ser., 3 (1854): 97–105.

Reveled that periodical literature was "one of the greatest in a day when feats are common," a medium that speedily communicated knowledge. The progenitor *Gentleman's Magazine* was engrossing, but periodicals should have a theme, not appear as "bundles of sticks" tied by a cause, conductor, sect, or bent. Neither able writers nor secret puffs and pans passing for criticism unified. Periodicals should commit to a Christian creed but tolerate "minor diversities" and should contain light and serious material. They should be independent and national, unlike the English editor of the *Edinburgh Review* [George Cornewall Lewis] who gave little space to Scotland. Serials should print the names or initials of writers in order to help novices, ensure responsibility, and root out "cliques of small scribes who make up for their insignificance with malice." Aside on Francis Jeffrey's editorial style at the *Edinburgh*.

62. "Letters from Paris. No. 4: Alexandre Dumas and His Mosquetaire Papers." 3[d] ser., 4 (1855): 35–48; No. 6, 215–24.

Publicized that in July 1853, Dumas, *père*, started the *Journal d'Alexandre Dumas*, enlisting friends to pen for it. The French law that required all journalists to sign their columns would "destroy the power and prestige of the press" but might leash *Charivari*, a paper that did "pander to the popular taste."

63. "Gilfillan's *Literary Portraits*: Some Hints on Criticism." 3[d] ser., 4 (1855): 85–93.

Review of George Gilfillan's *Third Gallery of Literary Portraits* referred to the *Edinburgh Review* and *Blackwood's Magazine*.

64. "Photographs of London Business. No. 3: The Wonders of Printing-House Square." 3[d] ser., 5 (1855): 25–34.

Concentrated on *The Times*, production and distribution (60,000 copies daily), its editorial and printing staffs, and its vendors. Leaders were the "thunderbolts of today and oracles tomorrow," columns whose subjects management set and then shaped by giving the leader-writer information. Reporters, under pressure to be "intelligent" and "[s]harp," had parliamentary rooms that were comfortable and three cabs available for the 20 men to get to the office. Advertisements were in every *Times* edition, but the second (6,000/7,000 copies) about noon had more telegrams and foreign correspondence. Aside that the triweekly *Evening Mail* had news and leaders but no advertising because it went to the country and abroad.

65. "The Pulpit and the Press." 3[d] ser., 6 (1856): 1–12.

Decried the popular belief that the "newspaper has superseded the pulpit" and the consequent "public laudation of the influence of the press." There should be a "division of labour" between the two because journalism, a trade where honesty was not a priority, was morally inferior to the pulpit.

The Home and Foreign Review, 1862–1864

Succeeding the *Rambler*, the sophisticated *Home and Foreign* spoke about the intersection of religion and journalism.

1. [Acton, J. D., Richard Simpson, and T. F. Wetherell]. "Cardinal Wiseman and the *Home and Foreign Review*." 1 (1862): 501–20.

Worried that Nicholas Wiseman's address (5 August 1862) to Catholic clergy, in which he referred to the *Home and Foreign*, could "paralyse one of the few organs of Catholic opinion in England." Although committed to Catholicism, the *Review*, like the *Rambler*, addressed a general, not a religious audience. Essays on politics and science would open minds, not threaten faith.

2. [Simpson, Richard]. "Thackeray." 4 (1864): 476–511.

Flipped through W. M. Thackeray's "Snob Papers" in *Punch*, pointing out that he admired the styles of Joseph Addison, Richard Steele, and Jonathan Swift.

3. Acton, J. D. "Conflicts with Rome." 4 (1864): 667–90.

Explained that the *Home and Foreign*, which never pretended to represent the Catholic majority but to speak for science and religion, could not continue as a Catholic journal in the face of papal opposition to the *Review*.

Household Words, 1850–1859

Edited by Charles Dickens and followed by *All the Year Round*, the popular six-penny *Household Words* assessed the French press and petitioned for inexpensive reading rooms for the British "unknown public" described in its pages by Wilkie Collins.

1. [Dickens, Charles and W. H. Wills]. "Valentine's Day at the Post Office." 1 (1850): 6–12.

Announced that 70 million newspapers passed annually through the post office because some were sent more than once. Demand came from press coverage of births and deaths, crimes and accidents, current vanities and social changes.

2. [Forster, John]. "Francis Jeffrey." 1 (1850): 113–18.

Reminisced about the start of the *Edinburgh Review*, intended by founders Jeffrey, Francis Horner, Sydney Smith, and Henry Brougham to stimulate serious thinking on serious subjects. Editor Jeffrey inaugurated the "forcible style of criticism" by paid contributors (10 guineas a sheet, later 20), setting "the all-important principle of a perfect independence of his publisher's control."

3. [Crowe, Joseph Archer]. "A Paris Newspaper." 1 (1850): 164–67.

Chose the *Constitutionnel* (40,000 copies daily) as the prototype of Paris newspapers. Their offices were neater than London ones cluttered with foreign gazettes, parliamentary reports, and reference books. The French preferred to sell their tribunes by subscription, so forms were available in the post office. The Advertising Company of Paris bought the last page of every paper of any consequence. On other pages were "polemics," which the French favored over news. Although France, like the United States, had "the personal system of journalism," French editors did not need swords or guns, as did Americans, to protect themselves from angry readers. Newspapers sired revolutions in 1830 and 1848, and editors continued to lead the masses who read or listened to news in "cheap newspaper clubs," albeit 1848 had shaken confidence in the press.

Newspaper staffs were small. French legislative reporters took notes for a couple of minutes, then transcribed; British, allegedly less biased, took notes for 30–45 minutes so they needed three hours to write their paragraphs. France had no penny-a-liners. News stories were gathered in general offices, and lithographic reproductions folded and labeled by women were sent to local and foreign journals.

4. [Wills, W. H.]. "The Appetite for News." 1 (1850): 238–40.

Agreed with F. Knight Hunt's *The Fourth Estate* that where there were newspapers, people were free. The press was "the engine of public liberty" because it promptly espoused the public's ideas. Distribution of news by 150 papers in London and 238 in the country and a serial for every interest guaranteed circulation of diverse views.

From the 1712 stamp until 1782, there were only 79 papers, but the number rose as concern about American and French matters grew. By 1790 there were 146 newspapers, most weeklies, in Britain and Ireland. Sales dropped after 1815, only to rise again as autodidacts and reduction of the stamp made an impact. Quoted the *Edinburgh Review* (32: 192) about differences between English and French journalism. Britain had bigger papers and more in the country, but the French and Americans read more.

5. [Wills, W. H.]. "Newspaper Antecedents." 1 (1850): 270–74.
History of news transmission proceeded from early societies dependent on oral sources to the reign of James I, when news writers even hired reporters. Nathaniel Butter's *Weekely News*, 1622–40, was the antecedent of the Civil Wars' "Mercuries" springing from army and royalist presses. In 1665 the *Oxford Gazette*, later *London Gazette*, emerged. When censorship eased in the 1690s, papers burgeoned. Among the important were the *Universal Intelligencer* (a two-page biweekly of news and advertising). During Anne's reign, "journalism had improved," and the *Daily Courant* appeared. Even after the 1712 stamp duty, the number and influence of newspapers expanded.

6. [Wills, W. H.]. "The Golden City." 1 (1850): 313–17.
Chuckled that in San Francisco an old *New York Tribune* could be resold for a dollar.

7. [Wills, W. H., E. C. Grenville-Murray, and ? Thomas Walker]. "German Advertisements." 2 (1850–51): 33–35.
Sampled matrimonial advertisements in Cologne's *Zeitung* and Vienna's *Zeitung*. Such inserts told more about life than treatises, especially in Britain where citizens were not public about passion.

8. [Morley, Henry]. "Views of the Country." 2 (1850–51): 169–72.
Rhapsodized that "[o]pinion is King of England" where a free press secured peace and progress by ending readers' parochialism and religious and political biases. The press was also the "direct agent in producing social reforms" by laying out facts.

9. [Hunt, F. Knight]. "Wings of Wire." 2 (1850–51): 241–45.
Connected telegraphy to news dissemination.

10. [Morley, Henry and ?Lynn]. "Free Public Libraries." 3 (1851): 80–83.
Contrasted the slow growth of free libraries in English towns to the rapid spread of reading rooms full of newspapers in France. Aside that the French *Charivari* had "stinging humour." *See* 8: 88.

11. [Hannay, James and W. H. Wills]. "Edward Baines." 3 (1851): 414–19.
Applauded Baines, who started as a printer's apprentice at the age of 16, bought the *Leeds Mercury* at 27, and later sat in Commons.

12. [Morley, Henry]. "The Labourer's Reading-Room." 3 (1851): 581–85.
Mused about one reading room that a few handloom weavers opened in London in 1848 and in 1851 held two dailies, 13 weeklies, and 15 periodicals for its 112 members.

13. [Jerrold, W. B.]. "The Constant Reader." 3 (1851): 599–600.
Satirist of writers of letters to the editor and readers of domestic, imperial, and Parisian newspapers confessed to scribbling about the arcane for many tribunes.

14. [Keene, John or James and W. H. Wills]. "A Golden Newspaper." 4 (1851–52): 207–08.

Compared the *Sydney Morning Herald* before the gold discoveries, when it contained government news, advertisements, vignettes, and letters, and after, when it doubled in size due to advertising the gold fields and headlining the exploits of miners.

15. [Grenville-Murray, E. C. and Henry Morley]. "Advertisements." 4 (1851–52): 359–60.

Characterized personal advertisements in Vienna newspapers as "ridiculous."

16. [Costello, Dudley]. "Picture Advertising in South America." 4 (1851–52): 494–98.

Pirated from Buenos Aires' newspapers, advertisements about slaves, male sports, and quack medicines.

17. [Thomas, William Moy]. "Sentimental Journalism." 4 (1851–52): 550–52

Trumpeted that the French press was inaccurate except for the *Gazette des Tribuneaux*, which published judicial reports. The papers' common column, "Various Facts," detailed so many accidents and catastrophes that no further embellishment was possible. Aside that Eugene Guinot, of *Ordre*, was "a journalist of some celebrity."

18. [George, Frances and Henry Morley]. "From a Settler's Wife." 4 (1851–52): 585–88.

Noted two Auckland newspapers, the government *New Zealander* and the *Southern Cross*.

19. [Thomas, T. M.]. "Margaret Fuller." 5 (1852): 121–24.

Recalled that Fuller edited the "*Dial*, an American Quarterly Review."

20. [Napier, ?]. "Bombay." 5 (1852): 181–86.

Broadcast that three morning journals, each "conducted with much spirit and vigour," served the "English gentry" in Bombay.

21. [Morley, Henry, ?Ossian Macpherson, and ? Mulock]. "The Harvest of Gold." 5 (1852): 213–18.

Earmarked the 'Gold Circular,' a column one Sydney daily printed to lure diggers while other papers promoted colonization.

22. [Dixon, Edmund Saul]. "French Provincial News." 5 (1852): 440–44.

Distinguished "voluminous" and ably done English local papers from small French ones with "scraps of news," births and deaths, advertising, and the "small-talk" necessitated by "political restrictions." Yet, because French journalists signed columns, they reaped more glory than their British counterparts.

23. [Blanchard, Sidney L.]. "Dining with the Million." 5 (1852): 489–93.

Surmised that French journals barred from political themes turned to social ones.

24. [Sala, George Augustus]. "The Sporting World." 6 (1852–53): 133–39.

Tagged *Bell's Life in London* "a very honestly and respectably conducted weekly paper."

25. [Sidney, Samuel]. "Lost and Found in the Gold Fields." 7 (1853): 84–88.
Differentiated British and Australian advertising about gold fields. The British entries sought information about missing kin; the colonial listed jobs, services, goods, and leisure activities.

26. [Lang, John]. "Starting a Paper in India." 7 (1853): 94–96.
Outlined how to begin a paper in Meerut. A press, usually hard to find, and type cost 2,500 pounds. An owner needed ten able compositors. Those of Portuguese paternity were very capable but allegedly unreliable, lazy, and alcoholic. Essential staff members were an editor-writer, two pressmen, and five distributors. Subscriptions by East India Company personnel should finance everything.

27. [Dickens, Charles and Henry Morley]. "H.W." 7 (1853): 145–49.
Fussed about editing *Household Words*. The "Voluntary Correspondent," habitually without patience, study, and punctuality, sent sloppy manuscripts penned in a style that did not match the serial. Correspondents further disturbed the editor by posting articles to his home and visiting his office, though women were less belligerent than men. In 1852 *Household Words* received 900 submissions of which it printed 11 after rewrites. Notwithstanding this circumstance, five current staff started as "Voluntary" authors.

28. [Dickens, Charles]. "The Spirit Business." 7 (1853): 217–20.
Assayed New York's *Spiritual Telegraph*.

29. [Morley, Henry]. "Country News." 7 (1853): 426–30.
Purported recipient of the wrong country paper conceded that the arrival, like his regular one, had local news and advertisements for medical remedies.

30. [Dodd, George and Henry Morley]. "Accommodation for Quidnuncs." 8 (1853–54): 88–91.
Continued 3: 80 on the subject of penny newsrooms. Paris had 400 successful facilities, most with numerous periodicals and good furnishings. London was slow to recognize the benefits of reading rooms, but a few were open. One in Cheapside put all the London dailies, morning and evening, and the "leading weekly" neatly on stands and retained the last for six months. This newsroom also displayed most country gazettes and a few foreign, but readers had to request quarterlies and monthlies. Although it was attached to a pub, it attracted the "respectable." Another newsroom, furnished like a home, had dailies, weeklies, a few magazines, and half the French tribunes. A third place had available (6 a.m. – 3 p.m.) all the morning and evening dailies, 32 weeklies, 32 country, 12 Scottish and Irish, and 12 foreign papers as well as 16 quarterlies and magazines. This site kept dailies framed on walls, other papers on tables, and quarterlies and magazines on boards. Back copies were stored but not filed systematically. Because its original Oxford Street space was small and hot, the newsroom had recently relocated to Holborn. Unlike Edinburgh newsrooms, London locales did not provide refreshments for workers as they read. News vendors also allowed readers to scan their papers for a penny.

31. [Lowe, James]. "The *Deseret News*." 8 (1853–54): 252–55.
Described the *Deseret News* as a small, single page journal of good print and paper, one with stories on Mormon governance, letters, poems, and advertising.

32. [Martineau, Harriet]. "Mr. Wiseman in Print." 8 (1853–54): 339–43.
Identified Mr. Wiseman as a man invited by an editor, who heard him speak, to write a leader.

Visited a morning daily about 10 p.m. when "the sense of wit, energy, and toil on the part of many to supply the matter of one day's newspaper" was awesome. The editor, surrounded by manuscripts, letters, proof-sheets, and new books, still would have to deal, at 5 a.m. the next morning, with early dispatches and late telegrams. The subeditors were busy culling material from the country press, though "everything of importance" was sent directly by local correspondents. The first round of parliamentary reporters, those assigned shifts of 45, then 30 minutes, were well into the four hours it would take to transcribe notes. The last group, with a 20-minute turn, had to condense speeches given after 3 a.m. so that the paper could make the early train. The music reviewer and law reporter had a separate pleasanter room, which like most others was healthy and airy. About 50 compositors were already dealing with births and marriages and trials. Proofreaders were reading aloud to each other. Like the rest of the staff, they had a "fresh and cheerful appearance."

33. [Jerrold, W. B.]. "Broken Language." 9 (1854): 331–32.
Spotted Gallic-English "even in the important journals of France," as the *Journal des Débats* and *Siècle*.

34. [Dickens, Charles]. "To Working Men." 10 (1854–55): 169–70.
Recommended *The Times* to working-class readers because it took seriously its "responsibility" to speak on social concerns.

35. [Sala, George Augustus]. "Numbers of People." 10 (1854–55): 221–28.
Borrowed from the 1851 census, data on journalism: 1,320 editors and writers, 207 newspaper reporters and shorthand writers (v. 5,444 artists).

36. [Morley, Henry]. "Mr. Whittlestick." 10 (1854–55): 287–88.
Pegged H. C. Willeston as the author of a series, "California Characters and Mining Sketches," for San Francisco's newspaper, the *Wide West*. The columns discussed newsboys (not in this article).

37. [Costello, Dudley]. "Misprints." 11 (1855): 232–38.
Excerpted some errors in British and Continental journals.

38. [Morley, Henry]. "Latest Intelligence from Spirits." 11 (1855): 513–15.
Ridiculed the *New England Spiritualist* for the "nonsense" and "foolery" in its advertising of elixirs, Rappers, and clairvoyants and for printing correspondence validating such inserts.

39. [Morley, Henry]. "Our Wicked Mis-Statements." 13 (1856): 13–19.
Responded to Harriet Martineau's pamphlet (published by the Lancashire Association to Prevent the Fencing of Machinery) that resorted to "personal invective" in charging *Household Words* with inaccuracy and advising its editor, Charles Dickens, to transfer his idealism from his serial to his fiction or to study all sides before being a journalistic "social reformer." (Dickens published an article on 26 July that dealt with a report not circulated until 7 August 1855.)

40. [Delepierre, Joseph Octave]. "The *Domestic Mercury*." 13 (1856): 445–48.
Summarized the titled gazette, which surfaced on 19 December 1679 as the *Mercurius Domesticus; or Newes from both City and Country*. "Published to prevent false reports," it nonetheless was mistaken

about the death of Nell Gwynn and the Popish Plot. The paper printed gossip, crime news, promises of reward for information about criminals, and advertisements for sales of or lost and found items.

41. [Fawkner, John Pascoe]. "A Colonial Patriot." 14 (1856): 130.

Cited a Melbourne resident who imported "six newspapers, six magazines, three quarterlies, and three annuals" in 1842–43, not unusual in pre-gold rush days in Victoria when colonists subscribed to many British newspapers and periodicals. Aside that the local *Argus* praised a column, "Old and New Squatters," in *Household Words* (December, 1855).

42. [Dodd, George]. "John Houghton's Wisdom." 14 (1856): 453–56.

Recognized Houghton, an apothecary, who edited and published *Collection for Improvement of Husbandry and Trade*, "a newspaper of universal knowledge." The serial circulated as a monthly from September 1681 until it suspended operation, 1685–92; was a two-page biweekly, 1692–93, then a penny weekly, 1693–1703. Its early motifs were "husbandry, trade, productive industry, or political economy," but as a weekly it specified commodity markets, shipping, and share prices. Houghton showed "frankness and straightforwardness" as an editor and foresight as a publisher by pioneering in London the "commercial newsroom," a site where all the information he had amassed was in reference books. *See* 14: 490.

43. [Dodd, George]. "John Houghton's Advertisements." 14 (1856): 490–93.

Amended 14: 453 by focusing on Houghton's addition, in his paper's second year, of advertisements for books, lotteries, goods, services, and matrimonial opportunities. The listings he wrote displayed "brevity, clearness, and precision of outline," not the "roundabout verbiage and hollow quackery" of their peers, and were a good source for writing social history.

44. [Dickens, Charles]. "Curious Misprint in the *Edinburgh Review*." 16 (1857): 145–48.

Rejected the idea of James Fitzjames Stephen in the *Edinburgh* (July 1857) that novelists should amuse and avoid "social and political questions" but acknowledged that the *Edinburgh* rendered "great services…to good literature and good government" and that Dickens benefited from the "loving affection" of Francis Jeffrey and "the friendship" of Sydney Smith.

45. [Capper, John]. "A Very Black Act." 16 (1857): 293–94.

Capper, who claimed to be the armed editor of a local paper in "one of the disturbed districts" of India, raged against restriction of the press in India. He planned to pen reactions to the "Mutiny" in hope that they would be as useful as those of William Howard Russell's in *The Times*. But the press was "gagged" because Calcutta newspapers, both Bengali and Persian, sowed treason. Local gazettes could not criticize the British government even by copying leaders from *The Times* or the *Daily News*. Aside that an editor in India had responsibility for finance, printing, answering correspondence, and gathering gossip.

46. [Lang, John]. "Wanderings in India." 17 (1857–58): 112–18.

Part of a series denounced Indian editors for deriding British rule.

47. [Ede, Joseph]. "Old Times and New Times." 17 (1857–58): 251–54.

Traversed *The Times* from 1 January 1785. The first issue had four small folio pages with foreign and court news, a law report, and a letter on newspapers. John Walter's goal was to serve 'something suitable to every palate.' In 1788 he changed the paper's name but not his aim. *The Times* soon had more advertising and shorter parliamentary reports. Published early (6 a.m.) using "Logography," 'a work of inconceivable difficulty,' it cost a halfpenny less than its competitors. By 1858 the paper was full of advertising on theatres and books, clothes and servants, individuals and commerce, but nothing that evidenced the "mysterious and sentimental" elements of the age.

48. [Collins, Wilkie]. "The Unknown Public." 18 (1858): 217–22.
This famous article separated known and unknown readers. Known readers were easy to classify. Those who read for religion scanned books, newspapers, and reviews; for information, essays; for amusement, material from libraries and railroad book stalls; for news, newspapers. However, the majority of readers were not book-club and library members, buyers and borrowers of newspapers or reviews, but were scanners of "penny-novel Journals."

Explored five of these journals, with lives of three months to 15 years, the largest selling 500,000 and the rest 4.5 million together. With three readers for each copy, they reached a huge but unknown audience. "Answers to Correspondents" bared writers of "[i]nconceivably dense ignorance, inconceivably petty malice, and inconceivably complacent vanity" and generated some serious, many stock responses. Other pages contained serials and short tales that were banal, strong on melodrama but not wicked. Scraps, such as poems, anecdotes, and woodcuts, came from outside sources. Journals serving neophyte readers should print quality so that they could learn discrimination and thus appreciate the next generation of good writers. "The largest audience for periodical literature, in this age of periodicals, must obey the universal law of progress, and must, sooner or later, learn to discriminate." *See Nineteenth Century* 9: 145 and 13: 279.

49. [Dixon, Edmund Saul]. "Literary Small Change." 18 (1858): 404–08.
Premised that almanacs were once the "major literary food of fifteen million Frenchmen." After 1855 *Les Cinq Centimes Illustrés*, a serial akin to the *Penny Magazine*, and many short-lived rivals replaced the almanacs. The most successful were the *Journal pour Tous*, costing two sous, and the *Journal du Dimanche*, one sou. Both reprinted British and American novels for those accustomed to feuilletons "at the foot of newspapers." Other periodicals, whose audiences were people of income, appealed to particular constituencies. The *Ami du Sciences*, conducted by Victor Meunier, charged ten francs for an annual subscription in Paris, 12 in departments, and 14 in England and was "well worth taking." The French also favored illustrated magazines, such as the *Univers Illustré*; comics, such as the *Petit Journal pour Rire*; fashion, such as the *Toilette de Paris*; music, such as the *Album des Concerts*; and theatre, such as the *Théâtre Contemporain Illustré*. Unlike the British, cheap French magazines had no letters. "The French are too sensible of ridicule, if not of shame, to commit themselves by such exposures," so they filled empty space with a rebus.

50. [Collins, Wilkie]. "Douglas Jerrold." 19 (1858–59): 217–22.
Highlighted Jerrold's career as a printer, then an essayist in *Blackwood's Magazine* and *Punch* for which he wrote with wit and originality while editing the affiliated *Illuminated Magazine*. He was also "most honourably and profitably" associated with newspapers, notably *Douglas Jerrold's Weekly Newspaper*, where his leaders demonstrated "signal ability." When that gazette ceased because of "defects of management," he went to *Lloyd's Weekly Newspaper*, 1852–57. "Jerrold conducted the paper with such extraordinary success as is rare in the history of journalism." His alleged "bitterness" was really honesty tempered by humor.

51. [Collins, Wilkie]. "A Breach of British Privilege." 19 (1858–59): 361–64.
Satire of new theatre seating was cast as a letter from John Bull, who refused to subscribe to *Household Words* because it was "not English to the back-bone."

Howitt's Journal, 1847–1848

Howitt's Journal, launched by Mary and William Howitt, soon engaged in a journalistic war with their former partner and then competitor, John Saunders.

1. [Howitt, William and Mary]. "Address to Their Friends and Readers." 1 (1847): 1–2.

Planned *Howitt's* for "entertainment" and "advancement."

2. [Howitt, William]. "Author versus Critic." 1 (1847): 109–12.

Loathed anonymous criticism because it was cowardly, leaving a critic's victim no means to retaliate. Editors of weeklies, such as the *Athenaeum*, should not hire "nameless and irresponsible agents of critical injustice."

3. "George Sand." 1 (1847): 128–30.

Divulged that Sand co-owned the *Revue Indépendante* and wrote regularly for the *Monde*.

4. Charles, C. M. "The Movements of the Italian Refugees." 1 (1847): after 154.

Bruited that Italians living in Britain published the *Eco di Savonarola*, a cheap but "well got up" organ for Italian "Reformed Christians."

5. "William Lovett." 1 (1847): 254–57.

Acclaimed Lovett, the publisher of *Howitt's* and earlier of the *Poor Man's Guardian*. He set up a "victim's fund" for those prosecuted for selling the unstamped paper, not unusual in the 1830s when government jailed about 500 people for opposing the stamp duty.

6. "Félicité [de] Lamennais." 2 (1847): 18–22.

Probed Lamennais' work for the *Avenir* in association with Count C. de Montalembert and J. B. Lacordaire. After the pope suppressed the *Avenir*, Lammenais became "a principal writer" and coconductor, with George Sand, of the *Revue Indépendante*.

7. Smiles, Dr. [?Samuel]. "Colonel Thompson." 2 (1847): 66–68.

Biography of Perronet Thompson verified that he penned for the *Westminster Review*, "set on foot" by Jeremy Bentham and John Bowring. In 1829 Thompson joined Bowring as co-owner and authored three or four articles for each number until the *Review* changed hands in 1836.

8. [?Howitt, William]. "To the Readers of the *People's* and *Howitt's* Journals." 2 (1847): 143–44; letters, 175–76, 191–92.

Chronicled a dispute between William Howitt and John Saunders when they were partners in the *People's Journal*. Saunders originally paid 100 pounds for the *Apprentice*, which he recaptioned the

People's Journal. Howitt invested 800 pounds in the press and other machinery and lost even more before he withdrew because Saunders, the editor and manager, lied about the paper's circulation. When Howitt took the equipment for his new *Journal*, Saunders appealed to editors of London and "influential" local heralds for capital, but they were unresponsive. *See* 3: 15, 224, 365.

9. Reynolds, George. "A Day and Night at the General Post Office." 3 (1848): 10–12, 26–28, 36–39.

Lectured that processing newspapers for mailing was slow work because they were bulky and numerous, about 40,000 arriving at 6 p.m. daily in the London post office.

10. [Howitt, William and Mary]. "The Editors' Address to Their Friends and Readers." 3 (1848): 15–16.

Revisited the dispute with John Saunders (2: 143) and stressed *Howitt's* goal to amuse. *See* 3: 224, 365.

11. "Sale of the *People's Journal*." 3 (1848): 224.

Insisted that the circulation of the *People's Journal* peaked at 8,000, never reaching the 20,000 it needed to survive. *See* 2: 143; 3: 15, 365.

12. Barmby, [John] Goodwin. "Letters from Paris. No. 3: The Placards of Paris." 3 (1848): 247–48.

Testified that the 1848 French Revolution produced "numberless" newspapers.

13. "Excellent Use for Newspapers When Read." 3 (1848): 256; letters, 288.

Proposed donating newspapers to the libraries, mechanics' institutes, and coffeehouses frequented by workers in order to keep them informed and to help them develop a habit of reading.

14. [Howitt, William]. "Address to the Readers of *Howitt's Journal*." 3 (1848): 365.

Admitted that the controversy with John Saunders (2: 143, 3: 15, 224) cost Howitt money and literary reputation. Aside that Harriet Martineau supported Saunders.

15. "Frederick Douglas's [*sic*] Newspaper." 3 (1848): 366.

Grieved that the *North Star* published by Douglass was experiencing financial difficulties because it was "conducted with rare ability."

The Leisure Hour, 1852–1900

Meant for enjoyment after work, *Leisure Hour*, affiliated with the Religious Tract Society, offered a mix of snippets and treatises on the press. It celebrated newspaper history, reporters, newsboys, and the "Great London Dailies" as seen by H. W. Massingham.

1. "A Few Remarkable Advertisements." 1 (1852): 44–45.
Excerpted advertisements from seventeenth- and eighteenth-century English and Scottish newspapers.

2. "A Visit to *The Times* Office." 1 (1852): 289–92.
Guaranteed that printing from "type in a vertical position," an important innovation in newspaper technology, allowed *The Times* to produce 10,000 copies per hour. The paper paid for a sick fund for employees and government taxes of 16,000 pounds on paper, 70,000 on stamps, and 20,000 on advertising that excluded the "disgusting quack notices" found in most local and some metro tribunes. *The Times* without advertising, the *Evening Mail*, went to the country. Leaders, though written under pressure of time, evinced "great research and extensive acquaintance with men and manners."

3. "Shades of the Departed: Joseph Addison." 1 (1852): 449–53.
Guessed that the *Tatler* and *Spectator* were well received.

4. "Refreshment and Reading-Rooms for the Working Classes." 1 (1852): 526–27.
Petitioned for reading rooms with snacks and a "liberal supply of newspapers" for workers.

5. "'Our Own Correspondent.'" 1 (1852): 661–62.
Took from Michael Homan, in Italy as "a correspondent for a leading morning journal," examples of reporters who were "ingenious, though sometimes unscrupulous" in news gathering.

6. "Following a Speaker." 2 (1853): 20–24.
Centered on parliamentary reporting from Edward Cave's *Gentleman's Magazine*, originally a monthly abstract of newspapers. After 1735 paragraphs on parliamentary speeches, with speakers' names or not, increased sales "immensely." Soon newspapers had reporters in Commons, the most famous, William Woodfall. In 1783 James Perry, then editor of the *Gazetteer*, commenced the practice of having reporters in Parliament every night. By 1853 there were about 70 who took shorthand in 45-minute shifts, returning to their offices to transcribe their notes.

7. "The Australian File." 2 (1853): 340–43.
Limned Melbourne's *Argus*, a daily with 56 columns, of which 43 were advertisements. The *Argus* in 1853 needed paper, type, compositors, proofreaders, and "strong fellows to turn the machines."

8. "A Reporter on the British Senate: The House of Commons." 2 (1853): 715–19; "The House of Lords," 746–48; "Pencillings in Both Houses," 764–66; "Telegraphing the Debates," 3 (1854): 586–89; "Another Session," 5 (1856): 182–83.
Disclosed that being a parliamentary reporter for a daily supplemented the income of a literary man. These reporters, some "authors of long standing" or "contributors to reviews and periodicals," were joined by law students and "editors of acknowledged ability," once reporters. They worked in relays in the galleries where Charles Dod, long reporter for *The Times*, was now their superintendent. Only those who knew shorthand took down everything. To condense a speaker's "verbiage" required "judgment" and "knowledge of the subject" and the ability to write under pressure in a hand a compositor could read. Good local reporters often failed when they moved to Parliament because they lacked these skills. Country journals should rely on short, readable telegraphic abstracts to complement the texts of their London correspondents.

9. "The Mails to the Antipodes." 2 (1853): 813–15.
Imagined that the reason the Melbourne post office handled so many newspapers from Britain (206,674 copies in 1851) was because they cost nothing to mail.

10. "Robert Nicoll." 2 (1853): 822–24, 837–39.
Admired Nicoll, editor of the *Leeds Times*, because he saw the newspaper as a venue to displace prejudice. Paid 100 pounds per year to edit, he supplemented his income by penning leaders for a Sheffield gazette.

11. "Newspapers from China." 3 (1854): 166–69.
Profiled the *North China Herald*, a Shanghai weekly that was English in format and advertising but plagiarized the *Peking Gazette* on crime, society, and the weather.

12. "Hints to Our Contributors." 3 (1854): 316–18.
Mandated that, in justice to the editor and compositor, manuscripts submitted to *Leisure Hour* should be written in black ink on one side of cream paper and checked for accuracy of quotations and names. All authors should include their addresses, and women should remember to sign their work.

13. "A London Railway Station." 3 (1854): 412–14.
Vividly painted the newsboy, with "his shrill treble."

14. "Edgar Allan Poe." 3 (1854): 427–29.
Judged that the only "creditable period" of Poe's journalistic career was at *Graham's Magazine*.

15. "The Newspaper Press of Victoria." 3 (1854): 606–07.
Borrowed from the *Literary Gazette*, which quoted a book by W. Westgarth, that Victoria acquired its first newspaper in 1838. The manuscript *Settlement* had local news and advertisements. When a printing press arrived from Britain, the paper was reborn as the *Melbourne Advertiser*. By 1840 Victoria had biweeklies, the *Port Phillip Gazette* and *Port Phillip Herald*. Melbourne in 1849 had three dailies for its population of 8,000. The *Argus*, which was akin to *The Times*, commenced in 1848. At first a biweekly of 625 copies with advertising revenue of 13 pounds and expenses of 30 pounds, by 1849 it was a daily and by 1851 printed 1,500 copies with advertising revenue of 80

pounds per week. During the gold rush, it went from 3,500–4,000 copies to 10,500 as advertising income soared to 800 pounds. In 1854 it was better than the *Sydney Morning Herald*, "a long established daily." Also profiting from the gold rush was the *Daily News*, a merger of the *Melbourne Advertiser* and *Port Phillip Patriot*. A "fast printing machine" that produced 1,000 pages per hour and gold advertising that generated 250–300 pounds soon raised circulation from 600 to 1,500.

16. "The Philadelphia Printer." 3 (1854): 772–75, 788–91.
Mentioned Benjamin Franklin's articles as "Busy Body" and his roles as newspaper publisher and editor, one who decried "personal abuse" in the press.

17. "Seventeen Hundred and Fifty-Five." 4 (1855): 238–40.
Probed an unnamed eighteenth-century news magazine that publicized international affairs and domestic society, births and deaths, the law courts, lottery, and literature.

18. "The Queen of a Literary Coterie." 4 (1855): 357–60, 373–75, 396–97.
Crowned Countess Marguerite Blessington for her essays in the *New Monthly Magazine*, her society columns in the *Daily News* that paid 500 pounds for six months, and her editing of annuals in the 1830s and 1840s for which she usually received 2,000 pounds per year.

19. "The Life and Poetry of D. M. Moir." 5 (1856): 90–93, 107–10.
Honored David M. Moir, a poet and physician who first penned for the *Scots Magazine* and then as Delta for *Blackwood's Magazine*.

20. "Cheapest News." 7 (1858): 477–79.
Featured the penny newspaper hawked by the newsboy who "pushes and puffs, and bawls and declaims incessantly" until people bought his sheet. He might be young or old, crippled, or an unemployed craftsman. His paper was not 'trash,' contrary to the belief of supporters of a stamp, because it contained telegraphic news and investigative reporting. Most penny papers had huge circulations that allowed them to raise the price of advertisements. The cheaper weekly halfpenny parish gazettes offered abstracts of Parliament, neighborhood news and advertising, and a "well-digested leader or two" with a good moral tone. The country papers got "wet" sheets from London on Friday with a blank page to add their district's happenings.

21. "The Day of a Newspaper Editor." 7 (1858): 636–38.
Outlined editorial qualifications to run a daily: "clear-sightedness, firmness, impartiality, and a love of truth," "great judgment," "conscientiousness," "solid acquirements," and "taste." The editor's day consisted of meetings and review of submissions, whether foreign correspondence, prose, or poetry, the last often accompanied by the scented letters of women. The subeditor scanned the country heralds for cuttings and ideas for leaders and maintained contacts with the paper's political party.

22. "The Atlantic Telegraph." 7 (1858): 695–99, 710–14, 726–30.
Predicted that telegraphy would whet the "appetite for news," take space from Parliament, letters, and advertising, and kill the "word-grinding fraternity" of penny-a-liners.

23. "Edinburgh about Sixty Years Ago." 8 (1859): 43–47.
This section of a series emphasized that the *Edinburgh Review* "created a new political and literary era" thanks to the "extraordinary ability" and command of language of founders Francis Jeffrey, Sydney Smith, and Henry Brougham. Success bred the opposition *Quarterly Review*.

24. "Inside the Post Office." 8 (1859): 429–31.
Blared that in 1858 the post office delivered 71 million newspapers in the kingdom. Sorting this volume sometimes involved guesswork about addresses, much to the chagrin of country subscribers who missed an issue or received the wrong journal.

25. "A Parisian Newspaper Office." 8 (1859): 783–84.
Observed that most Paris newspapers, unlike London dailies, had spacious offices and that French editors were neater but less powerful than British. In London, anonymity made the editor a tsar ready to censure the government. Paris journals, like London evening ones, were a double sheet. The *Moniteur* had access to official information, so others copied from it. Most concentrated on commerce and feuilletons instead of acting like a "safety-valve" for discontent with government.

26. "American Copyright." 9 (1860): 85–86.
Revealed that *Blackwood's Magazine* and other British periodicals got a United States copyright by recruiting an American to write an article.

27. "*The Times'* Reporter in India." 9 (1860): 172–74.
Grumbled that salaries were low in the newspaper "profession." The best field for "Reporters" in 1860 was foreign correspondence, as exemplified by William Howard Russell, lately dispatched to India.

28. "Reporters and Shorthand Writers." 9 (1860): 291–94.
Differentiated between shorthand writers who took down speeches verbatim and reporters only penning for the press who condensed. Reporters had a variety of assignments, but specialization was growing.

29. "Smith's Express Newspaper Office." 9 (1860): 664–67.
Inspected the W. H. Smith office where newspapers were delivered for outbound sales. *The Times* arrived in parts, advertising and supplements first, then news. Although the British press was "free and cheap," satisfying the demand for news required better printing and transport.

30. [Jerdan, William]. "Men I Have Known: Gifford of the *Quarterly*." 10 (1861): 165–66.
Alluded to William Gifford's connections with the "brilliant short-lived *Anti-Jacobin*" and the "more stable *Quarterly Review*."

31. "Literature and the Press Sixty Years Ago." 10 (1861): 421–23.
Detailed that in 1801 Britain had nine well-capitalized but poorly staffed morning papers selling 14,000 copies; seven evening selling 12,000; 22 Sunday selling 26,000; and a few other weeklies selling 29,000. Income came from sales and advertising, but government duties kept profits modest. Local papers employed 1,500 to produce 250,000 copies per week. There were 47 monthlies, all committed to anonymity.

32. "Count Cavour." 10 (1861): 518–22.
Labeled Camillo di Cavour a journalist in the 1840s because he wrote for a French periodical and cofounded the *Risorgimento* in 1847.

33. "Curiosities of Advertising." 10 (1861): 797–800.
Chastised newspapers that were largely advertisements supplemented by trash or that resorted to gimmicks to sell papers, as when the *New York Ledger* took space in rival gazettes for a chapter of a book but retained the rest of the text for the *Ledger*.

34. "The Penny-a-Liner." 11 (1862): 90–92.
Rooted penny-a-lining, "a peculiar vocation" requiring no special training, in the "endless craving for news." While a staff reporter covered important stories, the pushy liner scribbled wordy if less worthy articles on flimsy dispatched to at least six papers because length and simultaneous publication were key to a liner's income.

35. "Sensational Advertising." 11 (1862): 102–03.
Posited that a variety of advertising styles, from the erudite to the shocking, flavored a newspaper.

36. "The Newspaper Printing Office." 12 (1863): 76–78.
Delineated the process of producing a weekly of 48 columns, each six inches. On Tuesday, the editor read dailies and letters, wrote the leader, and assigned reporters while the subeditor scissored other tribunes. On Wednesday and Thursday, both read reporters' and reviewers' submissions and approved the advertising. On Friday, the paper was finalized unless a calamity occurred. A weekly lived on advertising more than sales, but they were crucial for the reputation that would lure advertisers.

37. "London Coffee-Houses, Past and Present." 12 (1863): 183–88.
Opined that coffeehouses lost their status as news sources as the press grew in the eighteenth century. In 1863 they subscribed to periodicals, dividing them into four-page packets so that each patron had something to read.

38. [Jerdan, William]. "Men I Have Known: Perry of the *Morning Chronicle*." 12 (1863): 206–07.
Memorialized James Perry, owner and editor of the *Morning Chronicle*. In his day "popular and influential journals" were the voices of a political party in contrast to *The Times*, "the greatest journal" in 1863, which voiced public opinion.

39. [Jerdan, William]. "Men I Have Known: Robert Southey." 12 (1863): 410–13.
Noted that Southey earned 400 pounds for four reviews in the *Quarterly Review* but other journals paid less.

40. "'98 and Its *Times*." 12 (1863): 511–12.
Concluded from *The Times* of 3 October 1798 that newspaper advertising was not important but that news of politics, the law courts, the Crown, and crime, interspersed by witty paragraphs, counted.

41. "*The Times* Newspaper." 12 (1863): 541–43.

Lifted from *The Times* news of current issues and of books by Edmund About and A. W. Kinglake. About dubbed the paper 'the King of journals.' Kinglake noticed its political sway, its 'enterprise' in news gathering, and its readiness to hire 'able writers' who confirmed and shaped opinion.

42. "A French Newspaper Office." 12 (1863): 675–77.

Compared London and Paris newspapers. The French had fewer advertisements and reports on the law courts, crime, and accidents because they had no penny-a-liners. News agencies collected information from the provinces and the world, then created a lithograph of what government would approve. Because French journalists signed their work, they were consistent and famous. They were sometimes powerful, as in 1830 and 1848, and often petty, fighting duels to save face. Their offices were more orderly than British ones because everything was outsourced, even advertising. The French produced 15,000–20,000 copies per hour using American presses. Women prepared issues for mailing to subscribers, as the French had no newsboys or companies for distribution.

43. [Jerdan, William]. "Men I Have Known: Archdeacon Robert Nares." 12 (1863): 727–28.

Unmasked Nares as a cofounder of the *British Critic* in 1793 and long its "principal editor."

44. "Duck Lane Working Men's Club." 13 (1864): 68–70.

Headlined a London club where workers could peruse newspapers and magazines except on Sunday when other material was available.

45. "The American Newspaper Press. I. The Northern States." 13 (1864): 477–80; "II. The Southern States," 493–95.

Trumpeted that the American press was more influential than the European because in the United States everyone read and every interest had a newspaper. Although many gazettes were short-lived, their prevalence prevented one from dominating. Secular and religious serials had big circulations in big cities. Town tribunes were cheap to run, and "honest and high-principaled" editors were the most honored citizens where local governments changed frequently. Exceptions were the California editors whose failure as prospectors led them to start newspapers.

Northerners liked cheap magazines with fiction (examples cited in this article). Among the quality magazines were the *Atlantic Monthly*, with original matter, and *Harper's Monthly*, which pirated from the British. The best quarterly was the *North American Review*. The penchant for haste favored magazines and especially newspapers. Major ones, as New York's *Herald*, *Times*, and *Tribune*, had "capable" reporters and foreign correspondents, some knowledgeable and some mere translators of foreign papers. American correspondents were "less scholarly and more personal" than their British peers.

In the South, the *Southern Literary Messenger* was "ably conducted." Newspapers in New Orleans, Richmond, and Charleston paralleled those in the North. "The profession of journalism" paid better because the South depended on expensive subscriptions; the North, on advertising. The author related experiences while working for the Richmond *Inquirer* when Northern printers and compositors left at the inception of the Civil War, which also brought shortages of paper and ink.

46. "Boston Celebrities." 13 (1864): 540–43.

Included as eminent Bostonians Oliver Wendell Holmes, "an originator" of the *Atlantic Monthly*; J. R. Lowell, its editor and a "frequent contributor"; George Field, a writer and junior partner in the serial's publishing firm; and Benjamin Shillaber, an editor of "the *Boston Saturday Gazette*, the oldest and the best literary journal of Boston."

47. [Jerdan, William]. "Men I Have Known: John Britton." 13 (1864): 698–701.
Portrayed Britton as a "self-made man" who penned criticism for one magazine and humor for another.

48. "William Makepeace Thackeray." 13 (1864): 774–80, 790–91.
Glanced at Thackeray's work as a correspondent for British and American papers and his articles in *Fraser's* and other magazines.

49. "Bishop Monrad." 13 (1864): 807–09.
Unveiled Ditler G. Monrad, a Dane who edited newspapers (*Foedrelandet* in 1841 and *Dansk Folkeblad* in 1843), before he became a bishop.

50. "The *Peking Gazette*." 14 (1865): 119–22.
Depicted the *Peking Gazette* as 9x4 inches with 15–20 single-sided printed pages and a decorated title page. The paper circulated daily to officials and on alternate days to others who paid two pence for an expurgated version. News of the court and officials was common; language was sometimes "bold," as when censors exposed local misgovernment. The Chinese invented printing but may not have used moveable type. Footnote identified author as the "late editor of the *North China Herald*, Shanghai."

51. "The Royal Literary Fund." 14 (1865): 315–19.
Relayed that in 1864 the titled fund awarded seven grants, totaling 280 pounds, to help literary periodical writers in need.

52. "Hints on Legal Topics: Copyright, II." 14 (1865): 788–91.
Explained that serials, except newspapers, were subject to the Copyright Act, 1842. If a proprietor commissioned an author, the owner held the copyright for 28 years. Legal cases arising from the statute involved several periodicals, among them *Welcome Guest* and the *London Journal*.

53. "John Leech." 14 (1865): 791–94.
Biography with a picture of Leech stressed that he was "the leading artist" of *Punch* within a year of its birth in 1841.

54. Macgregor, John, Esq. "Ragamuffins." 15 (1866): 455–60.
Separated decent workers, such as "busy" newsboys, from beggars and tricksters. The British should emulate Philadelphia, which had organized homes to shelter and educate newsboys.

55. "The Arts of Advertising." 15 (1866): 635–37.
Set off earlier newspapers, which underscored politics and business, and gazettes in 1866, which existed on advertising because competition forced dailies to lower prices. As advertisements proliferated, readers skimmed them, overlooking the needy and forcing sellers to improve style or eschew all but local papers.

56. "Recollections of Edinburgh Journalism." 16 (1867): 85–88.

Dated Edinburgh journalism from the 1661 *Caledonian Mercury* and the 1680 official *Edinburgh Gazette*, revived in 1699 by James Donaldson without its former political influence. Alexander Donaldson's eighteenth-century biweekly *Edinburgh Advertiser* pre-dated *The Times*. When his printers produced a "seditious" handbill in 1794, he fired them. The *Advertiser's* competitors were the *Mercury* and *Edinburgh Evening Courant*, a triweekly of David Ramsay, Esq., both in 1867 "highly respectable and well conducted." The *Mercury*, resuscitated in 1720 as a six-page paper "on fine paper and in very bold type," sold for three and a half pence. The original *Courant*, 1705–10, preceded Daniel Defoe's in 1710. Charles Maclaren and William Ritchie later launched the *Scotsman*, a weekly until 1855. J. R. M'Culloch, the economist, was an editor, then a contributor. In 1840 the *Witness* began with Hugh Miller, a self-taught man, as editor.

57. "Isaac Taylor." 16 (1867): 215–20, 235–39.

Commemorated Taylor, who penned after 1818 for the *Eclectic Review*, edited by his friend Josiah Conder. Taylor's sister Anne was an author for the *Youth's Magazine*.

58. "The Rascal Column in the Newspaper." 16 (1867): 277–80.

Deplored advertisements for patent medicines and easy loans intended to trick or trap readers.

59. "Thomas Hood." 16 (1867): 344–38.

Spelled out Hood's editorial career. When *London Magazine* editor John Scott died in a duel, the serial passed to friends of Hood's father. They hired him as subeditor, and he also wrote many articles, 1821–23. In 1840 he edited the *New Monthly Magazine* for 300 pounds per year and in 1844 started *Hood's Magazine*, a victim of mismanagement while he was ill.

60. "Errors of the Press." 16 (1867): 388–90.

Caught journalistic errors in spelling and grammar due to printers' misunderstandings of handwriting.

61. "Ephemerae of the Press." 16 (1867): 800.

Regretted that recent attempts to establish London dailies had failed. After the stamp duty ended, 23 surfaced; in 1866 there were 28. The penny press had driven out "influential party organs" in the capital and the country.

62. "Thomas Carlyle." 17 (1868): 38–42.

Cited Carlyle's essays in the *London Magazine*, 1823–24, the "short-lived" *New Edinburgh Review*, and *Fraser's Magazine* in 1840.

63. "'Our Own Correspondent.'" 17 (1868): 53–55.

Categorized as "our own," the writer or illustrator who faced danger covering conferences and wars. The correspondent had to transmit news by telegraphy but enhance it with "graphic details," so scribes should be knowledgeable about European politics, worldly, "energetic and enterprising," "fearless," good at observing people, and not too moral about getting information.

64. "Peeps Through Loopholes at Men, Manners, and Customs. II. Newspaper Magic and Modern Witchcraft." 17 (1868): 117–19; "VI. Newspaper Readings," 394–97.

Reckoned that the basis of newspaper power was cheaply conveying much information intelligently. In 1868 there were 200 metropolitan and 1,000 country gazettes. Many locals filled the blank pages of London sheets with area events and oddities. As the "thirst for news" and literacy grew, individual copies of newspapers available from faster presses and swifter railroads would replace public readings. Rural workers were learning to read from penny weeklies, and townspeople utilized reading rooms. Aside that *The Times* printed "lithographically."

65. "The Post Office." 17 (1868): 309–12.

Commented on postal newspaper distribution, primarily the sorting of weeklies on Friday because dailies went by rail.

66. Author of "Men I Have Known" [William Jerdan]. "Characteristic Letters: William Blackwood, the Publisher." 17 (1868): 757–58; "Editors of Daily Newspapers," 18 (1869): 411–14; "David Macbeth Moir," 617–19.

Thought that publishers of education, taste, and judgment, as William Blackwood, swayed opinion and helped meritorious writers. Among them was David M. Moir, the Delta of *Blackwood's Magazine*, where he was a valued and frequent contributor. However, daily newspaper editors of ability and judgment were the "real rulers" of Britain because they expressed the "national will." Good examples were Thomas Barnes of *The Times*, who excelled at leader-writing, and John Black of the *Morning Chronicle*, a hard worker undermined by the interventions of owners.

67. T., G. M., An American Consul. "The New York Newsboys." 18 (1869): 716–19.

Congratulated the newsboy, a "feature of New York life." His sales accounted for the most revenue, after advertising, of the city's leading papers, the *Herald*, *Tribune*, *Times*, and *World*. The majority of newsboys were immigrant children, although the Irish were adults. The hard lives of juveniles could train them in self-help if they did not waste money on cigars and liquor. Some worked regularly, earning a commission for every copy sold. They carried 20–40 copies on a route that finished by noon. They resumed at 3 p.m., continuing until 7 p.m. except in times of wars and elections.

68. "Reviews and 'Review Books.'" 19 (1870): 427–29.

Castigated reviews with a political or religious bias or without principles for disseminating brief literary critiques done by critics who relied on publishers' blurbs.

69. "M. Thiers." 19 (1870): 502–06.

Applauded Adolphe Thiers for his courageous and pithy editorials in the *Constitutionnel* and his cofounding of the *National*.

70. Whately, Miss E. J. "Charles Dickens." 19 (1870): 728–32.

Aired that Dickens considered editing, chiefly the *Daily News* but also the weekly *Household Words* and *All the Year Round*, as "distasteful."

71. "Newspapers and the War." 19 (1870): 774–76.
Starred higher sales by newsboys of Belgian and British journals during the Franco-Prussian War. On Sunday afternoons in Brussels, where the *Indépendance Belge* was the "leading paper," newsboys were very active. London newsboys fresh from ragged schools were out very late, except during heavy rains, peddling evening heralds, but all British gazettes profited from war news. War correspondents, dispatched by the metros and locals, proved that "[a]s usual, British gold and British pluck have triumphed" in news exclusives.

72. "An Old Newspaper; or Glimpses of England Seventy Years Ago." 20 (1871): 11–13.
Poured over the *Stamford Mercury* of 12 June 1801. Its four pages of poor paper and type, with advertising at the front and news after, cost six pence stamped. In 1871 the 28-page edition, still with news and advertising and without leaders, sold for two pence.

73. Lord, J. K., F.Z.S. "Pigeon Post." 20 (1871): 29–31.
Marginalized the use of pigeons to carry news during the Franco-Prussian War.

74. "A Thousand and One." 20 (1871): 133–34.
Title referred to the current number of *Leisure Hour*. Originally scanned by workers, it attracted other readers, so it survived on sales alone. Like periodicals generally, its taste improved commensurate with that of its audience; unlike many, it promoted "evangelical religion."

75. The Editor [James Macauley]. "First Impressions of America and Its People. XIII. American Newspapers." 20 (1871): 234–37; "XXII. Philadelphia," 535–41.
Tallied British newspapers. There were 1,450 newspapers in the kingdom of which 261 were in London. Dailies numbered 120, up from 35 in 1856; 61 sold for a penny and 34 for a halfpenny.

The United States had 5,200 newspapers, 550 dailies with 32 in New York. Many dailies had big circulations and large staffs (editorial, reporting, printing). Editors earned 25–60 dollars per week; reporters earned 20–30 dollars. Most editors maintained good moral and intellectual standards, but the *New York Herald*, which "panders" to immigrants, was not respected. Other journalism was better, as in some of Philadelphia's 200 newspapers and serials (plumbed here). The vices of the American press were personal abuse of politicians and exaggeration by and identification of journalists, who concentrated like the French more on their own wealth and power than on the reputation of their papers.

Sunday readers chose the religious press, unlike in Britain where crime was popular. The diverse ethnic press was Irish (Catholic and nationalist), German (not very good), Scandinavian, Spanish, Italian, Welsh, Scottish, and Chinese.

The United States also had periodicals for every religion and interest, such as farming, music, temperance, and women's rights. There were a few literary magazines whose audiences also perused British reviews.

76. "Sir William Thomson, F.R.S., D.C.L." 20 (1871): 532–35.
Recalled that Thomson edited the *Cambridge (and Dublin) Mathematical Journal* in 1845 and published in the *Quarterly Mathematical Journal*. Aside that in August 1858, people could read the news on the same day in Europe and the United States thanks to a momentary transatlantic cable.

77. "What's the News?" 20 (1871): 717–20.
Realized that timely news was critical for "Turfites" and "stock-jobbers." Telegraphy was vital, whether Reuters' abstracts or Press Association paragraphs of London papers sent to locals, but other ways to get news were available. War could not interrupt transmissions, as *The Times* return to pigeons during the Franco-Prussian War proved.

78. Timbs, John. "Thirty Years of the Reign of Victoria: Personal Recollections." 21 (1872): 100–04, 157–60, 293–95, 396–400, 549–52, 621–23, 821–23.
Timbs reminisced about his career in journalism with the *Mirror of Literature, Amusement, and Instruction*, the "earliest of cheap periodicals presenting any approach to a literary character"; the *Saturday Magazine*, which was livelier than the *Penny Magazine*; *Chambers's Journal*; the *Illustrated London News*, which stimulated the thirst for illustrated news; and the "*Literary World*, a weekly sheet with fine illustrations."

Revisited the youth of *Punch* and its predecessor, "*Cosmorama*, a sort of journal of fashion." Douglas Jerrold penned "his most popular works" for *Punch*. Tom Taylor, the art critic, contributed to the *Illuminated Magazine* before joining *Punch*. Editor Mark Lemon, a man of "judgment," "method," and "sympathy," kept *Punch* inoffensive, the secret of its success.

Raced through newspaper history from the *acta diurna* and Venetian gazettes to Roger L'Estrange and illustrations. Highlighted by name numerous newspaper journalists and periodical contributors, among them James Silk Buckingham, who started the *Athenaeum*. Albert Smith, who wrote for *Blackwood's Magazine* and *Punch* and was a theatre critic for the *Illustrated London News*, represented the range of many contributors.

79. "The Walter Printing Press." 21 (1872): 237–40.
Quoted the *Scotsman* on the newest *Times* printing press.

80. ?D[ennis], J[ohn]. "Reminiscences of Professor Wilson." 21 (1872): 693–95.
Rated John Wilson's "Noctes Ambrosianae" in *Blackwood's Magazine* the most popular magazine series to date.

81. "Dr. Norman Macleod." 21 (1872): 727–30.
Recognized Macleod as editor of the *Edinburgh Christian Magazine* for ten years but ignored his tenure at *Good Words*.

82. "The Post-Office Report." 21 (1872): 730–32.
Registered that the newspaper press sent 70,000 telegrams in 1871.

83. ?D[ennis], J[ohn]. "Recollections of Jeffrey and Cockburn." 22 (1873): 77–80.
Glided over the roles of Francis Jeffrey and Henry Cockburn at the *Edinburgh Review*.

84. "Names of Newspapers." 22 (1873): 133–35.
Mulled over the captions of "the most able and upright" press in the world. The "Daily News" was the clearest, but titles could be attention-getting, cosmopolitan, denominational, reflective, protective, defensive, observing, and illustrating.

85. "An Old Newspaper." 22 (1873): 442–46.
Analyzed the contents of the *Stamford Mercury*, January–June 1716, "one of the oldest real newspapers" still circulating. Originally it was an 11-page weekly with information about government, crime, weather, and foreign and local affairs alongside advertising.

86. Mackeson, Charles, F.S.S. "Curiosities of the Census, III." 23 (1874): 205–07; IV, 390–92.
Drew from the census that newspaper sellers were increasing, with some 5,000 men vending gazettes as a trade like tobacconists, and newsboys and girls flooding the streets. Newspapers contained too many "sensational" leaders, and "high-class reviews" published too many "sterner articles" by doctors, lawyers, and clerics.

87. ?D[ennis], J[ohn]. "An Old 'Academic Annual.'" 23 (1874): 716–17.
Sketched the *Edinburgh Academic Annual*, 1840 (the only volume published), whose contributors were later famous mostly in science. George Wilson, a chemist, also penned for the *North British Review*.

88. H., J. "The Right Hon. William Edward Forster, M.P." 24 (1875): 153–58.
Indicated Forster's essays in the *Edinburgh Review* and *Westminster Review*.

89. M., S. "English Newspapers in China." 24 (1875): 295–96.
Investigated the *North China Herald* (weekly) and *North China Daily News*, both published in Shanghai by the same company and both with news and advertising. The *Herald's* paper and type could match any English weekly, but it cost six times more for a journal of the same size.

90. "Caricature and Caricaturists." 24 (1875): 760–63, 793–95.
Series (other segments irrelevant) pinpointed John Leech's drawings for *Punch*, where he was the most popular and prolific artist; C. Keene, whose subjects were more serious; and *Vanity Fair*, read by those it satirized who were chiefly in the professions and government. French caricature, even under Napoleon III, was more powerful than British as *Figaro* and *Charivari* evidenced. French illustrations were impudent; German, exaggerated.

91. "The Life of Lord Macaulay." 25 (1876): 427–30, 445–48.
Tagged T. B. Macaulay "a leading writer" of the *Edinburgh Review*.

92. "The General Post-Office." 25 (1876): 636–40.
Boasted that the postal news staff (5 p.m. – 2 a.m.) could handle a high volume of press telegrams, even 220 *Times* columns a night.

93. Whitaker, J. V. "American Caricatures." 25 (1876): 759–62.
Credited better art and burgeoning periodicals for the influence of American caricaturists. *Gleason's Pictorial* (NY, 1851) was followed by the *Lantern* (NY, 1852) and Frank Leslie's *Illustrated Weekly* (1857), the equal of *Harper's Weekly*. Most of the genre was unsuccessful because American dailies ordinarily printed humor.

94. Whitaker, J. V. "Thomas Nast." 25 (1876): 807–11.
Named Nast, whose cartoons appeared in almost every issue of *Harper's Weekly*, "the champion of morality and justice." His caricatures of the Tweed ring and the Franco-Prussian War gave him more power than any English illustrator.

95. Masson, Gustave. "The Rainbow Coffee-House." 26 (1877): 180–82.
Mourned a Fleet Street coffeehouse that had recently closed. Among its eighteenth-century habitués was Pierre Desmaizeaux, a scribe for London and Amsterdam newspapers.

96. "Mr. and Mrs. S. C. Hall." 26 (1877): 407–11.
Silhouetted S. C. Hall but not his wife, Anna M. (Fielding) Hall. He began as a parliamentary reporter and "rapidly rose to eminence in that onerous profession." In 1825 he started the *Amulet* and in 1830 edited the *New Monthly Magazine*. Later he introduced the *Art-Union* (1839), known in 1877 as the *Art Journal*, which featured art and a "higher class of literary contributors."

97. "William and Mary Howitt." 26 (1877): 583–89.
Literary biography of the captioned couple encompassed their association with the *People's Journal*, its problems and losses, and their creation of *Howitt's Journal* and its failure due to their debts from the earlier enterprise.

98. "Village Clubs." 27 (1878): 11–13.
Conjectured that club readers in the country preferred illustrated magazines because of their pictures and short texts, other popular magazines, and neighborhood newspapers. Only "a few of the more intelligent" villagers opted for London gazettes.

99. ?D[ennis], J[ohn]. "Recollections of Thomas Campbell and David M. Moir." 27 (1878): 156–59.
Concentrated on Campbell's ideas of a free press and Moir's articles, penned as Delta, in *Blackwood's Magazine*.

100. "George Cruikshank." 27 (1878): 262–66.
Contended that Cruikshank's drawings always helped a periodical's circulation, whether for an 1821 serial of "slipshod dialect" that would "degrade public taste," the *Morning Herald*, 1825–26, or *Bentley's Miscellany*.

101. "The Telephone." 27 (1878): 318–20.
Tied the telephone to news transmission.

102. "Robert Carruthers, LL.D., Editor of the *Inverness Courier*." 27 (1878): 533–36.
Stamped Carruthers a "veteran journalist." He first penned for the *Dumfries Courier*, "the foremost paper" in southern Scotland. In 1828 he began editing the *Inverness Courier*, which Christian Johnstone once skillfully directed. After purchasing the paper with a loan of 500 pounds, he transformed it into "a model of provincial journalism" by recruiting Shirley Brooks and Edmund Yates.

103. "Rome in 1878." 27 (1878): 541–42.
Quoted *The Times* on Rome's press: the "grave *Opinione*," "racy *Fanfulla*," and "ranting *Capitale*," all maturing in their news delivery.

104. "The Cafés of Paris." 27 (1878): 660–664.
Linked some Paris cafés, such as Brébant's, to journalists.

105. "Curiosities of the Post Office." 28 (1879): 205–07.
Bragged that the post office handled 128 million newspapers in 1877.

106. "Elihu Burritt." 28 (1879): 357–60.
Praised Burritt for his editing of the *Christian Citizen*, "the first journal in America which was specifically devoted to the cause of peace." The Worcester (MA) publication sent columns on peace to other newspapers. Burritt's other serials, the *Bond of Brotherhood* and *Fireside Words*, a juvenile magazine, did not thrive.

107. "Don Emilio Castelar." 28 (1879): 392–96.
Remembered that Castelar started a republican Spanish weekly in 1864.

108. Kaufmann, Rev. M[oritz], M.A. "Utopian Experiments in the United States." 28 (1879): 618–23.
This section of a series on utopian socialism section mentioned Horace Greeley's *New York Tribune*.

109. Tallack, W. "Gothenburg." 28 (1879): 793–96.
Saluted S. A. Hedlund, owner and editor of the *Handels Tidningen* in Göteborg, Sweden. He was a man "who recognizes his responsibility as an influential leader of public opinion." The paper had an excellent reputation at home and abroad because it reported commercial news accurately, maintained a "high literary and aesthetic standard," and displayed a breadth in coverage that went beyond Scandinavia.

110. "Sir John Gilbert, R.A." 29 (1880): 183–85.
Bruited that Gilbert did many drawings for the *Illustrated London News*, 1845–54, while he was also the "mainstay of at least a dozen weekly or monthly magazines."

111. "Three of Our Old Contributors." 29 (1880): 824–28.
Singled out Charles Manby Smith, a writer for *Leisure Hour* since 1852, who went from printer's apprentice to periodical contributor and editor of *Tait's Edinburgh Magazine*. W. H. G. Kingston penned sea stories, and Frances Brown was a scribe for many serials.

112. "Memorable Scenes in the House of Commons. V. The Episode of John Wilkes." 30 (1881): 299–303.
Paired Wilkes and press freedom.

113. "Looking Back; or, Glimpses of the Eighteenth Century." 30 (1881): 642–46.
Touched on mid-century newspapers, the *York Courant*, *Leeds Intelligencer*, *St. James's Chronicle*, and *General Evening Post* (London).

114. Hood, Rev. E. Paxton. "The Kings of Laughter. II: Is Ridicule the Test of Truth?" 31 (1882): 119–23.
Earmarked the *Anti-Jacobin* as a model of "subtle satire."

115. Wolf, Lucien. "Notes on Modern Jews, I." 31 (1882): 372–76.
Sidelined the *Jewish World*, a London newspaper.

116. "Newspaper Advertisements in the Eighteenth Century." 31 (1882): 408–12.
Sampled eighteenth-century newspaper advertisements on jobs, lost and found articles, and spurious medical remedies.

117. "The Rev. Prebendary Harry James, M.A." 31 (1882): 674–76.
Memorialized James, a long-time contributor to *Leisure Hour*.

118. "How the Newspaper is Made." 32 (1883): 38–42.
Contrasted dailies in 1883 to the small early nineteenth-century newspapers, with their brownish paper and inartistic typography, narrow circulations, and heavy taxes. The new were "organs or guides of opinion" with "fresh, full, and accurate intelligence." Their value was in their details, not startling news, and their paid staffs of "educated gentlemen" who wrote well. Most honored was the parliamentary reporter who had to understand politics. Competition replaced "mere reproduction of spoken words" with "objective reporting" done in Charles Dickens' descriptive style. The foreign correspondent needed "social acceptability, discretion, and knowledge"; the war correspondent, courage, a sense of justice, and ingenuity. Other staff handled local meetings and foreign telegrams (usually in French). The editor was the "soul" of a daily, the person who knew his readers and their milieu. Being an editor was a "vocation" that required meetings with politicians or perusal of reports about politics followed by conferences with leader-writers. The subeditor, who began around 6 p.m., had to be careful about placing stories.

119. P., H. V. "Some Fashion-Gleanings, from 1744 to 1768." 32 (1882): 373–75.
Copied earlier fashion news from the *London Gazette* and unnamed periodicals.

120. Crane, Agnes. "Eastward by the Union Pacific." 32 (1883): 539–44.
Aside that a Mr. Cannon, "a shrewd and well-educated Englishman, a journalist," represented Utah in the United States Congress.

121. Levi, Professor Leone, F.S.A., F.S.S. "The British People: Their Income and Expenditure, Their Virtues and Their Vices, VI." 33 (1884): 377–82.
Classified the newspaper as an educational expense.

122. Macauley, James, M.D. "Popular Literature, with Reference to Infidelity and Public Morality." 33 (1884): 653–57.

Recorded that in 1824 there were many two-penny publications, such as the *Mechanics' Magazine* with a circulation of 15,000. Readers in 1884 opted for newspapers. Most were run well and upheld "order and freedom" but occasionally headlined vice and crime. Juvenile periodicals concerned with the sensational were "pernicious," but the *Boy's Own Paper* and its ilk were good antidotes.

123. "Italian Statesmen." 34 (1885): 187–88.

Talked about Marco Minghetti, who established and edited Bologna's *Felsineo* newspaper before he entered politics.

124. Massingham, H. W. "Johnson as a Journalist." 34 (1885): 484–85.

Acknowledged that journalism was a "vocation" in 1884 but had not been for Samuel Johnson. He came after "the giants of journalism," such as the "born journalist" Richard Steele. Johnson's work at the *Gentleman's Magazine* evolved from "occasional sketches" to essays on Parliament.

125. Heath, Richard. "Victor Hugo." 34 (1885): 809–16.

Bared that Hugo lived on his pay for articles in the *Conservateur*, c. 1822.

126. Chesson, F. W. "William Lloyd Garrison." 35 (1886): 20–25.

Trailed Garrison from local printer to editor of the *Philanthropist* (an 1826 Boston temperance journal) to the *Journal of the Times* and *Liberator*. Horace Greeley, "the foremost journalist in the United States," called the *Journal* "the ablest and most interesting ever issued in Vermont."

127. Gordon, W. J. "A Day at the Post Office." 35 (1886): 31–38.

Explicated, with excellent illustrations, postal handling of newspapers.

128. Gordon, W. J. "The Post in Many Lands." 35 (1886): 161–66.

Catalogued pigeons as news carriers in British counties without telegraphy.

129. "Mudie's Library." 35 (1886): 187–89.

Swore that the "most read" periodicals of the day were the *Nineteenth Century*, *Fortnightly Review*, and "American illustrated magazines."

130. ?P[utnam], Rev. G. H. "The Beginning and End of the Nineteenth Century." 35 (1886): 626–32.

Chronicled that Georgian era "editors were worried with state prosecutions for trivial offences" and "handicapped by the three-penny stamp duty." Papers of those decades that survived were the *Morning Post*, *Morning Advertiser*, *Globe*, and *The Times*. They cost six pence until 1802 when the price went to six and a half pence because the cost of paper rose 50 percent, the cost of ink rose 35 percent, and the cost of journeymen's wages rose 10 percent. In 1806 the *Post* had 5,000 subscribers when Parliament sat, so "horn-boys" were unnecessary. *The Times* sold 7,000–8,000 per day by employing this "noisy nuisance." The *Courier*, an evening paper during the French war, circulated 10,000 copies.

131. "*Through the Long Day*: Fifty Years of a Man of Letters." 36 (1887): 532–35.
Review of Charles Mackay's book associated him with the "*Morning Chronicle*, the leading journal of that time," and with "literary articles" for other newspapers and magazines. After training at the *Sun*, he was an assistant editor of the *Chronicle* in 1834 and in 1836 beat out W. M. Thackeray for the subeditor's job. Among Mackay's *Chronicle* contemporaries were owner John Easthope, editor John Black, subeditor George Hogarth, "Paris correspondent" E. E. Crowe, and parliamentary reporters John Payne Collier and Charles Dickens.

132. "An Old Man's Jubilee Grumble." 36 (1887): 554–55.
Blustered that English newspapers, even the 'leading journals' of 1887, were "polluting their pages" with personal news that the earlier *Age* would never print. Aside that Charles Mackay, John Payne Collier, and Charles Dickens were all parliamentary reporters.

133. "The Advertisements of the Day." 36 (1887): 627–69.
Summarized advertisements in "leading London newspapers" on 9 March 1887. *The Times* ran 1,558 and the *Daily Telegraph*, *Standard*, *Morning Post*, *Daily Chronicle*, and *Daily News* together had 7,421. These inserts covered personal, legal, and financial matters; employment opportunities; goods for sale; and information on education, theatres, exhibits, and periodicals.

134. Mason, James. "A Gallery of Illustrious Literary Characters. I. Goethe – Carlyle – Coleridge." 36 (1887): 690–95.
Nodded to Thomas Carlyle's essays in *Fraser's Magazine* and the *Edinburgh Review* where he amazed editor Francis Jeffrey with his "eccentricities of style."

135. "Some Experiences as an Editor." 37 (1888): 39–41.
Author claimed to be an illustrated magazine's editor about to resign. A periodical editor had to read and "consider honestly" all scribbling submitted by contributors, many with bad handwriting. Unlike an editor of a daily who had "an elaborate staff," the magazine editor had only a subeditor to assist in preparing copy printed two months in advance.

136. Capper, Samuel James. "A Visit to John Greenleaf Whittier." 37 (1888): 611–15.
Referred to William Lloyd Garrison's journalism but not that of Whittier.

137. Sergeant, Lewis. "F. W. Chesson." 37 (1888): 677–80.
Eulogized an anti-slavery activist who depended on his job as subeditor of the *Morning Star* from 1855 until its demise to support himself.

138. ?P[utnam], G. H. "Newspapers and Journalists: Past and Present." 37 (1888): 735–39.
Review of H. R. Fox Bourne's *English Newspapers – Chapters in the History of Journalism* testified that it was full of "striking details and piquant anecdotes." Nathaniel Butter and Roger L'Estrange, "a sort of inquisitor-general of the press," were important in early journalism as were Daniel Defoe, Joseph Addison, Richard Steele, and William Cobbett. Equally significant was the *Gentleman's Magazine*, initially known for its paragraphs from the newspapers, then Samuel Johnson's essays on Parliament. Henry Simpson Woodfall's *Public Advertiser* was home

to Junius, and Woodfall's brother, William, was the first parliamentary reporter for the *Morning Chronicle* as well as an early editor of the *Morning Post.* One of his successors, Henry Bate, was "a fast liver." James Perry made the *Morning Chronicle* profitable, and John Walter put *The Times* on the road to power.

Under George III, the press was still the victim of many libel suits. William Pitt the Younger tried to manipulate the press, as Robert Walpole had once done, at a time when the newspapers paid several duties. In 1828 they cost *The Times* 1,300 pounds per week. Although several nineteenth-century papers disappeared quickly, the *Daily News*, *Daily Telegraph*, and *Standard*, the first to issue a double sheet for a penny, endured. Only recently had British evening papers blossomed, although they had been popular in France for years.

The first country paper was the 1690 *Berrow's Worcester Journal.* Many other locals with large circulations and much influence surfaced, but the real impact of this press was after 1855 when the stamp duty ended. They numbered 50 in 1788, 200–300 in 1855, and 1,200 in 1888. Generally, press language was better, but gazettes had too many sports columns and lottery advertisements.

In 1888 there were about 4,000 newspapers circulating 22 million copies and 21,746 periodicals circulating 57 million copies. There were 2,403 dailies in Europe, 154 in Asia, 25 in Africa, 1,136 in North America, 208 in South America, and 94 in Australasia.

139. Mayo, Isabella Fyvie. "A Recollection of Two Old Friends: Mr. and Mrs. S. C. Hall." 38 (1889): 303–07.

Discussed the *Art Journal*, which was full of "exquisite engravings." It was launched by S. C. Hall who also edited the *New Monthly Magazine*, annuals, and other periodicals. His wife, Anna M. Hall, edited *St. James's Magazine* where she helped aspiring scribes.

140. Rees, J. Rogers. "Trifles." 39 (1890): 53–55.

Sighed that newspapers spread the gossip readers loved.

141. Gordon, W. J. "The Centenary of the Rotary Printing Press." 39 (1890): 167–71.

Evaluated, with illustrations, the technological innovations of William Nicholson of the *Journal of Natural Philosophy*. He consulted on the development of the König press. John Walter II, the "inventor of the leading article," had the original idea, and in 1804 a *Times* compositor built the press only to see it smashed by pressmen. Better-paid workers were less resistant to the steam press that *The Times* introduced in 1814.

142. Gordon, W. J. "The Newspaper Printing Press of To-Day." 39 (1890): 263–68, 332–37.

Delved into printing technology even though most journals were still set by hand. Aside that *The Times* had 96 columns (69 news and 27 with 1,264 advertisements) and used the telephone for transmitting parliamentary news.

143. "The Story of a Journalist." 39 (1890): 485–87.

Review of W. Robertson Nicoll's *James Macdonell, Journalist* stated that Macdonell, who died at 37, began at the *Aberdeen Free Press*. A leader-writer by age 20, he went to Edinburgh's *Daily Review* where he "became a professional journalist." He next edited Newcastle's *Daily Express*, penning five leaders and some columns weekly. He joined the *Daily Telegraph* at 24 years old before he became a leader-writer for

The Times, a job that was "the blue ribbon of the Press." Macdonnell also wrote for the *Spectator*, *North British Review*, and *Fraser's Magazine.*

144. Welldon, Rev. J. E. C., M.A., Head Master of the Harrow School. "Some Aspects of Popular Literature." 39 (1890): 702–05.

Expressed two concerns about journalism. First, too many sports pages, purportedly read to improve the body, and sporting gazettes, some 51 from dailies to monthlies in 1890, encouraged gambling. Second, all newspapers, even *The Times*, had too much personal information. The stories that invaded privacy by displaying intimacies pained victims but sold papers. "The scandal-hunger, like the land-hunger, is universal."

145. Buck, W. E. "'Yankee Dodges': Business Life and the Press." 40 (1891): 204–07.

Itemized some American journalistic faults, such as telephoning, bylining, insulting competitors, excessive interviewing by men and women, and, in New York, printing Sunday papers of over 50 pages.

146. "Statesmen of Europe: France." 40 (1891): 405–12, 460–66.

Covered Léon Gambetta and the *Réveil*; Napoleon III and control of the press; Emile Ollivier and Clément Duvernois who penned for the *Presse* as had Jules Ferry, also a scribe for the *Temps*; George Clemenceau, owner of *Justice*; and Henri Rochefort and the *Lanterne.*

147. Macauley, James, M.D. "*A Publisher and His Friends*: John Murray the Second." 40 (1891): 521–27.

Review of Samuel Smiles' book certified that the *Representative* (1826), which Benjamin Disraeli maneuvered Murray to publish, cost him 26,000 pounds. Asides on *Quarterly Review* editors William Gifford, J. T. Coleridge, and J. G. Lockhart and the "less sedate" contributors in the early years of *Blackwood's Magazine.*

148. Massingham, H. W. "The Great London Dailies – *The Times*." 41 (1891–92): 231–37, "The *Daily News*," 304–09, "The *Standard*," 378–81," "The *Daily Telegraph*," 455–60, "The *Daily Chronicle*," 525–29, "The Penny Evening Papers – the *Pall Mall Gazette*," 607–10, "The Penny Evening Papers – the *St. James's Gazette* and the *Globe*," 674–77, "The Half-Penny Evening Press," 740–43.

Survey of contemporary newspapers juxtaposed journalism and the "nobler craft of literature." The early *Times*, "coarse" in tone and full of gossip, typically sold 1,000 copies. Gradually, thanks to Henry Crabb Robinson, it added foreign correspondence. Its premier foreign correspondent was H. G. A. Opper de Blowitz in Paris. The model for war correspondents was William Howard Russell of Crimean fame. Qualified men, such as Edward Sterling whose "Thunderer" paragraphs gave *The Times* its nickname, made leaders "a force" as long as they reflected the views of the governing class. Men of this sort made *The Times* a major influence from the 1830s and the top paper in 1891. It showed the "more cultured side of journalism," still excelled in foreign correspondence, and was "cock-sure" in the spirit of William Cobbett. *Times* employees were not members of the London Society of Compositors but had benefits from the paper.

The *Daily News* had many editors. Charles Dickens was the first, but Thomas Walker, who left for the *Literary Gazette*, was the most "able, cultivated and genial." Among its writers were Harriet Martineau and the war correspondents Archibald Forbes in the Franco-Prussian War and J. A. MacGahan in Bulgaria. Henry W. Lucy, "Toby, M.P." at *Punch*, supervised the parliamentary reporters. W. Moy Thomas did the theatre criticism, which others copied. The paper also covered sports and foreign affairs, posting a woman, Emily J. Crawford, in Paris. She also wrote for *Truth* and the *New York Tribune*. Circulation of the *Daily News* was 100,000.

The *Standard* was the "most solid of British newspapers" with an "excellent appearance, substantial paper, and faultless printing." Once an evening gazette edited by William Maginn, it moved to the morning in the 1850s. Circulation rose after 1878 when W. H. Mudford, formerly a parliamentary reporter, became editor. T. H. S. Escott, "an accomplished, versatile" journalist, wrote some leaders before Alfred Austin and "G. A. Henty, the veteran war correspondent," penned commentary. Advertising paid for high staff salaries.

"The *Daily Telegraph* is pre-eminently the 'cockney' newspaper." It published the concerns of average Londoners, local advertising, crime news, abstracts of Parliament, and leaders without politics but with gossip. The paper struggled until it was acquired by Edward Levy, a good businessman ready to pay for a good staff. He hired a former parliamentary reporter as editor-manager and sent reporters to cover the Franco-Prussian War when British dailies were in a "race for news." George Augustus Sala, "the most learned journalist," wrote leaders. Edward Dicey and Thornton Hunt were early staffers. The paper's best feature was "Paris Day by Day," but the *Telegraph* liked 'booms,' inspired by Henry Stanley's African reports in the *New York Herald*.

The *Daily Chronicle* was originally a weekly for workers known as the *Clerkenwell News*. With faster presses and fewer advertisements, the *Chronicle* in 1891 printed more news, especially of London. The *Chronicle's* foreign correspondents were outstanding, as was its chief parliamentary reporter. Many of its leader-writers specialized. Among its other staff was George Bernard Shaw.

The *Pall Mall Gazette* drew its style from its editors, Frederick Greenwood, John Morley, W. T. Stead, and E. T. Cook. Morley lacked a "*flair* for news," and Stead was more "flamboyant," but both made the *Gazette* "a power." Stead introduced the interview, "now common to the English press." The paper favored illustrations and engravings, although the *Newcastle Weekly Chronicle* was the star in this area because of its technology. For the *Gazette*, Frank Gould did some excellent caricatures of Parliament. In "a concession to the New Journalism," the paper printed a gossip column but not a feuilleton, which Stead once tried. Other columns were on sports, literature, and the arts. Known for thoroughness in newsgathering and reporting, the *Gazette* had a fact-checking office headed by a woman. Although gifted with the best subeditor in London and a solid young staff, the paper had less overall quality of late.

St. James's Gazette was born when Frederick Greenwood left the *Pall Mall Gazette*. *St. James's* format was similar to the *Pall Mall*. A new editor, Sidney J. Low, lightened its tone with help from J. M. Barrie, but it was never as 'surly' as the *Saturday Review*. *St. James's*, with its arts, fashion, and gossip, was a child of New Journalism, but among its scribes was an "investigator," A. Shadwell.

The *Globe*, begun in 1803, had before 1850 absorbed five other papers and won a reputation for humor and leaders on social or literary topics. Its halfpenny children, the *Evening News* and *Star*, outsold competitors by headlining murders. The *Globe* published five editions between 12:30 and 6:30 p.m., the last the largest with much on sports.

The halfpenny papers commenced with the *Echo* in 1868. It was popular with London workers who read only cheap evening and sporting gazettes. Passmore Edwards, owner and editor, tried to give laborers "a keener civic interest and a higher intellectual standard." The *Echo* had columns on the arts and sciences that made it the favorite of the middle classes but lost sports fans to the *Evening News* and *Star*. The *Evening News* editor was "a shrewd, capable, gentleman of wide American experience" whose paper sold 100,000 copies per day. Evening papers lured buyers with fresh and varied news. Although the leader was a constant, content changed for each edition bringing more sensational paragraphs and putting more pressure on subeditors and printers.

American reporters worked harder, observed more, and penned more cleverly than the British. The Americans were pictorial; the British, too literal. The adoption of the American descriptive headline was a welcome addition. Newspapers needed good judgment in business managers because half of all sales were uncertain. Rapid distribution to newsboys, agents, and railroads helped.

New Journalism did not overshadow the old but catalyzed a "social synthesis" because party influence was still strong and journalists were still without the "culture, gravity, enthusiasm" to dominate.

149. "Statesmen of Europe – Germany." 41 (1891–92): 809–15.

Branded Wilhelm Liebknecht "by profession a journalist."

150. "The People of Europe: How They Live, Think, and Labour – France." 42 (1893): 548–54; "Russia." 43 (1894): 795–800.

Bellowed that the French read and edited fourth-rate newspapers that had to be amusing to succeed. The only serious dailies were the *Temps* and *Journal des Débats*, but *Figaro* and the widely-circulating *Petit Journal* were adequate. Comic papers that dealt with politics were coarse but had clever drawings.

Hypothesized that the costs of operating newspapers and the illiteracy of peasants limited a Russian press in the provinces.

151. "An Old Volume of *Punch*." 42 (1893): 824–28.

Rated *Punch* drawings of the 1840s less offensive and "cruel" than their forebears and "clean and wholesome" compared to French satire in 1893.

152. "*Letters of James Russell Lowell*." 43 (1894): 221–24.

Review of a book edited by Charles E. Norton mentioned that Lowell undertook "much newspaper and magazine work," including writing for Boston's *Courier* and the tribune of the American Anti-Slavery Society, the *Standard*, as well as editing the *Atlantic Monthly*.

153. Mayo, Isabella Fyvie. "William Alexander, LL.D." 43 (1894): 432–38.

Divulged that Alexander saw himself as a journalist seeking truth and newspapers as organs of sound principle. He began at the *North of Scotland Gazette* before reporting for and subediting other Scottish papers and editing the *Aberdeen Daily and Weekly Free Press*.

154. Noble, James Ashcroft. "Oliver Wendell Holmes." 44 (1895): 82–88.

Peeped at Holmes' work for the *Atlantic Monthly* and "short-lived" *New England Magazine*.

155. Hopkins, Tighe. "Books in Prison." 44 (1895): 444–47.

Whispered that American convicts not only read newspapers but edited and printed their own in some prisons.

156. Macauley, James, M.D. "*George Augustus Sala: His Life and Adventures*." 44 (1895): 512–15.

Review of Sala's autobiography spoke of his columns in short-lived publications until Charles Dickens brought him to *Household Words*. He later penned for *All the Year Round*, *Welcome Guest*, and *Once a Week* before becoming a regular contributor in the 1860s to the *Daily Telegraph*, then "the most prosperous paper." He was a foreign correspondent for the *Telegraph* but also scribbled for the *Echo*, *Illustrated London News*, *Cornhill Magazine*, and *Temple Bar*, which he christened and of which Edmund Yates was subeditor. Paid per article, Sala was not a member of the Institute of Journalists.

157. Collings, T. C. "The Settlements of London: Where They Are, and What They are Doing." 44 (1895): 600–06.

Gushed that "the illustrated papers are eagerly read" in libraries established in working class neighborhoods.

158. J. "Reviews and Reviewing by One Who has been and has Reviewed." 45 (1896): 458–59.

Insisted that literary criticism was harsh for two reasons. Critics, swamped by many books, only skimmed the lot or condemned a few in order to appear superior.

159. Newland, F. W. "A Panorama of London Life." 46 (1896–97): 285–88.

Echoed Charles Booth's *Life and Labours of the People of London* that there were 500 daily or weekly newspapers published within a half mile of Fleet Street.

160. Dennis, John. "Sydney Smith." 46 (1896–97): 666–69.

Review of Stuart J. Reid's *The Life and Times of Sidney Smith* credited Smith with the idea for the *Edinburgh Review*, an idea developed by Francis Jeffrey, Henry Brougham, and Francis Horner. At a time when "journalism was treated as a degrading pursuit," so low that Lincoln's Inn excluded those who scribbled for dailies, the *Edinburgh* and the *Quarterly Review* rehabilitated it.

161. "Critics and Criticism." 47 (1897–98): 88–91.

Deemed the *Edinburgh Review* partisan under editor Francis Jeffrey and deemed John Wilson the "life and soul" of *Blackwood's Magazine*.

162. "Sir John Gilbert, R.A." 47 (1897–98): 424–30.

Commented that the "artist-journalist," except for the caricaturist, emerged in the Victorian era. Gilbert was the chief artist for the *Illustrated London News* in its youth and sketched for *Leisure Hour* and other serials. In 1897 magazines were "picture books," and the "best artists are content to turn newspaper reporters."

163. C. "Mrs. Oliphant and 'Maga' on the Thames." 47 (1897–98): 556–60.

Revived Margaret Oliphant's 1877 essay on the relationship of John Wilson and William Blackwood.

164. "The Life of a Famous Journalist." 48 (1898–99): 95–98.

Review of John Knox Laughton's *Memoirs of the Life and Correspondence of Henry Reeve, C.B., D.C.L.*, emphasized that he was by "profession" a journalist. An anonymous leader-writer for *The Times*, 1840–55, then long-time *Edinburgh Review* editor, Reeve was "a product of the nineteenth century" who knew many "men of note" in England and France. He epitomized the journalist who could be "influential and masterly" and could "speak with freedom and authority...while in correspondence with statesmen."

Until the 1760s the press, saddled by government interference, did not produce an "organ of influence." Thereafter, the *Morning Chronicle* (1769), *Morning Post* (1772), *Morning Herald* (1780), *The Times* (1785), *Edinburgh* (1802), and *Quarterly Review* (1809) arrived, and by 1850 reviews had great sway. In 1771 Parliament summoned six printers for reproducing Commons debates, the last time it tried to restrict reporting.

165. Dennis, J[ohn]. "A Great Publishing House." 48 (1898–99): 250–52.

Reviewed *Annals of a Publishing House: John Blackwood*, by Mary Porter. Narrated that Blackwood, John Delane of *The Times*, and William E. Aytoun, a contributor of *Blackwood's Magazine*, were great friends. Blackwood continued his family's custom of engaging great writers, with whom he enjoyed good relations. He endorsed anonymity because it gave unknown authors an opportunity to publish in elite periodicals.

166. "French Presidents." 48 (1898–99): 395–98.

Repeated the view that "[a]s a journalist, [Adolphe] Thiers is supposed to have had an important influence upon events which resulted in placing Louis Philippe on the throne."

167. Dennis, John. "Mrs. Oliphant." 48 (1898–99): 572–74.

Called attention to the *Autobiography and Letters of Mrs. M. O. W. Oliphant* edited by Annie Coghill. Margaret Oliphant was a long-time author in *Blackwood's Magazine.*

168. Dennis, John. "*Richard Holt Hutton*." 48 (1898–99): 664–66.

Review of J. Hogben's *Richard Holt Hutton of the Spectator* paralleled his weekly article in that journal and Joseph Addison's work for an earlier *Spectator* because Hutton resisted the recent temptation to journalists "to write for effect."

169. "*The Abbé de Lamennais*." 48 (1898–99): 701–05.

Review of W. Gibson's booked yoked F. de Lamennais to the *Avenir*, a popular French paper whose attacks on Louis Philippe and Catholic bishops resulted in episcopal prohibition and consequent drop in circulation. When the pope called the *Avenir* "dangerous to society," it closed. Aside that the French press had "a brief spell of freedom" after 1815.

170. Bryce, Right Hon. James, D.C.L., M.P. "On Reading." 49 (1899–1900): 15–23.

Pronounced the newspaper "a necessity of life" because it pictured the world. Most people read the newspaper because it was a cheap source of information. For instance, commuters looked for business and perhaps politics. Magazines, frequently better written, also covered these topics.

171. Hay, William. "Thomas Pringle: A Forgotten Chapter of South African History." 49 (1899–1900): 158–68.

Introduced Pringle as an editor of the *Scots Magazine*, then Edinburgh's *Star*. In Cape Colony, he attempted to start an English-Dutch monthly, but when the governor rejected the proposal, Pringle launched the *South African Commercial Advertiser* with his friend, John Fairbairn. When the printer resisted government censorship, the *Advertiser* press was sealed and its owner sent home. Pringle successfully fought to keep the paper open for a time, and the case catalyzed freedom for the Cape press in 1828.

172. Massingham, H. W. "Archibald Forbes." 49 (1899–1900): 724–26.

Portrayed the owner of the *London Scotsman* who made his name as a reporter for the *Daily News* during the Franco-Prussian War. Forbes, "the most brilliant of war correspondents," was energetic and a good observer and writer but was surpassed in political acumen by his colleague, J. A. MacGahan. Wondered how Forbes would react to the censorship of the press during the war with the Boers.

173. W., G. "Gleanings from Some Eighteenth-Century Newspapers." 49 (1899–1900): 806–09.

Plumbed John Bagnall's two-penny *Ipswich Gazette*, 1734–36, that contained foreign news, a few health advertisements, obituaries, and crime and commercial reports.

The London Quarterly Review, 1853–1900

Rooted in Methodism, the *London Quarterly* alternated between moral and analytic perspectives in its texts on the press.

1. "Joseph Addison." 4 (1855): 99–122.
Review of *Johnson's Lives of the English Poets*, edited by Peter Cunningham, classed the *Tatler* as a popular penny paper with "a regard for decency." It had a "worldly good nature" and "sparkling fluency" but not "correctness of style." Addison "charms" readers, and Samuel Johnson awed them. Addison "threw all his energy and talent" into the *Spectator*. His "aim was alike to improve, not only morals, but language." However, William Cobbett set the standard for English in newspapers.

2. [McNicoll, Thomas]. "Popular Criticism." 4 (1855): 179–203.
Selected George Gilfillan as the exemplar of the faults of periodical literary criticism, writing as he did for "four or five of the popular serials."

3. [Rule, William Harris]. "Jesuitism: Its Political Relations." 5 (1855–56): 363–403.
Cited the *Civiltà Cattolica* as the Jesuits' tool to build their power in Naples.

4. [McNicoll, Thomas]. "Popular Authorship – Samuel Warren." 5 (1855–56): 464–80.
Saw no need for periodical compilations while quality essays appeared regularly. Those in *Blackwood's Magazine* and its ilk were classics.

5. [McNicoll, Thomas]. "*Memoirs of James Montgomery*." 6 (1856): 178–204.
Review of a book by John Holland and James Everett narrated that at age 21 Montgomery answered an advertisement for a printer. Joseph Gales, the owner and editor of the *Sheffield Register*, hired him. In 1794, after the government issued a warrant against Gales for his 'democratic ideas,' he left England. Montgomery took control of the paper under the caption *Sheffield Iris*. As editor he was prosecuted twice for libel, each time resulting in a fine and prison time (20 pounds and three months; 30 pounds and six months).

6. [Young, Archibald]. "Cuba: Its State and Prospects." 7 (1856–57): 98–118.
Counted six dailies in Havana in 1847. Its *Faro Industrial* was "the largest printed" in the Spanish Empire. Most small towns had newspapers, but editorial freedom was doubtful. "[A]n able monthly review" encompassed politics, industry, and literature, but some periodicals were "trashy in the extreme."

7. [Arthur, William]. "Christian Missions and the *Westminster Review*." 7 (1856–57): 209–61.
Complimented the *Quarterly Review* as "[o]ne of the highest members of the periodical press," a rank shared by the *Westminster*. The *Chinese Missionary Gleaner* was "valuable" to spread missionary ideas.

8. "Crime and Criminal Law in France." 8 (1857): 92–107.
Snapped that the French press contained many fewer stories on crime, the "thefts, frauds, and assaults which stain the columns of an English newspaper."

9. [Arthur, William]. "Kansas." 8 (1857): 517–40.
Review of seven books cited author-journalists who reported on Kansas: G. Douglas Brewerton, *New York Herald*, William Phillips, *New York Tribune*, and Thomas H. Gladstone, *New York Times*. Alluded to Atchison's *Squatter Sovereign*, edited by the speaker of the Kansas House, and the abolitionist press.

10. [Monsell, R. W.]. "The Danubian Principalities." 10 (1858): 213–65.
Claimed that Romania had a free press before 1830. Following their occupation of the principalities, the Russians prohibited local news and permitted only excerpts from St. Petersburg and Odessa journals. Moldavia in 1858 had no paper except an "official gazette." In Wallachia, censorship left "whole columns blank." Merchants supported publications abroad, the *Bucimal* and *Opinione* in Paris and the *Etoile du Danube* in Brussels.

11. "Illustrated Works." 11 (1858–59): 474–92.
Resurrected annuals, as the *Landscape*, *Oriental*, and *Keepsake*, none of which had stories "equal to those contained in our penny weekly numbers" and "far inferior" to those in *Household Words*. The *Keepsake*, whose pictures and tales were not even coherent, owed its success to "titled contributors."

12. [Spender, Edward]. "Rome and the Papal States." 12 (1859): 544–75.
Reported that the Papal States lacked a free press capable of shaping public opinion.

13. "Literature of the People." 13 (1859–60): 1–31.
Prioritized the newspaper, a medium improving in "moral tone" and "intellectual power," whose "influence over the popular mind surpasses that of any other class of publications." Its British history went from Nathaniel Butter's *Weekely News* to the avalanche of mercuries in the Civil Wars when the *Impartial Intelligencer* in 1648 purportedly carried the first advertisement. In the early eighteenth century E. Mullet published the *Daily Courant*, which promised accuracy without resorting to "private sources" for its sheet mostly of foreign news. The *Craftsman* was "the most notable newspaper," reaching 10,000–12,000 copies. Because tribunes survived on party support, "writers were as abusive as they were venal." Limits on parliamentary and trial reporting did not stop newspapers, which grew as "the public voice steadily demanded their emancipation." By 1800 the *Morning Post* had many preeminent literary scribes. Shortly after, in 1814, *The Times* went to the steam press. The 1859 large circulation penny gazettes, the *Standard*, *Daily Telegraph*, and *Morning Star*, had "leaders of great ability" with a "marked absence of violence in language…very little that is inflammatory." By means of an "improved tone of leaders, and stricter accuracy in their information," these dailies "gradually and fairly won the immense power which they at present wield." Weeklies were also prospering. The major Sunday papers were the *Observer* for the "upper orders" and the *Weekly Dispatch*, *News of the World*, and *Lloyd's Weekly Newspaper* for the "operative class." After the stamp duty ended, London parish papers blossomed. The oldest, the *Clerkenwell News*, was about three-quarters advertising and sold 14,000 copies. Provided data on the circulation of several London dailies and weeklies as well as William Cobbett's *Political Register* and on the advertising revenue of *The Times*.

Special and general periodicals also multiplied. The *Family Herald* and its kin varied except for answers to correspondents. While some of the inexpensive offerings were "obscene," "the evil was greatly exaggerated." Questionable data indicated that the young bought many penny serials from which they formed the bad reading habits that the Pure Literature Society detested. The tastes of children and servants, and perhaps those of "young women in factories," could be improved. The *British Workman*, unsuitable for "really intelligent artisans," was acceptable for their families. Better journals had a circulation comparable to the old *Penny Magazine*. Stories were a staple but did not always teach the public. A good model was *Leisure Hour*, which carried interesting articles about the kingdom and the empire to the lower and middle classes unlike the religious press that was too grave.

American newspapers, cheaper and bigger than British, had gone from 200 in 1801 to about 4,000 in 1859.

14. [Pope, W. B.]. "Lord McCaulay [*sic*]." 14 (1860): 1–24.
Recognized T. B. Macaulay's "valuable criticism" and essays of a "thorough and exhaustive character" in the *Edinburgh Review*.

15. "England at the Accession of George III." 15 (1860–61): 213–26.
Painted eighteenth-century England as an "age of magazines and reviews" thanks to the inferiority of newspapers and the quality of the *Gentleman's Magazine*. That serial, as well as the *Rambler*, showcased Samuel Johnson's talent. Asides on the *Connoisseur* and *St. James's Chronicle*.

16. "Henry Drummond." 15 (1860–61): 255–84.
Limelighted an MP who defended the stamp duty because he thought that newspapers and the national welfare were "incompatible." Drummond believed that journalism represented "individual honesty and collective profligacy, political and literary." Anonymous reporters frequently fed readers the 'political gossip' they craved and selective news items, but *The Times* knew that profits rested on good writing.

17. [Arthur, William]. "The American Crisis." 17 (1861–62): 252–76.
Grieved that even "foremost journalists" could be unfair. "It is a melancholy feature of newspaper information, that it gives all the bad things, and all the irritating ones, but omits the greater part of the good." For example, stories in top London dailies repeated biased American paragraphs on the 1861 Civil War; "inferior" metro and country papers paraphrased those dailies.

18. [Arthur, William]. "The Struggle in America." 17 (1861–62): 513–40.
Indicted the "loud-mouthed [*New York*] *Herald*" for "abuse" and "ravings."

19. [Arthur, William]. "Great Britain and Her West India Colonies." 17 (1861–62): 540–83.
Charged the British and American press with disseminating biased information.

20. "High Church Literature for the People." 18 (1862): 124–56.
Listed several Anglican periodicals.

21. "Greece and the Greeks." 20 (1863): 130–58.
Referred to *Elipis* as "the court newspaper" in Greece.

22. "The American War." 20 (1863): 225–44.
Asides on Thurlow Weed of the *Albany* (NY) *Journal* and Horace Greeley, the "anti-slavery journalist *par excellence*."

23. "Thomas Hood." 21 (1863–64): 90–127.
Synopsized Hood's work as a contributor to *Punch* and the *Athenaeum*, as editor of the *New Monthly Magazine*, and as father of *Hood's Magazine*, 1844.

24. "The General Post Office." 21 (1863–64): 209–38.
Estimated that the post office carried 73 million newspapers in 1862: 45 million with an "impressed newspaper stamp," 28 million with postage stamps or paid in cash. Transmittals had risen by 500,000 over 1861. About the same number were not delivered because of "imperfect addresses" and one in 5,000 "escapes from its cover, because carelessly folded." Revenue from the impressed stamp was 130,415 pounds. Aside that the *Weekly Dispatch* attracted "rabid, radical" readers.

25. [Marzials, Frank T.]. "Mexico." 21 (1863–64): 387–419.
Conveyed that Mexico had no newspapers except "the solitary and very dreary example of the *Official Gazette*, which appears at irregular intervals." The country had "until very recently" a single magazine, which contained reprints from foreign periodicals and "a few native articles of very slender merit."

26. "Benjamin Franklin." 23 (1864–65): 483–514.
Review of James Parton's *Life and Times of Benjamin Franklin* remarked that his *Pennsylvania Gazette* was "incomparably the best paper published in the colonies." *Poor Richard's Almanack* averaged 10,000 copies annually.

27. [Marzials, Frank T.]. "John Leech." 24 (1865): 105–26.
Essay based on Leech's autobiography put him first among English caricaturists. He drew primarily for *Punch*, which, unlike the French *Charivari*, had no "prurient jest." Leech also sketched for the *Illustrated London News* and *Once a Week*.

Ventured that a really interesting book would be "the secret history of some of our leading periodicals," but it would be hard to write because of the anonymity that empowered authors.

28. [Arthur, William]. "Sala's *America in the Midst of War*." 24 (1865): 147–71.
Review of Geoge Augustus Sala's book shared that "cheap dailies" captured buyers by effective use of news vendors' boards.

29. [Rigg, J. H.]. "*The Gay Science*." 28 (1867): 140–66.
Review of E. S. Dallas' book pegged him as the one-time "chief" of *Times* literary critics but who in 1867 penned its political leaders.

30. "The English Language." 28 (1867): 269–92.
Argued that in 1867 many newspaper scribes and the best in magazines and reviews were better than Junius. The "principal reviews" particularly distanced themselves from "political favouritism" in making literary judgments.

31. "New Paris." 29 (1867–68): 330–62.

Presented the French press as "flourishing," if "sorely fettered" by government and limited by advertising that was hardly "lucrative" even by the standards of English country papers. Unlike British gazettes where opinion was direct, the French veiled commentary to elude prosecutions even though they frequently culminated in small fines and big publicity. Foreign papers were subject to censorship except *The Times*, read daily by Napoleon III who considered it "innocuous."

In 1867 France had 21 "political journals," the largest anti-government. "The most widely read daily paper is undoubtedly the *Siècle*." Its circulation was 40,000–50,000 under editor Léonor Havin, who sat in the Chamber of Deputies. Next among political heralds was the recent *Liberté*, whose circulation rose to 30,000 after Emile de Girardin bought it. The oldest paper, the *Gazette de France*, had a small circulation, and the *Moniteur*, the "official organ," survived on government money. By 1867 the *Presse* was a "semi-official" paper. The *Univers* had been suppressed because of the "violence of its editor, M. Louis Veûillot." The *Temps*, whose London correspondent was Louis Blanc, had "some of the best writing in French journalism." The *Journal des Débats* hired scholars (listed) who did not write for the public but made the paper popular in England. The *Constitutionnel* had been saved by feuilletons and the essays of Charles Sainte-Beuve, "some of most valuable contributions to the art of criticism ever published." *Figaro* had accurate information, but its readers and those of the inferior *Petit Journal* liked gossip and fiction. The *Monde Illustré* was a "beautiful weekly."

Most European papers had Paris correspondents: *Indépendance Belge*, 22; *Allgemeine Zeitung*, eight; Cologne's *Zeitung*, three. *The Times* and *Daily News* men were past their prime, the *Globe* writer was an ex-Jesuit, and the *Morning Star* sent a woman.

32. "*Lives of the Lord Chancellors of England*." 32 (1869): 177–97.

Review of John Campbell's study regarded the birth of the *Edinburgh Review* as "a great event" of its time. It may not have had an editor initially, but it soon had many articles by Henry Brougham.

33. [Moore, John]. "Life of Sir William Hamilton." 33 (1869–70): 1–32.

Analyzed some of the 16 articles that Hamilton wrote for the *Edinburgh Review* after editor Macvey Napier recruited him.

34. [Spender, Edward]. "The *Diary* of Henry Crabb Robinson." 33 (1869–70): 297–329.

Review recapitulated Robinson's career as a *Times* foreign correspondent, then its foreign editor for six months, "the happiest of his life." He worked with Peter Fraser, the chief leader-writer, and William Combe, hired straight from debtors' prison. After *The Times*, Robinson "dabbled a little in magazine writing." John Walter allegedly asked him to offer Robert Southey the paper's editorship, which the latter declined.

35. [Paton, J. B.]. "Sainte-Beuve and Renan." 33 (1869–70): 457–80.

Rooted Charles Sainte-Beuve's reputation as a literary critic in his articles in the *Globe* and *Revue des Deux Mondes*.

36. [Spender, Edward]. "Fall of the Second Empire." 35 (1870–71): 21–64.

Assessed the role of journalism in the run-up to the Franco-Prussian War when the "ablest" journals tried to "allay agitation" and when a French press with "full liberty" soon witnessed restraint of the "democratic," then other papers.

37. "American Newspapers." 36 (1871): 390–408.
Reviewed *Henry J. Raymond and the New York Press for Thirty Years: Progress of American Journalism from 1840 to 1870* by Augustus Maverick, a *New York Times* staffer. Rhapsodized that newspapers were the "lungs" of liberty essential in "free countries." Tracked those in the United States from the *Boston News-Letter* to the revolution, a period when the Northern press reputedly developed more extensively than the Southern. Thereafter, limited technology slowed news. By the 1840s New York's Dutch gazettes were boring, and the rest were "indescribably offensive." The "unscrupulous and unprincipled" James Gordon Bennett raised interest and circulation. Horace Greeley exerted valuable pressure for reform but should not have attacked family and property. Henry Raymond expected the *New York Times* to be "temperate, but not time-serving; progressive, but not radical; orthodox, but not sectarian." The New York papers created the constituency that sustained them, making newspapers a business driven by public opinion. In 1871 the city's 150 publications served the mass of readers spawned by American education, readers who enjoyed "rowdy journals." Editors, whose columns exposed their competition, left to subeditors supervision of the Night, City, Finance, and Literary desks. A typical New York paper employed 100 men with a total outlay of 500,000 dollars per year, but only ten were editorial staff and ten were reporters on morning papers. The Associated Press, started by dailies' owners, cost 8,000 dollars per year. These papers earned, from advertising, 2.5 million dollars of their annual revenue of 8.7 million dollars.

The Massachusetts press was better; the Washington, "the contrivance of political adventurers." The influence of the *Chicago Tribune* was "generally for the good." Frontier gazettes had "sharp, short, lightning sentences," humor, and sensation. The United States had no comic organ akin to *Punch* because Americans had "extreme sensitiveness," equality eliminated class humor, newspapers had humor columns, and country editors jokingly demeaned rivals in order to enhance their own advertising. The Sunday papers were the least religious, and the religious mirrored sectarian animus. Even though the American press was vulgar, insensitive, irreverent, and commercial, it was improving.

Aside that *The Times* covered the "ruling powers" and displayed breadth in news, a "tone of authority," and "strict impartiality."

38. "British Journalism." 38 (1872): 87–123.
Review of James Grant's *The Newspaper Press* deplored its "slovenly style" and inaccuracy but stole its data on London's press. Commenced newspaper history with Catholic, then government censorship; Nathaniel Butter's newsletters, and Marchamont Nedham's *Mercurius Britannicus*. By 1700 heralds were "purveyors of news and critics of opinion." The "outrageous license and calumny" bred by partisanship led to stamp and advertising duties. The stamp killed cheap newspapers, adversely impacting their vendors. Daniel Defoe, as subeditor of *Mist's Journal*, softened its criticism of government. Jonathan Swift in the *Examiner* was "venomous" as was John Wilkes in the *North Briton*. Junius popularized anonymity and a style that persisted in the columns of Theodore Hook in *John Bull* and the Thunderer (Edward Sterling) in *The Times*. Attack was justifiable when the press was fighting for its existence but not later. One battle was about reporting Parliament. MPs resisted originally because they spoke for themselves, not their constituents, and in 1871 because they hated outsiders listening to debate on sensitive issues. Another struggle, about libel law, dated from the time when publishers were liable for printing others' speeches and writings.

Easing of taxes and greater freedom had helped the press but so had technology from steam to electricity. (Asides on labor's reaction to the steam press and the pros and cons of the Hoe press.) Telegraphy was pivotal in the technology of the press, notably after P. J. Reuter. His service and then nationalization of telegraphy centralized news collection and, through the aegis of the Press Association, benefited locals. They gained power by mentoring readers about politics and securing advertising. To survive, independent London papers were adding "periodical" material and sporting news to their pages but were not "licentious."

The British press was outstanding, with "vigour of style and loftiness of aim," unlike the American, which spent more money and had more energy. Asides that from 1832 men of "higher character and purpose" began to offer unstamped periodicals to workers and that in 1872 reporters, often barristers and contributors to quarterlies and monthlies, left Parliament at 1 a.m.

39. "The Post Office." 38 (1872): 265–300.
Endorsed low postal rates for newspapers because their diffusion was beneficial to the "community at large."

40. [Clarke, John A.]. "The Agricultural Labourers' Union." 40 (1873): 327–46.
Encompassed several periodicals for agricultural workers, among them the *Labourers' Union Chronicle* and those that covered the walls of workers' homes.

41. "Japan." 42 (1874): 83–120.
Enlightened that the *Kyoto Gazette* was the official paper in Japan.

42. [Forman, H. Buxton]. "Charles Wells." 46 (1876): 121–36.
Nodded to a Wells' 1845 story in the *Illuminated Magazine* and his articles in the *People's Journal*.

43. "The Great Social War." 46 (1876): 452–83.
Catalogued newspapers "called into existence by the movement" to repeal the Contagious Diseases Acts.

44. [Forman, H. Buxton]. "Thomas Wade." 48 (1877): 104–23.
Aside on the policies of the *Literary Gazette*.

45. "Thomas De Quincey." 49 (1877–78): 35–74.
Skimmed De Quincey's work for the *Quarterly Review* but dwelt on his contributions to *Blackwood's Magazine* and *Tait's Edinburgh Magazine* and his association with publisher James Hogg. De Quincey's 1821 articles in the *London Magazine* "first established his fame," although he had already edited the *Westmoreland Gazette* in 1819.

46. [Mayer, S. R. Townshend]. "The Brothers Chambers." 51 (1878–79): 1–28.
Review of William Chambers' *Memoir* of his brother, Robert, praised their journalistic endeavors. Their first collaboration was *Kaleidoscope*, a three-penny fortnightly, 1821–22, with Robert as editor and author and William as publisher and printer. Their most successful publication was *Chambers's Edinburgh Journal*. Half the price of *Kaleidoscope* the *Journal* circulated 80,000 copies by its third number.

47. "China and the Chinese." 51 (1878–79): 136–77.
Opined that Chinese newspapers printed "audacious lies."

48. [Aubrey, W. H. S.]. "The Immediate Future of the United States." 51 (1878–79): 346–71.

Castigated American newspapers because journalists "pander to the ignorance and selfishness of the lower strata of society and to discourse in the strain known as 'high fallutin' on their rights." "[T]he tone of the public press, with a few honourable exceptions, is low and unworthy. The hateful system of 'interviewing,' and of raking up, with a view to publication, all the details of a man's past life, with exceedingly free and personal comments thereon, has led to an amount of license and of libertinism in journalistic matters, a parallel to which can only be found in the very darkest and worst days of the French Revolution. All this has helped to create and foster a morbid love of sensationalism and of highly seasoned newspaper dishes."

49. "Lessing's Life and Works." 51 (1878–79): 425–48.

Revisited G. E. Lessing's work as editor of the "*Vos Gazette*, a literary journal of repute still in existence" for which he also was a critic of first rank.

50. "An Editor's Portfolio." 52 (1879): 398–426.

Review of *Selections from the Correspondence of Macvey Napier* assumed that his articles in the *Quarterly Review* and the *Edinburgh Review* prepared him to edit the latter. Among the contributors with whom he worked were Henry Brougham, Thomas Carlyle, and T. B. Macaulay, who sometimes objected when Napier trimmed the "tinsel" from an article. His predecessor as editor, Francis Jeffrey, aimed for "readableness," essays more suitable for "lighter forms of literature" than for the *Edinburgh*.

51. "Father Curci." 57 (1881–82): 281–322.

Headlined Carlo Maria Curci, a sire of "the well-known periodical, the *Civiltà Cattolica*." Its editor for seven years, Curci supervised such able contributors as Taparelli d'Azeglio, who wrote on politics and philosophy; Giambattista Pianciani, on science; and Antonio Bresciani, on literature.

52. "Fiji." 57 (1881–82): 323–44.

Noticed that "Levuka, the commercial capital" of Fiji, had two newspapers, each issued biweekly.

53. "Daniel Defoe." 57 (1881–82): 345–70.

Compared the "pamphlets and broadsheets" of Defoe's day to the newspapers and leaders of Victorians with respect to the "literary warfare of party politics." Defoe was a "master of the craft" of political pamphleteering before he commenced his *Review* while he was a prisoner in Newgate. His newspaper commented on "current politics" to those who "listened to and paid for his advice." Although sometimes hired by government, he pledged to be unbiased, "an independent but friendly critic." After 1715, supposedly retired from journalism, he manipulated Jacobite organs, as *Mist's Journal*, "to render them politically harmless" but "financially successful."

54. "Life and Works of Heinrich Heine." 58 (1882): 411–38.

Glanced at Heine's work for the *Allgemeine Zeitung* and *Revue des Deux Mondes*.

55. "Half a Century of Literary Life." 60 (1883): 390–419.

Asserted that in 1820s journalists died from fast living; in the 1880s, from hard work under daily pressure to offer a fresh approach to the same topics. Both generations authored magazine articles to support themselves while writing novels. George Augustus Sala and Edmund Yates chose this route and earlier, E. G. Bulwer-Lytton, the allegedly unsuccessful editor of the *New Monthly Magazine*. William Maginn was "a man of vast learning and manifold powers, a valued contributor to *Blackwood's* [*Magazine*] and *Fraser's* [*Magazine*] in their palmist days," and the author of "slashing articles in the Tory *Age* and the Radical *True Sun*."

In 1882 *Punch* maintained its "wit and wisdom," and the newest periodicals presented preeminent men addressing both sides of controversial subjects. Aside on S. C. Hall, editor of the *Art Journal* for 40 years.

56. [Rigg, J. H.]. "*The London Quarterly Review*: New Series." 2d ser., 1 (1883–84): 1–15.

Described the *London Quarterly* before 1883 as "respectable and dull," without resources to compete with other periodicals in the areas of "general literature and science" and ignoring or tardily including matters of "vivid passing interest." Hereafter, the *Review* would continue as a Methodist publication, "a kind of censor of the press" but not of all publications because of their "portentous prodigality," and would accommodate family reading.

Inaugurated "Summaries of Foreign Periodicals," a feature that lasted through 1900.

57. "*Thomas Carlyle*." 2d ser., 4 (1885): 1–25.

Review of J. A. Froude's book paraphrased that Carlyle unsuccessfully negotiated with J. G. Lockhart to write for the *Quarterly Review*. Carlyle refused to pen for the *Westminster Review* but did so for the *London Magazine*. He also would not write leaders or literary criticism for *The Times* because he objected to the paper's politics. His *Sartor Resartus* in *Fraser's Magazine* added "much to the injury of the magazine."

58. [Keeling, Annie E.]. "Khartoum and General Gordon." 2d ser., 4 (1885): 145–63.

Thanked "the English consul and *Times* correspondent" for his "vivid picture" of the Sudan campaign.

59. "George Eliot." 2d ser., 4 (1885): 197–222.

Review of Eliot's *Life as Related in Her Letters and Journals* mentioned her connection to the *Westminster Review* where she was "a solitary, hard worked" figure as writer, then assistant editor, and her offer to pen for *Blackwood's Magazine*.

60. [Keeling, Annie E.]. "Eminent Women." 2d ser., 5 (1885–86): 21–43.

Flagged Mary Wollstonecraft at the *Analytical Review* and Margaret Fuller at the *Dial* before being the "assistant to Horace Greeley" at the *New York Tribune*.

61. [Kaufmann, Moritz]. "Socialism." 2d ser., 5 (1885–86): 205–27.

Lectured that the *Neue Rheinische Zeitung*, Karl Marx's paper in 1848 Cologne, was quickly suppressed and that the *Christian Socialist*, the organ of the Social Democratic Federation, was the child of William Morris and others.

62. [Noble, James Ashcroft]. "Leigh Hunt: His Life, Character, and Work." 2d ser., 7 (1886–87): 331–54.

Shadowed Hunt from his 1805 *News*, with "a short life and little influence," to "more profitable journalistic work." In 1807 he was a theatre critic for *The Times* and in 1808 he introduced the

Examiner, where he earned a reputation "as the fiery irreconcilable who had been sent to prison for libeling a prince." After the *Examiner*, with the literature of P. B. Shelley and John Keats, he established the *Liberal*, with which Lord Byron had ties. Charles Dickens and Macvey Napier both evaluated his work.

63. "Richard Jefferies." 2[d] ser., 11 (1888–89): 225–39.
Review of Walter Besant's *The Eulogy of Richard Jefferies* delineated his career from 1866 reporter for the *North Wilts Herald*. In 1872 he sparked a controversy with a *Times* letter on agricultural labor that opened doors to newspaper jobs on that topic, jobs he rejected to write bad novels. In 1873 and 1874 his articles appeared in the *Fortnightly Review*, *Fraser's Magazine*, the *New Quarterly Review*, and elsewhere. After modest literary success he died young and poor.

64. "The Life of a Journalist." 2[d] ser., 14 (1890): 1–27.
Prefaced that "[i]n England, the ablest and most accomplished newspaper journalists have almost always lived secluded lives and been unknown to the general public" yet "have influenced the world."

Review of *James Macdonell: Journalist*, by W. Robertson Nicoll, contrasted Macdonell, a man of this mold, with the well-known personnel of 'new journalism.' He was a foreign correspondent and leader-writer for the *Daily Telegraph* for nine years before going to *The Times* as a leader-writer for four years until he died at 37 years old. Macdonell, a "first-class English journalist" though a Scot, was not university educated unlike *Daily Telegraph* colleagues Edward Dicey and Edwin Arnold. They regarded him as a man of culture who wrote in "singularly pure, polished, and easy English." His early mentor was William McCombie, "farmer-editor and founder of the *Aberdeen Free Press*." Macdonell was his clerk before he began writing for the paper. At 20 he took a job at the Edinburgh *Daily Review* and met Hugh Gilzean-Reid, editor of the *Edinburgh News* and 1890 president of the Institute of Journalists. By 1863 Macdonell was editor of Newcastle's *Northern Daily Express* where he earned 150 pounds per year. To compete with Joseph Cowen's *Chronicle*, Macdonell worked "with great ability and thoroughness, and with marvelous energy and elasticity of spirit." In 1865, when the *Express* was sold, he refused a job at the *Scotsman* for one at the *Telegraph*. To support his eight siblings he also penned for the *Spectator*, *Macmillan's Magazine*, *Fraser's Magazine*, the *Saturday Review*, and *Leeds Mercury*. His articles in the *Spectator* were "thoughtful and polished."

Particularized Macdonell's workday at *The Times* even to the paper and ink he used. He apparently admired its editor, John Delane, a man with "the remarkable sagacity, the practical business faculty, the range of general knowledge, and the swift and almost unerring judgment and insight" essential for a successful editor even though he never wrote leaders.

65. [Davison, W. T.]. "Current Ethical Problems." 2[d] ser., 15 (1890–91): 114–29.
Review of W. S. Lilly's *On Right and Wrong* drew from his chapter, "The Ethics of Journalism." The "Fourth Estate" had "immense" and "still rapidly increasing importance" as a literary and political pulpit. The inaccuracy of the "new journalism" corrupted readers intellectually and morally, undermining the ethics that drove self-sacrifice for the sake of duty.

66. "Lord Houghton." 2[d] ser., 16 (1891): 91–111.
Applauded R. M. Milnes, 1st Baron Houghton, for his "gratuitous literary work" for *Hood's Magazine* when Thomas Hood was dying.

67. "John Murray." 2[d] ser., 16 (1891): 326–47.

Stressed Murray's journalistic life from his association with the *Edinburgh Review* (whose London circulation accounted for 5,000 of its 7,000 total). He was determined to counter "the bitterness of its criticisms" and "its extreme views on politics" by establishing the *Quarterly Review*. It lured contributors Walter Scott, alienated from the *Edinburgh*, and Robert Southey, paid 100 pounds per article, and editor William Gifford, earlier of the *Anti-Jacobin*. The *Quarterly*, which "scooped" the *Edinburgh* about the end of the French war, slowly emerged as "a power in the literary and political world and proved a steady source of revenue." J. G. Lockhart was "a most capable ruler, refined in taste and sound in judgment," an "accomplished editor…with a brilliant staff." Murray later launched less successful periodicals and the daily *Representative*, notorious because of the machinations of Benjamin Disraeli.

68. "*An Englishman in Paris*." 2[d] ser., 19 (1892–93): 78–102.

Review of A. D. Vandam's book pinpointed "Dr. Louis Véron, founder of the *Revue de Paris* – the precursor of the *Revue des Deux Mondes*"; Eugene Delacroix, essayist in the *Revue des Deux Mondes*; and Louis Blanc, whose *Homme Libre* "was scrupulously exact in ascertaining the truth of the statements" even in the advertisements it published, unlike the English press.

69. [Simon, John S.]. "The Methodist Agitation of 1835." 2[d] ser., 19 (1892–93): 129–54.

Indicated several titles of the religious press.

70. "John Greenleaf Whittier." 2[d] ser., 19 (1892–93): 224–44.

Condensed Whittier's ties to William Lloyd Garrison, first at the *Newburyport Free Press*, then the *Liberator*. By 1838 Whittier was editing the *Pennsylvania Freeman* in a building constructed by and for abolitionists. He contributed to the *National Era* from its inception in 1847.

71. "A Literary Chronicle." 2[d] ser., 20 (1893): 241–60.

Reviewed *John Francis: Publisher of the Athenaeum*, (1831–32) by his son, John Francis. Explained that James Silk Buckingham, the father of the *Athenaeum*, soon left to start a daily. The *Athenaeum* then incorporated the *London Literary Chronicle* and hired major writers of the period. Charles Wentworth Dilke, editor from 1830, shaped the *Athenaeum* "as an independent organ of literary and scientific criticism and intelligence." He was "the real founder of the paper, inasmuch as his judicious and spirited editorship, in conjunction with Mr. Francis's able management, first brought it success and power."

Swept past J. G. Lockhart as "the accomplished editor of the *Quarterly*" [*Review*]; John Bowyer Nichols, the "laborious author, printer, and editor, whose name was for many years connected with the *Gentleman's Magazine*"; the Great Exhibition that "gave ample employment to the descriptive talent of the periodical press in 1851"; and the newspaper duties (stamp, advertising, paper in 1830).

72. "Old New England." 2[d] ser., 22 (1894): 130–50.

Recorded that advertisements in the *Boston News-Letter* and other "early New England newspapers" often dealt with runaway servants and slaves.

73. [Forbes, U. A.]. "The Egyptian Patriotic Movement of 1893." 2d ser., 23 (1894–95): 111–27.

Perceived the "development of the Public Press" in Egypt as "a significant manifestation of the educational movement," but one focused more on political factionalism than instruction. Most European journals in Egypt were inferior except the recent *Progrès*. *Al Ahram* was "the oldest Arabic paper in the country, conducted by an Egyptian 'patriot,' who is a native of Syria and a French protected subject." The *Bosphorus Egyptien* was the most rabid of the anti-English tribunes, but *Al Moqattam* countered some of its opinions. The serials dependent on "native official sources," the *Journal Egyptien* and *Moayyad*, had too much influence.

74. "Coleridge's *Letters*." 2d ser., 25 (1895–96): 58–76.

Review of a book edited by Ernest H. Coleridge disclosed that S. T. Coleridge's work for the *Morning Post* was so impressive that its owner offered him shares in the newspaper to continue.

75. "*The Table-Talk of Shirley*." 2d ser., 26 (1896): 58–75.

Reviewed book wherein John Skelton reminisced about his first editor, T. S. Baynes of the *Edinburgh Guardian*. Baynes, who then moved to the *Daily News* as assistant editor, was "a man so cultured, so clear-headed, so wise in judgment, so eloquent with his pen, and, above all, so pure and unselfish in character."

76. "The Memoirs of Lady Eastlake." 2d ser., 26 (1896): 98–114.

Review of Elizabeth Rigby Eastlake's *Journals and Correspondence* spoke of her contributions to the *Foreign Quarterly Review* and the *Quarterly Review* when it and the *Edinburgh Review* "divided the empire of criticism, and wielded an influence such as no periodicals have since attained." However, during J. G. Lockhart's tenure as editor, the *Quarterly* was "sometimes marked by an inexcusable insolence of tone."

77. "*Life and Letters of Oliver Wendell Holmes*." 2d ser., 27 (1896–97): 77–94.

Examined Holmes' work for the *Harvard Collegian*, Boston's *Daily Advertiser*, and the *Atlantic Monthly*, which J. R. Lowell agreed to edit if Holmes consented to contribute.

78. "Henri Rochefort's *Adventures*." 2d ser., 28 (1897): 69–83.

Review of Rochefort's book spanned his journalism. He was a penny-a-liner in the 1850s for *Charivari*, where authors had to pay for every line over a hundred. Rochefort then penned for some "forgotten journals" before joining *Figaro*. When the paper fired him in 1867 for satirizing Napoleon III, he created the *Lanterne*, a weekly akin to a pamphlet that gained "world-wide notoriety" for its anti-Bonapartism and forced him to relocate to Brussels. In 1869 his *Marseillaise* also attacked the emperor.

79. "Mrs. Oliphant: An Appreciation." 2d ser., 29 (1897–98): 85–98.

Eulogized Margaret Oliphant as "a characteristic product of the Victorian age," chiefly because of her "admirable critical work" in *Blackwood's Magazine* and her observations and style as "The Looker-on."

80. [Rigg, J. H.]. "*The London Quarterly Review*." 2d ser., 29 (1897–98): 108–12.

Editor asserted that the *London Quarterly*, "the property, and the literary organ, of the Wesleyan Methodist Church" in 1897, was "the only high-class quarterly which represents orthodox Protestant

Nonconformist views and culture." The *North British Review* once served the Free Church of Scotland with "great distinction." The *British Quarterly Review*, the journal of Congregational Nonconformists, became less wise and more political over time. The *Dublin Review* and *Church Quarterly* published theology, literature, and science, but the first was Catholic and the second had "too many narrow and shallow High Church articles." Religious monthlies catered too much to current opinions and tastes, so the field for serious thought belonged to the *London Quarterly*.

81. "The Making of New South Wales." 2d ser., 29 (1897–98): 231–52.
Devoted pages to Henry Parkes, from 1850 the owner and editor of the *Empire*. The newspaper originally succeeded because he had "spirit and intelligence" that gave it "political significance." "It was the first journal to send a commissioner to the gold fields."

82. "France as It Is Today." 2d ser., 30 (1898): 102–19.
Raged that French newspapers were full of "defamatory clamour" against all authority and "gross libels" of politicians that forced them to resign.

83. Smith, Franklyn G. "Spain after the War." 3d ser., 1 (1899): 289–304.
Denounced the "rigid censorship" that meant only a "demagogue press" survived in Spain.

84. Jones, Dora M. "George Borrow." 3d ser., 2 (1899): 18–33.
Review of Borrow's *Life, Writings, and Correspondence* silhouetted the long-past editor of the *Monthly Magazine*, Sir Richard Phillips, as "a freethinker, a vegetarian, and, with all his eccentricities, an able man of business, the pioneer of Chambers and Knight in the field of popular literature." Like Robert and William Chambers and Charles Knight, he opened journalism to "obscure pens."

85. Drage, Geoffrey. "The War in South Africa." 3d ser., 3 (1900): 193–213.
Peeked at the *Express*, a newspaper of "a few Germans and Afrikanders at Bloemfontein" in 1875. Under its German editor, Carl Borckenhagen, it was particularly influential, 1888–98, partly because it was the only journal in the area.

86. Salmond, S. D. F. "*Horace Bushnell*." 3d ser., 4 (1900): 310–26.
Review of Theodore T. Munger's biography of Bushnell, an American theologian who was "early on the editorial staff of the *Journal of Commerce* (NY)," sighed that after ten months, he decided that "the work of a journalist was too heavy for him" so departed to law, then theology school.

The London Review, 1829–1830

While introducing itself, the *London Review* summarized the press of 1829.

1. [White, Joseph Blanco]. "Journals and Reviews." 1 (1829): 1–9.
Paralleled the contemporary press and the ancient agora or forum because each spread opinion. Newspapers in 1829, issued weekly and daily, disseminated useful advertising of goods and services as well as poetry and stories of the "peculiarly bloody murder" and "domestic intrigue" that distracted readers from opinion columns. The "daily journals" were different from the "dignified periodicals" only in degree. Even the reviews resorted to poems and tales in order to sell. "The love of amusement is the leading tendency of a refined society, and the higher the refinements, the more are men inclined to seek their amusement with the least possible exertion" of the mind. By satisfying this bent, the serious press was weakening the power of concentration "necessary to attain excellence in any one branch of information." The goals of the *London Review* were "to stimulate instead of palling curiosity" and to be politically impartial because in calmer social times, readers preferred independence.

2. "Social Life of England and France." 1 (1829): 171–98.
Posited that Joseph Addison in the *Spectator* set the precedent for addressing "light literature" to both sexes, thus making it purer.

Longman's Magazine, 1882–1900

Seeking a mass market, Charles J. Longman's endeavor scanned the press of several nations.

1. Howells, W. D. "Lexington." 1 (1882–83): 41–61.
Observed that American men read mostly newspapers; women, books; both sexes, magazines.

2. Freeman, Edward A. "Some Points in American Speech and Customs, II." 1 (1882–83): 314–34.
Admitted that American newspaper interviewing could be unpleasant when a reporter posed unfair questions.

3. Boyes, John Fred[erick]. "In Memoriam – Dutton Cook." 3 (1883–84): 179–87.
Honored Edward Dutton Cook who lived in the era when journalism emerged as a "career." He published his first article in *Chambers's Journal* and others in the *Gentleman's Magazine*, *All the Year Round*, and *Temple Bar*. Once acting editor of the *Cornhill Magazine*, he achieved his greatest fame as theatre critic of the *Pall Mall Gazette* and *World*.

4. Layard, Gertrude. "Armand Carrel." 5 (1884–85): 48–53.
Saluted Carrel, "the great French journalist," whose early newspaper columns were on the military. He then wrote about politics for gazettes and magazines until January 1830 when he began the *National* with Adolphe Thiers. In July, when the king cancelled press liberties, journalists assembled at the *National* offices planning a resistance that subsequently helped to drive Charles X from power. Carrel, who knew the power of the daily, soon made the *National* "the ablest and most influential political journal." He condemned Emile de Girardin for turning the newspaper from "political instruction" to "financial speculation" dependent on advertising and volume sales. In their duel, Carrel died.

5. B[oyd], A. K. H. "Sir Henry Taylor's *Autobiography*." 5 (1884–85): 624–32.
Perused more carefully the contributions of Taylor's father, George, to the *Quarterly Review* than those of Henry to other periodicals.

6. Hervey, Charles. "Some Personal Recollections." 5 (1884–85): 634–40.
Recalled Countess Marguerite Blessington, who displayed "a certain literary talent" as editor of the *Keepsake*, and Charles Lever, the editor of the *Dublin University Magazine*, who published some of Hervey's articles.

7. Evans, Beriah Gwynfe. "The Peasantry of South Wales." 6 (1885): 286–302.
Warranted that the majority of Welsh newspapers were politically biased but otherwise "rank with the best-conducted English papers." Welsh gazettes and magazines stimulated peasants' interest in the outside world.

8. Prothero, R. E. "Oliver Wendell Holmes." 8 (1886): 300–06.
Remembered that Holmes attended Cambridge Port School with Margaret Fuller, later of the *Dial*, but omitted her connection to the *New York Tribune*.

9. Nelson, W. F. "Early Newspaper Sketches." 8 (1886): 499–513.
History of the origins of the "mighty influence" of the 1886 press wondered if "newes" came from noise. Precursors of the modern newspaper were the *acta diurna*, Venetian *gazetta*, and Frankfurt's *Journal* (1615), the first weekly. In England newsletters gave way to Nathaniel Butter's *Weekely News* and a legion of Civil War mercuries, many with advertising. Marchamont Nedham inserted a leader in his *Moderate* (1648), and Roger L'Estrange symbolized censorship. Other seventeenth-century landmarks were the emergence of the *Oxford*, later *London Gazette*, published since 1665, and perhaps the first country paper, the *Stamford Mercury* (1695).

Daniel Defoe's *Review* was important early in the next century as was the enactment of the 1712 stamp duty that apparently ended "a multitude of low-class newspapers with their wretched record of prodigies and wonders." Yet the 1731 prospectus of the *Gentleman's Magazine* said that there were so many serials it was impossible to read them all. The *General Advertiser* (1748) was the first all-advertising paper. In the 1760s the controversies about John Wilkes' *North Briton* and the *Public Advertiser's* Junius fueled interest in the press. When the *Daily Universal Register* arrived in 1785, it showed no signs of stardom even after changing its title to *The Times* in 1788. By 1803 it sold only 1,000 daily compared to the 4,000 of the *Morning Post*.

In 1760 9,464,790 newspapers were sold in England. By 1777 London had 17 newspapers producing 13,000,000 copies annually. The stamp duty rose dramatically during the French Revolution.

10. Matthews, Brander. "The Ethics of Plagiarism." 8 (1886): 621–34.
Discussed cases of plagiarism, including those of the *Atlantic Monthly* and *Cornhill Magazine*, and commentary on the subject published in the *Saturday Review*.

11. Prothero, R. E. "John Greenleaf Whittier." 9 (1886–87): 182–89.
Prefaced that Whittier "disliked journalism" even though he published in William Lloyd Garrison's *Newburyport Free Press* and edited Boston's *American Manufacturer*. He allegedly abandoned the press after a stint as editor of the *Hartford Review*. Meanwhile, "Garrison started the *Liberator* in a small, dingy, ink-bespattered office on the third storey of the Merchants' Hall in Boston."

12. Russell, George W. E. "Count Vizthum's Journals." 10 (1887): 34–43.
Review of Georg Vizthum's *Reminiscences of St. Petersburg and London Between 1852 and 1864* despised "the long articles in the *Quarterly Review* and letters to *The Times*, conceived in the most vehemently warlike spirit" by Lord Robert Cecil, later Lord Salisbury.

13. Besant, Walter. "The Endowment of the Daughter." 11 (1887–88): 604–15.
Guessed that middle-class women were entering journalism "by ones and twos. Before long, they will sweep in with a flood."

14. Pollock, Walter Herries. "Théophile Gautier." 16 (1890): 391–409.
Labeled Gautier a novelist, a poet, and "a journalist of the most steadygoing and punctual kind." His copy, done "thoroughly and conscientiously," was always on time. He published in the *Revue de Paris* and *Figaro* but excelled in literary criticism for the *Presse*.

15. The Author of *Letters from the Baltic* [Elizabeth Rigby Eastlake]. "Reminiscences of Edinburgh Society Nearly Fifty Years Ago." 21 (1892–93): 250–64.
Memorialized Francis Jeffrey, John Wilson, and J. G. Lockhart, the last two in relation to *Blackwood's Magazine*.

16. B[oyd], A. K. H. "Dean Church of St. Paul's." 25 (1894–95): 604–21.
Review of *Life and Letters of Dean [R. W.] Church* voiced that he was responsible for the "review department" in "the admirable ecclesiastical paper," the *Guardian* (1846).

17. Pollock, Walter Herries. "Marseilles." 26 (1895): 583–87.
Alerted aspiring journalists that they could submit material to editors of dailies but should not expect payment until they had a name.

18. Dobson, Austin. "Thomas Gent, Printer." 27 (1895–96): 572–85.
Biography of Gent, the eighteenth-century printer of the *York Journal*, aired that its competitor, the *York Courant*, was printed by his wife's uncle.

19. B[oyd], A. K. H. "Oliver Wendell Holmes." 28 (1896): 344–56.
Review of *Life and Letters of Oliver Wendell Holmes*, by John T. Morse, Jr., avowed that Holmes "suggested the title for the *Atlantic Monthly*" and editor J. R. Lowell "insisted he become a contributor."

20. P[arker], E. H. "The *Peking Gazette* and Chinese Posting." 29 (1896–97): 73–81.
Bruited that before the Europeans arrived in China, the *Peking Gazette*, or "as the Chinese call it, the *Metropolitan Reporter*," was the only newspaper there. The outsiders taught the Chinese the merits of "rapid, precise, and regular information." For 35 years the "leading" Shanghai journal published excerpts in English, but the *Gazette* also had competition from tribunes that got information directly from the capital by telegraph. Foreign editors who bought secrets from bureaucrats faced imperial censure if their columns caused problems. The *Shanghai Reporter*, accepted by the court and circulated also in Korea, Japan, Siam, and Burma, was "as well managed an organ as any European newspaper." The *Peking Gazette* was still important for news of the court, official promotions, provincial government, and decrees respecting missionaries.

21. Maxwell, Herbert. "Blackwoodiana." 31 (1897–98): 117–30.
Review of Margaret Oliphant's *Annals of a Publishing House* blared that the *Edinburgh Magazine*, with "a brace of utterly incongruous and equally incompetent editors," quickly failed. William Blackwood then created *Blackwood's Magazine*, whose "brutality" resulted in sales of 5,000 per month by 1827 and 8,000 by 1831. The "craze for anonymity" generated much "umbrage." Blackwood valued William Maginn's work before he was famous, but the founder's sons rejected good articles, causing quality authors to depart, such as W. M. Thackeray to *Fraser's Magazine*. Other important contributors were

G. H. Lewes, E. G. Bulwer-Lytton, and Archibald Alison. Paraphrased J. G. Lockhart, the *Quarterly Review* editor, that J. W. Croker was never a careful reviewer.

22. K. [Leonora B. Lang]. "Trials of the Wife of a Literary Man." 32 (1898): 126–32.
Fussed that magazine editors burdened their wives when they entertained prospective women contributors at home.

23. Lang, L[eonora] B. "Two Centuries of American Women." 35 (1899–1900): 323–35.
Pointed out that eighteenth-century American "[w]omen publishers and women printers were numerous." For example, Anna Katharine Green continued the *Maryland Gazette* after her husband died, while "the "Goddards, mother and daughter, were the most business-like."

Macmillan's Magazine, 1859–1900

Alexander Macmillan's monthly examined journalism frequently. Anonymity and technology, the London correspondent and the war correspondent, the penny press and its elite siblings all cropped up in *Macmillan's*.

1. Y., A. [Alexander Macmillan]. "The *Quarterly Review* on Mr. Tennyson's *Maud*." 1 (1859–60): 114–15.
Reacted to a *Quarterly* review (10/59) by saying that it was not in "the smart and slashing style" that critics often employed to display their own cleverness and hide their lack of insight.

2. Cairns, Rev. John, D.D. "The Late Dr. George Wilson, of Edinburgh." 1 (1859–60): 199–203.
Obituary of Wilson resurrected his work in a "manuscript weekly newspaper" while at the High School of Edinburgh and his later essays in the *British Quarterly Review*.

3. Maurice, Rev. F[rederick] D[ension]. "Lord Macaulay." 1 (1859–60): 241–47.
Rumored that T. B. Macaulay expected anonymity to die in magazines but not newspapers. The *Edinburgh Review* had "established the *WE* ascendancy," but its talented writers, with a new and dashing style of writing, still won renown.

4. Hughes, Thomas. "Italy Resurgent and Britain Looking On." 1 (1859–60): 494–95.
Envisioned *The Times* as "a mirror – and a wonderfully sensitive and accurate mirror – of the England of to-day."

5. Masson, David. "Thomas Hood." 2 (1860): 315–24.
Recapitulated Hood's journalistic career from the *Comic Annual* in 1829. After "casual contributions to other periodicals" he scribbled for, then edited the *New Monthly Magazine* (1841) before launching *Hood's Magazine* in 1844.

6. Norton, Hon. Mrs. [Caroline]. "Books of Gossip: Sheridan and His Biographers." 3 (1860–61): 173–79.
Judged that the *Age* showed "wit" and "vitality."

7. [Masson, David]. "The Chinese Capital, Pekin." 3 (1860–61): 248–56.
Pirated data from the *Chinese Repository* "published at Canton."

8. Hughes, Thomas. "Opinion on American Affairs." 4 (1861): 414–16.
Tagged the *New York Herald* "one of the most scurrilous journals of the whole States."

9. Dicey, Edward. "The Naples Question." 4 (1861): 499–504.
Assigned "little importance" to English press coverage of Italy because all papers with news from press agencies, as Reuter and Havas, used the same language. Aside on Naples' *Populo d'Italia*, Turin's *Armonia*, and the *Gazetta di Verona*.

10. Smith, Alexander. "Hugh Macdonald." 5 (1861–62): 17–23.
Unmasked poet Macdonald as subeditor of the *Glasgow Citizen* under editor "James Hedderwick, an accomplished journalist."

11. Coleridge, John Duke. "The Late Herbert Coleridge." 5 (1861–62): 56–60.
Pointed to the work of philologist Coleridge in the *Eton School Magazine* and *Macmillan's*.

12. One Who Knew It Well [J. M. Ludlow]. "Paris Revisited." 5 (1861–62): 65–72, 119–28.
Yearned for the small Paris news-shops that once sold the "cheaper, democratic papers." Napoleon III curbed this press, leaving only "worthless little halfpenny papers" fit only for children. *Figaro*, the *Monde Illustré*, and *Ami de la Religion* distributed "scandalous gossip, woodcuts, and a seasoning of bigotry." Among the elite press the "monthly *Revue Chrétienne* occupies a really distinguished place among the higher order of periodicals." The French read the British press but objected to its inability to differentiate between the people and the ruler.

13. Hughes, Thomas, Author of *Tom Brown at Oxford*. "Anonymous Journalism." 5 (1861–62): 157–68.
Reminded that the British press, except for one *Times* leader, was silent when France first required journalists to sign newspaper columns. Since journalism had great influence in a free society, it was important to consider its role. A free press should mean that leader-writers had the option to sign. Anonymity conferred power beyond the intrinsic worth of an article and deceived with its "we." The practice only benefited owners by making their papers more valuable, editors by inflating their importance, and journalists who catered to readers looking for the "spicy article," whether in the *Saturday Review* or *Reynolds's Miscellany*. Papers that ran counter to public opinion aimed to direct it, while the majority echoed views, shifting with them. One column did not reflect a journal, merely a journalist. Signed articles would allow the public to choose whom to read, would lessen abuse even in the "so-called religious newspaper," and would perhaps slow the drift of the *Saturday Review* to gossip, ridicule, and ultimately libel. The "highest class of writers" could be anonymous but mandating the rest to sign would limit "license." An end to secrecy would not harm the reputations of journalists, many with other professions, and might spur standards of practice. Signed essays in periodicals were increasing, and signed letters in newspapers were more effective than anonymous leaders.

14. Our Special Correspondent in America, E[dward] D[icey]. "Three Weeks in New York." 5 (1861–62): 453–63.
Pontificated that "in a free country the condition of the press is a correct index of its state of civilization." The United States newspaper resembled the English gazette "in the immense amount of news given, in the great space occupied by advertisements, and in the fact that the leaders are practical comments, not abstract essays," but the American model was "a sort of cross between a country newspaper and a penny paper." With higher literacy in the Northern United States, where

people yoked education and suffrage, every village had a journal. In the towns a far "lower class" than in Britain read the gazettes sold by street vendors rather than by subscription. "The inevitable consequence of such conditions is to encourage the 'sensation' system of newspaper headings and paragraphs which offend our taste so constantly."

Most dailies were local in scope. New York tribunes circulated widely but were not national unlike those in London and Paris. Philadelphia, for example, had no *New York Herald*, *New York Tribune*, or *New York Times* for sale on its streets. The American country press was better than the British; the metro, worse. If "the New York press is taken…as proof of the absence of high mental culture in the United States, the relatively high standard of the local press ought fairly to be taken as evidence of the extent to which education is diffused." However, people tended to measure American journalism by New York's papers, notably the *Herald*, which sold 100,000 copies daily because it was the most readable. The *Times* lacked the *Herald's* 'verve' but was as "unscrupulous" in reporting foreign affairs. The *Tribune* had "more weight by its individual opinion" and was "better written, better printed, and more carefully got up" but had a "doctrinaire" tone that made its articles difficult to peruse. "The most respectable-looking, to English eyes…are the *Post*, of which [William Cullen] Bryant is editor, and the *World*, which is the organ of the mercantile community. But neither…has a very extensive circulation." Most newspapers were careless about style. Short paragraphs with big headers lured hasty readers but were "fatal to good writing." Advertisements, in a "diversity of type and variety of space," were unattractive, and the *Herald's* personal inserts were "questionable."

15. Our Special Correspondent in America [Edward Dicey]. "Washington During the War." 6 (1862): 16–29.

Believed that the ideas of Henry Brougham, Francis Jeffrey, and Sydney Smith in the *Edinburgh Review* shaped the views of W. H. Seward, American Secretary of State.

16. Our Special Correspondent in America [Edward Dicey]. "The Free West." 6 (1862): 177–91.

Blared that Racine (WI) was an important town with several newspapers. In its more prosperous days it had three dailies. By 1860 there were three weeklies, the *Advocate, Press*, *Democrat*, and "a German paper, the *Volks-Blatt*." The *Advocate*, an example of a "Western country newspaper," had four pages (two advertising, two letters and some news) and cost six shillings per year. Although it was an "unwieldy English size," it had "sensible and moderate" language. When the *Advocate* built a new home, the *Press* constructed another close enough to block its rival's light.

17. K[innea]r, [A. S.]. "Leigh Hunt's Poetry." 6 (1862): 238–48.

Checked Hunt's work in his *Examiner* and the *London Journal*.

18. Collins, Charles Alston. "The Morning Paper." 6 (1862): 375–81.

Enthused that the morning paper was one of the "immense pleasures and sources of gratification." Leaders exhibited careful thought, and letters exhibited sound views. Provision of domestic and foreign news was so fast and thorough that it was hard to assimilate everything. Other columns went to crime, law courts, theatre, and finance, which like sports had a special language. Advertisements provided social commentary as did birth, marriage, and death notices.

19. Wright, Thomas, F.S.A., Etc. "The History of Almanacs." 7 (1862–63): 173–85.

Sped through the history of almanacs from Rome to the seventeenth century.

20. [Rowe, Nicholas]. "The Russian Political Press." 7 (1862–63): 393–400.
Outlined the Russian press from the *Moscow Gazette* (1703) and *St. Petersburg Gazette* (1711), both published irregularly until the latter became a biweekly in 1728. It was not a real newspaper but a record of ukases and official appointments. In 1745 a monthly literary review surfaced.

Easing of censorship by Alexander II brought a flood of periodicals, so "the Press now forms a real power in Russia." Reviews carried literary and theatre criticism, feuilletons, and essays on social customs. Among the chief periodicals, excluding the scientific and professional, was the *Russian Messenger*, edited by Michael Katkoff, "one of the most accomplished scholars and journalists." This monthly of excellent reputation had 9,000 subscribers. The *Contemporary*, with "great ability" in its literary articles, had recently lost Ivan Turgenev to the *Russian Messenger* but kept 7,500 subscribers. *Our Time*, pro-government, had 4,000; *National Notes*, an old and respected literary and political serial, had 3,000.

The "leading dailies," the *Moscow Gazette* and *St. Petersburg Gazette*, which had a "monopoly" on political information, had 9,000 subscribers each. The owners of the *Moscow Gazette* wanted to make it the dominant daily. The *Northern Bee* was a clever radical journal with 5,000 subscribers; the *Invalide*, with 2,000, featured personalities; the *Northern Post*, the official paper of the Interior Ministry, was "carefully conducted"; the *Journal de St. Petersbourg*, the organ of the Foreign Ministry "conducted with great ability," had 8,000 subscribers, many of them foreigners. St. Petersburg also had a *Police News*. The *Odessa Messenger* was the only good local paper. Most dailies cost a halfpenny but were half the size of the English. Without newsboys, they depended on subscriptions. Among the papers from abroad, the "most famous" was *Kolokol*, produced by Alexander Herzen in London. This widely circulated sheet was reputedly read by Alexander II. The secret press in Russia preached revolution.

21. Masson, David. "Dead Men Whom I Have Known – William Thom of Inverury." 9 (1863–64): 337–43.
Section of a series pictured buyers of the *Aberdeen Journal* waiting for it as it arrived "wet."

22. Stack, J. Herbert. "The New Irish Difficulty." 13 (1865–66): 506–18.
Discerned that British papers, even the top, scattered biased news among advertisements.

23. P[oole], E.S[tanley]. "Travellers and Critics." 13 (1865–66): 518–28.
Decried the reappearance, in the *Quarterly Review* and *North British Review*, of "the worst features" of literary criticism of prior decades. Readers of the 1860s expected "fairness," not "blows," so critics did greater damage than earlier.

24. "Penny Novels." 14 (1866): 96–105.
Imagined that mid-century penny magazines thrived from stories of "seduction, adultery, forgery, and murder" that pushed the *London Journal*'s circulation in 1849 to 500,000. When the *Journal* published the work of Charles Reade and excerpts of great novelists, circulation slipped to 250,000 until Pierce Egan stressed morality. By the 1860s the *London Journal* and *Family Herald* had a "strong moral tone" best evident in their answers to correspondents. Letters came principally from the poor, the ignorant, and those without recourse to other sources of information about medicine, law, and etiquette.

25. Gurney, Rev. Archer. "Reminiscences of Vienna." 14 (1866): 417–24.
Accented sensuality in such French serials as *Figaro*, the *Petit Journal*, and *Humorist*, an "amazingly clever paper" that was a Gallic version of *Punch* without illustrations.

26. M[aurice], C. E. "Life and Writings of Joseph Mazzini: Translated – Vols. I–III." 16 (1867): 54–61.
Indicated Mazzini's contributions to the *Indicatore Genoese* but nothing else of his journalism.

27. Sidgwick, Henry, Fellow, Trinity College, Cambridge. "The Prophet of Culture." 16 (1867): 271–80.
Essay on Matthew Arnold reiterated his view that however good, "bold," and "vivacious" anonymous criticism was, it was irresponsible. The prediction of others that signature would bring dullness was disproved by his writings.

28. Seeley, J. R. "Milton's Political Opinions." 17 (1867–68): 299–311.
Glanced at John Milton's ties to journalism and ideas on a free press.

29. The Author of *John Halifax, Gentleman* [Dinah M. Mulock]. "A City at Play." 18 (1868): 40–47.
Scoffed at Parisian periodicals that were "so limp as to their paper, so florid and grandiose in their style."

30. Ralston, W. R. S. "The Experience of a Russian Exile." 19 (1868–69): 107–14.
Article on Vasily Kelsiev singled out the Russian exile press: *Polar Star*, "known all over Europe" after 1855, and *Kolokol*, launched by Alexander Herzen in 1857, "which soon acquired immense weight and popularity" in Russia.

31. MacDonald, George. "Stephen Archer." 19 (1868–69): 235–43.
Related that Archer, "a stationer, bookseller, and newsmonger in one of the suburbs of London," kept his journalistic wares on racks at the door, shifting them as buyers' tastes changed.

32. A British Author [Arthur Helps]. "International Copyright Between Great Britain and America: A Letter to Charles Eliot Norton, Esq." 20 (1869): 89–95.
Categorized the use of another's work as theft, including American publication of books based on their serialized parts in British magazines.

33. Dicey, Edward. "The Italy of To-Day." 20 (1869): 114–23.
Rejoiced that Italian journalism was "becoming more of a profession." Only "a few years ago" Milan had the *Gazetta Ufficiale* and "a few literary and dramatic broadsheets." In 1869 the city had as many dailies as London, all selling well. One, *Perseveranza*, could "rank in the first class of Continental journals." Florence's *Nazione* was influential and profitable. However, many Italian papers, like French, contained little news and few advertisements but much personal abuse in violent language. Penned by recent graduates or scribes of no consequence, these cheap papers flourished because Italian readers, though less educated, were like Americans in craving news.

34. Yonge, Miss [Charlotte]. "Children's Literature. III: Class Literature of the Last Thirty Years." 20 (1869): 448–56.
Bowed to the *Magazine for the Young*, which "wonderfully contrives to avoid *flabby* stories," but not *Aunt Judy's Magazine*, whose quality varied.

35. Smiles, Samuel. "Frederick Koenig, Inventor of the Steam Printing Machine." 21 (1869–70): 135–45.

Congratulated John Walter II for transforming *The Times* from a news provider to a public opinion guide with political influence. His addition of leaders led to a loss of Customs printing, but "independence, the ability of its criticisms, and the vast mass of information...from correspondents abroad and effective reporting at home" won subscribers. His management skill averted a strike by compositors and pressmen opposed to installation of the steam press. Besides *The Times*, the *Literary Gazette*, *Journal of Natural Philosophy*, and *Weekly Dispatch* also adopted the König press. *The Times* subsequently went to the Applegarth, the Hoe, and then the Walter, an "entirely original" press. *See* 31: 309.

36. The Author of *Mary Powell* [Anne Manning]. "Mary Russell Mitford: An Epitome." 21 (1869–70): 346–54.

Lamented that the 40 pounds due Mitford for articles in the *Lady's Magazine* was not paid.

37. Badeau, General [Adam]. "Our Relations with England." 21 (1869–70): 455–64.

Aside on the possible demise of the *Spectator* in the 1860s.

38. Fyfe, J. H. "Sir George Cornewall Lewis." 21 (1869–70): 465–74.

Peeked at Lewis' editing of and articles in the *Edinburgh Review.*

39. "The Duel of the Nations." 22 (1870): 321–33.

Recorded that Berlin's "comic paper, *Kladderadatsch*" was "hardly second in importance to our own *Punch*."

40. Seeley, J. R. "The English Revolution of the Nineteenth Century. II." 22 (1870): 347–58.

Reckoned that nineteenth-century newspapers organized public opinion by providing information and a forum for discussion. By mirroring and molding views they were akin to Parliament except that they were in constant session throughout the kingdom. The danger was that this activity might breed readers who accepted rather than formulated ideas.

41. "M. Guizot and *The Spectator*." 23 (1870–71): 347–52.

Painted *Spectator* commentary on an article by François Guizot as "spluttering, and screaming, and menacing."

42. A Military Contributor. "England's Place among the Nations." 23 (1870–71): 358–68.

Grumbled that some journalists "writing for their daily bread used flippant language in speaking of the military world," 1854–56, language that hurt the army's reputation.

43. Goadby, Edwin. "England's Defence Against Herself." 23 (1870–71): 408–16.

Worried that average citizens underestimated British preeminence because dailies and weeklies overemphasized it.

44. "An Age of Lead." 24 (1871): 63–68.
Described morning papers in the reign of George IV as light and varied. Although journalism in 1871 was "*par excellence* the mirror of the age," it was drowning in "a sea of lead," full of foreign correspondence and lengthy parliamentary debates. Summaries of speeches, except those of key politicians, would still educate readers politically. The impressions of the reporter, an "impartial listener," helped readers more than verbatim copy. As country journals multiplied, MPs spoke to their audiences, conducting less business and boring readers of London morning dailies.

45. Barry, William. "The Current Street Ballads of Ireland." 25 (1871–72): 190–99.
Unearthed much local news in the titled ballads.

46. Bryce, James. "The Legal Profession in America." 25 (1871–72): 206–17.
Boasted that American lawyers had more status than other "learned professions, or their new sister, journalism."

47. Author of "Friends in Council" [Arthur Helps]. "A Conversation." 25 (1871–72): 286–94.
Contended that the increase in press power was "perfectly enormous," 1771–1871, and that journalistic "mischief" came from manipulation, not proliferation.

48. C[ross], J[ohn] W. "Social New York." 26 (1872): 117–25.
Stereotyped the *New York Herald* as "blatant nonsense."

49. W. "Charles James Lever." 26 (1872): 337–44.
Recited Lever's contributions to the *Literary Gazette*, *Cornhill Magazine*, and *Dublin University Magazine*, which he also edited, 1842–45, the "halcyon days for the corps of the Irish periodicals."

50. Cole, Charles A. "Vermont." 28 (1873): 171–80; 34 (1876): 69–75.
Denounced American local gazettes because their reviews were invariably judgments that dishonored the reviewer and debased the paper. Papers also promoted products and services indirectly, as when the physician and publisher of Burlington's *Bulletin* printed letters from patients he treated. Aside that Grace Greenwood was a "lively writer" for the *New York Tribune*.

51. Grove, George. "Mr. Deutsch and the *Edinburgh Review*." 28 (1873): 382–84.
Exemplified periodicals' disputes. Responded to a July 1873 *Edinburgh* article by F. R. Conder, itself in rebuttal to an October 1867 *Quarterly Review* essay by Emmanuel Deutsch, so widely read that copies of the *Quarterly* "on the tables of the Athenaeum Club are said to have been black with finger-marks."

52. Arnold, Matthew. "A Speech at Westminster." 29 (1873–74): 361–66.
Quoted the *Revue Suisse*, "one of the most seriously conducted and trustworthy reviews in Europe" that the American newspaper was 'ephemeral' reading. With "politics, poetry, advertising, criticism, novels, scandal, horrors, marvels" scattered indiscriminately in its pages, it spread ignorance.

53. Wilson, A[lexander] J. "The Walter Press." 31 (1874–75): 309–17.
Reveled that the daily was "a wonderful thing...a product of modern civilisation." Education, wealth, and wants spawned public demand for "*recent* news." Pressure of time meant news widely gathered and rushed by rail, telegraphy, and steamship had to be sorted. Putting the news in "perfect order" was the job of the newspaper. With more readers able to afford it and the ease of transporting it, speed in printing was essential.

The Walter press was the "newest and most perfect method of newspaper printing." *The Times* was a pioneer in technology from the König press (*see* 21: 135). Printing, unlike newspaper operations, sought to reduce labor by being "efficient." The Walter press, much better than the "old Hoe," printed from a continuous roll of paper constantly inking stereotypes to ensure consistent impressions. This process benefited penny dailies, expensive to establish and run in London where costs of other journalism departments and competition from gazettes like the *Scotsman*, the "most enterprising of the provincial papers," were rising.

While the legions of newspapers might account for the "literary superficiality" of audiences with leisure and could become an "annoyance," worthwhile dailies had "an enormous influence in widening people's ideas" on a variety of topics. Newspapers also "level up" knowledge and "prevent the spread of abuses." Those that were "vehicles of intercommunication" rather than representatives of class or party would endure. The leading country gazettes had a monopoly of local news; the London penny press had more constituents; and *The Times* had status, "imperial, it stands for the English race." Sales paid for paper; advertising paid for all other costs.

54. Routledge, James. "Indian Notes. I: The Political Situation." 32 (1875): 223–36.
Contrasted the attitudes of the Indian viceroy, "markedly fair and just" toward the Indian press, and the English in India, proponents of liberty only when indigenous gazettes applauded the Raj.

55. Edwards, H. Sutherland. "Self-Government in Russia." 32 (1875): 314–23.
Alluded to St. Petersburg's *Golos* and Kalouga's *Gazette.*

56. Keary, C. F. "*The Germ*." 34 (1876): 439–47.
Warranted that contributors to the captioned Pre-Raphaelite magazine significantly affected art and literature.

57. Edwards, H. Sutherland. "The Byways of Bookmaking." 34 (1876): 457–64.
Glimpsed George Augustus Sala's "interesting column" weekly in the *Illustrated London News.*

58. Dilke, Charles Wentworth. "English Influence in China." 34 (1876): 557–68.
Averred that the *China Mail* and *North China Herald* were biased in their reporting of Chinese affairs.

59. Smith, Goldwin. "A Word More about the Presidential Elections." 35 (1876–77): 375–85.
Conceptualized journalism as "a calling which is of almost fearful importance in any free country." The United States press was generally "moderate, reasonable, and loyal to the public good." Thanks to "increased ascendancy of native over foreign writing and management," "the level, both intellectual and moral, of American journalism has been visibly rising during the last ten years."

60. Lagardie, H. de [Caroline de Peyronnet]. "French Novels and French Life." 35 (1876–77): 386–96.

Broadcast that French journalism was frequently the road to a political career, and the newspaper feuilleton was the only "literary food" of many French readers.

61. Fitzmaurice, Edmond. "Hungary and Croatia." 36 (1877): 34–42.

Noticed two Croatian gazettes, *Zatocnik*, published on the frontier to escape the censors, and *Zastava*, whose imprisoned owner criticized government.

62. M[orley], J[ohn]. "Harriet Martineau." 36 (1877): 47–60.

Deemed Martineau's "Biographic Sketches," which first appeared in a London newspaper, "masterpieces in the style of the vignette." In 1852 she commenced leader-writing for the *Daily News*, sometimes scribbling six columns a week. Her 1,600 leaders greatly impacted "some of the most important social, political, and economical matters of five and twenty years."

63. Crawford, Emily [J.] "M. Thiers: A Sketch from Life." 37 (1877–78): 1–32.

Revealed that Adolphe Thiers, when a critic for the *Constitutionnel*, had "permanent and well-paid employment" because his reviews made the paper "the leading organ of the bourgeoisie." He also wrote "regularly" for the *Globe*. Thinking that "timid" shareholders controlled the *Constitutionnel*, he left it to start the *National* with Armand Carrel. They mobilized 40 of the 43 Paris newspaper editors as the prelude to the July Revolution.

64. N. [Wedell, Baron ?J. G.]. "Panslavists and the Slav Committees." 37 (1877–78): 68–73.

Exposed *Russi-Mir* correspondent, Peter Petroff, as Col. Monteverde of the Russian staff.

65. Edwards, H. Sutherland. "The Reform Period in Russia." 37 (1877–78): 161–70, 304–14.

Dated the Russian press from 1859 because under Nicholas I there were no political papers. Monthlies, such as the *Russian Messenger* and the *Contemporary*, initially flourished, but then newspapers, such as the *Novoe Vremia*, *Golos*, and "a dozen others" were born. The *Moscow Gazette* and *St. Petersburg Gazette*, originally government organs, were "papers of real importance" in the 1860s. Michael Katkoff, editor of the *Moscow Gazette*, was "more popular and more powerful than any journalist has ever been in a free country." *Kolokol* had some money from officials pro-reform or anti-superiors, men who visited Alexander Herzen in London where he published the serial. Among its important readers was Alexander II, and among its important contributors was the "revolutionist" Michael Bakunin. The *Day*, a "Slavonian organ," was later suppressed.

Reviews published the works of "native writers" and translations of foreign literature. Their contents evidenced a reading audience of "good taste" and serious interests.

66. Butler, W. F. "The War Campaign and the War Correspondent." 37 (1877–78): 398–405.

Highlighted two *Daily News* correspondents, Archibald Forbes, famous in the Franco-Prussian War, and J. A. MacGahan, a reporter with "a keen and trenchant style," known from the Afghan campaign. As mass journalism spread, the role of the war correspondent did likewise. The job was hard even with telegraphy, and military authorities could make it more difficult.

67. Evans, Arthur J. "The Austrians in Bosnia." 38 (1878): 495–504.
Correspondent complained about Austro-Hungarian control of telegraphy and Official Press Bureau restrictions on British republication of extracts from the imperial press.

68. Blades, William. "John Walter and the Birth of *The Times*." 39 (1878–79): 17–22.
Characterized John Walter I as a failed merchant when he borrowed 'logotype' from compositor Henry Johnson and modified it. Other newspapers ignored this printing technology, but his *Universal Daily Register* validated it and made him the father of the "greatest journal the world has ever seen." Aside that the *London Gazette* was the oldest newspaper in Britain.

69. Minto, William. "An Editor's Troubles." 40 (1879): 397–404.
Review of *Selections from the Correspondence of the Late Macvey Napier, Esq.*, edited by his son, M. Napier, discussed his tenure as *Edinburgh Review* editor, 1829–47. Although an "editor in his life-time gets but scant justice," whether his letters should be published was debatable. Francis Jeffrey, an earlier *Edinburgh* editor with whom Napier was "thoroughly in accord," counseled every editor to think about the effects of his work on readers, contributors, and the "advancement of what he believed to be right." By Napier's time the *Review* already had status and paid well, attracting many submissions that he showed "caution in accepting, and courtesy in declining." Usually the great writers responded politely to requests for rewrites. Napier needed men like T. B. Macaulay and Henry Brougham to keep the *Edinburgh* from being "intolerably dull." Brougham was something of a problem, publicly advocating reform but privately exhibiting "unscrupulousness." For example, he leaked the story of his own death to check newspaper coverage of it. Napier had to deal with Brougham's persona, his conflicts with Macaulay, and his advice and that of the Whigs on what direction the *Review* should take.

70. [Dasent, G. W.]. "John Thadeus Delane." 41 (1879–80): 267–72.
Biography of *Times* editor Delane reported that his father was financial manager of the newspaper. The son was 23 when he became editor in 1841 and was assisted for many years (1845–70) by his brother-in-law, George Dasent. Delane edited leaders but left the writing to a "devoted staff." He was a man of "courage" with "a profound knowledge of men and society," a man who had wide contacts whom he pumped for information and counseled. He led the newspaper with "political sagacity" in an era of many changes and, with his long tenure, had more power than most men in government.

71. Reid, T. Wemyss. "'Our London Correspondent.'" 42 (1880): 18–26.
Traced the evolution of the London correspondent who by 1880 was important in forming public opinion. At mid-century the correspondent, collecting mostly gossip for "second-rate country journals," was the "butt of journalists." Yet he satisfied curiosity, as eighteenth-century diaries and letters had earlier, by portraying the personal side of public figures to "country readers." After 1865, as more Scottish gazettes relied on telegraph wires and set up branch offices in London, a new correspondent was born. This person might talk to government clerks but was not above rifling desks to get news. The bizarre tactics of some journalists caused officials about 1869 to brief country reporters and to give them access to the Lobby. In 1880 these people and their confreres from London dailies and news associations crowded the Lobby, but the London correspondent, sometimes a politician, had status there and in the clubs. The "society" gazettes served metro and local readers material that was "not wholly vulgar and frivolous" but was akin to the work of Horace Walpole.

John Delane, *Times* editor, received tips from politicians but pretended that he had not. Using leaders to endorse action he knew government would take enhanced the paper's prestige.

72. Hughes, Thomas. "Dr. Channing, the Abolitionist." 42 (1880): 59–64.
Swept past W. E. Channing's letters to the *Liberator* and Boston's *Daily Advertiser* but stopped at the 1836 rifling of the *Philanthropist* when a mob drove the editor from Cincinnati and the 1837 sacking of the *Alton* (IL) *Observer* when a crowd killed the editor.

73. "*Journaliste Malgré Lui*." 42 (1880): 270–79.
Purported to be a story by an Englishman, living in a French province, who published a paragraph in the press about a local accident and later retracted it under threat of libel. Aside that the French did not distinguish between scribes for newspapers and reviews.

74. Quilter, Harry. "The New Renaissance; or, the Gospel of Intensity." 42 (1880): 391–400; responses by W. M. Rossetti and Harry Quilter, 43 (1880–81): 80.
Despaired that criticism to promote a new art movement, though at first notable and scholarly, soon substituted "personal feelings" of the critic for standards. The result was that the "new criticism" filled the press with "eloquently incomprehensible articles." *See Contemporary Review* 67: 761.

75. M., W. "A New Antipodean Periodical." 43 (1880–81): 114–21.
Spotlighted the *Victorian Review* (Melbourne), produced by "leading men" who wanted a magazine reflecting colonial culture and ideas on great problems of the region. It achieved its goal with "clear statements of the main issues...in calm, unrhetorical arguments." The *Review*, which compared favorably with other periodicals in English, was "strikingly free from the provincial spirit which characterised the beginnings of magazine literature in America." Its articles were original and scholarly, but its poetry and fiction came from Britain. Critiques of books and the arts were good, though tardy. The *Review* hoped to attract European and American readers.

76. Walpole, Spencer. "Mr. Frank Buckland." 43 (1880–81): 303–09.
Logged that Buckland, a naturalist, wrote for *Field*, a newspaper, and started *Land and Water*, a periodical that depended on his pen for "its existence and reputation."

77. Hitchman, Francis. "The Penny Press." 43 (1880–81): 385–98.
History opened with the early 1830s when philanthropists dreamed of regenerating society using a penny press that workers lacked money to buy or energy to read. What was necessary was a good businessman who could produce something without the aura of a tract.

In 1880 penny weeklies and monthlies burgeoned. "Their number is enormous, and their circulation almost fabulous." They sold 5 or 6 million weekly in London. Some bordered on vice, but most displayed merely "senile imbecility" or "irrational sensationalism," both "equally destructive to anything like masculine vigor of thought." These escapist serials diminished the value of reading. The worst, among them the *Illustrated Police News*, had the best circulation.

Many people only perused newspapers, of which the "largest circulation are those Sunday papers which are chiefly distinguished by the objectionable violence of their tone, by their frequent selection of disgusting law reports, by their attacks upon the reigning family, and by otherwise pandering to the worst instincts of the uneducated classes."

Philanthropic serials without advertising were rather dull. The *British Workman*, stressing temperance, and others were not as popular among workers as were *Lloyd's* or *Reynolds's* newspapers.

The religious papers bordered the secular with their "penny prints of very large circulation, half magazine and half newspaper." Of the several probed here, the *Christian Herald* issued 195,000 copies for about a million readers. The *Christian World*, akin to the *Daily News* in its news summaries, also disseminated religious tidings, an installment of a "floridly sensational religious novel," and advertisements for quack medical remedies.

The best representative of the secular press was the *Family Herald*, a "creditable specimen of penny magazine," with leaders, serial fiction, reprints, and letters. The *London Journal*, with good illustrations and many letters, was also popular.

Boys' literature was important because 14–15 papers sold 1–1.5 million copies weekly. Most were "simple and vulgar," but a few were "positively vicious." The best were the *Union Jack* and *Boy's Own Paper*; the worst, *Our Boys' Journal* and its ilk. *See Dublin Review* 3d ser., 6: 1.

78. Odell, W[illiam], Jr. "Free Libraries and Their Working." 43 (1880–81): 439–51.

Promoted newsrooms in order to reduce misery and crime among workers. Even if they read sensational newspapers, they would spend leisure hours in libraries, not in drink and vice, and would be ready for education.

79. Turgenev, Ivan. "Sketches and Reminiscences." Trans. C. E. Turner. 44 (1881): 306–20.

Turgenev remarked that he wrote feuilletons for the new Russian daily *Poriadok.*

80. Hare, Augustus J. C. "Arthur Penrhyn Stanley." 44 (1881): 353–71.

Referred to Stanley's "many articles" in the *Edinburgh Review*, *Quarterly Review*, *Nineteenth Century*, *Good Words*, and *Macmillan's*.

81. Masson, David. "Carlyle's Edinburgh Life." 45 (1881–82): 64–80, 145–63, 234–56.

Part II covered Thomas Carlyle's forays in periodicals, including an article neither returned nor printed and those in *Fraser's Magazine*. He also penned for "the *New Edinburgh Review*, a quarterly intended in July 1821 as a successor to the *Edinburgh Monthly Review*."

Part III plumbed Carlyle's essays in the *Edinburgh Review*, *Westminster Review*, *Foreign Review*, *Foreign Quarterly Review*, and *Blackwood's Magazine*.

Aside on the "*College Tatler*, a small satirical magazine of the Edinburgh students for the session 1823–24."

82. A Staff Officer [John Frederick Maurice]. "Hot Haste for News." 47 (1882–83): 130–39.

Questioned whether newspapers in wartime should "supply you with the facts" or, "in eager competition," provide fiction, not the incomplete or erroneous versions produced in haste but copy without basis that would sell papers. Answered that a free press had to make an "honest effort to arrive at truth," which the speed of telegraphy and the correspondents who invented drama jeopardized. Dailies, pushing war correspondents to send "lively" copy suitable for a special edition, printed "hot-haste despatches" without checking rather than wait out the day and be scooped. False stories could be profitable, since their corrections sold more papers. The worst was the "hasty message of some impetuous correspondent, or the scarcely more accurate telegraphic summary which a general is compelled to send off to satisfy the home craving for news." Equally guilty were the illustrated papers of low repute that published "sketches" of battles before their occurrence, but "adulteration" of illustrations extended even to *The Times*.

83. Masson, David. "Dr. John Brown of Edinburgh." 47 (1882–83): 281–95.
Tapped Brown's "various and frequent" articles in periodicals, notably the *North British Review*, which his friend, William Hanna, once edited.

84. Shorthouse, J. Henry. "The Humorous in Literature." 47 (1882–83): 363–76.
Bemoaned that in 1882 newspapers formed "all men's minds...into one fashion." Asides on the eighteenth-century *Spectator* and *Poor Robin's Almanack.*

85. Turner, Godfrey. "The Vulgar Tongue." 47 (1882–83): 390–97.
Attributed vulgarization of English in part to journalism's "hot haste, its indifference to all but the business of the hour." For example, repetition was regular, demonstrated by newspapers' constant use of the word 'alleged' in 1882.

86. Porter, James Neville. "Libel Law Reform." 47 (1882–83): 437–42.
Ruminated about the Select Committees of Commons (1879–80) that dealt with libel in newspapers. The law should not hold owners liable for printing correct reports of public meetings because the public had a right to know. Alternatively, owners' apologies for mistakes did not speak to accuracy. The newspapers should be required to publish the speaker's explanation or contradiction, which would eliminate concerns that injured parties had no redress and journalists had no reason to be careful. Libel suits, mainly those without merit brought by "low and pettifogging solicitors," were expensive even when damages were nominal. Recommended legal changes, some of which the recent Newspaper Libel and Registration Act incorporated: 1) the truth defense should allow a showing of public benefit; 2) the law should clarify whether owners were criminally responsible for libels published without their knowledge; 3) ownership should be publicly registered; 4) defendants should be able to be witnesses.

87. W[ard], M[ary] A[ugusta]. "French Souvenirs." 48 (1883): 141–53.
Review of *Literary Souvenirs*, the autobiography of Maxime du Camp, clarified that in 1851 he was editor and proprietor of the *Revue de Paris*. Among his colleagues was Théophile Gautier. The *Revue* welcomed young talent unlike the "*Revue des Deux Mondes*, with its staff of established and well known contributors." The government suppressed the *Revue de Paris* and others after the Orsini Plot. Aside that the *Presse* did not pay Gautier well for his feuilletons.

88. Bent, J. Theodore. "Two Turkish Islands To-day." 48 (1883): 299–309.
Objected to suppression of the press in Khios and Samos.

89. [Hill, G. Birbeck]. "On a Neglected Book." 48 (1883): 414–23.
Article on the eighteenth-century *Rambler* stated that it was not as immediately successful as were the *Tatler* and *Spectator*. They sold 3,000–4,000 daily to the biweekly *Rambler's* 500 copies. Joseph Addison authored 240 of the 555 *Spectator* articles; Samuel Johnson, 203 of 208 much longer *Rambler* pieces.

90. [Morley, John and Mary Augusta Ward]. "Anthony Trollope." 49 (1883–84): 47–56.
Review of Trollope's *Autobiography* cited his work in the *Cornhill Magazine*, *Fortnightly Review*, *Pall Mall Gazette*, and *Saint Pauls*, of which he was editor. "NO periodical was ever less intelligently edited."

91. T[raill], H. D. "Wilkes and Lord Sandwich: A Dialogue." 50 (1884): 334–43.
Satirized the career of John Wilkes.

92. T[raill], H. D. "Newspapers and English: A Dialogue." 50 (1884): 436–45.
Traced the dull, cumbersome, and stale language of newspaper writing to the substance of news and the incessant public demand for it.

93. [Morley, John]. "The Croker Papers." 51 (1884–85): 108–19.
Repeated that Benjamin Disraeli's *Conningsby* (ch. 5) evaluated J. W. Croker's contributions to the *Quarterly Review.*

94. R[yder, H.] I. "Irresponsible Opinion." 51 (1884–85): 346–49.
Surmised that irresponsible opinions in leaders were the product of partial information and/or rash judgment of writers. Newspapers encouraged everyone to form opinions but not to examine both sides of an issue.

95. W[ard], M[ary] A[ugusta]. "French Views on English Writers." 52 (1885): 16–25.
Graded Edmond Scherer of the *Temps* the best French literary critic since Charles Sainte-Beuve.

96. [Morris, Mowbray]. "Some Random Reflections." 53 (1885–86): 278–88.
Weighed anonymity, which accommodated bias and vindictiveness, weakened responsibility, and deprived the reviewer of fame, against signature, which exposed the critic to "the profane mob" whose demand for praise or censure undermined impartiality.

97. Smith, Goldwin. "William Lloyd Garrison." 53 (1885–86): 321–31.
Supposed that Garrison's printing work supported him from his days with Benjamin Lundy's *Genius of Universal Emancipation*. *See* 62: 18.

98. Smith, Goldwin. "The Capital of the United States." 54 (1886): 161–70.
Lauded George W. Curtis, of *Harper's Weekly*, because he and men of his type with an "active and patriotic interest in public affairs" were assets for journalism.

99. Saintsbury, George. "Christopher North." 54 (1886): 171–83.
Essay on John Wilson's writings as Christopher North did not regard him as a good reviewer because he digressed. At *Blackwood's Magazine*, 1825–35, he had a "quasi-editorial position which included the censorship of other men's work and an almost, if not quite unlimited right of printing his own." *Blackwood's* "early numbers were extremely local and extremely personal."

100. [Morris, Mowbray]. "The Terrific Diction." 54 (1886): 361–67.
Disagreed with those who thought that journalistic style was improving given the prose of Joseph Addison generally and of Samuel Johnson in the *Rambler*.

101. Smith, Goldwin. "England Revisited." 54 (1886): 401–12.
Verified that the "ability and power" of the English newspaper were increasing, so important matters had more debate in the press, particularly local papers, than in Parliament. "To a great extent the future

of England will be in the keeping of its press, and who are the masters of the Press becomes a question every day of greater importance." Country halfpenny locals could be unsatisfactory, "sporting" journals were not more "wholesome," the great dailies preserved the "balance of power," and the labor gazettes revealed "social bitterness." What was needed was more "Cottage journalism."

102. [Morris, Mowbray]. "An Alexandrian Age." 55 (1886–87): 27–35.
Guaranteed that literature was improving, "even in its most rifling and ephemeral work, the work of its daily newspaper."

103. Ritchie, Anne. "Mrs. John Taylor, of Norwich." 55 (1886–87): 106–15.
Article on Susanna Taylor, the grandmother of Henry Reeve, editor of the *Edinburgh Review*, theorized that it "toned down with time, but in its early days it was somewhat over vigorous and unsparing in measure."

104. Lomas, John. "Dostoïewsky [*sic*] and His Work." 55 (1886–87): 187–98.
Posted that Feodor Dostoevsky was "bitten by a love of journalism" and late in life opened two Slavophile newspapers.

105. S[aintsbury], G[eorge]. "William Hazlitt." 55 (1886–87): 429–41.
Delineated Hazlitt's contributions to several daily and weekly papers, the *Edinburgh Review*, and the *New Monthly Magazine*. Early on, he had "written ordinary press-work" in the 'gallery.' The scribes of *Blackwood's Magazine*, "the whiskey drinkers of the Noctes," criticized Hazlitt's drinking because he had a "life-long war" with them and their *Quarterly Review* peers.

106. Rees, J. D. "Persia." 55 (1886–87): 442–53.
Divulged that Iran's shah and princes were "more or less influenced by the European press."

107. Saintsbury, George. "Francis Jeffrey." 56 (1887): 256–67.
Review of Francis Jeffrey's *Contributions to the Edinburgh Review* returned to its founding. Its first articles were "violently partizan, unhesitatingly personal, and more inclined to find fault the more distinguished the subject was," but other serials were worse, the output of low-paid "hacks." The "far from perfect" early content subsided once T. B. Macaulay wrote for the *Review*.

108. [Morris, Mowbray]. "The Profession of Letters." 56 (1887): 302–10, 450–62; 57 (1887–88): 380–90.
Asserted that newspapers were valuable to owners and shareholders but of dubious worth to the population. The public was asked to believe that a press, the "chief engine of power," guided by men driven by profit was in the state's best interests. Yet the press did not control the national destiny. While no paper, not even *The Times*, could influence everybody, it could create a tyranny of opinion. Its reporters could harm the public, such as by publicizing police methods to control crime. Its editors, pressured by competition, had little time to select or reflect, so much that appeared was "rash and foolish" or helpful only to "unscrupulous persons abroad." Editors were not ready to suppress material that hurt the state because they answered to owners and buyers.

Journalism was "the work of the daily Press," and the journalist was someone "whose livelihood depends on that work," not on supplementary income. Writing in dailies was not literature, but journalism was one of the literary professions, the only one where a member "can never set up for himself." The journalist, "merged in his paper," spoke "in tones not his own." Many found it "the most congenial outlet for their energies, the readiest satisfaction of their literary ambitions, and the surest means of earning a living." They would be good journalists bringing "the greatest credit to themselves and their employers with no thought of intellectual degradation or wasted talents." As serials multiplied, there were jobs for men as reporters and women as readers. Men were typically not well educated, but some who specialized were "surprisingly good," producing "sound, honest, intelligent journeyman work."

For those who treated it as preface to a literary career, journalism was "hack-work," which "hinders, delays, and finally destroys a man's power of achieving the best in Literature." The pressure shattered writers' health or wasted their talent as editors drove their staffs like slaves.

To be a reviewer, a writer needed leisure to fill knowledge gaps. No editor allowed "complete license of opinion," but the quality periodicals offered more freedom. Newspaper critics treated books as news, letting readers decide their merits.

109. Hill, G. Birbeck. "Dr. Johnson's Style." 57 (1887–88): 190–94.
Assessed Samuel Johnson's writing in the *Rambler* and elsewhere.

110. [Manston, A. C.]. "Lessing's *Dramatic Notes*." 57 (1887–88): 448–54.
Investigated G. E. Lessing's Hamburg weekly, 1767, a serial whose goal was serious theatre criticism, not "light theatrical gossip."

111. Saintsbury, George. "Sydney Smith." 58 (1888): 17–29.
Pondered the relationship of Smith and Francis Jeffrey at the *Edinburgh Review*. While Jeffrey was the editor, Smith's articles were the "most distinct and original" and the most interesting until T. B. Macaulay arrived. Yet other periodical scribes never copied Smith's style.

112. Wheeler, Stephen. "The Indian Native Press." 58 (1888): 377–84.
Ranted that India presented "the spectacle of a national Press devoting a large share of its energy to reprobating the measures of Government and to traducing the character of individuals." If India were "a purely Asiatic state," such information would be ignored or controlled by "purely Oriental methods – by private retaliation or by summary execution." Press liberty left government to hope that the press was a safety value for discontent in a society where "the credulity of the uneducated Asian is omnivorous" and each paper had many readers.

India had about 350 vernacular newspapers: 170 printed less than 300 copies; 100 printed 300–700 copies; 50 printed 700–1,000 copies; 27 printed over 1,000 copies. These numbers were fuzzy since it was sometimes hard to distinguish newspapers from magazines. The vernacular press flourished best in Bengal, with *Bangabasi* at 20,000 copies. All the journals were anti-government, and the Bombay press was also anti-Christian.

Establishing a publication was easy because of lithography. Editors registered and paid one pound per month to print news from Britain and the bazaars. Their total expenses were about four pounds, with each copy priced at a farthing. Editors blackmailed subjects who paid to keep their problems out of the limelight. There was little recourse: a civil case was a "hopeless endeavor"; a criminal case was too expensive. Editors did not learn the benefits of British rule from British education but did know the style that sold papers in India. Government should license only moderate journals and prosecute libels.

113. [Moore, A. S.]. "On a Tennessee Newspaper." 58 (1888): 460–66.
Remembered 1883 days as a journalist in Nashville covering a candidate the local paper favored. The city-editor, "a young man with a straw hat, gauzy habiliments, and a cigarette," promptly took the neophyte

for a drink and dispensed some hints on how to report. The editorial room was awash with "conversation and hilarity," presided over by the editor in underwear, chewing a cigar, and "half-drunk." This kind and "brilliant" lawyer had "long, wildly disordered hair," "eyes, fervid with a kind of reckless intelligence," and "a large, sensual, but far from stupid mouth." Since the whole staff drank, typos were frequent. When printers struck for higher pay, replacements came from Chicago protected by a threat to harm anyone who interfered with them. After the paper "collapsed," the author went to a "more creditable" one.

Tennessee gazettes, regularly chastised for "fervid language, jocose familiarity, and political vituperation," were very different from British leaders of "cool, measured subtlety" or "stately tedium," no doubt the consequence of the "damp, sunless climate." Tennessee articles were supposed to be 'sassy, spicy...and spunky' and to "puff your friends in florid language, to suffocate your enemies beneath accumulated invective."

114. Smith, Goldwin. "*The American Commonwealth.*" 59 (1888–89): 241–53.
Review of James Bryce's book maintained that the "American press is not yet so free as the Press of England," perhaps because "[n]othing can be more miserable than the bondage of the American Press to the Irish vote."

115. Saintsbury, George. "Leigh Hunt." 59 (1888–89): 426–38.
Article on Hunt's periodical essays peeked at the *Examiner*, particularly the circumstances that led to his imprisonment for libel, and the *Indicator*, his weekly paper of 66 numbers. Hunt's work was "not low in actual merit" but not something to be read at length. Aside that no one had studied the evolution of the eighteenth-century periodical essay into the nineteenth-century magazine article.

116. Cornish, C. J. "A Turkish Democrat." 59 (1888–89): 452–57.
Starred Kemal Bey, who wrote most of the newspaper of the Young Turks on thin paper easily mailed.

117. [Morris, Mowbray]. "Critics in Court." 60 (1889): 134–40.
Text on legal actions against critics propounded that they were as essential to newspapers as editors and printers. Because of the many newspapers, some criticism was probably too friendly or too hostile. Fair discussion, even if adverse, should not be libel. Attacks on criticism came from those concerned about "the growing license of our newspaper press," but it only mirrored the times. For instance, a music-hall owner sued a newspaper "for publishing reflections on the morality of his entertainments."

118. Dunlop, R[obert]. "Archibald Prentice: A Page in the History of Journalism." 60 (1889): 435–43.
Trailed Prentice from 1815 columns in Cowdray's *Gazette*, which influenced "more intelligent working-men" but like other local papers had little London news, to ownership of the *Manchester Times* in 1828.

119. Saintsbury, George. "Twenty Years of Political Satire." 61 (1889–90): 336–47.
Surveyed satire in the 1780s and 1790s, with some examples from Eton's *Microcosm* and the *Anti-Jacobin*.

120. Smith, Goldwin. "A Moral Crusader." 62 (1890): 18–26.
Continued the story (53: 321) on William Lloyd Garrison, whose *Liberator* "barely paid its way."

121. Saintsbury, George. "De Quincey." 62 (1890): 101–12.
Emphasized Thomas De Quincey's influence on *Blackwood's Magazine* and the *London Magazine* with a gloss on his work for *Tait's Edinburgh Magazine* and *Hogg's Instructor*.

122. [Sellers, Edith]. "An Obscure Sect and Its Founder." 62 (1890): 286–94.
Headlined the Christadelphians, established by physician John Thomas. He published in the *Lancet*, edited the *Apostolic Advocate*, and planned another journal for St. Charles (IL), but all its supplies burned before an issue appeared.

123. H[ubbard], W[ilfranc]. "The Story of a Revolution." 62 (1890): 393–400.
Nodded to the *Mosquito*, "the comic print" of Buenos Aires.

124. Saintsbury, George. "Thomas Hood." 62 (1890): 422–30.
Itemized that Hood was a contributor to comic annuals, subeditor of the *London Magazine*, and editor of the *New Monthly Magazine*.

125. [Benson, Arthur C.]. "Brotherhoods." 63 (1890–91): 358–63.
Declared that "the telegraph has made the Daily Press" whose editors were men of concentration akin to early monks.

126. Jennings, L. J. "Laurence Oliphant." 64 (1891): 175–81.
Review of Margaret Oliphant's *Memoir of the Life of Laurence Oliphant* named him as *The Times* correspondent during the Franco-Prussian War. Though always in demand by the paper, he also wrote "a good deal for *Blackwood's Magazine*, where his contributions had for years been welcome." Aside that John Delane was "the great editor of *The Times*, whose journal I had then (1867) had the honour of representing in the United States."

127. Saintsbury, George. "William Cobbett." 65 (1891–92): 95–109.
Underlined the influence and profit Cobbett received from the *Political Register*, which sometimes had a deputy editor. In 1816 the paper reduced its price but retained its original direction. Aside on his *Porcupine*.

128. Roylance-Kent, C. B. "France and the Papacy." 67 (1892–93): 179–86.
Bowed to the *Avenir*.

129. Saintsbury, George. "Three Humourists: Hook, Barham, Maginn." 69 (1893–94): 105–15.
Distinguished humorists of "the second or lower classes," people without reputations, from the three captioned. Eyed the work of Theodore Hook and R. H. Barham briefly before turning to William Maginn's periodical essays. For *Fraser's Magazine* he penned "one of the earliest and one of the best examples of a kind of journalism for which there has since been greater and even greater demand, the brief biography, smart in style and somewhat swaggering in manner." At *Blackwood's* Maginn worked well with J. G. Lockhart, who was more knowledgeable and competent but not so versatile. Some of Maginn's essays in the *Magazine* "contain a great deal of the tedious and obsolete newspaper mannerism of the time, a mannerism of knowing and

braggart assumption." Irrespective of his learning and wit this "brilliant journalist" was more showy than solid.

130. [Moriarty, Gerald P.]. "The Political World of Fielding and Smollett." 69 (1893–94): 215–21.
Tied Henry Fielding to the *True Patriot.*

131. [Morris, Mowbray]. "A Vision of India." 70 (1894): 100–08.
Fretted about India's free press.

132. Nichol, John. "Louis Kossuth." 70 (1894): 153–60.
Recalled that Kossuth, in England for about a decade, edited newspapers there.

133. Himself [Walter Low]. "The Complete Leader-Writer." 70 (1894): 359–64.
Regarded the leader as "a survival from the time when the reading public was small, educated, and leisured, and really took an interest in such things." Leader-writers in 1894 should be young because they would have the stamina to work odd hours, the conviction that they knew everything, and the flexibility to write against their own beliefs. Leader-writers who now penned for a mass audience should not be too clever or profound or interested in anything but very current events. Although owners often interfered with editors, even the well-educated, they did not meddle in leader-writing. Editors assigned themes for leaders that had little influence since few read them. Writers need not be versed in topics because they could glean ideas by skimming the newspaper or repeating earlier ideas. Leaders could be sarcastic, "prosy," "dogmatic," "illogical," or "original" but never late. Everyone was in a hurry in a newspaper office, especially the "ink-begrimed, linen-aproned" printer.

134. Saintsbury, George. "Robert Southey." 71 (1894–95): 346–57.
Unveiled that Southey was forced to leave Westminster when his periodical, the *Flagellant*, condemned corporal punishment at the school. Later, on the matter of his succeeding William Gifford as editor of the *Quarterly Review*, Southey thought the job was his "to take or to allot."

135. [MacDonagh, Michael]. "Some Humours of Parliamentary Reporting." 71 (1894–95): 365–71.
Blamed the frequent errors in parliamentary reporting on speakers who were unclear; reporters who could not read their own shorthand or hurried in transcribing notes; telegraphers who garbled messages; subeditors who blue-penciled texts; and compositors and proofreaders who misread them. Most mistakes resulted from time constraints. Parliament no longer questioned reporters' integrity as Daniel O'Connell had at an earlier time, surprising when three-fourths of reporters were Irish.

136. An Indolent Reviewer [W. P. James]. "The Irresponsible Novelist." 72 (1895): 73–80.
Defended periodical reviewers against the charge that "hostile criticism" was the result of "personal malice." The anonymous and responsible reviewer was preferable to the known irresponsible novelist who embarrassed people chosen as archetypes for fictional characters.

137. A Lobbyist [Michael MacDonagh]. "From the Lobby of the House of Commons." 72 (1895): 195–202.

Exulted that Parliament no longer viewed journalists as impertinent or spies. "In these days, when the craze for notoriety is so widespread, and the appetite for news so insatiable, the journalist is a welcome visitor to the Lobby." There were "about thirty Lobbyists, who represented the London and the leading provincial daily papers…picking up every crumb of gossip (social as well as political)." Columns usually surfaced as a London Letter in a country gazette or as Political Notes in a metro one. Even though key politicians were not usually in the Lobby, journalists were "ubiquitous and vigilant." They cultivated sources for tips or listened to conversations for nuances. When news was slow, reporters resorted to jest and imagination. "The ethics of journalism is still a somewhat strange and inexplicable thing" but was better than when journalists went through scraps of documents and letters that they paid cleaners to gather from the House floors or eavesdropped on Members and bribed their clerks. Most newspapers cared about authentic information, not how it was secured.

138. A[inger], A[lfred]. "Alexander Macmillan: A Personal Reminiscence." 73 (1895–96): 397–400.

Claimed that Macmillan was "the first to project a shilling magazine in place of the old quarterlies at five shillings and magazines at half-a-crown." There was much discussion in his office, where many gathered weekly for "social chat," about what to christen the new periodical.

139. [Whibley, Charles]. "French and English." 75 (1896–97): 15–21.

Aside on Paris journalists, notably Jacques St. Cère of *Figaro*.

140. [Jones, H. E.]. "From Far Cathay." 75 (1896–97): 258–66.

Reviewed Hugh Clifford's *East Coast Etchings*, a collection of his articles in the *Straits Times*.

141. [Whibley, Charles]. "A New Academy." 77 (1897–98): 20–26.

Welcomed the academy of Edmond de Goncourt, open to the journalist because signature made him a "man of letters." Among the first recognized were Julien Geoffroy, "a critic of knowledge and discernment" for a "widely read" weekly who had "never risen higher than the highest journalism," and Octave Mirabeau, who "despite his courage, pertinacity, and insight, is nothing more nor less than an accomplished journalist."

142. [Morris, Mowbray]. "American Diplomacy." 77 (1897–98): 67–80.

Singled out, among "the more respectable of the American press," the *New York Tribune* and *New York Herald*.

143. [MacDonagh, Michael]. "Some Humours of the Composing Room." 77 (1897–98): 120–24.

Sampled typos in newspapers and magazines, some of which led to "libel actions and other unpleasant consequences." Problems arose from misspelling, incorrect punctuation, and "*mixes*, produced by the accidental running together of different items of news, and distinct paragraphs that ought to have begun on separate lines." There were few errors in light of "the amazing number of newspapers printed in the United Kingdom," and those few were due primarily to pressure of time.

144. Hadden, J. Cuthbert. "Some Friends of Browning." 77 (1897–98): 196–202.
Nominated – as a friend of Robert Browning – Benjamin Flower, editor of the *Cambridge Intelligencer*, who was imprisoned for libel in 1799. He also edited the *Political Register*, 1807–11, and paid some of the startup costs of the *Westminster Review*. He was the father of Sarah Flower, who penned for the *Monthly Repository*.

145. Gwynn, Stephen. "William Morris." 78 (1898): 153–60.
Logged Morris' articles in the "short-lived" *Oxford and Cambridge Magazine* and his launch of the newspaper *Commonweal* after the Social Democratic Federation split.

146. Greenwood, Frederick. "Public Opinion in Public Affairs." 79 (1898–99): 161–70.
Presumed that newspapers depended on events, omens, informers, and the "discerning and discriminating eye" of editors. Independent journalism did not undermine government because editors suppressed news in proportion as it injured the public interest. Officials protested the usually harmless "indiscreet revelation." When they said that the newspaper thwarted diplomacy, they were uninformed, exaggerating, or searching for an excuse to explain their own blunders. Only the "partisan journalist" echoed the party line and bosses even when they were wrong. *See* 79: 303.

147. Bradley, A. G. "America's Problem." 79 (1898–99): 232–40.
Mentioned *Harper's Weekly*, "one of the most sober and respected of American journals," and the "prodigious ignorance" of the average French journalist.

148. [Whibley, Charles]. "The Press of Paris." 79 (1898–99): 286–95.
Postulated that a reader could ordinarily discover a sense of a place from its newspapers. The Parisian combined a variety of political opinions and "a common character of gaiety and carelessness." "French journals preserve a literary point of view, wholly lost in our larger machines contrived chiefly for the dissemination of news." French paragraphs on "current events" were "brief, pointed, and not too serious," and "short-hand reports of speeches and such-like trash" were missing altogether. The French aimed to amuse, not improve. British newspapers were "more practical, but less amusing." They spent money on telegrams; the French, on writers. The British wanted news "horribly mauled, in Yankee-fashion, with headlines," and gossip. The French tolerated errors in papers whose "style and arrangement" were better than the British.

"In England, the newspapers grow rich upon advertisement." In France, profit and wages for high-paid staffs came from "modified blackmail." People paid to get social and financial news published, whereas in Britain a financier bought a page of "facing matter" in exchange for an editorial puff about a new company. Journalistic blackmail was more acceptable in France because politicians, police, and business already engaged in bribery.

Figaro addressed a "middle class" audience that was "respectable, half-informed, semi-cultured." It attracted the top writers, so its criticism was "amicable," its news no less accurate than its rivals, and its language not pretentious about its political and moral influence. Its founder, A. de Villemessant, like *Times* editor John Delane, never wrote leaders but proposed motifs. Penning the "first article" or being criticized in *Figaro* conferred status. The paper occasionally supported truth, as in the Dreyfus case, but when circulation dropped, it switched its position.

Unlike the halfpenny heralds meant to entertain without much news, the major newspapers, the *Temps* and *Journal des Débats*, had leaders that were as "heavy" and "barren" as the British and criticism that was "sedate, well-informed, and never sensational." The *Petit Journal* was "the best organized paper in France, with its million subscribers and its correspondents in all the provinces." It charged four pounds per line for advertising. Sports gazettes were numerous but not knowledgeable.

149. Templar [Spencer Brodhurst]. "Diplomacy and Journalism." 79 (1898–99): 303–08.
Controverted 79: 161 by balancing the values of secrecy in diplomacy and press reflection of popular support for policies. An editor, unlike a minister, served both "the country's welfare and the reading public." Although the press was beneficial, it could hamper foreign policy, so a joint committee of the Houses of Parliament should decide what to hide.

150. Brodhurst, Spencer. "The Outlook in France." 81 (1899–1900): 43–52.
Deplored the language in British and French gazettes on the Dreyfus case. Unlike "the most widely circulating and influential journals in France," the *Journal des Débats, Temps*, and *Figaro*, smaller French papers lied to the public and aroused hatred instead of airing the truth, "the most important function of a national Press."

151. [Gwynn, Stephen]. "A Child of His Age." 81 (1899–1900): 379–85.
Eulogized George Warrington Steevens, a war correspondent who died during the war with the Boers. A "highly trained university man," he was "already one of the most outstanding and characteristic figures in that too large field of contemporary literature which goes by the name of journalism." He was "the best special reporter of his day," first the *Daily Mail* correspondent for the Greco-Turkish War and then with Lord Kitchener in the Sudan. His dispatches on that campaign were his best. He could size up a situation and get the facts, as when he covered the Dreyfus case. His journalistic style, one of "exaggerated emphasis, colloquialism pushed to excess," was less obvious in his articles in *Blackwood's Magazine.*

152. King, Bolton. "England and Italy." 82 (1900): 208–16.
Conjectured that the Italian *Antologia* was modeled on the *Edinburgh Review* and on Giuseppe Mazzini's *Apostolato Populare.*

153. Fortescue, J. W. "Our Army and Its Critics." 83 (1900–01): 70–80.
Raged that war correspondents ordinarily had no military background yet saw themselves as "omniscient and infallible," belied by their inaccuracy.

The Modern Review, 1880–1884

The *Modern*, the offshoot of the *Theological Review*, opened with a thoughtful essay on periodical literary criticism.

1. The Editor [Richard A. Armstrong]. "The Story of Nineteenth Century Reviewing." 1 (1880): 1–33.

Commenced with Daniel Defoe's *Review*, "the father of the *Tatler* and the *Spectator*" but not the *Gentleman's Magazine*. The last was "the first great literary review" even though it was initially a serial summary of newspapers. Soon MPs brought their speeches for publication, which Edward Cave printed at the risk of 'fearful penalties.' Between the *Gentleman's* and the early nineteenth century's "great outburst of Review literature," a few other periodicals started. The *Monthly Review* was its "only respectable English rival." The *Scots Magazine* was as good but not other Scottish productions. The intellectual *Monthly Magazine* had some "pleasant banter." Other periodicals, 1760–1800, were "trivial to a degree that now would be intolerable."

Recounted the birth of the *Edinburgh Review*, attributing its success to the "splendid ability" of early writers and its reflection of audience political interests. The *Edinburgh* pioneered reviewing as an "independent essay" rather than as a recitation of contents. Editor Francis Jeffrey "slashed" articles as circulation grew, from 750 at birth to 12,000 in 1813. The *Review* had "extraordinary influence over policy and letters," but its literary criticism could be "not only unjust, but sometimes pernicious." It shot "stinging sarcasm against all things mean and base" making enemies in the process.

The *Quarterly Review* was the "great rival" of the *Edinburgh*. William Gifford, an editor of "singular ability," was the first of other editors discussed. J. G. Lockhart, the most famous, and Macvey Napier, editor of the *Edinburgh*, moved their reviews from "vivacious pugnacity" to "more ponderous decorum."

Blackwood's Magazine learned that "ridicule and vituperation" caused libel suits but used anonymity to mar literary reputations.

The early *Westminster Review* had John Bowring as editor and John Stuart Mill, Henry Brougham, and Francis Jeffrey among its distinguished contributors. Circulation grew under editor John Chapman.

When the *New Monthly Magazine* surfaced, other monthlies declined. Its later competitors were *Fraser's Magazine*, with its first generation of "brilliant writers"; *Tait's Edinburgh Magazine*, which touted a wide circulation; the *Foreign Quarterly Review*, educating readers about Continental literature; *Bentley's Miscellany* and *Ainsworth's Magazine*, then *Macmillan's Magazine* and the *Cornhill Magazine*.

In 1880 the *Fortnightly Review* was famous for broadcasting opposing opinions; the *Contemporary Review*, for doing the same with a more Christian spirit. Abstracted the religious press.

Aside that a new series is the "despair of bibliographers," akin to "the false hair and teeth of an antiquated beau."

2. Dorling, William. "William Lloyd Garrison." 1 (1880): 355–74.

Tracked Garrison's journalistic career from an apprenticeship at the *Newburyport Herald* while he sent anonymous articles to a "Boston journal." He edited the *Newburyport Free Press*, which had a "high moral tone" but no profit, then the temperance *National Philanthropist* and next, the Bennington (VT) *Journal of the Times*. He took over the *Genius of the Universal Emancipator* from Benjamin Lundy, its printer and publisher, and converted it to the larger weekly *Liberator*. Aside that John Greenleaf Whittier edited the *New England Review* published in Hartford (CT).

3. Rauwenhoff, L. W. E. "France and the Jesuits." 1 (1880): 559–73.
Perceived Cologne' *Zeitung* as "an authoritative journal."

4. Channing, William Henry. "*George Ripley*." 4 (1883): 520–57.
Review of O. B. Frothingham's book recorded that Ripley was coeditor, with Ralph Waldo Emerson and Margaret Fuller, of the *Dial*. Ripley was "the wisest, most equitable, and keenly discriminating while generous critic of his nation," writing "literary columns" for the *New York Tribune* and *Harper's Weekly*. He also edited the *Christian Register* and penned for other serials.

5. Gordon, Alexander. "Modern Quakerism." 5 (1884): 701–18.
Footnoted the *British Friend*, "a Glasgow monthly."

The Monthly Chronicle, 1838–1841

Reaching out to recent autodidacts, the *Monthly Chronicle* condemned annuals, newspaper taxes, and superficial art and literary criticism.

1. [Bulwer-Lytton, E. G. and Dionysius Lardner]. "Advertisement." 1 (1838): v–vi.

Pledged that the *Monthly Chronicle* would not rival competitors because it would focus on topics usually considered of "too grave a nature for periodicals that rather contribute to the amusement of a peculiar class than represent the interests of the general community." The *Chronicle* would publish articles on politics of interest to the middle classes and on the arts and science, criticism as a guide to reading, and some fiction.

2. [Bulwer-Lytton, E. G.]. "The Life and Writings of Scott." 1 (1838): 202–19.

Review of *Memoirs of the Life of Sir Walter Scott*, edited by J. G. Lockhart, repeated that Scott's anger about *Edinburgh Review* criticism of his work motivated him to support the *Quarterly Review*, intending to challenge the *Edinburgh's* authority and steal its profits. The *Quarterly* allegedly welcomed "cutting and severe sarcasm."

3. [Bulwer-Lytton, E. G.]. "Lord Brougham." 1 (1838): 249–58.

Briefly probed Henry Brougham's defense of a Durham newspaper editor prosecuted for libel.

4. [Bulwer-Lytton, E. G.] "Letters by an English Member of Parliament to M. De –, of the Chambre des Députés. No. 1: On Public Opinion." 1 (1838): 337–47.

Insisted that "journals, as they have grown up into their present importance, address a wide range of miscellaneous readers," primarily families and juveniles. Cheap weeklies, including Sunday, were the papers that circulated "most among the masses." Because the press shaped "the taste of the public," "[d]ecorous words and common-place affectations of morality" were "always safe and often useful" to eliminate "coarseness" from the language.

5. "The Influence of the Annuals upon Art." 3 (1839): 63–67.

Labeled annuals a "pestilent visitation of gilded flies." Tolerable when "they were limited in size and numbers," they were by 1839 "a heap of tawdry rubbish." The worthless drove the better from the market and "corrupt and debase the taste of readers." Although annuals were a "register of events," their "highly-finished engravings" required "enormous circulation." Anything less meant the art was inferior. In painting, annuals "encourage only the most vulgar, superficial talent, and employ only those artists who labour cheapest and quickest – that is, with the least expenditure of mind, and at the smallest risk of reputation." As to engraving, annuals begot a "race of mechanics" whose work displayed "sameness" and "dullness" compared to that of their French and German peers. To publish a successful annual, an owner needed a 'manufactory' of art and wide "channels of distribution."

6. "Austria and the Italian Liberals." 3 (1839): 153–66.
Averred that the *Italiano*, published by Young Italy in Paris c. 1831, "contained articles remarkable for the elevation of their ideas and the brilliancy of their style."

7. [?Crowe, E. E.]. "The Press of the Revolution." 3 (1839): 267–83.
Delighted that the "daily papers of France from 1787 till 1798 offer a mine of precious information to the historian of that gloomy era." Each revolutionary faction had a gazette, with excerpts from ten "leading revolutionary publications" here. Important men of the National Convention were journalists, among them Jean-Paul Marat and Camille Desmoulins.

8. [Mazzini, Joseph]. "Lamennais." 3 (1839): 317–28.
Resurrected the *Avenir*, a Catholic daily begun in 1830, of which F. de Lamennais was one founder. When "[s]elf-styled religious journals vied with each other in heaping abuse and calumny" on Catholicism, the pope suppressed them, including the *Avenir*. Lamennais later penned for the *Monde*.

9. Mazzini, Joseph. "Letters on the State and Prospects of Italy." 3 (1839): 401–13, 514–23; 4 (1839): 123–33, 226–37.
Enlightened that "no press exists" in the Italian states except the *Precursor*, the organ of the Austrian government. *Giovine Italia* surfaced in Marseilles, a place "favorable for communication," and a "secondary journal," devoted to Lombard affairs, started at Ticino. Other papers ceased when prosecuted.

10. [Michelsen, Edward H.]. "Benjamin Constant." 3 (1839): 436–49.
Disclosed that in his speeches Constant's "favourite topic was the *liberty of the press*."

11. [Blanchard, Laman]. "The Influence of Periodical Literature on the State of the Fine Arts." 4 (1839): 502–08.
Characterized the influence of newspapers on the "public mind" as "one of the most striking characteristics of our times." "The newspaper habitually...operates with gradual and irresistible force in producing and modifying our feelings and opinions." If the Fourth Estate was intellectually homogeneous, it would conquer the other three. Generally, it "exercised its irresponsible authority with fairness and integrity."

The press often ranked fine arts as "one of the least important subjects" because too many readers considered works of imagination "humbug." Newspapers swamped with news and concerned about important government issues did not allocate much space to theatre and book reviews. Journalists should exercise "honest watchfulness" of the arts, chiefly theatre, as "the most effective means for reviving and purifying public taste." They should condemn "minor theatres" for their "representation of some horrible and atrocious crime" but should refrain from the anonymous criticism that was inconsistent with "a higher and more conscientious tone." *See* 5: 33.

12. "The Coming Session." 5 (1840): 1–14.
Bemoaned that "the daily metropolitan press of England," which in 1830 supported "public improvement," was by 1840 "fostering all the worst passions of the populace" because it was so elitist. London had 13 dailies in 1830; ten in 1839. In 1830 there was no Tory gazette; in 1839 the party controlled two-thirds of the journals by buying shares in older papers, not commencing new ones. The *Morning Post*, for example, went from a "paltry and despised print" to "a paper of influence and of wide circulation." By publishing

the stamp returns, the government promoted certain papers, ones the public had to read even if they did not respect them. The more prestige a paper had, the more advertising it captured. Advertising paid for leaders, written by "twenty or thirty gentlemen of liberal education," and drove small competitors out of business.

13. [Blanchard, Laman]. "Novel Writing and Newspaper Criticism." 5 (1840): 33–38.
Reiterated some ideas of 4: 502. Novels were in vogue because readers cried for "literary productions." Newspaper criticism gave "authors by the grace of booksellers…a showy, though transitory popularity." Critics, with too many volumes and too little time to review, quoted "striking passages" and employed stock phrases. This style, best for travel books, was "pernicious" for fiction, notably fashionable and criminal that caught their eye. Anonymity, appropriate to protect an infant press, was by 1840 "cowardly." The press had money and talent; it did not need the "inquisitorial secrecy" that undercut "moral guidance." Anonymity shielded venal critics who could be dangerous. Signature would not affect reputation because fame was transitory, the curse of penning for an "ephemeral" press.

The newspaper was "the chief, if not the only intellectual ailment, of a large portion even of what are called the educated classes." Otherwise, it was "the great purifier, the prime agent of improvement in modern society." The newspaper benefited people by unmasking falsehood and championing the innocent and oppressed. To sustain "an intelligent, free, and honest press," it was important to correct its mistakes.

14. "Influence of Eloquence on English Freedom." 5 (1840): 127–34, 256–62, 366–75, 509–17; 6 (1840): 55–63, 179–84.
Indicated numerous libel cases, including that of John Wilkes.

15. "Thraldom of the British Press." 5 (1840): 138–50.
Admitted that reduction of the stamp duty in 1836 did not break the monopoly of London dailies. Starting a new metro paper required 50,000 pounds. To challenge *The Times* would cost more in order to pay for the mercantile information that readers sought. The big London dailies were crushing neophytes by reducing costs, through actions such as sharing the expenses of reporters and "post-office expresses." The Dover express, for example, was 1,600 pounds per year, but sharing was 320 pounds. The *Constitutional* and *Morning Gazette* had already failed because of this tactic. Parliament aided the metros by becoming a "court of inquisition for the investigation of all the most secret details connected with the management of each individual newspaper." The "newspaper stamp returns, in which the exact number of stamps taken out by each paper is set down," favored the dominant even when the figures were inaccurate. Circulation, crucial for advertising revenue, increased after 1836, but fewer papers existed between 1829 and 1839, mainly in the country. The London dailies set the opinions for the kingdom and "perhaps all over the world." Abolition of the stamp duty and substitution of penny postage or a tax based on pages would solve the problem.

16. "The Editor's Room." 5 (1840): 481–96.
Delineated the functions of the staff of a morning daily. Editors penned original leaders or checked the columns of leader-writers lest "the tone and character" conflict with those of the paper. The subeditor scissored the evening heralds and reviewed stories by penny-a-liners and letters. Parliamentary reporters loved the "dunce," the speaker whose comments were long but easy to summarize; the MP who sent his speech ahead; divisions; and the 'count out' to ensure that 40 were present. They hated long orations by those with shares in their paper or by ministers since their words had to be taken down verbatim. Correspondents forwarded "foreign flimsy" that condensed overseas gazettes or reflected European officials' tips in order to keep them as informers. Major heralds used foreign expresses but shared

the expenses. Literary and theatre reviews, penned by reporters without extra pay, were typically congratulatory. The printer, who received copy on small slips of paper, passed them to compositors. (48 slips = 1 *Times* column). Copy then went to proofreaders, leader-writers, and the editor but not reporters. If a penny-a-liner arrived late with hot news, the printer decided whether to include it. Second editions were primarily for late-breaking foreign events.

Evening papers were more accurate about Parliament because they had the day to check facts and were more important in moments "of great commercial excitement" on the exchanges. The evening plagiarized, as did weeklies and locals, from the London morning dailies that were "the key-note to the whole press."

Men accustomed to a routine, "retired officers or functionaries," read the dailies completely every morning and the reviews for information about books and plays.

17. Laing, Samuel. "Sweden and Norway: Mr. Laing's Reply to a Pamphlet." 6 (1840): 385–97.

Laing replied to an official pamphlet questioning his books on Norway (1836) and Sweden (1838) by citing cases to prove his thesis that the Swedish press was not free. One case was of a newspaper "suppressed twenty-four times by an arbitrary censorship." He chose to respond in the *Monthly Chronicle* because its audience was "the educated of the middle and upper classes, who read with intelligence and reflection."

18. "Inedited Facts Respecting the French Revolution of 1789." 7 (1841): 97–109.

Silhouetted the *Journal des Guillotines*, an evening daily that listed executions, "a daily register of the revolutionary tribunal, and a very exact and detailed one."

19. "Young Europe." 7 (1841): 467–70.

Broadcast that "literature is the ready emanation of the popular spirit. Newspapers, pamphlets, and periodicals form the very atmosphere of thought and action by at once stimulating and giving it expression. Perhaps there is no stronger proof of the advancement of the present age than the prodigious fertility of the periodical press, and the opinions which daily spread over the civilised world from this source: the beneficial influence it necessarily obtains is extended to every branch of social intercourse." Among important journalists were F. de Lamennais, William Howitt, Armand Carrel, and the men of the "liberal journals of France."

Murray's Magazine, 1887–1891

From the same house as the *Quarterly Review*, *Murray's* surveyed British, Irish, and American journalism.

1. [Arnold, E. A.]. "Editorial Announcement." 1 (1887): 1–2.
Confirmed that the "place once occupied by Monthly publications, as direct and powerful organs of Party, is now filled by Daily and Weekly newspapers; but the influence of Periodical Literature has been transferred to a wider and more independent sphere. In the pages of a Review or Magazine, carefully matured opinions may still be expounded by acknowledged authorities with greater completeness and deliberation than is possible in the Daily Press." "Political Articles will invariably be signed by their Authors, who alone are to be held responsible for the opinions they express."

2. Bunsen, George von. "What Germany Is About." 1 (1887): 115–27.
Balanced a new German (unnamed) fortnightly on poetry against German fiction that ignored journalists.

3. G., M. "Some Odd Numbers." 2 (1887): 481–90.
Flipped through a batch of 1834 periodicals, among them the *Monthly Repository*, the *Edinburgh Review*, and *Fraser's*, *Tait's*, and the *New Monthly* magazines. Quoted *Leigh Hunt's London Journal*, an eight-page weekly "clearly printed triple-columned," on the variety of periodicals in that year. Periodicals in 1887 spanned more subjects at a low price but lacked the quality of the *Journal* because the pace of contemporary life diminished interest in "high thought." Instead, British serials aped the vices of the American, such as slang, trivia, personality, so that "the journalism of to-day is the apotheosis of the infinitely petty." Newspapers mixed news and literature; magazines, though catering to every taste, meted out half-thoughts and gossip by scribes intent on "jubilant self-contemplation."

4. "Samuel Morley." 2 (1887): 792–802.
Review of Edwin Hodder's *Life of Samuel Morley* told that in 1841 Morley opened the *Nonconformist*. By 1868 Morley was "largely interested" in the *Daily News* (after it absorbed the *Morning Star*) giving its owners the benefit of his "prudent counsel and administrative skill."

5. Acworth, W. M. "The London and North-Western Railway." 3 (1888): 1–18, 160–77.
Tracked newspaper transmittal from arrival at the railroad to sorting by destination. Every day railroads carried 30,000–40,000 morning papers. Monday was easy because there were no weeklies. Tuesday was the society papers and Wednesday, the comic press.

6. Grain, R. Corney. "A Little Music." 3 (1888): 178–90.
Satirized being interviewed in "an age of interviewing." "Society papers" flourished even though many deprecated gossip.

7. Bird, Isabella L. "A Lady's Winter Holiday in Ireland." 3 (1888): 467–78, 622–36, 819–35.

Summarized the Irish press: the "daring political cartoons in *United Ireland*; the "arrest of the foreman printer of the *Cork Examiner*, one of the most pronounced of the Nationalist papers"; the *Cork Constitution*, with its "feeble squeak" for Protestants; the trial of T. Harrington, alleged co-owner of the *Kerry Sentinel*.

8. Acworth, W. M. "The South-Eastern and the Chatham Railways." 4 (1888): 209–25.

Specified the process and costs of moving newspapers by rail.

9. Roosevelt, Theodore. "Some Recent Criticism of America." 4 (1888): 289–310.

Deemed Matthew Arnold's critique of American newspapers a "denunciation" that was "too sweeping." American newspapers might offend decency and propriety but were publications of "sound common-sense, much shrewd humour," and morality, "potent forces for right" in public causes. Although Arnold admired the *Nation*, "its influence has been thoroughly unwholesome" with its "sour, spiteful dishonesty."

10. Arnold, F. "The Late Dean Burgon." 4 (1888): 472–88.

Alluded to the articles of J. W. Burgon in the *Guardian* and *Quarterly Review*.

11. Shand, Alexander Innes. "The Multiplication of Books." 4 (1888): 721–35.

Certified that at mid-century "the two-column review of a novel in the leading journal" could fuel a new edition of 1,000 for the book. In 1888 the dailies were too busy to review books at publication, but the literary journals also delayed so that the press had no effect on sales.

12. "Jools [*sic*] on London." 6 (1889): 542–50.

Review of Jules Dégregny's *Londres, Croquis Réalistes*, quoted him that London dailies were "ponderous" but inexpensive because of their advertising; periodical illustrations were inferior to the French, and *Punch* was not English or provincial enough for readers.

13. Smiles, Samuel. "Authors and Publishers." 7 (1890): 48–61, 207–19.

Imagined that a newsletter and the *London Gazette* satisfied eighteenth-century country readers. In the era of Alexander Pope, who penned for the *Grub-street Journal*, writers feared reviewers. As their criticism became more vehement, their reputations sank. Evaluated Samuel Johnson's work for the *Gentleman's Magazine*.

14. "Mad Tipperary." 7 (1890): 577–601.

Accused *United Ireland* of publishing a "hysterical leader" and the *Tipperary Nationalist* of libel.

15. Gladstone, William E. "Memoir of John Murray." 9 (1891): 577–87.

Mused about Murray's publishing career, his connection with the *Edinburgh Review*, which he thought was a model of 'higher criticism,' and the commencement of the *Quarterly Review*. Because of the "powerful direction" of editors William Gifford and J. G. Lockhart, it surpassed the *Edinburgh* in circulation. Murray's newspaper, the *Representative*, in which Benjamin Disraeli had a hand, was a failure.

16. Belloc, Marie Adelaide. "Two Brothers and Their Friends: the De Goncourts." 10 (1891): 541–53.

Confided that Théophile Gautier worked in the *Moniteur* office because he liked the pressure of the printer's devil waiting to get copy and to return proofs.

The National Review, 1855–1864

The successor of the *Prospective Review*, the *National* presented solid evaluations of leading press publications.

1. [Greg, W. R.]. "On the Just and the Unjust in the Recent Popular Discontent." 1 (1855): 1–30.

Outlined the "many high reform functions and many solemn obligations" of the "periodical press." Among these were to expose national grievances and, after "conscientious sifting," individual wrongs; protect the weak against oppression; reveal charlatans, "incapacity," and "corruption" in government; "allay popular passions" but identify legitimate discontent; save victims; and unmask criminals.

2. [Bagehot, Walter]. "The First *Edinburgh* Reviewers." 1 (1855): 253–84.

Classed review writing as "one of the features of modern literature," demonstrating its "casual character…temporary and fragmentary." Reviewers had to "instruct so many persons"; all, sure they were "competent to think," had to learn "to think rightly." Essays in the *Tatler* and *Spectator* were too short to accomplish this goal. The *Edinburgh Review* introduced longer articles with "suitable views for sensible persons," chiefly in the columns of Sydney Smith and Francis Horner.

3. [Powell, Baden]. "The Life and Writings of Dr. Thomas Young." 2 (1856): 69–97.

Cited the articles of Young, a physician and scholar, in the *Quarterly Review* and the *Transactions* of the Royal Society.

4. [Greg, W. R.]. "The Present State of France." 2 (1856): 123–56.

Approved the 'gagging' of journalism by Napoleon III because "some of the most widely circulated daily journals" were anti-British or Russian pawns. A free French press would ignite a newspaper war because British gazettes would retaliate. Further, many French newspapers displayed a "reckless spirit" and "violent language" that abetted popular unrest. Of the quality press the best were the *Journal des Débats*, the paper of the "middle class aristocracy"; *Siècle*, the "journal of the *cafés* and *cabarets*," and *Constitutionnel*, the herald of traders and shopkeepers. In the second class were the *Presse* and *Gazette de France*. François Guizot penned anonymously for the *Presse*, an evening paper that sold for three sous. Emile de Girardin, its conductor, kept it politically impartial and emotionally fascinating with "superior and exciting" feuilletons. The *Moniteur* was the "official organ," the *Univers* "priest-ridden."

Periodicals as the *Revue des Deux Mondes*, with temperate criticism and educated readers, should not be censured. The *Revue* was the most eminent, independent, and "lucrative" journal in France. Established as a fortnightly in 1830, it operated initially at a loss. Not until 1849 did it have the 6,000 subscribers necessary for profit. By contrast, the *Revue de Paris* had 1,300, *Revue Britannique*, 2,000, and François Guizot's *Revue Contemporaine*, 1,300.

5. [Greg, W. R.]. "The Political Tendencies of America." 2 (1856): 433–68.
Depicted American newspapers as "numberless and low-priced," with advertising accounting for five-sixths of their contents. Low startup costs spawned many cheap heralds whose small profit could not pay able writers but whose plan was to "gratify" their audience, to support prejudices, and to "inflame passions."

6. [Richmond, George]. "Pictures and Picture-Criticism." 3 (1856): 80–107.
Chastised the *Edinburgh Review* and *Quarterly Review* for their "fierceness which we had hoped was banished from respectable periodical literature."

7. [Masson, David]. "The *Noctes Ambrosianae*." 3 (1856): 175–200.
Review of John Wilson's *Noctes Ambrosianae* narrated the establishment of *Blackwood's Magazine* and its early conflicts with the *Edinburgh Review*. *Blackwood's* complemented the *Quarterly Review* by serving the Scottish wing of the Tories but was often wrong in its literary judgments and unpopular on social questions. It was better in "humour, in exuberant and jolly manliness," than was the *Edinburgh* because of Wilson's *Noctes*. They were "a novelty of the first order in British periodical literature...ephemeral writings calculated for immediate impression." They ignored "conventional decorum" but not the Tory-Whig polarization that made literary "levity" abusive.

8. [?Roscoe, W. C.]. "The Literature of Spirit-Rapping." 4 (1857): 131–51.
Referred to London's *Spiritual Herald* and the *Yorkshire Spiritual Telegraph*.

9. [Taylor, Tom]. "The Clubs of London." 4 (1857): 295–34.
Verified that Joseph Addison and Richard Steele got information and contributions for their serials from club members.

10. [Greg, W. R.]. "Louis Napoleon at Home and Abroad." 6 (1858): 472–95.
Averred that when Napoleon III first came to power he restricted but did not censure or suppress the press but manipulated it in 1858.

11. [Greg, W. R.]. "The True Difficulties of the Italian Question." 8 (1859): 488–502.
Nodded to the "*Mémorial Diplomatique*, an Austrian journal published in Paris."

12. [Greg, W. R. and James P. Lacaita]. "Italy: Its Prospects and Capacities." 9 (1859): 229–68.
Noted that the Italian idea of a free newspaper press was different from the English idea.

13. [Trollope, T. A.]. "Political and Religious Phases of the Roman Question." 15 (1862): 136–67.
Named the *Armonia*, *Civiltà Cattolica*, and *Mediatore* in Rome.

14. [Grant Duff, M. E.]. "The Crisis in Prussia." 16 (1863): 40–61.
Tagged the *Neue Preussische Zeitung*.

15. [Bagehot, Walter]. "Bolingbroke as a Statesman." 16 (1863): 389–426.

Thundered that Henry St. John, Lord Bolingbroke was "an unscrupulous writer" in the press. That he sanctioned licentiousness in government newspapers was evidenced by his recruiting Jonathan Swift, "the most bitter writer of libels."

16. "Wits of the French Revolution." 17 (1863): 38–60.

Held that the *Politique National*, "the organ of the most enlightened Conservatives," countered comic scribbling in the *Moniteur Universal* during the French Revolution.

17. [Pearson, Charles H.]. "Poland as It Is." 17 (1863): 366–84.

Complimented Vienna's *Presse* as *The Times* of Austria.

18. [Cobbe, Frances Power]. "What Annexation has Done for Italy." 18 (1864): 19–51.

Petitioned for better and braver leader-writing, more letters, and less political partisanship as Italian newspapers multiplied. The *Nazione* (Florence) was the most respectable because its news was clear and current and its columns were well written. The daily contained foreign telegrams, a leader "sometimes of very fair ability," local items, a feuilleton, and advertising. The paper was better than the *Giornale di Roma*, "the chief periodical of the Neri." Florence had three well-illustrated humor magazines: *Chiacchiera*, *Arlecchino*, and *Lampione*, which employed Mata, a lithographer known for his artistry and satire.

Itemized "the whole periodical press of Italy at the close of 1863" as "political newspapers, 17; "literary and scientific periodicals," 31; "miscellaneous," ten.

19. [Freeman, Edward A.]. "Mediaeval and Modern Greece." 18 (1864): 78–114.

Registered that Greece gained a free press with independence.

20. [Harrison, Frederic]. "The Destruction of Kagosima." 18 (1864): 270–93.

Contrasted the accuracy of *The Times* and the *Japan Commercial News*. Rued the jargon, copied from the *New York Herald*, of many British newspapers.

21. B[agehot], W[alter]. "Wordsworth, Tennyson, and Browning; or Pure, Ornate, and Grotesque Art in English Poetry." 19 (1864): 27–67.

Aside that the *Edinburgh Review* no longer reached the young and women.

22. Arnold, Matthew. "The Functions of Criticism at the Present Time." 19 (1864): 230–51.

Championed literary critics but not their publications. The *Edinburgh Review* was the captive of the Whigs; the *Quarterly Review*, of the Tories; the *North British Review*, of the "political Dissenters." The *Dublin Review* was too Catholic; the *Church and State Review*, a "High Church rhinoceros"; the *Record*, an "Evangelical hyena"; and *The Times*, the paper for the "common, satisfied, well-to-do Englishman." The only outstanding serials were the recently ended *Home and Foreign Review*, for "in no other organ of criticism in this country was there so much knowledge, so much play of mind," and France's *Revue des Deux Monde*, without parallel in England in its aim "to understand and utter the best that is known and thought."

The National Review, 1883–1900

This *National*, dedicated to Conservatism, scrutinized journalism and journalists at length. Among those in its spotlight were magazine editors and war correspondents.

1. Austin, Alfred. "'Above All, No Programme.'" 1 (1883): 24–39.
Promised that the *National Review* would "'promote deliberation, not…multiply opportunities for dogmatism" in pages that would be a "glass hive of Conservative thought." Aside that the Paris *Temps* was "the most able, the most moderate, and the most independent Liberal journal published on the Continent."

2. Carnarvon, [H. H. M. Herbert, 4th Earl]. "The First of March, 1711." 1 (1883): 40–50.
Marked the birth of the *Spectator* after 271 numbers of the *Tatler*. The *Spectator* used "gentle satire" compared to the 1883 leader, which "abounds in research and ability" but was often sarcastic. The *Spectator* reflected the move from a "rough to a more refined society." Its daily circulation reached 14,000 in an era when "the Press had become a formidable engine of political warfare." Joseph Addison was the genius behind its success with his style that was "a model of English writing."

3. Balfour, Arthur James. "Bishop Berkeley's *Life and Letters*." 1 (1883): 85–100, 299–313.
Review of A. C. Fraser's book on George Berkeley mentioned that he penned for the eighteenth-century *Guardian* and *Examiner* and that Daniel Defoe was paid for political writing but Joseph Addison and Richard Steele were not.

4. Tantivy, Thomas [Alfred Austin]. "Our Critics." 1 (1883): 161–74.
Abridged the reactions of several newspapers to the inauguration of the *National Review*.

5. Seton-Karr, W. S. "Lord Ripon's New Indian Policy." 1 (1883): 208–23.
Alerted that "a native journal, the *Reis and Rayyet*," in India printed an important report that other publications ignored.

6. Pembroke, [G. R. C. Herbert, 13th Earl]. "Liberty and Socialism." 1 (1883): 336–61.
Remarked that *The Times* research on political philosophy was not deep, so its leaders were full of "caution" and "vagueness."

7. Tantivy, Thomas [Alfred Austin]. "On the Literary Advantages of Grub Street." 1 (1883): 376–86.
Regretted that *Truth*, owned by Henry Labouchere, graded the *National* mediocre. *Truth* did not reflect the eighteenth-century *Spectator*'s style, one which drove Grub Street's into "corners." In 1883 a free

press allowed another Grub Street to publish private information that satisfied "the taste for scandal." *Truth* paid well for stories on the personal lives of others. The fascination with the excessive in *Truth* and its ilk was perhaps part of "social evolution."

8. Mallock, W. H. "The Radicalism of the Market-place." 1 (1883): 507–30.
Defined the marketplace as the newspaper.

9. Dennis, John. "The Art of Essay Writing." 1 (1883): 744–57.
Studied the *Tatler*, *Spectator*, and *Rambler* with aside that between 1750 and 1760 about 20 papers circulated, including those of Henry Fielding and Oliver Goldsmith.

10. Siewers, Carl. "Will Norway Become a Republic?" 2 (1883–84): 376–92.
Informed that Soren Jaaboek's paper, *Folktidende*, had the largest circulation in Norway c. 1860.

11. Bagenal, Philip H. "The International [Exhibition], and Its Influence on English Politics." 2 (1883–84): 422–36.
Encompassed the *Beehive*, the *Cooperative*, and the *Social Economist* as well as New York's *Irish World*, and Peter Kropotkin's *Révolte*.

12. Johns, B. G. "The Literature of Seven Dials." 2 (1883–84): 478–92.
Stumbled upon odd copies of periodicals, from the *Quarterly Review* to the *Gospel Missionary*, in the same bookstalls as halfpenny ballads.

13. Tantivy, Thomas [Alfred Austin]. "Will Party Government Continue to Work?" 2 (1883–84): 516–31.
Underscored that the nineteenth-century *Spectator* was known for "its honesty and candour, and its originality."

14. Blackburn, Henry. "The Art of Illustration." 2 (1883–84): 558–72.
Surmised that the press in 1883 had a "mass of illustrations" because of photography and telegraphic transmissions from war fronts. Many London papers were even putting pictures ahead of words. In the United States, *Harper's Monthly* and the *Century Magazine* excelled in illustrations.

15. Humphreys, J. T. C. "Two Aspects of the Irish Question. No. I: Is England Going to Keep Ireland?" 2 (1883–84): 653–67.
Categorized the Irish "National Press" as weeklies "conducted with very considerable ability" except *United Ireland*. They all had "immense circulation" and were "the sole political and literary food" of "the masses."

16. Austin, Alfred. "The Aristocracy of Letters." 3 (1884): 61–77.
Sighed that writers frequently did "task-work" in "the quarterly reviews, the monthly magazines, the weekly papers, and the daily press" to earn a living.

17. Kennard, N[ina] H. "Why Women Write." 3 (1884): 694–706.
Quoted an unnamed editor of a "first-class magazine" that women did some of its best work, a fact he would never admit in public. Postulated that women were "often unsound and extreme in their views," so they were "open to the mistrust and ridicule of the other sex." They needed "soberness and liberality of judgment," "patience and industry" to succeed in journalism.

18. Saintsbury, George. "John Gibson Lockhart." 3 (1884): 745–62.
Painted Lockhart as "eminently a journalist" whose work was never "slovenly" and always "consistent" with his principles. His essays for *Blackwood's Magazine*, where one of his articles was "literature," another "only capital journalism," preceded his *Quarterly Review* career. During his 28 years as its editor, he penned 100 essays while simultaneously contributing to *Fraser's Magazine*. There was some tension between Lockhart and Theodore Hook when he edited *John Bull*.

19. Browne, G. Lathom. "The Burning of Bristol: A Reminiscence of the First Reform Bill." 4 (1884–85): 45–62.
Juxtaposed the violent language of 1831 newspapers and the more moderate tone of 1884 gazettes.

20. Brabazon, [Reginald, 12th Earl Meath]. "A Woman's Work." 4 (1884–85): 86–90.
Centered on the Girls' Friendly Society, one of whose three magazines, *Friendly Leaves*, "has a monthly circulation of 50,000 copies."

21. Durie, James. "India, 1880–4: An Unofficial Retrospect." 4 (1884–85): 266–81.
Stationed the *Bombay Gazette*, *Madras Mail*, and *Times of India* among the "leading Anglo-Indian newspapers."

22. Marzials, Frank T. "A French Critic: M. Edmond Scherer." 4 (1884–85): 546–59.
Appraised the work of *Temps* critic Scherer.

23. Kent, Armine T. "Della Crusca and Anna Matilda: An Episode in English Literature." 4 (1884–85): 607–19.
Aside on the eighteenth-century morning daily, the three-penny *World,* "which in more than one respect resembled its modern namesake."

24. Tilley, Arthur. "Ivan Turgénieff [*sic*]." 4 (1884–85): 683–97; 5 (1885): 829–41.
Divulged that Turgenev in 1846 published in *Sovremennik*, Alexander Pushkin's journal, at the invitation of the editor.

25. Kebbel, T. E. "Tory Prime Ministers. III: Mr. Canning." 4 (1884–85): 801–18.
Rated George Canning's *Anti-Jacobin* "a brilliant success," one that came after he sold the copyright of his earlier journal, Eton's *Microcosm*, to Charles Knight for 50 guineas.

26. Katscher, Leopold. "Some Aspects of the Salvation Army." 5 (1885): 71–93.
Denigrated the *Little Soldier*, the Salvation Army's "detestable" weekly for juveniles that had an enormous circulation. Aside that Paul Leroy-Beaulieu was "the well-known editor" of the *Economiste* and contributor to the *Journal des Débats* and *Revue des Deux Mondes*.

27. ?B[orthwick, Algernon]. "The Conservative Political Press." 5 (1885): 634–45; with a letter by H. Byron Reed, 866–68.

Chronicled that the National Union of Conservative Associations had, at its July 1885 conference, urged the party to give "immediate and serious consideration" to expanding its local press. The country had few Tory tribunes with any influence because the party never cultivated the press, indeed disdained it. Local papers did not cost much, but Conservatives did not endow their prints with enough money to hire competent editors. Rather than offering amateur productions at a cheap price, it was better to bankroll a more expensive morning paper whose advertising would support it by the second or third year. Local magnates should not interfere but should treat editors with "courtesy and civility."

Letter countered that the country press spent funds recklessly and news agencies were not pro-Conservative, so a better solution was a daily London Letter akin to Joseph Cowen's for the *Newcastle Chronicle*. *See* 5: 818.

28. Traill, H. D. "What Is Public Opinion?" 5 (1885): 652–64.

Opined that London had six or seven "first class" morning dailies with high circulations. Most had two political leaders, each of three paragraphs. Since a newspaper had to be profitable, this material had to address matters of public concern. Before 1855 the newspaper supposedly directed public opinion, perhaps truest of *The Times* which shared the views of readers. After the paper duty ended, many cheap papers reversed this direction, putting the public in control. In either case, newspapers gave some a greater voice than others in shaping opinion.

29. A Conservative Journalist. "The Establishment of Newspapers." 5 (1885): 818–28.

Supplement to 5: 634, by person claiming to be 25 years a journalist (reporter, editor, owner), advised on building size, space allocation, equipment, and printing for a new paper. Startup costs, without the building, were 12,000 pounds. London staff, telegraphy, and printing would cost 25,500 pounds per year; paper, 8,000 pounds. Because it was wise to have a reserve of two years and to cover the purchase of a building, a prospective owner needed 200,000 pounds. To avoid begging for advertising and to counter "petty pilfering" by employees, owners had to maintain financial stability while hiring able journalists. Even if established rivals were dull and stupid, they had reputations and commensurate profits.

30. Greg, Percy. "Some Uses of a Parliamentary Seat." 6 (1885–86): 112–22.

Warned that partisan political journals were ordinarily ineffective because opponents did not read them and proponents discounted them.

31. Traill, H. D. "The Plague of Tongues." 6 (1885–86): 616–30.

Opted for a newspaper of information rather than of stump politics.

32. [Norman, C. B.]. "France: Its Finances and Its Freedom." 7 (1886): 325–42.

Announced that all newspapers were forbidden in French military barracks and that any officials seen reading the royalist press were dismissed.

33. Hitchman, Francis. "Social Aspects of the Revolution of 1789." 7 (1886): 392–412.

Despised French Revolutionary journalism. "The press reflected the general depravity. Anything viler than the newspapers of the Revolution it would be hard to imagine." Among the worst was *Père Duchesne*. The satire in the *Anti-Jacobin* was not in this mold.

34. Austin, Alfred. "The Revival of Common Sense." 7 (1886): 552–65.
Fumed that editors of "powerful journals" saw "their highest duty…rather to seem than to be right, to be prophets rather than arbiters of our fate."

35. Cotgreave, Alfred. "Free Libraries under the 'Act,' and Their Promotion." 7 (1886): 571–76.
Letter-essay on the Free Libraries Act stressed the value of library newsrooms for workers. Newspapers provided information about the trades, advertising about goods and services, and columns of light reading for rest and relaxation while educating opinion. A local editor, recognizing these assets, sponsored the library in Richmond.

36. Colchester, [R. C. E. Abbot, 3rd Baron]. "Mallet du Pan." 7 (1886): 668–77.
Scanned the 1790s correspondence of Jacques Mallet du Pan, editor of *Mercure*, a French pre-revolutionary monarchist journal.

37. A Conservative Journalist. "Why Is the Provincial Press Radical?" 7 (1886): 678–82.
Guessed that since 1836 the "opinionated journal" had replaced the pamphlet. In the country, papers had grown from one sheet to several pages, but printer-owners still spoke to the masses. To challenge this reputedly Radical press, its opponents needed money because readers in 1886 wanted less politics and more personalities. Since "the genius of the newspaper is to publish to the million what the individual desires to kept secret," it was not surprising that the paper with the 'largest circulation in the world' spotlighted the Divorce Court. This press was hard for respectable hopefuls to overtake, but the greatest success came to papers with a single owner, not a company. Journalists, often Radical in youth, were less so as logic and prosperity affected them.

38. Bradley, A. G. "Alexander Hamilton." 7 (1886): 796–815.
Speculated that Hamilton used the newspapers before 1775 to mobilize American colonists. Later Federalists started *Fenno's Gazette*, and Thomas Jefferson began the *National Gazette*, edited by one of his "clever, unscrupulous" clerks.

39. Lang, [Leo]nora [B.] "Paul de St. Victor." 8 (1886–87): 296–312.
Starred Frenchman de St. Victor who "succeeded Jules Janin as theatrical critic" at the *Presse*.

40. A Parisian. "France as It Is and Was: Government and Society." 8 (1886–87): 455–76.
Despaired that the French *Nouvelle Revue* was full of "vulgar frivolous calumnies" and secondhand information.

41. Dennis, John. "Robert Southey." 8 (1886–87): 765–76.
Called Southey "for years the ablest writer for the *Quarterly* [*Review*]."

42. Sharp, William. "Rossetti in Prose and Verse." 9 (1887): 111–24.
Whispered about "that exceeding scarce magazine the *Germ*."

43. Hoare, E. Brodie. "Notes on New Zealand." 9 (1887): 499–512.
Reported that "local newspapers deal ably with local affairs, but seem to regard contemporary history outside New Zealand with something approaching to contempt. The English and European telegrams are meagre, and often inaccurate."

44. [Sharp, William]. "The Royal Academy and the Salon." 9 (1887): 513–24.
Called for signing of art and book reviews.

45. Shore, H. N. "Recent Literature in China." 10 (1887–88): 112–24.
Testified that newspapers were still novel in China, which had five dailies in 1887. The much older official *Peking Gazette* was useless to inform the masses. It had three editions: two, on yellow paper, covered government and commerce; one, on red paper, covered the provinces. A committee edited the *Gazette*, which printed 15,000 copies daily. The *Shanghai Gazette*, launched in 1882, printed 10,000 daily. Its Chinese staff had a reputation for exposing government abuses. Its owners also produced the *Shanghai Illustrated News* using lithography. The Hong Kong *Universal Circulating Herald* likewise bared official misdoings.

The "most important magazines" were the *Scientific Magazine*, a monthly of the Chinese Polytechnic in Shanghai that had general as well as science articles and advertisements; the weekly *Globe Magazine*; and the "*Monthly Educator*, a Chinese *Leisure Hour* edited by missionaries." There were also other missionary magazines.

46. Banfield, Frank. "The Eruptive Force of Modern Fanaticism." 10 (1887–88): 268–80.
Pointed to newspaper war coverage as one cause of fanaticism because it had an "exciting effect on the nervous system."

47. Kaufmann, M[oritz]. "French Socialism." 10 (1887–88): 355–75.
Mused that the best writers on French socialism were journalists, yet socialist gazettes were not outstanding. To win large circulations, the *Cri du Peuple* and its brethren depended on feuilletons and scandal like the general papers. Still, the "revolutionary press" could occasionally rouse the masses.

48. Adams, Coker. "Lord Macaulay and Madame D'Arblay." 10 (1887–88): 461–77.
Documented the "warfare" between periodical writers of an earlier age.

49. Shand, Alexander Innes. "The Centenary of *The Times*." 10 (1887–88): 841–56.
Celebrated *The Times* anniversary with a history of its offices, personnel, and influence now streaming from the 70,000 copies it printed every hour. Its editor held "the blue ribbon of the profession," and its foreign correspondents were akin to ambassadors. The paper had a stellar staff complemented by a "brilliant flying corps of outsiders" and a variety of letter-writers. They all sustained the journal's reputation for fairness in economic and political affairs.

50. Heaton, J. Henniker. "Two Centenaries: The Centenary of Australia." 10 (1887–88): 857–65.
Memorialized "George Howe, the first editor and printer of the *Sydney Gazette*, now merged in the *Sydney Morning Herald*." Howe worked for *The Times* until he was transported.

51. Holmes, T. R. E. "Sir Herbert Edwardes." 12 (1888–89): 208–23.
Biography of a military commander believed that his 1845 weekly essays in the *Delhi Gazette* sparked reader interest in the paper.

52. Vincent, Edmund. "The Vernacular Press of Wales." 12 (1888–89): 318–25.
Detected similarities between Welsh and Indian journalism even though the government did not monitor the Welsh press as it did the Indian. The Welsh upper classes did not know Welsh, so the sects controlled the press. Welsh journalists, like their Indian colleagues, goaded readers to violence but were unwilling to participate in it.

53. A Scottish Conservative [James Ferguson]. "Scottish Conservatism." 13 (1889): 1–21.
Saw newspapers as "the artillery of political warfare," particularly evil when editors of the same party attacked each other.

54. Smith, G. Leslie. "The Congress and Modern India." 13 (1889): 202–19.
Essay on the Indian National Congress lamented that "the licence of the native press is now unbridled." Young men who could not find jobs and desired status established local gazettes that earned money from publishing sensation and libel or from blackmailing subjects who paid to avoid publicity. The Raj should restrict the "degraded press" because Indian readers, unlike British, were "ignorant, credulous, and easily inflamed," all prerequisites for sedition. *See* 13: 526.

55. Sylvester, Paul [Pauline Schletter]. "The First Special Correspondent." 13 (1889): 226–45.
Focused on Melchior Grimm, a talented journalist known for his honest and accurate criticism. About 1750 he founded *Correspondance Litteraire*, "a fortnightly manuscript journal," and restricted circulation to royal subscribers from Prussia and other German states, Sweden, Poland, and Russia. Grimm's serial was the forerunner of the *Nouveau Mercure de France* in 1775.

56. Pincott, Frederic. "The Indian National Congress: The Other Side." 13 (1889): 526–38.
Response to 13: 202 touched on the *Pioneer*, *Tribune*, and *Advocate* among the Indian press.

57. Waters, Cyril A. "William Gifford." 13 (1889): 677–87.
Tracked Gifford's editorial career from the *Anti-Jacobin*, whose management he shared with George Canning. Gifford, known as a tough editor, reached the pinnacle when he took the reins of the *Quarterly Review* because it was then, with the *Edinburgh Review*, a very important political and literary organ. In 1889 newspapers critiqued politics; weekly reviews and monthly magazines critiqued literature.

58. Keene, H. G. "The Age of Reason: Some Literary Aspects of the French Revolution of 1789." 14 (1889–90): 109–24.
Spotted the rise of the French press in the 1790s. In 1789 Paris had two newspapers, the *Gazette de France* and *Journal de Paris* until the *Moniteur* emerged. Next to surface were the *Journal des Débats* and the "Terrorist papers…breathless, bloody, and illiterate." An opponent of the latter was the *Mercure Français*, "an organ of constitutional democracy," 1793–94.

59. Conybeare, F[rederick] C. "Armenia and the Armenians." 14 (1889–90): 295–315.

Stated that Michael Katkoff, when editor of the *Moscow Gazette*, was "the most influential journalist in Russia."

60. Anglo-African. "Africa South of the Equator." 15 (1890): 1–17.

Aside on the *Zuid Afrikaan*, "the Dutch organ," and the *Cape Times* in South Africa.

61. Gaye, Arthur. "The Centenary of White's *Selborne*." 15 (1890): 101–13.

Alluded to Gilbert White's articles in the *Gentleman's Magazine*, 1780–90.

62. Hill, Charles. "A Plea for Sunday Observance." 15 (1890): 506–17.

Grumbled that London had "too many" weeklies that sold 12 to 16 "pages of close reading" for a penny.

63. Baden-Powell, George. "Mr. Gladstone and Malta." 16 (1890–91): 289–302.

Titled *Public Opinion* "the Maltese 'Liberal' newspaper."

64. Oldham, Alice. "The History of Socialism." 16 (1890–91): 310–34, 460–85, 621–49.

Logged the journalism of some socialists. Karl Marx edited and penned for the *Rheinische Zeitung* in 1842 and later, while living in London, wrote for eight years for the *New York Tribune*. Also in London Alexander Herzen published *Kolokol*, which was "widely circulated and eagerly read in Russia." More recently the Social Democratic Federation published *Justice*; the Socialist League, *Commonweal*; the Christian Socialist Society, *Christian Socialist.*

65. Watson, [John] William. "Critics and Their Craft." 16 (1890–91): 789–93.

Evaluated George Saintsbury's magazine articles. In the days of William Gifford, Francis Jeffrey, Henry Brougham, and J. G. Lockhart, critics were literary solons. In 1890 they were no longer "responsible guardians of law and order in literature" because a critic's own preference replaced the "rule in matters of taste and aesthetics." Neither the old "dogmatic" style nor the new "appreciation" served literature well.

66. Benson, Arthur C. "Eton." 17 (1891): 593–607.

Selected as one of the best Eton magazines (several listed here) the 1820 *Etonian* even though it was always in the shadow of the more famous 1786 *Microcosm*.

67. Lowe, Charles. "The New Emperor and His New Chancellor." 18 (1891–92): 19–42.

Blared that Wilhelm II had "a deep aversion" to journalists, so he refused to receive foreign correspondents at court. He reputedly read only the Press Bureau's daily extracts of German and European newspapers. To avoid the charge of manipulating the press, a charge against Otto von Bismarck, new chancellor George von Caprivi had no relations with it except the official *Reichsanzeiger*.

68. Ridge, W. Pett. "Club Life in East London." 18 (1891–92): 135–39.
Acknowledged that the primary role of workingmen's clubs was not to supply members with journals. Nevertheless, the typical club subscribed to some, and the Club and Institute Union circulated a "frank, queerly written little newspaper."

69. Low, Sidney J. "A Word for the Reviewers." 18 (1891–92): 799–808.
Swore that book authors in 1890 were sure of the "general unworthiness of contemporary reviewing as it is practised in the English periodical press." Yet literary critics tended to pad less than social or political journalists, and "editorial responsibility and equity" were better than the halcyon days of reviewing in the 1820s. Newspaper reviews were not universally "stupid, vulgar, or malignant." Some were "genuine attempts to express an honest opinion," albeit "often weak and unscholarly" because many writers had no literary education. Critics were poorly paid tyros with "enthusiasm" for literature or "busy professional men" caught up in their other careers who reviewed only for love of it. Authors should not take the ignorant and venal seriously and should not blame critics because "the public buys trash and neglects good work."

70. A London Editor. "Authors, Individual and Corporate." 19 (1892): 476–87.
Article on the Society of Authors and Institute of Journalists ranked press writing not only literature but often a more "artistic" form than books. *The Times*, *Spectator*, *Saturday Review*, *Temple Bar*, *Blackwood's Magazine*, *Longman's Magazine*, and the *Cornhill Magazine*, among others, represented quality, but all serials were recruiting great authors. Even the evening press showed "imagination." Editors who refused to review books from vanity presses checked the "unmeritorious," but the Society of Authors had no mechanism to measure quality. *See* 19: 626.

71. Besant, Walter. "Authors Individual and Corporate: A Reply." 19 (1892): 626–35; A London Editor. "Rejoinder," 635–38.
Retort to 19: 476 conceded that journalism was "one form of literature." Rejoinder again questioned the function of the Society of Authors.

72. Low, Sidney J. "Newspaper Copyright." 19 (1892): 648–66.
Opponent of copyrighting news because that was not in the public interest comprehended that the copyright of newspapers was not clear in statute or in case law. The Copyright Act, 1842, and a recent case involving *The Times* and the *St. James's Gazette* demonstrated this fuzziness. Complying with copyright was easier for a magazine than for a newspaper whose authors were "vast, varied." *See* 19: 855.

73. Hardy, Harold. "Newspaper Copyright: Letters." 19 (1892): 855–59; Spencer Brodhurst, 859–64.
Said in answer to 19: 648 that the Copyright Act, 1842, adequately distinguished between newspapers and other periodicals. Brodhurst cited cases to prove that the law protected newspaper articles.

74. An Old Journalist. "The Institute of Journalists." 20 (1892–93): 274–78.
Vetoed requiring prospective journalists to pass an examination of the Institute of Journalists because there were no educational standards for journalism. A reporter was someone "able to hear and see what no other body hears or sees." "Unless university training is to be made indispensable to journalism," no test was possible. Because the "Newspaper Press is great in its social standing, moral power, and

still expanding range," the institute should concern itself with protecting novices and monitoring nonprofessionals, such as clerics and lawyers, who wrote for newspapers.

75. Wicks, Frederick. "Authors, Publishers, and Reviewers." 20 (1892–93): 640–50.
Counseled literary critics to tell readers what to read, not "coin sentences for publishers' advertisements."

76. Waugh, Arthur. "The Tyranny of the Paragraph." 20 (1892–93): 743–48.
Carped that new journalism, evidenced by the "American passion for 'pithiness,'" was adversely affecting literature. Newspapers full of paragraphs bred a taste for the timely and diminished the value of criticism by converting reviews into abstracts. *See* 21: 38.

77. Fry, Oliver A. "In Defence of the Paragraph." 21 (1893): 38–43.
Interpreted 20: 743 as dismissing the 'leaderette,' "a short article of news and original comment," and confusing short reviews with book advertisements or the cuttings of a subeditor from the text. The paragraph, "in its best form…constitutes, probably, the highest flight of journalism." The style was not American but British, existing at least since the *Owl* of the 1860s. *Vanity Fair* adopted the format in 1868, and others, such as the *World* and *Truth*, copied it. Paragraphs allowed publication of more news, important because the "object of a newspaper is, or should be, to instruct on all things current." Paragraphs also fit telegraphy. The result was that "the Press was never cleaner, never more rightly enterprising than it is to-day." Dailies had good leaders. Weeklies, as the *Saturday Review* and *Spectator*, "make clear the strength, scholarship, and critical ability of our best journalists." Elite reviews were still "good" and still "dull" but had less influence because leisured readers were already well informed. The Americans had affected style otherwise, as by exporting the "blatant" headline.

78. Gardner, FitzRoy. "The Tory Press and the Tory Party: A Complaint." 21 (1893): 357–62.
Journalist Gardner deduced that Liberal newspapers were more appealing than Tory because of their "smart interviews, suggestive headings, rough cartoons and portraits, signed articles, interesting chit-chat, and general up-to-datedness." Tory gazettes tended to be "steady old-fashioned journalism" that was losing readers. *See* 21: 363.

79. Cust, Henry. "The Tory Press and the Tory Party: An Answer." 21 (1893): 363–67; Walter Herries Pollock, 367–68; W. E. Henley, 368–71; Sidney J. Low, 371–74.
Cust dated the revolution in journalism from the appropriation by the *Pall Mall Gazette* of an American "presentation of news with vigour and vivacity." To reach new voters, the press should stoop to personal gossip and paragraphs of information while "unobtrusively injecting Toryism." Pollock denied the value of sensationalism to attract Tory readers who might conclude that the party's goal was to be popular. Henley hated using popular culture, the "conspiracy of public bad breeding and individual prurience," to serve a "self-respecting party." Low intimated that the tactics of the Radical papers, "gulling voters" or "hitting below the belt," might sell in places London dailies never reached.

80. One Who Knows. "In Defence of the Post Office." 21 (1893): 647–58.
Peered at the cost of transmitting newspapers and other periodicals.

81. Martin, A[rthur] Patchett. "Robert Lowe as a Journalist." 22 (1893–94): 352–64.

Saluted Robert Lowe as a *Times* leader-writer who, while an MP, did not employ "the powerful engine of the Press for personal objects." Excerpted some leaders previously not attributed to Lowe.

82. Bunce, J. Thackray. "Church and Press." 22 (1893–94): 387–93.

Broadcast that country dailies were burgeoning and London ones were selling more copies as readers demanded news. Yet there was "an air of suspicion and standoffishness" between church and press, both agencies to improve the community. "As the profession of journalism rises in its personal and in its intellectual standard," there was less cause for complaint about the treatment of church matters, particularly in the more influential papers.

83. Stephen, Leslie. "The Duties of Authors." 23 (1894): 319–39.

Reminded that anonymous journalism in the early nineteenth century, when the British press was the freest in Europe, did not reap the respect of other professions. "In the year 1809 benchers of Lincoln's Inn passed a resolution that no one should be called to the Bar who had written for money for a newspaper," perhaps because politicians of the age utilized journalists as "mercenary guerillas." In 1894 journalists should never publish anonymously what they would not with signature. They could pen to amuse or inform, but they must be honest. They should not sacrifice their individuality to echo the style or sentiments of their journals. They should "try to know something," to put problems in historical context, and to ensure that their solutions were not "reproductions of exploded fallacies." Leader-writers should base their opinions on principle but acknowledge that the journalist's frame of mind was not conducive to serious political analysis.

84. Beck, Theodore. "The House of Commons and the Indian Civil Service." 23 (1894): 372–89.

Designated *Bangabasi* as "the most widely-read vernacular paper" in Bengal.

85. Lorac, Luis de. "The Situation in Belgium." 24 (1894–94): 334–46.

Branded the *Diable du Corps*, a Brussels newspaper, "a disreputable and indecent, but often clever journal."

86. Beck, Theodore. "Native India and England." 24 (1894–95): 375–91.

Feared that Bengali newspapers were sometimes seditious.

87. Lane-Poole, Stanley. "Sir Charles Newton, K.C.B., D.C.L., LL.D." 24 (1894–95): 616–27.

Recognized Newton's contributions to professional journals, such as the *Archaeologia*, and to general periodicals, such as the *Edinburgh Review*.

88. Spielmann, M[arion] H. "The Present Condition of Wood-Engraving in England and America." 25 (1895): 48–58.

Technical essay referred to illustrated publications and their personnel in England and the United States. *See* 25: 343.

89. Stephen, Leslie. "The Choice of Books." 25 (1895): 165–82.
Glimpsed "forgotten corners of social life" in eighteenth-century periodicals such as the *Rambler* with an aside on Junius.

90. Pennell, Joseph. "The True Condition of Wood-Engraving in England and America." 25 (1895): 343–50.
Hinted, in response to 25: 48, that Spielmann was biased because he was the literary editor of the *Magazine of Art.* The quality of wood engraving depended on how much money the publisher invested in it.

91. Quilter, Harry. "The Relation of Criticism to Production in Art." 25 (1895): 466–81.
Sermonized that art criticism did not get adequate space in most newspapers because editors prioritized "fashionable intelligence" (gossip) and sports. Those journalists who judged art by a school or were "recruited at random" without concern for credentials and those owners who would not tolerate offense to advertisers of art books were devaluing criticism.

92. Dobson, Austin. "'*Polly Honeycombe.*'" 25 (1895): 623–31.
Shared that many forgettable tales were in the eighteenth-century *Novelist's Magazine*, in demand in 1895 only for "its graceful old 'coppers' by Thomas Stohard," and in other obscure periodicals. Aside on the work of Oliver Goldsmith in the *Public Ledger*.

93. Spielmann, M[arion] H. "The Rivals of *Punch*: A Glance at the Illustrated Comic Press of Half a Century." 25 (1895): 654–66.
Surveyed editors and artists of comic publications. The *Fly* and *Ass* anticipated the taste for the comic journalism of *Punch* but died because they were less good-humored. Among the rivals of *Punch* were the *Great Gun* (1844–45) with some "strangely coarse" cartoons; the "exceedingly clever" *Diogenes* (1853–55); *Echoes from the Clubs* (1867–68), edited by war correspondent Frank Vizetelly, who disappeared during the Egyptian campaign; and several others in Britain and elsewhere in the 1870s and 1880s.

94. Maxse, Frederick A. "'Fraternal France.'" 25 (1895): 851–64.
Roared that the "popular Paris press is a truly terrible engine of mischief." Lower-class newspapers resorted to "vilification and blackmail," but the respectable papers found in restaurants and railroad stations, such as the *Petit Journal* and *Figaro*, did more damage. *Figaro* was "probably the most widely-read newspaper in France," more popular than the "serious papers," as the *Temps* and *Journal des Débats*, which were "too well informed to descend to gross caricature." By monopolizing information, newspapers not only shaped opinion but "intimidate the Government." *See* 26: 258, 28: 180.

95. A Resident in Paris. "French Journalism." 26 (1895–96): 74–82.
Explained that France had fewer reviews and magazines than Britain and the United States. The smallest were monotonous. However, Paris had 50 dailies, most selling for a sou to people with little money and literary taste. Contents varied, from the "reasonable" publications to those that published "false news" penned by "an apostle of hatred." Even Italy, "the land of the Mafia and the Camorro," had no such press. Paris journalists took money for influence, their "puffs" in news columns and

leaders. "This utilization of vice as a commercial agency has only within a few years invaded the domain of legitimate journalism, but it has already made serious ravages." Treating bribery lightly fathered blackmail. Ironically, French newspapers attracted many talented journalists who covered "news, politics, and literature" well, the last better than their British colleagues. About 35–40 journalists sat in the Chamber of Deputies.

96. Fitzgerald, C. C. P., Rear-Admiral. "'Fraternal France.'" 26 (1895–96): 258–66.

Reply to 25: 851 concurred that French journalism was "hot-headed, unreasoning," but discounted its often humorous commentary as a measure of serious opinion. It merely contrasted with the humorless, "cool-headed, reasoning" in British leaders.

97. Banfield, Frank. "Interviewing in Practice." 26 (1895–96): 367–78.

Validated the interview, earlier tainted by its American style. A good interview required more than the subject's cooperation. The "practiced journalist" could supply the right amount of "friction and guidance" to make a readable and relatively accurate column, but serious papers expected evidence of an intellectual exchange. Reporters should ask specialists to clarify answers for the benefit of readers.

98. Frewen, Moreton. "American Politics." 26 (1895–96): 595–608.

Averred that the Eastern press "created" Grover Cleveland's personality in his first term, so New York's *Tribune*, *Herald*, and *Sun* seemed immune to White House coercion.

99. An Editor. "Advertisement as a Gentle Art." 26 (1895–96): 650–56.

Inspired by Walter Besant's essay on the Literary Agent (*Nineteenth Century* 38: 979), this article linked the job to the press. Agents were partly responsible for the "enormous flood of rubbish" penned by authors in new periodicals.

100. Stephen, Leslie. "The Evolution of Editors." 26 (1895–96): 770–85.

Dated the term editor, meaning "the commander of a periodical," from the eighteenth-century *Post Boy* because Daniel Defoe's *Review* was a pamphlet. Defoe's *Daily Post* and William Cobbett's *Political Register* used the "I," not the "We." Although the *Gentleman's Magazine* in 1731 reproduced articles from weeklies and printed "book notices" and "miscellaneous literature," owner Edward Cave had a "true editorial spirit," supervising all details of the journal. Publishers then started periodicals of literary criticism, the *Monthly Review* of Ralph Griffiths and the *Critical Review* of Archibald Hamilton. The *North Briton* made John Wilkes famous, and Junius drove the *Public Advertiser* circulation to 3,000 daily during Henry Sampson Woodfall's tenure as editor. He depended on unpaid contributors and letters to fill the paper of which he was also business manager. Finally, John Walter II of *The Times* set the standard for hiring an editor as well as a foreign correspondent, the first being Henry Crabb Robinson. By John Delane's era the editor had "a position of high political importance." Another distinguished editor was James Perry, *Morning Chronicle* owner. The *Edinburgh Review* did not plan on an editor because its founders were a committee.

101. G[riffith]-Boscawen, A. "A Recent Visit to Japan." 27 (1896): 424–34.

Observed that the Japanese relaxed press censorship when "a Japanese paper partly published in the English language" circulated anti-British cartoons.

102. A Contributor. "Editors." 27 (1896): 505–15.
Author purported to be a contributor to 20 periodicals. Proprietors "with commercial instincts" were "the curse of honest journalism." Editors generally respected the journalist's "property in ideas," but rejections were not always polite or prompt. Acceptances often forced the writer to deal with "fussy" or "careless" editors rather than the "judicious." Some editors cared only about space; others never sent proofs. Although editors had more responsibility for unsigned stories, they should not alter anything, even titles, without notice. Payment scales varied, but most editors did not pay immediately for contributions solicited or submitted. Among ideal editors named here were those at *The Times*. *See* 27: 793.

103. An Editor. "Contributors." 27 (1896): 793–801.
Decided that the author of 27: 505 was not a "finished or perfect writer." The comments were anecdotal, prejudicial, and representative only of the "army" of contributors who sent the same piece to many periodicals. These troops paid no attention to a journal's standards for length or tone, for example offering gossip to a "serious" review. It was unreasonable to expect an editor to acknowledge all "casual contributions." An editor usually returned a rejected article unless the writer failed to give an address or posted additional work after the editor told the person not to do so. Sometimes editors filed stories for later publication. Potential contributors should not visit editorial offices because most editors were busy and impatient with egoists. An editor suspected that those who presented introductions from another editor were people a colleague was trying to dump. The chief flaws of contributors were "want of consideration, illegible hand-writing," writing much more than asked, using technical or foreign phrases unknown to readers, tardiness, and vanity. Offered a "plain truth for small fry contributors…In subjects of current interest, it is farcical that any man or woman should claim copyright" though perhaps the author had a "moral copyright" to be treated fairly. Aside that assistant editors once had "responsibility, trust, and power" but in 1896 were more akin to secretaries.

104. Maxse, Frederick A. "Anglophobia." 28 (1896–97): 180–88.
Repeated some ideas of 25: 851 and added that the press interfered with international relations because newspapers monopolized dissemination of information. British gazettes represented the opinions of owners or editors, not readers but had to have enough "original matter"' to be quoted and therefore to sell. The Paris *Petit Journal* had an "enormous circulation," but the French press was not as powerful as it considered itself. In the United States, as E. L. Godkin said in the *North American Review*, journalism was "war-like," relying on the "startling" conflict to 'renew the rage for extras' that inflated profits. Likewise, though British journalism was "a profession," its "success depends on the excitement it can stir." Yet *The Times*, which resisted "startling headlines," retained its "supremacy and prestige."

105. Colomb, P. H. "The Patriotic Editor in War." 29 (1897): 253–63.
Questioned how patriotic editors would behave in war, especially given access to telegraphy and news agencies. The answer was significant because the press formed public opinion but expressed novel concepts primarily to sell. Specifically, war editors should support military policy or consult experts before condemning it. Generally, they should preach "caution, patience, hope," mainly to workers who would likely be the "chief sufferers" from shortages and who might panic about price and wage changes.

106. Statham, E. Reginald. "The Case for the Transvaal." 29 (1897): 325–51.
Referred to several papers in Southern Africa: the *Rhodesia Herald*, edited by W. E. Fairbridge; *Natal Mercury*, "a thoroughly representative British journal"; *Natal Witness*, formerly edited by Statham; *Transvaal Observer*, edited by Statham since 1892; *Free State Express*, for which Statham

wrote; *Cape Times*, edited by F. E. Garrett; *Cape Argus*; Kimberley's *Diamondfields Advertiser*; and Barberton's *Gold Field News*, "an essentially English paper."

107. Foreman, John. "Europe's New Invalid." 29 (1897): 721–34.
Narrated that Spain's "newspapers live more by polemics than the publication of news" because its citizens were "passionate." Aside on the political bent of several Spanish gazettes.

108. Stephen, Leslie. "Johnsoniana." 30 (1897–98): 61–76.
Portrayed Samuel Johnson as "struggling for employment on the *Gentleman's Magazine*" and succeeding at the *Rambler*.

109. Stephen, Leslie. "The Importation of German." 30 (1897–98): 619–35.
Noticed William Taylor, who penned for the *Monthly Review* and the *Critical Review*, where he pioneered the detailed critique later characteristic of the *Edinburgh Review*.

110. Circumspecte Agatis. "The Tragedy of Arthur Crawford." 30 (1897–98): 900–17.
Essay on the trial of a civil servant rated the *Times of India* and the *Pioneer* "important newspapers" in the subcontinent.

111. "The Sorrows of Scribblers – Being the Confessions of a Magazine Contributor." 31 (1898): 63–74.
Author claimed to be one of the "army" of contributors in 1898 taxing editors' patience. Although the person's first manuscript was neatly penned, it received 20 rejections, from polite to bizarre, before publication earned its author one pound. Most magazines paid by scale, but scribes could barely survive on these wages in contrast to "[n]ewspaper journalism" that "offers daily bread." To succeed in magazines, tyros should not submit material to editors who were acquaintances, and all contributors should write on what was currently popular. Editors might change or cut texts for space but ordinarily returned those rejected.

Capsulated 22 periodicals. For example, the "anecdotic" *Temple Bar* paid "five pounds for a short article." The *Cornhill Magazine* and *Macmillan's Magazine* were best for "old-fashioned 'essay articles.'" The *Family Herald* was "addicted to adjectives."

112. Reeves, W. P. "Two Foreign Criticisms of Australasian Democracy." 31 (1898): 587–601.
Paraphrased E. L. Godkin that Australasian newspapers were not so trivial as American, but Reeves thought that the imperial press overemphasized sports. Most Australasians read British magazines and newspapers or local gazettes that scissored from these imports.

113. Maxse, L. J. "M. Cavaignac's Vindication of Captain Dreyfus." 31 (1898): 814–34.
Explicated the role of French newspapers in the Dreyfus case, among them the *Jour*, "one of the most impudent organs of the War Office."

114. Shadwell, Arthur. "Journalism as a Profession." 31 (1898): 845–55.
Trumpeted that journalism was a "recognized profession" in 1898. The expansion of newspapers provided decent employment that attracted the talented, but the situation of journalists was "amorphous." They needed a "self-governing organization" like other professions to monitor conduct,

to curb the false news that was common and the blackmail that was not. The mission of the press was "to tell the truth about current events" and to instruct with honest commentary.

London journalists, even with more education, were finding it harder to rise because so many people "drift" into journalism from other fields and news agencies reduced the job pool. Journalists should study modern history and literature rather than attend 'schools of journalism,' "which will never furnish editors, leader-writers, special correspondents, and critics," though they might train subeditors and reporters. Anonymity maintained the "exceptionally high tone of the English Press."

The top journalists earned 500–1,000 pounds per year, but others averaged 150–500 pounds. These wages were sufficient for young men. Editors, who received a set salary, were typically older and married, men ready to undertake the drudgery of the job. Leader-writers were "well-paid, agreeable" people who had to scribble very well because the leader was a "feature of serious journalism." Reporters were "the backbone of serious domestic journalism," doing work that was "easy and dull." Although shorthand was still useful, it was no longer necessary because of the "love of snippets." Special correspondents had more freedom to cover a variety of topics, but their wages were irregular unless they had a foreign base. Most were "discontented" except those in Paris. War correspondents had the "most exciting" assignments. Music and theatre critics were monotonous and trivial. Book reviewers were somewhat better. Interviewing, "odious" 'chats' with the famous, was the "lowest stage" of journalism. *See* 32: 211.

115. De Viti de Marco, [Antonio]. "The Recent Insurrections in Italy." 31 (1898): 902–13.

Assumed that further legislation suppressing journals would provoke sedition in their pages since existing press laws were not enforced in Italy.

116. A Veteran Journalist [Sidney J. Low]. "Journalism as a Career: A Reply to 'Journalism as a Profession.'" 32 (1898–99): 211–19.

Reaction to 31: 845, a "careful, conscientious, and sincere" statement, agreed that journalism was no longer a "casual employment of leisure hours." Differentiated management from the "literary" staff (editors, leader-writers, special correspondents, critics) and news collectors and arrangers (reporters, subeditors) while excluding the "Amazonian regiments of lady-journalists."

Journalism offered a comfortable living doing interesting work but few prizes, such as top editorial posts. Most editors worked hard for modest wages. Leader-writers also had a steady income but more regular hours and engrossing labor. Foreign correspondents and critics were satisfied if they had sufficient pay, but there were too many competitors for these jobs. Many newspapers did not have leader-writers, foreign correspondents, or critics. These job markets would probably shrink as telegraphic summaries increased and the British press aped the American prioritization of editors and reporters. Staff who were "quite old – of 55 or so" – lacked the vigor for journalism.

117. Conybeare, Frederick C. ("Huguenot"). "Side-Lights on the Dreyfus Case." 32 (1898–99): 250–67.

Articulated that the French press "reflects the mood of the people as a whole." The *Petit Journal*, "the most widely read paper in France, and also the most false and virulent," sold a million copies daily, primarily to "the mass of the *bourgeoisie*." The Jesuit *Libre Parole* had a wide circulation but was not among the "leading Catholic journals," as were the *Croix* and *Univers*. The *Libre Parole*, which employed Major M. C. Esterhazy as the columnist "Dixi," and its kin were full of invective, exemplified by columns on the Dreyfus case, but the *Temps* and *Journal des Débats* were "serious" gazettes. The *Revue des Deux Mondes* offered "dull paragraphs" by its editor, the "flabby Freethinker [Ferdinand] Brunetière."

118. Maxse, L. J. "The Key to the Mystery." 32 (1898–99): 268–83.
Swept past the *Petit Journal*, one of the "most repulsive and powerful rags in Paris," which mirrored "the real public opinion of France," as on the Dreyfus case.

119. Conybeare, Frederick C. "French Military Justice." 32 (1898–99): 337–56.
Essay on the Dreyfus case catalogued the *Médecine Moderne* as a "high-class scientific journal," the *Croix* as "the Parish Magazine of France," and journalist E. A. Drumont as a "Catholic Anarchist."

120. Maxse, L. J. "Russia and Captain Dreyfus." 32 (1898–99): 357–73.
Mentioned the "*Eclair*, one of the inspired and subsidized organs of the French War Office"; the "*Law Journal of St. Petersburg*, which is as strictly supervised as any Russian newspaper"; and the *Novoe Vremya* and *Novosti*, both part of the "authorised Russian Press."

121. Conybeare, F[rederick] C. "Treason in the French War Office." 32 (1898–99): 496–513.
Grouped the "Jesuit Press in France," *Petit Journal*, and *Gazette de France* as influential journalism, notably in the Dreyfus Case.

122. Morrow, F[orbes] St. John. "The New Irish Revolutionary Movement." 32 (1898–99): 719–30.
Declared that in 1899 the Irish press did not reach most local readers who apparently liked *Reynolds's Newspaper* and *Lloyd's Weekly Newspaper*, both with "a fair and increasing circulation." Asides on the *Irish Felon*, an 1848 newspaper of James Fintan, and Chicago's *Irish World*.

123. Maxse, L. J. "Some International Aspects of the Dreyfus Scandal." 32 (1898–99): 731–41.
Accused several French journalists of bias. One of the "gutter journals" of France was the *Gaulois*, but the 3 million readers of the *Petit Journal* meant that it represented the "real public sentiment of France."

124. Conybeare, Frederick C. "The Dreyfus Case. No. II: A Clerical Crusade." 32 (1898–99): 787–806.
Scrutinized the clout of the French Catholic press, such as the widely circulating *Croix*.

125. Maxse, Frederick A. "My Two Chiefs in the Crimea." 32 (1898–99): 835–49.
Indicted William Howard Russell for making "pernicious disclosures" to the enemy during the Crimean War when *The Times* "exercised an enormous power." "There was in those days, however, no public opinion to correct the Press, and the dismissal of a newspaper correspondent would have excited an uproar." *See* 33: 62, 33: 246.

126. Thomson, H. C. "The Misgovernment of the Transvaal." 33 (1899): 25–38.
Perceived the Press Law as "a great and needless irritation" for such local papers as the Transvaal's *Advertiser*. Aside on Natal's *Mercury* and *Afrikander*, "a Dutch newspaper published in Pieter-Maritzburg" and the Orange Free State's *Friend*.

127. Maxse, Frederick A. "Lord Raglan's Traducers." 33 (1899): 62–73.
Rebutted an article by William Howard Russell in the *Army and Navy Gazette* (2/99) that replied to 32: 835 because "the campaign of calumny that disgraced *The Times* of the winter of 1854–55" was so serious. Journalists abused anonymity when they hid behind 'We,' the 'Country,' the 'People,' or 'Public Opinion' in order to "vilify public men." *See* 33: 246.

128. Conybeare, Frederick C. "The Dreyfus Affair. No. II: *Il Caso Dreyfus*; or, the Jesuit View." 33 (1899): 140–58.
Chastised the Jesuit press, notably Rome's *Civiltà Cattolica*.

129. Maxse, L. J. "The Dreyfus Affair. No. III: The Sins of the Syndicate." 33 (1899): 158–68.
Destroyed a myth created by the *Patrie*, a Paris evening paper of wide circulation. Its editor, Lucien Millevoye, rumored that a British syndicate planned to buy French newspapers. The *Libre Parole*, which sold 250,000–500,000 copies per day, spread the word. Even when readers learned that the evidence for the story was forged, Millevoye's reputation as a journalist and a Deputy did not suffer.

130. Maxse, Frederick A. "The War Correspondents at Bay." 33 (1899): 246–53.
Rejoinder to a second article by William Howard Russell in the *Army and Navy Gazette* (3/99) echoed 32: 835 and 33: 62 that Russell, during the Crimean War, did "traduce" officers without giving them a way to reply and did leak "information of the utmost value to the enemy" in a decade when *The Times* symbolized the "whole power of the British Press." Yet he had "never seen an army in his life before his work in the Crimean War. By what amazing farce was it that his letters became accepted as the official despatches from the seat of the war."

"These newspaper correspondents take themselves so seriously. They spend their lives in a delirium of print. In campaigns, unless they are favored by Headquarter information, they are generally wrong." "Of course, there are sober, trustworthy correspondents whose writings are marked by a sense of responsibility and prudence," as the Reuters reporter in the Sudan. "The position of newspaper correspondents during a campaign should be officially determined. Their presence is already semi-official in that they are allowed rations, forage, and transport. Who are they that they should have the power of making or ruining reputations?"

"The greater number of the people do not realize that print – or whatever is called the Press – may be the vehicle of slander and falsehood." Worsening the problem was that the "doctrine of infallibility is claimed by the Press much the same as it is claimed by the Pope."

131. Maxse, Frederick A. "The Civil War in France." 33 (1899): 734–39.
Aside in a recapitulation of the Dreyfus case recited that the *Petit Journal* was "the most widely circulated journal in France."

132. Wise, B. R. "The Commonwealth of Australia." 33 (1899): 823–44.
Earmarked press power, instanced here by its role in shaping the new Australian government. Asides that merchants owned the *Sidney Daily Telegraph* and anti-unionists controlled the country gazettes.

133. Ignotus [H. W. Wilson]. "The Rapprochement Between France and Germany." 33 (1899): 892–901.

Communicated that a Munich magazine, the *Deutsche Französische Runschau*, polled "eminent Germans" about the French. British correspondents in France took information from the *Journal des Débats* and *Temps*, not the papers the French read most.

134. Gothier, Urbain. "Anglophobia: A French Warning to England." 34 (1899–1900): 26–46.

Singled out the French *Croix* and *Petit Journal*, with a combined total of 7 million readers who perused nothing else. The *Croix*, owned by the Assumptionists, was pro-Catholic; the *Petit Journal*, the property of Enrico Marinoni, was corrupt.

135. Owen, George S. "The Reform Policy of the Chinese Emperor." 34 (1899–1900): 119–31.

Heralded that the Chinese government adopted "the ablest and most progressive" journal, the *China Times*, as its official organ, although the *Peking Gazette* was "veracious." The empire also stopped arresting editors and confiscating papers, giving rise to 70 new ones.

136. Conybeare, F[rederick] C. "Sword and Cassock." 34 (1899–1900): 203–19.

Story on the Dreyfus case revealed that the military banned the *Avenir des Rennes* from their club but not the *Petit Journal* and others. The anti-Dreyfus press outside France, including Ireland's *Freeman's Journal* and Montreal's *Patrie* but not England's *Tablet*, demonstrated the impact of journalism.

137. Gothier, Urbain. "The Role of the Roman Catholic Church in France." 34 (1899–1900): 358–77.

Arraigned the French Catholic press for lying.

138. Stephen, Leslie. "The Cosmopolitan Spirit in Literature." 34 (1899–1900): 378–91.

Concentrated on the eighteenth century when Daniel Defoe, "a thoroughly trained journalist, had found out the secret of successful journalism: the charm of a straightforward circumstantial narrative."

139. Wilson, H. W. "Democracy and the War." 34 (1899–1900): 506–14.

Fretted that British newspapers divided about the war with the Boers might miss the trend of public opinion or endanger combatants by press leaks.

140. Bagot, Richard. "The Vatican at Work." 34 (1899–1900): 515–31.

Stamped Don Albertario, of Milan's *Osservatore Cattolico*, a "Socialist priest" whom the Vatican opposed as a candidate for parliamentary office. *See* 35: 400.

141. Conybeare, Frederick C. "Popular Catholicism in France." 34 (1899–1900): 767–80.

Disrespected French Catholic journals that promoted moneymaking schemes.

142. Horton, Robert F. "The Roman Danger." 34 (1899–1900): 932–43.
Signaled that too many British dailies and weeklies hired Catholics. Aside that the *Croix* was "the most widely circulated of the religious papers" in France.

143. Blennerhassett, Rowland. "Great Britain and the European Powers." 35 (1900): 28–39.
Esteemed Frankfurt's *Generalanzeiger* because it "exposed with much courage the degradation and mendacity of so large a section of the German press," such as Munich's *Neuste Nachrichten*. The German government influenced newspapers, and its Foreign Office subsidized St. Petersburg's *Zeitung*. Aside that the *Petit Journal* had the largest circulation in France.

144. Martin, A[rthur] Patchett. "An Australian's Reflections on the War." 35 (1900): 122–27.
Centered on Dr. W. H. Fitchett, editor of the Australian *Review of Reviews*.

145. Stephen, Leslie. "John Ruskin." 35 (1900): 240–55.
Aired that editors W. M. Thackeray (*Cornhill Magazine*) and J. A. Froude (*Fraser's Magazine*) rejected Ruskin's work.

146. Massingham, H. W. "The Ethics of Editing." 35 (1900): 256–61.
Distinguished between the "journal of opinion," for example the *National Review*, and the "journal of fashion," supported by tradesmen with columns of puffery. "Of a somewhat different *genre* is the 'great daily paper.' It is an organ both of opinion and of advertisement." The daily's profit came from advertising. Leaders in the major dailies addressed those "who own property…and accept, without much question, most English institutions as they exist," but other readers were of the same mind, "similarity of views among Englishmen, rich and poor, being one of the sources of our national strength." The "successful promoter of the business of journalism" in Britain, like the American editor, knew that the newspaper had to reflect readers' ideas. Even if the press was the new pulpit, journalists had to give the public what it wanted. The result was that editors were "debarred from the work of intellectual guidance."

American editors, however, were not required to be consistent. As the *New York Journal* showed, they had to "focus a great body of light-minded but fairly represented opinion in regard to a policy which…jumps with the mood of the hour." It was "difficult, unpleasant, and unprofitable to hold back an impulsive people" who might, especially in war, have an "unwise and imprudent, but natural and often uncontrollable, impulse of revenge." American papers preferred to serve this impulse rather than let rivals do so and thus steal advertising. Once the Americans abandoned sincerity for capitalism, the editor became a news gatherer rather than "an exponent and superintendent of critical work." Great dailies prioritized the value of writing differently. British anonymity, which undermined good writing, guaranteed homogeneity in outlook; French signature guaranteed individuality. *See* 35: 592.

147. Scythicus. "The Russian Press." 35 (1900): 301–18.
Tracked strategies of Russian press censorship from Alexius to 1900. The *Novoe Vremya* and the *Novosti* resembled British gazettes with respect to news and leaders. However, both dailies included many imperial notices and letters on minor matters and excluded most telegraphic dispatches. The *St. Petersburg Gazette* devoted its pages to essays on "social and economic interests" and foreign affairs, penned by a large staff of foreign correspondents. The *Sviet* "as a

purveyor of news" was "beneath contempt." These tribunes and several others displayed no signs of editing and parroted the authorities. *See* 35: 521.

148. Bagot, Richard. "Anglophobia at the Vatican." 35 (1900): 400–15.
Noted French Catholic papers, such as the *Univers* and *Croix*; Cologne's *Zeitung*; and the international *Osservatore Romano* although it was not the official organ of the Vatican. Plumbed Genoa's *Voce della Verità* but not Milan's "Clerico-Socialist organ, the *Osservatore Cattolico*," the paper of Don Albertario. *See* 34: 515.

149. Finnicus. "Russian Officialdom and the Finnish Press." 35 (1900): 521–24.
Supplementatry letter-essay to 35: 300 accentuated that the Finnish press was subject to "*preventive censorship*, from which the most important Russian journals are exempt." The Finns had to secure pre-publication approval of internal gazettes and clearance of outbound telegrams from censors who were "ship-wrecked individuals." The burden of censorship was heavy in Finland where peasants were regular readers of the 227 journals that circulated in 1899.

150. Maxse, Frederick A. "A Glimpse of South Africa." 35 (1900): 569–79.
Muttered that "[a]t Cape Town, there is no exciting Press: the news dribbles out, and there is no sensational writing." The morning *Cape Times* had little news, the morning *South African News* published without official intervention, and the evening *Cape Argus* was full of telegrams.

151. Shadwell, A[rthur]. "Proprietors and Editors." 35 (1900): 592–601.
Respondent to 35: 256 warranted that the 1900 press was "the newspaper and nothing else. No one can ignore or escape its influence." Indeed "the amount of faith actually placed" in newspapers by readers, particularly the uneducated, was "almost pathetic." A public "that demands conventional pablum" and not owners limited the scope of the newspaper. It was "a business concern," but the picture of "proprietors – capitalists, of course – with their damned commercial instincts that debase the Press and make it subservient to the mob" was false. Some owners abandoned principles for profits, but in a free market there was room for tribunes of all kinds. "All vary in each case with the requirements of the reader…but the primary business of the newspaper is to purvey news…and in dealing with news the ethics of editing come into play to a very important degree." Mercenary editors were rather casual about accuracy but were at least less partial than their French counterparts. Editors should be more independent but should not "diverge too widely" from their readers' ideas. As news increased, leaders should instruct.

152. Conybeare, Frederick C. "The Conspiracy Against the French Republic." 35 (1900): 727–45.
Cautioned that the French Catholic press, such as the *Croix* with 100 provincial editions, was a threat to the French government. Other "rags" had varying degrees of influence.

153. Stephen, Leslie. "Walter Bagehot." 35 (1900): 936–50.
Recognized Bagehot as "an energetic journalist" for the *Inquirer*.

154. Hofmeyr, Adrian. "An Africander's Reflections on the Future of South Africa." 36 (1900–01): 128–38.
Snarled that Transvaal's *Diggers' News* and *Volksstem* were untruthful but published without restraint during the war with the Boers.

155. An English Catholic. "The Roman Catholic Hierarchy in Australia." 36 (1900–01): 286–90.

Decided, based on the New South Wales *Freeman's Journal* and *Catholic Press*, that Australian Catholic papers with Irish editors fostered sedition. The secular press feared that criticizing these serials would lose them subscribers, as the *Sydney Morning Herald* experienced.

156. Battersby, H. F. Prevost. "The War Correspondent: A Suggestion for the Future." 36 (1900–01): 420–29.

Pronounced war correspondence modern but already "accepted as in the natural order of a campaign." The reporter, "an impartial spectator," had to "attract attention" so quickly learned to pen "not to enlighten the public, but to sell his wares." The military accredited inconsistently, licensing some who were irresponsible or ignorant, and censored arbitrarily. Only those of "proven ability" from major papers and news agencies should be certified for the front. Telegrams should be stopped: they led to bribery, confined journalists to wired regions, and encouraged competition that resulted in cut or clogged lines. Access to telegraphy should be granted to a staff writer who had "military knowledge, literary powers, and the habit of discipline." Others should have complete liberty, limited only by a "sense of decency," to publish their letters, preferable because they were more thoughtful than telegrams. Correspondents who broke the rules should be sent home and their employers prohibited from replacing them. The procedure might also reduce the swarm of journalists from news agencies, the "large users of the road, great consumers of forage, and often the biggest horse thieves in camps."

The New Monthly Magazine, 1821–1854

With bonds to *Ainsworth's Magazine* and *Bentley's Miscellany*, the *New Monthly* underscored the literary side of the press. Nonetheless, official restraint of its liberty, chiefly by taxation, did not escape observers.

1. C[ampbell], T[homas]. "Preface." 1 (1821): iii–xii.

Editorial on the *New Monthly*'s first year acknowledged that "no important periodical publication can be supported by gratuitous contributions." Readers were not interested in shortened articles, "the scrap-system of literature." Publishing 1: 145 was a mistake because its exaggerations provoked American critiques of British press taxes. These columns, pirated by Albion's cheap newspapers, reinforced the discontent of the poor.

2. [Curran, W. H.]. "On the Complaints in America Against the British Press." 1 (1821): 145–55.

Stereotyped Americans in response to an essay by A. H. Everett in the *North American Review* (#11, 1820) about the British press.

3. C., D. "The Proof-Sheet." 1 (1821): 232–36.

Distinguished between the printer, "who *consummates* the author's conceptions," and the critic, "the malicious and indelicate wretch, who delights to unstrip the dandy." Aside that John Wilkes was important in the achievement of press liberty.

4. "Germany – Past and Present." 1 (1821): 294–304.

Saluted the "bold political journalist," the man suppressed in one German state who opened a journal in another.

5. [Matthews, Henry]. "Jonathan Kentucky's Journal." 1 (1821): 430–35, 568–78, 693–700; 2 (1821): 104–12, 212–19, 522–32.

Contrasted British and American ideas of press freedom, notably ideas about political libel unknown in the United States. Aside that the Bank of London had a complete set of the *Oxford (London) Gazette* since the reign of Charles II.

6. X. [T. C. Morgan]. "Morality of Newspapers." 1 (1821): 630–36.

Defined advertisements as "a moving picture of the world." Some distorted morality, such as those on the generosity of moneylenders, the gratitude of recently-elected MPs, and the benefits of unnecessary goods.

7. “Specimen of a Prospective Newspaper: *The North American Luminary*, 1st July, 4796.” 2 (1821): 129–35.

Summarized news on the captioned future date.

8. W[ade, John]. “Hints to Young Authors.” 2 (1821): 589–92.

Guided junior contributors on how to prepare a periodical article, stressing preliminary investigation, analysis, and style.

9. T., S. M. “Dublin in 1822.” 4 (1822): 503–11.

Enlightened that in Dublin “the sweeping, slapdash, discursive, colloquial style common in the newspapers is very characteristic.” “The writing is, in point of literary merit, greatly inferior to that of the London journals.” Irish newspapers, cheaper than London, had fewer subscribers, but alehouses bought some heralds.

10. V. [Cyrus Redding]. “London and the Country.” 5 (1822): 273–77.

Commented that “country newspapers have neither novelty, life, nor independence, with a few exceptions, and are mere copyists,” whereas the London tribunes “excite and keep up a spirit of inquiry, besides giving information.”

11. M[organ, T. C.]. “Letter to the Editor.” 7 (1823): 1–4.

Categorized the press: the morning newspaper was a habit, “weekly literary journals” were for amusement, and magazines and reviews were intellectual food.

12. [Smith, James]. “*Annus Mirabilis*! Or, a Parthian Glance at 1822.” 7 (1823): 21–27.

Chuckled about the “magnificent prospectuses from divers new Utopian magazines” that arrived each December.

13. I. [Cyrus Redding]. “The Philosophy of Fashion.” 7 (1823): 238–44.

Ridiculed men of fashion who ordinarily got their political information from “the skim-milk of some obscure newspaper.”

14. [Smith], H[orace]. “The Library.” 7 (1823): 430–34.

Prophesized that most contributors to monthly magazines would be forever anonymous unless their essays were collected in books or the symbols that they substituted for signature were decoded.

15. M[organ, T. C.]. “On Giving Advice.” 7 (1823): 476–80.

Counseled periodical writers assigned a “single half-sheet” to be readable and novel because high-priced magazines certified journalists’ words as valuable.

16. [Smith], H[orace]. “Printed by Mistake.” 7 (1823): 529–32.

Fussed about the pressure in penning a monthly article, this one printed in error. As periodicals multiplied, there was not enough new material for undistinguished authors. Payment by the sheet caused them to pad a text in a stale style.

17. I., Y. [Cyrus Redding]. "The Bench and the Press." 10 (1824): 169–75.
Theorized that laws on the press were structured so as "to master its free spirit, and to confine it to the most narrow and petty regulations." This circumstance was due partly to the "opposite characters of the press and of the law," the first, one of action, and the second, one of thought. Lawyers envied the "power of the press," its wide influence in forming the public opinion that was the "expression of society, of the wise and the considerate – not of the unthinking." The bench blamed the press for abetting crime by publicizing it, but the press actually reduced it by ensuring it was punished and by preserving open courts. The press impacted primarily the middle classes: it expanded knowledge, spurred "reflection," protected freedom against official intrusion or enemies, and gave readers a sense of stake in government. "The citizen feels himself a party concerned in preserving peace at home, and in resisting foreign aggression, wherever there is a free press." The law should not "carp" at or censure the press for "trivial aberration."

18. M[organ, T. C.]. "Gamesters and Gaming." 10 (1824): 256–62.
Urged newspapers to be cognizant of public opinion but avoid erroneous views even if they sold copies.

19. M[organ, T. C.]. "The Literary World." 10 (1824): 364–68.
Trumpeted that many reviews and magazines were "thriving" and the periodical press was "daily growing in consequence and consideration."

20. "The Colonial Press." 11 (1824): 442–49.
Scolded imperial officials, as in Cape Colony and India, because they suppressed newspapers. Local authorities hated journalists who challenged them in leaders, news items, and advertising. A "degraded press" could not raise morals and manners. Freedom of the press, at least for "Englishmen" overseas, was "indispensably necessary." Governors should not have more power to control the press than the king at home. "[O]n minute local questions residents are capable of judging…the opinions and advice (not all on one side, but from every side)" in the journals.

21. Y. "The Canadian Emigrant." 13 (1825): 160–65.
Rued that Canadians received the *Edinburgh Review* and *New Monthly* later than clerics and lawyers in the American West who got them within two months of publication.

22. "Old Pages and Old Times." 13 (1825): 273–76, 379–83.
Revisited two publications of the 1690s, the *London Spy*, whose variety paralleled modern magazines, and the *English Lucian, or Weekly Discoveries of the Witty Intrigues, Comical Passages, and Remarkable Transactions in Town and Country.*

23. "Authors and Editors." 14 (1825): 92–96.
Former periodical editor groaned about the job's burdens, such as penning reviews, answering letters, recruiting contributors, and dealing with those who resented changes to their manuscripts.

24. Stendhal. "Sketches of Parisian Society, Politics, and Literature." 16 (1826): 98–110, 313–23, 508–18; 17 (1826): 81–90, 184–92, 284–88, 296–304, 416–24; 19 (1827): 374–81; 25 (1829): 199–200.
Lengthy series randomly hit the French press (only relevant pages cited). Charles X tried to suppress "the two most independent and best-conducted journals, *viz.* the *Courrier* and the *Constitutionnel*,

each of which has 24,000 readers." These newspapers were two of only five independent papers, so they drew much attention from French readers who got most of their opinions from talented writers of knowledge and style. Alternatively, the *Gazette de France* was one of "the dullest journals in the world." Since many officials (named here) originally were journalists, the press was feared and its reporters flattered.

The *Journal des Débats*, previously with highest circulation, suffered when the *Globe*, a serious herald for the upper classes run by able young men with money, commenced. Political journals like these papers had the same sway in France as literary reviews had in Britain. French periodicals with "extensive" circulations were the *Gazette des Tribunaux*, an "accurate picture of the state of France"; the *Frondeur*, witty and scandalous about "personalities"; and the *Revue Britannique*, excerpting British reviews even though the *Edinburgh Review* did well in Paris. Parisians also perused *The Times* and *Morning Chronicle*.

Content analysis showed that the monthly *Catholique* was similar in format to English reviews though somewhat obtuse. Another important religious serial was *France Chrétienne*. Every literary group had a journal that critiqued books except those published by its owner. The only honest book reviews were in the *Courrier Française*; the rest were puffs as were so many theatre reviews in the newspapers.

The income gap in journalism was wide. For example, the proprietor of the *Constitutionnel* had a profit of 30,000 francs per year while a journeyman printer earned five francs per day.

25. H., C. [John Neal]. "Character of the Real Yankees: What They Are Supposed to be and What They Are." 17 (1826): 247–56.

Nodded to the American "multitude of newspapers" springing up across the country.

26. [Redding, Cyrus]. "Death of Mr. Canning." 20 (1827): 269–80.

Eulogized George Canning, who penned in Eton's *Microcosm* as "B," the *Anti-Jacobin*, *New Monthly*, and other periodicals. Himself the victim of the "ribaldry and obscenity" of opposition papers, Canning "was a true friend to the liberty of the press, because he understood its uses and effects."

27. "Cunningham's *New South Wales*." 20 (1827): 393–400.

Review of P. Cunningham's *Two Years in New South Wales* paraphrased it on newspapers, unstamped in the colony. The *Sydney Gazette* carried much colonial news and "interesting and entertaining advertisements." The *Australian*, a nine-penny biweekly, and the *Monitor*, a one-shilling weekly, had as much ability as any London herald. The three together printed 70–80 advertisements per issue and 3,250 copies per week.

28. [?Smith], H[orace]. "Evils of Measurement in Literature." 23 (1828): 204–08.

Argued that paying for periodical articles by length and not by "intrinsic value" caused the "degeneracy of our contemporary literature." *See* 23: 323, 25: 98.

29. "Advertisements Extraordinary." 23 (1828): 209–14.

Excoriated the "atrabilious scribe" whose leaders denounced everything, whereas advertising mirrored "the character of public taste." Listings on medicines and medical advice, employment, and real estate also demonstrated that British newspapers were far more entertaining than foreign ones.

30. [?Smith, Horace]. "Good Living the Cause of Bad Writing." 23 (1828): 323–27.

Supplemented 23: 204 with two notions: a contributor of limited means, and therefore diet, produced more quality writing than a wealthy person with a liberal education and leisure; and food affected styles of scribes in different countries. *See* 25: 98.

31. "The 'Annuals.'" 23 (1828): 461–69.

Credited R. Ackermann for the first annual, *Forget-Me-Not* (1823), soon followed by *Friendship's Offering* (1824), A. A. Watts' *Literary Souvenir* (1825), the *Amulet* (1826), *Bijou* and the *Keepsake* (1828), and the *Anniversary* and *Gem* (1829).

32. ?M[organ, T. C.]. "Opinions for 1829." 25 (1829): 1–9.

Cautioned that magazines, unlike dailies, were unable to correct mistakes or change positions quickly.

33. ?M[organ, T. C.]. "Good Living Essential to Good Writing." 25 (1829): 98–101.

Modified the thesis of 23: 323 because, in a market oversupplied by writers, it was appropriate to pay by length for better pieces.

34. ?M[organ, T. C.]. "An Article for the *New Monthly*." 25 (1829): 421–27.

Anticipated that more periodical contributors would mean better style but repetitive topics. Since readers in 1829 were "less fastidious" about originality, the same article might appear in more than one magazine. However, too much duplication could drive audiences away. Contributors searching for ideas should watch fads, lie about subjects unfamiliar to the public, or reheat the news.

35. C., S. "John Bullism." 25 (1829): 466–72.

Judged sufficient the material that reviews and newspapers printed on art and literature because writers were usually no better informed than readers.

35a. "Art and Artists: A Conversation." 25 (1829): 567–73.

Aside that the Scots and Irish made good parliamentary reporters and bad art critics.

36. "The Present Times, with Remarks on a Late Article in the *Quarterly*." 25 (1829): 573–82.

Chided the *Quarterly Review* for publishing (4/29) an essay by Robert Southey that contained "assertions…unqualified and without explanation."

37. "Parliament and the Ladies." 26 (1829): 41–48.

Story on visitors to Parliament placed Henry Dudley Bate, editor of the *Morning Herald* in 1829, as the first to print the names of women in newspapers when he was editor of the *Morning Post*. Women were regularly in print thereafter when London papers detailed the parties and dinners of public figures.

38. "The 'Annuals.'" 26 (1829): 478–87.

Flipped through religious, juvenile, and literary annuals.

39. "Parliamentary Anecdotes." 28 (1830): 217–24.
Identified William Woodfall, who depended on memory and not notes, as "the father of newspaper Parliamentary reporting in a full and satisfactory manner." In 1830 reports were more accurate but lacked the personality of his day.

40. M[organ, T. C.]. "Law as It Is." 28 (1830): 255–61.
Contemplated the law of libel.

41. [?Kirwan, A. V.]. "Parisian Journal." 28 (1830): 383–86, 474–82.
Recognized the *Journal de Paris* for its study of the British press, the *Revue Encyclopédique* for its international information, and British journalists' sympathy for French colleagues restricted by government.

42. [Chamier, Frederick]. "Anecdotes of Russia." 29 (1830): 73–81.
Confirmed Russian censorship of local and foreign serials.

43. [?Kirwan, A.V.]. "The Revolution in France." 29 (1830): 284–93.
Narrated the role of journalists in the July Revolution.

44. B., J. [B. W. Procter]. "My Recollections of the Late William Hazlitt." 29 (1830): 469–82.
Synopsized Hazlitt's work for the *Morning Chronicle*, where he was the theatre critic, other papers, and the *New Monthly*.

45. [?Hall, S. C.]. "A Word or Two with the Public: From the Manager's Room." 31 (1831): i–iv.
Revised the goals of the *New Monthly*: it would expand its outreach to the public and exclude "*smaller* domestic doings (after the fashion of modern periodicals)." The *New Monthly* would seek scribes who could pen "sensible and agreeable" pieces on diverse subjects. Generally, it was "the duty of the journalist to adapt himself, in no inconsiderable degree, to the exigencies of the times. We do not mean that he should pander to its vices, but that he should administer to its wants." "The Press is, or ought to be, the ECHO of *Public Opinion*; – not of the clamorous, but of the honest and intelligent portion of the people, whose objects are Truth and the Common Good." Publications represented opinion, the truth derived from discussions among the "intelligent…not mass of men."

46. [Landon, L. E.]. "Living Literary Characters. No. 5: Edward Lytton Bulwer." 31 (1831): 437–50.
Deduced from their contents that "two pseudo-called great Reviews, the *Edinburgh* and the *Quarterly*," neglected Bulwer-Lytton's work because *Edinburgh* editor Francis Jeffrey was as partial as seventeenth-century Judge George Jeffreys and the *Quarterly* snubbed popular literature. Since politics preoccupied reviews, Britain had no great literary serials. Quoted Bulwer-Lytton that "the great body of critics are made up of unsuccessful writers" and "the inferior magazines and journals are truly the refuge of the literary destitute" where, according to Landon, anonymity paired a "want of principle" and a "want of responsibility." See *Fraser's Magazine* 3: 713.

47. P* [John Poole]. "No Article This Month." 32 (1831): 81–84.
Satirized the pressure of writing articles incessantly.

48. [?Bulwer-Lytton, E. G.]. "Literature Considered as a Profession." 32 (1831): 227–32.
Sought status for literature as a profession even though "a false system of education," compared to the French, left English scribes "mere caterers to amusement." To win respect, writers in dailies and elsewhere should cease quarreling and "join solid information and principles to powers of light and imaginative writing."

49. [Bulwer-Lytton, E. G.]. "Address to the Public." 32 (1831): 393–94.
Blared that "THE PRESS have done their duty!" The newspaper provided immediate information, and the "rapidity" of events also made monthlies more significant than quarterlies. What the *New Monthly* needed was "greater singleness of design."

50. [Bulwer-Lytton, E. G. and S. C. Hall]. "Ourselves, Our Correspondents, and the Public." 32 (1831): 445–54.
Centered on the novice contributor. Asides that American criticism, as in the *New England Magazine* and *Southern Review*, was "improving"; essays in the *Edinburgh Review* were sound but not timely, and John Bowring was a good editor for the *Westminster Review*.

51. "The Annuals for 1832." 32 (1831): 455–61.
Segregated annuals, in a periodical press that ranged from penny newspapers to bound tomes, as "the receptacles for our own lighter literature." The annuals published good engravings and bad poetry, as the seven reviewed here evidenced.

52. [Bulwer-Lytton, E. G.]. "The New Year." 34 (1832): 1–7.
Faulted the stamp tax for the absence of quality newspapers for the poor who then purchased the illegal cheap papers of "dishonest men" ready to stir the passions of the ignorant.

53. A. [E. G. Bulwer-Lytton]. "Upon the Spirit of True Criticism." 34 (1832): 353–57.
Honored weekly literary reviewers because their columns were frequently "fairer and truer," innovative and more influential than quarterlies. Although styles of reviews might differ, every critic should be moral and learned.

54. [Bulwer-Lytton, E. G.]. "The Wilful [*sic*] Misstatements of the *Quarterly Review*." 34 (1832): 385–91.
Impugned J. W. Croker and J. G. Lockhart for a *Quarterly* essay (3/32) that was "neither fair nor manly." *See* 37: 82.

55. [Hunt, Leigh]. "*The Indicator*." 34 (1832): 457–68.
Hunt borrowed from his own newspaper.

56. [Bulwer-Lytton, E. G.]. "Asmodeus at Large." 35 (1832): 24–32.
Catchall essay welcomed the *Penny Magazine*, pleaded for abolition of newspaper duties, and approved newspaper proliferation in the United States but not its periodicals, which were part of the inferior literature of that nation.

57. Pelham, Henry [E. G. Bulwer-Lytton]. "Letter from Paris." 35 (1832): 295–99.
Disclosed that one road to power in France was journalism, whereon journalists proceeded by intellect and merit.

58. Atticus [Isaac D'Israeli]. "On the Present State of Our Literature." 35 (1832): 340–43.
Lauded Joseph Addison, who "rescued periodical composition from the dregs of politics and polemics, in giving a more elevated direction to the national taste, by morals and literature" because the *Spectator* sold 20,000 copies per day. Contributors in 1832 only focused on amusement, practicing "the Art of writing on Nothing."

59. [Bulwer-Lytton, E. G.]. "To Our Friends, On Preserving the Anonymous in Periodicals." 35 (1832): 385–89.
Underscored that the *New Monthly*, less venomous than its peers, was for a long time the only periodical to print the editor's name. Anonymity of scribes gave critics "greater freedom" to issue unfair reviews because it conferred power without responsibility. The custom was useful in societies with despotic press laws. Cancellation of the remaining British restrictions on the press would awaken the "moral feeling" of writers faced with the glare of publicity. French signature discouraged papers that "live upon lies" and amplified respect, hence greater influence for journalists. *See* 39: 2.

60. [?Bulwer-Lytton, E. G.]. "The *True Sun*: Another Argument Against the Taxes on Knowledge." 35 (1832): 399–400.
Hoped that the *True Sun*, "a sincere, enlightened, and honest teacher," would not close lest workers would buy cheaper but illegal papers by angry scribes. The death of the *True Sun* would end "political instruction…by men of education and wisdom" and spur sedition.

61. A. [E. G. Bulwer-Lytton]. "Proposals for a Literary Union." 35 (1832): 418–21.
Proposed a union of journalists (newspaper or periodical), whose "written" work was above ten pages, in order to empower them and inspire fellowship.

62. The Author of *Pelham* [E. G. Bulwer-Lytton]. "Letter to the Editor of the *Quarterly Review*." 37 (1833): 82–87.
Resumed the attack, begun in 34: 385, on the veracity of the *Quarterly* generally and particularly of J. G. Lockhart in a recent (12/32) essay.

63. [?Colburn, Henry]. "A Few Words from the Proprietor." 39 (1833): 1–2.
Planned (on the departure of editor E. G. Bulwer-Lytton) to shift the *New Monthly* from a political to its original literary course.

64. "On the Anonymous in Periodicals." 39 (1833): 2–6.
Retort to 35: 385 defended anonymity of literary critics because it muzzled favoritism and malice but not good articles. Known writers would talk about themselves, not the book being reviewed, and would demand more money. Anonymity did not shield libel, and signature would not prevent it. Similarly, anonymous editors concentrated on their periodicals' interests, not personal fame.

65. H[all, S.] C. "Notes on Periodicals." 39 (1833): 424–31.
Assured that there were enough periodicals for every taste. Cheap serials, such as the *Penny Magazine*, often resorted to plagiarism and profited from the poor. Cheap newspapers, such as the *Crisis*, covered the same topics as their stamped brethren and circulated widely. "There is a rude energy in their style, added to a profligate dereliction of morality in their principles, which renders them acceptable to all the discontented men in the country." *See* 40: 65, 175.

66. H[all, S.] C. "The Chartered Booksellers." 40 (1834): 65–75.
Article on the Society for the Diffusion of Useful Knowledge reiterated notions in 39: 424 about the *Penny Magazine*. Affiliation of the two meant high sales but not representation of the society's views. The *Penny* was a sham principally perpetrated by publisher Charles Knight, whose regular plagiarism deprived its book reviews of any "weight." *See* 40: 175.

67. ?H[all, S.] C. "The Penny Press." 40 (1834): 175–84.
Renewed attack (39: 424, 40: 65) on the *Penny Magazine*, an attack that the *Literary Gazette* and "other periodical journals of great ability and influence" joined. The *Penny Magazine* was "an ill-conducted and very worthless work" whose circulation topped 150,000 per week. Publisher Charles Knight's *Companion to the Newspaper*, with "considerable merit" but without the endorsement of the Society for the Diffusion of Useful Knowledge, was struggling.

The *Crisis* and other unstamped tribunes, such as the *Poor Man's Guardian*, injected poison into the minds of the "manufacturing classes" who learned to read but not to develop the "power of reflection which might serve them as an antidote." Attempts to unionize, organized through the "cheap press," did not deal with labor and hours but "subversion." Abolition of the stamp duty would not restrain the cheap press, but legislation could curb its sedition, libel, and piracy.

68. H[all, S.] C. "Literature in 1834." 40 (1834): 497–505.
Conceded that the cheap press reduced ignorance but not bad writing by low-paid scribblers.

69. [Bacon, R. M.]. "The Democracy of England." 41 (1834): 409–27.
Avowed that "the periodical press forms opinion and publicizes that which it forms" but mined public views to do so.

70. J. "Coleridge." 42 (1834): 55–63.
Asides on the few buyers of the *Watchman* of S. T. Coleridge and the sound principles of the *Morning Chronicle* for which he wrote.

71. [?Bacon, R. M.]. "Taxes on Necessaries *Versus* Taxes on Knowledge." 44 (1835): 485–99.
Presumed that abolition of taxes on essential items, such as soap, was more important than imposts affecting the press. The end of press duties might catalyze cheap newspapers catering to "the terrific

passions which idleness and pauperism have engendered, and ever will." Already widely circulated were "sporting, slang, thimble-rig, race-course, gambling, prize-fighting, police-reporting, slanderous Tom and Jerry journals" that abetted bad morals. The *Penny Magazine* was not a good example of a cheap publication because it was entertainment.

Newspaper profits came from advertising because people shared newspapers in public and in private. Each local paper probably had 20 or 30 readers. Repeal of the stamp and paper tariffs would result in gazettes selling for only a halfpenny less because more pages, "for the million love quantity dearly," would raise costs. Country tribunes, published chiefly by printers whose equipment was their only real startup expense, could survive on local news, but no London weekly could compete with the metro dailies. Disputed Henry Brougham's theory in the *British and Foreign Review* (1: 157) about the impact of competition on advertising. *See* 46: 487.

72. [Laman Blanchard]. "The Blunders of the Remarkably Skilful [*sic*]: With a Little Praise of the Press, and a Word on Behalf of the World." 45 (1835): 17–20.

Noticed that newspapers, in reporting calamities, always comforted victims but rarely headlined private parties responsible. Instead, the press "traduces public men and stabs at private character… construing harshly and dealing in libel."

73. "Taxes on Necessaries v. Taxes on Knowledge." 46 (1836): 487–93.

Addendum to 44: 485 preached that "the tax on newspapers, amounting to four-sevenths of the whole cost, is heavy, very heavy," but it sustained the responsible press, a bulwark against revolution. Quality personnel, "persons of property, character, education, and ability," did not come cheap. Journalists had to have "nerves of iron…unflinching integrity of purpose…almost unassailable powers of intellect," yet they were often "regarded with suspicion and distrust" because they put their duty to society ahead of their feelings for individuals. A cheap press would debase them further. The government should punish publishers of the unstamped, not their vendors.

74. "Reform in European Turkey." 47 (1836): 475–78.

Review of *A Residence at Constantinople* by Rev. R. Walsh, LL.D., described the city's Turkish, French, Greek, and Armenian weeklies "as liberal in their opinion and as enlightened in their matter as any other periodical on the Continent, and more so than many of them."

75. [Blanchard, Laman]. "Portraits of Notorious Characters. No. III: 'Penny-a-Liner'" 48 (1836): 88–89.

Disdained penny-a-liners for their stock phrases.

76. [?Bacon, R. M.]. "The Journals of the Provinces." 48 (1836): 137–49.

Scored the reduction of the stamp duty, from four pence to one penny, as a victory for proponents of a cheap inflammatory press unless country papers blossomed. From April 1832 to March 1833 there were 181 local papers, the majority of which had circulations below 1,000. Owners were typically printers with 4,000–5,000 pounds for startup expenses, capital it would take five years to recoup because people were reluctant to abandon an established newspaper. Meantime, costs were rising because editors hired "active and able reporters" as public meetings and the general desire for news increased. If prosperity grew advertising, and local news and the more thorough criticism of weeklies lured buyers, the failure of the majority of locals, revealed in the *Leeds Mercury*, should stop.

The survivors could dilute the effects of a cheaper press. In 1796 no local editor would pen anything on "public affairs" but merely scissored London dailies. In 1836 country editors were known, and many were renowned for their ability unlike anonymous London editors and leader-writers. Locals read in many public places reached a bigger and more varied audience than metros, which only addressed wealthy Londoners. Country editors spent less time on personal attacks and more on political contemplation, so they had substantial power during elections. The editor should "act fearlessly and conscientiously" because he could be "the benefactor or the corruptor of his readers" but should be a political moderate, unlike William Cobbett.

77. "Horace Smith, Esq." 48 (1836): 348–51.
Aside on Smith's pieces in the *New Monthly*.

78. Editor [Theodore Hook]. "Memoir of the Rev. G. R. Gleig." 49 (1837): 221–22.
Touched on Gleig's work for *Blackwood's Magazine* and the *Edinburgh Magazine*.

79. μ. [T. C. Morgan]. "Plagues of Popularity." 51 (1837): 31–38.
Scorned writers who longed for "newspaper immortality" or envied the 'bright particular star' of a magazine.

80. A Near Relative. "Biographical Notice of the Late John Home, Esq." 57 (1839): 289–304, 471–83; 58 (1840): 164–78.
Recollected that in the reign of George III, Home wrote on politics for John Wilkes' *North Briton* and other newspapers. His pen names were "A Friend of the Constitution," "A Retired Officer in the Army," "A Foreigner," and "Tom Payne."

81. μ. [T. C. Morgan]. "On the Uses and Abuses of Truth." 59 (1840): 85–92.
Suspected that the "paragraph-grinder" of a "scandalous journal" lost the ability to recognize truth as time passed, but other journalists also did not prize accuracy. Cited the *Quarterly Review* 65: 283.

82. "A *Soirée* at Monsieur Guizot's." 60 (1840): 441–47.
Aside on the official French press bureau manned by "the ablest and most conscientious writers... well paid by government" and devoted to replying to false statements in the dailies, replies they were legally required to print.

83. "An Evening with M. Thiers." 61 (1841): 120–28.
Tapped Adolphe Thiers' press career, chiefly at the *National* in Paris.

84. "The French Press." 61 (1841): 371–81.
Located the "French" press primarily in Paris, where newspapers ranged from political and judicial to "theatrical and gossiping." Journals were small because they had less to say than British gazettes. The Parisians molded opinion, whereas British dailies represented views of readers able to "think, compare, probe, discuss, and investigate." Compared the formats, prices, and circulations of *The Times* and Paris *National* with glosses on the *Journal des Débats*, *Moniteur*, and the all-advertising *Petites Affiches*.

Most papers had less amusing advertisements than Paris and far fewer ones than London. Gallic provincial tribunes likewise were no match for the "wit, information, research, statistics, and local knowledge" of the British country press. The French locals displayed "a good deal of genuine talent, and sometimes sound reasoning" but had little influence because Paris papers dominated.

85. "An Hour or Two with Berryer." 62 (1841): 228–38.
Spoke about "the Abbé [A.-E.] de Génoude, the accomplished, learned, profound, and eloquent proprietor, editor, and everything else of the *Gazette de France*," the evening companion of *Quotidienne*, and Emile de Girardin, a "clever" journalist.

86. "Memoir of the Late Theodore Edward Hook, Esq." 63 (1841): 137–41.
Bowed to Hook's editing of *John Bull*, where he had "influence as a political writer," but ignored his other press endeavors.

87. Hood, Thomas. "A Tête-à-Tête with the Editor." 63 (1841): 153–56.
Outlined how to be a magazine editor, stressing that politics belonged in dailies.

88. Morgan, Lady [Sydney]. "Courts and Court Journals." 64 (1842): 544–53.
Evaluated the writing and advertising in the *Court Journal*. "[T]his periodical, however, like all such emanations of the press, is but a *census* of the tastes, wants, and social state of the market it is called on to supply," namely female aristocrats.

89. Dickens, Charles. "The Whispering Gallery: Letter." 65 (1842): 583–84.
Maligned American newspaper editors and owners as "men of very low attainments, and of more than indifferent reputations" who reprinted English works as they attacked their authors "coarsely and insolently."

90. The Editor [Thomas Hood]. "Boz in America." 66 (1842): 396–406.
Review of Charles Dickens' *American Notes* echoed him on the Lowell (MA) *Offering*, a serial by factory girls that could "compare advantageously with a great many of the English Annuals."

91. [Hood, Thomas]. "The Advertisement Literature of the Age." 67 (1843): 111–16.
Ruminated about content and style in periodical advertising.

92. [Colmache, Edouard]. "The Late Prince Talleyrand." Ed. Georgina A. Colmache. 70 (1844): 1–16, 182–95.
Alluded to the role of journalists in the 1830 July Revolution in France.

93. Redding, Cyrus, Esq. "Recollections of the Author of *Vathek*." 71 (1844): 143–58, 302–19.
Essay on William Beckford considered J. G. Lockhart "one of the ablest of our living writers," better than many *Quarterly Review* contributors. Aside that the *Morning Chronicle* "copied from the [*Morning*] *Herald*."

94. "Diplomatic Doings." 73 (1845): 153–66.
Thought that diplomats read the Paris press and the *Allgemeine Zeitung*. While Britain had "envoys collecting news at enormous expense in all the great capitals of Europe, the arts of 'foreign policy'

are negligently written" by men who never traveled. Aside that Armand de Richelieu, who sponsored the *Gazette de France*, was the sire of the French press.

95. Catellus. "A Discourse of Puppies: Part II." 73 (1845): 178–91.
Mocked periodical critics from the *Athenaeum* and *Westminster Review* to the "Minute Unknowns."

96. "The Late Mr. Laman Blanchard." 73 (1845): 428–30.
Elucidated Blanchard's journalistic career, from founder of the *True Sun* to editor of several magazines. He also penned "light essays" for the *New Monthly*, to which he was a "constant contributor," and for other "leading periodicals."

97. B[arnett], M[orris]. "Passages in the Lives of Celebrated Statesmen of Europe. No. III: Metternich." 74 (1845): 1–13.
Confided that Clemens von Metternich read even "the smallest journal" in the Habsburg Empire but chose *Punch* and the French *Charivari* for relaxation.

98. Reach, Angus B. "The Pleasures of Grumbling." 74 (1845): 49–54.
Among Reach's "grumbles" were letters to newspapers signed with a pseudonym.

99. Amicus. "Literary and Familiar Reminiscences of Thomas Campbell, Esq." 74 (1845): 163–73, 559–66.
Tribute to Campbell told of his gratitude for Henry Colburn's giving him 600 pounds per year and an assistant to edit the *New Monthly*. One of the *Magazine's* printers testified that Campbell's name caused circulation to double. Aside that his son, who died young, penned for the *Morning Chronicle*.

100. Hughes, John, Esq. "Sketch of the Late Rev. R. H. Barham: with a Few Lines to His Memory." 74 (1845): 526–34.
Indicated Barham's articles in *John Bull* and *Bentley's Miscellany*.

101. Bulwer-Lytton, E.[G.] "Confessions and Observations of a Water-Patient." 75 (1845): 1–16.
Reminded that periodical articles faded fast, even those in the styles of Thomas Campbell, Thomas Hood, and Theodore Hook. Because "the literary craft" was "a restless, striving brotherhood," it could adversely affect health.

102. The Author of "Jacob Omnium." [M. J. Higgins]. "The Man Most of Us Know." 75 (1845): 32–33.
Skipped through a typical gentleman's day, from reading "the lighter parts of the *Morning Herald*, the police reports, fashionable news, murders, and horse advertisements," and the police reports in *The Times* and *Morning Chronicle* to the "vacuum" before the evening papers arrived.

103. Reach, Angus B. "Oracles." 75 (1845): 228–35.
Laughed at "political oracles" who heard news in their clubs before it made the newspapers.

104. [Ainsworth, W. H.]. "Laman Blanchard and His Writings: With a Selection from His Correspondence with Mr. Ainsworth." 76 (1846): 131–40.
Excerpted from Blanchard's letters and his *Sketches from Life* that he edited George Cruikshank's *Omnibus* and subedited *Ainsworth's Magazine*, where he supported anonymity and wrote many reviews, none "hostile."

105. "George Canning." 77 (1846): 89–92.
Review of Robert Bell's *The Life of the Right Hon. George Canning* justified his use of ridicule in the *Anti-Jacobin* since it neutralized revolutionary ideology.

106. Redding, Cyrus. "Life and Reminiscences of Thomas Campbell." 77 (1846): 332–47, 399–406; 78 (1846): 81–90, 202–12, 312–22, 427–38; 79 (1847): 51–63, 241–48, 318–27, 423–31; 80 (1847): 66–74, 189–96, 313–20, 418–25; 81 (1847): 46–53, 99–206, 332–43, 397–405; 82 (1848): 173–79; 83 (1848): 28–42; 84 (1848): 300–10, 454–65.
Biography of the *New Monthly* editor, "when it stood alone among the periodical works," featured Redding as much as Campbell. During his tenure, the *Magazine* had writers who were "the first among literary men" and a wide circulation. The *New Monthly* was modeled on the *Gentleman's Magazine* and *Monthly Magazine*, but they were more aristocratic than this child of Henry Colburn.

Campbell's early work for the *Morning Chronicle* showed that he was ignorant about politics and unskilled in the "art of rapid composition." When he began editing the *New Monthly*, he was inexperienced but smart enough to avoid the scandal surrounding Queen Caroline. He was neither an innovator nor well organized. Yet he attracted competent scribes, among them theatre critic Thomas Noon Talfourd and William Hazlitt, who together with their colleagues lent the *Magazine* more literary taste and scholarship, but universities never supplied "one single contributor worthy of the notice."

By early 1830 the *New Monthly* had lost its early and valued writers to death or distraction authoring novels for money. The *Magazine* needed articles that were concise and varied, penned by people of "extensive reading, deep reflection, and a particular tact in the handling of subjects." Instead, the next batch of *New Monthly* contributors catered to the "sickly taste for excitement" of the less educated. Campbell, who was "incapable of acting with vigour," resorted to anonymous publications that deprived the periodical of its stature and range. He resigned to start the *Metropolitan* without sufficient capital, leaving a legacy of reviews by experts, not the typical 'notices' of the 1840s "penned by raw youth from Scotland and Ireland."

Aside that the "*South African Journal* was a very excellent periodical" due to the efforts of John Fairburn and Thomas Pringle, who had penned for *Blackwood's Magazine*.

107. "Extracts from the Diary and Letters of a Diplomatist." 78 (1846): 323–31.
Aside on an earlier leader-writer for the *Morning Post*.

108. "*Lucretia* – by Sir E[dward] Bulwer Lytton." 79 (1847): 124–31.
Deprecated the hypocrisy of newspapers that "croak loudest against fiction founded on crime" but publicized lawbreaking in "obnoxious" detail.

109. Mariotti, L. [Antonio Gallenga]. "Present State and Prospects of Italy." 79 (1847): 249–61.

Balanced the facts that newspapers were flourishing in Naples and Turin and that the *Penny Magazine* appeared in Italian in Piedmont and Lombardy against the political and ecclesiastical censorship that limited the influence of the press in Italy. Aside that the *Allgemeine Zeitung* was the "father of lies."

110. "The Rev. Richard Harris Barham." 79 (1847): 273–77.

Mentioned Barham's articles in *Blackwood's Magazine* and *Bentley's Miscellany*.

111. [Smith, Horace]. "A Greybeard's Gossip about His Literary Acquaintance." 79 (1847): 303–08, 515–22; 80 (1847): 38–48, 137–43, 290–97, 461–68; 81 (1847): 83–87, 227–40, 288–94, 415–24; 82 (1848): 14–20, 250–57, 329–41.

Opened with *Pic-Nic*, established in 1802 to "vindicate" theatre and "check" the scandalizing of aristocrats. Among its contributors were Smith and J. W. Croker. By the time its masthead was the *Cabinet*, it lacked aim, money, talent, and political intelligence.

Periodical writing was more lucrative in 1847, more even than penning a novel because articles could be gathered into a book. British serials, unlike French, published the best literature. British booksellers once sponsored periodicals to puff their books, but the *Edinburgh Review* and its progeny abandoned that goal.

Reminisced about several editors, among them Thomas Barnes at *The Times*; Theodore Hook, "a sort of literary gladiator" at *John Bull*; John Scott at the *London Magazine* where his attacks on *Blackwood's Magazine* led to the duel that killed him; John Taylor, owner of the *Sun* and editor of the *Morning Post*, who never became sour in the face of human "folly, depravity." *See* 86: 399.

112. [Ainsworth, W. H.]. "Sketches of Charles Hooton, Esq., and the Rev. J. T. Hewlett, A.M." 79 (1847): 397–99.

Memorialized Hooton and Hewlett, two contributors to the *New Monthly*.

113. "Recollections of Leman Rede." 80 (1847): 102–09.

Biography of Rede, a novelist and theatre critic who was "in high favour" during his lifetime, stated that his essays in the *New Monthly* and elsewhere were "pleasantly written."

114. "Santa Anna [*sic*] at Vera Cruz." 80 (1847): 361–63.

Granted that "English newspapers keep you tolerably *au courant du jour* concerning political events."

115. "A Year in Portugal During the Late Rebellion." 81 (1847): 127–44.

Marginalized Portuguese newspapers, as the *Nacional* and *Estrella do Norte*.

116. Mariotti, L. [Antonio Gallenga]. "The Italian Crisis." 81 (1847): 240–46.

Conjectured that the free press in Rome inspired a similar one in Florence while the "*Piedmontese Gazette* derives fresh boldness from the tone of *Alba* or *Contemporaneo*."

117. Mariotti, L. [Antonio Gallenga]. "The Italian Programme." 81 (1847): 253–59.

Preferred holding journals to ordinary law rather than special censure.

118. "Fisher's Annuals." 81 (1847): 297–98.
Fixed on the publishing stable of Fisher, Son and Company.

119. "Gossip on Parisian Authors." 81 (1847): 327–32.
Profiled Henri Berthoud, who "fills a prominent station in French literature." He launched *Litterature Pittoresque* and "a sort of *Penny Magazine, Musée de Famille*," as well as seven or eight other serials, of which three or four were profitable. Pointed out that famous French writers introduced their protégés to editors and reviewers to spark young careers.

120. "French Almanacs." 81 (1847): 456–65.
Logged several of the many French almanacs. Until the nineteenth century they disseminated general information or superstition to peasants but by 1847 specialized, as by craft or age. Among almanac editors were Léon Gozlan (*Almanach Comique*), Louis Huart (*Pittoresque*), and Henri Monnier (*Drolatique, Critique, et Charivarique*).

121. Hervey, Charles. "The Drama in Paris." 81 (1847): 484–88.
Lamented that "the small fry of Parisian newspapers, professedly theatrical, which appear, some daily, some twice, and some once a week, are positive nuisances." These "literary vampires" praised performers who were subscribers to their publications. The *Revue* was more "respectable, but dull," while *Entr'Acte* was a mere playbill. By contrast, the gazette with the highest circulation, the *Coureur des Spectacles* edited by Charles Maurice, printed articles "ably and fearlessly written." The *Corsaire's* theatre criticism was "invariably clever and generally impartial," but it was a more general paper.

122. [Ainsworth, W. H.]. "Subjects in Season." 82 (1848): 53–58.
Retrospective of the *New Monthly* trusted that circulation would rise every year.

123. "Revolutionary Paris." 82 (1848): 474–94.
Marked the *National* as the organ of the 1848 republican government. Its editor, Armand Marrast, also wrote for the *Constitutionnel.*

124. "Prince Metternich." 82 (1848): 495–501.
Broadcast that, as a result of the 1848 revolutions, "[t]he press throughout Germany is to be free."

125. "The French Model Republic." 82 (1848): 502–11.
Grieved that Emile de Girardin, "the noblest expositor" of the French press, had no impact on the French 1848 provisional government.

126. "The New Order of Politics." 83 (1848): 104–17.
Announced some effects of the 1848 revolutions on journalism. The German states were under pressure to grant press liberty just as the French government tried to silence the *Presse*.

127. "The Kaffir War." 83 (1848): 251–54.
Review of Harriet Ward's *Five Years in Kaffirland* included her "interview" with a chieftain but not the title of the periodical where it appeared.

128. "Ireland and the Repeal of the Union." 83 (1848): 347–57.
Bellowed that newspapers were multiplying in Ireland, from 25 in 1800 to 89 in 1846. The expansion was due "as much to an increase in political excitement" as to the "spread of intelligence." "The liberty, or rather license of language granted to the newspaper press in Ireland, far exceeds anything that has ever been permitted to the British press, or has been accorded to the newspapers of Europe or America by their respective governments."

129. "Chateaubriand." 83 (1848): 464–70.
Recounted that René de Chateaubriand penned for the *Journal des Débats* after he was dismissed from government. Aside on the "brutality and blasphemy" of French Revolution papers.

130. "The Siege of Vienna." 84 (1848): 429–40.
Relayed that in 1848 the Austrians prohibited dailies except Vienna's *Zeitung*, but the *Presse*, the Austrian version of *Lloyd's Weekly Newspaper*, and others emerged once the ban was relaxed.

131. "Jellachlich, Ban of Croatia." 85 (1849): 28–43.
Biography of Baron Joseph Jellachlich thanked Croatian journalists for their "dignity and self-control" in 1848 irrespective of Hungarian press "arrows" shot at Croatia.

132. "Theodore Hook." 85 (1849): 66–74.
Review of R. H. Barham's *The Life and Remains of Theodore Edward Hook* indexed the establishment of *John Bull* in 1820 as an "important event" in Hook's life. It was a vehicle for his journalism and a prelude to his editing the *New Monthly*, "that long-established favourite."

133. "The 'Rebel' Boers." 85 (1849): 74–78.
Catalogued *The Times* as the 'leading journal' in 1849 and the *Colonial Gazette* as a "periodical peculiarly devoted to the colonial interests of Great Britain."

134. "The Downfall of the Republic." 85 (1849): 122–25.
Bared that Louis Blanc, "the journalist and historian of republicanism," Armand Marrast, "the republican editor of *National*," and some *Réforme* journalists were in the 1848 French government while the *Presse* was in jeopardy because of its moderation.

135. "Beattie's Life of Campbell." 85 (1849): 234–39.
Review of *Life and Letters of Thomas Campbell*, edited by William Beattie, dubbed Campbell a "brilliant" editor. His inventive planning and kindliness to contributors made the *New Monthly* a success unlike his own *Metropolitan*.

136. "The Ionian Islands in 1849." 86 (1849): 105–12.
Endorsed the recently granted free press and the first newspaper, which was "impartial and independent," in the Ionian Islands.

137. "French Anti-Socialist Publications." 86 (1849): 185–90.
Peeked at the French organ of the Communists, the *Commune Socialiste*.

138. Wrottesley, Walter. "Hints to Emigrants to New South Wales." 86 (1849): 191–98.
Aside on Sydney dailies crammed with columns of goods for sale.

139. "Legitimist Revelations of the Late French Revolution." 86 (1849): 372–82.
Linked Paris' *National* and *Réforme* in 1848.

140. "Horace Smith." 86 (1849): 399–402.
Condensed Smith's journalism, including his Greybeard series for the *New Monthly*. *See* 79: 303.

141. Blundell, J. W. F., Esq. "The Swan River – Fremantle – Perth." 86 (1849): 475–83.
Conveyed that Perth, with no press censorship, had two weeklies, the *Inquirer* and *Gazette*.

142. "Lamartine's *History of the Revolution of 1848*." 86 (1849): 484–99.
Review of Alphonse de Lamartine's book echoed his ideas on the *National* and *Réforme* during the 1848 revolution. *See* 87: 64.

143. [Redding, Cyrus]. "The Authors of the *Rejected Addresses*." 87 (1849): 23–30.
Celebrated the work of Horace and James Smith for the *New Monthly*. Horace, "of no small value" to the *Magazine*, ended his connection in 1826 and James, in 1830.

144. "[Alphonse de] Lamartine and the Provisional Government." 87 (1849): 64–83.
Took more from Lamartine's *History* of the 1848 Revolution (86: 484), commenting that George Sand promulgated "incendiary doctrines" in the official paper, the *Bulletin de la République*.

145. "Railways." 89 (1850): 31–44.
Gleaned from Dionysius Lardner's *Railway Economy* the assets of railroads, such as bringing London morning papers to rural areas. "[T]he cheapness, promptitude, and rapidity" of this delivery and the speedy transmission of news by telegraphy largely accounted for the 'immense commercial, social, and intellectual power wielded, and benefits conferred, by these daily publications.' The "most widely circulating London journals" printed 40,000, each read by ten who talked to many more, giving the dailies an audience of about a million people.

146. "Revelations of Republican Life." 89 (1850): 94–109.
Spotlighted one de la Hodde, a "literary spy" paid by government to write for Paris' *Réforme* where he already earned 1,500 francs annually. Yet he satirized officials in *Charivari*.

147. Editor N. M. M. [W. H. Ainsworth]. "Notes and Queries." 89 (1850): 160–67.
Introduced a series triggered by *Notes and Queries*, a "very excellent weekly journal."

148. "*Lancashire Authors and Orators*." 89 (1850): 184–96.
Review of John Evans' book silhouetted W. H. Ainsworth and Archibald Prentice among others.

149. "The Romance of the Electric Telegraph." 89 (1850): 296–307.
Enthused that telegraphy benefited local journals by transmitting early abstracts of London morning papers. The act nationalizing telegraphy, "9th Vic., c. 44...prohibits favour and preference in the transmission of intelligence," but the Electric Telegraph Company apparently favored *The Times* over the *Morning Herald* because *The Times* spent more on usage.

150. "Paris in June." 89 (1850): 324–39.
Mourned that "[a]lmost all the leading organs of democracy have been silenced" in France, from the *Réforme* to the *Démocratique Pacifique*, a Socialist paper. Other gazettes, such as the *Siècle*, *National*, *Presse*, and even the *Journal des Débats*, were under varying degrees of pressure. Only the Bonapartist *Assemblée National* was secure.

151. "The Outrage upon General Haynau." 90 (1850): 241–43.
Charged the *Red Republican* with motivating an assault by an "English mob."

152. "French Almanacks." 90 (1850): 283–98.
Observed that French almanacs were either dedicated to Napoleon III or traced his career and the *Almanach pour Rire* was not very witty.

153. "The Great Exhibition of 1851." 92 (1851): 103–26.
Praised the *Art Journal* and *Journal of Design* for promoting the practical arts, such as lacemaking and ironworks.

154. Redding, Cyrus. "The Right Honourable Richard Lalor Sheil." 92 (1851): 254–62.
Revered Sheil, a playwright, attorney, and contributor to the *New Monthly*.

155. "Hartley Coleridge." 92 (1851): 276–85.
Skimmed Coleridge's essays in *Blackwood's Magazine*, 1826–31.

156. "Hodge-Podge." 92 (1851): 314–15.
Sputtered that on politics, the press could be "a stupid hireling" full of "dull bungles."

157. "De Barante's *History of the Convention*." 92 (1851): 402–20.
Review of Baron Amable de Barante's book on France, 1792–95, singled out the execution of the editor of the *Ami du Roi* and the suppression of dailies.

158. [Tartt, W. M.]. "The Late Mr. Edward Baines." 92 (1851): 431–34.
Review of *Life of Edward Baines* by his son and namesake followed the senior Baines. Emulating his hero, Benjamin Franklin, he was at age 16 a printer's apprentice for Thomas Walker, a newspaper publisher who acquainted the youth with "the mysteries of editorship" that culminated in his long career with the *Leeds Mercury*.

159. "[Alphonse de] Lamartine's *History of the Restoration*." 93 (1851): 48–65.
Applauded Louis XVI for restoring a free press, which did not exist in France in 1851.

160. "Unreciprocated Copyright." 93 (1851): 122–26.
Asserted that cheap periodicals, "the literature of Rail," could instruct the masses and raise their tastes. However, printing excerpts of quality writing created legal problems in Britain though not the United States, which constantly plagiarized British serials.

161. "French Almanacs for 1852." 93 (1851): 330–44.
Explored French almanacs, "receptacles of fun and wisdom" such as the *Journal pour Rire* and *Almanach Comique*, publications that turned to other subjects when officials "tabooed" politics.

162. [Ainsworth, W. Francis]. "Gold in Australia." 93 (1851): 353–64.
Nominated the *Bathurst Free Press* as the first paper to print a story on the discovery of gold in Australia.

163. "Louis Napoleon Bonaparte." 94 (1852): 111–26.
Referred to columns penned by *The Times* Paris correspondent.

164. Surtees, W. E., D.C.L. "Recollections of North America, in 1849–50–51, No: II." 94 (1852): 208–35.
Registered that the "leading newspapers of Washington – the *Intelligencer*, the *Union*, and the *Republic* – are ably and honourably conducted and cost six cents each. The *New York Herald*, remarkable for early information, costs two cents." New Orleans' *Picayune*, which purportedly drew its name from Spanish money as Venice's *Gazetta* had Italian, carried less news at a higher price.

165. "*Lord Palmerston, England, and the Continent*; Austrian Views of English Foreign Policy." 94 (1852): 253–68.
Review of a book by Count Carl von Ficquelmont, a French ambassador, disagreed with his idea of the press as a "tyranny."

166. [Ainsworth, W. H.]. "Things in General; An Epilogue to the Present Number." 94 (1852): 372–78.
Perceived advertisements in dailies as a form of "consolation or enjoyment."

167. Bushby, Mrs. [Mary Anne S.]. "A Survey of Danish Literature, from the Earliest Period to the Present Time." 94 (1852): 452–61; 95 (1852): 40–54, 139–56, 253–72.
Dated the Danish press from the 1785 monthly *Minerva* (Copenhagen) with political and literary essays. Its founder, Prof. Knud Rahbek, "stood high as a critic and a reviewer, and was the principal editor" as well as the editor of the *Danish Spectator*. Historian Rasmus Nyerup penned for another literary magazine, *Learned News*, and other periodicals and edited *Nyerup's Magazine of Voyages and Travels Performed by Danes*. Gustav Ludwig Baden, a professor of history and law, edited the *Northern Spectator*. Mëir Aron Goldschmidt, "a Jew" born in 1819, edited the *Corsair*, a "clever" weekly, "something between *Punch* and the *Athenaeum*." It reviewed books, music, and theatre and "ridiculed men and manners," but its illustrations were not as good as *Punch*. The *Corsair* declined when Goldschmidt left to become editor of "a monthly magazine – the best in Copenhagen," *North and South*.

"In England, the Bar supplies the greater proportion of what may be called *working* literary men – reviewers, magazine writers, newspaper writers" and others, but in Denmark many of these people came from the theatre.

168. [Jacox, Francis]. "Hartley Coleridge's *Northern Worthies*." 95 (1852): 177–82.
Esteemed Coleridge's essays in *Blackwood's Magazine*.

169. "'*Our Own Correspondent*' *in Italy*." 95 (1852): 284–94.
Reviewed a book by Michael Burke Honan of *The Times*. "The life of a newspaper correspondent, as may naturally be supposed, is one of alternate cloud and sunshine." Honan's anecdotes were lively, but his serious tips came from ministers. A foreign correspondent might accrue fame and wealth because he could make officials "turn pale," cause cabinets to fall, and shape the "destinies of nations," but his health suffered from his work.

170. Sir Nathaniel [Francis Jacox]. "Literary Leaflets. No. II: A 'Splendid' Writer." 96 (1852): 265–74.
Spotlighted George Gilfillan of Dundee who was "a liberal contributor" to periodicals, such as the *British Quarterly Review*, *Eclectic Review*, and *Hogg's Instructor*. He achieved his reputation as a "splendid writer" from the "half-educated…who crave stimulants." Examples of his style proved that he had "lawless taste" in language. The *North American Review* and *Athenaeum* disdained his work, though the latter's criticism may have sprung from jealousy.

171. "French Almanacks for 1853, and Parisian Literary and Political Chit-Chat." 96 (1852): 323–45.
Rhapsodized about the new *Almanach de la Littérature du Théâtre et des Beaux Arts* of the "renowned critic and feuilletonist," Jules Janin. In Paris as well as London, "cheap and inferior" literature blossomed, especially in women's periodicals. They increased circulation by promising gifts to subscribers. Aside on G. Wagner, editor of the *Almanach Prophétique*.

172. Sir Nathaniel [Francis Jacox]. "Literary Leaflets. No. III: Kingsley's *Phaethon*." 96 (1852): 424–32.
Review of Charles Kinsgley's work flitted past his essays in the *Christian Socialist* and *Leader*, which G. H. Lewes edited.

173. Hengiston, J. W., Esq. [John W. Oldmixon and Cyrus Redding]. "New York – Its Hotels, Waterworks, and Things in General." 97 (1853): 80–94.
Calculated that "newspapers are quite a drug" everywhere in the United States. New Yorkers bought them every morning for one or two cents from "little Pats in rags." Newspapers copied each other's columns except advertising. Most of the "chief articles" in periodicals came from English serials.

174. Sir Nathaniel [Francis Jacox]. "Literary Leaflets. No. VI: Sir William Hamilton:*Discussions of Philosophy*." 97 (1853): 374–82.
Ruled that the "metaphysical department of the *Edinburgh Review* owes whatever *prestige* it enjoys to the contributions of Sir William Hamilton."

175. Scoffern, Dr. [John]. "The Paradise of Spain." 98 (1853): 64–76.
Toured Motril, which had "no newspaper-rooms," so men heard information at the barber shop.

176. Sir Nathaniel [Francis Jacox]. "American Authorship. No. II: Richard Henry Dana." 98 (1853): 77–83.
Starred Dana as a writer for, then editor of the *North American Review* who also published articles and verse in the *New York Review*, edited by Willam Cullen Bryant.

177. Hengiston, J. W., Esq. [John W. Oldmixon and Cyrus Redding]. "More of the Ohio – the Mississippi and New Orleans." 98 (1853): 232–53.
Visited Cincinnati, which had a lone daily in 1793 and 13 in 1853 as well as 25 weeklies and four monthlies.

178. [Jacox, Francis]. "Thackeray's Lectures on *The English Humorists*." 98 (1853): 262–70.
Review of W. M. Thackeray's *The English Humorists of the Eighteenth Century* echoed him on Joseph Addison in the *Spectator* and Richard Steele.

179. "Reminiscences of Paris." 98 (1853): 309–19.
Protagonists were a Paris family. "Bertin *l'aîné*" published *Eclair* after the Directory restored press liberty. That freedom was narrow because "newspapers were frequently stopped and the proprietors arrested." When *Eclair* was suspended, Bertin and his brother, Bertin De Vaux, purchased the *Journal des Débats* for 20,000 francs. They recruited talented writers, such as René de Chateaubriand and other contributors (listed here). In 1804 the brothers left the *Débats* for the *Journal de l'Empire* but later returned. By 1811, when the paper was "flourishing," it was confiscated and its shares given to the supporters of Napoleon I and the police. From 1818 to his death in 1841 "*l'aîne*" managed the *Journal* and with his brother sustained journalism's power in France in the 1820s.

180. Sir Nathaniel [Francis Jacox]. "Literary Leaflets. No. XI: Sir Thomas Noon Talfourd." 99 (1853): 27–34.
Scanned Talfourd's periodical articles, as in the *London Magazine*, where he was one of its "once brilliant staff." He also penned for the *New Monthly* but judged Thomas Campbell unfit to edit it.

181. "A German's Impressions of England." 99 (1853): 95–101.
Review of book by Dr. [?Joseph] Gambilher seconded his belief in press freedom but not his idea that the libel law was "faultless."

182. "The Chinese Revolution." 99 (1853): 180–98.
Barked that "the official *Gazette* of Peking condescended to notice the Chinese insurrection" only after rebel successes were too obvious to omit.

183. "The French Almanacks for 1854." 99 (1853): 312–26.
Pronounced French almanacs derivative.

184. "A Political Conversazione of the Year 1848: Metternich, Guizot, Louis Philippe, Palmerston." 99 (1853): 343–49.
Blurted out that François Guizot "feared the journalists in France."

185. [Ainsworth, W. H.]. "Prologue to the Hundredth Volume." 100 (1854): 1–5.
Remembered many editors and writers of the *New Monthly*. Thomas Campbell favored literature and E. G. Bulwer-Lytton favored politics. The latter, whose editorial tenure was relatively short, brought in "first-rate contributors." Theodore Hook and Thomas Hood enlisted other quality journalists who kept the *Magazine* fresh and lent it variety, the essential elements of a "carefully-conducted" periodical. The owner as editor came in 1845 and, more recently, the *New Monthly* emphasized the United States.

186. "German Almanacks for 1854." 100 (1854): 90–99.
Inferred from seven German almanacs that tales and poetry were the only contents possible because of censorship.

187. "The Bourgeois of Paris." 100 (1854): 99–106.
Review of Louis Véron's *Memoires* claimed that at least one French editor rejected articles by coughing.

188. [Jacox, Francis]. "Gotthold Ephraim Lessing." 100 (1854): 127–37.
Imparted that Lessing launched and penned for the *Library of Belles Lettres*, 1757, a journal that with help from Moses Mendelssohn was a "signal success."

189. "The War with Russia." 100 (1854): 253–66.
Labeled the *Soldaten-Freund* "the Austrian military organ."

190. Pinch, Doctor. "About Lord Brougham." 100 (1854): 368–78.
Alleged that Sydney Smith would not let Henry Brougham publish in the first three numbers of the *Edinburgh Review* because of his 'indiscretion and rashness.'

191. Redding, Cyrus. "Sir Thomas Talfourd." 100 (1854): 407–15.
Paean to Talfourd, a former *New Monthly* theatre critic, depicted him as kind and "high-minded." He thought a magazine should welcome diversity, but Redding realized that anonymity was a tool for homogeneity.

192. Sir Nathaniel [Francis Jacox]. "Literary Leaflets. No. XIX: John Gibson Lockhart." 101 (1854): 56–64.
Delineated at length the products of *Quarterly Review* editor Lockhart's "trenchant pen."

193. Sir Nathaniel [Francis Jacox]. "Literary Leaflets. No. XX: Professor Wilson." 101 (1854): 162–79.
Grounded Wilson's "true fame" in his work in *Blackwood's Magazine*. "No such influence as his has been exercised on our popular periodical literature." Christopher North had "renown world-wide," but Wilson's beautifully written critical essays were original, imaginative and insightful.

194. [Jacox, Francis]. "De Quincey's *Miscellanies*." 101 (1854): 338–43.

Review of Thomas De Quincey's *Selections, Grave and Gay* (vol. 3) wished that his essays on German literature, published in *Tait's Edinburgh Magazine*, *Blackwood's Magazine*, and the *London Magazine*, were available in a book.

195. Pepper, Thomas [Ellen Wood]. "Stray Letters from the East." 101 (1854): 344–54.

Castigated *The Times* correspondent (William Howard Russell) who leaked the story of military mismanagement in Crimea. Although "no reporters are to be allowed to accompany the army," these "ferrets" would somehow get the news.

196. Pepper, Thomas [Ellen Wood]. "More Stray Letters from the East." 102 (1854): 41–52.

Raged about "interfering newspapers and their leading articles" with respect to war correspondence.

197. Andrews, Alexander. "The Eighteenth Century: or Illustrations of the Manners and Customs of Our Grandfathers." 102 (1854): 308–20, 478–88.

Part of a series sampled advertisements in the *Tatler* and other eighteenth-century newspapers.

The New Quarterly Magazine, 1873–1880

Targeting the educated, the *New Quarterly* commented on literary and theatre criticism and Continental journalism from Portugal to Russia.

1. Latouche, John [Oswald Crawfurd]. "Notes of Travel in Portugal." 2 (1874): 443–65, 667–705; 3 (1874–75): 399–415.

Part of a series quoted Charles Dana that ocean travel, by depriving people of "their daily dose of newspaper reading," left them little to say. Agreed that he was correct about the English and Americans but not others, who "seldom read newspapers."

"The newspaper fills but a small part of the life either of Spaniards or Portuguese. Religious, literary, scientific, legal, and social life in Portugal are hardly reflected at all in the journals." People only read the newspapers for politics, but the parliamentary speeches were "scantily reproduced," and "deliberate discussion of home politics" was rare. The gazettes were replete with "rumours that fill the columns of European journals." The Portuguese tribunes were tiny, about the same size as early "English *News Letters*" and "*Flying Mercuries*," and like those sheets, concentrated on foreign events and appealed to the emotions. The Portuguese aped the French, reporting everything, even the weather, "with literary artifice." Obituaries were "exquisitely pompous and stilted," probably because relatives paid for them. Critics earned money for puffs. By contrast, the British press had news and views. Thanks to a "free and cheap press" the British press was immense, whereas in Portugal, "newspapers are scarce and small."

2. Arnold, F[rederick]. "On the Personal History of Lord Macaulay." 2 (1874): 706–31.

Reminded that T. B. Macaulay's early work for *Knight's Quarterly Magazine* was so valuable it had been reprinted. Anglo-Indian "journalists considered themselves slighted by him; probably Macaulay considered that there was immeasurable difference between a Calcutta journalist and an 'Edinburgh Reviewer.'"

3. Smith, George Barnett. "Nathaniel Hawthorne." 3 (1874–75): 274–303.

Unearthed Hawthorne's "short experience" as an editor in 1836 when he conducted the *American Magazine of Useful Knowledge* in Boston. He earned 600 dollars per year until the owners went bankrupt. Hawthorne had the opportunity to write many pieces and the "drudgery" of picking extracts from other heralds to fill space.

4. The Editor [Oswald Crawfurd]. "De Quincey." 4 (1875): 257–87.

Prefaced an article on Thomas De Quincey that the early nineteenth century was "an age of periodical writing of a kind that had never before existed." The eighteenth-century essays of Joseph Addison and Richard Steele in the *Spectator* and Samuel Johnson in the *Rambler* were "short rhetorical exercises." "The new periodical literature took the form of real monographs." "In the Quarterlies, under the thin disguise of Reviews, the men best qualified to form and express opinions on particular subjects favoured the world with concise and brilliant expositions of their views, and three or four magazines followed suit. No literary movement in this country has ever done so much to excite and to promote literary culture."

"As a Review writer, [T. B.] Macaulay was unquestionably the first man of his age – before [Francis] Jeffrey, [Henry] Brougham, or Sydney Smith: as a writer of Magazine articles of the higher kind, De Quincey was quite as conspicuously eminent." "De Quincey's Magazine papers are, as a whole, in power as well as in range, very far above those of any writer of the century." "That department of literary labour in which he did the best work was criticism," although a recent critic branded it "respectable 'padding.'"

Aside that "a conscientious Magazine Editor" read as much past magazine literature as possible.

5. Buchanan, Robert [W.]. "The Modern Stage." 4 (1875): 325–62.

Singled out theatre critics, "as we facetiously call these gentlemen who 'do' the dramatic reviews for newspapers." Critics "arrogate pretensions and try to adjudicate claims" even though they were often ignorant. The bias of the unsuccessful often drove reviews. One example was John Oxenford of *The Times*. Oxenford was a playwright who produced "stuff merely written for the market" while he assessed the work of others. Dutton Cook, the *Pall Mall Gazette* man who loved theatre, was "about the best" in the dailies. The "notorious incompetence and carelessness" of the majority "hardened the managers" and "alienated the public." More charitable managers tolerated critics of good will even if "their knowledge may be inadequate, their taste questionable," but readers discounted theatre reviews. Aside that *The Times* published book reviews by staff on slow news days.

6. Arnold, Rev. Frederick, B.A. "Lord Bute, the Premier." 4 (1875): 444–74.

Touched on John Wilkes and the *North Briton*.

7. Cobbe, Frances Power. "Backward Ho!" 5 (1875–76): 231–62.

Posted "several monthly and weekly periodicals, among them *Human Nature*, the *Spiritualist*, the *Medium*, and *Daybreak*," that espoused spiritualism.

8. Collins, Mortimer. "Almanacs." 5 (1875–76): 409–30.

Rooted nineteenth-century "periodical light literature" in eighteenth-century almanacs. They provided news only in very rural areas because a local press already existed. In 1875 the country gazette lasted the average farmer for a week, but urbanites demanded dailies.

9. [Crawfurd, Oswald]. "Current Literature and Current Criticism." 5 (1875–76): 448–92.

Swept over the *Cornhill Magazine*, which "probably commands the most cultivated circle of readers in the United Kingdom"; *Good Words*, whose "literary rank and excellence are admirably sustained" and whose illustrations were superior to the *Cornhill*'s and other serials.

10. Turner, Matthew Freke [Oswald Crawfurd]. "Artemus Ward and the Humourists of America." 6 (1876): 198–220.

Paralleled Charles Brown (known as Artemus Ward) and Charles Dickens, whereas Washington Irving aped Joseph Addison and Richard Steele. Humor writers in the mode of W. M. Thackeray seemed to be flourishing. Publishers in New York and Boston initially profited from selling British humor "under cost price" to readers who were ready to pay. Since the Civil War cultivated an interest in Americana, humor in stories authored with originality by Americans had a "sudden and unexpected rise." Brown, first at the *Cleveland Plain Dealer*, moved to *Vanity Fair*, "a sort of New York *Punch*. Within a week every journal from Boston to San Francisco" printed his work. Bret Harte and Mark Twain not always ably imitated Brown. Twain's "The Killing of Julius Caesar," written "in the style of a Western newspaper," typified the genre but was not very good.

11. [Crawfurd, Oswald]. "Current Literature and Current Criticism." 6 (1876): 230–83, 488–533.

Calculated that the "number of critical journals of weight and authority" had trebled in the last 20 years, showering the public with evaluations. "Much of the old critical acrimony" had gone, and scribes were less "dictatorial," more advisory, allowing the public to compare their ideas. The *Athenaeum* was a "discerning journal." The *New Quarterly* was so committed to objectivity that it refused to review a novel by someone "permanently engaged upon the staff."

12. Latouche, John, Author of "Travels in Portugal" [Oswald Crawfurd]. "The Tourist in Portugal: The Lost City of Citania." 6 (1876): 387–412.

Witnessed that politics, literature, and science interested Portuguese townspeople, so they awaited French and English periodicals. The *New Quarterly* arrived in Braga within a week of publication.

13. Carr, J. Comyns. "The Academy and the Salon." 6 (1876): 413–39.

Despaired that *The Times* treated the "interests of art…with proud indifference."

14. Browne, C. Elliot. "A Wit of the Last Generation." 6 (1876): 440–62.

Starred Joseph Jekyll, who wrote "political lampoons in the newspapers." Early in the nineteenth century, "when the epigram and parody were still real and effective weapons of political warfare," Jekyll did some of his best work. Aside that the *Monthly Review* was "the great arbiter of literary distinction" in the eighteenth century.

15. [Crawfurd, Oswald]. "Current Literature and Current Criticism." 7 (1876–77): 200–82.

Bewailed that "[w]hen the critical journals of London…find that their contents are somewhat heavier than usual," they selected "some miserable novelist of the more ignoble or the more idiotic type… for trial and execution."

16. Hueffer, Francis. "The Literary Aspects of Schopenhauer's Work." 8 (1877): 352–78.

Regarded Arthur Schopenhauer's witticisms, observations, and aphorisms as "sufficient to make the fortune of half-a-dozen able journalists."

17. Jefferies, R[ichard]. "The Future of Country Society." 8 (1877): 379–409.

Hypothesized that the press could sway the barely literate who attached "importance to anything written." Most rural workers read neighborhood weeklies in "ale-houses or elsewhere." Laborers looked for "sensational topics," local gossip, and leaders that attacked the powerful. The *Illustrated Police News* was available in even "the most outlaying hamlets."

18. Zimmern, Helen. "Count Giacomo Leopardi." 9 (1877–78): 1–33.

Aired Leopardi's youthful endeavors for the *Spettatore* (Milan) and "other newspapers; editors complimented him." He penned for the *Spettatore* for "several years" and then for its successor, *Nuovo*, where he "contributed regularly" essays and poems.

19. Evershed, Henry. "Sir John Sinclair, and Some Other Scotch Improvers." 9 (1877–78): 143–68.

Bruited that Sinclair scribbled for the *Caledonian Mercury*, 1776, before authoring 367 books and pamphlets. Aside on the *Transactions of the Society of Improvers in the Knowledge of Agriculture in Scotland*.

20. Browne, C. Elliot. "Early Literary Journals." 9 (1877–78): 324–41.

Ranked the *Gentleman's Journal, or Monthly Miscellany*, 1692–95, the "first English magazine" because France already had the *Mercure Gallant*. Peter Motteux, founder of the *Journal*, modeled it on manuscript newsletters that were interrupted "very awkwardly and abruptly" by verse and fiction. He added essays and chat about music and drama. The editor's introduction solicited news and contributions because he had a "hard task…I must set up for a Journalist." Among the contributors were John Dryden and Charles Wesley. Apparently, there were problems getting fiction because later issues repeated earlier material or stole new material. Most books the *Journal* endorsed were long forgotten by 1877.

The decades following the Restoration "were especially remarkable for the great development of periodical literature." "The press teemed with cheap journals which brought knowledge within the reach of classes to whom literature was only known by the popular broadside and chapbook." Among the specialized were the *Weekly Collections for the Improvement of Trade*, 1682, by "John Haughton, one of the earliest members of the Royal Society"; the *Monthly Memorials for the Ingenious*, a 1691 science publication of "M. De La Crose, a Huguenot refugee"; the *Jockey's Intelligencer*; and *Observations upon the Weekly Bills of Mortality*, a medical serial. After the pioneer *Mercurius Democritus*, 1652, other satirical entries were the *Athenian Mercury* that laughed at readers' questions, and the *Diverting Post*, 1704, the forerunner of the "Society Journal" and "probably also the last periodical written entirely in verse."

Once the *London Gazette* commenced, newspapers "began to make comments and to express opinions." The "political journals were gradually developing from weekly news sheets; critical journals grew out of the bookseller's list." The *Weekly Advertisement of Books*, 1679, listed titles for a shilling each; the *Mercurius Librarius*, 1680, for six pence. The *Weekly Memorials of the Ingenious*, 1682, with book criticism by "John Pettiver, the botanist," was the "first English review" but lasted barely nine months because Pettiver's criticism was "solid and dull."

21. Ingram, John H. "Unknown Correspondence by Edgar Poe." 10 (1878): 1–30.

Deconstructed Poe's letters on his submissions to the *American Review* and *Metropolitan* and on his regular column, "Marginalia," in the *Southern Literary Messenger*. His need for money spurred him to negotiate with many other serials, including "a weekly paper of Boston…not a very respectable journal, perhaps in a literary point of view, but one that pays as high prices as most of the magazines." "I have also made permanent arrangements with every magazine in America (except Peterson's *National*), including a Cincinnati magazine called *The Gentleman's*." Poe's problems multiplied when the *Columbian Magazine* "failed" and then the *Union*, "taking with it my principal dependence." He complained that the *Whig Review* and *Democratic Review* no longer paid authors and the *Messenger* owed him money, but he hoped to survive on submissions to *Graham's Magazine*.

22. Edwards, H. Sutherland. "Panslavonianism." 10 (1878): 110–32.
Glanced at St. Petersburg's *Novoe Vremya* and *Standard.*

23. Lucy, Henry W. "Parliamentary Forms and Reforms." 10 (1878): 133–57.
Warranted that Commons in 1642 and 1694 and Lords in 1698 excluded news writers without a license. In 1878 the press not only had its own parliamentary gallery but other rooms as well.

24. [Hueffer, Francis]. "Current Literature and Current Criticism." 10 (1878): 213–40, 432–60, 655–84.
Affirmed that the *New Quarterly* did not "assume an air of superiority" over daily, weekly, and monthly critics. The purposes of a quarterly's review, which had the advantage of time, were to indicate the impression a book created and to correct errors in earlier assessments.

25. Latouche, John [Oswald Crawfurd]. "Country Life in Portugal." 10 (1878): 292–314.
Deduced that Portugal, because "too limited in population," could not have "a periodical press of any power." The people did not need "a great periodical press, such as ours or the American, because the Portuguese are a talkative and sociable race" who formulated and disseminated ideas orally much like the West Africans.

26. Blind, Mathilde. "Mary Wollstonecraft." 10 (1878): 390–412.
Acknowledged Wollstonecraft's "many essays for the *Analytical Review*."

27. Arnold, Arthur. "Socialism." 10 (1878): 413–31.
Traced the "socialist character" of the 1848 German revolutions to the pages by Karl Marx and other Socialists in the *Neue Rheinische Zeitung*.

28. "The Vernacular Press of India and the Afghan Crisis." 10 (1878): 614–33.
Vetoed a proposed Press Act because the Indian press, irrespective of the perceptions of MPs, was small. For example, the *Oudh Akhbar* circulated only 820 copies in a large and largely populated area. This press, which officials in 1878 accused of stirring unrest, was "[f]rom the journalistic viewpoint…outside the larger towns…an intellectual waste." Many papers still used lithograph stone, not even moveable type or a hand press. Gazettes born in the 1830s grew slowly because of fear of the penalty for sedition. It was true that since 1873 they had multiplied rapidly, numbering 200 in 1878. Each copy had subscribers from "among the most intelligent of the population" and many more readers. Government did not comprehend that tolerating a press presenting the rights of locals and the benefits of British rule would strike a balance between despotism and citizenship.

29. "Prince Bismarck." n.s., 1 (1879): 1–23.
Decried Otto von Bismarck's notion that newspapers "produce airy nothings, which appear solid and of value."

30. "Selected Books: *Hours in a Library*." n.s., 1 (1879): 463–66.
Review of Leslie Stephen's book zeroed in on his essay, "The First *Edinburgh* Reviewers." Believed that it was not as good as Walter Bagehot's study and "was unjust to Sydney Smith, who was a great deal more than a mere humourist."

31. "The Poetic Phase in Modern English Art." n.s., 2 (1879): 150–65.
Spurned art critics who flattered their friends too highly while they stigmatized others as 'oafs and puppies.' The art of 1879, hardly the stuff of genius, should not trouble any "social journalist."

32. [Sully, James]. "George Henry Lewes." n.s., 2 (1879): 356–76.
Guaranteed that when "Lewes entered the critical arena the quarterlies were still the great organs of higher criticism." People were willing "to read through a goodly article" rather than "to be coached up in a few minutes by a couple of columns in a weekly review." The *Edinburgh Review* "produced a certain manly vigour and directness" but also made criticism "rude and wanting in delicate insight." Its critics were often "dictatorial," giving an "individual impression" without reasons.

Lewes' essays had "a dash and a vigour...rare in contemporary journalism." They showed "penetrating insight" based on "philosophical studies" and "habits of reflection." Eschewing jargon, he wrote on many topics in many reviews (cited here) but was especially good on theatre. Editor of the *Leader*, 1851–54, he later focused on science, 1853–64, and on philosophy and psychology, 1865–78.

33. "Italian Affairs." n.s., 3 (1880): 67–91.
Recommended from Italy's free press Florence's "*Rassegna Settimanale*, an independent weekly review in which political and social questions are treated with admirable knowledge and ability, and which should be read by all persons wishing to acquaint themselves with Italian affairs." Aside on the *Nuova Antologia*.

34. Pattison, Mark. "Middle-Class Education." n.s., 3 (1880): 150–57.
Sighed that "[a] large percentage, disqualified by their literary education for the rougher occupations of practical business, join the struggling crowd of competitors for employment in the periodical press."

35. "Selected Books: *France since the First Empire*." n.s., 3 (1880): 216–19.
Review of James Macdonell's book quoted his wife that he was 'a journalist, and no man was prouder of his profession, no man ever strove harder to put his conscience into all that he did.'

36. "Russia." n.s., 3 (1880): 384–410.
Contended that press censorship fanned conspiracy in Russia. Officials of Alexander II confiscated a "new secret socialist journal," *Will of the People*.

37. "Jacobins and Levellers." n.s., 3 (1880): 411–31.
Sermonized that in 1793 the publications of the London Corresponding Society made the government nervous about 'sedition.' "Respectable booksellers and journalists were cast in terms of imprisonment for various periods, their sole crime being, in some cases, the republication of writings which Mr. Pitt had formerly approved." The fear of revolution was so great that even the opposition urged the public "to discourage the circulation of disloyal newspapers."

The New Review, 1889–1897

Reinventing itself regularly, the *New Review* expounded on anonymity and "new journalism."

1. Coleridge, [John Duke, 1st Baron]. "Matthew Arnold." 1 (1889): 111–24, 217–32.
Rated some of Arnold's columns on the American press "absurd and contemptible" but not unusual in journalism. The French regularly blasted the brutality of British newspapers.

2. Bigelow, Poultney. "The German Emperor." 1 (1889): 243–57.
Personified Wilhelm II as a man with "little patience" for his supposed enemies in journalism. For example, the "*Deutsche Rundschau*, the leading literary review, was seized by police because it published a section of the late Emperor's diary."

3. O'Connor, T. P. "The New Journalism." 1 (1889): 423–34.
Configured New Journalism as "more personal in tone." Reporting the "appearance, the habits, the clothes, or the home and social life" of an individual had previously been "an impertinence and almost…an indecency." "Personal journalism" in 1889 was "healthy…rational" because it gave to history a picture of a whole person, but it should be selective, which was not a trait of the American press. Gossip should never extend to "slander, scandal… personal attack." Still, it was better to be outspoken because "the public suffer a great deal more from the cowardice than from the audacity of journalism, from the suppression than from the publication of awkward facts." Newspapers should not hesitate to expose fraud, as in advertisements, because editors were timid or needed money. Good taste and the law would protect private individuals; libel, public persons.

Newspapers' language had to be "clear, crisp, sharp" because people read them quickly. Being independent in politics might generate the suspense that attracted more readers, but it was "fair and honourable" to articulate the bias of a gazette, "a weapon in the conflict of ideas."

4. Hopkins, Tighe. "Anonymity?" 1 (1889): 513–31; 2 (1890): 265–76.
Quoted John Morley (*Fortnightly Review* n.s., 2: 287) and 30 others polled on the worth of anonymity. Among them were journalists Eliza Lynn Linton, George Augustus Sala, T. P. O'Connor; the editors of the *Manchester Guardian* and *Liverpool Daily Post*; an editor of the National Press Agency; and the London correspondent of the *New York Tribune*. Fans thought that anonymity shielded those not well known; enemies thought that signature improved quality and reinforced responsibility.

Only about newspapers did people talk of "the tremendous power and dignity of anonymous writing." Although the public commonly regarded the press as "the wisest and most authoritative voice of the country," it was impossible to know if editors hired the best minds. Anonymous political leaders carried no greater weight than signed leaders and suffered from a lack of candor, perhaps the result of bias or profit. Signing leaders would not detract from their influence because these columns should be judged on their merits. The French system of signature would lessen inaccuracies and confer a degree of fame on journalists. Articles by tyros could be anonymous, but those "expressing individual opinions" by more senior journalists should not be.

5. Morgan, George Osborne. "The New Method in Electioneering." 1 (1889): 552–60.
Measured the improvement in the political "tone and temper" of newspapers against the diminishing influence of the *Edinburgh Review* and *Quarterly Review*. The local press particularly was one of "the readiest engines for creating and directing public opinion." London's halfpennies might be cheaper, but the "bulk" of readers "think twice about buying" them. "Leading journals," with "the pick of literary talent," were still abusive in politics, thus enhancing those they insulted. Society journals served "highly spiced morsels" but lowered public taste. Yet Belgravia matrons were willing to crowd London drawing rooms in July to get their names in the *Morning Post*.

6. Linton, E[liza] Lynn. "Candour in English Fiction, II." 2 (1890): 10–14.
Segment of a series roared that the publication of "the most revolting details in the daily Press" belied public concern for juvenile readers.

7. Hardy, Thomas. "Candour in English Fiction, III." 2 (1890): 15–21.
Dismissed magazine fiction because it did not foster the novel but merely tales for youthful audiences. The "newspapers read mainly by adults" should print feuilletons in order to overcome "English prudery."

8. Aïdé, Hamilton. "The Deterioration in English Society." 2 (1890): 112–19.
Bewailed readers' curiosity about the personal lives of others even though the "respectable portion of Our Press" did not descend to the level of the American newspaper reader.

9. Bradlaugh, Charles. "The Indian National Congress." 2 (1890): 242–53.
Aside that the former editor of the *Calcutta Review*, H. D. Phillips, was an undersecretary in the Bengal government.

10. "Studies in Character. No. 3: Henry M. Stanley." 2 (1890): 385–98.
Inferred that the *New York Herald* was the ideal employer for Stanley, a "newspaper correspondent" who equated success with scooping others. A man who gave "careful attention to minute details," he was a momentary celebrity before returning to the life of an "ordinary" journalist.

11. Coleridge, [John Duke, 1st Baron]. "Thinking for Ourselves." 3 (1890): 15–28.
Weighed anonymity in journalism. In 1890 statesmen signed their periodical essays and initialed their newspaper columns, assuming that readers knew them by theme or style. The problem was that most magazine and gazette journalists were not statesmen but unknowns with few talents. The press generally used "its enormous power" for good, ending abuse and injustice and stimulating interest in "public affairs." Nonetheless, the average journalist under pressure spun too many opinions. Since people in 1890 read few periodicals, perhaps only the *Review of Reviews*, they failed to challenge half-truths.

Aside that Daniel Defoe was "perhaps the earliest regular newspaper writer."

12. Linton, E[liza] Lynn. "Modern Topsy-Turveydom." 3 (1890): 427–37.
Loathed the "prurient and suggestive" journals that propagated "the New Morality." The "omniscient Able Editors of a few penny papers," men without real learning, dedicated "their minds and souls to the destruction of responsibility." Their only goal was to sell papers by favoring the individual over society. They demeaned the law by promoting "flabby humanitarianism" toward criminals and vandalism by day-trippers in contrast to champions of frail women who were merely "hysterical."

13. Matthews, Brander. "The Whole Duty of Critics." 3 (1890): 455–63.
Set out guidelines for literary critics, among them to review a book honestly, to conceal its denouement, and to avoid the extremes of severity or puffery in which the *Athenaeum*, *Spectator*, and *Saturday Review* specialized. The critic should help the reader understand and enjoy the best literature and should emulate the "model review," exemplified in the *English Historical Review* and *Political Science Quarterly*.

14. Besant, Walter. "The Science of Fiction, II." 4 (1891): 310–15.
Grumbled that short notices of new books in most newspapers did not separate masterpieces from fluff.

15. James, Henry. "The Science of Criticism, I." 4 (1891): 398–402; Andrew Lang, II, 403–08; Edmund Gosse, III, 408–11.
James discounted Anglo-American periodical reviews because they printed an "ocean of talk" to fill space unlike the French, which were more discerning. Lang contrasted eternal criticism from the "ignorant," "careless," and "spiteful" varieties. Gosse accepted the anonymous descriptive reviews that poured from the newspapers if they were fair. Higher criticism should analyze, not judge or carp about minor matters.

16. Grundy, Sydney. "The Science of the Drama, II." 5 (1891): 89–96.
Alerted that a playwright had to please "the Press" to succeed.

17. Lanin, E. B. [E. J. Dillon]. "Jewish Colonisation and the Russian Persecution, II." 5 (1891): 105–17.
Concluded from reading the *Novoe Vremya* that it shared the Russian government's antipathy to a Jewish press.

18. Geffcken, [Friedrich H.]. "Russia under Alexander III." 5 (1891): 234–43
Affirmed that in the Russian Empire "the Press is fettered." Aside on Cracow's *Czas*.

19. Lathrop, George Parsons. "Literature in the United States." 5 (1891): 244–55.
Deplored that in the United States people "maintain in opulence a daily Press which defies propriety and privacy, and revels in filth to an extent not matched by any other Press in the world." The nation lacked a body of criticism and trained readers because this quasi-despotic press closed out nonconformist authors who might irritate audiences.

20. Birrell, Augustine. "Authors and Critics." 6 (1892): 97–105.
Suspected that 'press notices' no longer had as great an impact as word-of-mouth, except harsh criticism that frequently increased a book's sales. Most criticism was "hack-work." Editors directed

reviewers to pen "lively 'copy,'" something suitable for those not planning to read the book but seeking amusement from "an independent, substantive, literary production." Instead of "hasty judgments," critics should learn "principles of taste" from the "immortal dead."

21. Marlborough, [G. C. S. Churchill, 8th Duke]. "The Telephone and the Post Office." 6 (1892): 320–31.

Noticed that the telephone, by speeding transmission of parliamentary speeches from the House to "the printing establishment of the Central News," replaced shorthand writers and telegrams.

22. Mallock, W. H. "Le Style C'Est L'Homme." 6 (1892): 441–54.

Essay on literary style endorsed anonymity in newspapers because a gazette should have a single style.

23. Lilly, W. S. "The Temporal Power of the Pope." 6 (1892): 484–97.

Stamped the *Moniteur de Rome* a "very respectable journal."

24. Stepniak [S. M. Kravchinsky]. "The Dynamite Scare and Anarchy." 6 (1892): 529–41.

Attributed the dynamite scare primarily to "sensational journalism" because interviewers of perpetrators gave them undeserved importance in the eyes of a public of depraved taste.

25. Wingfield, Lewis. "The Drama in the Antipodes." 7 (1892): 217–26.

Declared that in Australia, the "single branch of literature which is strong and healthy is, as may be guessed, the Press since the newspaper is a necessary accessory, in these days, to commerce." Melbourne's "*Argus* would be a credit and an honour to any country."

26. Mackenzie, Morrell. "The Relation of General Culture to Professional Success." 7 (1892): 323–34.

Believed that general cultural knowledge was as essential for success in journalism as in any profession. About 1860 it was "mainly in the hands of semi-literate penny-a-liners" but in 1892 was "largely recruited from the Universities."

27. Copping, Edward. "Douglas Jerrold." 7 (1892): 358–64.

Tracked Jerrold's journalistic career from his early days as a printer's apprentice. He later penned for such "leading magazines" as the *New Monthly* and *Blackwood's* and for "various newspapers," but his greatest acclaim came for his contributions to *Punch*. Envisioning him as a "snarling cynic" was incorrect.

28. Dolman, Frederick. "George Meredith as a Journalist." 8 (1893): 342–48.

Focused on Meredith's years as a journalist, "the late fifties and the early sixties." He penned political columns for a "Tory" newspaper, social and literary ones for the *Morning Post*, and leaders, "mostly on political subjects," as editor of the *Ipswich Journal*. "It is worthy of notice that in his capacity of newspaper editor Mr. Meredith gave to woman and her affairs an attention which thirty years ago was really remarkable in journalism," publishing articles on "the subtle qualities of the sex" and on "fashion."

29. Massingham, H. W. "Press and Parliament." 8 (1893): 527–35.

History of journalists in Parliament opened in 1729 when "the House of Commons passed a resolution to the effect that the reporting of its proceedings constituted a breach of privilege." This motion was reaffirmed in 1738. After their admission, one MP could rid the House of reporters. When they stayed, they were liable to the special jurisdiction of Commons, used to "fine, imprison," and cause "personal degradation," and they sat in quarters that were the "worst allotted to the Press in any civilised country." Although in 1893 only a formal vote of the majority could clear the House, which had "all but abandoned its penal powers against journalists," there still lingered the sense that journalists were intruding on a club. Yet "every member of the Press…is, with his colleagues, the only instrument through which the thing we call public opinion is formed and maintained." Indeed, *The Times* editor was probably "far more powerful" than most MPs. Hence, a press director, not the Sergeant-at-Arms, should "check gross personal misconduct" in the House.

Hinted that political bias was behind assignments in the Press Gallery, for example admitting the *Newcastle Daily Chronicle* but excluding the *Newcastle Leader* and the foreign press. Allocations were absurd: the *Globe* had six tickets, but the *Star*, with treble its circulation, had a single seat. The *Morning Chronicle*, not in the "front rank," and the *Daily Chronicle*, the "authoritative organ of Radicalism," each had nine tickets. The *Manchester Guardian*, "in many senses the best paper in England," had two, but its less competent rival, the *Manchester Chronicle* had three places. The *Liverpool Post*, a paper of "influence and high literary standing," had one, but two went to the *Liverpool Courier*. English and Scottish towns had about the same number of tickets, but the Irish had more.

30. Fullerton, William Morton. "The Significance of the Newspaper in the United States." 8 (1893): 655–64.

Pontificated that "the newspaper in the United States is not a satisfactory production" because it did not represent the best of the nation as the English press did. The American press was "a vital influence" even though it had no paper with the political sway of *The Times*. In days of "political excitement," editors had to determine the mood of a country whose geography deterred "well-considered" discussions of international affairs. The American newspaper focused on news, so it was "black with headlines." "The paper is edited to sell, not as a medium for the results of a budding literary aspiration. In order to sell, it must not be found napping in its great function of collecting news." Therefore, the editor's goal was "to furnish the largest amount of fresh matter daily in the most readable form." Editors ordered reporters "to pluck out the soul of the news and to express it in two or three lines," then headed the material by a "series of graduated types." Interviews and 'story' writing with many paragraphs kept papers lively, but columns "padded to Falstaffian repletion with undigested and often unwholesome verbiage in a style of inimitable bombast" also appeared because campaigns against local abuses sold papers.

In England, the newspaper was only just becoming a "*news*paper" and reaching a large constituency. Proofreading, typography, and style were better in England than the United States, but the Americans were more organized by department. The American press mirrored the "morbid love of excitement in its readers, an artificially exaggerated curiosity, a blatant individuality that knows little respect, an eager and versatile alertness of mind, a peculiar humour, a sensitive and facile temper. Wisdom, sanity, discretion are not its common characteristics. In a word, intellectual ability and dignity of tone are lacking in the newspapers in America," unlike those in Britain. The reason for this inferiority was that American gazettes spoke to a "transiently ignorant majority," not a "minority of brains, culture, refinement." Britain would probably shift to this discourse as the masses asserted themselves.

Reporters in the United States were the most important personnel, so they earned more than leader-writers and critics. American reporters were better than anywhere else because "no profession is more exacting." It required "self-poise, promptness, intelligence...wise and gentlemanly courage." Although Americans had a reputation for "impudence" and "vulgar cleverness," they were "mentally alert, unprejudiced, generous-minded, and with a proper sense of their responsibilities."

31. Stephen, Leslie. "William Cobbett." 9 (1893): 362–72, 482–93.

Concurred with Francis Jeffrey, in the *Edinburgh Review* (10: 386), that "Cobbett has more influence than all other journalists put together." His *Political Register* was "the voice of the English peasant." Cobbett thought that all other journalism was a "mischievous institution." While he was in jail for libel (1810), he continued the *Register* by dictating to his children. When people discovered that he had offered to stop, he denied it. "He was a journalist bound to keep himself before the public eye by assaulting someone, even, it might be, his own old friends or his former self."

32. Z. [A. G. F. Griffiths]. "Anarchists: Their Methods and Organisation, I." 10 (1894): 1–9; Ivanoff, II, 9–16.

Griffiths referred to an unnamed English anarchist paper as "a very dangerous sheet" because it incited crime. Ivanoff insisted that Russian Nihilists published "sensational paragraphs" against the Russian government in the English press. The stories were especially harmful in 1891–92 when they paralleled the "unbridled licence of the Russian revolutionary Press" and *Free Russia*, the gazette circulated by Stepniak (S. M. Kravchinsky) in London. He and his subeditor traveled to the United States and the Continent to collect money and slander. *See* 10: 215.

33. Archer, William. "French Plays and English Money." 10 (1894): 86–94.

Pointed out that many British theatre managers read press reviews before bidding on French plays.

34. [Grove, Archibald]. "*The New Review*." 10 (1894): 127–28.

Inaugurated a new series, differentiating the *New* from other periodicals. British illustrated magazines suited "the requirements of an educated people who are unable to spend large sums of money in the purchase of periodical literature." These serials were cheaper and more popular than those that pondered "more seriously and authoritatively." The "old quarterlies have been in a great way replaced by monthly reviews" because of the ease of postal and rail transmission. Monthlies addressed the educated not satisfied by the "mere interview...personal gossip...ephemeral fiction" but were expensive and often specialized. The *New* pledged to deliberate "great burning questions" in more depth than the dailies and weeklies at a cost less than most quarterlies.

35. Stepniak [S. M. Kravchinsky]. "Nihilism: As It Is (A Reply)." 10 (1894): 215–22.

Replied to 10: 1 that the *Moscow Gazette* discredited the Russian Free Press Publishing Company.

36. Quilter, Harry. "Apologia Pro Arte Meâ: Being a Comment on Some Contemporary Literary Criticism." 10 (1894): 324–36.

Charged that art critics abetted mediocrity by encouraging artists to create what journalists liked or understood, what could 'make copy.' The "gentlemen (and ladies) of the Press" should instead broaden their taste and knowledge.

37. Hawke, John, Hon. Secretary of the National Anti-Gambling League. "Our Principles and Programme." 10 (1894): 705–17.

Blamed the press for the spread of gambling. "The Press is accessory to the evil" by printing for pay the betting odds of horseraces. Since this printing was revenue for the newspapers, legislation to bar this information was essential.

38. Shaw, G[eorge] Bernard. "A Dramatic Realist to His Critics." 11 (1894): 56–73.

Complained that theatre critics knew little of life. London correspondents had a better understanding of the real world than "the hopelessly specialised critics."

39. Escott, T. H. S. "Edmund Yates: An Appreciation and a Retrospect." 11 (1894): 87–97.

Lectured that Charles Dickens, at *Household Words*, taught Yates how to manage a magazine and to satisfy its readers. Later he wrote 'The Flâneur,' "a column of weekly gossip" in the *Morning Star*, and edited *Temple Bar* and his "own newspaper," the *World*, with "substantial success." The *New York Herald* hired him as European correspondent-in-chief, from which post he accrued the capital to start the *World*.

Among Yates' contemporaries was E. C. Grenville-Murray, who penned the second feuilleton in the *World* and was also a pupil of Dickens at *Household Words*. Among colleagues (others named) who gathered at the Savage Club in the late 1860s were: James Macdonell (*Daily Telegraph*), one of the foremost London journalists, who was trained by Alexander Russel, editor of the *Scotsman*; Thornton Hunt, "one of the shrewdest and ablest of newspaper men"; Andrew Halliday, a chief writer for *All the Year Round*; and James Hannay, editor of the *Edinburgh Courant* and active in many areas of the press.

40. Barth, Theodor. "The Three Chancellors." 11 (1894): 557–70.

Noted Otto von Bismarck's previous contacts with the *Kreuz Zeitung*, the organ of the Junkers.

41. Montagu, Irving. "The Experiences of a War-Artist." 11 (1894): 624–36.

Artist explained, with samples from the *Illustrated London News*, how to illustrate a war.

42. Diplomatist. "The Armenian Question." 12 (1895): 62–66.

Reckoned that diplomats and journalists were "natural enemies" with respect to "reserve." Journalists were always seeking information, 'copy.' Searching reference books sometimes led them to incorrect analogies.

43. Clerk, A. "In Praise of Convention." 12 (1895): 260–69.

Listed as one convention, referenced in the title, newspapers' attempts to balance general and specific news, as on sports. Such material was vital to readers who skimmed gazettes to find facts, not to exercise their minds.

44. Street, G. S. "The Theatre in London." 12 (1895): 558–69.

Fussed that theatre critics were too specialized, each favoring a particular theme or the "modern" in plays. *See* 12: 654.

45. Runciman, John F. "The Gentle Art of Musical Criticism." 12 (1895): 612–24.
Drew from Sidney Thomson's talk, sponsored by the Society of Women Journalists, ideas about journalistic musical criticism. The 'old critics' and the "new" had much in common. The earlier generation, at the *Daily Telegraph* and elsewhere, was inaccurate or addicted to stale phrases. The new men, from the *Standard* to the *Musical Times*, were not much better. They had neither knowledge nor literary skill as their hasty pieces indicated.

46. Archer, William. "The Criticism of Acting." 12 (1895): 654–64.
Supported 12: 558 with evidence that theatre newspaper critics in 1895 relied on stock phrases in contrast to Leigh Hunt and William Hazlitt.

47. Phillipps, Evelyn March. "The New Journalism." 13 (1895): 182–89.
Defined "New Journalism" as "that easy personal style, that trick of bright colloquial language, that wealth of picturesque and intimate detail, and that determination to arrest, amuse, or startle, which has transformed our Press during the last fifteen years." The result was easier reading with a range of prices and interests.

The interview, once justified for its insight into a person or to supplement information, was in 1895 trivial and sensational, having drifted from "intelligent curiosity" to "impertinent, prying curiosity." Society papers badgered, but personal descriptions elsewhere were insulting, even "cruel and vile."

Ladies' pages stressed fashion, not the "low tone taken of what is known as the Woman's Movement by most existing journals." Some criticism of these pages was appropriate because they did not have writers who gave "a fair share of intelligent attention to the doings of women."

In order to satisfy the "craze for novelty and excitement," however, "journalists have created a monster who tyrannises the Press, and forces them to slave and strain against each other, and to have recourse to unworthy methods." Too many journalists hated work in which they took no pride because it stifled originality. Bad journalists needed better training; good wanted better editors. The press had power but no conviction. To resume its station, it must cease to "prey upon and pander to the more paltry side of human nature."

48. Morris, Martin. "American Traits." 13 (1895): 296–303, 434–42.
Denigrated American journalism, the consequence of the "openness of life," as "totally wanting in taste, either literary, social, or moral." Many journalists were "scandal-scavengers" who spied on people. Stories replete with slang and vulgarity unearthed the "lowest practices of mankind" while conferring notoriety cheaply.

49. Watt, Francis. "New Scotland." 13 (1895): 640–50.
Proclaimed that Scottish newspapers, with their penchant for "new ideas," shaped the "easier manners and wider views" of the decade. The *Glasgow Herald* and *Dundee Advertiser* were "extremely liberal." Only the *Scotsman*, with its "great ability and ample means," was a paper for "the best educated."

50. Steevens, G[eorge]W[arrington]. "The Indiscretion of the Kaiser." 14 (1896): 176–84.
Relayed that the German press knew what it could and could not print.

51. Harris, F. Rutherfoord. "The Fate of South Africa." 14 (1896): 331–48.
Thumbed through *Ons Land*, "the leading Dutch newspaper of the Cape Colony," the *Cape Times*, *Johannesburg Critic*, and Pretoria's *Land en Volk*.

52. Leonard, Charles. "The Case for the Uitlanders." 14 (1896): 454–72.
Purported Uitlander opposed the proposed Press Law, which was contra to the 1881 Constitution, and official subsidies for pro-government journals that were unpopular. Aside that *Volkstem* was a newspaper subsidized by "a group of Amsterdam financiers and politicians."

53. Whibley, Charles. "Edgar Allan Poe." 14 (1896): 612–25.
Bowed to Poe's journalism, especially his criticism that was "the terror of the incompetent."

54. Fitzmaurice-Kelly, James. "The Cuban Question." 15 (1896): 144–53.
Aside on American "journalistic fire-eaters."

55. C. de Thierry ("Colonial") [Mrs. J. Weston Campbell]. "England and Her Colonies." 16 (1897): 436–52.
Rued that journalists no longer acquainted readers with imperial geography and resources but misrepresented territories.

56. Roylance-Kent, C. B. "The Literature of Anarchism." 17 (1897): 281–90.
Underscored that anarchist literature was primarily journalism, although most serials were short-lived and penned by volunteers. Peter Kropotkin's *Révolte* appeared initially in Geneva, then Paris. Jean Grave reputedly brought it the "literary merit" that made it successful, i.e., 8,000 subscribers. *Père Peinard*, launched in 1888, exceeded this circulation by 500 under the direction of Emile Pouget, "a vigorous writer" who injected emotionalism but nothing like the extremism of the *International*.

57. Dalgleish, John. "The Bounder in Literature." 17 (1897): 409–17.
Critique of Richard Le Gallienne's *The Quest of the Golden Girl* disdained critics, especially in the dailies, for their banal language.

58. Fisher, W. E. Garrett. "Letters of Genius: A Human Document from the Waste Paper Basket." 17 (1897): 469–84.
Satirized an alleged correspondence between a subeditor of the *Liverpool Guardian* and a potential columnist.

59. Steevens, G[eorge] W[arrington]. "The Monotype." 17 (1897): 564–70.
Flagged the effect on journalism of the Langston Monotype Machine.

60. Millar, J. H. "William Blackwood and His Men." 17 (1897): 646–56.
Review of Margaret Oliphant's *Annals of a Publishing House* agreed that William Blackwood combined "the turn for business with a genuine feeling for literature," which made *Blackwood's Magazine* "a conspicuous example of brilliant journalism." "Everybody, apparently, was ready to write for *Maga*...which evoked in her contributors...a feeling of proud and devoted attachment." Among the regulars was J. G. Lockhart, dedicated to its interests because it published his first articles even though they contained errors and "lacked taste." He later earned 2,500 pounds per year as editor of the *Quarterly Review*.

The Nineteenth Century, 1877–1900

The *Nineteenth Century* of James T. Knowles, once of the *Contemporary Review*, was an agora for deliberative citizens. Among its highlights were studies of French, German, Turkish, Egyptian, and American journalism.

1. Grant Duff, M. E. "Russia." 1 (1877): 72–96, 298–314.
Aside on Michael Katkoff, editor of the Moscow Gazette.

2. Ralston, W. R. S. "Russian Revolutionary Literature." 1 (1877): 397–416.
Alluded to the *Polar Star*, *Kolokol*, which first circulated in manuscript, and St. Petersburg's *Vyestnik Evropy*, "one of the best periodicals of which any country can boast."

3. Spedding, James. "Teaching to Read." 1 (1877): 637–45.
Assured that in the *Phonetic News* "all the proper names were carefully spelt."

4. Greg, W. R. "Harriet Martineau." 2 (1877): 97–112.
Stated that Martineau the journalist never wrote for fame or wealth and never reconsidered her opinions.

5. Vogel, Julius. "Cheap Telegrams." 2 (1877): 783–95.
Coupled telegraphic information in the press and education of the public. Cheap telegraphy delivered to local gazettes British political speeches and foreign news, which the "chief newspapers" and Reuter's collected at "vast expense."

6. Arnold, Matthew. "A Guide to English Literature." 2 (1877): 843–53.
Review of Stopford Brooke's *Primer of English Literature* mentioned *The Times*, *Morning Chronicle*, *Morning Post*, *Morning Herald*, *Edinburgh Review*, *Quarterly Review*, and *Blackwood's Magazine*.

7. Chesney, George Tomkyns. "The Value of India to England." 3 (1878): 227–38.
Snapped that educated Indians who could not secure government jobs published "seditious newspapers…which the Government tolerates with scornful yet lazy indifference."

8. Chesney, George Tomkyns. "Russia and India." 3 (1878): 605–16.
Alerted that Indian courts learned information and the value of gossip from British newspapers.

9. Rae, W. Fraser. "Political Clubs and Party Organization." 3 (1878): 908–32.
Catalogued by name political dailies and weeklies of all stripes available at the Westminster, a Liberal club, in 1834.

10. Wedderburn, David. "Protected Princes in India." 4 (1878): 151–73.
Applauded *Native Opinion*, "a newspaper published in English and Marathi" that was an example of "intelligent and vigorous criticism" in the Indian press.

11. Montefiore, Leonard A. "Liberty in Germany." 4 (1878): 222–39, 735–51; 5 (1879): 264–84.
Guessed that *Nemesis* was widely read in 1816 when the *Rheinische Merkur* was the voice of republicans. In 1820 other German political papers were the *Allgemeine Zeitung* and Wurtemberg's *Deutscher Beobacter*, both suppressed by Clemens von Metternich. In 1830, Germans who attributed the July Revolution in France to journalists established the Society for the Promotion of a Free Press. George Büchner thereafter commenced the *Journal of the People* in Hesse. The press policies of Otto von Bismarck aped the Carlsbad Decrees.

12. Wilson, Edward. D.J. "The 'Friends of the Foreigner' Seventy Years Ago." 4 (1878): 327–46.
Commented on the influence of the *Edinburgh Review* and *Moniteur* in the age of Napoleon I.

13. Tyrwhitt, R. S[t. J.]. "The Limits of Modern Art-Criticism." 4 (1878): 512–16.
Counseled newspapers to avoid scandal, which "turns epigram into libel" by including intimate information.

14. Traill, H. D. "The Democracy and Foreign Policy." 4 (1878): 910–24.
Postulated that newspapers no longer formed opinion but still organized it. In 1878 they covered domestic news satisfactorily, but not foreign news because government limited international releases.

15. Trollope, Anthony. "Novel-Reading." 5 (1879): 24–43.
Confessed that novels, like magazines and theatre, occasionally achieved "a temporary success" from "scurrility and lasciviousness."

16. Blennerhassett, Charlotte. "Felix Antoine Dupanloup, Bishop of Orleans." 5 (1879): 219–46.
Summarized many French religious serials, among them the *Univers* and *Avenir*.

17. Hunt, W. Holman. "Artistic Copyright." 5 (1879): 418–24.
Bemoaned "flippant" newspaper stories on copyright protection for engravings and photographs.

18. Payn, James. "The Critic on the Hearth." 5 (1879): 1003–12.
Swore that 1879 critics, "at least in the higher literary organs," were more honest, less prejudiced, and less controlled by their publishers than their predecessors. Too many of the current crop were novices, but a good review was nonetheless a wonderful advertisement for a book.

19. Arnold, Matthew. "The French Play in London." 6 (1879): 228–43.
Saluted *The Times*, *Daily News*, and *Pall Mall Gazette* for their "interesting" and "good" theatre criticism in depth.

20. Montefiore, Leonard A. "Alsace-Lorraine since 1871." 6 (1879): 819–31.
Nodded to the *Journal d'Alsace.*

21. Payn, James. "The Literary Calling and Its Future." 6 (1879): 985–98.
Classified journalism in magazines and London and local newspapers as a "literary calling." Journalists were adequate, low-paid writers, who could be better if they were more broadly educated and trained in style rather than "largely recruited from failures in other professions." Aside that magazines in 1879 were stuffed with travel and newspapers, with fiction.

22. Cunliffe-Owen, Fritz. "Russian Nihilism." 7 (1880): 1–26.
Examined *Kolokol*, edited by Alexander Herzen, and the "Nihilist" paper, *Will of the People*, printed on "secret presses." This herald hinted that other Russian journals curried favor with government by condemning Nihilism.

23. [Canning], Stratford, [1st Viscount Stratford] de Redcliffe. "George Canning: His Character and Motives." 7 (1880): 27–42.
Labeled George Canning's work in the *Anti-Jacobin* "entirely ludicrous and satirical."

24. Forbes, Archibald. "War Correspondents and the Authorities." 7 (1880): 185–96.
War correspondent contended that this reporting, a noble and patriotic "craft" since Crimea, remained open until after the Afghan campaign but then was subject to regulations (reprinted here). These rules, introduced in India, met "with contemptuous derision" because they effectively excluded the reporter from the army in the field. Fans were certain that regulation would prevent an enemy from getting information and the army and readers from becoming disgruntled. Opponents thought a free press enabled readers to learn the truth, but an enemy did not usually peruse the British press, although Cetshwayo allegedly read the *Natal Witness*, and journalists could not undermine a competent military. The Germans maintained press freedom during the Franco-Prussian War, instead counting on control of field telegraphy and journalists' ignorance as restraints. The Russians employed a press officer to limit the news in the Russo-Turkish War. *See* 7: 434.

25. Payn, James. "Sham Admiration in Literature." 7 (1880): 422–33.
Mused about literary critics in Leigh Hunt's *Indicator* and elsewhere who told readers what was important.

26. Melgund, [Viscount, G. J. M. K. Elliot, 4th Earl Minto]. "Newspaper Correspondents in the Field." 7 (1880): 434–42.
Replied to 7: 185 that newspapers took the regulations on war correspondence as "a personal insult to the press," but they were necessary. Reporters were heretofore "guests" whose copy came from what they saw or heard in the camps. The public overvalued such news, accepting the correspondent as a "capable critic" of the army. Forbes was correct about the hazards of freedom, of which there were two others, the undocumented "parading" of certain officers for public admiration and "sensational writing." The English press, unlike that of many countries, had "great power" over the public mind, so it could not afford to indulge journalists. Signature would lessen the authority of war correspondents.

27. Mackay, Charles. "Burns and Béranger.´7 (1880): 464–85.
Judged the *Lounger*, edited by John Moore, "the last of the periodicals modeled on the style and plan of [Joseph] Addison and [Richard] Steele in the *Tatler* and *Spectator*" and P. J. de Béranger's work appropriate for the *Journal pour Rire* or *Charivari* but too erotic for most British readers.

28. Holyoake, George Jacob. "A Stranger in America." 8 (1880): 67–87.
Lectured that American readers were not as upset as British audiences when newspapers did not display "integrity" and that interviewing was "the most amusing and useful institution conceivable." "There is no appointment on the press to be more coveted than that of being an interviewer to a great journal" even though the "art of interviewing" was not yet fully developed. Giuseppe Mazzini and George W. Smalley, London correspondent of the *New York Tribune*, were paradigms of this "art."

29. [Liu, Ta-Jên]. "Diary of Liu Ta-Jên's Mission to England." Trans. F. S. A. Bourne. 8 (1880): 612–21.
Chinese visitor in 1876 delineated *The Times* printing operations and their costs.

30. Hyndman, H. M. "The Dawn of a Revolutionary Epoch." 9 (1881): 1–18.
Supported French press freedom for political analysis but not for inciting the masses, which cheap newspapers born in 1848 exemplified.

31. Payn, James. "Penny Fiction." 9 (1881): 145–54.
Explored fiction in two forms in cheap serials, tales and "Answers to Correspondents" dreamed up by some editors to fill space. Discounted the prediction of Wilkie Collins (*Household Words* 18: 217) that the public would eventually learn "in this age of periodicals" what was or was not good literature. Local penny heralds hired "eminent novel writers," but the masses eschewed most newspapers. Penny periodicals, the likely choice of "female domestic servants" though sellers were no guide, showed no improvement. *See* 13: 279.

32. Simcox, Edith. "George Eliot." 9 (1881): 778–801.
Glimpsed Eliot's critical essays in the *Westminster Review* and *Fortnightly Review.*

33. Adler, Hermann. "Recent Phases of Judaeophobia." 10 (1881): 813–29.
Categorized Russian journalists as anti-Semites. *See* 12: 687.

34. Blind, Karl. "The Conflict in Germany." 11 (1882): 254–74.
Disclosed that the weekly Literary Gazette in the *Vossiche Zeitung* "exerts much influence among the cultured classes," but the paper flip-flopped on politics.

35. Arnold, Matthew. "A Word about America." 11 (1882): 680–96.
Ranked New York's *Nation* the best American newspaper. *See* 17: 219.

36. Holyoake, George Jacob. "Theory of Political Epithets." 12 (1882): 84–97.
Recalled working for a "militant editor" of a journal who thought libel would attract readers.

37. Godkin, E. L. "An American View of Ireland." 12 (1882): 175–92.
Bruited that American perceptions of Ireland, 1840–80, came not from Irish serials but from *Punch* engravings.

38. Reinach, Joseph. "Parisian Newspapers." 12 (1882): 347–60.
Scrutinized the politics, styles, and staffs of numerous Paris papers. Contrasted English and French newspapers, the latter's "licence" rooted in its liberty. "In England, journalism is a profession; in France every one has been, is, or will be, a journalist." The English press was informative; the French, "appreciative." English journalism was "generally earnest and serious"; French, "light and rather frivolous." Gallic papers were typically smaller than British because there was little advertising. It was in separate gazettes, such as the *Petites Affiches* and *Journal des Gens de Maison*. French papers also had few leaders and less official and foreign news than English gazettes. "Emile de Girardin was the founder of the cheap French press." The poor paper of new cheap publications, led by the *Petit Journal*, did not halt their rise in circulation. However, people readily paid 20 centimes, 25 in the provinces for the *Journal des Débats*.

39. Smith, Goldwin. "The Jews: A Deferred Rejoinder." 12 (1882): 687–709.
Retorted to 10: 813 that the press was "the great benefactor and the great peril of society" depending on who controlled it. Newspapers and "agencies for the transmission of intelligence" in many countries were "becoming Jewish," a fact hidden because Jewish journalists assumed Christian names.

40. Wright, Thomas. "Concerning the Unknown Public." 13 (1883): 279–96.
Compared the penny novel serials of the 1850s and 1880s. In the 1850s, fine writers educated the "Penny public" in two-penny weeklies. In the 1880s, education was available in venues other than the cheap serial. Its readers were lower middle-class girls who devoured the fiction and probably the music. Men only read the jokes or answers to letters. *See* 9: 145 and *Household Words* 18: 217.

41. Reinach, Joseph. "The Unmounted Bucephalus." 13 (1883): 338–56.
Explicated how the French press affected politics.

42. McKenzie, John. "England and South Africa." 13 (1883): 700–28.
Tabulated that Cape Colony had 50 newspapers, the first in 1824; Natal had six or seven; the Orange Free State had two; and the Transvaal had one or two.

43. Traill, H. D. "The Politics of Literature: A Dialogue." 14 (1883): 610–21.
Equated journalists and barristers insofar as both advocated the positions of those who hired them.

44. Taylor, Henry. "An Academy of Literature for Great Britain." 14 (1883): 779–93.
Vilified biased, untalented, and ignorant literary critics. These journalists, scarcely qualified to pen "ephemeral books," used their columns to puff their own works.

45. Brodrick, George C. "The Progress of Democracy in England." 14 (1883): 907–24.
Announced that newspapers, whether shaping or reflecting opinion, "created a healthy community of political ideas between the people and the so-called governing classes." Leader-writers respected the political judgment of even the humblest voter.

46. Parkes, Henry. "Our Growing Australian Empire." 15 (1884): 138–49.
Blared that Australian colonists read not only local papers but more English newspapers and reviews than British audiences.

47. Rossiter, William. "The Continental Sunday." 15 (1884): 933–44.
Synopsized the international press. Denmark had many readers; St. Petersburg had 12 tribunes in a country where the population was largely poor and illiterate; Bucharest had 12 newspapers; Patras' poor did read; Constantinople had a variety of heralds; Teheran had three papers, but the poor could not afford any; Boston, San Francisco, and Baltimore had many "widely-read" gazettes; New York, where even the poor read extensively, had 32 dailies, 14 biweeklies, and 200 weeklies as well as other periodicals; New Orleans had six newspapers, all of a "poorer tone" and none perused by the masses.

48. Norton, [C. B. Adderley], 1st Baron. "Imperial Federation: Its Impossibility." 16 (1884): 505–16.
Foe of federation asserted that the British Empire already had a "great council," the press, which allowed "free, full, and constant interchange."

49. Rae, W. Fraser. "The Centenary of *The Times*." 17 (1885): 43–65.
Paean to *The Times* abridged its founding, early contents, and the roles of John Walter I and II. Its success was "not rapid," but its circulation of 4,000 in 1800 was relatively large for a daily even though the *Morning Post* reached 7,000 with S. T. Coleridge on staff. The younger Walter sent special correspondents abroad, first commissioning Henry Crabb Robinson. Walter II also dealt with the 1810 pressmen's strike and inaugurated the König press, replaced by the Applegarth, then the Hoe and the Walter. Shifting technology, whether in printing or telegraphy, showed *The Times* was ready to spend money on news. Competitors had niche readerships based on style or politics, but *The Times* reached everybody. People bought it, paid a vendor a weekly rate to read it daily for an hour, passed it amongst the family, or mailed it. Some other gazettes were very good, but *The Times* was a unique symbol of British civilization and John Delane was its most outstanding editor.

50. Arnold, Matthew. "A Word More about America." 17 (1885): 219–36.
Purported supplement to 11: 680 affirmed that British journalism was as influential as Parliament, notably when journalists, as John Morley, had a foot in each arena.

51. Archer, William. "The Duties of Dramatic Critics." 17 (1885): 249–62.
Nominated the "dramatic critic of an influential daily paper" as holding one of the most "responsible" offices in literature because the almost instantaneous review affected sales and reputations. Theatre critics should be objective and catholic. Initial columns written under pressure should merely report; later ones should evaluate a production. Critics were different from the "theatrical paragraphist" who collected news and gossip. Exemplars of their different roles were Auguste Vitu, the "serious and able" critic of *Figaro*, and Arnold Mortier, the paper's drama gossipmonger.

52. Acton, [J. D.]. "George Eliot's *Life*." 17 (1885): 464–85.
Review of *George Eliot's Life as Related in Her Letters and Journals*, edited by J. W. Cross, cited her work for the *Westminster Review*.

53. Kropotkin, P[eter]. "Finland: A Rising Nationality." 17 (1885): 527–46.
Heralded that the Russians suppressed the eighteenth-century Finnish press but since 1863 tolerated the rise of many cheap and widely read papers if they did not criticize the government or print in Russian.

54. Goldsmith, Isidor. "Why I Left Russia." 17 (1885): 883–904.
Limned the problems of publishing a periodical, *Znanie*, in the face of censorship and an underground press. Since *Znanie*, a review, published articles from contributors outside Russia, officials watched it closely. After they censured *Molva*, a Liberal paper started by a rich landowner and suspected of having a subversive staff, Goldsmith bought it. He then ended both serials, replacing them with *Slovo*, "a large review" that he opened to "young men of talent" and left Russia when the government suppressed it.

55. Smith, G[eorge] Barnett. "James Russell Lowell." 17 (1885): 988–1008.
Peeked at Lowell's editing of the *North American Review*.

56. Godkin, E. L. "An American View of Popular Government." 19 (1886): 177–90.
Speculated that American newspapers "prevent mental stagnation" and parochialism because they were so widespread.

57. Gaskell, Charles Milnes. "William Cobbett." 19 (1886): 238–56.
Narrated how Cobbett furthered his sociopolitical agenda in a *Political Register* with average sales of 75,000–100,000 weekly.

58. Jordan, J. N. "Modern China." 20 (1886): 40–50.
Anointed China's *Peking Gazette*, in existence for 800 years, as the oldest newspaper. This official paper contained announcements, decrees, and some foreign information. Another significant Chinese gazette was the *Shenpao*. An Englishman published one of the two papers in Shanghai with the aid of correspondents throughout the Empire. This sheet, in its tenth year, was able to "stir up the inert mass of Chinese indifference."

59. Katscher, Leopold. "Taine: A Literary Portrait." 20 (1886): 51–73.
Bowed to H. Taine's "literary and biographical essays" in the *Revue des Deux Mondes*, *Journal des Débats*, and *Revue de l'Instruction Publique*.

60. Salmon, Edward G. "What the Working Classes Read." 20 (1886): 108–17.
Intoned that once the paper duty was gone the Chambers' family and other publishers used the press to educate workers and improve their condition by calling attention to abuses that affected them. Enfranchisement made workers the "spoilt child of the press." In 1886 many newspapers and magazines addressed them, and London dailies published letters and articles by them. Workers perused morning and evening papers in their clubs, pubs, eating-houses, coffeehouses, and work-places, where employees pooled the cost of a subscription. They scanned the advertisements carefully and skimmed the rest but bought Sunday heralds. *Lloyd's Weekly Newspaper* sold 750,000 per week but was not "amusing." The *Weekly Dispatch* was fairer than *Reynolds's Newspaper* about upper class privileges. The *Penny Illustrated Paper* was popular for its satire and sports as were local gazettes.

Workers also liked the religious press, such as *Leisure Hour* and *Sunday at Home*, as well as others replete with scraps of information. The *London Journal*'s "Penny novelette," by 1886 the "veriest trash," and its worsening illustrations did not slow sales. *All the Year Round* and *Chambers's Journal*, once in many homes of the lower middle and working classes, were declining because of price. Workers opted for *Ally Sloper's Half Holiday* for fun.

Most periodicals for workers were inferior because journalists wrote down to their audiences instead of improving them, but these serials were less "vulgar, sensuous, and unwholesome" than their peers in Paris and New York. Women read serials with fiction; men chose those with crime.

61. Reid, Arnot. "How a Provincial Paper is Managed." 20 (1886): 391–402.
Presumed that the country press had a larger readership than the metro because locals carried neighborhood news and advertising as well as details on Parliament, commerce and shipping, and sports. Workers typically looked at only one newspaper, the halfpenny evening.

Big gazettes outside the capital rented two post office telegraph wires (6 p.m. – 6 a.m.) for 1,000 pounds. They paid 4,000 pounds in expenses to a corps of local reporters and 1,000 pounds to a London correspondent. Many had reporters in Paris and New York but depended on Reuters for foreign news and formed syndicates to cover a war. Specialists in editorial rooms with telegraphic access to Parliament should compose the leader, which was "not an essay, but a statement, an explanation, and a criticism of current facts." Editors should pay two guineas for each of the three leaders required daily (about 2,000 pounds annually) to attract "capable" people with brains and "industry," such as lawyers, professors, and clerics. Anonymity abetted irresponsibility, dangerous because journalism had influence even when it merely broadcast the news.

Analyzed the contents of *The Times*, *Standard*, *Daily Telegraph*, *Scotsman*, and *Scottish News*.

62. Salmon, Edward G. "What Girls Read." 20 (1886): 515–29.
Spotlighted only two sheets, the *Girl's Own Paper* and *Every Girl's Magazine*, because girls preferred to read trash or the *Boy's Own Paper*. *Every Girl's Magazine* was "healthy in tone" but very general. The *Girl's Own Paper* was more popular because of its prize competitions.

63. Gregory, W. H. "Loyalty of the Indian Mohammedans." 20 (1886): 886–900.
Estimated that there were more Hindu than Muslim papers in India.

64. Smalley, G[eorge] W. "Notes on New York." 21 (1887): 206–26.
Spoke about the architecture of newspaper buildings in New York, where Irish influence on the press was supposedly akin to that of Jews in Europe. The first was by the pen; the second was by money. *See* 22: 285.

65. Rossiter, William. "Artisan Atheism." 21 (1887): 262–72.
Indexed workers' preferences in reading journalism.

66. Reinach, Joseph. "The True Position of French Politics." 21 (1887): 340–50.
Indicated that Paris had at least six "conscientiously edited newspapers," but few Londoners read them. Most Britons got their news of France from *Figaro*, a "charming, exciting" journal of "gossip."

67. Reid, Arnot. "Twenty-Four Hours in a Newspaper Office." 21 (1887): 452–59.
Centered on the production, hour-by-hour, of a morning daily. The manager dealt with the publisher, advertisers, typesetting, and all other business. The editor had an assistant to coordinate leaders and other opinion pieces by people not journalists. The hardworking subeditor, with a "ready brain,"

handled news. The chief reporter supervised a staff of four to 12 people. The pressures of time and extra work could interrupt this rhythm.

Aside that journalism was a "calling" without regulations or an apprenticeship, so it was open to all.

68. Arnold, Matthew. "Up to Easter." 21 (1887): 629–43.
Noted that the "new journalism" was "full of ability, novelty, variety, sensation, sympathy, generous instincts: its one great fault is that it is *feather*-brained." It spouted assertions and confessed no errors.

69. Otway, Arthur. "Fallacies of the French Press." 21 (1887): 719–25.
Observed that the *Temps* was "one of the ablest and most respectable of the French newspapers," but the *Petit Journal* had the largest circulation. The French did not spend enough to maintain competent reporters around the world, so newspapers substituted style for knowledge, although John Lemoinne of *Figaro* was an exception.

70. Gladstone, Herbert J. "A First Visit to India." 22 (1887): 133–48.
Commended Indian journals for their political moderation, whereas the Anglo-Indian press had a style similar to the "low partisan papers" in England. Although India had many newspapers, it needed an official one to correct the inaccuracies of the others.

71. Reid, Arnot. "The English and the American Press." 22 (1887): 219–33.
Essay on British newspapers for a week in April 1886 and American, in March 1887 guaranteed that the newspaper in both countries was the chief reading, "the creature and the creator of national character."

The United States had 11,000 newspapers and periodicals; the British had 4,000 publications, from newspapers to annuals. The American and British local papers contained two pages of regional news and two pages of advertising and light reading. Cities in the United States had a newsy and humorous Sunday press. Also active were ethnic gazettes. No American paper had the influence of *The Times* even though Americans had a wide interest in the news. Americans could copy much of it from the British because of the time difference. American papers had more pages on Europe than the British had on the United States. American newspapers were less intellectual and literary than British. "The English newspaper tries to be dignified; the American tries to be smart" with "short paragraphs interspersed with portraits, and sensational head-lines." Good print and paper balanced small type.

Unlike British editors, Americans began as reporters. The American editor was a businessman; the British, a "man of letters." Hence American editorials were not "literary essays on impersonal subjects" but "short, light, and pithy," often personal and humorous columns, as those in the *Cincinnati Enquirer*, *Louisville Commercial*, *Boston Herald*, and *Chicago Tribune*. New York's *Sun* would be one of the best if not "disfigured by 'bunkum.'"

"The English press belongs to the leader-writers, and the American to the reporters." The Americans were better at finding news that sold papers, so they were better paid. Reporters penned "bright, racy, trivial" pieces, whereas the unoriginal British depended too much on shorthand.

72. Godkin, E. L. "American Opinion on the Irish Question." 22 (1887): 285–92.
Contradicted 21: 206. Most New York newspapers did not have Irish editors or leader-writers. Although there were many Irish reporters, their numbers were down from the 1840s as other Americans entered journalism.

73. Salmon, Edward. "Literature for the Little Ones." 22 (1887): 563–80.
Probed some of the "now overwhelming supply of really good children's magazines" (several listed) and traced the genre's evolution from the *Children's Magazine* (1799), the 1830s *Juvenile Forget-Me-Not* edited by Anna M. Hall, *Aunt Judy's Magazine* edited by Margaret Gatty, and *Chatterbox* (1866) to *Little Wide-Awake* (1875) of Lucy Sale Barker. *Little Folks* was one of the few British magazines that matched, in "beauty and general merit," the American *St. Nicholas* and *Harper's Young People*.

74. Gosse, Edmund. "The French Society of Authors." 22 (1887): 844–49.
Celebrated the half century of the Société des Gens de Lettres established by the "energetic and untiring journalist, Louis Desnoyers." He was the owner and editor of a "sort of society-journal," the *Sylphe*, in the 1820s, but it, like his *Aigle*, was confiscated. He next introduced *Charivari*. Desnoyers was always interested in protecting Paris editors and writers from pirating by the provincial press. The Société addressed this issue but allowed journalists to settle their disputes privately.

75. Acland, Emily A. "A Lady's American Notes." 23 (1888): 403–13.
Revealed that most Americans did not approve of the "tone" of their newspapers but appropriated journalistic opinion.

76. Arnold, Matthew. "Civilisation in the United States." 23 (1888): 481–96.
Averred that every nation had the newspapers it deserved. Although the United States had many valuable heralds, most contravened American notions of being elect and civilized people. Newspapers where news was gossip did not elevate readers. "The absence of truth and soberness in them, the poverty in serious interest, the personality and sensation mongering, are beyond belief." Americans denied that their press was "a scandal"; they considered it "one of their most signal distinctions," but most British country sheets were better than any of the American press. An exception was New York's weekly *Nation*, akin to the *Saturday Review* at its peak, but it was "conducted by a foreigner" and had few buyers.

77. Rothschild, Ferdinand. "Century for Century." 23 (1888): 589–602.
Concentrated on famous contributors to the *Revue des Deux Mondes* (established by François Buloz in 1830), which had "undisputed supremacy in French periodical literature."

78. Stanley, Maude. "Clubs for Working Girls." 25 (1889): 73–83.
Recognized the power of newspapers to disseminate any idea.

79. Gladstone, W[illiam] E. "Italy in 1888–89." 25 (1889): 763–80.
Acknowledged that every journalist had some sway and that associations of journalists protected press freedom, "a note of constitutional liberty alike indispensable and invaluable."

80. Knight, William. "Criticism as a Trade." 26 (1889): 423–30.
Articulated that the press served society well but sometimes published uninformed or biased articles on politics and literature. Leader-writers who perverted political ideas and literary reviewers who penned in ignorance and haste were equally dangerous. Critics who exposed an author's weaknesses might spur improvement but should differentiate between quality and fad and avoid cruelty. *See* 26: 833.

81. Church, Alfred J. "Criticism as a Trade: A Reply." 26 (1889): 833–39.
Respondent to 26: 423 claimed to have reviewed thousands of volumes. Most reviewers read the book, if only to prevent being exposed as frauds. Their work did not require expertise but had to be descriptive. Their chief flaw in 1889 was not "slashing" but flattering.

82. Stutfield, G. Herbert. "Modern Gambling and Gambling Laws." 26 (1889): 840–60.
Chastised the press for facilitating gambling. The burgeoning racing papers accepted advertisements by "touts and tipsters." The dailies' telegrams updated odds, and "sporting correspondents" often "hopelessly wrong" called winners.

83. Bamberger, L[udwig]. "The German Daily Press." 27 (1890): 24–37.
Hypothesized that nations in 1890 talked more through their newspapers than their diplomats, making the press a part of government and conferring on it influence at home "from value set on it abroad." German dailies were blossoming. Towns of 1,000–500 often had two heralds of the scissors variety. Unlike the French, the Germans read only one daily, so leaders were very important and German news increasingly so. Berlin had no great influence because the German press was regional. In fact, the largest circulating organ in Germany was Vienna's *Neue Freie Presse*.

The press was historically a strong weapon for government because of censorship. Yet "learned journalism" flourished from 1815 to 1866, excepting 1848, thanks to its "superior class of readers," as those of the *Allgemeine Zeitung*. In 1890 the journals were either partisan with a "peevish spirit" or independent with a caution characteristic of the Second French Empire. Only the "semi-official" organs had real liberty, but it was not appropriate to discuss complaints about them outside Germany. Whatever corruption existed was less than in other countries.

84. Mackay, Charles. "The Ascertainment of English." 27 (1890): 131–44.
Admonished the "multitudinous writers of our too prolific journalism," among others, for debasing English.

85. Blackburn, Henry. "The Illustration of Books and Newspapers." 27 (1890): 213-24.
Registered that London illustrated papers, with 30–40 pictures daily, generated many jobs for artists. These papers' chief concern was to keep pictures simple and accurate. In 1873 a Canadian company started New York's evening *Daily Graphic*. Around 1875, the city's *Tribune* had illustrations that outweighed any descriptive language in a British organ, which was typically supplemented only by maps. The press knew the technique for telegraphing pictures but was slow to employ it. Reporters should send sketches with their columns.

86. Greenwood, Frederick. "The Newspaper Press." 27 (1890): 833–42.
Exclaimed that in 1890 newspapers and their readers were generally rising "at a prodigious rate." In 1840 the kingdom had 12 dailies; in 1890 there were 180 of a total of 2,220 published (of which 470 were in London). London morning papers were strong, evening were selling 300,000 per day, and cheap weeklies sprouted in the neighborhoods. Country tribunes, also multiplying, were no competition. The capital had the best press in the world, except for style where the French and Germans excelled.

Government still gleaned public opinion from the press, but it did not have the political influence of mid-century. The "stump" competed with journalism, social issues were less confused in 1890, legions of publications reduced authority, and journalists did not match the caliber of the "great," as James Perry of the *Morning Chronicle*, John Delane of *The Times*, and Alexander Russel of the *Scotsman*. Compulsory education should revivify press political power, but for the moment newspapers featured the gossip that readers demanded and that discouraged quality writing even as signed articles were popular.

87. Greenwood, Frederick. "The Press and Government." 28 (1890): 108–18.
Worried that the press was a "rival influence to government" rather than fulfilling its mission to critique officials. However, more newspapers meant less influence for each, and able politicians refused to patronize journalism. Gazettes should eschew partisanship. Inside information was useful, but major papers could get their news elsewhere. Such a course would allow them to maintain the independence essential for cachet with the public.

Aside that journalism was not a profession but rather an occupation of those with "quick perceptions."

88. Wilde, Oscar. "The True Function of Criticism." 29 (1891): 123–47, 435–59.
Premised that periodical criticism was as valueless as the literature and art it judged. Critics of the "higher class," those who wrote for "sixpenny papers," might be more cultured than the authors they reviewed but were merely "reporters of the police-court of literature, the chroniclers of the doings of the habitual criminals of art."

England may have "invented and established Public Opinion," but "the English mind is coarse and undeveloped." Hence "modern journalism…justifies its own existence by the Darwinian principle of survival of the vulgarest." The difference between journalism and literature was that "journalism is unreadable, and literature is unread."

Aside that journalism in the United States was so bad that "no parallel can be found for it anywhere."

89. Aïdé, Hamilton. "Social Aspects of American Life." 29 (1891): 888–903.
Fretted about an American press "indifferent" to truth or cruelty when most Americans only read the newspaper that was in every town.

90. Forbes, Archibald. "A War Correspondent's Reminiscences." 30 (1891): 185–96, 414–29.
Remembered that most war correspondents before the Franco-Prussian War had no access to telegraphy, so they labored less and lived longer. Among the more outstanding thereafter were the American, J. A. MacGahan, *Daily News*, and artist Frederic Villiers, *Daily Graphic*, who covered the entire Russo-Turkish War. War correspondents in 1890 should speak many languages; ride; know warfare; and be calm, affable, intuitive, physically strong, very energetic, and ready to take risks.

91. Linton, Eliza Lynn. "The Wild Women: As Social Insurgents." 30 (1891): 596–605.
Journalist detested "pestilent papers" that challenged traditional ideas.

92. Lowe, Charles. "The German Newspaper Press." 30 (1891): 853–71.
Reported that the German emperor did not respect journalists and Otto von Bismarck disdained them. Only Cologne's *Zeitung* embodied the British ideal of an enlightened, independent, well-written

newspaper because others lived in the shadow of censorship, pre-publication until 1848 and post-publication until 1874. Even in 1891 gazettes faced libel and confiscation unless they printed "rectifications" of official stories.

There were many Berlin papers (named here), but they had fewer readers combined than a major London daily. Several specialized: the *Tagblatt* for Jews; *Volkszeitung* for workers; *National-Zeitung* for the middle classes; and the *Norddeutsche Allgemeine Zeitung* (which Bismarck manipulated for years) for government. All excluded gossip lest the police close them. The morning dailies, with leaders, essays, and fiction, survived on subscriptions. The evening papers could not afford telegrams or correspondents, so their news was stale. Regional papers, such as Cologne's *Zeitung* and Frankfurt's *Zeitung*, were often better than those in Berlin. Wolff News Company distributed pro-government news to which it had inside access.

Purported that Jews were pivotal in journalism. They invested in many tribunes and epitomized the journalist because they were newshounds, good writers, self-assured, and unscrupulous. British papers often hired them as correspondents in Berlin and Vienna.

93. Delille, Edward. "The French Newspaper Press." 31 (1892): 474–86.
Confined the French press to Paris (providing contents and buyer profiles here). All morning dailies had the same layout, three leaders of three paragraphs in the middle of the two center pages; reports from correspondents, the courts, and the police; racing notes; theatre and book reviews; financial news; and advertising. The serious *Temps* was exceptional; the "light, smart" *Figaro*, with its fiction, gossip, telegrams, theatre, and sports, was French. The *Petit Journal* had a million buyers and 3 million readers per day, but no Paris paper matched the British for advertising. The French were shriller about politics because their liberty was newer, but even when restricted they were "eloquent." Most organs excelled in literature because editors were constantly looking for new talent for which they paid well. Whatever their subject, all journalists signed their names.

94. Delille, Edward. "The American Newspaper Press." 32 (1892): 13–28.
Declared that the United States had a plethora of newspapers. New York had more than London with one-fourth of the population. The New York gazettes, housed in big buildings, were for New Yorkers but were "the most interesting and typical" of the nation. Among them was the *Herald*, three cents for 12 pages. A recent rival, Joseph Pulitzer's *World*, was "sidewalk journalism." Both had graphic language and pictures. Charles Dana's *Sun* was another competitor. *New York Times* editorials were "superior" in style and length. The *New York Tribune* thankfully had only modest headlines. Other American papers were similar thanks to telegrams and news agencies, but the dailies emphasized news irrespective of cost. Supplementing them were specialized serials and very large weeklies of 30–60 pages that were a "hodge-podge of rubbish." The spectrum went from the "dignified" *Nation* to the *Police Gazette*. Most featured sports, not literature. Of the illustrated press, *Harper's Weekly* was "decent" but "insipid"; *Frank Leslie's Illustrated Weekly* was "vulgar." Since the Civil War push for news, American papers made good use of telegraphy but lacked quality editing. The result was that this press was "not artistic, not literary, not didactic, not even political" but "infects" others.

95. Rae, W. Fraser. "The Egyptian Newspaper Press." 32 (1892): 213–23.
Relayed that Egyptians did not read newspapers regularly, but foreigners in Egypt did. There was no press freedom, yet Egypt had more journals than most of the Ottoman Empire, many scandalous ones in Arabic and French. The official paper appeared in French and had a French editor. Dailies and weeklies numbered 46: 28 in Cairo, 14 in Alexandria, four in Port Said. Of these, 20 were in Arabic,

12, in French, eight in Greek, five in Italian, and one in English, the *Egyptian Gazette*. Only 21 were authorized; the rest printed "falsehoods."

The best Arabic paper was Alexandria's pro-French *Al Ahram*, but the most widely read was Cairo's *Al Moqattam*. This independent four-page daily offered political, financial, and foreign news and advertising for about two-plus pence. Its staff of 40 included London, Paris, and New York correspondents who telegraphed stories. Its owners also published *Al Muqtataf*, which for 160 years had been the only magazine in Arabic and "exercises a civilising as well as an educational influence."

96. Meath [Reginald Brabazon, 12th Earl]. "A Britisher's Impressions of America and Australasia." 33 (1893): 493–514.

Postulated that some American Sunday and religious papers "written for a serious or leisured public are excellent in style and matter, as also are a few which appeal to a refined and literary class, and are content with a comparatively small circulation; but the average daily…is not of a high order." Most dailies printed "sensational accounts under startling headlines" of "crimes," "disasters," and "personalities." Protests of African Americans about their oppression resonated in some "leading newspapers," as the *Cleveland Plain Dealer*, but dailies usually did not have the "instructive and thoughtful articles" found in European gazettes. Newspapers of the frontier, without "dignity and refinement," were the nadir. Australian and New Zealand newspapers were less vulgar than American.

American magazines, "well known and read" in Europe, had better engravings, paper, and print than their Continental counterparts.

97. Humphery, George R. "The Reading of the Working Classes." 33 (1893): 690–701.

Lamented that newspapers cluttered pages with inappropriate information on complicated legal cases and messy divorce suits. Even the "leading journals," not just "certain abominable illustrated" ones, "pander to the worst propensities, play upon ignorant prejudices" to sell. The young took news as gospel but treated the rest as diversion.

98. Heaton, J. Henniker. "Post Office 'Plundering and Blundering.'" 33 (1893): 994–1008.

Roared that postal rates for transmission of periodicals favored news journals published weekly or less in Britain and discriminated against religious, scientific, and educational titles. Some serials, such as the *British and Colonial Druggist*, added news to get the cheaper rate. If a publisher put an address on the serial's cover, it was subject to the letter rate.

99. Kay, J. Taylor. "How to Catalogue Books." 34 (1893): 101–09.

Itemized the problems of cataloguing periodicals, especially those with the "best literature," because they had no subject index except *Poole's*. Would organize journals using the subject system of the United States Patent Office rather than the British Library, one of listing by location published.

100. Macintyre, James. "Théophraste Renaudot: Old Journalism and New." 34 (1893): 596–604.

Dubbed Renaudot the "Founder of the French Press," to whom a statue had recently been dedicated in Paris. He commenced the *Gazette de France* in 1631 under the aegis of Cardinal Armand de

Richelieu. The *Gazette*, like the "New Journalism," glorified the personal, unveiled scandals, and promoted moneymaking schemes. Just as the "New Journalism" supported one party in the morning, another in the evening, Renaudot started a second paper, the *Courrier Française*, to critique the court that supported him. "New Journalism" gave prizes and bargains to subscribers; Renaudot operated pawnshops for them.

The French press of the seventeenth and eighteenth centuries was more reputable than the British press. In the nineteenth century, the reverse was true because the French press was the creation of journalists, whereas British journalism was "a reflection of the public mind." French press decline began in the 1850s when anonymity, which journalists opposed, ended. Since that decade, the best people capitalized on fame to leave journalism. Britain's anonymous scribes had better salaries and benefits, and their work was more accurate. The French "star-system" could ruin the British press, chiefly its leaders, because signature would deprive writers of their independence and open them to corruption.

101. Traill, H. D. "The Anonymous Critic." 34 (1893): 932–43.

Agreed with Emile Zola that anonymity in political journalism kept it independent and honest but went beyond him to say that the best factions or schools in literature and art also benefited from anonymous criticism. Zola reckoned that literary anonymity licensed the unqualified and cowardly, boosted gossip, and expanded the contributor lists of lesser serials. Traill believed that anonymity might lower standards, sustain puffery, and conceal malice, but it shielded literary reviewers from the outside influence and personal pressures that the theatre critic, already known, experienced. The chief reason to end it was honesty, even though only "small fry" authors challenged a critic rather than a periodical.

102. Ackland, Joseph. "Elementary Education and the Decay of Literature." 35 (1894): 412–23.

Deprecated major monthlies because they "stimulate superficial, cursory, and scrappy reading." But the "extraordinary growth of weekly papers of a scrappy character," which fostered gambling and sensationalism, was the principal reason for the disinterest in literature. Even those with much fiction, such as the *Family Herald*, had big audiences that cared little for quality writing.

103. Parker, George F., Consul of the United States, Birmingham. "Intellectual Progress in the United States." 35 (1894): 729–45.

Boasted that American newspaper development had been "phenomenal," with more than 19,000 publishing in 1894. "Their sensationalism, scrappiness, and dogmatism produce something of a mental dissipation in cases of overindulgence." Nevertheless, the majority were run with "honesty and conscience by men who have learned both what the public wants and in what they can hope to lead it." The press, the "great engine of civilization," presented the "history of a day" and developed a taste for learning by covering "the most important and interesting topics."

104. Chesney, G[eorge Tomkyns]. "India – The Political Outlook." 35 (1894): 890–904.

Situated the Indian press as "unique in journalism" because it had no internal differences; its only goal was "to disparage and discredit the Government." The editors of most Indian serials were the "'advanced' Bengalis" who abandoned the customs of caste except as a tool to excite readers. The bulk of vernacular gazettes were "seditious," but a few were accurate, chiefly those in Western India where their tone symbolized "a more manly and straightforward race." Although most locals produced fewer than 100 copies, they circulated widely among those who saw no other print. The government should cease translating and thus making locals' hyperbole significant, even if it demonstrated their recognition that British governance was superior. The Press Act of 1878 should never have ended; similar legislation should be enacted to punish the seditious and to deter potential traitors until the locals were ready for a free press.

105. Salmoné, H. Anthony. "The Press in Turkey." 36 (1894): 716–26.
Howled that the Ottoman Empire censored the press. When it was young, it was freer; restrictions accompanied growth. The government, intent on impressing other states, could afford to sanction new papers because the censors scanned every issue before distribution. Editors borrowed uncontroversial items from foreign tribunes, then added telegrams from Havas and local personal pieces. Beirut's 15 Arabic journals all extolled the government because no free opinion was possible. In Constantinople, "one or two [papers] in English and French" ran against the tide, but most able writers were afraid to censure officials. Educated Turks read Egyptian journals, but their delivery was sporadic, or the foreign press, but its pages were scissored. *See* 37: 719.

106. Stott, David. "The Decay of Bookselling." 36 (1894): 932–38.
Grounded the decline in book sales partly in the "enormous increase of periodical literature." Newspapers left little time for other reading, so magazines, easier to skim, displaced books.

107. MacDonagh, Michael. "A Night in the Reporters' Gallery." 37 (1895): 516–26.
Admitted that every reporter wanted a seat in the Commons Gallery, which had 250 tickets for newspaper reporters, London correspondents, leader-writers, sketch-writers, and artists. Some tickets were transferable among staff, but the narrow gallery only held 80. *The Times* had the best location; other morning papers also had separate boxes, but two evening gazettes shared. London had the most seats because the assignments were done before the locals were important. Some tickets went to the agencies, as the Press Association, Central News, and Reuters. Reports, telegraphed to those not represented, might be summaries, full records of ministers, or targeted for a country paper. Transmission was also by telephone. Reporters, who prized speakers of "lucid thinking and direct utterance" at a reasonable pace, had two rooms in which to work, one with "a useful library." They also had access to such amenities as tea and smoking facilities. Aside on the names and schedules of *The Times* staff.

108. Banks, Elizabeth L. "Some American 'Impressions' and 'Comparisons.'" 37 (1895): 634–45.
American journalist living in London propounded that American editors showed more prudery than English editors, citing as evidence censorship of language in her article on fashion for an American serial.

109. Salmoné, H. Anthony. "The Real Rulers of Turkey." 37 (1895): 719–33.
Reiterated ideas in 36: 716. The Porte prohibited the local press from discussing government policies and objected to criticism in foreign papers. Officials banned 'Arab free newspapers,' mostly from Egypt, but some circulated secretly even under threat of heavy fines and imprisonment. The Turkish charge that the British funded new organs in Egypt was false.

110. De Viti de Marco, [Antonio]. "The Political Situation in Italy." 38 (1895): 548–60.

Rued that the legion of Italian newspapers, without the financial support of the politically uneducated Italians, was forced to survive on secret government funding.

111. Besant, Walter. "The Literary Agent." 38 (1895): 979–86.

Held that a novel's success depended initially on its publication in magazines. *See National Review* 26: 650.

112. Tuttiet, M[ary] G. "The Advantage of Fiction." 39 (1896): 123–31.

Opined that the prosperity of some newspapers and magazines was "partly the result of literary decadence." Magazines ready to beat rivals deserted good verse and fiction and played to readers' "[b]ase curiosity, vulgar craving for personalities, morbid love of the ugly, the revolting, and the commonplace." Still, bad fiction was not so "ruinous to the intellect" as "the dreary question and answer of the verbose interviewer, a creature with no sense of humour," the endless gossip, or the deadly articles on fashion and furnishings in newspapers.

113. Knight, William. "Criticism as Theft." 39 (1896): 257–66.

Assumed that serials were multiplying because people liked the short article. The goal of new ones was to please, not to educate. The 1890s were not years of greatness for periodical criticism, which in 1896 displayed ignorance and indiscriminate praise. Critics who did not read books but glossed reviews of others or who reviewed too many volumes did no justice to authors. Shallow summaries, a "disgrace to journalism," satisfied editors who wanted a column with enough extracts to allow readers to talk about the book without touching it. The pressure at a morning daily precluded thoughtful criticism, so dailies stole ideas from literary weeklies that had already pirated from monthlies. Aside that *Tit-Bits* was originally judged "the *ne plus ultra* of literary degradation" but made a fortune for its owner, George Newnes.

114. Comyn, Francis. "The Seamy Side of British Guiana." 39 (1896): 390–98.

Despaired that whenever Parliament was not sitting, and "any remarkable event occurs," the newspapers received a flood of letters from pseudo-experts.

115. Harrison, Frederic. "Matthew Arnold." 39 (1896): 433–47.

Separated Arnold from the 'lightning reviewer' of 1896, frequently a woman without his "vast knowledge, keen taste, and serene judgment."

116. Banks, Elizabeth L. "Self-Help among American College Girls." 39 (1896): 502–13.

Noticed that women attending the University of Chicago sometimes worked in the city's newspaper offices.

117. Purcell, Edmund S., The Author of the *Life of Cardinal Manning*. "Poisoning the Wells of Catholic Criticism." 39 (1896): 514–26; letters from William E. Gladstone, 526–28 and Sydney F. Smith, S.J., 694–96.

Inferred that the Roman Church pressured some Catholic newspapers to advance the faith at the expense of free expression. The papers were small, but the *Universe* and *Catholic Times*, both with "wide circulation," printed biased columns anonymously.

118. Mahaffy, J. P. "International Jealousy." 39 (1896): 529–43.
Suspected that editors promoted international rivalries to sell papers to a "thoughtless public." A free press could do as much harm as a controlled one. For example, American papers roused jealousy with "vulgar license"; the French blackened character; and the Irish were a forum for "the conspiracy of a small party." In England, "in spite of much foul stuff let loose weekly from our press," there were "at least a dozen journals" that were moderate and fair.

119. Fort, G. Seymour. "The True Motive and Reason of Dr. Jameson's Raid." 39 (1896): 873–80.
Alluded to the German press.

120. Shaylor, J[oseph], Simpkin, Marshall, and Company, Ltd. "On the Selling of Books." 40 (1896): 937–43.
Granted that a plethora of reviews hiked a book's sales but not as much as previously when a *Times* or *Spectator* column ensured the success of the first edition.

121. Palmer, H. J. "The March of the Advertiser." 41 (1897): 135–41.
Appreciated the interdependence between the press, "the most powerful engine" to sell goods, and advertisers who sustained its prosperity. They permitted a journal to be independent, to reflect opinion while serving the public. The latest rotary press allowed gazettes to expand from eight to 12 pages, so even the best ones accepted big advertisements after 1892. More advertising meant more money to pay newsgatherers. Format usually divided news and advertising, but business in 1897 wanted to set advertisements on news pages for which it was ready to pay more. The "cream" of the dailies refused, but many reputable ones printed the quasi-article from inexperienced sellers or disreputable agents. This insert could trick readers and impede editorial exposure of bad products. Equally fraudulent were letters of endorsement, a device to secure free advertising.

122. Bennett, Ernest N. "Side-Lights on the Cretan Insurrection." 41 (1897): 687–98.
Derided Greek journalists who habitually sent incorrect telegrams, obvious when they were compared to those of others. Most European correspondents did not speak Greek or Turkish so depended on local sources, some of whom were biased and many of whom controlled the wires.

123. Reid, [T.] Wemyss. "Some Reminiscences of English Journalism." 42 (1897): 55–66.
Reid recounted his career from an "apprenticeship to journalism" in the small office of the *Northern Daily Express* (1857), either the first or second local daily. The editor of the four-page penny herald was a "man of genius" and a talented writer.

Technology was a major force in journalism during Reid's tenure as editor of the *Leeds Mercury*, 1870–87. When government nationalized telegraphy, news was more accessible and, in the minds of many owners, more trustworthy. The use of special wires meant country papers carried more foreign news. The telephone and pneumatic tube later sped transmission, but pressure for immediacy detracted from the level of thought and writing of earlier decades, a trend in columns from leaders to book reviews.

Equally troublesome was that new journalists did not merely record great events but injected their own reactions. The editorial use of "we" had become personalized, a technique to enhance one's own ideas. No one in the Reporters' Gallery of the 1860s would accost an MP, but, as the country tribunes grew, Members wanted coverage in their home press so encouraged lobbying. Open contact with Members and ministers spawned journalists who were aggressive, familiar, and vain, vaunting their sense of superiority over a submissive public. Nonetheless, the new generation was better equipped and informed, "more earnest and sincere," than its predecessors.

124. Adams, George, Indian Civil Service (retired). "India (No. 1): A Remediable Grievance." 42 (1897): 486–92.

Warranted that the Indian press did not represent the views of the majority of Indians.

125. Ahmad, Rafiuddin. "India (No. 2): Is the British 'Raj' in Danger?" 42 (1897): 493–500.

Tagged most of the Indian press loyal, so its restriction would foment sedition.

126. Bentwich, Herbert. "Philo-Zionists and Anti-Semites." 42 (1897): 623–35.

Graded the *Jewish Chronicle* "the leading organ of the anti-Zionists in this country."

127. Pennell, Joseph. "Art and the Daily Paper." 42 (1897): 653–62.

Outlined trends in 1890s newspapers: "the editorial 'we' no longer leads a gullible public," and the uninteresting reporter who only described his own perceptions, the untutored war correspondent, and the critic by patronage were all gone. Dailies contained more illustrations following the lead of the pioneer New York *Daily Graphic* and the unrivalled London *Daily Graphic*. Pennell claimed a part in the premier of drawings in the *Daily Chronicle*, akin to ones in the illustrated weeklies. Technology was a factor, but the *Chronicle* also sought out quality artists, unlike its American counterparts, absent a school that trained journalism illustrators.

128. MacDonagh, Michael. "In the Sub-Editor's Room." 42 (1897): 999–1008.

Designated the subeditor's office as the "heart of the mighty machinery of the daily newspaper office." While "[e]xcellent reporters and brilliant leader writers are always obtainable without difficulty," a good subeditor was rare. Owners did everything in their power to retain the qualified. The subeditor, known in the United States as the news editor, allocated space. This person also dealt with news agencies; checked telegrams for accuracy and copy for libel; read letters; and monitored stories of penny-a-liners. The subeditor left to assistants the scanning of other periodicals for republication possibilities. Subeditors had to choose carefully what went on newsboys' posters because good headlines bumped up sales by the thousands. Later editions only updated news.

129. Chesney, G. M. "The Native Press in India." 43 (1898): 266–76.

Prefaced that the British were reaping what they had sown in India. Exporting inappropriate ideas, such as press liberty, was dangerous in a place where a minority managed papers that did not reflect British interests. Lord Charles Metcalfe freed the press in 1835 before there were Indian journals and Indian education. Control and liberty thereafter alternated. The British left the press alone after 1882, so the recent convictions of journalists for fanning unrest in the wake of famine were unusual. By 1898 gazettes subordinated foreign news, the arts, finance, and sports in order to talk about shared governance, preferring British rule to Russian dominion or anarchy. Officials paid too much attention to a press that resorted to distortion and misrepresentation but was not seditious. Aside that British press freedom in 1695 was not desired by the public and not confirmed until after John Wilkes.

130. Wedmore, Frederick. "The Short Story." 43 (1898): 406–16.
Painted the reading public as undemanding consumers, so the "ideal journalist" did not need to know much about any subject.

131. Heaton, J. Henniker. "A Postal Utopia." 43 (1898): 764–79.
Petitioned for revision of postal rates for transmitting periodicals.

132. Knowles, James, Editor. "Mr. Gladstone as a Contributor to the *Nineteenth Century*." 43 (1898): 1043–46.
Revisited William E. Gladstone's contributions to the *Nineteenth Century*.

133. Banks, Elizabeth L. "American 'Yellow' Journalism." 44 (1898): 328–40.
Enlightened that all yellow journalism, "a power for evil in the main," was American because New York papers had the money to buy the brains behind it. The appellation, incorrectly attributed to the Yellow Kid in the *New York World*, attached to the press of W. R. Hearst after he outbid Charles Dana for its artist and then hired other illustrators. In 1898 the label referred to the "sensational" press, about 15–20 dailies with large circulations. European correspondents borrowed from these heralds, which in 1898 focused on war headlines that guaranteed extra editions. Before the Spanish-American War erupted, "intelligent, clear-headed Americans" deemed the yellow papers "vulgar" but in 1898 wondered if they had pushed the United States into war. To counteract their influence, millionaire proprietors should steal the best reporters from the yellow papers for their own sober ones.

American women covered more than fashion and society; they were assigned "exposures," sometimes for their "tactfulness" and other times for shock value. Radical editors liked female reporters for moral stories; conservative editors, for stunts. Women did "the most difficult, the most enterprising, the most sensational, and the most original work" in the yellow press. Men were asked to risk their lives; women, their lives and honor.

134. Clarke, G. S. "The Tsar's Proposed Conference and Our Foreign Affairs." 44 (1898): 697–706.
Warned that ignorant journalists could irritate "international sentiment" because their telegrams and short paragraphs in papers of large circulation too frequently misrepresented matters.

135. Guyot, Yves, Ex-Minister of Public Works. "The Dreyfus Drama and Its Significance." 45 (1899): 149–72.
Guyot swore that he was the only person to take public exception, in an article in the *Siècle*, to the trial of Alfred Dreyfus. Thereafter the anti-Semitic journals featured the case joined in 1896 by the *Eclair*, with the same military "patronage" as the *Libre Parole* and *Intransigeant*.

136. Wallis, J. P. "Liberty of the Press in France." 45 (1899): 315–26.
Corroborated that since 1815 the French press vacillated between freedom and repression, which peaked in the Second Empire. The 1881 *Loi sur la Presse* put French journalists on the same footing as British, with the same rights and responsibilities as other citizens. The *Loi* covered criminal libel and slander but gave a "large measure of impunity" to newspapers because it did not effectively protect private character. Further, the legislation did not prevent the press from "interfering with the free course of justice" unlike the British contempt of court. The only limit on the press was that it

could not publish official documents pre-trial. The legislative gaps were particularly troublesome in a country with a widely circulated press perused by emotional readers.

137. Low, Frances H. "A Woman's Criticism of the Women's Congress." 46 (1899): 192–202.

Denounced the recent Congress of the International Council of Women because it did not "protest against the silliness, frivolity, and vulgarity of the women's journals and women's columns, with their tittle-tattle and extravagance in dress and illiteracy in tone." Congress speakers advised the woman reporter "to sink her personality" and praised her for the "lightness of tone" she brought to gazettes. People should read Joseph Addison to learn how journalism could be lively without being "illiterate…silly…vulgar." Meanwhile, papers trying to educate women, especially in preparation for suffrage, were "flat failures."

138. Elsdale, H[enry]. "Why Are Our Brains Deteriorating?" 46 (1899): 262–72.

Answer to captioned question was that reading primarily light periodicals discouraged thinking. *Tit-Bits*, "a pernicious hop-skip-and-jump style of literature," and its kin did not tax the mind.

139. Reid, [T.] Wemyss. "The Newspapers." 46 (1899): 848–64, 1020–34; 47 (1900): 157–72, 350–64, 526–40, 698–712, 866–80, 1036–50; 48 (1900): 159–72, 315–29, 496–509, 670–84, 842–56, 1024–39.

Reid's goal was to study newspapers, which provided "variety and veracity" as they influenced. In diary format, he opened with an analysis of stories in London dailies. Telegrams were often half gossip that unobservant readers did not detect; placards of evening tribunes frequently offended decency; both were too sensational. However, unlike European comic papers that were "savage and indecent," British columns on the struggle with the Boers showed "sobriety and moderation" except for the Jingo press. Military defeats should bring it to reality, notably about printing items garnered from censored reports. The editors of the *Echo* and *Daily Chronicle* resigned because of differences with their owners about war coverage, underscoring the threat to press liberty when "capitalist-ridden" newspapers insisted on unanimous opinion. Diversity was especially important given the secrecy of some telegrams. Equally troubling was the "newspaper-strategist" who hinted about his expertise and influence on the military or published personal views of a conflict.

The British "Yellow Press" was "a bad imitation of a bad original." For instance, the "wild gossip of Shanghai" was only fit for the wastebasket. British journalists once expressed "pious horror" about the "sensational lies" in the American heralds but were emulating their style in the reports from China. Even the more moderate "New Journalism" occasionally strained credulity. Reid decried "panic mongers in the halfpenny newspaper"; "red-hot reviewing" of books filled with "nuggets" that critics pirated from authors in other papers; theatre criticism that, in morning papers, was a long essay in "technical jargon" that had no impact on playgoers; and attempts to capture readers with competitions that were really "gambling transactions."

The Institute of Journalists defined "professional usage" but should enforce self-censure to keep the public's respect and should somehow control reckless statements and sensational news "pandering…to the mob." *The Times*, "which has never been inspired by any consuming love for associations of journalists," dealt "rather severely" with the Institute. When the *Belfast News-Letter* borrowed a letter from *The Times* without acknowledgement, and then apologized, an act "no honest journalist" would defend, *The Times* should not have blamed the institute.

140. Paul, Herbert. "The Prince of Journalists." 47 (1900): 73–87.
Headlined Jonathan Swift but thanked the Institute of Journalists for securing publicity for his "profession."

141. Bettelheim, Paul. "The Jews in France." 47 (1900): 116–20.
Bared anti-Semitic journals intended as a counterweight to the many Republican papers "in Jewish hands" after 1879. Aside that the *Nation*, owned by Camille Dreyfus, was anti-Jesuit.

142. Douglas, Robert K. "The Intellectual Awakening of China." 47 (1900): 988–92.
Tallied 19 Chinese newspapers in 1895 and 76 in 1898, but an edict of the Dowager Empress checked this growth.

143. Thring, [Henry, 1st Baron]. "The Copyright Bills, 1900." 47 (1900): 1005–19.
Pondered a provision of the copyright bill protecting news for 18 hours, a clause that would affect evening dailies' coverage of foreign events.

144. Skelton, Reginald A. "Statistics of Suicide." 48 (1900): 465–82.
Believed that stories on the "really vile crime or pathetic suicide" conferred notoriety because the newspaper, the "product of modern civilization," was everywhere.

The North British Review, 1844–1871

Of Free Church and Scottish parentage, the *North British* assigned space to secular reviews and foreign as well as domestic newspapers.

1. [Moncrieff, James]. "Lord Jeffrey's *Contributions to the Edinburgh Review*." 1 (1844): 252–84.

Construed Francis Jeffrey's articles in the *Edinburgh* as "parts of a great and gradually matured system of criticism" unlike those of others of its reviewers, among them T. B. Macaulay. Jeffrey was also effective as the *Review*'s editor. That position required being "a mark for every disappointed friend or foe to fling at – daily devoured by the petulance of authors – the jealousies and intolerable delays of contributors, and the grumblings of publishers."

The goal of the *Edinburgh* was "to induce on the public mind habits of calm and just thinking, and a spirit of unprejudiced inquiry after truth and justice in politics." It succeeded because of talented scribes who extended its influence without the severity often attributed to them. In other serials of the day, such as the *New Monthly Magazine*, there was too much information to notice good writing.

2. [Moncrieff, James]. "Recent Novels." 1 (1844): 545–79.

Conceded that periodicals in 1844 had a "better tone" than before even though "a flood of nonsense, childishness, false morals, and infidelity…flows from this copious fountain."

3. [Cunningham, William]. "The United States of North America." 2 (1844–45): 136–74.

Announced that every small town in the United States had a newspaper, which everyone read. Large towns usually had two dailies, a respectable penny and disreputable halfpenny. The result was that most Americans had opinions on public questions. American journals generally disseminated "sound moral and religious principles." The "recklessness in abuse of public men" and "outrages upon public decency in the shape of advertisements of quack medicines" were no worse than "some of the widely-circulated Sunday Journals of London." "The more intelligent and educated classes" supplemented this reading with British reviews republished and sold cheaper in the United States.

4. [Robertson, T. C.]. "Thornton's *History of British India*." 2 (1844–45): 324–59.

Review of Edward Thornton's *History of the British Empire in India* condensed press restrictions and their relaxation. At first, a "totally unshackled press" met with "indifference by the great bulk of the native community," but 1844 India had many varieties of journalism.

5. [Wilson, John]. "The Baron Hügel's *Travels in Kashmír and the Panjáb* [*sic*]." 2 (1844–45): 444–70.

Review of Charles Hügel's book filed the *Calcutta Review* as a periodical that "evinces high talent." "It bids to secure no small portion of favour, even in this country, particularly among the retired members of the public services of India." Many of its articles were of "first-rate quality."

6. [Chalmers, Thomas]. "Savings Banks." 3 (1845): 318–44.
Cautioned readers that "newspapers teem with eloquence of the highest order," so leaders, especially in the best journals, could easily mold opinion. Those in *The Times* were the "ablest and most influential." Nonetheless, the press was a bulwark against tyranny and a champion of the weak.

7. "Engraving." 6 (1846–47): 141–69.
Glanced at the impact of lithography on caricature, which had quickly become popular in France. *Caricature* commenced in 1830, and *Charivari*, which had the "most amusing prints," surfaced in 1832.

8. [?Patmore, Coventry]. "Popular Serial Literature." 7 (1847): 110–36.
Cited *Punch*, the *Christian's Penny Magazine*, and *Churchman's Monthly Penny Magazine* as examples of the breadth and variety of religious periodicals in 1847.

9. [Paul, William]. "The French Revolution of 1848." 9 (1848): 1–42.
Yoked the French press, notably the *National* and *Réforme*, to the 1848 Revolution and the government that followed.

10. [De Quincey, Thomas]. "Forster's *Life of Goldsmith*." 9 (1848): 187–212.
Review of John Forster's book bewailed that struggling young writers of Oliver Goldsmith's generation and of 1848 had to hire out to monthlies to survive.

11. [Masson, David]. "Recent French Social Philosophy – Organization of Labour." 9 (1848): 213–51.
Appraised the Saint-Simonian *Organisateur* and the *Globe*, the Fourierist *Phalange*, and the *Presse*, operating on a "co-operative principle" since the 1848 Revolution.

12. [Brewster, David]. "Mr. Britton's *Authorship of Junius Elucidated*." 10 (1848–49): 97–143.
Review of John Britton's book and ten others on Junius stamped him "a patriot and a moralist," a "public censor…defending, at the risk of his life, the laws and constitution." He fought for "'liberty of the press,' – the palladium of all the civil, political, and religious rights of Englishmen."

13. [Masson, David]. "The Socialist Party in France." 10 (1848–49): 261–92.
Broadcast that the *National*, under Armand Marrast, sponsored Republicanism and the *Démocratie Pacifique*, Fourierism before the 1848 Revolution. In February, hundreds of new journals began in Paris alone, among them several Socialist papers (titles and contributors here) and sheets by "fools."

14. [Burton, John Hill]. "Socialism in Britain." 12 (1849–50): 86–114.
Essay on the Owenites overlooked their periodicals but not the "respectable" *People's Journal*.

15. [Patmore, Coventry]. "F. K. Hunt's *Fourth Estate*." 13 (1850): 159–88.
Described Hunt's *The Fourth Estate: Contributions Towards a History of Newspapers and of the Liberty of the Press* as a "good general acquaintance" with "English newspaper history." The newspaper was a "chronicler" of the day, one that had the habit of praising itself, perhaps to conceal a dark side. The newspaper publicized the advantages of power that were the bases of despotism, the

'original' thinking that eroded custom, and the religious controversies that undermined faith. Because newspapers were "partial and distorted" and reading them "in excess is so common a form of mental debauchery," the "popular lust for news" was "one of the mightiest elements of our national decay."

Trailed the press from the Roman *acta diurna* to the Venetian gazettes, then to Nathaniel Butter's *Weekely Newes* (1622). It was the first English newspaper because prior sheets were not "regularly numbered and continuous." Butter, previously a "news-writer" for "private country gentlemen," preceded Théophraste Renaudot, who started the *Gazette de France* in the next decade with the blessing of government. The Civil Wars inspired mercuries, and John Milton's *Areopagitica* in the years before Charles II authorized publishing the news. Important was Roger L'Estrange, "licenser and journalist." Soon the post was carrying newspapers. Anne's reign witnessed the first daily, copyright legislation, and the stamp and advertising duties. The stamp silenced smaller papers momentarily, but they reappeared under George II. John Wilkes and Junius were problems for George III.

Quoted Hunt on the operation of a London daily. Among its expenses were yachts to collect steamers' news offshore. Newsmen then cabled the capital where notices went by cab to offices manned by subeditors ready to assign someone to pen a column before a rival.

16. [Anster, John]. "Southey's *Life and Correspondence*." 13 (1850): 225–63.
Review of Robert Southey's work, volumes II and III, logged his efforts for the *Annual Register*, where he did "slave-work," and for the *Quarterly Review*, where editor William Gifford deleted passages from his essays. Aside on the *Edinburgh Review*'s circulation, 9,000 when the *Quarterly* emerged.

17. [Kaye, J. W.]. "*Pendennis* – The Literary Profession." 13 (1850): 335–72.
Review of W. M. Thackeray's *The History of Pendennis* perceived mid-century as "an age of periodical literature" that was proliferating. "The literary man converses now through the medium of the Press, and turns everything into copyright at once," whether an article in a review, page in a magazine, leader in a top daily, or column in "a cheap weekly." Many authors could not write for newspapers, chiefly leaders. Leader-writers need not share the politics of a proprietor because most newspapers let them pick from the "jumble" of opinions. However, "[i]t is not enough to think and to know" because newspaper writing was a unique style. Writers also tended to be "improvident and irregular," traits not suitable for the business of editing or publishing. Other professionals likewise did not make good journalists, so journalism should not be their fallback. Literary critics puffed because publishers' advertising frequently supported a paper. Theatre and music critics were even more biased, taking seats for raves, supporting performer friends, and castigating competitor playwrights and musicians. To keep newspapers fresh, owners had to pay enough so that journalists did not have to pen for more than one sheet. Owners could balance their losses as book publishers against their profits from successful tribunes.

18. [Anster, John]. "*Autobiography of Leigh Hunt*." 14 (1850–51): 143–68.
Regarded Hunt's *Examiner* as "an exceedingly clever paper" in which his articles were the best. The quarterly *Reflector* ended after four issues because he ran out of money and was in prison for libel.

19. [Hanna, R. M.]. "Rome and the Italian Revolution." 14 (1850–51): 319–49.
Concurred that Rome's free press, 1848–49, "exceeded all bounds of liberty," but it was unfair to measure it by the "staid and sober journalism of constitutional countries." Aside on Giuseppe Mazzini's *Giovane Italia* and *Apostolare Populare*, which he published in London for 12 issues until he ran out of money.

20. [Hanna, R. M.]. "The Five Wounds of the Holy Church." 15 (1851): 497–528.
Ranked the *Civiltà Cattolica* "by far the ablest organ of the Papacy in Italy" even though it was edited by a "clique of old ladies."

21. [Greg, W. R.]. "France in January 1852." 16 (1851–52): 559–600.
Decreed that restricting French newspapers was dangerous and unnecessary since their readers only looked for a 'brilliant' leader and an "exciting" feuilleton and Paris gazettes, with circulations much higher than London's, were a vent for "the restless intellects and fiery tempers of the cultivated classes."

22. [Masson, David]. "Lord Cockburn's *Life of Jeffrey*." 17 (1852): 283–326.
Review of Henry Cockburn's book emphasized how Francis Jeffrey's editing of and writing more than 200 articles for the *Edinburgh Review* shaped it. Under his direction, it excelled as a "critical organ" and reflected his "taste as a critic." He told readers, in essays of honesty if not depth, what to think about new books. In 1852 literary criticism in "higher periodicals" was "deeper and more laborious"; reviews akin to Jeffrey's were in literary weeklies and dailies. Asides on the Christopher North articles in *Blackwood's Magazine* and the absence of a truly Scottish periodical.

23. [Greg, W. R.]. "The Prospects of France and the Dangers of England." 18 (1852–53): 303–50.
Bellowed that all French governments had "warred against journalism," but the 1848 law requiring signature was "the most fatal blow to the press." The press had forfeited respect, so the public accepted its repression by Napoleon III. By contrast, from 1815 to 1830, "able, instructed, honourable men" ran such papers as the *Globe*, *National*, and *Constitutionnel*. After the July Revolution journalists went into government, replaced at newspapers by lesser men whose rivalries demeaned journalism. It went from "an honourable profession...to the ignominy of a trade." Emile de Girardin hired inferiors who wrote down to readers. Adding to the coarseness were "feuilletons of Eugene Sue's stamp." By 1848 journalists were not persons of principle or ability but "assassins" and "panderers" for cash. Their papers were similar to Ireland's *Nation*. The problem was that French gazettes could still rouse the masses. When Napoleon III leashed the press, he gave it the opportunity for rebirth once emotions quieted. Soon reviews, then weeklies, and finally dailies should engage in political education and "rational and reflective criticism" of government.

24. [Brewster, David]. "*The Grenville Papers*." 19 (1853): 475–518.
Reviewed captioned papers and other materials, such as D. T. Coulton's essay in the *Quarterly Review* (90: 91), on the identity of Junius. *See Dublin University Magazine* 40: 1.

25. [Masson, David]. "Kaye's *Life of Lord Metcalfe*." 22 (1854–55): 145–78.
Review of J. W. Kaye's biography of Charles Metcalfe studied his tenure as governor-general of India when the issue of a free press arose. During Warren Hastings' time, papers were "reckless, scurrilous, and licentious in the extreme – mere literary garbage." People stopped their libels by bribery or force. In the Cornwallis era, "more respectable" tribunes with "local news and weak politics" had commenced, but in the Wellesley years the "newspapers were an intolerable nuisance to the men of power." Because John Adam deported British editors, papers had to be issued in the names of Indians. William Bentinck relaxed restrictions, and in 1835 Metcalfe abolished the Press Regulations, which led to a "new press-law similar to that of England."

26. [Kaye, J. W.]. "Literary Coteries." 23 (1855): 232–65.
Review of R. R. Madden's *The Literary Life and Correspondence of the Countess of Blessington* reckoned that Marguerite Blessington "reigned supreme" as an editor of annuals in the 1830s and 1840s. Editing in those decades involved working with publishers, artists, and contributors as well as authoring articles. Critics in 1855 were "a vagabond race" who came from many backgrounds and consequently had no recognition as a profession. Although most were competent, the partiality of coteries hurt periodical reviewing. Excessive flattery or detraction cloaked by anonymity made it hard for uninstructed readers to measure a book's merits. Yet those without time had no other recourse but to accept critics' statements.

27. [Blaze de Bury, Marie]. "Reign of the House of Orleans in France." 24 (1855–56): 91–116.
Linked the French press to the 1848 Revolution.

28. [Hayward, Abraham]. "Life and Writings of the Late Mr. Justice Talfourd." 25 (1856): 47–78.
Judged Thomas Noon Talfourd an able and fair critic during "his management...of the dramatic department of the *New Monthly Magazine*."

29. [Masson, David]. "Samuel Rogers and His Times." 25 (1856): 399–436.
Scanned Rogers' work for the early *Edinburgh Review*, years when it and the *Quarterly Review* "vindicated literature." Aside on John Wilkes.

30. [Hayward, Abraham]. "Rémusat's *English Statesmen* – Bolingbroke." 26 (1856–57): 185–208.
Reviewed Charles Rémusat's *England in the Eighteenth Century: English Statesmen*. Aired that it was a compilation of his articles in the *Revue des Deux Mondes*, which employed fine writers. British reviews, 1800–25, were better than French because Paris dailies offered the talented the opportunity to influence government. Their "capricious tyranny" sired quality French reviews.

This development was opposite to that in Britain, where newspapers gained in reputation, even for literary criticism. Newspapers were "the indispensable instrument of self (or popular) government, the medium through (or the stage on) which the nation discusses its affairs and transacts its business." The press was Parliament's reporter and the public's voice. Signature "would lessen the wholesome influence of journalism." During Lord Bolingbroke's age, a campaign to mandate signature in order "to check violence and personality" did not succeed because libel law and the stamp duty effectively restrained the press. By 1856 the best dailies had writers of talent and character and editors of responsibility. Aside on the *Craftsman* and eighteenth-century *Examiner*.

31. [Thomson, John Cockburn]. "Modern Style." 26 (1856–57): 339–75.
Blamed newspapers for the "lack of courage" of literary critics. The press formed opinion on books, as on other matters, "with their daily ukases from a dirty printing-office." Reviewers were afraid to challenge newspapers. The *Edinburgh* set the bar for criticism, a standard of taste and education in contrast to the eighteenth century. Faced at mid-century with newspaper competition, the *Review* and its peers shifted from the style of Sydney Smith and Francis Jeffrey to long treatises.

32. [Brewster, David]. "*Memoirs of John Dalton*." 27 (1857): 465–97.
Review of Dalton's book unveiled him as a scribe for the *Gentleman's Diary* and the *Ladies' Diary*, both periodicals that "often called forth the talents of some of our best mathematicians."

33. [Stebbing, William]. "Stanhope's *History* – Walpole and Pulteney." 28 (1858): 1–31.
Review of Lord P. H. Stanhope's *History of England, 1713–83*, covered the *Craftsman*'s directors and contents.

34. [Patmore, Coventry]. "Decay of Modern Satire." 29 (1858): 506–18.
Grieved that newspapers echoed prejudices under the guise of teaching. They drew their power from their popularity but resisted individual excellence in contrast to the *Anti-Jacobin*.

35. "Modern Literary Life – Douglas Jerrold." 30 (1859): 337–66.
Review of *Literary Adventure*, by Jerrold's son Blanchard, followed the father's press career as a theatre critic and subeditor as well as a contributor to the *Athenaeum*, *Monthly Magazine*, and *Punch*. In 1843 he edited the *Illuminated Magazine* and in 1845, *Douglas Jerrold's Shilling Magazine*. As an editor, he sometimes published bad writing because an author needed money. In 1846 he started *Douglas Jerrold's Weekly Newspaper*. Jerrold never had "any noticeable weight as a political writer," perhaps because of a "want of calmness and deliberative capacity."

36. "The British Press: Its Growth, Liberty, and Power." 30 (1859): 367–402.
Rejoiced that a "FREE Press is a blessing which we have enjoyed in this country, and in so ample a measure" unlike the French. Only "the intelligence and good feeling of readers" controlled newspapers.

Dated the newspaper from the printing press and press liberty from John Milton's *Areopagitica*. Scribbled newsletters of coffee-house scribes and news sheets of the Civil Wars abated with censorship. After it died, political criticism was so intense that it provoked stamp and paper duties. The stamp drove out the "worthless," but the case of John Wilkes and the beginning of parliamentary reporting were more crucial to press history. The attempt to curb gazettes during the French Revolution failed. Meanwhile, papers like the *Edinburgh Courant* (content and format cited in this article) blossomed, and improvements in the post, transportation, and printing boosted newspapers' annual sales, from 7.5 million in England and Wales in 1753 to 29 million in 1836. The end of the stamp had a dramatic effect, pushing sales to 72 million after 1855, 14 million of which were *The Times*. Remaining problems were the paper duty and locals' scissoring.

Periodicals also grew steadily during the nineteenth century: 372 in 1800, 842 in 1828, 2,530 in 1853, but their sales varied dramatically.

37. [Levi, Leone]. "*Works of Henry, Lord Brougham*." 30 (1859): 417–40.
Peeked at Henry Brougham's work for the *Edinburgh Review*.

38. [Morris, W. O'C.]. "Canning and His Times." 31 (1859): 304–38.
Recollected George Canning's connection with the *Anti-Jacobin* and its "wit and piquancy" under editor William Gifford, later of the *Quarterly Review*.

39. "Redding's *Reminiscences* – Thomas Campbell." 32 (1860): 287–20.
Review of Cyrus Redding's *Literary Reminiscences and Memoirs of Thomas Campbell* tabbed his editing of the *New Monthly Magazine*. He purportedly depended on Redding to handle the business aspects of the job but attracted contributors who made the *New Monthly* more profitable and Campbell worth his annual salary of 1,500 pounds.

40. [Kinnear, A. S.]. "Leigh Hunt." 33 (1860): 356–80.
Skimmed Hunt's essays in his papers, among them the *Indicator* and *Examiner*, which was "arrogant… in plan and conduct."

41. [Kaye, J. W.]. "India Convalescent." 34 (1861): 1–32.
Growled that the Anglo-Indian press fueled "irritation" between Britons and local peoples.

42. [Blaze de Bury, Marie]. "The Political Press – French, British, and German." 34 (1861): 184–209.
Supposed that half the world wanted to abolish and half to manipulate the press. It was "a manifestation of our collective self – therefore not to be feared; but the press is also the manifestation of the entire external public – therefore not to be absorbed by any unit, whether party or individual." The British press, the model for the impersonal because of anonymity, was shaped by the "thoughts and feelings latent in the public mind"; the French, by cliques, and the German, by ideology. French papers directed, whereas the British reflected the public mind. French political journalists often became politicians who could not govern.

The *Revue des Deux Mondes* was known for its "political excellence"; the *Journal des Débats*, for its writers. *The Times* was unique, truly embodying "public thought" while taking responsibility for its influence. Famous for its independence in domestic affairs, it presented solid arguments in a "high moral tone," but its foreign columns were inferior to Continental papers. The *Allgemeine Zeitung*, like *The Times*, was read by its enemies to find out what was afoot. The *Zeitung*'s Hermann Orgès and the *Revue*'s Eugene Forcade exemplified "a journalist superior to a journal."

43. [Blaze de Bury, Marie]. "Montalembert, and Parliamentary Institutions in France." 35 (1861): 31–60.
Related that French officials challenged by journalists in 1835 proposed repression to which Count C. de Montalembert objected. In 1848 newspapers were the weapons of workers in a revolution.

44. [Downes, John]. "Edmund Burke: His Life and Genius." 35 (1861): 445–79.
Recorded that an MP (Col. George Onslow), seeking Commons support in 1770 for a motion to reprimand printers of a newspaper that ridiculed him, provoked a debate on a free press. With the motion's failure, "THE FOURTH ESTATE WAS BORN!"

45. [Smith, Alexander]. "Essayists, Old and New." 37 (1862): 132–69.
Reassured that "extensively read" reviews and literary magazines were not deleterious but incorporated "much of our best thinking and writing." Some, such as the *Cornhill Magazine*, published authors above readers' levels, but periodicals generally would sell if they were able to "amuse, instruct, and refine" audiences. Writing for periodicals did not detract from authoring books, and worthwhile articles were frequently republished in a volume. Periodical style suited some scribes, such as Douglas Jerrold and Theodore Hook, better. Tyros could practice and test it without stigma in serials

committed to anonymity. Among the paradigms of good writing were Joseph Addison, Charles Lamb, William Hazlitt, Leigh Hunt, Thomas Carlyle, and T. B. Macaulay as well as the new generation's James Hannay and others named.

46. [Kaye, J. W.]. "Lord Canning." 37 (1862): 222–48.
Avowed that the press in India "rendered essential service to the cause of good government" except during the "Mutiny." Then, the Indian gazettes were "unscrupulous in the extreme"; the Anglo-Indian, "guilty of grave indiscretions." Even journals of "high character," such as the *Friend of India* and the *Hurkaru*, "a leading Calcutta journal," were guilty. Charles Canning, the governor-general, worried more about the effects of quasi-seditious statements in the Anglo-Indian heralds, especially "an English paper of good repute," because they spread "mischief" even when "well-intentioned." Hence, he cut off this press from Government House sources, whether for confirmations or leaks, a prelude to the Press Act.

47. [Greg, W. R.]. "The American Conflict." 37 (1862): 468–504.
Castigated American journalists for the "outrageous language of the daily organs of the public press, which have an enormous circulation and a profitable trade." Newspapers, which reached a much larger audience than the British press had, showcased "their wonderful ignorance, their inflated bombast, their reckless calumnies against all that are eminent and good, their ludicrous canonization of many that are mean and bad." Urban tribunes hired Irish writers because the United States had no moderate, "truly American" journalists. Though not so influential as their brothers in England, they pandered to the very lowest class. An example was the *New York Herald*; an exception, the *New York Times*.

48. [Downes, John]. "Professor Wilson." 38 (1863): 75–106.
Delineated John Wilson's work for *Blackwood's Magazine*, "one of the ablest Tory periodicals of the time." Wilson's commitment to *Blackwood's* was strong: he promised two articles in every issue but in 1827 penned 27 and in 1830, 30. *Blackwood's* authors of many interests were all famous for offending taste. J. G. Lockhart was a prime culprit.

49. [Hallard, Frederick]. "Royer Collard – Philosopher and Politician." 39 (1863): 1–28.
Documented that Collard opposed French press liberty in 1814 but supported it in 1827 because curbing "good journals" to rid the state of bad was illogical.

50. [Lancaster, H. H. and John Brown]. "Thackeray." n.s., 1 (1864): 210–65.
Tracked W. M. Thackeray's press career from the *National Standard*, "a weekly literary journal" that he edited from its nineteenth number in 1833–34. He joined *Fraser's Magazine* when it was in its "youth," "full of vigour and genius" and "brilliant with scholarship and originality and fire." He also penned for *Punch* when it was young and the *New Monthly Magazine* when it was in its "great glory," 1838–40, as well as for *The Times*, *Examiner*, and other newspapers (listed).

51. [Grant Duff, M. E.]. "Russia under Alexander II." n.s., 2 (1864): 134–69.
Accented that the Russian press was "still subjected to a severe censorship," but the government recently tried to persuade Europeans otherwise by granting "a great deal of latitude" to some. "M. [Michael] Katkoff, editor of two very important periodicals at Moscow, is perhaps at this

moment one of the most popular persons in the whole Empire." Aside that [Serge] Aksakov, a Slavophile, was a "remarkable" Russian journalist.

52. [Moncrieff, James]. "The Late John Richardson." n.s., 2 (1864): 463–501.
Eulogized a college friend of the *Edinburgh Review* founders and of Thomas Campbell, who paid Richardson to write for the *New Monthly Magazine*.

53. [Grant Duff, M. E.]. "Spain." n.s., 3 (1865): 65–106.
Scrutinized the major Spanish political newspapers and their ties to specific parties or interests as well as three editors, Madrid University professor Emilio Castelar of *Democrazia*; Joàn Maño de Flaquer, "a man of intelligence and ability," of the *Diario di Barcelona*, "an old-established journal;" Francisco Pi y Margall, until recently of *Discussion*. Spain had 265 journals (62 "daily and political"; 52 Catholic; 58 government; 93 specialized) but no reviews in 1865, "not one of the happiest moments of the Spanish periodical press" because there were few talented and knowledgeable writers.

54. [Lancaster, H. H.]. "*Essays in Criticism*." n.s., 3 (1865): 158–82.
Review of Matthew Arnold's book snatched up some periodical comments on the nature of literary criticism.

55. [Brown, John]. "John Leech." n.s., 3 (1865): 213–44.
Profiled Leech, a major periodical illustrator, alongside some of his drawings. By 1862 he had published 3,000 sketches in *Punch* alone.

56. [Merivale, Louisa A.]. "Three Women of Letters." n.s., 3 (1865): 327–56.
Headlined Lucy Aitken, Joanna Baillie, and Caroline Cornwallis. Aside that Aitken's father, a physician, edited several periodicals in the eighteenth century.

57. [Shairp, J. C.]. "Samuel Taylor Coleridge." n.s., 4 (1865): 251–322.
Narrated that Coleridge failed in conducting the *Watchman* in 1796, produced "brisk but barren" criticism for the *Edinburgh Review*, and penned for the *Morning Chronicle* and then the *Morning Post*.

58. [Merivale, Louisa A.]. "On the 'Gothic' Renaissance in English Literature, and Some of Its Effects on Popular Taste." n.s., 4 (1865): 461–86.
Spoke about style in the *Spectator*, *Rambler*, and other eighteenth-century publications.

59. [Hannay, James]. "Recent Humorists: Aytoun, Peacock, Prout." n.s., 6 (1866): 75–104.
Sampled the work of William E. Aytoun, Thomas Love Peacock, and Francis Mahony (Father Prout) in the *Edinburgh Review*, *Westminster Review*, *Blackwood's Magazine*, *Fraser's Magazine*, the *Examiner*, and the *Pall Mall Gazette*. Mahony was also a foreign correspondent for the *Daily News* and *Globe*.

60. [Hallard, Frederick]. "M. Prévost-Paradol." n.s., 7 (1867): 488–503.
Portrayed Lucien Prévost-Paradol as a major French journalist. In 1856 he alternated with Louis Alloury writing leaders for the *Journal des Débats*. Prévost-Paradol's columns of "thoughtful

eloquence and wit" criticized the government and led to his dismissal. He moved to the *Courrier du Dimanche*, a "brave but ill-fated paper," and then to the *Revue des Deux Mondes*.

The British daily press was a "reminder of our public liberties, our national strength and wealth, our living, restless, indomitable energy in every field." *The Times* was the principal herald, one "densely printed" and packed with advertising, a paper that presented the "core of political discussion in… a clear, strong editorial voice, in bold and able language." It printed reports of government and meetings, literary criticism, and "accurate and full" foreign correspondence. Above all, it symbolized the wants and feelings of civilization. The British presumed that if news was "early, full, and accurate," a daily would prosper.

In France, where signature was mandated, journalists used guarded and more "prudent and courteous" language than their British colleagues. The Briton, "a public functionary fulfilling a public duty," had more freedom but sacrificed prestige by anonymity. British editors, in contrast to French, did not usually seek office so had more time to think. "The wit, the eloquence, the logic" of these people passed away with them.

61. [Grub, George and Cosmo Innes]. "*Concilia Scotiae.*" n.s., 8 (1867): 63–93.
Review of Joseph Robertson's book indicated that he edited Glasgow's *Constitutional* and Edinburgh's *Courant* and contributed to the *Quarterly Review*. He considered the triweekly *Courant* a burden but was very conscientious about his responsibilities there.

62. [Grant Duff, M. E.]. "Italy in 1867." n.s., 8 (1867): 463–96.
Deplored the "very poor" writing of Italian journalism except in Milan's *Perseveranza*, Florence's *Opinione*, and Venice's "*Unità Cattolica*, a fierce clerical journal." Among second-tier serials were Florence's *Diretto* and *Italie* (in French). Rome's *Giornale di Roma, Osservatore Romano*, and *Correspondance de Rome* (in French) were not even mediocre.

63. [Simcox, G. A.]. "French Criticism – M. Renan." n.s., 9 (1868): 63–85.
Branded the *Revue des Deux Mondes* the "ablest organ of French criticism."

64. [Russell, C. W.]. "Montalembert's *Monks of the West.*" n.s., 9 (1868): 163–95.
Review of Count C. de Montalembert's book believed that his goal for his *Avenir* was to win press liberty in order to advance Catholicism. The periodical survived state prosecution but not papal opposition. After its demise, friends of Montalembert lent "tone" to *Correspondant* columns on French Catholic literature.

65. [Rae, W. Fraser]. "Henry Crabb Robinson's *Diary.*" n.s., 11 (1869): 357–80.
Review of *Diary, Reminiscences, and Correspondence of Henry Crabb Robinson, Barrister-at-Law, F.S.A.*, edited by Thomas Sadler, paraphrased Robinson on his tenure as *Times* correspondent in Spain during the Napoleonic era, his subsequent promotion to foreign editor of the paper, and his confreres, Peter Fraser, 'a powerful writer,' and W. Combe, more a consultant to John Walter than a journalist.

66. [Nicolson, Alexander]. "*Memoir of Sir William Hamilton, Bart.*" n.s., 11 (1869): 475–515.
Review of John Veitch's book divulged that Hamilton, who had many friends at *Blackwood's Magazine*, penned politics for the *Edinburgh Review*, 1829–39. During the editorial tenure of another friend, Macvey Napier, Hamilton prepared 14 articles for the *Review*.

67. [Acton, J. D. and T. F. Wetherell]. "Note to the 100th Number of *The North British Review*." n.s., 11 (1869): 602–05.

Comprehended that a literary periodical had to have a wide range of interests and commitments to "genial tolerance" and "scientific truth" acquired by impartial methods. The *North British* always welcomed views while avoiding "actual controversy."

68. [Sigerson, George]. "Literature of the Irish Land Question." n.s., 12 (1869–70): 173–95.

Pointed to a single Irish newspaper, Wexford's *People*.

69. [Buddeus, Aurelio]. "Parties and Politics of Modern Russia." n.s., 13 (1870): 153–81.

Theorized that the "official *Journal of St. Petersburg*" set the style and language of the Russian press, even the "organs of partial opposition." The *Moscow Gazette* had "intellectual supremacy" and tremendous influence "over the whole national Russian world." Still, Alexander Herzen's *Kolokol* was "imported in great numbers" from London because its doctrines were "popular."

The Oxford and Cambridge Magazine, 1856

In its brief career, the *Oxford and Cambridge* alluded to literary journalism.

1. [Heeley, Wilfred L.]. "Mr. Macaulay." 1 (1856): 173–84.
Opined that T. B. Macaulay wrote well from his youth, as his work in *Knight's Quarterly Magazine* showed. Aside that the British "newspaper press…evolved out of chaos," namely the Civil Wars.

2. [Lushington, Vernon]. "Carlyle: As A Writer." 1 (1856): 193–211, 292–310, 336–52, 697–712, 743–71.
Believed that Thomas Carlyle was not ordinarily interested in "single combats" with other periodical contributors.

3. [Morris, William and Edward Burne-Jones]. "Ruskin and the *Quarterly*." 1 (1856): 353–61.
Reacted to Elizabeth Rigby Eastlake's review, in the *Quarterly Review* (March 1856), of John Ruskin's *Modern Writers* by accusing her of "malice and petty spite, utterly unaccountable, even in the lowest man." Her article demonstrated the "reckless, somewhat meaningless, and utterly untrue things, with which critics are in the habit of fishing for praise for originality."

The Prospective Review, 1845–1855

Sponsored by Unitarians and the precursor of the elder *National Review*, the *Prospective* situated the press in a variety of contexts.

1. [Thom, J. H.]. "Sydney Smith." 1 (1845): 171–207.
Designated Smith as the first editor of the *Edinburgh Review*, 1802–03, and a contributor until 1829. Quoted him on the *Review's* impact.

2. "Benjamin Constant." 1 (1845): 356–91.
Denominated Constant a "Newspaper Editor" because he launched the French *Constitutionnel.*

3. [Gallenga, Antonio]. "Italy, the Pope, and the Jesuits." 3 (1847): 423–60.
Vetoed Vincenzo Gioberti's proposal for limited censorship in the face of official behavior in Italy. Tuscany, obeying an Austrian order, suppressed the *Antologia*, and Rome restricted its papers generally.

4. "*David Copperfield*, and *Pendennis*." 7 (1851): 157–91.
Essay on the styles and themes of Charles Dickens and W. M. Thackeray thought that Thackeray undermined respect for periodicals in his *Pendennis*. He painted Pendennis as a man scribbling "trifles for annuals and magazines" or reviewing books "only half read, in a flippant presumptuous way in a weekly," a character more dominant than Dickens' Warrington, an "honest" guide of opinion with "valuable facts and ideas" based on study.

5. [Beard, Charles]. "*Uncle Tom's Cabin*." 8 (1852): 490–513.
Review of Harriet Beecher Stowe's book lamented that the "editor of a Free-soil paper" had recently been lynched, not surprising because public opinion was an effective censor of the press in the American South.

The Quarterly Review, 1824–1900

Writing at birth for aristocratic Tory buyers and springing from the same firm as *Murray's Magazine*, the *Quarterly* was nevertheless ecumenical in its remarks on the press. They indicated its numerous manifestations, often accompanied by attempts to limit its clout, and its practitioners.

1. [Jacob, William]. "Travels in Brazil." 31 (1824–25): 1–26.

Toured Brazil where the "few journals had a very limited circulation" and the chief news interest was trade.

2. [Blunt, J. J.]. "Tour in Germany." 31 (1824–25): 174–97.

Exclaimed that "Dresden is perhaps the only respectable capital in Europe where no newspaper is published." People either had "no political appetite" or had enough information from Leipzig and French and British gazettes, such as *The Times* and *Morning Chronicle.*

3. [Southey, Robert]. "Lisbon." 31 (1824–25): 378–90.

Communicated that Lisbon had "no literary journals."

4. [Barrow, John]. "South America." 32 (1825): 125–52.

Registered that the press was relatively free in Brazil, and "several gazettes or newspapers are published and respectably conducted in Buenos Aires."

5. [Barrow, John]. "The Australian Colonies." 32 (1825): 311–42.

Introduced the Sydney press as the *Australian Magazine*, *Australian Newspaper*, and *Sydney Gazette*.

6. [Croker, J. W.]. "Pichot's *Literary Tour*." 32 (1825): 342–55.

Review of A. Pichot's *Voyage Historique et Litteraire en Angleterre et en Europe* laughed at his notion that the *Morning Post* was the best newspaper for "regular, reasoned, literary criticism."

7. [Sumner, John Bird and J. T. Coleridge]. "Mechanics' Institutes and Infant Schools." 32 (1825): 410–28.

Alluded to the *Mechanics' Magazine*.

8. [Ellis, Henry]. "Government of India." 35 (1827): 32–66.

Review of Sir John Malcolm's *The Political History of India from 1784 to 1823* spelled out that government controlled newspapers, as the *Calcutta Journal*, by libel and censorship. Malcolm favored restriction lest European gazettes undermine necessary despotism and Indian, the army.

9. [Dodd, Charles Edward]. "Law of Libel – State of the Press." 35 (1827): 566–609.
Boasted that "the Press has naturally acquired a range and intensity of power altogether unparalleled in history" because "education and intelligence are everyday spreading more widely." More readers demanded a variety of newspapers, but the political predominated. In 1821 284 newspapers sold 23,600,000 copies in Britain. London had 14 dailies and two weeklies. By 1827 information and language were better, but an active press unsurprisingly resulted in libel suits. Although the law exempted criticism, the legislation needed amending.

Truth should be a defense in public as it was in private prosecutions, but it would never be available as long as libel was defined as "*an outrage upon the peace of society*." Defendants should be able to show that they thought their stories were true, or at least did not suspect that they were false. Even if truth exposed very private matters, it was the function of the press to censure "moral crimes." Still, newspapers must not contaminate readers or cater to their "basest passions." Excluding truth as a defense in defamation was acceptable because the law held responsible persons whose "licentiousness is unmitigated by any of the laudable motives, or useful ends which often go so far to redeem the exuberances of political and speculative writers." Journalists who agreed on nothing except "liberty of the press" yelled for truth in all circumstances, yet "news-writers" were not really at risk in 1827. Because anonymity might shield those with "sordid and malicious views" or transform exaggeration for effect into "persecution" of individuals, the law against "libelous falsehoods" should be strong.

10. "New South Wales." 37 (1828): 1–32.
Checked out the biweekly *Sydney Gazette* and *Australian* and the weekly *Monitor*. Taken together, they averaged 70–80 advertisements per issue and a circulation of 650. The *Australian*, conducted by the son of a dull London columnist, and the *Monitor* combined ability and scurrility.

11. [Lockhart, J. G.]. "May Fair and Whitehall." 37 (1828): 84–100.
Centered on literary annuals, such as the *Keepsake*.

12. [Barrow, John]. "United States." 37 (1828): 260–97.
Swore that American newspapers were "read by every class of society; they comprehend everything that is passing in all the states of the Union. Their number is immense."

13. [Lockhart, J. G.]. "*Lord Byron and Some of His Contemporaries*." 37 (1828): 402–26.
Review of Leigh Hunt's book explored his work on his brother's *News*, where he won a reputation as a theatre critic. At their *Examiner*, "one of the most profligate radical prints," he was surrounded by flatterers so had no incentive to "reach the upper ranks of literature," which his writing for the later *Liberal* confirmed. Quoted Hunt on the *Weekly Messenger* owner and editor.

14. [?Southey, Robert]. "State and Prospects of the Country." 39 (1829): 475–520.
Fretted that newspapers, which were "excessive in number," partisan, and often erroneous, impaired the formation of public opinion.

15. [Blunt, J. J.] "Southey's *Colloquies on the Progress and Prospects of Society*." 41 (1829): 1–27.
Review of Robert Southey's text attributed "the present degraded condition of the press" to journalists' defective education, a condition so serious that this "formidable…engine" might destroy itself.

16. [Southey, Robert]. "Political and Moral State of Portugal." 41 (1829): 184–226.
Summarized the Portuguese language press during the French Revolutionary era. The first political journal, the *Correio Braziliense*, was known for its "moderation." It was primarily commercial but later added scientific and literary articles. Its publication in London led Portuguese officials to start the *Investigador Portugal*. The *Gazette*, with information from British generals, gave newspapers "an authority which they had never before possessed." The Portuguese government allowed a degree of freedom if only to spur criticism of its "necessary but envied [British] allies," who saw "liberty of the press as a public right" even when journalists opposed officials.

17. [Hall, Basil]. "Political Condition and Prospects of France." 43 (1830): 215–42.
Defined newspapers as "merely the organs or mouth-pieces of the general will." In France "the journalists *direct* the public opinion." Parisians edited leaders carefully and practiced good style in long articles because they knew that they had nationwide influence. People looked to the editor for views in contrast to Britain, where the editor was "to find out what are generally held to be the soundest opinions of the sensible men of that party to which his subscribers are attached, and to put *their* actual views in a distinct and forcible shape before the public." "Our newspapers do not dictate to the nation – they are merely the servants, not the masters of the public. They take their cue from the opinions of those persons in society who, from superior talents, knowledge, or station, not only possess the best means of judging, but are, practically, most in the habit of influencing the thoughts and conduct of those about them." Newspapers varied, but the top ones tended to engage in self-censorship.

18. [Southey, Robert]. "Dymond – [*Essays*] *On the Principles of Morality*." 44 (1831): 83–120.
Review of Jonathan Dymond's book seconded him on press morality. Some newspaper editors were careless about harmful stories, others deliberately misled readers, and too many took profits from or contributed to indecent magazines.

19. [Southey, Robert]. "Moral and Political State of the British Empire." 44 (1831): 261–317.
Marked *The Times* as "the most influential, though, at the same time, the most notoriously profligate of the London newspapers, and the most impudently inconsistent in everything, except malice and mischief." Its editors, "reckless of right or wrong, always take the part which, by flattering public opinion, may best promote" sales. Whig-Radical heralds were "the professors of scurrility, the sedition-mongers," but any newspaper that publicized agitators abetted revolution.

20. [Fullarton, John]. "Parliamentary Reform." 44 (1831): 554–98.
Recognized the press as "that powerful functionary never to be neglected with impunity" by a political party.

21. [Southey, Robert]. "French Revolution – *Conspiration de Babeuf*." 45 (1831): 167–209.
Review of Philippo Buonarroti's book pointed out that several republican societies of the 1790s published newspapers, such as François Babeuf's *Tribune du Peuple*.

22. [Lockhart, J. G.]. "Croker's Edition of Boswell." 46 (1831–32): 1–46.
Review of J. W. Croker's edition of James Boswell's *Life of Samuel Johnson* complained that the steam press enabled magazine writers and parliamentary reporters to publish too many books of poor quality.

23. [Southey, Robert]. "Poetry by Mary Colling." 47 (1832): 80–103.
Disparaged cheap newspapers that "feed the discontented with sedition, and communicate to the world the newest and most approved modes by which murder and arson may be committed with the least probability of detection." Alternatively, the press devoted space to "extracts of literary criticism or poetry" that sired autodidacts.

24. [Blunt, J. J.]. "The Works of the Rev. Robert Hall." 48 (1832): 100–32.
Assessed Hall's essay, *Apology for the Freedom of the Press.*

25. [Southey, Robert]. "Prince Polignac – Revolution of the Three Days." 48 (1832): 234–85.
Placed journalists as pivotal in French political changes, sometimes "by suppressing, mutilating, or misrepresenting the facts." Activists since the days of Louis XVI were tools of "those governments whose interest it has been to delude and inflame the people."

26. [Lockhart, J. G.]. "M. Beaumont on the Americans." 53 (1835): 289–312.
Review of Gustave de Beaumont's *Marie* concurred with him that newspapers were 'the sole literature' of the United States. Busy and undiscriminating Americans wanted "reading which costs little either of time or of money" but cared nothing about style.

27. [Barrow, John]. "Quin's *Steam-Voyage down the Danube*." 54 (1835): 469–505.
Review of Michael J. Quin's book conveyed that there was no press censorship in Hungary. There was a newspaper in Pest with others likely to follow since an Englishman recently commenced a paper manufactory and "a type-foundry upon the most improved system."

28. [Barrow, John]. "The Chinese." 56 (1836): 489–521.
Stated that the Chinese press was "free," but both writers and printers were responsible for columns. If these misled or incited sedition, the penalty was death.

29. [Hall, Basil]. "Tocqueville on the State of America." 57 (1836): 132–62.
Review of Alexis de Tocqueville's *Democracy in America* stressed the "influence of the *cheap press*," notably on politics, and the sometimes negative effect of that power. On one occasion a mob murdered a rebel editor and escaped punishment.

30. [Hayward, Abraham]. "Germany and the Germans." 58 (1837): 297–333.
Review of John Strang's *Germany in 1831* denied that British periodical criticism was 'puffing' and 'quackery.' The German press was more impartial because reviewers signed their articles, but signature "cramps" criticism and deterred the qualified from writing it. Signed or not, journalistic criticism neither hurt the good nor elevated the bad book.

31. [Hayward, Abraham]. "Privileges of Parliament – Publication of Printed Papers." 61 (1838): 122–49.
Grounded newspapers' sway and respectability in the law that held them accountable for falsehood.

32. [Ford, Richard]. "*Oliver Twist.*" 64 (1839): 83–102.
Review of Charles Dickens' book scorned penny magazines of amusement or instruction. A free press spawned "libelers and satirists" in aristocratic serials. "This depraved taste of the better classes was imitated by the lower, who required their garbage." The "superficial acres of type called newspapers" were equally bad because they left little time for quality reading.

33. [Croker, J. W.]. "Post-office Reform." 64 (1839): 513–74.
Argued that the "unstamped periodical papers that now swarm in our towns" detracted from "good order" and "good morals." Cheaper postage in the empire would spread sedition. People should pay to repost stamped gazettes in order to cut postal costs.

34. [Head, Francis B.]. "The Printer's Devil." 65 (1839–40): 1–30.
Essay on compositors confided that they not only bought a newspaper but paid one of their own to read it aloud while they worked. The proofreaders, meanwhile, checked their mistakes and authors' style. The turning point for printing was *The Times* inauguration of the steam press in 1814. In 1839 the *Quarterly* could send from eight to ten articles to a printer on Monday and issue the *Review* on Saturday. Aside that the "*moral* force of the British press" would save "the glorious institutions of the British Empire."

35. [Hayward, Abraham]. "Travellers in Austria and Hungary – Turnbull – Paget – Gleig – Trollope." 65 (1839–40): 234–72.
Review of books by P. E. Turnbull, John Paget, G. R. Gleig, and Frances Trollope sketched Viennese and Austrian local papers. Domestic news was mostly official announcements; foreign was wider. Foreign newspapers could be imported for private use, but coffeehouses could only rack the authorized. "One of the best continental reviews" was the *Wiener Jahrbüchen*, a periodical of "independence in its tone."

36. [Croker, J. W.]. "Conduct of Ministers – Seditious Meetings – The Press – Socialism." 65 (1839–40): 283–314.
Catalogued most unstamped heralds before 1836 as "immoral and seditious." The reduction of the stamp duty increased their numbers, very troubling because the poor read them uncritically. One, the *Western Vindicator*, incited insurrection in Wales. Equally threatening was government identification with a newspaper. The *Observer* was "a kind of accredited organ of the ministry," whereas previous administrations merely took a particular paper into their confidence. *See New Monthly Magazine* 59: 85.

37. [Hayward, Abraham]. "Journalism in France." 65 (1839–40): 422–68.
Originated French journalism in the French Revolution, when each group had a journal. Consulate organs, chiefly the *Journal des Débats* and *Mercure*, were influential in politics and "distinguished" in literature. Conflicts developed between the Restoration monarchy and the press. The July Revolution was "effected by journalists" then rewarded with government posts. This success perpetuated the belief that journalism was "the new Eldorado," the fastest professional road to wealth and power. When journalists in government did not provide for their colleagues, the press warred on the authorities. Armand Carrel, cofounder of the *National* and later killed in a duel with Emile de Girardin of the *Presse*, was "far the most remarkable of the regular writers" of the July Monarchy. He represented "first-rate talent and unimpeached integrity."

In 1839 numerous Parisian and provincial newspapers mirrored the French, from courage to meanness. The owners and contributors of the *Journal des Débats* (studied here at length) were important. The *Presse* price revolutionized journalism; *Charivari* satire was the model for this genre. Evening and provincial papers had some merits. French reviews were not as good as British except for the *Revue des Deux Mondes* and *Revue de Paris*. French critics often blackmailed authors.

In England the editor was the chief writer; in France, the arranger of contents. The English spent money on reporters; the French spent money on the entire staff. English papers printed "prosy speeches by common-place people" for profit; the French printed political news for partisanship. "In England, the newspapers do little more than embody public opinion; in France, they dictate it." Since English tribunes could quickly organize "widely-scattered information into one lucid focus," they should be as respected as other periodicals and their personnel should have access to government positions.

38. [Croker, J. W.]. "Correspondence of the Committee of Public Safety." 67 (1840–41): 481–500.

Derided histories of the French Revolution as superficial. People thought "the public journals, and especially the *Moniteur*, supplied not merely copious but *all-sufficient* sources of historical information." Yet in 1789 only the political press covered significant matters. In 1797 the 42 papers that censured the authorities were suppressed and their owners and editors transported for life.

39. [Lockhart, J. G.]. "Buckingham and Combe on the United States." 68 (1841): 281–312.

Review of J. S. Buckingham's *America* and George Combe's *Notes on the United States of America* verified that Buckingham's view of the "bombast of newspaper editors" was not unique. Two-thirds of British leaders were "written upon the supposition that the public feel a profound interest about editorial squabbles." What was unique about the American press was its "editorial indulgence in a species of fun and drollery."

40. [Lockhart, J. G.]. "The Copyright Question." 69 (1841–42): 186–227.

Snarled that Robert Chambers was a "trafficker" who made a fortune from *Chambers's Journal*, an "ephemeral compilation" of the works of others.

41. [Croker, J. W.]. "Dickens's *American Notes* – Mann's *Anniversary Oration*." 71 (1842–43): 502–28.

Repeated Charles Dickens' thesis that the worst manners and character of the United States were "the *child and companion* of her political institutions – a licentious and uncontrollable newspaper press."

42. [Lockhart, J. G.]. "Theodore Hook." 72 (1843): 53–108.

Marginalized Hook's editing of the *New Monthly Magazine* but not of *John Bull*. His campaign about Queen Caroline worked well in a weekly with an anonymous editor who could "strike frequent blows" to earn his 2,000 pounds per year. *See Dublin University Review* 33: 81.

43. [Croker, J. W.]. "Horace Walpole." 72 (1843): 516–52; 74 (1844): 395–416.

Certified that Walpole's letters had more information on history and society than the *Gentleman's Magazine*, *Critical Review*, *Morning Post*, *London Gazette*, and an early *Hue and Cry*.

44. [Lockhart, J. G.]. "*Memoirs of William Taylor, of Norwich – Correspondence with Southey.*" 73 (1843–44): 27–68.
Sampled Taylor's leaders penned when he edited the *Norwich Iris*.

45. [Croker, J. W.]. "The Guillotine." 73 (1843–44): 235–80.
Barked about the "subservience of the press to the dominant tyranny of the day" during the French Revolution. Even the *Moniteur* acceded, albeit it preserved "moderation and tact." The Directory cancelled whatever liberty existed and immediately transported more than 40 journalists.

46. "Illustrated Books." 74 (1844): 167–99.
Speculated that the *Penny Magazine* gave the "greatest impulse" to illustrated periodicals. The *Saturday Magazine* was also one of the "pioneers" of woodcuts in serials that the *Illustrated London News* matured.

47. [Kinglake, A. W.]. "Milnes on the Hareem – The Rights of Women." 75 (1844–45): 94–125.
Review of several books, among them R. M. Milnes' *Palm Leaves*, concluded that women could not converse with men because they relied on serials that had "well-written but short critiques, interspersed with copious extracts" of books instead of reading the volumes.

48. [Brougham, Henry]. "Publication of Private Matters – *Memoirs of Lady Hestor Stanhope*." 76 (1845): 430–59.
Designated "an individual who keeps a diary" a journalist. The press could publish society news but should be wary of private intrusions and revelations of "state secrets."

49. [Croker, J. W.]. "Thiers' Histories." 76 (1845): 521–83.
Review of Adolphe Thiers' histories of France highlighted his journalism, particularly cofounding the *National* with Armand Carrel. Thiers contributed literary paragraphs of "vivacity and taste" and political ones of "vigour and boldness" to the *Consitutionnel*. When he worked for the paper in 1825, it had 16,250 subscribers, the most in Paris, while the more conservative *Journal des Débats* had 13,000.

50. [Lockhart, J. G.]. "Captain Neill's Narrative – General Nott in Affghanistan [*sic*]." 78 (1846): 463–510.
Reviewed J. M. B. Neill's *Recollections of Four Years Service in the East* and volumes by E. Thornton and Mohan Lal. Chastised the Anglo-Indian press for disseminating libel soon translated into local dialects and "greedily circulated by all the internal enemies" of the British.

51. [Cheney, Edward]. "Pius IX." 82 (1847–48): 231–60.
Bemoaned that the freedom of the press granted by Pius IX in the Papal States led to journalists' "malignant and unjust attacks" on neighboring territories.

52. [Croker, J. W.]. "French Revolution – February, 1848." 82 (1847–48): 541–93.
Posted that the 1848 French government closed several journals and pressured others but not the *Journal des Débats*, *National*, and *Réforme*.

53. [Cheney, Edward]. "Revolutions in Italy." 83 (1848): 227–49.
Welcomed Italian press liberty, exemplified by the *Contemporaneo* (Rome), *Alba* (Florence), *Risorgimento* (Turin), and *22 Marzo dell Independenza Italiana* (Milan), but with a caveat. Because proponents of "extreme democracy" dominated newspapers, they were more licentious than when restricted. The "decency and moderation essential to the respectability of the daily press" had not overcome "exaggeration and vehemence."

54. [Croker, J. W.]. "Political Prospects of France and England." 83 (1848): 250–304.
Pointed to the *National*, *Moniteur*, *Réforme*, and other Paris serials.

55. [Croker, J. W.]. "Jérome Paturot – On the French Revolution." 83 (1848): 516–52.
Review of a novel by Louis Reybaud dubbed him a journalist of talent and moderation who penned for the *Revue des Deux Mondes*, *Constitutionnel*, and *National*.

56. [Cheney, Edward]. "Lord Beaumont on Foreign Policy." 85 (1849): 225–59.
Review of *Austria and Central Italy* by M. T. Stapleton, Baron Beaumont, tabbed many European gazettes "mendacious," mainly when their editors were in government. British "foreign correspondents" were not much better because their hosts leashed them, their ignorance of the local language encouraged their sources' deception, and their own prejudices distorted their reports.

57. [Croker, J. W.]. "Democracy." 85 (1849): 260–312.
Perceived "the power of the Press, and especially the Newspaper Press." The French press begat the 1830 and 1848 Revolutions. In Britain, "inferior periodicals…inundate our great towns," newspapers that were "grossly immoral and seditious." The "respectable" ones affected government by forcing it to respond to the democracy of the press, the pressure of public opinion.

58. [Head, Francis B.]. "Mechanism of the Post-Office." 87 (1850): 69–115.
Delineated how the post office handled newspapers.

59. [Reeve, Henry]. "The Austrian Revolution." 87 (1850): 190–238.
Glanced at liberty of the press in Austria.

60. [Croker, J. W.]. "Lamartine's Refutation of the *Quarterly Review*: Escape of Louis Philippe." 87 (1850): 276–88.
Tracked a controversy from an article in the *Quarterly* (3/50) to its translated republication in the *Revue Britannique*, a response by Alphonse de Lamartine in his *Conseiller du Peuple*, a monthly "pamphlet-newspaper," and a further commentary in the *Courrier de la Somme* (6/50).

61. [Lockhart, J. G. and Whitwell Elwin]. "Life and Letters of Southey." 88 (1850–51): 197–247.
Review of Charles Southey's edition of the *Life and Correspondence of Robert Southey* tallied his contributions to periodicals (*Annual Register* 52; *Foreign Quarterly Review* 3; *Quarterly* 94).

62. [Coulton, D. T.]. "Junius." 90 (1851–52): 91–163.
Acknowledged the ongoing interest of periodicals in the identification of Junius. *See Fraser's Magazine* 76: 794 and *North British Review* 19: 475.

63. [Croker, J. W.]. "The French Autocrat." 90 (1851–52): 257–83.
Prayed that Napoleon III was "not rash enough to hope, or mad enough to try" to achieve the "total extinction" of the French press, "a representative body." He apparently tolerated a few "servile" and "lying" papers.

64. [Lockhart, J. G. and Whitwell Elwin]. "Lord Cockburn's *Life of Jeffrey*." 91 (1852): 105–59.
Review of Henry Cockburn's biography of Francis Jeffrey revisited a founder of the *Edinburgh Review*, previously "a pretty regular contributor to the *Monthly Review*." Like its peers, it was a pawn of booksellers who dictated subjects and paid little to inferior scribes. Because of the "low state of journalism," Jeffrey was nervous about the effect being a salaried editor would have on his reputation and his careers in law and politics. His criticisms, though "strictly reviews, and not essays," demonstrated "his power of seizing and delineating the prominent features of a book." More important, he had the knowledge and skill to edit, although some of his 'journeymen' were less skilled. These "degenerate suckers thrown up from his root mistook asperity for sarcasm, and pertness for wit." Aside on Jeffrey's relations with Walter Scott.

65. [Bowen, G. F.]. "Ionian Administration – Lord Seaton and Sir Henry Ward." 91 (1852): 315–52.
Thundered that local Ionian newspapers, from the first in 1849, used liberty to "publish atrocious slanders." Government banished "two of the most seditious journalists," but London's *Daily News* employed a declared outlaw (Papanicolas), who wrote as "Ionian."

66. [Brooks, Charles]. "The House of Commons." 95 (1854): 1–37.
Silhouetted parliamentary reporters, those "for whom and to whom" MPs spoke. Better educated than their sometimes distinguished forebears, as Charles Dickens, they were "the filter through which the senatorial eloquence is percolated to the public." The journalist "purifies" speeches, correcting grammar and removing "nonsense." Reporters initially sat with the public but well before 1854 had a separate and spacious area. They still took notes in turns averaging about 100 words per minute in shorthand, but the "masterly" summary, introduced by Horace Twiss, was preferable to whole, often dull speeches.

67. [Wynter, Andrew]. "The Electric Telegraph." 95 (1854): 118–64.
Asserted that telegraphy made journalism more concise because of the price of messages. Technology already facilitated transmission of information from London morning dailies to local news exchanges and would soon speed news across the Atlantic.

68. [Thackeray, W. M.]. "*Pictures of Life and Character*." 96 (1854–55): 75–86.
Review of John Leech's book explicated his illustrations for *Punch*. *See Blackwood's Magazine* 158: 866.

69. [Forster, John]. "Sir Richard Steele." 96 (1854–55): 509–68.
Review of T. B. Macaulay's *The Life and Writings of Addison* rehabilitated Steele as the "father of the English essay." His essay writing represented "canons of taste" and "moral truths." His periodicals glowed with "the bright wit, the cordial humour, the sly satire, the subtle yet kindly criticism, the good nature and humanity" of the man. Although Daniel Defoe's *Review* was the model for the *Tatler*, it was more popular than any prior periodical. Begun in April 1709, the triweekly was not sent by post until #26 because reader demand was unanticipated. The *Spectator* also had great success before Steele established the *Guardian* and *Crisis*. Drew on Macaulay for Steele's relations with Joseph Addison.

70. [Gladstone, William E.]. "Sardinia and Rome." 97 (1855): 41–70.
Blared that the Piedmontese press was free but the Roman was restricted from fear of revolution, not blasphemy.

71. [Elwin, Whitwell]. "Memoirs of Sydney Smith." 97 (1855): 106–42.
Tribute to Sydney Smith divulged that the *Edinburgh Review* would not have survived its first year but for "the able and prolific pen" of Henry Brougham. Contributors who consented to write "without remuneration" did not do so after "the immediate flush of novelty was past." The salary of editor Francis Jeffrey, 50 pounds per issue, was insufficient for his duties. Publishers previously sponsored reviews in order to promote their own books. These serials, with articles by "illiterate drudges or needy men of intellect," were "dull and vapid, devoid of talent, taste, or candour." They discredited the whole genre until the *Edinburgh* arrived. Its early "pungency" captivated some and irritated others, but Jeffrey set the standard for the independent review by those who were not "rash young men." Later reviewers were less moderate, notably about politics.

72. [Wynter, Andrew]. "Advertisements." 97 (1855): 183–225.
Searched newspaper advertising from its inception for "the pattern of the age." The first advertisement was in the *Mercurius Politicus*, 1652, one of the many heralds born in the Civil War. (This reference is *contra* A. Andrews, I: 49.) An early *Hue and Cry* had inserts about "runaway servants and lost or stolen horses and dogs." In 1659 the *Mercurius Politicus* first noticed "negro boys," lads likely brought from Portuguese territories. Advertisements for "blacks" referred to Indians until about 1700. About the same time, listings for coach travel surfaced. Patent medicines were the only goods for sale until tea advertising began. During the Restoration, the field sports that the Puritans disdained returned to favor and with them dog advertising, which joined that for other goods and lotteries until the plague. Thereafter, advertisements featured that "romantic felon, the highwayman," and liquor, whose sale was rising. From 1688 papers and advertisements multiplied, culminating in the 1692 *City Mercury*, an all-advertising sheet that was free but still failed because it had no news. Newsletters continued because the printed press did not tell "political and social chitchat." In Anne's reign, auctions were the stars, but theatres were not far behind. By the 1720s personals placed the duels of men and the fights of both sexes alongside blood sports involving cocks and bulls and assignations that showed little respect for women.

The 1745 *General Advertiser*, the first to profit from advertising, opened "a new era in the newspaper press." It betokened a shift away from advertisements for amusement to those for business (goods and shipping). After 1800, George Robbins developed well-written "commercial puffing." By 1835 inserts were illustrated, and by 1855 some business advertising budgets were quite large, for example, Holloway's Pills at 30,000 pounds per year. *Times* listings were enormous (2,575 on 24 May 1855). Advertisements varied enormously. They covered jobs, goods, auctions, and personal matters. Among the more unusual were those on "conscience money," offers to pay for some mishap or injury. Even though papers were careful, swindling slipped in, such as the promise of a good imperial marriage. Advertising costs differed dramatically: for the same insert *The Times* charged four shillings; *Illustrated London News*, one pound, eight shillings; *Punch*, 15 shillings; the *Examiner*, three shillings, six pence; the *Spectator*, seven shillings, six pence.

The Times was "the national paper and reflects more than any other the life of the people." Its circulation rose from 23,000 in 1845 to 60,000 in 1855, but the end of the stamp duty would surely spawn "mosquito-like cheap journals." Some papers already specialized: the *Morning Post* on "fashion and high life"; *Bell's Life in London* on sports; the *Era* on "theatricals." The largest weekly by far was the *Illustrated London News*.

73. [Tomlinson, Charles]. "The Supply of Paper." 97 (1855): 225–45.

Ascribed greater demand for paper in part to the growth of periodicals. Colonial dailies were burgeoning, and Americans were also buying from British suppliers. Wholesalers were proponents of the paper duty because it protected their monopoly.

74. [Elwin, Whitwell]. "Southey's *Letters*." 98 (1855–56): 456–501.

Review of *Selections from the Letters of Robert Southey*, edited by J. W. Warter, dealt with Southey's articles in the *Quarterly*, which paid him ten guineas per page, a rate akin to that of the *Edinburgh Review*. Southey remarked that for this fee he could afford to "write with care." He previously penned for the *Monthly Magazine* for one guinea per week and for the *Critical Review* regularly.

75. [Hannay, James]. "English Political Satires." 101 (1857): 394–441.

Flipped through some newspapers, among them the eighteenth-century *Examiner* and *Anti-Jacobin* and the more recent *Times, John Bull*, and *Punch*, for examples of satire.

76. [Masson, David]. "Tobias Smollett." 103 (1858): 66–108.

Examined the *Critical Review*, "a literary journal in opposition to the *Monthly Review*." Smollett, the original editor of the *Critical*, "creditably conducted" it with respect to book reviews but had other problems. He later started the *Briton*, a weekly newspaper opposed by John Wilkes.

77. [Elwin, Whitwell]. "Life and Writings of Johnson." 105 (1859): 176–233.

Review of J. W. Croker's *Boswell's Life of Johnson* regarded Samuel Johnson's work for the *Gentleman's Magazine* as "important."

78. [Tremenheere, J. H.]. "The Australian Colonies, and the Gold Supply." 107 (1860): 1–45.

Recorded that Melbourne had three dailies and 18 weeklies or other serials. The Australians also had eight monthlies, a quarterly, and several annuals.

79. [Layard, A. H.]. "Cavour." 110 (1861): 208–47.

Indicated Camillo di Cavour's journalism, first with the *Giornale Agrario* and then the *Risorgimento* in 1847.

80. [Cecil, Robert]. "Stanhope's *Life of Pitt*." 111 (1862): 516–61.

Review of P. H. Stanhope's book bruited that the United States utilized its postal system to repress free opinion in periodicals during its Civil War.

81. [Cecil, Robert]. "The Confederate Struggle and Recognition." 112 (1862): 535–70.

Underscored that the United States enforced "press censorship" during the Civil War.

82. [Gleig, G. R.]. "Life of John Wilson." 113 (1863): 208–40.

Review of Mary Gordon's *Christopher North* talked about Wilson's work in the *Edinburgh Review* and his role in the birth of *Blackwood's Magazine*. The *Edinburgh* was "supreme" in "literature and taste," but *Blackwood's* engaged "distinguished" contributors, such as Wilson and J. G. Lockhart, to compete. Its early warlike style was not acceptable in 1863, but Lockhart never displayed "malignity."

83. [Mansel, H. L.]. "Sensation Novels." 113 (1863): 481–514.

Avouched that periodicals were partly responsible for the sensation novel. Because they issued regularly, to hold readers they borrowed material of "transitory interest." Publishers counted on serial installments of "tales of a marketable stamp" for later reprints as books. Themes for these tales frequently came from crime reports in the dailies.

83a. [Marzials, Frank T.]. "Lacordaire." 116 (1864): 111–43.

Biography of J. B. Lacordaire noted that he penned many of the *Avenir*'s "most furious articles" and edited the *Ere Nouvelle*.

84. [Massey, Gerald]. "Life and Writings of Thomas Hood." 114 (1863): 332–68.

Resurrected Hood's ideas about his roles at the *London Magazine*, as subeditor and as contributor. From 1841 he edited the *New Monthly Magazine* for 300 pounds per year while also publishing in *Punch*. In 1844 he commenced *Hood's Magazine* with limited capital.

85. [Gleig, G. R.]. "Life of Lockhart." 116 (1864): 439–82.

Suspected that J. G. Lockhart was responsible, after its sixth number, for the success of *Blackwood's Magazine*. In 1826 he became editor of the *Quarterly*, which "claims to take part in forming public taste and directing public opinion on points of the greatest importance to the moral and intellectual well-being of society." "The editor has not only to master the spirit and temper of the age, keeping himself *au courant* for that purpose with the literature, the science, and the politics of the whole civilised world, but he must sit in judgment on the labours of others." Although the courteous Lockhart was a good editor, some authors objected to his changes of their manuscripts. *See Temple Bar* 105: 175.

86. [Hill, Alfred]. "Libel and the Freedom of the Press." 117 (1865): 519–39.

Dated press freedom from 1694 when the Licensing Act expired. In English libel law, a writing, not a publication, determined a civil or criminal offense done with malice. Privilege extended to "public officers in public matters" and courts. Comments about others might be "unfair, uncalled for, and in bad taste" but could not be challenged unless the writer was reckless about the truth. Newspapers were rarely found guilty because the victim usually wanted space to answer, not damages, but rarely got either. Libel law, by making the press accountable, also made the public take it seriously. The *Saturday Review* case, *Campbell v. Spottiswoode*, 1863, was a warning to journalists to "use every reasonable means of ascertaining…truth." The proposed amendment to exempt publishers from responsibility for printing speeches with libelous information was dangerous because press reach was so wide.

87. [Merivale, Herman]. "Caricature and Grotesque in Literature and Art." 119 (1866): 215–50.

Had fewer words on press caricature in the eighteenth and nineteenth centuries than on artists.

88. [Bulwer-Lytton, E. G.]. "Charles Lamb and Some of His Companions." 122 (1867): 1–29.

Spotlighted Lamb, William Hazlitt, and Leigh Hunt. Hazlitt was the "truculent assailant of the political opinions" in the *Quarterly*, but Hunt's essays in the *Indicator* were excellent.

89. [Yule, Henry]. "The Week's Republic in Palermo, 1866." 122 (1867): 100–36.

Unveiled a Sicilian government that "systematically suppressed news" of a short revolt by silence in the official gazette, although one of the dailies reported the event.

90. [Johns, B. G.]. "The Poetry of Seven Dials." 122 (1867): 382–406.

Chronicled that cheaply printed ballads once spread news quickly. In London, 20–30 dozen were formerly sold every day there was good weather. The penny daily slowed the circulation of halfpenny ballads of crimes "in their minute and hideous details."

91. [Hayward, Abraham]. "New Paris." 123 (1867): 1–35.

Warranted that French newspapers under monarchy had much influence. Unlike the English press, the French did "more than lead opinion." "It brought about one revolution after another." Because it did so with "an air of arrogant superiority…it consequently excited little sympathy when it fell." In 1867 French journalism was "unsatisfactory in the extreme." It could criticize only the enemies of government lest it face libel charges and suppression. Equally, the "influence of the English newspaper press, although eminently beneficial on the whole, and indeed indispensable to English institutions, is not and cannot be exercised without offending the feelings or prejudices of a large part of the community."

92. [Gleig, G. R.]. "Sir Walter Scott." 124 (1868): 1–54.

Surmised that by 1808 the *Edinburgh Review* was such a "strong party publication" that John Murray, with "energy and sagacity," reacted with his *Quarterly* for which Scott wrote. The *Edinburgh*'s war against the *Quarterly* was sounder politically than economically.

93. [Hayward, Abraham]. "Lord Macaulay and His School." 124 (1868): 287–333.

Expounded T. B. Macaulay's ideas on the identity of Junius.

94. [Hayward, Abraham]. "Lord Lyndhurst and Lord Brougham." 126 (1869): 1–61.

Review of John Campbell's *Lives of Lord Lyndhurst and Lord Brougham* noticed that Henry Brougham neither demanded a big advance for his *Edinburgh Review* essays nor claimed to pen an entire issue.

95. [Kebbel, T. E.]. "Era of George the Second." 128 (1870): 110–34.

Calendared "political journalism" from the *Craftsman*, conducted by "gentlemen and statesmen" who "reflected the spirit of the age completely." Its circulation of 12,000 made it "a real power in the political world."

96. [Hayward, Abraham]. "Lanfrey's *Napoleon*." 128 (1870): 342–86.
Review of P. Lanfrey's book iterated that Napoleon I controlled the press but permitted "a little venom" to prove that it was free.

97. [Wilson, John]. "Prévost-Paradol and Napoleon III." 129 (1870): 369–92.
Portrayed Lucien Prévost-Paradol as a diplomat well known for his journalism. He was "the most vivacious, the most pertinacious, and most formidable critic in the press of imperial policy from 1858 to 1866," with leaders in the *Journal des Débats* and fortnightly letters in the *Courrier du Dimanche*. Just as in 1807 René de Chateaubriand was censured for a *Mercure* column against Napoleon I, so Prévost-Paradol had to pay a fine and serve a short prison sentence for a *Courrier du Dimanche* column against Napoleon III.

"The gradual recovery of its freedom of late years by the French newspaper press has been due in great measure to the distinguished ability and independence of individual journalists; while the full recognition of those qualities has in like measure been due to the publication of the names of French newspaper-writers at the foot of their articles." Signature was a mandate since 1848.

98. [Smith, William]. "Evidence from Handwriting – Junius." 130 (1871): 328–50.
Reviewed Charles Chabot's *The Handwriting of Junius Professionally Investigated*.

99. [Wilson, John]. "The Third French Republic, and the Second German Empire." 130 (1871): 351–73.
Review of Emile Leclerq's *La Guerre de 1870*, a book of newspaper cuttings, maintained that the Paris press shaped the perspective of the entire French nation during the Franco-Prussian War.

100. [Brewer, J. S.]. "New Sources of English History." 130 (1871): 373–407.
Announced that the "liveliest materials of history have been banished now-a-days to newspaper paragraphs and special correspondents," whereas in earlier eras ambassadors' letters were a major source of information.

101. [Smith, William]. "The Life and Writings of John Hookam Frere." 132 (1872): 26–59.
Earmarked Frere's part in the launch of the *Quarterly* and his columns in the *Anti-Jacobin*. The style of *Anti-Jacobin* writers was appropriate for its time but not for 1872.

102. [Elwin, Whitwell]. "Forster's *Life of Dickens*." 132 (1872): 125–47.
Review of John Forster's biography proceeded from Charles Dickens' days as a parliamentary reporter and his initial article in the *Monthly Magazine* to his editing of *Bentley's Miscellany*. Dickens' support of international copyright offended a purportedly demoralized and tyrannical American press.

103. [Wilson, John]. "The Reign of Terror, and Its Secret Police." 133 (1872): 43–76.
Plumbed the *Nouvelles à la main*, French manuscript chronicles of the old regime that sold for six to nine francs monthly.

104. [Hayward, Abraham]. "Charles, Comte de Montalembert." 134 (1873): 415–56.
Guessed that the circulation of Montalembert's *Avenir* never hit 3,000.

105. [Palgrave, Francis]. "John Stuart Mill's *Autobiography*." 136 (1874): 150–79.
Confirmed that Mill, from age 16 to 22, "wrote copiously in newspapers and reviews."

106. [Hayward, Abraham]. "Political Caricatures: Gillray and His Successors." 136 (1874): 453–98.
Focused on illustrators James Gillray, Richard Doyle, and John Leech, the last two published in *Punch*.

107. [Smith, William]. "John Wilson Croker." 142 (1876): 83–126.
Classified Croker as both a contributor to the *Quarterly* and informal assistant of editor William Gifford.

108. [Hayward, Abraham]. "Ticknor's Memoirs." 142 (1876): 160–201.
Review of George Ticknor's *Life, Letters, and Journals* quoted his favorable impression of Francis Jeffrey, 'this Abraham of the *Edinburgh Review*.'

109. [Craik, Henry]. "*English Thought in the Eighteenth Century*." 143 (1877): 404–23.
Review of Leslie Stephens' captioned book glided over Joseph Addison's satires in the *Spectator*.

110. [Hayward, Abraham]. "Harriet Martineau's *Autobiography*." 143 (1877): 484–526.
Review of Martineau's book encompassed her refusal to edit the *Economical Magazine*.

111. [Hardcastle, J. A.]. "The Legislation of the Commonwealth." 145 (1878): 449–74.
Returned to the early British attempts to control the press that provoked John Milton to write in its defense.

112. [Burrows, Montagu]. "Rise of the Modern British Empire." 146 (1878): 331–61.
Testified that the "Press was making a rapid advance" in the eighteenth century.

113. [Hayward, Abraham]. "M. Thiers: His Life and Character." 146 (1878): 443–84.
Idolized Adolphe Thiers as "the life and soul" of the *National*, which he started with Armand Carrel in 1830. Thiers also penned for the *Constitutionnel* and *Globe* at a time when journalism was "a well-ascertained stepping-stone to fame and fortune" in France.

114. [Hayward, Abraham]. "Prince Bismarck." 147 (1879): 113–55.
Unmasked "Dr. Busch" as a "journalist *attaché*...in constant and confidential communication" with Otto von Bismarck during the Franco-Prussian War.

115. [Hayward, Abraham]. "Count Cavour." 148 (1879): 99–142.
Posited that Camillo di Cavour adopted Benjamin Constant's idea that the press was "the mistress of intelligence, and intelligence...of the world." Cavour's journalism from 1843 involved writing for numerous periodicals and cofounding the *Risorgimento* in 1847. As editor he wrote leaders, but his style was not suitable for newspapers.

116. [Collins, J. Churton]. "Lord Bolingbroke." 149 (1880): 1–47.
Judged that the early numbers of the eighteenth-century *Examiner* were "not distinguished by conspicuous ability." Daniel Defoe's *Review*, by contrast, was "the most influential paper in the kingdom."

117. [Morris, Mowbray]. "Thomas Chatterton." 150 (1880): 78–110.
Broadcast that Chatterton, whose hero was John Wilkes, tried to imitate the style of Junius. The authorities, upset by the "mysterious power" of Junius in the *Public Advertiser*, staged such a campaign of seditious libel against it, the *London Museum*, and *Evening Post* as to make every newspaper "cautious."

118. [Hitchman, Francis]. "The Newspaper Press." 150 (1880): 498–537.
Boomed that there was no history of the British newspaper but only books (cited) on specific aspects of this press.

Reduction of the stamp and introduction of the penny post in the 1830s began a growth that brought commensurate clout (with data from C. Mitchell's first *Newspaper Press Directory* in 1846 to the 1879 edition). Printing technology abetted circulation, and telegraphy, newsgathering. Telegraphy was crucial for the news agencies, Reuters, and the Central Press, which served the country gazettes. Stereotyping was also important. Since 1868 the Press Association impacted all local heralds.

Country papers (probed in alphabetical order here) changed after 1855. Dailies overtook weeklies. As they lost "power and prestige," they turned to serializing novels to survive. Meantime, newspapers in Wales, Ireland, and Scotland proliferated.

London dailies and weeklies in 1880 exceeded the quality of the entire eighteenth-century output, albeit literary excellence was ephemeral. Sunday papers, however, were notorious for "the violence and brutality of their tone" and their Radical politics. The parish newspaper, the trade journal, and serials of causes and of sects flourished in the capital.

More readers, thanks to national education, meant more newspapers making the "profession of journalism, a tolerably profitable one." The best London leader-writers earned 15–20 guineas per week. Junior reporters in the country, who had "capacity, intelligence, and industry," could become editors.

Aside that Liberal election success in 1880 was due to press coverage secured by flattering journalists. *See* 171: 150.

119. [Collins, J. Churton]. "Lord Bolingbroke in Exile." 151 (1881): 67–99.
Singled out Henry St. John as a major author of the *Craftsman*, which had "an influence on public opinion without precedent in journalism." His "Dissertation upon Parties" (1733–34) and the columns of Junius were the epitome of political journalism.

120. [Hayward, Abraham]. "Thomas Carlyle and His *Reminiscences*." 151 (1881): 385–428.
Revived Carlyle's articles in the *Edinburgh Review* and invitations of the *Foreign Review* and *Foreign Quarterly Review* to pen for them.

121. [Courthope, W. J.]. "Radical History and Tory Government." 152 (1881): 239–71.
Lamented that newspapers, unlike other publications, still had to pay a penalty for libel under the terms of 1819 legislation.

122. [Hayward, Abraham]. "*The Comte de Montlosier.*" 153 (1882): 203–40.
Reviewed A. Bardoux's book whose protagonist, Count F. de Montlosier, an émigré from the French Revolution, established the short-lived *Journal de France et d'Angleterre* in London in 1795. He then took over the *Courrier de Londres*, once edited by Abbé Charles Calonne and successor to Jacques Brissot's *Courrier de l'Europe* , and made it influential.

123. [Collins, J. Churton]. "Jonathan Swift." 153 (1882): 377–430.
Retold the story of Swift's "paper war" in which the *Examiner* fought the *Medley* and *Observator*, a conflict wherein both sides were "rancorous and unscrupulous." Richard Steele in the *Guardian* symbolized journalism of such "scurrility and intemperance" that Swift responded in a "cruel pamphlet," *The Importance of the "Guardian" Considered.* Aside on Swift's work for the *Tatler* and *Spectator.*

124. [Hayward, Abraham]. "Mr. Lecky's *England in the Eighteenth Century.*" 153 (1882): 489–529.
Review of W. E. H. Lecky's book considered the case of John Wilkes, the columns of Junius, and the struggle of the press to gain entry to Parliament.

125. [Hayward, Abraham]. "Sir Archibald Alison's *Autobiography.*" 155 (1883): 134–73.
Review of Alison's book contested his views of the early *Edinburgh Review*, perhaps due to the fact that he was "a constant and voluminous contributor" to *Blackwood's Magazine.* He often produced two political essays a month. Aside that the *Quarterly's* neglect of his *History of the French Revolution* was the result of charity, not the machination of J. W. Croker.

126. [Lee-Warner, William]. "The Indian Crisis." 156 (1883): 243–69.
Acknowledged that the "press of India, and in the last resort that of England, constitute the only remaining check upon the Viceroy." Yet Anglo-Indian journals were unable "to represent native opinion" because of the "weakness of their literary staff" and the barriers of language, custom, and distance. The Indian press also did not mirror popular ideas because it was "the organ of a small educated minority," mainly Brahmin editors. They were so committed to preaching libel that they swallowed losses. Their tribunes were "in a special degree the weapon of the political organizations, which are secretly sapping the foundations of British rule." The British Empire had 360 newspapers. Bombay had 120 for 17 million people; Madras, 35 for 31 million.

127. [Martin, Theodore]. "*The Croker Papers.*" 158 (1884): 518–66.
Review of the correspondence and diaries of J. W. Croker referred to his essays in the *Quarterly.*

128. [Morris, Mowbray]. "English Society, and Its Historians." 161 (1885): 142–71.
Observed that it was to the "magazines…one goes to for entertainment."

129. [Jennings, L. J.]. "The New Parliament." 162 (1886): 257–91.
Reasoned that, based on election results, "the Liberal press has been far more active than the Conservative."

130. [Jennings, L. J.]. "Travels in the British Empire." 162 (1886): 443–67.
Denigrated an Indian press "full of sedition."

131. [Prothero, R. E.]. "Cabot's *Life of Emerson.*" 166 (1888): 130–59.
Review of the works of James E. Cabot and others rebutted Thomas Carlyle's perception of the *Dial* as impractical and instead called it a "representative of a fresh, indigenous, and thoroughly American movement."

132. [Palmer, Roundell]. "The Monarchy of July, and Its Lessons." 166 (1888): 439–68.
Decried Irish attempts to intimidate jurors, a tactic allegedly learned from the French press of 1832.

133. [Hardcastle, J. A.]. "*Fifty Years Ago.*" 167 (1888): 186–217.
Review of Walter Besant's retrospective credited Samuel Warren's "Diary of a Late Physician," published in *Blackwood's Magazine*, 1830–36, for popularizing the 'monthly serial.' In 1888 newspapers contained book reviews in "true literary style" and often good theatre criticism.

134. [Whittle, J. L.]. "Daniel O'Connell's *Correspondence.*" 167 (1888): 303–34.
Review of titled volume edited by W. J. Fitzpatrick said of the 1842 *Nation* that "its style of writing and directness of policy went home to the popular heart."

135. [Strachey, Edward]. "Nonsense as a Fine Art." 167 (1888): 335–65.
Touched on contributors, chiefly those in *Punch*, who refined comic writing as well as comic art.

136. [Cartwright, W. C.]. "The Letters and Diary of Count Cavour." 168 (1889): 103–35.
Flagged Camillo di Cavour as *Risorgimento* editor.

137. [Boyle, Courtenay]. "Gambling." 168 (1889): 136–66.
Voiced that the many "sporting newspapers" had "more or less" accurate information and gossip on horse racing. "Even the highest class newspapers publish turf intelligence, and all but the very highest give a daily quotation of the odds."

138. [Mallock, W. H.]. "Mr. John Morley, and Progressive Radicalism." 168 (1889): 249–80.
Review of Morley's *Collected Writings* pirated his notion that the press kept discussion at a "low level" because the 'mind of the average journalist' was 'usually a degree or two lower' than the mind of an 'ordinary' reader.

139. [Hitchman, Francis]. "Penny Fiction." 171 (1890): 150–71.
Blasted juvenile papers whose serialized fiction was "foul and filthy trash." This material spurred youths who were the products of secular education to commit crime. Examples were the *Bad Boys' Paper*, *Boys of London*, and *Boys of New York*, printed in London from New York stereotypes. The *Boys of England*, in business for 14 years, was somewhat better, and the *Boy's Own Paper* and *Girl's*

Own Paper were much better. The last two would probably reap more sales if they removed the imprint of the Religious Tract Society.

The cheap press stole from British and American novelists or employed amateurs and hacks, "broken-down University men, unsuccessful reporters," to pen stories. "But if the literary level of the weekly press be low, its morals are irreproachable. Fortunately, it has been found out that immorality and indecency do not pay" because law and public opinion opposed them. The *Family Herald* was "a very creditable specimen of the popular literature of the day"; its fiction was good, but its essays were "trite." The *London Journal* and its competitors featured the "penny periodical romance." Reiterated concepts (150: 498) of the British Sunday press.

140. [Grey, W. E.]. "Twenty Years of Irish Home Rule in New York." 171 (1890): 260–86.

Investigated the relationship between New York machine politics and the press with evidence from newspaper columns and magazine cartoons, such as those in *Puck* and *Life*. New York dailies were all "party organs," but "serious and comic" weeklies might be independent.

141. [Jennings, L. J.]. "The Work of the House of Commons." 171 (1890): 532–64.

Rationalized that the London press except *The Times* no longer reported debates in full because editors assumed their readers cared nothing about Parliament. The local papers were much more detailed and accurate than the metros.

142. [Courthope, W. J.]. "Memoir of John Murray." 173 (1891): 1–36.

Review of Samuel Smiles' *A Publisher and His Friends* synopsized Murray's negotiations to transfer publication of the *Edinburgh Review*. These talks opened in 1805, when the *Edinburgh* already had 7,000 subscribers, and continued until the 1807 transfer. When the *Edinburgh* moved again, Murray started the *Quarterly*. He thought that the *Edinburgh's* able criticism should be balanced by a periodical of another party, one which made his name as a publisher. After the breach between Walter Scott and the *Edinburgh* because of its unfavorable review of *Marmion*, Murray offered him the editorship. When he declined because of pressure of other work, Murray hired William Gifford, once editor of the *Anti-Jacobin*. Gifford operated in the shadow of the *Edinburgh* and with the interference of his publisher except on book assignments. He did not initially create a "team of contributors," diversify contents, and publish on time. Among his early recruits was Robert Southey. He and others earned ten guineas a sheet for articles but not fame because the *Quarterly* resisted calls for signature.

143. [Courthope, W. J.]. "The History of Bookselling in England." 174 (1892): 158–91.

Premised that "Edmund Cave, the printer," launched the *Gentleman's Magazine* because by 1730 reading was "agreeable to the taste and imagination." The *Gentleman's* combined the poetry of miscellanies and the essays of the *Tatler* and *Spectator*. "In 1749 Ralph Griffiths established the first Review of current literature" and in 1756 Tobias Smollett, the *Critical Review*, which anticipated the *Edinburgh Review* and the *Quarterly*.

144. [Mallock, W. H.]. "Conservatism and Democracy." 176 (1893): 254–86.

Embedded democratic progress in the newspaper, itself the child of cheap printing, because leaders helped voters to form political opinions, the first stage of democracy.

145. [Sneyd, Henry]. "Viscount Sherbrooke." 177 (1893): 42–72.
Biography of Robert Lowe unearthed his articles in the *Quarterly* and his advice to R. E. Prothero to take the job as its editor. When Lowe penned for *The Times*, he was "one of that brilliant galaxy, which helped to create the continental impression" that the paper "was part of the Government of England."

146. [Hamilton, George F.]. "W. H. Smith." 178 (1894): 308–39.
Based Smith's business success on rapid and certain delivery of newspapers to vendors. He initially sorted dailies at 4 a.m. to ensure this delivery.

147. [Prothero, Michael E.]. "Public Opinion in India." 182 (1895): 429–53.
Signaled that the Indian "vernacular press" was "a weapon in the hands of the educated classes." An example was "*Bangabashi*, the most widely circulated, as well as one of the most scurrilously abusive, of the Bengali prints." Its recent prosecution should serve as a "well-deserved lesson" to "the whole Native press." Although each newspaper was relatively small, the aggregate influence of the Indian serials was great. Defended the Vernacular Press Act because Indians, without a "high sense of public duty and personal honour," would misuse freedom. Journalists, many who failed elsewhere or pursued only profit, enlisted abuse in the cause of blackmail.

148. [Shand, Alexander Innes]. "Children Yesterday and Today." 183 (1896): 374–96.
Located John Aiken's *Evenings at Home* as "the forerunner of the periodicals and journals which now cater indefatigably for the tastes of all sorts and conditions of juveniles."

149. [Barry, William]. "Lamennais." 185 (1897): 447–76.
Biography of F. de Lamennais logged that "a handful of journalists accomplished a revolution" in France in July 1830, and Lamennais and his friends soon after started the *Avenir*.

150. [Oakley, C. S.]. "On Commencing *Author*." 186 (1897): 88–110.
Review of an anonymous multivolume work wondered if journalism was literature. "Journalism is saying a thing of the hour in the manner in which a clique of the hour wishes to have it said." It could be literature, but literature could not be journalism even though "great men of letters from time to time have been considerable journalists" because literature was "independent of time and place."

151. [Dicey, Edward]. "The South African Committee." 186 (1897): 241–67.
Singled out W. T. Stead, "sometime editor" of the *Pall Mall Gazette*, who printed "rumors to create a new sensation in his *Review of Reviews*." Stead was "a writer of considerable though crude ability" who depended on "head-lines, leaded type, sensational paragraphs, and all the artifices of latter-day journalistic advertisement."

152. [Broadfoot, William]. "Indian Discontent and Frontier Risings." 186 (1897): 552–76.
Review of W. Crooke's *The North-Western Provinces of India* accepted its thesis that Indian journalists were semieducated employees of minor gazettes. They thrived on blackmail but were ready to "excite sedition." Even with small circulations they were dangerous. One reader could inform a whole village, so press restrictions were essential.

153. [Kebbel, T. E.]. "The House of Blackwood." 187 (1898): 234–58.
Commemorated the publishing house that in infancy respected the *Quarterly* and its editor, William Gifford. By 1817 the *Quarterly* was the equal of the *Edinburgh Review*. *Blackwood's*, even with an "aggressive" style, was significant because of its Scottish connection. Garnering a large circulation was not important to John Murray, who left in 1819. Afterwards, its articles were "vigorous" but without literary "comity," indeed frequently contradictory. J. G. Lockhart, John Wilson, and William Maginn were the "most dangerous contributors." Lockhart, while the "excellent editor" of the *Quarterly*, wrote for *Blackwood's* where his literary talents fit better. This was not the case for others. Douglas Jerrold was "neither morally nor intellectually of the Blackwood type"; Thomas De Quincey scribbled many pieces but was egotistical. With owners who were the real editors, *Blackwood's* gradually shifted from a literary to a political emphasis.

154. [Wilson, H. W.]. "*The Unpublished Letters of Napoleon*." 187 (1898): 357–83.
Deplored that Napoleon I confiscated and suspended newspapers or employed them to ridicule his enemies.

155. [Wilson, H. W.]. "The United States and Spain." 188 (1898): 216–41.
Noted the war cries of the "sensational press" after the *Maine*.

156. [Whittle, J. L.]. "The International Ferment." 188 (1898): 242–65.
Stressed that "sensational journalism…found ready acceptance" after the *Maine*.

157. [Preece, William H.]. "Wireless Telegraphy." 188 (1898): 494–503.
Paean to Guglielmo Marconi urged newspapers, already devotees of telegraphy, to assign "more space to scientific progress and less to political retardation."

158. [Baines, Talbot]. "Democracy and Foreign Affairs." 189 (1899): 241–65.
Suggested that journalists' determination to find news caused governments to think that there was more public "excitement than exists." British papers, unlike American, usually presented foreign affairs with "sobriety and information," but neither country's gazettes were accurate gauges of opinion. Quoted E. L. Godkin's *Unforeseen Tendencies of Democracy* that the American press used patriotism to sell papers.

159. [Baines, J. A.]. "India under Lord Elgin." 189 (1899): 313–36.
Blessed recent restriction of press freedom in India because it did not limit "legitimate criticism."

160. [Whibley, Charles]. "The Catholic Reaction in France." 189 (1899): 453–71.
Branded the *Libre Parole* as an anti-Semitic paper couched in patriotism.

161. [Moore, Norman]. "Whitwell Elwin." 191 (1900): 291–98.
Honored Elwin, the 1850s editor of and a regular contributor to the *Quarterly*.

162. Rodenburg, Julius. "Foreign Opinion." 191 (1900): 560–72.
Affirmed that the duty of the daily press was "to lead, control, and correct public opinion." The "greatest and most influential" newspapers in Germany did not engage in "violent abuse."

The Rambler, 1848–1862

Forebear of the *Home and Foreign Review* and beacon for enlightened Catholics, the *Rambler* displayed devotion to its church's journalism.

1. [?Capes, J. M]. "Preface." 3 (1848–49): iii–vi.
Recommitted the *Rambler* to political impartiality, the "strictest decorum of language," and a resistance to "offensive" personalization.

2. Our Own Correspondent [J. S. Northcote]. "Roman Intelligence: Agitation in the City – Attempted Assassination of Father Hearne, of Manchester." 3 (1848–49): 39–41.
Selected the *Epoca*, *Contemporaneo*, and *Giornale Romano* as the "radical journals" of Rome.

3. [Capes, J. M.]. "The Duties of Journalists – Catholic and Protestant Education." 3 (1848–49): 325–31.
Confessed that no periodical was always accurate in its facts, judgments, taste, and even "positive morality."

4. "Barham's *Life of Theodore Hook*." 3 (1848–49): 365–67.
Review of R. H. Barham's book recollected that Hook's "daring and witty personalities in the *John Bull* newspaper made even its hopeless Toryism brilliant and entertaining." *John Bull* was "a phenomenon in the annals of newspapers." It was selling 10,000 copies weekly by its sixth number and in its first year realized a profit of 4,000 pounds.

5. [?Capes, J. M.]. "Macaulay's *History of England*." 3 (1848–49): 420–33.
Paralleled T. B. Macaulay's style in the captioned work and his *Edinburgh Review* essays.

6. [Capes, J. M.]. "The Fourth Estate." 3 (1848–49): 471–77.
Maintained that the nineteenth-century press, notably in England, France, Germany, and the United States, was the "supreme authority" because it had the "practical power to control every other authority in a state." All "ephemeral literature" had great reach. London had 120 dailies and weeklies, 130 monthlies, 40 quarterlies, and 20 periodicals of societies. Ireland had 100 serials, though Scotland had fewer. In the future, newspapers and magazines would likely supplant books.

The moral and intellectual influence of newspapers derived from their participants' "ability, genius, and learning," people "thoroughly versed in all the arts of persuading, convincing, cajoling, and terrifying." In Britain, they came with talent and knowledge from many other professions. Nonetheless, journalism was not disorganized. The power of "WE" conferred on it a "corporate and anonymous character." Anonymity buttressed the "*prestige*" of the press and the popularity of any journal. Although it hid ignorance, bad judgment, and management trickery, it allowed leaders to stand on their merits. Libel checked abuses. Newspapers might differ globally, but all, "under the guise of giving information to the world, teach the world how to think and what to believe."

7. [Capes, J. M.]. "The *Quarterly Review* and Mr. Macaulay." 4 (1849): 97–106.
Described *Quarterly* reviewer J. W. Croker as "one of the most accomplished, the most clever, the most bitter, the most unrelenting, and the most personal among the whole class of professional or amateur reviewers." Literary critics could use strong language but should not resort to "misrepresentation, violent abuse, and the falsification of quotations," particularly in an age when more readers were skimming reviews and never opening books.

8. [Capes, J. M.]. "Cheap Books." 4 (1849): 409–16.
Sighed that "the slavery of those who write for the daily press is a proverb," and the leader-writer was one of the most overtaxed.

9. [Capes, J. M.]. "Literature for the Catholic Poor." 4 (1849): 417–19.
Responded to a letter in the *Tablet* on the subject of "periodicals for Catholic poor." There was a dearth because it was hard to fund a penny weekly "of respectable and attractive appearance and sterling worth." Such a serial should be eight pages and similar in size to *Chambers's Journal*, the only cheap and practical success in its genre. The Catholic version should have "an editor of independent vigorous character, varied acquirements, clear insights in the affairs of the time, and some degree of theological knowledge," a person who could stimulate thought or "excite an interest in fiction" as the Protestant periodicals did. Initial capital would have to be sufficient for paper, printing, the editor's salary, and contributors' stipends because advertising revenue would not flow until the serial had a reputation. Few donors were ready to support intellectual efforts for the poor, and most scribes wrote "*down to them*" because the Catholic masses preferred "vicious tales, horrible histories" to "mental cultivation."

10. [Capes, J. M.]. "Communism." 5 (1850): 109–24.
Chronicled that the "representative organs of the press" disseminated "popular opinion." Among "the more respectable portion," the "influential" papers were *The Times*, "with that exquisitely clever and ridiculous self-complacency which is its great characteristic," the *Morning Post*, *Morning Chronicle*, *Morning Herald*, *Daily News*, *Examiner*, and *Spectator*.

11. [Capes, J. M.]. "Church Reform." 5 (1850): 297–318.
Stamped Catholic periodicals, especially the important ones run by laymen, as "the most efficacious of modern and humanly-devised instruments for good which the Church can wield."

12. "Southey's *Life and Correspondence*." 5 (1850): 338–54.
Review of *The Life and Correspondence of Robert Southey* edited by his son, C. C. Southey, identified the father as a scribe for the *Monthly Magazine* and the "author of well-paid articles in the *Quarterly Review*." Once a senior writer, he conveniently forgot the views of his youth when his essays were a target in the *Anti-Jacobin*.

13. [Capes, J. M.]. "Wants of the Time." 5 (1850): 485–504.
Scanned Protestant serials, which in London alone numbered about 150 in 1850.

14. "Balmez." 6 (1850): 122–64.

Review of A. de Blanche-Raffin's *James Balmez, His Life and His Works*, compressed his journalistic career, which began when his manuscript was chosen for publication in an 1839 competition. In 1843 he established Barcelona's short-lived *Sociedad*, "one of the most interesting periodicals of the Spanish press." He then founded the Madrid weekly *Pensamiento de la Nacion*, a political newspaper with "no injurious language, no personalities, no violations of the law." In 1845 he inspired the launch of the daily *Conciliador*, "an organ of a young school of Catholic writers" but continued with the *Pensamiento* until its demise in 1847.

15. [Capes, J. M.]. "Theological Science: Protestant Preaching." 6 (1850): 238–51.

Complained that journalism, "deeply rooted in our social system," was superficial. Readers were abandoning serious treatises for "reviews, magazines, and newspapers," and every group had its organ "to lead" or "to arouse." The press once forced readers to think but not in 1850. "Everybody likes good articles, everybody reads them, everybody is influenced by them." "Articles just do what the age requires. They present 'views.'" They did not demand prior knowledge but hit the main points of an issue, enabling the reader to "take a side." They made "rapid glances" look like "profound investigations" as they mixed seriousness and jest, modesty and arrogance.

Aside that the "Pope is the special patron of a new Italian periodical," the *Civiltà Cattolica*, edited in Naples by the Jesuits, that sold 6,000 of its initial number.

16. [Capes, J. M.]. "A Socinian View of Catholicism." 6 (1850): 351–59.

Flitted past Unitarian periodicals, notably the "able" *Inquirer* and the courteous, fair, and thoughtful *Prospective Review*, and such influential weeklies as the *Spectator*, *Examiner*, and *Athenaeum*.

17. [Capes, J. M.]. "Rise, Progress, and Results of Puseyism." 6 (1850): 506–44; 7 (1851): 60–89, 144–61, 228–48.

Aired that the owners of the *British Critic* in 1843 thought it had too much Popery so ended it and substituted the "unscrupulous" *English Review*. The Puseyites published the "increasingly flippant" *Ecclesiologist*.

Aside that John Walter II of *The Times*, "one of the most accomplished watchers of public opinion," erred when he invited J. H. Newman to pen for *The Times* just before Tract #90 appeared.

18. [?Capes, J. M.]. "*Yeast*." 7 (1851): 525–33.

Review of Charles Kingsley's novel measured several serials in relation to religious bias.

19. "Leigh Hunt's *Autobiography*." 8 (1851): 46–57.

Outlined the goals of Hunt, "the caustic editor of the *Examiner*," for his paper.

20. [Capes, J. M.]. "The Protestant Criticising." 8 (1851): 471–86.

Complimented the *Guardian* for "a degree of tact and ability far beyond the ordinary run of what are called religious newspapers," such as the "Puseyite" *English Churchman*. "The *Spectator* is the pre-eminently candid, philosophical, reasoning, unimpassioned periodical of a generation which believes in nothing except its own critical acumen."

21. [Northcote, J. S.]. "The Roman Revolution." 9 (1852): 55–68.
Cited the *Italia del Populo* as the paper of Giuseppe Mazzini and the *Monitore* as "the mouthpiece of the government" of the Roman Republic.

22. Parisis, Pierre-Louis. "Monsignor Parisis on Catholic Journalism." 9 (1852): 87–100.
Prefaced a translation of part of Parisis' *Cas de Conscience* by saying that the press had a power "so pregnant for good or for evil, and to which a certain homage is paid, and a certain recognition is given." Parisis realized that the clergy could not possibly edit all Catholic serials. Lay journalists could review Catholic works on religion even if they lacked religious training and concentrated on immediate issues or personalities as long as they stimulated discussion.

23. [Capes, J. M.]. "The French in London." 9 (1852): 169–79.
Satirized the issue of freedom of the press.

24. [Capes, J. M.]. "The Struggles of Catholic Literature." 9 (1852): 255–64.
Revealed that the *Rambler* was "considered an unusually unsuccessful periodical, as Catholic matters go" irrespective of the fact that its circulation was greater than any Anglican monthly or quarterly, excluding the "*Edinburgh* and *Quarterly Reviews*, which are purely secular in their character." The *Rambler* was printed on good paper, but "the prices paid to the printer, paper-maker, and bookbinder are very moderate," its publisher took a lower percentage of profit than most, and its original authors penned for nothing. Yet the serial was down 400–500 pounds because its price was too low compared to that of the *Quarterly Review*. Urged Catholics to redirect money from buildings to intellectual projects.

25. [Northcote, J. S.]. "Manners and Customs of the Sardinians." 10 (1852): 306–22.
Identified Antonio Bresciana, S.J., as an editor of *Civiltà Cattolica*.

26. [Wallis, J. E.]. "Our Position and Prospects." 11 (1853): 1–15.
Regarded the newspaper as an "oracle" symbolized by *The Times*, "so formidable in strength, so unscrupulous in the use of its weapons." Aside on the "dreary dullness of poor doleful *Punch*."

27. [Stothert, J. A.]. "Catholic Novelists." 11 (1853): 251–62.
Gloried that there was a growing Catholic literature, a part of which was "weekly newspapers" and "periodicals, monthly and quarterly."

28. [Formby, Henry]. "Catholic Literature for the Poor." 12 (1853): 83–90, 169–74.
Admitted that attempts to publish cheap Catholic serials frequently failed because the poor preferred the murders and sensations of penny sheets sold door-to-door. Eight to ten journals had closed within six months, among them the *Catholic Weekly Instructor* "of really sterling merit."

29. [Northcote, J. S.]. "The Editor to the Readers of the *Rambler*." 12 (1853): 427–30.
Professed that the *Rambler* had a "miscellaneous class of readers," whereas many other periodical subscribers were "alike in profession, tastes, sex, and private pursuits." Most of the "teeming press" focused on a specific interest, but the *Rambler* devoted itself to Catholic "cultivation" generally. To be

a periodical "of first-rate merit," to "offer more adequate remuneration to our contributors and secure more interesting contributions," it needed an additional 200 subscribers.

30. [Capes, J. M.]. "How to Convert Protestants." 2d ser., 1 (1854): 1–19.
Glanced at the role of periodicals in differentiating religions.

31. [?Parsons, Daniel]. "The Religious Census of England." 2d ser., 1 (1854): 183–90; "Our Picture in the Census," 356–75.
Part one interpreted some press reactions to the captioned census.

32. [Capes, J. M.]. "Illustrated Books." 2d ser., 1 (1854): 462–72.
Remarked that the *Illustrated London News* was facing competition because a "speculative and puffing publisher, [John] Cassell by name, is issuing a *penny* sheet, crowded with illustrations, which, if not fully equal to those of its prototype, are by no means contemptible. Mr. Cassell boasts of an immense circulation…and considering that he clears nearly one farthing on each copy…it is very likely that he turns over a respectable sum of money weekly." Aside on cheap juvenile miscellanies.

33. [Northcote, J. S.]. "The Life of an Editor." 2d ser., 1 (1854): 510–19.
Recited the problems of editing a periodical. Unhappy or tardy contributors could cause an issue to be "dry" or a series to be interrupted. Candidates tried every device to get an editorial reading. Although the *Rambler*, as a Catholic journal, received fewer books to review than its peers known for their puffery, book publishers and authors were as bothersome, regularly quarreling about an article's length or reprint rights.

34. [De Vere, Aubrey]. "Chinese Civilisation and Christian Charity." 2d ser., 1 (1854): 552–57.
Applauded *Annals of the Holy Childhood*, a new Catholic French monthly intended to convert the Chinese.

35. [Capes, J. M.]. "Protestant Authors and Publishers, and Catholic Readers." 2d ser., 2 (1854): 93–105.
Estimated that the *Rambler's* circulation was higher in proportion to Catholics than any Protestant periodical was to Protestants. Monthlies had "advantages for exercising the functions of literary criticism in comparison with quarterly or weekly journals." Quarterlies were too late, and their essays were not true reviews. Weeklies marched with "breathless haste." All serials with reviews should sever connections to publishers.

36. [Capes, J. M.]. "The 'Civilisation' Argument." 2d ser., 2 (1854): 365–80.
Guessed that "the daily production of a London newspaper – that gigantic monument of the results of organization, regularity, readiness, and self-command," was not possible in countries with very hot climates.

37. "The Printing-Presses of the Abbé Migne." 2d ser., 2 (1854): 447–50.
Announced that Jacques Migne, with "scissors and paste," published "*La Voix de la Verité*, a newspaper of two editions," daily and triweekly.

38. "Hofer and the Tyrolese War of Independence." 2[d] ser., 2 (1854): 479–504.
Review of Andrew Hofer's *Memoirs* tapped the *Bavarian State-Gazette*.

39. [Capes, J. M.]. "The Editor to the Reader." 2[d] ser., 3 (1855): 1–2.
Exulted that the *Rambler's* new series increased circulation 50 percent as it "found its way into quarters where no such publication was ever before permitted to enter." This rise, which balanced one in paper costs, required that it be "every day more responsible."

40. [Capes, J. M.]. "Catholic Politics and Catholic M.P.s." 2[d] ser., 3 (1855): 85–96.
Muttered that life was so fast that monthlies could not compete with "daily and weekly journalists, whose vocation it is, whatever event turns up, to dash at it without a moment's hesitation, and to pronounce some opinion or other, no matter at what risk of misconception or error." However complex or passionate the issue, the "modern devourer of newspapers" wanted "views." Aside that Frederick Lucas, editor of the *Tablet* and reputedly the first influential Romanist MP, was the target of the "vehemently Catholic" *Dublin Weekly Telegraph*, "a journal which is sold at a very cheap price and has a large circulation."

41. "The Blind Leading the Blind." 2[d] ser., 3 (1855): 158–62.
Paraphrased Nicholas Wiseman that "the cheap literature of England, periodical and penny journals, some with a circulation of 400,000 copies weekly," did not dispense "wholesome knowledge" but "moral poison."

42. [Simpson, Richard]. "*The Englishwoman in Russia*." 2[d] ser., 3 (1855): 208–21.
Review of book by "a Lady" held that, unlike the Russian press, the British was open to all, whether in letters to a *Times* driven by "the steam-engine" or in paragraphs from "the garret of the penny-a-liner."

43. [Capes, J. M.]. "Catholic Politics Thirty Years Ago." 2[d] ser., 3 (1855): 421–32.
Evaluated the articles of Richard Lalor Sheil, originally in the *New Monthly Magazine* and recently published as a book.

44. "Mr. [Robert] Montgomery's 'Poetry': Religious Sentimentalism." 2[d] ser., 4 (1855): 94–107.
Denied that the press was "omnipotent" in its literary reviews. Whether in the early *Edinburgh Review* and *Quarterly Review* or the mid-century *Times*, adverse criticism was not fatal for a book.

45. [Capes, J. M.]. "Frederick Lucas." 2[d] ser., 4 (1855): 450–60.
Deprecated the style of Frederick Lucas, editor of the *Tablet*, whose "theory of journalising" was to damage opponents. Aside that the *Quarterly Review* was "that organ of all that is anti-Catholic, anti-Irish, and anti-popular."

46. [Capes, J. M.]. "Social Tyranny of Protestantism." 2[d] ser., 5 (1856): 241–58.
Inventoried social bias against Catholics that related to the press. Reading libraries restricted their access, and all journals portrayed readers of *The Times*, *Examiner*, *Edinburgh Review*, *Quarterly Review*, and *Westminster Review* as well-educated Protestants. Aside that the *Weekly Dispatch* was the "Sunday recreation" of London suburbanites.

47. [Capes, J. M.]. "On the Exaggerations of Modern Art." 2d ser., 5 (1856): 401–13.
Grasped that in an age of speed, people liked periodicals they could skim.

48. [Capes, Frederick]. "Scientific Evidence: The Trials of Palmer, Dove, Etc." 2d ser., 6 (1856): 226–31.
Juxtaposed *Times* leaders condemning the popular taste for criminal literature and the paper's stories on hangmen satisfying such a taste.

49. [Capes, J. M.]. "Catholicity and Despotism." 2d ser., 6 (1856): 418–34.
Averred that living in Protestant Britain with its free press was preferable to living in a Catholic tyranny.

50. [Wenham, J. G.]. "Principles of Education." 2d ser., 7 (1857): 37–52.
Bewailed that "common literature of the day," including newspapers, "contains a great deal that is both irreligious and immoral." Many serials did not seek to instruct or amuse but only to profit.

51. [Capes, Frederick]. "Critics and the Fine Arts." 2d ser., 7 (1857): 126–32.
Disliked "the tone and style which so many of our public journals and periodicals…adopt" on the fine arts. The critic should "guide popular taste" which, "for want of careful cultivation and technical knowledge…is apt to be warped." The intelligent and sincere critic should state reasons for judgment in terms that were not too technical.

52. [Simpson, Richard and J. M. Capes]. "The *Rambler* and the *Dublin Review*." 2d ser., 7 (1857): 140–44.
Retorted to the *Dublin Review*'s "unjust and uncharitable misrepresentations" of a *Rambler* article. *See* 2d ser., 8: 216 and *Dublin Review* 41: 441.

53. [Capes, J. M.]. "Modern Anglicanism – the *Union*." 2d ser., 7 (1857): 144–50.
Headlined "a new newspaper" of Anglicanism.

54. [Capes, J. M.]. "The Political Future." 2d ser., 7 (1857): 323–37.
Explicated how some of London's press overcame readers' antipathy to "dullness" in their leaders. *The Times* featured "smashing"; the *Morning Herald*, "brilliant stupidity and profound emptiness"; and the *Spectator*, "sentences of solemn instruction to a small knot of readers willing to pay a high price."

55. [Capes, J. M.]. "Protestant Criticisms on Catholic Morals." 2d ser., 7 (1857): 403–20.
Recognized the *Saturday Review's* "ability, good taste, and standards of cultivation…unsurpassed by any periodical" of the age.

56. [Capes, J. M.]. "The French Emperor." 2d ser., 8 (1857): 81–94.
Discerned the hostility of Napoleon III to the press in a 'warning' to the *Correspondant*, "the only French periodical which dares to remark on the dominant imperialism in a spirit of free, legitimate, and religious criticism."

57. [Capes, J. M.]. "Converts and Old Catholics." 2d ser., 8 (1857): 216–30.
Defended the *Rambler* policy of "freedom of remark" in a controversy with the *Dublin Review* (41: 441). *See* 2d ser., 7: 140.

58. [Capes, J. M.]. "Amusements for the People." 2d ser., 8 (1857): 233–45.
Postulated that "most men do not read much more than the newspapers and periodicals" and women only engaged in 'light reading.'

59. [Capes, J. M.]. "Ultramontanism and Despotism." 2d ser., 8 (1857): 272–90.
Premised that "[j]ournalism, whether in the daily and weekly paper, or the monthly and quarterly review, is clearly the phenomenon of the age. Its influence is great." Yet Britain had no Catholic daily, and Naples banned the *Civiltà Cattolica*. The French hierarchy blessed the *Univers* but "condemned" the *Avenir*, both Catholic. Catholic journals throughout Europe were mutually antagonistic.

60. [Capes, J. M.]. "A Retrospect." 2d ser., 9 (1858): 73–84.
Etched *Times* journalists as "accomplished writers whose pens *The Times* commands."

61. [Capes, J. M.]. "Liberty in France." 2d ser., 9 (1858): 157–68.
Snapped that Napoleon III "nailed up the lips of the French press."

62. [Maguire, John]. "German Jews and French Reviewers." 2d ser., 10 (1858): 104–20.
Pored over the collected periodical articles of Philippus Jaffé in a volume reviewed by Rome's *Analecta Juris Pontificii*.

63. [Capes, Frederick]. "*Novels and Novelists*." 2d ser., 10 (1858): 200–07.
Review of J. Cordy Jeaffreson's book exposed the "vaunted influence" of *The Times* as sham because it echoed, not shaped opinion.

64. [Eckstein, Ferdinand d']. "M. Guizot and His Contemporaries." 2d ser., 10 (1858): 217–29, 289–301.
Review of François Guizot's *Memoires* recalled that he was an activist with the *National* journalists in the July Revolution and an advocate of a free press while an official in the government of Louis Philippe. Aside on the *Consitutionnel*.

65. [Capes, Frederick]. "*China*." 2d ser., 10 (1858): 345–56.
Review of a book by George Wingrove Cooke, *The Times* man in China, thanked the 'leading journal' for sending a reporter to cover military operations "though the presence of a newspaper-reporter" in command areas "must grate" on the generals.

66. [Simpson, Richard]. "Belgium." 2d ser., 10 (1858): 388–99.
Enlightened that Belgian journals in French so depended on French buyers that they assigned three or four columns to Gallic news but only half columns to local items. The "*Indépendance*, which was once the declared enemy of France," was in 1858 "merely the trumpeter of the French government." Alternatively, the *Journal des Bruxelles* was "the most Catholic and the most patriotic of Belgian papers, and as such is frequently confiscated on the French frontiers."

67. [Acton, J. D.]. "The Count de Montalembert." 2d ser., 10 (1858): 421–28.
Rated C. de Montalembert's *Correspondant* "the chief Organ of Catholic opinion in France." This serial and the first Catholic journal of the German states, the *Historisch politische Blätter*, supported freedom of thought so were persecuted by the authorities, the one in France and the other in Bavaria.

68. [Acton, J. D.]. "The Catholic Press." 2d ser., 11 (1859): 73–90.
Surveyed the Catholic "periodical press in England." "If we except certain very elaborate essays in the *Atlantis*, there is hardly anything serious or durable in the productions of the Catholic literature of the day." The *Dublin Review* was declining even though it had the same competent conductors and could draw from the large pool of talented scribes available to "first-rate" journals. However, it was jealous of the *Rambler*. The *Tablet* was not current about Catholic thought and competed with the reviews for writers. Catholics did not prefer the *Edinburgh Review* or *Westminster Review* but did think that important topics were overlooked "by the most competent men" in Catholic journals. A new Catholic review would protect the faithful against "the ignorance, the malignity, and the mendacity of the Protestant press"; educate readers for political action; guide them in literature by setting "a high standard of learning and criticism"; and examine intellectual issues and social problems. The *Rambler* did not have space for this kind of coverage.

69. [Stokes, S. N.]. "The Royal Commission and the *Tablet*." 2d ser., 11 (1859): 104–13.
Answered *Tablet* castigation of the *Rambler* for sanctioning cooperation with the Royal Commission on Education, a cooperation that Catholic bishops opposed.

70. "To Readers and Correspondents." 3d ser., 1 (1859): i–ii.
Enumerated the *Rambler*'s new goals: "the refinement, enlargement, and elevation of the intellect in the educated classes" by means of "a manly investigation of subjects of public interest under a deep sense of the prerogatives of ecclesiastical authority." "All controversy will be conducted under anonymous signatures."

71. Eckstein, Baron [Ferdinand d']. "The Abbé de Lamennais." 3d ser., 1 (1859): 41–70; J. D. A[cton], 70–77.
Eckstein trailed F. de Lamennais' journalistic career from its inception to the *Avenir*. Acton reported that the French government in summer 1824 tried "to ruin hostile papers by vexatious litigation." When cases against the *Courrier Française* and *Quotidienne* failed, the authorities went to censorship, purportedly eased at the accession of Charles X. Meanwhile, the *Journal des Débats* led press protests against the dismissal of René de Chateaubriand as foreign minister. Aside on Count F. de Montlosier, who edited the *Courrier de Londres*, 1794–1800, then the weekly *Bulletin de Paris* before writing for the *Constitutionnel*.

72. [Eckstein, Ferdinand d']. "The Political System of the Bonapartes." 3d ser., 1 (1859): 289–332.
Decided that the "newspaper department of literature fared the worst" under Napoleon I. "Journalism had been an incendiary power in the Revolution, and the daily papers had acquired considerable ability. The emperor smothered them all." He set up a "bureau of the official press," which fed the *Moniteur*, and ordered the rest to print theatre criticism even when there was a demand for news. One paper revitalized after 1815, the *Génie du Christianisme*, or *Delphine*, centered on domestic and foreign policies. Napoleon III limited the press, except for the *Univers*, *Siècle*, and *Charivari*.

73. A[rnold], Thomas. "Mill, *On Liberty*." 3d ser., 2 (1859–60): 62–75, 376–85.
Review of John Stuart Mill's work rejoiced that the heyday of periodicals of the "rationalist" school was over. For example, the *Prospective Review* was dead, and the *Westminster Review* had "a stationary circulation and less than the old pugnacity."

74. Z., Y. [Victor de Buck]. "Belgian Politics." 3d ser., 2 (1859–60): 388–93.
Registered the narrow circulation of Belgian Catholic newspapers in France.

75. [Arnold, Thomas]. "Sir Walter Scott." 3d ser., 3 (1860): 39–67.
Remembered that Scott was first a contributor, then "a determined opponent" of the *Edinburgh Review*.

76. H., F. [Florence M. Bastard]. "Women, Politics and Patriotism." 3d ser., 4 (1860–61): 349–62.
Categorized newspapers as one of the "modern modes of thought and civilization," one that could "render notoriety" and "excite the exclusively masculine elements of patriotism," namely power, territory, pride, and career in contrast to feminine devotedness, loyalty, and duty.

77. [Acton, J. D.]. "Political Causes of the American Revolution." 3d ser., 5 (1861): 17–61.
Crowned Orestes Brownson "the most influential journalist of America" in 1844, although Benjamin Lundy, earlier editor of the *Genius of Universal Emancipation*, was also important.

78. [Acton, J. D.]. "Cavour." 3d ser., 5 (1861): 141–65.
Touched on Camillo di Cavour's "articles on agricultural and economical questions" in the *Giornale Agraria*. In 1847 he cofounded the *Risorgimento*, "which he conducted with great ability."

79. [Acton, J. D.]. "Expectation of the French Revolution." 3d ser., 5 (1861): 190–213.
Lectured that in 1762 the "*Gazette de France* owed its popularity not to its veracity but to its republican tone."

80. [Acton, J. D., Richard Simpson, and T. F. Wetherell]. "To Readers and Correspondents." 3d ser., 6 (1861–62): 147–48.
Promised that a change of publishers would not alter the *Rambler's* aim "to cooperate with Catholic periodicals of higher pretensions in a work of especial importance in the present day – the refinement, enlargement, and elevation of the intellect of the educated classes."

81. [Acton, J. D., Richard Simpson, and T. F. Wetherell]. "Enlargement of the *Rambler*." 3d ser., 6 (1861–62): 429–31.
Recounted that the *Rambler*, a monthly, 1 September 1848 – 1 February 1859, originally had "social and literary" topics, but it gradually "assumed a less ephemeral character than ordinarily belongs to a monthly periodical." It next appeared every two months (1 May 1859 to this volume) and was now switching to quarterly publication.

Saint Pauls, 1867–1874

Balancing entertainment and enrichment, *Saint Pauls*, initially captained by Anthony Trollope, dissected journalism and depicted journalists.

1. [Trollope, Anthony]. "Introduction." 1 (1867–68): 1–7.
Characterized a magazine's editor as a "man of letters," its contributors as those seeking recognition, and its owners as those pursuing profit. Monthlies in 1867 offered "the reading public the greatest part of the literature which it demands." The periodical press, originally a "humorous essay" alone on a "small sheet," became a "dry, critical review, joined with the occasional news," then "august quarterlies" that were often partisan, and finally the "mixed pages of the monthly," with serialized novels requisite for magazines. Public demand for this light literature did not preclude essays by noted authors. Magazines should not leave politics to newspapers but should eschew literary criticism, all too frequently of books that were an "easy mark for ridicule or for friendly praise."

Aside that the *Tatler* was primarily the work of Richard Steele and the *Spectator*, of Joseph Addison.

2. [Dicey, Edward]. "The Tourist at Home." 1 (1867–68): 163–71.
Confessed that newspapers repeated some leaders.

3. F[itzgerald], P[ercy]. "The Decay of the Stage." 1 (1867–68): 173–81.
Averred that press criticism "not altogether intellectual" was gospel to theatregoers.

4. [Dicey, Edward]. "The Trade of Journalism." 1 (1867–68): 306–18.
Defined journalism as an "independent and honourable trade." The "professional journalistic writing" in newspapers, magazines, and reviews was "a lower class of literature." Although "journalism, like law or physic, is of use to the community," its importance should not be exaggerated. "If a man can write a good report, or pen a neat paragraph, or compile news intelligently…he is entitled to credit…but he is not the benefactor of his species." Journalists typically wrote to earn a living and to increase sales, not to enhance their own reputations. Because of anonymity they had no name and few social perks.

The good journalist had to read extensively and have "knowledge of the world…considerable power of diction and a certain flow of fancy, intellectual tastes, and physical energy." Newspapers left no time to get background information. Magazines were easier for tyros. They only needed "access to a good library of reference," a table and chair, and money for pens, ink, and paper. A talented person who could write on demand could earn a "moderate income," about 2,000 pounds per year, which was more than many professions. Second-rate authors who fit a particular journal might get three to five pounds per week "without much trouble or difficulty." The really successful received 800–1,200 pounds per year for relatively short hours, but the competition to reach the top was tough. Pushing for more pay was useless since British journalists, unlike their peers in other professions or in French serials, had no cachet with readers. Only a few periodicals were "really valuable properties," so people aspiring to fame should be foreign correspondents. They had independence, could "associate with men of culture and education," and might influence their audiences merely be adding to their knowledge.

5. [Gielgud, Adam]. "The Panslavist Revival in Eastern Europe." 2 (1868): 18–33.

Bared that some journalists were campaigning to replace the German language in Galicia with the Russian, not the Polish tongue. Aside that Michael Katkoff went from able but unknown scribe of the *Russian Messenger* to powerful editor of the *Moscow Gazette*.

6. [Stephen, Leslie]. "Anonymous Journalism." 2 (1868): 217–30.

Explained that proponents of signature equated the "anonymous journalist" with the "hired assassin." Newspapers claimed omniscience, infallibility, prophecy, and consistency even when the facts changed. When they erred, they opened space for rebuttals, but pitting an individual against an organization was never equal. Two or three leading tribunes might articulate what became public opinion, but they merely organized rather than shaped "the confused utterances of what is called public opinion." The press was neither the voice of independents "employed from sheer public spirit in educating the public mind" nor "the oracular preaching of a race of superior beings." Journalists might agree with a paper's general tendency, but, whether "arrogant," "flippant," or "vacillating," they regularly mirrored readers' prejudices. Still, there was plenty of "honest and vigorous writing" and room for new ideas. Anonymity separated journalism from other fields, permitting men with something to say to avoid the disagreeable effects of notoriety. Contributors from other professions liked anonymity because journalism was not well regarded by their colleagues. Signature might improve modesty and coherence, but anonymity ensured a variety of views, some unpopular ones that authors would not otherwise express. When journalism became a profession, its old reputation would evaporate and its new "influence and dignity" would spur signature.

7. [Dicey, Edward]. "The Women of the Day." 2 (1868): 302–14.

Article on the *Saturday Review* series, "Girl of the Period," saw the serial as "a sort of literary lion's mouth for the reception of impeachments against established objects of worship." Like other "class journals," it understood the prejudices of its readers, many of them women, but also imagined that females prioritized any notice above oblivion for their sex.

8. [Trollope, T. A.]. "Giampietro Vieusseux, the Florentine Bookseller." 2 (1868): 727–35.

Saluted Vieusseux, the founder and publisher for 12 years of "*Antologia*, a periodical of liberal principles." It was an Italian periodical before there was an Italy, a journal where anonymity protected authors and masterly editing garnered respect. Established in 1820 with fewer than 100 subscribers, by 1829 it had 950. Austrian and papal censorship killed it in 1832.

9. [Dicey, Edward]. "Provincial Journalism." 3 (1868–69): 61–73.

Labeled the London press, led by a *Times* that was an "extraordinary achievement of intellectual and mechanical ingenuity," the press of the nation. Yet the capital had no press "of any weight" for its own doings. No local gazette "succeeds in – or even aims at – representing the public opinion of its particular district" but only some party or interest. Country people read the London heralds to learn opinion on major issues. Irrespective of telegraphy, even the "ablest" locals had little political impact. They carried general news and editorial comment on it, but they excelled in headlining local problems. The country papers farthest from London tended to be the best. Any region that could get the metros by breakfast had a weak press.

News of towns, whose coverage was growing, routinely came from people without much education and with low pay, people who required close editing. In the "profession" of journalism as elsewhere, it was "useless to struggle against manifest destiny." Journalists of talent and energy went to London. Editors did the same unless they owned their papers. Local editors might be lawyer-proprietors or reporters risen after "drifting into journalism" from another field. Many were London subeditors recruited because they were "high-minded and honest." A local editor, who customarily earned 200–400 pounds per year, had little status. Even an Edward Baines or an Alexander Russel did not have the clout of a London editor. Anonymity did not exist for journalists in the country, so they showed "reticence" lest they offend the powerful. Although country editors faced "corrupt influences" and "little prospect of future advancement," their papers were "singularly honest, very free from gross personalities, and conducted with considerable ability."

France had a national press, but the United States did not. Among the Germans, Cologne's *Zeitung*, Berlin's *Norddeutsche Allgemeine Zeitung*, Augsburg's *Allgemeine Zeitung* and Vienna's *Presse* all had influence; in Italy, Florence's *Nazione*, Naples' *Nazionale*, and Milan's *Perseveranza* had similar sway.

10. [Gielgud, Adam]. "Prussia, Germany, and France." 3 (1868–69): 147–62.
Attributed blank pages in many German newspapers to police deletions of articles that attacked the authorities.

11. [Hardman, Frederick]. "Spain under Its Last Bourbon Sovereign." 3 (1868–69): 277–89.
Disclosed that in 1867 four men were sent to the galleys for publishing the *Revolution* and *Flash of Lightning*, two Spanish newspapers that were akin to the *Bat*, a tribune that circulated in the streets and coffeehouses before the 1854 revolution.

12. [Merivale, Louisa A.]. "Ludwig Tieck." 4 (1869): 321–33.
Mentioned Tieck's "close literary connection with the Schlegels just as they began their famous critical journal, the *Athenaeum*."

13. [Gielgud, Adam]. "Beust versus Bismarck." 5 (1869–70): 29–44.
Recorded how German statesmen used newspapers to float their ideas.

14. [Trollope, Anthony]. "Formosa." 5 (1869–70): 75–80.
Critique of a *Times'* review of a play on prostitution (with a character named Formosa) opined that young women readers no longer skipped such columns as they had in the 1830s.

15. [Bayne, Peter]. "Lord Brougham." 5 (1869–70): 178–203.
Compared the early *Edinburgh Review*, a "startling meteor," to the 1869 version, "the most steady-paced of the planets."

16. [Levi, Leone]. "On Railway Economy." 5 (1869–70): 352–65.
Credited the railroad for more reading of newspapers because an "enormous number" of them were sold at railway stations.

17. [?Bayne, Peter]. "Our Rulers, as Described by One of Themselves." 7 (1870–71): 167–76.

Review of a study of the Lord Chancellors by Lord John Campbell conceived of newspapers and other serials as "the most influential organs – but they are not enduring records of opinion." Their "demigod of today" might be a has-been tomorrow.

Aside that Henry Brougham and Francis Jeffrey each penned six articles and Sydney Smith penned seven for the inaugural number of the *Edinburgh Review*.

18. Hoey, Frances Cashel. "'Red' Paris on Easter Sunday." 8 (1871): 163–76.

Alleged that newspapers flourished in Paris in 1869 because the press was "emancipated."

19. Browne, Matthew [William Brighty Rands]. "The Literary Life." 8 (1871): 365–70, 450–57; 9 (1871): 82–86, 295–99.

Focused on the typical young tyro who sent an article to the "discriminating" editor ready for "fresh talent" only to receive a rejection. Success in periodical publishing depended on chance rather than great ability. Novices needed the "talent of the usual journalistic or magazine kind, combined with adequate culture and knowledge of the world." To produce quickly, they must not tire easily. They must not be discouraged because editors first turned to "known and tried contributors" or the friends they recommended. Editors also selected items that fit their periodical's "character" and returned those that echoed a previous article or one commissioned on the same subject. They only allowed established contributors to choose their topics. Therefore, neophytes chasing glory and wealth should "[p]ay careful attention to the special character and requirements" of a periodical, learning from back issues. The inexperienced should develop their own style slowly in "humble" gazettes and should not expect an editor to accept something because they appealed for money. Living from this work was not easy. Most first articles were offerings; later ones were paid tardily, if at all, depending on the circumstances of the journal.

Quality writing was almost impossible in journalism. The chief handicaps were pressure of time; editors and readers who accepted "bad writing…full of base mannerisms"; conflicts between one's personal and a periodical's beliefs; and shifts in public views that required rapid response or accommodation. The "ordinary journalist" was busy covering public meetings and club talk, with its "gas" and tobacco. Leader-writers had to generate columns that seemed to "begin from nothing" and "lead nowhere." They leaned toward "*bourgeois* journalism," which merely reiterated the ideas of the average person. Reviewers could not abridge a book but had to pen a column or two, often on a volume that had "no particular life." Money came from detailed descriptions, "the kind of article which teaches one-half of the world how the other half lives," the kind of article in *All the Year Round*. Descriptive paragraphs could be "trash" but were more commonly "simple, naïve, truly autobiographical…or wrought with literary art of *some* kind." They appeared to be the creation of someone drunk the day before who missed what people said or saw.

20. Holbeach, Henry [William Brighty Rands]. "Female Culture in the Eighteenth Century." 9 (1871): 195–200.

Posited that topics, letters, and a taste for the "sensational" were the same in ladies' magazines of the eighteenth and late nineteenth centuries. However, the earlier serials had "more coarseness of speech," more disdain for "men's persons and their dress," and more news.

21. Hutcheson, Walter [Robert W. Buchanan]. "Criticism as One of the Fine Arts." 10 (1872): 386–95.

Cautioned that the qualifications of many critics were weak and the journals in which they published were not "quite free of undue influence." Signature would end distortion, whether the "editorial tone" of a G. H. Lewes or the "deep-seated prejudice" of a Richard Holt Hutton.

22. Hutcheson, Walter [Robert W. Buchanan]. "Pity the Poor Drama!" 10 (1872): 505–13.

Denigrated London theatre critics who praised bad plays and puffed what they despised. For example, John Oxenberg (*The Times*) bowed to "degraded tastes," guaranteeing worthless works a good run. Because newspapers printed "venal and dishonest puffs" or "insincere 'slurring over' of wretched failures," the public "distrusts" them.

23. Holbeach, Henry [William Brighty Rands]. "Literary Legislators: Mr. Vernon Harcourt." 10 (1872): 633–39.

Tagged *Punch*, the *Pall Mall Gazette*, and *Saturday Review* "powerful organs" and explored Harcourt's work in the last publication.

24. A Disgusted Journalist. "Editors and Correspondents." 11 (1872): 363–66.

Excerpted letters to the editor that asked for personal advice or carped about text and typos.

25. Greenwood, James. "'Penny Awfuls.'" 12 (1873): 161–68.

Highlighted penny weeklies that printed information from the Newgate calendar. As these publications prospered, they proliferated.

26. Camden, Charles [Richard Rowe]. "Seaside in Winter." 12 (1873): 186–89.

Reassured that "[r]eviews, magazines, newspapers, quarterlies, monthlies, weeklies, dailies" in local reading rooms kept the isolated tourist informed about the world.

27. Aubrey, W. H. S. "The Central Telegraph Station." 12 (1873): 339–46.

Tabulated that telegraphy, nationalized since 4 February 1870, transmitted 350,000 words daily for the press. Most messages on "great political gatherings," the stock exchanges, racing, accidents, and important meetings of "learned bodies" went at night to newspapers "in London and in all the leading provincial towns." News quickly gathered by Reuters, Central News, and the Press Association always made the morning dailies. Some locals paid 500 pounds per year for special wires from 6 p.m. to 3 a.m.

28. An Irreconcilable [William Brighty Rands]. "The *Penny Magazine*." 12 (1873): 542–49.

Petitioned for a reprint of the *Penny Magazine* because recent cheap periodicals that instructed now specialized and the rest merely amused. What was missing was the variety of the *Penny*, a "serial of miscellaneous entertaining *knowledge*." Charles Knight was its "capital" editor because of his "neutral docility of mind," never introducing his own ideas except in the sense of "catholic liberalism." The "titles and models of some of our worst periodicals have come from America – that land of national education, free institutions, and diffused popular culture." The German model, inexpensive "wholesome" serials, did not survive in a British market governed by "the immense multiplication of the lower types of readers."

29. Forbes, Archibald. "How I 'Saved France.'" 14 (1874): 24–32.
Reminisced about fellow correspondents during the Franco-Prussian War, among them William Howard Russell and French journalists.

30. A Journalist. "The Cap That Fits." 14 (1874): 82–89.
Lamented that journalists were sued for libel because the details of their stories sometimes matched people's lives. A plaintiff invariably jumped on the similarities and overlooked the differences.

31. Holbeach, Henry [William Brighty Rands]. "Mr. [James] Fitzjames Stephen and Mr. Leslie Stephen." 14 (1874): 193–220.
Review of James Fitzjames Stephen's *Liberty, Equality, Fraternity* and Leslie Stephen's *Essays on Free-Thinking and Plain-Speaking* condemned the "macadamised scarcely-human Leading-Article-ism" of journalism.

The Scottish Review, 1882–1900

The *Scottish*, irrespective of its caption, unveiled the press in Britain and beyond, closing with a telling prediction about the United States.

1. [Lewin, Walter]. "Letters in America." 1 (1882–83): 30–51.
Speculated that magazines were more in demand in the United States than in Britain because "this class of literature" was suitable for "railroad reading." "America far surpasses us in the excellence of its Magazines – 'get up' and contents alike being of the best." In the top ranks were the *Atlantic Monthly* for literature and the *Century* for art. The American newspaper, which every town had, was "usually scrappy and entertaining. Items of grave news are enlivened with descriptive and facetious comments, and that solemnity which marks the British 'Editorial' is little known." Aside on Margaret Fuller's work for the *Dial* and *New York Tribune*, where she was the "chief literary critic."

2. [Brown, James]. "Thomas Carlyle's Apprenticeship." 1 (1882–83): 72–100.
Revealed that acquaintance with Francis Jeffrey, editor of the *Edinburgh Review*, gave Carlyle "fairly regular work as a contributor to the quarterlies and monthlies," but his income was uneven in his early days.

3. "Charles Dickens." 3 (1883–84): 125–47.
Deemed Dickens "the best reporter in the gallery of the House of Commons," work about which he reminisced in a speech for the Newspaper Press Fund in May 1865. His days as an editor varied. Briefly at the *Daily News*, he wanted to publish a cheap "first-class" paper. At *Household Words*, he printed a "morbid justification of himself" when he left his wife. When *Punch* refused to circulate this column, he broke with its editor, "his old friend, Mark Lemon," and launched *All the Year Round.*

4. [Metcalfe, W. M.]. "Frederick Denison Maurice." 3 (1883–84): 336–56.
Recollected that Maurice began and edited a magazine that lasted for only four numbers in 1825 even though John Stuart Mill saw in it 'considerable literary merit.' By 1827 Maurice was writing for the *Westminster Review*. He next edited the *Athenaeum* although "he had scarcely the requisite qualifications." The *Athenaeum* was "already in bad odour with the public," but under Maurice circulation dropped. He left the post in 1829, continuing as a contributor.

5. [Veitch, Sophie F. F.]. "George Eliot." 5 (1885): 250–64.
Stressed that Eliot's appointment as assistant editor of the *Westminster Review* was "an event of the deepest importance to her" because it led to her "acquaintance" with G. H. Lewes.

6. Ker, Robert, Trinity Church, Quebec. "The Prospects of Canadian Confederation." 7 (1886): 330–40.
Glanced at the Quebec *Presse* and *Etendard* and at "*Toronto Week*, a journal remarkable for its literary ability, its perfect independence, and its thorough impartiality in dealing with public questions."

7. Stewart, George, Jr. "Life and Times of Longfellow." 8 (1886): 101–26.
Indicated periodicals that printed the poetry of H. W. Longfellow, among them the *Portland Literary Gazette*; *United States Literary Gazette*, edited by Theophilus Parsons; and *Harper's Monthly*, which paid 1,000 dollars for his 'Keramos.'

8. Bourinot, John George. "Canada and the United States." 16 (1890): 1–29.
Asserted that the Canadian press was more aware of public issues than the American, which did not even report Congress fully.

9. [Metcalfe, W. M.]. "Mr. Lecky on Ireland." 17 (1891): 171–208.
Review of W. Lecky's *History of England in the Eighteenth Century* guessed that the *Northern Whig*, the paper of the Society of United Irishmen, had a large circulation.

10. [Metcalfe, W. M.]. "A Publisher and His Friends." 18 (1891): 24–53.
Review of Samuel Smiles' *A Publisher and His Friends: Memoir and Correspondence of John Murray* followed his career from 1805 when he became London agent for the *Edinburgh Review*. Murray, uncomfortable with its politics, and Walter Scott, disgruntled by its criticism of his work, joined forces to launch the *Quarterly Review* with shaky financing. Murray labored to keep its editor, William Gifford, on schedule and to locate writers. In 1815 William Blackwood became Murray's agent in Scotland. Because *Blackwood's Magazine* was disdained for its personal attacks, Murray shared some of that rebuke. With the "skilful management" of editor J. G. Lockhart, the *Quarterly's* "reputation…was soon greatly enhanced." Of its contributors, J. W. Croker's reputation improved after his death. Robert Southey received 100 pounds for each of his 94 essays, earning him more than any of his other endeavors.

11. [Metcalfe, W. M.]. "Laurence Oliphant." 18 (1891): 175–97.
Alluded to Oliphant's tenure as *Times* correspondent in the Franco-Prussian War and his work for the *Owl* and *Blackwood's Magazine*.

12. Cockburn, James D. "Beginnings of the Scottish Newspaper Press." 18 (1891): 366–77; 21 (1893): 399–419.
Acknowledged that Scotland was slow to develop a press because it had "little commerce to support, and scant science and art to enlighten," and the "reformed church" resisted "the very appearance of liberty of thought." The Scots looked to English newspapers and newsletters, though they had little interest in Scotland before 1637. In 1642 the *Scots Scout's Discoveries* and in 1643 the *Scots Intelligencer* and *Scots Dove* appeared. These papers descended to "startling depths of scurrility and obscenity" but were the sires of others in 1644, 1651, and 1652. In 1652 Christopher Higgins allegedly sold "facsimiles of English sheets," among them *A Diurnal of Some Passages and Affairs*, "the official organ of Parliament," and *Mercurius Politicus*, "edited by that splendid turncoat, Marchamont Nedham." He and John Birkenhead were the only "noteworthy diurnal-writers" of the era. In 1659 Higgins issued the *Mercurius Britannicus* with information from other diurnals and some Edinburgh news. The same year he launched "the first original newspaper published in Scotland," the *Faithful Intelligencer from the Parliament's Army in Scotland*," which preceded Thomas Sydserf's *Mercurius Caldeonius* of 31 December 1660. Both were "desperately ugly specimens of typography," but Sydserf's was the first attempt "to establish a permanent Scottish newspaper." He was previously a "literary hack" in London. His scribbling did not attract advertising, so the paper died in a year. Between 1660 and 1700, three more Scottish newspapers were born and died quickly. In 1699 James

Donaldson commenced Edinburgh's *Gazette* as a folio, and in 1705, Adam Boig began the *Edinburgh Courant*, which undersold the *Gazette*.

After the Act of Union London assigned supervision of the press to the magistrates just as competition developed. Unlike in England, in Scotland authors rather than printers owned the tribunes. As in England, owners used scissors but in Scotland "produced their quaintly-worded paragraphs of 'home news.'" These proprietors were "a dejected race, sordid in views, incapable of heroism, and destitute of education; they were creatures of an uncongenial environment," yet it was "from them and not from the printers of Edinburgh that Scottish journalism slowly evolved." The *Courant* had no literary matter but had foreign, English, and local news, and "a goodly show of advertisements." When Boig died in 1710, Daniel Defoe was named editor, but the paper ended when he left in 1711. Defoe's appointment was not a tactic to muzzle the Scottish press or to give him a job. He took little interest in the *Courant*, perhaps because he was too busy spying for the authorities. Other heralds surfaced, 1706–12, but the *Scots Courant*, 1710–20, was rather long-lived. The modern press commenced with the *Evening Courant* in 1718 and the *Caledonian Mercury* in 1720.

Listed papers, 1652–1799, some with paragraphs identifying owners or summarizing contents. Asides on Nathaniel Butter, the Civil War press, John Milton as press censor, 1651–52, and the Venetian *Gazetta* (1536) as the first newspaper.

13. Millar, A. H. "Sir Walter Scott." 23 (1894): 225–51.

Reminded that Scott wrote "several articles" in the early *Edinburgh Review* before he switched to the *Quarterly Review*, intended "as an opposition journal."

14. Wallace, William. "A Journalist in Literature." 24 (1894): 157–72.

Analyzed the essays of Richard Holt Hutton, "the high water mark of self-respecting journalism." He focused on opinion about facts, not the recording of them.

If anonymity persisted, the press of the future would retain "the power of pure reason." However, readers in 1894 wanted the 'graphic,' making the interviewer and the artist as important as the reporter and the leader-writer. Literature was in "the clutch of journalism" because of "the present adoration of the snippet." Soon the space once allotted to long leaders in newspapers would go to short fiction and criticism.

15. White, T. Pilkington. "The Malcontent Woman." 25 (1895): 270–90.

Deemed "the avocations of literature and journalism" appropriate employment for the "New Woman."

16. [Wallace, William]. "Journalism from the Interior." 28 (1896): 354–72.

Boasted that journalism was "one of the greatest feats of allied money and brains in modern days." Newspapers might appear to certify opinion, and their minutiae might destroy "the intellectual vitality" of readers, but the British were unlikely to accept leaders based on "cooked news." Competition prevented gazettes from being dictatorial, and the charter of the Institute of Journalists barred it from being a union. According to journalist Henry W. Lucy, there were few blackmailers in the British press. Thanks to the standard of anonymity, purportedly set by John Delane of *The Times*, the newspaper was "the most effectual subordination of labour to capital that the world possesses at the present moment."

Because of anonymity, "journalism is the least honoured of the professions; strictly speaking, it is not a profession at all." Journalists lacked status and endured low salaries. They could not afford to cultivate the external community and could not accept its gifts lest they be charged with bias. There was also no "real community" internally among leader-writers, subeditors, reporters, and business managers. Leader-writers might become editors and reporters might become subeditors, but reporters and subeditors, usually without the ability to form opinions, did not become leader-writers. Reporters, whose job it was "to record accurately, impartially," left a paper for higher pay elsewhere. An editor rarely moved because he could only go to a herald of the same party else his "professional, political, and personal reputation would, in all probability, be irremediably ruined." Editors, under the pressure of time, had to balance the race for news caused by competition and the ideas of owners. If newspapers abandoned partisanship and anonymity, owners could hire noted writers and thus make journalism a profession.

As newspapers devoted more space to events, their "literary quality" declined. To sell, the newspaper had to tell the public what to think, and it was easier to pen an emotional rather than a rational column. The new 'leaderettes' were better than spinning sentences for length, but real writers could not develop their ideas in a paragraph, particularly when they were under pressure to respond to news. Likewise, the interview, "borrowed from the go-ahead but not specially dignified journalism of the United States," was eroding literary quality. As journalists specialized, short pieces should improve. Until then, "[s]econd-rate writers and thinkers, more or less of the all-round type, though no doubt quite conscientious, must for many years to come perform the regular work of ordinary newspapers."

Magazines and weeklies had better writing than dailies and could "check the demagogues" of the daily press. Magazines with brief but thoughtful articles on narrow subjects already affected evening dailies.

Aside that to start a new tribune in Scotland in 1896 would cost 500,000 pounds, up from 50,000 pounds in 1846.

17. [?Wallace, William]. "*An Editor's Retrospect.*" 29 (1897): 128–51.
Reviewed a book by Charles A. Cooper of the *Scotsman* that *The Times* scorned as "a violation of journalistic and social propriety." Yet Cooper's paper was renowned for "its steadfast adherence to the higher ethics and better traditions of the Press," unlike the "want of reticence and dignity which is usually associated with the 'New Journalism.'"

In 1897 the editor of "a great daily newspaper" worked under constant pressure in contrast to the more leisured man who printed a weekly on a wooden press in 1850. Cooper was a "reporter, art-critic, London correspondent, subeditor in London, and subeditor in Edinburgh" before he became editor of "the leading newspaper north of the Tweed." In 1861 he was a parliamentary reporter for the *Morning Star* and in 1862, its subeditor. In the 1860s subeditors supervised the numerous penny-a-liners who could significantly rouse readers, as in the garroting scare. In 1868 the *Scotsman* hired Cooper as subeditor and promoted him to editor in 1877 after he had been their London correspondent. The *Scotsman* was already important for inaugurating the 'Special Wire' and 'Private Correspondence' and fighting for the admission of local journalists in the Reporters' Gallery. Its high circulation was due to its use of special newspaper trains and agents in big towns.

18. Bourinot, Jno [John] Geo[rge]. "Literary Culture in Canada." 30 (1897): 143–63.
Grumbled that "the chief literary ailment of large classes of our best population is the newspaper press." Produced under the pressure of Canadian life, "Canadian journals, however, have not yet descended to those depths of degraded sensationalism for which some New York papers have become so notorious." Aside that several American periodicals published Canadian literary work.

19. "*Annals of a Publishing House.*" 31 (1898): 51–81.
Review of Margaret Oliphant's book esteemed *Blackwood's* as "a great and popular Magazine," one which had "remarkable success" because it recruited "some of the most brilliant minds." These authors shared readers' interests so could mold their views. Repeated William Blackwood's conclusion that the *Quarterly Review* effectively countered the *Edinburgh Review*. *See* 33: 83.

20. [Cochran-Patrick, Neil K.]. "R. W. Cochran-Patrick." 31 (1898): 106–26.
Memorialized Scottish MP Cochran-Patrick who was "a frequent contributor to the *Numismatic Journal*."

21. [Wallace, William]. "The New Departure in British Humour." 31 (1898): 329–49.
Distinguished current "frank and easy" journalistic humor from prior writing that was so severe no "reputable magazine" would publish it in 1898. Unlike Sydney Smith and Charles Dickens, most of the younger journalists had "little time and less inclination" for humor, leaving it to *Punch* or specialists. Serious monthlies and weeklies, seeming to echo Matthew Arnold, printed the words of the "unsmiling literary exquisite of today, whose mission is apparently to be politely contemptuous of 'common people' and 'common things' in a 'column' of gentle and even stoical ridicule." Such scribes put literature inside "the whale's belly of journalism."

22. W[hite], T. P[ilkington]. "The Vaunts of Modern Progress." 32 (1898): 81–113.
Conceded that "the higher class of periodicals" exhibited "excellent, vigorous, and scholarly writing," but the rest was "literary tinfoil." The "vulgar, restless vanity of the seekers of notoriety, which has given birth to a new industry – that of the journalistic interviewer," spawned newspapers stuffed with "petty details." Equally offensive were the signatures and portraits of writers in women's periodicals. However, journalism was one of only two prose fields that paid in 1898.

23. Blaze de Bury, Fernande. "The Abbé Prévost in England." 33 (1899): 27–52.
Logged that Antoine Prévost's eighteenth-century journal, "*Le Pour et Contre*, published in Paris by the Didots, contained information about everybody and everything," that is gossip, reviews, adventure, science.

24. "Further Annals of a Publishing House." 33 (1899): 83–94.
Reviewed Mary Porter's *John Blackwood*, which was the third volume of the work cited in 31: 51. Among contributors to *Blackwood's Magazine* were experts on the military and Charles Lever. He wrote essays on politics and society, "wild stories," and a "racy series" as Cornelius O'Dowd.

25. [Wallace, William]. "The Agony in French Politics and Literature." 33 (1899): 263–86.
Submitted that the French peasant's mind was "something better than a mere echo of a halfpenny press," but the rustic was not likely to read the *Revue des Deux Mondes*, edited by Ferdinand Brunetière, "the leading critic" in French journalism.

26. "*The American Revolution*." 33 (1899): 328–53.
Review of G. O. Trevelyan's book posited that colonial newspapers "contributed much to the extreme virulence of the opposition" to British rule.

27. Wallace, William. "The Life and Limitations of Stevenson." 35 (1900): 13–35.
Reviewed books by R. L. Stevenson who detested 'personal writing,' that journalism which he saw as "the root of all literary and much other evil."

28. [Metcalfe, William]. "The South African Crisis." 35 (1900): 59–69.
Noticed that the *Cape Times* lifted "some amusing extracts from the [Boers'] seminary magazines" and that newsboys were active in Boer areas.

29. [Metcalfe, W. M.]. "Yiddish Literature." 36 (1900): 44–62.
Starred Alexander Zederbaum, who founded "a Hebrew periodical, the *Hameliz*, in 1861, as an organ for advanced ideas and culture." In 1863 the weekly added a supplement, the *Kol-mewasser*, printed in "Judeo-German," but this "rallying point" for all who could write Yiddish was suppressed in 1873. In 1881 Zederbaum published a Yiddish weekly, the *Jüdisches Volksblatt*, more popular after Mordechai Spektor and Solomon Rabinowitsch joined its staff in 1883. In 1887 Spektor started his own serial in Warsaw, the *Hausfreund*, "a purely literary periodical, the first of its kind in Judeo-German."

30. Cockburn, James D. "Daniel Defoe in Scotland." 36 (1900): 250–69.
Depicted Defoe as a "patriotic journalist" under William III; a "tongue-tied partisan, changing his colours with each ministry" under Anne; and a detective, "Whig and Tory simultaneously" under George I when papers paid by the Tories, as *Mist's Journal*, could be "disabled and enervated" by him. In 1864 documents showed him "as the secret, wily instrument of the Government employed in gagging a Tory Press." At the end of his career, Defoe could find no periodical to publish his work. Even though the press had a "habit of vilification," he deserved the "outpouring of Grub Street" against him.

31. Wallace, William. "The Coming War of American Dreams." 36 (1900): 269–92.
Bemoaned that the newspaper in the United States, "even the very 'yellowest,' reflects the moods and aspirations, the 'ideas' and the crazes of present-day America." In the United States, the status of books and newspapers was similar, whereas in Britain books were above gazettes in the hierarchy of print. American books conveyed the 'philosophy' of the newspaper to "half-articulate masses." While "[s]ensational journalism" was an expression of American adolescence, "the tyranny of newspapers" caused some citizens to look to the state for protection against them and might motivate more people in the twentieth century if, as Wallace anticipated, the nation moved to democracy, socialism to achieve equality, and world supremacy.

Tait's Edinburgh Magazine, 1832–1855

With a penchant for politics, William Tait's magazine denounced press taxes for three decades. Items in which it compared itself to contemporaries included valuable data but disappeared quickly.

1. [Tait, William]. "A Tête à Tête with Mr. Tait." 1 (1832): 9–16.
Pledged that *Tait's* would be different from 1832 periodicals of "prosing disquisitions, spoony tales, pointless epigrams, and endless twaddle" and be more like the generation of John Wilkes when serials featured "the livingnesses of the day."

2. [Lauder, T. D.]. "The Revolution." 1 (1832): 17–25.
Pleaded for the end of newspaper duties so that knowledge could spread.

3. [Tait, William and Christian Johnstone]. "To Correspondents." 1 (1832): 139 (verso), 383, 515.
Notified contributors that *Tait's* failure to publish submissions was not always due to their "inferior merit" but also to tardy arrival, repetition of ones already printed, and unavailable space. Long articles, which "generally proceed from dullness, carelessness, or enthusiasm," were unsuitable for readers of periodicals. "The readiness of writers of established fame and the eagerness of young volunteers full of talent and enthusiasm" to pen for *Tait's* was "gratifying." At the request of the majority of contributors, replies were sent privately.

4. [Tait, William]. "Keep Him Down." 1 (1832): 220–23.
Understood that in the hierarchy of periodicals there were "many most useful and popular kinds of literature, which the quarterly people would sooner die than acknowledge."

5. [Johnstone, Christian]. "British Writers on America." 1 (1832): 229–34.
Digressed that the *Quarterly Review* had "a bit of learning for the scholar and a bit of fine feeling for the lover of humanity" but was mostly "falsehood" and "sophistry."

6. "The Botheration of the 'Personnel.'" 1 (1832): 286–90.
Lamented that name or physical appearance could inhibit a journalistic career and consign a person to poverty. Dependence on journalism did not guarantee security. Even the few London daily editors with influence on public affairs earned 500 pounds per year, except *The Times* paid 1,000 pounds.

7. "The Fourth Estate." 1 (1832): 356–59.
Singled out Samuel Johnson as the sire of the Fourth Estate, which London daily newspaper editors, with "clear-sighted, profound, and statesmen-like views," embodied in 1832. "The direct and indirect influence of the newspaper press, from the tact, ability, and integrity with which it is at present

conducted, and the astonishing facility and rapidity with which it reports the debates in Parliament and the proceedings of all public assemblies, and indicates every change in the public interest, is a stronger safeguard of freedom, and check against corruption, than all the statutory enactments that ever legislative wisdom devised."

8. [Bowring, John]. "Louis Philippe of France." 1 (1832): 610–12.
Bewailed that the French government constantly prosecuted the press, "the invincible bulwark of modern liberty."

9. [Johnstone, Christian]. "To Correspondents." 1 (1832): 651 (verso).
Advised contributors to *Tait's* that unless a submission was clearly inappropriate, editors took a month to decide whether to publish it, especially if it came from an unknown. Legible handwriting usually speeded review.

Aside that the charge by the *Brighton Gazette* that *Tait's* attacked the *Athenaeum*, "that clever and impartial Journal" for which it had "a particular respect," was incorrect. The *Athenaeum*, unlike other London weekly literary organs, was not a "Publisher's Puffing Machine" or overpriced.

10. [Weir, William]. "On the State and Prospects of Germany." 1 (1832): 689–703.
Roared that most Continental states had no freedom of the press.

11. [Johnstone, Christian]. "Cheap Periodicals." 1 (1832): 721–24.
Identified Daniel Defoe as the father of cheap periodicals. "Defoe is the first author of the whole class of periodical literature which rises above a mere gazette or bulletin, and endeavours to reason and joke as well as to disseminate the news or lies of the day. His *Review* was the prototype of the *Tatler*," which "carried the kind of paper started by the *Freeborn Englishman* to perfection." The *Spectator* had a greater reputation "less perhaps for its intrinsic merits than because of its more ambitious pretensions." Readers tolerated its serious essays because they were surrounded by "interesting gossip." Newspapers in 1832 were the "successors" to the *Tatler* and *Spectator* without their partisanship.

The press abetted progress not by ideas but as a medium for their exchange. By enlightening readers, it prepared for the "moral nation." Newspaper taxes were an anomaly in an age which favored liberty of the press. *Chambers's Journal*, which sold 28,000 each issue before London and New York reprints, confirmed that people wanted variety in information. "As a repertory of solid instruction and delightful illustration of fire-side morals, it is invaluable." Unhappily, it did not discuss the newspaper duties. The *Penny Magazine* was badly managed by a committee whose members had "second or third rate intellects." Its lack of quality was also true of "its ape and would-be rival, the genteelly sanctified *Saturday Magazine*."

12. [Tait, William]. "The Reform Act and the Ministry." 1 (1832): 781–84.
Categorized the *Morning Chronicle, Sun, Morning Herald*, *Globe*, *True Sun,* and *Examiner* as "newspapers of talent and extensive influence." Equally significant was the *Edinburgh Review*, which purportedly put the Whigs in power and kept them there.

13. [Nichol, John Pringle]. "The Ministry and the People." 2 (1832–33): 5–19.
Accused the authorities of stalling abolition of taxes on the press.

14. [Tait, William]. "To Correspondents." 2 (1832–33): 137 (verso), 269, 413, 685.
Appreciated the "distinguished writers" who were steady contributors to *Tait's*. Tyros should not expect return of articles: they were either held for space or discarded because they were unsuitable. *Tait's* was a good place to advertise because many circulating libraries and book clubs bought it. Sales in the kingdom were third to *Blackwood's Magazine* and the *New Monthly Magazine* and in Scotland, to *Blackwood's* and the *Edinburgh Review*.

The new *Dundee Chronicle* and the established *Dundee Advertiser* were newspapers conducted with "vigour and talent." The new *Dundee Times*, to be run by a recruit from the *Spectator*, should emulate them.

15. [Mill, John Stuart]. "Austin's Lectures on Jurisprudence." 2 (1832–33): 343–48.
Review of John Austin's *The Province of Jurisprudence Determined* said that the newspaper was the key to the "world's business" but that it hurt good books by encouraging hasty reading. *See Westminster Review* 3/25: 1.

16. [Murphy, Denis]. "The Present State of Ireland." 2 (1832–33): 518–23.
Corroborated a government "war against the press" in Ireland with examples of prosecutions of the *Freeman's Journal*, *Pilot*, and other papers.

17. "The Annuals." 2 (1832–33): 524–26.
Essay on the "graphic art" of annuals dealt with illustrations in general.

18. [Doubleday, Thomas]. "Taxes on Knowledge – Duty on Paper – Direct and Indirect Taxation." 2 (1832–33): 608–17.
Announced that *Tait's* joined other journals in campaigning for reduction of duties affecting newspapers. These indirect taxes were unequal for rich and poor, hurt business, and abetted smuggling. Supporters called for a penny stamp duty and no tariff on literary journals, but Doubleday wanted to eliminate the stamp and substitute a penny fee for every time a newspaper went through the post office even though that might leave country readers to local papers, "with their narrow views, timid speculations on politics, and inferior literary merit." The paper duty was also onerous. Newspaper owners had to raise prices commensurately to make a profit.

19. [Tait, William]. "To Our Readers." 3 (1833): ix–x.
Rejoiced that newspapers welcomed *Tait's*.

20. [Tait, William and Christian Johnstone]. "Notice to Correspondents." 3 (1833): 137 (verso).
Communicated that Tait's, unlike *Blackwood's Magazine*, might arrive late in Scottish towns because it included a monthly register.

21. [Lauder, T. D.]. "The Budget." 3 (1833): 137–40.
Regretted that the government did not reduce the newspaper stamp duty when it lowered the one on advertising. As advertising poured in, owners would raise their space rates.

22. "London Sights." 3 (1833): 298–302.
Chose the newspaper, which left out many details in its hurry to report the news, as a London sight.

23. "On the Review of Miss Martineau's *Illustrations of Political Economy* in the Last *Edinburgh Review*." 3 (1833): 337–41.

Filed the *Edinburgh* as "the sceptic's" review because it was "always sneering at man's highest hope" and the *Quarterly* as "the bigot's review" because it defended "established principles and practices, however false and mischievous."

24. [Mill, John Stuart] "Writings of Junius Redivivus: *The Producing Man's Companion*." 3 (1833): 347–54.

Article on William Bridges Adams cited his breadth of knowledge and incisive style evident in his work in the *Mechanics' Magazine, New Monthly Magazine*, *Monthly Repository*, and *True Sun* and his "personal attacks on public characters" in the *Examiner*.

25. [Johnstone, Christian]. "On Periodical Literature." 3 (1833): 491–96.

Recorded that magazines developed about 1750 to serve either an interest, as literature or science, or the leisured but not well-educated reader. Serials for the latter were a jumble but prepared the public for periodical reading. The American and French revolutions spawned newspapers and reviews penned by those whose "[r]apid production, energy of style, strong and brief description, and keen research into the workings of passion and thought, distinguish their writings." But writers in 1833, in what looked to be an easy trade, lacked depth, and "capricious" magazine readers caused them to follow whims in columns measured by marketability. The result was columns that seemed trivial or mediocre. This perception was unfortunate because periodicals were no longer "unimportant" or "ephemeral." They answered serious questions, guarded or shaped public taste, promoted the truth, and usually avoided venality.

26. [Tait, William and Christian Johnstone]. "*Johnstone's Edinburgh Magazine* – New Radical Newspapers." 3 (1833): 551.

Spotlighted an inexpensive new periodical, *Johnstone's Edinburgh Magazine*, to be "written and selected" by Christian Johnstone. It should suit "the most cultivated minds" because of her "imagination…rich sense of humour…delicate female gentleness."

New gazettes, the *Leeds Times*, *Devonport Independent*, and *Newcastle Press* were "distinguished for talent, no less than for boldness and honesty." The *Newcastle Press* promised to be "among the first" of country papers.

Aside that contributors to *Tait's* should send manuscripts well before deadlines or tell the editor the article's expected posting and length.

27. [Bowring, John]. "French and English Authorship." 3 (1833): 727–28.

Opted for British anonymity rather than French signature in periodicals. In France, "every fifth-rate contributor to a sixth-rate journal" earned a name. In Britain, 'Everybody' knew contributors, so there was no need to brand articles like sheep.

28. [Johnstone, Christian]. "Fashionable Novelism." 3 (1833): 729–31.

Spotted the *Examiner*, *Spectator*, *Westminster Review*, and *Tait's* among the "unbiased critical journals."

29. [Tait, William and Christian Johnstone]. "*Johnstone's Edinburgh Magazine*." 3 (1833): 783–94.

Commended the "correct, clear, and vigorous" style of John Johnstone and the skill of Christian Johnstone in "works of fancy" in a promotional for the captioned serial. In an "age of periodicals, and, above all, of cheap periodicals," inexpensive monthlies, the pets of the "higher classes of retail booksellers," were going to replace weeklies unable to develop a full story or a book review. Monthlies were better for fiction than weekly penny parts. Illustrated publications were for children, not adults.

30. [Tait, William]. "To Our Subscribers." 4 (1833–34): i–iii.

Affirmed the incompatibility of fighting for the rights of the people and selling at a high price, yet *Tait's* had a good circulation. Among monthlies priced at two or three shillings, sixpence, *Tait's* was third in circulation and second in profit. In 1833 cheap periodicals, thanks to the rapid "printing-machine," were outdistancing expensive serials, so *Tait's* was reducing its price to a shilling. There would be no deterioration in quantity and quality because contributors would continue to be "liberally remunerated." Higher sales should compensate for price reduction. Although workers might read *Tait's* in libraries and clubs, middle-class readers, who first skimmed it in reading rooms, soon bought and "carefully perused" it.

31. [Tait, William]. "The Libel Cases." 4 (1833–34): iv.

Theme was that "the Libel Law reached the ultimate point of injustice, caprice, and absurdity" in December 1833 cases involving the *True Sun*, Dublin's *Pilot*, and Brighton's *Guardian*, whose editor was penalized for ideas expressed in a letter to him. *See* 4: 389.

32. "The Libel Cases." 4 (1833–34): 389 (verso).

Added to 4: iv that the *Pilot* merely republished a letter from a London newspaper. The case of the *Guardian* had already demonstrated that the law was "oppressive, tyrannical, and dangerous to freedom."

33. [Johnstone, Christian]. "*Johnstone's Edinburgh Magazine*: The Cheap and Dear Periodicals." 4 (1833–34): 490–500.

Sketched *Johnstone's* as a cheap monthly with "literary merits" and a circulation of 5,000 in Scotland, a figure that rivaled the *Edinburgh Review* and *Blackwood's Magazine* in the north. *Johnstone's*, which matched "the best of the expensive monthly periodicals in the excellence of its literary contents," needed buyers "whose intelligence and means correspond with the contents and price."

Cheap weeklies, such as the *Penny Magazine*, *Saturday Magazine*, and *Chambers's Journal*, accelerated reading. They were "welcomed as the genial shower by the parched land." The *Penny* had "beautiful wood cuts." Booksellers preferred these journals to the "cheap trash" available in booths. Inexpensive monthlies, which addressed a "higher class" in terms of wealth and "intellectual attainments," counted on the "*flash* article" to lure library readers of elite periodicals, but not their buyers who were "more intellectual." The *Quarterly Review* was already down from 14,000 to 9,000–10,000 and the *Edinburgh Review* from 12,000 to 6,000–7,000. The circulation of the *New Monthly Magazine* was also lower. The *Westminster Review* was steady at 3,000, the *Foreign Quarterly Review* at 2,000, and the *Metropolitan* at 1,000 because their circulations were not large enough to be impacted. *Blackwood's Magazine*, with 9,000 subscribers, was probably going to lose readers to cheaper rivals. *Fraser's Magazine* had a talented staff, the "piquant unscrupulous sort of article," the favor of newspapers, but not a high subscription rate.

Costs for writers, printers, and stereotyping were the same for most periodicals, but some saved money by resorting to thinner paper or fewer but larger pages with double columns.

34. [Johnstone, Christian]. "*Exposure of the Spy System*, and English Libel Law." n.s., 1 (1834): 77–78.

Centered on a case against *Tait's* London agents. The libel law held news vendors to the same standard for liability as it did periodical owners, editors, and contributors. *See* n.s., 1: 152, 785, 805; 2: 1.

35. [Wallace, Robert]. "Abuses of the Post-Office." n.s., 1 (1834): 96–101.

Thanked France for proposing free exchange of newspapers, which Britain rejected.

36. [Johnstone, Christian]. "O'Connell's Libel Bill: Richmond the Spy." n.s., 1 (1834): 152–59.

Backed a new libel bill for "Liberty of the Press," a bill which disallowed a suit if no slander existed, absolved a publisher if the author was known, and permitted truth as a defense. The suit against *Tait's* was a case study. *See* n.s., 1: 77, 785, 805; n.s., 2: 1.

37. [Wilks, John]. "Letters from O.P.Q. No. III: French Prospects at the Close of April 1834." n.s., 1 (1834): 221–27.

Highlighted the hundred prosecutions of Paris' *Tribune* that culminated in its closing and the arrest of its editor, subeditors, printers, and some workmen.

38. "Sir James Mackintosh's *History of the Revolution of 1688*." n.s., 1 (1834): 247–58.

Introduced Mackintosh as the editor of the *Oracle* who, paid by quantity, printed very long columns until he received a fixed salary. Aside on Benjamin Flower, editor of the *Cambridge Chronicle*.

39. [Tait, William and Christian Johnstone]. "To Our Subscribers." n.s., 1 (1834): 289.

Trumpeted the merger of *Tait's* and *Johnstone's Edinburgh Magazine*. *Tait's* was three times more popular in Scotland than the *Edinburgh Review* and *Blackwood's Magazine* and was gaining an audience in England. *Johnstone's* subscribers would have to pay more but would have more articles on better paper.

40. [Wilks, John]. "Letters from O.P.Q. No. V: A Bird's-Eye View of the Political State of Europe and the Progress of the Movement." n.s., 1 (1834): 449–58.

Deplored that a French press, albeit uncensored, still had to deposit security money and to endure many prosecutions that resulted in fines and imprisonments.

41. "On National Manners." n.s., 1 (1834): 487–89.

Ranted that the *Quarterly Review*, "the Delphian oracle of the world of do-nothingness," escaped libel suits while serials with caricatures were not so lucky.

42. [Johnstone, Christian]. "What Shall We Do with Our Young Fellows?" n.s., 1 (1834): 527–30.

Answered the title question by guessing that young men without fortunes and with some ability would be good newspaper subeditors and reporters.

43. Author of "The False Medium" [R. H. Horne]. "The 'Unstamped Press' in London." n.s., 1 (1834): 614–25.

Comprehended that the popular view of the unstamped press was uncomplimentary, seeing it as seditious and edited by "drunken, demoralized outcasts." The cheap weeklies, such as *Leigh Hunt's London Journal* or *Chambers's Journal*, "which are of an intellectual, scientific, or amusing character," did not fit this casting. The misperception about treason came from penny political serials beginning with the *Black Dwarf* and William Cobbett's *Political Register*; the image of journalists, from the "worthless" *Weekly Police Gazette*, quasi-criminal *Hue and Cry*, and their ilk. The *Poor Man's Guardian*, which was not really a newspaper, saw its sellers jailed. Publications, as the "well got up" *Conservative* and *Reformer*, had merit. They averaged 30,000–40,000 copies weekly, but with four readers each reached many more. Robert Owen's *Crisis* promoted "intelligence" among workers and demonstrated the "march of intellect," but its circulation dropped once he was no longer editor. His *Pioneer, or Grand National Consolidated Trades' Union Magazine*, exhorted workers to act. Its circulation once hit 20,000–25,000 weekly. Other unstamped offerings ranged from the violent to the humorous (listed here). The "able leading articles of political and social science, dialogues, and original papers" in the *Official Gazette of the Trades Unions* exemplified its "moderation" and "superior quality." Not a newspaper but "an exclusive magazine," it made the workers' case by displaying "knowledge, reason, and a thorough command of temper." *See* n.s., 1: 733.

44. [Tait, William]. "Lord Brougham's Evidence on the Newspaper Stamp Duty." n.s., 1 (1834): 625–28.

Essay on the newspaper stamp, "this impolitic and slavish tax," excerpted at length Henry Brougham's ideas on the value of a cheap press to help "the people" form political opinions and recognize that some more expensive weeklies, as *John Bull*, were trash. More cheap papers would also mean fewer libelous ones.

45. [Roebuck, J. A.]. "Lord Durham and the *Edinburgh Review*." n.s., 1 (1834): 643–48.

Remarked that with a "political press so vigilant as that of Britain," any maneuvering by people in power was impossible to hide.

46. [Darling, J. J.]. "Fatherhood of the Unstamped." n.s., 1 (1834): 733–34.

Tagged William Carpenter's *Political Letters* as the immediate father of the unstamped press. It circulated 63,000 weekly until he was imprisoned for publishing it. William Cobbett's *Political Register*, the *Black Dwarf*, and others named were forerunners that, except for Cobbett's paper, disappeared after the Six Acts. Among the more than 100,000 unstamped pages circulated every month in 1834, the *Weekly Police Gazette* (correcting text in n.s., 1: 614) did "much to humanize and inform the people," but the *People's Police Gazette* was "a disgusting mass of trash and depravity."

47. Tait, William. "To the Readers of *Tait's Magazine*." n.s., 1 (1834): 785–88.

Revisited the libel case in n.s., 1: 77, 152 with emphasis on the truth defense. Aside that *Tait's*, whose circulation purportedly equaled that of the *Edinburgh Review*, gave the "same quantity of letter-press as London monthlies and quarterlies for one-third the price."

48. "Private History of the London Newspaper Press." n.s., 1 (1834): 788–92.

Tried to reconcile the "vast" influence of London dailies, particularly the "all-powerful" *Times*, with owners who speculated in newspapers for profit and editors paid to write in "the profession of literature," who winked at lies. The press often betrayed public trust while disguised as a medium of truth and honesty.

The Times was a joint-stock company of 24 shares (each originally priced at 100 pounds and worth 1,200 in 1834), of which John Walter owned 16 shares. Editor Thomas Barnes was a "very learned and accomplished" man who worked hard for 1,000 pounds per year and one-half of a share in the paper. He directed parliamentary reporters and correspondents from whom he expected "obedience to his will." Leader-writer Edward Sterling, known as "Vetus," deserved his high salary of 1,500 pounds because he penned quickly and well, if without consistency, about politics. For the "city article," Thomas Alsager earned 800 pounds per year, merited by his expertise in business. *The Times*, irrespective of recent errors, was incomparable even if it scorned the "advancing spirit of the age."

The *Morning Chronicle* had declined after James Perry because the new owner had less money and ability. Once it had trouble paying for paper and foreign correspondents, it resorted to 'windows' and bigger type to save money but was recently sold for 17,000 pounds by an owner who had paid 30,000 pounds.

The *Morning Herald*, a political cipher, was a profitable 'family paper' with a good police reporter. The *Morning Post*, circulating primarily to aristocrats who liked its "rabid" leaders," survived on high-priced advertising.

In the evening, the *Globe* and *Sun* stressed politics. The *Standard*, even with William Maginn, was "mere style."

Among the weeklies, the *Weekly Dispatch* was the colossus. It had a leader-writer named Williams, a former navy man and son of an American Loyalist. (He did not write as "Publicola" as stated here. That journalist was W. J. Fox.) The *Sunday Times* was "pleasant and inoffensive" but down from the 10,000 copies it once sold. *John Bull*, edited by Theodore Hook, was the puppet of government. The *Spectator* excelled in style but was expensive. Workers preferred the *True Sun* and *Examiner*.

49. [Johnstone, Christian]. "Exposure of the Spy System: Richmond the Spy *versus Tait's Magazine*." n.s., 1 (1834): 805–50.

Printed the transcript of a libel trial discussed above (n.s., 1: 77, 152, 785) with comments on the case's progress. *See* n.s., 2: 1.

50. [Johnstone, Christian]. "Richmond v. Simpkin and Marshall." n.s., 2 (1835): 1.

Celebrated the successful conclusion of the libel case in n.s., 1: 77, 152, 785, 805.

51. "Manchester." n.s., 2 (1835): 11–16.

Relayed that Manchester had five Saturday morning newspapers: the *Chronicle*, *Courier*, *Guardian*, *Times*, and *Advertiser*. The oldest was the *Chronicle*, but after 1821, the *Guardian*, with "superior industry and ability," led in circulation and advertising. All were politically partisan, but as "channels of communication and vehicles of discussion" in the city and beyond, they printed many copies. Asides that London's *Globe* served retirees, the *Examiner* served Radicals, and "the licentious *John Bull*" served parsons.

52. [Johnstone, Christian]. "*The United States and Canada in 1832, 1833, and 1834*." n.s., 2 (1835): 114–28.

Review of C. D. Arfwedson's book noted that Cincinnati had "sixteen daily journals and periodicals."

53. The Author of the "Exposition of the False Medium," Etc. [R. H. Horne]. "The Stamped Press: The Mighty Organ of Good and Evil." n.s., 2 (1835): 167–75.

Rhapsodized that the newspaper was "a flying omnibus, licensed to carry the opinions of the world." Appearing regularly, crossing time and space, and seeming ubiquitous, it could be a mirror or distributor but never a designer of opinion. Seeing all, this "terrestrial telescope" justified its existence by informing about everything and controlling tyrants. The ideal paper should be "well-varied and *well-timed*" with material of "novelty and excitement." Columns other than news need not always be truthful, which limited circulation, but should never engage in "slander of private character." However, the stamped press should be the "public instructor."

Rome's *acta diurna* was the first press, but the term "gazette" came from the Venetian coin or the Italian magpie (*gazzera*). The British papers evolved from newsletters (though not the forged *English Mercurie* cited here) to Nathaniel Butter's *Weekely Newes*, the Civil Wars' mercuries, Roger L'Estrange's *Public Intelligencer*, and the *Oxford* (soon *London*) *Gazette*. In 1690 there were nine newspapers, one an unnamed daily in 1696. During the early eighteenth century, there were three dailies, ten triweeklies, and six weeklies, and the *Gentleman's Magazine*, originally with extracts from newspapers. In 1753 7.5 million pages were published; in 1760, 9.5 million; in 1833, 30.5 million. Benjamin Flower's *Cambridge Intelligencer* and William Cobbett's *Political Register* later emphasized press liberty.

In 1800 newspapers paid six pence per joke. By 1833 newspapers had "a certain position in literature," so columns on "important matters" prevailed. Many newspapers, though not the *Examiner* and *Spectator*, turned "serious subjects to a burlesque" because authors knew little and had little time to write. Since country heralds quoted these two papers, their circulation and influence expanded. Although *The Times* was anti-labor, some laborers read it as well as the friendlier *True Sun*. Aside on the nature of advertising.

54. [Johnstone, Christian]. "The Thoughts of Isaac Tomkins and Peter Jenkins upon the Aristocracy of England." n.s., 2 (1835): 295–98.

Confided that aristocratic contributors to "a political journal" demeaned it. Echoed Henry Brougham that the upper class did not read papers that defended rights and rejected license. The nobility was less interested in information on a "useful or important subject" than in "buffoonery."

55. Murphy, Denis, Esq. "O'Connell and the Catholic Association." n.s., 2 (1835): 299–309.

Pinpointed the *Morning Register* as the "first example of a regular reporting establishment in Ireland." Other papers, such as the *Freeman's Journal* and *Evening Post*, were the tools for the Catholic Association to publicize its message.

56. [Johnstone, Christian]. "The Life and Writings of William Cobbett." n.s., 2 (1835): 491–506, 583–97.

Agreed with the *Edinburgh Review* (10: 386) that as "a periodical political writer," Cobbett was 'first in power and popularity,' a man whom all serials "of name" "assailed." In contrast to the press of his era, that of the 1830s used its power for right.

57. "On Advertisements, and Advertising, Considered as One of the Fine Arts, in which the Theory and Practice are Combined." n.s., 2 (1835): 575–82.

Realized that advertising in a newspaper or magazine should fit "*the class*" of its readers. For example, subscribers of the *Edinburgh Review*, *Quarterly Review*, *Westminster Review*, *Monthly Repository*,

Fraser's Magazine, *Blackwood's Magazine*, and *Tait's* were book buyers. Advertisers likewise should read the periodical where they proposed to list. Most British serials would reject advertisements in the typical American gazette because they were "little more than impudent nasal announcements," but Americans doted on them. New York's *Morning Courier* had 12,000.

58. [Johnstone, Christian]. "*Letters, Recollections, and Conversations of Coleridge.*" n.s., 3 (1836): 113–23.

Borrowed, from S. T. Coleridge's book, information about his work for the *Morning Post* and *Blackwood's Magazine*, for which he scribbled fast and thought little.

59. [Johnstone, Christian]. "Mrs. Trollope's *Paris and the Parisians.*" n.s., 3 (1836): 174–89.

Review of Frances Trollope's book doubted her statement that Paris penny-a-liners were ready to write for any rebellion. Aside that British servants scanned the *Westminster Review* and the upper class scanned the *Age* or *John Bull.*

60. [Tait, William]. "Advertising in Scotland." n.s., 3 (1836): 190–200.

Analyzed the advertising and other content of major Scottish newspapers. Also noticed the all-advertising *North British Advertiser*, some London newspapers, and Scottish magazines purchased by booksellers and "keepers of circulating libraries" in Scottish towns.

61. [Johnstone, Christian]. "Bulwer's Work on France." n.s., 3 (1836): 209–22.

Review of H. Bulwer's *The Monarchy of the Middle Classes* referred to Armand Carrel's role at the *National* and Jules Janin's move from a "popular" to an "aristocratic" journal.

62. [Johnstone, Christian]. "*Literary Remains of* [*the Late William*] *Hazlitt.*" n.s., 3 (1836): 501–10.

Learned from the titled work that, upon arrival in 1811 London, Hazlitt "wrote political and theatrical criticisms for the leading newspapers." Subsequently, he penned for the *Edinburgh Review*, "the finest in critical felicity," the *New Monthly Magazine*, and *London Magazine.*

63. [Darling, J. J.]. "Public Opinion as Indicated in the Newspaper Press." n.s., 3 (1836): 661–62.

Growled that the stamp duty limited newspapers to reflecting opinions of the wealthier on great questions but not always on "less exciting" ones. Indicated the number of newspapers in England, Ireland, Scotland, Wales, and the Channel Islands committed to each of the major parties and London newspapers with increased and decreased circulation.

64. [Darling, J. J.]. "The Liberal Newspapers: Effects of the Reduction of Stamp-Duty." n.s., 3 (1836): 685–92, 799–808.

Attributed the higher circulation of Liberal papers (such as the *Scotsman*, from 1,400 to 2,000) and the birth of new ones (such as the *Perth Chronicle*) in Scotland to reduction of the stamp duty. The same trends were true of London and English locals (named). London's morning *Constitutional*, the most important new morning herald, was promising. New weeklies at three pence would not steal buyers from the old unstamped because their price was too high and their advertising too unappealing for workers. No stamp but a penny post would bring the news to all laborers. Data on circulation, pre- and post-duty reduction, was updated in the second part of the essay.

65. [Johnstone, Christian]. "[James] Prior's *Life of Goldsmith.*" n.s., 4 (1837): 238–58.
Examined Oliver Goldsmith's work for the *Monthly Review* and it rival *Critical Review* as well as for several other magazines and newspapers.

66. [Johnstone, Christian]. "Cottle's *Recollections* of Coleridge." n.s., 4 (1837): 341–48.
Review of Joseph Cottle's book spoke of S. T. Coleridge's commencement of the *Watchman*. A four-penny weekly, then a daily at #10, it functioned as a review and a newspaper.

67. [Johnstone, Christian]. "Miss Martineau's *Society in America* and Grund's *American Society.*" n.s., 4 (1837): 404*–24.
Review of books by Harriet Martineau and F. J. Grund postulated that newspapers in Britain and the United States served "to promote the pecuniary and party interests of their proprietors." According to Martineau, American editors behaved like lawyers; they were honest in private life but tolerated falsehood in print to protect owners.

68. [Johnstone, Christian]. "Serjeant Talfourd's *Letters and Life of Charles Lamb.*" n.s., 4 (1837): 575–86.
Review of Thomas Noon Talfourd's book glimpsed the styles of criticism in the *Edinburgh Review* and *Quarterly Review.*

69. [Johnstone, Christian]. "The Books of the Season." n.s., 4 (1837): 678–88.
Reckoned that the cheaper the price of an annual, the worse its illustrations. Johnstone once derided annuals but then decided that they were better gifts than food and more valuable than jewelry for "a woman of taste and refinement." Annuals in 1837 were moral, unlike their "frivolous" forebears. *Fisher's Drawing-Room Scrap Book* was "tasteful and elegant," and *Findan's Tableaux* was a good example of light literature.

70. "The Progress of Society in India." n.s., 4 (1837): 765–69.
Broadcast that educated Hindus "published magazines and newspapers in the English language, which came into fair competition with similar works under European editors." There were seven Bengali papers in Calcutta.

71. "Decline of the Drama." n.s., 5 (1838): 112–15.
Blamed the "multiplication of newspapers" partly for neglect of the theatre.

72. [Cobden, Richard]. "The Affair of the *Vixen*: Circassia and England." n.s., 5 (1838): 120–25.
Essay on a diplomatic crisis ruminated about how quickly foreign correspondents disseminated facts and their own opinions and how governments used this information.

73. [Johnstone, Christian]. "*Diary Illustrative of the Times of George IV*, Etc., Etc." n.s., 5 (1838): 177–93.

Aside that the titled book led the London press to be "seized with one of its periodical fits of moral indignation."

74. Elliott, Ebenezer. "A Letter to Mr. Tait." n.s., 5 (1838): 253–56; with a footnote by W. Tait, 253.

Footnote proposed a bureau of public opinion to collect the ideas in newspaper leaders.

75. [Johnstone, Christian]. "*The Poetical Works of Thomas Pringle*." n.s., 5 (1838): 280–83.

Chronicled that Pringle coedited the *Edinburgh Monthly Magazine*, edited Edinburgh's *Star*, and wrote for the *New Monthly Magazine* before he went to South Africa. There, he established and coedited, with John Fairbairn, the *South African Journal*, a short-lived small magazine, and the weekly *South African Commercial Advertiser*. When an issue arose about the *Advertiser*'s coverage of Governor Charles Somerset, the two men resigned. The printer and owner could not produce the paper so closed it pending a decision of the Home Office. The governor then sealed the press and deported the owner.

76. [Johnstone, Christian]. "[J. G.] Lockhart's *Life of Sir Walter Scott*." n.s., 5 (1838): 307–27.

This segment of a series illuminated Scott's connections with the *Edinburgh Review* and *Quarterly Review* and his ownership of the "silly and scurrilous *Beacon*."

77. [Johnstone, Christian]. "*Speeches of Lord Brougham*." n.s., 5 (1838): 475–90.

Revived Henry Brougham's speech in the libel case of John and Leigh Hunt, when their *Examiner* allegedly copied from a *Stamford News* column penned by John Scott.

78. [Johnstone, Christian]. "Australian Emigration." n.s., 6 (1839): 168–76.

Review of T. Hatton James' *Six Months in Australia* quoted him that the "fearless and independent" if irregularly published *South Australian Gazette* ran afoul of the authorities.

79. [Johnstone, Christian]. "Laing's Sweden and Norway." n.s., 6 (1839): 307–27.

Review of S. Laing's books on Norway and Sweden eyed the latter's journalism. "The press is under a rigid censorship in Sweden, and the government is perpetually and capriciously interfering with it." Exemplifying this interference was the 25th *Aftonblad*, a Stockholm paper whose first 24 attempts had been suppressed.

80. [Johnstone, Christian]. "Continuation of Captain Marryat's *Diary in America*." n.s., 7 (1840): 95–103.

Review of Frederick Marryat's book accented that he and other travelers to the United States concurred that "if not more dishonest than the press of other countries, the American press is the most gross and scandalous that is tolerated among civilized men."

81. "Advertisements and Advertisers." n.s., 7 (1840): 384–85.
Suggested that social news sent to "popular" newspapers by "ladies of rank" and "fashionable mamas" was really advertising. Charging for such inserts, and letters by the socially overlooked or politically partisan, might add to this source of revenue on which newspapers depended.

82. [De Quincey, Thomas]. "Sketches of Life and Manners: From the Autobiography of an English Opium-Eater." n.s., 7 (1840): 765–76; n.s., 8 (1841): 97–109.
Segments of a long series rambled across many subjects: the unmasking of Junius; the *London Magazine*, 1821–23; the preeminence of *The Times* in London and on the Continent; and Kendal's press. Its *Gazette* was "generous in its treatment of private character," and its *Chronicle* showed the spillover of material from reviews to magazines and then to newspapers.

83. [Johnstone, Christian]. "Memoirs of the Late James Smith, Esq." n.s., 8 (1841): 92–96.
Watched the journalistic careers of James Smith and his brother, Horace, from their days with *Pic-Nic*, "a kind of half-dramatic, half-political or satirical newspaper." They and their colleague, J. W. Croker, worked without pay for editor George Combe, "an able and eccentric" writer. Excerpted the brothers' contributions to other serials.

84. [Johnstone, Christian]. "*The Life and Literary Remains of L. E. L.*" n.s., 8 (1841): 445–55.
Review of Laman Blanchard's book on L. E. Landon mused about her influence on William Jerdan, editor of the *Literary Gazette* to which she contributed. She also penned for the *Court Journal* and other magazines as well as for annuals, among them *Fisher's Drawing-Room Scrap Book*.

85. [Johnstone, Christian]. "Recent Travellers in Russia." n.s., 9 (1842): 118–31.
Sidelined Russian press censorship that excluded all British newspapers except the *Morning Post* and even "the harmless *Galignani's Messenger*," without which Russians had no "current gossip" about Europe.

86. [Johnstone, Christian]. "*Memoirs of Jeremy Bentham.*" n.s., 9 (1842): 443–54.
Review of a book edited by John Bowring appraised Bentham's role in the early *Westminster Review*, including his relations with Henry Brougham.

87. "Madden's History of the United Irishmen." n.s., 9 (1842): 578–97.
Review of R. R. Madden's *Lives and Times of the United Irishmen* reprised the group's newspaper, the *Press*, for which John Sheare wrote "intemperate and inflammatory addresses."

88. [Johnstone, Christian]. "Borrow's *Bible in Spain*." n.s., 10 (1843): 161–74.
Review of George Borrow's book admired the "*sang-froid*" of the Madrid correspondent of the *Morning Chronicle* during the late Spanish revolution.

89. Hooton, Charles. "Texiana: Rides, Rambles, and Sketches in Texas." n.s., 10 (1843): 185–92.
Disdained Texas literature because it was "embodied in some twenty newspapers of the most miserable description" edited by printer-owners. They clipped from other gazettes or penned "drivel" but survived on advertising.

90. [Johnstone, Christian]. "*Memoirs and Correspondence of Francis Horner*." n.s., 10 (1843): 296–311.

Review cast Horner as a key player in the early days of the *Edinburgh Review*. After the *Quarterly Review* began, he wanted the *Edinburgh* to "eschew newspaper-like political leaders and flippant personalities" and to display "decorum."

91. [Johnstone, Christian]. "Hood's *Australia and the East*." n.s., 10 (1843): 586–99.

Lifted from John Hood's book that John D. Lang, owner of and regular scribe for Sydney's *Colonial Observer*, was "a man of a superior order of mind."

92. [Johnstone, Christian]. "The Marquis de Custine's *Empire of the Czar*." n.s., 10 (1843): 637–48, 693–701.

Aside that Nicholas I read one newspaper daily, the *Journal des Débats*.

93. "Lord Brougham and His Detractors." n.s., 10 (1843): 681–85.

Headlined the press attacks on Henry Brougham but marked the early *Examiner* "venomous" and *John Bull* "ferocious."

94. [Johnstone, the Christian]. "Recent Biographies: Mr. Sidney Taylor." n.s., 10 (1843): 729–32.

Review of John S. Taylor's *Writings* located him as a scribe for the *Morning Chronicle* and *Morning Herald*, which he also edited.

95. "An Irishman's Thoughts on Repeal." n.s., 10 (1843): 803–09.

Emphasized the clout of Irish newspapers, principally the *Nation* and the *Pilot*, even in villages.

96. [Johnstone, Christian]. "Lord Jeffrey's *Contributions to the Edinburgh Review*." n.s., 11 (1844): 12–15.

Review of Francis Jeffrey's work graded him a master of the "profession" of journalism. He steered the *Edinburgh Review* around early obstacles and secured its '[p]lace' in literature and politics as a symbol of "a new and brighter era in periodical literature." *Edinburgh* critics, unlike Jeffrey, were not guided by "moral tendency" but rather by the assumption that they were superior to authors.

97. [Johnstone, Christian]. "*Memoirs and Correspondence* of Mrs. Grant of Laggan." n.s., 11 (1844): 174–81.

Biography of Anne Macvicar Laggan, born in Glasgow, had more paragraphs on the *Edinburgh Review*, mainly the critical style of editor Francis Jeffrey.

98. [Johnstone, Christian]. "*A Summer at Port Phillip*." n.s., 11 (1844): 213–18.

Review of Robert Dundas Murray's book cheered Port Phillip's three newspapers.

99. "*Memoirs and Recollections* of the Late Abraham Raimbach, Esq." n.s., 11 (1844): 223–31.

Profiled Raimbach, a newspaper theatre critic and engraver, and engravings in the *English Theatre* and *Novelist's Magazine*.

100. [Johnstone, Christian]. "Grant's *Impressions of Ireland*." n.s., 11 (1844): 766–74.
Review of James Grant's book touted its data on Dublin newspapers, their owners, editors, tone, circulation, and management. Dublin had two dailies, six triweeklies, one biweekly, and five weeklies at the time of writing. The *Nation* printed 120,000 copies per week, but many more people probably read each copy.

101. "Thiers' *History of Napoleon*." n.s., 12 (1845): 310–23, 566–79.
Review of Adolphe Thiers' book chastised him for condoning the efforts of Napoleon I, notorious for his press restraints, to persuade George III to censor British newspapers critical of the emperor.

102. "The Novels of Zschokke." n.s., 12 (1845): 435–44.
Remembered that Heinrich Zschokke from 1804 conducted the *Swiss Messenger*, "a newspaper of great influence."

103. [Johnstone, Christian]. "*Servia, the Youngest Member of the European Family*." n.s., 12 (1845): 510–17.
Review of A. A. Paton's book hailed a recent Serbian journalistic endeavor, the *Servian Moniteur* published in Pest.

104. "Bell's *Life of Canning*." n.s., 13 (1846): 276–82.
Review of Robert Bell's book unveiled that George Canning was instrumental in the creation of Eton's weekly *Microcosm* and the *Quarterly Review*. In 1846 "every manufacturing town" produced decent "*penny* literature," so different from Canning's savage wit in the *Anti-Jacobin*, language beneath contempt.

105. Gilfillan, George. "Sir Edward Bulwer Lytton." n.s., 13 (1846): 409–13.
Declared that the *New Monthly Magazine*, under E. G. Bulwer-Lytton's editorship, "approached our ideal of a perfect Magazine, combining as it did impartiality, variety, and power." However, his stand against anonymity was wrong. The practice gave critics time to hone style, promoted better writing by neutralizing egotism, and piqued readers' curiosity.

106. Gilfillan, George. "Leigh Hunt." n.s., 13 (1846): 655–60.
Contrasted Hunt's "dashing, slashing, free and fearless style" in the *Examiner* with his "meek and almost mawkish tone" in his *London Journal*, a cheap periodical with a "catholic and genial spirit." This shift was likely the consequence of "the tear and wear, the fret and fever, the squabbling and heart-burning of a newspaper life."

107. Gilfillan, George. "*Life and Correspondence of John Foster*." n.s., 14 (1847): 4–11.
Review of John Sheppard's book tabbed Foster's critical articles for the *Eclectic Review*, articles that revealed a style of "generosity and width."

108. "The Late James Calder." n.s., 14 (1847): 269–73.
Saluted Calder for his independence while co-owner and editor of the *Englishman*, "the principal Sunday paper" about 1815.

109. "*Russia's Internal Life*." n.s., 14 (1847): 320–24.
Review of a book by an anonymous author averred that severe Russian press censorship positioned the *Imperial Gazette* as the only source of information.

110. "The Late Robert Mackenzie Daniel." n.s., 14 (1847): 468–71.
Eulogized Daniel who, as editor of the *Jersey Herald* 1845–46, was a victim of personal abuse from political opponents.

111. Gilfillan, George. "Leigh Hunt on the Pension List." n.s., 14 (1847): 522–26.
Considered Hunt's pension a deserving reward for his achievements, including his work in journalism, and a valuable precedent for the field.

112. De Quincey, Thomas. "Schlosser's Literary *History of the Eighteenth Century*." n.s., 14 (1847): 575–83, 690–96.
Review of F. C. Schlosser's book glanced at Jonathan Swift, Joseph Addison, Richard Steele, and Junius.

113. Gilfillan, George. "Thomas Macaulay." n.s., 14 (1847): 765–74.
Singled out Macaulay's articles in *Knight's Quarterly Magazine* and the *Edinburgh Review*, where his essays were "studded with facts" but "eminently clear" so that "[t]heir immediate effect is absolutely intoxicating."

114. "*Australia Felix*." n.s., 15 (1848): 11–16.
Review of William Westgarth's book sermonized that in the empire a newspaper could be both the "organ of some mischief" and "great instrument of good." It was "the moral censor as well as the political intelligencer, the theatrical and literary critic and commercial advertiser. Above all, it is the daily letter, the Reporter from Home."

115. Barmby, [John] Goodwin. "Louis Blanc." n.s., 15 (1848): 249–51.
Narrated Blanc's career as a journalist for the *Bon Sens*, where, after a series of rapid pay raises, he became editor. At the same time, he penned for the *National*. When the *Bon Sens* changed hands in 1838, he started and edited the *Revue du Progres*.

116. [Troup George]. "The Chartists of Britain and Repealers of Ireland." n.s., 15 (1848): 295–300.
Attested that the "fiery language" in *Times* leaders was "associated with its fame."

117. St. John, Percy B. "France – Political History of the Month." n.s., 15 (1848): 316–42.
Reasoned that French journals did not have timely news because they had "few reporters" and "no correspondents." Even with little advertising, papers managed to survive. When the *Presse* introduced its 3 p.m. edition, it quickly hit 70,000 copies. A recent aborted mob attack on the *Presse* offices was insignificant.

118. [Troup, George]. "Taxes on Knowledge and the Newspaper Press." n.s., 15 (1848): 351–56.

Gushed that the newspaper was "a marvel of the age" because of its "brief and universal" accounts. For the press to be "the palladium of all national privileges," it had to be free of taxes and stamps, the "fetters" worn by the "fourth estate." A free press was an important first step in the education of the masses. Journalists, who worked very hard, could do the job. "Very probably there is no other profession that, during the last twenty or thirty years, has increased more rapidly in efficiency and respectability than 'the press.'" Even a local herald, commanded by an "ignorant, conceited, ill-natured, or careless" editor and stuffed with columns of "trash," was useful. In 1848 the stamp left workers two choices: reading the costly stamped papers in pubs or buying the amoral unstamped ones that did not benefit the treasury. A statement by owners and editors condemning the stamp would catalyze its demise, but the established papers liked it because it nipped new rivals. Without a stamp and with steady base costs, they might draw people away from unstamped tribunes and flourish as did the penny gazettes in New York and Paris. The publications of Edward Lloyd and G. W. M. Reynolds already had big audiences.

119. St. John, Percy B. "General View of the Revolutions in Europe." n.s., 15 (1848): 451–84.

Focused on the French press. France had many cheap newspapers, popular because of their political coverage and feuilletons for which they paid well. Eugene Sue, for example, earned 10,000 francs per novel at the *Constitutionnel.* Most journals divided the work among a principal editor, political editor, and literary editor. Prior to the 1848 Revolution, Paris had 26 dailies; in 1848, 150 (several editors cited). Before 1848 the anonymous editors of the *Assemblée National* were "able" journalists of "spirit and talent." They and their peers had little political influence after the revolution, but journalists' reputations might land them a job in government. Since the revolution occurred, paid street 'criers' sold papers. Once the *Presse* inaugurated an afternoon edition, others followed. Circulations jumped, for instance the *Presse* from 30,000 to 70,000 and *Réforme*, from 20,000 to 40,000. While dailies burgeoned, weeklies, as *Charivari*, lagged. Postal arrangements were no help, and advertising dropped because few could afford it and layouts were "disagreeable." Although magazines multiplied, they attracted few subscribers. Among the new organs were the *Voix des Femmes*, on women's rights, and *Gamin*, with humor.

Aside that the Austrian government jailed the editor of the *Constitution* and some newspaper writers for their republicanism.

120. [Troup, George]. "Taxes on Knowledge." n.s., 15 (1848): 499–503.

Separated very old papers silent about the newspaper stamp from younger ones anxious for its abolition. Many journalists would not speak out because they had a personal interest in the matter. Because the stamp inflated the price of newspapers, the majority of people did not read them regularly, perpetuating ignorance or "bluster."

121. St. John, Percy B. "France – The Revolution of June and July." n.s., 15 (1848): 523–40.

Linked the French press to the February 1848 Revolution.

122. [Troup, George]. "Seditions of August." n.s., 15 (1848): 575–83.

Alluded to the trial of an Irish Catholic printer and journalist acquitted by a Catholic jury of penning for a 'felon' journal.

123. St. John, Percy B. "Revolution in Europe." n.s., 15 (1848): 686–700.
Indexed the political loyalties of France's *Presse*, *Gazette de France*, and other newspapers in the wake of the 1848 Revolution.

124. [Troup, George]. "*Life and Letters of Thomas Campbell.*" n.s., 16 (1849): 31–45.
Review of William Beattie's book stated that Campbell did not excel in journalism, whether as editor of the *New Monthly Magazine* or owner and editor of the *Metropolitan*.

125. Searle, January [George Searle Phillips]. "Huddersfield – Its Physical, Social, Manufacturing, Commercial, and Religious Characteristics." n.s., 16 (1849): 233–40.
Deduced from the *People's Journal*, *Chambers's Journal*, and others of "a like stamp" that the literary taste of the masses was improving although many people still read the periodicals of Edward Lloyd and G. W. M. Reynolds.

126. Hurton, William. "Winter Pictures from the North of Europe. No. II." n.s., 17 (1850): 88–97.
Disclosed that Denmark had a single literary magazine, *North and South*. There were no cheap journals, but many Danes subscribed to British and French monthlies and quarterlies. The country had 70–100 newspapers, of which *Fatherland* circulated broadly. Copenhagen's ten dailies and four weeklies contained some news, much political talk, and feuilletons. *Berling's Gazette* was the mouthpiece of government. The weekly illustrated papers were rather "puerile," although the *Corsair* was similar to *Punch* and *Charivari*.

127. [Troup, George]. "Taxes on Knowledge." n.s., 17 (1850): 234–39.
Scrutinized the taxes on paper and advertising, the newspaper stamp, and the security payment for "seditious" libels. All stifled the cheap newspaper, which the government needed to reach the people. *The Times* and other senior papers feared that competition would kill them without the taxes. The penny post, advanced as a compromise, was unfair because many papers were not mailed. A case study of an average country paper showed the impact of the stamp. Given the costs of composing, reporting, and management, even a penny stamp would inhibit inexpensive newspapers. An unstamped press would not be revolutionary and would raise the literary quality available to workers. They were already opting for "good and unstamped weekly publications" and should have the same access to newspapers as the rich and colonists. More gazettes also meant more jobs and better wages for press personnel, notably the "generally deserving class of men, connected with the literary and reporting department."

128. "Francis Jeffrey." n.s., 17 (1850): 239–48.
Credited Jeffrey's editing and writing for the initial success of the *Edinburgh Review*. Its early contributors "exalted periodical journalism from a subordinate and ancillary, to a paramount and independent place in literature, and made it a popular vehicle, not only of criticism, but of original speculation."

129. [Venables, G. S.]. "Revolutionary Revelations." n.s., 17 (1850): 299–305, 414–23.
Glided over the French press in the reign of Louis Philippe, notably the Communist *Humanitaire*, and in the 1848 Revolutions. The *National*, with its 4,000 subscribers, was no match for *Réforme* with its 20,000 and agenda of "insurrection."

130. [?Mansfield, Horatio]. "A Chapter on Provincial Journalism." n.s., 17 (1850): 424–27.

Hypothesized that established country papers counted on customers' buying habits to survive so relied on scissors and omitted the expensive and bothersome leader. Because new locals usually underestimated the costs of production and taxes, many were soon the prey of capitalists. Locals prospered if their journals were "*written down* to the public taste." Stories about murder and seduction and "vast gooseberries" generated profit. Where printers were owners, educated men resisted being editors. The rest, enduring time constraints and readers' complaints, worked hard on the content and layout of their tribunes because their staffs were ordinarily ill-trained and tactless. Scribblers were willing to begin at low pay in order to gain enough experience to move up. All country journalists had "little regard for the intrinsic respectability of the vocation." Each rank slighted those below, especially bad because the editor and reporter represented the journal and journalism to the public. When journalists insulted each other, they demeaned the profession.

131. [?Mansfield, Horatio]. "*Autobiography of Leigh Hunt.*" n.s., 17 (1850): 563–72.

Review of Hunt's book honored him as a "martyr" for press liberty, chiefly the consequence of columns of "boldness and pugnacity" in the *Examiner*.

132. [Mansfield, Horatio]. "A Little 'Difficulty' in French Literature." n.s., 18 (1851): 151–56.

Presumed that the new French law requiring signature by journalists would produce more duels, as the recent conflict between men of the *Evènement* and *Corsaire* foreshadowed.

133. [Paget, John]. "The Philosophy of Murder." n.s., 18 (1851): 171–76.

Observed that penny-a-liners liked 'terrible,' 'shocking,' and 'frightful' murders because they were good for half a column in the press of "newspaper-loving readers" in barber shops on Sundays.

134. [Bayne, Peter]. "Carlyle's *Life of Sterling*." n.s., 18 (1851): 699–707.

Review of Thomas Carlyle's biography of John Sterling said that he "animated" the *Athenaeum* and later wrote "excellent magazine-articles" for *Blackwood's Magazine* and other serials.

135. [Lushington, Franklin]. "*The Times* and the Poets." n.s., 19 (1852): 18–21.

Crowned *The Times* "the acknowledged leader of the public mind on every subject" in a society where the press "educates the public."

136. Vindex. "Bribery and Corruption in the Press: A Letter to Lady Bulwer Lytton." n.s., 19 (1852): 145–51.

Barked that the "great journals" consistently reviewed the work of Rosina D. Bulwer-Lytton with "much diffidence and some coyness." She, like other female authors, expected social standing to guarantee press critiques. When they were unfavorable, she fantasized that her husband bribed London papers to "malign" her.

Journalism was generally less corruptible than other professions, exceptional because of its great influence. Its goals were to guide government, ensure liberty, address grievances, and protect the poor and helpless. Journalists were "a phalanx of chosen men, all pre-eminent for genius, talents, learning, and an extensive and varied knowledge of the world." To benefit their readers, they must be honest and "impartial."

137. [Mansfield, Horatio]. "Edgar Poe." n.s., 19 (1852): 231–34.
Opined that Edgar Allan Poe authored some of his "finest" criticism while editing *Graham's Magazine*, although in the mid-1840s he penned for "several of the chief periodicals."

138. [Macgregor, John]. "The Governments of Continental Europe. No. III." n.s., 19 (1852): 257–64.
Nodded to French press censorship in Louis Philippe's reign.

139. [Mansfield, Horatio]. "David Macbeth Moir (Delta)." n.s., 19 (1852): 327–30.
Review of *The Poetical Works of David Macbeth Moir*, edited by Thomas Aird, recalled that Moir published significant prose and poetry in the *Edinburgh Literary Gazette* and *Blackwood's Magazine* but declined an offer to edit the *Quarterly Journal of Agriculture*.

140. [Mansfield, Horatio]. "Modern Journalism." n.s., 19 (1852): 353–57.
Prefaced a history of journalism with word that the "newspaper, as now constituted and conducted in the United Kingdom, is one of the great wonders of a wonderful age." It also used the great inventions of the era, such as the *Times'* printing press producing 10,000 copies per hour.

Drew data from *The Fourth Estate* by F. Knight Hunt, a "recent historian of the Press, himself a Journalist." Nathaniel Butter's *Weekely News*, seven pages of "coarse print" of notepaper size, was translated from Dutch. The Stuarts were "deadly foes" of newspapers, but by the early eighteenth century, the first daily was circulating. The *Daily Courant's* only page had foreign news on the front and advertising on the back. *The Times*, born in 1788 after 939 numbers of the *Universal Daily Register*, had four pages of four columns each. They contained editorial notices, "facetious and gossiping articles," shipping news, and advertisements but little foreign news. The paper succeeded thanks to the efforts of John Walter II and editor Thomas Barnes, albeit editors rarely wrote at "a first-class daily paper." In 1851 *The Times* sold 38,000 copies per day, "nearly double the aggregate daily sale of all the other morning and evening papers published in London." Special occasions, such as the opening (1 May 1851) of the Great Exhibition, raised the number to 52,000. This circulation won *The Times* the major share of London's press advertising. Asides on the *Morning Chronicle*, *Morning Post*, and *Morning Herald*.

141. [Mansfield, Horatio]. "*Money and Morals*." n.s., 19 (1852): 518–27.
Review of John Lalor's book gloried that England had "a newspaper-press characterised by a high moral tone, consummate ability, and the fullness and accuracy of its records." Gazettes not only excelled in reporting news but acted as "a perfect mechanism, through which everyone who has the ear of the public can act upon its moral condition."

142. [?Mansfield, Horatio]. "Our Own Correspondent." n.s., 19 (1852): 727–33.
Reviewed *The Personal Adventures of 'Our Correspondent' in Italy* by Michael Honan of *The Times*. Honan covered the 1830 July Revolution in France, then went to Italy, Spain, Constantinople, Mexico, and beyond. Imagined that by 1852 he must have retired or been fired, or else publication of this book would be a breach of confidence. Because he was an Irish Catholic, he may have been the tool of the Jesuits, "an agent admirably adapted for carrying out their designs."

The foreign correspondent was "the stormy petrel of the press, or the jackal of journalism" who scavenged for inside information in places in turmoil. Like the anonymous newspaper editor who issued leaders that could "mould the destinies of peoples and nations," the masked correspondent helped to make the press a "leviathan."

143. "A Newspaper Afloat." n.s., 20 (1853): 76–81.
Limned the *Great Britain Times*, published by passengers aboard *Great Britain* en route to Cape Colony in 1852.

144. "Gossip on Newspapers, Criticism, and the Free List." n.s., 20 (1853): 93–95.
Condemned the free list, tickets allotted to theatre critics who determined the fate of a play. These gifts, which enabled newspapers to print many reviews, indubitably biased critics. Criticism was clearer in the eighteenth century when Samuel Johnson penned for the *Gentleman's Magazine* and Oliver Goldsmith "or poor Ned Purdon wrote petty critiques in the *Ledger*." When gazettes passed their free tickets to potential advertisers, theatre owners cancelled the list. This gesture should motivate book publishers to desist from puffing and spur critics to read books.

145. [Macgregor, John]. "How to Lose a Colony." n.s., 20 (1853): 275–79.
Shared that Bloemfontein had a weekly newspaper, the *Friend of the Sovereignty and Bloemfontein Gazette*. Launched in 1850, it appeared in Dutch and English with many advertisements and letters on business and public affairs.

146. [Beard, J. R.]. "Last Echoes of a Public Hall." n.s., 20 (1853): 350–54.
Aside that newspapers were "the paper columns that sustain the modern Temple of Fame."

147. "Bribery and Corruption." n.s., 20 (1853): 354–56.
Warned that the press could be corrupt or "the engine" of corruption.

148. [Ritchie, James Ewing]. "The House of Commons, from the Strangers' Gallery." n.s., 20 (1853): 488–93.
Toured the Reporters' Gallery, with "those three boxes in the middle" for *Times* personnel. Several MPs had ties to the press, such as Charles Gavan Duffy of the *Nation* and W. J. Fox, 'Publicola' of the *Weekly Dispatch*.

149. [Ritchie, James Ewing]. "The Reporters' Gallery." n.s., 21 (1854): 146–50.
Situated the Reporters' Gallery directly below the Ladies' Gallery. Journalists had 30 seats, but only 12 or 13 men were present at a time. The gallery was comfortable, and reporters were less "roysterous" in their reactions to dull speeches. Note-takers rotated after 30 minutes, but the summary reporter remained throughout. Each paper usually had nine or ten men on call, but their hours varied. Most reporters were young and not intellectual. Those who wrote well hoped to emulate Charles Dickens, earning a healthy income until they succeeded as novelists or editors. Some even aspired to joining the House. Members had initially reacted to reporters with fear, then annoyance about inaccuracy, but in 1854 the "fourth estate" safeguarded their liberties.

150. "Professor Wilson." n.s., 21 (1854): 332–35.

Described John Wilson's contributions of "brilliancy, freshness" in *Blackwood's Magazine*. In his era they "commingled profanity, wit, learning, and buffoonery" as weapons against the *Edinburgh Review*, which pioneered attacks on authors of quality literature.

151. [Bayne, Peter]. "Genius, Literature, and Devotion. II: John Foster." n.s., 21 (1854): 513–20.

Biography of Foster scanned his work for the *Eclectic Review*.

152. [?Mansfield, Horatio]. "The Late Professor Phillips, F. K. Hunt, and J. G. Lockhart." n.s., 22 (1855): 41–45.

Commemorated men with links to journalism. Samuel Phillips published a novel in *Blackwood's Magazine* and literary reviews in *The Times*. His work was "not particularly accurate or profound" but had a "manly and vigorous form." F. Knight Hunt worked for the *Morning Herald*, then commenced the *Medical Times* and *Ladies' Newspaper*. He was also subeditor of the *Illustrated London News* and editor of the *Pictorial Times*. In 1846 he became assistant editor of the *Daily News* on the recommendation of Charles Dickens and in 1851, editor. The author of *The Fourth Estate* was a man of "[s]ound intellect and good business-habits." J. G. Lockhart initially penned for *Blackwood's Magazine* before serving as *Quarterly Review* editor for many years (inaccurately dated here), for which he earned 1,200 pounds per year.

153. [Mansfield, Horatio]. "The Great American Humbug." n.s., 22 (1855): 73–81.

Unearthed that P. T. Barnum in 1831 opened a newspaper, *Herald of Freedom*, but was soon jailed for libel.

154. [Donne, W. B.]. "The Coffee-Houses of the Restoration." n.s., 22 (1855): 104–11.

Listed periodicals, among them the *Tatler* and *Gentleman's Magazine*, conventionally available in eighteenth-century coffeehouses.

155. "Life of James Montgomery." n.s., 22 (1855): 159–65.

Proceeded from Montgomery's youthful journalistic career, as a tyro at the *Bee* in 1791 and clerk for the *Sheffield Register* in 1792, to his role as co-owner and editor of the *Iris* at mid-decade and as contributor to the *Eclectic Review* in the early 1800s.

156. [Rands, William Brighty]. "Reading Raids. IV: The Cheap Press." n.s., 22 (1855): 222–29.

Moved from the 1830s penny press, as the *Penny Magazine* and *Chambers's Journal*, to the 1850s. The *Penny* was "always *well* written," but the *Mirror* and the *Apollo Magazine*, with its "namby-pamby contents," were both more literary. The *Mirror* was a favorite of "theatrical folk and gentlemen of the fourth estate: it presupposed a better culture in its readers than did the *Penny Magazine*, and charged a halfpenny more." *Chambers's Journal*, "addressed to the middle classes," increased in importance because it looked at social questions, "while the *Penny Magazine* was teaching the million prudence, self-denial and the duty of self-training." Between 1830 and1840, cheap weeklies devoted to fiction were also popular. Thereafter, the *Family Herald* and *London Journal* aimed to entertain and edify.

The *Family Herald* always had at least a page of original writing on a serious topic. Both it and the *London Journal* printed many letters (sampled here). *Household Words* was the 1850s equivalent of the *Penny Magazine*.

Removal of the newspaper stamp would spawn many penny gazettes and removal of the paper duty, many cheap monthlies. Because leader-writing required "a peculiar training," serious newspapers would still be expensive. New penny papers would avoid slander because the English respected "the *amenity* of the Press" as well as "its *freedom*" and "its *purity*." Should these predictions prove inaccurate, editors should sign their columns. As masses of men read about politics, they would probably seek the vote. Cheap apolitical weeklies would likely lure women readers from cheap monthlies. To balance the inexpensive press, a few "Literary Organs...free, fair mediums of communication between literary men and women and the public," were desirable.

157. [?Mansfield, Horatio]. "Horace Greely [*sic*], the Hero of Cheap Journalism." n.s., 22 (1855): 229–37.

Review of J. Parton's *Life of Horace Greeley, Editor of the New York Tribune*, recapitulated his career from typesetter at the *Northern Spectator* (VT) to editor of his own weekly *New Yorker* and daily *New York Tribune*. This paper proved that a cheap press could have "perfect independence and high morality" even with intense competition. The new unstamped British papers should reject theatre advertising and support international copyright to maintain this level.

158. [Donne, W. B.]. "Printing and Printers." n.s., 22 (1855): 390–98.

Parroted that F. Köenig, a Saxon clockmaker, developed the "first printing-machine" for *The Times*.

159. "*The Life of James Montgomery*." n.s., 22 (1855): 744–47.

Review of a book by John Holland and James Everett treated Montgomery's newspaper leaders as "essays by a gentleman, a poet, and a scholar," notwithstanding that he was "harassed by the weekly duties of journalism" at Sheffield's *Iris*. Aside on the influence of the *Leeds Mercury*.

Temple Bar, 1860–1900

Striving to beguile and benefit the affluent among the middling class, *Temple Bar* roamed the journalistic world. Information about local, imperial, French, and American newspapers filled many paragraphs.

1. [Jerrold, W. B.]. "The Father of the French Press." 1 (1860–61): 38–44.
Denominated Théophraste Renaudot the father of French journalism. Before France had a press, newsmongers scribbled for their rich patrons and "hawkers of scandalous and seditious news sold their illegal bits of paper." Renaudot, a physician, wanted to start "a political organ" with the truth. With the supposed blessing of Armand de Richelieu, the *Gazette de France* began in 1631. Denis Sallo's more literary *Journal des Savants* followed in 1665 and Jacques Loret's *Mercure Gallant*, "social" or "little journalism," in 1672. Many periodicals emerged in the early 1700s, some "clandestine" that criticized the throne. In 1860 French evening gazettes were "gray little papers" with "scraps of news...lively criticisms on opera or drama...quotations of the Bourse...divers facts," advertising, and serial romances but not politics because government considered the subject disruptive.

2. J[errold, W.] B. "Madame Doublet's News-Saloon." 1 (1860–61): 473–82.
Envisioned the eighteenth-century salon of Madame Doublet as a place where "all the clever and daring thinkers and gossips of her day...met to supply the news that the government press dared not print." News was put in two registers, "one for facts, one for mere rumours," both more intriguing than the *Gazette de France*. The registers also had reports of legal proceedings, criticism, "notices of new prohibited books," poems, "scandal," and "anecdotes." Doublet's servants copied extracts and sold them notwithstanding police efforts to control their circulation. Another secret press was the *Gazetier Cuirassé*, a print of Charles Théveneau de Morande that challenged the official practice of subsidizing leaders, which "elevated second-rate famished men to the front of the scribbling army."

Once the Estates-General convened, many journals surfaced in towns and the countryside. About 1,000 were born between 1789 and 1793. In October 1790, for example, Paris had 60–70 sheets. Some were never sold but only posted. They had "eccentric titles" and a "vehemence of expression and audacity of principle." Comic and verse papers also developed. All revolutionary journals omitted the names of proprietors, printers, and editors. In 1792, sure that a paper shortage was an aristocratic plot to stop them, these journalists embarked on a "coarse and blasphemous" campaign against the authorities. Thereafter every revolutionary government had its own herald and tried but failed to silence opponents. Citizens, meanwhile, burned the gazettes of their press enemies.

3. [Thornbury, George W.]. "American Hotels and American Food." 2 (1861): 345–56.
Witnessed that Americans were the "most voracious and miscellaneous newspaper readers" because the format suited "their quick and too generally...superficial minds." Many American hotels held a "litter of provincial papers each padlocked to its own mahogany file-staff" because every small town

had a newspaper. Gazettes were "all rather violent and personal, excessively editorial, and too fond of laborious fine writing, often wasted on small local events." The best American journals were New York's *Herald* and *Tribune*.

4. "In the Name of the Prophet – Smith!" 4 (1861–62): 181–94.
Aside on the *Missouri Inquirer* (1833), a newspaper advocating the "doctrines" of Joseph Smith.

5. "The Morals of the Decade." 4 (1861–62): 288–94.
Accepted newspapers as the Fourth Estate. It could retain power if it shifted from instruction, as readers became more knowledgeable, to representation of their opinions. Journalists had to abandon early-century bombast, in 1861 "consigned to the limbo of disgust." "Common sense, enforced by ability, is the great strength of a free and independent press" and would suit readers "enlightened" about politics and religion.

6. [Sala, George Augustus]. "Notice." 5 (1862): ii.
Clarified that manuscripts rejected by *Temple Bar* were not returned to contributors because silence was "merciful and considerate."

7. J[errold, W.] B. "Pens and Ink in the Reign of Terror." 5 (1862): 287–95.
Bound the French Terror press to the 1830s British unstamped because both roused the masses.

8. [?Wilberforce, Edward]. "A Popular Paper in Munich." 6 (1862): 34–41.
Headlined the *Neueste Nachrichten*, a popular Munich daily with scissored news but valuable original advertising. Its inserts, unlike those in *The Times*, were not well-organized columns. Some were a half or whole page costing a penny a line. They were similar in content to the British except that there were no births, marriages, and deaths. Germans used advertisements as paeans and policy statements in lieu of letters.

9. [Hutton, James]. "An Indian Newspaper." 6 (1862): 502–11.
Inspected the *Delhi Gazette*, a ten-page triweekly. Of its 40 columns, 18 were advertising. Subscribers, for a print run of 1,400, paid five pounds a year including postage. Its business management was good, but its "editorial incapacity" was apparent. In addition to advertisements for banks, books, house and personal goods, and food and drink, it printed many letters (sampled here), news summaries, telegrams, and leaders of "monumental imbecility." If the *Delhi Gazette* was the best of Anglo-Indian journalism, then that journalism desperately needed improvement.

10. K[empt], R[obert]. "The Newspaper Press of America." 7 (1862–63): 190–201.
Fixed on James Gordon Bennett, founder of the *New York Herald*, because the British press had recently discussed at length his "gross misrepresentations of the laws and institutions of England, and his foul calumnies upon her people." He was a hard worker but unscrupulous. From its onset the *Herald* faced the hostility of the city's press and business because Bennett relied on scandal and abuse of contemporaries to sell papers. Their 'moral war' against him was futile. In 1844 the *Herald* printed 20,000 copies daily; in 1855, 55,820; in 1861, 105,000. While Horace Greeley's *Tribune* was "democratic" and Henry Raymond's *Times* was a "reliable paper for general information," the *Herald* was successful because it was "the mouthpiece of the mob…the mob is king in the United States."

The United States had "ably conducted newspapers." Beginning in Boston in 1690, American gazettes multiplied rapidly: in 1775 there were 34; 1800, 200; 1830, 1,000; 1860, 5,253 against Britain's 1,250. The United States had 300 dailies, 72 published in New York. Many editors were former soldiers and statesmen (examples here); all were self-centered, vilifying each other unlike their peers in Britain. Although American papers had "plenty of smart, clever, talented writing... their egoism, personality, and coarse familiarity are their bane." They lacked the "scholarly, dignified, tasteful leader-writing" of *The Times* or *Daily News*. Their inferior paper, small type, and disorganized format, in which advertising was more like placards, were unappealing. "[T]he American press wants that high moral tone, that true enlightenment, and that sterling independence, which make the British press the palladium of the people's rights, and the glory and happiness of the country."

11. "Sitting Up." 7 (1862–63): 349–58.

Satirized the inspirations for and distractions to penning periodical articles.

12. [Sala, George Augustus]. "Breakfast in Bed; or Philosophy Between the Sheets. No. VII." 8 (1863): 70–79.

Defended penny-a-liners, "the meritorious and useful individuals whose more courteous designation is 'occasional reporters,' men paid in the penny to two and one-half penny range." Although they were an "exceedingly industrious, inoffensive, and intelligent class," certainly better than "more pretentious scribblers," the public saw liners as "poor and miserable," "humble and obscure," apt targets for ridicule. By contrast, war correspondents, as William Howard Russell, were famous.

13. Sala, George Augustus. "Cloudy Memories of an Old Passport, I." 8 (1863): 111–18.

Sighed that the *Westminster Review* was "that respectable but somewhat senile organ of mild atheism and genteel sedition."

14. "Truth in Art." 8 (1863): 358–69.

Certified that "pictorial newspapers and magazines, of which the *Illustrated London News* was the first and is still the chief," educated the public about art.

15. [Scoffern, John]. "The Public Press in Matters of Science." 8 (1863): 447–53.

Contended that newspapers were so partisan in politics that they were unable to deal with its intersection with technology. When gazettes did dwell on technology, they discredited themselves in the eyes of the expert and the general reader. This outcome was particularly bad because newspapers were "almost omnipotent" in political education.

16. C[ollins, Mortimer]. "Bohemia." 8 (1863): 551–63.

Article on a cultural movement and its newspaper, the *Teaser*, commended William Maginn for the success of *John Bull* and *Fraser's Magazine* "in their early days of brilliant and reckless Toryism." The 1863 leader-writer, acting mechanically to fill space, merely "catches the caprice of the hour, and sets it down in the stereotyped style of the leading papers."

17. W[raxall], L[ascelles]. "François Marmontel." 9 (1863): 141–53.

Starred Marmontel, the eighteenth-century editor of the *Mercure de France* who was imprisoned for refusing to identify one of its authors.

18. [?Yates, Edmund]. "Comic Literature." 9 (1863): 590–99.

Warranted that comic periodicals were "in great demand" in 1863. *Punch* previously had few rivals, but the penny *Fun* and *Comic News* were new competitors. None of the three "appeal to education or refinement." Instead of "wit, humour, and pointed sarcasm" they distributed "wild exaggeration, vulgar anti-climax, and outrageous punning." During its "golden age," *Punch* printed Thomas Hood, Douglas Jerrold, and W. M. Thackeray, but 1863 comic writing was drivel, affected by the burlesques of theatres and comic songs of music halls. Such humor "destroys all seriousness of thought, induces frivolity, weakens the perception of the true and the beautiful, degrades the taste, and corrupts the language." Comic journalism was not a career for young men of talent.

19. C[ollins, Mortimer]. "Country Newspapers." 10 (1863–64): 128–41.

Rued that local gazettes were struggling under the impact of railroads, which brought *The Times* and "those terrible penny papers" to the country. Bigger towns, such as Manchester, were already transforming the penny daily to serve regions. Most small dailies failed because they underestimated costs and published too many telegrams, trivial village news, and illogical and ill-written leaders. Yet speculators persisted in financing them.

Early country weeklies, such as the *Stamford Mercury*, chronicled borough and county news well. They understood that dullness, not feeble attempts to copy the *Saturday Review*, attracted English farmers. In 1863 locals aping London publicized circulation to attract advertising and printed gossip and letters of "exquisite trash" from London correspondents. Country journals edited by ill-paid men who were also reporters would eventually be driven out of business by London.

Aside that the *Edinburgh Review* inaugurated a new era in criticism, but it and *Blackwood's Magazine* were London periodicals except in name.

20. [Hutton, James]. "'Young Bengal' as a Newspaper Correspondent." 11 (1864): 295–303.

Newspaper editor reminisced about letters, on education, gossip and taxes, sent by Bengalis "trained to a greater or lesser extent in the English language and literature." Evidenced racism by saying that Bengali correspondents were "fully aware of the moral inferiority of their race."

21. "Two Cuttings from the Advertisement Sheet." 11 (1864): 551–57.

Ridiculed the typography and spacing in newspaper advertisements. Those in the dailies were a "mass of rank jobbery"; in the weeklies, a service for job hunters.

22. Sala, George Augustus. "Manners to Mend." 12 (1864): 91–97.

Segregated the "most foul and petty libel" of John Wilkes in the *North Briton*, the coarseness of William Cobbett's sheets, and the prose of the early *Examiner, Blackwood's Magazine*, and *Fraser's Magazine* from the more moderate language of 1864 journalism. Although the comic press "commendably abstained from cruel, personal satire," it was dull.

23. [Timbs, John]. "Modern Eccentrics." 16 (1865–66): 558–66.

Designated William Cobbett as an eccentric because of his choice of the gridiron as the emblem for the *Political Register*.

24. [Devey, Joseph]. "Literary Forgeries: Rowley's Poems and Tragedies." 17 (1866): 132–44.
Recorded that the eighteenth-century *Felix Farley's Journal* printed false columns by Thomas Chatterton.

25. Escott, T. H. S. "Intellectual Flunkeyism." 17 (1866): 539–45.
Balanced pride in the power of the "Cheap Press," the daily penny newspaper, and anxiety that its 'sensational leaders' and tendency to pry into politicians' lives would transmogrify it into "an Americanized periodical literature."

26. [Robinson, J. R.]. "A Week with the Fenians." 18 (1866): 177–95.
Spotlighted a special correspondent dispatched by his managing editor to cover the Fenian "invasion of Canada."

27. D[oran], J[ohn]. "Quite Beneath Notice." 18 (1866): 259–70.
Denounced "*Belgique*, a *religious* paper," for its "reckless mendacity."

28. [Skinner, J. Hilary]. "Is He a Spy?" 19 (1866–67): 405–10.
Remembered covering the 1866 Austro-Prussian War when the Prussians were suspicious of the "newspaper correspondent."

29. [Escott, T. H. S.]. "Cliques and Criticism." 20 (1867): 321–26.
Chose dominance by cliques as the key flaw of newspaper literary criticism. Coteries, shielded by anonymity, engaged in "mutual puffing" because they feared that attacks would trigger counterattacks, but conceded that many "*popular critics*" did good work.

30. Hannay, James. "Recollections of a Provincial Editor." 23 (1868): 175–85.
Mused about experiences as a journalist: a cathedral town weekly was dull because of the local duke's interference; a London comic paper closed when one partner absconded with its treasury; a West Country gazette was originally owned by railroad speculators; a tribune in the manufacturing districts lured capitalist readers not aware of "style, taste"; a Scottish herald was partisan in politics and religion and very parochial.

31. Sala, George Augustus. "Lord Brougham." 23 (1868): 421–32.
Esteemed Henry Brougham who penned the "opening address for the *Penny Magazine*" and many articles for the *Edinburgh Review* edited by Francis Jeffrey, whose style was "more refined and self-contained." Brougham was one of *Punch*'s victims. The serial, with a front piece by Richard Doyle, was "one of the funniest papers ever printed" but not for the "soured and envious" who perused the *Saturday Review*.

32. Hannay, James. "From Pittenweem to Barcelona." 25 (1868–69): 27–39.
Snubbed Paris' *Lanterne* because it lacked "delicacy, subtlety in its satire."

33. Atom [H. E. H. Jerningham]. "Paris Gossip." 25 (1868–69): 138–44, 429–32, 524–26.

Avouched that *Figaro* was losing its popularity to *Gaulois*, "the best informed and best written paper" of a French press that was generally "detestable" because of editors' constant "bickering and quarreling."

34. Ecroyd, Henry. "Spain in the Throes of Revolution." 25 (1868–69): 487–502.

Noted *Euscalduña Iaungoicoa eta Fornac*, "a neo-Catholic Basque newspaper."

35. Ralston, W. R. S. "Alexander Hertzen [*sic*]." 29 (1870): 44–58.

Logged Herzen's journalistic career. He edited the *Vladimir Gazette* in 1838 after the government ordered a newspaper in every department. Next he created *Polar Star* and *Kolokol*, smuggled into Russia where its popularity roused the jealousy of Michael Katkoff.

36. Shuldham, E. B. "Heine's Life and Writings." 29 (1870): 210–27.

Detailed that Heinrich Heine was hired by Baron J. F. Cotta, editor of the *Allgemeine politische Annalen*, to do "well-paid literary work." Heine also was the Paris correspondent for the *Morgenblatt* and a political columnist for Cotta's *Allgemeine Zeitung*.

37. [Borlase, J. S.]. "Melbourne in 1869." 30 (1870): 225–35.

The author, a former editor of the *Australian Journal*, a serial similar to the *Family Herald*, testified that Melbourne had six dailies, 12 weeklies "including a capital *Punch*," and two monthlies. The city's *Argus* was "the leading newspaper of Australia" and "superior in every respect to the *Sydney Morning Herald*." Reporters and proofreaders made less than compositors because too many men from the "poorest class" were seeking jobs in journalism. Parliamentary reporters who were "first-classmen on a first-class paper" might do better but would still earn less than their London confreres.

38. An Eye-Witness [Otto Corvin-Wiersbitzki]. "Strasburg after the Siege." 30 (1870): 534–53.

The author, covering the Franco-Prussian War, met "Hermann Vogel, the talented special correspondent of the *Frankfurt Gazette*"; W. T. Rae, special correspondent for New York's *Daily News*; and F. J. Jackson of the city's *Evening Post*.

39. Andersen, Hans Christian. "A Visit to Charles Dickens." Trans. Augusta Plesner. 31 (1870–71): 27–46.

Visited *The Times* whose departments were organized "almost with military discipline" and printing operations were awesome. "The power of mind reigns here along with the power of steam" giving the paper influence "from Lapland to Hindoostan."

40. [Corvin-Wiersbitzki, Otto]. "Life at Versailles." 31 (1870–71): 195–205.

Correspondent during the Franco-Prussian War unearthed that the subeditor of Cologne's *Zeitung*, on special assignment in France, published the daily *Moniteur Officiel du Département de Seine-et-Oise*. This four-page evening folio had to contend with Germans "ridiculously narrow-minded" about the press. They kept reporters on a tight leash, as the "rising journalist" Hoff, who represented the *Allgemeine Zeitung*, Vienna's *Presse*, and Berlin's *National Zeitung*, learned. He was sent to report on French prisoners after his story that the Germans favored British correspondents over their own displeased authorities.

41. [Austin, Alfred]. "Our Neighbours and Ourselves." 32 (1871): 54–69.
Complained that politicians were less accurate and more biased than war correspondents.

42. [Corvin-Wiersbitzki, Otto]. "Aspect of Paris after the War." 32 (1871): 91–107.
Broadcast that some Paris newspapers refused to publicize the German occupation of the city after the Franco-Prussian War. Others printed the news surrounded by a black border.

43. The Author of "Robespierre" [H. B. Baker]. "Marat: 'The Delirium of the Revolution.'" 32 (1871): 358–69.
Analyzed the contents of J. P. Marat's *Ami du Peuple* and its successor, the *Journal de la République*.

44. [Gillard, Hardy]. "From San Francisco to Niagara." 33 (1871): 233–46.
Traveler located 12 dailies in San Francisco.

45. [Austin, Alfred]. "The Present State of the English Stage." 33 (1871): 456–68.
Pondered the effects on theatre of the "daily newspapers, those very lowest and latest channels to which the waters of thought, observation, and just criticism descend." Journalists facing deadlines scribbled "hasty and indiscriminating" theatre reviews. "No other branch of journalism is so badly done," so readers held reviewers in "universal and merited contempt." Critics usually puffed every play because theatre advertising was "too lucrative" to lose, but some leader-writers were finally exposing reviewers' exaggeration.

46. O[sborne], S[idney] G. "Stray Thoughts on Coming Political and Social Upheaval." 34 (1871–72): 240–51.
Despaired that the lower class perused "a portion of the Press" that was "cheap, violent, and very nasty," and full of "racy obscenity." Such papers accented scandal and scoffed at religion, perhaps prompting the masses to become a mob.

47. [Austin, Alfred]. "Modern Manners." 34 (1871–72): 453–62.
Whined that the press, a "useful and certainly necessary institution," undermined respect for public and private men by ridiculing them in order to amuse readers. Journalism's motto seemed to be "Nothing is sacred."

48. An English Lady [?Antoinette K. Crichton]. "Narrative of an Escape from the Conflagration of Paris." 34 (1871–72): 497–516.
Verified the basis of Communard newspapers.

49. The Author of "Mirabeau." [H. B. Baker]. "Richard Steele." 34 (1871–72): 518–32.
Regarded Steele as the sole father of the *Tatler* and the *Spectator* because Joseph Addison was neither a regular contributor nor an original thinker. The *Tatler* was "the first periodical work ever published in this

country…the precursor of the modern magazine and the modern novel." Soon with a large circulation, it pirated the name "Isaac Bickerstaff" from Jonathan Swift. The *Spectator*'s "success was immediate and enormous," printing 1,000 daily until the stamp duty. Steele also published the *Guardian*, for which Addison wrote. Steele's other serials, *Town Talk, Chit Chat*, and the *Tea Table*, were short-lived. He followed these with a triweekly political journal, the *Englishman*, then the *Theatre* and *Plebian*, a foe of Addison's *Old Whig*. Steele's writing was not as good as Addison's or Swift's.

50. [Trollope, Frances E.]. "About Charles Lamb." 35 (1872): 21–36.
Cited Lamb's work for the *London Magazine*. Aside that the *Quarterly Review* was "a Pandora's box of heart-burnings, friendship-breakings, resentments, and discontents" but a "majestic periodical."

51. [Baden-Powell, George]. "Postal Universities." 36 (1872): 518–27.
Article on distance education pictured newspapers as "essentially the mouthpieces of the wants and feelings of everybody."

52. [Bentley, George]. "How the World Wags." 36 (1872): 540–44.
Bragged that the *Quarterly* was "a review still, as ever, edited with remarkable ability, which maintains its eminence amongst the publications of Europe."

53. [Doran, John]. "A Hundred Years Ago." 37 (1872–73): 240–54.
Peeked at satire in the eighteenth-century *Public Advertiser.*

54. Dent, John C. "America and Her Literature." 37 (1872–73): 396–406.
Declared that American periodical literature "affords unquestionable evidence of the learning, acuteness, and breadth of thought of the writers who furnish it." The best quarterly was the *North American Review*; the best magazine, the *Atlantic Monthly*. Among other magazines good in the East were *Scribner's*, *Putnam's*, and *Harper's Monthly*, and in California, the *Overland Monthly*. The United States excelled in "legal, medical, and science magazines." Americans also read British quarterlies.

As for newspapers the "standard of American journalism – more especially New York journalism – is low…below that of any other country in the world." The most popular newspapers were the worst, with a "slovenly" style and a determination "to create a sensation." Many journalists were talented and honorable but were pressured to follow the crowd instead of leading "popular feeling." American "sporting journals," "vile repositories of wickedness," were "a disgrace, not to civilization only, but to humanity itself."

55. [Cudlip, Annie]. "James Hannay." 38 (1873): 89–94.
Referred to Hannay's "brilliant scholarly articles" in the *Quarterly Review* and his editing (1860–64) of the *Edinburgh Courant.*

56. [Hoey, Frances Cashel]. "The Life of Charles Dickens." 38 (1873): 169–85.
Glimpsed Dickens' editorial tenure at the *Daily News.*

57. [Doran, John]. "Artists and Critics." 38 (1873): 542–56.
Traced the evolution of periodical art criticism from letters to editors in eighteenth-century serials. The *London Post* soon had an art critic, and an artist headed the "Fine Arts" column of the *Examiner.*

58. Camus [?John George Francis]. "Junius and Sir Arthur Gordon." 39 (1873): 335–46.

Disputed Gordon's thesis, in a letter to *The Times* (22 May 1871), that contemporaries knew the identity of Junius.

59. [Doran, John]. "Henry Fothergill Chorley." 40 (1873–74): 93–101.

Biography of Chorley, a London music critic and friend of Charles Dickens, watched newspaper criticism move from the "axe and scalpel school" to "severity" during the nineteenth century.

60. [Kingsley, Henry]. "Richard Steele." 40 (1873–74): 103–21.

Concentrated more on Joseph Addison than Steele. Addison penned for the *Tatler*, "one of the greatest English classics," from #18. He also aided Steele with the *Guardian*. Asides on the *Plebian* and *Old Whig*.

61. [Baker, H. B.]. "Chateaubriand and His Times." 40 (1873–74): 194–208, 373–89.

Stated that René de Cheateaubriand as a journalist "stood in the first and most influential rank, as the pages of the *Conservateur* testified." He also penned for the *Journal des Débats*.

62. [Kingsley, Henry]. "Addison." 41 (1874): 319–37.

Profiled Joseph Addison with a gloss on the *Spectator*.

63. Ingram, John H. "Edgar Poe." 41 (1874): 375–87.

Evaluated Poe's "poems, tales, and reviews" in Richmond's *Southern Literary Messenger*, which he edited for 500 dollars per year. His stories and "trenchant critiques" raised circulation from 300 to 4,000. "In 1837 Poe wrote some slashing critiques for the *New York Review*" and in 1838 joined Philadelphia's *Gentleman's Magazine* becoming editor in 1839. Although he was "unreliable," he went on to edit *Graham's Magazine* in the early 1840s. By 1844 he was writing for New York's *Mirror*, and in 1845 he bought the *Broadway Journal*, a serial of quality but few readers that ceased in 1846.

64. [Austin, Alfred]. "A Burning Question." 42 (1874): 22–34.

Aside that *Saturday Review* writers "apparently make a profession of imperfectly polished scurrility."

65. [Besant, Walter]. "Writers and Reviewers." 42 (1874): 100–10.

Inventoried preferences of literary critics. Contributors to reviews read a variety of books to produce articles that lifted "the standard of excellence." Among the weeklies (several listed), *Saturday Review* critics chose "scholarship and antiquarian research"; *Spectator* reviewers opted for "theological" texts; and *Athenaeum* folks read parts of books, "especially of last-century gossip." Morning dailies in London and the country should expand their short notices "to raise the national standard of taste."

Selection of a book for review always implied favoritism, so the *Saturday Review* and *Spectator* set a uniform length. Slashing may have amused a former generation, but in 1874 most critics praised their friends as was common in any profession. The *Saturday Review* published the best criticism in its "palmy days" in the 1860s, but its 1874 columns were "bright and clever." *Athenaeum* critics showed "literary correctness and care," and *Spectator* reviewers "appreciated" a book. People who cared about a topic typically read a volume irrespective of its reviews.

66. [Austin, Alfred]. "The Vice of Reading." 42 (1874): 251–57.
Pontificated that the "modern newspaper is to the full as noxious as the modern novel; but it, too, is ubiquitous and universal." The purpose of newspapers was no longer to spread news but to make money. "It is impossible for newspaper-writers to be exact, the conditions under which they write forbidding such a result," yet readers adopted their ideas without question. Reading newspapers was harmful for men who should think independently and for women who should abandon it for physical exercise.

67. The Author of *Authors at Work* [Charles Pebody]. "Southey in His Study." 42 (1874): 370–86.
Condensed Robert Southey's journalistic career. In 1795 he scribbled criticism for the *Courier* for five shillings per column and "spicy paragraphs" for the *Morning Post* for six pence each. He then penned "seditious odes" for the *Citizen* for one and a half guineas per week. He was best known for his pieces in the *Quarterly Review*, where he earned 100–50 guineas for each one, which subscribers "read with great zest," and his "skits" in the *New Monthly Magazine*. He rejected *The Times*' offer of 2,000 pounds per year to replace Thomas Barnes as editor. Aside that the *Morning Post* had a staff poet paid 75 pounds per year.

68. [Austin, Alfred]. "Is the National Spirit Dead?" 44 (1875): 167–81.
Contemplated the foreign and domestic press: Paris' *Journal des Débats*, whose John Lemoinne was an "accomplished but accidental journalist"; Cologne's *Zeitung*, Augsburg's *Allgemeine Zeitung*, Berlin's *National Zeitung*, Vienna's *Abendpost*, Milan's *Perseveranza*, Rome's *Opinione*, and Naples' *Pungolo*. In 1870 the *Courrier de Versailles* switched from official paper of Napoleon III to journal of news and "short but telling leaders" under a Prussian editor.

At home *The Times* had had "enormous power" for over two decades; the *Standard* was "the most vigorous, the most influential, and the most independent of the Conservative organs"; the *Pall Mall Gazette* was "manly"; and the *Daily Telegraph* was a "buffoon."

69. [Baker, H. B.]. "How Jules Janin Became a Journalist." 45 (1875): 71–75.
Trailed Janin's long career from the *Lorgnette* to *Figaro* to the *Journal des Débats* where he was the theatre critic for 40 years.

70. [Escott, T. H. S.]. "O'Connelliana." 45 (1875): 234–42.
Ranked Benjamin Disraeli's "Runnymede" letters in *The Times* (1836) as inferior in style and argument but fiercer in invective than those of Junius.

71. [Baker, H. B.]. "A Neglected Humourist." 45 (1875): 448–64.
Biography of Samuel Foote referred to his comedy, *The Patron*, whose protagonist was a hack scribbling paragraphs for the *Farthing Post*.

72. Horne, R. H. "John Forster: His Early Life and Friendships." 46 (1876): 491–505.
Imparted that in 1833 Forster headed the theatre section and Laman Blanchard headed the literary section of the *True Sun*, which "qualified and energetic editors" William Carpenter and John Bell directed. Forster then moved to the *Examiner* as literary and theatre editor where his energy and intellect outweighed the indolence and wit of owner and editor Albany Fonblanque. Forster made the *Examiner* a power in the arts, and Fonblanque made it a force in politics.

73. [Pollock, Walter Herries]. "The Literary Hades." 46 (1876): 525–29.
Damned periodicals that printed superficial, misleading, and sometimes malicious literary reviews and newspapers that printed literary scandal. Yet a *Times* critic recently threatened someone who rebuked him.

74. Mayer, S. R. Townshend. "Leigh Hunt and Lord Brougham: With Original Letters." 47 (1876): 221–34.
Borrowed from W. J. Fox the opinion that the early *Examiner* was "the champion of every good object" at a time when libel was a serious menace to the press. John Scott, later editor of the *London Magazine*, was prosecuted while editor of the *Stamford News* because he reprinted an article against army flogging. The libel trial of the Hunts, for the *Examiner*'s ongoing denunciations of "the character, the conduct, and the companions of the Prince Regent," was more famous.

75. [Forrest, G. W.]. "Lord Macaulay." 47 (1876): 251–65.
Determined that T. B. Macaulay first achieved literary fame from his *Edinburgh Review* articles, not his earlier pieces in *Knight's Quarterly Magazine*. Paraphrased him on the birth of the *Edinburgh*.

76. [Baker, H. B.]. "Churchill, the Satirist." 47 (1876): 528–48.
Recounted that Charles Churchill once supervised poetry for the *Library* but was notorious for his attack on the *Critical Review* edited by Tobias Smollett. Churchill, an acquaintance of John Wilkes, escaped an arrest warrant issued in connection with the *North Briton*. Aside on the reasons for the failure of the eighteenth-century *St. James's Magazine*.

77. [Smith, George Barnett]. "James Hannay." 49 (1877): 234–47.
Bowed to Hannay as editor of the *Edinburgh Courant*, 1860–64, and the author of a host of newspaper articles as well as "brilliant essays" in the *Quarterly Review*. He also penned for the *Cornhill Magazine*, *Temple Bar*, *Punch*, and the *North British Review*.

78. F[onblanque], A. de. "The Young Man from the Country." 50 (1877): 392–96.
Recollected that in 1847 London had four dailies.

79. [Graves, A. P.]. "An Irish Poet and Novelist: Joseph Sheridan LeFanu." 50 (1877): 504–17.
Portrayed LeFanu as owner and editor of the Dublin newspaper, the *Warder*, in the 1830s when he also penned for the *Dublin University Magazine*. He later purchased the *Dublin Evening Packet*, the *Dublin Evening Mail*, and the *Dublin University Magazine*, which he also edited. LeFanu's "learning and brilliancy, and the power and point of his sarcasm…made the *Dublin Evening Mail* the most formidable of Irish press critics."

80. Jerrold, Evelyn. "Alexandre Dumas the Younger." 51 (1877): 392–408.
Remarked on the poems of Dumas, *fils*, in the *Journal des Demoiselles* and his father's significance for journalism's feuilleton.

81. J[eaffreson], J. C[ordy]. "Dr. Doran, F.S.A." 52 (1878): 460–94.
Plumbed John Doran's articles in the *Literary Chronicle* and his poetry and literary columns in the *Bath Journal*. As literary editor and proofreader of the *Church and State Gazette*, he earned 100 pounds per year but more as editor. He was a regular contributor to the *Athenaeum*, 1854–69, and edited it when Hepworth Dixon was away. Doran expected to succeed Dixon but moved to *Notes and Queries*, a better fit for his talents, at the invitation of Charles Dilke.

82. Wedmore, Frederick. "Cruikshank." 52 (1878): 499–516.
Resurrected George Cruikshank's drawings for *Fraser's Magazine* "in its great days" of the 1830s and for *Oliver Twist* in *Bentley's Miscellany*.

83. [Hoey, Frances Cashel]. "The *Memorials* of Miss Martineau." 53 (1878): 457–74.
Marginalized, from Harriet Martineau's *Memorials* (attached to her *Autobiograph)*, her articles in the *Westminster Review* where "she aired her grievances" and her 1,600 leaders in the *Daily News* where she was probably overrated.

84. [Morris, Mowbray]. "About Joseph Addison." 55 (1879): 33–52.
Assessed Addison's writing in the *Spectator*, *Free-holder*, and *Whig-Examiner*. He was so scrupulous about his work that he would stop the *Tatler* press to edit, whereas Richard Steele wrote more on the spur of the moment.

85. Buchanan, Robert [W.]. "Sydney Dobell: A Personal Sketch." 56 (1879): 80–91.
Biography of a poet reported that the *Athenaeum* had sued critic Alexander Smith for plagiarism.

86. Pollock, Lady [Juliet]. "Criticism Past and Present." 57 (1879): 367–71.
Fussed that the "short time and narrow space" of newspapers did not allow for the cogitation necessary for literary criticism even when journalists were knowledgeable about the subject.

87. [Berger, Florence K.]. "Théophile Gautier." 58 (1880): 58–70.
Expounded on Gautier's work for George Sand's *Chronique de Paris* and for the *Presse*, which paid him 12,000 francs per year for 60 articles on "musical, dramatic, or fine-arts criticism." Aside that François Buloz, editor of the *Revue des Deux Mondes*, was "mean, avaricious."

88. [Bentley, George]. "Recent Materials for Future Memoirs." 58 (1880): 524–35.
Review of the letters of several authors insisted that Sydney Smith's "wit" made the reputation of the *Edinburgh Review*. In 1880 the virulence of papers of "high character," such as the *Spectator*, was a sharp contrast to *Punch*, which was "fair-hitting."

89. [Bagenal, Philip H.]. "The National Press of Ireland." 60 (1880): 326–36.
Surmised from official ongoing surveillance of the captioned press that government imagined it a "power for evil." The National papers began with the 1842 *Nation* of Thomas Davis, John B. Dillon, and Charles Gavan Duffy. This press, "loved by the masses" and "ignored and hated by the upper class," promulgated new political and social ideas and facilitated the election of extremists to Parliament. Irish dailies, often conducted with great ability, were nevertheless "inflammatory,"

distributing "suggestive illustrations" to rouse the 'rustic' population against the British. However, unlike the 1840s when writers made a "bold and brilliant attempt to awake" the people, scribes of the 1880s were engaged in "hopeless guerilla warfare between pen and power, between inkpot and imperialism" because that sold. Both the Parnellites' *Irish World*, published in New York and circulated without cost, and the Fenians' *Irishman* evidenced this trend.

90. [Oliver, J. A. B.]. "Lord Brougham's Eccentricities." 62 (1881): 183–90.
Commented on Henry Brougham's articles in the *Edinburgh Review*, which he saw "as his own peculiar and all-powerful engine" and where he enjoyed a "reign of terror as a critic."

91. [Betham-Edwards, Matilda]. "A Recent History of the Second Empire." 63 (1881): 55–81.
Averred that Napoleon III was anti-press because he created the Sixth Chamber of Justice to deal with "press offences." The office meted out the fines, imprisonments and other penalties that ruined journalists. Among those deported were Charles Ribeyrolles, "an esteemed journalist" of *Réforme*, and Amédée Jacques, founder of the *Revue démocratique*. In a six-week period, the *Siècle* and six other Paris papers as well as over 30 provincials were punished. When the *Lanterne* spoke against the empire, it was forced to relocate to Brussels. What angered the press most was the acquittal of Pierre Bonaparte, a cousin of the emperor, for the murder of journalist Victor Noir.

92. [Bentley, George]. "Mr. Froude's *Life of Carlyle*." 65 (1882): 519–30.
Review of J. A. Froude's book unveiled Thomas Carlyle's antagonism toward William Hazlitt because he was 'selling his soul' to periodicals. Aside on Dr. William Cooke Taylor, "a principle writer of the *Athenaeum*."

93. E[ngel], L[ouis]. "Meyerbeer." 66 (1882): 61–75.
Reviled French critics who took money for favorable reviews or for contradictory ones, signing one column authentically and another with an alias. For example, P.-A. Fiorentino was himself in the *Constitutionnel* and DeRovray in the *Moniteur*.

94. [Hervey, Charles]. "Charles Monselet." 67 (1883): 431–36.
Featured Monselet, a French humorist for Bordeaux's *Courrier de la Gironde* where he was also the theatre critic. In 1846 its editor, Felix Solar, invited Monselet to Paris to write for the *Epoque*. After its quick death, Monselet moved to the *Artiste*, edited by Arsène Houssaye, then the *Siècle* where Louis Desnoyers was a "part editor." Monsalet wrote no humor when he went to the *Presse* but, hired by Louis Véron for the *Constitutionnel*, returned to this genre. Monsalet, theatre critic for *Monde illustré*, based his reviews on "the opinions of fellow-journalists" who saw the plays.

95. Richards, James Brinsley. "Mr. Gladstone's Oxford Days." 68 (1883): 29–47.
Tabbed William E. Gladstone as editor of the *Eton Miscellany* when it was staffed by "lads of talent" and as writer for the *Oxford University Magazine*.

96. [Hervey, Charles]. "Some Reminiscences of Literary Paris." 68 (1883): 431–37.
Sketched some French theatre critics. Jules Janin, "the wittiest of journalists, and the pleasantest and most genial of men," was the outstanding reviewer of the *Journal des Débats* and wrote for the

Revue de Paris and *Artiste*. P.-A. Fiorentino, who penned theatre and gossip columns, was accused of blackmail as was his colleague, Charles Maurice, owner and editor of the *Courrier des Spectacles*.

97. [Richards, James Brinsley]. "The Eton Days of Sir Stafford Northcote." 70 (1884): 83–96.

Graded the 1832 *Eton College Magazine* as good as its predecessor, the *Eton Miscellany*, thanks to editor John Wickens, assisted by Thomas Phinn and G. W. Lyttelton. Noted that the British Library copy of the serial had the names of contributors in pencil.

98. Martin, Arthur Patchett. "An Australian Novelist." 71 (1884): 96–110.

Shadowed Marcus Clarke from 1867 when he wrote for Melbourne's daily *Argus* and "its weekly offshoot the *Australasian*." Clarke scribbled paragraphs and "sub-leaders," then literary articles because "a good colonial weekly" functioned as a magazine and newspaper. At the same time, he started the *Colonial Monthly*, which was similar to "lighter English periodicals," but it was a financial failure. Later, because of 'a violation of journalistic etiquette,' he had to leave the *Argus* and *Australasian*. He then worked for the *Sydney Herald*, *Age*, and *Leader*. His "witty diatribes" won him a job as the Melbourne correspondent for the *Daily Telegraph* while he also contributed to the *Melbourne Review*, an "[e]clectic quarterly," and the *Victorian Review*, owned by Americans.

99. [Archdale, George]. "Hayward's [*Selected*] *Essays*." 71 (1884): 169–87.

Review of Abraham Hayward's columns in the *Edinburgh Review*, *Quarterly Review*, *Fraser's Magazine*, and *Morning Chronicle* quoted *Edinburgh* editor Macvey Napier's *Correspondence* that early reviewers were unkind and added that Henry F. Chorley, the *Athenaeum's* music critic, had many enemies.

100. Coleman, John. "Personal Reminiscences of Charles Reade, Extending over Twenty Years." 71 (1884): 465–82; 72 (1884): 72–86.

Shared that Reade clipped articles from the British and American illustrated press for reference in his own writing.

101. [Archdale, George]. "Edmund Yates." 72 (1884): 460–75.

Article on the editor of *Temple Bar* cited his work for *Town Talk* but not other periodicals.

102. [Richards, James Brinsley and E. C. Grenville-Murray]. "Prince Bismarck's Character." 73 (1885): 114–31.

Underscored Otto von Bismarck's hostility to the press. Aside on Hanover's satirical *Floh*.

103. [Richards, James Brinsley]. "M. Jules Ferry and His Friends." 73 (1885): 401–16.

Rooted Ferry's early political success in "writing for a newspaper which had a witty editor," August Nefftzer. He hired Ferry in 1865 to pen leaders for the *Temps*. Other friends were Léon Say, owner of the *Journal des Débats*, and Adolphe Guéroult, editor of the *Opinion Nationale*.

104. [Kennard, Nina H.]. "George Sand." 73 (1885): 480–95.

Conjectured that Sand's conversion to republicanism motivated her to found the *Cause du Peuple* and write for the *Commune de Paris* in 1849.

105. Jerrold, Evelyn. "On George Sand." 75 (1885): 177–200.
Inferred that *Figaro* editor Henri Delatouche had no qualms about employing Sand because the paper was always open to novices. Sand also penned for the *Revue de Paris*, *Revue des Deux Mondes*, and the "ultra-journal," the *Commune de Paris* in 1849, shortly after she commenced the weekly *Cause du Peuple* with "sentimental Radical views." Among her journalistic peers were "Capo de Feuillier, a forgotten critic of *l'Europe Littéraire*, a forgotten journal," and Gustave Planché of the *Revue des Deux Mondes*. Aside that *Figaro*, renowned for its "political ferocity," symbolized the French press in British eyes.

106. Shilleto, A. R. "The Year 1785: A Retrospect." 75 (1885): 235–42.
Differentiated dissemination of society news in 1785, when its only source was the *Gentleman's Magazine*, and 1885, when the *World*, *Queen*, *Vanity Fair*, *Truth*, and others circulated.

107. [Berger, Florence K.]. "The Newspaper-Boy and the Wax-Lady." 75 (1885): 539–42.
Painted the newsboy as "dirty and ragged" with "the same kind of expressive hungry look that the wandering street dogs had." The typical newsboy lived in an attic and worked a half-day "on the edge of the curb-stone, beside the summary of the evening's news, which was printed on a big sheet in three-inch capitals," and a half-day running without shoes no matter what the weather. "Though he was one of the active distributors of the world's intelligence, the very news that he was instrumental in conveying to others was a dead letter to him" because he was usually illiterate.

108. [Archdale, George]. "The *Hayward Letters*." 79 (1887): 190–206.
Analysis of the *Selections from the Correspondence of Abraham Hayward* alludes to the *Edinburgh Review* when Macvey Napier was editor.

109. [Smith, H. Greenhough]. "Wit and Wits." 79 (1887): 283–90.
Quoted several periodical humorists, among them Sydney Smith, Theodore Hook, Douglas Jerrold, and Thomas Hood.

110. K[itton], F. G. "The True Story of *Pickwick*: A Jubilee Biography." 79 (1887): 373–82.
Abstracted periodical reactions to Charles Dickens' *The Pickwick Papers*, penned while he "had a handsome salary for his duties as a reporter on the staff of the *Morning Chronicle*."

111. Jerrold, Evelyn. "Léon Gozlan." 79 (1887): 435–40.
Acclaimed author and journalist Gozlan who eschewed money for quality, unlike 1887 newspapers dominated by advertising. Gozlan trained at *Figaro* when Alphonse Karr and Jules Janin were "giving the journal that free, fanciful tone" and "brilliant independence of idea" that were its hallmarks.

112. W[otton], M[abel] E. "With an Old Magazine." 79 (1887): 567–74.
Concentrated on the 1820s *London Magazine* edited by John Scott. He was "a man in the prime of life, of good average ability, and with the courage of his opinions. He was shrewd and conscientious, with an immense capacity for work, and...with an enviable power of reconciling conflicting interests" among his staff. Scott quarreled with J. G. Lockhart, then penning for *Blackwood's Magazine*, about Leigh Hunt. In the subsequent duel, Scott died, killed by Lockhart's second. The *London Magazine*

then recruited Thomas Hood as subeditor. His "fresh young verse, delicious little essays, and witty answers to correspondents" sparked the serial. "Hood's name came to be associated with a quality tolerably rare in those hard-hitting times – he wrote amusingly, and he hurt no one's feelings." Charles Lamb, a contributor, introduced Thomas De Quincey to the *London* owners who agreed to publish his "Confessions of an Opium-Eater." Among the other staff at the monthly 'magazine dinners' were B. W. Procter ("Barry Cornwall"), William Hazlitt, notorious for his 1821 account of Queen Caroline at Covent Garden Theatre, and T. G. Wainwright, who wrote as Janus Weathercock until transported.

113. Praed, Mrs. [Rosa] Campbell. "Some American Impressions." 80 (1887): 315–26, 482–91; 81 (1887): 61–75.

Encountered American 'interviewing,' in "perhaps one of its highest phases of development," when a *New York Herald* reporter boarded Praed's ship by tug. At the dock were "a perfect mob of reporters" who were generally "kindly and considerate…courteous and obliging." One told her that all "great public men begin as newspaper men" in the United States. "Everyone reads the papers here, from the children upwards, and the Americans know how to make their papers interesting," first by "sensational headings."

Toured the *New York Tribune* building, remarking on its views, composing-room, library, offices conducive to good work, and its "Tombstone editor" who supervised obituaries. A Western editor later told Praed that frontier papers existed in a violent environment.

114. Merivale, Herman. "About Two Great Novelists." 83 (1888): 188–204.

Essay on W. M. Thackeray and Charles Dickens flitted past Thackeray's editing of the *Cornhill Magazine* but ignored his other journalism as well as all of that of Dickens.

115. [Richards, James Brinsley]. "Our Diplomatists." 84 (1888): 179–98.

Assured that "[t]he nation is abundantly informed about foreign affairs by the newspapers, and the Government is bound to ascertain promptly how much of what the press reports is true." Aside that "political adventurers" in France circulated "jackal newspapers."

116. Ward, Charles A. "Memoir of Alexander Cruden." 84 (1888): 242–51.

Posited that Cruden, hired in 1754 "to correct the press for the *Public Advertiser*," may have had a hand in "those wonderful 'Letters of Junius.'" His confrere, John Wilkes, was a "profligate though witty self-seeker" in the *North Briton*.

117. [Brice], Arthur Montefiore, F.R.G.S. "New York and New Yorkers." 84 (1888): 343–57.

Discovered New York's "only Jewish paper in existence, printed in a sort of Judeo-German tongue." Found it "[p]ainful" to see "the unblushing way in which people ventilate their domestic grievances" in New York's other journals. Most editors were American born, but Irish immigrant reporters were as able to capture "the national spirit." Powerful men "dabbled" in journalism; women were "numerous and successful." "The Journalists' Club is the rendezvous of a set of thoroughly amusing, rather than interesting men and women."

118. [Salt, H. S.]. "Thomas Campbell." 85 (1889): 87–102.

Considered Campbell's early journalism at the *Morning Chronicle* unsuccessful, but he nonetheless went on to publish in the *Edinburgh Review*. When he edited the *New Monthly Magazine* in the 1820s, he displayed "forgetfulness and unbusiness-like habits." Cyrus Redding, the subeditor, muttered that he did all the work while Campbell had the prestige and a salary of 500 pounds per year. Campbell later launched his *Metropolitan*.

119. [Caine, T. Hall]. "Charles Whitehead." 87 (1889): 99–110.
Positioned Whitehead in the mid-1830s as "contributing pretty largely to current periodicals," such as the *Monthly Magazine*, *New Monthly Magazine*, and *Bentley's Miscellany*.

120. Rae, W. Fraser. "Sir Philip Francis." 87 (1889): 171–91.
Searched for the identity of Junius with some words on his publisher, Henry Sampson Woodfall, printer and editor of the *Public Advertiser*.

121. [Brice], Arthur Montefiore, F.R.S.G. "Among the Americans." 87 (1889): 493–507.
Repeated the *Herald*'s perception of itself as "on top" among New York newspapers.

122. [Richardson, Robert]. "Sydney in September." 90 (1890): 111–17.
Conveyed that Sydney journalists spent leisured afternoons at the Athenaeum Club.

123. Rae, W. Fraser. "*The Journal of Sir Walter Scott*." 90 (1890): 477–99.
Paraphrased Scott's views on the appointment of J. G. Lockhart as *Quarterly Review* editor and on his style. Scott's 1827 letters to the *Edinburgh Weekly* signed Malachi Malagrowther were apparently as influential as Jonathan Swift's earlier "Drapier Letters."

124. Wilkinson, W. H. "Through Chinese Spectacles." 92 (1891): 98–111.
Earmarked the *North China Herald* as "the principal Shanghai newspaper."

125. [Hervey, Charles]. "Notes of a Book-Collector." 92 (1891): 124–29.
Registered that French newspapers paid substantially for feuilletons. For example, Eugene Sue received 16,000 francs from the *Journal des Débats* for *Mystères de Paris*, and the *Presse* paid one shilling per line for *Mathilde*.

126. Rae, W. Fraser. "The ’΄Ana Ξ [Lord] of Publishers." 92 (1891): 343–61.
Elucidated how the *Quarterly Review* made John Murray's reputation as a publisher. He was previously London man for the *Edinburgh Review* and an agent for *Blackwood's Magazine*, the personality of whose scribes he disliked. When he started the *Quarterly*, the "*Edinburgh* then held the field." Reviewers in both serials tried to prove that they were cleverer than authors. William Gifford's reputation as a "venomous and merciless editor" came from his days at the *Anti-Jacobin*, not the *Quarterly*. His "scholarship" set him apart from Francis Jeffrey as editor of and contributor to the *Edinburgh*. J. G. Lockhart, a later *Quarterly* editor, declined an offer to edit Murray's short-lived daily *Representative*.

127. [Wright, John Preston]. "William Cobbett." 93 (1891): 175–88.
Abbreviated Cobbett's journalism from his American "political newspaper" that ended in a fine of 5,000 dollars for libel to his *Political Register*, 1802–25, which "very rapidly became popular and successful." Since it was a "discussion of the burning questions of the day written in a tone of

arrogant dogmatism by one who was a master of simple, clear and resonant English," Cobbett lived with libel.

128. Kitton, F. G. "Dickens as an Art Critic." 93 (1891): 319–29.
Flipped through Charles Dickens' columns in *All the Year Round* and the *Examiner*.

129. Rae, W. Fraser. "A Modern Mystic." 93 (1891): 413–28.
Article on Laurence Oliphant touched on his trip to New York, c. 1857, with John Delane of *The Times* but nothing else on his journalistic career.

130. Crosse, Mrs. Andrew [Cornelia]. "Alexander Knox and His Friends." 94 (1892): 495–517.
Thought that Knox "found his literary and professional vocation" in journalism. He was a leader-writer for the *Morning Chronicle* before going to *The Times*. Among his associates was Rev. Thomas Mozley, who had "a profound sense of the responsibility of the journalist." Knox was a contemporary and friend of William Howard Russell (on staff since 1843). Wingrove Cooke, *Times* special correspondent in China in 1857, was another "distinguished colleague." Knox, a Metropolitan Police Magistrate after 1860, contributed to the *Edinburgh Review* when G. C. Lewis was editor and to *Blackwood's Magazine*.

131. Kitton, F. G "*John Leech*." 95 (1892): 207–21.
Review of W. P. Frith's book spotted Leech's drawings in the 1830s in "that famous sporting chronicle, *Bell's Life in London*." His cartoons, which appeared in *Punch* from its fourth number, were personal but "never coarsely or aggressively so."

132. Layard, George Somes. "A Stroll Through a Great Cruikshank Preserve." 96 (1892): 47–63.
Stressed the pressure on artists to produce timely and authentic plates for a monthly, such as *Ainsworth's Magazine*, which George Cruikshank illustrated. His drawings were also in *Punch*. *See* 99: 560.

133. [Jones, Harry]. "Glimpses Back: A Hundred Years Ago." 99 (1893): 104–12.
Picked up, in the *New Annual Register*, information about eighteenth-century libel suits against the owner of the *Morning Post* and the printer of the *Argus*.

134. [Lathrop, Lorin A.]. "Walt Whitman." 99 (1893): 252–59.
Recapitulated Whitman's journalistic career. In 1832 he penned for "George P. Morris' then celebrated and fashionable [*New York*] *Mirror*." In 1839 he wrote and printed the *Long Islander* before doing "free lance" work for New York's daily *Aurora*. He was a regular for the evening *Tattler* and edited the *Brooklyn Eagle*, losing the job because of politics. By the 1850s he was on the staff of New Orleans' *Crescent* but returned to Brooklyn to launch the *Freeman*, a weekly, soon daily. In the 1860s he contributed to a Washington war hospital paper, the *Armory Square Gazette*, and to Colorado's *Jimplecute*.

135. [Meetkerke, Cecilia]. "Théophile Gautier." 99 (1893): 541–48.
Guessed that "Gautier became a journalist because he could not afford to remain a poet." Hired in 1836 by the *Presse* as art critic, he avoided "the baser side of journalism."

136. Layard, George Somes. "George Cruikshank: A Defence." 99 (1893): 560–67.
Responded to a *Daily Graphic* refutation of 96: 47.

137. Sellers, Edith. "Théophraste Renaudot: A Seventeenth Century Social Reformer." 101 (1894): 209–23.
Acknowledged physician Renaudot as the father of the French newspaper. His goal in his 1631 *Gazette de France* was to nip gossip and potential sedition. He later started the *Courrier Français*, which his sons edited.

138. [Linton, Eliza Lynn]. "The Decay of Discipline." 102 (1894): 191–97.
Accused "democratic journals" of undermining respect for authority.

139. Tweedie, Mrs. Alec [Ethel B.]. "A Chat with Mrs. Lynn Linton." 102 (1894): 355–64.
Counted Eliza Lynn Linton among the pioneer women journalists. She penned "social leaders" based on Commons debates and Blue Books for the *Morning Chronicle*, which paid her 20 pounds per week for six columns. She later contributed to the *Saturday Review*, *Queen*, and other publications where her "essays are full of fire – critical, analytical, clear-sighted as a man's, and written as unflinchingly."

140. [Smith, George Barnett]. "Theodore Hook, Satirist and Novelist." 103 (1894): 465–78.
Addressed Hook's journalism. "The most important event in Hook's literary career…was the establishment of the *John Bull* newspaper at the close of 1820." His "sarcastic wit and fiery and unscrupulous zeal" about news and his "satirical onslaughts" in book reviews spurred a rapid rise in circulation. In 1836 he became editor of the *New Monthly Magazine* with a salary of 400 pounds per year.

141. [Courtney, William P.]. "A Manchester Man of Letters." 104 (1895): 563–74; 105 (1895): 68–79.
Lauded John Byrom who in 1715 developed shorthand, which he advertised as a service in the *Post Boy* and which some quickly used for parliamentary reporting.

142. Frith, Walter. "Spring in New York." 105 (1895): 83–97.
Thundered that Americans were so "slave-ridden" by newspapers that people had a "mortal dread of the press."

143. [McClymont, William]. "Notes on J. G. Lockhart." 105 (1895): 175–85.
Defended Lockhart as a critic in *Blackwood's Magazine* and the *Quarterly Review*. Referred to a G. R. Gleig essay in the *Quarterly* (116: 439).

144. Stuart, Esmé [Amélie C.Leroy]. "Only the Advertisements." 106 (1895): 220–30.
Concluded from scanning several reviews, magazines, and local newspapers that a reader could derive as much pleasure from a book's advertising as from the volume itself.

145. [Mayer, Gertrude]. "Thomas Hood." 110 (1897): 186–204.
Talked about Hood's days at the *London Magazine*, *Comic Annual*, and *New Monthly Magazine*. After Theodore Hook died, Hood edited the *New Monthly*, earning 300 pounds per year for the job and stipends for articles.

146. [Phipps, Ramsay Weston]. "Prospects of Literature." 110 (1897): 552–62.
Grouped newspapers with literature because everyone read them and "in the country districts they often contain tales of considerable merit." However, many local gazettes were inaccurate and partisan, and most religious heralds did not enhance faith. The general press, confronted by people who read too slowly or too lazily to absorb whole columns, purloined the large headline from the United States. British readers also had a "prurient curiosity for details, often evil details, of the lives of persons" who were strangers. Since the 1860s those "who would recoil from books" spawned an "enormous increase in the number of magazines." This trend was "injurious" because serials, except for the *Edinburgh Review* and *Quarterly Review*, lacked the space to develop important topics.

147. Mackenzie, Gertrude. "The Story of the New South Wales Contingent." 111 (1897): 202–18.
Eyed the *Sydney Morning Herald* and Melbourne's *Argus*.

148. Hillier, Arthur Cecil. "'Christopher North.'" 116 (1899): 64–75.
Essay on John Wilson confined his generation to the "old bad style of criticism" in periodicals, although his judgment was "on the whole beneficently exercised."

149. [Mayer, Gertrude]. "A Successor of Samuel Pepys." 117 (1899): 327–50.
Named J. W. Croker the heir to Samuel Pepys, particularly because of Croker's writing in the *Quarterly Review*, his "most congenial and influential literary channel."

150. Sanders, Herbert M. "Literature in Captivity." 118 (1899): 20–32.
Catalogued cases of imprisoned journalists. Daniel Defoe, while in Newgate in 1704, commenced *A Review of the Affairs of France*, which achieved a "vigorous circulation" after he was released. Leigh and John Hunt were incarcerated for their *Examiner* article in 1812 on the Prince Regent. "They had the courage of their opinions," so Leigh edited the paper from jail.

151. Sanders, Herbert M. "Parodies." 119 (1900): 237–53.
Glanced at W. M. Thackeray's "*Punch's* Prize Novelists," "pieces of the broadest kind."

152. Diplock, A. H. "M. Anatole France." 119 (1900): 363–74.
Studied 'Causerie,' France's weekly column of literary criticism in the *Temps*.

153. MacDonagh, Michael. "Counsellor [Daniel] O'Connell." 120 (1900): 331–51.
Mentioned the satire in Cork's *Freeholder*, published by "a journalist named John Boyle."

The Theological Review, 1864–1879

Antedating the *Modern Review*, the Unitarian *Theological* pointed out the religious press in Western Europe.

1. [Gordon, John]. "Scotch Religious Liberality." 1 (1864): 180–98.
Observed that *Good Words*, though published in Scotland, was a religious magazine that circulated "over the whole island." With Norman Macleod as editor, it carried religious instruction and "literature of a generally attractive kind."

2. [Cobbe, Frances Power]. "Religion in Italy in 1864." 1 (1864): 198–214.
Synopsized Italian religious journalism: Turin's Catholic *Pace*, a daily, and Rome's *Mediatore*, a weekly, edited by Carlo Passaglia. In Naples the Protestant *Coscienza* had "no great merit," and *Civiltà Evengelica* had no attention. In Florence the Waldensian *Eco della Verità*, with a circulation of 750, was "a very respectable controversial paper of a popular character, its tone good, and the ability of some of the articles very fair." The Florentine *Scuola della Domenica* sold 2,500 copies for children, and *Letture di Famiglia*, which spoke for evangelicals, sold 500. This "moral and literary periodical" was akin to *Leisure Hour*. Appended that in Britain, religious information about Italy came from *News of the Churches*, *Evangelical Christendom*, and *Voice from Italy*, which was "privately distributed."

3. [Beard, Charles]. "Ecclesiastical Chronicle." 1 (1864): 236–54.
Bowed to the British Catholic *Home and Foreign Review*, "ably and honestly conducted," and the French Protestant *Lien*, edited by Athanase and Etienne Coquerel.

4. Un Pasteur de l'Eglise Réformée de Paris [Athanase Coquerel]. "Protestantism in France: 1789–1864." 2 (1865): 353–78.
Part of a series starred the *Archives du Christianisme*, with essays by Albert Stapfer; *Mélanges de religion* and *Revue Protestante*, with pieces by Charles Coquerel, and *Revue de Théologie*, which revitalized French Protestantism from mid-century.

5. "The Weakness and Strength of the Pulpit." 1 (1864): 423–37.
Grieved that the newspaper was replacing the pulpit because "leading articles," available in every reading room, were not "raising men…above the passion of the moment, and inducing them to substitute principle for worldly policy."

6. *** "Religion in Denmark." 2 (1865): 322–34.
Touched on the British *Theological Monthly*.

7. *** "Religion in Sweden." 2 (1865): 645–64.
Discovered "the Swedish *Watchman*, a Church Review," and that Swedish farmers advertised their grain and cattle from the pulpit, not in the press.

8. Paul, C. Kegan. "Edward Irving." 3 (1866): 89–116.
Nodded to Irving's work for "the *Morning Watch*, a quarterly Journal of Prophecy."

9. Bowring, John. "W. J. Fox." 3 (1866): 413–48.
Reviewed the *Memorial Edition of Collected Works of W. J. Fox*, who in the 1820s applauded the burgeoning of two-penny magazines, "some of them respectfully got up." In 1866 the thousands of copies of these weeklies had given way to the hundreds of thousands of penny dailies, "creditably edited...conducted by many of our wisest heads and contributed to by our ablest pens; not only providing food for the multitudinous labouring classes, but finding a welcome reception among the most cultivated." The press was a major power, aiding the 'servile many' and swaying the 'ruling few.'

10. Smith, J. Frederick. "Lessing as Theologian: A Study." 5 (1868): 311–34.
Tagged G. E. Lessing's cousin, "Mylius, the editor of *Freigeist*...a man of loose thought and loose life."

11. Rathbone, P. H. "The Progress of the Working Classes." 5 (1868): 357–73.
Review of *The Progress of the Working Class, 1832–1867*, a book by J. M. Ludlow and Lloyd Jones, contended that "cheap periodical literature" in 1868 was better than in prior decades. "With all its defects, the tone, temper, ability, and, let us add, purity of the penny press throughout England, is what any nation may be proud of" irrespective of the sometimes strong language and inappropriate advertising of baby farmers. Compared to 1843 political commentary, "the improvement in taste, fairness, and purity has been very remarkable."

12. DeM[organ], A[ugustus]. "Henry Crabb Robinson." 6 (1869): 376–400.
Review of Robinson's *Diaries, Reminiscences, and Correspondence* stated that in 1800 he was writing "on German matters" for the *Monthly Register*. By 1807 he was the *Times* correspondent in Spain and then penned the paper's leaders. When he became foreign editor, Peter Fraser, formerly of the *Anti-Jacobin*, took over the leaders. Robinson also published in the *Christian Reformer*.

13. Beveridge, H[enry], Bengal Civil Service. "Christianity in India." 6 (1869): 465–82.
Review of Norman Macleod's *Address on India Missions* pointed out that his time in India inspired some of his articles in *Good Words*.

14. Gordon, John. "John Wesley." 8 (1871): 193–221, 374–406.
Raved that the *Arminian Magazine* was "wonderful for the variety and interest of its contents."

15. Howse, Edward S. "Saint-Simon and Enfantin." 9 (1872): 39–64.
Broadcast that Auguste Comte, Auguste Blanqui, and Armand Carrel wrote for the *Producteur*, started by Olinde Rodrigues, a disciple of C. H. de Saint-Simon. The serial, though widely read in southern

France, was never profitable even as a penny monthly nor was the later *Organisateur*, a weekly. The daily *Globe*, "owned and conducted with rare ability by Michel Chevalier," perhaps succeeded because it was free. When the government in 1832 accused the *Globe* of printing columns dangerous to public morality, it charged a penny.

16. A Liberal Catholic. "The Alt-Katholik Movement in Germany." 9 (1872): 65–102.

Aside on Florence's *Rinnovamento Cattolico* and Cologne's *Rheinische Merkur*.

17. Reville, Albert. "The Religious Situation in France Subsequent to the War of 1870–71." 10 (1873): 115–35.

Situated *Figaro* among the minority of French newspapers with an immoral bent. This "contemptible periodical with more wit than conscience" was taken seriously because it was "freely circulated and largely bought, especially in the streets and places of amusement. No doubt this journal is generally read, but this is merely on account of its wit, and without involving the admission that it has any claim on public esteem."

18. Beard, Charles. "A Group of French Friends." 10 (1873): 339–64; 11 (1874): 70–98.

Headlined F. de Lamennais, C. de Montalembert, and J. B. Lacordaire, who started the *Avenir* because they believed in "the power of the press to affect general opinion." It was a literary success, if somewhat heavy on "invective" and light on humor. Its campaign for civil liberties led to a state prosecution, the animus of the Catholic clergy, and its death when it submitted to the papacy on the issue of religious freedom. Lamennais, who opted for liberty over faith, published in the *Peuple Constituant* and *Réforme* in 1848. Lacordaire, who became a saint, endorsed the 1848 Revolutions in "a radical paper, the *Ere Nouvelle*" but later changed his mind. Montalembert, who tried to balance civil liberty and religious dictate, endorsed "restrictive laws against the press" in 1849.

19. [Thom, J. H.]. "In Memoriam: William James Lamport." 12 (1875): 111–26.

Mourned Lamport, a contributor, the business manager, and a "familiar friend" of the editor of the *Theological Review*.

20. Beard, Charles. "Heinrich Heine." 13 (1876): 174–201.

Bared Heine's friendship with "the celebrated publisher, Baron J. F. Cotta," who owned the '*Times*' of Germany, Augsburg's *Allgemeine Zeitung*. This friendship resulted in Heine's appointment as the paper's Paris correspondent on art and literature.

21. Smith, William C. "Norman Macleod." 13 (1876): 274–96.

Review of *Memoir of Norman Macleod* by his brother, Rev. Donald Macleod, discussed *Good Words*. Norman Macleod's goal as editor was "to compete with that dreary literature in which children talk 'like Eastern patriarchs,' and the supernatural is vulgarized and made ridiculous." Because it was Sunday reading, its fiction "alarmed the righteous."

22. Cox, G. W., "Presbyter Anglicanus." "The Range of Christian Fellowship." 13 (1876): 499–508.

Review of G. R. Gleig's *The Great Problem* disdained the *Edinburgh Review* and its kin "for which a reputation for orthodoxy has a commercial value."

23. Smith, J. Frederick. "Heinrich Lang." 14 (1877): 299–323.

Identified Lang as the editor of the *Zeitstimmen*, "the periodical of the rationalistic party of the Swiss Church." In 1872 the serial merged with the "*Reformblätter* of Bern and appeared as the *Reform*," but Lang stayed on as a coeditor.

24. Patrick, David. "Two English Forerunners of the Tübingen School: Thomas Morgan and John Toland." 14 (1877): 562–603.

Focused on Morgan, who wrote "reviews of English works" for a German publication edited by his professor and friend, [A. G.] Baumgarten in 1749–51, a periodical with several competitors.

25. Upton, Charles B. "James Hinton and His Philosophy." 15 (1878): 572–94.

Unearthed that Hinton, a physician, wrote on physiology and ethics for the *Medico-Chirurgical Review* and *Christian Spectator*.

26. Smith, J. Frederick. "Social Democracy in Germany." 16 (1879): 44–73.

Alluded to the German *Socialist Review*.

27. Upton, C[harles] B. "Thomas Elford Poynting: In Memoriam." 16 (1879): 487–507.

Memorialized a cleric who penned for the *National Review*, *Theological Review*, and *Inquirer*.

Titan: A Monthly Magazine, 1856–1859

James Hogg replaced his *Hogg's Instructor* with *Titan*, which pictured Parisian journalism in detail.

1. "Paris Journals and Journalists." 2 (1857): 1–14.
Prefaced a study of Paris journalism that "[t]here is no one thing which more distinctly represents and expresses the character of a nation, than does the character of its newspaper press." The French press was national, not international in contrast to the Belgian, which included newspapers of Russian, German, and French refugees and of "fallen dynasties." A good source to learn about French journalists, who did not deserve freedom because of their licentiousness, was Edmond Texier's 1851 *Biographie des Journalistes*.

During the French Revolution many new gazettes sprouted, but the *Moniteur* and *Journal des Débats* survived. The last was so "preeminent," with so many famous contributors, that it required no comment (though a footnote detailed Bertin family control.) Because the *Moniteur* supported the empire, it had little nonofficial news. It did have outstanding critics, Théophile Gautier on theatre and Charles Sainte-Beuve on literature. The owner of the *Patrie* was a French Deputy, and one of its writers, Amédée de Cesena, also penned for the *Représentant du Peuple*. The *Siècle* was the first paper to circulate widely among the petit bourgeoisie. Although it was "dull," it was "honest and respectable." Among its staff was Louis Jourdan, who previously ran a French paper in Athens. Emile de Girardin modified the feuilleton for his *Presse*. He once had great sway because of his "specious arguments" and "effrontery" but now suffered under press curbs. The *Constitutionnel*, edited by Bernard Granier de Cassagnac, was even "less respectable." He penned for the *Journal des Débats* until its "sagacious editor," Bertin *l'aîné*, saw through him. Other *Constitutionnel* editors, "though literary hacks," were "highly respectable men," a far cry from the time under Louis Philippe when the paper masked "selfishness and sensuality" by a claim to urbanity. Among the other press cited, the *Univers* directed by Louis Veûillot was ultra-Catholic, and *Charivari*, the French *Punch*, had "witty drawings" by Charles Vernier. The *Illustration* was "a very good weekly" but not equal to the *Illustrated London News*. Paris had few other weeklies.

2. "A Magazine a Hundred Years Ago." 2 (1857): 491–96.
Itemized the contents of the *Gentleman's Magazine* (March 1757): essays, "Historical Chronicle," births, marriages, and deaths, and mortality data.

3. "A French Celebrity on Social Changes." 4 (1858): 693–702.
Profiled Bernard Granier de Cassagnac, who recently commenced the *Réveil* to resume his war against light literature. He thought that newspapers' political partisanship was "an obstacle to their being the vehicle of grand ideas." Journalists who knew no history or no literature were "easy and fluent phrase-makers" without originality and style. "These men who live and die in journalism are like mites in cheese...like damp wood that burns without a flame." They made journalism a trade or a pulpit, scribbling for money or ideology. Without the press the first would be "commercial travelers or street-rioters"; the second would be "historians, economists, and poets."

4. “The Modern English Pulpit.” 5 (1858): 257–66.
Juxtaposed the decline of pulpit power and the rise of press power.

5. “The Story of an Exile: Memoir of M. Alexandre Thomas.” 5 (1858): 385–410.
Glanced at Thomas’ columns in the *Journal des Débats* and *Revue des Deux Mondes*.

6. “Who Reads All the Novels?” 6 (1859): 666–77.
Disclosed that the *London Journal* and *Family Herald* had “enormous sales” but excluded serials otherwise.

7. “Douglas Jerrold and the *Punch* School.” 7 (1859): 23–29.
Dubbed *Punch* contributors the greatest cluster of wits in contemporary periodicals but not on a par with Joseph Addison, Richard Steele, John Wilson, and William Maginn. The power of *Punch* came from its timely engravings, which contrasted with the less relevant essays in *Blackwood’s Magazine*, *Fraser’s Magazine*, and their ilk. The goal of *Punch* was to improve the world by mirth. However, as it aged, it lost the quality of its youth. If *Punch* was dull or trivial, it was still moral, always ready to expose humbug. Douglas Jerrold exemplified its “earnestness.”

The Westminster Review, 1824–1900

Grounded originally in Benthamite radicalism, the *Westminster* incorporated the *London Review* molded by John Stuart Mill in the 1830s and the *Foreign Quarterly Review* in the 1840s. Before and after these amalgamations, the *Westminster* broadcast insightful appraisals of the newspaper, of eminent periodicals, and of the status of journalists.

1. [Fox, W. J.]. "Men and Things in 1823." 1 (1824): 1–18.
Estimated that two-penny magazines, "some of them respectably got up," were "circulating to the amount of several thousand weekly." "Periodical literature has enlarged its boundaries," so it attracted those of "higher talent."

2. [Bowring, John]. "Politics and Literature of Russia." 1 (1824): 80–101.
Hoped that the intellectual progress of Russian women, already evidenced by those active in the country's periodical writing, might diminish despotism. *See Foreign Quarterly Review* 16: 445.

3. [Mill, James]. "Periodical Literature: *Edinburgh Review*." 1 (1824): 206–49; [John Stuart Mill], 505–41; [James Mill]. "*Quarterly Review*." 2 (1824): 463–503.
The senior Mill limited his essays to criticism, notably in the *Edinburgh* and *Quarterly*, because the scope of periodical literature was so wide. Periodicals that aimed for "immediate effect" echoed "opinions in vogue," usually those of the powerful. The *Edinburgh* and *Quarterly* addressed the "aristocratic classes" from different perspectives. Although *Edinburgh* authors were people of "higher intellect," the *Review* seemed unwilling to take a stand on press freedom (22: 72) but was ready to pander to prejudice. The *Quarterly* was less for instruction than amusement. Its contributors were "compilers from books of travel" or "mere *litterateurs*, men, who almost rank with the lowest class of artizans." The *Edinburgh* usually supported good ideas; the *Quarterly* opposed them. The younger Mill echoed Henry Brougham in the *Edinburgh* that the greatest benefit of press freedom was its check on misrule by examining official conduct. *See Edinburgh* 27: 245 and *Cornhill Magazine* 38: 218.

4. [Coulson, Walter]. "Newspapers." 2 (1824): 194–212.
Review of *The Periodical Press of Great Britain and Ireland* (1824) by a Scotsman singled out newspapers. "A newspaper is a modern machine which has grown up, as the British constitution is said to have done. It has not been the fruit of an original design; but has been adapted to the wants of society by a series of improvements, insignificant individually, but striking in the aggregate." This development continued even after William Pitt, seeking more revenue in 1797, imposed a direct tax on newspapers that lasted until 1815. "The newspapers…are the heart and surest civilizers of a country. They contain within themselves not only the elements of knowledge but the inducements to learn." The reader could always find "something which enlarges his mind or exercises his reason," material that would "instantly and necessarily dissipate mischievous prejudices" and spark careful deliberation and discussion. The newspaper was also "the

instrument which enables an individual to avail himself of the experience of the whole community." The press exposed "absurd general opinions" and stopped "false and injurious rumours." When it erred, it confessed in its own pages. Newspapers were born of "commercial ingenuity" but lived by protecting "justice."

"The daily newspapers of London, the most remarkable of periodical literature for the greatness of their effects – for the quantity and intensity of labour bestowed upon them – and for the cheapness of the rate which (taxes excepted) their advantages are offered to the public," were paradigms. *The Times*, full of advertising to offset taxes, published 6,000 per day but could not compare to the *Journal des Débats* (14,000) and *Constitutionnel* (18,000) in Paris. The stamp impacted size because no sheet, even free supplements, could exceed "32 inches long by 22 inches."

British readers liked leaders so dismissed useful other copy as "mere leather and prunella." "It is an axiom, which the experience of all periodical works established beyond quarterlies, that every unpaid contributor is an ass." Therefore, dailies had to pay for journalists as well as for production, foreign serials, and fast reports from the courts, police, and the country, all of these costs in order to perform "with a zeal and fidelity beyond all praise." This standard divided British newspapers from American, in which legal news was "very irregular…very rude" and legislative reports were "very brief." The French gazettes also neglected the legislature because it did not act "with good faith and impartiality" as did Commons.

James Perry first conceived the system of reporting teams in Parliament. These men had no need of shorthand because they had "well-trained minds and considerable knowledge" so they could grasp the concepts in debates. In 1824 reporters had "an esprit de corps," respect for good work, "professional morality," and a "horror of garbling and mis-representation." They had full access to the House, and though sometimes could not hear clearly, performed "conscientiously" and "ably." The columns in *The Times* and *Morning Post* were the best because other papers could not afford their level of coverage or did not have readers with such an interest.

John Walter II of *The Times* "has contributed more than any individual living to the correctness and utility of newspapers" by relying on the König press capable of producing 2,000–500 impressions per hour.

5. [Mill, John Stuart]. "Periodical Literature: *Quarterly Review* – Political Economy." 3 (1825): 213–32.

Murmured that *Quarterly* essays frequently favored the powerful.

6. [Hogg, T. J.]. "Periodical Literature – *Quarterly Review* – Articles on Greek Literature." 3 (1825): 233–61; 4 (1825): 233–60.

Chastised the *Quarterly* for inhibiting free speech and exhibiting bias.

7. [Mill, John Stuart]. "Law of Libel and Liberty of the Press." 3 (1825): 285–321.

Defended a free press. The *Morning Chronicle*, "a journal in which we have now been long accustomed to look for excellence of all sorts," spearheaded a review of the libel law.

8. [?Buckingham, James Silk]. "The British in India." 4 (1825): 261–93.

Endorsed a free press in India to "check misrule" and to inform Britons about their empire. The regulation of 14 March 1823 "annihilated" a press that gave "abundant light" when it was relatively free, 1818–23, a span when many papers in local languages emerged.

9. "Periodical Literature: *Parliamentary History and Review, for the Session of 1825*." 5 (1826): 263–68.

Calculated that periodicals multiplied rapidly after 1800 as a consequence of the advances in knowledge. The early *Gentleman's Magazine* did not satisfy serious readers, but the *Edinburgh Review* met their needs. It was informative and intellectually stimulating, and its "most eminent writers" helped to eliminate prejudices.

10. "Biography of French Ministers." 5 (1826): 457–504.

Glanced at French ministers who were journalists and official attempts to control the press of the First Empire.

11. [Bowring, John]. "Greek Committee." 6 (1826): 113–33.

Essay on the British Committee for Greek Independence said that there was no newspaper in Greece "until the Committee sent types and presses."

12. [Southern, Henry]. "*Travels in Chile and La Plata*." 6 (1826): 202–30.

Review of John Miers's book excerpted that Chile had pre-publication censorship of serials.

13. "Puffing, and *The Puffiad*." 9 (1828): 441–50.

Asserted that the "grand medium of puffing is the periodical press: traders have long known it as a means of communicating the existence of their wares at particular places." Advertising in dailies was useful, and occasionally an editor highlighted a product. Because newspaper owners were profit-minded, they would accept all advertisements. Among the earliest were those for quack remedies and auctions, chiefly of horses and wines. In the 1820s inserts by booksellers, couched as announcements, increased. They corrupted the press and literature, but, because of the costs of the stamp and paper duties, proprietors welcomed the repetitious notices of publishers. Editors might be paid well for their independence and their papers might promise impartiality, but such advertising was "prostitution of the press," money to dominate the competition. Lowering the duties on advertising and paper would increase circulation and advertising. The press could be pure if the rich alone published newspapers or an outside group, such as the Society for the Advancement of Useful Knowledge, vetted them.

14. [Merle, Gibbons]. "Newspaper Press." 10 (1829): 216–37.

Gloated that the "daily press is undoubtedly one of the great powers of society, a power constantly interfering with, and controlling every other. It has an omnipresent vision – there is nothing too high for its grasp – nothing too minute for its attention." It "occupies itself with all public affairs – and with all private concerns as soon as they come within the circle of public interest; and perhaps of all the great machinery, it is that which is most constantly improving – and presenting from year to year new evidence of what wealth and industry and mind can do, when coalescing for any important object." "The general character of the Newspaper Press is high and honourable," although it had the potential for despotism, vulgarity, and bias.

The kingdom had 308 newspapers: of London's 55, 13 were dailies printing (process explained here) 40,000 copies, with 10,000 from *The Times*. To succeed in this business required capital; investors put 250,000 pounds into London's seven morning papers. "The best property in newspapers is that where the talent of the political writers, and the general care and good taste of the managers and selectors have secured the approbation of discerning readers." London gazettes employed 1,100 people, 500 at dailies and 600 at weeklies. Salaries for major morning newspapers typically were: editors 600–1,000 pounds per year; subeditors 400–600 pounds per year; reporters (ten to 14 in number not counting penny-a-liners) four to six guineas per week; compositors (usually 30–35) two pounds, 8 shillings plus overtime; proofreaders (typically one to two) 2.5–3.5 guineas; printer four to eight guineas, and "supernumeraries" one pound, three shillings, six pence. The wages of reading-boys and business clerks were additional. Morning dailies costing about 250 pounds per week to produce derived their profits from advertising. The six evening tribunes, together smaller than *The Times*, had less advertising but were cheaper to publish. They had fewer employees (editor, subeditor, three or four court reporters) but spent money on couriers of international news.

Editors ordinarily penned leaders; subeditors scissored from the country heralds. Reporters for the courts and Parliament were frequently law students, while penny-a-liners were crude writers whose paragraphs were "mawkish and affected" and replete with bad grammar and spelling. Thanks to flimsy, this style infiltrated many papers. "The penny-a-line men are to the press what the Cossacks are to a regular army."

15. [Merle, Gibbons]. "Weekly Newspapers." 10 (1829): 466–80.

Focused on London papers, published for the country on Saturday and for the capital on Sunday until paying a double duty on advertising forced some to the cancel the Sunday edition. Three-quarters of the Sunday press had more than 100 advertisements, perhaps because the day had no post. The double sheet, inaugurated by *The Times*, allowed a supplement without extra stamp duty. Weeklies usually had expenses of 20 pounds per issue. The registered proprietor might be a straw man making libel suits difficult. Together, weeklies employed about 400 and were "conducted with a degree of talent." They printed about 110,000 copies. The circulation of weeklies, unlike dailies, was not rising, but they produced a "marked intellectual improvement of the metropolitan masses." About one in 18 people outside London read a weekly gazette, a sign of the 'March of Intellect' in a country where there was one paper per 400 people. However, this reading could be hazardous if a person perused "those newspapers only in which appeals are made to the weak and malevolent passions."

16. [Merle, Gibbons]. "Provincial Newspaper Press." 12 (1830): 69–103.

Prefaced that many local papers began as a "public means of announcing the mercantile changes and wants of the population, upon the express understanding that all opinions on political questions should be excluded." In 1830 some of the largest country gazettes copied those of London even though local editors had more skill and talent than men of 1800. Locals were relatively expensive to start and difficult to maintain. Illiterate compositors might come cheap, but printers were scarce, and audiences suspicious of new heralds were slow to abandon the metros they perused in reading rooms. Owners, often printers whose other worked funded the newspaper, needed about half the capital necessary to launch in London. Country organs returned about 100–250 pounds annually, lower than the 400–1,000 pounds of some London ones.

Liverpool's eight papers were good. Manchester's seven were "polished and urbane in their conduct towards each other," but neighboring towns with journals prevented a regional readership. Brighton's three were relatively new. Birmingham had only two, which was surprising. Bristol's four lacked "taste and industry in the getting-up." Leeds and Exeter also had newspapers, as did many other places (noted here by day of publication).

Edinburgh's press mirrored the "peculiar habits of the inhabitants, from which there is an absence of that excitement which necessarily promotes a newspaper circulation in more bustling cities." The triweekly *Courant* printed 1,700 copies each issue. The *Weekly Journal* produced 2,500 and had more advertising, perhaps because "its opinions have substantial weight from the character of political integrity which it has gained." It was also the first to cover literature and the arts. The *Caledonian Mercury* was the "bold exposer of abuses of all kinds," a paper known for its early reports and "exclusive information." The *Saturday*

Evening Post also had timely London news but was not strong in original commentary. The *Scotsman* was outstanding in statistical and philosophical articles and in literary criticism. The *Advertiser* did not "enjoy a high reputation," and the *Observer* was losing money. Using the Applegarth and Cowper machines to print, an all-advertising journal outdistanced other Edinburgh papers in this department.

"The IRISH press may be said to reflect the real condition of the country, full of politics and destitute of capital and commercial enterprise." Irish heralds were similar to those in England and Scotland in composition and typography but not content, with less literature and science. Moreover, the Irish had few magazines or reviews to fill the gap. Irish circulation was rising. The number of sheets of the island's 59 journals was 3,779,097 in 1829, up by 100,000 from 1827. Dublin's 13 newspapers accounted for 2,203,025 of this total. The morning *Saunders' News-Letter* had the largest circulation and most advertising but "not reputation for talent." It purportedly survived because of its "pretended neutrality" about religion. The *Morning Register*, the organ of the Catholic Association, covered the association's meetings in depth so had less space for advertising. Dublin had three triweekly evening papers. The *Evening Post*, with its "unsullied reputation," had a stable circulation. The *Evening Mail* had many advertisements but was not capable of doing analyses or statistical research. Its Joseph T. Hayden had "done more for the Irish press in regard of typography (a department which needed large and radical improvement) than any other man." The *Evening Packet*, exhibiting "clumsiness of style and want of knowledge," had no "intellectual ability." Dublin also had five weeklies. "The Irish provincial journals are forty-five in number and at least the half of them so worthless and contemptible as scarcely to deserve the name of newspapers," but those in the North were better in newsgathering and typography.

The *Scotsman*'s thesis that reducing stamp and advertising duties would increase circulation was correct. The results would be more revenue for government and more towns with newspapers. Britain had 334 for a population of 23 million, whereas the United States, without duties, had 800 for a population of 12 million. Philadelphia had 70 per week compared to Liverpool's eight publications.

17. "Rose's *Southern Africa*." 12 (1830): 232–46.

Review of Cowper Rose's *Four Years in Southern Africa* cited the *Anti-Slavery Reporter* and an unnamed newspaper of Cape Colony.

18. [Thompson, T. P.]. "Taxes on Literature: The Six Acts." 12 (1830): 416–29.

Viewed the laws on libel and the newspaper stamp as despotism. Their enforcement, as seen in cases noted here, was to make "perilous, troublesome, and unprofitable" newspapers for the poor. Official efforts to control "a nation's news" were wrong. While every American town of 8,000–10,000 had a daily, in Britain there were none outside London and only 12 there.

19. [Thompson, T. P.]. "*Le Représentant des Peuples*." 12 (1830): 518–25.

Introduced a new French periodical, titled here, with its prospectus and its first-issue contents.

20. "Sabbath-breaking and the Bishop of London." 13 (1830): 135–47.

Paraphrased London bishop, C. J. Bomfield, that "wicked newspapers," with accounts of the Sunday parties and concerts of the rich, tempted the poor to break the Sabbath.

21. [Peacock, Thomas Love]. "Randolph's *Memoirs, Etc. of Thomas Jefferson*." 13 (1830): 312–35.

Review of T. J. Randolph's book reiterated Jefferson's belief that a free press was essential for 'honest and unoppressive government' even though newspapers lied about him. He did object to material that was false, slanderous, or in depraved taste because such work was more harmful than official censorship.

22. [?Sedillot, Louis P. E. A.]. "Events of the Three Days in Paris." 13 (1830): 475–88.

Referred to the July Revolution. After government "suspended" press freedom in 1830, newspaper owners decided to publish. Printers refused to print dailies for fear that the authorities would destroy their presses. When the Tribunal of Commerce condemned the printers, it legitimized resistance. The printers then held off attempts to seize presses until the police broke through the gates of offices.

23. [Bulwer, W. H. L.]. "Belgian Insurrection." 14 (1831): 161–74.

Approved the 1814 guarantee of liberty for the Belgian press, although it subsequently attacked the rights of society and individuals. Failure to appoint the promised judiciary intended to protect press independence was supposedly a factor in the recent Belgian revolution.

24. "*Basil Barrington and His Friends*." 14 (1831): 224–32.

Review of R. P. Gillies' book argued that booksellers' advertising was so extreme that even "the simplest of newspaper readers" recognized its hyperbole. Repealing the advertising duty would multiply such listings.

25. [?Bowring, John]. "Brissot." 14 (1831): 332–58.

Chatted about Jacques Brissot's friendships with periodical scribes and the editor of the *Courrier de l'Europe* and his unsuccessful venture in periodical publishing.

26. [Chadwick, Edwin]. "Taxes on Knowledge." 15 (1831): 238–67.

Premised that newspapers were useful to educate the masses, signal readers about emergencies, acquaint people with law, and expose ignorant officials. Taxes on newspapers, chiefly the stamp duty, clipped circulation because most of the middling class could not afford them and created a business monopoly of serious import. Because only large London dailies could support parliamentary reporters, they were the "fourth estate," the conduit for conveying legislation to the public in reports that were not full text but abridgements done with "discretion" and "responsibility." The major journals conformed to the "public sentiment" on great topics but tended to lead, or even falsify, on others. Smaller heralds lifted information from other publications without recompense. This practice sanctioned immoral behavior and cheated gazettes that spent money on collecting news. A cost analysis proved that reduction of the stamp duty would sire a cheap press whose competition would solve these problems. Trade journals especially would benefit.

27. [Thompson, T. P.]. "*Quarterly Journal of Education*." 15 (1831): 495–506.

Analyzed the contents of the titled serial.

28. [Bannister, Saxe]. "Civilization of Africa." 15 (1831): 506–22.

Bemoaned that London nowhere launched journals to provide "a regular and full view of its proceedings with the uncivilized people." "In all the colonies in which the chief intercourse is had with native tribes, a sturdy opposition has been maintained by the government against a free press in private hands." Consequently, false information circulated in African territories ruled by the British.

29. [Stephen, George]. "Jeremie on Colonial Slavery." 16 (1832): 522–34.
Review of John Jeremie's *Four Essays on Colonial Slavery* credited "an enlightened press" in Jamaica.

30. "Present State of France." 17 (1832): 211–41.
Explained that the Bourbon Restoration met no resistance from the public or journalists when it censored all dailies and some other gazettes because, from 1800 to 1814, there had been no free press. After the July Revolution, which many printers of the royal press apparently joined, there was a "prodigious amount" of newspapers in France, most Republican. The *Journal des Débats* remained profitable by "selling itself to the ministry."

31. [Merle, Gibbons]. "Journalism." 18 (1833): 195–208.
"Journalism," Merle ordained, "is a good name for…[t]he intercommunication of opinion and intelligence…by means of journals." "'Newspapers,' and 'newspaper-writing', not to mention that they have a bad odour, only imperfectly describe the thing intended." "The Press is, however, a new power; and it is neither arranged on a right footing as yet, nor is it properly appreciated, nor has time settled or sanctioned the names or the conditions of the persons who take part in its government."

Unlike the French, who prized journalists, the British disdained them even though newspapers were everywhere accepted. Napoleon I gave dignity to the press by controlling it. The stricture against anonymity conferred status on those who influenced opinion and a lower duty improved the "information, style, tone" of papers. French politicians built reputations in journalism but not British journalists, some of whom were people of ideas, ability, and morality.

London gazettes contained many items: reports of Parliament, meetings, courts and crime; extracts from country and foreign papers; advertising, and scribbling of penny-a-liners. These serials had little for "a person of education and intelligence." The morning press reported everything in "absurd style" and sometimes "bad English." Editors decided contents and penned "the dicta that are to guide the opinions of the British world." However, many able men were unwilling to submit to a "trading proprietor" or mix with "the rags and fragments of the basket of the literary scavenger." Lesser editors tolerated inaccurate reporters who penned in "haste, indifference, uncertainty" or "caprice," and the hoaxes of penny-a-liners without "the education of decent butlers." The key to success was profit, not authenticity. While the average writer was probably capable of addressing ordinary people about their prejudices and vanities, anonymity was popular with owners who were ashamed of those they hired and with occasional contributors embarrassed by having a press association. "The journalist" who was "an instructor and a representative" deserved higher pay for talent and honesty.

The size of the enterprise and the cost of the stamp meant profit depended on monopolies and minimal staffs. Ending the stamp would likely breed specialized papers and "accredited channels of news." Most important, the newspaper would be "the political university." Education would draw workers to the new serials, albeit weeklies stuffed with "frivolity, indecency, and slander" would probably persist for the "depraved" rich.

32. [?Stephen, George or ?Saxe Bannister]. "Stuart's *Three Years in North America*." 18 (1833): 317–53.
Review of James Stuart's book disclosed that in many American newspapers advertising and political sermonizing trumped news and law reports. Editors sometimes feared their readers, notably in slave states where newspapers did not thrive. In 1810 New York had 66 gazettes and Georgia, 13; in 1833 New York had 221, and Georgia still had 13 publications.

Aside that abolition of the stamp should promote proliferation of British newspapers.

33. [Thompson, T. P.]. "Musical Periodicals – *Harmonicon* and *Giulianiad*." 18 (1833): 471–74.

Named *Harmonicon* the most informative musical magazine, partly because *Giulianiad* was devoted to the guitar.

34. [Symonds, Arthur]. "Legal and Fiscal Trammels of the Press." 18 (1833): 474–93.

Enumerated press handicaps, primarily laws of libel, partnership, and copyright, taxes, and postal rates. Partnership law prevented any interest group from organizing to publish a journal. Copyright raised the issue of theft of information. The stamp, originally meant to suppress periodicals, was a revenue source in the 1830s. If the mail could not handle the anticipated volume of new serials, the post office should expand. The country press had additional problems. Contributors paid the cost of mailing news, so they sent less. Locals copied London heralds, mainly the columns of penny-a-liners, not the best source of information. The advertising "patronage of local magistrates" kept journals alive but dependent. The British had to decide the scope of the press, whether it should serve the powerful or everyone, in light of these barriers.

35. "Turkish Empire." 19 (1833): 163–78.

Noticed the recent *Moniteur Ottoman*, a newspaper in French authorized by Sultan Mahmud II to verify his commitment to the enlightenment of his subjects.

36. [Thompson, T. P.]. "*London University Magazine*: Note on Austin's *Jurisprudence*." 19 (1833): 329–32.

Review of John Austin's *The Province of Jurisprudence Determined* greeted the new magazine of London University students. It would be a "stimulus for exactness" and an opportunity to measure success with the public if writers cultivated good style and appropriate material and avoided flippancy and personal pronouns.

37. "Rush's *Residence at the Court of London*." 19 (1833): 372–87.

Review of Richard Rush's book purloined his view of London newspapers as thorough and fearless because the libel law was vague enough to give them latitude. Articulated that dailies spoke to the educated who ignored a paper if it did not agree with their ideas. Other urbanites adopted an opinion by conversing with neighbors, not gleaning it from a gazette. Weeklies, penned with more deliberation, catalyzed more informed judgments.

38. [Symonds, Arthur]. "Statistical Information: Department of Government." 20 (1834): 87–100.

Underscored that all interests could get the information "proper to each" if the newspaper stamp went.

39. [Bannister, Saxe]. "Regency of Algiers." 20 (1834): 132–41.

Failed to link the spread of the printing press in Algeria to its periodicals (cited).

40. "French Reporting." 20 (1834): 371–78.

Compared journalistic coverage of the Chamber of Deputies and Parliament. Although British reporters had unlimited access, their newspapers had less space to devote to the legislature and less inclination to pay the price for shorthand coverage. By contrast, the *Moniteur*, legally bound to give transcriptions to speakers, coped with Deputies who modified as often as they corrected texts.

41. [Richards, Thomas]. "Van Diemen's Land." 21 (1834): 18–52.

Blared that Van Diemen's Land had "two Annual Almanacks, one Monthly Magazine conducted with spirit, and nine newspapers, seven of which are published in Hobart Town and two at Launceston."

42. "Influence of the Press." 21 (1834): 498–505.

Opposed the preference of *Blackwood's Magazine* (36: 373) for an "Established Press" of the best writers bought to "write down democracy." Political debates in the press were better than those in Parliament because the press reflected, not molded opinion. In 1834 taxes and competition among gazettes that were "the waste of paper and resources" burdened the "People's Press." Its organs should "unite," using common publishers, local agents, reference libraries, and advertising solicitations to lower expenses and raise circulations. Savings from cheaper costs of print, paper, and coach delivery could fund more talented scribes who should have the same stature and rewards as other professions.

Urged newspapers to archive back issues.

43. "Germany." 22 (1835): 131–62.

Grieved that the Frankfurt Diet in 1819 enacted "a law of repression" that continued for 12 years instead of the liberty of the press pledged in 1814.

44. "Heinrich Heine's *Germany*." 23 (1835): 291–303.

Sampled Heine's critiques of German press censorship.

45. [Bannister, Saxe]. "South Africa." 23 (1835): 415–23.

Diverted to the *Watchman*, "a weekly newspaper devoted to disseminating intelligence among the Wesleyan Methodists."

46. [Wade, John]. "Works of William Cobbett." 23 (1835): 451–71.

Shadowed Cobbett's journalistic career, in which he "was never successful," from his 1797 American *Porcupine*. Loss of a slander suit in 1799 brought a fine for Cobbett and an end to his herald's reputation. His *Rush-Light* was full of abuse relating to his trial. When he returned to London, he started a new *Porcupine* that had government funding but wasted little on newsgathering. His later *Political Register* validated that he was more suitable as a news commentator than a reporter.

47. "Quin's *Steam Voyage down the Danube*." 23 (1835): 471–93.

Review of Michael J. Quin's book appropriated his description of Magyar magnates gathering at a club in Pest to read English, German, and French reviews, magazines, and newspapers. Pest also had its own newspaper in Hungarian. Journalists, who had to sign their names, corrected "some national prejudice" or taught "some wholesome principle of legislation" in a society without censorship. The city's academy published a Magyar quarterly.

48. "*My Note Book*." 24 (1836): 231–44.

Review of John Macgregor's book aired that the *Penny Magazine* was everywhere on the Continent. The German edition, printed in Paris with English woodcuts "stereotyped," numbered 18,000 copies.

The London Review

49. Q., P. [James Mill]. "The State of the Nation." 1/30 (1835): 1–24.
Averred that newspapers "enforce the topic of the day" rather than promulgating new ideas. Most other periodicals overlooked novice readers of politics but parroted gazettes in a "more wordy" fashion.

50. B[ulwer-Lytton, E. G.]. "Prose Fictions and Their Varieties." 1/30 (1835): 476–87.
Praised weekly reviews for printing literary criticism. However, their readers wanted variety, so columns were more "clever" than "accurate" with little analysis.

51. H[ickson], W. E. "Reduction, or Abolition, of the Stamp-Duty on Newspapers." 2/31 (1836): 336–55.
Reasoned that the newspaper, as "the great instrument of civilization," should be cheap. The stamp and advertising tariffs should go, and the paper duty should be lower. Even a reduction of the stamp duty would spur more newspapers, adding to the revenue from paper and advertising duties. London top dailies were silent on the issue, probably because their owners were anxious about the rivalry repeal might spawn and the impact of reduction on stamped Sunday editions. Because the *Morning Chronicle* historically fought for the people, its muteness deceived Parliament about public opinion. Proprietors of unstamped papers also worried that a change might destroy them. Their tone was better, thanks to such talented editors as John Bell, formerly of the *True Sun*, and their circulation could reach 30,000–40,000 copies per week. Cheap tribunes deterred demagogues by educating the masses and providing a vent for grievances. If their language was not refined, they were no more "malignant" than *John Bull*. It was wrong to imagine that most people sought "political disquisitions": what they wanted was news, as the 40,000 weekly copies of the *Police Gazette* verified. Reduction would still favor London because of free postage and would encourage locals to address regional matters simply.

Aside that newspaper copyright was essential to end anonymity, the source of the "real licentiousness of the press." *See* 3/25: 264.

52. A. [John Stuart Mill]. 'State of Society in America." 2/31 (1836): 365–89.
Interpreted the *Quarterly Review* acknowledgment of an error in one article and of the unpleasant tone of others as "an example of candour…highly laudable, and almost new in the morality of the periodical press."

The London and Westminster Review

53. A. [John Stuart Mill]. "Civilization: Signs of the Times." 3/25 (1836): 1–28.
Returned to a theme, in *Tait's Edinburgh Magazine* (2: 343), that newspapers hurt the publication of good books because gazettes were quicker to read though they were sometimes erroneous. London newspaper editors were powerbrokers in 1836. Abolition of the stamp duty would break their monopoly and bring more diversity. Meantime, because reviews were too dense, people turned to magazines.

54. H[ickson], W. E. "Proposed Reduction of the Stamp Duty on Newspapers." 3/25 (1836): 264–70.
Refuted arguments for reduction of the stamp duty because only repeal would stimulate cheap local newspapers and weaken the domination of London ones sustained by advertising. *See* 2/31: 336.

55. B[isset, Andrew]. "The *Quarterly Review* for April, 1836: Article on French Novels." 3/25 (1836): 300–10.

Growled that the "*Quarterly Review*, as every knows, is not famous for the strict honesty of its criticisms."

56. A. [John Stuart Mill]. "Fonblanque's *England under Seven Administrations*." 5/27 (1837): 65–98.

Review of Albany Fonblanque's book marked him a "proud eminence among English journalists." His work for the *Examiner* was only equaled by Armand Carrel's for the *National* in Paris.

57. C., J. "Norway." 5/27 (1837): 164–95.

Review of S. Laing's *Journal of a Residence in Norway* documented that the country had a free press without a tax. Most of its 20 newspapers were full of advertising and official notices. The daily *Morgenbladet* in Christiana, with the biggest circulation of the six in the capital, carried domestic and foreign news. Its leaders were penned with "great ability," and its advertising was voluminous. The paper and type of Norwegian gazettes were better than those in France and the German states.

58. A. [John Stuart Mill]. "Parties and the Ministry." 6/28 (1837–38): 1–26.

Counseled London newspapers to be sensitive to public opinion rather than sycophants for party.

59. A. [John Stuart Mill]. "Armand Carrel." 6/28 (1837–38): 66–111.

Lauded Carrel, who as editor and chief writer of Paris' *National* made it outstanding as political literature and confirmed the value of signed journalism.

60. U[siglio], A[ngelo] and [Giuseppe Mazzini]. "Italian Literature since 1830." 6/28 (1837–38): 132–68.

Indexed Italian periodicals whose goal was to instruct. One example (others cited) was the *Educator of the Poor* (Tuscany), edited by Raphael Lambruschini, which had 1,100 subscribers.

61. R[obertson, John]. "Works of Theodore Hook." 6/28 (1837–38): 169–98.

Observed that periodical literary critics substituted verbiage for reason.

62. C[ole], M. [Henry]. "Uniform Penny Postage." 7/29 (1838): 225–64.

Studied periodicals, such as the *Penny Magazine*, *Saturday Magazine*, and *Chambers's Journal*, distributed cheaply by private agencies. The *Penny* paid only a farthing for delivery, so government should be able to carry any periodical for a penny.

63. X. [Henry Cole]. "Modern Wood Engraving." 7/29 (1838): 265–78.

Technical essay named the *Penny Magazine* as the impetus for illustrations in periodicals and credited wood engraving (unlike copper) for giving lower class readers access to art.

64. T[hackeray, W. M.]. "Parisian Caricatures." 32 (1838–39): 282–305.

Surveyed French prints and drawings in the press. *Charivari* always published political illustrations, but by 1838 most were "roguery." The journal cost 40 francs per year or half the price of the *National*.

British Sunday papers relieved upper class "Sabbath *ennui*." Aside that the honesty of the English press changed as fast as French politics.

The Westminster Review

65. [Thackeray, W. M.]. "George Cruikshank." 34 (1840): 1–60.
Illustrated essay on Cruikshank's style theorized that his work for the first number of the *Comic Almanac* made it "at once…a vast favourite with the public," which it had "so remained ever since."

66. R[obertson, John]. "Rebellion of the Kirk: The Kirk and Political Parties." 34(1840): 461–88.
Essay on the Scottish Kirk swore that the "Moderates" were "best able to support, buy, and write newspapers." A press was essential for any group in 1840 because "a deficiency in newspaper power really means a want of the power of creating that public opinion which it is the humbler function of Parliament to embody and enact in laws."

67. L[eeds, W. H.]. "Russian Literary Biography." 36 (1841): 35–57.
Asides on the *Foreign Review* and *Foreign Quarterly Review*.

68. The Editor [W. E. Hickson]. "The *Westminster Review*, Nos. 66 to 71." 36 (1841): 456–72.
Vowed that the *Westminster* was nonpartisan. The use of initials indicated that an author's views were not necessarily those of the editor.

69. L[ewes], G. H. "Authors and Managers: Regeneration of the Drama." 37 (1842): 71–97.
Chose the popularity of "cheap literature," including magazine fiction, as a factor in the decline of drama.

70. [Hickson], W. [E.]. "Political Retrospect: 1830 to 1841." 37 (1842): 394–427.
Judged Parliament's "refusing to repeal the taxes on knowledge" a "blunder…putting down the unstamped press with a strong hand." *The Times* had "10,000 subscribers" and "50,000 daily readers" not likely to abandon the newspaper that shaped opinion and consequently government.

71. [?Hickson, W.] E. "The Philosophy of *Punch*." 38 (1842): 265–318.
Graded *Punch* as better than the *Age* and *John Bull* with its "obscene journalists." *Chambers's Journal* and the *Penny Magazine* relied on "some of the first writers of the day" to enlighten readers. Many periodicals of 1842, not just the quarterlies whose subscribers "belong to the aristocracy of the literary world," looked to experts for contributions.

72. N., S. [Charles Brinsley Sheridan]. "The Ionian Islands." 38 (1842): 413–29.
Vetoed a free press for the Ionian Islands. "The population in that small space, with a free press furnishing them daily excitement, would find a bushel of moral *cowitch* clinging beneath the close clothing of England's protection."

73. L[ewes], G. H. "Errors and Abuses of English Criticism." 38 (1842): 466–86.
Deemed anonymity of critics "the parent evil" of literary criticism. An author, even if less influential than a periodical, should sign since a review was an individual's opinion. Boosting egos was less harmful than shielding the mediocre and the puppets of editors' views. Anonymity also allowed a critic to commend and to damn the same work in different serials. Signature would make critics more responsible, as Paris' *National* evaluation of George Sand, a "friend of its remarkable editor Armand Marrast," proved. Flattery in signed columns would be no worse than severity in the anonymous. Signature would demand better educated critics, but writers would then be more likely to accept their "just and earnest criticism."

74. R[obertson, John]. "Sir Lytton Bulwer." 39 (1843): 33–69.
Essay on E. G. Bulwer-Lytton rejoiced that journalism was no longer disreputable. "To be a high-minded journalist asks more virtue than perhaps any other profession requires." Journalists were the "authors of the moral life of nations," and their work was "the highest done by men," always using their "great power" for "good." "Men wincing under the whips of journalists certainly speak ill of them. But in the real opinion entertained by intelligent persons no profession is more honoured in England at this hour that that of the Press." The journalist was, in any gathering, "the Lion" whose autographs would "fetch high prices." Young men went to the law for wealth or title, but journalists had more influence. "The Legislature does what the Press bids it." The journalist was likewise "the instructor of the most intelligent minds," whereas the Bar fostered bullying and lying. The journalist's audience was also larger than those of the courts or Parliament.

75. H[ickson, W. E.]. "Dickens's *American Notes*." 39 (1843): 146–60.
Quoted Charles Dickens that American newspapers were 'licentious,' filled with 'slander,' and the only reading of many citizens. *The Times* warned that democracy and a popular press were a dangerous combination, but a cheap press was not necessarily immoral. The *New York Herald* was better than an *Age* or a *John Bull* and their kin, although the Americans and the British had "much to deplore" about their gazettes. The style of American editors might be "coarse and vulgar," but people bought penny papers not for their "scurrilous libels" but for "early commercial intelligence… and a great number of advertisements." The stamp duty did nothing to correct journalism's flaws but did limit its sway. Newspapers would improve when anonymity ceased, copyright commenced, and a "just and honest law of libel" protected "honest reporting." *See Foreign Quarterly Review* 30: 197, 31: 250.

76. H[ickson, W. E.]. "Porter's *Progress of the Nation*." 40 (1843): 425–45.
Review of G. R. Porter's book excerpted his "comparative circulation of stamped newspapers," 1831–32 and 1841–42. After Parliament reduced the stamp duty, circulation of the stamped press rose, but no new daily started in London. Retaining the duty connoted "distrust" of a free press and stifled penny and halfpenny tribunes. Imposing this indirect censorship was less desirable than promoting a quality cheap press.

77. [Hickson], W. [E.] "Trials of Hardy, Tooke, and Thelwall." 40 (1843): 474–506.
Spotlighted the trials of Thomas Hardy, John Horne Tooke, and John Thelwell in the French Revolutionary era. Government then controlled the press by strict enforcement of libel law and penalty for offering a paper for hire.

78. N[ewmarch], W[illiam]. "Mechanics' Institutions." 41 (1844): 416–45.
Pointed out that "the more influential public journals" ignored mechanics' institutes. If more of these places subscribed to local newspapers, workers might abandon pub reading. Country journals would also complement the politically biased "literary periodicals" that mechanics' institutes commonly purchased.

79. [Hickson], W. [E.]. "Mazzini and the Ethics of Politicians." 42 (1844): 225–51.
Condemned government for opening letters of Giuseppe Mazzini because he was purportedly politically dangerous. Yet he merely used the free press to achieve his goals. He was best known as editor of *Giovine Italia*, published in Marseilles, but he worked for Genoa's "weekly literary gazette," *Indicatore*, in 1828 and Livorno's *Indicatore* in 1829 before they were suppressed.

80. P[owell], B[aden]. "*Life of the Rev. Jospeh Blanco White*." 44 (1845): 273–325.
Review of J. H. Thom's book said that White edited the *Español* "to promote that cause of freedom and liberal institutions in Spain" around 1810 and conducted a short-lived British quarterly in 1828.

81. [Hickson, W. E.]. "Railway Investment." 44 (1845): 497–521.
Indicted *The Times*, the 'leading journal,' for its capacity for "panic producing" (in this instance in its columns on railway speculations).

82. D., N. [?John Ward]. "The Affairs of New Zealand." 45 (1846): 133–222.
Starred the *New Zealand Journal*, a six-penny fortnightly first published in 1840, which was in 1846 "a storehouse of information respecting the colony."

The Westminster and Foreign Quarterly Review

83. [Hickson, W. E.]. "Editorial." 46 (1846–47): vi.
Justified the merger of the *Westminster* and *Foreign Quarterly Review* because both advocated an independent press. The *Edinburgh Review* and *Quarterly Review* each "deservedly take a high place in the ranks of periodical literature," but they were partisan. The *Westminster*, whose "Foreign Literature" would be supervised by the former editor of the *Foreign Quarterly*, published "free and fearless discussion."

84. "Louis Blanc." 49 (1848): 103–19.
Aside on "trifling periodicals [that] save the indolent crowd from the trouble of thought and examination, flatter their readers with the belief that they belong to, and form part of, a literary age and people, and ensure a profit and a notoriety for those who concoct them."

85. [Hickson, W. E.]. "The French Revolution of February, 1848." 49 (1848): 137–98.
Reminded that the government of Louis Philippe prosecuted many journalists and enacted a stamp law (September 1835) that killed the press of the masses. The higher priced, as the *National* edited by Armand Marrast, the "ablest journalist of France," survived because they did not challenge the authorities.

British reduction of the stamp duty also adversely affected cheap serials, the medium of mass education. They averaged 200,000 copies weekly, but they shrank with a lower stamp duty that was a "boon" to expensive papers and a disincentive to new dailies.

Aside on a new French free-trade journal, the *Libre Echange*.

86. [Hickson, W. E.]. "Draft of a Proposed National Address to the Queen, on the Present State of the Representation, and the Grievances of Misgovernment, as Affecting the People of Great Britain and Ireland." 49 (1848): 483–503.

Among the titled grievances was restriction of the press. Taxes sustained the monopoly of "a few capitalists, proprietors of London daily journals." Yet the British colonies as well as France and the Italian and German states were free of taxes. Pleaded for an end to the stamp (in a long footnote) and for newspaper copyright "to raise the character of the press, while extending its influence."

87. S. "*Essays*, Etc. by Lord John Russell." 50 (1848–49): 1–33.

Review of Russell's works echoed his ideas that pre-publication review impeded freedom of the press but curbing "licentiousness" after publication was proper and that partisan dailies were acceptable as long as readers had access to papers of many persuasions.

88. [Hickson, W. E.]. "The French Republic." 50 (1848–49): 188–236.

Registered that in the June Days of 1848 the government suppressed "ten of the most disaffected journals" in France and jailed Emile de Girardin, editor of the *Presse*. The National Assembly revived "caution-money," a large pre-publication deposit, in order to lock papers in capitalists' hands.

89. [Martineau, James]. "Life of Channing." 50 (1848–49): 317–48.

Review of W. E. Channing's *Memoir* revealed that his periodical essays, though very serious, were widely read. He was a vigilant guardian of freedom of the press. Channing believed that it was "the chief instrument of the progress of truth and of social improvement, and is never to be restrained by legislation, except when it invades the rights of others, or instigates to specific crimes." Consequently, in 1834 he defended a journalist (one Kneeland) who had been accused of blasphemy because of his atheistic opinions. Aside on the murder of an unnamed anti-slavery journalist.

90. "English Spelling Reform." 51 (1849): 63–92.

Highlighted the *Phonotypic Journal* and *Phonetic Journal*, both printed in phonetics, and the arrival of the weekly *Phonetic News*.

91. "*Popular Life in Berlin*." 51 (1849): 216–23.

Review of an Adolph Brennglass book imagined that all Berliners read newspapers. "The great confectioners' shops take from sixty to seventy journals and periodicals of various kinds."

92. W[ard], J[ohn]. "Hungary." 51 (1849): 419–65.

Alluded to Louis Kossuth's early reporting on the Diet and editing in 1841 "*Pesti Hirlap*, the first liberal newspaper published in Hungary."

93. [Hickson, W. E.]. "Louis Napoleon: The French Elections." 51 (1849): 465–96.

Logged that in Paris, every corner had a stall hawking penny newspapers, whose sales were "immense." For example, P. J. Proudhon's *Peuple* sold 95,000 copies, only a few by subscription. Louis Napoleon did not retain the stamp duty but did keep caution-money. About 100 papers paid the fee, which he lowered to 800 pounds. The violent language associated with "ultra-democratic" opinion and the "ignorant intolerance" of reactionaries would likely doom the popular press. Already, "six popular journals" were "suppressed, and their presses broken." The government threatened the *National*, *Presse*, and *Siècle* with similar treatment if they criticized the government. Alternatively, periodicals were easily accessible. People could read magazines and reviews in coffeehouses and 6,000 'salons de lecture' costing three pence. Aside on Hippolyte Dussard, the first editor of the *Journal des Economists.*

94. "*La Revue Comique.*" 51 (1849): 524–31.
Predicted the end of the captioned review, "the French *Punch*, and the ablest of the journals published in Paris adopting the weapons of satire and caricature," because it attacked the authorities.

95. "*Histoire Morale des Femmes.*" 53 (1850): 516–30.
Review of Ernest Legouvé's book attested that French newspapers, "one branch of the literary profession," supplied a "tolerably steady" income for those of average talent. Yet women were excluded from this area of journalism even as clerks.

96. "Revolution and Counter-Revolution." 55 (1851): 92–134.
Admired Hungary's *Pesti Hirlap* for hiring talented writers whose frank political debates in decent language thwarted Habsburg censors. The paper circulated widely in the 1840s, tolerated by a government that needed Magyar money and troops.

The Westminster Review

97. [Chapman, John and George Eliot]. "Prospectus of the *Westminster and Foreign Quarterly Review* under the Direction of New Editors." 57 (1852): iii–vi.
Committed the *Westminster* to "that untemporizing expression of opinion, and that fearlessness of investigation and criticism which are the results of a consistent faith in the ultimate prevalence of truth." Planned to invite "Independent Contributors," "men of high mental power and culture," at variance "with particular ideas or measures," though not the "general spirit" of the *Review*; and to allocate more space to literary articles to elevate readers' taste because "minor and miscellaneous notices" appeared in newspapers by 1852.

98. [Fox, W. J.]. "Representative Reform." 57 (1852): 1–41.
Intoned that the 'Fourth Estate,' if free, mirrored the will of the majority and ensured the responsibility of legislators by reporting their deliberations.

99. [Griswold, R. W.]. "Contemporary Literature of America." 57 (1852): 305–22, 663–77.
Announced that the popularity of British literary periodicals in the United States left little room for the American, although the *North American Review* "enjoyed a distinguished reputation for culture and criticism."

100. [Chapman, John]. "The Commerce of Literature." 57 (1852): 511–54.
Specified the newspaper stamp, paper duty, and ignorance of the masses as obstacles to press circulation in Britain. New York had 15 dailies with an average aggregate issue of 130,000; London had ten with 65,000.

101. [Weir, William]. "Lord Jeffrey and the *Edinburgh Review.*" 58 (1852): 95–110.
Decided that the early *Edinburgh* had a "monopoly of popularity" because of its many gifted contributors, one of whom was editor Francis Jeffrey. As an author, he was more suited by knowledge

and style to be an essayist than a critic. As an editor, he excelled in selecting articles and handling writers. His *Review* was not a "great enlightener," but it introduced readers to some great literature of England and France. Still, Jeffrey worried that this job would "compromise his gentility."

102. [Hannay, James]. "The Poetry of the *Anti-Jacobin*." 58 (1852): 459–79.
Scrutinized the *Anti-Jacobin*, renowned for its satire that was similar to political "squibs" and caricature. Its poetry had "no value as a protest," so it should "not rank with high satire, but properly with conventional and squib-satire." William Gifford, John Hookam Frere, and George Canning were important contributors, the last two quite "elegant" writers.

103. "The Profession of Literature." 58 (1852): 507–31.
Review of William Jerdan's autobiography trailed him from his early newspaper reporting. He also penned for magazines before editing a country gazette, next the *Sun*, and finally the *Literary Gazette*. His egotism blocked him from admitting his failings and fueled his anger about the low pay of literary critics.

Many scribes of "doggerel in a weekly" or a "fantastical article in a magazine" were "not by nature or education" going to succeed. They came to London with a "facility for scribbling" and swam in "the stream of vagrant journalism" by learning its lingo and making contacts, but they had no diligence. They might move from paragraphs to leaders or criticism, from newspaper to newspaper, but their work lacked depth. Those eventually "worn out" retired without savings, never having made a real contribution to journalism. One needed talent and interest to prevail in this as in any profession.

104. [Sinnett, Jane]. "Contemporary Literature of Germany." 58 (1852): 598–614.
Rated German serials generally healthier for the public than those of England and France. The *Illustrirte Zeitung* was adequate, and the *Haus Chronik* was "homely, but not unpleasant."

105. "Our Army: Its Conditions, and Its Wants." 63 (1855): 368–97.
Essay on Crimea decried that William Howard Russell "should have had the indiscretion to betray the movements of the army, by which future operations may be impeded, and that the *Times* should have been impudent enough to print them." The paper ordinarily "rendered…great services" but in its war coverage was guilty of "serious injury."

106. [Newman, Francis William]. "International Immorality." 64 (1855): 37–73.
Contrasted British official behavior at home and in the empire. The "editor of a newspaper was banished from Malta for printing in Italian an address of [Giuseppe] Mazzini" previously published in *The Times*. If the government took the same action in the kingdom, there would have been an outcry.

107. [Forster, W. E.]. "The Foreign Policy of the United States." 64 (1855): 170–204.
Aside that the American press was so free that any slander could find an outlet if it did not "run counter to the prejudices of an overwhelming majority."

108. "The London Daily Press." 64 (1855): 492–520; John Chapman, 521.
History from the forged *English Mercurie* (1588) placed Nathaniel Butter's *Weekely Newes* as the first English newspaper. Thereafter, biweeklies, triweeklies, and dailies began. Most papers were not done well. For example, the *New State of Europe* was "two pages of thin, coarse paper very inferior to the worst American newspaper of the present day." Its peers were often "a folio or quarto sheet" with blank pages for people to write about their "private affairs." The *Daily Courant*, at first a triweekly,

drew from many foreign tribunes, among them the *Gazette de France*, the *Haarlem Courant*, and the *Amsterdam Courant*. The *Daily Courant* had no leaders because the original owner thought these columns "mis-lead" and no editors because they were "ignorant or unprincipled." Soon a new proprietor, Sam Buckley, "a printer with 'general learning,'" added domestic news and advertising. The 1712 stamp and advertising duties impacted circulation, and many weeklies died. The *Spectator* did not oppose these taxes but realized they would require a price hike for its 1,200–1,500 educated subscribers.

Most dailies born in the eighteenth century were morning papers. The *Morning Chronicle* (1769) was famous for printer and editor William Woodfall, whose fabulous memory made him an ace parliamentary reporter. His brother, Henry Sampson Woodfall, was responsible for printing the columns of Junius in the *Public Advertiser*. James Perry bought the *Chronicle* for a high price, and he and John Black made it important. Contemporaries of the *Chronicle* were the *Morning Post* and *Morning Herald*, but neither was distinguished. *The Times*, under John Walter, published parliamentary information, home and foreign news, and advertisements but hardly neared the influence it had in 1855. These dailies, intensely partisan because of political funding, had no style. Their nineteenth-century heirs seemed as venal, ready to sell themselves to the highest bidder, political at first and then commercial. *The Times*, under John Walter II, had more interest in profit than in ideas. *The Times*, *Morning Chronicle*, and *Morning Herald* led in circulation, 1833–35. Then *The Times* declined but recovered in the 1840s as the *Chronicle* lost buyers. Party papers, among them the *Standard*, were small in 1850 compared to the allegedly independent *Times*. Based on the stamps of nine London papers, *The Times* accounted for 75 percent of London's circulation. In 1822 London tribunes accounted for 60 percent of all sales, but as country ones emerged, the metro share dropped to 25 percent in 1855. Chapman appended that *The Times* had a "distrust of abstract right" because it was hard to champion morality and principles and turn a profit. *The Times* was "the reflex rather than the originator of public opinion."

Aside that every newspaper had key men who shaped its success: Edward Baines at the *Leeds Mercury*, J. R. Macculloch and Charles Maclaren at the *Scotsman*, and John Edward Taylor at the *Manchester Guardian*.

109. [Masson, David]. "Edinburgh Fifty Years Ago." 66 (1856): 407–42.

Recorded that the dominant parent at the birth of the *Edinburgh Review* was Sydney Smith. The *Review* was soon a power in "thought and literature," later in politics. Aside on the "the Whig-Radical editor of the short-lived *Edinburgh Gazetteer*," 1792–93.

110. [Hannay, James]. "Literature and Society." 67 (1857): 504–25.

Rued that "unimportant peers" and "important middle-class people" still disdained the 'newspaper fellow.'

111. "France under Louis Napoleon." 70 (1858): 301–50.

Suspected that Napoleon III restricted the French press quickly because it had more influence than the Chamber of Deputies. "A number of influential and respectable journals" were immediately suppressed, and an 1853 press law prohibited inauguration of new journals or appointment of editors without official sanction. Serials had to publish an "official reproof" after challenging the government. Three reprimands resulted in a suspension, which could also come from copying error from a foreign periodical or omitting the stamp. Eleven papers, including the *Progrès du Pas de Calais* for which Napoleon III once scribbled, had already suffered reprimands, suspensions, or suppressions. The law also limited street sales. The authorities chose where their decisions were published, a requirement for validity, so they ruined papers not selected. Officials also forbade coverage of some news, from grain price quotations to imperial architecture. The government had its own *Gazette des Instituteurs*, a "trifling" organ full of propaganda, to challenge Hachette's 25-year-old weekly *Manual Genéral de l'Instruction Primaire* for "country schoolmasters." This periodical, recently a monthly, eliminated its news summary to survive.

112. [Prentice, C.]. "De Lamennais: His Life and Writings." 71 (1859): 512–34.
Revisited F. de Lamennais' journalism from his stints in the 1790s at "short-lived journals," among them the *Thé* of Bertin d'Antilly and *Actes des Apôtres* of Augustin Barruel-Bauvert. By the 1820s Lamennais was writing for the *Mémorial Catholique* before joining the *Avenir*. Long after its papal censure, he penned for *Peuple Constituant* in 1848.

113. [Hippisley, J. H.]. "The Realities of Paris." 73 (1860): 30–65.
Avouched that the French political press, when free, was more influential than the British because French readers were less politically educated and "more impressionable." French gazettes stirred revolutions when discontent was not apparent. Journalists had more liberty than they realized, as Louis Jourdan in the *Siècle* exemplified. In 1860 *Figaro* and other papers were full of "personal scurrility."

114. "The Post Office Monopoly." 74 (1860): 50–84.
Muttered that postal charges for letters were high to offset the low price for newspapers. Justifications based on the talent of journalists or the merits of journals were not persuasive. Both transmissions should come from "general taxes" as they did in Sweden.

115. "The French Press." 74 (1860): 193–224.
Review of Eugene Hatin's *Histoire Politique et Littéraire de la Presse en France* determined that the roots of the French press were foreign. Since the press relied on printing, the *acta diurna* and Venetian gazette were irrelevant but not the *Zeitung* of sixteenth-century Augsburg. Théophraste Renaudot's weekly *Gazette de France*, perhaps licensed by Armand de Richelieu, was popular, but this "court chronicler" could hardly criticize officials. The keystone of the French press, from the reign of Louis XIV, was fascination with "individuality." Bias, initially about religion and later persons and governments, was particularly troubling once French became the international language. The biweekly *Muse Historique* (1650–53) was an early satirical "rhyming" paper. The *Journal des Savants*, begun in 1665, featured serious criticism but was frequently curbed by official "despotism." Examples of important periodicals were the *Nouvelles de la République des Lettres* (1684) and *Nouvelles Ecclestiastiques* "from a clandestine press." Other "literary and ephemeral" serials were sporadic.

The modern French press commenced about 1750 with the *Encyclopédie* and *Année Littéraire*. The "speculating publisher, [Charles] Panckoucke," invited satirist Benjamin Linguet to edit the new *Journal de Bruxelles* in 1774, shortly before the first daily, the 1777 *Journal de Paris*, surfaced. Linguet later started the *Annales Politiques* in England, but it "created an immediate sensation in France" because of its critiques of government. A press of personality was already in place well before the French Revolution. Thereafter, no paper could claim to be the "efficient leading journal," not even the *Journal des Débats*. Only the *Revue des Deux Mondes* displayed "calm and dispassionate evenness." Although the French press had "literary talent," the prominence of personality weakened its impact.

In Britain, Anne's press served the government. The United States press served one or another candidate, though a few newspapers held "a high and patriotic view." "The press of England owes its singular power to its impersonality," meant not to conceal "cowardly stabs" or "shameless puffs" but to demonstrate "aggregate feeling." British journalists of "honesty and ability" gathered and circulated information in an organized way, restrained only by the "intuitive moral sense of our country."

116. [Teleki von Szék, Jane F.]. "The Organization of Italy." 74 (1860): 386–410.

Stamped the *Gazette of the Kingdom* "the official paper" of the united Italy.

117. [Ellison, Thomas]. "American Slavery: The Impending Crisis." 75 (1861): 152–71.

Testified that the American South had no free press, only "tainted" newspapers. The slave states circulated 704 papers, 12.5 newspapers per person (excluding slaves). The free states circulated 1,790 papers, 25 newspapers per person.

118. [Rae, W. Fraser]. "The Critical Theory and Writings of H. Taine." 76 (1861): 55–90.

Mentioned Taine's articles, "which revealed great solidity and range of knowledge," in the *Revue des Deux Mondes* and *Journal des Débats*.

119. [Teleki von Szék, Jane F.]. "Count de Cavour." 76 (1861): 417–48.

Recalled that Camillo di Cavour once edited the *Giornale Agraria*. In 1847 he was a founder, then "chief writer and responsible editor" of the *Risorgimento*, "a paper of moderate and constitutional liberal views." Aside that *Armonia* was the "clerical organ of Turin, usually known for its violence."

120. [Binns, William]. "The Religious Heresies of the Working Classes." 77 (1862): 60–97.

Unmasked three current periodicals of "extreme unbelief." The *Counsellor*, around for 25 years, originated as the *Herald of Progress*. The new *Barker's Review* was "more tolerant, thoughtful, and reputable" than the *National Reformer*, which represented a "violent section."

121. [Newman, Francis William]. "English Rule in India." 78 (1862): 112–39.

Aside on the *Oudh Gazette*.

122. [Goldstrücker, Theodor]. "The Religious Difficulties of India." 78 (1862): 457–89.

Surmised that the growth of an Indian press since 1857 showed the political awareness of Indians.

123. [Mill, John Stuart]. "*The Slave Power*." 78 (1862): 489–510.

Review of J. E. Cairns' book boomed that several of the most influential literary and political organs, among them *The Times*, were not always impartial.

124. [Noel, Robert R.]. "Austrian Constitutionalism." 79 (1863): 333–75.

Charged "the Vienna liberal press," c. 1860, with engaging in the "free use of claptrap" to foment discontent, perhaps because their editors were Jews. They directed "a considerable portion of the press" in Austria and other German states and in Prague. Although Austria had no press censorship, those who criticized the government were prosecuted. Among them were Dr. E. Gregr, "the editor of the popular Czechish [*sic*] newspaper, *Národní Listy*," and Canon Stulc, editor of a "Bohemian paper," *Pozor*, as well as the conductors of Vienna's conservative *Fatherland* despite its calm articles.

125. "Lady Morgan." 79 (1863): 471–502.
Tapped Sydney Morgan's articles in the *New Monthly Magazine*.

126. "Saint-Simon and His Disciples." 80 (1863): 109–37.
Remembered C.-H. de Saint-Simon as the founder of France's *Producteur* and inspiration for the *Organisateur* and *Globe* directed by Michel Chevalier. After 1832, with Chevalier gone, the *Globe* was a model of "pacific language and indifference to party."

127. [Thornton, W. T.]. "Strikes and Industrial Co-operation." 81 (1864): 349–83.
Skimmed the *Co-operator*, "a penny monthly paper, designed to record and promote the progress of Industrial Associations, and of which the contents are, for the most part, contributions by working men. Perfect freedom of discussion is permitted in its pages."

128. "The Anti-Slavery Revolution in America." 84 (1865): 43–76.
Put anti-slavery periodicals, from Charles Osborne's 1817 *Philanthropist* where Benjamin Lundy was the "chief writer," in the limelight. Osborne went on to edit Tennessee's *Emancipator* and Lundy went on to edit Ohio's *Genius of Universal Emancipation*, which he carried on his back to readers. William Lloyd Garrison, a "journeyman printer," joined Lundy when he moved the paper to Baltimore. In 1830 Garrison opened the *Liberator* in Boston. When Georgia legislators pushed for his trial in 1831, the Boston mayor resisted their demand.

129. "The Principles of Our Indian Policy." 84 (1865): 185–219.
Classed both the *Englishman* in Calcutta and the *Delhi Gazette* in the Northwest Provinces as a "leading journal."

130. [Noel, Robert R.]. "The Situation in Austria." 85 (1866): 358–89.
Aside on Vienna's *Abendpost* and *Presse*.

131. P[robyn], J. W. "Italy, Venice, and Austria." 86 (1866): 147–83.
Divulged that Piedmont previously permitted a free press for domestic but not foreign affairs dealing with rulers and their governance.

132. [Probyn, J. W.]. "Italy and the War of 1866." 87 (1867): 275–325.
Painted Milan's *Perseveranza* as an "influential and moderate organ of the Italian press."

133. [Wilson, Edward D. J.]. "M. Louis Blanc's *Letters on England*." 88 (1867): 381–405.
Review of Blanc's book parroted him that opinion and not law protected press freedom in England. Writers who mirrored the majority had few restraints. Blanc was sure that signature would check the tendency to echo. John Morley (*Fortnightly Review* n.s., 2: 287) conceded only that it might stimulate independent thinking. The *Economist* temporized that anonymity made editors servants of owners and signature made journalists celebrities ready to depart to rival gazettes for higher pay.

134. [Noel, Robert R.]. "Dualism in Austria." 88 (1867): 431–58.
Pictured Vienna's press, like others in Europe, as "controlled to a considerable extent by a Government press-bureau." Nonetheless, the capital's conservative *Fatherland* and "democratic" *Reform* critiqued government as did their colleagues in other German states.

135. [Amos, Sheldon]. "Dangers of Democracy." 89 (1868): 1–37.
Comprehended that the daily press could be a force for spreading "civilizing or degrading influences," so journalists should be accurate and honest.

136. [Robinson, John]. "South Africa." 91 (1869): 307–59.
Lectured on bias in Natal's *Mercury* and the Cape's *Argus* and *Standard*. Conversely, Transvaal's *Argus*, though "constantly threatened with suppression," exemplified "courage and moral excellence."

137. "The Imperial Library of Paris." 93 (1870): 429–60.
Communicated that the captioned library had "a complete set" of the *Westminster* and several other British periodicals but few British newspapers, not even *The Times*. This gap was woeful because the French so often leashed their press. Even though the *Moniteur* was "not the *most* trustworthy in Europe," the British Museum held it.

138. [Noel, Robert R.]. "The Nationality Question in Austria." 94 (1870): 35–46.
Authenticated that all Czech political newspapers were banned, 1848–59, and editors faced fines or prison for violations of official guidelines, 1867–70. In 1869 the Czechs had 22 newspapers, four in the provinces. Two-thirds were dailies, and three were illustrated weeklies. The journals and reviews encompassed 12 on theology, seven on education, five on science, two each on agriculture, industry, commerce, and "ladies," and one each on "Pomology," chemistry, medicine, natural history, theatre and music, and jurisprudence. There were also four Czech newspapers in the United States.

139. [Pantaleoni, Diomede]. "Roman Catholicism: Present and Future." 94 (1870): 116–60.
Characterized the *Civiltà Cattolica* as "an official *Moniteur* of the Papacy."

140. "American Literature." 94 (1870): 263–94.
Raved that the "essays in the *North American Review* and the *Atlantic Monthly*, for instance, are in every sense equal to the best of our own reviews." Americans combined "occasional tartness" with knowledge and "critical acumen."

141. "The American Republic – Its Strength and Weakness." 95 (1871): 322–37.
Differentiated freedom of the press in the United States from its restraint in France. The French newspaper printer had to have "a special license"; the owner, editor, and printer had to list their names and addresses in the paper, and journalists had to sign copy. Attacks on government and "false news" resulted in stiff penalties.

142. "Thomas Hood." 95 (1871): 337–54.
Examined Hood's journalistic career from his days at the *Dundee Advertiser*. He was subeditor at the *London Magazine* before editing the *New Monthly Magazine* for 300 pounds per year. He also

published in *Punch* and owned *Hood's Magazine*. This venture had articles by "well-known literary men" but failed when Hood, already short of funds, fell ill.

143. [Robertson, James Barr]. "France, the Jesuits, and the Tientsin Massacre." 95 (1871): 404–41.

Nodded to Shanghai's *Evening Courier*, the *North China Herald*, *London and China Express*, and *North China Daily News*.

144. "Ste. Beuve [*sic*]." 95 (1871): 442–84.

Extolled Charles Sainte-Beuve as the "first literary critic" of his age, a man famous for his articles in the *Globe*, "a celebrated literary journal of the period." The paper, originally an organ of intellectuals of the late Restoration, became the mouthpiece of the Saint-Simonians after 1830. Sainte-Beuve then penned for Armand Carrel's *National* and the *Revue des Deux Mondes* from its inception in 1831 until 1846. In 1850 he moved to the *Constitutionnel* and later to the *Moniteur*.

145. [Wilson, John]. "The Authorship of Junius." 96 (1871): 406–24.

Summarized the attempts to identify Junius.

146. [Osborn, Robert D.]. "India: The Musalman Panic." 97 (1872): 359–80.

Titled the *Pioneer* "the leading journal of the North-West Provinces."

147. [Curwen, Henry]. "André Chénier: Poet and Political Martyr." 98 (1872): 124–65.

Glanced at Chénier's writings in the *Journal de Paris*, February–August 1792. He disavowed a tie to the editors and paid to publish his own ideas, a "common practice" of the day.

148. [Henderson, James Scott]. "France: Her Position and Prospects." 98 (1872): 414–43.

Clarified French press liberty as "free discussion" as long as there was no "abuse of public men" because that led to disorder. Aside on the *République Française* of Léon Gambetta.

149. [Curwen, Henry]. "Henry Murger, the Bohemian." 99 (1873): 404–49.

Silhouetted a Parisian poet who scribbled verses for the *Gazette de la Jeunesse* before getting a "berth upon the *Journal de Commerce*" in 1844 where he earned 50 francs per month for his eight-hour days. In 1845 he penned "romantic copy" for the short-lived *Moniteur de la Mode* and *Castor*. Neither had many subscribers, so low wages caused him to switch to the *Artiste*, where Arsène Houssaye helped any "struggler." Murger next went to the "*Corsaire*, a lively little journal originally named *Satan*," that combined politics and literature. There he developed his style. He tried editing, for *Evénement* where he assisted Charles Hugo and for *Dix Décembre*, but Murger was a better writer than editor. The *Moniteur* and then François Buloz, "the autocratic editor of the *Revue des Deux Mondes*," printed Murger's work.

150. "Our Ocean Steamers." 101 (1874): 355–76.

Designated the 1790 *Federal Gazette and Philadelphia Daily Advertiser* as the first American paper to publish a steamboat advertisement and the 1874 "*New York Evening Post*, one of the most respectable and influential journals in the country."

151. "Home Life: English Dwellings." 103 (1875): 173–92.
Paused at "a well-written article in the *Queen*...written, we suppose, by the hand of a lady."

152. "Our Position in India." 103 (1875): 346–85.
Certified that in India "[t]he tone of the Native Press was more or less unhealthy," but no government action occurred until an 1857 "extremely stringent penal law." This regulation, which also affected the Anglo-Indian papers, was not enforced, so "mischievous misstatement has become the rule rather than the exception" in the gazettes. Either censorship or a "semi-official journal" would balance the Indian papers, an essential "channel of communication." *See* 104: 126, 391.

153. "The Guicwar of Baroda." 104 (1875): 126–59.
Stressed the "enormous value and assistance" to London of "a Native Press, even tolerably well-conducted," such as the "Indian vernacular newspaper" directed by R. Caldwell. The top English gazettes in Bombay were the *Times of India* and *Bombay Gazette*. *See* 103: 346, 104: 391.

154. "The Baroda Blunder." 104 (1875): 391–414.
Amplified talk (in 103: 346, 104: 126) about the Indian press. Anticipated that "the task of properly controlling the Press in India will, owing to the spread of education and the growth of Native public opinion, be one of increasing difficulty and importance." The official decision to permit civil servants to write for the press was wrong, even on conditions that their tone was moderate and their articles without information obtained by virtue of their jobs. Anonymous columns scribbled by those whose journalism and job interests differed would prevent the press from being a watchdog on government.

155. [Whitehurst, E. C.]. "Lord Macaulay." 106 (1876): 1–28.
Review of G. O. Trevelyan's *Life and Letters of Lord Macaulay* gleaned from it that T. B. Macaulay in 1814 compiled an index for the *Christian Observer*, which his father edited. While the index was useful, the son's letter to the editor defending novels upset many readers. In 1823, over the objections of his father, young Macaulay penned for *Knight's Quarterly Magazine* and in 1825 for the *Edinburgh Review* where he encountered a jealous Henry Brougham.

156. "Sunday in England." 106 (1876): 29–43.
Recommended reading *Good Words* and its ilk as appropriate "intellectual activity" on Sunday.

157. "The Turkish Question: Russian Designs and English Promoters of Them." 107 (1877): 93–163.
Spotlighted the role of the London papers in swaying public opinion for or against a government.

158. "Harriet Martineau." 108 (1877): 65–101.
Trailed Martineau from the *Monthly Repository* for which she first wrote without pay and then for 15 pounds per year. In 1852 she promised a leader a week to the *Daily News* but was soon authoring six columns as well as essays in the *Westminster Review* and *Household Words*. She allegedly severed her connection with the latter because editor Charles Dickens was "bigoted" about Catholicism. This attitude was different from the "independent" *Westminster* and even from the "scoffing" *Quarterly Review* and the "skepticism" of the *Edinburgh Review*.

159. [Whitehurst, E. C.]. "Sir John Bowring." 108 (1877): 387–426.
Reminisced that Jeremy Bentham funded the early *Westminster Review*, which Bowring edited. Bentham was political editor and Henry Southern, literary. W. J. Fox, later "Publicola" of the *Weekly Dispatch*, penned the first article.

160. [Morfill, W.R.]. "Russian Literature." 108 (1877): 446–65.
Sidelined a Russian magazine, *Old and New Russia*.

161. "Democracy in Europe." 109 (1878): 1–33.
Opined that France had a "manacled public press."

162. [Jaff, A. H.]. "Lessing: His Life and Writings." 109 (1878): 91–139.
Probed the journalism of G. E. Lessing during the reign of Frederick the Great, who purportedly opened the press to allow attacks on religion and to make newspapers 'more interesting.' Lessing penned literary criticism for Berlin's *Rudiger's Gazette*, the *Vossische Zeitung* after 1752, but refused to edit the paper.

163. [Whitehurst, E. C.]. "Charles Sumner." 109 (1878): 159–207.
Bowed to Sumner's articles in the *North American Review* and *American Jurist*, "a law periodical of high rank."

164. "Russia Abroad and at Home." 110 (1878): 150–80.
Flagged the *Temps* and *Journal des Débats* among the "organs of enlightened French opinion."

165. "The Situation in the East and the Future of Russia." 110 (1878): 469–99.
Noted that the *Standard* had a "well informed" correspondent in Constantinople. His colleagues were from the *Manchester Guardian*, *Pall Mall Gazette*, and *Daily Telegraph* as well as Berlin's *Vossische Zeitung*.

166. "India and Our Colonial Empire." 110 (1878): 589–616.
Insinuated that *The Times* correspondent in Calcutta was a spokesperson for the Indian government. Aside on southern Africa's *Guide*, published in King William's Town.

167. "The Russians in Turkey." 111 (1879): 57–76.
Categorized the *Journal of the Revolution* as part of the "clandestine" Russian press and the *Russian World* as the pawn of a Russian general.

168. [Morfill, W. R.]. "Polish Literature." 111 (1879): 359–86.
Noticed the *Bohemian Journal*.

169. "Our South African Colonies." 111 (1879): 386–420.
Extracted material from the *South African Mail* and *Cape Argus*.

170. "Prince Bismarck." 112 (1879): 444–79.
Synopsized Otto von Bismarck's press policies. Although Prussia abolished censorship in 1848, Bismarck controlled the press through the Central Press Bureau. It wrote leaders, stories, and telegrams

for papers in and outside Germany. He also paid the press directly from his 'Reptile Fund,' while police seized journals and officials prosecuted their conductors.

171. [Whitehurst, E. C.]. "Lord Brougham." 112 (1879): 480–539.
Rehashed the launch of the *Edinburgh Review* by Francis Jeffrey, Sydney Smith, and Francis Horner. Henry Brougham, a contributor (1802–42), claimed that he wrote 80 articles in the first 20 numbers. He also defended John and Leigh Hunt, editors of the *Examiner* who were prosecuted for libel when they republished a leader from the *Stamford News*. The brothers were acquitted but not the *News* editor. (The Hunts were later convicted for their *Examiner* language about the Prince Regent.)

172. "Russia and Russian Reformers." 113 (1880): 160–80.
Generalized that Alexander Herzen's *Kolokol*, established in London in 1856, was "a Russian paper of the most democratic kind." However, when Michael Bakunin began to write in 1861, his "lust for destruction" undermined *Kolokol*'s influence well before it relocated to Geneva in 1865.

173. [Whitehurst, E. C.]. "*The Letters of Charles Dickens*." 113 (1880): 423–48.
Quoted Dickens that 'every vile, blackguard, and detestable newspaper' in the United States excerpted his books. He thought American heralds were too reckless, much more so than former British sheets.

174. "India and Our Colonial Empire." 113 (1880): 504–42.
Aside that Paris' *Moniteur* and New York's *Herald* were "high authorities" in the press.

175. "India and Our Colonial Empire." 114 (1880): 193–216.
Mused that "[j]ournalism" conveyed English ideas to India's "'educated' natives," who then developed "powerful and able organs in the Press."

176. [Whitehurst, E. C.]. "Lord Campbell's Memoirs." 115 (1881): 360–402.
Reviewed *Life of John Lord Campbell, Lord High Chancellor of Great Britain*, by Mary S. Hardcastle. Recollected that Campbell, while a law student, was a parliamentary reporter for the *Morning Chronicle*, then jointly edited by Robert Spankie and James Perry and "the leading Liberal newspaper."

177. [Call, W. M. W.]. "Thomas Carlyle: His Life and Writings." 115 (1881): 457–93.
Catalogued Carlyle's essays in the *London Magazine*, edited by John Scott, *Foreign Review*, *Edinburgh Review*, *Westminster Review*, and *Fraser's Magazine*.

178. [Call, W. M. W.]. "George Eliot: Her Life and Writings." 116 (1881): 154–98.
Returned to 1851 when John Chapman invited Eliot to assist him with a new series for the *Westminster Review*. She wrote several articles but resigned as assistant editor in 1853. G. H. Lewes, a scribe for *Blackwood's Magazine*, supposedly secured her entry into that magazine.

179. "India and Our Colonial Empire." 116 (1881): 199–220.
Distinguished "the diatribes of the *Hindu Patriot*" from a new "Service monthly, the *Canadian Military Review*."

180. [Morfill, W. R.]. "The Latest Bohemian Literature." 116 (1881): 372–91.
Scanned the *Journal of the Czech Museum*; the "literary journal *Lumir*," edited by J. V. Sládek in Prague, and *Casopis*, a quarterly that was "a *thesaurus* for the Slavonic student."

181. [Whitehurst, E. C.]. "Richard Cobden." 117 (1882): 98–136.
Named Cobden as "Libra," a correspondent of the *Manchester Times*. His "Letters" on "subjects of public interest" displayed "thought and ability."

182. "Canada as a Home." 118 (1882): 1–28.
Aside on "English illustrated papers."

183. Bower, George Spencer. "Camille Desmoulins." 118 (1882): 28–58.
Denominated Desmoulins "before all things, a journalist." He owned the *Révolutions de France et de Brabant*, 1789–92, and edited the *Tribune des Patriotes* for its four numbers in 1790.

184. [Call, W. M. W.]. "Shelley: His Friends and Critics." 119 (1883): 1–54.
Portrayed P. B. Shelley "boiling with indignation" when John and Leigh Hunt were sentenced to two years imprisonment and fined 1,000 pounds for "the bitter philippic against the Prince Regent in the *Examiner* newspaper."

185. [Cabot, James Elliot]. "The Carlyle-Emerson Correspondence." 119 (1883): 451–93.
Commented on Ralph Waldo Emerson's articles in the *North American Review*, *Atlantic Monthly*, and *Dial*, where he was responsible for many pieces in its four-year history.

186. "*Young Ireland: Four Years of Irish History*." 120 (1883): 71–94.
Review of Charles Gavan Duffy's book pointed out that his *Nation* was the core of Young Ireland, 1845–49. Aside on other related newspapers.

187. [Robertson, James Barr]. "Great Britain, the United States, and the Irish Question." 120 (1883): 315–48.
Situated John Morley, former editor of the *Fortnightly Review* and in 1883 editor of the *Pall Mall Gazette*, "in the very front rank" of writers on "philosophical politics."

188. [Whitehurst, E. C.]. "John Wilson Croker." 123 (1885): 150–87.
Drew from the letters and diaries of Croker, a "constant contributor" to the *Quarterly Review*. "He was neither a sound nor a genial critic." As an MP, he penned for newspapers, but anonymity cloaked his columns.

189. [Whitehurst, E. C.]. "The Weakness of Russia." 124 (1885): 135–60.
Signaled that Russia's already "censured press" was experiencing more suppression of newspapers and magazines.

190. "George Eliot." 124 (1885): 161–208.
Flitted over Eliot's work as "assistant-editor of the *Westminster*" *Review* and her "brilliant articles" for this periodical, the *Leader*, *Saturday Review*, and *Fraser's Magazine*.

191. "*William Loyd* [*sic*] *Garrison: The Story of His Life*." 125 (1886): 366–93.
Review of a book by "His Children" followed Garrison, who had a "clear and trenchant journalistic style," from his days as a "printer's boy with Mr. Ephraim W. Allen, editor of the Newburyport *Herald*." Garrison also scribbled anonymous columns for this biweekly before he edited the Newburyport *Free Press* in 1826. In 1828 he edited the *National Philanthropist* but left the same year to direct the *Journal of the Times* in Bennington (VT). In 1829 he was associate editor of the *Genius of Universal Emancipation*, which Benjamin Lundy moved from Ohio to Baltimore. The *Universal Emancipation* contained a "Lady's Repository," edited by Elizabeth Margaret Chandler, a Quaker. The paper's last page was in French for Haitian readers. When the serial died in 1830, Garrison was in jail for libel. By 1831 he launched the *Liberator* with type borrowed from a friend, the print office foreman of the *Christian Examiner*. The *Liberator* from #17 had an "ornamental heading." The Georgia legislature offered 5,000 dollars for Garrison or any seller of the *Liberator*. Aside that the *African Repository* was the organ of the New England Anti-Slavery Society.

192. White, Z. L. "A Decade of American Journalism." 128 (1887): 850–62.
Estimated that the United States and Canada published 15,420 periodicals with an aggregate circulation of 30,165,250. Thirteen, mostly weeklies, sold 150,000 copies. The majority of American families bought a weekly; about half, a monthly, and a third, a daily.

New York witnessed major shifts in the 1880s. James Gordon Bennett Jr., desperate to compete with the *Sun* also printing 120,000 copies per day, dropped the *Herald* from four to three cents. The *World*, the pioneer quarto, previously lowered its price in 1882 from three to two cents. In 1883 Joseph Pulitzer, the new owner, introduced methods unknown in "Eastern journalism." He hired the "brightest, most active and persistent reporters" to find trivia and to conduct interviews that could make headlines. He stationed well-paid correspondents who telegraphed news from around the United States. He used the Atlantic cable to pick up gossip as well as news. The *World's* popularity soon impacted other papers. The *Times* and *Tribune* quickly went to two cents, selling more papers as the *Herald's* sales dropped. A price of two cents sparked soaring circulation, from 150,000 in 1883 to 200,000 in 1887. Before 1883 the *Herald* excelled at newsgathering. By 1887, with a "depraved public taste," it discovered that rumors and trifles were more profitable. The *Times* and *Tribune* readers remained "better-informed, better-educated, more thoughtful people, who detest sensational gossip," but all New York papers in 1887 had short leaders. New York's *Sunday Tribune* had more news, letters, and articles by "writers of recognized talent and popularity…to give the paper variety and spice." Selling for three cents and offering delivery within 500 miles for 34 pages that were less than 50 percent advertising made it a major journal in the Sunday market.

Journalistic shifts were also obvious outside New York. Politically independent papers flourished in many cities. Country weeklies, also proliferating, improved thanks to stereotyping. Sunday editions filled space with syndicated news and commentary or telegrams from New York. An increase in personal advertising boosted circulation.

As some dailies declined in "good taste and literary excellence," weeklies and "popular monthly magazines" emphasized these qualities.

193. "Ralph Waldo Emerson." 128 (1887): 985–97.
Review of James Elliot Cabot's *A Memoir of Ralph Waldo Emerson* indicated that he edited the *Dial* (1842–44) after Margaret Fuller (1840–42).

194. McCoan, J. C. "Seven Weeks in Australia." 129 (1888): 52–76.
Ranked dailies and weeklies in Melbourne and Sydney equal in size and literary merit to those in London. Australian country papers were likewise similar to British locals. Melbourne's *Argus* was the best morning gazette, but Sydney's *Morning Herald* (the oldest) was a close second. Melbourne's *Age* and Adelaide's *Observer* were right behind them. The best evening offering was Melbourne's *Herald*. Australians also disseminated reviews, magazines, and "class publications."

195. "The South African Conference." 129 (1888): 490–99.
Purloined from the "*Northern Post*, a South African paper."

196. Brooks, George. "Anglophobia in the United States: Some Light on the Presidential Election." 130 (1888): 736–56.
Remarked that the *New York Times* was "perhaps the most able and impartial journal in America."

197. "Colonies and Colonization." 131 (1889): 13–25.
Gloated that most colonies had a "daily newspaper in the larger cities" and "semi-weekly and party prints swarm everywhere."

198. "Mr. Bryce's *American Commonwealth*." 131 (1889): 383–407.
Review of James Bryce's book relayed his theses that the United States press mirrored opinion better than the British and that the bad reputation of American newspapers was undeserved.

199. Ford, Sheridan. "Tzar-Tyrant or Tzar-Tribune?" 132 (1889): 204–12.
Review of W. T. Stead's *Truth about Russia* argued that Russian rulers were afraid of a free press because it could catalyze the grant of other constitutional rights faster than could dynamite. Aside that the *Pall Mall Gazette* reflected Stead's "catholic" concept of a newspaper.

200. Massie, John. "Middle Class Education." 133 (1890): 144–62.
Deplored that the only literature of interest to upper class boys was in the *Sportsman*, *Sporting Times*, and *Field*. Asides on the *Journal of Education* and *Manchester Guardian*, "no harum-scarum newspaper."

201. Miller, W[illiam]. "Prince Bismarck's Position." 133 (1890): 333–44.
Graded Cologne's *Zeitung* a "high-class journal" but more critical of government than "English journalism, even in times of great popular excitement, even in the heat of partisan strife."

202. Watson, Robert Spence. "The Friends of Russian Freedom." 133 (1890): 470–78.
Hinted that Russia wanted to close Finland's press.

203. Harrison, Henry. "Defoe's Political Career: Its Influence on English History." 135 (1891): 512–23.

Divided Defoe's career into official and literary activities, with his writings more responsible for his influence. The late seventeenth and early eighteenth centuries were "stormy periods of press warfare." Newspapers only had news; pamphlets had political opinion until Defoe's *Review*. This "first magazine of its kind" was very popular.

204. Morfill, W. R. "The Sufferings of a Bulgarian Patriot." 135 (1891): 524–31.

Paraphrased an article in the *Periodichesko Spisanie*, "the leading Bulgarian Review."

205. Barham, C. N. "Persecution of the Jews in Russia." 136 (1891): 138–47.

Tabbed Britain's *Jewish Chronicle*.

206. "The Italian Ministry." 136 (1891): 233–44.

Singled out Luigi Luzzati as a Jew who was "the editor of the widest read specialist paper that Italy possesses, *Il Sole*, an agricultural and commercial journal."

207. Lee, Randolph. "'Christopher North.'" 136 (1891): 309–20.

Assessed John Wilson's writings in *Blackwood's Magazine*.

208. Ritchie, David G. "The Logic of a Despot's Advocate." 137 (1892): 268–76.

Postulated that W. T. Stead, in the *Review of Reviews*, expressed "a very high ideal of the function of the journalist" because he "seeks religious and political significance" for his periodical. His tone was similar to that of the *Church Times*, "which may be read as a comic journal."

209. Hayes, A. A. "An Unknown Country." 137 (1892): 422–34.

Recognized *The Times* as "the great newspaper which tradition and common consent declare to be the leading exponent of British opinion."

210. Fairbairn, Evelina. "Laurence Oliphant." 137 (1892): 498–512.

Dealt with Oliphant as a correspondent for *The Times*, where he earned a name, and for some New York papers in the 1870s as well as an essayist in *Blackwood's Magazine*.

211. Leatham, James. "The Press and the Pulpit: some Thoughts on a Well-Worn Theme." 137 (1892): 601–07.

Assumed that the press had more sway than the pulpit because the "professional journalist" gave "undivided attention to journalism" whereas clerics had duties beyond preaching. A newspaper might represent the moods of readers, but its primary goal was commercial success. It fulfilled its functions, to chronicle and to discuss, when it was "informing, amusing, instructive, and improving."

212. Waters, Cyril [A.]. " 'Steadism' in Politics: A National Danger." 137 (1892): 618–26.

Sketched W. T. Stead as "a young, fresh, and ardent genius" when he edited the *Pall Mall Gazette*. He achieved even greater fame with the *Review of Reviews*, yet he was "boycotted" by much of the London press.

213. "Mr. Conway's *Life of Thomas Paine*." 138 (1892): 469–82.
Review of M. D. Conway's book plumbed Paine's work for the *Pennsylvania Magazine and American Museum*, which paid him 50 pounds per year as editor. Although the serial printed literature and science, religion and politics being forbidden, it was a 'seed-bed' for reform.

214. "Professions Accessible to Women." 139 (1893): 381–85.
Included journalism among the professions open to women.

215. "Wilkes." 140 (1893): 291–311.
Explicated John Wilkes' case with much material from the *North Briton*.

216. Fraser, G. M. "Shorthand Writing in Foreign Lands." 141 (1894): 189–94.
Associated shorthand with parliamentary reporting in some European countries but not France. Gallic reporters attended the "rowdy proceedings" but depended on shorthand specialists for details. Shorthand experts were increasing in Italy but did not dominate among reporters.

217. Stanton, Theodore. "A Franco-American's Notes on the United States." 141 (1894): 195–204.
Guessed that the American press in 1894 was at a new low point and sinking. Even "the best journals" were deteriorating, and the Sunday editions of big city dailies were getting "bigger and bigger."

218. "Ireland's Position in Literature." 141 (1894): 289–96.
Measured the *Nation* as "mediocre…from a literary point of view." Its editor, Charles Gavan Duffy, was "a struggling journalist but he possessed organising power" that served him well in the post. Aside on T. F. Meagher, the author of articles in "*Harper's* [*Monthly*] *Magazine* and other well-known American periodicals."

219. Hostell, J. Castell. "Mr. Goldwin Smith in Literature and Politics." 141 (1894): 539–52.
Featured the writings of Smith, a frequent contributor to British, Canadian, and American periodicals.

220. Robertson, John G. "The Beginnings of the German Novel." 142 (1894): 183–95.
Rooted British novels in journalistic prose, such as the *Tatler* and *Spectator*, which basis German fiction lacked.

221. Miller, W[illiam]. "Impressions of Greece." 142 (1894): 304–14.
Trumpeted that Greek newspapers were "intensely partisan" with journalists constantly on the attack against opposing gazettes. As a result, "political journalism in Greece is extremely amusing."

222. Indian. "Discontent in India." 142 (1894): 481–84.
Referred to Indian gazettes run by English-educated Brahmins. For example, the *Hindu* was "entirely edited, managed, and owned" by members of the caste.

223. Bradford, Jacob, Mus.D. Oxon. "Musical Criticism and Critics." 142 (1894): 530–36.
Objected to anonymous music reviews in newspapers because they concealed bias, encouraged puffs or blows, and tolerated snap critiques. Criticism in local papers was the worst, "a collection of ridiculous and absurd phrases." Many gazettes were ready to abandon anonymity, so a Council of Critics should monitor reviewers.

224. "Dr. John Chapman." 143 (1895): 1–4.
Obituary for a long-time editor of the *Westminster Review* outlined its characteristics and personnel.

225. Bradfield, Thomas. "William Cullen Bryant." 143 (1895): 84–91.
Recalled that Bryant edited New York's *Monthly Review* before owning and penning for the city's *Evening Post*. His nobility as a journalist made it "an influential commercial and political American gazette."

226. K., W. J. "Betting and Gambling." 143 (1895): 140–50.
Accused general and sports dailies, many with large circulations, of abetting gambling on horses. Among the chief offenders were the *Sportsman*, *Sporting Chronicle*, and *Sporting Life*, which together sold 350,000–400,000 copies per day. Tipsters' advertisements in late papers claimed to have called winners. Sporting weeklies were as important but tended to publish less in off-seasons. The predictions of sportswriters, "the greatest humbugs of modern journalism," usually were wrong.

227. Breslin, J. William "Democracy at Home." 144 (1895): 62–69.
Despaired that the lower classes only read "penny dreadfuls" and a "Radical weekly with its coarse invective and its foetid agglomeration of the crimes and horrors of the week."

228. Burton, Reginald George. "The Censorship of the Press in Russia." 144 (1895): 135–40.
Evidenced, with articles from 1827 to 1877, Russian censorship of the press.

229. Denison, George T. "Canada and Her Relations to the Empire." 144 (1895): 248–65.
Aside on bias in British journalism.

230. Miller, W[illiam]. "The Smallest Republic in the World: A Visit to San Marino." 144 (1895): 284–93.
Reported that San Marino had no newspapers but had a journal, the *San Marino Philatelist*, to advertise its stamps.

231. Bradfield, Thomas. "Enduring Characteristics of Macaulay." 145 (1896): 152–66.
Encountered, in T. B. Macaulay's essays in the *Edinburgh Review*, "fearless decision of opinion, extraordinary fullness of information, a clear and orderly arrangement of intricate details."

232. Wilson, Fred. "Journalism as a Profession." 146 (1896): 427–36.
Theorized that journalism was frequently the basis for political, social, and especially literary success. Charles Dickens excelled in the Parliamentary Press Gallery though not as editor of the *Daily News*. Douglas Jerrold went from printer to periodical contributor.

In 1896 London editors were the honored intimates of the powerful. Their country counterparts were mayors and judges. Journalism was respectable but still underpaid. The average reporter earned 100 pounds per year; an editor or subeditor, 120–130 pounds. The profession had other problems: oversupply clumped the really talented with the herd; papers publishing "horrors and sensations" in haste did not showcase a journalist's "literary grace and style" or even good grammar; apprenticeship was deadly. Apprentices, typically skilled in shorthand, spent five or more years covering local events. Boredom drove many to submit material to London serials in hope of getting a better job. Failure to advance left men dependent on the Newspaper Press Fund at the close of their careers. The Institute of Journalists was the "laughing-stock of the journalistic world" because owners ran it. What journalists needed was a union. *See* 146: 686.

233. Shansfield, W. N. "Journalism as a Profession: A Rejoinder." 146 (1896): 686–88.
Responded to 146: 427 that a newspaper was run for profit. Local reporters currently received three pounds per week and compensation for expenses, and London halfpenny gazettes were always ready to hire good writers. Once "educated journalism" developed, pay would increase.

234. Sibley, N. W., B.A., LL.M. "Mr. Lecky on Junius." 147 (1897): 57–70.
Weighed prior efforts in books and articles to identify Junius. *See* 152: 50.

235. C., A. "Crime in Current Literature." 147 (1897): 429–38.
Fumed that 243 of the 800 newspapers published weekly in Britain in 1893 printed the detective stories that raised urban circulations. Aside that the quality of Irish newspapers was better than English or Scottish gazettes.

236. Pratt, E. "India and Her Friends." 147 (1897): 645–52.
Memorialized Robert Knight, "long connected with the Press in Bombay and Calcutta," who edited the *Friend of India*, *Indian Economist and Statesman*, and *Times of India*.

237. H., K. G. "The Queen as Editor." 147 (1897): 656–57.
Focused on a March 1897 article in the *Review of Reviews* equating the British Empire with a newspaper of which the queen was permanent editor.

238. Lockhart, Robert Murray. "A Notable Publisher." 148 (1897): 665–71.
Aired that William Blackwood published the *Edinburgh Monthly Magazine*, the forerunner of *Blackwood's Magazine*. Contributors J. G. Lockhart and John Wilson helped to make it brilliant. Archibald Constable, the owner of the *Edinburgh Review* and *Scots Magazine*, "a feeble little periodical," was Blackwood's "rival." Aside on William Gifford as editor of the *Quarterly Review*.

239. X.M.P. [An Ex-Member of Parliament]. "Parnellism and Practical Politics." 149 (1898): 40–49.
Aside on several Irish newspapers.

240. Hopkins, T. M. “A Protest Against Low Works of Fiction.” 149 (1898): 99–102.

Accredited the newspaper as “one of the greatest, if not the greatest secondary educational power at the disposal of the public.” Reading news and “high class articles written by men of great intellectual power” would benefit those who customarily perused inferior fiction.

241. Sillard, R. M. “Concerning Theatrical Criticism.” 150 (1898): 634–40.

Broadcast that editors rarely checked theatre criticism. Magazines relied on capable critics, and newspapers regarded these columns as unimportant. Most newspaper critics were generalists or penny-a-liners whose reviews were secondary for gazettes selling politics, sports, and finance in 1898.

242. A Wellwisher of Ireland. “A Plea for Ireland’s True Progress.” 151 (1899): 681–90.

Acknowledged William O’Brien, editor of *United Ireland*, and his colleague, the owner of the *Freeman’s Journal*.

243. Sibley, N. W., B.A., LL.M. “A Theory of Junius.” 152 (1899): 50–63, 261–65.

Continued discussion of Junius’ identity. *See* 147: 57.

244. “The Dreyfus Case and the Future of France.” 152 (1899): 357–68.

Tagged the ongoing “rabid anti-Semite newspapers” in France.

245. A Leader-Writer. “The Lament of a Leader-Writer.” 152 (1899): 656–64.

Anguished that there were fewer leaders in 1899 than the average three in 1889 newspapers. The diminution was due to reassignment of space to sports, finance, and the colonies. Syndication and especially telegrams ruined “literary journalism,” but the ungrammatical leaders by peers accelerated its demise. Many dailies, led by the *Daily Mail*, substituted “short and snappy paragraphs” for people who had no interest in leaders even when they appeared in the light style of a George Augustus Sala. “High-class weeklies” with serious columns were declining because they did not pay well enough to attract the talented. By contrast, France was the “paradise of journalists” because papers subordinated news, telegrams, and advertisements to the style and signature that ensured fame. The British equated journalists with war correspondents and anonymous reporters.

246. “The War and After: Empire Wreckers – Parasites, not Patriots.” 153 (1900): 117–34.

Evaluated the impact of the “Yellow Press” but did not mention jingoism.

247. Freshfield, Frances Heath. “The Development of the Jingo.” 154 (1900): 392–97.

Paired jingoism and the “Yellow Press.”

Key to Indexes

Entries in author and subject indexes are listed alphabetically by periodical title, not key designation.

AM *Ainsworth's Magazine*, 1842–1854
AY *All the Year Round*, 1859–1895
BM *Bentley's Miscellany*, 1837–1868
BR *Bentley's Quarterly Review*, 1859–1860
BK *Blackwood's Edinburgh Magazine*, 1824–1900
BF *The British and Foreign Review*, 1835–1844
BQ *The British Quarterly Review*, 1845–1886
CJ *Chambers's (Edinburgh) Journal*, 1832–1900
CR *The Contemporary Review*, 1866–1900
CM *The Cornhill Magazine*, 1860–1900
DB *The Dark Blue*, 1871–1873
DR *The Dublin Review*, 1836–1900
DU *The Dublin University Magazine*, 1833–1880
ER *The Edinburgh Review*, 1802–1900
FQ *The Foreign Quarterly Review*, 1827–1846
FR *The Fortnightly Review*, 1865–1900
FM *Fraser's Magazine for Town and Country*, 1830–1882
GW *Good Words*, 1860–1900
HI *Hogg's (Weekly) Instructor*, 1845–1856
HF *The Home and Foreign Review*, 1862–1864
HW *Household Words*, 1850–1859
HJ *Howitt's Journal*, 1847–1848
LH *The Leisure Hour*, 1852–1900
LQ *The London Quarterly Review*, 1853–1900
LR *The London Review*, 1829–1830
LM *Longman's Magazine*, 1882–1900
MM *Macmillan's Magazine*, 1859–1900
MR *The Modern Review*, 1880–1884
MC *The Monthly Chronicle*, 1838–1841
MU *Murray's Magazine*, 1887–1891
NA *The National Review*, 1855–1864

NR *The National Review*, 1883–1900
NM *The New Monthly Magazine*, 1821–1854
NQ *The New Quarterly Magazine*, 1873–1880
NE *The New Review*, 1889–1897
NI *The Nineteenth Century*, 1877–1900
NB *The North British Review*, 1844–1871
OC *The Oxford and Cambridge Magazine*, 1856
PR *The Prospective Review*, 1845–1855
QR *The Quarterly Review*, 1824–1900
RA *The Rambler*, 1848–1862
SP *Saint Pauls*, 1867–1874
SR *The Scottish Review*, 1882–1900
TM *Tait's Edinburgh Magazine*, 1832–1855
TB *Temple Bar*, 1860–1900
TH *The Theological Review,* 1864–1879
TI *Titan: A Monthly Magazine*, 1856–1859
WR *The Westminster Review*, 1824–1900

Author Index

Subject Index

Lightning Source UK Ltd.
Milton Keynes UK
UKOW050424160312

189071UK00002B/29/P